J. C. Power

History

of the

Early Settlers

of

Sangamon County Illinois

"CENTENNIAL RECORD"

John Carroll Power
ASSISTED BY HIS WIFE
Mrs. S. A. Power

UNDER THE AUSPICES OF THE OLD SETTLERS' SOCIETY

HERITAGE BOOKS
2014

HERITAGE BOOKS
AN IMPRINT OF HERITAGE BOOKS, INC.

Books, CDs, and more—Worldwide

For our listing of thousands of titles see our website
at
www.HeritageBooks.com

A Facsimile Reprint
Published 2014 by
HERITAGE BOOKS, INC.
Publishing Division
5810 Ruatan Street
Berwyn Heights, Md. 20740

Entered according to Act of Congress, in the year 1876, by
John Carroll Power
In the office of the Librarian of Congress, at Washington, D.C.

This book was previously published as a two-volume set.

— Publisher's Notice —
In reprints such as this, it is often not possible to remove blemishes from the original. We feel the contents of this book warrant its reissue despite these blemishes and hope you will agree and read it with pleasure.

International Standard Book Numbers
Paperbound: 978-0-7884-1018-5
Clothbound: 978-0-7884-8863-4

OUR OWN PRELUDE.

It is with unfeigned satisfaction that I write these closing words, for that is what they are, although placed at the opening of the volume.

It will be found, by consulting the book, that in settling Saugamon county every one of the original thirteen States are represented, also every State organized before Illinois; and that the descendents of the early settlers of this county may be found in every State organized since Illinois; also in the District of Columbia, and in every Territory belonging to the United States government. Remarkable as it may appear, there is not a State or Territory in our whole nation but has some chord that centers in Sangamon county. Many European countries might be included also. Thus it will be seen that the homogeneous character of our whole people could not be more forcibly illustrated than by this volume.

It is my hope that it will be an educator, in suggesting the idea of how to arrange and continue a family history. There are family histories presented here that will be prized for many generations, and yet but few of them would ever have been written up by the families themselves. It is surprising that there are not more families who write up their own histories. Family pride is commendable, and, viewed properly, should be a powerful stimulant to right living, but it can have no reliable foundation without written history. Let a man rise to eminence and all are eager to learn something of his origin and history. I could not cite a more remarkable instance of this than has already been developed in this county, in the history of Abraham Lincoln. There are hundreds of families in the county from whom, to all human appearance, a great man is as likely to spring as in the case mentioned, and yet they have no family records, or if they do keep them, they only give dates without locating events. Look at your family Bibles and see if you can learn from them where any event connected with your ancestors took place. You must remember, however, that this all requires labor. If you wish to test it, go to work and prepare a sketch of a numerous family such as you find here.

I expected to complete this in one year, but when the magnitude of the work dawned on me I thought it might take two years. Nearly that time was spent in collecting the materials. The two years has doubled, and with four months added, I find myself putting on the finishing touches. Thus you have the result of more than four years labor on my part, and about two years by Mrs. Power. She has, during that time, written nearly two thousand letters of inquiry to the descendents of early settlers, and has incorporated the information obtained by their replies, in the family sketches to which they properly belong, besides rendering me much other valuable assistance, in all parts of the book.

To Edwin A. Wilson, not only thanks, but much more substantial tokens of approval are due. He has done that which none of the early settlers seemed disposed to do. Without his co-operation, in furnishing the sinews of war, I should not have undertaken the work.

To Messrs. Preston Breckenridge, N. W. Matheny and N. M. Broadwell, the committee of the Old Settlers' Society, who have so heartily entered into the spirit of the work, I not only tender my thanks, but venture to express the hope and belief that every family represented in the book will feel under lasting obligations to them for the impartial manner in which they have discharged the duties devolving upon them.

To the families of the early settlers, who so kindly and courteously responded to my inquiries, and extended to me the hospitalities of their homes, I cannot find words to express the thanks I feel; but ardently hope that the perusal of the book will return to you some of the pleasure I enjoyed in visiting your families. In the book we lay before you, we think all will admit that every pledge has been more than redeemed. What I say about myself and my associates will be seen the first time by them, as it is by you—here in print.

And last, though not least, I reverently bow with thanksgiving and praise to Almighty God, that He granted to me uninterupted health from the beginning to the end of this work.   J. C. P.

SPRINGFIELD, ILL., December, 1876.

FROM THE
UNITED STATES BIOGRAPHICAL DICTIONARY.
Illinois Volume, Page 86—1876.

JOHN CARROLL POWER was born September 19, 1819, in Fleming county, Kentucky, between Flemingsburg and Mount Carmel. His grandfather, Joseph Power, with six brothers older than himself, were all living near Leesburg, Loudon county, Virginia, at the beginning of the American Revolution, and all became soldiers in the cause of freedom. Some of the elder brothers served through the whole seven years' struggle for Independence, the younger ones entering the army as soon as they arrived at a suitable age. Joseph was but sixteen years old when he enlisted, and that was during the last year of the war. He was married a few years later, and, in 1793, started with his wife, children and household goods, on pack-horses, and in company with several other families crossed the Alleghany mountains to Pittsburgh. They descended the Ohio river in boats, landing at Limestone, now Maysville, and afterwards settled in what became Fleming county, Kentucky.

John Power, the second son of Joseph, born November, 1787,, in Loudon county, Virginia, was the father of the subject of this sketch. He was a farmer in comfortable circumstances and the owner of a few slaves; but with his numerous family he could not send his children from home to acquire that education which is now to be obtained in district schools, within the reach of all; consequently this son of whom we write grew to manhood without having mastered more than the simplest rudiments of the English language.

Like many other men who have struggled against adverse circumstances, he commenced his education at a period of life when he should have been in possession of it. He takes pleasure in attributing to a great extent the measure of success he has attained, both morally and mentally, to his selection of a wife. He was married May 14, 1845, to Miss Sarah A. Harris. The marriage was solemnized about twenty-six miles below Cincinnati, in Aurora, Indiana. Miss Harris was born there October 1, 1824, of English parentage.

Her grandfather, on the maternal side, was the Rev. John Wadsworth, who was rector of a single parish of the Protestant Episcopal church near Manchester, England, more than a third of a century. His daughter Catalina was the mother of Mrs. Power.

On her father's side the history reaches back to her great-grandfather, William Cox, who was a wholesale merchant in London. He was also deacon of a Baptist church in that city. By his business travels he became conversant with the illiterate and destitute condition of the poor people of the kingdom, and made an effort to induce Parliament to establish a system of free schools; but failing in that, he next undertook to persuade his friends to unite with him in organizing and supporting a system of week-day instruction so extensive that "every person in the kingdom might be taught to read the Bible." When he had gone far enough to realize that the magnitude of the work was almost appalling, his attention was providentially drawn to the consideration of Sunday schools, in order to determine whether or not they would answer the same purpose. Becoming convinced that they would, he zealously adopted the latter plan, and on the 7th of September, 1785, he organized in the city of London the first society in the world for the dissemination of Sunday schools. That society stood for eighteen years without a rival, and during that time it was instrumental in establishing Sunday schools wherever Christian missions had unfurled the banner of the cross.

William Fox had two sons and three daughters. The eldest daughter, Sarah, became the wife of Samuel Harris, a druggist of London. They had a son and daughter. The son, William Tell Harris, was married April 24, 1821, in England, to Catalina Wadsworth, daughter of Rev. John Wadsworth, as already stated. They came to America soon after their marriage, and settled in Aurora, Indiana. They have both been dead many years. Their only living child, Sarah A., was educated at private schools, and a four years' course in Granville Female Seminary, an institution under the auspices of the Protestant Episcopal church, at Granville, Ohio, from which she graduated in 1842. After her marriage to Mr. Power, in 1845, at his request she directed his studies, and when he began to write for publication she became his critic; in that way rendering the best possible assistance, which she continues to the present time.

Mr. Power was brought up a farmer, but engaged in other pursuits a number of years, always cultivating habits of study and occasional writing, but without any thought of becoming an author until well advanced in life. He met with serious reverses about the beginning of the great rebellion; and at its close, finding himself in possession of a few thousand dollars, determined to return to agricultural pursuits. He accordingly removed to Kansas, purchased a farm and prosecuted the tilling of it for three years. The grasshoppers destroyed the crops of 1866 and 1867, and the drought of 1868 made almost a total loss of those three years, with all the expense of farming. In April, 1869, he accepted the first and only offer he ever received for his farm, returned to Illinois, and since that time has devoted himself almost exclusively to literary pursuits.

His prize essay on Self-Education, for which the Illinois State Agricultural Society awarded him a premium in 1858, was revised and published in "Harkness' Magazine;" the editor expressing the opinion that those who read it would find it "one of the most profitable, instructive and mentally and morally invigorating essays they ever read."

His "History of the Rise and Progress of Sunday Schools," published in 1864, by Sheldon & Co., New York, was his first publication in book form. It is the only connected history of that noble branch of Christian work ever attempted, and appears by common consent to be accepted as the standard authority on that subject. Mr. Power has written several books and pamphlets on various local subjects; also magazine articles on a great variety of topics.

An open letter by him to the Postmaster-General, on the subject of addressing mail matter, is a brief and interesting magazine article. Some of his ideas are quite novel, and will bear investigation. The main point he aims to enforce is, that all mail matter should be addressed by first writing the name of the state in full, next the county, then the postoffice, and end with the name of the person or firm expected to receive it; thus reversing the order practiced from time immemorial. He considers that essay his contribution to the great American Centennial.

Perhaps his most finished work is the latest—his monumental edition of the "Life of Lincoln." It is a fitting tribute to the nation's martyred dead. His style is peculiarly clear, concise and original. He treats every subject most thoroughly and comprehensively, yet with an ease and grace of manner that charms the reader. A gentleman of the highest literary attainments, connected with Madison University, Hamilton, New York, in a note to the publishers, says: "I have read your 'Life of Lincoln' by Power. It has the charm of a novel."

Mr. Power is now engaged on a history of the early settlers of Sangamon county, Illinois, which, of course, includes the city of Springfield, his place of residence. This work, upon which he has spent more than four years' constant labor, will be issued in 1876. It is awaited with expectant interest by his numerous friends. He has other literary work laid out, sufficient to keep him employed for years to come, and will doubtless continue in that pursuit the remainder of his days.

CONTENTS.

	PAGE.
Additions, Omissions and Corrections	16
Letter A	75
" B	87
" C	165
" D	242
" E	274
" F	293
" G	321
" H	346
" I	397
" J	406
" K	421
" L	435
" M	471
" N	537
" O	549
" P	552
" R	591
" S	633
" T	699
" U	733
" V	735
" W	745
" Y	789
" Z	796
Deep Snow	62
Extract from Ill. Vol. United States Biographical Dictionary	5
Historical Prelude	25
Long Nine	494
Miscellaneous	62
Note of 101 citizens	48
Old Settlers Society	9
Ordinance of 1787	27
Our own Prelude	3
Railroads	43
Sangamon County	31
Springfield	44
State Capitals	45
Sudden Change	65
Trayler Brothers	720
Wars—Black Hawk	54
" Winnebago	53

ORGANIZATION

OF THE

OLD SETTLERS' SOCIETY OF SANGAMON COUNTY.

ITS MEETINGS AND MOVEMENTS TO HAVE A
HISTORY OF THE EARLY SETTLERS
WRITTEN AND PUBLISHED.

A call for a meeting of the early settlers of Sangamon county, Illinois, was drawn up May 25, 1859, by Pascal P. Enos, and circulated by him until sixty-one signatures were obtained, proposing a meeting of all those who were citizens of the county previous to the winter of the "deep snow," 1830-31; for the purpose of organizing a society to preserve the history of Springfield and Sangamon county. The call was published in the *Journal* and *Register* of May 27th, and the meeting was held June 1st, and adjourned to June 15, 1859.

The OLD SETTLERS' SOCIETY OF SANGAMON COUNTY was then organized by adopting a constitution, in which it was declared that all persons were old settlers who came to the county previous to the "deep snow." Thomas Moffitt was chairman, and Pascal P. Enos secretary of the meeting. It was declared that October 20th of each year should be celebrated as Old Settlers' Day, in honor of the first cabin in the county having been raised by Robert Pulliam, October 20, 1817. It was also declared that until the first Monday in June, 1860, the officers of the society should be Thomas Moffitt, President, and Pascal P. Enos, Secretary.

The old settlers and their descendents assembled on the morning of Oct. 20, 1859, in the vicinity, formed in procession, and, headed by a band of music, marched to where the first cabin stood. Two wagons had been drawn together on the spot to serve as a platform. The President, Judge Moffitt, called the meeting to order, and the exercises were opened with prayer by Rev. Wm. S. Prentice, the presiding elder of the Springfield district of the M. E. church. The band then played the red, white and blue, after which the Hon. James H. Matheny was introduced and delivered an oration, suitable to the occasion. Several other brief speeches were made after which they held a festival in picnic style, and thus passed the day, to the general satisfaction of all who assembled there.

It was fully expected that those meetings would be held annually, but nine long and eventful years passed before the early settlers of the county held another reunion. The next year, at the proper time for holding the meeting, the whole country was ablaze with the political excitement of the campaign that terminated in the election of Abraham Lincoln—one of the least pretentious of the early settlers of Sangamon county—to the office of President of the United States. Then followed war, that terminated in the abolition of slavery and the death of President Lincoln.

RE-ORGANIZATION OF THE SOCIETY.

July 28, 1868, a call appeared in the *Journal* and the *Register*, proposing to hold a meeting at Clear Lake, seven miles east of Springfield, on the 20th day of August. The call was signed by thirty-two of the early settlers.

CLEAR LAKE, August 20, 1868.

The meeting was called to order by the chairman of the committee of arrangements, Strother G. Jones, Esq. Exercises were opened with prayer by Rev. C. B. Stafford. Speeches were made by Munson Carter, Rev. John England, Gen. M. K. Anderson, and Samuel Williams, when they adjourned for dinner, which was taken in pic-nic style. After dinner Preston Breckenridge gave an account of his three first years in the county, 1834–5–6. The year 1835, has always been remembered as a time of great suffering. Other speeches were made and the meeting adjourned.

CLEAR LAKE, Aug. 20, 1869.

The annual meeting of the Early Settlers' of Sangamon County was called to order at 12 o'clock by S. G. Jones, the President. After prayer by Rev. Mr. Holton, of Springfield, speeches were made by Rev. Dr. Bergen, Revs. C. B. Stafford and David England, and adjourned for dinner. After that, more speeches by J. Wickliffe Taylor, P. Breckenridge and J. H. Matheny. The meeting was then closed for the purpose of effecting a more permanent organization, which was done by enrolling eighty-six names of early settlers, of both sexes. They provided for future business by the election of P. Breckenridge, President; Samuel Preston and Strother G. Jones, Vice Presidents; John F. King, Secretary.

CLEAR LAKE, Aug. 31, 1870.

Mr. Breckenridge not being present, Vice President S. G. Jones called the meeting to order. Prayer was offered by Rev. Francis Springer, who followed that with an address. Brief speeches were made by Elisha Primm, David England and Samuel A. Grubb, and after dinner, Samuel Williams read a paper full of historical reminiscences. Speeches were made by Col. Thomas Bond of Taylorville, Joab Wilkinson of Macon county, and John Fletcher of Sangamon, and adjourned.

IRWINS GROVE, Sept. 23, 1871.

Mr. Breckenridge called the meeting to order, and the exercises were opened with prayer by the venerable Daniel Wadsworth of Auburn. Thomas S. Parks, the secretary, read the minutes, followed by a brief speech from Samuel Williams. Governor Palmer was then introduced and made a speech depicting many scenes and incidents in the lives of the early settlers, not forgetting his own experience in courting, by taking his girl behind him on horseback to camp meetings, picnics, etc. It was regarded as the most mirth provoking speech ever delivered at an old settlers' meeting. After that came dinner, followed by a letter from General McClernand and speeches from J. H. Matheny and Hon. John T. Stuart. Then came the election of officers, as follows:

P. BRECKENRIDGE, President.
NOAH MASON, Vice President.
THOMAS S. SPARKS, Secretary,

Oak Ridge Park, adjoining Springfield on the north, SEPTEMBER 29, 1872.

The meeting of the Old Settlers was called to order at eleven o'clock. As a change in the usual programme, the Society proceeded at once to the election of officers for the ensuing year. Job Fletcher was elected President, with seventy Vice Presidents, and Noah W. Matheny, Secretary. After dinner, General John A. McClernand was introduced and spoke about three-fourths of an hour in a chaste and eloquent style. The next speech was by Rev. William J. Rutledge. He said that thirty-three years before he had run a saw mill on Spring creek and sawed stringers used in laying the track of the first railroad ever built in the State of Illinois. The latter part of his speech was exceedingly humorous and closed amid a roar of laughter. Major Elijah Iles then took the stand and in a conversational way related many interesting incidents of his experience among the early settlers. He was followed by Revs. J. D. Randall, of Edwardsville, and William S. Prentice and F. H. Wines, of Springfield. George R. Weber made the closing speech, and the meeting adjourned.

PLEASANT PLAINS, August 29, 1873.

The Old Settlers assembled in full force. A long train of cars well filled, came from Springfield, bringing the old settlers from all other parts of the county. The President, Captain Job Fletcher, called the meeting to order, and an address of welcome ws delivered by Rev. John Slater, of Pleasant Plains. The exercises were formally opened with prayer by Rev. Mr. Lyon of the M. E. church. Governor Palmer was then introduced and made an excellent old settlers' speech in his usual mirth provoking style. Next came dinner, after which several more speeches, and then the following officers were elected for the ensuing year: Rev. Samuel M. Wilson, of Pleasant Plains, President; James Parkinson, Vice President; and N. W. Matheny, Secretary.

Crow's Mill, or Cotton Hill, SEPTEMBER 10, 1874.

The Old Settlers assembled in large numbers to-day, in Stout's Grove, to find that the most ample provision had been made for their comfort by the local committee, William Burtle, Philemon Stout, Davis Meredith and Job Fletcher. The President, Mr. Wilson, not having arrived, the meeting was called to order by Captain Fletcher. After a few short speeches, dinner was announced and partaken of with a keen relish by all. More speeches were then made, and a vote of thanks was tendered the retiring President, Rev. S. M. Wilson. The following officers were then elected: William

Burtle, President; Alexander B. Irwin and Davis Meredith, Vice Presidents; Noah W. Matheny, Secretary.

CANTRALL, ILL., Aug. 21, 1875.

The Old Settlers' of Sangamon and Menard counties held a union meeting here to-day. William Burtle, President of the Old Settlers' Society of Sangamon county assumed the chair, and the meeting was opened with prayer by Elder Vawter of Cantrall. Speeches and feasting occupied the time until just previous to adjournment, when the following were elected as officers for the ensuing year: Alexander B. Irwin, President, E. C. Matheny, Secretary.

Fair grounds, near SPRINGFIELD, ILLS., Aug. 31, 1876.

The Old Settlers' of Sangamon county, assembled here to-day by thousands. They came by the Chicago & Alton Railroad, in wagons and carriages, on horseback and on foot. Alexander B. Irwin, the President, being detained by sickness, the assembly was called to order by Gen. M. K. Anderson. Brief speeches were made, but the principal one was by Hon. William H. Herndon. It was rich in incidents and anecdotes, and flashed with brilliant thoughts throughout. After this speech one hour was devoted to dinner in pic-nic style. A few more short speeches were made and then the following were elected as officers of the society for the next year: Alexander B. Irwin, President; Gen. M. K. Anderson, Vice President; E. C. Matheny, Secretary.

OLD SETTLERS HISTORY.

In June, 1872, I was called upon by Hon. Preston Breckenridge, who was then serving his third term as President of the Old Settlers' Society of Sangamon County. He stated, in substance, that the early settlers of the county had for some years been talking of having something written and published that would serve as a history of the county and biographical sketches of themselves; that thus far they had not found any person qualified for the work who was willing to undertake it. He further stated that a copy of the small pamphlet history of Springfield, prepared and published by myself, under the auspices of the Springfield Board of Trade, had fallen into his hands, and that after perusing it, and conversing with some of his friends who knew me, he determined to form my acquaintance, and see if I could be induced to engage in the enterprise. He very frankly told me there was no fund to defray the expense, that the only inducement they could offer would be their co-operation in collecting information and giving their subscriptions for the book. The following communication was the result of that interview:

Hon. P. Breckenridge, President of the Society of Old Settlers of Sangamon County:

SIR:—You, as the representative of your society, having expressed to me a desire to have a book written and published, to preserve, as far as possible, the biographical, historical and other reminiscences of the early settlers of Sangamon county, and having requested me to suggest a plan upon which I would be willing to undertake such a work, I offer the following as my views upon the subject: The materials are so abundant, that I would not be willing to engage in it if I were required to compress all in a very small, cheap volume. I propose to undertake to write and publish a book upon that subject, to contain not less than five hundred octavo pages, with a small map, showing all the townships, villages, towns and cities, with other objects of interest, in the county—all to be printed on the best quality of book paper, and bound in the finest of English cloth, provided I can obtain subscriptions for one thousand copies at five dollars per copy.

If this plan should meet the views of your society, I should expect old settlers to co-operate with me, by furnishing all the information they may respectively possess. It would be more satisfactory for those interested, if you would appoint a committee of three—a majority of whom shall reside in Springfield—to whom I can submit all copy for their approval, before publication.

J. C. POWER.

Springfield, Aug. 14, 1872.

At a meeting of a committee of the Society of Old Settlers, on the fifteenth of August, the above communication was laid before them, whereupon the following resolutions were adopted:

Resolved, That this society heartily endorses the proposition of Mr. Power, and we hereby pledge ourselves, as a society and as individuals, to co-operate with him in obtaining the requisite number of subscribers and in collecting information and compiling the book.

Resolved, That the President of this society, Hon. P. Breckenridge, is hereby requested to appoint two old settlers of this county, who reside in Springfield, to act with himself, the three to form the committee to point out sources of information to Mr. Power, and examine his manuscript, for the purpose of correcting all errors before publication.

Resolved, That for the purposes of this book, all persons are considered old settlers, who were citizens of Sangamon county previous to December 31, 1840.

Mr. Breckenridge appointed Noah W. Matheny and Judge N. M. Broadwell as his colleagues so that the committee is composed of Hon. P. Breckenridge, Hon. N. W. Matheny, and Hon. N. W. Broadwell.

The Old Settlers' Society by this action did all that was necessary to place the subject in its true light before the public, but the undertaking was one involving so much time, labor and money, that nearly two months elapsed before I decided to go on with the work, when the following was added, and the canvassing commenced:

With the view of rendering the book of general interest to all the citizens, I shall make the history of the county as full as possible, to the date given in the third resolution. In this history all old settlers will be incidentally mentioned, but for those who take sufficient interest in it to subscribe for one or more copies of the book, a concisely written biographical sketch will be given of themselves and families. The order of arrangement will be, first, the history, then the biographical sketches.

At a meeting of the Old Settlers' Society in Springfield, August 22, 1874, for the purpose of agreeing on the time and place of holding the next annual festival, and for the transaction of any other business that might come before it, the following report of special committee was read, and on motion ordered to be included as part of the proceedings of the meeting:

GENTLNMEN:—We, the undersigned, committee appointed by your honorable body two years ago this day, to co-operate with Mr. J. C. Power, and so far as necessary, direct his movements in preparing a history of the old settlers of Sangamon county, beg leave to report that we have examined his work, and find that he has canvassed the whole county outside of Springfield, and that we are highly pleased with the progress made. Mr. Power has collected a much greater quantity of material than we had expected; and the work, when completed, we believe will be a source of much pleasure to the surviving Old Settlers, and of increasing interest to their descendents in all coming time. He is more than redeeming every promise made at the commencement, and it will amply repay all the patrons of the work to wait with patience the few months longer that will be necessary to complete it.

In view of the fact that there is such a vast fund of interesting information, we have advised Mr. Power that if there be any families of old settlers who do not take sufficient interest in the subject to aid by their subscription in carrying forward the work, that he omit any extended sketches of them, in order to devote more space to historical matters of general interest.

PRESTON BRECKENRIDGE,
N. W. MATHENY,
N. M. BROADWELL.

My time was fully occupied for nearly two years in writing up and arranging the materials in my hands, and incorporating additional matter constantly coming in. This brought us to our "Centennial" year, and the following Joint Resolution was passed by the Senate and House of Representatives of the United States, and approved by the President, U. S. Grant, March 13, 1876:

Be it resolved by the Senate and House of Reprvsentatives of the United States of America, in Congress assembled, That it be, and is hereby recommended by the Senate and House of Representatives to the people of the several States that they assemble in their several counties or towns on the approaching centennial anniversary of our national independence, and that they cause to have delivered on such a day an historical sketch of said county or town from its formation, and that a copy of said sketch may be filed, in print or manuscript, in the Clerk's office of said county, and an additional copy, in print or manuscript, be filed in the office of the Librarian of Congress, to the intent that a complete record may thus be obtained of the progress of our institutions during the first centennial of their existence.

Hon. J. L. Beveridge, Governor of Illinois, issued a proclamation April 25, 1876, recommending to the people in every county and town in the State, that they take measures to carry out the recommendations of the Joint Resolution of Congress. The following correspondence was in compliance with the recommendations:

MR. J. C. POWER:

Sir:—As Congress has, by joint resolution, recommended to the people of the several States, that they cause to be prepared and preserved in a certain manner, histories of the different places, "to the intent that a complete record may thus be obtained of the progress of our institutions during the first centennial of our existence;" and as the Governor of Illinois has, by proclamation, called upon the people of this State to prepare such record, we, as Advisory Committee of the "Old Settlers' Society," of Sangamon county, in the absence of any action on this subject by the city or county authorities, suggest that your "History of Sangamon County" be supplied by you in compliance with the requirements of the resolution of Congress, as the Centennial record.

Having examined two hundred and fifty pages of the advance sheets of your work, it appears to fill the requirements both as to Sangamon county and the city of Springfield, and is more complete and full than any similar work could be, if gotten up and prepared in the brief time yet remaining for such business.

NOAH W. MATHENY,
N. M. BROADWELL,
PRESTON BRECKENRIDGE.

Springfield, Ill., May 8, 1876.

On behalf of the officers of Sangamon county we heartily concur in the foregoing suggestions, believing that the object desired will be completely attained thereby.

JAMES H. MATHENY, County Judge.

JOHN J. HARDIN, County Clerk.

Messrs. Matheny, Broadwell, Breckenridge, Matheny and Hardin:

Your note of the 8th instant is before me. In reply, I would say that my work of nearly four years' incessant toil on the history of the Early Settlers of Sangamon County is drawing to a close. I very willingly acquiesce in your suggestion that it be adopted as the "Centennial record." It is passing through the press as rapidly as possible; two hundred and fifty of the six or seven hundred pages are already printed. It may not be entirely finished by the arrival of the Centennial anniversary, but when completed I will have copies bound in the most durable manner, and deposited at the places designated in the joint resolution of Congress, with special reference to the pleasure it may afford your descendents in perusing its pages at our second Centennial anniversary.

Respectfully yours,
J. C. POWER.

Springfield, Ills., May 9, 1876.

SPRINGFIELD, ILL., Dec. 21, 1876.

J. C. POWER, ESQ.:

Sir:—Having given your book entitled, "History of the Early Settlers of Sangamon County, Illinois," a somewhat careful examination, we are free to say that it more than fulfills the promises made by you in undertaking the execution of the work.

N. M. BROADWELL,
N. W. MATHENY, } Committee.
PRESTON BRECKENRIDGE,

ADDITIONS, OMISSIONS AND CORRECTIONS.

ABEL, ROSWELL, Sen., His wife, Mrs. Elizabeth Abel, died Aug. 9, 1876, in Rochester, Ill.

ALEXANDER, JOHN S., See his name, page 77. His son WILLIAM, died Aug. 21, 1876, at Williamsville, Ill., and was buried at Oak Ridge Cemetery, Springfield.

AMOS, Mrs. SARAH See her name, page 81. The name of her son, Judge Samuel K. Swingley, is there erroneously spelled Swinley.

ANDERSON, Gen. MOSES K. See his name, page 82. His son, WILLIAM WILKES, was married Aug. 14, 1876, near Hillsboro, Fleming county, Ky., to Emma L. Jones, a native of that county. He continues his studies at Transylvania University, Lexington, Kentucky.

BEAM, JACOB H. See his name, page 105. He died Dec. 1, 1876.

BENNETT, Rev. WILLIAM T. See page 111. His daughter, REBIE H., was married June 6, 1876, to Geo. W. Freto, and resides in Mechanicsburg, Illinois.

BRADLEY, WILLIAM, was born in 1786, in Green county, Ky., and was married there Sept. 20, 1810, to Elizabeth Crowder. They moved to Sangamon county, arriving September, 1831, in what is now Ball township, bringing eight children, and had three born there. Of their children, the eldest—

MARY, born Aug. 4, 1810, in Green county, Ky., was married there to Jacob Greenawalt. See his name, page 339. He died and she was married Oct. 29, 1863, to Michael Fay, as his third wife. He was born July 18, 1824, in Baden, Germany, and was brought by his parents to Sangamon county, in 1831. Mr. and Mrs. Fay reside in Cotton Hill township, southwest of New City, Sangamon county, Ill. Mrs. Fay is the only one of her father's family living in the county.

William Bradley died Dec. 20, 1849, in Sangamon county. His widow lives with her son, Thomas, near Owaneco, Christian county, Illinois—1874.

BROWN, ROBERT T., See his name, page 150. His daughter, MARGERY I., was married Sept. 6, 1876, to Thomas S. Sawyer, and lives near Cantrall, Illinois.

BULLARD, WESLEY. See his name, page 158. His son, JAMES R., born Oct. 10, 1846, died July 16, 1876, in Mechanicsburg, Illinois. His son, JOHN N., was married May 10, 1876, in Springfield, to Lillie May Pinckard, daughter of Thomas Pinckard, of the State Journal office.

CALLERMAN, EVAN H., page 169. He died September, 1876, in Williamsville, Illinois.

CANTRALL, JULIA, was married June 17, 1876, in Buffalo, Ill., to William Campbell.

CANTRALL, ZEBULON P., died April 24, 1876, at Chesnut, Illinois.

CLAYTON, JOHN C., was born March 10, 1810, in Caldwell county, Ky. He came to Sangamon county in 1829, with his cousin and brother-in-law, John S. Clayton. See his name, page 205. John C. Clayton was married Jan. 24, 1830, in Beardstown, Illinois, to Ginsey (Jane) Clack, who was born March 17, 1815, in Caldwell county, Ky., also. They had four children who lived to maturity. Mr. Clayton was a soldier in a company from Sangamon county, in the Black Hawk War of 1832. Early in 1856, he moved his family to the vicinity of Urbana, Champaign county, Illinois. Of their four children—

HUMBERT, born August 17, 1839, in Alton, Madison county, Ill., brought up in Sangamon county, married April 14, 1867, in Decatur, Illinois, to Marietta Fry. They reside near Chatham, Sangamon county, Illinois.

ELIAS W., born Oct. 6, 1843, in Sangamon county. In the war to suppress the rebellion, he became first lieutenant of Co. B, 3d Mo. Cav., and was killed in battle at Little Rock, Arkansas, in 1864.

JOHN HARDIN, born June 16, 1847, in Sangamon county, brought up in Champaign county, Illinois, and married at Neosho, Newton county, Missouri, May 7, 1875, to Justie E. Webster, who was born Nov. 19, 1854, at Pleasant Hill, Cass county, Missouri. She is a graduate of Central Female College, Lexington, Missouri. Since 1874, J. H. Clayton has been a member of the mercantile firm of Whitsitt & Clayton, and resides at Nevada, Missouri.

ANNA E., born May 26, 1851, in Sangamon county, brought up in Champaign county, Illinois, and in 1868 went to make her home with an uncle in Missouri. She was married Sept. 21, 1871, to C. E. Whitsitt. They have one child, LENA A. He is a member of the mercantile firm of Whitsitt & Clayton, and resides at Nevada, Vernon county, Missouri.

John C. Clayton died April 7, 1856, near Urbana, Illinois. Mrs. Clayton was married June 2, 1859, to William Craig. She died Dec. 18, 1868.

CONSTANT, JONATHAN. His son, LEWIS A., was married Dec. 17, 1875, to Augusta J. Elder, and lives in Springfield, Illinois.

CONSTANT, THOMAS, was born August 14, 1776, erroneously printed 1796, on page 219.

DARNEILLE, JAMES W. See page 242. He moved from Chicago to Belvidere, Illinois, where his wife, Mrs. Belle Moulton Darneille, died in November, 1876.

CULLOM, SHELBY M. See his name, page 298. He was elected Governor of the State of Illinois Nov. 7, 1876, and will be inaugurated Jan. 3, 1877.

DIXON, JAMES M. See page 252. His daughter—

HESTER D., married Thomas Stoker. They moved from Buffalo to the vicinity of Illiopolis, Illinois. His son—

RICHARD Dixon, was married May 6, 1874, to Elizabeth E. Logan. They have one son, and reside near Mechanicsburg, Sangamon county, Illinois.

DODDS, F. EWING. See page 225. His daughter, Virginia E., was married Nov. 15, 1876, to Ninian E. Kenney.

DRENNAN, WILLIAM. See his name, page 264. He died Sept. 28, 1876. He had been for several years, and was at the time of his death, the oldest citizen of Sangamon county. His funeral sermon was preached by Rev. J. C. Van Patten, from Psalms 23-4: "Yea though I walk through the valley of the shadow of death, I will fear no evil; for Thou art with me; Thy rod and Thy staff they comfort me."

ELKIN, GARRETT. See page 282. His son, CHARLES N., born April 12, 1846, near Springfield, Illinois, enlisted May, 1864, for one hundred days, in Co. K, 133d Ill. inf., and served full term. In June, 1865, he enlisted for one year in Co. E, 154th Ill. Inf., and served full term. He was married May 16, 1867, to Harriet Regin, who died Jan. 16, 1873. He was married Sept. 1, 1874, to Ella Welsh. He is conductor on the Springfield City Railway, and lives in Springfield, Illinois. EDWARD S. was with his brother, Charles N., in the three months service, and after that served two years in Co. A, 10th Ill. Cav. He married Mary A. Brown, has one child, LEE, and lives in Springfield, Illinois.

ELLIOTT, TEMPLE, was elected Nov. 7, 1876, sheriff of Sangamon county for two years. See page 285.

FERGUSON, Mrs. LUCY. See her name, page 295. Her son, WILLIAM H., left four children. J. H., ELLEN, WILLIAM and MARTHA, now living near Decatur, Illinois. Her daughter, LUCY C., born in 1809, in Culpepper county, Virginia, married there in 1831 to Rev. Isaac Haines, of the M. E. Church, who was born in 1806, in Rappahannock county, Virginia. They lived a short time in North Carolina, returned to Virginia, and from there to Sangamon county in 1836. They had two children, WILLIAM C., born Sept. 21, 1832, in Wilmington, North Carolina, brought up in Sangamon county, married Dec. 14, 1859, in Christian county, Illinois, to Lucy E. Young, who was born Jan. 12, 1840. She died Dec. 16, 1865, leaving one child, DORA E. William C. Haines was married Jan. 1, 1866, in Missouri, to Margaret Hancock, who was born in 1846, in Henderson county, Kentucky. They have two children, LUCY R. and WILLIAM C., jun., and reside near Taylor-

—3

ville, Illinois. LUCY A. Haines, born in 1835, in Albemarle county, Virginia, married in 1854 in Taylorville, Illinois, to J. V. Clark. They have one child, MARY A. In 1859 they moved to Charleston, Missouri, and now reside in Mississippi county, opposite Cairo, Illinois. Rev. Isaac Haines died in 1838, near Rochester, Sangamon county, Illinois, and Mrs. Lucy C. Haines died August, 1850, near Taylorville, Illinois. PHILIP C. Ferguson's son, EZEKIEL, born August 5, 1839, in Sangamon county, married January, 1869, to Hester Kelly. They have two children, PHILIP C. and HIRAM R., and live near Taylorville, Illinois, Dr. Philip C. Ferguson died Feb. 28, 1864. His widow and four children, the eldest of whom is THOMAS J., reside near Wathena, Doniphan county, Kansas.

FORTUNE, THOMAS E. See his name, page 306. His daughter, ELIZABETH, J. B., married Samuel Odor Butts, who was born in February, 1809, and died August 26, 1840, leaving three children. JULIA F. was married in 1852 to Isaac Allen, have four children, JESSIE, BENJAMIN, CHARLES and HERMAN, and live in Jacksonville, Illinois. ANNA E. married Josiah Burrows, have three living children, ALBERT S., E. LEE, and HELEN G., and live near Jacksonville, Illinois. THOMAS S. lives in Colorado. Mrs. E. J. B. Butts married Barnabas Barrows. They had one child, CHARLES, born Jan. 3, 1854, near Jacksonville. Barnabas Burrows died May 18, 1876, and his widow and son reside near Jacksonville, Illinois.

FOSTER, JOHN S. See page 307. His wife's maiden name is erroneously spelled. It should be Eliza A. Corson.

FOSTER, THOS. VEATCH, was born Sept. 25, 1788, in Harrison county, Kentucky. He was a brother to Ivins Foster. See page 309. Thomas V. Foster was twice married and had four children who lived to maturity by each marriage. He moved to Sangamon county, Illinois, in 1826, and settled seven miles southwest of Springfield, where he died of cholera November 15, 1832. His youngest child by the first marriage, THOMAS VEATCH FOSTER, Jun., was born July 29, 1821, in Harrison county, Kentucky, was married June 24, 1847, in Sangamon county, to Polly E., daughter of Augustine E. Foster, a younger brother of Ivins Foster. Two years later Thomas V. Foster, Jun., and wife moved to the vicinity of Elkhart, Logan county, Illinois. They had five children. Their second child, WILLIAM A. Foster, born June 27, 1849, in Sangamon county, Illinois, five miles west of Chatham, and brought up in Logan county. He took a three years literary course in the Illinois Wesleyan University at Bloomington, and graduated Feb. 10, 1876, at the Hahnemann Medical College, Chicago. He is now—December, 1876—a druggist in Springfield, Illinois.

FOUTCH, JOHN, was elected Nov. 7, 1876, to represent Sangamon county for two years in the Legislature of Illinois. He resides at New Berlin. Page 310.

GALT, THOMAS, was born Sept. 12, 1805, in Lancaster county, Pennsylvania. He received his literary education at Jefferson college, Canonsburg, Penn., and his theological education at the Presbyterian Theological Seminary at Allegheny City, Penn. He was licensed to preach June 18, 1834, by the Presbytery of Ohio. He was married Oct. 6, 1834, in Washington county, Penn., to Sarah Happer, who was born in that county Sept. 11, 1809. They moved west in the spring of 1835, and after spending a few months in Peoria, came to Springfield in the autumn of that year. Rev. Dr. John G. Bergen introduced Rev. Mr. Galt to the Farmington Presbyterian church, of which he soon after became pastor. Mr. and Mrs. Galt had four living children, namely—

JAMES J., born Sept. 28, 1835, in Sangamon county, was married October, 1857, to Mary A. Brown. They have eight children, and live near Palmyra, Nebraska.

JOHN, born Nov. 30, 1838, in Sangamon county, married Feb. 11, 1862, to Margaret A. Epler, who was born July 30, 1841, in Morgan county, Illinois. They had six children, MARTIN E. died young, WILLIAM A., CHARLES E., ANNABEL, CARRIE and LILLIE live with their parents. John Galt and family resides at the family homestead where his parents settled in 1835, and where he was born. It is one mile east of Farmingdale, Sangamon county, Illinois.

MARTIN H., born Sept. 9, 1841, in Sangamon county, married Nov. 19, 1865, to Clara Spillman. They have three living children, and live near Manti, Fremont county, Iowa.

THOMAS, Jun., born July 10, 1844, in Sangamon county. He was married August, 1869, at Otisville, New York, to Jennie McFarlane. They have three children. Rev. Thomas Galt, Jun., is pastor of the First Presbyterian church of Aurora, Illinois, and resides there.

Mrs. Sarah Galt died Jan. 25, 1849, near Farmingdale, and Rev. Thomas Galt, Sen., married Margaret S. Moore. They had one living child.

ELIHU L., born Feb. 13, 1856, in Sangamon county, married April 9, 1872, in Petersburg, Illinois, to Lou Bergen. They have one child, and reside in Petersburg.

Rev. Thomas Galt, Sen., died Sept. 12, 1857, near Farmingdale, Sangamon county, Illinois. Mrs. Margaret S. Galt resides in Petersburg, Menard county, Ill.

GARRETSON, THOMAS P. See his name, page 324. He was born Sept. 18, 1818, in Anne Arundel county, Maryland, came in 1839 to Sangamon county, was married July 2, 1845, in Menard county, Illinois, to Martha M. Harrison, a native of Kentucky. They had two children, both of whom died in infancy, and Mrs. Garretson died April 26, 1848, in Springfield. He was married Feb. 22, 1854, in Menard county to Phebe Campbell, who was born April 26, 1831, in Butler county, Ohio. They had ten children. The three eldest, VINCENT, AMANDA and ALBERT died of scarlet fever from the 24th to the 28th of September, 1858. The other seven, CORNELIUS, BEAUREGARD, LOURENA MAY, JAMES T., SARAH J., WILLIAM L. and ANNETTA, live with their parents. Thomas P. Garretson is a carpenter by trade, and was working within six feet of the Winchester House, on the steeple of the First Presbyterian church in Springfield, in 1842, when Mr. House was thrown from the steeple by lightning and killed. Mr. Garretson and family reside ten miles west of Lincoln, Logan county, Illinois.

GREENING, ZACHARY T. See page 339. His wife, Mrs. Mary Greening, died in February, 1876.

HAINES, CHRISTOPHER. His son, FRANCIS A., was born March 22, 1832, in Sangamon county. In 1852 he went overland to the Pacific coast, and in 1856 and '7 was a volunteer soldier against the Indians in the north of Oregon. In November, 1858, he started for Illinois, arriving in Springfield January 1st, and was married in Bureau county Jan. 17, 1859, to Zerelda G. Britt. They had two children, ELLA BELLE and MINNIE, both died young. Mr. Haines enlisted Jan. 13, 1864, in Co. C, 2d Ill. Artillery, served to the end of the rebellion, and was mustered out with the regiment Aug. 3, 1865. He and his wife reside at New City, Sangamon county, Illinois.

HAND, ELIAS, was born about 1770, in Cape May county, New Jersey. He was married there to Miss Sayre. They had four children in New Jersey, and moved to Sangamon county, arriving May 30, 1838, in what is now Gardner township. Of their children—

DANIEL died, aged thirty years.

MARIA married John Robinson, and lives in Minnesota.

JESSE married Mary Hagin, and lives in New Jersey.

ELIZABETH, born in New Jersey, married in Sangamon county to Franklin Bradley. They had one son, FRANK, who is a minister in the M. E. Church, and in 1873 lived in Davisville, Michigan. Franklin Bradley died Sept. 14, 1845, and his widow married John G. Ransom. See his name.

Elias Hand died November, 1856, and his widow died in 1869, aged eighty-seven years.

HARBUR, LEVI. See page 354. He died Nov. 27, 1876.

HARDIN, JAMES T. Page 356. His son, Benjamin, was married August 2, 1876.

HARROWER, WILLIAM. Page 360. His daughter, AGNES E., widow of Dr. James B. Smith, died Nov. 5, 1876, in Springfield, Illinois.

HEDRICK, ALFRED, was born near Greenville, Tennessee, came with his father, Charles Hedrick, to Sangamon county among the early settlers. Alfred Hedrick lives in Taylorville, Ill., Of his two sons—

WILLIAM, born Jan. 25, 1844, in Sangamon county, married April 8, 1865, to Martha M. Kimball, who was born Jan. 18, 1844, in Vermont. They now—1874—have four children, MARION C., NATHAN K., ALFRED C., and ROBERT A., and live four miles south of Rochester, Illinois.

HENRY R., born Feb. 25, 1848, in Sangamon county, married Dec. 30, 1869, to Laura J. Johnson, has two children and lives four miles south of Rochester, Illinois.

HEDRICK, JONATHAN, born in Kentucky, and married there to Julian Holland, a native of Maryland. They had two children in Fleming county, Ky., and moved to Sangamon county, Illinois, arriving in the fall of 1830, at Buffalo Hart grove, thence to what is now Clear Lake township, where they had four children. Of their six children—

REBECCA, born Oct. 8, 1828 in Fleming county, Ky., was married Oct. 16, 1847, to Joshua Cantrall. See his name.

ROSETTA, born in Fleming county, Ky., married in Sangamon county to Abner Clark. She died, leaving a son, WILLIAM Clark.

BARTON, died, aged twenty-five years.

NARCISSA, married McDonald Cantrall. See his name.

FLEMING, died aged fifteen years.

MUNSON, born in Sangamon county, enlisted in 1862, for three years in Co. C, 114th Ill. Inf., and died at Vicksburg, a short time after it was captured in 1863.

Jonathan Hedrick and wife reside in Athens, Illinois.

HICKMAN, GEORGE T. His son, WILLIAM H., enlisted Aug. 5, 1862, in Co. B, 130th Ill. Inf., and died Jan. 19, 1863. Another son, JAMES F., married Sophia C. Burns, and lives near Buffalo Hart, Sangamon county, Illinois—1876.

HOUGHTON, ALVIN, born June 12, 1810, in Madison, Somerset county, Maine, was married Sept. 6, 1835, at Skowhegan Falls, Maine, to Betsy Hilton, who was born June 17, 1815, at Anson, Maine. Alvin Houghton came to Springfield, Illinois, in June, 1837, and brought his wife in the spring of 1840. He was a carpenter by trade, and worked at that business for about twelve years, after which he kept a dairy until 1851, when he moved twenty miles east of Springfield, on a farm, and remained there until the fall of 1869, and then moved to Washington county, Kansas.

Alvin Houghton and wife had five children—

AMELIA, died in her second year.

ERVIN, O., born Dec. 14, 1841, in Springfield, Ill., was married Sept. 13, 1866, in Sangamon county to Sarah Jane Wall, who was born Feb. 6, 1842, in Allegany county, Pennsylvania. They have two children, LAURA E. and LILLIAN, and live four and a half miles northeast of Illiopolis, Illinois.

AUSTIN E., born May 29, 1844, in Illinois. Lives with his parents.

CLIMENA B., died in her second year.

AVILLIA B., born Jan. 1, 1853, lives with her parents, near Butler, Washington county, Kansas.

HUDSON, JOHN. See his name, page 385. His son, JOHN M., died Oct. 12, 1876. His son, ANDREW J., having been married fourteen years, has an only child, MARGARET MARIA, born Feb. 11, 1876.

ILES, ELIJAH, Sen. His wife, Mrs. Melinda Iles, died in May, 1866.

INSLEE, JOSEPH. His son—NEWTON JASPER, born Dec. 31, 1832, in Sangamon county, married May 16, 1852, to Eliza A. Keys. They had five children. ANN E., died in her second year. EMMA J., MARY L., MELISSA and JOSEPH W.; the four latter live with their parents near Cotton Hill postoffice, Sangamon county, Ill.

JAYNE, Dr. GERSHOM, page 406. His daughter, JULIA M., married Hon. Lyman Trumbull. Their son, Walter Trumbull, was married Sept. 27, 1876, in Chicago, to Hannah M. Slater.

JOHNSTON, ADAM, was born April 14, 1816, in Glasgow, Scotland. When he was four days old his parents embarked on board a vessel, and after a short stay at Belfast, Ireland, sailed for America, landing during the summer of that year in Philadelphia, Penn. He was brought up in that city and learned the business of a marble mason. During that time he assisted in building Girard College. He went in 1837, to Jefferson city,

Missouri, and after filling a contract on the State House, then in course of construction there, he came to Springfield, in the spring of 1839, and worked as a journeyman on the State House of Illinois. Mr. Johnson was married July 3, 1846 to Barbara A. Wolgamot. He has been continuously and successfully in business in Springfield, nearly thirty-eight years. Adam Johnson and wife now—December, 1876—reside in Springfield, Illinois.

JOHNSON, LUE. See his name, page 413. His son, ORSON D., born April 23, 1827, in Vermont, was married in Rochester, Sangamon county, Ill., to Lydia Eggleston. They have four living children, ELLEN, born Sept. 16, 1848, in Rochester, was married in Mount Pulaski, April 16, 1865 to Aaron G. Green, and have four children, FLORA, LUE, GEORGE, and MINDRED, and live in Mt. Pulaski, Illinois. OLLIE, born Aug. 6, 1851, in Rochester, Ill., was married in Mt. Pulaski, Jan. 6, 1868, to Walter McGraw, and died April 30, 1874, leaving one child, RALPH. BETTIE, born July 6, 1858, and WILLIAM, born Dec. 11, 1861, both in Mt. Pulaski. Orson, D. Johnson and family, live in Mt. Pulaski, Logan county, Illinois.

JONES, HASKINS, was born in Maryland, and married in Jefferson county, Tenn., to Lucy Tolley, and came to Sangamon county, in 1835, settling in Sand Prairie, five miles east of Rochester. They had thirteen children—

JOHN F., married Lucinda Pike and died, leaving one child, CHARLES T.

ELIZABETH, married John L. Firey. See his name.

DAVID C, married Ann Griffith and lives near Breckenridge, Ill.

NANCY, married James Campbell, and lives in Edinburg, Ill.

MARY P., married John B. Eaton. See his name.

CARTER T., born Aug. 17, 1834, in Jefferson county, Tenn., married in Sangamon county, April 23, 1863, to Theresa Talbert, has four children, FANNY, LUCY, BETTY and CARTER T., Jun., and lives four miles south of Rochester, Illinois.

HASKINS, Jun., married Lettie Sweet, who died, and he married again, and lives near Breckenridge, Illinois.

LUCY J., married John H. Martin, and lives near Taylorville, Illinois.

PRISCILLA, married Thomas Stokes. See his name. He died and she married James Lay, and lives in Kansas.

Haskins Jones died in 1842, and his widow died April, 1873, he in Sangamon, and she in Christian county, Illinois.

KENNEY, NINIAN E. See page 425. He was married Nov. 15, 1876, to Virginia E. Dodds, daughter of F. Ewing Dodds. See his name, page 255.

KEYS, ISAAC, Jun. See page 426. His son, EDWARD D., was married Oct. 10, 1876, to Lulie Todd, in Springfield, Illinois. His daughter, ANNIE E., was married Dec. 7, 1876, in Springfield, to Alvin B. Hoblet, of Pekin, Ill. Mr. Hoblet is cashier of the Farmers' National Bank of that city.

KEYES, CHARLES A. See page 427. His infant daughter, ELIZABETH M., died July 18, 1876.

LAMB, SUSAN M. See page 435. Her daughter, Hannah M. Slater, was married Sept. 27, 1876, in Chicago, to Walter Trumbull.

LANTERMAN, PETER. Page 443. He died Oct. 9, 1876, near Elkhart, Illinois.

LINCOLN, ABRAHAM. Page 456. An attempt was made on the night after the Presidential election, Nov. 7, 1876, to steal his body from the sarcophagus, in the National Lincoln Monument. The thieves were detected in the act but escaped. Two men are under arrest charged with the crime, and are now—December, 1876—in jail at Springfield, awaiting trial. Their reputed object was to secure a large reward in money, and the release of an engraver, who is serving a ten years term in the Illinois Penitentiary, for engraving and issuing counterfeit money.

LINDSAY, JOHN, was born in 1773 at Fort Pitt, now Pittsburgh, Penn. He was taken by his parents to Fleming county, Kentucky. He was married there in the year 1800 to Mary Glass. She died January, 1811, leaving five children, and Mr. Lindsay was married there in September, 1811. They had one child in Kentucky, and moved in 1817 to St. Clair county, Illinois, where they had one child, and moved to what is now Sangamon county in 1819, settling in what is now the western part of Springfield. Of his children—

REBECCA, born September, 1802, in Kentucky, married in Sangamon county to Andrew Orr, and died within one year.

POLLY, born September, 1804, in Kentucky, married James Smith, and died there, leaving one child, AMANDA.

DAVID H., born February, 1807, in Fleming county, Kentucky, married in 1832, in Sangamon county to Mary A. Dorrance. They had four children, MARY S., born March, 1833, died Jan. 6, 1869, in Shelby county, Illinois. MARGARET A., born March, 1836, married B. F. Sinard. She died, leaving a son, MILTON SINARD, who lives in Mt. Auburn, Illinois. MARQUIS D., born March 23, 1839, enlisted August 9, 1861, for three years, in Co. B, 30th Ill. Inf., served full term, and was honorably discharged Aug. 27, 1864. He was married in Sangamon county Oct. 31, 1866, to Margaret Kinney, who was born April 6, 1839, in Cazenovia, New York. They had two children. LOGAN L. lives with his parents. IDA MAY died in her fourth year. M. D. Lindsay lives near Loami, Illinois. MARTHA, born March, 1842, married Daniel Young. Mrs. Mary A. Lindsay died in 1846, while her husband was in Mexico. David H. Lindsay was a soldier in the 4th Ill. Inf., under Colonel E. D. Baker. He served one year from June, 1846, returned home and died in 1847, of disease contracted in the army.

GEORGE G., born November, 1808, in Kentucky, married in Sangamon county to Margaret Ward, and died there, leaving one child, JAMES.

AMANDA L., born December, 1810, in Kentucky, married in Sangamon county to John Morgan, and died, leaving four children, ELIZABETH, SALLY ANN, JOHN W. and SOPHIA S.

By the second wife:

JOHN P., born July, 1814, in Fleming county, Kentucky, married in Sangamon county in 1839, to Virginia B. Young. They had six children in Sangamon county. MARY J., born July 22, 1840, married Seth Moore, and lives in Lawndale, Illinois. MELISSA G., born Dec. 23, 1841, married Charlie E. Morton, and lives near Centerville, Iowa. James N., born July 30, 1842, is unmarried, and lives in Centerville, Iowa. ELIZABETH born Feb. 15, 1846, died aged seven years. ELIZA ANN, born Sept. 15, 1848, married William A. Smith, and lives in Colfax county, Nebraska. JOHN W., born March 22, 1850, is unmarried, and lives Russell county, Kansas. Mrs. Virginia B. Lindsay died May 2, 1850, in Sangamon county, and J. P. Lindsay married Eliza A. McCandless, and in 1853 moved to Logan county, where they had six living children. SOPHIA BELLE, FLORENCE P., ALMA M., CHARLES E. and WINNIE M. John P. Lindsay resides near Lincoln, Logan county, Ill.

ABRAHAM L., born April 10, 1814, in St. Clair county, Illinois, was married in Sangamon county to Ann Wise. They have seven living children. JOHN D. married and lives in Ottawa, Kansas. NANCY J. married B. H. Lake and lives in Mount Pulaski, Illinois. SOPHIA MAY, married N. Elkin, and lives near Elkhart, Illinois. WILLIAM H., EVA E., GEORGE B. and HARRIET C. live near Elkhart, Logan county, Illinois. Mrs. Ann Lindsay died January, 1865, near Elkhart, Illinois, and Abram L. Lindsay now—1876—lives Russell county, Kansas.

LORD, JOSEPH T., was an early settler of Sangamon county. His son, WILLIAM N. Lord, lives near Breckenridge, Sangamon county, Illinois

McCLELLAND, JOHN. His son, Dr. Robert McClelland, was married Sept. 8, 1874, to Susan Turley, near Williamsville, Illinois.

McGINNIS, JOHN J. See his name, page 499. His widow, Mrs. Elizabeth McGinnis, was married in December 1874, to Y. B. Clark, and lives at Clarkdale, Christian county, Illinois.

McGRAW, ABSOLOM D. See his name, page 501. He died in the autumn of 1876 near Springfield, Illinois

McKINNIE, WILLIAM A. Page 504. His wife, Mrs. Emma M. Kinnie, died Nov. 22, 1876.

McMURRY, ARTHUR B. His daughter, MARTHA J., married Robert Elder, and live near Girard, Crawford county, Kansas. His son, LEWIS S. lives near Girard, Crawford county, Kansas

McMURRY, LOGAN. His daughter Mary E., married Hiram F. Robbins, who was born in Warren county, Pennsylvania came to Ogle county, Illinois, enlisted March, 1862, in Co. A, 12th Ill. Cav., for three years, and was honorably discharged March, 1865, went to Maple Grove, Kansas, in May, 1866, and was married there July 26, 1868.

NUCKOLLS, JOHN. See his name, page 548. His widow, Mrs. Ann Nuckolls, died Sept. 30, 1876, aged nearly ninety years.

ORR, ROBERT, was born in Wythe county, Virginia, and was there married to Sarah Messersmith. They moved to Ohio in 1817, to Connersville, Indiana, in 1818, and to Springfield, Illinois, in 1826. They had ten children— *ANDREW, MELINDA; ALEXANDER S.* married Eliza J. Wallace, and lives near Auburn, Illinois. *ELIZABETH, NANCY J.; HIRAM* married Savilla Ranch, and both died. *ROBERT; MARGARET; SAMUEL* married Jane Laswell, and lives near Auburn, Illinois.

Robert Orr and his wife both died near Auburn, Sangamon county, Illinois.

POWER, GEORGE. See his name, page 578. He was awarded the premium of a gold headed cane for the most skillful feat of horseback riding, by an elderly gentleman, at the fair of the Sangamon county Agricultural Society, in September, 1876. He was in his seventy-ninth year, and the eldest of five competitors. The cane was presented in presence of the largest number of visitors during the fair, by the president of the society, ex-Governor John M. Palmer.

PRICKETT, Mrs. CHARLOTTE G. See page 581. She died Nov. 2, 1876, in Springfield.

PURSELL, WILLIAM. See his name, page 590. His daughter, ALICE BELLE, was married Nov. 2, 1876, to William T. Kincaid, near Farmingdale, Sangamon county, Illinois.

RIDGELY, CHARLES, was born Jan. 17, 1836, in Springfield, Illinois. He is the eldest son of N. H. Ridgely—*page 616*—by his second wife, who was the daughter of Jonathan Huntington, and was born in Boston, Mass. Her brother, Hon. George L. Huntington, deceased, was mayor of Springfield in 1861-2. Charles Ridgely entered the preparatory department of Illinois College at Jacksonville, in October, 1849, and in March, 1852, withdrew from the college to accept a position in Clark's Exchange Bank, which was organized at that time in Springfield by his father in connection with some eastern capitalists. June 22, 1853, he became cashier of the bank, which position he occupied until it was wound up, March 29, 1855. His father, N. H. Ridgely, succeeded to the business of Clark's bank, as a private banker. Charles took the place of cashier with him, where he continued until April 1, 1859, when he was admitted into partnership with his father in the banking business; the new firm name being N. H. Ridgely & Co. Charles' brother, William was admitted as a member of the firm April 1, 1864, and its business continued until Oct. 1, 1866, when it was merged into the Ridgely National Bank. Chas. Ridgely became vice president at the organization, and now—December, 1876 —continues to hold that position. In 1871, he was mainly instrumental in organizing the Springfield Iron Company, and building the Rolling Mill at Springfield. He became, and continues to be the President of that company. As a compliment to the President of the company, the new postoffice at the mills bears the name of Ridgely. Charles Ridgely is also a member of the firm of Beard, Hickox & Co., proprietors of the North Coal Shaft. In 1870 he was honored with the nomination of the Democratic party as candidate for the office of state treasurer of Illinois, but the party being in the minority, he, in common with the entire ticket, was defeated. He has served two terms as a member of the Board of Education of the city of Springfield. He was married June 10, 1857, to Jane M., youngest daughter of James W. Barret. She was born in Island Grove, Sangamon county. They have four children; WILLIAM BARRET, EDWARD, FRANKLIN and MARY LEE. Chas. Ridgely, wife and children reside in Springfield, Ill.

SHORT, CALEB. His grandson, JOHN R., died Feb. 24, 1876, in Nodaway county, Missouri.

SMITH, DEWITT C., was elected Nov. 7, 1876, to represent Sangamon county two years in the Legislature of Illinois. He resides at Bates.

SMITH, GEROGE M. See his name, page 666. His son, JACOB H., was marri d, not in Hennepin, but in Washington, Tazewell county, Illinois, to Joanna Higgins, who was born Oct. 26, 1819, in Cumberland county, Kentucky. They have eight children, namely, GEORGE D., was married Sept. 3, 1874, in Missouri, to Mattie Foree, and now lives in Hope, Hempstead county, Ark. MARY J. was married June 21, 1866, in Saline county, Missouri, to Dr. Robert S. McNutt. They have four children, SAMUEL, JOANNA, MARY and ROBERT, and live in Rocheport, Boone county, Missouri. WILLIAM T., born April 28, 1850, in Saline county, Missouri, and now—1876—lives in Berlin, Sangamon county, Illinois. MATILDA J. was married Dec. 2, 1871, to John H. Herring, have one child, WILLIAM S., and reside near Herndon, Saline county, Missouri. ANNA E., ALICE W. and MATTIE F. live with their father, near Marshal, Saline county, Mo. FREDERICK N. lives with his brother, George D., in Arkansas. George M. Smith's son, JOHN W., left five children, namely, AMANDA, married George W. Parrish, and has one child, DAISEY MAY. MARY M. and CARRIE live with their sister, Mrs. Parrish, in Oshkosh, Wisconsin. JOSEPH B. and WILL A. live with their uncle, Fox, in Quincy, Illinois. George M. Smith's daughter, ELSIE A., born Dec. 20, 1830, in Jennings county, Indiana, married in Sangamon county, Illinois, July 4, 1842, to Stephen Butler, who was born Nov. 13, 1815, in Adair county, Kentucky. They have ten children, namely, JOHN, born May 5, 1843, MARY C., born Oct. 8, 1844, in Sangamon county, was married May 7, 1864, to D. A. Russell, and live in Harrrison county, Iowa. H. G., born Sept. 20, 1846, married March 11, 1876, to Ida Willes. MARTHA M., born Feb. 19, 1848, married Dec. 2, 1868, to Alfred H. Fairchilds, and lives in Jefferson county, Iowa. SOPHRONIA, born Feb. 23, 1850; ELIZABETH, born July 1, 1852, in Sangamon county, Illinois. HARRIET, born Sept. 7, 1855; OWEN, born Sept. 16, 1857; BASSETT, born July 16, 1859, and SAMANTHA, born July 7, 1863, the four latter in Jefferson county, Iowa. Stephen Butler and family now—November, 1876—reside near Missouri Valley postoffice, Harrison county, Iowa.

Smith, Lawson H. See *his name, page 108*. He died Dec. 12, 1876, near Rochester, Illinois.

STEPHENSON, JAMES. See *his name, page 684*. He was born July 3, 1872. His son, *WILLIAM C.*, born Oct. 10, 1812. *HANNAH A.*, born Oct. 12, 1814, married Jacob Zwingle. He died Feb. 8, 1876. Their son, WILLIAM M. Zwingle, was married May 25, 1876, to Eliza Graham. *JAMES W.*, born May 20, 1816, moved from Audrain county, Missouri, to Pike county, Illinois. *FINIS E.*, born Sept. 29, 1818. He moved from Chandlerville, Illinois, to Wichita, Kansas. *HARRIET* married William N. Spears. She moved from Lincoln, in 1876, to Tallula, Menard county, Illinois.

THAYER, WILLIAM P. See *his name, page 710*. His daughter, *BERTIE*, was married Nov. 30, 1876, to Lee Hickox, in Springfield, Illinois.

WALLACE, WILLIAM. See *his name, page 747*. His son, BENJAMIN F., moved from Keokuk, Iowa, to Macon, Macon county, Illinois. His daughter, JANE ELIZABETH, married Dr. John F. Sanders. See *his name, page 637*.

WEBSTER, BELA C., was one of the early merchants of Springfield. A sketch of him was expected but had not arrived when this record closed, Dec. 15, 1876.

WHITESIDES, NICHOLAS B. Page 764. His daughter, EMILY C., was married Nov. 21, 1876, to James F. Demmit, of Logan county, Illinois.

WILKISON, CARY, was born in Kentucky, and married there to Nancy Moon. They came to Sangamon county, Illinois, among the early settlers. They had four children. Their son, *REUBEN*, resides in Taylorville, Illinois.

Cary Wilkison died in 1834, and his widow married James Snodgrass, Jun. See *his name, page 671*.

YOCOM, SAMUEL. Page 792. His daughter, REBECCA, married John W. Ham, not Horn. See *his name, page 352*.

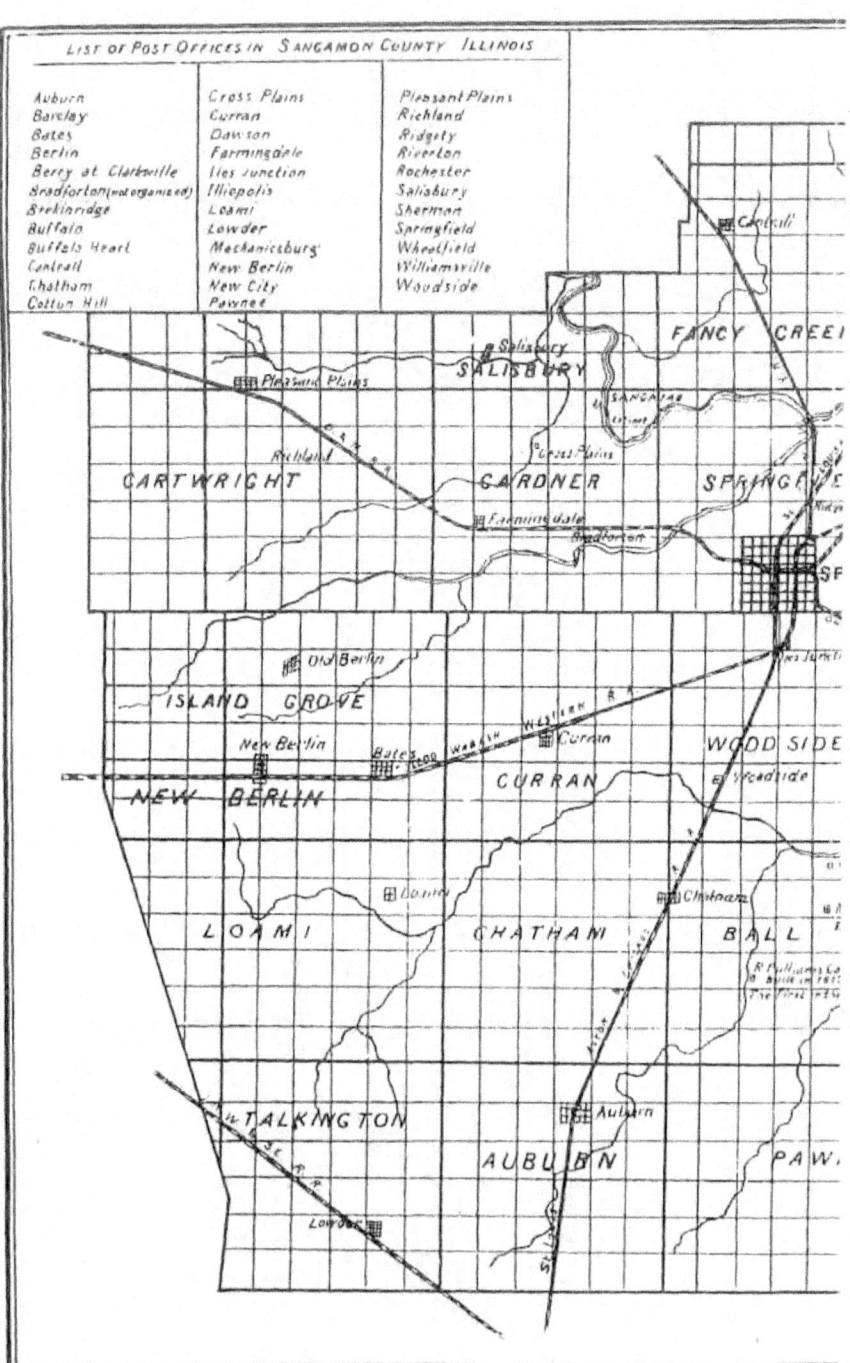

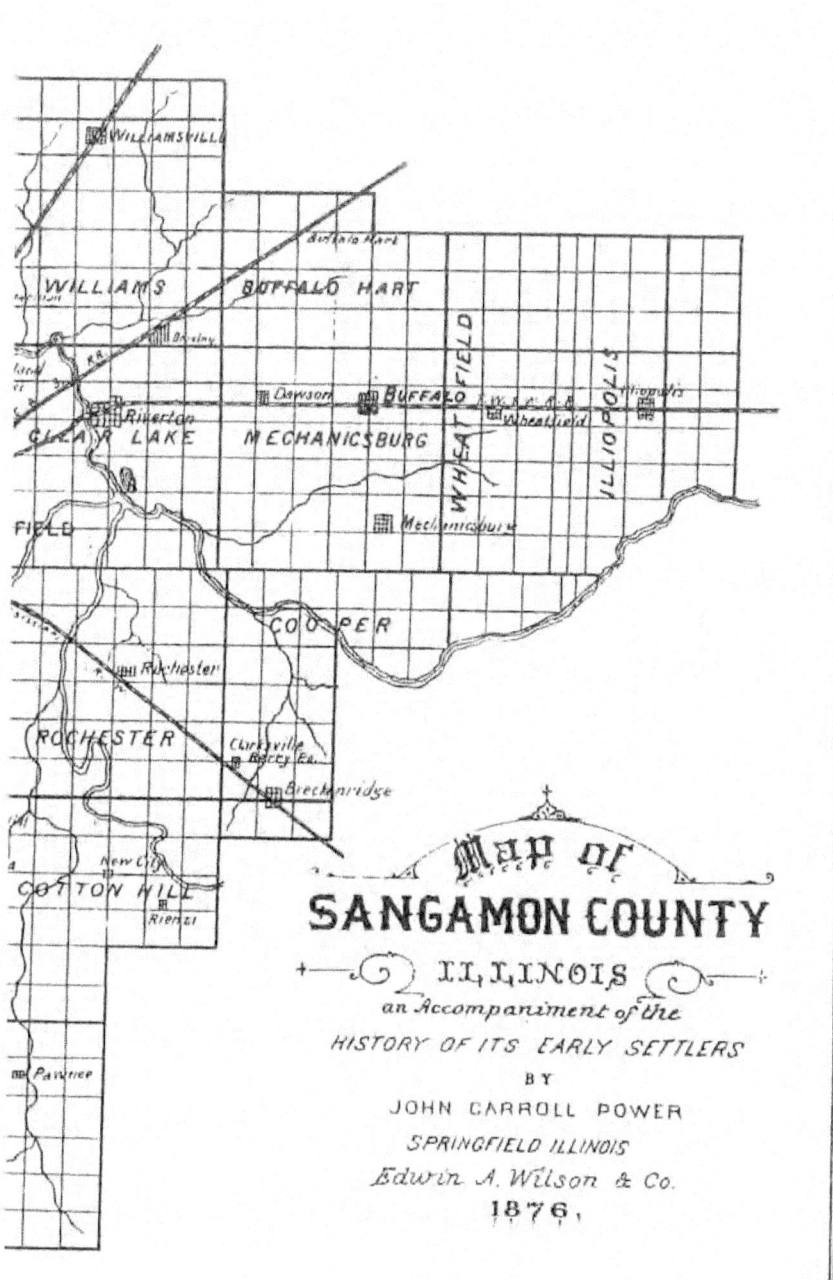

HISTORICAL PRELUDE.

THE first white men who explored the upper Mississippi valley were Jesuit missionaries from New France—now Canada. They visited the southern shores of the great northern lakes, for the purpose of communicating a knowledge of christianity to the aboriginal natives.

Jacques Marquette, a Roman Catholic priest, and Louis Joliet, a merchant from Quebec, with two canoes and five men, left Green Bay and went down the Wisconsin river to the Mississippi, entering the latter stream June 17, 1673. They floated down the "father of waters," making frequent stoppages among the Indians, and passed below the mouth of the Ohio river. Here they found the savages disposed to be hostile, which caused them to return. On approaching the mouth of the Illinois river, on their way up, they were told by the aborigines, that if they would follow the course of that stream their route to the lakes would be much shorter. Accepting this advice, the party reached Lake Michigan, at a point where Chicago now stands. Other Frenchmen came by the way of Canada and the lakes, and in a few years all this region of country was considered a part of New France. The French being entitled to it by right of discovery, their possession was undisputed for about ninety years.

Difficulties arising between France and England, at home, the British government sent an army of one thousand regular soldiers under Gen. Edward Braddock, to make war against the French and their native allies in the new world. General Braddock landed at Alexandria, Virginia, and after increasing his army to twenty-two hundred men, by the addition of provincials, or citizens of the country, he marched to attack Fort DuQuesne, where Pittsburgh now stands. Colonel George Washington, who was well acquainted with the Indian character, accompanied the expedition as a volunteer aid. General Braddock refused the counsels of Colonel Washington, and the result was the surprise and defeat of his whole army by the French and Indians. The commander was slain in the engagement, which took place July 9, 1755.

In 1758 the English government sent another army, which was more successful. It took Fort Duquesne, and the war raged until 1763, when the fall of Quebec left the English victorious; and by the treaty which followed, the whole of New France was ceded to Great Britain.

Previous to the year 1673 the upper Mississippi valley was known only to the aborigines or Indians. From the year of its discovery by the explorations of Marquette and Joliet, for more than half a century there was no attempt at organized government. The first effort was made in 1718, when the "Company of the West" was formed in Paris for the government of the New World. In that year the building of Fort DeChartres was commenced, and when completed was occupied as the military headquarters of the French. It was about sixteen miles above Kaskaskia, in the American bottom, three miles from the bluff and three-fourths of a mile from the river. At the time New France was ceded to England, in 1763, Fort DeChartres was occupied by M. St. Ange de Bellerive, as commandant and Governor of the Illinois country. He continued in possession of the fort until 1765, when Captain Sterling, of the forty-second Royal Highlanders, was sent out and took possession of the fort and country, in the name of the British government. He died about three months after his arrival. Fort Chartres continued to be the headquarters of the British until 1772, when part of the fort was destroyed by a great rise of water in the Mississippi river. The English garrison was then removed to Kaskaskia.

In 1763 the population of what is now the State of Illinois, did not exceed three thousand. About one-third left the country upon its change of masters; so that when the English took possession, the entire population, including French, English and negroes, was about two thousand. Speaking of their new seat of government, Rev. John M. Peck says: "In olden time, Kaskaskia was to Illinois what Paris is at this day to France. Both were, at their respective days, the great emporiums of fashion, gayety, and I must say, happiness also. In the year 1721 the Jesuits erected a monastery and college in the village of Kaskaskia, and a few years afterwards it was chartered by the French government. Kaskaskia for many years was the largest town west of the Alleghaney mountains. It was a tolerable place before the existence of Pittsburgh, Cincinnati or New Orleans."

The English government became fairly settled in their occupation of the country wrested from France, and then commenced that series of parliamentary enactments for the taxation of the American colonies, without permitting them to have any voice in her national councils, which led to the revolutionary struggle. Open hostilities commenced at Lexington, Massachusetts, April 19, 1775. Couriers were despatched, on the most fleet-footed horses, and in a very few days the infant colonies were ablaze with excitement, and the call to arms was responded to from Maine to Georgia. The first Congress met in Philadelphia, Sept. 5, 1774, and continued its meetings by successive adjournments, until July 4, 1776, when the American colonies were declared to be free and independent States. The familiar events of the war for independence, followed each other in quick succession, until all parties were engaged in the conflict along the Atlantic coast; but there were British outposts in the west which had until 1778 remained undisturbed. It was known that these posts were depots for supplying the Indians with arms and ammunition, that they might practice deeds of cruelty and murder against the frontier settlers. The general government had not power to command without consent of the States, even the limited resources of the country; but what there was, in the way of soldiers, seemed imperatively demanded on the seaboard. Under these circumstances, Colonel George Rogers Clarke, of Virginia, volunteered to lead an expedition against the British garrison west of the Alleghanies; and the Governor and Council of Virginia took the responsibility of sending him out. Two sets of instructions were given him: One, which was public, was for Col. Clarke to raise seven companies, and proceed west. The secret and real instructions were for him to raise seven companies, of fifty men each, proceed to Kaskaskia, and take and destroy the garrison of Fort Gates at that place; and that the object of the expedition must be kept a profound secret. The instructions were given January 2, 1778, by the Governor at Williamsburg, then the Capital of Virginia. Col. Clarke left Virginia on the fourth of February for Pittsburgh. He took with him twelve hundred pounds in depreciated currency to defray the expenses of the expedition, and raised three companies in Pittsburgh. He procured boats, and with his supplies, arms and ammunition, descended the Ohio river to "Corn Island," opposite the present city of Louisville, Kentucky, where he was met by Captain Bowman, who had gone down through Kentucky to raise a company of men. When all were assembled on the island, Col. Clarke first declared to them that his point of destination was Kaskaskia, in the Illinois country. From Corn Island he descended with his forces to Fort Massac, at the west side of the Ohio river, about forty miles above its junction with the Mississippi. The party left their boats at this point, and marched across the country to Kaskaskia, a distance of one hundred and twenty miles, through an unbroken wilderness.

They arrived within sight of the village on the morning of July 4, 1778. He concealed the main body of his men, and sent out spies to reconnoitre. At night the men were divided into two bodies, one to take the village and the other, Fort Gage. After all was in readiness, with the soldiers drawn up in line on the banks of the Kaskaskia, Col. Clarke delivered a short address to his troops, in which he reminded them that it was the anniversary of the Declaration of Independence, and that they must take the fort and village at all hazards. Fort Gage was a work of considerable strength, mounted with cannon and defended by regular soldiers. So secret had been the movements of the attacking party, and so little were they expected, that they reached the very gates of the fortifications unperceived. In addition to this, they were so fortunate as to get into communication with an American belonging to the fort, who led a detachment of soldiers, under the celebrated Simon Kenton, inside, through a back gate. The first intimation the Governor had of their presence, was by Kenton giving him a shake to arouse him from his slumbers. The conquest was achieved without the shedding of a drop of blood. The mortification of Governor Rocheblave was so great when he found himself a prisoner in the hands of so small a body of raw malitia, without having an opportunity to fire a gun, that he refused to acknowledge any of the courtesies extended to him on account of his official position. The only alternative for Colonel Clarke, was to send him in irons to the Capital of Virginia.

Soon after the capture of Kaskaskia Colonel Clarke communicated the result of his expedition to the Governor, and expressed a desire to have civil government extended over the conquered territory. An act was passed by the law-making powers of Virginia, in October, 1778, to establish the county of Illinois. "It embraced all that part of Virginia west of the Ohio river, and was probably the largest county in the world, exceeding in its dimensions the whole of Great Britain and Ireland." To speak more definitely, the county of Virginia, called Illinois, embraced the territory now included in the States of Ohio, Indiana, Illinois, Wisconsin and Michigan.

After capturing Fort Gates, the next point to be reduced was Fort St. Vincent, now Vincennes, Indiana. This fortification, with Governor Hamilton and seventy-nine men, fell into his hands February 24, 1779.

Until this stage of its history, the Illinois country had been successively under savage, military, and monarchial rulers; but the time for another change was at hand. The first republican Governor of Illinois was no less a personage than the renowned Patrick Henry, the great orator of the American Revolution. He became the Governor of Virginia in 1776, and by re-election continued to hold the office until 1799. The law of Virginia establishing the county of Illinois having been enacted in October, 1788, it was in this way that he became the first republican or democratic Governor of Illinois.

On the twelfth of December, 1788, Governor Henry appointed John Todd civil commandant and Lieutenant Colonel of the new county. He wrote Commandant Todd a lengthy letter of instructions, in which he says: "The grand objects which are disclosed to your countrymen, will prove beneficial or otherwise, according to the nature and abilities of those who are called to direct the affairs of that remote country. * * * One great good expected from holding the Illinois is to overawe the Indians from warring against the settlers on this side of the Ohio." Near the close of his letter, Governor Henry says: "I think it proper for you to send me an express once in the month with a general account of affairs with you, and any particulars you may wish to communicate."

The headquarters of Commandant Todd, or the seat of government for the county, was at Kaskaskia. The stay of Colonel Todd in Illinois was not of long duration. Being under orders to return to Virginia, he made it convenient to visit his family at Lexington, Kentucky, on the way. While at Lexington, news came that the Indians west of the Ohio were crossing over into Kentucky. He returned at the head of his command, to assist in repelling the savages, and was killed at the battle of Blue Licks. *See sketch of the Todd family in this volume.*

In 1780 Congress recommended to the several States having waste or unappropriated lands, in the western country, to cede it to the United States government for the common benefit of the Union. In January, 1781, Virginia responded to the overture of Congress, by yielding her claims to the territory northwest of the Ohio river, with certain conditions annexed. By an act of Sept. 13, 1783, Congress proposed to comply in the main with the wishes of Virginia, but suggested some modification of the terms. On the 20th of Dec. following, the General Assembly of Virginia passed an act accepting the modified terms proposed by the United States Congress. By this settlement the United States was to refund to Virginia all the money that had been expended by that State in her military operations in conquering and holding the territory. It was also stipulated that a quantity of land, not exceeding one hundred and fifty thousand acres, promised by the State of Virginia, should be allowed and granted by the United States to General George Rogers Clarke, and to the officers and soldiers of his regiment who marched with him when the forts, Gates, at Kaskaskia, and St. Vincent, now Vincennes, were reduced; and to the officers and soldiers who were afterwards incorporated into that regiment. By this act the representatives of that State, in Congress, were instructed and empowered to transfer the territory, by deed, to the United States. The deed was executed March 1, 1784, and signed by Thomas Jefferson, Samuel Hardy, Arthur Lee, and James Monroe. By Virginia protecting the frontier settlers from the cruelties of Indian warfare, she very justly goes down to posterity with the honor of having donated to the general government, territory from which has grown five of the very best States of the American Union. But while she was generous to the public, she failed to be just to the man who was instrumental in bringing so much honor upon herself. In Butler's history of Kentucky it is said of George Rogers Clarke: "The government of Virginia failed to settle his accounts. Private suits were brought against him for public supplies, which ultimately swept away his fortune, and with this injustice the spirit of the hero fell, and the General never recovered his energies, which had stamped him as one of nature's noblemen. At the same time it is feared that a too extensive conviviality contributed its mischievous effects." The latter was, most likely, the real cause of his misfortunes.

THE ORDINANCE OF 1787.

July 13, 1787, an ordinance for the government of the Northwestern Territory, ceded by Virginia to the United States, was enacted by Congress, and General Arthur St. Clair appeared at Marietta, on the Ohio river, and put the new government in operation. Washington county was the first organized, and included a considerable portion of the present State of Ohio. In February, 1790, Governor St. Clair and his Secretary, Winthrop Sargeant, arrived at Kaskaskia and organized the county of St. Clair, which embraced more than half the present State of Illinois. The first legislative body for the Northwestern Territory assembled at what is now Cincinnati, September 16, 1789. On the third of October, General William H. Harrison was elected the first delegate to represent the Northwestern Territory in the Congress of the United States, and for more than ten years its government continued without change.

May 7, 1800, an act of Congress provided for the organization of a territorial government to be called Ohio. November 29, 1802, it was admitted to the Union as a State, with its seat of government at Chillicothe.

From the time the territorial government of Ohio was organized, the remainder continued to be governed as the Northwestern Territory. The same year Ohio was admitted as a State—1802—the Territory of Indiana was organized, with William Henry Harrison as Governor. In 1803 the first legislature of Indiana Territory assembled at Vincennes. Illinois being then a part of Indiana Territory, St. Clair county sent three representatives. Indiana was not admitted as a State into the Union until 1816, but seven years previous to that time had lost more than half its area.

By an act of Congress, approved February 3, 1809, Illinois was separated from Indiana, and provision made for organizing a Territorial Government. Hon. Ninian Edwards, Chief Justice of Kentucky, was appointed by President Madison, to be the first Governor of the Territory of Illinois. The government was organized, in the absence of Governor Edwards, by Nathaniel Pope, Territorial Secretary, April 28, 1809. Governor Edwards arrived at Kaskaskia early in June, and on the eleventh of that month took the oath of office. He was Governor during the whole territorial existence of Illinois. His first commission was dated March 7, 1809; re-appointed November

12, 1812; again re-appointed Jan. 16, 1816. From 1809 to 1812 all the legislation was done "By authority of the Governor and Judges." They did not enact laws, but selected from the territorial laws of Indiana, and from the State of Kentucky such as were suitable to the situation, and declared them to be the laws of the Territory of Illinois. During those three years the Territory was without a voice in Congress.

The first election in Illinois was held by order of Governor Edwards, March 14, 1812, for the purpose of ascertaining if the people generally desired to take part in the government and relieve the Governor and Judges of so much responsibility. The result of the election was favorable to the change. That involved the necessity for another election, which was ordered for October ninth, tenth and eleventh, for the purpose of choosing a delegate to Congress and members of the Territorial Legislature. The members thus elected assembled at Kaskaskia November 25, 1812, being the first legislative body in the territory. From that time to 1818, all business was done in the name of the "Legislative Council and House of Representatives." That body assembled annually in December.

By an act of Congress, approved April 18, 1818, the people of Illinois were authorized to advance from a Territorial to a State Government. In August an election was held for State officers and a representative in Congress. The State was admitted into the Union Dec. 3, 1818. Shadrach Bond, who had been a delegate in Congress from 1812 to 1815, and receiver in the land office from that time until the State was admitted to the Union, was elected the first Governor under the State organization. Ex-Governor Edwards and Jesse B. Thomas were chosen by the legislature to be the first United States Senators.

SANGAMON COUNTY.

When Illinois was admitted to the Union it was composed of thirty-three counties, but Sangamon county and Springfield were unknown. The county was created, by a law of the State, entitled:

"An act establishing the County of Sangamon"—Approved January 30, 1821.

SECTION 1. *Be it enacted by the People of the State of Illinois, represented in the General Assembly*, That all that tract of country within the following boundaries, to-wit:—Beginning at the northeast corner of township twelve north, on the third principal meridian, thence north with said meridian to the Illinois river, thence down the middle of said river to the mouth of Balance or Negro creek, thence up said creek to its head, thence through the middle of the prairie which divides the waters of the Sangamon and Mauves Terre, to the northwest corner of township twelve north, range seven west, of the third principal meridian, thence east along the north boundary of township twelve to the place of beginning, shall constitute a separate county to be called Sangamon.

SECTION 2. *Be it further enacted*, That so soon as the county commissioners of said county shall be elected and duly qualified into office, they shall meet at some convenient place in said county, and determine on some place as near the centre of the population of said county as circumstances will admit, and such place, when selected by said county commissioners, shall be the temporary seat of justice for said county, until otherwise provided by law: *Provided, however*, that if any settler or settlers, owner or owners, of the place so selected as aforesaid, shall refuse to have the temporary seat of justice fixed on his, or her or their improvements, then the said commissioners may determine on such other place contiguous thereto as they may deem proper.

SECTION 3. *Be it further enacted*, That said county commissioners shall be allowed the same compensation for the time necessarily employed in fixing the temporary seat of justice as in other cases.

SECTION 4. *Be it further enacted*, That the citizens of Sangamon county are hereby declared in all respects entitled to the same rights and privileges as are allowed in general to other counties in this State; *Provided, always*, that in all cases where free holders only are capable of performing any duty, or are entitled to any privilege; housekeepers shall, for all such purposes, be considered as free holders in the said Sangamon county, and shall and may do and perform all duties appertaining to the different offices in the county.

SECTION 5. *Be it further enacted*, That the county of Sangamon shall compose a part of the first judicial circuit of the State.

That all may understand the difference between the boundaries of the county when organized, and the present boundaries, it is only necessary to spread before you any late township map of the State and trace the following boundaries: Commencing at the northeast corner of Locust township, in Christian county, thence north to a point on the Illinois river, about two miles west of the city of Peru, thence down the middle of said river to what is now the boundary line between Cass and Morgan counties, thence east to the northeast corner of Morgan county, thence south on the line between Morgan and Sangamon counties, to the northwest corner of Otter township, in Macoupin county, thence east to the place of beginning. It will be seen that the boundaries between this county and Morgan, Macoupin and Montgomery, are unchanged. The original metes and bounds of Sangamon county, as given, embraced the following counties and parts of counties, as at present constituted: Part of Christian, a small part of Macon, all of Logan, part of McLean, all of Tazewell, part of Woodford, part of Marshall, part of Putnam, all of Mason, all of Menard, and all of Cass.

The territory constituting the county was thus set apart by law, but it was without officers. For the purpose of supplying them an election was held Monday, April 2, 1821, at the house of John Kelly. At this election William Drennan, Zachariah Peter, and Rivers Cormack were elected county commissioners. They met the next day, each took the oath of office, and at once entered upon the discharge of their duties. The following is a transcript from the original records of their first term of court:

APRIL 3, 1821:

At a Special Term of the County Commissioners' Court for the County of Sangamon, begun and held at the house of John Kelly, on Spring creek, on the third day of

April, 1821: Present, Zachariah Peter, Rivers Cormack, and William Drennan, commissioners. Ordered by the Court that Charles R. Matheney be appointed Clerk of the County Commissioners Court for the county of Sangamon; who thereupon took the oath prescribed by law, also the oath of office, and entered into bond, as the law directs, with James Latham his security. Ordered that court adjourn.

ZACHARIAH PETER,
WM. DRENNAN,
RIVERS CORMACK.

The Commissioners met again in Special Session, April 10, 1821, at the same place. Present: Z. Peter and Wm. Drennan. John Spillers was allowed ten dollars for conveying election returns to Vandalia. James Sims was appointed County Treasurer. John Lindsay, Stephen Stillman, and John Robinson, were appointed to the office of Justice of the Peace. The following report was made with reference to the location of the county seat:

WHEREAS, the Act of the General Assembly, entitled An Act, establishing the county of Sangamo, required of the County Commissioners when elected and qualified into office, to fix a temporary seat of justice for said county: Therefore, we, the undersigned, County Commissioners for said county, do certify that we, after full examination of the situation of the population of said county, have fixed and designated a certain point in the prairie near John Kelley's field, on the waters of Spring creek, at a stake marked Z. & D., as the temporary seat of justice for said county; and do further agree that the said county seat be called and known by the name of Springfield.

Given under our hands this 10th day of April, 1821.

ZACHARIAH PETER.
WM. DRENNAN.

There is no explanation of letters used in marking the stake, but it is probable that the only two commissioners present agreed to use one initial from each of their names.

The point chosen was near what is now the northwest corner of Second and Jefferson streets. The first court house in the county was built on the same spot.

We find the county of Sangamo organized, and the county seat temporarily located and named. It may be interesting to note some of the incidents that influenced the selection of that particular spot. Towns and cities are born, live, and die, subject to the contingencies of birth, life, and death, analagous to that of human beings. About the year 1818, an old bachelor by the name of Elisha Kelly emigrated from North Carolina to this State, stopping first in Macoupin county. Mr. Kelly was exceedingly fond of the chase, and in prospecting for good hunting grounds, wandered in between two ravines, a couple of miles apart, running in a northwesterly direction, and emptying into Spring creek, a tributary of the Sangamon river. The deer with which this country abounded before the advent of civilization, made their homes in the timber along the larger water courses. In the morning they would leave the heavy timber, follow up the ravines, along which the trees became smaller, and finally ran out on the open prairie. They would pass the day amid the tall and luxuriant grass, roaming about and grazing at pleasure, and as nightfall approached, return down the ravines, to the places they had left in the morning, each to seek its lair for repose. The deer in passing down these ravines, gave Mr. Kelly an opportunity for the full gratification of his ambition for game. It seemed to him so much like a hunter's paradise, that he returned to his old home and induced his father, Henry Kelly, and his four brothers, John, older than himself, and Elijah, William and George, younger, to emigrate with him, those who had families bringing them. He induced other families among his acquaintances to emigrate also. More families continued to move into the country, and generally settled at long distances from each other, but the principal settlement clustered around the Kellys. When the commissioners came to locate the county seat, it was discovered that the Kelley settlement was the only place in all the county, large as it was, where enough families could be found in the vicinity of each other to board and lodge the members of the court and those who would be likely to attend its sessions.

The records do not show that anything more than locating the county seat was done that day, but in another part of the book we find a copy of a contract that was evidently entered into after adjournment, and before they separated. There is no evidence of any advertising for proposals to build a court house, but here is the contract:

Article of agreement entered into the 10th day of April, 1821, between John Kelly, of the county of Sangamo, and the undersigned, county commissioners of said county. The said Kelly agrees with said commissioners to build, for the use of the said county, a court house of the following description, to-wit: The logs to be twenty feet long, the house one story high, plank floor, a good cabin roof, a door and window cut out, the work to be completed by the first day of May, next, for which the said commissioners promise, on the part of the county, to pay the said Kelly forty-two dollars and fifty cents. Witness our hands the day and date above.

JOHN KELLY,
ZACHARIAH PETER,
WM. DRENNAN.

As the temple of justice approached completion the commissioners found that it would be a very nice summer building, but they evidently had some doubts about it for winter. So we find another contract, of which the following is a copy:

Jesse Brevard agrees with the county commissioners to finish the court house in the following manner, to-wit: To be chinked outside and daubed inside. Boards sawed and nailed on the inside cracks, a good, sufficient door shutter, to be made with good plank and hung with good iron hinges, with a latch. A window to be cut out, faced and cased, to contain nine lights, with a good, sufficient shutter hung on the outside. A fire place to be cut out seven feet wide, and a good, sufficient wooden chimney, built with a good, sufficient back and hearth. To be finished by the first of September, next.

JESSE BREVARD.

June 1, 1821.

June 4, 1821, the court assembled in the court house for which they had signed the contract twenty-four days previous. A contract was entered into that day to build a jail, first drawing up the specifications and then writing the contract on the back, of which the following is a copy:

Robert Hamilton agrees to build the within named jail for the county of Sangamo, and to have the same completed by the first Monday in September, next, for the sum of eighty four dollars and seventy-five cents, for which the commissioners agree, on the part of the county, that the said Hamilton shall be entitled to a warrant on the county treasury for the sum of eighty-four dollars and seventy-five cents, as aforesaid.

ROBERT HAMILTON.

June 4, 1821.

The following is a "description of a jail for Sangamo county," to-wit: The timber to be cut twelve feet long, hewed twelve inches square, raised seven feet between the floors, the upper and also the under floor to be of the same kinds of timber, hewed and fit on the sill with a shoulder of at least three inches. The under sill to be let in the ground so as to let the floor rest on the surface of the earth. The logs to be matched with a half dove-tail, and made to close. The building to be covered with a good cabin roof, a window cut eight inches square, half cut out of the timber above and half below. A bar of iron let into the log above and one below, one-half inch thick and two inches wide; three bars of iron standing upright one inch square, let in through the top and bottom bar and into the timber. One door cut three feet in width and five feet high, to be faced, or checked, with good timber, three inches thick, put on with good spikes; a strong door shutter, made of good oak plank, put together crossing and angling, with rivets, at least four in each cross of the plank, and fourpenny nails, drove from each side of the door, not more than one-half inch apart. To be hung with three good, strong, iron hinges, so turned as not to admit of the door coming off, and a good, strong bolt lock. The building to be completed by the first Monday in September, next.

June 4, 1821:

At the meeting of June 4th John Hamblin and David Black were appointed constables. To this time the records show that the name of the county had been written Sangamo, but without any apparent reason, we find a letter added, making it Sangamon.

June 5, 1821:

At a meeting of the commissioners under this date, we find that John Kelly was allowed $42.50 due him on contract for building the court house, and he was allowed $5.00 for extra work. At a meeting September 1, 1821, Jacob Ellis was allowed $4.50 for Judge's seat and bar in the court house. The meeting of December 4, 1821, shows that Jesse Brevard was allowed $20.50 for finishing the court house, making a total of $72.50 as the total cost of the first court house of Sangamon county, but even here we see that the cost nearly doubled the original contract of $42.50.

Continuing the business done on June 5th, we find that the county was divided into four election districts, or townships, called, respectively, Sangamon, Springfield, Richland and Union. Overseers of the poor were appointed, two for each township, and a board of three trustees to look after the overseers of the poor. It does not appear that any one was appointed to look after the trustees. At that meeting James C. Stephenson was appointed county surveyor, and George Hayworth county treasurer, in place of James Sims, who refused to qualify. Provision was made for levying a tax on houses, neat cattle, wheel carriages, stock in trade and distilleries.

July 16, 1821. Ordered, that one-half of one per cent. be levied on all property for the purpose of paying for the public buildings, and for other purposes.

December 4, 1821. John Taylor came into court and entered his protest against the sufficiency of the jail. At the same term it was ordered that Robert Pulliam be allowed to keep a tavern, or public house of entertainment, upon his executing a bond and paying to the county the sum of three dollars, and that he be allowed to charge the following rates, to-wit: Meal of victuals, 25 cents; bed for night, 12½ cents; feed for horse, 12½ cents; keeping horse all night, 37½ cents; whisky, for half pint, 12½.

March term, 1822. Erastus Wright was authorized to keep a ferry across the Illinois river, opposite Fort Clark, now Peoria. Rates of charges were fixed in the license. We learn that he never kept the ferry.

Elijah Slater, on filing his bond, with Dr. Gershom Jayne as security, was granted license to keep a tavern, or public house of entertainment, in the town of Springfield, and a schedule of charges fixed similar to that annexed to Mr. Pulliam's license.

George Hayworth, the county treasurer, made what was probably intended as his annual report, although the county had been organized only about eleven months. The amount of taxes collected for 1821 was $407.44; fines collected, $40.00, making the total receipts $447.44. The amount paid out was $420.18¾. This included the payment of all the officers, and of all bills connected with the building of the court house and jail, leaving $27.26¼ cents in the treasury, and no public debt. From the official papers it appears that the entire salary of the county treasurer for that year was $22.26¼.

July 29, 1823, the amount of taxable property returned to the court was $129,112.50. After reducing the territory of the county to about one-seventh of the original area, we find that the taxable property now—1876—amounts to about *thirty-five millions* of dollars.

Adam Hamilton, county treasurer, reported at the May term, 1824, total amount of collections was $875.87½, and the disbursements $753.90½ leaving a balance of $121.97 in the treasury.

After the temporary location of the county seat, a contest sprang up, looking to the permanent location of the same. At an election of members of the legislature, two opposing candidates went before the people on the merits of two localities. I. S. Pugh was the candidate for Springfield, and William S. Hamilton, a son of the distinguished statesman, Alexander Hamilton, represented Sangamo, a beautiful site for a town on the banks of the Sangamon river, about seven miles west, bearing a little north from Springfield. Hamilton was elected, but Pugh went to Vandalia, the capital, as a lobby member, and succeeded in having commissioners—named in the next paragraph—appointed, who proved to be favorable to Springfield.

An act of the General Assembly, approved December 23, 1824, provided for reducing the boundaries of the county, and named James Mason, Rowland P. Allen, Charles Gear and John R. Sloo, as a board of commissioners who should permanently locate the county seat. A proviso in the law forbade its being located unless thirty-five acres of land was donated on the spot. The commissioners assembled March 18, 1825, and confirmed the former location. More than the requisite donation was made, forty-two acres being conveyed for that purpose by Elijah Iles and Pascal Enos. The land conveyed was parts of sections thirty-four and twenty-seven, in town sixteen north, range hve west, of the third principal meridian. The work of the special commission was consummated when the county commissioners accepted the deeds. They soon after ordered all the land to be laid out into town lots, and, after reserving one square for county buildings, had the remainder sold. Wm. S. Hamilton was appointed to lay off and map the town lots. At the same meeting it was ordered that the sale of lots should begin on the first Monday in May, 1825, and that it should be so advertised in the Edwardsville Spectator, and in the Intelligencer, at Vandalia. Mr. Hamilton failed to lay out the lots, and Tom M. Neale did the work. At a meeting of the commissioners, May 2, 1825, Mr. Neale was appointed crier to sell the lots, and Erastus Wright to clerk at the sale. The following report of two days' sales will show the contrast between the value of Springfield real estate then and now:

		Lots.	Block.	Amount.
FIRST DAY.				
Garret Elkin	bought	1	22	$25.75
James C. McNabb	"	3	22	12.00
James Adams	"	5	22	13.75
Robert Hamilton	"	7	22	16.50
SECOND DAY.				
Garrett Elkin	bought	2	22	31.00
Elijah Iles	"	4	22	20.00
"	"	4	23	40.00
"	"	5	23	14.00
James Adams	"	6	22	17.25
Garrett Elkin	"	8	22	17.56¼
T. M. Neale	"	3	23	21.00
"	"	2	23	17.25
Thomas Cox	"	1	23	14.00
C. R. Matheny	"	8	23	10.25

At the June term, 1825, of the county commissioners' court, John Taylor, sheriff, made the following return or report:

Taxes collected for 1824	$600.00
Fines collected same year	23.00
Total	$623.00
Amount paid out	549.97
Balance in favor of the county	$73.03

July term, 1825. The county commissioners began to think the time had arrived for building a larger and better court house. They passed an order that the county proceed to build a court house, not to exceed three thousand dollars, provided one-half the expense be made up by subscription. It was to be of brick, two stories high. The failure to raise the money by subscription defeated the whole project.

It will be remembered that the court house built in 1821 cost, on the original contract, $41.50; for extra work, $5.00; for a seat for the Judge, $4.50; and for finishing the building, so as to make it habitable for winter, $20.50, making a total of $72.50.

SANGAMON COUNTY.

Coming down from their project to build a $3,000 court house, we next find a contract in the office of the county clerk, made September, 1825. Log buildings could no longer be tolerated, and this was to be a frame. The contract price was $449.00, which did not include the flues. That was let to another party for $70.00, making a total of $519.00. The old log court house was sold at auction to John Taylor for $32.00, nearly half the original cost. The new frame court house was built at the north-east corner of Adams and Sixth streets. It must have been a magnificent structure, judging from the fact that at the term of the court in June, 1826, Robert Thompson was allowed two dollars and twenty-five cents for the plan of the court house.

It may be a matter of some interest to say a few words here about the method of raising revenue to keep the machinery of government moving. At a term of commissioners' court, March 23, 1827, a schedule was made of the kinds of property to be taxed, beginning: "On slaves and indentured or registered negro or mulatto servants, on pleasure carriages, on distilleries," etc., etc.

Only a few years elapsed until the frame court house was thought to be inadequate to the growing wants of the people. It is recorded in the county archives that in February, 1830, the county court appointed three agents or commissioners to superintend the erection of a brick court house. On the third of March the commissioners reported to the court that they had entered into contracts with two parties. One for the brick work, at $4,641, the other for the wood work, at $2,200, making a total of $6,841. This edifice was completed early in 1831, and stood in the centre of the public square, bounded by Washington and Adams, Fifth and Sixth streets. It was a square building, two stories high, hip roof, with a cupola rising in the centre. From the time that court house was erected, all the business of the town collected around the square.

In 1837, when Springfield was selected as the future capital of the state, with a pledge to raise fifty thousand dollars to assist in building the state house; also to furnish the site upon which it should stand, it was not an easy matter to agree upon a location. If land was selected far enough from the existing business to be cheap, the fifty thousand dollars could not be raised. Those already in business around the square refused to contribute, because the state house, being so much larger and more attractive, would draw the business after it, thus depreciating the value of their property. After discussing the question in all its bearings, it was found that the only practicable way to settle the matter was to demolish the court house and use the site for the state house. Under that arrangement the business men around the square pledged themselves to contribute to the fifty thousand dollar fund to the extent of their ability. The court house was accordingly removed, early in 1837, and work on the state house commenced. This square, with the court house and other buildings on it, were valued at sixteen thousand dollars, about one-third of which was lost in the destruction of the buildings.

Having thus summarily disposed of their court house, and having engaged to do so much towards building the state house, the people of Sangamon county were unable to undertake the building of another. In order to supply the deficiency, the county authorities rented a building that had been erected for a store house by the Hon. Ninian W. Edwards. It is at the west side of Fifth street, five doors north of Washington, and was used as a court house for about ten years. Mr. Edwards still owns it, and it is yet used as a business house. After the state house was built, the fifty thousand dollars paid, and the county emerged from the general wreck caused by the financial crash of 1837-8, Sangamon county began to take measures for erecting another court house. In the month of February, 1845, a lot of ground was purchased at the southeast corner of Washington and Sixth streets, as the site for the building. On the twenty-second of April a contract was made by the county commissioners for the building, according to plans and specifications previously adopted. The edifice was to cost $9,680, to be paid in county orders. It was completed according to contract, and was used as the court house of Sangamon county nearly thirty-one years, until January, 1876.

When the movement for building a new state house was made, early in 1867, it was deemed politic on the part of the friends of Springfield that Sangamon county should purchase the old state house, erected from 1837 to 1840, and make it the court house of the county. The law providing for the building of a new state house, which was approved by Gov. R. J. Oglesby, February 25, 1867, with a supplementary act two days later, contained a clause for the transfer of the state house to Sangamon county and the city of Springfield, which was afterwards changed, making the county alone the purchaser. It was stipulated that the Governor should convey the public square, containing two and a half acres of land, with the state house upon it, to Sangamon county, in consideration of two hundred thousand dollars, to be paid to the state of Illinois, and for the further consideration that the city of Springfield and the county cause to be conveyed to the State a certain piece of land, described by metes and bounds in the bill, and containing between eight and nine acres, upon which to erect the new state house. The law also provided that the state should have the use of the old state house until the new one was completed. The land was secured at a cost to the city of seventy thousand dollars, and conveyed to the state; the two hundred thousand dollars was paid by the county, and the property conveyed by the state to the county. That was done in 1867, but the county did not come into possession of the property for seven years. During that time the simple interest, at ten per cent., on the two hundred thousand dollars purchase money, would have amounted to one hundred and forty thousand dollars, making the cost of the old state house to Sangamon county three hundred and forty thousand dollars. The state vacated the house in January, 1876, and the county authorities at once took possession. It will thus be seen that in fifty-five years the county has had five court houses, and been ten years without any. The first one cost forty-two dollars and fifty cents, and the last three hundred and forty thousand dollars.

CIRCUIT COURT.

While the commissioners were busy putting the machinery of the county in working order, we find that the Circuit Court for the county was organized also. The following is the complete record for the first term:

Sangamon Circuit, May Term, 1821:

At a Circuit Court for the county of Sangamon, and State of Illinois, begun and held at the house of John Kelly, on the first Monday of May, (7th day), in the year of our Lord, one thousand, eight hundred and twenty-one.

Present: JOHN REYNOLDS, Judge.
         CHARLES R. MATHENY, Clerk.
         JOHN TAYLOR, Sheriff.
         HENRY STARR, Prosecuting Attorney, *pro tem.*

The following list of Grand Jurors were empanneled and sworn:

Daniel Parkinson, foreman.	George Hayworth,
Claybourn James,	William Eads,
Henry Brown,	Thomas Knotts,
John Darneille,	James McCoy,
Archibald Turner,	James Tweddell,
William Davis,	Aaron Hawley,
Abraham Richey,	Field James,
Abraham Carlock,	Mason Fowler,
Levi Harbour,	Isaac Keys,

Elias Williams.

Charles R. Matheny presented his bond and security as clerk, which was approved by the court.

John Taylor presented his bond as sheriff, with security, which was approved by the court.

Suit was commenced by Samuel L. Irwin against Roland Shepherd, for trespass, and dismissed at plaintiff's cost.

The Grand Jury came into court and returned two indictments for assault and battery and one for riot. Trial deferred until next term, and court adjourned.

The next term was October 8, 1821; held but one day, and proceedings covered two pages of the record.

Next term commenced May 6, 1822; lasted three days, and proceedings covered nine pages of the record. Now, in 1876, with the county reduced to about one-seventh of the territory it then occupied, the Circuit Court continues about eighteen weeks, annually, or three terms of about six weeks each, and the proceedings of each term cover from three to five hundred pages of the record.

In those days, when the electric telegraph was unknown, and it required from twenty days to one month for a letter or newspaper to be brought from the Atlantic coast, the early settlers were under the necessity of giving an amusing turn to passing events when it was at all practicable. An incident illustrating this is related by men who witnessed the facts. When the court was held in the first log court house, an attorney by the name of Mendel violated the rules of decorum as understood by his Honor, Judge John York Sawyer, who ordered Mendel to be arrested and sent to jail for a few hours. On repairing to the court house next morning, the Judge, lawyers and others were surprised to find the court in session before the hour to which it had adjourned. A large calf was on the platform usually occupied by the Judge, and a flock of geese cooped up in the jury box. Mendel, having been released from jail, was inside the bar; bowing first to the calf and then to the geese, he commenced his pleading: "May it please the Court, and you gentlemen of the jury."

The first three or four years of the records of the Circuit Court reveals nothing more than the ordinary routine in such tribunals. The most startling event in the community occurred August 27, 1826. A murder was committed that day near the Sangamon river, in what is now Menard county, about five miles above where Petersburg now stands. A blacksmith named Nathaniel VanNoy had, in a fit of drunken frenzy, killed his wife. He was arrested and lodged in jail the same day. The sheriff, Col. John Taylor, notified Judge Sawyer, who at once called a special session of the Circuit Court. A grand jury was empanneled and sworn, consisting of the following citizens:

Gershom Jayne, foreman,	Jesse M. Harrison,
Stephen Stillman,	Robert Cownover,
John Morris,	James Turley,
John Stephenson, Jr.,	Aaron Houton,
James White,	John Young,
Thomas Morgan,	John Lindsay,
James Stewart,	Charles Boyd,
Jacob Boyer,	Wm. O. Chilton,
Robert White,	Job Burdan,
John N. Moore,	Hugh Sportsman,
Wm. Carpenter,	Abram Lanterman.

Upon hearing the evidence a true bill was found against the accused, and a petit jury called, consisting of the following persons:

Boling Green, foreman,	Wm. Vincent,
Samuel Lee,	Philip I. Fowler,
Jesse Armstrong,	John L. Stephenson,
Levi W. Gordon,	Levi Parish,
Thomas I. Parish,	James Collins,
Erastus Wright,	Geo. Davenport,

A foreman was appointed, the jury sworn, and the trial commenced on the 28th. Attorney-General James Turney acted for the people; James Adams and I. H. Pugh, for the defendant. A verdict of guilty was rendered on the 29th, and sentence was pronounced the same day, that the condemned man be hung November 26, 1826. Thus, in less than three days was the murder committed, the murderer tried and condemned to be hung. The sentence was carried out at the time appointed, in the presence of almost the entire community. Many are yet living who witnessed the execution. Having already sold his body, it was delivered to the surgeons, who immediately commenced dissecting it in an old open house. The spectacle was so revolting that they were compelled to desist and remove it to a more private place. In a country so new, the settlers so widely separated, and so little that was interesting or exciting to furnish topics for conversation, the excitement caused by that event cannot be imagined by the people at the present time. The writer has, time and again, had the dates of events, such as the advent of families in the community, marriages, births, deaths, and incidents too numerous to mention, all settled beyond a doubt by its having occurred "the fall VanNoy was hung!"

PROBATE COURT.

Having given an account of the organization of the Commissioners' Court and of the Circuit Court, the department of justice would not be complete without a Probate Court. The following from its records will show when and by whom that court was organized:

SPRINGFIELD, SANGAMON COUNTY,
STATE OF ILLINOIS, *June 21, 1821.*

Agreeable to an act of Assembly establishing Courts of Probate, approved February 10, 1821, the court was opened at Springfield, Sangamon county, on the 4th day of June, 1821. Present, James Latham, Judge.

The court proceeded to issue letters of administration to Randolph Wills on the estate of Daniel Martin, deceased. After which the court adjourned until court in course.

JAS. LATHAM, *Judge.*

After which court met and adjourned three times without transacting any business, until August 26, 1821, when the filing and recording the will of Peter Lanterman occupied the attention of the court one entire term.

October, 1821, we find the following will recorded:

Before the witnesses now present, Louis Bennett, in perfect memory, does give to the daughters of Kakanoqui, Josett Kakanoqui and Lizett Kakanoqui, two thousand livres each, and six hundred livres for praies for his father; also, six hundred livres for him, if for prayes, and thirty dollars for prayes promised, and one hundred dollars for Kakanoqui, the rest of his money to be given to his brothers and sisters of Louis Bennett. After duly hearing read over before the witnesses now present, and signing the same will, he does voluntarily appoint Joseph D. Portecheron and Louis Penconneau, Senr., as exaequators of his will.

LOUIS + BENNETT.
His mark.

JOSEPH D. PORTECHERON, }
JOSEPH DUTTLE,   His   } Witnesses.
FRANCOIS + BARBONAIS, }
   mark.

NEWSPAPERS.

During the winter of 1826-7 the "*Sangamo Spectator*" was established in Springfield by Hooper Warren. He says, in a letter to the old settlers' meeting, October 20, 1859: "It was but a small affair, a medium sheet, worked by myself alone most of the time, until I made a transfer of it, in the fall of 1828, to Mr. S. Meredith." Mr. Warren is yet residing at Henry, Illinois.

The *Sangamo Journal* was established by Simeon and Josiah Francis. *See their names.* The first number of the paper was issued November 10, 1831, and has con-

6—

tinued to the present time, and is now known as the *Illinois State Journal*, and has been published weekly and daily since June 13, 1838. Its present proprietors are the "Illinois Journal Company," composed of D. L. Phillips, Prest.; E. L. Baker, Sec.; J. D. Roper, Treasurer; and Charles Edwards and A. J. Phillips.

The *Illinois State Register*, first established at Vandalia, was removed to Springfield in 1836, by Walters & Weber. It has been published as a weekly and daily since January 2, 1849. Its present proprietors are E. L. & J. D. Merritt.

SANGAMON RIVER NAVIGATION.

The transportation question will always be a leading one in civilized communities, and especially so in their early settlement. To the first settlers of Illinois it was of unusual importance, on account of the vast extent of undrained soil, so rich and soft as to be almost impassible, in its natural state, for half of every year. For the transportation of heavy articles long distances, no other mode was thought of except by water. They could be conveyed three or four times the distance in that way, much cheaper than on a straight line by any known method. Consequently, efforts were made to navigate every stream to the highest point possible. In the *Sangamo Journal* of January 26, 1832, there appears a letter from Vincent A. Bogue, written in Cincinnati and addressed to Edward Mitchell, Esq., of Springfield. Mr. Bogue says he will attempt the navigation of the Sangamon river if he can find a suitable boat, and expresses the opinion that if he succeeds it will revolutionize the freight business. This is an editorial paragraph from the *Springfield Journal* of February 16, 1832:

"NAVIGATION OF THE SANGAMO.—We find the following advertisement in the *Cincinnati Gazette* of the 19th ult. We hope such notices will soon cease to be novelties. We seriously believe that the Sangamon river, with some little improvement, can be made navigable for steamboats for several months in the year." Here is the advertisement:

"FOR SANGAMO RIVER, ILLINOIS.—The splendid upper cabin steamer, *Talisman*, J. M. Pollock, Master, will leave for Portland, Springfield, on the Sangamon river, and all the intermediate ports and landings, say Beardstown, Naples, St. Louis, Louisville, on Thursday, February 2. For freight or passage, apply to Capt. Vincent A. Bogue, at the Broadway Hotel, or to Allison Owen." The same boat was advertised in the St. Louis papers.

After the above notices appeared in the *Journal*, the citizens of Springfield and surrounding country held a public meeting, February 14, 1832, and appointed a committee to meet Mr. Bogue with a suitable number of hands to assist in clearing the river of obstructions. Another committee was appointed to collect subscriptions to defray the expense. The *Journal* of March 8 announces the arrival of the steamer at Meredosia, where its further progress was obstructed by ice. The *Sangamo Journal* of March 29, 1832, says: "On Saturday last the citizens of this place (Springfield) were gratified by the arrival of the steamboat *Talisman*, J. W. Pollock, Master, of 150 tons burthen, at the Portland landing, opposite this town. (Portland was at the south side of the Sangamon river, between where the bridges of the Chicago & Alton and the Gilman, Clinton & Springfield railroads now stand.) The safe arrival of a boat of the size of the *Talisman*, on a river never before navigated by steam, had created much solicitude, and the shores for miles were crowded by our citizens. Her arrival at her destined port was hailed with loud acclamations and full demonstrations of pleasure. When Capt. Bogue located his steam mill on Sangamon river, twelve months ago, and asserted his determination to land a steam boat there within a year, the idea was considered chimerical by some, and utterly impracticable by others. The experiment has been made, and the result has been as successful as the most enthusiastic could expect; and this county owes a deep debt of gratitude to Captain Bogue for getting up the expedition, and his never tiring and unceasing efforts until the end was accomplished. Capt. Pollock, who is naturally warm and enthusiastic, entered fully into the feeling of our citizens, who visited the mouth of the river to render any and every assistance in their power; and much credit is due him for his perseverance and success. The boat experienced some difficulty from drifts, and leaning timber on shore, which made her trip somewhat tedious. The result has clearly demonstrated the practicability of navigating the river by steamboats of a proper size; and by the expenditure of $2,000 in removing logs and drifts and standing timber, a steamboat of 80 tons burthen will make the trip in two days from Beardstown to this place. The citizens of Beardstown manifested great interest for the success of the enterprise, and some of them accompanied the boat until the result was no longer doubtful. They proposed the cutting of a communication or canal from the bluffs to their landing—about five miles—whereby seventy-five miles of navigation may be saved, and offered one thousand dollars to assist in completing it. It is to be hoped that the next Legislature will afford some aid in making the river safe and pleasant in its navigation. Springfield can no longer be considered an inland town. We have no doubt but within a few months a boat will be constructed for the special purpose of navigating the Sangamo river. The result which must follow the successful termination of this enterprise to our county, and to those counties lying in its neighborhood, it would be impossible to calculate. Here is now open a most promising field for the exercise of every branch of honest industry. We congratulate our farmers, our mechanics, our merchants and professional men for the rich harvest in prospect, and we cordially invite emigrating citizens from other states, whether rich or poor, if so be they are industrious and honest, to come hither and partake of the good things of Sangamo."

A ball was gotten up in honor of the arrival, and several yards of machine poetry appeared in the next number of the *Journal*, detailing the various incidents connected with the wondrous event. The boat was unloaded, and immediately started on its return, but the river had so fallen and brought the water within so narrow a channel, that it was impossible to turn it around, and they were compelled to back it out the entire distance. The only mention ever made of her afterwards was a newspaper report that the *Talisman* was burned at the wharf in St. Louis in the latter part of the next April. No attempt was ever made after that to bring a boat up the river. Thus ended the dream of navigating the Sangamo, across which a man may walk almost dry shod for nearly half of every year.

RAILROADS.

The navigation of the Sangamon river being a failure, left the problem of transportation still unsolved. Brains and hands were at work in another land, that were destined to revolutionize all former ideas on the subject in this, but their labors had never been heard of by the people, with the exception, probably, of an occasional extensive reader of the news. The railroad was then in its very infancy in England. The steam locomotive, about that time, found its way to this side of the Atlantic, but it required a few years more for it to reach Illinois. The first rail laid in the state was at Meredosia, on the Illinois river, May 9, 1838, on what was called the Northern Cross Railroad. The first locomotive arrived at the same place September 6, 1838, on the steamboat Chariton, and was put on the track and first turned its wheels on the 8th of November following. It required more than three years to complete the road to Springfield. The first locomotive was run into Springfield, February 15, 1842, on what is now the Toledo, Wabash and Western Railroad. George Gregory—*see his name*—was the engineer, and Thomas M. Averitt—*see his name*—was the fireman, both of whom are yet living in this county. The State of Illinois has now over six thousand miles of railroad, and Springfield has railroads by which travelers may enter and leave the city in eight different directions.

SPRINGFIELD.

We have already said that a temporary county seat was chosen for Sangamon county, April 10, 1821, and called Springfield. The first survey of public land in the county took place that year. The Rev. John M. Peck, in his Pioneer History of Illinois, says that Springfield was laid out in February, 1822, referring, no doubt, to Calhoun, which was the name given to the first plat of what is now a part of Springfield. It is in the northwestern part of the city. The first sale of public lands in Sangamon county took place November 7, 1823. At that sale the lands were purchased upon which Calhoun had been laid out. Four different parties entered each a quarter of as many sections cornering together. The town plat of Calhoun was recorded December 5, 1823. It was under a law approved December 23, 1824, that the county seat was permanently located by the commissioners, who assembled March 18, 1825, and confirmed the former location at Springfield. The land donated by Elijah Iles and Pascal Enos was laid out into lots, making the streets correspond with those of Calhoun. There was great prejudice against the name of Calhoun, (afterwards the great nullifier of South Carolina,) many refusing to recognize it, and it soon ceased to be used except in the conveyance of lots.

The first legislation on the part of the state, with reference to Springfield, was approved February 9, 1827. By this act the court of county commissioners was required to appoint street commissioners for the town, and levy a tax for improving the same. A general law for the incorporation of towns was enacted and approved February 12, 1831. April 2, 1832, Springfield was incorporated under that law. October 18, 1832, the county court ordered a re-survey of the town, in order to adjust the discrepancies between the plats of Calhoun and Springfield. The survey was made and acknowledged June 18, 1833, and recorded November 9, 1836.

The first board of trustees after the town was incorporated, April 2, 1832:

C. R. Matheny, President,   Elisha Tabor,
Cyrus Anderson,   Mordecai Mobley,
John Taylor,   Wm. Carpenter.

1833:   John R. Gray, President.
1834-5-6-7-8: C. R. Matheny, President.
1839:   Peleg C. Canedy, President, and Abraham Lincoln a member of the town board.

By an act of the General Assembly, approved February 3, 1840, a city charter was granted to Springfield. This law provided for an election to be held the first Monday in April, being the sixth day, to adopt or reject the proposed charter. It was adopted, and the first election for city officers was held April 20, 1840.

Benjamin S. Clements was elected Mayor, and James R. Gray, Washington Iles, Joseph Klein and William Prentiss, Aldermen. The following were the successive Mayors from that to the present time: For 1841, Wm. L. May; 1842, David B. Campbell; 1843, Daniel B. Hill, who resigned and Andrew McCormick was elected to fill the vacancy; 1844, Andrew McCormick; 1845, James C. Conkling; 1846-47 and '48, Eli Cook; 1849-50 and '51, John Calhoun; 1852, William Lavely; 1853, Josiah Francis. In 1854 the number of Aldermen was increased from four to twelve, and William H. Herndon was elected Mayor; 1855, John Cook; 1856-57 and '58, John W. Priest; 1859, William Jayne; 1860, Goyn Sutton; 1861-62, Geo. L. Huntington; 1863, John W. Smith; 1864, John S. Vredenburgh; 1865, Thomas J. Dennis; 1866, John S. Bradford; 1867, Norman M. Broadwell; 1868, William E. Shutt; 1869, N. M. Broadwell; 1870, John W. Priest; 1871 and '72, John W. Smith; 1873, Charles E. Hay; 1874, the wards were increased from four to six, and Obed Lewis elected Mayor; 1875, Charles E. Hay; 1876, this is printed in February, and the election takes place in April.

SPRINGFIELD, THE STATE CAPITAL.

From the discovery of the country by the French in 1673, there was no attempt at organized government in the territory now composing the State of Illinois, until 1718, when the "Company of the West" was formed in Paris, for the new world. Kaskaskia had been settled between 1680-90, and is regarded as the oldest permanent settlement in the Mississippi Valley.

Judge Caton, in his oration at the laying of the corner stone of the new state house, October 5, 1868, described the building which was used as the capitol when the territorial government was organized, in the following language: "It was a rough building in the centre of a square in the village of Kaskaskia, the ancient seat of the western empire for more than one hundred and fifty years. The body of this building was of uncut limestone, the gables and roof of the gambrel style of unpainted boards and shingles, with dormer windows. The lower floor, a long, cheerless room, was fitted up for the House, whilst the council sat in the small chamber above. This venerable building was, during the French occupancy of the country, prior to 1763, the headquarters of the military commandant. Thirty years ago the house was a mass of ruins, and to-day, probably, there is not a stone left to designate the spot where it stood." That building was the capitol during the territorial existence of Illinois, and the state government was organized in it also.

The state constitution of 1818 required the General Assembly to petition Congress for a grant of land upon which to locate the seat of government for the state. In the event of the prayer of the petitioners being granted, a town was to be laid out on said land, which town should be the seat of government of the state for twenty years. The land was granted. "At the session of 1819, in Kaskaskia, five commissioners were appointed to select the land appropriated by Congress for the state capital." The commissioners made their selections further up the Kaskaskia river. Having selected the site, the commissioners were sorely puzzled in their efforts to select a name that should be so euphonious as to attract the attention of the whole world. Governor Ford, in his history of Illinois, gives the following humorous account of the way it was done: "Tradition says that a wag, who was present, suggested to the commissioners that the 'Vandals' were a powerful nation of Indians, who once inhabited the banks of the Kaskaskia river, and that 'Vandalia,' derived from the name, would perpetuate the memory of that extinct but renowned people. The suggestion pleased the commissioners, the name was adopted, and they thus proved that the cognomen of their new city—if they were fit representatives of their constituents—would better illustrate the character of the modern, than the ancient inhabitants of the country."

Having located and named their town, it was at once laid out, and the dense growth of timber cut away and a two story frame building erected on the square set apart for the State capitol. The building was placed on a rough stone foundation in the centre of the square, and was of very rude workmanship. The lower floor was for the House of Representatives, and the upper divided into two rooms, the largest one for the Senate and the smaller one for the office of Secretary of State. The State Auditor and Treasurer occupied detached buildings. The archives of the State were removed from Kaskaskia to Vandalia in December, 1820. That wooden State house was burned a few years later, and a much larger one built of brick on the same ground. The rapidity with which emigration filled up the northern portion of the State made it apparent, long before the twenty years it was to remain at Vandalia expired, that it would be necessary to remove the capital further north, and as early as 1833 the question began to be agitated in the General Assembly.

In the Legislature of 1836-7 Sangamon county had two Senators and seven Representatives. They were the most remarkable delegation from any one county to the General Assembly, being much taller than the average of human stature. Some of them were less and some more than six feet, but their combined height was exactly fifty-four feet. They were then and are yet spoken of as the "Long Nine." The names of those in the Senate were Archer G. Herndon and Job Fletcher; in the House, Abraham Lincoln, Ninian W. Edwards, John Dawson, Andrew McCormick, Dan Stone, Wm. F. Elkin and Robert L. Wilson. One or two were as tall, but none taller, than Abraham Lincoln, who, quoting his own language, was "six feet, four inches, nearly." It was known that a movement would be made to re-locate the State capital. The "Long Nine" were united for securing it, and nothing could turn one of them from their purpose. They were ready to yield anything else, but when any other point was yielded, it secured votes for Springfield as the capital. Their opportunities were great. The people of Illinois were, at that time, almost insane on the subject of internal improvements. Not one in ten thousand of them had ever seen a railroad, but they had heard of them, and thought the prairies of Illinois the best place in the world to build them. The first movements began in the General Assembly in 1833, but the first charter was: "An act to incorporate the Chicago and

Vincennes railroad company with an authorized capital of $3,000,000," and was approved January 17, 1835. Within one year and four days from that time, charters were granted for building railroads in the State, of which the combined capital authorized was $18,200,000. In this legislation the State did not propose to furnish any capital, only authorized capitalists to invest their money. Not a mile of railroad was ever built under any of those charters. Before the next session, the Legislature realized that there were no capitalists to build railroads, and a new system was inaugurated. The most remarkable act ever passed by a legislative body in the State was approved February 27, 1837, and was entitled "An act to establish and maintain a general system of internal improvements." Two supplementary acts were approved March 4, 1837. The three acts fill thirty-two octavo pages. The object was to construct public works at the expense of the State, in all parts of the same. Under this law appropriations were made for canals, and the improvement of rivers, to the amount of $650,000; also, for the building of railroads, $9,550,000, making a total of $10,200,000. During the month of February and March, 1837, bills were passed chartering twenty-two railroad companies with authorized capital stock to the amount of nearly $8,000,000, making an aggregate of about $30,000,000 involved in the vain endeavor to legislate railroads into existence in the State of Illinois before their time.

While the internal improvement bill was pending, the "Long Nine" were busy. They said little or nothing in locating proposed railroads, but would assist other localities, where votes could be secured for locating the capital at Springfield. The result was the passage of "An act permanently to locate the seat of government for the State of Illinois," which was approved at Vandalia, February 25, 1837. This law provided for a joint session of the two houses, on the twenty-eighth of the same month, to select a situation. An appropriation of fifty thousand dollars was made, to commence building the State house. The law also declared that no place should be chosen unless its citizens contributed at least $50,000 to aid in the work, and not less than two acres of land, as a site for the capitol. When the two houses assembled on the twenty-eighth, the question was decided by the following—

BALLOTINGS.	1st.	2nd.	3rd.	4th.
Springfield	35	43	53	73
Jacksonville	14	15	9	1
Vandalia	16	15	16	15
Peoria	16	12	11	6
Alton	15	16	14	6
Scattering	25	7	15	7
Illiopolis		10	3	

That settled the question, and Springfield was declared to be the future capital of the State.

A supplemental act was passed on the third of March, authorizing the commissioners of Sangamon county to convey the land, as a site for the new edifice, to the State. It also named Dr. A. G. Henry, of Sangamon; Archibald Job, of Cass, Wm. Herndon, of Sangamon, as commissioners, who were authorized and instructed to superintend the work of erection. It was expected that the new capital would be completed in time for the first meeting of the Legislature in Springfield, which was fixed for the special session of 1839-40. Finding that the building could not be sufficiently advanced, the Second Presbyterian church, on Fourth street, was secured as Representatives' Hall. The building was then quite new, and was, by far, the largest church edifice in the central and whole northern part of the State. It was built of brick, stood a few feet north of the site of the present magnificent Second Presbyterian church, until the latter was erected. The old building was torn down in the summer of 1875. The Methodist church was used for the Senate chamber, and the Episcopal church for the Supreme Court, both wooden buildings. The Legislature first convened in special session December 9, 1839.

It was thought by many to be unreasonable to require a little town of eleven hundred inhabitants, struggling with the disadvantages of a new country, to pay the $50,000 pledged. During that special session, Hon. Stephen A. Douglas, then a member from Morgan county, proposed to bring in a bill, releasing Springfield from the payment of the same. The sterling honesty of Abraham Lincoln manifested itself on this, as on all other proper occasions. He interposed his objections, although he fully appreciated the kindly feelings that prompted the proposal, but he insisted that the money should be paid. Arrangements were entered into for paying it in three instalments. The two first payments were made without any great difficulty; but the third pressed more heavily, as the financial crash that swept over the whole United States, while the new State house was in course of construction, impoverished many. Under these circumstances, it became necessary to borrow the money to make the last payment, from the State Bank of Illinois. A note for the amount was signed by one hundred and one citizens, and deposited with the bank, the money drawn, with which internal improvement scrip or stock was purchased and paid into the State treasury, thus paying the last instalment in the State's own evidence of indebtedness. From that time it was a matter between the State Bank and the citizens who signed the note. Soon after the note was given, the State Bank failed, and some of the payments were made in the depreciated paper of the bank, for which it had received par value when it was paid out. The original note is preserved in the Ridgely National Bank, but the following is a copy of the same:

$16,666.67. SPRINGFIELD, *March 22, 1838.*

One year after date, we, the undersigned, or either of us, promise to pay to the President, Directors and Company of the State Bank of Illinois, sixteen thousand, six hundred and sixty-six dollars and sixty-seven cents, for value received, negotiable and payable at the bank, in Springfield, with interest until paid, at the rate of six per centum per annum, payable semi-annually.

John Hay,	Thomas Mather,	C. R. Matheny,
L. Higby,	Tho. Houghan,	William Butler,
Joseph Thayer,	D. Prickett,	P. C. Canedy,
William Thornton,	J. Calhoun,	Jos. Klein.
M. O. Reeves,	Josiah Francis,	P. C. Latham,
W. P. Grimsley,	Washington Iles,	A. G. Henry,
William Wallace,	Joel Johnson,	Ninian W. Edwards,
John B. Watson,	C. B. Francis,	John T. Stuart,
C. H. Ormsby,	Wm. S. Burch,	Jonas Whitney,

Moses Coffman,
Geo. Pasfield,
B. C. Webster,
S. M. Tinsley,
Ephriam Darling,
Jona. Merriam,
Ira Sanford,
Charles Arnold,
John L. Turner,
Joshua F. Amos,
Sullivan Conant,
And. McClellan,
Alexander Shields,
A. Trailor,
C. C. Phelps,
R. B. Zimmerman,
William Hall,
James L. Lamb,
M. L. Knapp,

J. M. Shackleford,
B. Ferguson,
Benjamin Talbott,
Jesse Cormack,
B. C. Johnson,
Thomas Moffatt,
John F. Rague,
Simeon Francis,
Nathaniel Hay,
Robert Irwin,
Virgil Hickox,
George Trotter,
Stephen T. Logan,
Robert Allen,
James R. Gray,
J. Adams,
J. S. Britton,
W. B. Powell,
F. C. Thompson,
E. M. Henkle,
James W. Keyes,
Wm. Porter,
Wm. H. Marsh,
W. Ransdell,
Joshua S. Hobbs,
John G. Bergen,
B. S. Clement,

Erastus Wright,
John Todd,
E. D. Baker,
A. Lincoln,
Garrett Elkin,
John Capps,
Alexr. Garrett,
Gershom Jayne,
T. M. Neale,
William G. Abrams,
Dewey Whitney,
M. Mobley,
Foley Vaughn,
Abner Y. Ellis,
N. A. Rankin,
S. H. Treat,
Elijah Iles,
Henry F. Luckett,
James P. Langford,
Henry Cassequin,
J. M. Cabaniss,
James Maxcy,
Z. P. Cabaniss,
E. G. Johns,
Amos Camp,
Thos. J. Goforth,
Benj. F. Jewett,
W. M. Cowgill.

From a footing up of the principal and interest on one side of the note, the final settlement appears to have been made February 19, 1846. The principal and interest to that time was $17,918.

Soon after the Legislature adjourned at Vandalia, in March, 1837, and the members returned to their homes, a public festival was given in Springfield in honor of the new legislation for the removal of the capital. Among the toasts and speeches that followed the dinner, were the two following:

By Abraham Lincoln, Esq: "All our friends—they are too numerous to mention now, individually, while there is no one of them who is not too dear to be forgotten or neglected."

By S. A. Douglas, Esq.: "The last winter's legislation—May its results prove no less beneficial to the whole State than they have to our town."

A tradition still lingers here that something stronger than water was used in drinking the toasts on that occasion, as there was not a man to be found after the festival that could tell who made the last speech, and that important fact is lost to history.

The commissioners appointed to superintend the building at once entered upon the discharge of their duties, and on the fourth of July, 1837, the corner stone of the State house was laid with grand civic and military demonstrations. After it had been lowered to its place in the wall, it was mounted by E. D. Baker, afterwards United States Senator from Oregon, and the lamented Colonel of Balls Bluff memory, who delivered one of those thrilling and eloquent speeches, for which he was so famous. It was estimated that the building would cost $130,000, but $240,000 was expended before it was completed according to the original design. When the State house was completed it was looked upon with wonder and admiration by the people. It was thought to be so enormous in size that it would answer all the purposes of the State for all time to come; but from the time it was built until the breaking out of the great rebellion the growth of Illinois was beyond anything that could have been imagined by the early settlers.

When the rebellion came to an end, and what was left of the *two hundred and fifty-six thousand men* from Illinois, who assisted in carrying the stars and stripes until there was no armed foe to conquer, returned to their homes, furled their banners, and assumed their accustomed places in the peaceful avocations of life, it soon became apparent to all who had occasion to visit Springfield, that the building of another State house could not be delayed for any great length of time. The State had so far outgrown the edifice, which had been regarded as a wonder of magnificence and architectural beauty only a brief quarter of a century before, that its records were unsafe, and many branches of its official business had to be transacted in rented buildings, where much of its valuable property was exposed at all times to the danger of being destroyed by fire. The question had been very generally discussed in a quiet way, and soon after the Legislature assembled in January, 1867, Hon. James C. Conkling presented a bill providing for the erection of a new State Capitol at Springfield, and laid it before the House of Representatives. It passed both houses, and was approved by Governor Oglesby February 25, 1867, with a supplementary act two days later. That law provided for the conveyance by the Governor of the square containing two and a half acres of land, with the State house upon it, to Sangamon county, for a court house, in consideration of $200,000, to be paid to the State of Illinois, and for the further consideration that the city of Springfield, and Sangamon county, cause to be conveyed to the State a certain piece of land, described by metes and bounds in the bill, and containing between eight and nine acres, upon which to erect the new State house. The law also provided that the State should have the use of the old State house until the new one should be ready for occupancy. The land was secured at a cost to the city of $70,000, and conveyed to the state; the $200,000 was paid by the county, and that amount, with $250,000, to be drawn from the State treasury, making $450,000, was appropriated to commence the work. The total cost of the building was limited to $3,000,000. The design by J. C. Cochrane was adopted July 15, 1867, and Jan. 14, 1868, he was appointed architect and superintendent. Excavation commenced early in the spring, and the first stone was laid June 11. On the fifth of October the corner stone was laid by the Grand Master of Free Masons of the State of Illinois, with the imposing ceremonies of the order, and surrounded by members of the craft from all parts of the State.

The ground plan is in the form of a great cross. The grand outlines are, total length from north to south, 359 feet, exclusive of porticos; and from east to west, 266 feet, with twenty feet additional in the grand portico at the east end, which is the principal front. The body of the edifice above ground consists of the FIRST STORY, PRINCIPAL STORY, SECOND PRINCIPAL STORY and GALLERY STORY.

July 2, 1870, the people of Illinois voted on the question of adopting or rejecting a new constitution, that had been prepared by a convention legally called for that purpose. It was adopted by a large majority. A clause in the new constitution prohibited the legislature making appropriations for the State house, then in course of construction, beyond a total amount of three and a half millions of dollars, unless the question of additional appropriations was first submitted to a vote of the people. The money within the constitutional limit has all been appropriated. The dates of approval by the Governor, and amounts, are given below. The fourth appropriation was to be expended equally in the years 1873-4:

February 25, 27, 1867	$450,000
March 11, 27, 1869	650,000
June 14, 1871	600,000
March 19, 1873	1,000,000
March 24, 1875	800,000
Total	$3,500,000

There is much work yet to be done, but whether an additional appropriation, requiring a vote of the people, will be necessary to complete the grand edifice, is a question for a future legislature to determine. The building was so far advanced that the State archives were removed thereto, and the State officers took possession of it in January 1876, and in that way the State of Illinois inaugurated the great American Centennial.

GOVERNORS OF ILLINOIS.

TERRITORIAL.

Ninian Edwards ....from 1809 to 1818

STATE.

Shadrach Bond...1818—1822
Edward Coles..1822—1826
Ninian Edwards..1826—1830
John Reynolds...1830—1834

Lieutenant-Governor Casey, elected with Gov. Reynolds in 1830, was elected to Congress in 1832. Wm. L. D. Ewing, a member of the Senate, was chosen President of the Senate. Gov. Reynolds was elected to Congress in August, 1834, and left the State for the national capital about the middle of November. Wm. L. D. Ewing, as President of the Senate, was Governor fifteen days, until the assembling of the Legislature in December, and the inauguration of the governor elect.

Joseph Duncan..from 1834 to 1838
Thomas Carlin..from 1838 to 1842
Thomas Ford..from 1842 to 1846

The constitution of 1848 changed the time of the assembling of the Legislature from December to January, and ordered a new election in November, 1848, for four years. Consequently—

Augustus C. French was Governor ....from 1846 to 1853
Joel A. Matteson...from 1853 to 1857
Wm. H. Bissell..from 1857 to 1860
　He died March 18, 1860, and—
Lieutenant-Governor John Wood...................................from 1860 to 1861
Richard Yates...from 1861 to 1865
Richard J. Oglesby..from 1865 to 1869
John M. Palmer..from 1869 to 1873
Richard J. Oglesby, inaugurated in 1873, but immediately elected to the U. S. Senate, when the Lieutenant-Governor—
John L. Beveridge...from 1873 to 1877

TOWNSHIP ORGANIZATION.

A law was enacted by the General Assembly of Illinois, and approved by the Governor, February 10, 1849, providing for township organization, but leaving it optional with counties to adopt it or not. Sangamon county never took any action under that law.

Another law was enacted and approved February 17, 1851, providing for township organization, and differing from the law of 1849 in some of its provisions. Under that law a petition was laid before the commissioners' court, June 5, 1860, praying the court to cause to be submitted to the voters of the county the question of township organization. The court, having heard the petition, ordered that the prayer of the petitioners be granted, and the subject be submitted at the next general election, which was held Tuesday, November 6, 1860. The vote was canvassed by the court on the tenth of December following, when it was ascertained that there was a majority of 859 votes in favor of township organization, on a total vote of 7,241. The following action was then taken: "Ordered by the Court, that John S. Bradford, John Gardner, Sen., and Joseph Campbell be appointed commissioners to divide Sangamon county into towns or townships, in accordance with the fifth and sixth sections of the General Law of the State of Illinois, in relation to township organization." March 1, 1861, the commissioners submitted their report, and the following are the names of the townships:

Auburn,	Island Grove,
Ball,	Loami,
Buffalo Heart,	Mechanicsburg,
Campbell, now Chatham,	Power, now Fancy Creek,
Cartwright,	Pawnee,
Clear Lake,	Rochester,
Cooper,	Sackett, now Salisbury,
Cotton Hill,	Springfield,
Curran,	Talkington,
Gardner,	Williams,
Illiopolis,	Woodside.

New Berlin has since been formed from part of Island Grove, and Wheatfield from part of Illiopolis, making a total of 24 townships.

An election was held for choosing supervisors, Tuesday, April 2, 1861. The first meeting of the Board of Supervisors was held April 29, 1861, on a call of eight members, which was the method pointed out in the law. From that to the present time the business of Sangamon county has been transacted by a Board of Supervisors, elected annually.

POST OFFICES IN SANGAMON COUNTY.

Auburn,	Illiopolis,
Barclay,	Loami,
Bates,	Lowder,
Berlin,	Mechanicsburg,
Berry,	New Berlin,
* Bradfordton,	† New Harmony,
† Breckenridge,	Pawnee,
Buffalo,	Pleasant Plains,
Buffalo Heart,	Richland,
Cantrall,	Riverton,
Chatham,	Rochester,
Cotton Hill,	Salisbury,
Cross Plains,	Sherman,
Curran,	Springfield,
Dawson,	Wheatfield,
Farmingdale,	Williamsville,
Iles Junction,	Woodside.

* This is a new office authorized by the post office department, but not yet organized. Feb., 1876.
† The original name of this office was New Harmony, but is about being changed to Breckenridge.

SANGAMON COUNTY IN THE INDIAN WARS.

I shall have occasion, all through the biographical part of the work, to make frequent mention of the part taken in the Winnebago and Black Hawk wars by the early settlers of the county; for that reason I deem it best to give a brief account of them here.

THE WINNEBAGO WAR: When the war of 1812-14, with England, drew to a close, there were many Indians in the territory of Illinois. They generally gave way as civilization advanced, yielding the ground, sometimes reluctantly, but peaceably, until the summer of 1827. It was known to the white settlers that the different tribes of Indians along the northern and western frontier were at war among themselves. After the discovery of lead around what is now Galena, the white people flocked to that region in great numbers. In their search for minerals they encroached upon the lands of the Winnebago tribe. Being thus irritated, a small party of their tribe surprised a party of twenty-four Chippeways and killed eight of them. The United States Commander, at Fort Snelling, on the upper Mississippi, caused four of the offending Winnebagoes to be arrested and delivered to the Chippeways, by whom they were shot for murder. Red Bird, the chief of the Sioux, though acting with the Winnebagoes in an attempt to obtain revenge for the killing of the four members of their tribe, was defeated by the Chippeways. He then determined to wreak his vengeance on the white people who had assisted his enemies and invaded his country. June 27th two white men were killed near Prairie DuChien, and on the thirtieth of July two keel boats, carrying supplies to Fort Snelling, were attacked and two of the crew killed. The news soon spread among the settlers, and upon a call from Gov. Edwards, four companies of infantry and one of cavalry were made up in Sangamon county. The cavalry company was commanded by Edward Mitchell, and the four infantry companies by Captains Thomas Constant, Reuben Brown, Achilles Morris and Bowlin Green. The whole under command of Col. Tom. M. Neale, with James D. Henry as adjutant, (the latter was at that time sheriff of Sangamon county,) marched to Peoria, where the regiment was more fully organized, and continued to Galena. Before their arrival in the Indian country, Red Bird with six of his warriors, voluntarily gave themselves up to the U. S. forces under Gen. Atkinson, to save their tribe from the miseries of war. Thus ended the campaign, and the Sangamon county soldiers returned to their homes.

Of the six Indians held as prisoners, some were acquitted and others convicted and hung, more than a year after they were captured. Red Bird, whose proud spirit could not endure the humiliation and confinement, sickened and died in prison. His fate was much deplored by the whites, for he had been a true friend to them until the United States Government compelled his Winnebago friends to give up the four men to the Chippeways to be shot.

THE BLACK HAWK WAR: The Sac and Fox Indians were first recognized by the United States Government in 1787, in a treaty at Fort Harmer, negotiated by Gov. St. Clair, in which the Indians were guaranteed protection. In 1804, in a treaty conducted by Wm. H. Harrison—afterwards President of the United States—their title to a large scope of country on Rock river was extinguished, but they were permitted to occupy the country as a hunting ground, their principal village being at the north of Rock river, near where the city of Rock Island now stands. A third treaty was entered into in 1830, by the terms of which they were to remove from the lands they had sold, east of the Mississippi, and peaceably retire to the west side of the river.

The two principal chiefs of the nation were Keokuk and Black Hawk, the latter of whom was born in 1767, at the largest village of their tribe, at the mouth of Rock river. He had fought on the side of the British in the war of 1812, at the head of 200 savages, for which he annually received payment to the time of their removal west of the Mississippi. Consequently, their band was always called the British Band. Black Hawk moved reluctantly, claiming that his tribe had been injured by the people of the United States. Keokuk determined to abide by the treaty, and drew the larger part of the tribe after him, but Black Hawk declared all the treaties void, and in the spring of 1831, at the head of 300 warriors, crossed to the east side of the river and engaged in a series of acts exceedingly annoying to the few settlers who had purchased the sites of the former homes of the Indians, from the government. The Indians would throw down fences, destroy grain, throw the roofs from their houses, and declared that if the settlers did not leave they would kill them. Governor John Reynolds, on being informed of the state of affairs on Rock river, determined to expel the Indians. He issued a proclamation, May 27, 1831, calling for volunteers, and named June 10th as the time, and Beardstown as the place of rendezvous. More than twice the 700 men called for volunteered. Finding so many willing to go, it was decided to accept the services of the whole 1,600 men. They were organized into two regiments, one spy and one odd battalion. James D. Henry, of Springfield, who had been the adjutant in the Winnebago war, was appointed to command the first regiment. I will now confine myself to the part Sangamon county took in the campaign. James Campbell, Adam Smith, and Jonathan R. Saunders each commanded a company. When the Indian town was reached at the mouth of Rock river, it was found to be deserted. The Indians had taken advantage of the darkness and fled to the west side of the Mississippi river, near where the cities of Davenport and Rock Island now stand. The savages having escaped, the soldiers took vengeance by burning the village. Gen. Gaines, who commanded the United States soldiers, sent an order to Black Hawk, requiring him and his band to return and enter into a treaty of peace. He failed to come, when a more peremptory order, with the threat of following them with all the troops at his command, brought in about thirty chiefs, including Black Hawk, and a treaty was signed on the 30th of June, 1831. By that treaty the Indians agreed to remain west of the river, and never to cross it without permission from the President of the United States. After distributing the food intended for sustaining the soldiers, among the Indians, the volunteer army disbanded and returned to their homes, without the loss of a single person by disease, accident, or otherwise.

Before the Indians were forced to leave their village and return to the west side of the river, Naopope, a chief of the British band, and next to Black Hawk in authority, had started on a visit to Malden, Canada, to consult his English father—some commander there, probably—concerning the right of the Indians to retake possession of their lands on Rock river. On his return he also visited White Cloud, the prophet of the Winnebagoes, at Prophetstown, 35 miles from the mouth of Rock river. White Cloud assured his visitor that not only the British but the Ottawas, Chippewas, Potawattomies and Winnebagoes would assist his tribe in regaining their village and the lands around it. When Naopope returned, in the summer, he found his tribe west of the river, and bound, by a new treaty, not to interfere with the whites in possession of their former homes. Notwithstanding this, he communicated to Black Hawk the encouragement he had received. Black Hawk immediately commenced recruiting to increase the number of his braves, and sent a messenger to Keokuk, requesting his co-operation. The latter refused, and counseled Black Hawk to abstain from any hostile movement, assuring him that the promises of support could not be relied on. Black Hawk rejected such good advice, and resolved to bid defiance to the whites. He spent the winter of 1831-2 in recruiting, and raised about 500 warriors. His headquarters were at what is now the city of Fort Madison, Iowa. In the spring he started, with his warriors, on horseback, while the squaws, papooses and baggage were loaded in canoes, and all moved up the river. April 6, 1832, the whole party crossed the Mississippi, opposite the mouth of Rock river, and commenced ascending that stream, ostensibly for the purpose of entering the territory of the Winnebagoes and raising a crop with them, but the real object was to secure them as allies.

Gen. Atkinson, in command of Fort Armstrong, on Rock Island, sent messengers ordering them to return west of the Mississippi river. Black Hawk positively refused to go. When this became known in the settlement the greatest consternation prevailed, and the settlers fled from their homes in search of safety. Messengers were dispatched to Vandalia, and Gov. Reynolds issued a call, on the 16th, for volunteers to assemble at Beardstown on the 22d of the month. Gen. Atkinson at the same time called for volunteers to aid the regular soldiers at Rock Island. Gov. Reynolds, at the time of issuing the call for volunteer soldiers, addressed an open letter to the citizens in the northwestern counties, and sent influential messengers among the people, and in every way endeavored to encourage enlistments. Eighteen hundred men rallied under this call at Beardstown, on the 22d of April. Among them were three regularly organized companies from Sangamon county. One was commanded by Thomas Moffitt, one by Jesse Claywell, of which Rezin H. Constant afterwards became Captain, and one by Abraham Lincoln. They were divided into four regiments and a spy battalion. The First regiment was commanded by Col. DeWitt, the Second by Col. Fry, the Third by Col. Thomas, the Fourth by Col. Samuel M. Thompson. In the latter Abraham Lincoln commanded a company. Col. James D. Henry commanded the spy battalion. The whole brigade was put under the command of Brigadier-Gen. Samuel Whitesides, of the State militia, who had commanded the spy battalion in the first campaign.

On the 27th of April Gen. Whitesides began his forward movement, accompanied by Gov. Reynolds. The army proceeded by way of Oquawka to the mouth of Rock river, where it was agreed between Generals Whiteside and Atkinson, in command of the regulars, that the volunteers should march up Rock river to Prophetstown, and there feed and rest their horses. On arriving there the volunteers burned the town, and Gen. Whiteside continued the march in the direction of Dixon, arriving at the latter place, the General ordered a halt, and sent out parties to reconnoitre. Here he found two battalions, consisting of 275 mounted men, from the counties of McLean, Tazewell, Peoria and Fulton, under the command of Majors Stillman and Bailey. Major Stillman was from Sangamon county. (*See his name.*) The officers of this force had previously been ordered in advance of the main body to protect the settlers, and now they asked to be put forward on some dangerous service, in which they could have an opportunity to distinguish themselves. They were accordingly ordered further up Rock river, to spy out the Indians. The forward movement began on the 12th of May, Major Stillman being chief in command. He moved up Rock river, on the southeast side until they came to a small stream that rises in Ogle county and empties into Rock river. This stream was then called Old Man's creek, but from that date has borne the name of Stillman's run. There he encamped for the night, and in a short time a party of Indians were seen on horseback about a mile from the camp. A party of Major Stillman's men mounted their horses, without orders or commander, and were soon followed by others, and in this helter skelter manner pursued the Indians, who, after displaying a red flag, endeavored to make their escape, but were overtaken and three of them slain. This brought on an attack from the main body of Black Hawk's army, numbering about 700 warriors. Those who, by their insubordination, brought on the fight, retreated, and, with their horses on a full run, dashed through the camp of Major Stillman, who did all that was possible by ordering his men to retreat in order and form on higher ground, but they never found a rallying point until they reached Dixon, thirty miles distant. Both Ford, and Davidson & Stuve, in their histories of Illinois, exonerate Major Stillman and his men from all blame, and rightly attribute the disaster to want of discipline and that experience which is necessary to give soldiers confidence in their officers and in each other.

That opened the war, and there could be no cessation of hostilities until one side or the other yielded the ground. It is not my purpose to attempt following out all the details of the war, but will hasten to a close. For a time the Indians scattered themselves over the country: They would lay in ambush and shoot down detached bodies of armed men, or murder and scalp unprotected women and children. Men were generally enlisted for short terms, and sometimes, when the main body of the Indians were almost in their grasp, the term of enlistment would expire, and they would insist on being discharged. To fill their places with new recruits required time. At the time of the repulse of Major Stillman and his men, there were about twenty-four hundred men under arms, including the volunteers from Illinois and the regular soldiers from Fort Armstrong, under Gen. Atkinson. They could have killed, or driven every Indian across the Mississippi river in one month, but the term for which they had enlisted had nearly expired, and they were anxious to be discharged. The Governor had previously issued orders for raising two thousand men. He then called for a volunteer regiment from among those whose time had expired, to hold the Indians in check until the new recruits could be brought to the scene of conflict. It was soon raised and put under command of Col. Fry and Lieutenant-Col. James D. Henry. Gen. Whiteside volunteered as a private. This body of men had a number of encounters with the savages before the new recruits were brought into the field. The new levy assembled at Beardstown, and were at once ordered to Fort Wilburn, on the south bank of the Illinois river, about one mile above the town of Peru. There the volunteer forces were organized into three brigades. The first and second were organized June 16, 1832, with 1,000 men each. Alexander Posey was elected General of the first and Milton K. Alexander, General of the second brigade. The third brigade was organized June 18th, with 1,200 men, and Col. James D. Henry was elected General. This made the volunteer force consist of 3,200 men, exclusive of the regular soldiers under Gen. Atkinson. Many weeks were spent in trying to find the main body of Black Hawk's warriors. They were all the time working their way further north, hoping to elude their pursuers. The army was continually undergoing changes. July 15, 1832, found Gen. Henry, Gen. Alexander and Major Dodge far up in Wisconsin, at a place called Fort Winnebago. Some Winnebago chiefs came in and reported that Black Hawk was encamped on Rock river. The three officers above named held a council and, although it was in violation of orders, they decided to march directly for the Indian camp, hoping to take them by surprise. General Alexander soon announced that his men refused to go, and Major Dodge that his horses were too much disabled to go, but a body of men soon after arrived from Galena to join Major Dodge's battalion, which made his effective force 120 men. Gen. Henry's brigade was by this time reduced to between five and six hundred men, but only about four hundred and fifty had horses. While making arrangements to start, Gen. Henry discovered that his own men, influenced by association with those of Gen. Alexander, were on the point of open mutiny. Lieutenant-Col. Jeremiah Smith, of one of his regiments, presented to the General a written protest, signed by all the officers of his regiment except Col. Fry, against the expedition. Gen. Henry quietly but firmly ordered the men under arrest for mutiny, assigning a body of soldiers to escort them back to Gen. Atkinson. Col. Smith begged permission to consult a few moments with the officers before anything further was done. In less than ten minutes they were all at the General's quarters, pleading for pardon and pledging themselves to return to duty. Gen. Henry replied in a few dignified and kindly remarks, and all returned to their duty. Gen. Alexander's men marched back, and the others started in pursuit of the enemy, under the direction of competent guides. Three days' hard marching brought them to Rock river. Here three Winnebagoes gave intelligence that Black Hawk was further up the river. Preparations were made for a forced march the next morning, and Dr. Elias Merriman, of Springfield, in company with W. W. Woodbridge, of Wisconsin, and a chief called Little Thunder, for a guide, were started about dark that evening to convey dispatches down the river to Gen. Atkinson. They had gone but a few miles to the southwest when they fell into a fresh broad trail of the enemy endeavoring to escape. Little Thunder hastened back in terror to the camp to warn the Indians that their efforts to deceive the commanding General were detected. They were all arrested by Major Murrey McConnell, of Jacksonville, and taken to the tent of Gen. Henry, and confessed that they had come into camp and given false information to aid the Indians in their retreat. On the next morning, July 19, a forced march commenced in pursuit of the Indians. On the third day, about four o'clock in the afternoon, the advance guard was fired upon by the savages secreted in the grass. The fight continued until dark, and the men lay on their arms until morning, when it was discovered that the Indians had all crossed the Wisconsin river during the night. Sixty-eight Indians were left dead on the field, and twenty-five more were found dead along the line of march. Only one white man was killed and eight wounded. This has always been known as the battle of the Wisconsin.

The next day Gen. Henry found his men too much worn down by fatigue and want of food to pursue the retreating Indians. After two days march he joined Gen. Atkinson at Blue Mounds, with the regulars, and Alexander's and Posey's brigades. It was soon apparent to General Henry and his officers that General Atkinson and all the regular officers were deeply mortified at the success of the militia, who they did not intend should have any credit in the war. After two days' preparation, the whole force, under direction of General Atkinson, took up their line of march, July 25th, in pursuit of the Indians. Crossing the Wisconsin river, and striking the trail of the Indians, the regulars were put in front, Dodge's battalion and Posey's and Alexander's brigades came next, and Gen. Henry, with his command, was placed in the rear, in charge of the baggage. All parties clearly understood this to be an insult to Gen. Henry and his brave volunteers for having found, pursued and defeated Black Hawk and his warriors, while the regulars, and Alexander's brigade, who had refused to accompany Henry, were taking their ease at a long distance from the scene of danger. Gen. Henry's brigade keenly felt the insult, and claimed the right to be placed in front, but the General never uttered a word of complaint, and his men, following his noble example, quietly trudged on in the rear. After a full week of weary marching, at ten o'clock on the morning of August 2d, the army reached the bluffs of the Mississippi river, which, at that point, was some distance from the margin of the stream. Black Hawk had arrived at the stream a day or two before, and the Indians were crossing as fast as they could. On the first day of August the steamboat *Warrior*, which had been employed to convey supplies up the river for the army, was coming down, and notwithstanding the Indians displayed a white flag, the captain affected to believe it was only a decoy, gave them fifteen minutes to remove their women and children, when he fired a six-pound cannon, loaded with cannister, into their midst, followed by a severe fire of musketry. In less than an hour twenty-three Indians were murdered, it might almost be said, in cold blood. Black Hawk now turned all his energies to reach the opposite bank of the river. With that object in view he sent twenty warriors to the high bluff. When Gen. Atkinson reached the bluffs on the morning of August 2d, his men were greeted by firing from behind trees. The tall grass made it impossible to learn anything of the force they had to contend with. According to instructions from Black Hawk, when all became engaged they were to retreat to a point three miles up the river. Dodge's battalion led in the chase after the twenty Indians, followed by the regulars and Alexander's and Posey's brigades, all under the immediate direction of Gen. Atkinson. In the hurried pursuit Gen. Henry was called on for a single regiment to cover the rear of the pursuing forces. Otherwise his whole brigade was left without orders.

Despite the intention to disgrace Gen. Henry and his men, fortune now seemed to favor them. The men under Major Ewing, of the latter brigade, discovered that the trail by which the main body of Black Hawk's forces had reached the river was lower down, and that they were much nearer than the point to which the twenty decoy Indians were leading the main forces. He who had been placed in the rear as a mark of special disfavor, by the strategy of a few savages, who had thus far triumphed over the veteran General, was now thrown again to the front, and well did he make use of this favorable circumstance. Gen. Henry, being notified of the discovery of the main trail, descending to the foot of the bluff, and there leaving his horses, prepared for an attack. The trail from there to the river was through drift wood, brush and weeds. Eight men were ordered forward to the perilous duty of drawing the fire of the Indians, to ascertain where they were. Fully aware of their dangerous mission, they moved boldly forward until they were in sight of the river, when they were fired upon by about fifty Indians. Five of the eight fell, either killed or wounded. Gen. Henry immediately ordered the bugle sounded for a charge. The fifty Indians fell back to the main body, amounting in all to about three hundred warriors. This made the force about equal on both sides. The fight became general along the whole line; the inspiring strains of the bugle cheering on the volunteers; the Indians were driven from tree to tree until they reached the bank of the river, fighting with the most sublime courage, and contesting every inch of ground. At the brink the struggle was desperate, but of short duration. The bloody bayonet in the hands of the excited soldiers drove them into the surging waters, where some tried to swim to the opposite shore, others only aimed to reach a small willow island.

All this was done before the commanding General was aware that the volunteer General and men, whom he intended to punish for having found and defeated the Indians at the battle of the Wisconsin river, had again found and almost exterminated the main body of the enemy, while he was leading the largest portion of his army after twenty straggling Indians, whom he had not been shrewd enough to detect in their false movements. After the Indians had been driven into the river, Gen. Henry despatched Major McConnell to give intelligence to Gen. Atkinson of his movements; but while pursuing the twenty Indians he had heard the firing of Gen. Henry's brigade, and hastening to share in the engagement, met the messenger near the scene of action. Some of the newly arrived forces charged through the water to the island and kept up the fight until all were killed, drowned, captured, or made their escape to the opposite shore of the river. It was estimated that the Indian loss amounted to one hundred and fifty killed, and as many more drowned, including women and children. But fifty prisoners were taken, mostly squaws and papooses. The largest portion of the Indians escaped across the river before the battle commenced. The American loss was seventeen killed and twelve wounded. This was called the battle of the Bad Axe, because it was fought in Wisconsin, a short distance below the mouth of the river Bad Axe. It was above Prairie DuChien.

That Black Hawk brought that great calamity on his people there can be no question, but that he was devoted to their interests his last move testifies beyond a doubt. Finding himself and followers almost in a starving condition, pursued by a foe well fed, and otherwise stronger than his own forces, he approached the brink of the river, hoping to reach the opposite bank before his pursuers could overtake him. His means of transportation being inadequate, he finds it impossible to escape. Knowing that his fate is sealed, he doubtless gives hasty orders that the canoes be plied as fast as possible, and looking for the last time upon many who had trusted their all to his guidance, he places himself at the head of a handful of faithful followers, and boldly sallies out to meet the foe one hundred and fifty times stronger than himself, his only hope being to turn them aside until his own people should escape. How his heart must have sunk when he heard the firing and knew there was but one way for it to terminate. When Gen. Atkinson, discovering the ruse, ceased the pursuit of the few and marched to where the battle was raging, Black Hawk, with his twenty followers, made their escape up the Mississippi and passed over to the Wisconsin river. They were finally captured, far up that stream, by a party of Sioux and Winnebago Indians, who professed to sympathize with Black Hawk and his followers, but were ready, like blood hounds, to hunt them down when they most needed friendship, and when there was a seeming opportunity to gain favor with the strong and victorious party. Black Hawk and his friends were delivered to Gen. Street, the United States Indian agent at Prairie DuChien, and sent by Col. Zachary Taylor down to Rock Island. Upon arriving there the cholera was raging, and they were sent down to Jefferson Barracks, Mo., where a treaty was made. Black Hawk and his party were held as hostages for the good behavior of their tribe. They were taken to Washington City, and from there to Fortress Monroe, where they remained until July 4, 1833. They were then released, by order of President Jackson, and escorted to Baltimore, Philadelphia, New York, and other cities, and returned by way of the New York canal and northern lakes, thence to their own people, west of the Mississippi river. Black Hawk died, October 3, 1840, on the Des Moines river, in Iowa.

Many of the men engaged in that campaign acquired state and some of them national reputation. Among them may be mentioned Joseph Duncan and Thomas Ford, who became Governors of Illinois, Henry Dodge, who became Governor of Wisconsin, and Zachary Taylor and Abraham Lincoln, who became Presidents of the United States.

The most remarkable man of all engaged in that campaign was Gen. James D. Henry, and if that had been an age of newspapers and reporters, he would have acquired a national reputation at once. That he was the hero of the two principal battles fought in expelling the Indians in that campaign, was known beyond a doubt, and so well understood by the Illinois soldiers from all parts of the State, that the opinion was freely expressed that if he had lived he would have been elected Governor by an overwhelming majority, against any other man. Strange as it may seem, he was scarcely heard of outside of the State. This was all owing to the fact that there was but one paper in the State north of Springfield, and that was edited and published by the kind of man that brings odium on the press whenever he touches it.

Dr. Addison Philleo was one of the men who almost publicly commenced dissecting the body of VayNoy, who was hung in Springfield in November, 1826. He was compelled by the citizens to desist from the disgusting spectacle until the body was removed to a more private place. Dr. Philleo had removed to Galena, and at the time of the Black Hawk war was publishing a paper there, called the *Galenian*. He attached himself to the battalion of Major Henry Dodge, of Wisconsin. Major Dodge's battalion was a part of Gen. Henry's brigade when Black Hawk and his forces were discovered by Gen. Henry. Gov. Ford, in his history, describing the chase of Gen. Henry after Black Hawk, says: "On the third day, about noon, also, the scouts ahead came suddenly upon two Indians, and as they were attempting to escape, one of them was killed and left dead on the field. Dr. Addison Philleo, coming along shortly after, scalped this Indian, and for a long time afterwards exhibited the scalp as an evidence of his valor."

That was the kind of man the world was dependent upon for a history of the Black Hawk campaign. He was the only newspaper man with the army. After the battle of the Wisconsin, Dr. Philleo wrote an account of it for his paper, and that being the first paper it was published in, was copied all over the United States. He chronicled the doings of Major Dodge only, and always spoke of him as General Dodge. Gen. Henry, the real commander, was never mentioned except as a subordinate. By this deception many histories now assert that Dodge was the commander in that war. General Henry never made a report of any part of the campaign, and those errors were never officially contradicted. In that campaign he contracted disease of the lungs, and afterwards went south, hoping that the climate and medical treatment would restore his health, but he gradually sank until March 4, 1834, when he died in New Orleans. *See his name in the biographical department.*

I have been thus minute in this sketch of the Indian wars, because almost every family among the early settlers of Sangamon county were represented in the army; and, although they were at a comparatively safe distance from the scene of conflict, yet their sympathies were naturally drawn out towards those who were in danger. Another reason why I have given the subject such prominence is that there is no recent history of those wars accessible to the public.

The mention I shall make of the part taken by the descendents of the early settlers of Sangamon county in suppressing the great rebellion will partake of a much wider range, but the comparatively recent date of that event, and the publications in almost every house concerning it, precludes the necessity of my attempting any extended account of it here.

MISCELLANEOUS.

Under this head I shall record some events that will occasionally be referred to in the biographical part of the work. By describing them fully here, a bare reference to them hereafter will be understood. The two most important were the "deep snow" and the "sudden change."

THE DEEP SNOW:—What is here spoken of as the "deep snow" must be taken relatively. Snows fall almost every winter much deeper in New York, the New England States, Canada and in the northern latitudes generally. This, however, is distinguished from all others as the "deep snow," because, in this latitude, the like of it was not known before, and has not been known since. A description of it by Rev. J. M. Sturtevant, President of Illinois College, in an address before the Old Settler's Society of Morgan county, at Jacksonville, a few years ago, is the best authority I can find. Having been brought up where such snows were nothing unusual, he would be less likely to be deceived in his judgment than one who had never witnessed the like before. President Sturtevant says:

"In the interval between Christmas, 1830, and January, 1831, Snow fell all over central Illinois to a depth of fully three feet on a level. Then came a rain, with weather so cold that it froze as it fell, forming a crust of ice over this three feet of snow, nearly, if not quite, strong enough to bear a man, and finally, over this crust of ice, there was a few inches of very light snow. The clouds passed away, and the wind came down upon us from the northwest with extraordinary ferocity. For weeks, certainly not less than two weeks, the mercury in the thermometer tube was not, on any one morning, higher than twelve degrees below zero. This snow fall produced constant sleighing for nine weeks."

The recollection of some of the early settlers is that rain fell for some days, until the earth was saturated with water, and the day before Christmas the rain turned to snow, and the flakes were so large that in a few hours it attained a depth of six inches. I have, time and again, heard this snow described as much more than three feet deep, and no doubt the experience of those making the statements justified them in it. The situation was rather alarming, even to a New England man. There, a few hours of wind blows all the snow from exposed places, and deposits it in valleys and behind hills, where the wind cannot reach it. It is only where the roads cross these receptacles that it is necessary to break a track. It is made the occasion for a frolic with New England people to turn out with ox teams and sleds to break a road, and then there is no more trouble until the next snow storm. Such work here would have been useless. In this level country the drifting never ceases as long as the snow lasts. Any number of teams might break a track, but it would fill behind them in a few moments. The only way they finally made roads here was by wallowing through it, and going as near the same place as they could, until the snow was trodden hard and rounded up like a turnpike road. Many instances have been related where teams, attempting to pass each other on these raised roads, found it too narrow, and the result was that one if not both the vehicles would be upset, leaving the occupants and teams floundering in the snow. To regain the proper position on the road was not always an easy task. Long after the great body of the snow melted off, these roads remained. One man, describing them, said they looked like silver threads, stretching over the prairies as far as the eye could reach.

Railroads were not then dreamed of, but they would have been, for several weeks, as utterly useless as though they were sunk out of sight in the earth. Snow plows would be of no avail in such a storm as that, for the track would fill, in less than an hour, behind any train that might force its way though. Quoting again from President Sturtevant, he says: "It is a consolation that such a winter has never occurred but once in the memory of man. But what has happened once may happen again. If it does we shall get a very definite idea how important our railroads are to us, and we shall be very glad that the snow is not over the telegraph wires." In the latter clause he no doubt had reference to the fact that in those days, when everything was right, they did not have or expect a mail more than once a week, but even that was interrupted for several weeks during the "deep snow."

That snow come so early in the season that it caught nearly all their corn in the fields, and it was very difficult to obtain enough of it to keep stock from perishing. Few had any milling done, and the devices were numerous to reduce the grain to a condition fine enough to be baked into something resembling bread. Some of them will be described. I will here give a few incidents illustrating some of the straits the people were put to in order to preserve life and property.

Among the earliest settlers on Sugar creek was a man by the name of Stout—no relation to any of that name now in the county. He had raised a family, but his wife had died, and his children had married and left him alone. He built a small cabin in the woods, and in that he did his own cooking, slept, and worked at making bread trays, wooden bowls, rolling pins, wooden ladles, and such other implements as every household was in need of. He traded the products of his labor for something to eat or wear, seldom receiving or expecting any money. He lived very comfortably until the "deep snow" come. Then his open cabin and scant supply of bedding was not sufficient to keep him warm. He went around among his neighbors and tried to obtain some addition to his bedding, but found them all deficient in that respect themselves. He finally solved the difficulty by felling a large tree near his cabin, took a cut from it of suitable length, and made a trough inside, the full length of his body, and hewed it off on the outside until it was light and thin enough for him to handle easily. He would then make his bed on some chips or shavings, as he had done before, first bringing his trough along side, and when snugly covered up, he would take the trough and turn it over himself for covering. As soon as the warmth of his body filled the space he would be comfortable, and could lay snug and warm until morning. There was neither floor nor chimney to his cabin, so he made the fire on the ground. When the weather was extremely cold he would move his fire just before retiring, scraping the coals and ashes carefully away, and then make his bed where the fire had been during the day. This is a new proof of the oft repeated adage, that "Necessity is the mother of invention."

DEATHS IN THE SNOW:—Very many cases occurred of persons being lost in the snow, ending in death. I will mention a few here, but others will be referred to in the succeeding parts of the work.

A man named William Saxton lived on Lick creek, above Loami. He went hunting, and failing to return, his friends and neighbors went in search of him, and found his body about one mile from his home, where he had sunk down, and appeared as if asleep.

Samuel Legg started from Sugar creek, not far above where the C. and A. railroad now crosses, intending to go to Richland timber, near where Pleasant Plains now stands. He was not heard of until the next April, when the remains of himself and horse were found, nearly consumed by wolves. He had gone but a few miles, as the body was found on what is now the farm of John B. Fowler, a few miles west of Chatham. A bottle with a small quantity of whiskey was found near his remains.

A man started from the timber on Horse creek to chase a wolf while the snow was falling. He was not seen nor heard of until the next spring, when his body was found at a place called Willow grove, in Shelby county. His horse and dog were found with him, and all had perished together. The distance was about forty miles from where he started. It was thought that he became bewildered by the falling snow, and continued his efforts until his horse, dog and himself sank down to die.

William Workman went hunting in the Lick creek timber, south of Loami. He walked on the crust of the snow, and was approaching a deer for the purpose of shooting it. Without being aware of it, he was over a ravine of considerable depth. The crust broke and he went down. Raising his rifle gun he could barely reach the crust with it. By tramping the snow under his feet until it became solid, he found himself gradually rising with the slope of the ground, and by reaching up with his gun and breaking the crust, he finally escaped, but he says it was a long and laborious operation. Simeon Vancil relates an experience very similar.

So completely did the snow cover everything that wild game was accustomed to feed upon, that the deer, turkey, and some other kinds of game, were almost exterminated. There was another reason why it was destructive to the deer. That animal runs by a succession of leaps, and, as a natural consequence, the faster they ran the greater would be the force with which they struck the snow. When pursued by dogs, a few vigorous leaps would stop them short, their small, sharp hoofs breaking through the crust, would leave them helpless, with their bodies resting on the snow. At the same time a dog or wolf of equal weight would pass safely over, because, by their manner of running, they did not strike the snow with such force, and even if they had, their soft, pad-like feet would be less likely to break the crust.

It required but a short time, thus shut off from food, for the deer to become too lean for venison. All thoughtful people then abstained from killing them, but there were others who thought only of the sport, and destroyed them where and when they could. Dogs and wolves, learning that they could be made to break through the crust and become disabled, chased down and destroyed great numbers of them. From all these causes the deer were almost exterminated, and they never become plentiful afterwards.

Mr. Simeon Vancil, who came to the county in the fall of 1818, says that it was very common to see large quantities of buffalo bones on the highest points of land. In explanation of that there was a tradition among the Indians who remained in the country to hunt, after the white settlers come in, that there had been a "deep snow" about thirty years before, say about 1800, and that the buffalo, herding together on the highest ground, because the snow was thinnest, remained there and perished with cold and hunger. Of course this was only given as a tradition, coming from the Indians. There could be no corroborative testimony from civilized men, for the simple reason that there were none in the country.

THE SUDDEN CHANGE:—Soon after commencing the collection of materials for this work, I was frequently asked the question, "Has any person told you about the sudden change?" My answers at first would, for obvious reasons, be in the negative. The interrogator would then undertake to give me an account of it, but I was never able to learn that any person in the county had kept a record of the indications of a thermometer at that time, or that there was a thermometer in the county; and for a long time I could not ascertain the year in which it took place.

In an interview with Mr. Washington Crowder, the date was settled in his own peculiar method. Mr. Crowder remembers that on the morning of December 20, 1836, he started from a point on Sugar creek about eight miles south of Springfield, to the latter place, for the purpose of obtaining a license for the marriage of himself and Miss Isabel Laughlin. He had finished his courting on the nineteenth, with the understanding that the marriage was to take place on the twenty-first, leaving the twentieth for obtaining the license. There were several inches of snow on the ground, but rain was then falling slowly, and had been, long enough to turn the snow to slush. Every time the horse put his foot down it went through the slush, splashing it out on all sides. Mr. Crowder was carrying an umbrella to protect himself from the rain, and wore an overcoat reaching nearly to his feet. When he had traveled something like half the distance, and had reached a point about four miles south of Springfield, he had a fair view of the landscape, ten or twelve miles west and north. He saw a very dark cloud, a little north of west, and it appeared to be approaching him very rapidly, accompanied by a terrific, deep, bellowing sound. He thought it prudent to close his umbrella, lest the wind should snatch it from his hands, and dropped the bridle reins on the neck of his horse for that purpose. Having closed the umbrella and put it under his arm, he was in the act of taking hold of the bridle rein, when the cold wave struck him. At that instant water was dripping from every thing about him, but when he drew the reins taut, ice rattled from them. The water and slush was almost instantly turned to ice, and running water on sloping ground was congealed as suddenly as molten lead would harden and form in ridges if poured on the ground. Mr. Crowder expressed himself quite sure that within fifteen minutes from the time the cold blast reached him his horse walked on top of the snow and water, so suddenly did it freeze.

When he arrived in Springfield he rode up to a store at the west side of Fifth street, between Adams and Monroe, a few doors south of where Bunn's bank now stands. He there attempted to dismount, but was unable to move, his overcoat holding him as firmly as though it had been made of sheet iron. He then called for help, and two men come out, who tried to lift him off, but his clothes were frozen to the saddle, which they ungirthed, and then carried man and saddle to the fire and thawed them asunder. After becoming sufficiently warm to do so, Mr. Crowder went to the county clerk's office, obtained his license, and by driving his horse before him, returned to where he had started in the morning. The next day he started on horseback, but found the traveling so difficult on the ice that he dismounted, tied up the bridle, left his horse to

—9

find the way back home, and went on foot to the house of his affianced, where he was married at the time appointed. Mr. Crowder admits that it was a very thorough test of his devotion, but it must be conceded that he proved himself equal to the emergency.

Other evidences of the suddenness and intensity of the cold are numerous. Rev. Josiah Porter, of Chatham—*see his name*—remembers that the cold wave reached Chatham about half past twelve o'clock, noon; that he consulted his watch at the time, and knows he is correct. His recollection of the suddenness and intensity of the cold corroborates the account given by Mr. Crowder. Although Mr. Porter was in Chatham at the time of the sudden change, and resides there now, he was then doing the work of an evangelist, which led to his traveling over a large portion of Illinois and Indiana. In the discharge of his duties he became acquainted with a remarkable circumstance that occurred in what is now the west part of Douglas county, near the corner of Piatt and Moultrie counties. Two brothers by the name of Deeds had gone out to cut a bee tree, and were overtaken by the cold and frozen to death. Their bodies were found ten days later, about three miles from home.

The extent of that cold wave may not be generally known. That it first touched the earth west or north-west of here is highly probable, from the fact that it reached here at half past twelve, noon, according to the time noted by Mr. Porter. He also learned that it was nearly sundown when the cold reached the point in Douglas county where the two brothers perished. I also learned from a gentlemen in this county that at the time, his father kept a hotel at Labanon, Ohio, and although his account would indicate that the cold wave had spent some of its force, yet when it arrived there it froze some wagons fast in the mud in an incredibly short time, while some travelers were discussing the terms for staying all night. It reached there at nine o'clock. Putting the statements as to time and place together, it would appear that the cold wave traveled something near three hundred miles in eight and a half hours, or about thirty-five miles an hour. These statements have been given to me altogether from memory, more than thirty-five years after the event, and no doubt vary greatly from what a scientific report at the time would have presented.

A great many instances have been related to me, in all parts of the county, of the suffering by men and animals. It has been told me time and again that chickens and geese, also hogs and cows, were frozen in the slush as they stood, and unless they were extricated by cutting the ice from about their feet, remained there to perish.

Andrew Heredith was a merchant miller and pork packer in Cincinnati, Ohio. Through misfortunes incident to business he failed. Among other misfortunes, he had a pork house burn there. Preston Breckenridge, of this county, happened to be in Cincinnati, and remembers being an eye witness to the burning. After his failure, Mr. Heredith was aided by friends to commence business in Sangamon county. He built a flouring mill about three miles west of Loami, near what is called Lick creek, and called the place Millville. He bought wheat and made flour; also bought and drove fat hogs to St. Louis. In the fall of 1836 he bought and drove two lots to St. Louis, and made some money each time. He used all the capital at his command, and all the credit his successes gave him, and collected a third drove of between 1,000 and 1,500 hogs, and was driving them to St. Louis. The country was so sparsely settled that he found it expedient to start with three or four wagons, loaded with corn to feed the hogs. When a load was fed out there were generally a sufficient number of hogs exhausted by traveling to load the wagon. Mr. Heredith had reached a point on the open prairie eight miles south of Scottville, Macoupin county, when the cold wave overtook him. Finding that men and animals were likely to perish, he called the men together, upset all except one of the wagons, in order to leave the corn and hogs together, righted up the wagons, and with all the men in them, drove to the nearest house, and before they could reach there all became more or less frozen, but none lost their lives.

The hogs, thus abandoned, piled on each other. Those on the inside smothered, and those on the outside froze. A pyramid of about 500 dead hogs was thus built. The others wandered about and were reduced to skeletons by their sufferings from the cold, the whole proving a total loss. Mr. Heredith was a man of good business qualifications, and of great energy. He was making superhuman efforts to retrieve his fortunes, but that blow crushed him; he never rose again, but sank down and in a short time died. In the biographical part, *see his name.*

JAMES HARVEY HILDRETH:—At the time Rev. Mr. Porter gave me his recollections connected with the "sudden change," he told me that some years later he met a man in DeWitt county, by the name of Hildreth, who was crippled in his hands and feet. He said Mr. Hildreth informed him that it had been caused by his being caught away from shelter at the time of the "sudden change." Mr. Hildreth then gave him a detailed account of his sufferings and experience, which Mr. Porter gave to me from memory. This made such an impression on my mind that I was anxious to know more of the incident. In the course of my travels over the county, I was at the house of Mrs. Thomas J. Turley. *See the Turley and Trotter names.* How the subject came up I do not remember, but I learned from Mrs. Turley that Mr. Hildreth was her cousin. She gave me additional information, and referred me to another cousin— of herself and Mr. Hildreth—Mr. Moses Kenny, of Kenny, Logan county. I deferred writing to that gentleman until I was drawing my work to a close, and when I did so, was answered by Mr. John Kenny, of the same place, who informed me that his brother Moses was dead. Mr. John Kenny answered all my inquiries, and referred me to Mr. A. L. Barnett, of Clinton, DeWitt county. He, also, kindly responded. All the parties consulted bear the very highest character for truthfulness. It is from this mass of information that I give the following account of the case. Although the particular event I am about to relate did not occur in this county, it illustrates an atmospheric phenomena that affected this entire region of country, and was so remarkable that the like of it is not on record, nor known by any person now living, and it is to be hoped that it may never be known again. It is to be regretted that there is no scientific knowledge on record of the event. The country was so new, and the settlers of a class generally of limited education, so much so that I have been unable to learn of a family in the county who owned a thermometer at the time. But now to the subject.

James H. Hildreth was born about 1812, in Bourbon county, Ky. He came to Illinois about 1833 or '4, and settled on Vermilion river, near Georgetown, Vermilion county, and engaged in cattle trading. Mr. Hildreth, then twenty-four or twenty-five years of age, was a very stout and rugged young man. He left home on the nineteenth of December, 1836, in company with another young man by the name of Frame, intending to go to Chicago, both on horseback. On the second day out, December 20th, they entered the border of a large prairie, and the next timber was many miles distant, on Hickory creek, a tributary of Iroquois river, and now in Iroquois county. It rained all the forenoon, and the earth was covered with water. They encountered a slough containing so much water they did not like to attempt passing through it. In order to head the slough they rode some miles in a northeast direction, and having crossed it, turned northwest to regain their course. That was about the middle of the afternoon. It suddenly ceased raining and the cold wave came in all its fury from the northwest, striking them square in the face. They were then out of sight of any human habitation, and their horses became absolutely unmanageable, and drifted with the wind, or across it, until dark closed in upon them. How long they were discussing what to do is not stated, but they finally agreed to kill each the others horse. They dismounted and Hildreth killed Frame's horse. They took out the entrails, and both crawled into the carcass as far as they could, and lay there, as near as Hildreth could judge, until about midnight. The animal heat from the carcass having become exhausted, they crawled out, intending that Frame should kill Hildreth's horse, and both crawl into it. Just then the one having the knife dropped it, and it being dark, they were unable to find it. Being thus foiled in their purpose, they both huddled about the living horse as best they could, until about four o'clock in the morning. Frame by that time was so benumbed with the cold that he became sleepy, and notwithstanding Hildreth used every exertion to keep him up, he sank down in a sleep from which he never awakened.

The feelings of Hildreth at this juncture can only be left to the imagination. He managed, by jumping about, to keep from freezing until daylight, when he got on his horse and started in search of shelter. In mounting he dropped his hat, and was afraid to get off, fearing he would never be able to mount again. Thus, bare headed, he wandered about for some time, until he reached the bank of a stream, supposed to be Vermilion river. Seeing a house on the opposite shore, he hallooed as best he could until he attracted the attention of the man, who, after learning what he wanted, said he could not assist him. A canoe was lying at the opposite shore, but he affected to be afraid of the running ice. Hildreth then offered him a large price if he would cut a tree and let it fall over the stream so that he could cross. The man still refused, and directed Hildreth to a grove which he said was a mile distant, where he would find a house. He went, but it was five miles, and the house proved to be a deserted cabin. He returned to the river opposite the house, called again for help, and was refused. He then dismounted, crawled to the bank, and found that the ice had closed and was sufficiently strong to bear him, and he crawled over. Arriving at the fence, the brutal owner of the place refused to help him, and he tumbled over it, and crawling in the house, laid down near the fire. Hildreth lay and begged for assistance, and when the man would have relented and done something, his wife restrained him. The frozen man lay there until four o'clock that afternoon, when some hog drovers came along and moved him to another house, where he was properly cared for. The name of the inhuman wretch was Benjamin Russ. After learning of his inhumanity, a movement was made to punish him, but he fled. Mr. Hildreth always expressed the belief that his offering to pay liberally for cutting a tree across the river, led them to think that he had a large amount of money, and that if, by their neglect, he perished, they could obtain it. Such a being was very rare among the early settlers of central Illinois, who were remarkable for their readiness to divide their comforts with all new comers, and especially those who were in affliction.

Mr. Hildreth met with a heavy loss, financially, by his failure to go to Chicago. He was conveyed back to the house of his brother in Vermilion county, where all the toes were taken from both feet, and the bones of all his fingers, except one joint of the thumb on his right hand, which enabled him to hold a pen or a drover's whip. Soon after recovering sufficiently to enable him to travel, he removed to DeWitt county, where he continued trading in cattle. He was married, April 7, 1847, in DeWitt county, to Adaline Hall. His left foot never healed entirely, and nearly twenty-two years after his misfortune, it became alarming, and he had the leg amputated below the knee. It soon healed, but his lungs, already diseased, caused his death about the middle of June, 1858, near Mt. Pulaski, Illinois.

He has three children now living. Henry resides near Chesnut, Logan county. John lives in Logan county, near Kenny, DeWitt county. His daughter Sarah married William Weedman, and resides near Farmer City. Mrs. Adaline Hildreth married Harrison Meacham, and resides near Clinton, DeWitt county, Illinois.

Notwithstanding his great calamity, James H. Hildreth was a useful man in the community where he lived. Most men would have given up in despair, and become a charge upon their friends; but he was active and energetic, and continued in the business of a farmer and stock dealer until he was physically unable to do more.

Mr. Preston Breckenridge expresses the opinion that the velocity of the cold wave, given in another part of this sketch, is too slow. He thinks it must have moved at least seventy miles an hour, judging from his present knowledge on the subject. He had just taken his dinner, and was sitting near a window, between one and two o'clock in the afternoon, in view of a pool of water, ten or twelve inches deep. He heard a terrific roaring sound. Suddenly the rain ceased, and it became quite dark. The first touch of the blast scooped all the water out of the pool. Some of it returned, but in a moment it was blown out again, and scattered in frost and ice, leaving the pool empty, and the bottom frozen dry. He says it had been raining slowly all the fore part of the day, and so warm that he thinks a thermometer would have stood as high as forty degrees above zero, possibly higher, and that the first touch of the tempest would have brought it down to zero in a second of time. Mr. Breckenridge is well acquainted with many incidents illustrating the unparalleled suddenness and severity of the cold. He relates a case of two young men who lost their lives near Paris, Edgar county, Illinois, after efforts to save themselves similar to those made by Hildreth and his friend. I might cite any number of incidents illustrating the intense suffering caused by the cold in Sangamon county, but the number of those who perished was comparatively small, for the reason that it was more thickly settled than the county north and east. There must have been about ten thousand inhabitants in the county at the time.

A REMARKABLE INCIDENT:—The following incident was related to me by Benj. F. Irwin, who received the statement from Rev. John M. Berry, a Cumberland Presbyterian Minister, who resided a short distance northeast of Pleasant Plains. Families coming into the new settlements were many times put to great inconvenience to pro cure food, and especially breadstuff. Stealing was seldom resorted to, as there was a general desire to divide with new comers. A man who owned a mill, occasionally missed meal and flour, and concluded to lay in wait and see what would be the result. Soon after dark one evening, he placed himself under the bolting chest, and had not long to wait. A man entered the mill, and the first thing he did was to kneel down and pray fervently for pardon for what he was about to do. He laid his whole case before the Lord; told him of his willingness to work, his inability to obtain employment by which he could earn bread, and asked the Lord to open the way for him, and as though he fully expected his prayer to be answered, he took only a sufficient quantity of flour to supply his immediate necessities, and was about to depart. The owner of the mill recognized the man as one for whom he had formed a feeling of great respect, and would have been willing to help if he had known that he was destitute. He called out from his place of concealment for the man to stop. A real thief would have run, but the man with the flour halted without hesitation, when he was told to fill his sack, and when that was gone to come and get more. They were friends before, but were much warmer friends after, to the end of their lives. The facts were kept quiet, and the names of the parties were never known except to a small number of persons; but the miller ever after asserted that he had more confidence in that man than any other he ever saw. The sequel proved that the miller must have been a man of sterling principle, for if he had been like ordinary mortals, the other would have been ruined.

PANTHERS:—John Harlan was among the earliest settlers. He heard a coon making a piteous noise, went out with his gun and found a panther trying to catch it. He shot that and two other panthers in succession, and that gave the name to Panther creek, or Painter creek, as it was generally spoken.

A boy by the name of Jordan, at the age of 14 years, shot a panther in the Lick creek timber, in what is now Loami township. When dead it was found to measure eleven feet from the tip of its nose to the tip of its tail.

A Mrs. Brown, wife of Henry Brown, who was an early settler on Lick creek, in what is now Chatham township, had been to one of her neighbors, and was returning, late in the afternoon, on foot, accompanied by two large dogs. The dogs ran to her, one on each side, which caused her to look, when she saw a huge panther on each side of the road. She walked quietly forward, the dogs keeping close to her side, and so passed the danger. She regarded her escape as almost miraculous, and never could speak of it without a shudder.

MILLS AND MILLING:—Before mills were built here the settlers had to go to Edwardsville for grinding; but sixty or seventy miles was too far to take a grist every day, and it was necessary that something should be more readily obtained. A piece of tin that can now be had anywhere for a few cents, was then an object of great interest. Every old tin vessel was saved, torn in pieces, cut to a suitable size, punched full of holes, and nailed to a board for a grater. While the corn was soft, meal could be grated in a very short time, sufficient to make bread for a whole family, by rubbing an ear of corn back and forth on the grater. That implement is always pronounced by the old settlers "*gritter.*"

Mr. William Drennan remembers that the first mill in Sangamon county was built by Daniel Liles on the farm where Daniel G. Jones now resides, near Horse creek, and on the line between Ball and Cotton Hill townships. It was erected in the fall of 1819, and was made on the plan known as a band mill. That was a horizontal wheel, with arms fifteen feet or more in length, and of sufficient height for the horses to pass under the arms. Several holes would be bored near the outer end of these arms. One wooden pin was placed in each one of the arms. A band of rawhide stretched around those pins and the trunnel head would communicate the power to the burrs, which were usually made of any loose stone picked up on the prairies. A mill of that kind would grind eight or ten bushels a day. Liles' mill never had any roof, and when it rained the track became very muddy. If his customers complained, he would assume an air of injured innocence and ask if they expected him to work in the rain. If they said no, but that he should do it when the weather was fair, his invariable reply was, that they did not need it then. The people came to this mill thirty or forty miles, and although it was kept running day and night, sometimes they would have to wait several days for a turn at the mill. One man told me that when he was a boy his parents started him to mill, supplied with an extra quantity of feed for his horses and some meat for himself, with the understanding that he was to parch corn as a substitute for bread. He had to wait so long for his turn that when it came he had nothing to grind, himself and horses having consumed all the corn, and he would have been compelled to lose his turn, but the miller kindly loaned him a grist, which he repaid the next time he went to mill.

The earliest mills were only intended for grinding corn, and at first no effort was made for bolting flour, but those who raised the first wheat would cut it with the old fashioned reap hooks, called sickles, thresh it on the ground with a flail, separate the chaff and wheat by a man taking a measure of wheat, standing on an elevated place, and pouring it out slowly, with a shaking motion, while two others stood below with a common bed sheet, folded double, and taking hold of each end and giving it a quick motion toward the failing wheat, would thus blow the chaff away, while the wheat, being heavier, would fall perpendicular. The wheat thus cleaned would be taken to the corn mill and ground, of course very imperfectly. The next point was to separate the bran from the flour. At first this was done by making a light frame, three or four feet long, and one and a half by two feet wide, and stretching a piece of the thinnest cloth that could be obtained, over it. Some of the wheat meal would be put on this cloth and the frame shaken from right to left, after the manner of a sieve or meal sifter, and the finest part of the wheat meal would go through. That was made into bread, usually biscuit. That implement was called a search, usually pronounced *sarch*. Some of the earliest settlers will tell you that the sweetest morsel they ever tasted in their whole lives was the first piece of wheat bread thus made, after having been a whole year, and sometimes longer, living on the coarsest of corn bread.

HONESTY OF THE EARLY SETTLERS:—John Sims remembers that a few years after they came to the settlement their corn was all frost bitten, and he went to Madison county to obtain corn for seed and bread. He had to pay $1.00 per bushel for it, and wishing to haul all he could, he filled some sacks and laid them across the corn in the wagon bed. He stalled in the mud, in Macoupin county, and left his wagon there, several miles from any house, and where people traveling hundreds of miles had to pass it. When he went home for more teams, some unexpected obstacles presented themselves, and it was two weeks or more before he returned. When he did so, some of his corn was gone, but closer examination revealed the fact that money was tied in the sacks from which the corn was taken. Some was tied with horse hairs and some with strings, in small bunches, in all between eight and ten dollars; sufficient to fully compensate for the corn taken. He has hauled dry goods and groceries, in large and small packages, has stalled and left his wagon for days and weeks, and never knew anything to be stolen.

When the land office was opened, in 1823, in Springfield, the receiver was ordered to send the coin to Louisville, Ky. The route was so difficult to travel and so long, that he was permitted, after one effort, to send it to St. Louis for safe keeping. Mr. Sims had a good team, and was called on to do the hauling. On more than one occasion he has loaded his wagon with boxes of gold and silver, amounting to from thirty to fifty thousand dollars. He has gone without any guard, been two or three nights on the road, would feed his horses tied to the wagon, sleep on some straw thrown over the boxes, and was never molested, and never thought there was danger.

A SNAKE STORY:—Gen. James Adams was bitten by a rattlesnake in 1821, and wishing to obtain some rattlesnake oil, he advertised that he would pay fifty cents for the first one brought to him, and in order to make sure of getting one, he offered twenty-five cents for each additional one. A man by the name of Barnes found a den near the mouth of Spring creek, killed all he could, loaded them in a wagon, drove to Springfield, and left his wagon in an out-of-the-way place. He first took one snake and received fifty cents, then two, and received twenty-five cents each. He then took Gen. Adams to the wagon and showed him the whole load. Adams refused to pay for them. Barnes then called his attention to the advertisement, but he still refused. Barnes then called on two men, Reuben Burden and John White, who counted the load, and there were 122 snakes. He then demanded his money, $30.75. This brought the General to a compromise, and the matter was settled by his paying $5.00 extra. Joseph E. McCoy is my authority.

Albion Knotts says that when they come to the country, in 1819, his father soon learned that the next supply of shoes for his family would have to be manufactured by himself, although he had never made a shoe. This discovery was barely made when he found that he must produce the leather also, as there were no tanners in the country. He first cut down a large oak tree, peeled off the bark and laid it up to dry. He dug a trough in the log, as large as it would make, for a tan vat. He then gathered up all the hides he could obtain. The next question was how to remove the hair. It was known that it could not be done by regular tanners' process, both for want of the proper materials, and the knowledge in using them. Some person suggested that it might be done with water and ashes, but great caution would be necessary, lest the solution be made too strong. In that event it would ruin the hides. In his extreme caution he did not make it strong enough, and so removed but a little more than half the hair. In place of grinding the bark he beat it up on a stump with the poll of an axe. He then put the hides in the trough, covered them with the pulverized bark, put on weights to keep the mass down, and filled the trough with water, changing the bark several times during the summer. As winter approached he took the hides out, though not more than half tanned, and made them into shoes. He made them on what was called the *stick down* plan. That is, in place of turning the upper leather under the last, it was turned outward and sewed with a straight awl through the upper and sole. This would make a walk all around the shoe that a mouse might travel on. It was frequently the case that awls could not be obtained. Then they would take a common table fork, break off one of the tines, and sharpen the other for the awl. Shoes made as I have described, with the upper leather hair side out, not more than half of it removed, and without any blacking, would certainly look very odd. There can be little doubt that the above is a fair description of the first tanning and shoe making ever done in Sangamon county.

When the first settlers came there were no stores filled with dry goods, as there are now, and if the goods had been in the country there was no money to buy them. The only way families could supply themselves with clothing was to produce the materials and manufacture their own goods. Those who first came from the Southern States—as most of them did—brought their cotton, flax and hemp seed, raised the fibre and did all the work. They at first picked the seed by hand, carded it on hand cards, spun it on wheels designed for spinning wool or flax, wove it into cloth, and made it into garments for men and women's wear. That which was designed for underclothing was prepared without coloring, as a matter of course, but for outer garments, and particularly ladies' dresses, something better was required. Some among the earliest brought a little indigo, madder, and same other drugs, but for greater variety and economy, a large number of barks were used, such as black walnut, butternut, several varieties of oak, hickory, etc. When peach trees grew the leaves were used for making one of the brightest colors. Some of the cotton yarn, dyed with each of those colors, skilfully arranged in weaving, and made into dresses, looked remarkably well. Some of the *old* boys now living say that the young ladies of their time, thus attired, looked equally as charming in their eyes as those of the present era, with their flounces made of goods from the looms of Lyons and the shops of Paris, do to our young men. Flax and tow was never colored, and was mostly used for men and boys' wear in the summer. A tow shirt, with a draw string around the neck, and reaching below the knees, was a full dress in summer for boys up to ten or twelve years of age. Some of our most substantial farmers were thus attired in their boyhood days.

Elisha Primm says that his father built a cotton gin in 1822. He says that from the time the first settlers came into the county until the winter of the "deep snow," 1830 and '31, this was as good a cotton country as Georgia. He says that this was attested by men familiar with cotton growing in the Southern States. Elisha attended the gin built by his father, which was run by horse power. The people brought cotton to be ginned, from all distances up to twenty miles. Sometimes it would accumulate on his hands until he would have as much as 3,000 pounds. The price for ginning was a toll of one pound in every eight, after the cotton was ginned. It sold from 12 to 16⅔ cents per pound, and occasionally higher. After the "deep snow" the seasons appeared to shorten, and cotton was generally bitten by the frost before it had time to mature, and cotton raising was finally abandoned. It seemed as though the seasons were overruled so as to be adapted to the wants of the pioneer settlers, when there was no other way for them to be supplied with clothing, but when roads were opened and capital came in, bringing merchandise, the seasons gravitated back to their normal condition.

FIRST PRODUCE MARKETED:—Mr. William Drennen believes that the first produce marketed in the county was on Sugar creek, in the Summer of 1818. George Cox sold half a dozen small green pumpkins to an Indian for twelve and a half cents.

—10

This note was written while I was standing on the spot, a few yards north of the Sulphur Springs, south of Loami, where once stood a sycamore tree in which A. E. Meacham took a ten foot rail, held it in a horizontal position against his waist, and turned entirely around inside the tree. It was about eighteen feet in diameter outside, and was long used as a wigwam by the Indians. The entrance was at the east side. It was safe when there were only Indians in the country, but some vandal, claiming to be civilized, set fire to it and burned it down.

The Sulphur Spring spoken of above, bubbles up at the foot of a hill near Lick creek, and in its natural state, when animals approached it to drink the water, was a quagmire, but the early settlers made an excavation, eight or nine feet deep, and walled it up, so that the water flows out over the top of the wall, clear and pure. Soon after it was thus improved two old topers, on a very hot day, visited the spring, taking with them a jug of whisky, intending to have a good time laying in the shade near by, drinking their whisky, and for variety, taking an occasional sip at the sulphur water. One of them undertook to cool the whisky by holding the jug in the water, and while doing so let it slip from his grasp. To cut a forked limb from a tree and make a hook of it would be too much work. In order to rescue the jug, the one who let it slip consented that the other should take him by the heels and let him down head foremost. The whisky was secured in that way, at the imminent risk of drowning one or both of the men. It must have been liberally watered or it would not have sunk.

There are at least one hundred and fifty grave yards and burial places in Sangamon county, and nine-tenths of them are so much neglected that, so far as marking any particular locality or grave, the following lines, taken from a Scottish grave yard, are peculiarly applicable:

> "In this church yard lies Eppie Coutts,
> Either here or hereabouts;
> But whaur it is none can tell,
> Till Eppie rise and tell hersel."

The first death of a white man in Sangamon county was that of an Indian ranger. The Sulphur Spring near Loami was known to the Indians, and was very early a camping ground for the whites. When the settlements had not extended farther north than the vicinity of Alton, Indians, according to their custom, killed some of the frontier settlers, and were pursued by some Rangers. While camped at the sulphur spring one of them died, and was buried by his comrades on a beautiful knoll near the spring. It was known to the very earliest settlers as the grave of the Indian Ranger, and was the nucleus of the present Sulphur Springs Cemetery. The land was entered by Jonathan Jarrett, who intended a small part of it for a cemetery and church purposes, but died without making a deed. A regular company has been organized, according to law, and it is now handsomely fitted up and well cared for. There ought to be a monument over the grave of the Indian Ranger, to show that it was the first burial of a white man in the county.

EXPLANATION.

The names of early settlers, or heads of families, in LARGE LETTER; Names of the second generation in *ITALIC CAPITALS*; third, in CAPITALS; fourth, in SMALL CAPITALS; fifth, in *Italics*.

A.

ABEL, ROSWELL, was born July 23, 1785, on Sharon Mountain, Litchfield county, Conn. Three brothers by the name of Abel came from England about 1750. One of them settled in Connecticut, one in Virginia, and what became of the other is unknown. Jonathan, who settled in Conn., brought up a family of five sons and two daughters. His son David was the father of the subject of this sketch. David Abel, and two of his brothers, William and Andrew, were Revolutionary soldiers. William settled in Canada after the Revolution, and brought up a family there. This branch of the family has lost sight of Andrew. David was born on Sharon mountain, married and lived on the same farm until four children were born, and then moved to Washington county, N. Y., where six children were born. Each brought up families. David Abel presented the gun which he carried through the Revolution, to his son Roswell, with instructions to present it to *his* son, if he had one, but if not, to a brother's son. He has it yet in his possession, at the home of his son Roswell P., to whom he bequeaths it. The brass breech bears the inscription "Liberty or Death," every letter of which is yet distinct.

Roswell Abel, whose name heads this sketch, was married Oct. 22, 1807, to Betsy Mason. She was born Oct. 22, 1790, at Fort Ann, Washington county, N. Y. Her father, Coomer Mason, was a Revolutionary soldier, also. He had two brothers, Shubal and Hail, who fought at the battle of Benington. Roswell and Betsy Abel had three children, born at Granville, Washington County, N. Y. They moved to Springfield, Ill., arriving July 15, 1836. Of their children—

LIZETTE, was born December 4, 1809, married Oct., 1829, in Essex county, N. Y., to Calvin Peabody. They came to Springfield in 1838. They had five living children, namely: CHARLES P., born Feb. 25, 1837, married April 5 1866, to Jane Cheeseman. They have three children, HARRY, IDELLA L., and MARY. HELEN, born Jan. 28, 1835, married Oct. 24, 1865, to Amos Atwood. They have two children, HELEN M., born Jan. 18, 1867, and EMMA C., born August 14, 1869, and reside near Farmington, Dacotah county, Minnesota. JOHN C., born March 13, 1843, married Feb. 4, 1868, in Enterprise, Mo., to Emily Kinsman. They have four children, BURTON, FRANKLIN, WILLIAM and HARRY, and reside in Brookfield, Mo. SARAH E., born in Sangamon county, married July 11, 1857, to Dr. Orlando Lent. They had one child, CHARLES J. He died Nov. 4, 1874, in his 17th year, and Dr. Lent died while on duty at Paducah, Ky., Military Hospital, in 1863. His widow married T. M. Elliott, and resides near Grantsville, Linn county, Mo. EDWIN R., born Dec. 12, 1844, enlisted Dec. 14, 1863, in Vaughn's Battery 3d Ill. Art. He was married Jan. 24, 1867, in Missouri, to

Clara Sockman. They have three children, ORLEY, FRANCIS and TRUDELLA, and reside near Browning, Linn county, Missouri. Calvin Peabody moved from Sangamon county, Illinois, to Linn county, Missouri, in 1865, and died there, Sept. 7, 1870. His widow resides near Browning.

CHLOE E., born April 19, 1812, in New York. Married Nov., 1839, in Springfield, to John Armstrong. *See his name.*

ROSWELL P., born June 30, 1815, in Washington county, New York; came to Sangamon county, Illinois, with his parents in 1836. Married September 30, 1846, at Greencastle, Pa., to Margaret J. Loose. She was born there, Jan. 22, 1820. They reside at Rochester, Ill.

Roswell Abell and wife have been married more than 69 years. They reside with their son, Roswell P., at Rochester, Sangamon county, Illinois.

ABELL, JEREMIAH, was born in 1770, in Rockingham county, Va. He was there married to Hannah Aiken, who was born in 1771. They emigrated to Adair county, Ky. Mr. Abell was the owner of some slaves, but he liberated them in Kentucky, and moved with his family to Sangamon county, Ill., arriving in 1829, in what is now Auburn township. Their daughter—

PENELOPE, married in Adair county, Ky., to Samuel McElvain. *See his name.* They come to Sangamon county with her parents.

Their son, Dr. J. R. Abell, resides at Taylorville.

Rev. Jeremiah Abell was regularly educated for the ministry, preached many years in connection with the Presbyterian church, and received the title of Doctor of Divinity. After coming to Illinois he severed his connection with the Presbyterian church and united with the Methodists. He moved, about 1846, to McDonough county, and died there in 1852.

ADAMS, JAMES, was born Jan. 24, 1783, in Hartford, Conn. Harriet Denton was born Jan. 31, 1787, in Hartford, also. They were there married about 1809, and moved to Oswego, N. Y., where they had five children. They moved to Springfield, Illinois, arriving in the spring of 1821, soon after the place was declared to be the county seat of Sangamon county. Of their four living children,

LOVENIA E., born May 3, 1813, at Oswego, N. Y., married in Springfield, to Peter Weber. *See his name.* They both died in the north part of the State. She died Sept. 5, 1838.

CHARLOTTE B., born May 2, 1815, in Oswego, N. Y., and died Jan. 10, 1832.

LUCIAN B., born Dec. 10, 1816, in Oswego, N. Y.; married in Springfield, March 14, 1847, to Margery A. Reed, who was born July 9, 1824, in Williamsport, Penn. They have four children. JAMES L., born Jan. 22, 1848, in Springfield, graduated in a commercial college in Chicago, and is employed in a railroad office in Vallejo, California. ELDORA J., ENOLA A. and HARRIET L., reside with their parents in Springfield. Lucian B. Adams studied law and obtained license to practice in 1840. For twenty years he discharged the duties of a justice of the peace, and the greater part of that time acted as police magistrate, U. S. commissioner and notary public. He is now U. S. commissioner.

VIENNA M., born July 10, 1818, in Oswego, N. Y.; married in Springfield, to Charles G. McGraw. *See his name.*

James Adams was a lawyer, and engaged in practice when he came to Springfield, in 1821. He was elected justice of the peace in 1823 or '4 and was elected successively for many years. He took part in the Winnebago and Black Hawk Indian wars of 1827, and 1831 and '2. He was elected Probate Judge of Sangamon county, and died in office, August 11, 1843. His widow, Mrs. Harriet Adams, died August 21, 1844, both in Springfield.

ALEXANDER, THOMAS, was born about 1768, in Ireland, and his parents came to America when he was about four years old, landing at Charleston, S. C. Lynna Goodlett was born Oct. 11, 1780, in Greenville District, S. C. They were there married, and had three children, all of whom died under eight years. In 1806 they moved to Christian county, near Hopkinsville, Ky., where they had two children, and moved to Sangamon county, Ill., arriving in Oct., 1828, three miles east of Auburn. In 1829 they moved to what is now Chatham township, south of Lick creek. Of their two children,

MARY ANN, born in 1810, in Kentucky; married in Sangamon county to John L. Drennan. (See his name.)

DAVID, born Oct. 3, 1814, in Christian county, Ky.; came to Sangamon county in 1828; married March 13, 1833, to Catharine Darnielle; had 14 children, all born in Sangamon county, six of whom died in infancy, and LYNNA died at 13 years. Of the other seven, JOHN T., born Dec. 25, 1835, enlisted on the first call for 75,000 men, April, 1861, for three months, in Co. A., 2nd Kansas Cavalry, served full term, and enlisted Nov., 1861, in Co. D., 2nd Mo. Art., for three years. Re-enlisted as a veteran Jan., 1864. He lost his right hand April 13, 1865, at St. Charles, Ark., by the premature discharge of a cannon, while firing a salute on hearing of the surrender of the rebel forces under Gen. Lee. He now (1873) resides with his parents. DAVID S., born Nov. 20, 1842, enlisted August 13, 1861, in Co. B., 30th Ill. Inf., for three years; served until August 9, 1862, when he was discharged on account of physical disability, at Memphis, Tenn. He was brought home, and, after a lingering illness, died, March 10, 1866. CATHARINE, born Dec. 20, 1844; married May 29, 1862, to Lafayette Beach. (See his name.) Had one child, CHARLES D. HIRAM, born March 30, 1847; enlisted March 14, 1864, in Co. C., 11th Mo. Inf., for three years. Served until July 14, 1865, when he was discharged on account of physical disability. He was married March 9, 1873, to Mary M. VanDoren. They reside five miles southwest of Chatham. WILLIAM, born Oct. 1, 1849; married March 14, 1872, to Emma Price, and reside in Chatham township. MARY BELLE and CYRUS reside with their parents, six miles southwest of Chatham, on the farm where the family settled in 1829.

Thomas Alexander died Dec. 18, 1835, and his widow died August 12, 1844, both in Sangamon county.

ALEXANDER, HENRY, was born June 10, 1802, in Fleming county, Ky. His father moved to the adjoining county of Bath when he was a child. He was married June 24, 1827, to Polly Gragg, of Nicholas county, and lived in Bath county until 1833, when he moved to Montgomery county. They had four children in Kentucky, and moved to Sangamon county, Ill., arriving Oct. 22, 1835, in what is now Rochester township, where four children were born. Of their children,

JESSE F., born Dec. 10, 1828, in Bath county, Ky., married in Sangamon county, Ill., March 4, 1852, to Nancy A. Hendrix, who was born April 22, 1829, in Fleming county, Ky. They had five children; one died young. LUCRETIA, their second child, born June 26, 1855, married March 12, 1874, to James A. Walker. The other three, LAURA, GEORGE and REBECCA reside with their parents, near Appleton City, St. Clair county, Mo.

HIRAM, born in Kentucky; married in Sangamon county to Eliza Hendrix. They have seven children, and reside in Jefferson county, Iowa.

LUCINDA A., born in Kentucky; married in Sangamon county to Isaac Groves. (See his name.) Their daughter Susan married John W. McClelland. (See his name.)

WILLIAM G., born in Kentucky; married in Sangamon county to Julia McIntyre. They have four children, and reside near Illiopolis.

JAMES O., born in Sangamon county; married Sarah Ham. They have three children, and reside in Champaign county.

REBECCA and HENRY H., (twins) born in Sangamon county.

REBECCA married John W. Smith, had four children, and she died in 1870. Two of the children died also, near Williamsville.

HENRY H. married Emily Sargent, and resides in Illiopolis.

POLLY S., born in Sangamon county; married Benjamin Keck; have three children, and reside in Illiopolis.

Mrs. Polly Alexander died August 25, 1868, and her husband, Henry Alexander, resides with his children.

ALEXANDER, JOHN S., was born Sept. 24, 1793, near Lexington, Ky.; married Mary Simpson, who was born April 16, 1799, in Fayette county, Ky. They were there married, and had four children. The family moved to Sangamon county, Ill., arriving in the fall of 1826, in what is now Fancy creek township, where six children were born. Of their children,

SARAH S., born Nov. 7, 1820, in Kentucky; married March 6, 1837, to Samuel D. Cantrall. (See his name.)

JAMES H., born March 19, 1822, in Kentucky; married in Sangamon county to Ann E. Hardin. They live in Washington Territory.

HANNAH H., born June 1, 1824, in Kentucky; married James Kilgour, and died. (See his name.)

WILLIAM, born June 12, 1826, in Fayette county, Ky.; married in Sangamon county to Eveline Lacey; had three children, and she and all the children died. He married Catharine Hill. They have three children, FREDIE, FRANKIE and a babe, and reside at Williamsville.

ASA C. and MARGARET C., (twins), born March 15, 1829, in Sangamon county.

ASA C. married Mary J. Tabor, and resides in Ford county.

MARGARET C. married Harrison Blue; had two children, and he died, April, 1852, and she married George Martin, and resides in Iroquois county.

GEORGE, born Feb. 13, 1831, in Sangamon county; enlisted in a Kansas regiment in 1861 or '2, and died in military hospital at Springfield, Mo.

JOHN S., Jun., married Dorcus A. Mills.

SAMUEL C., born Jan. 31, 1838; married Amanda Hall, and lives in Ford county.

MARY J., born April 15, 1840, in Sangamon county; married August 7, 1856, to Andrew J. Hedrick, who was born August 23, 1834. They had three children, HARRISON H., RUTH A. and ALICE V. Mr. Hedrick enlisted August 15, 1862, in Co. I., 34 Iowa Inf., for three years. He was discharged on account of physical disability, March 13, and died May 8, 1863, in Menard county. Mrs. Hedrick married, Oct. 12, 1864, to William Reesburg. They have one child, WILLIAM H., and reside near Illiopolis.

Mrs. Mary Alexander died Nov. 1, 1852, and John S. Alexander died July 15, 1853, both in Sangamon county.

ALKIRE, HARMONAS, was born in 1804, in Bourbon county, Ky. His parents moved, when he was quite young, to Pickaway county, O. In 1826 he visited Sangamon county on business for other parties. Returning to Ohio, he went to Lafayette, Ind. The next year he came to Sangamon county again, on business, and was married in Springfield, Dec. 31, 1829, to Martha McLemore. She was born July 10, 1810, in Burke county, N. C. Her parents moved, in 1811, to Knoxville, Tenn., and moved from there to Sangamon county, Ill., arriving, Dec. 23, 1828, at Springfield. Soon after marriage Mr. Alkire returned to Lafayette with his wife. They had two children born there, and then moved to Sangamon county, arriving, August, 1832, in what is now Fancy Creek township, where they had eight living children. Of the other ten children,

MARY ANN, born at Lafayette, Ind., is unmarried, and resides with her parents.

JAMES V., born Feb. 3, 1832, at Lafayette, Ind.; married, Oct. 4, 1866, to Addie H. Ross, who was born March 6, 1838, in Miami county, O. They have two living children, ANNIE M. and MARGARET A. J. V. Alkire is farming and practicing medicine. Resides three miles west of Sherman.

MARGARET J., born Dec. 17, 1833, in Sangamon county; married Isaac Mull, who was born March 2, 1820, in Mason county, Ky. They have five children, IDA M., HENRY E., JENNIE, MATTIE E. and CHARLES C., and reside four miles north of Springfield.

CAROLINE M., born Jan. 24, 1835, in Sangamon county; married April 6, 1865, to Conrad Shamel. They have three children, CHARLES H., CLARENCE A. and JOHN Y., and reside near Springfield.

WILLIAM W., born July 26, 1837, in Sangamon county; married Judith S. Lightfoot. They have three children, HERBERT, EMMETT and ARTHUR, and reside four miles southwest of Troy, Doniphan county, Kan.

DANIEL, born in Sangamon county, is a traveling preacher in the M. E. church, at present, 1873, resides with his parents, recruiting his health.

ALBERT H., born in Sangamon county, is a traveling preacher in Illinois Conference, M. E. church, 1873.

PRISCILLA E., married George W. Neer, and resides near Taylorville.

MATTIE E., married Edward J. Myers. They have two children, MARY

A. and EDWARD L., and reside in Fancy Creek township.

LEANDER died June 5, 1871, in his 18th year.

Harmonas Alkire and his wife are living on the farm where they settled in 1832. It is three miles west of Sherman. He confirms the statement of Washington Crowder that the sudden change took place December 20, 1836, because he entered a piece of land that day, and the papers bear the above date.

ALLEN, ROBERT, was born in the year 1800, in Greensburg, Green county, Ky. He was married there to a Miss Anderson, and came to Springfield, Ill., in 1831. Col. Allen engaged in the mercantile business as a member of the firm of Allen & Blankenship, soon after coming to Springfield. He also became a mail contractor on a very extensive scale, and brought a large number of fine stage coaches from Nashville, Tenn., being the first ever introduced into the State. He made Springfield his headquarters, and on some occasions had as many as five hundred horses on hand at one time. Col. Allen was one of the directors of the old State Bank. He was connected with the army in the Mormon war in 1845, and in the Mexican war of 1846-7. Not long after coming to Springfield, Mrs. Allen died, and Mr. Allen was married in April, 1833, to Jane Eliza Bergen. They had two children, one of whom died young. Their son,

ROBERT, Jun., born Feb. 28, 1837, in Springfield, and brought up in the city. When the rebellion broke out he was commissioned, August 28, 1861, as Captain of Co. —, 30 Ill. Inf., and served as such until May 25, 1863, when he was promoted to Major of the regiment, in front of Vicksburg. He served part of the time in the Quartermaster's department; also acted as Assistant Inspector-General of the 3d Div. 17th Army Corps, and resigned August 8, 1864. Major Robert Allen was married Dec. 5, 1865, in Springfield, to Anna M. Purdy, who was born May 12, 1838, in Trenton, N. J. They had three children. GEORGE B., the youngest, died August 12, 1872, in his second year. HENRY T. and FANNIE M. reside with their parents in Springfield. Major Allen is a practicing attorney.

Col. Robert Allen died Dec. 1, 1854, and his widow, Mrs. Jane Eliza Allen, died March 18, 1857, both one mile north of the old State house in Springfield.

ALLEN, WILLIAM S., was born June 16, 1774, in Bourbon county, Ky. He was married to Abigail Snedegar. They had five children in Kentucky. Mr. Allen came to Sangamon county in 1835, purchased land and prepared a house. He returned to Kentucky and brought his family, arriving Nov. 1, 1836, in what is now Ball township. Of their children,

MARIA L., born in Bourbon county, Ky., was married there to Shelton Watts. They had three children there, and moved to Sangamon county in 1839. Of their children, NANCY J. married John Drennan, and resides near Tolono, Champaign county, Ill. WILLIAM S. married Sarah Knotts, and resides near Tolono, Ill. BENJ. FRANKLIN married Isabel F. Thompson. *See R. B. Thompson sketch.* Shelton Watts died July 16, 1843, and his widow married John Brownwell. *See his name.*

MARY E., born Feb. 28, 1819, in Bourbon county, Ky., was married in Sangamon county, Ill., June 16, 1841, to James W. Stephenson. They had nine children. MARGARET A., born July 16, 1842, was married Sept. 2, 1875, to Andrew Little. They reside near New Canton, Ill. JAMES A., born June 30, 1843, WILLIAM E., born July 24, 1845, FINIS E., born Oct. 18, 1849, and PRESLEY B., born March 14, 1851, reside with their parents. MARY E., born Nov. 7, 1854, was married June 6, 1872, and resides in Mexico, Mo., and ELLEN, born Sept. 9, 1856, resides with her parents. Two children died in infancy. James W. Stephenson and family reside near New Canton, Ill.

NANCY died in Kentucky, aged 19 years.

WATERMAN P., born Jan. 8, 1820, in Bourbon county, Ky., was married in Sangamon county, Feb., 1849, to Louisa Watts. They have four children. MARIA L. and WILLIAM S. reside with their father. MARY E. was married Oct. 29, 1873, to John L. Clayton, and resides in Ball township. JULIA A. resides with her father. Mrs. Louisa Allen died Nov. 26, 1857, and W. P. Allen was married Oct. 18, 1858, to Catharine Vaughn. They have six children, MARGARET E., HARRIET R., LOUISA J., JOHN, JOSEPH F. and ALPH. R., and reside in Ball township, on the farm settled by Mr. Allen's father, in 1836.

JOHN W., born in Kentucky, brought up in Sangamon county, was married in Menard county, Illinois, to Jane Watkins. They reside near Atlantic, Cass county, Iowa.

Mrs. Abigail Allen died Sept. 10, 1843, and William S. Allen died Dec. 11, 1848, both in Sangamon county, Ill.

ALLISON, ISAAC F., was born July 2, 1801, in Virginia, and his parents moved to Mason county, Ky. He was married about 1827, to Deborah Callerman. They lived in Fleming county, Ky., a short time, and moved to Sangamon county, arriving in the fall of 1829, on Spring creek, where seven children were born.

JOHN, born in 1828, in Fleming county, Ky., raised in Sangamon county, enlisted in the 4th Ill. Inf., under Col. E. D. Baker, in 1846, and died the same year at Matamoras, Texas.

JOSEPH, born in Sangamon county; married Hannah Knudson and died, leaving a widow and three children.

SUSANNAH, died, aged twelve years.

ELIZABETH is unmarried, and resides in Kansas.

JAMES M., born April 13, 1840, in Sangamon county; enlisted August 5, 1861, in Co. A., 38th Ill. Inf.; discharged on account of physical disability, March 29, 1862. He re-enlisted, in Sept., 1862, for three years, in Co. K, 115 Ill. Inf.; was transferred, in 1864, to Co. A., First U. S. Engineers, and was honorably discharged with the regiment, Sept. 19, 1865. He was married Nov. 18, 1866, in Sangamon county, to Julia A. Dunham. They have two children, MARTHA D. and ALICE M., and reside five miles northeast of Springfield.

ELIJAH and MINERVA reside near Jacksonville, Neosho county, Kan.

JOHN W., born in Sangamon county, died June 29, 1868; aged 21 years.

Mrs. Deborah Allison died May 29, 1860, in Sangamon county, and Isaac F. Allison died December 22, 1869, in Crawford county, near Jacksonville, Neosho county, Kan.

ALLISON, MARGARET, came to Sangamon county as one of the family of Thomas Black. See his name. She arrived in 1819. Her parents lived in Philadelphia. She died within one year after arrival, in the 29th year of her age.

ALSBURY, REV. CHAS. D., was born Oct. 25, 1817, in Indiana. He came to Sangamon county, Ill., and was married March 14, 1839, to Ann Cordelia Cloyd. They had five living children, namely:

THOMAS, born Feb. 12, 1840, and died Nov. 6, 1860.

ANN, born in 1841 or '2; married April 4, 1861, to John W. Anderson. They have four children, CHARLES W., MINNIE A., JOHN C. and MELISSA J., and reside in Woodside township.

CAROLINE, married, Dec., 1870, to Leander L. Little; have one child, and reside in Montgomery county.

MARTHA, married, Jan. 3, 1867, to John D. Smith. See his name.

JOHN C. resides with his mother.

Rev. Charles D. Alsbury was a preacher of the gospel in connection with the Baptist church. He died, and his widow resides one and a half miles northwest of Woodside.

AYLESBURY, CHARLES, was born in North Carolina and married in Virginia, to Mrs. Jane Huggins. They moved to Kentucky, and from there to Springfield, Ill., in 1823. Mr. Aylesbury entered the land south of the public square. They brought some children with them. Mrs. Aylesbury's daughter, by her first marriage,

JANE HUGGINS, born in Virginia, married William B. Jarrett. See his name.

Of the Aylesbury children,

CHARLES, born in Greenbrier county, Virginia, and married there to Mary Reay. They had two children, and came to Sangamon county in 1823, and settled on Spring creek, where they had nine children. JOHN, born in Virginia; married in Sangamon county to Sarah West, and reside in Piatt county. ELIZABETH, born Jan. 8, 1822, in Greenbrier county, Va.; married in Sangamon county, August 9, 1849, to George W. Buchanan, who was born Nov. 27, 1823, in Morgan county, Ill. Mr. and Mrs. Buchanan had six children. MARY J. married B. F. Nurbonn, and resides with her father. JAMES F. died in 1871, aged 19 years. SUSANNA, ELIZABETH, ALBERT and ISAAC, reside with their father. Mrs. Elizabeth B. died, and G. W. Buchanan resides west of Loami. BRICE died in Sangamon county, aged 20 years. EDWARD and NANCY are married, and live in Missouri. Charles Aylesbury, wife and three children reside in Piatt county.

ALEXANDER, born in Virginia; married in Sangamon county, to Ginsey Jordan, raised a family, and moved to Decatur. He enlisted in an Illinois regiment, served three years, re-enlisted as a veteran, was furloughed home, and died in Springfield.

LEVI, the youngest son, is married, and resides in Macon county.

Charles Aylesbury, Sen., died in 1861, in Loami township. His widow resides with her son Levi, in Macon county. She is now—1873—more than 96 years old.

ALVEY, WILLIAM, was born Sept. 16, 1799, in Washington county, Ky. He came to the southern part of Illinois in 1824, and to Springfield in May, 1825. He was married Nov. 6, 1825, near Springfield, to Madaline Watson. They had six children, all born in Springfield.

MELVINA, born July 22, 1826, in Springfield; married there to Samuel B. Fisher. See his name.

SIMON B., born Oct. 16, 1827, in Springfield, went to Oregon in 1849, was married in Yamhill county, Oregon, August 30, 1853, to Dollie V. Elder, daughter of A. R. Elder, formerly of Springfield, Ill. They have five children, viz: ALICE M., born Oct. 10, 1854, in Yamhill county; married, August 30, 1873, to James H. Downey, of Steilacoom City, W. T. WILLIAM A., born June 25, 1864, in Oregon. EDITH S., born Sept. 17, 1867. EDWARD B., born Feb. 28, 1873, and JUNIA AFTON, born June 24, 1874; reside with their parents in Steilacoom City, Pierce county, Washington Territory.

ELIZA A., born Oct. 17, 1829, in Springfield; married at Marengo, Iowa, to Dr. George W. Wallace, who was born in Columbiana county, Ohio. Studied medicine with Dr. McCook, one of the celebrated McCook family. Moved to Iowa in the spring of 1848. They had seven children, namely: GEORGE W., MARY E., FLORENCE, WILLIAM A., CLARA, ALFRED F., and LINCOLN. Dr. W. died April 4, 1865, at Salisbury, Sangamon county. Mrs. Wallace and family reside in Springfield.

MARY E., born July 12, 1831, in Springfield, married, about 1859, to Josiah Hickel. They reside in Kansas.

J. WILLIAM, born March 12, 1834, in Springfield, was married there, May 20, 1860, to Alzina A. Brown, (daughter of Ira A. Brown.) They have six children, viz: MELVINA, HELEN B., JAMES W., HENRY P., HOMER W. and ———. Mr. J. Wm. Alvey is a merchant in Mechanicsburg, Sangamon county, Ill.

ALFRED resides in Springfield.

William Alvey moved to Marengo, Iowa, in 1848, and Mrs. Madeline Alvey died there, May 12, 1849. He was married April, 1850, to Eleanor Penny. He died May, 1855, at Marengo, Iowa.

AMOS, MRS. SARAH, was born June 13, 1793, in Washington county, Md. Her maiden name was Friend. She first married Phillip Swinley; had two children, and Mr. Swinley died. Mrs. Swinley was married the second time, August 2, 1810, to James Amos. They had two children, and James Amos died Feb. 6, 1823, in Maryland, also. Mrs. Amos came with her children to Sangamon county, arriving March 1, 1838, in Springfield. Of her children,

BARBARA E. SWINLEY married in Virginia to Thomas Lemon, who died, and Mrs. Lemon came with her child to Sangamon county in 1839, and died in Decatur, April, 1865. Her daughter VIRGINIA married Joseph Strong, in Decatur, moved to Hannibal, Mo., and died there, June, 1872, leaving three children.

SAMUEL K. SWINLEY, born April 21, 1802, in Washington county, Md.; married there to Maria Rice, and came to Springfield with his half brother, Joshua F. Amos. Mr. Swinley settled near where Woodside station now stands. While there he served as one of the county judges with J. Wickliffe Taylor and Armstrong. His wife died there in the fall of 1852. Judge Swinley moved to

Decatur in 1857 or '8, was there married to Ruth Prather, of Washington county, Md. He died early in 1872, and his widow resides in Decatur.

JOSHUA F. AMOS, was born Jan. 28, 1812, in Washington county, Md., and came to Springfield, Ill., June 10, 1835. He was married March 1, 1838, in Springfield, to Julia A. Hay, daughter of John Hay, Esq. They had three children born in Springfield. SARAH E., born Oct. 30, 1839, married Oct. 30, 1861, to Levin W. Shepherd, who was born in Loudon county, Va., Sept. 3, 1836. He served one year each, 1860 and 1861, as clerk and comptroller of the city of Springfield; was a member of the Board of Supervisors of Sangamon county in 1868 and 1869. In 1862 he was appointed by President Lincoln Assistant Quartermaster in the U. S. Army, and stationed at Fort Ridgely, Minn. Transferred to Keokuk, Iowa, where he commanded that Fort for six months. Thence to Columbus, Ky., as Depot Quartermaster; thence to Chicago, as Disbursing Quartermaster; thence to Tennessee, thence to Fort Kearney, Nebraska, at which place he resigned, Oct., 1865, and became a lumber merchant in Springfield, Ill. Afterwards removed to Kansas; was first President of Peoples National Bank of Ottawa. Resides now in Denison, Texas, which place he laid out in 1872, and sold the first lot there. Col. Shepherd was twice brevetted for faithful services during the war. GEO. A., born Sept. 4, 1841, married, Oct. 30, 1866, to Josephine A. Andrews, eldest daughter of Col. George W. Andrews, at Wapakoneta, Auglaize county, Ohio. She was born there, May 29, 1844. They have two children, GEORGIA and ROBERTA, and reside in Humboldt, Kansas. Mr. George A. Amos is engaged in the practice of law. JOHN M., born August 18, 1844. He enlisted in Col. Phillips' three months regiment. Stationed at Rock Island, Ill., in 1864. He was married Oct. 30, 1867, to Caroline J., youngest daughter of Oramel Clark, Esq. They have four children, JOHN J., GEORGE O., JULIA R., and CURTIS H., and reside near Springfield. Mr. Joshua F. Amos and wife reside adjoining Springfield, on the west. Mr. Amos spent six years, from 1845 to 1851, in Lagrange, Mo. In 1852 he, with Nathaniel Hay, established the well known firm of Amos & Hay, which continued until the decease of Mr. Hay. Mr. Amos has retired from active business.

ROBERT J. AMOS, was born March 2, 1815, in Washington county, Md. Came to Springfield June, 1835, and settled in Woodside township. He went to Decatur in 1850, and was there married, in 1856, to Mrs. Mary Packard. They have two children, ANNIE and ROBERT, born in Decatur. They moved, in 1869, to Humboldt, Kansas, where they now reside.

Mrs. Sarah Amos died Feb. 15, 1847, at the residence of her son, Robert J. Amos, in Woodside township, Sangamon county.

ANDERSON, JAMES, was born in 1784 in Botetourt county, Va. Nancy Fletcher was born in 1786, in Rockbridge county, Va. They were there married, in 1802, and had two children in Virginia. They moved, in 1808, to Kentucky, where they had three children, and in 1813 moved to Indiana, where one child was born. They moved to Sangamon county, Ill., in 1820, and settled in what is now Ball township. Of their six children—

ROBERT N., born in Virginia, married, in Sangamon county, to Rebecca Wilson, who died, and he married Clarissa Woods, moved to Wisconsin, and both died there.

MARGARET L., born March 28, 1806, in Virginia, married in Sangamon county to William Drennan. (See his name.)

JOB F., born in Kentucky, died unmarried, at 55 years of age.

JOHN N., born in Kentucky, raised in Sangamon county, married in Arkansas, and died there.

NANCY, born in Kentucky, married in Sangamon county to John Caldwell, and died in Texas.

REBECCA, born in Indiana, raised in Sangamon county, went to Arkansas, married and died there.

James Anderson died in 1828 and his widow died in 1845, both in Sangamon county.

ANDERSON, MOSES K., was born Nov. 11, 1803, in Butler county, Ky. His parents died when he was ten or twelve years of age, and he was taken by a relative to that part of Davidson which is now Cheatham county, on Hanpeth river, Tenn. Cassariller Stroude was born Nov. 25, 1812, in Dickson county, Tenn. M. K. Anderson and Cassariller Stroude were married in her native county, Sept. 13, 1827, and moved to Sangamon county, Ill., arriving March 2, 1829, in what is now Cartwright township, four miles east of Pleasant Plains, and south of Richland creek, where they had nine children. Of their children—

THOMAS F., born Sept. 11, 1829, in Sangamon county, married Dec. 25, 1852, to Martha L. Child. They had five children. LAURA died, aged two years. CHARLES, EDWARD, HENRY and TAVNER reside with their parents, one mile north of Richland Station.

WILLIE ANN, born Sept. 17, 1831, in Sangamon county, married Francis Corson, who died, leaving one child, MOSES E, and she married George Springer. They have five children, MARY, CLARA, ANNA, REUBEN and CHARLES, and reside in Parsons, Kan.

SARAH J., born March 14, 1834, in Sangamon county, married John D. McCullough. They have four children, LAURA, WILLARD, EDWARD and LILLIE, and reside at Franklin, Morgan county.

MARY E., born April 17, 1836, married John L. Child. *See his name.*

MELINDA E., born Nov. 4, 1838, married Joseph Potter. They have five children, CHARLES, EUGENE, NELLIE, HATTIE and LULU, and reside at Palmer Ill.

CYNTHIA A., born Dec. 10, 1840, married Edward D. Ballard. They have three children, HARRIET, JAMES A. and CLIFTON D., and reside one and a half miles north of Richland station.

GEORGE W., born April 3, 1843, in Sangamon county, married near Athens, June 12, 1862, to Melinda F. Moran, who was born May 16, 1845. They have five children, FRANK, MOSES W., JAMES W., JENNIE and GEORGE, and reside two and a half miles north of Richland station.

MARENA A., born July 26, 1845, married William P. Mitchell. They have four living children, MINNIE, WILEY, JOHN, and a boy babe, and reside near Humboldt, Richardson county, Neb.

WILLARD WICKLIFFE, born April 28, 1848, married April 8, 1869, to Susan Moran, who was born Dec. 14, 1848, in Menard county. They have two children, HARRY and CASSARILLA, and reside two miles north of Richland station.

Mrs. Cassarilla Anderson died August 17, 1850, and M. K. Anderson was married Dec. 31, 1850, to Mrs. Marena T. Hall, whose maiden name was Stroude. They had three children. JOHN T. and ELIZA F. died between seven and nine years.

WILLIAM WILKES, born Sept. 8, 1857, resides with his parents in Springfield, but is now a theological student at Lexington, Ky.

Moses K. Anderson taught a military school in Dickson county, Tenn., and the old system of military training being in vogue when he came to Illinois, he was very soon elected captain of a company, and in a short time was promoted to Colonel and Brigadier-General. He was appointed, about 1838, by Gov. Carlin, Adjutant-General of the State, and continued to hold the office by successive appointments, until 1856. During the time, Gen. Anderson was called upon to discharge the duties of his office in connection with the Mormon war, at Nauvoo, and the Mexican war.

When Gen. Anderson came to Sangamon county he borrowed of Eli Blankenship the money to enter his first 80 acres of land, and paid fifty per cent. for the use of the money. He has since given each of his children a good farm, and has 500 acres left. He has been four years county judge, six years alderman in Springfield, and 20 years justice of the peace. He is of the opinion that the "deep snow" of 1830-31 was five feet deep on a level in the timber.

ANDERSON, TAVNER B., born Nov. 30, 1809, in Butler county, Ky., went with his brother Moses K., to Tennessee, and from there to Sangamon county, Ill., arriving March 2, 1829, in what is now Cartwright township. He was in the Black Hawk war, was married Dec. 9, 1834, to Polly Pirkins. They had six children, in Sangamon county.

AMERICUS, born Dec. 29, 1835, was married Oct. 5, 1856, to Emily Thompson. They had two children, and one died. Mr. A. died Oct. 2, 1860.

FRANCIS J., born Sept. 28, 1837, died young.

JOSEPH O., born April 23, 1840, died April 15, 1847.

RUFUS B., born Oct. 1, 1841, in Sangamon county, married Martha Young. They have two children, and reside near Palmer, Christian county.

MELINDA M., born May 23, 1844, married Y. B. Clark. They had seven children; all died but one. Mrs. Clark died Sept. 3, 1872. Their child is in Texas. Mr. C. resides at Clarksdale, Christian county, Ill.

HARRIET F., born Jan. 7, 1846, in Sangamon county, was married Dec. 5, 1868, to William H. McDonald. They had four children, two died. They reside near Clarksdale.

GEORGE E., born Dec. 24, 1849, in Sangamon county, was married Sept. 23, 1874, to Mollie Boyd. They have one child, and reside near Clarksdale, Ill.

CHARLES T., born August 4, 1852, and resides at Williamsville, Sangamon county.

Tavner B. Anderson and wife reside five miles southwest of Taylorville, and near Palmer City, Christian county, Ill.

ANTLE, REV. JOHN, was born April 15, 1789, in Cumberland county, Ky. Elizabeth Buchanan was born in Cumberland county, Pa. Her parents moved to Lincoln county, Ky., when she was seven years old. Her father died in that county, and she went to live with a married sister in Cumberland county. John Antle and Elizabeth Buchanan were there married. They had five children. The family then moved to Morgan county, Ill., in 1829, and from there to Sangamon county, arriving Jan. 9, 1830, in what is now Salisbury township. Of their children—

POLLY, born in 1810, in Kentucky, married in Sangamon county to Henry Hadley, and she died.

SALLY, born Jan., 1811, in Kentucky, married in Sangamon county, Sept., 1833, to Marshall Bragg. Mr. Bragg died, and his widow and three children reside in Keokuk county, Iowa. A married daughter resides in Logan county, Illinois.

HENRY, born Sept. 12, 1813, in Cumberland county, Ky., married in Sangamon county, Jan. 18, 1837, to Nancy Duncan. They have eight living children. SARAH A. married Charles Bottroff, and resides in Cartwright township. SIDNEY D., ELY ANN, JAMES S., NATHAN McC., LURANA, MARTHA F. and MARSHAL B., reside with their parents, adjoining Salisbury on the west.

ANDREW J., born in 1815, in Cumberland county, Kentucky, married in Sangamon county to Ann Dardon, Oct., 1840. They have one child, and reside near Seio, Linn county, Oregon.

MARTHA, born August 8, 1818, in Kentucky, married in Sangamon county, March, 1839, to Simon Stevens. They had five children, one died young. JOHN enlisted August, 1862, in Co. H., 114 Ill. Inf., for three years, and died in the army in 1863. MARSHALL A., GEO. S. and WILLARD T., reside with their mother. Mr. Stephens died in 1863, and his widow resides in Salisbury township.

Mrs. Elizabeth Antle died Sept., 1844, and John Antle died August 30, 1864, she in Menard county and he in Salisbury.

Rev. John Antle preached to five churches, called Separate Baptists. One each at Salisbury and McKinnie Settlement, in Sangamon county, Baker's Prairie and Sand Ridge, in Menard county, and one in Morgan county. The only pay he received or expected was the hope of reward in a better world.

ARCHER, WILLIAM, was born July 30, 1793, in North Carolina, and in 1807 his parents moved to Tennessee, where he was married to Elizabeth Jackson. They had one child, and moved to Madison county, Illinois, where they had one child, and Mrs. A. died, and he married Elizabeth Holt, Dec. 20, 1818. She was born Dec. 3, 1793, in Oglethrope county, Ga., and, losing her parents when quite young, she was taken by an uncle, Robert White, to Madison county, Ill., in 1811. Wm. and Elizabeth Archer had twins in Madison county, and moved to Sangamon county, arriving April 30, 1820, in what is now Curran township, where they had nine children. Of all his children—

WINSTON, born Sept. 12, 1814, in Tennessee, raised in Sangamon county, married Mary Robinson, moved to California, and died in 1866, leaving a widow and six children, near Petaluma, Sonoma county, California.

MARTHA, born Sept. 24, 1817, in Madison county, Ill., married in Sangamon county to John Riddle. *See his name.*

By the second wife—

JACKSON and *CARROLL*, twins, born Sept. 30, 1819, in Madison county, Ill.

JACKSON, married Oct. 7, 1844, to Eley F. Meacham. They had three children. ELIZABETH J. was killed in her eighth year by a fall from a wagon. MARY A. born May 14, 1848, married Feb. 16, 1865, to Andrew Alson, who was born March 6, 1838, in Sweden, and came to America in 1855. They had three children. The second, CHARLES, died in his fourth year. ANNA E. and CLARA A. reside with their parents, six miles west of Springfield. GEORGE R. born August 13, 1851, resides with his mother. Jackson Archer died April 7, 1852, in southwest Missouri, while on a journey for his health. His widow married Wm. Duff. *See his name.*

CARROLL, married Nov. 24, 1842, to Delilah Renshaw. They had three children. MARTHA T., born May 27, 1847, married to Lorenzo Stillman, have three children, and reside near Curran. ANN E., born August 5, 1849, married Sept., 1870, to Edward Robison, and reside in Linden, Kan. SARAH C., born Feb. 8, 1851, married November 21, 1872, to Henry Gaines, and resides near Odell, Ill. Mrs. Delilah Archer died May 31, 1865, and Carroll Archer was married Sept. 4, 1866, to Elizabeth Houghton, who was born Oct. 25, 1830, in Menard county. They have two children, EDWIN and MARIA BELLE, and reside three miles northwest of Curran.

MARY, born May 24, 1822, in Sangamon county, married Nov. 11, 1840, to Alexander Penny; had one child, WILLIAM, born Nov. 3, 1844, enlisted August 14, 1862, for three years, in Co. F., 144th Ill. Inf., was captured at the battle of Guntown, Miss., June, 1864, and died in Andersonville prison, Feb. 24, 1865. Alex. Penny died in 1868, and his widow married Mathew Redman, who was born May 1, 1828, in county Wexford, Ireland. They reside five miles west of Springfield.

SARAH, born Dec. 24, 1823, resides with her mother.

NANCY, born Nov. 13, 1825, in Sangamon county, married Samuel O. Maxcy. *See his name.*

JOHN, born Oct. 3, 1826, married Susan Taylor. They have one child, AMERICA, and reside in McDonough county, near Fandon. He was a soldier in a cavalry regiment from that county in suppressing the rebellion.

MADISON, born August 27, 1828, married Margaret Dixon, who died Dec. 29, 1863, leaving three children, WILLIAM B., MARY J. and SARAH E.

THOMAS J., born August 3, 1830, and resides near Rossville, Kan.

WASHINGTON J., born July 19, 1832, married Dec. 29, 1861, to Mrs. Melinda Hammond, whose maiden name was Cox. They have five children, GEORGE W., THOMAS C., MINNIE L., MARY A. and WILLIAM, and reside three miles north of Curran.

ELIZABETH, born Nov. 1, 1838, married Jan. 18, 1865, to Peter VanOrman. Mrs. VanOrman and her child, LIZZIE, reside with her mother.

William Archer died August 31, 1867, from the effects of being thrown from a horse, and his widow resides at the farm where they settled in 1820.

In the fall of 1873 Mrs. Elizabeth Archer, then eighty years of age, gave to the writer a piece of a dress made with her own hands more than sixty years before. The family of her uncle, with whom she moved from Georgia to St. Clair county, Ill., in 1811, brought some cotton in the bolls, for the purpose of using the seed in growing cotton in their new home. Miss Holt, as her name then was, obtained the consent of her uncle to apply the cotton to her own use. She picked it from the bolls and separated the cotton from the seed with her fingers, and spun it on a wheel, borrowed from a neighbor more than thirty miles distant. She had a rude loom constructed for the purpose, and had just commenced weaving, when the first assassination among the white settlers by Indians took place, as the beginning there of the war with England. That occurred in June, 1812. She, with her uncle's family, fled to Fort Bradsby, a rude wooden fortification near by. Appealing to the Lieutenant in command for protection, he reported the case to Governor Edwards, who authorized him to grant her request. A guard was accordingly placed around the cabin, and kept there until the weaving was completed. The design was unique and beautiful. The cloth was carefully preserved, some of it bleached to snowy whiteness, and made into a dress. She wore it the first time to a quarterly meeting in 1815, just after the close of the war, and attracted universal attention as the finest dressed lady in all that region of country.

ARCHER, MOSES, came to Sangamon county with his brother William. He was four times married, and died at Galena before the rebellion. His son—

ROBERT, died in 1870 or '71, leaving a widow and three daughters in Christian county.

ARCHER, MICHAEL, came to Sangamon county two years later than his brother William, and married Effy Duff, moved to Missouri, raised a large family, returned to Sangamon county during the rebellion, and Mrs. Archer died in Sangamon county. He returned to Jasper county, Mo., and died there in 1871.

ARCHER, ROBERT, was born Sept. 17, 1801, in Tennessee, and came with his brothers, Moses, Michael, Obadiah, their sister Jemima, and their mother, in 1821, to Sangamon county, where their brother William had settled the year before. Robert Archer and Matilda Duff were married Feb. 6, 1825, and had three children in Sangamon county.

ELIZABETH J., born August 1, 1827, married Nov. 15, 1850, to Reuben Brown. See his name.

BENNETT, C. D., born July 13, 1828, died Sept. 28, 1846.

MARTHA T., born April 15, 1830, in Sangamon county, married Leadbetter Bradley. See his name.

Robert Archer died October 17, 1859, and Matilda, his wife, died July 20, 1863, both in Sangamon county.

ARCHER, JEMIMA, came to Sangamon county in 1821 and married George Duff. See his name.

ARCHER, OBADIAH, came with his mother, sister and brothers to Sangamon county in 1821. He has been twice married, and resides at Galena, Ill.

Mrs. Martha Archer, mother of William, Moses, Michael, Obadiah and Jemima, came with her children to Sangamon county, in 1821, and died at the house of her son Moses, several years later.

ARMSTRONG, HUGH M., born Feb. 13, 1839, in Warren county, Ky., and moved with his father and family to Madison county, Ill., in 1816. Hugh came to Springfield Nov. 8, 1829. He was married in Springfield June 3, 1830, to Lavina M. Dryer, daughter of John Dryer. See his name. They had ten children, in Springfield; five died young. Of the others—

CATHARINE L., born July 20, 1830, was married in Springfield, July 18, 1853, to Samuel M. Culver, who was born in New York. They had five children. CARRIE M. died aged seven years. CHARLES A., HUGH M., WILLIAM H. and GILBERT R., reside with their parents in Springfield.

CYNTHIA J., born Nov. 1, 1839, was married in Springfield, July 11, 1865, to H. F. Hollingsworth, a native of Carroll county, Ill. They have one child, MAHLON F., and reside near Freeport, Stephenson county, Ill.

ALBERT H., born July 22, 1845, in Springfield, was married Dec. 19, 1868, to Jennie Merriweather, who was born July 19, 1845, in Green county, Ill. They have four children, KATE M., ANNIE, HARRIE HALE and ALBERT D., and reside in Springfield. Mr. A. is a machinist.

JOHN D., born August 7, 1852, and JULIA M., born August 8, 1856, both in Springfield, reside with their parents.

Hugh M. Armstrong was brought up a hatter and engaged in that business with his brother Hosea in Springfield, in 1829. He was afterwards interested in wool carding, and, in connection with Joseph and E. R. Thayer, originated, and for some years conducted, the Springfield Woolen Mills. He now resides on a farm near Batavia, Kane county, Ill.

ARMSTRONG, JOHN, was born Nov. 14, 1814, in Chester county, Pa., came to Springfield, Ill., August 1, 1837, and was married Nov. 14, 1839, to Chloe E. Abel. They had eight children, two of whom died young.

WILLIAM P., born Sept. 7, 1840, married Frances E. Maxon. He died Feb. 12, 1874, and she died in June of the same year, both in Springfield.

ROBERT R., born Feb. 20, 1844, died Jan. 1, 1860.

LUCY E., born Jan. 5, 1846, in Springfield, married Jan. 5, 1870, to C. H. Foster. They have two children, GERTRUDE E. and FREDRICK F., and reside in Pawnee. Mr. Foster is a merchant there.

HENRY R., born March 27, 1848,

CHARLES A., born Feb. 10, 1850, and—

EDWARD R., born Feb. 20, 1852; the three latter reside with their parents.

Mr. Armstrong has been a contractor and builder for many years. He was appointed by President Lincoln, in 1861, to the office of Post Master in Springfield, and held the office until August 5, 1865. He now resides in Springfield.

ARMSTRONG, THOMAS, was born Jan. 27, 1785, in Augusta county, Va. He was there married, Nov., 1815, to Jane Burgess, who was born June 3, 1796, in Greenbrier county. They had seven children in Augusta county, and moved, in 1827, to Logan county, Ohio, where they had two children, and moved to Sangamon county, Ill., arriving Oct. 21, 1830, in what is now Cotton Hill township. Of their children—

MARY W., born March 24, 1816, in Virginia, married in Sangamon county to James I. Dozier. See his name.

SARAH J., born May 11, 1817, in Virginia, married Daniel Keys; had one child, SARAH. She married Robert Jones, and resides in Kansas. Mrs. Keys died Sept. 28, 1844. See his name.

ABEL, born Oct. 30, 1818, in Virginia, came to Sangamon county in 1840. Is living with his third wife, near Newton, Jasper county, Ill.

ELIZA, born August 8, 1820, in Virginia, married in Sangamon county, March 1, 1849, to George Brunk. See his name. She died Oct. 4, 1860.

THOMAS D., born April 4, 1822, in Virginia, married in Sangamon county, January, 1849, to Jane Woozley. They reside in Christian county.

NANCY, born Feb. 13, 1824, in Virginia, married in Sangamon county, in 1846, to Moses A. Jones. See his name.

CAROLINE A., born Dec. 14, 1826, in Virginia, married in Sangamon county, March 1, 1849, to Rape Funderburk. See his name.

ANGELINE, born Nov. 15, 1833, in Logan county, Ohio, married in Sangamon county, to David Hall. They have three children, and reside near Newtonia, Newton county, Mo.

JOHN B., born June 9, 1839, in Logan county, Ohio, raised in Sangamon county, married near Pana, to Sarah King, and resides in Christian county.

Mrs. Jane Armstrong died Feb. 13, 1843, and Thomas Armstrong died Feb. 15, 1859, both in Sangamon county.

AVERITT, THOMAS M. See his name in connection with George Gregory and the first railroad locomotive ever run into Springfield.

B.

BAKER, EDWARD DICKINSON, was born Feb. 24, 1811, in London, England. His father, Edward Baker, was an educated gentleman, and his mother a sister of Capt. Thomas Dickenson, of the British navy, who distinguished himself at the battle of Trafalger. Edward D. was the eldest of five children. About the close of the war with England, in 1815, his father and family emigrated to America, landing at Philadelphia, Penn. Here Mr. Edward Baker engaged in teaching. On account of the financial embarassments of the family, as soon as Edward D. was old enough, he was apprenticed to a weaver. In 1826 his father moved to Belleville, Ill., where he opened a select school, and young Edward D. Baker evinced such a taste for literature that the late Gov. Edwards, then a resident of Belleville, gave him free access to his library. From Belleville young Baker went to St. Louis, and to procure funds for necessary expenses, drove a dray for at least one season. From St. Louis he went to Carrolton, Ill., and began the study of law and at the same time acting as deputy in the county clerk's office. He was married April 27, 1831, to Mrs. Mary A. Lee, a widow with two children. In the spring of 1832 Mr. Baker enlisted in the Black Hawk war, and in 1835 moved to Springfield, and soon after became a law partner of Stephen T. Logan. He delivered the oration at the laying of the corner stone of the old State house, July 4, 1837. In the latter year he was elected to the General Assembly to fill the vacancy caused by the resignation of Hon. Dan Stone, and was re-elected the following year. In 1840 E. D. Baker was elected State Senator for four years, and elected to Congress in 1845. When the war broke out with Mexico, Mr. B. hastened home, raised a regiment, which was accepted by the government as the 4th Ill. Inf., Col. E. D. Baker, commanding. Arriving on the Rio Grand, he discovered that the troops were in need of additional tent equipage, munitions of war, etc., and for a few months accepted the position of bearer of dispatches to the war department, and repaired to Washington. Congress was in session, and not having resigned his seat in the House, availed himself of his privilege as a member, and made a speech of great and almost magical power in favor of a vigorous prosecution of the war, and in behalf of the volunteers then in the field, and rejoined his regiment. After the battle of Cerro Gordo, the term of Col. Baker's enlistment expired, and his men not wishing to re-enlist, he reluctantly left the field, and, returning home, resumed the practice of his profession. In the spring of 1848 he moved to Galena, Ill. As one of the Whig electors for the State at large, he took an active part in the Presidential campaign of 1848. He took his seat as Representative in Congress, the second time, in Dec., 1849. In 1851 he entered into an agreement with the Panama Railroad Company to grade a portion of that road, but after several months exposure to a tropical sun, he and his men fell sick and abandoned the country. In 1852 he emigrated with his family to California, establishing himself in practice in San Francisco. There he delivered the funeral oration of two of his early friends, fallen by the fatal bullet of the duelist, Ferguson and Broderick. The latter stands alone as the most brilliant funeral oration ever delivered on the continent of America. After the death of Boderick, Col. Baker moved to Oregon, and was elected U. S. Senator from there in 1860. For the first time in his life he was placed in a position congenial to him. The decorum and courtesy that usually marks the intercourse of Senators, was most grateful to his habits of thought and feeling.

Col. Baker was a man of action as well as of words, and soon after the fall of Fort Sumter he recruited a regiment in Philadelphia and vicinity, which was called the California regiment, and soon after, President Lincoln tendered him a Brigadier-General's commission, but he declined it, probably because it would have vacated his seat in the Senate. At the first session of the 37th Congress, convoked by President Lincoln, July 4, 1861, Col. Baker was in his seat, and participated prominently in the passage of those important measures which became necessary to place the nation on a war footing. On the adjournment of this special session, Col. Baker rejoined his regiment, which was attached to and formed a part of the army of observation on the Potomac. He, however, was restless in camp, and a vague presentiment of his approaching fate seemed to haunt him wherever he went, and he said to a friend that since his campaign in Mexico he could never afford to turn his back on an enemy. He returned to Washington, settled his affairs, and called to bid the President and family farewell, when the lady of the Executive Mansion, who, in her, then, high position, was gracefully mindful of early friendship, gave him a boquet of late flowers. As though partially soliloquizing, he said: "Very beautiful; these flowers and my memory will wither together." He pressed with quiet earnestness on his friend, Col. Webb, the measures which might become necessary in regard to the resting place of his mortal remains, then mounted his horse and rode gaily away to his death. He was leading his men at Ball's Bluff, and, when ten feet in advance of them, fell, pierced by eight bullets, Oct. 21, 1861. His body was borne tenderly away, embalmed, and removed to Washington City, where appropriate funeral honors were paid to his remains; then sent to New York City, and from there by steamer to

San Francisco, where he was buried in Lone Mountain Cemetery, of that city. Of the two children of Mrs. Baker by her first marriage—

MARIA L. LEE, born in 1827, was married Feb. 11, 1845, to James H. Matheny. *See his name*.

FRANK LEE went to California, and died there.

Hon. Edward D. Baker and wife had four children, namely:

LUCY S., born about 1832 in Carrolton, Ill., brought up in Springfield, was married in San Francisco to Charles Hopkins. They have four children, CHARLES, CAROLINE, ROBERT and RALPH, and reside at Olympia, Washington Territory. Mr. Hopkins is U. S. Marshall for that Territory.

CAROLINE C., born in Carrolton, Ill., brought up in Springfield, was married in San Francisco to Robert J. Stevens. They have two children, ROBERT and CARRIE, and reside in Washington City.

ALFRED W., born in Springfield, resides in San Francisco.

EDWARD D., Jun., born in Springfield, married Saccha Alma Bradshaw. He is a Captain in the U. S. Army, and is on duty at some western military post.

Mrs. Mary A. Baker died in San Francisco.

The great and fatal mistake of Col. Baker was one that did honor to his noble and chivalrous spirit. He had fairly and honorably reached the highest position in our government that any adopted citizen could attain. In the Senate of the United States he was the peer of any man in the nation, and his counsels there were worth a hundred fold more than it could have been in the field. When he volunteered to lead a regiment, he was liable to become subordinate to men far, very far, inferior to himself, and that proved to be his destruction; but he had, no doubt, weighed well the step he was about to take, and thereby laid the most costly sacrifice on the altar of his adopted country that it was possible for any citizen to make, even though he were to the manor born.

BAKER, JOHN L., was born June 20, 1805, in Campbell county, Ky. He is a brother of Thomas, and was married in 1828, in Butler county, Ohio, to Rachel Biggs, who was born in that State,

Oct. 6, 1804. They had three children there and moved to Shelby county, Ind., where they had two children, and from there to Sangamon county, Ill., arriving in 1835, in what is now Loami township, where they had two children. Of their eight children two died young.

MARGARET, born April 27, 1829, in Ohio, was married in Sangamon county, Ill., to Henry Westfall. They have seven children, SMITH M., ANN E., HELEN, INA, LEONA, GEORGE and CHARLES, and reside near Elkhart Logan county, Ill.

THOMAS N., born Jan. 28, 1831, in Ohio, was married in Sangamon county to Frances Preddy. They have six children, all born in Sangamon county, namely: SIBYL, JOHN L., ALICE, MARY, DON CARLOS and ETTA, and reside near Ottawa, Kansas.

SARAH J., born April 25, 1832, in Ohio, was married in Sangamon county to Jonathan Jarrett. *See his name*.

REUBEN F., born Jan. 24, 1834, in Shelby county, Ind., was married in Sangamon county to Elizabeth Mahard. They have seven children, JOHN, GEORGE, JAMES, ORTHELLO, HORATIO, ALICE and ARMINDA, and reside near Nebraska City, Neb.

EPHRIAM, born March 31, 1835, in Indiana, was married in Sangamon county to Anna Mahard. He died in Sangamon county, leaving a widow and two children, EBEN and CHARLES. The widow and children reside in Missouri.

JOHN W., born Dec. 13, 1837, in Sangamon county, Ill., was married there to Sarah Mahard. They have four children, JAMES E., ELIZABETH, THOMAS and M. ALICE, who reside with their parents, near Ottawa, Kansas.

PAULINE L., born Sept. 22, 1844, in Sangamon county, married James S. Cloud. They have four children, M. ALICE, DORA, MINNIE E. and JESSE M., and reside in Ottawa, Kansas.

John L. Baker and wife reside in Ottawa, Kansas.

BAKER, THOMAS, was born March 3, 1794, in Campbell county, Ky.; brother to John L. Nancy Robertson was born Oct. 9, 1806, in Harrison county, Va. They were married Dec. 29, 1823, in Kanawha county, West Va., at the house of Jonathan Jarrett, Sen. Mr. and

Mrs. Baker had two children in West Virginia, and moved to Sangamon county, Ill., arriving Nov. 1826, in what is now Loami township, where they had eight children. Of their ten chilldren—

JOHN, born March 16, 1825, in West Virginia, died in Sangamon county, Aug. 29, 1835.

CHARLES, born April 12, 1826, in West Virginia, married in Sangamon county, August 11, 1844, to Lucretia Minter. They moved in the fall of that year to Tarrant county, Texas. He died there in 1871, leaving a widow and ten children.

WILLIAM, born Feb. 11, 1829, in Sangamon county, married Jan. 10, 1850, to Margaret Morris. They have ten children, and reside near Bancroft, Daviess county, Mo.

MARY A., born Dec. 27, 1831, in Sangamon county, married Nov. 8, 1853, to Barnard A. VanDeren. See his name. They had two children, THOMAS N. and MAGGIE L. Mr. VanD. died, and she married, Nov. 2, 1868, to John Lowery, who was born Sept. 15, 1837, in county Down, Ireland. They had two children, MARY A. and BARNARD A.; the latter died in infancy. Mr. and Mrs. Lowery reside four miles south of Loami.

MARGARET, born Oct. 27, 1834, in Sangamon county, married Dec. 18, 1857, to James W. Greenwood. See his name.

THOMAS, Jun., born Oct. 1, 1836, in Sangamon county, married April 23, 1861, to Mary J. Hall. She died August 21, 1866, leaving one child, GEORGE W. Mr. Baker was married March 19, 1867, to Mrs. Harriet Cosser, whose maiden name was Hall. They have two children, JOSEPH F. and HATTIE, and reside three and a half miles southwest of Loami.

NANCY, born March 28, 1839, in Sangamon county, married William G. Miller. See his name. She died, leaving two children with their father, who is married and resides in Loami township.

CYRUS W., born May 19, 1842, in Sangamon county, married April 13, 1862, to Sarah A. Jarrett. They have three children, HENRY, BARNARD A. and JO. C., and reside one and a half miles southwest of Loami.

SARAH J., born Dec. 7, 1846, in Sangamon county, married Nov. 2, 1865, to Joseph O. Joy. They have three children, CHARLES W., WILLIE A. and JOHN W., and reside three miles southwest of Loami. Mr. Joy was a soldier in suppressing the rebellion.

ISAAC N., born Dec. 11, 1849, in Sangamon county, married April 21, 1870, to Sarah E. Post. They have one child, HARRY O., and reside at the homestead settled by his parents.

Thomas Baker, Sen., died Jan. 5, 1852, and his widow resides at the homestead settled by herself and husband in 1826. It is one and a half miles southwest of Loami.

BAKER, ISAAC, was born near Fredericktown, Md. He served as a lifer in the Revolution, the last two years of the war. Phœbe Waddell was born near Baltimore, Md. They were married there in 1787, and moved to what became Bourbon county, Ky., where twelve children were born, eight of whom married there. The parents and four youngest children came to Sangamon county in the fall of 1829, in what is now Rochester township. Of their children—

JAMES, born July, 1788, in Bourbon county, Ky. It is believed he was the first white child born in the county. He was married Sept. 17, 1813, in Nicholas county, Ky., to Nancy Squires, who was born Oct. 22, 1794, in Fauquier county, Va. They had eight children in Nicholas county, and moved to Sangamon county, Ill., arriving Nov., 1828, at Springfield, and a week later left for what is now Logan county. In Jan., 1831, he moved to Rochester, Sangamon county. They were five days moving twenty miles, through what is known as the "deep snow." Mr. B. was a soldier in the Black Hawk war. Two of his children were born in Illinois. Of his ten children, S. WILLIS, born Oct. 10, 1814, in Kentucky, died unmarried, in Illinois, June 25, 1850. THOMAS J., born March 1, 1816, in Kentucky, died in Sangamon county, Oct. 17, 1832. MARGARET J., born Dec. 20, 1817, in Kentucky, married in Sangamon county, Nov. 15, 1838, to Daniel S. Stafford. She died in less than a year. MARTIN E., born Jan. 27, 1820, in Nicholas county, Ky., married March 4, 1852, in Springfield, to Mary C. S. Williams, who was born Feb. 3, 1826, in Montgomery county, Md., and came to Springfield in 1839. They have eight children, JAMES W., CORNELIA A., MARGARET E., MARTIN E., jun., NANCY E., HORACE W., MARY F. and CHARLES O., and reside four miles southwest of Illiopolis. ELIZA E., born Nov. 7, 1822, in Kentucky, died July 3, 1835, in Sangamon county. KITTY A., born Jan. 22, 1824, in Kentucky, married in Sangamon county, in 1848, to Oliver Stafford; have seven children, and reside in Mt. Pulaski. JOHN S., born Nov. 7, 1826, in Kentucky, taught school in Sangamon county many years; went to California in 1854, and died July 30, 1873, in San Francisco. WILLIAM F., born June 29, 1828, in Kentucky, brought up in Sangamon county, married, Feb. 7, 1860, in Christian county, to Elizabeth Green; have four children, and reside near Grove City. MARY E., born Oct. 22, 1830, in Logan county, married, Nov. 4, 1852, to Leander Green. (*See his name.*) MARTHA A., born August 11, 1833, in Sangamon county, married Dec. 29, 1859, to William Crenshaw; have two children, and reside in Georgetown, Ky. James Baker died Feb. 14, 1869, and Mrs. Nancy Baker died Oct. 3, 1872, both in Christian county.

JACOB, born August 9, 1790, in Bourbon county, Ky., was a soldier from that county in the war of 1812. He was married in Nicholas county, Ky., to Jane Branch, sister of Edward Branch. *See his name.* Four of their children were born in Kentucky, and he came to Sangamon county with his father, arriving in 1829, near Rochester, where five children were born. Of his seven children, JULIAN, married first to Alfred Waddell, who died, and she married Willis Runnels, and both died. Her sons, ALFRED Waddell, resides in Greenfield, Mo., JESSE and WILLIS reside near Nashville, Mo. SUSAN, born in Kentucky, married in Sangamon county to James Virden, who died, and his widow resides seven miles east of Springfield. They had five children. PLEASANT, born April 25, 1819, in Nicholas county, Ky., married in Sangamon county, June 24, 1846, to Lavina Waddell, who was born in Kentucky. They had five children; two died in infancy. JULIAN and WILLIAM H. reside in Clear Lake township. ALVIN resides with his father. Mrs. Lavina Baker died April 20, 1857, and Mr. B. married Mary E. Cook, a native of Scioto county, Ohio. They have five children, MARY, SUSAN J., ELIZA A., PLEASANT and LAURA E., and reside in Clear Lake township. ISAAC, born Oct. 6, 1821, in Kentucky, married in Sangamon county to Almyra Pike. He died, leaving one child, ISAAC, who resides south of Rochester. POLLY A., born in Kentucky, married in Sangamon county to Daniel Barr. JANE, born July 15, 1827, in Kentucky, married in Sangamon county to John M. McCune. *See his name.* ALVIN, born in Sangamon county, married Hester Hornbaker. He died in 1856, leaving two children, EDWARD and ALONZO. Mrs. Jane Baker died, and Jacob Baker afterward married twice, and died May 18, 1872.

THOMAS, born about 1792, in Kentucky, married there to Sarah Delay. They had four children, and came to Sangamon county in 1828, with his brother, James, and settled near Rochester, where one child was born. Of his children, ISAAC resides near Medoc, Mo., ELIZABETH, born in Kentucky, married in Sangamon county to Jabez Capps. *See his name.* JOHN resides near Medoc, Mo. WILLIAM resides in Virginia City, Montana. JEMIMA married and died in Mt. Pulaski. Thomas Baker died March, 1874, and his widow resides near Medoc, Mo.

JOSEPH, born in 1796, in Kentucky, came to Sangamon county in 1828, and died in Medoc, Mo.

SUSAN, born March 15, 1799, in Bourbon county, Ky., married Robert Bell. *See his name.*

ISAAC, born in Kentucky, never came to Sangamon county. He resides near Medoc, Mo.

SQUIRE, born Jan. 8, 1803, in Kentucky, came to Sangamon county in 1829, and resides near Mapleton, Kansas.

WILLIAM, born in 1805, in Kentucky, and resides near Mapleton, Kan.

GREENBURY, born in Kentucky, married in Sangamon county to Anna Payne, who died, and he married Mrs. Mary Johnson, formerly Mrs. Barker, and whose maiden name was Williams. They had four children. MOSES was a Union soldier in the 11th Mo. Inf., and was killed while aiding in the arrest of a deserter. THOMAS J. was a member of the 16th Ill. Cavalry, and died in Andersonville prison. S. WILLIS served three years in the 11th Mo. Inf.; was honorably discharged, and married in Sangamon county to Matilda Mear. He died early in 1874, leaving a widow and two children, near Medoc, Mo. EFFIE was married in Sangamon county, to Joseph Brunk, and resides near Medoc, Mo. Mrs. Mary Baker died May 22, 1842, in Sangamon county. Greenbury Baker died March 4, 1873, in Sangamon county.

HARRISON, born in Kentucky, married in Sangamon county, to Nellie Bowles. They had eight children, born in Sangamon county, and moved to the vicinity of Medoc, Mo. Mr. and Mrs. Baker died there in 1872, and were buried in one grave.

POLLY, born in Kentucky, married in Sangamon county to Elias Williams. See his name.

PHOEBE, born April 5, 1816, in Kentucky, married in Sangamon county to Josiah B. Williams. See his name.

Mrs. Phœbe Baker died July 3, 1845, and Isaac Baker died in Sept. 1848, both in Sangamon county, south of Rochester. He was about 100 years of age.

BAKER, WILLIAM, was born about 1798, in Sevier county, Tenn. He came to St. Clair county, Ill., when a young man. Phebe Neeley was born Dec. 14, 1799, near Nashville, Tenn., and was taken to St. Clair county, Ill., when she was a young woman. Wm. Baker and Phebe Neeley were married about 1818, near Belleville. They had one child born there, and the family moved to Horse creek, in what became Sangamon county, in the spring of 1819, in what is now Cotton Hill township, where seven children were born. They then moved to a mill on Sangamon river, three miles north of Rochester, where one child was born. Four of the children died under two years. Of the other five—

JAMES, born Jan., 1819, in St. Clair county, and raised on Horse creek, on the farm now owned by Samuel Galloway. William Enyert, who went to school with him, remembers having heard him say frequently, in their boyhood days, that he would join some Indian tribe at 18 years of age. Between 1837 and '40 he went west, and came back in 1844, to see his mother, who then lived in Rochester. He said he had joined the Snake tribe of Indians, and after a stay of about six months, he returned to that tribe. But little was known of him until 1849, when a party of eight persons left Springfield for the gold regions of California. William Enyert says they found him at the crossing of Green river, keeping a ferry. He recognized Mr. Enyert readily, and treated him kindly. Mr. Enyert learned from him that he was a chief in the Snake tribe; had two wives, one with him and one at Fort Bridger, and two children by each. His daily receipts were from $500 to $600 at the ferry. He is yet living among the Indians, and is occasionally heard from by his friends. Mr. Enyert says that when he saw him he was full six feet tall, wore his hair long and straight, stood erect as any Indian, wore buckskin clothes, and in his general appearance looked very much like an Indian. Mr. Enyert had been a school-mate of his in this county. E. C. Matheny saw him under similar circumstances.

ADELIA, born in Sangamon county in 1821, died at 15 years of age.

JOHN, born in Sangamon county, resides among the Indians, near Fort Bridger, Wyoming territory. Went there a few years later than his brother James.

ELIZABETH, born in Sangamon county, Cotton Hill township, is unmarried and resides in Rochester; is the only member of the family residing in Sangamon county.

ELIZA, born in Sangamon county, died at 15 years of age.

William Baker went to Texas previous to 1844, started from there to California about 1852, and died on the road. Mrs. Phebe Baker died, August, 1861, in Rochester.

BALDWIN, JOHNSON, was born March 25, 1797, in Scott county, Ky.; was married in Gallatin county, Oct. 24, 1822, to Betsy Kendall. They had one child born in Kentucky, and moved to Sangamon county, Ill., in company with her father, William Kendall, arriving Oct. 17, 1824, in what is now Curran township, where eleven children were born; one died in infancy. Of their children—

MARY A., born Sept. 19, 1823, in Kentucky, married in Sangamon county to Richard Bradley. See his name.

ALISSA, or *ALICE*, born Nov. 17, 1824, in Sangamon county, married John Wesley Elliott. *See his name.*

HARRIET, born March 4, 1827, in Sangamon county, married John M. Smith. *See his name.* Resides near Curran.

ELIZA, born Nov. 6, 1828, in Sangamon county, married Edward D. Campbell, and resides near Lancaster, or Mansfield, Texas.

WILLIAM, born Jan. 23, 1831, in Sangamon county, married Dec. 22, 1853, to Mary J. Parkinson. They had seven children. ADDIE C. died August 22, 1871, in her seventh year. LIZZIE died in infancy. ELLA M., EUNICE P., JAMES O. and OTIS J., (twins), and WILLIE O., reside with their parents, six miles west of Springfield.

NANCY, born May 4, 1833, in Sangamon county, married August 20, 1872, to John Mull, who was born Dec. 5, 1821, in Kentucky. They reside six miles southwest of Springfield.

EDITH, born Feb. 26, 1837, in Sangamon county, married Feb. 13, 1873, to Wm. Dyer, and resides four miles northwest of Curran.

AGNES, born Dec. 18, 1838, died Oct. 5, 1864.

EMILY, born August 15, 1841, resides with her sister, Mrs. Dyer.

SUSAN, born Sept. 15, 1843, married Wm. B. Gilbert. They have two children and reside three miles north of Springfield, on Athens road.

ELIZABETH died August 29, 1856, in her eleventh year.

Mrs. Betsey Baldwin died August 13, 1847, and Johnson Baldwin died Dec. 4, 1871, both in Sangamon county.

BALL, JOHN S., born about 1795, in Madison county, Ky. Went to Clarksville, Tenn., and from there to Eddyville, Ky., from there to Sangamon county, and after spending several years, returned to Kentucky; back to Sangamon county, then to JoDaviess county; from there to Missouri, where he left his family, went to California, and at the end of three years returned to his family in Missouri. Now resides with his sons in Morgan county. His son—

THOMAS H., married in Morgan county to Eliza A. Hodgson, has two children, COLUMBUS A. and IDA BELL, and reside in Ball township.

BALL, JAPHET A., was born July 5, 1800, in Madison county, Ky. When a young man he went to Clarkesville, Tenn., where he learned the trade of a blacksmith with his brother John S. From there he went with his brother to Eddyville, Caldwell county, Ky., and from there to Sangamon county, arriving late in Dec., 1825, in what is now Woodside township. He was married Dec. 2, 1828, to Sarah Henderson. They had two children—

CLARISSA J., born in Sangamon county, married Jeremiah Penicks. They had four children, and Mr. Penicks died. Mrs. Penicks and her children reside at Palmer, Christian county.

JAMES H., died in his fourteenth year.

Mrs. Sarah Ball died March 12, 1832. Japhet A. Ball was married May, 1834, to Marinda Davis, who died April 12, 1855. Mr. Ball was married Sept. 30, 1863, to Melissa Morison. They have two children—

JOHN M. and

FANNIE M., and reside east of Sugar creek, in Ball township, four miles southeast of Chatham.

Japhet A. Ball enlisted July, 1827, in Col. Tom M. Neal's Battalion of mounted volunteers, to fight the Indians in the north part of the State. This was known as the Winnebago war. He again enlisted, and was commissioned by Gov. Reynolds as First Lieutenant, June 18, 1831. A treaty with Black Hawk, the chief, terminated hostilities. The Indians commenced depredations again, in the spring of 1832. J. A. Ball was commissioned by Gov. Reynolds, April 28, 1832, as Capt. of a Company in Long's Odd Battalion of Inf. It was mustered out in June, 1832, for the purpose of changing to a mounted organization, but that ended his military career. Mr. Ball served from 1843 to 1856 as Justice of the Peace. He was elected and commissioned by Gov. Bissell, Nov. 14, 1857, as Associate Judge of Sangamon county, for four years. The township organization being adopted in 1860, terminated his official career. The township of Ball was named for him.

Judge Ball says that on the first day of Jan., 1831, while the "deep snow" was falling, he killed fourteen deer. They would founder in the snow, and were easily taken. He built a saw mill on Sugar creek, and sold a large quantity of lumber at the mill, and at times kept teams running to Springfield. The scarcity of money for a few years after the financial crash of 1837, was very severe on the new settlements. The Judge says that during one of those years he did an extensive business in the lumber trade, and his total receipts in cash was exactly seventy-five cents.

BALL, SMITH, was born July 10, 1810, in Madison county, Ky., came to Sangamon county, Ill., arriving at the house of his brother, Japhet A., in 1829. He was married June 13, 1837, to Rebecca Moffatt. They had one child in Sangamon county, and in the fall of 1839 moved to Mt. Pleasant, Iowa. In the spring of 1840 he moved to Jefferson county, where they had six children. Of their seven children—

EMILY A., born March 27, 1838, in Sangamon county, was married in Iowa to William Case. They have six children, and reside in Marshall county, Iowa.

MARY M., born March 25, 1840, in Iowa, was married there to George B. Phillips. They have six children, and reside near Wooster, Iowa.

NANCY J., born August 30, 1842, died aged 22 years.

GEORGE W., born June 7, 1847, in Jefferson county, Iowa, is a practicing lawyer, unmarried, and resides at Iowa City.

MARGARET C., born Dec. 10, 1847, in Iowa, was married there to Richard Fisher. They have two children, and reside near Wooster.

LEWIS C., born Jan. 18, 1852, and

FRANK P., born Feb. 25, 1854, reside with their parents, near Wooster, Jefferson county, Iowa.

BALL, WILLIAM, born in Madison county, Ky., came to Sangamon county about 1835, and moved to Jo Daviess county.

BALL, JANE, born in Madison county, Ky., married William Richardson, came to Sangamon county in 1829, and died in this county. Lewis B. Richardson, of Auburn township, is her son.

BALL, BETHANY, born Aug. 13, 1796, in Madison county, Ky., married John Brawner. *See his name.*

BALL, POLLY, born in Kentucky, married in Sangamon county to John Rames, moved to Missouri, and both died there.

BALL, ELIZABETH, born in Madison county, Ky., married William Brawner. *See his name.*

BALL, LUCY, born in Kentucky, married in Sangamon county to Daniel Morris, moved to Texas, and after residing there ten years, returned to Sangamon county, and both died, leaving several children.

Mrs. Nancy Ball, mother of John S., Japhet A., Smith, William, Jane, Bethany, Polly, Elizabeth and Lucy, came with the last of her children to Sangamon county in 1829, and died at the house of her son, Japhet A., in 1846.

BANCROFT, ISAAC, was born April 29, 1776, near Boston, Mass. Mercy Coburn was born March 12, 1781, in Massachusetts, also. They were married March 5, 1799, and had two children in Massachusetts. They moved to St. Lawrence county, N. Y., where they had ten children, and moved to Springfield, Ill., arriving August 10, 1839. Of their children—

MERCY and

BETSY married and raised families. One of them died in Massachusetts. The other resides in Hainesville, Lake county, Illinois.

PRUDENCE, born in New York, died May 3, 1824, aged twenty-four years.

JONATHAN C., born Feb. 2, 1809, in New York, married Frances Stone. Mr. Bancroft died June 2, 1845, leaving a widow and three children in Springfield. His son, Coburn, died in 1870, in Springfield.

ALMA S., born August 20, 1811, and died aged 23 years.

ISAAC, Jun., born May 6, 1815, in New York, married Mary Blackman. He is now e Congregational minister, and resides in Green county, Wis.

JOSEPH, born April 5, 1817, died Oct. 16, 1851.

TIMOTHY, born Feb. 26, 1819, in St. Lawrence county, N. Y., is unmarried, and resides in Springfield.

BENJAMIN, born March 3, 1821, in St. Lawrence county, N. Y., married September 19, 1854, to Elizabeth C. Cass, who was born March 13, 1836, in Montgomery county, Ill. They had five children, three of whom died young. EDWARD T. and LUCINDA A. reside with their father. Mrs. E. C. Bancroft died Feb. 3, 1871, and Benj. Bancroft resides in Fancy Creek township.

HARMAN H., born Feb. 1, 1823, died in Springfield in his 23d year.

Isaac Bancraft died Oct. 8, 1844, and his widow died Feb. 10, 1868, both in Springfield.

BARBRE, ELI, was born July 25, 1798, in Kentucky. He was married about 1819, in Posey county, Ind., to Nancy Wilkinson, a native of Kentucky, also. They had four children in Indiana, and Mrs. Barbre died there, in 1828. Mr. Barbre moved to Edgar county, Ill., and was married there Jan. 17, 1829, to Anna Wilson. They had two children in Edgar county, and moved to Sangamon county, Ill., arriving in the fall of 1835, in what is now Island Grove township, where they had two children. Of their nine children—

ISAAC, born August 10, 1820, in Ind., came to Sangamon county with his parents, returned to Indiana, married Nancy Bennett. He served three years in an Indiana regiment, for the suppression of the rebellion, and resides in Posey county, Ind.

WILLIAM, born Nov. 10, 1822, in Posey county, Ind., married in Sangamon county, Jan. 15, 1845, to Rebecca Smith, and had two children. She died, Oct. 18, 1847, leaving one child. He was married, Feb. 6, 1849, to Lucy M. Smith. They had nine children. Of all his children, NANCY J., by the first wife, married James McKee, has two children, LUCY A. and MARY H., and reside in Nodaway county, Mo. MARY A., married James A. Trimble. *See his name.* MARTHA, the twin mate to Mary, died in infancy. JOHN E., JAMES W., THOMAS F., GEORGE L., RICHARD S., SAMUEL M. and MARTHA C., reside with their parents, two miles east of Curran. William Barbre enlisted Sept., 1861, in Co. B., 10th Ill. Cav., for three years. He was wagon master and Veterinary Surgeon, and was honorably discharged in June, 1863.

CHARLOTTE, born 1824, in Indiana, married Wright Miller, has several children, and resides in Lynn county, Oregon.

CELIA D., born in 1826, in Indiana, married, successively, Edward Bennett, Charles Wiggins and James Cleveland, all of whom died, and she married Henry Atkinson, and resides in Clark county, Ill.

SARAH E., born July 5, 1831, in Edgar county, married in Sangamon county, to Harvey Withrow. *See his name.*

JAMES L., born March 4, 1834, in Edgar county, Ill., married, Dec. 28, 1854, to Lucinda Dixon. They had nine children, four of whom died under four years. The latter five, WILLIAM E., ALBERT F., MARY E., HARRIET C. W. and GEORGETTA, reside with their parents in Cooper township, three miles southwest of Mechanicsburg.

JOHN A., born Dec. 19, 1835, married March 5, 1857, to Margaret R. McKee, had six children, JAMES A., WM. E., EDWIN H., ANNAH L., JENNIE and GEORGE, reside with their parents, two and a half miles southwest of Mechanicsburg. John A. Barbre enlisted Dec. 23, 1863, in Co. B, 10th Ill. Cav., for three years, served until Nov. 22, 1865, and was honorably discharged at San Antonio, Texas.

MARY C., born in 1837, in Sangamon county, married Rev. Geo. Keller.

Eli Barbre died in the fall of 1846, and his widow married Wm. Withrow. (*See his name.*) She died in the fall of 1871.

BARGER, ADAM, was born April 8, 1784, in Botetourt county, Va. He went, when a young man, to Kanawha county, West Va., and was there married, August 12, 1810, to Lucinda Nolan. They had ten children in Virginia, and moved in a family boat to Shawneetown, Ill. He took a farm wagon and two yoke of oxen, and hired another team at Shawneetown, and thus brought his family and two loads of household goods, arriving Oct., 1826, in what is now Loami township, but then called Yankee Settlement, where they had three children. Of their children—

ALBARTES, born May 26, 1811, in Kanawha county, West Va., married, Dec. 23, 1829, in Sangamon county, to Margaret F. Patrick. They had 13 children,

JOHN A., born July 21, 1831, died in his 21st year. MAJOR E., enlisted, May 25, 1861, in Co. I., 14th Ill. Inf., for three years, served full term, and was honorably discharged, June, 1864, at Springfield. He is a lawyer, and resides at Loami. JANETTA, born June 2, 1834, married James J. Henton. (See his name.) SOPHIA, born Feb. 10, 1836, married Robert E. Berry. (See his name.) WILLIAM F., born Dec. 19, 1838, enlisted, May, 1861, in Co. I, 14th Ill. Inf., for three years, re-enlisted as a veteran in another regiment, served to the end of the rebellion, was honorably discharged, and resides near Loami. JULIA A., born Dec. 18, 1840, married Morrison Brown, have four children, and reside in Loami township. JAMES N., born March 20, 1842, enlisted, in 1861, in Co. C, 11th Mo. Inf., for three years, was discharged on account of physical disability, acted as deputy provost-marshal at Springfield for a time, and enlisted in 152d Ill. Inf. Served to the end of the rebellion, married Margaret Hunter, has three children, and resides one mile southwest of Loami. CHARLES H., born Nov. 18, 1845, enlisted in Co. —, 16th Ill. Cav., in 1862, for three years. Served full term, and was honorably discharged. LEROY, born Feb. 20, 1847, resides with his father. GEORGE W., born June 10, 1849, married Mollie McKinney, have one child, and reside near Berry Station, Sangamon county. ALBERT, LUCINDA J. and HARRIET E. reside with their father. Mrs. M. F. Barger died Feb. 25, 1876, and Albartes Barger resides where he settled in 1831, near Loami.

JULIA A., born Oct. 18, 1812, in West Virginia, married in Sangamon county to Dr. J. R. Abel. (See his name.) Have three children, and reside in Taylorville.

THERESA, born May 13, 1814, in Virginia, married Thomas Sowell. (See his name.)

ZEBULON, M. P., born Dec. 14, 1815, died in his 29th year.

SOPHIA, born April 12, 1817, married, her husband died, and the family reside in Cass county.

JOHN, born Oct. 31, 1818, married Elizabeth Eustace, had four children, and he died. His widow married and lives in Wisconsin.

OLIVIA, born Oct. 28, 1820, married Morris Sweet. (See his name.)

MARY A., born July 23, 1822, married Wm. Weir. Had five children. She was killed by a runaway team, in Nebraska City. Family reside there.

HARRIET, born Feb. 26, 1824, married John McClure, who died, leaving a widow and eight children in Cass county.

JAMES M., born Jan. 9, 1826, in West Virginia, unmarried, and resides in Loami.

LETHE, born March 29, 1831, married, March 24, 1856, to Daniel Cuppy, have two children, MARY E. and HARRIET V., and reside at Loami. Mr. C. served three years in 11th Mo. Inf.

WILLIAM F., born Feb. 12, 1833, in Sangamon county, went to California, in 1856, resides in Nevada City, Cal.

Mrs. Lucinda Barger died August 11, 1853, and Adam Barger married Mrs. Deborah Colburn, whose maiden name was Phelps. He died August 11, 1864, in Loami township. His widow resides with her children.

BARNETT, THOMPSON, was born Dec. 15, 1795, in Kentucky. Ann Patterson was born Sept. 29, 1803, in Holston county, Va. When she was two years old her parents moved to Adair county, Ky. Thompson Barnett and Ann Patterson were married there, Jan. 19, 1822. They had three children born in Kentucky, and moved to Illinois, arriving in the fall of 1829, at Irish Grove, Menard county, where one child was born. Thompson Barnett died Dec. 12, 1830, at Irish Grove. Mrs. Ann Barnett was married May 26, 1836, to Levi Cantrall, and brought her four children to his home in Fancy Creek township. Of her children by the first marriage—

NANCY J., born Nov. 25, 1822, in Adair county, Ky., married in Sangamon county to William D. Power. (See his name.)

ARMINTA M., born March 27, 1825, in Kentucky, married in Sangamon county, to Jefferson Vandergrift. They had four children, and she died. Mr. V. and his children reside in ————, Wis.

MARY E., born August 29, 1829, in Kentucky, married in Sangamon county to James Hibbs. Mrs. Hibbs died, leaving one child, NANCY J., who married Dorrell Primm, and resides in Menard county.

J. THOMPSON, born April 20, 1830, at Irish Grove. He married and has five children, JAMES, EDDIE, NATHAN, ANN and MARY, and resides in Fancy Creek township.

For Mrs. Ann Barnett's further history, see *Levi Cantrall*.

BARNES, EZRA, was born Sept. 6, 1806, at Groton, New London county, Ct. He started from Hartford with a team, and, in thirty-one days' driving, reached St. Louis, Nov. 13, and five days later came into Sangamon county, arriving Nov. 18, 1833. For 21 months he peddled clocks, after which he commenced farming, raising his first crop in 1836. He again peddled dry goods, and came near being drowned while crossing the Sangamon river north of Springfield. He was married, Dec. 6, 1838, to Elizabeth Mason. She was born Feb. 4, 1818. They had five children, all born in Sangamon county, namely:

EZRA, Jun., born April 30, 1842, in Sangamon county, married in 1872 at Preston City, Conn., to Prudence A. Browning. They reside five miles southwest of Chatham.

SETH A., born in Sangamon county, is a member of the firm of Barnes & Simpson, druggists, in Taylorville.

OLIVE F., born in Sangamon county, married Feb. 10, 1876, to George Bremer.

CHARLEY and ANGELINE, reside with their parents in Ball township, two and a half miles south of Chatham.

BARNES, DANIEL, was born Feb., 1807, in Bucks county, Pa. He was married in 1832, in Lancaster county, to Margaret A. Richardson, who was born Jan., 1810, in that county. Mr. Barnes kept a book store and bindery in Harrisburg, and was the State binder for Pennsylvania for five years. They had three children in Harrisburg. Mr. Barnes closed up his engagement as State binder in the spring of 1840, sold out his book store, and came west on horseback, looking for a location. He selected Springfield as his future home, and was soon followed by his family. They had four children in Springfield, two of whom died young. Of the other five children—

ALBERT G., born Sept. 4, 1835, in Harrisburg, Pa., was with his father in Springfield from 1840 to 1855, when he engaged in business in Taylorville. He was married August 27, 1861, near Mechanicsburg, Ill., to Henrietta Branson. They have five living children, BENJ. LINCOLN, ALBERT G., Jun., MARY H., CLARA MAY and HARRY R., and reside in Taylorville, Ill. Mr. Barnes is engaged in the mercantile business and banking.

ALMOND F., born in 1837, in Harrisburg, Pa., raised in Springfield and Taylorville, married in 1863, in Quincy, Ill., to Nellie Harvey. They reside in Quincy.

HARRIET A., born in Harrisburg and died in 1859.

CHARLES E., born Dec. 19, 1842, in Springfield, married in Taylorville, Jan. 25, 1871, to Jeanette Overand, who was born August 24, 1855, in Hartford, Conn. They have one child, RALPH, and reside in Taylorville. Mr. Barnes was in business with his father until the death of the latter, and is now a hardware merchant.

ANNA, born about 1844 or '5, in Springfield, married in St. Louis, Mo., to J. H. Pierson, and resides in Hearne, Robertson county, Texas.

Daniel Barnes sold dry goods in Springfield, from 1842 to 1849. He was in business with his son, Charles E., until Jan. 10, 1868, when he died, in Taylorville. His widow resides there.

Gilbert Barnes, the father of Daniel, was born in 1780, in Bucks county, Pa. He was a soldier from that county in the war of 1812. He married and had seven children in the same county. Gilbert Barnes, and other members of his family, came to Springfield with the family of his son, Daniel, in 1840, but I have not been able to obtain a full history of the family.

BARRETT, DR. R. F., moved from Green county, Ky., to Sangamon county about the time of the "deep snow" of 1830 and '31, and settled on Spring creek, in what is now Island Grove township. He had a son born there, and in 1839 Dr. Barrett accepted the position of Professor of Materia Medica, in the Medical College of Missouri, and moved to St. Louis. His son—

ARTHUR B., born August 22, 1835, on Spring creek, Sangamon county, married in St. Louis to a Miss Sweringen. He was for seven years President of the company managing the St. Louis Fair, and

—13

it was largely through his influence that it acquired a reputation unsurpassed by any other institution of the kind in America. He was also President of the Missouri Life Ins. Co. He was elected Mayor of St. Louis, was inaugurated April 13, and died April 24, 1875.

BARROW, ABRAHAM, was born Oct. 15, 1803, in Frederick county, Va. Mahala Larrick was born Nov. 14, 1809, in the same county. They were married there, Oct. 20, 1831. Two of their children were born in Berkley county, Va. They moved to Sangamon county, Ill., arriving Sept. 19, 1835, in what is now Cotton Hill township, where they had four children. Of their children—

JOHN T., born Feb. 27, 1833, in Berkley county, Va., was married, Dec. 12, 1861, in Christian county, Ill., to Eliza J. Ducker, who was born July 24, 1842, in Ohio. They had two children in Sangamon county. They moved to Sarpy county, Neb., Nov. 6, 1865. Three children were born in Nebraska. They moved to Texas in 1870, and settled in Dallas county, where one child was born. Thence to Fort Worth, in Tarrant county, where two children were born. Of their eight children, six died in infancy. FLORA A. and CHARLES H., reside with their parents, at Fort Worth, Tarrant county, Texas.

ORANGE P., born in Virginia, died in Sangamon county in infancy.

JOSEPH W., born March 11, 1837, in Sangamon county, was married April 12, 1860, to Susan E. Hardin. They have four children, MARY V., SARAH E., PRESLEY L. and MAHALA D., and reside near Taylorville.

MARY J., born March 16, 1840, in Sangamon county, married May 3, 1859, to Thomas W. Fleming. They had two children. MARY A. died July 27, 1874, and EMMA L. resides with her mother. Mr. Fleming died July 26, 1866. Mrs. Fleming was married Sept., 1871, to John L. Morgan, who was born in Sandusky, Ohio, and served three years in Co. E., 13th U. S. Inf. He was honorably discharged August 6, 1868. They reside near Zion Chapel, three miles north of Pawnee.

ANN E., born Feb. 13, 1842, in Sangamon county, married John Q. A. Husband. See his name.

ELIZA V., born March 30, 1851, in Sangamon county, married Feb. 9, 1870, to Nimrod Vickers. One child, FRANK, died in infancy. They reside in Christian county, four miles east of Pawnee.

Abraham Barrows died April 9, 1862, and Mrs. Mahala Barrows died Oct. 18, 1874, both at the family homestead, six miles south of Springfield.

BARROWS, JOSIAH, was born Sept. 17, 1793, in Thompson, Windham county, Conn. In 1798, his parents moved to Bridport, Vt., where Josiah was married Feb. 23, 1825, in Lebanon, New Hampshire, to Joanna Allen. She died Sept., 1826, in Vermont, and Mr. Barrows was married Jan., 1829, in Lebanon, N. H., to Emily Young. She died Nov., 1831, in Vermont, and he was married, July, 1836, in New Haven, Vt., to Mrs. T. M. Case, whose maiden name was Mills. They had two children in Vermont, and came to Illinois, arriving in Chatham, Sangamon county, Oct., 1839, where they had two children, and moved to Springfield about 1846. Of their children—

MARY P., was born in Vermont in 1837, and was married Jan. 1, 1861, in Springfield, to John H. Morse. They have three children, JOHN, GEORGE and HORACE, and reside at Morse's Mills, Jefferson county, Mo. Mr. Morse was an avowed abolitionist, and during the war to suppress the rebellion, was much annoyed by the rebels. His store was robbed, but being warned, he had time to remove some of the lighter goods. Amid all his troubles he continued to flourish, and has several times represented his district in the State Senate of Missouri. He is always engaged in some public enterprise.

SAMUEL M., born about 1838, in Vermont, raised in Sangamon county, Ill., married Sept. 1867, in Vineland, Jefferson county, Mo., to Ellen Morse. They have four children, JULIA, KATIE, ELLEN and ARTHUR. S. M. Barrows was a Union man, and subjected, like his brother-in-law, to annoyance during the war. He is Post Master, and resides at Morse's Mills, Mo.

LUCY, died in Springfield, aged about sixteen years.

ANNA, born in Springfield, resides with her sister, Mrs. Morse.

LOUISA CASE, daughter of Mrs. Barrows by a former marriage, resides with her half-sister, Mrs. Morse.

Mrs. T. M. Barrows left Springfield to visit her daughter, Mrs. Morse, in Missouri, and died there, Nov. 1865.

Josiah Barrows, after the death of his wife, spent his winters in Missouri, and summers in Springfield, Ill., until 1875. He now resides with his children in Missouri.

BARROWS, LUCY, sister of Josiah and Franklin, was born March 14, 1797, in Woodstock, Conn. Came west in 1838. She resided in Sangamon and Morgan counties until Jan., 1841, when she was married to Erasius Wright. *See his name.*

BARROWS, FRANKLIN, brother to Lucy and Josiah, came to Springfield Nov., 1855. They came too late to be classed as early settlers, Mr. Franklin Barrows and family continue to reside in Springfield.

Prentiss Barrows, the father of Josiah, Lucy and Franklin, was a soldier of the Revolution, under command of Benedict Arnold, and occupied the same building used as Gen. Arnold's headquarters. Prentiss Barrows was standing in the yard when Arnold left the Americans to join the British, and as he passed, something heavy in his pockets struck Barrows, and it was always believed that it was gold, a part of the price of his treason. Prentiss Barrows died in 1812, at Bridport, Vt., from disease contracted in the army of the Revolution.

BASHAW, MRS. ELLEN, whose maiden name was Reed, was born about 1774. Her parents were from Pennsylvania. Ellen Reed was married in Bourbon county, Ky., to William Bashaw. He was a native of Virginia. They had three children, and Mr. Bashaw died in Bourbon county. Mrs. Bashaw, with her three sons, moved to Sangamon county, Ill., arriving in the fall of 1830, and settled three miles north of Rochester. Of her three children—

JAMES, born Jan. 18, 1800, in Kentucky, married in Sangamon county, Jan. 17, 1832, to Mary McCune. They had seven children in Sangamon county, CINCINNATUS, ELEANOR, EMILY, HIRAM, CORDIANN, JAMES R. and WILLIAM M. James Bashaw died in 1850, and his widow resides two miles north of Rochester.

WILLIAM S., born Nov., 1805, in Bourbon county, Ky., married in Sangamon county, in 1834, to Isabel McCune. They had nine children; four died young. AMANDA, born April 6, 1835, married James A. James. *See his name.* JAMES, born Jan. 27, 1838, married Feb. 20, 1862, to Mary Bailey, who was born Jan. 26, 1844, in Hawkins county, Tenn. They have three children, LAURA I., GEORGE A. and DOLLY, and reside in Clear Lake township, eight miles due east of Springfield. HANNAH, married William Thomas, and resides one mile west of Dawson. CHARLES SPENCER and ALEXANDER reside in Clear Lake township. Mrs. Isabel Bashaw died July 27, 1861, and William S. Bashaw died Jan. 3, 1874, within one and a half miles of where he settled with his mother in 1830. Wm. S. Bashaw had been five years a Justice of the Peace, and was in office at the time of his death.

JAQUELIN, born Nov. 24, 1808, in Kentucky, married in Sangamon county to Eleanor Poor, had nine children, and he died in 1868. His widow married James McQuinn, and resides near Rochester.

Mrs. Ellen Bashaw died Sept., 1852, on the farm where she settle in 1830.

BATES, ISAAC, was born Oct. 14, 1796, in the town of Jaffrey, Cheshire county, New Hampshire, and when a young man, went to St. Lawrence county, N. Y. CHARLOTTE BRYANT was born Dec. 11. 1805, at Shoreham, near White Hall, Vt., and taken by her parents to St. Lawrence county, N. Y. Isaac Bates and Charlotte Bryant were married and had six children in St. Lawrence county. The family moved to Sangamon county, Ill., in wagons, arriving June 30, 1837, at Springfield, and the next week (July 4), witnessed the laying of the corner stone of the State house, the work on which had just commenced. In 1839 he entered land north of the Sangamon river, moved there, and made a home in what is now Fancy creek township. Two children were born in Sangamon county. Of their children—

JOSEPH, born June 16, 1822, in St. Lawrence county, N. Y., married in Sangamon county to Mrs. Rebecca Power, whose maiden name was Brown. Mrs.

Bates had one child by her first marriage, MARY J. POWER. She married John B. Brown, and lives in Jefferson county, Kan. Mr. and Mrs. Bates have six children. FIDELIA E. married Winfield S. Hay, and lives in Fancy creek township. ISAAC D., JAMES W., JOSEPH F., ZIMRI E., and JOHN CARROLL reside with their parents in Fancy Creek township, 12 miles due north of Springfield.

ORLANDO, born March 20, 1824, in St. Lawrence county, N. Y., married in Sangamon county to Sarah Brown. They have three living children, JANE and CHARLOTTE, (twins.) JANE married William Stienberger, and lives near Mt. Pulaski. CHARLOTTE married Abram Larue, and lives near Williamsville. EMMA lives with her parents in Williamsville.

NELSON, born April 13, 1826, in New York. He lost one arm by the explosion of a gun when he was 14 years old. He married Melinda Ferguson, has three children, MINNIE J., WILLIAM, and FREDERICK, and lives in Petersburg, Ill.

ALBERT, died, 1829, in infancy.

FIDELIA, died August 31, 1845, aged 15 years.

ZIMRI B., born Feb. 28, 1833, in St. Lawrence county, N. Y., enlisted, Nov. 25, 1861, in Co. G., 10th Ill. Cav., and was commissioned as 1st Lieutenant. He was promoted to Captain, Oct. 20, 1862. He served about four years, and resigned in Feb., 1865. He was married Sept. 23, 1866, in Sangamon county, to Hattie Stockdale, who was born April 2, 1846, in Pennsylvania. They have two children, NORA M. and HOWARD R., and reside in Fancy Creek township, at the home settled by his parents in 1839.

IRA, died in Sangamon county, Oct., 1858, in his twelfth year.

PARTHENIA, born March 12, 1842, in Sangamon county, married William S. Constant. *See his name.*

JAMES M., born June 19, 1844, in Sangamon county, married Julia Constant. They have one child, ETHEL, and reside in Williamsville.

Isaac Bates died April 23, 1855, in Fancy creek township. His widow resides with her daughter, Mrs. Constant. Mrs. Bates is a cousin to William Cullen Bryant, the poet, and editor of the *New York Post*.

BATES, JAMES, was born March 2, 1803, in Cheshire county, N. H., raised at Potsdam, N. Y., and came with his brother Oliver to Sangamon county in 1833. He was married in the fall of 1842, to Eunice Watts who died in June, 1846. Mr. Bates was married in May, 1852, to Mrs. Irena Holmes, whose maiden name was Watts. She died in April, 1865. James Bates resides one mile northwest of Farmingdale. He never had any children.

BATES, OLIVER, was born in 1796, in Cheshire county, N. H. Moved, about 1806, to Potsdam, St. Lawrence county, N. Y., where he was married to Charity Buckman, Sept. 8, 1824. She is a sister of Joel Buckman, and was born in Bethel, Vermont. They had three children in New York, two of whom died young. They moved in a colony of 52 persons to Sangamon county, Ill., arriving in 1833, and early in 1834 settled adjoining the present Farmingdale Station, on the south, where three children were born. Of the four children—

ROXANA, born Oct. 23, 1832, in Potsdam, N. Y., was married in Sangamon county, Ill., April 6, 1853, to Jacob Foster. *See his name.*

ZURA, born Jan. 12, 1836, in Sangamon county, was married to Mrs. Josephine Ellis. They have three children, CHAS. B., ELIZABETH A. and ROXANA L., and reside in Taylorville, Ill.

BUCKMAN, born Nov. 6, 1840, in Sangamon county, was partially educated at Jacksonville, Ill., and graduated at the State University, Bloomington, Indiana. He began the study of law in Pekin, Ill., where he died July 13, 1864.

ELIZABETH, born Feb. 25, 1839, in Sangamon county, died at the residence of her sister, Mrs. Foster. Oliver Bates died in 1865, where he settled in 1834. His widow died in March 1869, at the residence of her daughter, Mrs. Foster.

BATTERTON, AMOR, was born May 3, 1772, in Loudon county, Va. Nancy Guthrie was born about 1776, in North Carolina, and her parents moved, when she was a child, to Madison county, Ky. They were there married and had one child, who was drowned in Kentucky river. They moved to Adair county, where they had nine children, and moved to Madison county, Ill., in 1818, and from there to Rock creek, in what is now Menard county, in 1820, thence to what is now Salisbury township, Sangamon county, in the spring of 1822, and settled one and a quarter miles northwest of where Salisbury now stands. Of their nine children—

DAVID, born Nov. 5, 1796, in Kentucky, married Nancy Yoakum. They had eight children, and Mr. B. died in Menard county. His family moved to Cass county, and his widow died there. Their children reside in Menard and Cass counties, and in Kansas. Mr. B. was 1st Lieutenant in a Company in the Winnebago war.

NELSON, born July 27, 1798, in Kentucky, married Betsy Davenport, had four children, and Mr. B. died in DeWitt county. Their son WILLIAM was a soldier in an Illinois regiment, and died in 1863, in the army. MARY and NANCY are married, and reside in Minnesota. JAMES W. and his mother live in Missouri.

ANDERSON, born May 3, 1800, in Kentucky, married Polly Robinson, who died, and he married again and went to Arkansas.

WILLIAM, born Dec. 14, 1801, in Adair county, Ky., married Jan. 1, 1833, in Sangamon county, to Eliza Gaines. They had twelve children; two died young. MADISON, born Oct. 20, 1833, enlisted, August 13, 1862, for three years, in Co. B., 114th Ill. Inf., was captured at Guntown, Miss., June 11, 1864, was taken to Andersonville prison and escaped by falling in with Gen. Stoneman's men when they were about to be exchanged Sept. 14, 1864, and was mistaken for one of them. He left them at Atlanta, was furloughed home from Memphis, joined his regiment in Jan., 1865, served to the end of his term, and was honorably discharged, August 3, 1865. He was married April 24, 1864, in Sangamon county, to Cynthia S. Lemmon. They have three living children, MINNIE M., JENNIE, and a boy babe, and reside four and a half miles north of Salisbury. RICHARD, born July 19, 1836, married Permelia Miller, have three children, ADAM F., MURRAY, and ELIJAH, and reside in Menard county. AMY C., born Feb. 19, 1838, married John R. Wells, have seven children, and reside in Macon county, Mo. ROBERT, born August 4,

1839, enlisted for three years, August 13, 1862, in Co. B, 114th Ill. Inf., served full term, and was honorably discharged at Springfield, June 29, 1865. He died at home, August 16, 1868, from the effects of camp diarrhea and sun stroke. HENRY CLAY, born Nov. 12, 1843, married Jan. 20, 1870, to Maria Maltby, who was born May 27, 1850, at Petersburg, Ill. They have one child, IDA MAY, and reside one mile west of Salisbury. MILDRED P., born May 4, 1846, married Daniel C. Pelham. *See his name.* MARIA, SARAH E., CHARLOTTE and GEORGE W., reside with their parents, one and a quarter miles west of Salisbury.

LEVI, born August 20, 1804, in Kentucky, married in Sangamon county, March 3, 1831, to Dorcas Sackett. They had six children. MARY A. married Wm. Hines, have ten children, and reside two miles north of Salisbury. THOMAS S. married Lucy Duncan, have five children, JASPER N., ALLIE J., FRANCIS M., GEORGE W. and ANDERSON D., and reside one and a half miles north of Salisbury. ELIAS married Ellen Duncan; have two children, HARVEY and ANNIE, and reside five miles north of Salisbury. AMANDA J. married Ira Brown, and resides two and a half miles north of Salisbury. WILLIAM H. married Mary E. Duncan, has one child, NORA, and resides with his parents, two miles north of Salisbury. Levi Batterton served in a Sangamon county Company in the Winnebago war, and drew as a pension, twice, forty acres of land.

MARY, born Dec. 14, 1804, in Kentucky, married Willoughby Randolph. They had four children. Their youngest son, LEVI, was a soldier in an Iowa regiment, was wounded and died at the battle of Pittsburg landing. The family reside at Knoxville, Iowa.

PRISCILLA, born Feb. 9, 1809, in Kentucky, married June 16, 1836, to William Yoakum, who was born July 28, 1812, in Claiborne county, Tenn. They have one son, WILLIAM F., who married Mary Adams, and resides with his parents in Menard county, two miles north of Salisbury.

SUSANNAH T., born June 7, 1811, married Coleman Gaines. *See his name.*

E. GEORGE, born June 26, 1814, in Adair county, Ky., married Jan. 19, 1843, in Menard county, to Huberty Clark. They had ten children; one died young. JOHN C. resides with his parents. ELISHA C. married Farinda Duncan. They have three children, EMMA J., EDWARD L. and SYLVA V., and reside one mile southeast of Salisbury. PRISCILLA J. married Wm. Tozer, have three children, and reside five miles northwest of Salisbury. MARY A., MARTHA A., MORRIS M., LAURA A., GEO. M. and CHARLES L., reside with their parents, two miles north of Salisbury.

Mrs. Nancy Batterton died July 31, 1835, and Amor Batterton died August 4, 1835, both near Salisbury.

BEACH, JARED, was born Nov. 24, 1770, in Essex county, N. J., and was married there, Feb. 13, 1794, to Mary Harrison, who was born Sept. 18, 1775, in the same county. They moved to New York City, where they had five living children, and in 1835 moved to Springfield, Ill. Of their children—

ELECTA, married in New York City to Henry Howell, moved west, and died, Feb., 1859, in Centreville, Iowa.

CATHARINE, born Sept. 12, 1805, in New York city, married there, August 3, 1830, to Edmund R. Wiley. See his name.

RICHARD H., born March 11, 1808, in New York City, married there, in 1832, to Eliza H. Baldwin, who was born in 1814, in Cranberry, Middlesex county N. J. They had one child, and moved to Morgan county, Ill., where he taught school one year, and came to Springfield in 1834, and in 1835 united with E. R. Wiley in the mercantile business, as Wiley, Beach & Co. They established the first clothing store in Springfield, which they continued many years. Mr. and Mrs. Beach had four children in Springfield. Of their five children, SARAH, born in 1833, in New York City, married in Springfield to George H. Nolte. They had three children, GEORGE E., RICHARD B. and MINNIE G. Mrs. Nolte died in 1862, in Beardstown. CATHARINE E., born in 1835, in Springfield, died in 1848 in Beardstown. MARY B., born in Springfield, resides with her father. MATILDA B., born Feb. 28, 1839, in Springfield, married, April 14, 1868, to Rev. William E. Caldwell, of Lodi, Michigan. They have three children, JENNIE, MINNIE and EDWARD, and reside at Clio, Genesee county, Michigan. Mr. Caldwell is pastor of the Congregational church of that place. EDWARD P., born May 27, 1841, in Springfield, married May 11, 1865, to Julia E. Cone, and resides in Springfield. Mrs. Eliza H. Beach died Oct. 31, 1865, and Richard H. Beach was married, June 27, 1867, to Sarah Lavinia Pearson. They reside in Springfield.

ELIZA H., died April 14, 1865, in Centreville, Iowa.

AMELIA, born Sept. 21, 1816, married in 1843, in Springfield, to John Harris. She died May 22, 1845.

Mrs. Mary Beach died Dec. 17, 1836, and Jared Beach died March 4, 1852, both in Springfield.

BEACH, JOB A., was born April 5, 1780, in Morris county, N. J. Susan Hathaway was born Oct. 12, 1782, in the same county. They were married and had eight children in New Jersey, and in 1817 moved to Butler county, Ohio, and the next year to Dearborn county, Ind. Of three children born in the latter county, one died in infancy. Mrs. Susan Beach died there in Oct., 1822, and Job A. Beach was married, August 26, 1824, to Judith Connelly, who was born Dec. 2, 1805, in Washington county, Pa. They had five children in Indiana, and the family moved to Sangamon county, Ill., in the fall of 1835, and settled south of Spring creek, in what is now Gardner township, where five children were born. Of the twenty children of Job A. Beach—

CHARLES, born Dec. 16, 1801, in New Jersey, married in Ohio to Elizabeth McGilvey. She died, leaving one child, and, when last heard from, he lived in Rockville, Ind.

EUNICE, born April 7, 1803, in New Jersey, married in Indiana to Enoch Conger. They had six children, and moved to Oquawka, Ill., where the parents died.

J. MUNSON, born May 1, 1806, in Morris county, N. J., married near Carthage, Hamilton county, Ohio, August 27, 1835, to Christiana M. Robinson. They came to Sangamon county, Ill., arriving Sept. 19, 1836, in what is now Gardner township, where they had eleven children; two died young. CAROLINE, born June 3, 1837, married Jan, 15, 1857, to George Carr. She died April 5, 1860, leaving one child, BENJAMIN, who resides with his father, in Wisconsin. MARY A., born Jan. 23, 1839, married August 20, 1862, to Henry P. Hart. They have six children, HENRY E., WILLIAM M., MARY C., BENJAMIN S., JULIA P. and WALTER A., and reside five miles northwest of Springfield. Henry P. Hart enlisted August 9, 1862, for three years, in Co. H., 95th Ill. Inf., was corporal and postmaster in the Company, served until June 6, 1863, when he was promoted to Captain of a Company of U. S. colored troops. CORNELIA, born Jan. 15, 1841, married April 3, 1860, to Samuel Cook. They have four children, JAMES E., WILLIAM M., JOHN and JENNIE, and reside in Chandlerville, Ill. EDWARD M., born Oct. 6, 1843, enlisted August 20, 1862, for three years, in Co. B., 130th Ill. Inf. He was corporal and fifer the greater part of the time, served full term, and was honorably discharged August 15, 1865. He was married June 3, 1869, to Maggie Frazee. They have one child, LIBBIE G., and reside eight miles west of Springfield. VIRGINIA, born July 8, 1846, married Oct. 3, 1872, to Charles W. King. *See his name.* JULIA D., born April 6, 1848, married Oct. 24, 1870, to Hiram McC. Reed. Who was born Aug. 26, 1846, in Butler county, Ohio. They have one child, MAGGIE C., and reside near Berlin. JOSHUA M., born Oct. 4, 1852, died in his seventh year. JOSEPH W., born Dec. 14, 1855, and ALICE J., born Jan. 4, 1859, reside with their parents, eight miles west of Springfield.

MILTON, born April 25, 1808, in New Jersey, married, raised a family, and resides in Lawrenceburg, Ind.

EMELINE, born May 8, 1810, in New Jersey, married in Dearborn county, Ind., to Ezekiel Pettigrew, and both died in Park county, leaving seven children.

NANCY, born June 26, 1813, in New Jersey, married in Indiana to Jacob Daisy, moved to Arkansas, where he died, and she married again.

JANE, born August 24, 1814, in New Jersey, married Ephraim Lawler. She died in Clay county, Ill., leaving four children near Louisville.

PRUDENCE, born Sept. 25, 1816, in New Jersey, married Wm. Bullion, in Park county, Ind., and died there.

ELIZABETH, born Jan 22, 1818, in Indiana, died unmarried in 1869, at the house of her sister, Lavina, near Vandalia.

LAVINA, born Nov. 30, 1820, in Dearborn county, Ind., married in Springfield, Ill., to Stephen D. Perry. They have nine children, and reside near Shabonier, Fayette county. Of the second marriage—

ELIZA, born August 4, 1825, in Indiana, died, aged two years.

JOB ALLEN, Jun., born March 1, 1827, in Dearborn county, Ind., came with his parents to Sangamon county in 1835. He enlisted August, 1862, for three years, in Co. I, 130th Ill. Inf. He was under Gen. Banks in his expedition up Red River, was captured and taken to Camp Ford, at Tyler, Texas, and after six weeks imprisonment, news came that they were to be exchanged, and the rebel guards becoming less vigilant, he escaped and wandered 26 days before reaching the Union lines. His comrades remained fourteen months in the rebel prisons. Mr. Beach served to the end of the rebellion, and was honorably discharged in August, 1865. He is unmarried, and resides with his mother, eight miles west of Springfield.

MARY A., born June 25, 1829, in Indiana, raised in Sangamon county, married in Knox county, Ill., to Jonathan Cacebeer, have one child, and reside at Wilton Junction, Iowa.

LUCY, born April 29, 1831, in Indiana, died in Sangamon county, aged sixteen years.

BENJAMIN F., born May 31, 1833, in Indiana, raised in Sangamon county, married in Knox county, Ill., enlisted at Moline, served three years, re-enlisted as veteran, served to the end of the rebellion, and was honorably discharged. He moved to Springfield, Mo., and died there, May 18, 1869, leaving a widow and four children.

SUSAN, born March 17, 1836, in Sangamon county, resides with her mother.

HARLAN P., born Nov. 20, 1838, in Sangamon county, married in Fayette county, to Ellen J. Tharp. He served as First Sargeant three years in the 111th Ill. Inf., was with Sherman in his march to the sea, served to the end of the rebellion, was honorably discharged, and died

March 13, 1870, leaving a widow and one child in Fayette county.

MARTIN L., born Feb. 11, 1811, in Sangamon county, enlisted May, 1862, for three months, in Co. G., 68th Ill. Inf., and died of disease, Sept. 10, 1862, in Washington City.

FRANCIS, born Oct. 1, 1843, died in infancy.

LOUISA R., born May 10, 1846, in Sangamon county, married Thomas D. Barnhart, had one child, and Mrs. B. died, Nov. 28, 1871, in Kansas.

Job A. Beach died April 11, 1849, in Sangamon county, and his widow resides eight miles west of Springfield, with her unmarried children.

BEARDON, SAMUEL L., was born Feb. 27, 1827, in Christian county, Ky. His father moved to Christian county, Ill., in 1828. His mother dying soon after, his father gave him to John French, a friend of the family, who had moved to Chatham township, in Sangamon county. He was brought up by Mr. French. Samuel L. Beardon was married April 10, 1852, in Sangamon county, to Susan Gofor. They have four children—

GEORGE T., ISAAC N., SAMUEL E., and IRA, and reside two and a half miles northeast of Auburn.

John French died in 1854, in Chatham township.

BEAUCHAMP, JOSHUA, was born about 1782, in Washington county, Ky. He was married there to Catharine Payne. They had seven children in Kentucky, and moved to Sangamon county, Ill., arriving in what is now Woodside township, in the fall of 1827, where two children were born. Of the children—

MARIA R., born in Kentucky, married James H. Withrow. See his name.

The other children—

HENRY N., EDWARD, ELIZA, WILLIAM, JOSEPH and AMANDA, all married, some died, and the living are in Kansas and Missouri.

Joshua Beauchamp moved to Missouri, and died April 1, 1842, in the Platt purchase. His widow resides in Doniphan county, Kansas.

BEAM, JACOB, was born about 1762, in N. J., and when he was a youth, went to Lexington, Ky., which he found to be a very small village. Rachel McClure was born in Huntington county, Pa., in 1775, and taken by her parents to Fayette county, Ky., when she was quite young. Jacob Beam and Rachel McClure were married at Lexington, and had two children there. They moved to Manchester, Ohio, where they had eleven children, and from there to Clarke county, Ind., where one child was born, and from there to what is now Lincoln, Logan county, Ill., arriving the day before the election which made Andrew Jackson President, in 1828. Finding it impossible to obtain food and shelter for his family through the winter, after a stay of two weeks, Mr. Beam moved to Rochester, Sangamon county, in the latter part of Nov., 1828. Of their children—

JAMES, born near Lexington, Ky., married in Sangamon county to Susan Hyner, who was born Oct. 15, 1810. They had nine children, all of whom are dead, except RACHEL, born May 15, 1831, married Jacob Rape. See his name. James Beam died in 1855, in Sangamon county, and his widow died in 1858, at Mt. Auburn, Christian county.

JOHN, born in Kentucky, married in Sangamon county, to Ellen Williams. They have three children, and reside at Boscobel, Grant county, Wis.

ELIZABETH, born at Manchester, O., married in Sangamon county to Harvey Summers. They had six children. SIMON P. was accidentally shot in Marysville, California, about 1860. JOHN WESLEY, was a member of a California Cavalry regiment, and was killed by his horse running away with him on the march to the field of conflict, in 1862. GEORGE W. was a soldier in an Illinois regiment, captured and died in a rebel prison in South Carolina. MARY E. married a Baptist minister, and resides in Iowa. WILLIAM resides near Rockbridge, Green county. SARAH E., resides with her father. Mrs. E. Summers died, and Harvey Summers resides in Alton.

MARY, born in Ohio, is unmarried, and resides with her brother, Joseph Beam.

DAVID, born in Manchester, Adams county, Ohio, married in Sangamon county, to Rosanna Ebey, who was born near Columbus, Ohio. They had eleven children in Sangamon county, five of whom died young. GEORGE W. went to Washington Territory in 1854, married there to Sarah Wright, a native of Missouri. They went over the plains together. Mr. Beam died March, 1865, on Vancouver's Island, leaving a widow and three children. She is again married, and resides in San Francisco. JACOB H., born April 28, 1834, married Jan. 19, 1865, to Amanda Cummings, and resides in Springfield. LOUISA J. married Emery Raymond, and died March 17, 1863, leaving two children. NANCY A. married Lewis Williams, who died, and she married Geo. W. Dugger, and resides in Virden. WILLIAM T., born Sept. 22, 1844, married Sept. 25, 1872, to Margaret A. Sanders. They have one child, CORDELIA A., and reside in Rochester township, near where his grandfather Beam settled in 1828. JAMES HARVEY, born July 24, 1849, married Oct. 23, 1873, to Eliza J. Sanders, and resides on part of the farm near where his grandfather settled in 1828. It is in Cotton Hill township. David Beam died Feb. 28, 1853. His widow died April 16, 1860. Mr. Beam acted as Justice of the Peace for many years; was a farmer and miller.

SARAH, born in Ohio, married in Sangamon county, to John A. Maxcy. They have two children, and reside in Alton.

NANCY, born in Ohio, married in Sangamon county, to Jacob Miller, and both died. They left six children in DeWitt county.

THOMAS, born at Manchester, O., and came to Sangamon county with his parents. Some of his friends here relate an incident in his life that illustrates real life among the early settlers. He raised a good crop of corn in the summer of 1830, and in the fall determined to sell it and go to the Galena lead mines. After making it known in all the settlement, he was unable to get an offer for his crop at any price in money, but he traded it for a barrel of whisky, traded that for a three year old steer, and finally sold that for $10.00. He took a vow to use that for paying his expenses out of the county, and never to live in it again. He went to the lead mines, was married in Wisconsin to Catharine Reed. They had six children in Wisconsin, and moved to California in 1863. He is now a wealthy man, and resides at Crescent City, Del Norte county, California.

—14

JANE A., born in Ohio, married in Sangamon county to William Cable, moved to Wisconsin, and after spending twenty-four years there, moved to Iowa, and died there in 1872, leaving several children.

WESLEY, born in Ohio, married in Sangamon county, Dec. 25, 1840, to Amelia Rape. They had five children in Cotton Hill township; one died in infancy. NANCY J. married W. T. Williams; had two children, ALBERT L. and THEODORE L. Mrs. W. died and they live with their father, who married and resides in Cotton Hill township. MARY A. married James M. Sankey, have three children, and reside near Fairbanks, Ind. AMANDA E. married Wm. Z. Williams, have one child, and reside near Shelbourn, Ind. JOHN L. is unmarried, and resides 'in Cotton Hill township. Wesley Beam died in 1852, in Cotton Hill township, and his widow married Mr. Howlett. *See Rape family name.*

CORDELIA, born in Ohio, married in Sangamon county, to Daniel Fetters. They had four children, and she died in Cotton Hill township.

JOSEPH, born July 27, 1820, in Clarke county, Ind., married in Sangamon county to Mary P. Spicer. They had two children. NANCY J. A., married Henry Hertel, have one child, ADA LILLIAN, and reside three miles north of Pawnee, in Cotton Hill township. SARAH E. married Isaac Porter, who was born Dec. 29, 1836, in Monroe county, Ohio. They moved to Kansas City, Mo., and she died there, May 21, 1869, one month after marriage. Mr. Porter brought her remains back to the family cemetery for interment. He has since married Maggie Caldwell, and resides in Pawnee. Mrs. Mary P. Beam died Oct. 16, 1850, and Joseph Beam was married April 25, 1854, to Barbara Deardorff. They had four children. THOMAS W. and LINDSAY C., the eldest and youngest, died under three years. JOSEPH L. and WALDO P. reside with their parents in Ball township, ten miles southeast of Springfield. He has acted as Justice of the Peace for several years.

Jacob Beam died March 24, 1838, and his widow died April 21, 1851, both near where they settled in 1828.

BEDINGER, CHRISTIAN, was born Dec. 24, 1771, in Berkley county, Va. Sophia Taylor was born Sept. 24, 1776, in Maryland, they were married about 1798, in Maryland or Virginia, and made their home in Berkley county for a short time, then moved to Harrison county, near Cadiz, Ohio, where nine children were born. The parents and three of the children came to Sangamon county, Ill., arriving in the fall of 1836, in Island Grove. Of all their children—

PHILIP, born Nov. 8, 1799, in Ohio married in Cadiz to Sarah Hartman raised a large family, and resides near Nova, Ashland county, O.

JOSEPH, born June 16, 1801, in Ohio, married there to Deborah Metcalfe, had four children, and Mrs. B. died. Their daughter SOPHIA came to Sangamon county with her grandparents, and married James N. Eckler. JENNIE resides with her uncle, Wm. Bedinger. Joseph Bedinger has not been heard from for many years.

ISAAC, born June 18, 1807, married in Ohio, to Sarah Brown, came to Sangamon county, and died near Berlin, in 1851, leaving a widow and four children.

GEORGE, born Feb. 11, 1810, came to Sangamon county with his parents, remained four or five years, went to Missouri, married there to Eliza Carver. Both parents died, leaving four children near Lockridge, Jefferson county, Iowa.

WILLIAM, born June 11, 1812, near Cadiz, Ohio, came to Sangamon county in the spring of 1837, married Nov. 1, 1839, to Martha Carver, and had three children in Sangamon county. ELIZA J., born March 3, 1843, married in 1860 to George Wolfe, have four children, and reside near German Prairie Station. SARAH E., born Feb. 25, 1846, married in 1860 to John C. Robinson. They have one child, MARTHA A., and reside half a mile south of Camp Butler. ALBERT, born April 25, 1849, resides with his father. Mrs. Martha Bedinger died Nov., 1852, and Mr. B. was married Feb. 9, 1863, to Mrs. Sarah M. Greenslate, whose maiden name was Oliver. They reside half a mile south of Camp Butler.

HENRY, born June 5, 1814, in Ohio, married in Sangamon county to Sophia Carver, had one child, and he died. She married Job Dickenson.

MARY, born Jan. 6, 1818, in Ohio, arried in Sangamon county to Joseph Bumgardner. They had six children, four of whom died young. ADDISON and MATILDA F. reside with their parents, five miles east of Springfield.

Mrs. Sophia Bedinger died in 1840, and Christian Bedinger died Oct., 1851, both in Sangamon county.

BELL, ZEBULON, was born Nov. 18, 1799, in Gerrardstown, Berkley county, West Virginia. His grandfather, James Bell, was born and educated in Scotland. The exact date of his coming to America is unknown to his descendents. He landed in Philadelphia, and being a millwright, built a snuff mill in that city, said to have been the first machine of the kind in America. He went from Philadelphia to Frederick county, Va. According to traditions in the family, he must have been almost a Hercules in physical strength. In connection with his business as a millwright and miller, he is said to have carried nine bushels of wheat up three flights of stairs at a single load. James Bell was married in Scotland to Ellen Nelson. They brought two children with them to America, John and James. The latter, born March 18, 1770, in Scotland, was too young to remember crossing the Atlantic ocean. This would imply that they came before or during the Revolution. He married Margaret Fulton, a native of Chester county, Penn. She was of Irish descent. They settled in Gerrardstown, Berkley county, West Va., where they had nine children, three, only, of whom are living. John, born March 23, 1798, resides in Quincy, Logan county, Ohio. Launcelot, born Dec. 5, 1801, resides near Taylorville, Christian county, Illinois, and Zebulon, in age between the two latter, is the one whose name heads this sketch.

Zebulon Bell was married Sept. 20, 1821, in Gerrardstown, Berkley county, West Va., to Rachel Swingle, who was born Dec. 20, 1801, in the same county. They had five children there, and moved to Sangamon county, Ill., arriving May 6, 1834, in what is now Woodside township, west of Sugar creek, and six miles southeast of Springfield, where five children were born. Of their ten children—

BENONI, born July 24, 1822, in Berkley county, West Va., married in Sangamon county, March 21, 1847, to Eliza J. Wills. They had two living children. MARGARET C., born March

15, 1848, married, Nov. 25, 1868, to John M. Doake, who was born Oct. 3, 1844. They have three children, IVA, BENONI M. and MARY A., and reside six and a half miles southeast of Springfield. WILLIAM S. resides with his father. Mrs. Eliza J. Bell died Jan. 22, 1857, and Mr. Bell was married Oct. 12, 1859, in Madison, Ind., to Mrs. Anna Settle, whose maiden name was Taylor. She was born Dec. 17, 1833, in Lancaster county, Penn. They had five children, three died in infancy. CHARLES E. was killed by the kick of a horse, July 31, 1873, in his fifth year. ADA H. resides with her parents. Benoni Bell and wife reside within half a mile of where his parents settled in 1834. It is six and a half miles southeast of Springfield.

JAMES T., born Dec. 15, 1823, in Berkley county, West Va., enlisted in Sangamon county, Aug. 27, 1862, for three years, in Co. E., 114 Ill. Inf., served his full term, was honorably discharged, and now resides near Fountain, Colorado.

MARIA C., born June 29, 1825, in Berkley county, Va., married in Sangamon county, July 1, 1847, to John Bell, who was born Jan. 28, 1813, in Pittsburg, Penn. They have one child, RACHEL A., born April 9, 1848, married John H. Shoup. *See his name.* John Bell and wife reside with their daughter, Mrs. Shoup, in Cotton Hill township.

JOHN W., born May 2, 1828, in Berkley county, Va., married in Sangamon county, to Sarah E. Gatton. They have seven children, viz: MARY C., SAMUEL L., JOHN W., ALICE J., RACHEL E., EMILY E. and CARY L., and reside near Fountain, Colorado.

ZEBULON N., born April 19, 1830, in West Virginia, brought up in Sangamon county, is unmarried, and resides in Christian county, near Old Rienzi, Sangamon county.

MARGARET E., born May 31, 1834, in Sangamon county, was married Feb. 23, 1857, to Andrew Anderson, who was born in Garrard county, Ky., April 29, 1832. They have seven children, ARABEL, AGNES M., RICHARD Y., ZEBULON J., MARY S., JAMES and RACHEL, and reside in Cotton Hill township.

LAUNCELOT, born March 17, 1837, in Sangamon county, went to Pike's Peak in 1860, married there, March 21, 1865, to Lydia E. Roberts, who was born in Bourbon county, Ky., Dec. 26, 1846. Of their children, MARY M., CLARINDA M., IVY FORREST, GEORGE S. and FLORA E. The two latter died young. Launcelot Bell and wife reside near Fountain, El Paso county, Colorado.

STEPHEN, born April 19, 1839, in Sangamon county, enlisted August 27, 1862, for three years, in Co. E., 114th Ill. Inf., was taken prisoner June 10, 1864, at the battle of Guntown, Miss. He spent four months in Andersonville prison pen, two weeks at Savannah, Ga., one month at Millen, Ga., and was exchanged at Savannah, Nov. 24, 1864. He rejoined his regiment, served full time, and was honorably discharged with the regiment. He was married in Sangamon county, Jan. 20, 1869, to Louisa L. Womack. They have three children, CORA G., MAY S. and JAMES E., and reside five miles south of Springfield.

An incident, said to have taken place in Andersonville prison, went the rounds of the papers at the time, but its truthfulness was doubted. It had almost passed from my mind, until it was revived by Stephen Bell, who says that he was an eye-witness to the breaking out of a spring of pure water, under circumstances that seemed almost miraculous. It is not necessary to repeat the description of the prison, as that has been so often done. It is well known that inside the stockade there was a line, sometimes imaginary, called the "dead-line." If a prisoner crossed that line approaching the stockade, he was almost sure to be shot dead. A stream of water ran through the stockade from north to south. All the offal and filth from the camp of the rebel guards entered the stream above the stockade, and that was the only supply of water for the prisoners. About 100 yards east of and on ground 15 or 20 feet above that dirty slough, and four or five feet inside the dead-line, or between that and the stockade, a stream of water spouted up ten or fifteen feet, where there was not the least appearance of water before. Troughs were put up, and it was conducted inside the prison bounds. It took place about two o'clock in the afternoon, on a bright day in August, 1864. There had been a heavy rain the day before, accompanied by a terrific thunderstorm. The torrents of water broke down the stockade where it crossed the slough. The opening was so wide that the rebel authorities feared the prisoners would attempt to escape. They caused cannon to be fired and their soldiers to shout and halloo, and make all the noise they could, and in every way present as great an appearance of force as possible. No effort was made to escape, the breach was mended, the waters subsided, the clouds passed away, and it was the next day, when all was bright and clear, that the stream of pure water spouted up from the earth. Stephen Bell says he was as near it at the time as any other person. He thinks that of the 28,000 prisoners confined there at the time, the larger portion of them regarded it as a direct interposition of Providence in their behalf. Each one had his own way of expressing his feelings, some of them neither refined nor reverential, but none the less heart-felt and sincere.

James H. Pulliam and Benj. F. Fletcher, whose histories may be found in this book, were in the prison at the time, and testify to the truthfulness of the above statement. Mr. Samuel Lewis, of Auburn, was not there at the time, but saw the spring afterwards.

MARY L., born March 30, 1842, in Sangamon county, married Samuel Reaton. They have three children, IDA, JAMES E. and FRANK, and reside near Fountain, Colorado.

ARTHALINDA, born Sept. 2, 1844, in Sangamon county, married Jan. 7, 1859, to Alexander Shoup. *See his name.*

Mrs. Rachel Bell died Dec. 15, 1852, in Sangamon county, and Zebulon Bell moved west in 1859, and resides with his children, near Fountain, El Paso county, Colorado.

BELL, ROBERT, was born March 8, 1795, in Bourbon county, Ky. His father was born in Ireland, and had but four children, Robert, and three sisters. After his sisters were married, he had no knowledge of any relative in America, bearing his family name. He was a soldier from Bourbon county in the war of 1812. Robert Bell and Susannah Baker were married Feb. 12, 1818, in that county, and moved to Nicholas county, and from there they moved with their three children to Sangamon county, Ill., arriving in the fall of 1830, and settled four miles south of the present town of Rochester, where they had six children. Of their nine children—

ISAAC B., born June 25, 1820, near Carlisle, Nicholas county, Ky., married in Sangamon county, March 28, 1840, to Susan Stokes. They had six daughters in Sangamon county. CAROLINE M., born April 18, 1842, married March 29, 1868, to Lawson H. Smith, who was born Feb. 20, 1831, in Carlisle, Ky. They have three children, CORDELIA A., WM. RILEY and ANNA BELLE, and reside three miles southeast of Rochester. LOUISA J. resides with her parents. MARGARET A., born Sept. 30, 1846, married Jonathan G. Crouch. *See his name.* MARY E., EMILY T. and DEBORAH S. reside with their parents, one and a quarter miles west of Clarkesville.

JAMES H., born Nov. 30, 1822, in Nicholas county, Ky., married in Sangamon county, May 7, 1843, to Milla Dotson, who was born Nov., 1822, in Loudon county, Va. They had four children. JOHN W., the second child, died under two years. ELIZA A., born Feb. 25, 1844, married Sept. 4, 1864, to Benj. C. Gray, who was born August 12, 1832, near Hopkinsville, Ky. Mr. Gray has one child, CHARLES Y., by a former marriage. Mrs. Gray died Dec., 1874, and B. C. Gray resides near Clarkesville. HIRAM F., born Dec. 17, 1852, resides in California. JAMES M., born August 6, 1836, lives with his father. Mrs. Milla Bell died March 16, 1870, and James H. Bell resides in Springfield.

MARY J., born June 6, 1828, in Nicholas county, Ky., married in Sangamon county, August 31, 1847, to John S. Dickerson, who was born April 2, 1824, in Nicholas county, Ky., and came to Sangamon county in 1851. They have six children. JAMES H., born June 24, 1848, in Daviess county, Ind., raised in Sangamon county, graduated at the Eclectic Medical College of Philadelphia, and is a practicing physician near Taylorville. Dr. Dickerson was married in 1875 to Miss Humphreys. *See Humphreys' family sketch.* ISAAC S., born August 28, 1850, in Daviess county, Ind., married March 11, 1873, in Sangamon county, to Mary E. Bomhoff, who was born Sept. 20, 1848, in Sangamon county. They have one child, SINAI, and reside one mile west of Clarksville. ROBERT P., born Dec. 4, 1852, SARAH E., born Nov. 14, 1854, MARY S., born Nov. 2, 1856, and ALMARINDA, born Jan. 29, 1859, the four latter in Sangamon county, reside with their parents, one and a quarter miles west of Clarksville.

PHŒBE E., born Nov. 1, 1830, in Sangamon county, married March, 1849, to John Johnson. *See his name.*

ALMARINDA, born Sept. 25, 1832, in Sangamon county, married March 28, 1850, to James S. Galloway, who was born May 7, 1819, in Bath county, Ky. They had four children, two of whom died young. WILLIAM N. resides near Taylorville, and LIZZIE A. resides in Cotton Hill township. J. S. Galloway died Sept. 14, 1861, and his widow married, Nov. 7, 1865, to Benj. L. Auxier, and resides four miles south of Rochester.

SQUIRE J., born August 10, 1834, died July 17, 1847.

PRESTON B., born Feb. 26, 1837, in Sangamon county, married, August 9, 1863, to Mary Bond, and resides in Rochester township.

AUSTIN, born Feb. 13, 1839, was killed by the kick of a horse, March 10, 1850.

MELVIN, born Feb. 9, 1843, in Sangamon county, married, Oct. 12, 1865, to Rachel Martin, have two children, WILLIAM J. and ALICE, and reside at the Bell family homestead. He is a cripple for life, caused by a runaway team.

Robert Bell died June 25, 1872, near Illiopolis, from injuries caused by a runaway team four days previous. Mrs. Susannah Bell was made a cripple for life by the same accident. They had lived more than 54 years as man and wife. She resides on the farm where they settled in 1830, four miles south of Rochester.

BELL, BAILEY, was born Nov. 2, 1776, in Fauquier county, Va., and was there married to Nancy Foxworthy, who was born April 3, 1785. They had three children, and moved to Clarke county, Ky., in 1818, where two children were born, and thence to Sangamon county, Ill., arriving in Nov., 1834, at Buffalo Hart Grove. Of their five children—

BAILEY F., born Dec. 30, 1807, in Fauquier county, Va., was married in Clarke county, Ky., Nov. 27, 1827, to Mahala Burns. They had one child in Kentucky, and the family moved to Sangamon county, Ill., arriving in the fall of 1831, in Buffalo Hart Grove, where they had six children, and reside near Knoxville, Marion county, Iowa.

ARIE, born Oct. 11, 1811, in Fauquier county, Va., was married in Clarke county, Ky., Sept., 1834, to Thomas McGowan. They had five children, and reside near Buffalo Hart station.

JAMES, born Sept. 13, 1814, in Virginia, was married in Logan county, Ill., to Nancy Brown. They have seven children, and reside in Rosemont, Jasper county, Iowa.

BENJAMIN, born May 16, 1818, in Clarke county, Ky., was married in Sangamon county, Sept. 26, 1840, to Amanda Starr. They had six children. MARY E., born April 9, 1843, married Hugh McGorey, and died Oct. 14, 1865. EMILY, born Dec. 7, 1845, died Sept. 11, 1862. THOMAS J., born Sept. 28, 1848, died in his third year. WILLIAM, born Nov. 29, 1851, BENJAMIN, Jun., born March 29, 1856, and FLORENCE, born August 20, 1860, reside with their parents, in Logan county, three miles east of Buffalo Hart station.

THOMAS J., born June 18, 1821, in Clarke county, Ky., was married in Illinois to Ann Allen. They have six children, CHARLES, ALBERT, CLARA, EMMA, ARTHUR, died in his tenth year, and LESLIE. Thomas J. Bell and family reside at Cornland, Ill.

Mrs. Nancy Bell died August 6, 1843, in Logan county, and Bailey Bell died Feb. 6, 1846, in Sangamon county, at Buffalo Hart Grove.

BENHAM, JOHN T., born August 21, 1789, in Cheshire, New Haven county, Conn. In 1805 or 1806 his parents moved to Ferrisburg, Addison county, Vt. He was a soldier in the war of 1812, and was in the battle at Vergennes, early in 1814. John T. Benham was married Jan., 1818, at Ferrisburg, to Catharine Porter. They had six children; two died in Vermont. Mr. Benham moved with his family to Sangamon county, Ill., in wagons, arriving in the fall of 1830. He entered land, and settled two and a half miles northeast of Rochester, where seven children were born. All except five died unmarried. Of those five—

POLLY A., born Jan. 15, 1819, in Vermont, married Jonathan S. Rogers, and she died in Sangamon county.

JOHN W., born Oct. 10, 1824, in Vermont, married Mrs. Melissa E. Porter, and resides in Pontiac, Ill.

CATHARINE, born July 23, 1826, in Vermont, married in Sangamon county, Oct. 3, 1843, to John Robinson. They had four children; three died young. JOHN, Jun., accidentally shot and killed himself. John Robinson went to California in 1849, and was never heard of after 1851. His widow married Amos C. Derry. They have two children, and reside in Illiopolis.

HENRY W., born Oct. 30, 1830, in Sangamon county, married Almena Stafford. She died, and he married Mrs. Frances Austin, whose maiden name was Wood, and resides in Charlotte, Ill.

NOAH P., born April 14, 1836, in Sangamon county, was married March 9, 1861, to Elizabeth Stevens, who was born Feb. 4, 1847, near Sandusky, Ohio. They have four children, MARY C., ERMINNIE W., GERTRUDE J. and JOHN O., and reside two and a half miles east of Rochester.

Mrs. Catharine Benham died June, 1852, in Sangamon county, and Mr. Benham was married Sept. 7, 1852, to Mrs. Mary Rakestraw, formerly Mrs. Seavers, and whose maiden name was Wallin. She was born July 11, 1816, in Columbiana county, Ohio, and came to Illinois in 1837. Mr. Benham was in the Black Hawk war. Mr. and Mrs. B. reside two and a half miles northeast of Rochester.

BENHAM, WILLIAM A., was born Nov. 5, 1803, near Shepherdstown, Va. His father, Van Bennett, died in Virginia, and his two sons, William A. and Thomas L., with their three sisters, Luranah M., Ann Elizabeth and Mary, with their widowed mother, Mrs. Phœbe Bennett, all left Virginia, Oct. 2, 1833, for Illinois, arriving at Paris on the second of November. The two brothers came on to Springfield, bought land three miles east of the city, and returned to Paris just in time to be present at their mother's death, Dec. 12, 1833. The two brothers and three sisters moved to their farms in Sangamon county in March, 1834. The youngest sister, Mary, who was born Nov. 12, 1815, in Virginia, died April 17, 1834, near Springfield. William A. Bennett was married August 19, 1843, in Morgan county, to Sarah A. Stevenson. She was born Oct. 2, 1819, in Scott county, Ky., and was taken by her parents in 1829, to that part of Morgan county which is now Cass county. Mr. and Mrs. Bennett had three children, namely—

MARY E., born March 1, 1844, in Sangamon county, married May 26, 1869, to Charles F. Mills, who was born May 29, 1843, at Montrose, Pa. They have two children, MINNIE and WILLIAM HENRY, and reside with Mrs. Mills' parents, three miles east of Springfield. Charles F. Mills was attending Shurtleff College, at Alton, Ill., when the rebellion commenced. He enlisted August, 1862, for three years, in Co. C., 114th Ill. Inf. He was soon after appointed by President Lincoln, hospital steward at Camp Butler, and remained there nearly three years, when, at his own request, in the fall of 1864, he was ordered to Nashville, Tenn. Being in the regular service, his term did not expire with the suppression of the rebellion, but he continued until the fall of 1866, when he resigned, and was mustered out at Nashville, Tenn.

WILLIAM A., Jun., and

CHARLES S. died in infancy.

William A. Bennett and his wife reside on the farm where he settled in 1834, three miles east of Springfield.

BENNETT, LURANAH M., born March 7, 1807, in Jefferson county, Va., came with her brothers and sisters to Sangamon county, in 1834, remained several years, and returned on a visit, in 1842, to her native place, where she was married to Rev. Thomas P. W. Magruder, of the Presbyterian church, who moved with his family to Illinois in the spring of 1844. They have three children—

ALFRED W., resides at Central City, Colorado Territory.

CHARLES V. resides with his parents.

LIZZIE C. married Samuel S. Smith. They have two children, a son and a daughter, and reside near Rushville, Ill.

Rev. Thomas P. W. Magruder and wife reside near Rushville, Schuyler county, Illinois.

BENNETT, THOMAS L., was born July 6, 1809, in Jefferson county,

Va.—For family history, see the sketch of his brother, William A.—Thomas L. Bennett arrived in Sangamon county first in the fall of 1833. He was married Nov. 6, 1842, at Jubilee College, Robins' Nest, Peoria county, Ill., to Jeanetta S. Ingraham, a native of New York City. They had four children in Sangamon county—

AGNES, the youngest, died at ten years of age.

HENRY V. S., visited Greenwood county, Kansas, in the autumn of 1868, where his father and family joined him in the spring of 1869.

SUSAN C. and

SOPHIA went with their parents. The latter was married Oct. 12, 1871, in Kansas, to Alexander F. Crowe. They have one child, THOMAS B., and reside in Kansas, also.

Thomas L. Bennett and family reside near Line Postoffice, Lyon county, Kansas.

BENNETT, ANN F., born Dec. 10, 1813, in Jefferson county, Va., came to Sangamon county with her brothers and sisters, in 1834, was married in the Episcopal church, at Jacksonville, Ill., to Samuel H. Treat, now Judge of the United States District Court, and resides in Springfield.

BENNETT, REV. WM. T., was born Nov. 30, 1805, in or near Shepherdstown, Jefferson county, Va. He united with the M. E. church in Shepherdstown, in 1828, was soon after licensed to exhort, came to Springfield, Ill., in company with his brother, Van S. Bennett, in Dec., 1834. He was married June 6, 1836, in Ottawa, Ill., to Rebecca J. Roberts, who was born Oct. 5, 1811, in Virginia. When she was an infant her father liberated his slaves and moved to Washington county, Pa. She came with the family of her uncle, Dr. James Roberts, to Jacksonville, Ill., in 1833, and from there to Ottawa in 1834. Mr. and Mrs. Bennett made their home in Springfield. He was licensed as a local preacher, and in 1849 was appointed to take charge of the M. E. church in Springfield, to fill a vacancy. In 1850 he entered the traveling connection. They had seven children, all born in Sangamon county, namely—

EDWARD W., born August 5, 1837, in Springfield, enlisted at Danville, in April, 1861, on the first call for 75,000 men, in Co. E., 12th Ill. Inf., and served nearly six months. He enlisted June 24, 1862, at Mechanicsburg, for three years, in Co. A., 73d Ill. Inf.; was commissioned as 1st Lieutenant. After the battle of Stone's river he was transferred, Jan. 8, 1863, and promoted to Capt. of Co. F, same regiment. He served as such to the end of the rebellion, and was mustered out with the regiment at Springfield, June 15, 1865. He was married at Mechanicsburg, Dec. 23, 1869, to Harriet N. Fullinwider. They have two children, ANNA N. and JACOB H., and reside near Mechanicsburg.

EMMA R., born Dec. 18, 1838, in Springfield, married August 14, 1861, to Stephen A. Short, who was born Oct. 7, 1836, in Pickaway county, Ohio. He enlisted a few days before his marriage, for three years, in Co. A, 73d Ill. Inf.; was appointed Sergeant, and was wounded July 20, 1864, at the battle of Peach Tree Creek, Ga., which terminated in the amputation of his right leg, above the knee. Mr. and Mrs. Short have two children, LULU and EDITH L., and reside in Mechanicsburg.

ANN T., born Dec. 16, 1841, died in her second year.

ANNA L., born Nov. 13, 1842, in Springfield, died suddenly, Oct. 28, 1866, in Mechanicsburg.

JOHN A., born Dec. 28, 1844, in Springfield, enlisted Dec., 1863, in Co. F, 73d Ill. Inf., for three years. He was killed June 24, 1864, at Kennesaw mountain, Ga., by a stray shot, while sitting in his tent writing a letter. His remains were brought home in 1866, and interred at Mechanicsburg.

JULIA A. died Feb. 5, 1849, in her second year.

REBIE H., born in Sangamon county, June 30, 1850, resides with her parents.

Rev. Wm. T. Bennett continued in the effective work of the ministry until 1867, when he assumed the superannuated relation to Ill. Conf., and in 1871 was superannuated, and now resides in Mechanicsburg.

Edward Bennett, the father of Rev. Wm. T. Bennett, liberated his slaves and sold his land, with the intention of moving west, but died in Virginia in 1833. Edward was brother to Van S., who was the father of Wm. A. Bennett. See his name. It will thus be seen that Rev. Wm. T. Bennett and Mr. Wm. A. Bennett are cousins.

BENNETT, VAN S., was born Dec. 9, 1802, near Shepherdstown, Va., came to Springfield in 1834, with his brother, Rev. Wm. T. He never married, and died in Sangamon county, Aug., 1873.

BENNETT, MARGARET E., sister to Rev. Wm. T. Bennett, was born Dec. 24, 1800, near Sheperdstown, Va., came to Springfield, Ill., in 1836, remained five years, returned to Virginia, and came back to Sangamon county in 1841. She never married, and resides with her sister, Mrs. Kalb.

BENNETT, ELIZA, (sister of Rev. Wm. T. Bennett,) was born Dec. 27, 1810, near Hagerstown, Md. Her parents moved, when she was five years old, to Shepherdstown, Va., where they had previously resided. She was there married, May 20, 1832, to George W. Shutt. They had one child born in Shepherdstown, and Mr. Shutt died there in 1835. Mrs. Shutt, with her child, moved to Springfield, Ill., arriving in May, 1836. After a residence of five years in Springfield, she returned to Shepherdstown, Va., and was there married, Jan. 17, 1841, to Daniel G. Kalb, who was born Dec. 4, 1815, in Frederick City, Md. They had two children in Shepherdstown, and moved to Washington county, Md., where they had one child; thence to Loudon county, Va., where they had one child, and from there to Springfield, Ill., arriving in October, 1849, where one child was born, and in 1856 moved to Round Prairie, four miles east by south of Springfield. Of her children by her first marriage—

GEORGETTA, born July 18, 1835, in Shepherdstown, Va., was married Jan. 1, 1853, in Springfield, Ill., to Philip L. Shutt, who was born Nov. 18, 1829, in Loudon county, Va. They had eleven children, five of whom died young. The other six, FRANKLIN, MAGGIE, CHARLES, PAUL, HARRY and LAURA, reside with their parents in Paris, Edgar county, Ill.

Children of her second marriage—

MARY ABNER, born Dec. 12, 1841, in Shepherdstown, Va., resides with her parents.

ETHELBERT, born Sept. 18, 1843, in Shepherdstown, Va., brought up in Sangamon county, and enlisted at Springfield, August 20, 1861, for three years, in Co. B., 33d Ill. Inf. He served more than his full time, and was honorably discharged, Oct. 11, 1864. He is now in business in St. Louis.

WILLIAM E. B., born August 2, 1846, in Washington county, Md., brought up in Sangamon county, Ill., enlisted at Springfield, March 26, 1864, for three years, in Co. G., 114th Ill. Vol. Inf., and was killed in battle of Guntown, Miss., June 10, 1864.

GEO. BROOK, born Dec. 4, 1848, in Loudon county, Va., is a dealer in musical instruments in Springfield.

JULIA M., born Nov. 16, 1854, in Springfield, died June 10, 1859.

Daniel G. Kalb and wife reside at Willow Dale, one mile northeast of Sangamon Station. Mr. Kalb was a local preacher in the M. E. church from Feb. 6, 1847, until 1864. His license was signed at eight annual renewals by Rev. Peter Cartwright, but when it expired in 1864, he declined to have it renewed. He was engaged in teaching from 1837 to 1854. Mr. Kalb enlisted August 11, 1862, in Co. G., 114th Ill. Vol. Inf., for three years. Finding it quite oppressive to march with his knapsack and haversack, he obtained a wheelbarrow, and not meeting with opposition from officers, ran it hundreds of miles, and often carried the baggage of sick and disabled comrades. He has the wheelbarrow yet, and it will doubtless be handed down as a memorial of the war to suppress the rebellion, and the part he acted in it.

BENNETT, JOHN A., (brother to Rev. Wm. T. Bennett,) was born near Shepherdstown, Va., came to Springfield in 1835, with George R. Weber, and died Dec. 23, 1841.

BENNINGTON, JAS. M., was born May 20, 1826, in Owen county, Ind. His father died in 1838, and in his 13th year, he came to Sangamon county with his half brother, John Hartsock. They arrived Feb. 22, 1839, in what is now Ball township. James M. Bennington was married Sept. 30, 1869, to Mrs. Nancy Nuckolls, whose maiden name was Drennan. They have one son, JOHN, and reside four miles west of Pawnee.

John Hartsock, half brother to Mr. Bennington, married Susan Clemons, who died, and he married Mrs. Mary A. Pulliam, whose maiden name was Levi. They reside in Christian county.

Two brothers of Mr. Bennington, Samuel and Harrison, came to Sangamon county with their mother in 1841, and were consequently too late to be included as early settlers.

BEERS, PHILO, was born July 16, 1793, in Woodbury, Conn. When he was about fifteen years old he was put to live with an elder brother, probably on account of the death of his parents. They could not agree, and he ran away, and was gone twelve or thirteen years, without his relatives hearing from him. During his ramblings he became acquainted with Doctor Joseph Bennett Stillman, who introduced him to his mother and sisters, at Morganfield, Ky. Mr. Beers always said that he made up his mind, on their first acquaintance, to have Miss Martha Stillman for a wife. The Stillman family moved to Sangamon county, Ill., and Mr. Beers went to Carlyle, Clinton county, same State. He was first elected a justice of the peace, and after serving for a time, was elected to represent Clinton county in the Legislature of Illinois, when it assembled in Vandalia. While residing at Carlyle he was married in what is now Williams township, Sangamon county, on the farm of John Poorman. In response to a letter of inquiry, the author of this book received from the clerk of Madison county, Ill., a reply, dated April 29, 1874, in which it is stated that a license was issued at Edwardsville, Oct. 27, 1820, for the marriage of Philo Beers and Martha Stillman; that it was returned, endorsed by Elder Stephen England, with the statement that he had solemnized the marriage Nov. 2, 1820. The clerk also stated that it was the 279th license issued from that office. They are believed to have been the first couple ever married north of the Sangamon river in the State of Illinois; certainly the first in what is now Sangamon county. The first marriage under a license from Sangamon county was between Wm. Moss and Margaret Sims, April 20, 1821. Mr. Beers took his bride to Carlyle, where they had two children. They moved to Sangamon county, and settled three miles southwest of Williamsville, where one child was born. Of their three children—

—15

JOSEPH B., born and died at Carlyle in infancy.

HENRY CLAY, born in 1824, at Carlyle. Philo Beers was the only man living in Carlyle who voted for Henry Clay for President of the United States that year, and the citizens insisted that the babe should be named for his father's candidate. Henry Clay Beers was married in 1848, in Sangamon county, to Adelaide C. McNabb. They had one child, WM. PHILO, who died, aged two years. H. C. Beers died in 1851, in Springfield. His widow married Adolphus Rogers, and resides near Cincinnati. He is a merchant there.

CAROLINE M., born Feb. 20, 1827, in Sangamon county, married in Springfield, May 13, 1847, to Elder Andrew J. Kane. See his name.

Mrs. Martha Beers died in 1845, and Philo Beers died March, 1858, both in Springfield. Mr. Beers moved into Springfield and built a brick dwelling house at the northwest corner of Madison and Fifth streets, about 1830. It was among the first, if not the first, brick dwelling erected in Springfield.

BEERUP, ANDREW, born Dec. 12, 1812, in Canandagua county, N. Y., and raised in Canada, came to Springfield, Ill., in 1837 or '8. He was married July 2, 1840, in Sangamon county, to Mary A. Maltby, who was born Nov. 27, 1819. They had nine children in Sangamon county, five of whom died young. Of the other four—

CHARLES A., born April 27, 1841, married Jan. 14, 1864, to Mary Babcock, who was born Jan. 22, 1844, in Muskingum county, Ohio. They have three children, John R., ALICE J. and LEE C., and reside six miles west of Springfield.

THOMAS A., born June 27, 1843;
GEORGE E., born Oct. 10, 1854, and WILLIAM H., born June 10, 1858, all reside with their brother, Charles A.

Andrew Beerup died Nov. 26, 1872, and his widow died Sept. 27, 1873, both in Gardner township.

BEERUP, THOMAS, brother of Margaret, Andrew and William, was born Sept. 17, 1819, in Canandagua county, N. Y. Came to Springfield June 3, 1840, and witnessed a grand log cabin demonstration of the political campaign of that year to elect a President of the United States, as his introduction to the city. He was married July 26, 1843, to Sinai A. Neale. They had seven children born in Sangamon county, namely—

THOMAS N., born Oct. 12, 1844, in Sangamon county, enlisted Aug. 9, 1862, in Co. B, 114 Ill. Inf., at Springfield. He was wounded at the battle of Jackson, Miss., May 14, 1863. A rebel musket ball broke his arm (being the first man in the regiment to receive a wound). He was captured in hospital two days later, paroled at Richmond, Va., a month later, and was honorably discharged at St. Louis, Nov. 17, 1863. He now draws a pension, and resides with his parents.

HALLIE E., born April 15, 1846, in New Castle, Henry county, Ky., married Nov. 30, 1865, to Edward B. Winslow. They have two children, BDWIN M. and PRESTON A., and reside in Girard, Ill.

GEO. N., born June 20, 1848, in New Castle, Henry county, Ky., died Sept. 15, 1850.

PRESTON J., born Jan. 21, 1851, in Springfield, Sangamon county, Ill., died March 1, 1872.

EDWIN M., born in Waverly, Morgan county, Sept. 13, 1855, died Jan. 8, 1864.

MERRIAN E., born Jan. 11, 1858, in Waverly, Ill., died Oct. 8, 1869.

NEVILLE B., born Nov. 3, 1859, in Waverly, Ill., resides with his parents.

Thomas Beerup and wife reside one-half mile south of Chatham.

BEERUP, WILLIAM W., was born Sept. 6, 1822, at Sidney, Canada, and came to Sangamon county in 1843 to join his brothers, Andrew and Thomas. He married Catharine E. Tolley, *See the Tolley name.*

BEERUP, MARGARET, sister of Andrew, Thomas and William W., was born June 18, 1829, at Beamsville, Canada, came to Sangamon county, Ill., June, 1844, and was married at Havana, Ill., June 18, 1849, to Levi Harpham, who was born Dec., 1821, at Hartford, Ohio county, Indiana. They have five children, namely—

GEO. E., ALICE J., CHARLES F., LEE W. and *SILAS ELMER*, and reside near Havana, Ill.

BEERUP, JANE, sister to Andrew, Thomas and William W. Beerup, and to Mrs. Margaret Harpham. She married Marvin Pond. *See his name.*

BERGEN, REV. JOHN G., D. D., was born Nov. 27, 1790, at Hightstown, Middlesex county, N. J., ten miles east of Princeton, N. J. Of his ancestors the history is preserved for seven generations, which will be found designated by numbers. 1st. Hans Hansen Bergen was born in Bergen, Norway. He was a ship carpenter, and went to Holland; from there he emigrated to New Amsterdam, now New York city, arriving in 1633. In 1639 he was married to Sarah Rapalje (now Rapalye). She was born June 9, 1622, about where Albany, N. Y., now stands, and is believed to have been the first child of European parentage born in in the colony of New Netherlands, which then included the present States of New York, New Jersey and part of Connecticut. Hans Hansen Bergen and Sarah Rapalje, his wife, had four sons and four daughters. 2nd. Joris, Jores, or George, their fifth child, was baptized in New Amsterdam, July 18, 1649, and married Aug. 11, 1678, to Sara Stryker. They had nine children, and their fourth child. 3rd. Hans Jorise Bergen was baptized Aug. 31, 1684, and married Aug. 16, 1711, to Sytje Evert Van Wicklen. They had five children. Their eldest son (4th), Jores, or George Bergen, married Miss Hoagland. She had three children, and died. He married a second time, and had nine children. His eldest son (5th), John B. Bergen, born March 27, 1739, married June 8, 1763, to Sarah Stryker, who was born August 25, 1745. They had eight children. Their eldest son (6th), George I. Bergen, born June 16, 1764, married in 1789 to Rebecca Combs. They had ten children, all born in New Jersey. Their eldest son was (7th) John G., whose name heads this sketch. Both his parents being consistent Christians, he, under their training and example, became a member of the Presbyterian church, at thirteen years of age. He attended Baskingridge Academy, and when properly prepared entered the junior class at Princeton College, and graduated at seventeen years of age. Having chosen the ministry, he commenced a theological course of study under Rev. Dr. John Woodhull, who had been appointed by the Synod of New York and New Jersey, Professor of Theology, in the absence of a seminary for that purpose. At 20 years of age he was licensed to preach the gospel. It was his desire to mount his horse, go to the west and commence preaching, but he was induced to accept the position of tutor in Princeton College in 1810. In Sept., 1812, he resigned that position, and in Oct., 1812, accepted a call as pastor of the Presbyterian Church at Madison, N. J. Rev. John G. Bergen was married Nov. 10, 1812, at Freehold, N. J., to Margaretta M. Henderson, who was born in 1793 in that city. Her father, Dr. Thomas Henderson, was a Judge, member of Congress, and a ruling Elder in the old Tennent church at Freehold. The pastor of that church, Rev. William Tennent, to all human appearance died, and after laying three days in what proved to be a trance, he opened his eyes just as they were closing the coffin for the last time.

Rev. J. G. Bergen was pastor of the church at Madison for about 16 years, during which time his labors were greatly blessed. They had five children born at Madison. George I. Bergen, the father of Rev. J. G. Bergen, was a merchant, and sustained such losses during the war with England, beginning in 1812, that he closed his business, and in the summer of 1818 emigrated to Woodford county, Ky. In 1824 Mr. G. I. Bergen, in company with a married son and daughter and their father-in-law, Major Conover, six persons in all, set out to explore Indiana, and camped near where Indianapolis now stands. They made up their minds to remain there, and one night while they were around their camp-fire, they were startled with the cry of "Who's here!" coming out of the darkness. The words were run together, and seemed like a single word, "Hoosier," and this circumstance is believed to have been the origin of that appellation for citizens of that State. The traveler who had thus unceremoniously approached them remained all night, and before he left next morning had convinced them that it was better to go and see the prairies of Illinois. The result was that they settled in Jersey prairie, twelve miles north of Jacksonville, in Morgan, now Cass, county, Ill. George I. Bergen died in 1825, and his widow married Rev. Mr. Kenner, in 1827, and they visited Mrs. Kenner's old home in New Jersey. While there her son, Rev. J. G. Bergen, resigned his pastorate of the church at Madison, Sept. 10, 1828, for the purpose of accompanying his mother to Illinois. The party started Sept. 22, 1828, going by the way of Lexington and Frankfort, Ky., to visit friends. After a journey of nearly 1,500 miles, they arrived at Springfield, Nov., 1828, bringing their five children, namely—

JANE ELIZA, born 1813, in Madison, N. J., came with her parents to Springfield. Soon after their arrival, her father built a house on his own lot at the south side of Washington street, between Fourth and Fifth streets, and in that she taught school in 1829. That was believed to have been the first school taught by a lady in Springfield. She was married in April, 1833, to Col. Robert Allen. See *his* name.

CATHARINE H., born Sept. 21, 1816, in New Jersey, married in Springfield to Edward Jones. See *his* name.

AMELIA M., born July, 1818, in New Jersey, married in Springfield, May, 1840, to Joshua G. Lamb, a cousin of James L. Lamb. They are without family, and reside in Alton.

THOMAS H., born Dec. 15, 1820, at Madison, Morris county, N. J., brought up in Springfield, married March 29, 1849, at Trenton, N. J., to Mary G. Cooley. She was born in that city, July 20, 1823. Soon after they were married they left for Springfield, and while on board a small steamboat on the Ohio river, near Wheeling, West Va., it blew up, killing 17 persons. They escaped with their lives, but lost their entire baggage. They are without family, and reside one mile east of Springfield.

GEORGE, born April 5, 1824, at Madison, Morris county, N. J., brought up in Springfield, Ill., is unmarried, and resides one mile east of Springfield.

Mrs. Margaretta M. Bergen died Oct. 18, 1853, near Springfield, Ill. Dr. Bergen was married at the latter place, Nov. 9, 1857, to Mrs. Susan A. Vanhoff. Rev. Dr. J. G. Bergen died Jan. 17, 1872, and his widow resides in Springfield.

Dr. Bergen, describing Springfield as he first saw it, said it was composed of about thirty-five log cabins, two or three small frame houses, without a place of divine worship other than a log school house just built. That school house stood in the street at the crossing of Adams and Second streets, in a thicket of hazel and brier bushes, and a few tall oaks. It was built in the street because (he says) the town authorities and owners of the lots were too penurious to donate the land. Rev. J. G. Bergen found a Presbyterian Church that had been organized Jan. 30, 1828, by Rev. John M. Ellis, a missionary from the southern part of the State. It was without a house of worship. He took charge of the church, and on the second Sabbath after his arrival he gave notice to the little church and the people generally, that he came to Springfield, not to make an experiment, but to live, labor and die on the field with his armor on, and then said: "Come, let us rise up and build a house for God." A brick house was accordingly built at the east side of Third street, between Washington and Adams. He says that was the first church built in the central part of the State for any Protestant denomination. The Methodists of Springfield were building a frame house of worship at the same time, but they were a few weeks later in finishing it. The original members of the First Presbyterian Church were Mrs. Elizabeth Smith, widow of Rev. John Blair Smith, D. D., mother of Mrs. Dr. John Todd. The Presbyterian Church of Springfield was organized in her house. The other members were John Moore, John N. Moore, Andrew Moore, Mary Moore, Elizabeth Moore, Margaret Moore, Catharine Moore, Phœbe Moore, James White, Elijah Scott, Jane Scott, Samuel Reed, Jane Reed, William Proctor, Sarah Stillman, Nancy R. Humphreys, Ann Iles and Olive Slater, nineteen in all; five only lived in Springfield. Some lived forty miles distant. The Ruling Elders were John Moore, John N. Moore, Samuel Reed and Isaiah Stillman. Rev. J. G. Bergen preached, as stated supply, until 1835, when he received a formal call to become Pastor of the church, and was installed Nov. 15 of that year. That was the only Presbyterian Church in the country at that time. Six churches have been organized by colonies from that church (two of them in the city). During the ministry of Rev. Mr. Bergen, from 1828 to 1848, when he resigned the pastorate, five hundred were added to the church. When he came to Springfield he was the eighth Presbyterian minister in the State, and the farthest north of any of them. There were twenty-five churches under the care of these eight ministers. He lived to see, including both branches of the Presbyterian and the Congregational churches, 600 ministers and 800 churches in the State. He assisted in forming the first Presbytery and first Synod in the State; was the first Moderator of each. When the Old and New school churches were reunited in 1869, he was the first Moderator of the United Synod.

In 1854, without any previous intimation of their intentions, Center College, at Danville, Ky., conferred on the Rev. John G. Bergen the Degree of D. D.

After his resignation as pastor of the First Church, he devoted much of his time to writing for the religious press, over the signature of "Old Man of the Prairies." He has left two large scrap books full of these writings.

BERRY, ROBERT E., was born Dec. 3, 1823, in Davidson county, near Nashville, Tenn. When a child his parents moved, first into Madison, and then into Gibson county, in the same State. From there they moved to Williamson county, Ill., and from there to Christian county, in 1844. Robert E. left his parents in Williamson county, and come to Sangamon county, in what is now Cooper township, in Dec., 1840. He was married Sept. 8, 1850, to Elizabeth Stokes, who was born Aug. 6, 1832. They had one child—

AMANDA M., who died at the age of seven years. Mrs. Berry died Sept. 25, 1853, and Mr. Berry was married Oct. 8, 1856, to Sophia Barger. They have seven children, namely—

WILLIAM, FRANCIS M. and BENJAMIN F., twins—F. M. died in his sixth year—LAURA E., EMMA D., LIZZIE and CHARLES; the six living, reside with their parents.

Robert E. Berry resides at Berry postoffice, Clarksville, Sangamon county.

BETTIS, JAMES H., was born Oct. 18, 1811, in Lincoln county, Ky. His parents moved to Hamilton county, O., in 1818. James H. came to Sangamon county in 1839. He was married July 28, 1844, in what is now Auburn township, to Elizabeth Fletcher. They had six children in Sangamon county, and in 1855 moved to Missouri. In 1864 they moved back to Sangamon county. Of their children—

OLIVER F., born in Sangamon county, married June 20, 1866, to Jane Patterson. They reside in Auburn township.

REBECCA J., born in Sangamon county, married Franklin Nicholson, and reside near Virden.

JAMES W., MARTHA E., NANCY A. and JOHN R., the four latter reside with their parents in Auburn township.

The parents of J. H. Bettis moved from Ohio to DeWitt county, Ill., before he came to the State. After his father's death, his mother came to Sangamon county, in 1842, and died in 1850. She was born in Garrard county, Ky., in 1780, and is believed to have been the first white child born in that county.

BEVANS, JOHN, was born in Maryland, and married, near Snow Hill, to Mary Rounds. They had six children, and she died. He married Margaret Jones, and had one child in Maryland. The family moved to Woodford county, Ky., and from there to Sangamon county, Ill., arriving, in 1828, in Island Grove, south of Spring creek. Of his seven children—

MARTHA, born in Maryland, married in Kentucky to Alexander Montgomery, came to Sangamon county in 1828. They had six children, and the parents died in Berlin. Their only child living in Sangamon county, MARTIN, resides in Springfield.

WILLIAM, born in Maryland, married, had two children, and died near Chillicothe, O.

DRUZILLA, born in Maryland, married at Island Grove to Fielding Jones, have six children, and reside near Assumption, Christian county Ill.

BARSHEBA, born in Maryland, married in Kentucky to Hiram Bailey, and died in Indiana.

JOHN D., born Oct. 5, 1813 in Worcester county, near Snow Hill, Md., came to Sangamon county in 1828, married at Island Grove, Jan 2, 1842, to Nancy Foutch. They had eight children:

THOMAS F., born in Sangamon county June 19, 1843, married March 27, 1870, at Carbondale, to Carrie L. Collins, who was born Oct. 3, 1850, at Wheeling, Va. They have one child, EDDIE F., and reside in Berlin. The other seven were born in Wapello county, Iowa, two of whom died young. MARY R., born Sept. 24, 1847, in Iowa, married Hawes Yates. See his name. JOHN D., Jun., born Nov. 10, 1850, and HENRY K., reside with their mother. MARTHA resides with her sister, Mrs. Yates. RACHEL lives with her mother. John D. Bevans died Jan. 13, 1858, in Wapello county, Iowa. His widow resides in Berlin.

NANCY, born in Maryland, was married at Island Grove to Amon Blaney. Both died in St. Clair county.

By the second marriage—

SARAH, born in 1824, in Maryland, married near Berlin to Thomas G. Mendenhall, and reside at Berlin.

John Bevans died in March, 1837, and Mrs. Margaret Bevans died April, 1859, both in Island Grove township.

BICE, JOHN, born Nov. 4, 1808, in Henry county, Ky. He came to Sangamon county in 1834, and was married May 5, 1835, near Mechanicsburg, to Mary A. Pickrell. They settled in what is now Williams township, one and a half miles north of the present town of Barclay. They had six children there—

SARAH E., born Feb. 8, 1836, married James F. Hickman. See his name.

JESSE W., born Oct. 21, 1837, enlisted in Co. A. 3rd Ill. Cavalry, Aug. 14, 1861. He was promoted for meritorious conduct at Pea Ridge, to Lieutenant, afterwards to Captain, and the last ten months he served with the rank of Major. He was honorably discharged in Nov., 1865. In Dec. following he was appointed assistant assessor of internal revenue, until the office was abolished by Congress, May 20, 1873. J. W. Bice was married Sept. 19, 1872, to Belle Wariner, daughter of the late Dr. Wariner, of Bloomington. They have one child, JESSIE BELLE. Major Bice is now Deputy Sheriff of Sangamon county, and resides in Springfield.

BENJAMIN F., born June 28, 1840, enlisted in Co. B, 130th Ill. Vol. Inf., and was mustered in at Camp Butler, Aug. 1,

1862. He was appointed 2nd Sergeant of same company, at Memphis, Tenn., Nov. 26, 1862, and served until Aug. 11, 1865, when he was mustered out by special order at New Orleans, La., for the purpose of accepting a commission from Gov. R. J. Oglesby, dated July 26, 1865, as 2nd Lieut. Co. D, 30th Ill. Vol. Inf. He was honorably discharged Aug. 12, 1865. B. F. Bice was married in Dec., 1867, to Bertha Owen. They have three children, MARY, EMMA G. and EVA, and reside near Elkhart, Logan county, Illinois.

ABEL P., born Dec. 3, 1842. He was married in 1863 to Melissa C. Blue. They have three children, JOHN H., ARTHUR L. and NETTIE B., and reside two miles north of Barclay.

SUE E. resides with her sister, Mrs. J. F. Hickman, at the homestead where her parents settled in 1835.

JOHN H., born Feb. 11, 1848, enlisted in 1863 in 16th United States Inf. Served three years, and was honorably discharged in 1866. He was afterwards employed on the Toledo, Wabash & Western railroad, and was killed by an accident Jan. 31, 1871.

John Bice, died March 14, 1848, at the family homestead, and his widow resides with her sister, Mrs. Hall, at Buffalo.

BICE, SUSAN, born in Henry county, Ky., married there to Elijah Utterback. *See his name.*

BILLINGS, ROBERT, was born Jan., 1801, in Dorchester county, Md. Mary Dean was born April 6, 1810, in Somerset county, Md. They were married Oct., 1829, in Sussex county, Delaware, and had two children born in Summit county, Md. They moved into Baltimore county, where one child was born and died, and then moved to Sangamon county, Ill., arriving Oct. 1840, in what is now Rochester township, and had nine children in Sangamon county. Of their children—

NANCY E., born July 15, 1830, in Maryland, married in Sangamon county to John Short, had one child, and Mrs. Short died.

MARY E., born Feb. 15, 1833, in Maryland, married in Sangamon county to James Wilson, have two children, and reside in Cotton Hill township.

WILLIAM EDWARD, born in Sangamon county, died in his 23d year.

GEORGIANN, born in Sangamon county, married Samuel Long, had one child, and Mr. Long died, and she married Wm. Thompson. They have three children, and reside near Lincoln.

SUSAN JANE, born in Sangamon county, married John Popp, have three children, and reside in Cotton Hill township.

CHARLES H., born in Sangamon county, married Mrs. Martha Mortar. He died July 31, 1871.

JOANNA, born in Sangamon county, resides with her parents.

CHARLOTTE married John Miller, have two children, and reside two and a half miles south of Rochester.

CAROLINE married William Glenn. They have two children, and reside three miles south of Rochester.

JENNIE, born in Sangamon county, Oct. 29, 1853, resides with her parents.

Robert Billings and his wife reside two and a half miles south of Rochester.

BILLINGTON, JOHN, was born Sept. 29, 1819, in the town of Shrewsbury, Shropshire, England. He came to the United States, landing in New York in June, and arrived early in Aug., 1840, at Springfield. He lived several years in the family of Willard Tinney, on Richland creek, to learn farming. He had learned the business of baker and confectioner in England, and established himself in that business in Springfield. He was married, in Springfield, to Elizabeth A. Cannon. She died Nov., 1851, not leaving any children. He was married March 24, 1853, at Buffalo Hart grove, to Rachel Constant. They have one child—

MARY J., and reside at Dawson.

Mr. Billington erected a residence for himself, where Dawson now stands, in 1854, before there was any station or town laid out. When the postoffice was established in that year, he was appointed Postmaster, which he held about seven years. He was also the first station and express agent at that place, and is yet (1874) acting in that capacity. Mr. Billington's parents, four brothers and one sister, came later. These were William, the civil engineer, now deceased. Thomas resides at Mt. Pulaska, Henry at Waynesville, James and Mary A.

BILYEU, PETER, was born in 1777, in Alleghany county, Md., and was taken by his parents to Green river, Ky. He was there married to Diana Blackwill. They had two children in Kentucky, and moved to Overton county, Tenn., where twelve children were born; two died young. The family moved to Sangamon county, Ill., arriving Oct. 1, 1829, in what is now Loami township, where one child was born. Of their children—

SARAH, born Nov. 26, 1801, in Kentucky, married March 23, 1819, to William Workman. *See his name.*

JOHN, born in 1803, in Kentucky, married Elizabeth Workman in Tennessee, came to Sangamon county, raised a large family, moved to Christian county, and died there in 1867.

LYDIA, born in Tennessee, married David Workman. *See his name.*

NANCY, born in Tennessee, married Jacob Teeple, moved to Missouri, raised a family, and he died there. She died in Christian county, Ill.

ISAAC, born in Tennessee, married Polly Bilyeu, raised a family, and resides in Missouri.

GEORGE, born in Tennessee, married Elizabeth Workman, raised a family, and resides in Christian county.

ELIZABETH married Richard Bilyeu. He was killed in time of the rebellion, in Miller county, Mo., leaving a widow and several children there.

POLLY married James McMullen, have children, and reside in Missouri.

DIANA married Thomas Greening, who died, and she married Stephen Workman, Jun. He died, leaving a widow and four children in Christian county.

HANNAH married John Wyckoff. He died in Christian county. His family reside in Missouri.

CYNTHIA, born Aug. 29, 1827, in Tennessee, married in Sangamon county to Levi Harbour, Jun. *See his name.*

MINERVA married Robert Fowler, and resides in Kansas.

Peter Bilyeu died July 7, 1863, and his widow died Sept., 1865, both in Christian county, Ill.

BIRD FAMILY, John Bird was born Jan. 1, 1767, in Essex county, N. J., and when a young man, went to Washington, Mason county, Ky. Abigail Auter was born May 26, 1780, in Essex county, N. J., also, and in 1798 went with her widowed mother and two sisters to Washington, Ky. John Bird and Abigail Auter were married there in 1801. They had ten children in Mason county, Ky., and the entire family moved, in 1825, to Harrison county. John Bird died there, of cholera, July 15, 1833. Their daughter, Sarah, who was married to Jesse Folks, died six days before her father, and their son John, in his thirteenth year, died seven days after his father, all of the same disease. Mrs. Bird, with some of her children, came to Sangamon county, Ill., arriving Sept. 6, 1835, in what is now Mechanicsburg township. Her other children came the next year. Mrs. Abigail Bird died in Sangamon county. Of her eight children who came to the county—

BIRD, MORRIS, was born Feb. 19, 1803, in Mason county, Ky., married, March 29, 1827, in Harrison county, to Sarah Brannock, who was born July 24, 1808, in Bourbon county, Ky. They had four children in Harrison county; one died in infancy, and they moved to Sangamon county, Ill., in 1835, and settled near Mechanicsburg, where they had twelve children, eleven of whom died in infancy, and Margaret died, aged nine years. Of the other three—

MARY A. C., born Nov. 5, 1828, in Harrison county, Ky., married in Sangamon county, Feb. 21, 1856, to Miles H. Wilmot, who was born Jan. 5, 1825, in Caswell county, N. C., and came to Sangamon county in 1854. He has three children by a former wife; two daughters, married, and a son. All reside near Shelby, Iowa. M. H. Wilmot and wife have no children except an adopted daughter, ELLA WILMOT. They reside half a mile east of Illiopolis. Mr. Wilmot has been elected five years in succession, to represent Illiopolis township in the Board of Supervisors of Sangamon county, beginning with the election of April, 1870. He was chairman of the board for 1872 and '3. He also served five years as Justice of the Peace and Police Magistrate in Mechanicsburg and Illiopolis.

JOHN M., born April 23, 1834, in Harrison county, Ky., raised in Sangamon county, married in Griggsville, Pike county, Ill., Oct. 6, 1859, to Frances E. Greenleaf, daughter of Rev. Calvin Greenleaf, of the Baptist church. She was born in

Pike county, June 15, 1841. Mr. and Mrs. Bird had three children, CLARENCE I. died in his third year. NELLIE M. and CALVIN MORRIS reside with their parents, in Mechanicsburg.

GEORGE W., born Nov. 16, 1849, in Sangamon county, resides with his parents.

Morris Bird and wife reside at Mechanicsburg. He was commissioned as Postmaster at Mechanicsburg, March 28, 1848, during the administration of President Taylor, and has held the office under all administrations to the present time.

BIRD, RICHARD, was born Nov. 19, 1804, in Mason county, Ky. He united with the M. E. church, in 1824, and commenced preaching in 1827. His first circuit was in the southern part of the State, and extended into Tennessee. By a singular coincidence, his colleagues bore such names as to indicate that the trio belong to the feathered species of animated nature, Crow, Martin and Bird. Rev. Richard Bird was married, March 8, 1832, in Shelby county, Ky., to Lucinda N. Fullinwider. They had two children in Kentucky, and came to Sangamon county, Ill., settling near Mechanicsburg, and at once united with the Ill. Conf. M. E. church, and commenced the work of a traveling preacher. They had seven children in Illinois, three of whom died under seven years. The two born in Kentucky died in Illinois, one at five and the other at two years of age. Of the other four—

FRANCES M., born Aug. 23, 1836, in Sangamon county, married Thomas Scott, and had four children; two died in infancy. CHARLES W. and HARRIET B. reside with their mother. She was married Jan. 10, 1867, to Rev. Reuben Gregg, of the M. E. Church. They have three living children, ARTHUR B., EDA F., ALLEN C. and LURA R. They reside at Augusta, Ill.

RICHARD C., born August 8, 1838, in Tazewell county, Ill., married, Sept. 26, 1860, at Chatham, Sangamon county, to Addie Hesser. He enlisted in 1862, for three years, in Co. A., 73d Ill. Inf. He was injured, Sept. 26, 1862, in Louisville, Ky., by a drunken driver upsetting an army wagon, which fell upon him and came near causing his death. He was discharged on account of physical disability, Feb. 23, 1863. He lost his right hand by firing a salute at Mechanicsburg, July 4, 1864. Mr. and Mrs Bird had three children in Sangamon county, and in the fall of 1866 moved to Kansas, where they had four. Their names are EDWARD T., ALLISON E., HENRY E., RICHARD N., JOHN M., LUCINDA A. and HARRIET F., and reside near Ottawa, Kansas.

JACOB F., born August 5, 1846, in Sangamon county, married Sept. 16, 1873, at Payson, Ill., to Mrs. Anna E. Vickers, whose maiden name was Hughes. She was born Dec. 31, 1849, in Butler county, Ohio. They reside at the family homestead, adjoining Mechanicsburg on the south.

THOMAS M., born Sept. 10, 1848, in Sangamon county, married, Oct. 19, 1871, at Decatur, to Florence M. Wood, who was born Sept. 10, 1851, at Clarenceville, Lower Canada. They have two children, JOHN RICHARD and ETHEL LUCINDA, and reside one and a half miles southwest of Mechanicsburg.

Rev. Richard Bird considers the vicinity of Mechanicsburg his home, but continues to travel as a preacher in the M. E. church, in the Illinois Conference. His residence for the conference year of 1875-6 is Easton, Mason county, Ill.

BIRD, JOANNA, was born Nov. 20, 1807, in Mason county, Ky., married to James M. Dixon. See his name. He died and she married John C. Eckel. See his name.

BIRD, THOMAS, was born Dec. 25, 1809, in Mason county, Ky., came to Sangamon county in 1835. He never married, and died Sept. 11, 1858, near Mechanicsburg.

BIRD, ABRAHAM, born Aug. 30, 1813, in Mason county, Ky., came to Sangamon county in 1836, married, May 9, 1839, to Nancy Riddle. They had one child—

DAVID R., born April 26, 1841, in Sangamon county. He enlisted; was with his cousin, Dr. Riddle, all through the war to suppress the rebellion. Present residence not known.

Mrs. Nancy Bird died April 26, 1841, and Abraham Bird died Feb. 19, 1853, both in Sangamon county.

BIRD, HENRY, was born Dec. 15, 1815, in Mason county, Ky., came to

Sangamon county in 1836, was married Sept. 30, 1841, to Margaret J. Hussey, who was born April 5, 1821, in Sangamon county, Ill. Two children were born there, and in 1845 they moved overland in wagons, to Yamhill county, Oregon. Five children were born there, and they moved to Portland, Multnomah county, Oregon, where one child was born. Of their nine children—

CLARISSA, born August 30, 1842, in Sangamon county, Ill., married in Oregon, July 30, 1861, to Hiram Ransom, and resides in California.

MARY E., born June 23, 1844, in Sangamon county, married in Oregon, Dec. 29, 1869, to W. S. James. She died Feb. 19, 1874, in Portland, Oregon, leaving two children, viz: ELLA and MARY, the latter died August 9, 1874. Mr. James resides in Portland.

NATHAN H., born Dec. 12, 1846, in Yamhill county, was married March 15, 1870, to Alice Talbot. They have two children, WALTER and VIOLA, and reside near Bellvue, Yamhill county, Oregon.

RICHARD, born April 5, 1848, in Yamhill county, is unmarried, and resides in Portland.

JOHN, born Sept. 20, 1851, in Yamhill county, is unmarried, and resides in Portland.

CORNELIA E., born Nov. 20, 1853, in Yamhill county, resides with her mother.

STEPHEN, born Oct. 9, 1855, in Yamhill county, resides near Sheridan, Yamhill county, on a farm.

BENJAMIN M., born April 1, 1858, in Yamhill county, resides with his mother.

WILLIAM E., born Dec. 11, 1862, in Portland, resides with his mother.

Henry Bird died August 20, 1873, in Portland, and his widow resides there.

BIRD, HETTY E., was born July 9, 1818, in Mason county, Ky., came with her mother to Sangamon county in 1835. She was married near Mechanicsburg, Feb. 25, 1845, to Samuel Powers, who was born April 28, 1797, in Hampshire county, Va. They had one child, and Mrs. Powers died, March 16, 1851, in Sangamon county. Mr. Powers moved to Iowa with his daughter—

RHODA A., born Sept. 19, 1848, in Sangamon county, and married in Iowa, July 22, 1865, to Barzilla Reeves, who was born April 5, 1841. They had five children in Iowa. Their second child, ISAAC N., died in his fourth year. ANDREW J., DAVID M., GARRISON B. and HESTER A., reside with their parents, near Sidney, Fremont county, Iowa.

Samuel Powers resides in Atchison county, Mo.

BIRD, ABIGAIL, was born Sept. 27, 1824, in Mason county, Ky., came with her mother to Sangamon county, Ill., in 1835, married, Oct. 12, 1843, to Hugh Sutherland. He was born May 4, 1816, in Edinburgh, Scotland, came to America in 1827, remained in the Atlantic States until 1841, when he came to Sangamon county. Mr. and Mrs. S. had nine children, Charles W., next to the youngest, died in his third year. Of the other eight—

HESTER J., born Dec. 21, 1844, in Sangamon county, married March 17, 1869, to Joseph N. Burcham, have two children, REUBEN and JOHN L., and reside three and a quarter miles east of Mechanicsburg.

BETSY J., born Sept. 17, 1846, died Sept. 2, 1858.

JOHN G., born April 28, 1848, in Sangamon county, married, August 31, 1870, in his native county, to Mary J. Peak. They had two children, ARTHUR CLARK and CARLOS B. The latter died in his second year. Mrs. S. died March 12, 1875, in the twenty-seventh year of her age. John G. Sutherland resides at Warrensburg, Ill.

ELLEN R. born Jan. 30, 1850, in Sangamon county, married Feb. 14, 1875, to William Upton, and resides three and a half miles east of Mechanicsburg.

ABIGAIL ANN, born Dec. 23, 1851, in Sangamon county, married Feb. 7, 1875, to Charles Mussenden, and resides four miles east of Mechanicsburg.

THOMAS M., born Sept. 8, 1854,

HUGH A., born Dec. 12, 1856, and

CHARLEY B., born Dec. 29, 1861.

The three latter reside with their parents, adjoining Illiopolis on the east.

BLACK, SAMUEL, was born July 2, 1798, in Augusta county, Va. Mildred Gaines, a niece of Mrs. Peter Cartwright, was born Oct. 4, 1802, in Charlotte county, Va. They were married,

Feb. 20, 1822, near Hopkinsville, Ky., where their parents had emigrated when they were quite young. They had one child in Kentucky, and moved to Sangamon county, Ill., arriving Nov. 19, 1825, in what is now Cartwright township, where they had two children, and in 1828 moved to Morgan county, where seven children were born. Of their children—

ELIZA, born Dec. 31, 1824, in Kentucky, married George Ragen, have seven children, and reside in Cass county, Iowa.

JAMES R., born July 5, 1826, in Sangamon county, married Dec. 13, 1863, to Arvilla M. McMurphy, who was born Nov. 25, 1833, in St. Lawrence county, N. Y. They have four children, VICTOR C., JENNIE M., IONA C. and ALBERT C., and reside one and a quarter miles north of Pleasant Plains, within half a mile of where he was born, on the farm of his grandfather, Rev. Richard Gaines.

WILLIAM, born April 5, 1828, in Sangamon county, married Jane Short, and died in three months after marriage.

SARAH B., born May 1, 1833, in Morgan county, married Tilman Sharp, has one child, and resides in Morgan county.

JOHN, born Dec. 3, 1830, just before the "deep snow," married Sarah Vaughn, have three children, LOU ELLA, J. W. and J. R., and reside in Morgan county.

AMY, born Feb. 5, 1839, died Sept. 8, 1869.

MARTHA G., born Feb. 4, 1835, is unmarried, and resides with her parents.

SAMUEL, Jun., born June 27, 1837, married, Dec. 2, 1860, to Mary Self, have two children, W. E. and C. S., and reside in Morgan county.

MARY J., born March 9, 1842, married, Sept. 20, 1861, to James Phillips, who died, and she married Wm. Self, and resides in Cass county.

MILDRED, born Jan. 7, 1845, married Samuel T. Mattix, has one child, and resides in Morgan county.

Samuel Black and his wife reside six miles north of Jacksonville, surrounded by most of their children. Mr. Black made his first trip to Sangamon county to move the mother of Rev. Peter Cartwright. He made, altogether, seven round trips with a six horse team, when there were no roads, in moving the Cartwright, Gaines and Black families.

BLACK, WILLIAM, born about 1793, in Edinburgh, Scotland. He came to America when young, landing at Philadelphia. A stone cutter by trade, he was employed on some of the banks and other public buildings in that city, finishing with a contract on Girard College. Anna Young was born April 6, 1798, in the city of Philadelphia. William Black and Anna Young were there married, Dec. 7, 1820. Their nine children were born in Philadelphia, one of whom died young. Mr. Black came to Springfield in the fall of 1839, and April, 1840, his family arrived and moved to a farm he had purchased, six miles northeast of Springfield. Of their eight children—

JOHN, born April 12, 1822, is unmarried. He went to California in 1849, and now resides in San Francisco.

WILLIAM, Jun., born April 21, 1824, in Philadelphia, was drowned, April 9, 1849, in a slough near where the Gilman and Clinton railroad crosses the Sangamon river.

HENRY, born July 23, 1826, in Philadelphia, married, May 3, 1871, in Humboldt, Kansas, to Mrs. Artenecia A. Chambers, whose maiden name was Bradshaw. They have two children ANNA A. and BLANCHE, and reside at Humboldt, Kansas.

JAMES, born July 8, 1828, in Philadelphia, was married March 2, 1852, to Amanda A. Cartmell. They had one child, and Mrs. Black died, Jan. 11, 1854. Mr. Black was married, Feb. 5, 1862, to Eliza A. Cartmell. They have four children. Of his five children, WILLIAM L., by the first marriage, and the other four, WALTER B., ALVIN F., AMANDA M. and EMMA T., reside with their father, on the farm settled by his father in 1840, six miles northeast of Springfield.

GEORGE W., born August 15, 1830, married Sept. 21, 1858, to Sarah A. Mann. They had eight children, two of whom died young. MARY E., ELIZABETH, ANNIE L., HENRY F., THOMAS M. and CHARLES W., and reside on Round Prairie, five miles east of Springfield, between the mouth of Spring Creek and South Fork.

ANNA E., born Sept. 26, 1832, married, Jan. 1, 1852, to Marion F. Whitesides. (*See his name.*)

FRANCIS G., born Feb. 27, 1835, married, Oct. 4, 1859, to Elizabeth Hammond. They had two children, JOHN W. and ELIZA J., and Mr. Black enlisted August, 1862, in Co. G., 114th Ill. Inf., for three years, and died of disease at Vicksburg, just after the surrender by the rebels, July 4, 1863. His remains were brought home and interred near German Prairie Station. His children reside with their mother, who married A. R. Welch.

WALTER C., born Sept. 22, 1837, enlisted in Co. G., 114th Ill. Inf., for three years, August 5, 1862, was twice slightly wounded, served full time, and was honorably discharged, August 10, 1865. He was married, Feb. 5, 1866, to Permelia F. Cartmell. They have three children, ANNA C., FRANCIS E. and ORA EVA, and reside two miles southeast of Riverton.

Margaret Allison lived as one of the family of William Black, in Philadelphia. She came with the family to Sangamon county, and died Sept. 20, 1840, aged 29 years.

William Black died Dec. 15, 1858, and his widow died July 25, 1874, both on the farm where they settled in 1840. Mr. Black became a member of the Scots Thistle Society soon after his arrival in Philadelphia, and remained a member as long as he lived.

BLACK, THOMAS, was born Oct. 25, 1768, and went from South Carolina to Christian county, Ky., where he was married to Edith A. Pyle. They moved to southern Illinois just before the "Shakes"—meaning the earthquake of 1811, that sunk New Madrid, Missouri. They fled in terror back to Kentucky; but finding the earth did not all sink, they returned to southern Illinois, and moved to what became Sangamon county, arriving April 9, 1819, in what is now Auburn township. Of their children, viz:—

SARAH, born July 3, 1796, in Kentucky, married there to a Mr. Edwards. They had one child, SUSAN, who married Wm. Woods. Mr. Edwards died, and his widow married Bailey Taylor. They had three children, viz: AMANDA married Peter Wheeler. EMMA married Miller Bagby. THOMAS B. was married in 1866. He had three children; *one* is dead. Mr. Taylor died, and the family moved to McDonough county, Ill., and from there to Iowa, where she died.

DAVID, born Sept. 17, 1798, in Kentucky, married Jan. 2, 1823, in Sangamon county, to Sarah Moffitt. They had six children. WILLIAM married Millie Moore, and live near Belleville, St. Clair county. GEORGE married Viney Broom, and resides near Blue Mound, Macon county, Ill. EDITH A. married Wm. Simmons. He died, and Mrs. S. married Mr. Brown. They reside in Texas. The others are ANNE, LEANDER and FRANCIS. David Black died Oct. 7, 1856, in Chatham township, and his widow resides with her youngest son, in Macon county, near Blue Mound.

ELIZABETH, born March 6, 1803, in Kentucky, was married in Sangamon county to John Harris. They had one child, JAMES, who was drowned in a mill pond while fishing, aged fourteen years. Mr. and Mrs. Harris both died in Macoupin county.

NANCY, born Aug. 4, 1806, in Kentucky, married in Sangamon county, Aug. 18, 1833, to John N. Viney, who died Jan. 5, 1871, and Mrs. Nancy V. died May 23, 1871, without children. *See his name.*

JOHN, born Aug. 8, 1809, in Kentucky, married in Sangamon county, Aug. 4, 1831, to Sarah Myers. They had nine children; three died young. Of the other six, ELMINA died Feb. 23, 1858, aged 22 years. DRUSILLA, born Aug. 30, 1837, in Sangamon county, married June 10, 1856, to James Babcock. They had nine children; one died young. RICHARD J. D. died Aug. 4, 1875. WILLIAM died Aug. 23, 1875. LAURA, ELLEN, ALBERT M., ADDIE M., IRA J. and ANNETTA E. The family reside near Oreana, Macon county, Ill. THOMAS, born Oct. 6, 1839, in Sangamon county, was married April 12, 1863, to Mary M. Lewis, who died Dec. 21, 1865, and he was married Feb. 3, 1868, to Emily C. Graves, who died Aug. 10, 1871, leaving one child, FLOSSIE C. Mr. Black was married April 6, 1873, to Martha J. Dodds. They have one child, a son, and reside two miles east of Auburn. ALBERT M., born Sept. 14, 1843, in Sangamon county, was married June 24, 1865, to Salome T. Ham. They have two children, and reside near Pawnee. ADALINE M., born May 25,

1847, married Aug. 2, 1865, to Wm. D. Patton. *See his name.* She died Jan. 26, 1875, leaving two children. JOHN W., born Sept. 29, 1851, in Sangamon county, married Feb. 2, 1873, to Susan R. Kimble. They have two children, JOHN D. and EMILY, and reside three miles east of Auburn. John Black died Aug. 1, 1855, and his widow, Mrs. Sarah Black, died March 18, 1858, both in Auburn township.

THOMAS, born Sept. 3, 1813, in Christian county, Ky., married in Sangamon county, March 7, 1855, to Mary J. Wallace, who was born Nov. 1, 1831. They have three children, EDITH, MARY F. and MARCHIE, and reside in less than half a mile of where his father settled in 1819, about three and a half miles east of Auburn.

CARTER T., born Jan. 24, 1818, was married Oct. 8, 1840, to Mary C. Coberly, who was born Nov. 7, 1820. Of their six children, namely: ELLEN E., born in Auburn township, July 12, 1841, married July 1, 1858, to J. T. Graves. They have six children, ROBERT L., MARY N., ZILDAH S., WILLIAM J., MARK and CATHARINE, and reside in Butler, Bates county, Mo. JOSEPH C., born Aug. 29, 1843, in Auburn township, Ill., died in Missouri. CHARLES C., born Aug. 22, 1845, in Andrew county, Mo., died in Nodaway county, Mo. WILLIAM T., born May 21, 1848, in Andrew county, Mo., married in Nodaway county to Mary C. Crabtree, Dec. 29, 1869. They had one child, JAMES T. Wm. T. Black and son died in Bates county, Mo. GEORGE H., born March 11, 1858, in Nodaway county, Mo., and JOHN D., born Sept. 16, 1860, in Nodaway county, reside there.

Mrs. Carter Black died May 14, 1875, in Nodaway county, Mo. Carter Black is now (1876) in Sangamon county.

Mrs. Edith A. Black died April 15, 1822, and Thomas Black was married in 1823 or '4 to Mrs. Rebecca Viney, whose maiden name was Shiles. She died Feb. 13, 1851, and Mr. B. died Nov. 3, 1851, aged 84 years, both where he settled in 1819.

BLUE, JOHN, was born Sept. 9, 1777, in South Carolina. His father was a soldier in the Revolutionary army, and was taken prisoner by the British the very day of his birth. His parents moved to Fleming county, Ky., when he was quite young. Elizabeth McNary was born in South Carolina, and taken by her parents to Fleming county, Ky., also. They were there married about 1806, had seven children in that county, and then moved to Hopkins county, where they had four children. About 1823 they moved to Green county, O., where they had two children, and then moved to Sangamon county, arriving in the fall of 1830, in what is now Clear Lake township.

MARTHA married Robert Blue, had six children and died.

SAMUEL married Isabel Webb, had eight children, and resides in Missouri.

DAVID H., born Sept. 23, 1816, in Fleming county, Ky., married in Sangamon county May 19, 1844, to Fannie Webb. They had two children, one of whom died young. MELISSA C. married Abel P. Bice. *See his name.* David H. Blue resides two miles north of Barclay.

ELIZA married Adolphus Jones, had one child, and all died.

WILLIAM M., born in Fleming county, Ky., married in Sangamon county to Adaline Cline. They had five children. JAMES H. married Catharine Dunlap, had one child, DORA E., and live in Fancy creek township. GEORGE W., LUCY, DAVID and PARTHENIA, live with their mother. William M. Blue enlisted in Aug., 1862, in Co. C, 114 Ill. Inf., for three years. He was killed at the battle of Guntown, Miss., June 10, 1864. His widow married M. Hardman, and lives near Cantrall.

HARRISON married Margaret Alexander. They had three children, and he died in Fancy creek township.

CAROLINE married Stephen Cantrall. They have six children, and live near Kansas City, Mo.

AMOS went to Oregon when a young man, and resides in Jackson county.

John Blue died in 1842, and his widow in 1848, both in Sangamon county.

BONDURANT. The first known of the name in America was Dr. Joseph Bondurant, a Huguenot, who was banished from France on account of his religion, during the reign of Queen Anne, about the year 1700. He was wealthy in France, but could only bring his library with him. He and his companions, Ford,

Agee, O'Briant and Shatteen, all settled in Virginia.

BONDURANT, JOSEPH, the fourth generation from Dr. Joseph Bondurant, was born Sept. 15, 1801, in Bedford county, Va., moved to Kentucky in early life, and was married Oct. 27, 1823, to Martha Sharp. They moved to Sangamon county Oct., 1828. He was one of the early school teachers in the Dickerson neighborhood. They had eleven children, namely—

JOHN T., born June 5, 1824, in Kentucky, raised in Sangamon county, married near DesMoines, Iowa, in 1848, to Virginia Cooney. In 1850 he emigrated to California, and died in Sacramento, Dec. 23, 1850, of disease contracted while crossing the plains, leaving a childless widow.

LUCRETIA J., born Nov. 4, 1825, in Kentucky, married Nov., 1845, in Sangamon county, to Joel Churchill. *See his name.* They reside at DeLand, Piatt county, Ill.

ELIZABETH T., born April 28, 1827, in Kentucky, married in Athens, Ill., May 15, 1842, to William Miller, of that place, where they resided until 1852, when they moved to Mechanicsburg. They had nine children, namely: MARTHA E., married Jan. 16, 1872, to T. P. Lofland. She died June 14, 1873, leaving a son six months old, to be brought up by her aunt, Margaret D. Underwood. ANNIE M., JOHN T. and THOMAS B. died under ten years. ALBERT D., JOSEPH W., SARAH J., AMANDA B. and GEORGE L. live with their mother. William Miller died July 17, 1868. His widow and children live in Mechanicsburg.

ALEXANDER C., born Sept. 1, 1829, in Sangamon county. He went to Iowa in the winter of 1856, and was married there Oct., 1861, to Margaret Brooks, of DesMoines. They had seven children, namely: EMMA, FANNIE, LIZZIE, FRANK, FLORENCE, BURTON and NELLIE, and reside near Altoona, Polk county, Iowa.

THOMAS C., born Dec. 29, 1831, in Sangamon county, settled in Piatt county in 1856, near DeLand, Piatt county, Ill.

SAMUEL T., born Dec. 9, 1834, in Sangamon county, married Nov. 15, 1860, in Douglas county, to Sarah Ellen Barnett. They have two living children, and reside near Wabash, Wayne county, Ill. He enlisted August 7, 1862, for three years, in Co. E., 79th Ill. Inf. Dec. 2, 1862, he was detailed to the Pioneer Corps department of the Cumberland. March 19, 1863, he took charge of four saw mills, on Stone's river, Tenn., and put them in order. Sept. 15, 1863, he was ordered to Chattanooga, where he took charge of building water-works, on the 8th of October, doing the civil engineering with a common spirit level. He remained in charge until May 15, 1865, when he resigned for the purpose of perfecting some inventions of his own. He is now engaged in the lumber trade.

MARGARET D., born Jan. 31, 1837, married Oct. 28, 1858, to Thomas Underwood. *See his name.*

MARY E., born Feb. 3, 1840, is unmarried, and resides with her brother Thomas, near DeLand, Piatt county, Ill.

MARTHA F., born March 24, 1842, in Sangamon county, married Jan., 1864, to William Thornton, of DesMoines, Iowa. They have three children, namely: LILLIE, LUCY and HARRY, and reside near DesMoines.

JOSEPH N., born May 2, 1844. He went to Iowa in 1866, and married in 1867 to Sarah DeVore. They had three children, WILLIAM, EARNEST and FRANK. In 1871 Mr. J. N. Bondurant returned to DeWitt county, Ill., and resides near Farmer City.

AMANDA E., born April 25, 1847, in Sangamon county, died Oct. 4, 1858.

Mr. Joseph Bondurant died April 30, 1864, at his daughter's, Mrs. Lucretia Churchill, near Mechanicsburg. Mrs. Martha Bondurant resides with her son Thomas, near DeLand, Piatt county, Ill.

BOLL, VALENTINE J., was born April 22, 1807, at Flersheim, Nassau, Germany. He came to America in 1833, arriving June 29, at Baltimore, being forty-four days from Bremen. He went to New Philadelphia, O., to see a relative, thence to St. Louis, and from there to Sangamon county, and made pottery for Chistopher Newcomer two years. In the fall of 1836 he started back to Germany by way of New Orleans, and arrived at his native town Jan. 2, 1837. He was there married, April 2, 1837, to Elizabeth C. Heller. She was born Feb. 13, 1819, in the same town. They embarked June 12, 1837, at Amsterdam, and were forty-nine days on the passage to New York. He went via Albany, Buffalo, Cleveland, thence to Portsmouth, on the Ohio river, thence to St. Louis and back to Sangamon county, late in 1837. His father, step-mother and five children, a married sister and her husband, Garred Young, and others, making a total of seventeen persons, came with him. He made pottery in Ball township for about eighteen years, and then engaged in farming exclusively. They had nine children, all born in Sangamon county, two of whom died young. Of the other seven—

GARHARD, born Nov. 2, 1838, in Sangamon county, married Jan. 5, 1862, to Mary J. Greenawalt. They had five children, THOMAS H. and JAMES A., the first and fourth, died young; MARY E., AMANDA F. and SARAH M., reside with their parents, one mile northwest of Pawnee.

ELIZABETH, born in Sangamon county, married John T. Burtle, Jun. *See his name.*

PAUL A., born in Sangamon county, resides with his parents.

GEORGE P., born in Sangamon county, married Mary M. Mollihorn. They had two children, WILLIAM A. and CHARLES V., and reside in Ball township.

CATHARINE J. married Patrick McAnanry, have two children, MATTHEW and ROSA, and reside at Tallula.

MARGARET and EVA reside with their parents in Ball township, five miles southeast of Chatham.

BALL, JACOB, born about 1829, at Flersheim, Nassau, Germany, came to America, and to Sangamon county, with his half-brother Valentine, in 1837. He was married in 1867 to Sarah Conner. They have two children—

ELIZABETH and THOMAS, and reside in Ball township, six miles southeast of Chatham.

BOWEN, ZAZA, was born Oct. 24, 1806, in Guilford county, N. C. His father died when he was two years old, and his mother, with her four children, the eldest of whom was married, moved to Cabell county, West Va., in 1817. Zaza Bowen and Mary Knight were married June 25, 1827, in that county, and in the fall of that year moved to Sangamon county, Ill., arriving Dec. 4, 1827, in what is now Loami township. They had seven children in Sangamon county. The two eldest died under five years. Of the other five children—

REBECCA J., born June 28, 1831, married in 1850, to James W. George. They have three living children, and reside near Mt. Auburn, Christian county.

ABNER, born Feb. 24, 1833, in Sangamon county, married March 16, 1856, to Frances A. Cutter. They have four children. WALTER, N. C., and JOHN CALHOUN, twins; ZAZA A. and WILLIAM J. Not having a daughter, they adopted one, whom they call KATIE BOWEN. They reside on the farm settled in 1828 by Mrs. B.'s father, S. R. Cutter. It is two and a half miles northwest of Loami.

ELIZABETH, born Nov. 13, 1834, in Sangamon county, married Robert M. Park. *See his name.*

ISABEL A., born Dec. 26, 1836, married in 1855, to Charles W. Fisher. They had five children, MARY E., NANCY E., ELIZABETH C., WILLIAM Z. and JOHN N. Mrs. F. and her children reside three miles west of Loami.

WILLIAM A., born July 28, 1838, died Oct. 11, 1860.

Mrs. Mary Bowen died Dec. 31, 1839, and Zaza B. married, Jan. 7, 1841, to Sarah Park. They had four children; all died under nine years.

Mrs. Sarah Bowen died Sept. 28, 1860, and Zaza Bowen was married, Sept. 17, 1863, to Mrs. Lydia M. Light, whose maiden name was Patterson. They reside three miles west of Loami, on the farm where he settled in 1836. Zaza Bowen remembers Springfield when it was a collection of round log huts, covered with clapboards held on by weight poles. He remembers seeing the jail covered with a stack of hay.

BOWLING, JAMES, was born March 8, 1790, in Fauquier county, Va., was taken by his parents to Tennessee when he was nine years old, and from there to Logan county, Ky., in 1808. He was there married, Oct. 17, 1817, to Margaret Jones, who was born Nov. 18, 1793, in Mercer county, Ky. James Bowling and wife left, the day after their marriage, for Bond county, Ill. They moved on horseback, each riding a horse and leading a pack horse, to carry their goods. One child was born in Bond county, Ill., and they moved to Sangamon county, arriving in 1819, in what is now Rochester township, on the farm now owned by R. P. Abel, adjoining Rochester on the west. In 1830 they moved one mile north. They had six children in Sangamon county. Of their seven children—

ELIZABETH W., born Sept. 22, 1818, in Bond county, Ill., was married in Sangamon county, April 27, 1843, to James M. Logan. *See his name.*

ELVIRA P., born Feb. 25, 1820, in Sangamon county, was married April 28, 1844, to Daniel Barr. They had three children. JAMES THOMAS married Elizabeth Atkinson. They had two children, LOUIE and MATTIE, and Mr. Barr died, March 13, 1875, leaving his widow and children in Rochester. MARGARET E., born Oct. 16, 1846, married Samuel West. *See his name.* CHAS. E. born August 18, 1850, married, Dec. 2, 1873, to Louisa D. West, and lives in Rochester. Daniel Barr and wife reside in Rochester.

JOHN P., born Jan. 12, 1822, in Sangamon county, was married Oct. 14, 1846, in Green county, to Maria Lorton. They had three children. Their second child, SARAH M., died at Mt. Auburn in 1854, in her fourth year. WILLIAM K. was born Jan. 1, 1849, and married August 27, 1874, to Alice Jernigan, who was born in Greenville, Ky., and resides near Virden, Ill. JAMES R., born Aug. 10, 1859, resides with his parents, near Virden, Ill.

JULIAN F., born Feb. 5, 1824, in Sangamon county, was married Sept. 6, 1845, to Abraham E. Nickolls. He had previously been married, and had two children. They had seven children, and Mrs. Nickolls died, Feb. 28, 1867. Of their children, ANDREW T. resides at Rochester, Ill. MARGARET A. married William Morgan, and resides near Mt. Auburn. EMILY S. married John Shewmaker, and resides near Decatur. MARY J. married William Murphy, and resides at Topeka, Kansas. ELIZABETH A. married Wm. Meek, and resides at Central City, Colorado. JAMES B. and ELVIRA M. reside with their father, at Kingsville, Kansas.

JANE A., born Oct. 6, 1826, adjoining Rochester on the west. She was married, Feb. 2, 1854, to John Cassity, who was born Jan. 12, 1821, in Bourbon county, Ky., and came to Sangamon county in the fall of 1830. They had five children, three of whom died in infancy. WILLIAM, born May 4, 1857, and FRANK, born March 21, 1867, reside with their parents, in Rochester, within 200 yards of where Mrs. Cassity was born.

ARMIZA T., born Jan. 30, 1830, in Sangamon county, was married, Mar. 10, 1853, to John S. Highmore, who was born Sept. 22, 1828, in Somersetshire, England. He came to America in 1849, and to Sangamon county in March, 1850. They had two children. LAURA, born Jan. 27, 1854, married John F. Miller, (*see his name,*) and resides in Edinburg. ARMIZA resides with her aunt, Jane A. Cassity, who brought her up. Mrs. Highmore died August 27, 1856, and Mr. Highmore was married March, 1860, to Mary A. Cloyd. *See name of Cloyd.* They had three children, and Mrs. H. died, and Mr. Highmore was married the third time, to Mrs. Mary Price, widow of Dr. Price, who was born in Virginia. They reside in Rochester. He has been a member of the county board of supervisors from 1863 to 1867, and from 1872 to 1875.

Mrs. Margaret Bowling died Nov. 14, 1846, and James Bowling died April 12, 1853, both near Rochester.

BOYD, JOHN, was born Feb. 13, 1777, in Pennsylvania, and went to Botetourt county, Va., when a young man. Susannah Hiner was born Dec. 22, 1780, in Botetourt county, Va., and they were there married June 26, 1802. Two children were born in Virginia, and they moved to Franklin county, O., about 1806, where six children were born. The family then moved to Sangamon county, Ill., arriving in the fall of 1819 in what is now Ball township, where one child was born. Mr. Boyd was a millwright, and his services were in great demand. In the fall of 1830 he was at work on a mill on the Sangamon river north of Rochester, known afterwards as Baker and Darling's mill. Wishing to visit his family, and having some business at Springfield, he went there first, and then started home. A heavy sleet was falling at the time, which proved to be the precursor of the deep snow. The walking was laborious, and the next day his body was found by his neighbor, Christopher Newcomer. It was six miles southeast of Springfield, on what is now the farm of William Southwick. He was found just as the snow began to fall, and if he had lain another day would not have been seen until spring. Of his children—

HANNAH, born in Botetourt county, Va., was married in Sangamon county, Ill., to John Dillon. They both died near the town of Dillon, in Tazewell county, leaving six children residing there. JESSE went to Arkansas, married and died there. SUSANNAH was married Aug. 24, 1848, to Joseph Meredith, and died Dec. 24, 1868, in Christian county. MARY married Timothy Larramore, and resides near Tremont, Tazewell county, Ill. WILLIAM died in Sangamon county. JANE resides with her sister Mary. DANIEL served four years in an Illinois regiment, and died in Tazewell county. JOHN married, and resides in Iroquois county, Ill. ISAAC died in the Union army.

MARY, born Jan. 1, 1806, in Botetourt county, Va., was married to George Brunk. See his name.

JACOB, born Oct. 30, 1807, near Columbus, O., married in Sangamon county, Ill., Sept 1, 1833, to Rebecca Royal. They had nine children in Sangamon county. JOHN T., born in 1835, married Sarah E. Clayton. They had two children, GEORGE E. and EMERY A., and Mr. B. died April 5, 1874, in Taylorville. WILLIAM H., born May 1, 1837, was married March 31, 1859, to Mary A. Vigal. They have one daughter, FRANCES D., and reside in Cotton Hill township, between Brush and Horse creeks. GEORGE B., born Dec. 25, 1839, enlisted Aug., 1862, in Co. E, 114 Ill. Inf., for three years; served full time, and was honorably discharged at Springfield. He married Harriet Williams. They have three children, CLARENCE E., SUSAN R. and PHEBE C., and reside in Cotton Hill township. MARY married Alonzo Sparks. They have two children, MAUD and RAY, and reside near Girard, Kan. SUSAN married Harvey Alexander. They have four children, CHARLES M., JACOB W., LULIE M., and HATTIE E., and reside near Girard, Kan. JAMES O. served in Co. I, 7th Ill. Inf., from Feb., 1865, to the close of the rebellion. He married Marietta Reed. They had two children, REBECCA J. and JESSE M., and reside in Cotton Hill township. SARAH J. married Elijah D. Lawley. See his name. They have two children, LOUIS E. and FREDERICK G. DAVIS O. married Sarah A. Campbell. They have two children, OLIVE and CLARA A., and reside in Cotton Hill township. VINCENT C. died Aug. 22, 1871, in his eighteenth year. Jacob Boyd and his wife reside in Cotton Hill township.

THOMAS, born Oct. 25, 1809, was married, and resided in St. Louis at the close of the rebellion. He died about 1869.

JOHN, born Aug. 5, 1811, in Ohio, married in Iowa to Elizabeth Dyer. They reside near Ozark, Jackson county, Iowa. He was a soldier from Sangamon county in the Black Hawk war, and served in an Iowa regiment during the rebellion.

BENJAMIN died in his ninth year.

JOSEPH, born April 1, 1816, in Ohio, brought up in Sangamon county, was married in Iowa to Anna Ray. He enlisted in an Iowa regiment, and died at Louisville, Ky., leaving a widow and three children near Ozark, Iowa.

CATHARINE, born Oct. 26, 1818, in Ohio, died in Sangamon county, aged seventeen years.

SAMUEL, born Aug. 25, 1823, in Sangamon county, died in his seventeenth year.

Mrs. Susannah Boyd died Aug. 9, 1848, in Sangamon county.

BOYER, WILLIAM T., was born April 4, 1817, in Adair county, Ky. Sarah A. Jackson was born Dec. 7, 1820, in the same county. They were married Oct. 24, 1839, near Franklin, Morgan county, Ill. They had one child in Morgan county, and moved to what is now New Berlin township, arriving in 1840. They had ten children in Sangamon county. Four of their children died under ten years. Of the other six children—

SARAH A., born Oct. 19, 1843, in Sangamon county, married March 14, 1867, to John Mitchell. They had four children, EMMA M. and LAURA A. died under five years. RHODA E. and ANNIE, and reside in Talkington township, seven miles west of Auburn.

MARY F., born Sept. 8, 1845, in Sangamon county, married, March 30, 1863, to John H. Cox. They have three children, WILLIAM H., GEORGE W. and CHARLEY, and reside near Franklin, Morgan county.

WILLIAM A., born Dec. 5, 1849, resides with his parents.

ELIZA J., born March 11, 1851, married William A. Young, Nov. 11, 1869, have one child, INA, and reside in Talkington township, six and a quarter miles west of Auburn.

ANNIE M. and

JACOB C. reside with their parents, six miles southwest of Loami.

BOZARTH, WILLIAM H., was born about 1796, in Grayson county, Ky. Elizabeth Stewart was born in 1797, in the same county, and they were there married in 1819. They had four children born in Kentucky, and moved to Sangamon county, Ill., in Oct., 1825, on Spring creek, west of Springfield about two and a half miles. Mr. Bozarth was killed by a fall from a horse in December following, only two months after coming to the county. His widow returned to Kentucky, was there married to Rawley Martin, returned to Sangamon county in the fall of 1830, and settled on Lick creek. In 1840 Mr. Martin moved to Warren county, Iowa. Of the four Bozarth children—

HIGGINSON married Mary Bozarth, in Grayson county, Ky., and remained there.

OLVER H. P. married Elizabeth Brooks, and resides in Grayson county, Ky.

ELI L., born in Grayson county, Ky., married in Sangamon county to Artelia Peddicord. They had five children. ARMINDA and MINERVA P. died young. Eli L. Bozarth died Oct. 29, 1868. His son, WILLIAM W., was drowned in Sugar creek, April 21, 1869. The other two children, VIOLA E. and PHŒBE, reside with their mother at the house of her father, Jonathan Peddecord, in Ball township.

ISAAC H., born in Grayson county, Ky., married Rhoda Seybold, and resides at Blandinville, McDonough county.

BRADFORD, JAMES M., was born Sept. 28, 1795, in Culpepper county, Va. His parents moved to Scott county, Ky., when he was twelve years old. His commencement in business was trading down the Ohio and Mississippi rivers. He was married July 4, 1820, at Port Gibson, Miss., to Ann E. Barnes, who was born Sept. 10, 1802, in North Carolina, and in 1807 was taken by her parents to Mississippi, where they settled. She was educated at Port Gibson in a French Catholic convent. After a residence of three years there, they moved to Scott county, Ky., where they remained one year, and moved to Franklin county, near Frankfort, and within three miles of Dick Johnson's Indian school. They had four children in Kentucky, and moved to Sangamon county, Ill., arriving in the fall of 1834, in what is now Gardner township. Of their four children—

THOMAS A., born August 2, 1821, at Port Gibson, Miss., brought by his parents to Sangamon county, was educated at McKendree College, Lebanon, Ill., graduated at that institution, and was married in Lebanon to Jane Baker. He went to Missouri and there enlisted in Co. B., Col. Doniphan's regiment, and marched overland to Mexico, in 1846. Col. Doniphan had orders, on arriving at Chihuahua, to report to Gen. Wool. He was unable to learn the whereabouts of Gen. Wool, and Thomas A. Bradford was one of six men who volunteered to carry through the dispatches, which they delivered to Gen. Wool at Saltillo, having gone the distance of three hundred miles, through an enemy's country, without the loss of a man. He was, with John Calhoun, engaged in the survey of public lands for the U. S. Government, and died Dec. 25, 1856, near Wyandotte, Kan., his wife and only child having died before.

ELIZABETH E., born July 31, 1823, in Scott county, Ky., was married in Sangamon county, May 24, 1840, to David Madison. He died two years later, leaving a son, JAMES B., who died at fourteen years of age. Mrs. Madison resides near Bradfordton, Sangamon county.

SUSAN, born May 25, 1825, in Kentucky, married June 11, 1858, in Sangamon county, to William G. Hawkins, who was born Sept. 14, 1827, in Boone county, Ky., but resided in St. Louis at the time of his marriage. They live in Sangamon county.

—17

MARTHA A., born May 26, 1832, in Kentucky, died while attending school in Springfield, August, 1848. Mrs. Ann E. Bradford died in Sangamon county, July 8, 1835, and James M. Bradford was married, Dec. 27, 1836, to Arsenath Talbott. They had six children in Sangamon county, one of whom died in infancy. Of the other five children—

WILLIAM T., born June 8, 1838, was married Oct. 1, 1861, to Grizella A. Parkinson. They had six children. The eldest, JAMES, and the fifth one, SUE H., died under three years. ELIZABETH A., THOMAS P., LAURA M. and WILLIAM A., reside with their parents, in Gardner township.

HARRIET E., born Feb. 3, 1841, in Sangamon county, married Hiram E. Gardner. See his name.

ISABELLA M. resides with her mother in Springfield.

SARAH J., born Nov. 3, 1845, married William H. Parkinson. See his name.

EDWARD T., born May 19, 1850, was married, Feb. 17, 1870, to Carrie M. VanPatten. They have one child, EDWARD M., and reside at Bradfordton. James M. Bradford died March 3, 1852, and his widow resided on the farm which has become Bradfordton, on the Ohio and Mississippi railroad, until April, 1874, when she moved to Springfield, and lives on north fifth street. James M. Bradford was a soldier in the war of 1812, from Scott county, Ky. He served one term in the General Assembly of Illinois, elected in the fall of 1840.

BRADFORD, JOHN S., was born June 9, 1815, in Philadelphia, Pa. His father was a native of Delaware, and died in Philadelphia in 1816. John S. learned the trade of a book-binder in his native city, and in 1835 started on foot for the City of Mexico. He walked to Pittsburg, thence to Cincinnati by steamboat, from there to Dayton, O., and Richmond, Ind., working at his trade in all the places he passed through. At Richmond he was induced, in 1837, to join a corps of United States engineers who were then engaged in constructing what was called the National Road. It was a wagon road, built at the expense of the United States government. The law authorizing its construction was enacted when the Democratic party was in power, with one of its cardinal tenets: opposition to all internal improvements by the government; but President Jackson favored this because it was a military necessity. The road commenced at Cumberland, Md., crossed the Ohio river at Steubenville, passed through Columbus, O., Richmond, Indianapolis and Terre Haute, Ind., thence to Vandalia, Ill. At the latter point a determined contest arose between the people of the States of Illinois and Missouri, whether the point for crossing the Mississippi river should be Alton or St. Louis, the contestants fully believing that the future great city of the Mississippi valley depended on the decision of that question. Before it was settled the public mind became interested in railroads, and the National Road ended at Vandalia. The corps of engineers disbanded at the latter point. The State capital was then in transit from Vandalia to Springfield, and Mr. Bradford came here, arriving December, 1840. In the spring of 1841 he bought the interest of Mr. Burchell in the book-bindery of Burchell and Johnson, and became one of the firm of Johnson and Bradford.

John S. Bradford was married July 15, 1841, in Brandenburg, Ky., to Adaline M. Semple, who was born Oct., 1817, in Cumberland county, Ky. Her brother, Hon. James Semple, was at that time Charge de Affaires to New Grenada, afterwards United States Senator from Illinois, and still later one of the Judges of the Supreme Court of the State.

Soon after coming to Springfield, J. S. Bradford became Lieutenant in the "Springfield Cadets." They were ordered to Nauvoo by Gov. Ford in 1845, serving two months in the "Mormon war." In 1846 Mr. Bradford enlisted in Co. A, 4th Ill. Inf., under Col. E. D. Baker, and was appointed Quartermaster by Gov. Ford. As such he accompanied the regiment to Mexico, where he started to go twelve years before with a bookbinder's outfit. After his arrival in Mexico he was commissioned as commissary in the United States army. He was at the bombardment and capture of Vera Cruz, battle of Cerro Gordo and others, returning with the regiment to Springfield in 1847. The result of that war securing to us California and the discovery of gold,

Mr. Bradford started from Springfield Jan. 1, 1849, by the Isthmus of Panama to California, and was eighty-seven days on the Pacific ocean, reaching San Francisco May 20, 1849. He made Benicia his headquarters, and when the military commander of the department of the Pacific ordered a government to be formed for a new State, Mr. Bradford was elected to represent the district bounded by Oregon on the north, Sacramento river on the east, Bay of San Francisco on the south, and the Pacific ocean on the west. That Legislature organized the State without ever having gone through a territorial probation, and divided it into counties. Mr. Bradford was elected in 1850 to represent a district composed of the five counties of Solano, Napa, Sonoma, Mendocino and Marin, being a portion of the district he represented in the first Legislature. His family resided in Springfield, and he retained his business relations with Mr. Johnson also. He returned to Springfield in 1851, and since that has served the county of Sangamon, in 1857, as Superintendent of Public Instruction; was one of the Commissioners to divide the county into townships and name them, served the city of Springfield as Treasurer, Alderman and Mayor. When Illinois was called on for 6,000 of the 75,000 men to meet the rebels, Mr. Bradford was appointed by Gov. Yates as commissary, with the rank of Lieutenant-Colonel, his commission bearing date April 16, 1861, being the first commission issued by Gov. Yates in connection with the war to suppress the rebellion. He prepared quarters for the first soldiers rendezvoused by the State, and called it Camp Yates.

J. S. Bradford severed his connection with the firm of Johnson & Bradford in 1869, and opened a book store in Springfield, which he sold out in 1873, and moved to Aberdeen, Miss., returning to Springfield in Nov., 1875, where he now resides.

Mr. and Mrs. Bradford had seven children in Springfield, namely—

WILLIAM, resides at Lake Station, Newton county, Miss.

OSCAR, born Sept. 28, 1845, in Springfield, was married in 1871, in Owensboro, Ky., to Mary Crutcher. They reside in St. Louis, Mo.

SUSAN A. resides with her parents, in Springfield.

EUGENE S. resides in St. Louis, Mo.

JOHN, ANTRIM C. and DONALD, reside with their parents in Springfield.

BRADLEY, TERRY, was born in Rutherford county, North Carolina, and married there to Chloe Elliott, a sister to Andrew Elliott. See his name. They had eleven children born in Rutherford county, N. C., and moved to Sangamon county, Ill., arriving in what is now Gardner township, south of Spring creek, in 1834. Of their children—

SIMMONS, born March 3, 1811, in North Carolina, married March 28, 1839, in Sangamon county, to Jane Douglas. They had six children; three died young. WILLIAM H., born Jan. 5, 1840, married March 6, 1862, to Mary Rannebarger, who was born Jan. 13, 1842, near Columbus, O. They had three children. ELLA J. died, aged two years. EDWARD E. and LOTTIE B. reside with their parents, seven miles west of Springfield. THOMAS LEVI and JOHN ELI, twins, born Nov. 22, 1842. THOMAS L., married Nov. 24, 1864, to Hannah J. Smith, have two children, and reside in Curran township. JOHN E., married July 9, 1868, to Nancy A. Sims, had one child, HIRAM J., and she died April, 1869. He was married Dec. 16, 1869, to Sarah O'Hara, and reside at Philadelphia, Cass county, Ill. Simmons Bradley died Nov. 18, 1866, and his widow resides seven miles west of Springfield.

WILLIAM, born March 26, 1812, in Rutherford county, N. C., and came with his parents to Sangamon county in 1834. He was married Aug., 1846, in Jasper county, Mo., to Elizabeth Ragan, a native of Kentucky. They came to Sangamon county and had six children, one of whom died young. In 1857 they returned to Missouri, where two children were born. Of the seven children, three are married; MOLLIE, the third child, born in Sangamon county, and married in Missouri, July 4, 1875, to J. J. Gates, a native of Pike county, Ill. William Bradley died Dec. 13, 1875. His widow and seven children, married and unmarried, reside near Carthage, Jasper county, Mo.

SARAH, born in North Carolina, married in Sangamon county to Caleb Darden. They had three children. Their son THOMAS was a soldier in an Illinois regiment, and died at Memphis, Tenn. The entire family are dead.

WINNIE, born in North Carolina, married in Sangamon county to William Brundage. They had three children, and moved to Dallas county, Tex., in 1854.

RICHARD, born in Rutherford county, N. C., came with his parents to Sangamon county, was married in 1844 to Mary A. Baldwin. They had four children born in Sangamon county. Mrs. B. died Sept. 10, 1852, and the youngest child died soon after. Mr. B. moved in the fall of 1866, with his three children, to Kansas. Of his children, RICHARD J., born Dec. 8, 1845, in Sangamon county; SARAH C., born Feb. 9, 1848, in Sangamon county, married in 1870, in Kansas, to Franklin Campbell, and has one child, MARY E. WILLIAM B., born in Sangamon county. Richard Bradley and his three children reside near Fredonia, Wilson county, Kan.

JONATHAN, born in North Carolina, raised in Sangamon county, went to Texas, was pressed into the rebel service, and died there.

MELINDA, born in North Carolina, and died in Sangamon county at 26 or '7 years of age.

RHODA, born in North Carolina, married in Sangamon county to John Brundage, moved to Texas and died there, leaving two children, who reside in Kansas.

ELIZABETH, born in North Carolina, married in Sangamon county to Abraham Duff, son of Charles Duff, resides since 1866 near Neodesha, Wilson county, Kan.

LEADBETTER, born March 17, 1826, in Rutherford county, N. C., came with his parents in 1834 to Sangamon county, married April 22, 1856, to Martha J. Archer. They have seven children, BENNETT C., ANNA, ELIZABETH, LOUIE, WALTER L., LAURIETTA and JACKSON, and reside four and a half miles west of Springfield, on the farm settled by his father in 1834.

MYRA, born in North Carolina, married in Sangamon county to William King, who died, and she married Henry Morgan. See his name.

Terry Bradley died in 1835, and Mrs. Chloe Bradley died July 20, 1865, both in Sangamon county.

BRANCH, EDWARD, was born Dec., 1795, in Virginia, and when he was a child his parents moved to that part of Bourbon, which afterwards became Nicholas, county, Ky. He was there married Dec. 2, 1818, to Rebecca Cassity. They had four children in Kentucky, and the family moved to Sangamon county, Ill., arriving late in Oct., 1830, in what is now Rochester township, where they had two children. Of their six children—

ZERELDA E., born Nov. 19, 1821, in Nicholas county, Ky., married in Sangamon county May 16, 1839, to Joel Cantrill. See his name.

MARY J., born April 22, 1824, in Kentucky, married in Sangamon county to Robert Archer, son of Moses. See his name. He died April, 1872, leaving a widow and three daughters near Grove City, Christian county.

HONOR A., born March 24, 1827, in Nicholas county, Ky., married in Sangamon county to William A. Whitesides. See his name.

ELIZABETH A., born Jan. 9, 1830, in Nicholas county, Ky., married in Sangamon county, Sept. 25, 1848, to Joshua Graham. See his name.

LOUISIANA, born July 16, 1832, in Sangamon county, married Joseph Miller. See his name.

WILLIAM, born Feb. 28, 1835, in Sangamon county, died April 2, 1845.

Edward Branch died Aug. 1, 1835, and his widow resides with her daughter and son-in-law, Wm. A. Whitesides.

BRANSON, JOHN, was born Jan. 12, 1764, in North Carolina. He emigrated, when a young man, to the vicinity of Charleston, S. C., and married Sarah Jones. They had six children in South Carolina, and moved to Ross county, O. From there to the vicinity of Xenia, Green county, Ohio, before the Indians had entirely left. They had five children there. Some of the elder children married and remained in Ohio, but Mr. Branson with the younger members of his family, moved to Sangamon county, Ill., arriving Oct., 1822, in what is now Fancy Creek township. Of all his children—

ELI, born in South Carolina, married three times, died, leaving a family in Fulton county. His son, CALVIN, resides near Ipava, Fulton county.

ANDREW, born in South Carolina, and married Susannah Wilkinson. They both died, leaving several children near Athens, Illinois.

WILLIAM, born Jan. 9, 1791, in North Carolina, and was taken by his parents to South Carolina, in 1793. In 1811 the family moved to Chillicothe, Ohio, where he was married to Sally M. Graves, in 1815. He moved to Indiana, and from there to Sangamon county, Ill., about the time his father came; moved to Galena, and from there to DeWitt county, Ill. They had seven children, and Mrs. Sally M. Branson died May 10, 1840, in DeWitt county. In December, 1840, he was married to Martha Cooper, in Sangamon county. In March, 1847, he moved to Sangamon county, and March 28, 1848, he started overland with his family and arrived Sept. 15, 1848, in Polk county, Oregon. He had eight children by the second marriage. He died Nov. 16, 1860. His widow married Michael Shelley, and died Dec. 24, 1868, near Independence, Polk county, Oregon. Nearly all the descendents of William Branson reside in the vicinity of Sheridan, Yamhill county, Oregon. His son, B. B. BRANSON, Jun., born Sept. 4, 1830, went with his father to Oregon, in 1848, married there, Sept. 15, 1854, to Eliza E. Dickey, who was born Jan. 19, 1834, in Tenn. They have eight living children. SARAH A., born July 3, 1855, married Nov. 6, 1873, to C. O. Burgess, and resides near Sheridan. JOSEPHINE, ELIZA JANE, EPHRIAM N., ELNORA SHERMAN, LAURA V., IDA M. and ORLEY R. reside with their parents, near Sheridan, Yamhill county, Oregon.

CATHARINE, born in South Carolina, married in Green county, Ohio, to Frederick Stipp. They came to Sangamon county, and two of their daughters reside in Springfield, namely: Mrs. Wood and Mrs. Moody. Mr. and Mrs. Stipp died several years since.

KEZIAH, born in South Carolina, married in Green county, Ohio, to Jesse Sutton. They came to Sangamon county in 1823, moved to Iowa, and both died, leaving several children in VanBuren county, Iowa.

JOHN, Jun., born Oct. 15, 1795, near Charleston, S. C. He was a teamster from Ohio during the war of 1812, and has a crippled hand from an injury received while on duty. He was married, Sept. 12, 1817, in Clarke county, Ohio, to Ann Cantrall, daughter of Zebulon Cantrall, who was a brother of William G., Levi and Wyatt. They had one child, ZEBULON, born June 20, 1818, in Clarke county, Ohio, married August, 1840, in Sangamon county, to Rachel Braugher, and soon after moved to Fulton county, where five children were born, namely: EMILY, CAROLINE, ISAAC, MARION and ZEBULON, jun. Zebulon Branson enlisted in the 103d Ill. Inf. for three years, in 1862. He was 1st Lieut., and was killed June 27, 1864, while leading his company in a charge on the rebel fortifications at Kennesaw Mountain. His family reside near Ipava, Fulton county. Mrs. Ann Branson died, and *JOHN* Branson was married, Sept. 12, 1822, in Champaign county, Ohio, to Miriam Thomas. They had five children, namely: THOMAS and CATHATINE, twins, born Dec. 1, 1823; THOMAS married, Feb. 4, 1847, to Eliza C. Kiger, who was born March 13, 1830, in Winchester, Va. They had three children. MARIA T. died, aged ten years. CATHARINE W., born May 25, 1850, married March 25, 1869, to Thomas Neal. They had three children, namely: *Charles N.*, died in infancy; *Thomas* and *Coke* reside with their parents, in Mitchel county, near Cawker City, Kansas. CHARLES, born March 11, 1852, resides with his mother. Thomas Branson died March 5, 1864, and his widow resides eight miles northwest of Springfield. CATHARINE, the other twin, married Rev. Hardin Wallace. They have two children, namely: Mrs. E. M. Sharp, of Mason City, Ill., and Mrs. Carlton Gatton, of Middletown, Ill. Mr. and Mrs. Wallace reside at Bath, Mason county, Ill. CAROLINE married Giles Woods. They have seven children, and reside near Waverly. MARIA married Samuel C. Woods. They have one child living, and Mrs. W. died, August 20, 1875. Mr. Woods resides near Waverly. EMILY married Rev. Joseph H. Hopkins. They had one child, and mother and child died in 1848, at Whitehall, Ill. Mrs. Miriam Branson died, and John Branson married,

Nov. 8, 1840, to Mrs. Mary Humphreys, whose maiden name was McKinnie. They had two children. MINNIE married George P. Brahm. They had one son CLAUDE, and Mrs. B. died, May 17, 1872. Mr. Brahm, with his son, resides at Kinney, Logan county, Ill. JOHN L. enlisted in 1862, for three years, in the 13th Ill. Inf. Served about one year, and was discharged on account of physical disability. He married Nellie Cain. John Branson and wife reside one and a half miles northwest of Salisbury. He is in his eighty-first year.

THOMAS, born Feb., 1798, in South Carolina, was married Aug. 12, 1829, in Clark county, O., to Eleanor Thomas, and came to Sangamon county with his father in 1822. They had three children, and Mrs. B, died in Sangamon county Jan 24, 1840. Thomas Branson married Louisa Cole. They had five children, and in 1857 moved to Texas. Of Mr. B.'s children by the first marriage, ADALINE, born Oct. 9, 1833, was married Oct. 3, 1849, to W. S. Dunham, of Waynesville, DeWitt county, Ill., where she died May 29, 1852. ALIDA, born Sept. 21, 1837, in Sangamon county, Ill., is unmarried, and resides in Mansfield, Texas. REBECCA, born Nov. 30, 1839, in Sangamon county, married Lieut. Frank King, U. S. A., in Dallas county, Texas, Oct. 14, 1862. Lieut. King was killed in Louisiana, May 8, 1864. Mrs. King was married Nov. 2, 1865, to Rev. D. D. Leech, in Dallas county, Texas, and she died Aug. 23, 1866, in Ellis county, Texas, leaving one child, FRANK K., born Aug. 22, 1866, in Ellis county, and resides with his aunt Alida, in Tarrant county, Texas.

Of the children of the second marriage, ELEANOR, born March 10, 1842, was married Dec. 24, 1862, to Samuel Uhl, of the 12th Texan Dragoons. They have five children, viz: SUE E., ADDIE C., LOUISA, CHARLES and ALMA. and reside in Dallas county, Texas. EMILY, born May 21, 1844, in Sangamon county, married April 10, 1867, to Thomas Uhl, in Dallas county, Texas. They have one child, WILLIAM S., and reside in Dallas county. THOMAS C., born April 27, 1848, in Sangamon county, Ill., was married July 1, 1875, to Virginia Hill, in Dallas county, where they now reside. BENJAMIN L., born Oct. 7, 1850, in Sangamon county, is unmarried, and resides in Lancaster, Dallas county, Texas. AUGUSTA, born June 13, 1853, in Sangamon county, married Aug. 24, 1873, to F. Fox, and resides in Slate Spring, Miss. Thomas Branson died Oct. 21, 1864, and Mrs. Louisa Branson died July 5, 1865, both near Lancaster, Dallas county, Texas.

MARY, born in Green county, O., married in Sangamon county, Ill., Sept. 23, 1824, to Abraham Onstott. They have five children. Mrs. Onstott died June, 1875. The family reside in Clinton, DeWitt county.

REBECCA, born in Ohio, married Elijah Harper, and died, leaving several children in Clark county O.

BENJAMIN B., born Feb., 1810, in Ross county, O., married in Mechanicsburg, Sangamon county, Ill., May, 1837, to Mary Thompson. They have two children, viz: HENRIETTA, born Aug. 27, 1839, on Fancy creek, Sangamon county, married in Mechanicsburg, Aug. 27, 1861, to A. G. Barnes. See his name. HENRY, born Dec. 2, 1842, on Fancy creek, married June, 1867, in Jacksonville, Ill., to Clara L. Lathrop. They have two children, and reside at Ottawa, Kan. Benj. B. Branson and wife reside in Jacksonville, Ill.

NANCY, born June 4, 1806, in Ohio, married in Sangamon county to Dr. Charles Winn, who was born Aug. 13, 1800, in Virginia. He received his medical education at Transylvania University, Lexington, Ky. He came to Sangamon county and practiced his profession on Fancy creek; moved from there to Waynesville, Ill., and from there to Springfield, O. They had seven children. CORILLA died Nov. 8, 1855, aged twenty-five years. BYRON died March 16, 1854, at McKendree College, in his twenty-first year. RICHARD D. died in St. Joseph, Mo., March 15, 1872, in his thirty-eighth year. CHARLES L., born Nov. 11, 1838, married July 22, 1859, in Jackson county, Mo., and died, leaving a widow and two children in Kansas City. ROBERT B., born July 11, 1840, resides in Chicago. EMMA H., born Dec. 29, 1842, near Springfield, O., married in Sangamon county to A. G. Pickrell. See his name. FLORENCE M., born June 12, 1846, near Springfield, O., married

William T. Hall. *See his name.* Dr. Charles L. Winn died Aug. 17, 1847, near Springfield, O., and Mrs. Nancy Winn died Nov. 4, 1852, at Columbus, Adams county, Ill.

Mrs. Sarah Branson died in Ohio, and her husband, John Branson, Sen., died in 1845, in Sangamon county, Ill., aged eighty-one years.

BRAUGHTON, PETER, was born July 6, 1812, in Worcester county, Mass. His parents moved to Ross county, O., in 1816, and a few years later to Pickaway county, about ten miles south of Columbus. In 1836 Peter came to Springfield, Ill., and soon after settled in what is now Williams township. He was married in Sangamon county Sept. 30, 1846, to Mary D. Utterback. They have four children, all born in Sangamon county, namely—

SUSAN E., NANCY A., EMILY J. and THOMAS J.

Peter Braughton resides in Williams township, three miles each from Sherman and Barclay.

BRAUGHTON, JACOB, an elder brother to Peter, came with him to Sangamon county in 1836. He never married, but was engaged in farming for several years. He started overland to California, and died on the road, between 1850 and 1855.

BRAUGHTON, WILLIAM, a brother to Jacob and Peter, came to Sangamon county in 1846, too late to be included as an early settler. He resides one and a half miles north of Barclay. His son Adam married into the family of Simeon Taylor. *See his name.*

BRAWNER, JOHN, a twin brother to William, was born Aug. 9, 799, in Maryland. His parents moved to Fayette county, Ky., when he was a child. He was married May 20, 1819, in Madison county, to Bethany Ball. They had four children in Kentucky, and moved, in connection with her mother, brothers and sisters, to Sangamon county, Ill., arriving in the fall of 1829 in what is now Woodside township, where they had three children. Of their seven children—

NANCY, born in Kentucky, married in Sangamon county to R. M. Thompson. They moved to Iowa, had nine children, and she died. Of their children, HENRY resides with his aunt, Mrs. J. B. Ogden.

JOHN was a soldier in an Iowa regiment, and died in the army. THOMAS E. served three years in the 55th Ill. Inf., re-enlisted, and served to the end of the rebellion. He is married, and resides in Alton. The other children are scattered.

BASIL, born in Kentucky, married in Sangamon county to Sarah Pulliam, and live in Iowa. *See Pulliam.*

ELIZABETH A., born in Madison county, Ky., married in Sangamon county to Thomas Knotts, have six living children, and reside in Ball township.

MARY E., born in Madison county, Ky., married in Sangamon county to Joseph B. Ogden. *See his name.*

JOHN S., born in Sangamon county, married and died, leaving a widow and seven children.

LEWIS, born in Sangamon county, married Hannah Dragoo. He died, leaving a widow and three children in Cotton Hill township.

MARTHA J. married Abraham Bennington. They have four children, and reside in Montgomery county.

Mrs. Bethany Brawner died about 1839, and John Brawner died in 1841, both in Sangamon county.

BRAWNER, WILLIAM T. was born August 9, 1799, in Maryland. His father died when he was seven years old, and his mother moved to Madison county, Ky., when he was eighteen years old. He was there married, Dec. 25, 1822, to Elizabeth Ball. They had three children in Kentucky, and the family moved to Sangamon county, Ill., arriving in Oct., 1829, in what is now Curran township, where they had seven children, namely:

JOHN S., born Nov. 18, 1818, married in Sangamon county, to Nancy McCredy; have eight children, and reside in Adair county, Mo.

MARY born Oct. 23, 1825, in Kentucky, married in Sangamon county to William C. Hillerman; had six children, THOMAS A., JACOB, RUTH, HULDAH, FRANKLIN and MARY, and Mrs. Hillerman died, March 18, 1869. Mr. H. married in 1870 to Rebecca Drennan. They have one child, ANN E., and reside in Chatham.

COLUMBIA, born Dec. 18, 1827, in Kentucky, is unmarried, and resides with her mother.

MINERVA, born May 11, 1830, in Sangamon county, married William Duval, have eight children, and reside in Knox county.

JAMES H., born March 23, 1833, in Sangamon county, married Martha A. McGinnis. They have three children, SALLY, ROBERT S. and WILLIAM P., and reside in Chatham township.

ELIZA H., born Oct. 28, 1835, in Sangamon county, is unmarried, and resides with her mother.

CLARISSA, born April 1, 1838, married Nelson Combs, and died in March, 1864, about five months after marriage.

WILLIAM M., born Sept. 27, 1840, in Sangamon county, married April 7, 1870, to Isabel Works, who was born August 12, 1847, in Owen county, Ky. They have one child, JOHN H., and reside in Curran township.

LEWIS B., born Jan. 20, 1843, in Sangamon county, married April 18, 1872, to Laura F. Tippitt, who was born Sept. 12, 1856, in Owen county, Ky. They have one child, ELIZABETH, and reside in Curran township.

ISAAC, born Nov. 5, 1845, died at ten years of age.

William T. Brawner died Nov. 12, 1846, and his widow resides in Curran township, south of Lick creek.

BRECKENRIDGE, PRESTON, was born Aug. 5, 1807, near Paris, Bourbon county, Ky. The name of Breckenridge originated in a singular manner. In one of the wars in Scotland between the Protestants and Roman Catholics, a family by the name of McIlvain particpated on the side of the Protestants, who were defeated. Some of the McIlvain brothers saved their lives by taking refuge under a low shrub, called *brack*, which grows on the ridges in the Highlands of Scotland. This circumstance so impressed them, that they determined to give themselves a new name, hence Brack-on-ridge. As Protestants, the Breckenridges took part in some of the wars in Ireland at a later period, in which the great, great grandfather of Preston was a leader. The Protestants being again defeated, two of the Breckenridge brothers fled to America. One of them settled in Pennsylvania, and the other in Virginia. Their first names are not preserved, but the descendants of the one who settled in Pennsylvania have retained the original spelling: Brackenridge. The brother who settled in Virginia raised a family, among whom was one son Alexander, who had a son Robert, who had a son John, who had two sons, Robert Jefferson, known as the late Rev. R. J. Breckenridge, D. D., of Kentucky, and Joseph Cabell, the latter of whom was the father of John C. Breckenridge, ex-Vice-President of the United States. The first Alexander also had a son George, who had a son Alexander. He was twice married, and the eldest child by the second wife was Preston, whose name heads this sketch. Preston Preckenridge was married in Nicholas county, Ky., Nov. 17, 1827, to Catharine Moler, who was born in that county Aug. 30, 1804. They had four children born in Kentucky, and the family moved to Sangamon county, Ill., arriving Oct. 16, 1834, in what is now Cotton Hill township, east of Sangamon river, where eight children were born, one of whom died in infancy. Of their eleven children—

ALEXANDER, born Oct. 31, 1828, in Nicholas county, Ky., married May 25, 1852, to Martha H. Barnhill, who was born Aug. 19, 1833, in Wayne county, Ill. They had eight children, two of whom died in infancy. The other six, ELIZABETH C., MARY A., FELIX H., NANCY L., CHARLES A. and ROBERT CARROLL, reside with their parents, half a mile east of Breckenridge.

HUGH, born Dec. 9, 1829, in Kentucky, married Feb. 22, 1855, to Sarah M. Randolph, who was born June 20, 1837, in Logan county. They have two children, HERBERT C. and EDITH A. Hugh Breckenridge enlisted Oct. 10, 1861, in Co. B, 10th Ill. Cav., for three years; re-enlisted as a veteran Jan., 1864, served full term, and was honorably discharged Jan. 6, 1866, at Springfield. He resides at Breckenridge.

CORNELIUS, born March 12, 1831, in Kentucky, married Sept. 4, 1855, to Elizabeth L. Barnhill, who was born May 29, 1838, in Wayne county. They had five children, two of whom died in infancy. The other three, ELIZABETH F., WILLIAM R. and GEORGE E., reside with their parents near Breckenridge.

Yours Truly
Preston Breckenridge

JOSEPH, the last in Kentucky, born July 17, 1832, married March 28, 1855, to Sarah J. Matthew. They had two children; one died in infancy. The other, PRESTON, resides with his mother. Joseph Breckenridge enlisted Sept., 1862, in Co. E, 114th Ill. Inf., for three years. He was taken sick at Camp Butler, and died at home, Nov. 29, 1862.

ELMORE, born Nov. 4, 1834, the first of the family born in Sangamon county, married Nov., 1857, to Susannah Randolph, had six children, two died in infancy, and Mrs. B. died. The four children, LEANOR, MARY A., ELMER P. and SIMON F., live with their uncles and aunts in Missouri. He resides at Forest City, Neb.

CLEOPHAS, born Aug. 7, 1836, in Sangamon county, enlisted Aug. 18, 1861, for three years, in Co. D, 33d Ill. Inf. He was dangerously wounded at the siege of Vicksburg, but recovered, served to the end of his term, and was honorably discharged Oct. 18, 1864, at Springfield. He was married Jan. 30, 1868, to Lilian T. Cave. They have two children, INEZ and IDA, and reside with his father, three and a half miles west of Breckenridge.

CATHARINE, born June 19, 1838, in Sangamon county, married Jan. 30, 1856, to Simon P. Randolph. They had six children, three of whom died in infancy. The other three, PRESTON B., MAY and EDITH, reside with their parents at Seattle, Washington Ter.

ELIZABETH and *MARY* (twins), born Jan. 13, 1841, in Sangamon county.

ELIZABETH, married April, 1862, to James H. Abell. They had four children, EMMA J., WILLIAM A., JOHN P. and HENRY E., reside with their parents in Taylorville.

MARY, married March, 1863, to Thomas Rishton, and resides at Council Bluffs, Iowa.

PRESTON, Jun., born Dec. 11, 1842, enlisted Aug., 1862, in Co. E, 114th Ill. Inf., for three years; served full term; was honorably discharged at Vicksburg, Aug. 3, 1865; was sick at the time, but returned home with his comrades, arriving at his father's house on the 7th, and died the 8th of August, 1865, seventeen hours after his arrival.

JANE, born Feb. 9, 1845, in Sangamon county, was married August, 1864, to William Karnlage. They have three children living, LUCY J., ANNIE M. and WILLIAM, and reside at Lincoln, Ill. Mrs. Catharine Breckenridge died Feb. 4, 1847, and Preston B. was married March 29, 1849, to Lucy Robb. They had two children—

DAVID, born Dec. 28, 1850, in Sangamon county, is unmarried, and resides near Cedar Hill, Dallas county, Texas.

LUCY D., born Aug. 13, 1854, in Sangamon county, was married Oct. 13, 1874, to William H. Hunter, who was born Dec. 10, 1848, in Muskingum county, O. His grandfather, Charles Hunter, was born and married in Scotland; came to America, and settled in Muskingum county, O. His eldest son, William, was the father of William H. Hunter, the latter of whom, with his wife, reside in Cotton Hill township.

Mrs. Lucy Breckenridge died Nov. 18, 1854, and Preston Breckenridge resides on the farm settled by him in 1834. It is in the northeast corner of Cotton Hill township, three and a half miles west of Breckenridge.

Preston B.'s father was sixty-five years old when he was born. Their united ages to the present time (1876) is one hundred and thirty-four years. Preston Breckenridge was one of the representatives of Sangamon county in the State Legislature of 1851 and '2. Abraham Lincoln was a candidate before the convention, but Mr. B. beat him. Mr. B. was a member of the Sangamon county Board of Supervisors for 1873.

Preston Breckenridge remembers that the fall of 1834, when he came to the county, was dry, and continued dry through the winter; that May 12, 1835, a great rain storm set in, and rain continued to fall for about forty days and nights, which so seriously interfered with plowing and planting that but very light crops were put in. When the rain ceased, and hot weather set in, the stagnant water and decaying vegetation poisoned the atmosphere, and chills and bilious diseases prevailed to such an extent that in many cases there were not enough well persons to take care of the sick and bury the dead. That year has ever since been spoken of as the wet and sickly summer and fall.

The wheat crop looked well in the fall of '34, but it nearly all froze out, and in

—18

1835, '6 and '7, the wheat crop was a total failure, and wheat bread was so scarce that a biscuit became an object of interest, so much that women would send them to the children when visiting took place between the families.

The difficulty of obtaining food during the winter of 1835 and '6 was very great, there being nothing for bread in Central Illinois except frost-bitten corn. Good crops were raised in the southern part of the State, and those who could pay for it went there for corn. That is believed to have been the origin of calling the southern part of the State Egypt, and not because of any unusual darkness prevailing there.

BRIDGES, GEORGE, was born in 1793, in Montgomery county, Ky. He was married there in 1816, to Rebecca Lockridge. They had four children in Kentucky, and moved to Sangamon county, Ill., arriving Nov. 3, 1835, in what is now Curran township, eight miles south of Springfield, where they had five children. Of their children—

JOHN M., born in 1819, in Kentucky, died unmarried, in Sangamon county, Nov. 14, 1865.

WILLIAM, born July 15, 1821, in Kentucky, married in Sangamon county, Sept. 2, 1852, to Mary E. White. They had two living children, HORACE W. and ALICE M., and Mrs. Mary E. Bridges died Sept. 17, 1871, and William Bridges was married in Feb., 1873, to Mrs. Helen Bird, whose maiden name was Ransom. The family moved west in Sept., 1873, and William Bridges died, Jan. 30, 1874, at Grass Valley, Nevada county, California, leaving his widow and two children there.

MARGARET H., born in Kentucky, married in Sangamon county to J. M. Richardson, moved to Iowa, and died there, leaving three children.

ELIZABETH, born Oct. 14, 1827, in Kentucky, married in Sangamon county, to William Brownell. See his name.

MIRANDA, born March 27, 1831, in Kentucky, married George Brownell. See his name.

GEORGE H., born Nov. 14, 1840, in Sangamon county, married Nov. 22, 1860, in Sangamon county, to Rebecca Pyle, who was born in Sangamon county, July 6, 1850. They have four children, JOHN H., LAURA M., ADA A. and NORA L., and live in Springfield.

MARTIN C., born May 16, 1842, in Sangamon county. He enlisted August 15, 1862, in Co. B., 114th Ill. Inf., for three years. He was detailed as drummer at the organization of the regiment, promoted, Jan. 1, 1865, to drum-major, and was honorably discharged, Aug. 15, 1865. He was married, Oct. 3, 1866, in Sangamon county, to Sarah E. Drennan. They have one child, DAVID JOSEPH, and reside near Woodside, on the farm where his parents settled in 1835.

Mrs. Rebecca Bridges died in 1848, and George Bridges died in 1849, both in Sangamon county.

BRIDGES, MILTON A., was born July 20, 1810, in Montgomery county, Ky. He was there married to Mary Foster, and had two children in Kentucky. The family moved to Sangamon county, Ill., arriving Sept. 25, 1833, in what is now Chatham township, preceding his brothers, George and William. They had two children in Sangamon county. Of their four children—

THOMAS J., born Dec. 22, 1831, in Kentucky, died unmarried, in Springfield, Sept. 19, 1850.

AMANDA M., born July 10, 1833, in Kentucky, married Robert Crowder. He died, leaving a widow and three children in Christian county, two miles east of Pawnee.

CHARLES H., born Jan. 27, 1837, in Sangamon county, married to Frances A. Matthews. They had four children, MARY, the second child, died in her second year, JOSEPH M., MARSHALL and MONTE MAY, and reside in Illiopolis. Mr. Bridges is a merchant there.

MARTHA, born in Sangamon county, April 30, 1842, died in infancy.

Mrs. Mary Bridges died, and Milton A. Bridges married Mrs. Ellen H. Hatchet, who had previously been Mrs. Trumbo, and whose maiden name was Hill. Milton A. Bridges and wife live in Pawnee.

BRIDGES, WILLIAM, was born May 5, 1793, in Montgomery county, Ky. Isabella K. Lockridge was born in the same county, Nov. 10, 1796. They were there married, July 4, 1815, and had nine children in Kentucky. The family moved to Sangamon county, Ill., arriving in the fall of 1835, in what is now Woodside township, where they had two children. Of the eleven children—

MELINDA, born August 15, 1817, married H. Hathaway, who died, and she married Richard Wilkins, and they both died.

JOHN W., born June 4, 1819, died in his twentieth year.

BETSY A., born July 20, 1821, married Henry Gillen, and she died, Nov. 25, 1838.

AMANDA M., born Sept. 25, 1823, in Kentucky, married Alfred C. Malone. (See his name.)

MARILDA J., born Feb. 23, 1826, married Jacob C. Mitts. They had seven children, namely: WILLIAM, born Dec. 9, 1845, married Sarah Stroude, who was born August 24, 1844, in East Tennessee. They had two children, FRANK E. and WILLIAM J., and reside in Curran township, south of Lick creek. Of the other six children, COLUMBIA, died at eighteen years. HELEN V. and JAMES W. reside at the homestead, in Curran township. EMMA lives with her uncle, David Hermon. MARY and JOHN live with their aunt, Lucinda Neal. Mrs. Mitts died Nov. 6, 1862, and her husband died Nov. 12, 1865, both in Sangamon county.

LUCINDA, born Feb. 4, 1828, married June 14, 1849, to Erastus R. Whited. They had four children; two died young. ISABEL K. married, Dec. 29, 1869, to Jesse J. Martin. They have one child, JULIA M., and reside in Loami township. Mr. Martin was born Feb. 21, 1843, in Harrison county, West Va., enlisted Aug. 17, 1862, for three years, in 12th West Va. Inf. Served until the suppression of the rebellion, and was honorably discharged, June 16, 1865. FANNIE WHITED died Jan. 21, 1873, in the seventeenth year of her age. E. R. Whited died Jan. 4, 1860, and his widow married, April 8, 1862, to Stephen B. Neal. See his name.

EMMA B., born August 19, 1830, in Kentucky, married Isaac H. Trumbo. See his name.

JAMES M., born in Kentucky, Dec. 15, 1832, married Jan. 10, 1866, to Mary F. Drennan. They have three children, WILLIAM F., MARTHA A. and EVA MAY, and reside on the farm where his parents settled in 1835, in the southwest corner Woodside township.

WILLIS, born Oct. 20, 1836, in Sangamon county, enlisted in Co. B., 114th Ill. Inf., August, 1862, for three years. He was discharged on account of physical disability, in 1863, and died of disease contracted in the army, March 20, 1864, at home.

WILLIAM L., born Sept. 3, 1839, married Sarah Card. He died Oct. 6, 1867. His widow and one child, WALTER, reside in Menard county.

William Bridges died Jan. 3, 1873, and his widow died June 24, 1873, both on the farm where they settled in 1835. Mr Bridges was a soldier from Kentucky in the war of 1812, and drew a pension to the end of his life.

The date of birth of William Bridges and his brother George indicates that they must have been twins, or there has been a mistake in giving me the dates.

BRIDGES, WILLIAM, was born April 28, 1787, in South Carolina. The family moved to Tennessee, and when William was a young man, to Green county, O. Martha Martin was born March 11, 1784, in Clarke county, Ky. She was the third child of her parents. When they had two children the family were, with many others of the settlers, in Strode's Station, for protection against the Indians. When the savages attacked the fortification, which terminated in its destruction, the men were in the fields. The women and children collected in one of the block-houses. The men finding the fort at the mercy of the Indians, though it would be impossible to save their families, and each one looked out for his own personal safety. Mr. Henry Martin, of all the men, went alone to the block house, and by his earnest entreaties induced them to open the door. He then compelled his wife, against her protestations, to accompany him with their two children, and they at once entered a canebrake, eluded the Indians, and thus saved their lives. One old lady followed them until they crossed a stream, and when she could travel no further, concealed herself in a cave until the danger passed. The fort was burned, and all the others were slain. Henry Martin remained in Kentucky until after the birth of his daughter Martha, when he moved with his family to Green county, O. William Bridges and Martha Martin were married near Xenia, and r sided in that city until they had two children. Mr. Bridges served one year in the war with Great Britain, from the summer of 1812 to 1813. He then moved to Fayette county, Ind., where they had one child, and next moved to Sangamon county, Ill., arriving about 1824 in Buffalo Hart Grove. Of their three children—

SARAH, born Nov. 14, 1812, in Xenia, O., married in Sangamon county Feb. 12, 1829, to John Ridgeway, a cousin to Lindsay. See his name. He died, and she married Jonathan Constant. See his name.

MARGARET, born Feb. 15, 1816, in Xenia, O., married in Sangamon county to James Hill. They had two children. MARY M. married Mr. Harris, and reside at Staunton, Miami county, Kan. WILLIAM married Harriet Stafford, and reside at Clarksville. James Hill died April 17, 1844, and Mrs. Margaret Hill died Jan. 23, 1845.

ELIZABETH, born Nov. 9, 1819, near Connersville, Ind., married in Sangamon county to John C. Morgan. See his name.

William Bridges died March 12, 1833, and Mrs. Martha Bridges died Jan. 31, 1865, both in Sangamon county. They were not related to any other family of Bridges in the county.

BRITTIN, EVANS E., was born Oct. 28, 1791, in Bucks county, Pa. His father died when he was quite young. His mother, with her seven children, moved to Virginia, and from there to Ross county, O., in 1800. Evans E. was there married, Sept. 18, 1818, to Mary J. England. They had one child, and moved to what became Sangamon county, Ill., arriving in the spring of 1820, in what is now Fancy creek township, where they had eight living children. Of their children—

STEPHEN, born Aug. 20, 1819, in Ohio, married in Sangamon county to Jane McClelland. He died Nov. 28, 1862, and she died in 1864, both in Sangamon county, leaving several children.

MIRANDA, born Jan. 12, 1824, in Sangamon county, married John Canterberry. See his name.

ELIJAH, born Nov. 12, 1825, in Sangamon county, married Martha Canterberry. He died March 5, 1873, leaving a widow and two children in Marion county, Iowa.

JAMES M.

EVANS E., Jun., born Nov. 26, 1829, married Melissa Peeler, had two children, and she died. He married Elizabeth Ridgeway. They have four children, and reside near Williamsville.

WASHINGTON, born July 4, 1832, married Eliza Mallory. He died, leaving one child, LAURA E., and his widow married Thomas Glascock. See his name.

HENRY, born Jan. 8, 1835, in Sangamon county, married Dec. 9, 1856, to Nancy Mallory. They had twelve children, six of whom died young. JOHN E., HENRY E., ALBERT L., EMMA N., WILLIAM A. and ROGER E., reside with their parents. Henry Brittin lives near Cantrall, on the farm settled by his father in 1820.

MARY J., born Aug. 3, 1837, married Thomas Glascock, and she died. See his name.

ELEANOR.

Mrs. Mary J. Brittin died Aug. 11, 1846, and Evans E. Brittin resides with his children. He has twice been a pioneer. He remembers that when his mother's family moved to Ohio, they had to go into Kentucky, sometimes a hundred and fifty miles, for breadstuff. After raising grain, it was three years before they had a grist ground. All that time they beat hominy, and sifted out the finest for bread, or grated the corn and made bread in that way. Coming to Sangamon county was a renewal of that kind of life. St. Louis was the nearest point at which they could buy farming tools, salt and all other articles. For grinding meal and flour they went to the American bottom, east of St. Louis. Mr. Brittin has hauled wheat to Springfield and sold it for twenty-five cents per bushel, and has known corn to be hauled twenty-five miles and sold for six and a quarter cents per bushel in trade.

The Christian Church, organized May 15, 1820, the first in Sangamon county, built its first house of worship on Mr. Brittin's farm, near the present town of Cantrall.

BRITTON, BENJAMIN, was born June 2, 1797, in Virginia. When he was a youth his parents moved to Franklin county, Ohio. He was there married, in April, 1816, to Elizabeth Brunk. She was a sister to George Brunk, and was born Oct. 13, 1800, in Franklin county, Ohio. They had four children in Ohio, and moved to Indiana in 1824, and from there to Sangamon county, Ill., arriving in Oct., 1825, in what is now Cotton Hill township, where they had seven children. Of all their eleven children—

JOSEPH, born in Ohio, died in Sangamon county unmarried, at about fifty years of age.

REBECCA, born in Franklin county, Ohio, married in Sangamon county, to Nathaniel Duncan. Mr. D. died, and his widow married Joel Vandever, and resides in Pana. *See his name.*

James I. Dozier relates an anecdote illustrative of life among the early settlers. He remembers that Benjamin Britton hired Nathaniel Duncan to haul a load of corn to Springfield, which would be a day's work for the team. The price agreed upon was $1.37½. Twenty bushels was all he could haul. Mr. Britton went along to do his own selling. Arriving there, with all his efforts, *five cents* per bushel was the highest price he could obtain. He sold the load, paid over the whole proceeds, $1.00, but how they settled the other thirty-seven and a half cents, he does not remember. That was in 1836.

ELEANOR died, aged fourteen years.

MARGARET, born in Franklin county, Ohio, married in Sangamon county to Oscar F. Matthew. *See his name.*

HANNAH, born in Sangamon county, married Sterling Clack, moved to Nevada, Vernon county, Mo., where he died, leaving a widow and five children.

DAVID B., born and died in Sangamon county, aged 21 years.

ANDREW J., born in Sangamon county, married Sarah McDaniel, have four children, and reside near Princeton, Colusa county, Cal.

MARIA J. died at twelve years of age.

CAROLINE E., born June 6, 1834, in Sangamon county, married Geo. W. Spicer. *See his name.* He died, and she married Nathan Plummer, and resides in Cotton Hill township.

LORENZO D., born in Sangamon county, married Melissa Barfield. They had five children, and Mr. Britton died, Dec., 1872, leaving his widow and children near Clarkesdale, Christian county, Illinois.

LOUISA, born in Sangamon county, married Philip Clark, and died in Missouri.

Mrs. Elizabeth Britton died August 18, 1854, and Benjamin Britton died Jan. 21, 1868, both in Sangamon county.

BRITT, JOHN P., was born July 4, 1804, in Greenbrier county, Va. He came to Sangamon county in 1832, and was married, Dec. 1, 1833, to Sarah B. Wilson, who was born Feb. 17, 1815, in Union county, Ky. They had five living children, namely:

ZERILDA A., born Oct. 15, 1835, in Springfield, was married, Jan. 17, 1859, in Princeton, Ill., to Francis A. Haines. *See his name.*

MARY J., born August 24, 1840, in Springfield, married Feb. 19, 1868, to John G. English. They have two children, GRACE and PEARL, and reside near Taylorville, Ill.

JOHN W., born Oct. 22, 1842, in Hancock county, was married, August 17, 1862, in Springfield, to Caroline Haines. She died, and he went to China. He returned to America, and was last heard from in California.

JULIA A., born Nov. 3, 1846, in Springfield, and resides with her mother.

SARAH H., born Jan. 21, 1849, in Springfield, was married March 18, 1868, in her native city, to John Branch Gilliland, who was born Feb. 29, 1848, in Decatur, Ala. They have two living children, ALICE BELLE and MARY JOSEPHINE, and reside in Springfield. Mr. G. is a printer, and has been ten years employed in the Journal office. His father, Wm. A. Gilliland, is a printer in the Register office.

John P. Britt died July 7, 1852, in Springfield, and his widow married Wm. B. Yeamans, who died August 30, 1860, and she married, Jan. 19, 1863, to Larkin Bryan, who died in 1874, and Mrs. Sarah B. Bryan resides in Springfield.

Obadiah and William Britt, brothers to John P., came to Sangamon county, and a few years later moved to Bureau county, Ill. Mrs. Jemima Britt, mother of the three brothers, came with them to Sangamon county, and went with two of them to Bureau county, where she lost her life by falling from a wagon and the wheels passing over her.

BROADWELL, JOSIAH, was born July 14, 1795, in Morris county, N. J. His father, Simeon Broadwell, was a brother to Moses Broadwell, represented in this book. A cousin to Moses and Simeon — Baxter Broadwell — was the father of Judge Norman M. Broadwell, of Springfield, a sketch of whom may be found in connection with the name of his father-in-law, Washington Iles. Josiah Broadwell went to Dayton, O., in 1815, and married near the city May 31, 1827, to Priscilla Custid. She died, leaving one child. Mr. B. married the second time in Dayton, Jan. 13, 1835, to Ann Comfort Custer. She died June 5, 1836, without children. Josiah Broadwell came to Sangamon county about 1840, bringing his only son—

OLIVER, who remained two or three years in Sangamon county, went to Iowa, married there to Rachel Pearson. They had six children, and he died May 12, 1873, at Pleasant Hill, Saline county, Neb. His widow and children reside there.

Josiah Broadwell was married in Sangamon county, Oct. 25, 1842, to Mrs. Rachel L. Moore, whose maiden name was McCarty. They had five children, two of whom died young—

CYRUS F., born March 16, 1846, in Sangamon county. He was married Sept. 1, 1867, in Denver, Col., to Ella Goff, who was born Oct. 18, 1850, in St. Louis, Mo. They have four children. GEORGE W., born June 13, 1868, in Sangamon county; RACHEL A., born Aug. 25, 1870; DELIA E., born April 9, 1872—the two latter in Missouri—and CLINTON, born Feb. 24, 1874, near Guide Rock, Webster county, Neb., where the family now reside.

GEORGE and **JOSIAH,** Jun., live with their parents.

Josiah Broadwell and wife reside four miles west of Springfield.

BROADWELL, MOSES, was born Nov. 14, 1764, near Elizabethtown, N. J. Jane Broadwell was born Feb. 6, 1767, in the same neighborhood, and was Moses' second cousin. They were there married Nov. 5, 1788, and soon after moved to Hamilton county, O., to a fort situated where Columbia now stands, five miles above Cincinnati. In 1804 they moved to Clermont county, O. They had twelve children in Ohio, three of whom died young. They moved in a keel boat from Cincinnati to St. Louis in the spring of 1819, and the next spring came up the Illinois river on a steamboat, said to have been the first that ever ascended the latter stream. They landed at Beardstown in June, 1820, and came to Sangamon county in the latter part of June or early in July of that year, settling on the south side of Richland creek, about one mile east of where Pleasant Plains now stands. Of their nine children—

MARY, born April 27, 1791, in New Jersey, was married Dec. 19, 1807, to Henry S. Sweet, a native of New York. They had one child, and all the family died.

DAVID, born June 11, 1794, in Ohio, was married to Mrs. Mary A. Drake. She died in Menard county, Ill., and he died May 18, 1858, in Iowa.

SARAH, born Feb. 16, 1796, in Ohio, was married in Sangamon county, in 1837, to David Van Eaton. They had no family, and she is now a widow, residing with her niece, Mrs. A. B. Irwin.

JOHN B., born Sept. 27, 1797, in Hamilton county, O., was married March 29, 1817, in same county, to Betsy Pratt. They had one child at that place, and moved with his father to St. Louis, where one child was born, and from there to Sangamon county, arriving in Dec., 1819, on the south side of Richland creek, one mile east of where Pleasant Plains now stands, where one child was born. Of their three children, JANE S., born Dec. 19, 1817, in Clermont county, O., married in Sangamon county to John S. Seaman. They had six living children. JONATHAN went to New Orleans in 1857 with a drove of horses. He sold out, and expected to leave for home in a few days, but his friends never heard of him afterwards. DANIEL married in Indiana, moved to Iowa, and died May 28, 1871, in Michigan, while on his way to Mineral Springs for his health. WILLIAM enlisted at Springfield, in 1861, in what became the 11th Mo. Inf., for three years. Both his lower limbs were broken by a falling tree, while he was lying sick in tent; one limb was amputated. He went to Iowa, married, had one child, and his wife died. He resides near Jefferson, Green county, Ia. ISAAC was a sergeant in the 64th Ill. Inf. Served three years, re-enlisted as a veteran, served to the end of the rebellion, and was honorably discharged, and resides near Jefferson, Iowa. CHARLES was a Union soldier in two Illinois regiments; served out his enlistments with honor, and resides near Fredonia, Kan. CALISTA married Charles R. Pratt, and resides near Fredonia. John Seaman died in 1850, and his widow married Alexander B. Irwin. *See his name.* CINTHELIA, born Oct. 17, 1819, in St. Louis, was married in Sangamon county, Ill., to Alexander B. Irwin. *See his name.* DANIEL P., born Sept. 17, 1821, in Sangamon county, was married to Irene Holcomb. They had six children born in Sangamon county. EMMA C. married in Springfield to Benjamin Trumbull, and resides in Emporia, Kan. ALONZO was married March 6, 1874, in Bloomington, Ill., to Clara Furrow, and resides in Denver, Col. WILLIS married in Springfield to Sophronia Burge, and resides in Emporia, Kan. CHARLES resides near Pleasant Plains. HERBERT and ETTA reside with their father. Daniel P. Broadwell moved to Topeka, Kan., thence to Emporia, Kan., where Mrs. B. died, Dec. 25, 1869. Mr. B. married Mrs. Mary Kingston, and resides near Emporia. Mrs. Betsy Broadwell died Sept. 30, 1823, and John B. Broadwell was married March 10, 1825, to Elizabeth King, sister of John and Jeremiah King. They had six children. WILLIAM married Cynthia McMurphy, and died, leaving a widow and three children in Sangamon county. They reside in California. MOSES J., born March 6, 1827, was married in Iowa to Mary A. Cann, in Sept., 1862. They reside in Denver, Col. MARTHA married William Macon, and died in California. HARRIET married A. Poppeno, and died, leaving three children in Sangamon county. FRANCIS M., born May 15, 1836, in Sangamon county, was married in Davis county, Iowa, to Sarah Allen, moved to Denver, Col., and died there. HENRY C. is on the Pacific coast. Mrs. Elizabeth Broadwell died July 23, 1840, in Sangamon county, and John B. Broadwell resides partly near Fredonia, Kan., and with his daughter, Mrs. Irwin, in Sangamon county.

WILLIAM, born April 27, 1799, in Hamilton county, O., was married in Sangamon county, Dec. 15, 1821, to Margaret Stevenson. They had one son, WILLIAM B., born Jan. 3, 1825, in Sangamon county. He laid out the town of Broadwell, in Logan county. He was married, and resides in Hutchinson, Reno county, Kan. William Broadwell was killed at Old Sangamo, in Sangamon county, Ill., Nov. 22, 1824, while assisting in raising a barn. His widow married Richard Latham. *See his name.*

CHARLES, born Dec. 3, 1800, in Hamilton county, O., was married Jan. 9, 1825, in Sangamon county, to Ellen Carman, daughter of Jacob Carman. They had eight children, JACOB, SILAS, RACHEL, HELEN, ADELIA, MARGARET and MARY A. The latter married A. P. Brereton, and resides in Pekin. Charles Broadwell moved to Pekin, and died in 1854. His widow resides there.

JEFFERSON, born June 9, 1805, in Clermont county, O., died Dec. 10, 1830, in Sangamon county.

CYNTHIA, born Nov. 2, 1807, in Clermont county, was married, May 21, 1826, in Sangamon county, to William Carson. *See his name.*

EUCLID, born Oct. 7, 1809, in Clermont county, O., was married in Sangamon county Dec. 12, 1833, to Laura Farrington. They had eight children, some died young, and the family moved to Iowa. LOUISA, born Aug. 27, 1836, was married Feb. 21, 1861, in Van Buren county, Iowa, to D. S. Jamison, who was born Aug. 25, 1822, in Westmoreland county, Pa. They have four children, ELSWORTH, CORA, SHERMAN and HON. They reside at Keosauqua, Van Buren county, Iowa. ROSALINE, born March 1, 1839, was married Feb. 16, 1860, to Rev. J. W. Roe. They had six children, ALLEN, CLARA, WILLIAM, LAURA, CHARLES and JOHN. Mrs. Rosaline Roe died July 30, 1874, at Malvern, Mills county, Iowa. MARIA, born Sept. 21, 1841, married Aug. 3, 1863, to Ephriam Farrington. They have two children, ELSIE and EVA, and reside at Belle Plain, Sumner county, Kan. CHARLES, born April 28, 1846, died Oct. 1, 1875, in Denver, Col. MILLIARD F., born Aug. 16, 1850, resides at Niles, Van Buren county, Iowa. ELLA, born Aug. 5, 1853, in Macon county, Ill., was married March 31, 1872, to Dr. C. L. Crooks. They had two children,

CLARK and BESSIE, and reside at Cantril, Van Buren county, Iowa. Euclid Broadwell died Feb. 12, 1874, at Niles, and his widow resides there.

Moses Broadwell is said to have built the first brick house in Sangamon county. He died April 10, 1827, and his widow died March 8, 1836, both in Sangamon county, Ill., where they settled in 1820.

BROOKS, REV. JOHN F., was born Dec. 3, 1801, in Oneida county, N. Y. His parents were of New England origin, but emigrated to New York in 1792, when the whole region was a forest, with here and there a small settlement. Mr. Brooks graduated at Hamilton College, in that county, in 1828, and afterwards studied three years in the theological department of Yale college, New Haven, Conn. He was ordained to the gospel ministry by Oneida Presbytery, in the autumn of 1831, and was married soon after to a daughter of Rev. Joel Bradley. They immediately left for Illinois, under a commission from the American Home Missionary Society. They traveled by canal, lake and stage to Pittsburg, thence by steamboat, down the Ohio river to New Albany, Ind. Any route to Illinois by way of Chicago, in those days, was not to be thought of, as that place was just emerging from the condition of an Indian trading station. At New Albany Rev. Mr. Brooks purchased a horse and "Dearborn," as it was then called, which was a one horse wagon with stationary cover. In this they continued their journey, crossing the Wabash river at Vincennes. After passing a skirt of timber on the west side, they entered the first prairie of Illinois, in the midst of a furious storm. They were far from any house, with only the carriage as a protection, and that in danger of being upset by the gale. They weathered the storm, however, by turning the back of their carriage to it, but the prairie was covered with water, and they could only discern the path by observing where the grass did not rise above the water. They sought a house to dry their garments, and that night arrived at Lawrenceville, where Rev. Mr. B. preached his first sermon in Illinois, the next day being Sabbath. About three days after they arrived at Vandalia, the State capital, having been five weeks on the way from the vicinity of Utica, N. Y.

After visiting several towns and villages, Rev. Mr. Brooks located for the winter at Collinsville, in the southern part of Madison county, preaching, alternately, there and at Belleville. In the spring of 1833 he moved to the latter place, where he continued five years, preaching there, and at several other points in St. Clair and Monroe counties.

About the second year of his residence at Belleville, he and his wife opened a school, which increased so rapidly they employed an assistant. They taught all grades, from A, B, C, to the classics and higher mathematics. Several attended that school, who afterwards entered the halls of legislation, and other departments of public life. In 1837 Mr. Brooks was chosen principal of a Teachers' Seminary, which benevolent individuals were endeavoring to establish in Waverly, Morgan county. He taught there with success, but the general embarrassment of the country, caused by the financial disasters of 1837, compelled a relinquishment of that enterprise. During the time he was teaching he endeavored to preach one sermon every Sabbath, but the double labor induced bronchial affection, from which he has never fully recovered. In 1840 Mr. B. was called to Springfield to take charge of an academy for both sexes, though in different apartments, to be taught in a new brick edifice erected for that purpose on the west side of Fifth street, between Monroe and Market. Here he continued his labors, with the aid of two assistants, for two years and a half. Many persons now prominent in business or in domestic life, received a portion of their education there. After this he labored for two years under direction of Presbytery supplying vacant churches in this and adjoining counties. His health was now much impaired, and designing light labor, he opened a school for young ladies in a small room near his own house. The applications soon outran the size of the room, which he enlarged, and his wife again assisted him. His school increased, his health improved, and he purchased the property on the corner of Fifth and Edwards streets, re-arranging the two-story frame building internally to suit the purposes of a school. This he opened as a Female Seminary, the Autumn of 1849, with three assistants, and Mrs.

Brooks in charge of the primary department, held in the room he previously occupied. In addition to the usual course, Mr. Brooks added drawing, painting and music; two pianos were introduced, and this is believed to have been the first effort at teaching music in the schools of Springfield. This Seminary prospered for four years, when Mrs. Brooks' health failed, and it became necessary to close the institution. Since her death in 1860, Rev. Mr. Brooks has devoted a large part of his time to hearing classes, and giving private lessons.

He was one of seven young men who banded together, while in their theological course in New Haven, for the establishment of a college in this State. Illinois College, at Jacksonville is the result of their exertions. Mr. Brooks has been one of its trustees from the first.

He relates, as an illustration of the change of times in attending Presbytery in the State since he entered it, that a clergyman in those days must have his horse and saddle as certainly as his Bible and hymn book. The settlements were remote from each other, and a ride of three or four days to a meeting of Presbytery was a common experience. Once, in attending such a meeting, Mr. Brooks traveled in an easterly direction from Bellville, for two or three days, and found a sparse settlement, mostly of log cabins. They had erected a frame church building and roofed it, without siding or floor, with only a few rough boards for seats. The Presbytery opened its sessions, several sermons were preached, the sacrament administered, but rain came on before that body adjourned, and they moved to a private house, with only one room and a small side apartment. At meal time Presbytery adjourned, that the table might be spread, and after evening service, six or seven members lodged in the same room, on beds spread on the floor. People, in sustaining religious worship under such circumstances made as great sacrifices, according to their means as those who build their $50,000 churches do now. At this meeting Mr. Brooks was entertained at a cabin where the only light admitted was through an open door, or one or two sheets of oiled paper, in place of glass windows. He met a man, however, in that settlement, from his native town, in New York, and he had two glass windows, but his neighbors thought him extravagant, and somewhat aristocratic to indulge in such a luxury. Rev. Mr. Brooks resides west side of Fifth, between Edwards and Cook streets, Springfield, Illinois.

BROWNELL, JOHN, was born Aug. 14, 1800, in Rhode Island. During his infancy his parents moved to Seneca county, N. Y. He came west with the family of William Seely. Mr. B. and the other members of his family came by water to Shawneetown, and from there in wagons, arriving in what is now Ball township, July 5, 1819. John Brownell was married to Nancy Pulliam, in 1821. Of their eleven children born in Sangamon county, two died in infancy. Of the nine living—

WILLIAM, born Dec. 10, 1822, in Sangamon county, was married Jan. 20, 1848, to Elizabeth Bridges. They had four living children, and Mrs. B. died, Feb. 17, 1869. Mr. Brownell was married in Sangamon county, Dec. 29, 1869, to Sarah E. Vaughan, who was born Mar. 3, 1840, in Kentucky. They had two children. Of the children by his first marriage, MARGARET J., born Nov. 24, 1848, in Sangamon county, was married Nov. 3, 1866, to John M. Sutton, who was born July 29, 1845, in Michigan. They have three living children, WILLIAM N., DELLA M. and HURTIE E. J. M. Sutton resides in Auburn. JOHN W., MIRANDA I. and COLUMBUS V., and by the second marriage, ORAH V. and EDWARD, reside with their father. William Brownell and family reside in Auburn.

WILSON K., born Jan. 18, 1825, in Sangamon county, was married May 17, 1855, to Sarah Murphy, a native of Maine. They had two children, ELIZA and SARAH, and Mrs. B. died, Feb., 1859. Wilson K. married Polly A. Lawson. They had four children, who all died. Mrs. Polly Brownell died, and Wilson K. resides in Ball township.

GEORGE W., born July 16, 1827, was married Jan. 20, 1848, in Sangamon county, to Miranda Bridges. They had ten children. MARY ISABEL, born Nov. 5, 1848, was married May 26, 1864, to Henry Willard, who was born in Missouri in 1841. They had two children,

IDA A. and GEORGETTA. Mr. W. died, and she married May 20, 1869, to Calvin McClure, who was born in Ohio Feb. 10, 1829. They had one child, GERTRUDE. Mr. McClure died March 15, 1873, and Mrs. McC. married James McCulley, who was born Aug. 18, 1848, in Sangamon county. They have one child, ISAAC F., and reside in Chatham township. JOHN L., born June 7, 1850, was married Aug. 27, 1873, to Susanna Graves, who was born Feb. 14, 1849, in Macoupin county. They have one child, CLARENCE H., and reside near Taylorville, Ill. WILLIAM W., born Aug. 2, 1852. BEBECCA E., born Jan. 15, 1855, in Sangamon county, was married Nov. 13, 1872, to James Hurst. They have one living child, WILLIAM. MELISSA M., born Jan. 25, 1856, married Nov. 20, 1873, to Isaac Bowls, who was born in Ohio, in Dec., 1852. JOSEPH S., NANCY J., GEORGE H., VIOLA M. and CHARLES E.; the latter died in infancy. All the other unmarried children reside with their parents, near Taylorville, Christian county, Ill.

MARY A., born Dec. 12, 1829, was married March 13, 1849, to Pleasant Kent, who was born in Ohio. They had twelve children, seven living. One child, ELIZA, married William Miller. They have two children, and reside in Woodside township, Sangamon county.

IRRILDA J., born June 26, 1832, in Sangamon county, was married Feb. 22, 1853, in same county, to L. T. Porterfield, who was born May 16, 1833. They had eight children; two died young. Of the other six, JOHN H., MARIA M., AMANDA J., FRANCIS L., MARY L. and HATTIE J. L. T. Porterfield died April 26, 1869. His widow and children reside in Auburn, Sangamon county, Ill.

ELIZABETH M., born Dec. 9, 1835, in Sangamon county, was married July 29, 1856, in same county, to Milton Pike, who was born June 5, 1823. See his name. They had eight children; one died in infancy. ALICE and LILLIE, twins, born June 5, 1857; Lillie died June 13, 1867, and Alice died April 9, 1872. MARY M., EDDIE F., HATTIE T., FREDDIE B, and MINNIE A. Mr. Pike and family reside in Auburn, Sangamon county, Ill.

MARIA L., born July 24, 1838, was married June 2, 1857, in Sangamon county, to Joseph C. Campbell, who was born in Wayne county, Ill. He enlisted Sept. 6, 1861, in Co. I, 29th Reg. Ill. Vol. Inf., died Sept. 15, 1864. His widow married James Rape, and they reside near Taylorville, Ill.

FRANKLIN, born Aug. 23, 1843, married Sarah Reed. They had four children; two died young. They reside in Ball township.

FRANCIS M., born April 3, 1846, in Sangamon county, was married Sept. 4, 1871, in Macoupin county, to Emma Brooks, who was born Jan. 28, 1844, in Kent county, Delaware. They reside in Auburn.

Mrs. Nancy Brownell died Aug. 28, 1856, and John Brownell was married March 29, 1860, to Mrs. Maria L. Watts, whose maiden name was Allen. They reside in Ball township, on land entered by Mr. Brownell in 1822.

BROWN, WILLIAM, was born April 19, 1779, in Frederick county, Virginia. The family have a record reaching back through his father, James Brown, born April 19, 1742, O. S., in Spotsylvania county, Va., to his father, James Brown, born April 29, 1708, O. S., in Middlesex county, Va., whose parents emigrated from England. James Brown, the father of the subject of this sketch, emigrated from Virginia to Bourbon county, Ky., in 1784. William Brown was married in 1805, in Fayette county, Ky., to Harriet B. Warfield, who was born March 3, 1788. They had ten children; one died in infancy; all born at the family residence except the eldest, who was born at the Warfield homestead, near Bryan's Station, Fayette county, Ky. William Brown was a successful lawyer, and for several years before leaving Kentucky, his home was a country seat, overlooking the town of Cynthiana, and the valley of the Licking. He led a company of volunteers from Kentucky, in the war of 1812, in which he won the title of Colonel. He represented Harrison county in the Legislature of Kentucky, and later represented his district in Congress. He, in company with his son-in-law, James D. Smith, explored the central region of Illinois, and in 1832 made large purchases of land in and around Island Grove, in Sangamon county. He brought his family the year following, and after providing for the erection of a country residence, made his home in Jacksonville, Morgan county, where, after a brief illness, he died, Oct. 6, 1833. Of their nine children who accompanied them to Illinois, four never resided in Sangamon county, viz: *ELISHA W., ELIZA C.* and *SARAH H.* reside at Boonville, Cooper county, Mo. *WILLIAM* made Jacksonville his home, brough up a family of children, and died there, after a life full of usefulness and honor, in 1871. Of the other five children—

JAMES N., born Oct. 1, 1806, at Bryan's Station, Fayette county, Ky., was married near Cynthiana, Ky., to Polly A. Smith. They had three children in Kentucky, all of whom died in infancy. They moved to Sangamon county, Ill., where six children were born, one of whom died in infancy. JAMES N., Jun., born July 13, 1836, died Feb. 8, 1851. WILLIAM, born June 11, 1839, was married, Oct. 18, 1865, in Covington, Ky., to Sally R. Smith, who was born Feb. 1, 1847, in Harrison county, Ky. They had three children, all of whom died in infancy. Mrs. Sally R. Brown died May 6, 1870, at Island Grove. Mr. B. resides at the family homestead. CHARLES S., born Oct. 11, 1841, was married Jan. 15, 1874, in Middletown, Butler county, Ohio, to Sarah E. Bonnell, who was born there, May 30, 1843. They reside at the family homestead. BENJ. WARFIELD, born Oct. 10, 1844, resides at the homestead, three miles west of Berlin, Sangamon county. MARY H., born March 19, 1848, and was married Jan. 4, 1872, at Island Grove, to Samuel N. Hitt, who was born Sept. 20, 1834, in Bourbon county, Ky. He enlisted Sept. 21, 1861, at Camp Butler, in the 10th Ill. Cav., and was elected 1st. Lieut., was promoted through all the grades to Col., and was honorably discharged, Dec., 1866. Mr. and Mrs. Col. Hitt had two children; one died in infancy. MARY B. resides with her parents, half a mile east of New Berlin, Sangamon county. Capt. James N. Brown, Sen., represented Sangamon county in the Legislature of Illinois for the years 1840, '42, '46 and '52. During the session of the last named year he drafted a bill and secured its passage, which led to the organization of the Illinois State Agricultural Society. He was elected its first President, Jan. 5, 1853, and re-elected in 1854. He held, to the day of his death, offices of public trust, but whilst giving much of his time to the State, his love for agriculture was not abated, nor his active duties in her pursuits neglected, and to his sagacity and persistant life-time efforts is Illinois largely indebted for her prominence as a producer of short horn cattle. For more than a third of a century he was a member of the M. E. church, and his active christian life closed Nov. 16, 1868. His widow, Mrs. Polly A. Brown, died May 18, 1873, both where they settled in 1833. Their remains are interred in Wood Wreath Cemetery.

RUTH ANN, born April 29, 1812, married James D. Smith. *See his name.*

MARY, born March 3, 1814, was married in 1831, in Kentucky, to Barton S. Wilson. They moved from Jacksonville, Ill., to Island Grove, in 1835, and thence, in 1837, to Boonville, Mo., where Mrs. Wilson died, in 1858, but three children survive her, viz: Mrs. REBECCA Brand, JOSEPH and JOHN, all of whom, with their father, reside in Neosho, Newton county, Missouri.

REBECCA, born Jan. 4, 1819, was married in Jacksonville, Ill., to Charles W. Price. *See his name.*

LLOYD W., born Feb. 22, 1824, in Kentucky, graduated in arts at McKendree College, in 1842, and in medicine, from the University of Maryland. In 1847 he married Rebecca P. Warfield, of Lexington, Ky. He practiced medicine in that city one year, and came to Illinois Dec., 1848, and settled near the town of Berlin, in 1849, practiced medicine there until 1857, when he abandoned his profession for other pursuits, and moved to Boonville, Mo. He returned to Illinois in 1858, and after a brief stay in Jacksonville, settled on his farm at Lost Grove, on the line between Sangamon and Morgan counties. Of Dr. L. W. Brown's ten children, five died in infancy. The others are: HARRIET B., born May 1, 1852, died July 11, 1867, at her grand-father's, (Dr. Warfield) in Lexington, Ky. She is buried in Wood Wreath Cemetery, Ill. WILLIAM B., EDWARD F., REBECCA C. and LLOYD W., Jun.

Dr. L. W. Brown is a banker, and, with his family, resides in Jacksonville, Ill.

BROWN, WILLIAM B., was born Feb. 2, 1802, in Greensburg, Green county, Ky. Harriet L. Allen was born Dec. 17, 1804, in the same place. She was a daughter of Col. David Allen, a pioneer from Virginia. He took an active part in the Indian wars of Kentucky. William B. Brown and Harriet L. Allen were married in Greensburg, Dec. 31, 1822. They had five children in Kentucky, and moved to Athens, Ill., in Nov., 1833, where they had one child, and Mrs. Brown died Oct. 7, 1835. Wm. B. Brown was married in Athens, June 20, 1837, to Laura B. Buckman. They moved to Sangamo, in Sangamon county, in 1839. They had four living children. Of all his children—

DANIEL C. and *DAVID A.*, twins, were born Sept. 27, 1824, at Greensburg, Ky., and brought by their father to Sangamon county. At fifteen years of age they sawed all the lath used in building the first State House in Springfield, now the Sangamon county Court House.

DANIEL C. then served an apprenticeship to the drug business. He was married June 30, 1852, in Petersburg, to Catharine L. Cowgill. They have three living children, HARRIET CLEMANTINE, JOHN H. and ELIZA B. Daniel C. Brown has been for many years, and is now, a druggist in Springfield.

DAVID A., was reading law with Col. E. D. Baker in 1846, when the war with Mexico commenced. At the suggestion of Mr. Baker, Mr. Brown commenced raising a company. Before it was full, it was consolidated with another part of a company from Logan county, and became Co. I, 4th Ill. Inf. Mr. Brown was elected Second Lieutenant. He was with the regiment at the bombardment of Vera Cruz, and at the battle of Cerro Gordo, April 18, 1847. The next day Lieut. Brown was promoted for gallantry, as aid de camp to Col. Baker, then commanding the brigade. On returning from Mexico, Mr. Brown read law in the office of Lincoln & Herndon, and was admitted to the bar. He was then appointed Clerk of the Circuit Court of Menard county, to which office he was afterwards elected, and served in all six years, when he returned to Springfield, and practiced law for six years. He abandoned the practice, and in 1859 engaged extensively in farming at Bates, in this county. He was elected Vice-President of the State Board of Agriculture, and served four years, ending Sept., 1870, when he was elected President of the Board for two years. He was appointed by Gov. Beveridge as one of the three Railroad and Warehouse Commissioners, March 13, 1873, confirmed by the Senate the same day, and commissioned by the Governor on the 17th of the month. David A. Brown was married Dec. 8, 1852, in Sangamon county, to Eliza J. Smith. They have six living children, SALLIE C., WILLIAM J., HARRIET J. MARY E., JAY T. and CARRIE A., and reside at Bates.

WILLIAM J., born March 23, 1827, in Greensburg, Ky., raised in Sangamon county, was married at Clinton, Ill., Nov. 22, 1854, to Elizabeth M. Smith, and moved soon after to Decatur. They have three living children, HATTIE J., ANNIE and CHRISTOPHER N. In 1862 Wm. J. Brown became Capt. of Co. A, 116 Ill. Inf. He served through the battles of Chickasaw Bluff, Arkansas Post, and the siege and capture of Vicksburg. Capt. Brown resigned in 1863 on account of physical disability, took a trip to California for recruiting his health, and from that to the present time has been in the drug business in Decatur.

MARTHA T., born and died in Kentucky, in her sixth year.

JOHN H., born Feb. 17, 1832, in Greensburg, Ky., raised in Sangamon county, married in Decatur, Jan. 2, 1856, to Clara A. Stafford. They had three living children, DANIEL A., HARMON and MARY. John H. Brown was a druggist at Cairo, and was Treasurer of the city while residing there. He removed to Springfield, and continued in the same business, until failure of health induced him to visit California, where he died, at Grass Valley, April 11, 1866. His widow married Dr. Justus Townsend, and resides in Springfield.

CHRISTOPHER C., born Oct. 21, 1834, at Athens, Ill. He was married in Springfield to Bettie J. Stuart. They had three children, STUART, EDWARDS and PAUL. Mrs. Bettie J. Brown died March 2, 1869. Part of the buildings now occupied by the Bettie

Stuart Institute had been her home, and the institution was so named in honor of her memory. C. C. Brown was married June 4, 1872, in Chicago, to Mrs. Carrie Farnsworth, whose maiden name was Owsley. They have one child, ELIZABETH J., and reside in Springfield. Mr. Brown is a member of the law firm of Stuart, Edwards & Brown.

JOEL B., the eldest child of the second wife, was born March 9, 1840, at Sangamo, Sangamon county. He was married Jan. 12, 1865, to Ella S. Saunders. They have one child, BETTIE J. Mr. Brown was in the drug business in Decatur, from 1859 to 1864. He is now a member of the firm of D. & J. B. Brown, booksellers and druggists, in Springfield.

MARY L. was born Sept. 7, 1844, in Sangamon county, and married Albert H. Cowgill. See his name.

FRANKLIN B. was born Nov. 28, 1848, in Sangamon county, and resides at Minneapolis, Minn.

JAMES B. was born July 24, 1851, in Sangamon county, and resides in Springfield.

William B. Brown was a merchant in Kentucky, but on coming to Illinois he engaged extensively in land speculations. In connection with others, he took part in laying out many of the important towns in Illinois and Iowa. He died Dec. 14, 1852, in Petersburg, and his widow, Mrs. Laura B. Brown. resides with her daughter, Mrs. Cowgill, in Springfield.

BROWN, REV. JOHN H., D. D., brother to William B. Brown, came to Springfield too late to be included as an early settler. His son, Dwight Brown, is a member of the firm of D. & J. B. Brown, of Springfield. Dr. John H. Brown was Pastor of the First Presbyterian Church of Springfield for a number of years, and at the time of his death was pastor of a church in Chicago. He died in Chicago, Feb. 23, 1872, and was buried in Oak Ridge Cemetery. His widow resides on North Grand Avenue, Springfield.

BROWN, JAMES L., was born Oct. 20, 1786, in South Carolina. He was married there May 28, 1806, to Jane M. Berry, and soon after went to Union county, Ky., where they had eight children, and the family moved to Sangamon county, Ill., arriving, in 1824, in what is now Fancy Creek township, where they had three children. Of their children—

NANCY H., born Nov. 28, 1808, married George Levan, who died in 1843, and she married John D. McCumber, and she died March 6, 1872.

WILLIAM N., born May 25, 1810, in Kentucky, married Sarah Kilgour, who died, and he married Lucinda Ensor, and he died Feb. 19, 1872, in Sangamon county. His widow and six children reside in Montgomery county.

ELIZABETH C., born Dec. 23, 1812, married Enos Darnall. They had six sons, two of whom, JAMES L. and WILLIAM, are deaf and dumb, and were educated at Jacksonville. Mr. Darnall died near Wintersett, Iowa. His family reside there.

BENJAMIN F., born March 28, 1815, in Kentucky, married May 15, 1835, to Susannah Dunlap. They had seven children. MARY C. married George W. McClelland. See his name. ARMINDA M. married Owen G. Allen, and reside in Sullivan county, Mo. JOHN J. married Mary A. Short, have one child, and reside at Heyworth, McLean county. EDNA D. died Feb. 1, 1866, aged eighteen years. JAMES T. died Dec. 30, 1865, in his fifteenth year. ANNA F. married Martin McCoy, and reside in Fancy Creek township. Benjamin F. Brown died Feb. 21, 1866, and his widow resides four miles northwest of Sherman.

MARY H., born June 23, 1817, married James T. Dunlap. See his name.

THOMAS C., born Nov. 2, 1819, died, aged eleven years.

SARAH B., born April 3, 1821, married Orlando Bates. See his name.

EMILY A., born May 12, 1823, married John R. Dunlap. See his name.

MARTHA J., born April 29, 1825, married George Groves. See his name.

SUSAN F., born Aug. 27, 1827, married G. Willcockson, have six children, and reside in Lawrence county, Mo.

REBECCA H., born Feb. 24, 1832, married William D. Power, Feb. 8, 1847. They had one child, and he died March 15, 1848. His widow married March 22, 1849, to Joseph Bates. See his name.

James L. Brown died April 18, 1854, and his widow died twenty-seven days later—May 15, 1854. He was a soldier in the war of 1812, and was at the battle of New Orleans.

BROWN, THOMAS, was born Feb. 4, 1792, in South Carolina. Martha Thaxton was born May 4, 1791, in South Carolina also. They were married there, and moved to Allen county, Ky., where they had five children, and moved to Sangamon county, Ill., arriving Oct 7, 1827, in what is now Fancy Creek township, where they had one child. Of their six children—

JEMIMA, born June 1, 1811, in Allen county, Ky., married in Sangamon county to Thomas Sales. They had two children. MARGARET married William McClelland. See his name. GEORGE T. married Susannah Gardner. She died, and he married Mrs. Elizabeth Turley, whose maiden name was Cline. They have two children, THOMAS and MARGARET. George T. Sales enlisted in 1861 for three years, in Co. C, 7th Ill. Inf. He was a Lieutenant, served full term, and was honorably discharged. He lives near Athens, Ill. Thomas Sales died, and his widow married Philip Crickmour, who also died. Mrs. Jemima Crickmour now (1874) lives with her sister, Mrs. James McClelland.

Aunt Jemima—as she is called by the young people—related to the writer a good joke on herself, which serves to illustrate the manners and customs of the people at the time she come to the country. She says that when the weather was sufficiently warm to admit of it, the young people, upon going to any public meeting, would carry their shoes and stockings until they approached their destination, when they would stop and put them on. As soon as they passed out of view, on leaving, they would again stop, take them off, and carry them home in their hands. This was done in order to make them last as long as possible. She thought it a singular custom; but after seeing her associates practice it a few times, decided to try it herself. She was then about sixteen years of age. Religious meetings were held at private houses. She started on a Sunday morning to attend a meeting at the house of a neighbor, carrying her shoes and stockings in her hands. A short distance from the house she put them on, entered the meeting, and all passed off well until she started on the return, when a young gentleman accosted her at the door, and asked permission to accompany her home. This placed her in a quandary. If she wore her shoes the entire distance, it would wear them out so much earlier; if she stopped and took them off, there was reason to fear it would frighten her beau away. She was not long in deciding to wear the shoes and keep the beau. Economy in that line was thus brought to a sudden termination.

JAMES, born Nov., 1813, in Allen county, Ky. He was married in Sangamon county to Elizabeth Scott. They have three children, and live in Kansas. At the time of the "deep snow" he was but sixteen years old. It became necessary for him to carry a grist to mill on horseback. He found the traveling quite difficult, in consequence of the crust on the snow cutting the legs of his horse. A shawl belonging to some of the female portion of the family had been wrapped about his person to keep him from freezing. He tore that in two pieces, took off his suspenders, and with them tied a half of the shawl on each of the forward legs of the horse, about where the snow crust would strike them. In that way he was enabled to bring home a supply of breadstuff for the family.

JOHN, born March 4, 1815, in Kentucky, died in Sangamon county in 1842.

ELIZABETH, born in Kentucky, married in Sangamon county to William Cutwright. She died, leaving one son, DANIEL, who enlisted in the first call for 75,000 men, in 1861, and died in the army.

MARY, born Dec. 25, 1818, in Allen county, Ky., married in Sangamon county to James McClelland. See his name.

ROBERT T., born Aug. 21, 1831, in Sangamon county, married Dec. 28, 1848, to Edna M. Dunlap, who was born Jan. 13, 1832. They had seven children; the eldest died young. THOMAS, born Oct. 10, 1851, married Oct. 23, 1872, to Hattie L. Short, and live in Fancy Creek township. MARY E., JAMES F., ALEXANDER, MARGERY I., ROBERT U. and JOHN A., live with their mother. Robert T. Brown died Feb. 6, 1866, and his widow lives near Sherman.

Mrs. Martha Brown died Sept. 11, 1862, and Thomas Brown died July 23, 1868, both in Sangamon county. Their children remember that the first corn Mr. Brown raised in the county for sale, was hauled away by Abraham Lincoln, as the hired man of John Taylor, who owned the land where they lived.

BROWN, JAMES M., was born Sept. 28, 1812, in Davidson county, near Nashville, Tenn. He came to Sangamon county, arriving March 31, 1831, at the house of Gen. M. K. Anderson, east of Pleasant Plains. He was married Aug. 7, 1832, to Elizabeth Willis. They had eight living children in Sangamon county. Of their children—

MARTHA J., born Oct. 6, 1833, was married Sept. 14, 1856, to Daniel T. Hughes. They have three living children, ADA, LULIE and ARTHUR, and reside at Greenview, Ill.

CLARISSA M., born July 18, 1835, was married June 13, 1852, to J. S. Young, a native of Somerset county, Penn. They have seven living children. JOSEPHINE, born August 23, 1854, was married Nov. 20, 1873, to Charles A. Robinson, a native Michigan. They have one child, GERTRUDE L., and reside near Oak Grove, Seward county, Neb. JEREMIAH S., JAMES M., ROSA B., MARY F. DORA E. and CLARA M., and reside near Valparaiso, Saunders county, Neb.

SARAH E., born Dec. 5, 1837, was married April 20, 1856, to James K. VanDemark, a native of Ohio. They have one child, ROSA S., and reside near Valparaiso, Neb.

MARY J., born Sept. 20, 1841, married George W. Sampson. He died Oct., 1874, near Fairfield, Iowa. Mrs. Sampson and her children, JAMES and NELLIE, reside with her parents.

JOHN H., born Jan. 29, 1846, was married, August 13, 1865, to Adaline K Adams. He is now (1875) a widower, with three children, CHARLES N., JAMES W. and ZACHEUS K., and resides at Crowder, Saunders county, Neb.

JAMES T., born Dec. 13, 1848, married Amanda A. Pierce. They have one child, CHARLES E, and reside near Pleasant Plains, Sangamon county.

LAVINA F., born Jan. 19, 1854, was married Sept. 25, 1873, to Thomas Broderick. They have one child, and reside near Pleasant Plains, Sangamon county, Illinois.

JOSEPH C., born March 7, 1853, was married, Sept. 11, 1873, to Sarah A. Snook. They have one child, THEODORE O., and reside near Crowder, Saunders county, Neb.

James N. Brown and wife reside two and a half miles west of Pleasant Plains, Sangamon county, Ill.

BROWN, JOSHUA, was born May 20, 1792, in Davis county, Ky. Nancy Wilcher was born Dec., 1789, in the same county. They were there married, early in 1812. They had three children in Kentucky, and in Nov., 1818, moved to St. Clair county, Ill., and from there to what became Sangamon county, arriving April 18, 1819, in what is now Curran township, east of Archer's creek, and south of Spring creek, and later entered one hundred and sixty acres of land south of Spring creek, in Gardner township. They had five children in Sangamon county. Of their eight children—

REZIN D., born May 6, 1813, in Davis county, Ky., was married in Sangamon county, Ill., May 15, 1834, to Rachel Earnest. They had twelve children in Sangamon county. CATHARINE F., born March 7, 1835, was married Nov. 6, 1855, to John Childs, who was born Dec. 25, 1829, in Burlington, N J. They had ten children, LEONA L., JOSEPH H., NOAH H., KATIE A., JOHN D., TIMOTHY S., ANNIE R., CHARLES F., JESSIE B. and HATTIE, and reside near Warrensburg, Macon county, Ill. MARTIN V., born March 4, 1837, the day VanBuren was inaugurated President of the United States. He was married Sept. 26, 1869, to Helen M. Cecil. They have one child, and reside near Rose Hill, Henry county, Mo. MARY A., born May 7, 1838, was married Oct., 1857, to James M. Galt. They have eight children, and reside near Palmyra, Otoe county, Neb. CHARLOTTE, born Dec. 19, 1839, married Feb. 23, 1864, to Thomas B. Ray. See his name. She died Jan, 9, 1836, leaving one child, CHARLOTTE, who resides with her grand-parents, Brown. JOHN D., born March 1, 1842, married Nov. 6, 1867, to Louisa J. Cecil. They have one child, GERTIE, and reside near Mt. Rose, Mo. CHARLES F., born Sept. 14, 1843, died Sept. 30, 1853. PETER, born Aug, 6, 1845, resides in Alta City, Utah. ANNIS, born Aug. 16, 1847, married Nov 10, 1869, to

John Happer. They have two children, HOWARD H. and NELLIE, and reside near Maroa, Macon county, Ill. LUANNA, born April 8, 1849, married Oct. 17, 1872, to Frank Leverton, and reside five miles west of Springfield. EDWIN, born May, 1851, died Feb. 5, 1862. CHARLES, born Sept. 16, 1853, resides with his parents. JACOB J., born Jan. 15, 1856, died Jan., 1865. Rezin D. Brown and wife reside in the southeast corner of Cartwright township.

WILLIAM W. was born Feb. 6, 1815, in Kentucky, married in Illinois, Feb. 13, 1844, to Phœbe Poole. They had four living children. CLARINDA J., born Jan. 12, 1845, married William Ankrom, and reside in Curran township. ZILLA A., born July 5, 1848, married Henry Dewall. They have one child, and reside at Falls City, Neb. JOSHUA T., born Feb. 28, 1851, resides in Sacramento, Cal., (now, in 1873). MARY M., born Dec. 23, 1858, resides with her father. Mrs. Phœbe Brown died May 14, 1863, and William W. Brown was married Nov. 16, 1869, to Mrs. Almeda DeLaughta, whose maiden name was Parker. She was born in Livingston parish, near Lake Pontchartrain, La. They reside five miles east of Berlin.

JOHN B., born Oct., 1816, in Kentucky, brought up in Sangamon county, and died unmarried, in the spring of 1869, in Wisconsin.

JAMES M., born Jan. 1820, in Sangamon county, married Abigail Gilison. They had two children in Sangamon county, moved to Iowa, and from there to Portland, Oregon, thence to Silver mountain, California, where he was robbed and murdered, about 1867, leaving a widow and two children.

ZILLAH, born Nov. 14, 1821, in Sangamon county, was married, Jan. 12, 1840, to John Hillis, who was born April 30, 1814. They had four living children. JOSHUA W., born April 5, 1843, was married near Mt. Rose, Mason county, in 1870, to Birdie Meleane. They reside in Alma county, Colorado. MARY A., born June 29, 1845, was married April 17, 1870, to Byington Owens. They have two children, and reside in Waynesville, Ill. JAMES E. and JOHN R., born Sept., 1849. JAMES E. was married Oct. 24, 1871, to Frances N. Jennings.

They reside in Waynesville, Ill. JOHN R. is unmarried and resides in Waynesville. John Hillis died April 30, 1849, and his widow was married Dec. 30, 1856, to James Large. They had two children. Mr. Large died April 18, 1864, and Mrs. Zillah Large and family live in Waynesville, DeWitt county, Ill.

JOSHUA M., born July, 1825, in Sangamon county, married Elizabeth A. Brown. They had six children, and he died Jan. 7, 1867. His widow married William Mercer, and resides near Hamburg, Iowa.

ELMORE S., was born in 1827, in Sangamon county, enlisted in 1847, in the 4th Ill. Inf. Served one year in the Mexican war, returned home, and died in 1848.

REUBEN M., was born in Jan. 1829, in Sangamon county, was married Nov. 15, 1850, to Elizabeth J. Archer. They had six children, and Mrs. Brown died, Sept. 20, 1864. Mr. B. married Mrs. Jerusha Smith, whose maiden name was Sturtevant. The family reside in Fredonia, Kansas.

Mrs. Nancy Brown died June 2, 1847, and Joshua Brown was married May 11, 1848, to Mrs. Mary Robinson, whose maiden name was Mayhew. She died May 12, 1861, and he died Sept., 1863, on the farm where they settled in 1824.

BROWN, JACOB J., was born August 15, 1781, in Vermont. He was married Feb. 24, 1803, in Hartford, Conn., to Ann Bacon, who was born there, Sept. 19, 1786. They had four children in Hartford, and moved to Green county, Penn., where they had four children, then moved to the State of New York, and from there to Sangamon county, Ill., arriving in 1823 or '4, in what is now Gardner township, north of Spring creek, where they had two children. Of their children—

DELOS W., born Oct. 28, 1803, in Hartford, Conn., married in Sangamon county, to Ruth Morgan, and had three children. ELIZABETH married Abner Wilkinson, and died. Mr. W. and his children reside in Springfield. D. W. Brown moved, about 1856, to Atchison county, Mo., and from there to Fremont county, Iowa. He died, and his widow and two children reside near Sidney, Iowa.

AMOS W., born March 11, 1807, in Connecticut. He married three times. His second wife was Sophia Earnest. She died, leaving one child.

JAMES M., born May 16, 1809, in Connecticut. He was a soldier from Sangamon county, during the Winnebago war, came home sick, and died August 22, 1827.

MARY A., born April 27, 1811, in Connecticut. She was married three times, is now a widow Elliott, and, with two of her children, resides in Grundy county, Mo.

JULIA ANN, born August 9, 1812, in Green county, Pa., married in Sangamon county, to Jeremiah King. See his name.

LEANDER J., born March 19, 1815, married twice, and died, leaving a widow and five children near Oakford, Menard county.

HULDAH M., born April 18, 1817, in Green county, Pa., married in Sangamon county to Jesse Ankrom, and lives in Springfield.

LUCY M., born Feb. 13, 1820, in Pa., married twice, and died August 4, 1852, in Beardstown.

JACOB J., Jun., born March 8, 1825, in Sangamon county, married Nov. 4, 1850, to Emily M. Ralston. They have seven children, and live near Farmingdale.

ELIZABETH A., born Nov. 9, 1829, in Sangamon county, married Joshua M. Brown. See his name. He died and she married Wm. Mercer, and lives near Hamburg, Iowa.

Jacob J. Brown, Sen, died Oct. 11, 1839, and his widow died Oct. 21, 1873, both in Sangamon county.

BRUCE, BENJAMIN P., was born May 21, 1826, in Carroll county, Tenn. His parents moved to Morgan county, near Jacksonville, in the spring of 1830. His father died there, of cholera, in 1833. His mother, with six children, moved to Springfield in 1834, and in 1836 moved back to Morgan county, where she was married to George R. McAllister. While she lived in Springfield her son, whose name heads this sketch, was bound to Rev. Joseph Edmondson, of the M. E. Church, and taken to St. Clair county, thence to Bond county. In 1843 he went to Memphis, Tenn., and returned to Springfield in 1852, and was married June 18, 1854, to Ann Gunn, in Morgan county. He enlisted for three years, Aug. 6, 1862, in Co. H, 114 Ill. Inf. He was wounded in the right eye at the battle of Nashville, Dec. 15-16, 1864, recovered, served full term, and was honorably discharged Aug. 3, 1865. Mr. and Mrs. Bruce had four children; two died in infancy. SARAH A. died, aged twelve years. WILLIAM T. resides with his parents. Benjamin P. Bruce and wife reside three and a quarter miles northwest of Springfield.

His mother, Mrs. Mary W. McAllister, whose maiden name was Gunn, resides with him.

BRUNK, DAVID, was born Dec. 17, 1819, in Ohio, came with his brother George, his mother and stepfather, Thomas Royal, to Sangamon county, in Dec., 1824. He was married Nov. 5, 1833, to Maria Shoup. They had four children in Sangamon county, namely—

JACOB, born Nov. 5, 1834, married Emily J. Mason. They have three children, THOMAS M., CHARLES A. and ELIZABETH M., and live one half mile east of Crow's mill, in Ball township.

SARAH J. married Wm. H. Southwick. See his name.

ELLEN E. married Walter S. Carpenter. They had three children, CHARLES B. died, aged eight years, JACOB H. at three years. MARIA CATHARINE lives with her parents, in Ball township.

ANN MARIA married —— Southwick. See his name.

David Brunk died Jan. 23, 1855. His widow lives near Crow's mill, in Ball township.

BRUNK, GEORGE, was born Dec. 22, 1804, in Miami county, Ohio. At seventeen years of age he came to Sangamon county, Ill., arriving in the fall of 1821. He entered eighty acres of land in what is now Ball township, returned to Ohio, and brought his mother, and stepfather, Thomas Royal, with his brothers and sisters, to Sangamon county, and settled them on the land he had entered, where Dr. Shields now resides. He entered more land, built for himself a hewed log house, and was married Dec. 30, 1827, to Mary Boyd. She was born Jan. 1,

1806. They had eight children, three of whom died young.

AMANDA J., born April 7, 1830, married Daniel G. Jones. *See his name.*

MARY E., born Dec. 17, 1831, married Eugene Owens. They had six children. The third one, JOHN F., died at two years of age. The other five, GEO. B., DANIEL G., EMMA E., ULYSSES GRANT and ARTHUR R. reside with their mother, in Cotton Hill township.

SUSANNAH, born May 28, 1833, died March 15, 1847.

MARIA C., born Nov. 23, 1835, married Dow Newcomer. *See his name.*

EVELINE, born March 26, 1844, married Lockwood Rusk. *See his name.* She died, and left one child in Cotton Hill township.

Mrs. Mary Brunk died March, 1847, and Mr. Brunk was married March 1, 1849, to Eliza Armstrong. They had three children, namely:

MARTHA A., born Jan. 8, 1850, married Thomas J. Nuckolls. *See his name.*

THOMAS ALBERT, born July 30, 1853. He was educated under the guardianship of Philemon Stout, at Shurtleff College, and resides in Ball township.

GEORGE A., died at six years of age.

Mrs. Eliza Brunk died Oct. 4, 1860, and Mr. B. married Dec. 12, 1861, to Emily Talbott. They had two children, viz.: TALBOTT F. and JOSEPH C., who reside with their mother.

George Brunk died Sept. 2, 1868, near where he settled in 1824. His widow married Lindsay H. English, and resides two miles southeast of Springfield.

The first entry of land in Sangamon county was made Nov. 6, 1823, by Israel Archer, being the west half of the northwest quarter of section eight, town fourteen north, range fourteen west. It is in Cotton Hill township, and the Prot. M. E. church stands on a part of it now.

The second entry was made the same day, Nov. 6, by Mason Fowler. It was the east half of the southwest quarter of section twenty-seven, town fourteen, range four west, and is on Horse creek.

The next day, Nov. 7. Elijah Iles, Thomas Cox, John Taylor and Paschal P. Enos, entered the four quarters on which Springfield was laid out. This is from a newspaper article written by Geo. Brunk.

BRYAN, GEORGE, was born Feb. 15, 1758, in North Carolina. He went, or may have been taken by his parents, to Virginia, and from there to Kentucky with Daniel Boone, about 1780. There he either founded, or by his bold daring as a leader, gave the name to a primative fortification called Bryant's Station, in what became Fayette county, Ky., a few miles from where the city of Lexington was afterwards established. It will be observed that in applying the name to the fortification a letter has been added, making the name Bryant, which is erroneous. There is a tradition preserved by his descendants, that soon after the fort was established, the young women belonging to the families connected with it were washing clothes at a stream of running water on the outside of the stockade. George Bryan and some of the other young men stood guard. Not being apprehensive of danger, they permitted the Indians to place themselves between the girls and the fort. The guard quickly secured a position between the girls and the savages, and a skirmish ensued. After making the way clear, Bryan, in a loud voice, announced that he would marry the girl who would enter the fort first. They all escaped, and he, true to his word, after gaining the consent of the young lady, was married in the fall of 1781 to Elizabeth Ragan, who was born in 1760, in South Carolina. Mr. Bryan always claimed that it was first marriage of a white couple in what became the State of Kentucky. That was before the era of mills in that region of country, and his descendants have handed down the statement, in connection with the wedding festival, that he paid ten dollars for a bushel of corn meal, to make bread for the occasion. They had at least raised one crop, and Mr. Bryan rolled pumpkins into the fort as a substitute for chairs to seat the guests. They had ten or eleven children, four of them sons, and Mrs. Bryan died. Mr. Bryan was married in 1829, to Mrs. Cassandra Miller, who died in Kentucky, in 1833. In 1834 Mr. Bryan came to Sangamon county with some of his children and grand-children. Of his children, who came to this county—

NICHOLAS, born March 24, 1794, in Bourbon county, Ky. He was a soldier in the war of 1812, and was in the battle of New Orleans, Jan. 8, 1815. Soon after the close of the war, and within that year, he was married in his native county to Mary Delay Scott, who was born there Dec. 24, 1800. They had four children in Kentucky, and came to Sangamon county in 1833, settling in what is now Woodside township. Their son GEO., born in 1818, in Kentucky, married near Elkhart, Logan county, Ill., in 1839, moved to Texas and died there, leaving two children. ELIZA C., born Feb. 17, 1820, in Bourbon county, Ky., married July 25, 1837, near Springfield, Ill., to James Taylor. See his name. MARY J., born May 22, 1822, in Bourbon county, Ky., married in 1840 in Springfield, Ill., to Milton H. Wash. See his name. ROBERT A., born July 13, 1833, in Kentucky, married in Springfield, Ill., to Hannah Sperry. She died, and his residence is unknown, but it is somewhere South. Mrs. Mary D. Bryan died Dec. 25, 1843, in Springfield, Ill., and Nicholas Bryan was married in 1845 to Adelia Trumbull. They had one child, BRYANAH, and moved to the Pacific coast. Nicholas Bryan died in 1855, in San Jose, Santa Clara county, Cal., leaving his widow and daughter there.

MELINDA W., born April 11, 1797, in Bourbon county, Ky., married there in 1815 to Abraham Todd, who was born in Woodford county, Ky., in 1792. They had three children in Kentucky, and Mr. Todd died. Mrs. Todd married Thomas P. Pettus. See his name. Mr. Pettus and wife, with her three daughters by the first marriage, came to Sangamon county in 1838, and settled near what is now Woodside Station. Of the three children, ELIZA J. TODD, born April 29, 1816, in Woodford county, Ky., married in Sangamon county, April 16, 1840, to Stephen S. Ferrell. They have a family, and reside at Boscobel, Grant county, Wis. MARY A. TODD born Jan. 12, 1819, in Woodford county, Ky., married Aug. 12, 1835, in Sangamon county, to Thomas B. Morris. They have children, and reside near Wyoming, Iowa county, Wis. ANNA MARIA TODD, born Jan. 19, 1823, in Woodford county, Ky., married in Sangamon county to John B. Wolgamot. See his name. Also, see T. P. Pettus.

POLLY, born Aug. 20, 1797, in Bourbon county, Ky., married there to Thomas Jones. See his name. She died in Kentucky, but her family came to Sangamon county.

When George Bryan came to Sangamon county, in 1834, he was in his seventy-sixth year, but he continued visiting Kentucky, riding each way on horseback, annually for eleven years. He died Nov. 22, 1845, and was buried near Woodside Station, Sangamon county. He was eighty-seven years, nine months and seven days old.

It seems almost incredible that a man who was of sufficient age to have been a soldier in the American Revolution, and who took an active part in the stirring scenes of the frontier settlements in the second State admitted to the American Union, should have become an early settler of Sangamon county, and witnessed some of its earliest strides towards civilization: but the life of George Bryan extended over this long and eventful period. His grandson, William T. Jones, has a great fund of reminiscences of the life of his grandfather Bryan, as he received them from the lips of the venerable patriarch while living. I can only give place to two incidents, both of which occurred in Kentucky.

On one occasion, when the forests were swarming with hostile Indians, Mr. Bryan, with six other men, left the Station for a scouting expedition. Proceeding cautiously, they had gone but two or three miles when the seven white men were fired upon by just twice their number of Indians, who lay in ambush until the white men were very near them. The Indians were good marksmen with bows and arrows, but they had not been sufficiently accustomed to fire-arms to become expert in using them. In their haste they overshot their marks, and never hurt a man. The advantage would then have been decidedly in favor of the whites, but at this juncture three of the latter, supposing there was a large force of Indians, took to flight. The other three, with Bryan at their head, each took to a tree, and commenced firing at the Indians. The fight continued the whole day, and as the sun was sinking to rest, it was discovered that there were but two men on each side in fighting condition: the chief on one side, and Bryan on the other, with a single man each. The others were all killed or severely wounded. A parley ensued, which ended in an agreement that the one subordinate on each side should cease hostilities, for the purpose of taking care of the dead and wounded, and that the two leaders should fight until one or the other conquered. Each kept behind a tree, with his gun loaded, while they were parleying, and when ready to renew hostilities, each called the other by every epithet expressing cowardice that they could respectively command, and each dared the other to come out and engage in open combat. As it was growing dark, Bryan put his cap on the end of his ramrod, and moved it from the tree as though he was very cautiously preparing to shoot. The Indian fired at the cap, and finding himself deceived, he ran in a zig-zag course, cautiously looking back until he thought himself at a safe distance, when he took to a tree and began to load his rifle. The moment the chief fired, Bryan sprang from his tree, and, instead of following direct, he ran at an angle of about forty-five degrees from the course of the Indian, and was soon out of the line where the latter expected to see him. Bryan thus had the Indian in plain view, while the latter thought himself secure. As the chief raised both arms to ram down the load, Bryan fired, the ball entering under one arm, it passed out under the other, and he fell dead. His clothes were covered with silver brooches and other ornaments, that were kept in the families of Bryan's descendants for many years.

As the increasing number of the whites convinced the Indians that they must eventually give way, they became less hostile. About this time Bryan and a comrade spent several weeks in hunting, and had taken a large number of skins and furs. While the two were alone in camp, a considerable number of Indians encamped near them; and very soon two of the Indians came to their camp, and, without the least ceremony, commenced opening and examining the goods belonging to the two white men. Mr. Bryan made up his mind that the result of their winter's work was lost, for if the Indians chose to take their goods, it would be madness to resist with such odds against them. Unknown to Bryan, his partner was an expert in legerdemain, and the thought occurred to him that the Indians might be driven off by some deceptive movement. He asked one of the savages for his butcher knife, and at once went through the motions of swallowing it. The other Indian handed out his knife, which was swallowed with violent contortions. The two hurried away to their own camp, and soon returned with their chief, who held in his hand a much larger knife, having a very rough buck-horn handle, with a horn spike about three inches long at one side. The white man shook his head, make signs that the knife was too large, that the little horn on the side of the handle would be more than he could swallow. They insisted, and he made signs that he would try. He then indulged in contortions so violent as to bring tears to his eyes; but the knife disappeared. The red men felt of his body, and came so near finding where the knives were hidden, that he thought it would be safer to return them, and commenced casting up and handing each Indian his knife. They, one after another, received their knives, each taking his own very carefully by the point, between the thumb and finger, would smell of it, make a wry face, and throw it on the ground. The three savages withdrew together, leaving their knives where they had fallen, and before morning the whole company, afraid to steal anything else, stole themselves away.

Having said so much about his pioneer life, in which he was brought in contact with wild beasts, savages, and white men unused to the restrains of civilized life as we now enjoy it, would probably lead the reader to infer that he was a rough and harsh man; but such was not the case. He embraced christianity in early life, and was one of the most steadfast supporters of the ordinances of religion. He aided in building a Baptist church at Bryan Station, which a grand-daughter of his, now living in Springfield, visited in 1860, and found it still in use. He was a member of that church, and worshipped there as long as he remained in Kentucky. He always held family worship, in which the colored servants were expected to unite.

He continued the practice to the day of his death.

BRYAN, LARKIN, was born Nov. 2, 1800, in Woodford county, Ky. He was married there in 1820 to Mrs. Harriet Chapman, whose maiden name was Thornberry. They moved to the Missouri lead mines, and from there to Sangamon county, in the fall of 1821, and settled five miles northeast of Springfield. They had seven children in Sangamon county. Of their children—

WILLIAM C., born Jan. 29, 1822, married Anna Brennan, have three children, and reside near Charleston, Ill.

MARY F., born July 11, 1824, married Presley Chrisman. She died, leaving her husband and three children near Promise City, Wayne county, Iowa.

RACHEL J., born Dec. 7, 1825, married Willis Chrisman. They have four children, and reside in Sangamon county, near Waverly.

JAMES H., born March 7, 1827, is unmarried, and resides in Springfield. He has a saw mill on South Fork.

CINTHIA A., born Oct. 18, 1829, married John Kline, and resides in St. Joseph, Mo.

LARKIN A., born March 3, 1830, married Nov. 1, 1860, to Sarah A. Mitchell, who was born April 16, 1842, in Finedon, Northamptonshire, England. They had five childen. HARRIET E. died in her seventh year. JAMES W., JESSIE H., LAVINIA A. and CHARLES W. reside with their parents, near Waverly, Ill.

HARRIET M., born July 3, 1832, married DeWitt C. Marsh. *See his name.*

Mrs. Harriet Bryan died April 4, 1862, and Larkin Bryan was married Jan. 14, 1863, to Mrs. Sarah Yeamans, who had previously been Mrs. Britt, and whose maiden name was Wilson. He died two miles north of Springfield, in 1874. His widow resides in Springfield.

BUCHANAN, REUBEN, was born March 20, 1809, in Woodford county, Ky. His father moved, in 1819 or '20, to Morgan county, Ill. Reuben remained there until 1834, when he came to Sangamon county, settling at Salisbury, where he was married to Barbara Duncan, a step-daughter of Solomon Miller. She was born March 15, 1812, in Cumberland county, Ky. Mr. and Mrs. Buchanan had four children, three of whom died young. The only one living—

HARRIET A., born Dec. 3, 1838, at Salisbury, married Jan. 1, 1857, in Springfield, to Lafayette Smith. *See his name.*

Mr. Buchanan moved from Salisbury to Springfield in April, 1847, and was engaged in the grocery business until his death, which occurred Nov. 14, 1861. His widow resides with her son-in-law, Lafayette Smith, in Springfield.

BUCKMAN, JOEL, born Nov. 6, 1790, in Bethel, Vermont. He was the second child of Jeremiah Buckman and Ruth Banister, his wife. They were born in Springfield, Mass; he Sept. 11, 1762, and she March 20, 1771. Joel Buckman and Huldah Tilley were married in Vermont, and moved to Potsdam, N. Y., had six children, and Mrs. B. died, Dec. 17, 1828. He was married June 19, 1829, to Hannah Bowker. They had one child, and moved to Sangamon county, Ill., arriving Sept., 1834, at Old Sangamo. Mrs. Hannah B. died Nov. 6, 1838. Joel Buckman and Sally Watts were married in Sangamon county, March 5, 1839. They had one child. Of all his children—

JOEL, born Dec. 2, 1813, died July 5, 1835.

LORENDA, born Sept. 9, 1815, in Potsdam, N. Y., married in Sangamon county, June 20, 1837, to William B. Brown. *See his name.*

LEVINIA, born Dec. 22, 1819, in New York, married in Sangamon county, Dec., 1835, to Waters Carman. They had four children, and she died. He moved to Oregon.

CALVIN, born Jan. 31, 1822, in New York, married in Sangamon county, Nov. 1843, to Sophia Eastabrook. They have seven children, and reside at Delavan, Tazewell county.

HULDAH S., born Feb. 16, 1824, in New York, married in Sangamon county, Oct. 20, 1842, to Lucius Seeley. *See his name.*

SILAS T., born Feb. 19, 1828, in New York, married Anna Clemens. He resides near Farmingdale.

HANNAH W., born March 26, 1832, died in her third year.

BENJAMIN, born Sept. 6, 1841, in Sangamon county, resides with his mother, near Farmingdale.

Joel Buckman died March 13, 1872, in Sangamon county, and his widow resides two miles southwest of Farmingdale.

BULLARD, REUBEN, was born Dec. 22, 1792, in Caroline county, Va. He went to Woodford county, Ky., in 1787, and to Shelby county in 1790. He was there married in 1803, to Elizabeth Gill, who was born Oct. 30, 1779, near Charlestown, Va. They had eight children in Kentucky, four of whom, Eliza, Lucinda, Richard and Nancy J., died there, between the ages of fifteen and twenty-five years. Mrs. Elizabeth Bullard died Jan. 6, 1835, and Reuben Bullard, with three of his children, came to Sangamon county, arriving in Nov., 1835, in what is now Illiopolis township, one son having come before. Of the four children—

JOHN, born Feb. 10, 1805, in Shelby county, Ky., came to Sangamon county April 6, 1830, and made his home partly at Buffalo Hart Grove and partly in the vicinity of Mechanicsburg, and returned to Kentucky in 1833. Sarah S. Fallis was born Feb. 3, 1812, in St. Louis county, Mo., her parents having moved there from Kentucky. During the war with England the Indians became troublesome, and the family moved back, in 1813, to Henry county, Ky. John Bullard and Sarah S. Fallis were there married, Sept. 4, 1834, and came at once to Sangamon county, where they had ten children. JOHN W., born Oct. 21, 1836, died May 6, 1856. NANCY F., born May 29, 1838, married April 30, 1873, to Charles Howard, and reside near Neola, Iowa. WILLIAM S., born Jan. 7, 1841. He enlisted August 7, 1862, in Co. A, 73d Ill. Inf. for three years, was wounded at the battle of Franklin, Tenn., Nov. 30, 1864, served until the end of the rebellion, and was honorably discharged. He was married Dec. 28, 1871, to Elizabeth S. Zane. They have two children, LETHE IRENE and MARY, and reside four and a half miles east of Mechanicsburg. REUBEN S., born August 31, 1842, married Sept. 23, 1873, in Shelbyville, Ky., to Marian Saunders. She was born there, May 8, 1849. They have one child, ANNIE, and reside four and a half miles east of Mechanicsburg, where his father settled in 1834. EDNA E., born April 12, 1844, married Oct. 16, 1867, to Charles C. Radcliffe, a native of Frederick county, Md. They have three children, NORA A., AUBRA L. and SALLIE F., and resides in Mechanicsburg. JOSEPHINE, born Dec. 17, 1845, was married at Mechanicsburg, May 27, 1875, to Capt. George Ritchey, and reside in Boonville, Mo. MARY J., born Dec. 17, 1847, died Feb. 14, 1875. WILBER C., born Sept. 19, 1850; JACOB B. born Jan. 20, 1854; HENRY S., born March 18, 1858, all reside with their mother, except WILBUR C., who lives in Decatur. John Bullard died Dec. 26, 1872, and his widow lives in Mechanicsburg.

MARY A., born Sept. 25, 1810, in Shelby county, Ky., married there to Benjamin Fortune. *See his name.*

SARAH AGNES, born March 24, 1814, in Shelby county, Ky., married Jacob N. Fullinwider. *See his name.*

WESLEY, born July 28, 1816, in Shelby county, Ky., married March 23, 1843, in Sangamon county, to Sarah A. Foster, who was born July 18, 1824, in Montgomery county, Ky., and came to Sangamon county on a visit in 1842. Her parents lived, at the time, in Putnam, Ind. Mr. and Mrs. B. had eight sons in Sangamon county. WILLIAM H., born August 16, 1844, enlisted August 4, 1862, for three years, in Co. A, 73d Ill. Inf., was slightly wounded at the battle of Franklin, Tenn. He served to the end of the rebellion, and was honorably discharged, June 24, 1865, married in Sangamon county, Sept. 13, 1866, to Abbie P. Baldwin, who was born Nov. 21, 1847, near Monticello, Madison county. They have three children, SARAH L., WESLEY C. and MARY B., and live five miles east of Mechanicsburg. JAMES R. resides (1874) in San Francisco, Cal. JOHN N., FRANCIS B., SAMUEL A., GEO. W., BENJ. F. and SAY A. FOSTER; the six latter live with their father. Mrs. Sarah A. Bullard died Feb. 13, 1861, and Wesley Bullard was married August 6, 1863, in Sangamon county, to Mrs. Elizabeth Holsman, whose maiden name was Kidd. She was born May 7, 1828, in Fluvanna county, Va. Her home was in Circleville, Ohio, but she was on a visit to Sangamon county at the time of her marriage. They have two children, JULIA and ROBERT A., and live four miles east of Mechanicsburg, where he settled in 1835.

Reuben Bullard died Sept. 6, 1836, in Sangamon county.

His father's name was Reuben Bullard. He was in the Revolutionary army as a non-combatant, and lost his life by drinking too freely of cold water while he was over-heated. He made a gun, which he gave to his son, whose name heads this sketch. It is now (1874) in possession of a son of John Bullard—Reuben S.—the fourth generation from the man who made it. The brass plate opposite the lock bears the inscription, R. B., 1772. It is a smooth bore; the barrel is four feet eight inches long, and the whole gun is six feet one inch. An anecdote is related of it, that when the boys of a former generation used the gun, they always hunted in pairs, one to do the shooting and the other to see that the marksman did not get the muzzle beyond the game.

BURCH, JOHN, was born about 1770, in Georgia. He was married in 1800, in Gallatin county, Ky., to Elizabeth Hampton, who was born in 1780, in Loudon county, Va. They had six children in Kentucky, and Mr. Burch came to Sangamon county in the fall of 1828, with his son-in-law, James McKee. He went back to Kentucky for his family, and died there May 10, 1829. In the fall of that year his family moved to Sangamon county, and settled near Mechanicsburg. Of their six children—

SARAH, born about 1801, in Kentucky, married there to William Jack, and moved to Sangamon county. See his name.

BENJAMIN, born Aug. 1, 1803, in Gallatin county, Ky., married in Sangamon to Mary Smith. He died in McLean county in 1863. His widow married James Waite, and lives in Bloomington.

JANE, born in 1805, in Gallatin county, Ky., married there Jan. 9, 1828, to James McKee, and came to Illinois in the fall of that year, and settled near Mechanicsburg.

PRESTON H., born in 1807, in Gallatin county, Ky., married in Sangamon county in 1831, to Elizabeth Suter. They had five children in Sangamon county. SARAH E. married William H. Green, and lives at Dubuque, Iowa, with her only child, LULU. LEVARIAN, born Dec.

25, 1837, in Sangamon county, enlisted at Newport Barracks, April, 1861, in Battery G, 2nd Reg. U. S. Art. He was promoted to Second Lieutenant, was wounded at the battle of Gettysburg, and died of his wounds, late in 1863, at Washington City. JAMES M., born Feb. 18, 1839, in Sangamon county. He graduated at St. Louis Medical College in 1859, and enlisted as a private, June 20, 1861, in Co. C, 8th Mo. Inf.; was promoted in July, '61, to Asst. Surg., which he resigned in Aug., 1862, and was commissioned Captain of Co. K, 94th Ill. Inf. He resigned that office in Sept., 1863, and was promoted Lieutenant Colonel of the 16th U. S. Colored Troops, at New Orleans, which he resigned at Brazos, Texas, in Sept., 1864. Dr. J. M. Burch was married Oct. 8, 1860, at Bloomington, to Jennie L. McClunn, a native of that city. After the close of the rebellion he practiced medicine at Illiopolis, and died there July 26, 1874, leaving a widow and four children, FRANK P., ED. R., LEVARIAN and CORA. Mrs. Jennie L. Burch and children reside at Bloomington. JOHN S., born July 1840, in Sangamon county, went to California in 1861, and was drowned March 3, 1865, at San Juan, Nicaragua, while on his way home. ELIZA J., born March, 1842, in Sangamon county, is a teacher at Mt. Sterling. Preston H. Burch enlisted in 1862, at Peoria, in Co. —, 108th Ill. Inf., and died of disease at Young's Point, near Vicksburg, Miss., Feb. 18, 1863. His widow died at Mt. Sterling, Brown county, Ill., Dec., 1865.

ELIZA, born in 1810, in Kentucky, married in Sangamon county to James Smith. They had one child, MARY, born in Sangamon county, married Oct. 8, 1860, to Dr. Edward Stevens, and reside in Bloomington. James Smith died Sept., 1845, in Springfield, and his widow married Josiah Green. She died Feb., 1852, and he died July, 1855, both in Mechanicsburg.

WADE S., born Oct. 14, 1815, in Gallatin county, Ky., married in Sangamon county Jan. 8, 1845, to Mary E. Young. They had ten children, seven of whom died under seven years. SUSAN B., born July 26, 1850, married Jan. 8, 1868, to James Newton Moreland, who was born Dec. 17, 1840, in Bath county, Ky., served nearly four years—from Aug. 1,

1862—in Co. B, 10th Ky. Cav. (Union), and was honorably discharged in 1865. Mr. and Mrs. Moreland live in Illiopolis township. WERTER P., born March 11, 1861, and HARRY, born Feb. 10, 1864, live with their parents—W. S. Burch and wife, reside two miles south of Lanesville.

Mrs. Elizabeth Burch died Sept. 20, 1865, in Curran township.

BURKHARDT, JOHN M., was born Feb. 2, 1807, in Schwarzenberg, county of Nuremberg, Kingdom of Wurtemberg. He came to America in 1832, and spent two summers in Pennsylvania, and as many winters in Mississippi. He came to Springfield in 1836, and was there married, Aug. 18, 1843, to Mary E. Nagle, who was born June 24, 1827, in Bavaria, Canton Bergzabern. She sailed Oct. 20, 1841, in the ship Oceana. The vessel was wrecked off the island of Jamaica, Dec. 3, 1841. The passengers were all saved, but lost their baggage. They were transferred to another vessel, and arrived at New Orleans Jan. 8, 1842, to find the city in holiday attire in honor of Gen. Jackson's victory over the British, Jan 8, 1815. Her father died in St. Louis, while she was detained by shipwreck. She came on to Springfield, arriving in March, 1842, and joined her sister, Mrs. Catharine Lorch, then and now the wife of Charles Lorch. Mr. and Mrs. Burkhardt had eleven children; two died under three years, and Charles A. died, aged seven. Of the other eight—

JOHN, born May 20, 1844, enlisted July 4, 1862, for three months, in Co. D, 70th Ill. Vol. Inf., and served five months as a Corporal. He again enlisted March 22, 1864, in Co. G, 114th Ill. Vol. Inf., for three years. He was killed June 10, 1864, at the battle of Guntown, Miss.

BERTHA, born June 23, 1847, was married March 6th, 1874, to Walter F. Swift, who was born in New Bedford, Mass. They reside in Ottawa, Kan.

CHARLES A., EMMA, ANNIE L., JENNIE C., IDA B. and *LILLIE E.*, live with their mother.

John M. Burkhardt died Aug. 1, 1868, and his widow resides one mile east of Springfield, Ill.

BURNS, THOMAS, was born August 1, 1773, at Alexandria, Va. His father was a native of Scotland, and was killed by his team running away when Thomas was a child. Elizabeth Ridgeway was born Nov. 25, 1775, in Berkley county, Va. Thomas Burns and Elizabeth Ridgeway were married March 11, 1794, and had one child in Berkley county; and then moved to Washington county, West Va., where they had three children. They then moved to North Carolina, and after a short stay, moved to Jessamine county, Ky., where they had one child, and from there to Clarke county, where they had seven children. The family moved from there to Sangamon county, Ill., arriving in the fall of 1829, in what is now Mechanicsburg township. Some of their children had preceded them. Of their children—

RACHEL, born Jan. 30, 1795, in West Virginia, died Jan. 30, 1816, in Kentucky.

ELIZABETH, born Nov. 28, 1796, in West Virginia, died Feb., 1840, in Sangamon county.

ROBERT E., born March 28, 1799, in Washington county, West Va., married in Clarke county, Ky., Sept. 15, 1825, to Patsy Cass, and moved to Sangamon county, Ill., arriving Oct., 1825, in Buffalo Hart Grove. They were the first of the family to come to the county. They had four children in Sangamon county, two of whom died young. ROBERT FRANKLIN, born Dec. 9, 1830, died July 11, 1852. ELIZABETH C., born June 7, 1838, married April 16, 1854, to John T. Constant. *See his name.* Robert E. Burns and his wife reside at Buffalo Hart Station, very near where they settled in 1825. Mr. Burns had a neighbor, Wm. Bridges, who was a blacksmith and gunsmith. Wm. and Hiram Robbins came to Mr. Bridges to have work done, and he had no coal. They told him that they had seen coal cropping out of the ground in their hunting excursions, and gave him directions so that he could find it. Mr. Burns took his wagon and team, went with Mr. Bridges to the place and dug out a load, and found it good for blacksmithing. It was in a ravine about three-fourths of a mile northwest of where Barclay now stands. That was in 1826, and was the first coal found in that part of the country. Mr. Burns raised cotton for clothing, and it matured perfectly before the "deep snow" of 1830–31. After that he tried frequently, bringing seed from Tennessee several times, but all his efforts proved to be such failures that the seed ran out and was lost.

ANN T., born May 27, 1801, in West Virginia, married in Kentucky, August 6, 1817, to Abner Enos. *See his name.* She died there, June 13, 1829.

JOHN R., born Oct. 19, 1803, in Jessamine county, Ky., married in Sangamon county, April 17, 1828, to Lucy A. Cass. He was a soldier in the Black Hawk war. They had twelve children, all born in Sangamon county, three of whom died under five years. MARY J., born Mar. 26, 1831, married Feb. 28, 1847, to John Cass. *See his name.* THOMAS F., born Jan. 9, 1833, married Sept. 30, 1856, Ursula Greening. Thos. F. Burns enlisted July 25, 1862, in Co. F., 114th Ill. Inf., for three years. Served about one year, and was honorably discharged on account of physical disability. He now resides in Mt. Pulaski. WILLIAM A., born Nov. 28, 1839, married Dec. 24, 1867, to Lucy E. Jones. They have two children, WM. ELMER and IVA MAY, and live near Buffalo Hart Station. MARTHA A., born Feb. 27, 1843, lives with her parents. ARMINTA, born Dec. 30, 1844, married Feb. 21, 1867, to Wm. B. Robinson. *See his name.* SOPHIA, born Feb. 13, 1849, married Dec. 27, 1871, to James F. Hickman. *See his name.* IVA, born March 18, 1851, married Oct. 25, 1871, to James L. Wright, who was born in Lockmaben, Scotland, and resides in Buffalo Hart township. JOHN T., born Jan. 11, 1854, and ROBERT B., born Oct. 26, 1856, live with their parents, one mile south of Buffalo Hart Station.

Mrs. Lucy A. Burns says that they raised cotton in the summer of 1828; that she picked it from the bolls, picked the seed out with her fingers, carded it with hand cards, spun and wove it, and made it up into garments of various kinds. In 1829 they raised a much larger quantity, and had it ginned on a machine owned by William G. Cantrall. They paid toll, or part of the cotton, for ginning, the same as grinding is done by custom mills. When all was done they had eighty pounds of ginned cotton left. She says that after the "deep snow" it never would mature.

MAHALA, born May 10, 1806, in Clarke county, Ky., married there Nov. 27, 1827, to Bailey F. Bell. *See his name.*

MELINDA and LUCINDA, twins, born July 23, 1808, in Clarke county, Ky.

MELINDA, married in Sangamon county, Jan. 17, 1830, to Ambrose Bowen Cass. *See his name.*

LUCINDA, married in Sangamon county, Sept. 20, 1832, to John W. Robison. *See his name.*

EMILY, born June 14, 1811, in Clarke county, Ky., married in Sangamon county, Jan. 17, 1830, to Clemmon Strickland. They had three children. The parents and two of the children died. JOSEPH, the only living member of the family, married Emily Chance, and lives at Buffalo.

REBECCA, born Feb. 16, 1814, in Clarke county, Ky., married in Sangamon county to Bennett Wood, a native of Kentucky. They lived in Green county, Ill., until they had two children, namely: BAZZLE or BASIL M., born June 16, 1835, in Green county, enlisted July, 1862, for three years, in Co. E., 116th Ill. Inf. Served full term and was honorably discharged with the regiment, in 1865. He was married in Sangamon county, Jan. 25, 1866, to Nannie J. Graham, who was born July 4, 1843, in Morgan county. They had two children, FLORA and GRACIE, and Mrs. Wood died, Jan. 6, 1872. Mr. Wood resides one and a quarter miles east of Illiopolis, with his father-in-law, Mr. Graham. SARAH Wood, born March, 1834, in Green county, married in Sangamon county to John Stall. They have four children, and live at Niantic. Bennett Wood died in Green county, and his widow married James McGee. Mrs. McGee died in Sangamon county, leaving two children: JOHN T. and WILLIAM R. McGee reside in Williamsville.

FRANKLIN, born August 6, 1816, in Kentucky, married in Sangamon county, March 3, 1836, to Louisa Ridgeway. They had —— children. THOMAS J. married and resides in Kansas. PARTHENIA married George Sensbaugh, and lives near Whiterock, Jewell county, Kansas. LOUISA J. married Daniel Redman, and lives near Lone Oak P. O., Bates county, Mo. MAHALA resides with her sister, Louisa J. B. HARDIN lives with his uncle, Robert E. Burns. Franklin Burns and his wife are both dead.

PATSY, born Feb. 20, 1819, in Kentucky, married in Sangamon county, Dec. 26, 1837, to Baldwin Harper. They had one child, EVELINE. She married Theophilus Kirwood, and lives near Warrensburg, Macon county. Mr. and Mrs. Harper are both dead.

Mrs. Elizabeth Burns died Oct. 5, 1830, and Thomas Burns died August 11, 1836, both in Sangamon county.

BURTLE, WILLIAM, born July 1, 1780, near Montgomery Court House, Md. His parents moved, when he was a boy, to Washington county, Ky. Sarah Ogden was born in 1786, in St. Mary's county, Md. Her father died when she was a child, and her mother moved, with several children, to Washington county, Ky. William Burtle and Sarah Ogden were there married, about 1805. They had nine children in Kentucky. The family moved to Sangamon county, Ill., arriving October, 1826, in what is now Ball township. Mr. Burtle entered land, and made improvements for a permanent home, about two hundred yards east of where St. Bernard's Catholic Church now stands, and moved on it in the spring of 1828. Of their nine children—

JOSEPH, born in Kentucky, married in Sangamon county to Mrs. Maria Miller, whose maiden name was Gatton. They both died in Sangamon county, without children.

JOHN, born in Kentucky, was married there to Matilda Simpson. They had two children, one of whom died in infancy. His daughter married, moved to Texas, and died there. John Burtle died in Ball township. His widow married, moved to Missouri, and died there.

JAMES, born May 25, 1811, in Kentucky, was married in Sangamon county to Elizabeth Gatton. They had six children. JOHN T. married Eliza J. Simpson. They have six children, JAMES B., JOSEPH E., EMMA, SAMUEL, ANNA and JEROME. Mrs. Eliza J. Burtle died in May, 1875, and John T. Burtle and family reside in Ball township, seven miles southeast of Chatham. WILLIAM O. married Mary M. Speak. They have three children, MARIA, OSCAR E. and MARY M., and reside with his mother at the family homestead. SARAH E. married John Simpson. They had one child, and mother and child died. JOSEPHUS died in his twenty-fourth year. MARY A. died, aged nineteen years. James Burtle died, and his widow resides in Ball township, six and a half miles southeast of Chatham.

THOMAS, born Aug. 12, 1815, in Kentucky, married in Sangamon county to Louisa Simpson. They have four children. JAMES H. married Sarah E. Gatton. They have six living children: LOUISA A and MARY L. (twins), ANNA E., MARTHA F., WILLIAM J. and THERESA H. Mrs. Sarah E. Burtle died in Sept., 1873, and James H. Burtle resides in Ball township. JOHN T., Jun., married Elizabeth M. Boll. They have three children, EDWARD A., JACOB B. and ANN N., and live in Ball township. MARY A. married Joseph H. Berry. They have five daughters, SARAH L., ELIZA C., MAGGIE A., MARY A. and ADA F., and live in Ball township. ELIZA J. married John A. White. They have two children, JOSEPH H. and WILLIAM T., and reside with her father. Mrs. Louisa Burtle died April 2, 1875, and Thomas Burtle resides near St. Bernard's Catholic Church, in Ball township.

ELLEN died, aged fourteen years.

MARY, born in Kentucky, married in Sangamon county, Ill., July 24, 1834, to Josephus Gatton. *See his name.*

BENJAMIN, born in Kentucky, married in Sangamon county to Monica Gatton. They have six children living. MARY E. married William R. Greenawalt. *See his name.* The other children reside with their parents, in Pawnee township.

WILLIAM, Jun., born Aug. 9, 1822, in Grayson county, Ky., came with his parents to Sangamon county in Oct., 1826, was married Sept. 4, 1856, to Mrs. Elizabeth A. Simpson, whose maiden name was White. Mrs. Burtle had one child by her former marriage, JEROME SIMPSON. Mr. and Mrs. Burtle had two children. IDA F. died March 9, 1875, in her fourteenth year, and CHAS. E. lives with his parents. William Burtle has been a school teacher, Justice of the Peace, and for more than twenty years Treasurer and Collector of Ball township; also a member of the Board of Supervisors of Sangamon county. He was also elected President of the Old Settlers' Society, in 1874, for one year. He now lives in Auburn, engaged in mercantile business with his step-son, Jerome Simpson.

William Burtle, Jun., remembers that his father and James Simpson sent a request to St. Louis that a priest visit their neighborhood. Rev. Mr. Dusuaswa came in 1829, and held services at the residence of Joseph Logsdon. That was the first service ever held by a Catholic priest in Sangamon county, and long before anything of the kind took place in Springfield. William Burtle remembers that there were then but two Catholic families in Springfield. The next services were at the house of Wm. Burtle, Sen., by Rev. Joseph A. Lutz. The next priest to visit them was the Rev. Mr. Van Quickenbon. Services were held at the house of William Burtle, Sen., until 1849, when St. Bernard's Church was built. One edifice was burned, and the present one was built on the same ground. St. Bernard's church is associated with that at Virden in sustaining a priest.

Mrs. William Burtle relates, in a very amusing manner, some of her experience on coming to the county. She had listened to the descriptions of the flowers blooming on the prairies, and made up her mind that it would lend additional charms to those she was acquainted with to cultivate them on the prairie where the wild flowers could grow around them. She came prepared with seeds, and at the proper season armed herself with a hoe and sallied forth to indulge her taste for horticulture on the raw prairie. The romance all vanished at the first blow, as the hoe rebounded without making the slightest impression. Until that time she thought plowing with large ox-teams was overdoing the work, but then became fully satisfied that it was indispensable as a preparation for the cultivation of the soil.

ZACHARIAH, born in Kentucky, married in Sangamon county to Elizabeth J. Harper. They have five living children, JAMES W., SARAH E., EDGAR A., MARY M. and ROBERT E., and reside on the farm settled by his father in 1828, about two hundred yards east of St. Bernard's Catholic Church.

William Burtle, Sen., died July 24, 1860, and Mrs. Sarah Burtle died Feb. 11, 1868, and both were buried near St. Bernard's Church. About the time William Burtle, Sen., came to Sangamon county with his family, his father, Benjamin Burtle, came, and after remaining two or three years returned to Kentucky, and died there.

BURTON, EDWARD, was born Oct. 13, 1796, on Roanoke river, Va., and went to Rutherford county, Tenn. He was there married to Frances Hudson, who was born April 10, 1797, in Virginia also. They had five children in Tennessee, and moved to Sangamon county, Ill., in 1825 or '6, and settled on Lick creek, in what is now Chatham township, where they had four children. Of their children—

JOHN A., born in Tennessee, married in Sangamon county, Aug. 8, 1844, to Elizabeth H. Park. He died March 11, 1859, leaving two children. MARY F. married July 31, 1861, to William H. H. Harris, who was born July 8, 1841, in Macoupin county. They have three children, ALLIE F., VINETTIE and ZELMIE, and live four miles southwest of Loami. LEONARD F., lives with his sister, Mrs. Harris. Mrs. E. H. Burton married Wm. S. Morris. *See Park family.*

ELIZABETH G. died, aged twenty-five years.

ELLEN married Blaney Pitts, have nine children, and reside near Centralia.

MARY, born Dec. 21, 1822, in Rutherford county, Tenn., married in Sangamon county, Oct. 18, 1840, to William Edwards. *See his name.*

PERMELIA A., born Aug. 1, 1826, married Oct. 13, 1840, to Henry Edwards, who was born Jan. 6, 1820, in Garrard county, Ky. He is nephew to his brother-in-law, William Edwards. They had twelve children; nine died under seven years. GEORGE D. died at nineteen. ERVING lives with his parents. RICHARD S. married Margaret E. Adams, have two living children, HENRY P. and ADA M., and live in Talkington township. Henry Edwards and wife reside in Talkington township also (1884).

RICHARD S. married Sarah J. Edwards. He enlisted in an Illinois regiment, and died at home on sick furlough, leaving three children. His widow married, and resides in Texas.

JULIETTE married James Jordan Edwards. *See his name.*

BENJAMIN W. married Rachel G. Park. They have two children, NELSON M. and NANCY E. Mr. Burton died Jan. 4, 1861. His widow and children reside two and three-quarter miles west of Loami (1874).

LUCINA married James A. Edwards. *See his name.*

Edward E. (or D.) Burton died at Girard Ill., April 8, 1859, while attending Sangamon Presbytery of the Cumberland Presbyterian Church, to which he was a delegate. Mrs. Margaret Burton died Sept. 1, 1859, in Sangamon county.

BUTLER, NATHAN M., born Jan. 30, 1795, in Adair county, Ky. He was married in Green county, to Mary Harding, who was born in 1795, in that county. They made their home in Adair county until they had four children, when they left for the west, and after a detention of seven months in Indiana, arrived, Oct. 7, 1824, in Morgan county, Ill., where they had two children. In the spring of 1831 they moved to Sangamon county, and settled on the south side of Island Grove, two miles northeast of where Berlin now stands. Of their six children—

WILLIAM A., born July 23, 1817, in Adair county, Ky., married in Sangamon county, to Mrs. Jane Clark, whose maiden name was Trotter. She was born Feb. 2, 1827, in Indiana, and raised in Sangamon county. Mr. Butler was city Marshal of Springfield in 1861, and '2; is now farming four miles east of Springfield.

STEPHEN H., born Nov. 12, 1818, in Adair county, Ky., brought up in Sangamon county, married in Menard county Feb. 27, 1845, to Nancy J. Coats, who was born Dec. 6, 1825, in Warren county, Ky. They had twelve children; five died under six years. ISAAC E., born Jan. 27, 1846, married Feb. 13, 1873, to Emma J. Clark, and resides five miles east of Springfield. JULIA B., born Dec. 4, 1847, married Nov. 6, 1868, to James Simpson. *See his name.* MARY L., born June 5, 1849, married Joseph Donner. *See his name.* WILLIAM, born April 12, 1856, JOHN D., born Dec. 5, 1859. IRA and IDA, twins, born July 19, 1861, live with their parents. S. H. Butler resides four and a half miles east of Springfield.

JOSHUA C., born Nov. 26, 1820, in Adair county, Ky., brought up in Sangamon county, married April, 1857, in Jefferson county, Iowa, to Margaret J. Ristine. She died in Springfield in 1859, leaving one child. J. C. Butler was married in Sangamon county to Elizabeth Stitt, and has three living children, viz: CHARLES B., born June 6, 1850, married June 14, 1871, in Sangamon county to Ann Owen. They have one child, and live near Virginia, Cass county. MARGARET J., MARY E. and ROBERT L. live with their parents, two and a half miles northeast of Berlin. Joshua C. Butler was a member of Co. A., 4th Ill. Inf., and served under Col. E. D. Baker, in the Mexican war, from June, 1846, to June, 1847.

ELIZABETH E., born August 4, 1823, in Adair county, Ky., married in Sangamon county to William T. Barrett.

JOHN C., born April, 1825, in Morgan county, Ill., enlisted in the same company and regiment with his brother, Joshua C., and was discharged on account of physical disability. He married Frances Brown. They had two children, both of whom died, and Mr. Butler died in Springfield. His widow married John J. Hardin. *See his name.*

RACHEL R. born in Morgan county, married in Sangamon county to E. Riley Pirkins. *See his name.*

Mrs. Mary Butler died, and N. M. Butler married Mrs. Martha H. Stone, whose maiden name was Hunter. They had three children, viz—

SALLY H., born in Sangamon county, married Edmond E. Butler, of Kentucky. They had one child, and mother and child died at DesMoines, Iowa.

SAMUEL H., born in Sangamon county, enlisted in 1861, for three years, in the 10th Ill. Cav. Served until Nov., 1864, when he was honorably discharged at San Antonio, Texas. He remained there in the employ of the government and married in March, 1870, to Matilda Ann Blair. They had two children, a son and daughter. He was shot by an assassin, and died in the year 1872 or '3, in Texas.

JAMES E., born in Sangamon county, married March 31, 1869, to Molly

E. Oglesby. They have three children. He enlisted in 1861, for three years, in the 10th Ill. Cav., at Springfield. Re-enlisted as a veteran, promoted to First Lieut. Served to the end of the rebellion, and was honorably discharged. He resides near Dayton, Cass county, Mo.

Nathan M. Butler died April 4, 1842, in Sangamon county, and his widow died Oct. 14, 1851, in Menard county. N. M. Butler was a soldier in the war of 1812, and was in the battle of New Orleans. He was Col. of a regiment in the Black Hawk war of 1831-32.

BUTLER, WILLIAM, was born Dec. 15, 1797, in Adair county, Ky. During the war of 1812 he was selected to carry important dispatches from the Governor of Kentucky to Gen. Harrison, in the field. He traveled on horseback, and made the trip successfully, although he was but fifteen years of age. When a young man he was employed in the iron works of Tennessee, and after that was deputy of the Circuit Clerk for Adair county, Ky. While thus engaged, he made the acquaintance of a young lawyer, now the venerable Judge Stephen T. Logan, of this city. The friendship thus formed continued through life. Mr. Butler spent a portion of his time as clerk on a steamboat. In 1828 he came to Sangamon county, and purchased a farm in Island Grove. On that farm his father, Elkanah Butler, lived and died. William Butler came to Springfield, and was soon after appointed Clerk of the Circuit Court, by his early friend, Judge Logan, March 19, 1836, and resigned March 22, 1841. He was appointed, by Gov. Bissell, State Treasurer, August 29, 1859, to fill the vacancy occasioned by the resignation of State Treasurer Miller. He was elected to the same office in 1860 for two years. William Butler and Elizabeth Rickard were married Dec. 18, 1832. They had three children, namely—

SALOME E., born in Springfield, and now resides on South Sixth street, at the family homestead.

SPEED, born Aug. 7, 1837, in Springfield. He graduated at the Lutheran University in Springfield, in 1854, studied law, and was admitted to practice in 1860. When the rebellion came upon the country in 1861, Speed Butler was selected by the Governor of Illinois to carry a dispatch to Washington City, asking for an order to remove the United States arms from the Arsenal at St. Louis to Alton, Ill. Railroad and telegraphic communication to the Capital was cut off, but he managed to make his way through, obtained the order, and returned in safety. The arms were removed just in time to keep them from falling into the hands of the rebels. Soon after completing that service he was appointed Commissary, with the rank of Captain, but was at once assigned to duty on Gen. Pope's staff, and was with that officer during his campaign in North Missouri, at Island No. 10, &c. In Sept., 1861, he was appointed Major of the 5th Ill. Cav. For gallantry on the battle-field at Farmington, Miss., in June, 1862, he was promoted to Colonel in the regular army; but still, by permission from Gen. Wool, he remained on duty with Gen. Pope. He shared the fortunes of that officer during the Virginia campaign, as also in Minnesota against the Indians. He served until the close of the rebellion, in 1865.

Col. Speed Butler was married May 26, 1864, in Milwaukee, Wis., to Jeannie McKenzie Arnold, who was born Sept. 4, 1845, in Poughkeepsie, N. Y. They have three children, ANNIE L., ELIZABETH and ARNOLD W., and live near Springfield, on the southwest.

HENRY WIRT, born Feb. 11, 1840, in Springfield, graduated in 1859 at Brown University, Providence, R. I., and was married May 9, 1867, to Helen McClernand, daughter of Gen. John A. McClernand. She was born in Springfield, and died April 26, 1870, leaving one child, WILLIAM J. H. W. Butler and son live in Springfield.

Mrs. Elizabeth Butler died March 2, 1869, and Hon. William Butler died Jan. 11, 1876, both in Springfield.

C.

CALDWELL, WILLIAM, was born Dec. 15, 1779, in Nansemond county, Va. His father, Thomas Caldwell, was born in Ireland, and married there to Betsy Harris, a Welch lady. They emigrated to America, and landed at Charleston, South Carolina, where they remained a short time, and then moved to

Virginia. At the time of Thomas Caldwell's death, he and his wife had a home in the family of the son William. John C. Calhoun was related on the side of his mother to the Caldwell family, and there is the source from which that distinguished statesman obtained his middle name: John Caldwell Calhoun. When William Caldwell was a youth, his parents left Virginia and moved to Jessamine county, Ky. Nancy Roberts was born Sept. 24, 1782, in Goochland county, Va., and when young, went to Jessamine county, Ky. William Caldwell and Nancy Roberts were married Feb. 7, 1804. They had six living children in Jessamine county, and the family moved to Green county, Ill., in 1831, and in 1836 moved to Sangamon county, Ill., and settled in what is now Auburn township. Of their children—

GEORGE L., born Dec. 6, 1804, in Kentucky, married Sept. 10, 1829, to Polly Roberts. She inherited two negro slaves (a man and woman) from the estate of her father. On May 7, 1830, they took advantage of the absence of Mr. Caldwell, who was Sheriff of the county at the time, and strangled his wife to death with a small cord. They then placed her in a natural position in bed, bandaged her head, and placed such medicines on a stand, within her reach, as she would have been likely to use if she had been indisposed, and left her until it was discovered by other members of the family. The bruises on the neck excited suspicion, and the blacks being charged with the crime, confessed that they had taken her life, hoping by that means to be sent to their former home. The man was an old, trusted carriage servant, and forced the woman to assist him. They were tried, and, upon their own confession, convicted and hung. George L. Caldwell was married Sept. 27, 1831, to Eliza McDowell. They had one son, and Mrs. Caldwell died June 18, 1839, and Mr. Caldwell died Sept. 30, 1840. Neither of them ever came to Sangamon county. Their son GEORGE M. CALDWELL is the extensive stock-raiser near Williamsville, in this county.

JOHN, born Jan. 21, 1807, in Kentucky, came to Carrollton, Ill., in 1827. He was married there Jan. 23, 1834, to Mary J. Davis. She was born near Danville, Ky., Jan. 16, 1815. When a young lady, she rode on horseback from Danville, Ky., to Tallahassee, Florida, and returned to Danville, and after a short visit, continued her journey to Carrollton, Ill., a distance of at least two thousand miles. John Caldwell and wife had five children, namely: WILLIAM C., born March 15, 1835, married Jan. 14, 1864, to Sarah C. Bancom, who was born Nov. 16, 1840, in Sangamon county. They reside eight miles southwest of Springfield. JANE Y. died in her eleventh year; BETSY in her seventh year; HENRY died in infancy. BENJAMIN F., born Aug. 2, 1848, in Greene county, Ill., was married May 27, 1873, to Julia F. Cloyd, who was born March 7, 1856, in the southeast corner of Curran township, Sangamon county. Immediately after their marriage they left for New York, via Detroit and Suspension Bridge. At New York took steamer (June 4th) for Queenstown, Ireland, where they landed June 14th. Passed through Ireland to Belfast; thence to Scotland, down through the centre of England to London; from there through Holland, Belgium and smaller German States, to Berlin, in Prussia; thence to Vienna Exposition, across the Alps into Italy, meeting with the unexpected pleasure of an audience with Pius the IX. Returning, passed through Mt. Cenis tunnel, thence by Geneva to Paris; from Paris back to London, thence to Liverpool, taking steamer for Boston, where they arrived Oct. 6th, same year. Distance traveled in round trip, 14,000 miles. Mr. and Mrs. B. F. Caldwell have one child, MARY JANE, who was born March 20, 1874. They reside near Chatham, Sangamon county, Ill. John Caldwell died of heart disease, Aug. 1, 1863, after a painful illness, and his widow resides eight and a half miles southwest of Springfield, and one and a half miles north of Chatham.

JANE R., born April 15, 1809, married in Kentucky to Minor T. Young. Came to Illinois, and she died Jan. 21, 1844, in Curran township.

ELIZABETH, born Aug. 17, 1812, married Jan. 12, 1831, to Albert G. Talbott. She died April 29, 1838, leaving three children in Kentucky, namely: MARY A. married Dr. William Tomlinson. The sons are WILLIAM P. and ALBERT G., Jun.

CHARLES H., born March 18, 1818, in Kentucky, died May 24, 1833, at Jacksonville, Ill., while a student at Illinois College.

WILLIAM, Jun., born Aug. 14, 1820, in Kentucky, married Sept. 30, 1842, in Mercer county, Ky., to Mary J. Campbell. Mr. Caldwell died June 29, 1844. His widow married Mr. —— Moore, and resides at Pleasant Hill, Cass county, Mo.

William Caldwell, Sen., died Aug. 1, 1844, and his widow died Dec. 19, 1858, both at the southeast corner of Curran township.

When he moved from Auburn to Curran township, in 1841, there was not a place for holding religious worship near him. In order to afford temporary accommodations, he constructed his residence in such a manner that it could be used for that purpose. It consisted of a large central room, with three other large rooms opening into it. Plans were laid, before his death, for building a church, and on his death bed he requested that it be called Bethel, which was done, as the Christian Church near where he lived bears that name. Mr. Caldwell was a man of great public spirit all his life. He was Captain of a company from Jessamine county, Ky., in the war of 1812. A younger brother was a member of his company, and was taken prisoner at the battle of the river Raisin. He came near freezing to death while confined in a rail pen in Canada. William Caldwell was Sheriff of Jessamine county, Ky., and represented the county several times in the State Legislature. He represented Sangamon county two terms in the Legislature of Illinois.

CALHOUN.—The origin of the family in America was with Andrew Calhoun, who was born March 27, 1764, in Rye, Ireland. The family record speaks of his birth place as "Heland." That may have been a provincial name, or the original Gaellic name for Ireland. Andrew Calhoun was a near relative of the father of John C. Calhoun, of South Carolina. He came to America about 1792, and made his home in Boston, Mass. March 15, 1795, he was married at Chelmsford, Mass., to Martha Chamberlin, who was born at the latter place, Feb. 20, 1770. She was a descendent of the Puritans. They had eight children, all born in Boston. Their sixth child, *JOHN*, is the one of whom we wish to speak particularly, but will first briefly mention his brothers and sisters, that the reader may understand the character of the family.

WILLIAM B., was a lawyer, and stood high in the profession. He lived in Springfield, Mass.; was speaker of the house of representatives eight years, and President of the Senate a number of years. He represented the Springfield district in Congress eight years. CHARLES was, for twenty consecutive years, Secretary of the Senate of Massachusetts. ANDREW H., left his native State and became connected with journalism in the State of New York. He served seven years on the Board of Canal Commissioners, and one term as Clerk of the State Senate. HENRY was a merchant in Montgomery county, New York. Later in life he was, for many years, Deputy Collector of United States Customs in the city of New York. SIMEON HOWARD, born August 15, 1804, was educated at Harvard College, became a Christian minister, and joined a mission at Mount Lebanon, Syria. He was entrusted with translating the Bible into the native language, and subsequently established a native college near Beirut, of which he is now—1875—the President. JAMES, younger than John, was for thirty years an active business man in Cincinnati, O. There were two sisters, SUSAN, older, and MARTHA, younger. The father, Andrew Calhoun, after spending the prime of his life as an extensive merchant in Boston, retired to a farm in Montgomery county, N. Y., where he lost his wife, returned to Boston, married again, and died April 14, 1842.

CALHOUN, JOHN, was born Oct. 14, 1808, in Boston, Mass., and in 1821 accompanied his father to the Mohawk Valley, in New York. After finishing his studies at the Canajoharie Academy, he studied law at Fort Plain, both in Montgomery county. In 1830 he came to Springfield, Ill., and resumed the study of law, sustaining himself by teaching a select school. He took part in the Black Hawk war of 1831–2, and after its close, was appointed by the Governor of the State, Surveyor of Sangamon county. He induced Abraham Lincoln to study surveying, in order to become his deputy. From that time the chain of freindship between them continued bright to the end of their lives, although they were ardent partizans of different schools in politics. John Calhoun was married Dec. 29, 1831, in Sangamon county, to Sarah Cutter. *See Cutter sketch.* They had nine children in Sangamon county, and in 1854 Mr. Calhoun was appointed by President Pierce, Surveyor-General for Kansas and Nebraska, and he moved his family to Kansas. Of all their children—

JOHN, Jun., born Nov. 15, 1832, died in his third year, in Sangamon county.

ANDREW, born June 11, 1835, in Sangamon county, was killed Jan., 1860, by the explosion of a steam saw mill in Leavenworth county, Kansas.

ELIZABETH, born March 18, 1835, in Sangamon county, was married March 1, 1870, in the Catholic church at Leavenworth, Kan., to Henry Jackson, a native of England. He is a Lieutenant in the 7th Reg. U. S. Cav., and is now—1876—on detached duty in the signal service at Washington, D. C.

SETH J. was born March 4, 1839, in Springfield, Ill. He went with his father to Kansas in 1854, and when the rebellion commenced he enlisted in Battery H, 1st Mo. Art., It had been an infantry regiment under Col. Frank P. Blair, and after the battle of Wilson creek, changed to artillery. It was under Gen. Grant from the siege of Fort Donelson to the evacuation of Corinth, and under Sherman in his "march to the sea." Seth J. Calhoun was wounded July 22, 1864, in the battle of Atlanta, Ga., and soon a er promoted to second Lieut. of his Battery. He served one full term, re-enlisted as a veteran, served to the end of the rebellion and was honorably discharged. He now—1875—lives in Leavenworth, Kan.

ALBERT, born Feb. 10, 1841, in Springfield, and died in his fourth year.

MARTHA, born Jan. 9, 1843, in Springfield, resides with her mother.

SUSAN, born Sept. 8, 1844, in Springfield, Ill., married, August 29, 1866, in Leavenworth, Kansas, to Virgil W. Parker, who was born Dec. 16, 1840, in Rome, N. Y. They have one child, ADELIA, and reside in Atchison, Kansas.

MARY, born May 25, 1847, and *JAMES*, born Nov. 30, 1852, both in Springfield, Ill., live with their mother.

John Calhoun died Oct. 25, 1859, at St. Joseph, Mo. His widow and unmarried children now—1876—reside in Leavenworth, Kansas.

Hon. John Calhoun deserves more than a passing notice. He entered the political field in 1835, being the Democratic candidate that year for the State Senate of Illinois, but there being a large Whig majority in the county, he was defeated by Archer G. Herndon. In 1838 he was elected to represent Sangamon county in the State Legislature. In 1841 he, with John Duff, completed the railroad from Jacksonville to Springfield, being the first to reach the State Capital. In 1842 he was appointed Clerk of the Circuit Court of Sangamon county by Judge Treat. In 1844 he was one of the Presidential Electors of Illinois for President Polk. In 1849-'50-'51, he was successively elected Mayor of Springfield. In 1852 he was one of the Presidential Electors of Illinois for President Pierce, and was selected by his colleagues to carry the vote to Washington City. In 1854 he was appointed, by President Pierce, Surveyor General of Kansas and Nebraska, and moved his family to Kansas.

Here he entered a political field with new and exciting sectional elements. He was elected a delegate to the convention that framed what has passed into history as the Lecompton Constitution. He became the President of that body, which was composed of unscrupulous pro-slavery adventurers, with a small number of conservative members, among whom was the President. That odious instrument would have been adopted by the convention without submitting it to a vote of the people, had it not been for the determined opposition of President Calhoun, who threatened to resign, and opposed it by every method in his power, unless it was submitted; and when it came to the polls he voted against adopting the pro-slavery clause. That instrument provided that the President of the Convention should count the vote and report the result.

Soon after this duty was discharged he started for Washington City, leaving all the returns and papers relating to the election with one L. A. McLane, Chief Clerk of the Surveyor General's office. He has been described as "A brilliant clerk, but vain, vacillating, and ambitious of doing smart things, and economical of the truth generally." The instructions given to him by Gen. Calhoun before starting east, was to afford every facility to any body of respectable men to examine the returns, as evidences of dissatisfaction were already apparent, and the conviction soon became general that a stupendous fraud had been committed against the ballot. Soon the excitement became intense, endangering the lives of some of the conspicuous actors, and McLane became alarmed. Gen. Thomas L. Ewing, Jun., and Judge Smith called upon him, with a letter from Mr. Calhoun, instructing the clerk to let those gentlemen examine the returns. Mr. McLane falsely stated to Messrs. Ewing and Smith that the returns were not in his possession; that Gen. Calhoun had taken them with him when he left for Washington. A few evenings later, McLane attended a ball at Lawrence, where he was plied with good cheer, attentions and flattery, so grateful to his appetite and vanity, and after becoming mellow by the occasion, a Lawrence belle, acting the part of Delilah, drew from him the secret of the coveted papers. The next day he was called upon by a committee of the territorial legislature, who demanded the returns, when he again denied having them in his possession. He was then summoned before a committee of the legislature, and there stated under oath that Gen. Calhoun had taken the returns with him. The cross-questions revealed to him the fact that the Lawrence belle had betrayed him. Realizing his position, he returned that night to Lecompton, and with a few cronies, put the returns in a *candle box*, and buried it under a wood pile. A porter in the Surveyor-General's office, by the name of Charles Torrey, who had for a long time acted as a spy for the enemies of Gen. Calhoun, watched the operation, and gave the information. A company of men from Lawrence soon after unearthed the box, and bore away the prize.

The exposure of McLane's villainy was now complete, and he precepitately fled the Territory, with a mob in close pursuit. Thus the odium of the dastardly acts of this man were unjustly visited upon Gen. Calhoun. Unqualified abuse and misrepresentations were heaped upon him, and spread broadcast over the country by the press. That broke down his spirits, and he soon after left the Territory, went to St. Joseph, Mo., and died there. He deserved a better fate. He was a man of genial, hopeful, generous temperament; ever ready to serve or defend a friend, but rarely defending himself, except on the spur of the moment; of great ability, and for a time was the best political orator in the State of Illinois. He was brilliant, but deficient in practical application. President Lincoln has been heard to say that John Calhoun was the strongest man he had ever met on the stump; that he could manage Douglas, but that Calhoun always gave him his hands full.

CALLERMAN, DANIEL K., was born Dec. 10, 1806, in Fleming county, Ky. He came to Sangamon county, Ill., in company with his widowed mother, arriving Nov. 14, 1828, at Springfield. He was married Sept. 29, 1833, to Allie M. Henton. They had ten children in Sangamon county, two of whom died young. Of the other eight—

JOHN, born Aug. 9, 1834, married Nov., 1855, in Missouri, to Elizabeth Bunn. He is supposed to have lost his life in time of the rebellion, leaving a widow and three children in Vernon county, Mo.

EVAN H., born Oct. 2, 1836, in Sangamon county, and married Henrietta Drake. They had three living children, WILLIAM H., CHARLES M. and CORA. Mrs. C. died June 9, 1873, and he was married March 15, 1876, to Nellie Elder, of Sangamon county, a daughter of Dr. A. W. Elder, an early settler of Morgan county. E. H. Callerman lives in Williamsville.

URIAH W., born Jan. 14, 1839, in Sangamon county, married May 30, 1875, to Mary Curries. They live near Garnett, Anderson county, Kansas.

BARBARA ELEANOR C., born March 21, 1841, in Menard county, married March 11, 1860, in Sangamon county, to Andrew M. Whitenack, who was born Aug. 9, 1830, in Somerset county, N. J. They have one child, DANIEL C., and live near Edinburg, Ill.

MARTHA A., born Sept. 17, 1843, in Menard county, married Nov. 27, 1860, in Sangamon county, to Minard A. McClelland. They have five children, FRANCIS A., IDA A., MARSHAL A., MAUD M. and MATTIE, and live near Garnett, Kansas.

MARY, born Dec. 19, 1848, in Menard county, married Sept. 24, 1868, in Sangamon county, to John R. W. McNeill. They had two children. GEORGE died young. WALTER lives with his parents, near Edinburg, Ill.

GEORGE W., born Dec. 24, 1851, and

ANN, born June 20, 1857. The two latter live with their mother.

Daniel K. Callerman died Dec. 2, 1873, and his widow lives near Williamsville.

CALLERMAN, URIAH, was born Dec. 31, 1798, in Fleming county, Ky., and was married there to Eleanor McKinnie. They had one child in Kentucky, and moved to Sangamon county, Ill., arriving in the fall of 1822, four miles north of Springfield, where they had three children. Of their children—

JOHN L., born June 2, 1822, in Fleming county, Ky., married in Sangamon county, Sept. 18, 1845, to Frances Cole. They had one child, JOHN L., Jun., born in Sangamon county, married Jan. 8, 1874, to Susan M. Lightfoot, and live five miles northwest of Springfield. John L. Callerman died August 26, 1846, and his widow married Levi Branson, and lives near Cincinnati, Neb.

ELIZABETH, born Dec. 26, 1823, in Sangamon county, died Sept. 21, 1845.

NANCY, born March 3, 1826, in Sangamon county, married Goodrich Lightfoot. See his name.

JAMES W., born April 19, 1828, in Sangamon county, married March, 1856, to Emma Ash. They have six children, and live ten miles southeast of Springfield.

Uriah Callerman died Sept. 13, 1828, and Mrs. Eleanor Callerman died August 26, 1846, both in Sangamon county.

CAMPBELL, ANTRIM, was born Aug. 5, 1814, in New Jersey. He came to Springfield about 1838, and engaged in the practice of law. He was married May 12, 1841, to Mrs. Ann Farquar, whose maiden name was Cranmer. Mr. Campbell was appointed, Jan. 24, 1849, Master in Chancery for the circuit court of Sangamon county, and resigned the same, Oct. 28, 1861. He was appointed by the U. S. Circuit Court, Master in Chancery for the Southern District of Illinois. He died in office, August 11, 1868. His widow resides at the Leland Hotel, Springfield.

CAMPBELL, DAVID B., came to Springfield with his brother Antrim. He was Attorney-General from 1848 to 1856, and died in office, in Springfield.

CAMPBELL, ENOS, born about 1758, either in Scotland or near Trenton, N. J., soon after the arrival of his parents in America. He enlisted in the Revolutionary army at seventeen years of age, and served six or seven years, until the British army left the American shores. Mr. C. drew a pension to the end of his life. Enos Campbell and Damaris Nowee were married in New Jersey, and moved to Uniontown, Fayette county, Penn., where they had nine children, and moved, about 1806, to Butler county, O., where they had one child, and the family moved to Sangamon county, Ill., arriving in the fall of 1835, in what is now Gardner township. Some of the children had arrived before, and some never came. Of their children—

SARAH, born in Pennsylvania, married in Ohio to William Gard. They raised a family, and both died in Preble county, Ohio.

JOHN N., born April 10, 1794, in Uniontown, Fayette county, Pa., married Oct. 12, 1818, in Butler county, Ohio, to Phœbe Clarke, who was born April 30, 1791, in Uniontown, Pa., also. They had five children in Ohio, and moved to Sangamon county, arriving Oct. 3, 1824, in what is now Salisbury township, where they had four children. Of their children, ISRAEL, born in Ohio, married in Sangamon county to Mary Jacks, and lives in DeWitt county. CHRISTIANA, born June 27, 1819, in Ohio, married in Sangamon county, to Philip Clark, Jun. See his name. CLARKSON, born March 3, 1821, in Ohio, married in Sangamon county, to Ann Kyles. They had two children, and live in Minnesota. He was Lieutenant in an Illinois regiment in suppressing the rebellion. ENOS, born Nov. 22, 1822, in Ohio, married in Sangamon county, Feb. 12, 1851, to Rachel Duncan. They have two children, both married, and live near Clinton. BARZILLA, born July 22, 1824, in Ohio, married in Sangamon county, to Rosanna Sackett, moved to Clinton and was Sheriff of DeWitt county and Quartermaster of the 107th Illinois Infantry. They have five children, and live at Twin Springs, Lynn county, Kansas. LEWIS, born Nov. 17, 1826, in Sangamon county, married in Clinton to Philena Argo. They have six children, and live at Clinton, Ill. JOHN N. Jun., born March 24, 1829, in Sangamon county, married June 29, 1852, to Susan Hendel. He died Aug. 11, 1856, near Clinton. SARAH A., born May 30, 1831, in Sangamon county, married Sept, 21, 1854, to Robert Boyd, who died leaving one child, ADA. Mrs. Boyd married Albert Williams, and both died, leaving one child in Clinton. MARY A., born Dec. 22, 1824, in Sangamon county, married James Willis. They have four children, and live near Clinton. John N. Campbell was a soldier in the war of 1812, from Ohio, and the Black Hawk war from Sangamon county. He and his wife live in Clinton now—1874—both over eighty years of age.

LEWIS, married in Ohio to Leah Weaver, came to Sangamon county before the "deep snow," moved back to Ohio in 1832, where he lost his wife, returned to Sangamon county in 1836, married Clarissa Willis, had eight children, and lives near Athens, Menard county. His daughter, Leah, married John Slater. See his name.

RACHEL, married in Ohio to Henry Price, moved to Sangamon county, in 1835, moved, in 1841, to Iowa, and from there to the Pacific coast in 1854. They had ten children, and live in California.

ABIGAIL, married in Ohio to Jacob Mann, raised a large family, and lives near Paris, Edgar county, Ill.

MARY, born in 1790, or '91, in Uniontown, Penn., married in Ohio to William H. Fitz Freeman. They had five children in Ohio, and came to Sangamon county in 1837. She died July 21, 1854, in her 64th year, and Mr. Freeman died Jan. 19, 1856, in the 77th year of his age. Their son, Abraham Freeman, married Margaret Penny, has several children, and lives in Springfield.

JANE, born April 27, 1808, in Butler county, Ohio, married Jacob Gard. See his name.

Mrs. Damaris Campbell died April 23, 1837, and Enos Campbell died June 2, 1838, both in Sangamon county.

CAMPBELL, JOHN, was born Nov. 4, 1790, in Carter county, Tenn. His father, Jeremiah Campbell, settled there before the American Revolution, and was a soldier during the Revolution, under Gen. Francis Marion. He lived to be about 100 years old. His youngest son, Jackson, was the owner of the old homestead at the beginning of the great rebellion. The farm had then been in the family about 100 years. John Campbell enlisted in a company from Carter county, in the war with England, served six months, re-enlisted and served until March, 1815. He was an ensign in the last campaign, and drew a pension to the end of his life. He remained in Tennesssee until 1818, when he went to Madison county, Ill., and was there married Nov. 6, 1818, to Lavina Parkison, who was born Feb. 21, 1803. They moved to what became Sangamon county, arriving March 22, 1819, on Lick creek, in what is now Chatham township, and had seven children there, namely—

ALFRED C., was born July 22, 1819, in Sangamon county, Ill. He was the first white child born on Lick creek, and but two are known to have been born earlier in the county. They were Samuel Drennan, born May 5, 1819, on Sugar creek, and Joseph E. McCoy, born March 13, 1819, on Horse creek. Alfred C. Campbell was married May 3, 1838, in Sangamon county, to Polly Foster, a daughter of Peyton Foster. They had seven children, one of whom, WM. P., died young. JOHN P., born August 4, 1839, in Sangamon county, married Aug. 26, 1858, in Shelby county to Sarah Elliott. They have three children, POLLY, WILLIS, and ELEANOR G., and reside near Mowequa, Shelby county, Ill. John P. Campbell enlisted Oct. 2, 1861, in Co. E, 32d Ill. Inf. He arose by regular grades to the rank of Captain, was wounded at the battle of Hatchie, honorably discharged, and now draws a pension. ELZIRA, E., born April 23, 1844, in Sangamon county, married in 1862, to James W. Clark. They have one child, POLLY, and reside near Mowequa, Shelby county. SARAH C., born Mar. 27, 1846, in Sangamon county, married in 1865, in Champaign county, to F. Bechtel. They have one child, POLLY. LEONORA J., born April 15, 1848, in

Sangamon county, and reside near Mowequa. ALFRED C., Jun., born May 26, 1850, in Sangamon county, married in 1873 to Maggie Hunter. They have one child, CARRIE D., and live near Mowequa, Ill. GEORGE W., born May 9, 1853, in Shelby county, is a sailor, and when last heard from was in Germany. Mrs. Polly Campbell died Jan. 9, 1858, and A. C. Campbell was married June 17, 1859, to Miss Jane Hunt. They are without family, and reside near Mowequa, Shelby county, Ill. Capt. A. C. Campbell enlisted June 10, 1846, in Co. D., 4th Ill. Inf., under Col. E. D. Baker. He was commissioned 2d Lieut., and after the death of Capt. Achilles Morris, at Tampico, Mexico, Lieut. Campbell commanded the company at the siege and capture of Vera Cruz, and the battle of Cerro Gordo. When the rebellion broke out he raised a company, Oct. 2, 1861, and became Capt. of Co. E., 32d Ill. Inf., under Col. John Logan, and fought in all the battles from Fort Donelson to the sea. At Pittsburg Landing his company lost thirty-two men, killed and wounded, out of fifty-six in action. He served three years and four months, and was honorably discharged. Capt. Campbell moved, in 1851, to the vicinity of Mowequa, Shelby county, where he now resides.

WILLIAM P., born Nov. 4, 1820, in Sangamon county, married, March 12, 1843, to Elizabeth Carson. They had fourteen children, five of whom died in infancy, and one, JOSIAH W., was killed in May, 1859, by becoming entangled in the harness on a mule, which ran away with him as he was leaving his plow to escape from an approaching rain storm. Of the other eight, JEREMIAH, born Jan. 1, 1843, married Mary Wheeler, have two children. EARNEST L. and EARLEN R., and reside in Loami township. WILLIAM P., Jun., born April 7, 1846, married Sarah Dodd, who was born Dec. 11, 1847, in Bradley county, Tenn. They had one child, AMANDA, who died July 18, 1873, in her second year. They reside in Talkington township. JAMES S., twin to Josiah W., was born June 5, 1848, married Rebecca A. Hunter, who was born August 15, 1852, in Jersey county. They had two children; one died in infancy, and KITTIE MAY resides with her parents, in Talkington township. SIMON P., born May 17, 1854, married Mar. 6, 1873, to Kate A. Workman, and resides four miles south of Loami. LONELY ARIZONIA, ISAAC H., JACKSON and BEATRICE, reside with their mother. Wm. P. Campbell died August 24, 1868, and his widow resides three miles south of Loami. Mr. Campbell was a soldier in the Mexican war, where he contracted chronic diarrhea, which caused his death more than twenty years after.

JEREMIAH, born Dec. 22, 1822, married Luro Combs, and died in 1853, leaving a widow and two children in Shelby county. Mrs. Luro Campbell married Abner Smith, and resides near Mowequa, Shelby county, Ill.

JOSIAH W., born April 5, 1828, married Elizabeth Workman. They had two living children, and Mrs. C. died and he married Angeline White. They have three children, and reside in Vernon county, Mo.

PETER C., born Jan. 19, 1832, married May 5, 1852, to Amanda E. Carson. They had three children, two of whom died in infancy. RACHEL C. resides with her parents. Peter C. Campbell and wife live in Chatham township, within one mile of where he was born.

CAROLINE, born Oct. 23, 1834, married John Workman. See *his* name.

Mrs. Lavinah Campbell died Dec. 13, 1853, and John Campbell was married in 1855 to Mrs. Margery Carson, whose maiden name was Parkison, a sister of his first wife. She died March 5, 1870. John Campbell died Feb., 1875, on the farm where he settled in 1819, five miles west of Chatham, leaving a large estate which he had accumulated by industry and economy. He, as nearly all the earliest settlers, took part in the Black Hawk war. The first mill in the county, built by Daniel Lisle, was sold by him, and after changing hands once or twice, was bought by Mr. John Campbell, and moved to his farm on Lick creek, where he put it up and ran it for years, each customer bringing his own horses to run it. That kind of mills went out of use long ago, and one of the burrs was used by Mr. Campbell as a doorstep, to the day of his death.

CAMPBELL, LEVI, was born May 1, 1818, in Madison county, Ill., and came to Sangamon county when he was quite young. He was married March 4, 1841, to Susannah Staley. They had three living children, namely—

SARAH J. married John Hudson. See his name.

MARY F., married Kirk Lacey. They have three children, and live in Waverly.

STALEY D., lives west of Loami.

Levi Campbell was a soldier from Sangamon county, in the war with Mexico, in 1846 and '7. He died May 22, 1851, and his widow married Wm. B. McCray. They have three children—

ROBERT D., JAMES A. and STEPHEN W., and live west of Loami.

CAMPBELL, MAXWELL, was born Oct. 29, 1795, in Cabarras county, N. C. His grandfather, Robert Campbell, came from Scotland, bringing six sons: Robert, James, John, William, Samuel and George. Their arrival in North Carolina was not long before the American Revolution, and all the six brothers were soldiers in the Revolutionary army. The second Robert was the father of the subject of this sketch. Maxwell Campbell was married July 25, 1822, in North Carolina, to Nancy Plunkett. She was born June 15, 1806, in the same county. They came to Sangamon county, arriving in May 1823, and settled in the north side of Richland creek in what is now Cartwright township. They had six living children in Sangamon county—

ROBERT R., born August 13, 1823, married Dec. 13, 1847, to Cynthia S. Penny. They have eight children. SAMUEL lives with his parents. NANCY C. married J. Harnsberger. See his name. MATILDA C., GEORGE B., PETER A., IDA JANE, JOHN D. and CHAS. A., live with their parents, two and a half miles northeast of Pleasant Plains.

JOHN H., born May 19, 1828, married Feb. 28, 1851, to Minerva E. Bumgardner. They have three children. ISABEL M. married Aaron Thompson. NANCY E. and WILLIAM J. live with their parents. John H. Campbell enlisted Sept. 18, 1862, for three years, in Co. F, 114th Ill. Inf. Served his full term and was honorably discharged in July, 1865, at Trenton, N. J. He lives east of Pleasant Plains.

JAMES E., born Oct. 8, 1830, married Oct. 4, 1865, to Cordelia Valentine, who was born Dec. 20, 1847, in Pickaway county, Ohio. They live near Pleasant Plains.

MATILDA D., born April 3, 1833, married Jan. 25, 1851, to Wm. F. Irwin. See his name.

WILLIAM V., born May 2, 1836, married Feb. 13, 1862, to Mary E. Valentine, who was born Dec. 14, 1843, in Pickaway county, O. They had four children. OLIVER H. died young. MAXWELL M., JASPER S. and CORA V. live with their parents, at the family homestead settled in 1823.

JASPER J., born May 22, 1839, enlisted Sept. 18, 1862, for three years, in Co. F, 114th Ill. Inf. He was captured at the battle of Guntown, Miss., June 10, 1864, remained in Andersonville prison-pen until near the close of the rebellion, and was marching under rebel authority to the Mississippi river for the purpose of being exchanged. On the second day's march, he being emaciated by starvation, fell out of the ranks, and was never heard of after.

Maxwell Campbell and his wife live on the farm where they settled in 1823. It is four miles northeast of Pleasant Plains.

Maxwell Campbell says he raised the three first crops after he came to Sangamon county, with an ox. He used the ox for riding and all other purposes, the same as a horse. In working he used harness instead of a yoke. He could carry a grist of corn on the ox to mill, hitch him in, do his own grinding, and then carry it home. He made a cart, each wheel of which was a solid piece of wood, and with the ox, did his first hauling. Mr. Campbell says that for the first five years after coming to the county he never had a cent of money. He first built a very small cabin, then prepared hewn logs for a much larger house. They were hauled together and lay two years because he had no money to buy whisky for the raising. He then bought a blind horse for five dollars in trade. It had a bell on it, which Mr. Campbell sold for two gallons of whisky, and was thus enabled to raise the house in which he has lived more than forty years. Soon after trading for the blind horse, he put a sack of corn and a boy on the ox, and rode the horse to mill, hitched the horse and ox together, ground out the grist, and then started home. The ox threw the boy and sack off. The boy caught one foot in the traces, and the ox dragged him among the trees and stumps, and was likely to kill him. Mr. Campbell, seeing the perilous condition of the boy, ran ahead of the ox, caught it by the horns—and knowing him to be its master, rather than the physical strength he exerted—enabled him to hold it until help came and extricated the boy. At this point in the story, the old gentleman paused, looked wise, and with a comical expression of countenance, added in a trembling voice: "*The neighbors always said they knowed that ox afterwards by the prints of my fingers in his horns.*"

CAMPBELL, ROBERT, was born in 1798, in Caborras county, N. C., and married there to Mary Hill. They moved to Sangamon county, Ill., about 1828, and settled on Richland creek. They brought two children with them, and had eight in Sangamon county. In 1868 the family moved to Kansas. Of their children—

JAMES married Nancy H. Stubbs, and has two children, ALBERT T. and OSCAR, and live in Kansas.

NANCY married John E. King, and live in Kansas.

SAMUEL, WILEY, GREEN, JAMES, FRANKLIN, JOHN and CARROLL, the two latter twins, all, married and unmarried, live near Fredonia, Wilson county, Kansas.

Robert Campbell died Sept. 12, 1872, near Fredonia, Kansas, and his widow lives with their children.

CAMPBELL, HUGH, twin brother to Robert, was born in 1798, in North Carolina, married there and came to Sangamon county, Ill., in Sept., 1830, on Richland creek. They had nine children, and Hugh Campbell died August 28, 1865, and his widow died July 26, 1869, both in Rochester.

CAMPBELL, NELSON, youngest brother to Maxwell, Robert and Hugh. He was born in North Carolina, married in Tennessee to Themy Grady, and came to Sangamon county in 1830. They had three children. Their eldest son—

ROBERT, married Mrs. M. Gale, and had two children. He enlisted in 1862, for three years, in the 114th Ill. Inf. Served full term and was honorably discharged. He died Jan., 1873 near Rochester.

Nelson Campbell and wife died in Sangamon county.

CAMPBELL, ROBERT, was born Sept. 9, 1783, in Kanawha county, West Va. Mary Griffith was born there, Sept. 15, 1791. They were married June 30, 1808, and some of their children were born in that county. The family moved to Cincinnati, and from there to Sangamon county, arriving previous to 1835, near Loami. Of their children—

SIDNEY S., born May 4, 1810, in West Va., married in Sangamon county, March 30, 1836, to Barbara A. Neal. They had six living children in Sangamon county. ROBERT D., born Jan. 27, 1840, enlisted July 15, 1861, in Co. C, 11th Mo. Inf., for three years; re-enlisted as a veteran, Jan., 1864, served until Jan. 15, 1866, when he was honorably discharged. He was married Sept. 2, 1868, to Sarah Shryer. They have one child, JAMES E., and live one mile south of Bates. MARIA N., born Feb. 9, 1842, married Wm. H. Sowell. *See his name*. SAMUEL, born March 12, 1844, enlisted Sept., 1861, in Co. B, 10th Ill. Cav., for three years. He was wounded in the battle of Little Rock, Ark., from which he recovered, but died of disease in hospital at that place, Sept., 1863. HARVEY G. born July 7, 1846, lives with his mother. AMARINE, born Nov. 7, 1848, married Morris Lee. They have two children, and live near New Berlin. ELIZABETH, born Sept. 2, 1856, married James M. Williams, who was a Union soldier, also. They have two children, and live in Pleasant Plains. Sidney S. Campbell died in 1874. His widow resides at Loami.

HAMILTON, born June 12, 1812, in West Virginia, married in Sangamon county to Harriet Riddle. They moved to Oregon, where he was murdered.

MARY E. V., born Oct. 4, 1814, married Woodford Turpin, who died while a soldier in the Mexican war, leaving two sons, CHARLES and HAMILTON. Mrs. Turpin married Walter Nicholls and reside near Dundee, Rice county, Minnesota.

JOHN A., born Sept. 30, 1816, in Kanawha county, West Va., came with his parents to Sangamon county, and after spending a few years near Loami, came to Springfield. He was married Oct. 4, 1838, to Susan C. Short. They had five children, four of whom died young. MARIETTA, born July 25, 1841, in Springfield, Ill., was married there, Oct. 28, 1860, to Daniel Myers. They had one child, CAROLINE, and Mr. Myers died Oct. 30, 1863. Mrs. Myers lives with her father, in St. Louis. Mrs. Susan C. Campbell died April 3, 1852, and John A. Campbell married Mrs. Elizabeth Rusk, whose maiden name was Hawker. She died, and he married Nov. 9, 1856, to Elizabeth T. Rich. They have one living child, CYRUS W., and reside at 921 North Tenth Street, St. Louis, Mo.

CHARLES R., born Nov. 17, 1821, in West Virginia, married in Sangamon county to Mary Gibson. They have two children, and live at Oswego, Labette county, Kansas.

WILLIAM P., born Nov. 24, 1826, married Julia Slater. They have three children, and live in Springfield.

NANCY A., born April 27, 1830, married George Underwood, and both died, leaving three children in Buchanan county, near St. Joseph, Mo.

Robert Campbell died Dec. 10, 1845, and his widow died Jan. 26, 1862, both in Loami township.

CAMPBELL, THOMAS, was born Oct. 31, 1786, in Yorkville District, South Carolina. His father, James Campbell, was born in county Antrim, Ireland, and emigrated to South Carolina. Thos. Campbell went, in 1807, to visit his brother David, in Caldwell county, Ky. He was married in that county, March 22, 1810, to Elizabeth Robinson, a sister to Edward Robinson. *See his name.* She was born May 3, 1788, in Nelson county, Ky. Her father, George Robinson, was born in Bucks county, Pa., married in Maryland, to Elizabeth Griffith, moved to Loudon county, Va., and from there to Nelson county, Ky. Thomas and Elizabeth Campbell had eight children in Kentucky. He moved with his family to Sangamon county, Ill., arriving about Nov. 10, 1823. The first land sales took place in Springfield on the sixth of that month, and a few days later he entered some land south of Little Spring creek, and there made a home for his family. It is now in Island Grove township, three miles northeast of Bates, where they had four children. Of their twelve children—

JAMES R. was born March 4, 1812, in Caldwell county, Ky. He enlisted in a Sangamon county Light Horse Co. in the spring of 1831, for the Black Hawk war; served three months, enlisted in another Sangamon county company, in 1832, was in the battle of Wisconsin, and served until the surrender of the Indian chief, Black Hawk. Mr. Campbell enlisted at Galena in Co. K, 1st Ill. Inf., in 1846, for one year. He was in the battle of Buena Vista, Mexico, Feb. 22, 1847, in which Col. J. J. Hardin was killed. J. R. Campbell never married, and resides at the family homestead near Bates.

MARGARET A., born Nov. 8, 1813, in Kentucky, married in Sangamon county, to Allen Short. *See his name.* They had three children, and she died Sept. 23, 1845.

ELIZA J., born July 18, 1815, in Kentucky, married in Sangamon county to Pinckney Hughes. They had four children. MARY E. married Thomas Baker, and lives at Nilwood. THOMAS P. married Amanda Ross, and lives at Nilwood. ANNIE and NETTIE live with their mother. Mr. Hughes died in 1860, and his widow resides at Nilwood, Macoupin county, Ill.

NARCISSA D., born Dec. 9, 1816, is unmarried, and resides at the family homestead, near Bates.

DOROTHY M., and POLLY M., twins, born Oct. 9, 1818, in Kentucky.

DOROTHY M., married in Sangamon county, to Benj. T. Renshaw, moved to Iowa, and had three children, ELIZABETH L., MORGAN and ELIJAH C. Mr. Renshaw was a soldier in an Iowa regiment, and died in St. Louis. His family live near Clio, Wayne county, Iowa.

POLLY M., married in Sangamon county to Robert Wiggins. They have one child, CHARLES, and live near Nilwood, Ill.

WILLIAM B., born Jan. 28, 1821, in Kentucky, married Oct. 11, 1849, to Sarah L. Dunbar, who was born June 1, 1825. They have five living children, CHARLES V., MINNIE A. and WALTER L., (twins), VELMA A.

WILLIAM LINCOLN, and live Oskaloosa, Iowa.

DWARD DODDS, born May 29, , in Sangamon county, married Eliza win. They have two children, ZABETH and CHARLES J., and e near Hutchins, Dallas county, is.

ULIETTE, born June 13, 1827, in amon county, married Solomon idage, moved to Texas, and died in of the rebellion.

OHN B., born Oct. 26, 1829, in San- on county, went to Oregon, about , and from there to California. Last d from in 1867, at Petalouma, Cal.

THOMAS, Jun., born Nov. 2, 1834, angamon county, married Sarah A. y. They have one child, THOMAS nd reside near Hutchins, Texas.

homas Campbell was licensed to ch the gospel in 1818, by Logan bytery, of the Cumb. Presb. church, entucky, and was ordained after com- to Illinois. He preached at Irish ve, Menard county, to the church on ar creek, Sangamon county, and ched in his own neighborhood as long e lived. Rev. Thomas Campbell died 11, 1850, at the place where he set- in 1823, and his widow died there in ., 1876.

AMPBELL, THOMAS H., born May 21, 1815, in Pennsylvania, e to Henderson county, Ill., from e to Chester, in Randolph county, ice to Springfield. He came by the tation of his old friend, Gen. James lds, to discharge the duties of his e, Gen. Shields being then Aditor of e. Mr. Campbell was married Oct. 1845, in Jacksonville, Ill., to Catharine McDougall, a native of New York, sister of the Hon. James A. McDou- , late U. S. Senator from California. and Mrs. Campbell had four children pringfield, namely—

'EANETTE, born Feb. 18, 1847, died Feb. 16, 1862.

THOMAS H., born Dec. 1, 1849, in gamon county, is a lawyer, and resides pringfield.

AMES W., born Dec. 29, 1851, in ingfield, is a farmer, and lives with his her.

TREAT, born Jan. 23, 1855, in Springfield, is a student, and lives with his mother.

Mr. Campbell continued in the auditor's office until the expiration of Mr. Shield's term, and the election of Gen. W. L. D. Ewing, who died in 1846. Mr. C. was appointed to fill the unexpired term. He was elected to the same office in 1848, and again in 1852, thus serving in the State Auditor's office nearly twenty years, be- ing the chief officer ten years of that time. Mr. Campbell was appointed by Gov. Yates, special commissioner to audit accounts between the U. S. Government and the State of Illinois, in which work he was engaged at the time of his death, Nov. 22, 1862. His widow resides east side of Second, near Edwards street, Springfield, Ill.

CANFIELD, JOHN E., was born Jan. 12, 1802, in Morristown, N. J. He came to Sangamon county in 1831, re- turned to New Jersey, and was married in New York City, April 14, 1834, to Susan LaTourette, who was born Feb. 21, 1806, at Somerville, Somerset county, New Jersey. In May, 1834, they came to Illi- nois, and settled west of Springfield, in what is now Curran township. They had five children, one of whom died in infancy. Of the other four—

DANIEL L., born August 29, 1838, in Sangamon county, enlisted April 23, 1861, for three months, in Co. G, 7th Ill. Inf. He was commissioned 1st Lieut. at its organization, and afterwards appointed Quartermaster of the regiment. Served full time, re-enlisted Nov. 25, 1861, in Co. I, 10th Ill. Cav. He was appointed 1st Lieut., and afterwards made Battalion Quartermaster. That office was abolished, and he was mustered out, April 4, 1862. He resumed his position as 1st Lieut. of Co. I, and died May 7, 1863, at St. Louis, of disease contracted in the army.

HELEN M., born Dec. 11, 1840, in Sangamon county, was married in June, 1868, in Morristown, N. J., to Thomas H. Taylor, a son of the Rector of Grace church, New York City. They have one child, THOMAS H., Jun., and reside near Plainfield, N. J.

JOHN C., born Oct. 8, 1842, in San- gamon county, was married Feb. 15, 1865, in Springfield, Ill., to Ella L. Todd, who was born August 27, 1846, in Lexington,

Ky. They have two children, ELLA S. and MAI L. Mr. Canfield has been a merchant in Springfield for the last seventeen years, where he and his family reside.

JAMES F., born Nov. 4, 1844, in Sangamon county, is a clerk in the U. S. Postoffice department, at Washington, D. C.

Mrs. Susan Canfield died April 6, 1846, in Springfield, and John E. Canfield died Jan. 7, 1866, in Jacksonville, Ill.

John E. Canfield was one of the original members in the organization of St. Paul's Episcopal church, in Springfield, and continued a member of the same until his death.

CANEDY, PELEG C., son of Capt. Peleg and Silence Fobes Canedy, was born August 25, 1803, in Enfield, Hampshire county, Mass., partly raised at Middlebury, Vt., and spent most of his early manhood in Washington City, where he was accustomed to see Webster, Clay, Calhoun, and their compeers. There he also saw for the last time, his brother, Lieut. Philander F. Canedy, of the U. S. Navy, who, after having done important service in the harbor of Charleston, S. C., during the nullification excitement, and acted as sailing master of the sloop of war Florida, died Jan. 2, 1834, at Pensacola, Florida. Mr. P. C. Canedy visited New Orleans, Nachitoches and St. Louis, at the latter of which he engaged in business for a time, and came to Springfield, Ill., in Dec., 1830, just in time for the "deep snow." He began the drug business, and still later added books to his stock. This was the first establishment of the kind in Springfield. He was married in Morgan county, Illinois, August 8, 1838, to Sarah Camp, who was born Jan., 1815, in Vermont. They had three children—

CHARLES FOBES, born June 4, 1847, in Springfield. His early education was received in the preparatory department of Illinois University, and at the Central High School, both in Springfield. His preparation for college was continued by his private tutor, Rev. John F. Brooks, of same city. He graduated at Yale college, July 22, 1869, and graduated at the General Theological Seminary, New York City, June 27, 1873. While a student he had charge, as lay reader, of St. Mark's church, Baskingridge, N. J. He was ordained Deacon in the Protestant Episcopal church, by Bishop Potter, of New York, June 29, 1873. He was ordained Priest by the aforesaid prelate, Nov 23, 1873, and Yale college conferred the degree of Master of Arts on him, June 25, 1874. Rev. C. F. Canedy is unmarried, and Rector of St. John's church, Monticello, N. Y.

GEORGE P. died in his third year.

MARY P., born March 31, 1852, in Springfield, was partially educated there, but finished her education at the Chegaray Institute, Philadelphia, and St. Mary's school, New York City. She resides with her brother, the Rev. C. F. Canedy, at Monticello.

Mrs. Sarah Canedy died Jan. 12, 1855, in Springfield. P. C. Canedy was for many years deacon and trustee in the second Presbyterian church, Springfield, Ill., and before the latter place adopted a city government, was member and President of the Board of Town Trustees. He was also one of the committee to receive President Lincoln's remains. He has always been active and energetic in every undertaking which had in view the welfare and happiness of his fellow citizens. A local paper of March, 1863, speaks of him as an example of uprightness and integrity. Mr. Canedy travels much, and is often at Springfield, but considers his son's house his home. He is now, March, 1876, in Springfield.

CANTERBURY, ASA, was born March 7, 1788, in Virginia. His father died when he was a child, and his mother moved to Bath county, Ky. He was married to Peggy Hornback, who was born Feb. 6, 1791. She lived in Fleming county, on the opposite side of Licking river. There being opposition to their marriage, they went to Aberdeen, O., and were there married. It could there be solemnized on short notice, as no license was required by the laws of Ohio at that time, and runaway wedding parties from Kentucky were quite popular. They had four children in Bath county, and moved to the Fleming side of Licking river, where they had three. The family moved to Sangamon county, Ill., arriving in the fall of 1826, in what is now Fancy creek township, where they had four children. Of their eleven children—

—23

ISAAC, born in 1810, in Bath county, Ky., married in Sangamon county, July, 1830, to Elizabeth Morgan. They, with four other families, moved, in 1832, to Des-Moines county, Iowa, crossing the Mississippi river at Flint Hills, now Burlington. They were said to be the first white families that ever moved into Iowa. They had six children, and Isaac Canterbury died there in 1848. His widow and children still live in DesMoines county, Iowa.

MARIA, born in 1812, in Bath county, Ky., married in Sangamon county, May 14, 1829, to William Primm. See his name.

CARLISLE H., born Dec. 5, 1814, in Bath county, Ky., married, August 11, 1836, to Emily Morgan, who was born in Sangamon county. They had thirteen children, four of whom died under six years. Of the other nine: ASA married Margaret England, and lives in Ford county. SARAH married William Fuquay, and lives in Ford county. WILLIAM M. enlisted August, 1861, for three years, in Co. F, 28th Ill. Inf. He was sick when he left Camp Butler, and died at Camp Holt, Ky., Nov. 7, 1861. RUTH A. married Wm. H. H. Holland. See his name. OLIVER P., JOHN C., CARLISLE N., LINCOLN G. and LAURA E. live with their parents, in Menard county, two and a half miles west of Cantrall.

VALENTINE, born in 1816, in Bath county, Ky., died in Sangamon county, aged seventeen years.

JOHN F., born August 27, 1820, in Fleming county, Ky., married in Sangamon county, Feb. 22, 1842, to Miranda M. Brittin. They had six children. JOHN B., born March 24, 1843, died March 19, 1864. ASA M. married April 19, 1866, to Lucinda Fisk. They had five children; three died in infancy. The other two, MATTIE E. and ELLIS, live with their parents, at Cantrall. MARY J. married John J. Stevens. They have three children, CHARLES A., JOHN E. and FRANK E., and reside at Cantrall. MARGARET A. married Joseph S. Cantrall. See his name. EVANS E. resides with his father. WM. H. died in infancy. Mrs. Miranda M. Canterbury died Sept. 22, 1853, and Mr. C. married Sept. 24, 1854, to Harriet E. Purkins, of Menard county. They live near Cantrall. John F. Canterbury raised a good crop of wheat in 1842. He hauled sixty-five bushels of it to St. Louis, one hundred miles, and sold it for thirty-seven and a half cents per bushel. He drove three yoke of oxen, was twelve days, and his total receipts were $24.37½.

ELIZA J., born in Fleming county, Ky., married in Sangamon county, to William Cline. See his name.

OLIVER P., born July 21, 1824, in Fleming county, Ky., married in Sangamon county to Elizabeth Council. They have nine children. MARY E. resides with her parents. MARGARET J. married William Vandergrift. He served three years in an Illinois regiment in aiding to suppress the slaveholders' rebellion. They live in Fancy creek township. MARIA F., MELISSA M., JOHN H., ANNIE F., JULIA E., WILLIAM R. and NELLIE E. live with their parents, in Menard county, two and a half miles southwest of Cantrall.

MARTHA A., born in 1827, in Sangamon county, married Elijah Brittin. See his name. He died March 5, 1873, in Iowa.

MARGARET, born about 1829, in Sangamon county, married Stephen England. See his name.

ABRAHAM, born in 1831, in Sangamon county, died aged twelve years.

JULIA A., born about 1834, in Sangamon county, married Agustus J. Bronson, and reside in Menard county, six miles northwest of Williamsville. Mr. B. enlisted August, 1862, in Co. C, 114 Ill. Inf. for three years. He was a hospital steward from 1863, served more than full term, and was honorably discharged in 1865.

Asa Canterbury died Oct. 16, 1856, and his widow died July 8, 1857.

CANTRALL.—The origin of the family in America was with Zebulon Cantrall, who came from Wales, and settled in Philadelphia, Penn., about the year 1700. There is a tradition in the family that he built the first brick house ever erected in that city. Zebulon Cantrall had a son, Joseph. He had a son, Joshua, who was born August 8, 1748, either in Pennsylvania or Virginia, most probably the latter. He was a soldier in the war for American Independence. This Joshua Cantrall married and had nine sons, but

10 daughter. Four of his sons died without families. Of the other five, Joshua, born in Virginia, raised a family, and died August 11, 1840, in DeWitt county, Ill. The other four, Zebulon G., William G., Levi and Wyatt, are the subjects of the following sketches.

CANTRALL, ZEBULON G. was born June 29, 1773, in Botetourt county, Virginia. He was a brother of Joshua, William G., Levi and Wyatt. The family moved in 1789, to Bath county, Ky. Zebulon G. was married there, August 31, 1797, to Sarah McCallum. They moved to Clarke county, Ohio, from there to Sangamon county, Ill., arriving in the fall of 1833. In the spring of 1834 they moved to DeWitt county, Ill. They had fourteen children; two died young. Of the twelve—

ANN, born August 31, 1798, in Bath county, Ky., married John Branson. *See his name.* She died May 16, 1822.

JOSHUA, born April 3, 1802, in Kentucky, was married in 1828, in Butler county, Ohio, to Eliza Scott. He died Oct. 12, 1860, in DeWitt county, and Mrs. C. resides with her daughter, SARAH, the wife of Irvin Daniels, near Warrensville, Ill. Her son, John S., lives in Kansas.

AGNES M., born Sept. 12, 1806, in Kentucky, married John McIntire. She is a widow, and resides with her brother William.

JOHN M., born Feb. 22, 1808, in Kentucky, was married in Champaign county, Ohio, Nov. 13, 1830, to Joanna M. Jones. They had eleven children; two died in infancy. Of the nine children: WILLIAM J., ZEBULON D., ELIZABETH, IRA J., MARY A., (the latter died in Nov., 1875,) MILES T., ALMA J., EFFIE and JOHN C., the latter died in the spring of 1872. John M. Cantrall died Feb. 11, 1863, and his widow died Sept., 1870, both in DeWitt county, Ill.

JAMES M., born April 10, 1810, in Kentucky, was married August 9, 1832, to Eliza McLaughlin. They had three daughters; one died young. ELMIRA married Abner J. Lutz, and lives near Lincoln, Ill. ELIZA J. married Mr. Piatt, and lives in Lincoln. James M. Cantrall died April 27, 1866, and his widow lives in Lincoln, Ill.

SARAH, born March 14, 1812, in Clarke county, Ohio, was married in Sangamon county, Ill., Jan. 14, 1834, to Joshua M. Cantrall. *See his name.*

ZEBULON P., born Jan. 17, 1814, in Clark county, Ohio, was married in what is now Logan county, Ill., Oct. 16, 1838, to Elizabeth Paulk. They had six children; two died young. AMOS A., born May 11, 1845, in Logan county, enlisted Sept., 1861, in Co. L, 4th Ill. Cav. Served until June, 1866, when he was honorably discharged. He lives near Cisco, Piatt county. MARTHA J., born Oct. 3, 1842, was married June 9, 1862, to Samuel Mott. They have six children. GEORGE A., SARAH E., LEWIS A., JAMES A., EFFIE C. and ALVA, and live near Argenta, Macon county, Ill. SARAH A., born Dec. 25, 1844, was married March 23, 1871, to Theodore A. Funk. She died April 30, 1872. MARY E., born Jan. 8, 1848, was married Jan. 12, 1871, to Edwin C. Hunsley. They have two children, LAURA A. and INEZ, and live near Cisco, Ill. Mrs. Elizabeth Cantrall died June 12, 1852, and Z. P. Cantrall was married to Mrs. Rachel Doyle. She died Oct., 1865, and Z. P. Cantrall was married March 14, 1872, to Mrs. Mary Harp, whose maiden name was Everly. They reside near Chesnut, Logan county, Ill.

ELIZA, born July 4, 1816, in Clark county, Ohio, was married Oct. 5, 1834, to Jeremiah Duncan. She died Jan. 29, 1854, leaving seven children. MARY L., HELEN A., the latter born in 1840, in Logan county, was married to George Whiteman. They live at Waynesville, Ill. AMY L. married Mr. Condell, and he died. WILLIAM W. married Roxanna Cushman. They had two children. REBECCA S. married Mortimer Sampson. They have one child, and live in Waynesville. JEREMIAH P. lives in Waynesville.

REBECCA and RACHEL, twins, born July 25, 1818, in Ohio. REBECCA married in June, 1836, to Jacob F. Sampson. They had three children. Mrs. S. died March 24, 1849. The children live in Kansas.

RACHEL was married in 1842 to Chas. Graves, and resides with her daughter, FANNIE Storer, near Plum Grove,

Butler county, Kansas. Her son, John W. Graves, resides at Centralia, Ill.

WYATT, born May 11, 1821, in Ohio, married Louisa Stevens. She died, and he married Mary A. Day. He died Jan. 7, 1875, leaving a widow near Lane, Franklin county, Kansas.

WILLIAM L., born May 15, 1823, in Ohio, was married Oct. 26, 1843, to Melinda Stout. They had eight children. ANN, born in 1844, was married in DeWitt county to Joel Hopesberger. They have four children, and live near Kenney station. EMELINE, born in 1846, married Thomas Watson. They have three children, and live near Kenney Station. JOHN K., JESSE, WILLIAM and ADDIE. Mrs. Melinda Cantrall died March 10, 1864, and W. L. Cantrall was married in 1865 to Christine Everly, and lives near Chesnut, Logan county, Ill.

Mrs. Sarah Cantrall died May 26, 1843, and Zebulon G. Cantrall died Sept. 11, 1845, both in DeWitt county, near Waynesville.

CANTRALL, WM. G., was born Sept. 6, 1784, in Botetourt, Va. His parents moved to Bath county, Ky., in 1789. He was there married, in 1804, to Deborah Mitts, who was born Nov. 16, 1785, in Virginia. Soon after marriage they moved from Bath county to the vicinity of New London, Huron county, O., and then moved to Pickaway county. They had ten children in Ohio, and the family moved to Sangamon county, Ill., arriving Nov. 1, 1824, in what is now Fancy creek township, on what was then called Higgins creek, but now called Cantrall's creek. Two children were born in Sangamon county. Of all their children—

DOROTHY, born March 15, 1805, in Ohio, married in Sangamon county to Charles Snelson. They had seven children, moved to DesMoines county, near Burlington, Iowa, where Mrs. Snelson died. The family live there.

ANN, born Aug. 1, 1806, in Ohio, married in Sangamon county to John W. Snelson. They had eight children, and moved to Keokuk county, Iowa, where Mrs. Snelson died. The family live there.

ELIZABETH, born Aug. 29, 1808, in Ohio, married in Sangamon county to Joseph D. Langston. *See his name.*

JOSHUA M., born Dec. 17, 1810, in Pickaway county, O., was married in Sangamon county, Jan. 14, 1834, to Sarah Cantrall. She was born March 14, 1812, near Urbana, O. They had eight children in Sangamon county; six died under eight years. Of the other four: ZEBULAN G., born May 7, 1835, married Elizabeth J. Lilly, a native of Augusta county, Va. They have six children, MARY A., MELISSA E., ARMINTA and AMELIA (twins), CELIA J. and NOAH MATHENY, and live in Fancy creek township. WILLIAM G., Jun., born Feb. 20, 1837, married Mary J. Randall. They have four living children, MARCUS N., SARAH M., MARY L. and LOUISA M., and live in Fancy creek township. JACOB M., born Dec. 25, 1841, married Marian J. Tufts, who was born near Buffalo, N. Y. They have one child, ADDIE E., and reside in Fancy creek township. MAHALA E., born Oct. 4, 1845, married Oct. 9, 1873, to George W. Bailey, being his second wife. He was born in Hawkins county, Tenn. He was a soldier in the 5th Tenn. Inf. in the Mexican war, in 1846 and '7; came from Mexico to Sangamon county in 1848. He enlisted in 1862 for three years, in Co. H, 114 Ill. Inf.; was commissioned as Captain at the organization of the regiment. His health failing, he resigned in May, 1863, and lives in Salisbury township. Joshua M. Cantrall resides in Fancy creek township, eight miles north of Springfield.

THIRZA, or *THERESA*, born Nov. 8, 1812, in Ohio, married in Sangamon county, to Edward Guyott. She died Oct. 7, 1851, three months after marriage. He married again, and lives in Springfield.

ADAM M., born Feb. 27, 1815, in Ohio, married in Sangamon county to Delilah Smith. They had nine children. JEREMIAH married Etta Drone, and live in Fancy creek township. HARRIET married Wm. Brisentine; moved to Dallas county, Texas, in 1853. She died there, leaving one child. WM. L. BRISENTINE lives with his granduncle, Joshua M. Cantrall. *See his name.* Adam Cantrall and his wife live at Riverton.

DEBORAH, born Feb. 16, 1817, in Ohio, married in Sangamon county to Marshal S. Randall. They have twelve children, and reside near Blue Mound, Christian county. Their daughter, Mary J., married Wm. G. Cantrall, Jun. *See his name.*

MAHALA, born Dec. 4, 1818, in Ohio, married in Sangamon county to Newton Street. She died, and he resides in Montgomery county.

SUSANNAH, born Nov. 23, 1820, in Ohio, married in Sangamon county to Leonard Mitts. *See his name.*

WILLIAM M., born Dec. 22, 1822, in Ohio, married in Sangamon county to Adaline Claywell. They had nine children; two died under six years. JULIA A. married Leander Jones, have three children, and reside in Salisbury township. MIRANDA married Rollin V. Mallory. *See his name.* JAMES M., PERCY—DEBORAH J. is a cripple, having had eight inches of bone taken from one of her lower limbs — LEWIS E. and SARAH E. The latter is a deaf mute, and is being educated at the State Institution at Jacksonville. The five unmarried reside with their mother. William M. Cantrall enlisted July, 1862, for three years, in Co. C, 114 Ill. Inf.; was appointed Sergeant at the organization. Disease was brought on by over-exertion at the battle of Guntown, Miss., June 10, 1864, and he died in hospital at Memphis, Tenn., July 9, 1864. His widow and unmarried children live in Fancy creek township, eight miles north of Springfield.

MIRANDA J., born May 12, 1826, in Sangamon county, married William Snelson. They had one child, CHAS. H. SNELSON, and William S. died March 9, 1853. His widow was married March 4, 1858, to Samuel Mellinger, who was born Jan. 27, 1832, in Franklin county, Pa. They have four children, WILLIAM C., MAHALA A., DEBORAH A. and LUCY E., live with their parents in Fancy creek township. Mr. Mellinger had one child by a former wife, SAMUEL I. He lives with his father. Samuel Mellinger enlisted Aug. 12, 1862, in Co. C, 114 Ill. Inf., for three years; served full term, and was honorably discharged Aug. 3, 1865.

ANDREW J., born Jan. 4, 1829, in Sangamon county, died March 15, 1842.

Mrs. Deborah Cantrall died March 15, 1856, and William G. Cantrall, Sen., died March 6, 1867, on the farm settled by them in 1824, in Fancy creek township.

CANTRALL, LEVI, was born Oct. 1, 1787, in Botetourt county, Va. He was taken by his parents in 1789 to that part of Mercer which afterwards became Bath county, Ky. He was there married Nov. 30, 1809, to Fanny England. They had one child in Kentucky, and the family moved, in 1811, to Madison county, O., where five children were born. They then moved to Madison county, Ill., in Oct., 1819; moved on and arrived where Springfield now stands, Dec. 4, 1819, and reached the north side of the river, in what is now Fancy Creek township, on the fifth, made the selection of a location on the seventh, and commenced building a cabin Dec. 8, 1819. They had seven children in Sangamon county. Of their thirteen children—

THOMAS, born Oct. 11, 1810, in Bath county, Ky., married Oct. 3, 1831, in Sangamon county, to Priscilla D. McLemore, who was born Sept. 14, 1814, in Tennessee. They had nine children, namely: CLARISSA, born Jan. 20, 1833, unmarried, and resides at the house of H. H. Holland. TURNER H., born May 9, 1834, last heard from in Alabama. YOUNG M., born April 30, 1836, married, 1861, to Ellen Graham; had one child, THOMAS E., and Y. M. Cantrall enlisted in 1862 for three years, in Co. C, 114 Ill. Inf., and died in the army. His widow and son reside in Athens. LEVI, born July 16, 1838, died, aged nineteen. NANCY A., born March 25, 1840, married Egbert Mallory. *See his name.* THOMAS J., born Dec. 21, 1842, served three years in the 10th Ill. Cav., was honorably discharged, and lives in Nebraska. FANNY P., born March 2, 1843, married James D. Mallory. *See his name.* MARY E., born Dec. 8, 1844, is a teacher in Springfield. Mrs. Priscilla D. Cantrall died, and Thomas C. married June 12, 1848, to Elizabeth Estel. They had four children. MARTHA E., born June 12, 1849, married and died in Logan county. ROBERT H., born July 16, 1851, married Miss Goff, has one child, and resides near Athens. WILLIAM M., born April 16, 1853, and CHARLES H., born Dec. 29, 1855, reside with their mother. Thomas Cantrall lost his life by a runaway team dragging a saw-log over him, in 1858. His widow and unmarried children reside near Athens.

ANN, born July 17, 1812 in Madison county, O., married in Sangamon county to Edward Ridgeway. They had three children, and Mr. R. died in 1834. His widow married Ferdinand Meeker, and had several children. She died in Logan county. Her daughter, NANCY RIDGEWAY, married James Milam, and resides in Buffalo Hart, Ill. Her daughter, DULCINA MEEKER, married Jeremiah Lashbaugh, and resides in Illiopolis township.

NANCY, born Sept. 15, 1813, in Madison county, O., married in Sangamon county to Turner Holland. See his name.

STEPHEN L., born April 4, 1815, in Madison county, O., married in Sangamon county to Mary Ridgeway. They had three children. FANNY married George Provines, has seven children, and reside near Clinton. ALMYRA married Samuel Mellinger, and died, leaving one child. Samuel Mellinger married Mrs. Miranda Snelson, whose maiden name was Cantrall. GEORGE W. enlisted Aug., 1862, for three years, in Co. I, 114 Ill. Inf., and died in the army. Mrs. Mary Cantrall died in Buffalo Hart grove, and Stephen L. Cantrall died in 1874, at the house of his brother Joshua.

SELINDA, born Nov. 14, 1816, in Ohio, died in Sangamon county, at twelve or thirteen years of age.

ELEANOR, born Oct. 17, 1818, in Ohio, married in Sangamon county to John Jordan, and resides near Olathe, Kan.

ELIZABETH, born May 26, 1820, in Sangamon county, married James Driskell. Mrs. Driskell died. One son, DAVID, enlisted in Co. C, 114, Ill. Inf., in Aug., 1862, for three years, and died at home of disease contracted in the army. Another son, LEVI, resides in Menard county.

LEVI, Jr., born March 17, 1822, in Sangamon county, married to Elizabeth C. King, who was born July 11, 1828, in Tennessee. They had four children. JASPER H., born March 23, 1847, married Sarah E. Wagner, has three children, WILLIAM H., BERTRAM and JOSEPH, and resides near Paxton. WILLIAM M., born March 1, 1849, married Minnie Wells, has two children, ALVIN N. and

WILLIAM V., and resides near Illiopolis. MARY E. married Sept. 2, 1874, to Benjamin F. Warren, has one child, HARRY N., and resides near Illiopolis. ALFRED N. resides with his mother. Levi Cantrall, Jr., died March 14, 1868, and his widow married Sept. 2, 1874, to Enoch Primm.

RACHEL, born Feb. 29, 1824, in Sangamon county, married John Overstreet. See his name.

CHARLES S., born Jan. 6, 1826, in Sangamon county, married Jan. 7, 1845, to Emily M. Vandergriff, who was born Oct. 6, 1830. They had two children. MARY E., born June 13, 1848, married Jan. 25, 1866, to Stephen O. Price, has two children, and resides near Lincoln. MACDONALD, born Aug. 22, 1851, married Aug. 4, 1870, to Margaret Peden, has two children, and resides in Springfield. Mrs. Emily M. Cantrall died Jan. 29, 1852, and C. S. Cantrall married June 20, 1852, to Lucy Swearengin, who was born Oct. 15, 1828. She died April 14, 1853. C. S. Cantrall married April 26, 1855, to Harriet A. Graham, who was born Feb. 17, 1836, in Athens. They have nine children, CHARLES H., THOMAS D., ALICE, JOHN W., LEVI G., WILLIAM H., FANNY A., HOMER E. and IDA. Charles S. Cantrall had one leg amputated, caused by disease. It was done in Sept., 1871. He resides two miles west of Illiopolis.

JOSHUA, born July 28, 1828, in Sangamon county, married Rebecca Hedrick. They had thirteen children; three died in infancy. Of the other ten, LAFAYETTE was married July 23, 1874, to Gussie Chambers, and lives in Illiopolis township. FANNIE SELINDA married Benjamin Capps. See his name. CARLISLE, BARTON R., JULIA A., MACDONALD, LAURA E., CLARA P., LEVI and BENJAMIN, and reside one and a half miles west of Illiopolis.

JESSE, born April 7, 1830, in Sangamon county, married Eliza J. Humes. They had ten children. He enlisted Aug., 1862, for three years, in Co. C, 114th Ill. Inf. He was commissioned 2d Lieut. at the organization, promoted to Captain, and served as such to the end of the rebellion, and was honorably discharged. He moved with his family to Black Bob, Johnson county, Kansas.

MACDONALD, born April 5, 1833, in Sangamon county, married Narcissa Hedrick. They had one child, and Mr. Crantrall died Sept. 15, 1872. His widow and son, CHARLES, reside in Menard county, five miles northeast of Cantrall.

Mrs. Fanny Cantrall died Sept. 10, 1835, and Levi Cantrall married May 27, 1836, to Mrs. Ann Barnett, whose maiden name was Patterson. They had five children, three of whom died in infancy. Of the other two—

FANNY L., born Oct. 9, 1838, in Sangamon county, married Jan., 1857, to Henry Graham. They have four living children, MARY A., WILLIAM, ARMINDA D. and JOSEPH, and reside near Athens, Menard county.

JOSEPH S., born Oct. 16, 1841, in Sangamon county, married Jan. 14, 1869, to Margaret A. Canterbury. They have one child, DAISY E., and reside at Cantrall. He is one of the proprietors of the new town of Cantrall.

Levi Cantrall died Feb. 22, 1860, and his widow resides with their son Joseph S., at Cantrall. The town of Cantrall was laid out on land he entered soon after coming to the country, and was named in honor of his memory.

INCIDENTS.

From a statement in writing made by Levi Cantrall a few months before his death, I learn that in building the cabin he commenced Dec. 8th, 1819, about half a mile west of the present town of Cantrall, the mortar froze so that he could not plaster it. December 24, 1819, snow began to fall, and continued one snow after another until it was two feet deep on a level. The weather continued intensely cold, and a company of seven men started to the American Bottom for provisions. They were Levi and Wyatt Cantrall, Alexander and Henry Crawford, M. Holland, a Mr. Kellogg and John Dixon, who afterwards founded the city of Dixon, Ill. They loaded their wagons with flour and meal and started home on the eighteenth, and on the twentieth rain commenced falling. The rain and melting snow set the whole country afloat, and when they reached the Sangamon river it was too full to cross. They sent back to Kelly's—where Springfield now stands— for tools, and obtained an axe and grubbing hoe. With these they made a canoe, and reached home twenty-one days from the time of starting. On the 6th of May, 1820, the frost killed their growing corn. The settlers thought of moving back south, but they hauled up provisions before the next winter and lived through it.

Levi Cantrall built a horse mill in the fall of 1820. It was a band mill, with a wheel forty feet in diameter. It was the first mill ever built north of the Sangamon river, and people came thirty miles or more to mill. Mr. Cantrall built a water mill on Cantrall's creek, near the present town of Cantrall. It did sawing and grinding. He says the snow of 1830-31 was four feet on a level. Levi Cantrall kept a tannery where he lived for more than forty years.

CANTRALL, WYATT, was born Dec. 20, 1790, in Bath county, Ky., the same year that his parents moved from Botetourt county, Va. He was married in Bath county to Sally England, and moved to Clarke county, O., where they had three children, and then moved, in company with Mrs. Cantrall's father, Stephen England, to St. Clair county, Ill., in the fall of 1818, and in the spring of 1819 to what is now Fancy Creek township, in Sangamon county, where they had six children. Of their nine children—

ELIZA, born Sept. 8, 1813, in Ohio, married in Sangamon county to John McLemore. He died in 1871, leaving a widow and two children at Stirling, Whiteside county.

SAMUEL D., born Feb. 9, 1816, in Clarke county, O., married in Sangamon county, March 6, 1837, to Sarah S. Alexander. They had six living children. ALBERT A. married March 6, 1862, to Martha Hunt. He enlisted in Aug., 1862, in Co. C, 114 Ill. Inf., for three years, and was appointed Sergeant. He was captured at the battle of Guntown, Miss., in June, 1864, and was placed in the Andersonville prison pen, where he remained about five months, and after that was taken from one prison to another to prevent being released by the Union forces, and was paroled March 1, 1865, and died of starvation and exposure March 5, 1865, at Wilmington, N. C. WYATT E. married Grizella Holland. LUCINDA J. married B. F. Horn. HENRY married Emma E. Graham. ELIZA married Henry Lake, son of Bayless, and MARGARET A. married Isaac Bates, son of Joseph. S. D. Cantrall lives two miles north of Cantrall.

DAVID P., born May 7, 1818, in Ohio, married in Sangamon county to Eleanor McLemore, had three children, and she died. He married Ursula Bull, has three children, and lives in Iowa.

ZEBULON, born Aug. 11, 1823, in Sangamon county, and died in 1840.

WIATT E., born March 22, 1825, in Sangamon county, died in 1841.

STEPHEN E., born April 20, 1827, in Sangamon county, married Caroline Blue. They have seven children, and live at Black Bob, Johnson county, Kan.

WILLIAM J., born July 28, 1829, in Sangamon county, married Lucy Kingsbury, who died, and he married Calista Neil, have three children, and lives at Black Bob, Kan.

POLLY ANN, born Sept. 17, 1832, in Sangamon county, married Thomas Hethcote, have one child, and live at Stirling, Whiteside county.

JOHN H., born Oct. 1, 1834, in Sangamon county, married Eleanor Stratton, have six children, and live in Iowa.

Mrs. Sally Cantrall died Aug. 1, 1840, in Sangamon county, and Wiatt Cantrall married in the fall of 1841 to Mrs. Polly Kingsbury, whose maiden name was Foster. They had one child—

JOSHUA P., born in 1843 in Sangamon county, married Grace Winters. They have one child, and live in Chase county, Kan.

Mrs. Polly Cantrall died about 1859, and Wiatt Cantrall resides at Stirling, Whiteside county.

CANTRILL, THOMAS, was born April 4, 1775, and Elizabeth Murray was born Sept. 19, 1774. The place of their birth is not known, but probably in Orange county, North Carolina, where they were married and had one child. They then moved to Green county, Ky., where they had five children, and moved to Sangamon county, Ill., arriving Oct., 1828, in what is now Rochester township, three and a half miles east of Springfield. Of their children—

MARY, born in North Carolina, married in Kentucky to Thomas Perry, and came to Sangamon county before her parents. They had six children, but all the family are dead.

WILLIAM, born Jan. 17, 1800, in Green county, Ky., came to Springfield, Ill., in March, 1825, was married in Sangamon county Feb. 14, 1828, to Elizabeth Hall, who was born Dec. 8, 1809. They had two children, and moved to Decatur, April, 1833, where they had two children. Of their children: THOMAS H., born Nov. 1, 1829, in Sangamon county, raised in Decatur, and died in the spring of 1864, at Walla Walla, Washington Ter. JANE ELLEN, born Oct. 27, 1832, in Sangamon county, married in Decatur, April 4, 1857, to A. S. Keller, and lives at Sullivan, Moultrie county, Ill. MARY E., born Sept. 27, 1835, in Decatur, married Dr. William Dillon. *See his name.* SUSAN L., born July 3, 1844, married Feb. 3, 1863, to Harl P. Christie, and lives in Decatur. Mrs. Elizabeth Cantrill died August 4, 1868, and William Cantrill lives in Decatur.

SUSAN, married Robert Bird, had two children, and the parents died.

ANNA married William Black. They had six children. The parents and two of the children are dead.

ZEBULON, born April 8, 1807, in Green county, Ky., married in Sangamon county in 1829, to Elizabeth Enyart. They had four children, and he died Jan. 8, 1840. His widow lives near Mechanicsburg.

JOEL, born Jan. 8, 1811, in Green county, Ky., married in Sangamon county, May 16, 1839, to Zerelda E. Branch. They had ten children in Sangamon county; two died in infancy. LEWIS M., born April 9, 1840, married July 23, 1863, to Elmira M. Lee, who was born Oct., 1839, in the State of New York. They live at Joliet, Ill. EDWARD T., born Dec. 27, 1842, enlisted August, 1862, in Co. E, 114th Ill. Inf., for three years, and died July 11, 1863, at Vicksburg, Miss. His remains were brought home and buried near Rochester. LAURA J., the fifth child, died in her fifteenth year. WILLIAM B., JAMES N., HENRY A. and HENRIETTA, twins, and EMILY, live with their mother. Joel Cantrill died Sept. 4, 1866, and his widow lives on the farm where his parents settled on coming to the county, near Sangamon Station.

Mrs. Elizabeth Cantrill died Oct 1, and Thomas Cantrill died Oct. 3, 1836, both near what is now Sangamon Station.

CAPPS, MRS. MARY, whose maiden name was Devas, was a native of London, England. Her husband, Charles Capps, was for many years a merchant in London, and died there. His widow, whose name heads this sketch, came to America with her sons, John, Benjamin and Charles, leaving one son (Thomas) in England. They arrived in Springfield, Ill., Nov., 1830. Her sons Jabez and Ebenezer having preceded the other members of the family several years, Mrs. Capps brought some of her daughters, and others came later.

Mrs. Mary Capps died Nov. 8, 1857, at the residence of her son-in-law, Dr. Alexander Shields, in Sangamon county. Of her nine children who came to America, eight are now living.

CAPPS, JABEZ, born Sept. 9, 1796, in the city of London, England, came to America in the summer of 1817, arriving near what is now Springfield, Ill., in the spring of 1819, and is believed to have been the first school teacher in Sangamon county. He was married in 1828, near Rochester, to Prudence A. Stafford, who was born in Vermont. They had three living children, and Mrs. Capps died May 13, 1836. Jabez Capps was married near Rochester, Ill., Sept., 1836, to Elizabeth Baker. They had ten children, one of whom died young. Of all his children—

CHARLES S., born Jan. 31, 1830, in Springfield, was married May 3, 1854, to Eliza McGraw. They live in Mt. Pulaski.

EBENEZER S., born Feb. 15, 1834, in Springfield, was married in 1856 to Eliza Freeman, and live in Mt. Pulaski.

OLIVER T., born Feb. 13, 1836, in Springfield, was married in 1856 to Eliza Bush, and live in Mt. Pulaski.

By the second marriage—

JOHN H., born Nov. 15, 1839, in Mt. Pulaski, married Martha Pumpilly, and live in his native town.

PRUDY A., born Dec. 18, 1841, in Mt. Pulaski, was married March 8, 1860, to S. Linn Beidler, who was born June 23, 1837, at Mt. Joy, Lancaster county, Pa. Of their seven children, one died young. MONITOR C., FRANK X., JOHN LINN, SNOW FLAKE, IMOGENE and RELL C., live with their parents at Mt. Pulaski, Ill. Mr. Beidler is a druggist, and with the exception of one year during President Johnson's administration, has been Post Master there since 1857.

MARY, born Oct. 8, 1844, in Mt. Pulaska, married Michael McNattin.

WILLIAM, BENJAMIN, JABEZ B., EDWARD, HARRIE B. and *MAUD*, all live with their parents.

Mr. Jabez Capps was a merchant in Springfield from 1827 to 1836, when he formed a company and laid out the town of Mt. Pulaski. Brought his goods from Springfield, and continued in business until 1870. He is now engaged with his son in the nursery business. Mr. Capps was Post Master at Mt. Pulaski for fifteen years, and County Recorder four years. He and his family reside in Mt. Pulaski.

CAPPS, EBENEZER, was born May, 1798, in London, Eng. Came to Springfield in 1820. He returned to Europe in the spring of 1830. On his return he went to Vandalia, Ill., in the fall of same year. He was married in Morgan county, Ill., March 1, 1835, to Ann Norwood. They have five living children, namely—

SARAH, HANNAH, MARY A., CHARLES E. and *THOMAS.*

Mrs. Ann Capps died Sept., 1855, and Ebenezer Capps was married May 29, 1860, in Springfield, to Rosetta Iles. They had one child—

ROSETTA.

Mrs. Rosetta Capps died in Dec., 1861. Ebenezer Capps was married to Mrs. Elizabeth Snyder, at Lincoln, Ill., Oct., 1863. They had two children—

GEORGE B. and *SUSAN.*

Ebenezer Capps and family reside in Vandalia, Ill.

CAPPS, MARY, was born in 1801, in London, Eng.; died unmarried at Vandalia, Ill., Dec. 3, 1858.

CAPPS, ANN, was born in 1803, in London, Eng. She was married there to William Salisch. They came to America, arriving at Vandalia, Ill., in 1833, where Mr. Salisch died the year following, leaving a widow and two children, viz—

SALINA died, aged twelve years.

CHARLES W., born Jan. 24, 1832, in London, Eng., came with his parents to Vandalia, and after the death of his father, was brought by his mother to Springfield, Ill., where he was married, Oct. 31, 1861, to Anna C. Hughes. They had four children. CHARLES F. died in his fourth year. RALPH E., CHAS. E. and SCOTT A. C. W. Salisch is Post Master at Cotton Hill, Sangamon county.

Mrs. Ann Salisch was married in 1837, in Springfield, to Dr. Alexander Shields. *See his name.*

CAPPS, SUSAN, was born in 1805, in London, Eng. She was married in Springfield, Ill., to James Gobbett. He went to California, and died on his way home on the steamer, of Asiatic cholera. Mrs. Gobbett lives with her sister, Mrs. Dr. Shields.

CAPPS, SARAH, was born in 1807, in London, Eng., is unmarried, and lives with her sister, Mrs. Dr. Shields.

CAPPS, JOHN, was born Dec. 16, 1810, in London, Eng. Came to America with his mother, brothers and sisters, arriving at Springfield, Ill., in Nov., 1830. He was married there Sept. 5, 1833, to Nancy Clements, who was born Oct. 2, 1817, in Lincoln county, Ky. (She is a cousin of Mrs. Mathew Cloyd.) Mr. and Mrs. John Capps had five children in Springfield, and in 1844 moved to Mt. Pulaski, where they had four, and about 1855 moved to Decatur, where they had three; thence to Illiopolis, Sangamon county. Of their twelve children two died young—

MARY M., born Oct. 6, 1834, was married Jan. 19, 1853, to James Sims. They have six children, ADA, JOHN F., ELLA, HATTIE, RALPH LINCOLN and FANNIE, and live in Mt. Pulaski.

THOMAS W., born Dec. 26, 1838, in Springfield, enlisted in 1862 for three months, in Co. I, 68th Ill. Vol. Inf.; served full term, and enlisted in the United States Navy. He was married Dec. 29, 1869, to Nellie Van Hise, in Mt. Pulaski. They had one child, EARL, Mrs. Nellie Capps died, Oct. 23, 1873. Mr. T. W. Capps lives in Mt. Pulaski.

CHARLES R., born March 11, 1841, in Springfield, was married in Mt. Pulaski, May 29, 1862, to Lizzie Lushbaugh. They have four children, LOUIE E., ELMER LINCOLN, FRANK and MABEL, and live in Mt. Pulaski.

ALEXANDER S., born May 2, 1843, in Springfield, enlisted Aug. 9, 1862, for three years, in Co. B, 106th Ill. Vol. Inf., served until Aug. 1, 1865, when he was honorably discharged. He was married Sept. 3, 1867, to Maggie Ishmael. They have one child, KATIE E., and live in Illiopolis.

JABEZ M., born Aug. 19, 1845, in Mt. Pulaski, enlisted in 1863 for one hundred days, in Co. D, 145th Ill. Inf., served more than full time, and was honorably discharged. He was married June 17, 1867, to Sallie Bechtel. They have three living children, LONE, PEARL and GERTRUDE. J. M. Capps is engaged in milling at Mt. Pulaski, and lives there.

ANN S., born Jan. 22, 1848, in Mt. Pulaski, was married May 5, 1868, to James W. McGuffin. She died in Illiopolis, April 7, 1874, leaving three children, BENJAMIN F., WALTER and JOHN C.

BENJAMIN F., born July 21, 1850, in Mt. Pulaski, was married Aug. 12, 1870, to Fannie S. Cantrall. She was killed Oct. 8, 1870, near Illiopolis. She was mounting a horse, when it took fright, drew the rein in a noose around her hand, and dragged her until she was dead. B. F. Capps married Emma Snyder. They live at Mt. Pulaski.

ALBERT B., *JOHN C.* and *BUNN*, live with their parents. John C. had a twin mate, who died young.

John Capps and family reside one and a half miles west of Illiopolis.

CAPPS, CHARLES, was born Feb. 7, 1814, in London, Eng. Came with his mother, brothers and sisters to America, arriving at Springfield, Nov., 1830, and moved to Vandalia in December of the same year. He was married Nov. 11, 1852, in Sangamon county, Ill., to Elizabeth A. Gobbett, who was born Oct. 27, 1836, in Missouri. They had four living children—

MARY A., born Dec. 3, 1854, was married March 13, 1872, to George R. Wylie. They have one child, MAUDE E, and live in Mt. Pulaski.

SARAH F., JAMES A. and *AMY G.*, reside with their parents in Mt. Pulaski.

CAPPS, BENJAMIN, was born June 24, 1820, in London, England. Came to Springfield in 1830, and to Van-

dalia in 1831. He returned to England in 1844, and remained there until 1852, when he went to Australia, and returned to Vandalia in 1856. He was married in Mt. Pulaski in May, 1862, to Lucy McGraw. They have four living children—
IDA, JENNIE, BENJAMIN and *HANNAH N.*

Benjamin Capps has always faithfully served his adopted country, and votes the straight Republican ticket. He, with his family, reside in Vandalia, Ill.

CARPENTER, WILLIAM, born July 3, 1787, in the city of Philadelphia, Penn., was the eldest son of Samuel and Catharine Carpenter. He had two brothers, Charles and Samuel, Jun.; also two sisters, Elizabeth and Catharine. His father died when William was quite young, leaving the family dependent entirely on their own exertions for a livelihood. William was baptized in the German Lutheran church in Philadelphia, Sept. 23, 1787. Carl Linnensheet and Margreth, his wife, (grandparents), sponsors. Arrived at manhood, he and his brother Samuel came to Licking county, Ohio, then the "far west." In the fall of 1819 William C. was married to Margaret Pence, who is still living. She was the daughter of Peter and Catharine Pence, and was born Feb. 5, 1803, in Shenandoah county, Va. Her mother's maiden name was Godfrey, whose father fought in the Revolution, under Gen Wayne, and was killed by the Indians, near Wheeling, Va., in the summer of 1820. William Carpenter, his wife and Samuel, started for Illinois. The time occupied in coming was six weeks. They passed through what is now Springfield, crossed the Sangamon river, and built a cabin about two miles north of it. At that time the "Kelly cabins" constituted all the settlement at what is now the city of Springfield. Samuel C. soon tired of the west, and returned. When land came into the market, Wm. C. entered the land upon which he had settled, and erected a two story log house, which is still standing, although dilapidated. This afterwards became an important point for the stage line on the State road leading from Springfield to Peoria, and called the "six mile house." Their nearest neighbors then were three or four miles distant, and the Indians (friendly tribes) frequently visited the house for something to eat, and a matter of considerable alarm to the females when the men were away, as was frequently the case, "to mill," or "on a hunt." They grew cotton, picked, carded, spun and wove it into cloth for family use. These cards are still in the possession of some of the family. For a long time Edwardsville, Madison county, Ill., was the nearest mill and postoffice. It took two weeks to go and return with a grist, usually a sack of corn, on horseback. St. Louis, Mo., was the nearest market. About the year 1828, William Carpenter, with a family of five children, moved to Springfield, then grown to the dignity of a town, and called Calhoun. He there engaged in merchandizing. The farm was afterwards rented, and occupied by Hon. S. T. Logan, then just arrived from Kentucky. Six children were born in Springfield. Of their eleven children—

CATHARINE, born Sept. 28, 1820, in Sangamon county, was married June 8, 1843, in Springfield, to Adolphus Wood, who was born Nov. 8, 1806, in Chenango county, N. Y. They had six children; the two eldest died young. Of the other four, WILLIAM C., born in Springfield, Ill., Dec. 28, 1848, was married August 29, 1874, in Chicago, to Emma E. Wood, who was born in Springfield, Jan. 2, 1851. They have one child, CHARLES O., and live on the farm with his mother. ELIZABETH and GEORGE live with their mother. CHARLES is clerk in Diller's drug store, Springfield, Ill.

Mr. Wood died Jan. 12, 1861, and his widow resides three and a half miles north of Springfield.

CHARLES, born Nov. 12, 1822, in Sangamon county, was killed in Springfield by a fall from a horse, March 17, 1833.

SAMUEL, born Nov. 12, 1824, in Sangamon county, was married Nov. 27, 1851, to Mary E. J. Kerns, who died March 16, 1853, and Samuel C. was married Dec. 16, 1858, to Mrs. Martha J. Black, whose maiden name was Short, daughter of Rev. Daniel Short. She was born Sept. 25, 1831, in Butler county, Ohio. They had six children born in Sangamon county. ANNA S., WILLIAM D., CARRIE E., MARTHA J., MARY M. and LENA L. Mrs. Martha J. Carpenter died July 17, 1873. Samuel Carpenter and his children resides five miles north of Springfield, adjoining the farm where he settled in 1820.

ELIZABETH, born Jan. 19, 1826, in Sangamon county, was married Nov. 27, 1851, in same place, to Richard Cobbs, who was born in Cynthiana, Harrison county, Ky., May 22, 1822. They have four children, MARIETTA, JOHN W., ALBERT R. and MARGARET A. Mr. Cobbs is a tailor, and resides in Springfield.

WILLIAM, Jun., died in his third year.

MARGARET, born Feb. 27, 1830, in Springfield, was married June 5, 1848, to William A. Browning, who was born April 23, 1825, in Licking county, Ohio. They have seven children living; three died in infancy. AMELIA E. was married Dec. 28, 1871, to R. F. Gailey. Their only child, WILLIAM A., died in infancy. They reside in Pana. EVA O., MARGARET L., MARY J., WILLIAM O., LOUISA B. and FLORA M. reside with their parents. Mr. and Mrs. Browning reside in Pana, Ill.

JOHN, born Nov. 2, 1832, and
GEORGE, born March 28, 1835, in Springfield, both reside with their mother.

EMILY A., born August 8, 1837, died Oct. 5, 1854.

MARY E., born March 28, 1843, and
SARAH J., born Jan. 26, 1846. The unmarried children reside with their mother.

William Carpenter died August 30, 1859, in Springfield, and his widow resides at the corner of Seventh and Carpenter streets, Springfield, Ill. William Carpenter was elected Justice of the Peace in Ohio in 1820, held the same office in Sangamon county about fourteen years, and was the second Justice of the Peace in Sangamon county. May 15, 1830, he was appointed Quartermaster 20th Reg. Ill. Militia, Col. T. M. Neal commanding. April 12, 1832, he was appointed Paymaster 4th Reg. Mounted Vol. Inf., by Col. Samuel M. Thompson. In 1834 was elected to represent Sangamon county in State Legislature, when the Capital was at Vandalia. He was subsequently a member of the city council for a number of years. In 1837 was appointed by President Van Buren, Postmaster at Springfield, which office he resigned in 1840. In 1844 and '5 Mr. C. with his son-in-law, Adolphus Wood, erected a saw and grist mill on the Sangamon river, on the Peoria road, which has always been known as Carpenter's mill, although christened Rock Dam Mills.

CARSON, JOHN, was born Aug. 8, 1794, on Saluda river, S. C., and raised in Campbell county, Tenn. He was in a Tennessee regiment in the war of 1812. After the war he came to Madison county, Ill., with his father, and was there married to Margery Parkison, in 1818. She was born Oct. 19, 1799. They came to Sangamon county in 1820 or '21, and settled on Lick creek, in what is now Chatham township. They had ten children, all born in Sangamon county except one. Of their children—

JAMES S., born Oct., 1819, married Permelia Swanson. They had five children. He was accidentally shot and killed April 12, 1859, by another hunter mistaking his call for that of a turkey. That was in Fayette county. His only two surviving children, WESLEY McD. and ISAAC M., reside in Loami township.

RACHEL, born in 1823, in Sangamon county, married Ransom Youtsler. They both died, leaving five children. Her death took place Nov. 9, 1863.

ELIZABETH, born Dec. 25, 1824, in Sangamon county, married William P. Campbell. See his name.

AMANDA E., born April 17, 1829, in Sangamon county, married May 5, 1852, to Peter C. Campbell. See his name.

WILLIAM P., born Dec. 25, 1830, in Sangamon county, married April 5, 1855, to Minerva Workman. They have seven children, DAVID, SARAH, JOHN C., ELIZABETH, LYDIA A., LEE and AMANDA, and live in Loami township.

ISAAC C., born Feb. 7, 1833, in Sangamon county, married Martha Lawson, have one child, and live in Crawford county, Kan.

JOHN M., born March, 1836, in Sangamon county, married Elizabeth Workman. They have six children, and live in Crawford county, Kan.

LOUISA, born April 11, 1840, in Sangamon county, married William A. Barnes. He was born Aug. 2, 1836, in Talladega county, Ala. She died May 27, 1872, leaving four children with their relatives in Chatham and Loami townships. W. A. Barnes married Lucy A. Allen, and live in Chatham.

John Carson died in Fayette county, Nov., 1844, and his widow married John Campbell. *See his name.*

CARSON, WILLIAM, born July 8, 1799, in Westmoreland county, Pa. When he was four years old his father moved to Hamilton county, Ohio. William was never out of that county until he was twenty-six years old. He then came to Sangamon county, Ill., arriving Nov. 1, 1825, at Springfield. He walked the whole distance from Cincinnati to Springfield in eleven days. He spent the first winter at Sangamo, and was married May 21, 1826, to Cynthia Broadwell. They had fifteen children, seven of whom died young. Of the other eight—

SARAH J., born March 2, 1828, married Aaron Thompson. Mrs. T. died Oct., 1855, leaving two children in Missouri.

LEAH A., born July 30, 1829, married William De Armand, have nine children, and live in Atchison county, Kan.

ELIZABETH A., born Oct. 6, 1831, married Oct. 2, 1856, to Jacob King, and live in Nodaway county, Mo.

RACHEL C., born Dec. 22, 1832, married Nov., 1863, to Joshua Short, have one child, and live in Nodaway county, Missouri.

MARY M., born July 26, 1834, married Jacob Shawver. He was a soldier in an Iowa regiment, and died at Helena, Ark., in April, 1863. She married Josiah Culver, and live in Marion county, Iowa.

HELEN B., born April 30, 1837, married Feb., 1860, to Charles B. Miller, have six children, and live in Marion county, Iowa.

WINFIELD S., born May 27, 1843, married March 27, 1866, to Emma J. Taylor, who was born Oct. 30, 1844, in Somerset county, N. J. They have three children, WILLIAM E., JENNIE A. and CHARLES F., and live near Pleasant Plains.

WILLIAM L., born Nov. 6, 1846, married March 12, 1868, in Hamilton county, O., to Ella Carson, who was born there Sept. 17, 1844. They have three children, ROBERT B., ALICE M. and NELLIE B., and reside one and a half miles east of Pleasant Plains.

William Carson and his wife are living on the farm settled by her brother, John B. Broadwell, in 1819. Mr. C. has lived nearly half a century within one mile of where he now resides, one mile east of Pleasant Plains.

CARTER. PLATT S., was born June 29, 1815, in Warren, Litchfield county, Conn. He came to Waverly, Ill., in Nov., 1836, and in Jan., 1837, began to improve the farm where J. Milton Lockbridge now resides, one mile west of Auburn. He was advised to abandon the project, lest he should freeze to death, and was solemnly warned that he would be compelled to live without neighbors, his improvements being more than two miles from the timber. He returned to his native town, and was there married, July 25, 1839, to Flora M. Carter, who was born in the same place, July 25, 1815. They came at once to their new home, near Auburn, traveling the entire distance in wagons. At that time there were no improvements southwest nearer than fifteen miles, and the whole area a natural meadow. There was an abundance of grass for thousands of cattle and sheep. A year or two later Mr. Carter bought a flock of sheep, and that caused great uneasiness to some of the neighbors, who had a few head of cattle, lest the sheep would eat all the grass. Mr. and Mrs. Carter had four children in Sangamon county, namely—

ADONIRAM, born Nov. 5, 1842, enlisted August, 1862, in Co. C, 101 Ill. Inf., but was discharged on account of physical disability, without fully entering the army. He graduated at Michigan University, in the class of 1868, and is now a practicing attorney at 157, south Clark street, Chicago.

DARIUS, born June 6, 1845, enlisted May 2, 1864, in Co. C, 145th Ill. Inf., for one hundred days. and was honorably discharged, Sept. 28, 1864. He was married April 6, 1869, to Avice Pickett, who was born Nov. 9, 1848, at Hartland, Conn., and died May 14, 1870. He was married April 29, 1873, to Sarah Poor, who was born Oct. 1, 1850, in Sullivan county, Tenn. They reside in the southwest part of Loami township.

LUCINDA A., born August 31, 1848, in Sangamon county, married June 25, 1874, to Dr. Albert Brown, who was born

June 25, 1849, in Chicago, Illinois. He graduated at Bellevue Hospital Medical College, New York City, March, 1873, and resides in Waverly, Ill.

PLATT S., Jun., born Dec. 6, 1850, in Sangamon county, married near Waverly, Morgan county, Nov. 20, 1873, to Belle Woods, and resides in Sangamon county, near Waverly, Ill.

Platt S. Carter, Sen., is one of the many successful farmers of this county. He has always taken an active interest in every movement calculated to develop the resources of the country, and to elevate the intellectual standard of the cultivators of the soil, and has several times represented Loami township in the Board of county Supervisors. He has been an energetic worker in the interests of the Sangamon county Agricultural Society, and was President of the same for the year 1875. He resides in Loami township, two and a half miles north of Waverly.

CARTWRIGHT, PETER, was born Sept. 1, 1785, on James river, Amherst county, Va. His father was a Revolutionary soldier, and soon after our independence as a nation was acknowledged by Great Britain, his parents moved to that part of our country known as Kentucky, then inhabited by hostile Indians. There not being any wagon roads, the moving was done on pack horses. Their's was one of two hundred families that moved in a body, guarded by one hundred young men, well armed. On the night of the first Sunday after their departure, and while they were encamped with the women and children in the center, surrounded by part of the men guarding, while others slept, the father of Peter Cartwright heard something moving towards him and grunting like a hog. Knowing there was no swine with the company, Mr. C. had his suspicions aroused and kept a sharp look-out. He soon perceived a dark object much nearer him than the sounds at first indicated, and readily made up his mind that it was an Indian aiming to get as near as possible, and then spring upon and murder him in the dark. Mr. Cartwright took aim and fired. The crack of the rifle raised a great commotion in camp, and as soon as a light could be procured, an Indian was found dead, with a rifle in one hand, a tomahawk in the other, and a bullet-hole through his head. Their line of travel was marked by the dead bodies of white people slain by the Indians, with other evidences of hostility. As the moving party approached Crab Orchard, where a temporary fortification had been erected, the last day's march was a very long one. Seven of the two hundred families fell behind the main body, and worn down with fatigue, they encamped and went to sleep without guards. In the night they were attacked by twenty-five Indians, and all except one of them slain. The Cartwright family first settled near what afterwards became Lancaster, Lincoln county, Ky. After a stay of two years, in the fall of 1793 Mr. Cartwright moved his family to a place nine miles south of Russelville, Logan county, Ky., and within one mile of the Tennessee line.

While the family resided there Peter entered into the spirit of the rude sports and vices that prevailed in the community, such as horse-racing, card-playing and dancing. His mother had long been a member of the M. E. Church, and prayed for and plead with her son to turn from the error of his ways. He was converted, and united with the Ebenezer M. E. Church in June, 1801. He displayed such talents and fervor in speaking, that he very unexpectedly received the following paper:

"Peter Cartwright is hereby permitted to exercise his gifts as an exhorter in the Methodist Episcopal Church, so long as his practice is agreeable to the Gospel.

"Signed in behalf of the Society at Ebenezer.

"JESSE WALKER, A. P."

May, 1802.

In the fall of that year his father determined to move to Lewiston, near the mouth of the Cumberland river. Peter applied for letters for his mother, sister and himself. Upon receiving his own he found that it was not only a letter of dismissal to a sister church, and to exhort, but that it gave him authority to hold meetings, organize classes, and form a circuit. It also required him to report at the fourth quarterly meeting of Red river circuit the next fall.

In his new home he found an academy, or school of a high grade, and for a time prosecuted his studies with great success;

but in consequence of persecutions that arose, he abandoned the school and commenced organizing the circuit, which he reported in the fall of that year—1803. In October he became a regular traveling preacher, with a colleague, on the Red river circuit. His first sermon led to the conversion of an infidel. He received twenty-five members during the first quarter, and six dollars for his support at the end of the same. For the years 1805 and '6 he was appointed to Sciota circuit, in the State of Ohio.

At the meeting of the Western Conference, held in East Tennessee, Mr. Cartwright was ordained Sept. 15, 1806, as a Deacon in the M. E. Church, by Francis Asbury, the first Bishop of the church in America. He was next appointed to Marietta circuit. In the fall of 1806 he left that circuit, with a blind horse, almost destitute of clothing, and seventy-five cents in money, started to travel more than five hundred miles to see his parents. The next meeting of Conference was held Sept. 14, 1807, at Chillicothe, O. His appointment for 1807-8 was to Barren circuit, in Cumberland district, Ky. About the close of his labors in that circuit—

Rev. Peter Cartwright and Frances Gaines were married Aug. 18, 1808. She was born Aug. 18, 1789, in Charlotte county, Va. When she was in her seventeenth year her parents moved to Lincoln county, Ky. Her father died there, and her mother moved two years later to Barren county, where Frances was married.

The Conference was held at Liberty Hill, Tenn., commencing Oct. 1, 1808. At that meeting Mr. C. was ordained—Oct. 4, 1808—to the office of Elder of the M. E. Church, by William McKendree, who had become one of the Bishops of the M. E. Church. The ordination took place Oct. 4, 1808. His next appointment was to Salt Creek circuit, Ky. During that year his father died, and some time was spent in settling the estate. The next Conference was held at Cincinnati in the fall of 1809. His appointment was to Livingston circuit, Cumberland district, Ky. Mr. C. continued to preach in Kentucky until they had seven children. During that time he saw and understood the pernicious influence of slavery, and after consulting with his wife, who was of the same mind, they determined to remove to a free State. In the spring of 1823, he, in company with two friends, started to explore Illinois in search of a home. They ascended the Wabash valley, and crossed the prairie to the Illinois river above Fort Clark, now Peoria. They went west and south and then east, crossing the Illinois river at what is now Beardstown, where there was but one family in a small cabin. From there they ascended the valley of the Sangamon river to a settlement in Sangamon county, on Richland creek, where he found a family living in a double log cabin, with a few acres of land under cultivation. Mr. C. bought the claim, and entered the land when it came into market.

He returned to Kentucky and brought out his family, arriving Nov. 15, 1824, at the place he had purchased the year before, in what is now Cartwright township, three-quarters of a mile north of Pleasant Plains. They had two children in Sangamon county. Of their nine children—

ELIZA B., born in Livingston county, Ky., May 11, 1810, married Peyton L. Harrison. See his name.

MARIA H., born Sept. 20, 1812, in Christian county, Ky., married in Sangamon county, July 28, 1833, to Rev. W. D. R. Trotter, who was born near Bowling Green, Ky., and came to Sangamon county in 1830 or '31. Mr. Trotter was a traveling preacher in the M. E. church from the time he came to the State until 1872, when he became superannuated, and resides in Jacksonville. They have five children, all married.

CYNTHIA, born March 27, 1815, in Christian county, Ky., was killed Oct. 23, 1824, by a tree, near which they had encamped and kindled a fire, falling on her while they were all asleep on the ground. They carried the corpse of their child twenty miles, and buried it in Hamilton county, Ill.

MADISON A., born July 4, 1817, in Christian county, Ky., married Dec. 29, 1835, in St. Louis, to Matilda Purvines, both of Sangamon county. They had six children, namely: WILLIAM T. married Emma Slater; had one child, EVA A., and he married Florence Moore; had two children, EDGAR EVERETT and ASBURY L., and reside in Cartwright township. MARTHA J. married Daniel Harnett, and died August 8, 1862, at

Pleasant Plains. PETER S. married Frances Maria Irwin; have two children, JENNIE E. and ROBERT A., and reside near Chanute, Kansas. ELIZABETH F. married Peter L. Harrison. *See his name.* JOHN M. and ANNIE M. reside with their parents at Pleasant Plains.

WEALTHY M. J., born August 9, 1819, in Christian county, Ky., married March 17, 1840, to Gorham Eaton, who was born in Merrimac county, N. H. They had three children, EMILY F. married William G. Purvines. *See his name.* MARY A. married A. S. Nottingham. *See his name.* HORACE G. married Ella Allen, had one child, ELLEN, and Mrs. Eaton died. He resides near Pleasant Plains. Gorham Eaton died August 26, 1846, and his widow married March 26, 1850, to Elmer Mickel, who was born in Cape May county, N. J. They have six children, ANNIE, CHARLES H., CAROLINE M., ARMINDA B., MYRA E. and EDWARD LINCOLN, and reside two miles northwest of Pleasant Plains.

VALENTINE C., born May 19, 1821, in Christian county, Ky., married in Sangamon county, Feb. 9, 1841, to Cinthelia Scott. They have nine children. SARAH F. J. resides with her parents. THOMAS B. married Mary E. Cloud, daughter of Rev. Newton Cloud, of Jacksonville; have two children, MAUD and CLAUD, and reside near Waco, Sedgwick county, Kansas. CARRIE E. married Samuel D. Pallett, and resides near Waco, Kansas. HATTIE J. married David O. Williams; has one child, LESTER, and resides near Waco, Kansas. CHARLES A. resides near Waco, Kansas. ALBERT B., MINNIE P., NEWTON C. and WALTER D., reside with their parents. V. C. Cartwright lived near Pleasant Plains until 1874, when he moved to Sedgwick county, near Delano, Kansas.

SARAH M., born July 2, 1823, in Christian county, Ky., married Sept. 1, 1841, to Henry Smith, who was born in Cape May county, N. J. They had ten children; two died in infancy. MARIA F. married Frank N. Elmore. *See his name.* PETER C., born Oct. 24, 1844, married Margaret McDonnell, who was born Nov. 17, 1844, at Lexington, Ky. They have four children, HENRY, MARY O., NETTIE and CARROLL, and reside at Pleasant Plains. WILLIAM T. died Feb. 22, 1869, in his twenty-third year. MADISON N. resides west. CAROLINE E., HENRY D. and EDWARD P. reside with their mother. Henry Smith died March 20, 1873, and his family reside at Pleasant Plains.

CAROLINE M., born Sept. 9, 1826, in Sangamon county, married August 30, 1848, to Rev. Benjamin Newman. They had one child, PETER C., who married and resides at Mattoon. Mrs. C. M. Newman died May 23, 1853.

ARMINDA F., born Oct. 3, 1828, in Sangamon county, married Aug. 30, 1848, to Rev. Levi C. Pitner. They have one son, LEE PITNER, and reside at Evanston, Ill.

Rev. Peter Cartwright, D. D., died Sept. 25, 1872, and his widow died Feb. 7, 1876, both near Pleasant Plains, Sangamon county, where they settled in 1824. Mr. Cartwright had been a member of the M. E. Church more than seventy-one years, a preacher nearly three score and ten years, and a Presiding Elder more than half a century. To attempt a description of the man and his labors would be useless in a sketch like this. Nothing but his own "Autobiography" and "Fifty Years a Presiding Elder" could do justice to the subject. His system of theology does not admit of a belief in special providences; and yet, it would appear to others as though he was especially raised up to illustrate what one man can accomplish in mental and physical labors in a good cause, sustained by the power of God. He had just entered upon his eighty-eighth year, and his wife in her eighty-seventh year. At the time of her death she had fifty-three grand-children, sixty-two great-grand-children, and five great-great-grand-children, a total of one hundred and twenty-nine descendants.

The circumstances of her death were exceedingly impressive. She was attending a religious meeting at Bethel Chapel, about one mile from her home, in the opposite direction from Pleasant Plains. The minister conducting the services called on her as the first to give her testimony, which she did, remaining seated. She spoke with much feeling, closing with the words: "The past three weeks have been the happiest of all my life; I am waiting for the chariot." The exercises continued until sixteen persons had risen and spoken a few words each, the last of whom was her eldest son. The lady sitting nearest her thought she had fainted, and the windows were thrown open to admit fresh air; but "The chariot had arrived."

CARTMELL, ANDREW, was born March, 1766, in Greenbrier county, Va. He went to Bath county, Ky., when he was a young man. Nancy D. Brown was born Oct., 1772, in Culpepper county, Va., and in 1780 was taken by her parents to Bath county, Ky. A. Cartmell and Nancy D. Brown were married and had eight children in Kentucky, and they moved to Sangamon county, Ill., arriving Oct. 10, 1829, six miles northeast of Springfield. Of their children—

WILLIAM W., born Oct., 1800, in Bath county, Ky., married there in 1832, to Mary Crockett, moved to Sangamon county, and from there to Ralls county, Mo., raised a family of six children, and lives near Merton, Grundy county, Mo.

LUCINDA married in Kentucky to John Rudder, had two children, and died there. Her children came to Sangamon county with their grandfather Cartmell. LUCRETIA married Samuel Houston. *See his name.* THOMAS was a soldier in the 4th Ill. Inf., and was killed in 1847, in the Mexican war.

JOHN M., born August 25, 1802, in Bath county, Ky., was married there March 23, 1829, to Mildred R. Tacket, and came with his parents to Sangamon in the fall of that year. They had five children. AMANDA A., born April 29, 1830, married March 2, 1852, to James Black. *See his name.* JOHN W., born May 19, 1833, married in Missouri to Mary E. Chipps, have four children, and reside near Merton, Mo. He served three years in Co. C, 23d Mo. Inf., from Aug., 1861. JAMES H., born Oct. 14, 1837, married Martha Crane, who died April 19, 1871, leaving four children. He married Nov. 19, 1872, to Mrs. Zilpha Halbert, whose maiden name was Taylor. They live four miles east of Springfield. ELIZA A., born August 30, 1842, married James Black. *See his name.* MARION, born July 19, 1845, married Feb. 1, 1872, to M. O. James, have one child, ANNIE R., and live six miles north east of Springfield. Mrs. M. R. Cart-

mell died April 14, 1875, and John M. Cartmell lives where his father settled in 1830. It is six miles northeast of Springfield.

JAMES H., born in 1804, in Kentucky, married there to Elizabeth Duval. He died in Sangamon county, July 17, 1839, and his widow returned to Kentucky.

EVELINE, born July 22, 1807, in Kentucky, married in Sangamon county, Oct. 25, 1830, to Charles Harper. They had one child, and she died May 6, 1845. Her son ULYSSES lives in Texas.

NANCY, born August 11, 1810, in Bath county, Ky., married there to Willis Cassity. *See his name.*

ELIZA, born in Kentucky, married in Sangamon county, to Alex. Rigdon, who died, leaving a widow and seven children near Mt. Pulaski.

MARY A., born in Kentucky, married in Sangamon county to Samuel Harper, have four children, and live in Caldwell county, Texas.

ANDREW J., born in Bath county, Ky., came to Sangamon county with his parents, married in Logan county, in 1843, to Nancy Edwards. They had six children. LOUISIANA married P. O'Brannon, and resides near Mt. Pulaski. PERMELIA F., born Nov. 29, 1846, married Walter C. Black. *See his name.* MARY E. married George Hickman, and live near Lincoln. JAMES H. lives near Mt. Pulaski. TIMOTHY L. lives near Williamsville. ALVIN resides near Mt. Pulaski. Mrs. Nancy Cantrall died Sept. 6, and her husband Oct. 20, 1856, both in Logan county.

Andrew Cantrall died Sept. 12, 1832, and his widow died Dec. 5, 1858, both in Sangamon county.

CARVER, JACOB, born March 10, 1787, in Pennsylvania. Elizabeth Hoover was born Dec. 8, 1784, in Virginia. They were married near Dayton, O., and had nine children there. The family moved to Sangamon county, Ill., arriving in the fall of 1830 in what is now Clear Lake township, four miles northeast of Springfield. Of their nine children—

WILLIAM, ELIZA and *JOHN* died between thirteen and eighteen years of age. The other six are—

HIGHLY, born Jan. 13, 1806, near Dayton, O., was married there April 20,

—25

1826, to Philip Shaffer; came to Sangamon county with her parents; moved the same fall to Cass county, where Mr. Shaffer died, August 28, 1843, leaving six children. The widow married Feb. 1, 1836, to Daniel Lahmon. They have one child, and reside near Virginia, Cass county.

SARAH, born Nov. 26, 1810, near Dayton, O., married there to Jesse Smith, came to Sangamon county with her parents, had three children, moved back to Ohio, where two children were born and Mr. Smith died. The family reside at New Carlisle, Clarke county, Ohio.

REBECCA, born Sept. 21, 1812, in Ohio, married in Sangamon county to Benjamin Hooton, had four children, and moved to Ozark county, Mo., where she died.

SOPHIA, born Aug. 19, 1820, in Ohio, married in Sangamon county to Henry Bedinger. They had one child, and Mr. B. died, and she married Job Dickson. They had two children, and both parents died. Their son, JOHN DICKSON, married Mary Collins, and resides in Sherman. SARAH DICKSON married Edward Workman. He was shot dead, Oct. 4, 1865, by a drunken man, because he would not drink with him. The widow married Wm. Howard. She had one child by each marriage— WM. H. WORKMAN and JOHN E. HOWARD. Mr. and Mrs. Howard live four miles east of Springfield.

JAMES, born Dec. 13, 1825, near Dayton, Montgomery county, O. He was married in Sangamon county, Jan. 16, 1863, to Martha Workman, who was born May 23, 1847, in Rush county, Ind. They have four children, WILLIAM W., JOSEPH B., JAMES F. and GEORGE H., and live at the homestead settled by his parents in 1830. It is four miles northeast of Springfield.

FELIX, born Oct. 4, 1828, near Dayton, O., married in Sangamon county, Jan. 22, 1857, to Rachel Donner. They had five children. FLORA died young. LIZZIE, ALBERT, HENRY and FRANK. The four latter live with their parents, near where Mr. Carver's parents settled in 1830.

Jacob Carver died in 1833, in Ohio, having returned there on business. Mrs. Elizabeth Carver died Nov. 8, 1857, on the farm where the family settled in 1830.

CASSITY, ALEXANDER, was born in 1793, in Bath county, Ky. The father of Alexander and Willis Cassity built a stockade with block houses inside, on Slate creek, in Bath county, in the early settling of Kentucky. It was called Cassity's station, and was a place of refuge from the Indians until they were forced out of the country. Remains of that station are yet visible. Alexander Cassity was married in Bath county to Eliza B. Groves. She died there in 1832, leaving three children. He was married in the same county to Elizabeth Lockridge, had one child, and moved to Sangamon county, Ill., arriving Oct. 26, 1835, and purchased a farm in what is now the southeast corner of Chatham township, where they had five living children. Of their children—

JOHN F., born in 1826, in Bath county, Ky., enlisted in Sangamon county, Aug. 10, 1861, for three years, in Co. B, 30th Ill. Inf., and was promoted to Sergeant-Major. He was mortally wounded at the battle of Atlanta, Ga., July 22, and died July 26, 1864.

WILLIS H., born March 23, 1828, in Bath county, Ky., married Sept. 26, 1865, in Sangamon county, to Ella McGriff, a native of Preble county, Ohio. They had two children. CARRIE E. died young, and MINNIE L. lives with her parents, in Auburn.

JAMES L., born in Kentucky, raised in Sangamon county, and died in Iowa.

MARGARET E. married Andrew Rauch. See *his name*.

EMMA C. married Jacob Rauch. See *his name*.

FRANCIS M. born in Sangamon county, and died unmarried.

AMANDA I., born in Sangamon county, married James T. Hutton. See *his name*. They live on the farm where she was born, in Chatham township.

ALEXANDER M., born in Sangamon county, and enlisted July, 1862, for three years, in Co. I, 73d Ill. Inf., was wounded Dec. 31, 1862, at the battle of Stone's river, and discharged on account of physical disability. He was married to Mary A. Hutton, and lives in Gentry county, Mo.

LOUISA G. died young.

MARTHA L. born in Sangamon county, married Sept. 5, 1866, to John T. Welch. The have two children, EDWIN H. and HARRY K., and reside in Auburn. Mr. Welch was born June 30, 1842, in McDonough county, Ill. He enlisted April, 1861, for three months, in Co. D, 16th Ill. Inf. May 24, 1861, the whole regiment enlisted for three years. Dec. 23, 1863, the regiment re-enlisted as veterans. J. T. Welch served through all the enlistments to the end of the rebellion. He is now a merchant in Auburn.

Alexander Cassity died March 12, 1851, and his widow died Nov. 16, 1861, both on the farm where they settled in 1835.

CASSITY, WILLIS, brother to Alexander, was born Jan. 2, 1805, in Bath county, Ky. He was married there Jan. 24, 1827, to Nancy Cartmell. They had two children in Kentucky, and moved to Sangamon county, arriving at Springfield Oct. 10, 1829. They had one child in Sangamon county. Of their children—

JAMES W., born in Kentucky, died at twenty years of age.

ELIZABETH, born in Kentucky, married John Parsons. He died August, 1872, leaving a widow and six children, near Salisbury.

LEVI, born Jan. 1, 1836, in Sangamon county, enlisted Oct. 20, 1861, in Co. B, 10th Ill. Cav., for three years. As a non-commissioned officer he commanded a section of one of the batteries attached to the regiment at the battle of Prairie Grove, Ark., Dec. 7, 1862, and lost his left arm in that engagement. He was discharged on account of physical disability, Dec. 31, 1862. Levi Cassity was married April 23, 1863, to Nancy Drennan. They have one child, JOHN F., and live three and a half miles southeast of Chatham.

Willis Cassity, after coming to Sangamon county, lived a few years in Logan county, and a few years in Missouri. He and his wife now live in Ball township.

CASSITY WILLIAM, cousin to Alexander and Willis, was born in Bath county, Ky. He was married in Nicholas county, Ky., to Honor Wells, a native of Pennsylvania. They had five living children in Kentucky, and moved to Sangamon county, Ill., arriving in the fall of 1830, in what is now Rochester township. Of their children—

GEORGE died in Kentucky, at twenty-two years of age.

JEREMIAH died in Kentucky, at sixteen years of age.

REBECCA, born Feb. 14, 1802, in Nicholas county, Ky., married Edward Branch. *See his name.*

LEWIS, born in Kentucky about 1805, and died in Sangamon county, unmarried, in 1852.

MARY, born Aug. 28, 1806, in Nicholas county, Ky., married there Jan. 4, 1827, to James W. Neill. *See his name.*

William Cassity died in 1844, and Mrs. Honor Cassity died Aug., 1854, both in Rochester township.

CASS, ROBERT, was born in 1768 or '9, in Iredell county, N. C. His father, James Cass, was born in England, and when he was six or seven years of age was pressed into the British navy, and trained to a sea-faring life. Being separated from his relatives at so early an age, he never understood his own name, and called himself James Cast. He came to Philadelphia, and finally settled in Iredell county, N. C. After raising a family there, he moved with his children to Clarke county, Ky., and there met two Englishmen by the name of Cass. After becoming acquainted, he found that one of them was his brother, and the other his cousin, and for the first time learned that the family name was not Cast, but Cass. His son Robert, whose name heads this sketch, having always been called Cast, did not think it prudent to resume the original name, but related the facts in the case to his children, and his descendants have very generally returned to it. Robert Cass was married Feb. 26, 1790, in Iredell county, N. C., to Lucy Riley. They had one child there, and moved to Clarke county, Ky., where they had four children, and Mrs. Lucy Cass died, Feb. 13, 1809. Robert Cass was married in Clarke county, April 26, 1810, to Mary Boggs, and had two children there. The family then moved to Sangamon county, Ill., arriving Oct. 2, 1826, in Buffalo Hart grove. Of his seven children—

AMON, born Sept. 6, 1792, in North Carolina, married March 18, 1813, in Kentucky, to Patsy Simpson. He raised a family, and remained in Clarke county, Kentucky.

JAMES, born Aug. 12, 1697, in Clarke county, Ky., and married there Nov. 20, 1817, to Ann Hood. They had eight children, and came to Sangamon county in 1829. Mrs. Ann Cass died, and James Cass married Amanda McKinney. They had four children, and he died. His widow and living children reside near Mt. Pulaski. His son JOHN, born Sept. 22, 1820, in Kentucky, was married Feb. 28, 1847, in Sangamon county, to Mary J. Burns. They had thirteen children. ARTANECIA, born Feb. 5, 1849, was married April 15, 1873, to G. W. Edwards, and lives at Buffalo Hart Grove. AMON, born Sept. 3, 1851, lives with his mother. ALEXANDER, born Nov. 6, 1853, was married near Springfield, Ill., Nov. 3, 1875, to Delia Fenton, and lives at Farmer City, DeWitt county, Ill. LUCY A., born April 30, 1855, was married March 13, 1872, to Herbert White. They have one child, *Olive May*, and live at Farmer City. ALVI, JOHN L., ISABEL, IDA, ANNA E., SOPHIA, ROBERT F., HATTIE J. and THOMAS F. W., live with their mother. John Cass died Jan. 17, 1872. His widow and children live near Buffalo Hart station, or Farmer City, Ill. FRANK D, born Dec. 6, 1832, in Sangamon county, was married April 29, 1858, to Sarah G. Landis, who was born April 8, 1833, in Indianapolis, Ind. They have one child living, EDWARD K. F. D. Cass studied medicine in Mt. Pulaski, teaching school in the meantime. He graduated at Rush Medical College in 1864. Was appointed assistant surgeon of the 151st Ill. Inf. in 1865, served a short time and resigned. Dr. Frank D. Cass resides at Mt. Pulaski, Ill., and is engaged in practice there.

ARCHIBALD, born Dec. 1, 1799, in Clarke county, Ky., married there to Deborah Mershon. They had three children in Kentucky, and came to Sangamon county, Illinois, arriving Oct., 1828, at Buffalo Hart Grove, where they had three children. Of their children: ROBERT, born Nov. 20, 1821, in Kentucky, married in Sangamon county, Aug. 20, 1840, to Sarah J. Lawson. They had four children. MINERVA J. and ORLANDO W. died under two years. FLORENCE F., born May 17, 1852, died August 24, 1869. NOAH MATHENY, born July 9, 1857, lives with his parents, near Buffalo Hart Station. SARAH J., born Oct. 27, 1826, in Kentucky, married in Sangamon county, in 1842, to George Ridgway, have four living children, MARY C., ROBERT, JOHN and ALLEN, and live near Lockhart, Texas. WILLIAM L., born Aug 15, 1829, in Sangamon county, died Aug. 20, 1846. The other children all died under six years. Archibald Cass died Sept., 1852, and his widow died later, both in Sangamon county. He was a soldier from Sangamon county in the Black Hawk war in 1831-2. He was also a member of Co. D, 4th Ill. Inf., and served one year in 1846-7, in the war with Mexico. He was a nurse in the army, and practiced medicine the latter part of his life.

PATSY, born Dec. 28, 1802, in Clarke county, Ky., married there Sept. 15, 1825, to Robert E. Burns. *See his name.*

NINIAN R., born April 8, 1806, in Clarke county, Ky., married in Sangamon county to Mary Wade, They had seven children. THOMAS F. died in 1849 at Mt. Pulaski, aged twenty-three years. GEORGE W., married Martha J. Turley, have nine children, and live near Lincoln. EMILY married Daniel Dunn, had two children, and died in Missouri. Her children: THOMAS A., resides at Mt. Pulaski. MARY E. resides with her aunt, Mrs. Jones. LUCY E., born March 28, 1836, in Logan county, married Strother G. Jones. *See his name.* CAROLINE A., born August 16, 1838, is unmarried, and resides at Lincoln. SARAH AGNES, born in 1840, married Simpson Constant, had one child, CASS CONSTANT, and she married Frederick Bush. They have two living children, NELLIE E. and CARRIE B., and reside at Mt. Pulaski. ROBERT enlisted for three years, in 1862, in an Illinois regiment, and died August, 1863, at Murfreesboro, Tenn. Mrs. Mary Cass died Dec. 31, 1848. N. R. Cass married Mrs. Elizabeth Swing, whose maiden name was Laughney. She had one child, Belle W. Swing, by a former marriage. She married T. T. Beach, who is a practicing lawyer, and lives in Lincoln. Ninian R. Cass died August, 1872, at Mt. Pulaski, and his widow resides with her daughter, Mrs. Beach, at Lincoln.

A. BOWEN, born Feb. 11, 1811, in Clarke county, Ky., came with his parents to Sangamon county in Oct., 1826, married Jan. 17, 1830, to Melinda Burns. They had nine children in Sangamon county, namely: ELIZABETH E., born Nov. 14, 1830, married Nov. 8, 1849, to Michael Finfrock. He was born May 3, 1820, in Chambersburg, Pa., went to Miami county O., with his parents in 1836, and came to Sangamon county in 1843. Mr. and Mrs. Finfrock have seven children, BOWEN C., HELEN M., CHARLES M., PAUL H., IRVING G., WILLIS and ERNEST S. reside with their parents, four miles southeast of Buffalo Hart Station. Mr. Finfrock was a member of the Sangamon county Board of Supervisors at the first term in 1861-2, and again from 1872 to 1876. MARY C., born May 8, 1833, married March 31, 1858, to Benjamin F. Edwards, who was born July 12, 1823, in Madison county, N. Y. They have four children, GAYLORD C., JOHN F., BENJAMIN F., Jun., and MARY R., and reside two miles southeast of Buffalo Hart Station. LUCY A., born August 31, 1835, married April 20, 1869, to Dr. Leslie Gillette. They have three children, LESLIE B., FANNIE T. and GEOGIANA, and reside at Buffalo. LEWIS, born March 10, 1838, married Dec. 24, 1862, to Christiana Lawson. They had four children. The eldest, WILLIAM S., and the youngest, ALFRED, died in the second year of their ages. CLARENCE F. and ARTHUR F. reside with their parents, five miles southeast of Buffalo Hart Station. PAULINA J., born Oct. 4, 1843, married Oct. 13, 1864, to Alfred Shrieve, and resides near Elkhart. HARDIN, born Sept. 16, 1845, married Oct. 10, 1866, to Hattie N. Landis, have two children, PHILIP and LEWIS B., and reside one and a half miles southwest of Buffalo Hart Station. SCOTT, born Nov. 20, 1847, MARION, born April 12, 1850, and HARRY, born born Feb. 3, 1854, live with their parents. Ambrose Bowen Cass and his wife reside half a mile southwest of Buffalo Hart Station, and within one fourth of a mile of where his father settled in 1826. He was a soldier in the Black Hawk war, both in 1831 and 1832, from Sangamon county, and was in the battles of Bad Axe and Wisconsin.

LUCY A., born Jan. 15, 1813, in Clarke county, Ky., married April 17, 1828, to John R. Burns. *See his name.*

Mrs. Mary Cass died Sept. 14, 1840, and Robert Cass died July 9, 1852, both near where they settled in 1826.

CHAMBERS, HENRY B., born Jan. 1, 1809, near Dover, Del. He was married in Delaware to Elizabeth Bodie, and moved to Adams county, Ill., in 1831, and from there to Springfield, in 1840, where Mrs. C. died, April, 1854. He was married Jan. 25, 1855, to Mrs. Elizabeth A. Turner, whose maiden name was Earnest. They had seven children— *ELIZABETH E., JAMES H., JOHN B., WILLIAM R., JACOB J., KENDALL* and *MAGGIE J.*

H. B. Chambers died May 26, 1871, and his widow resides four miles west of Springfield.

CHANDLER, ROBERT, was born about 1812, in Kentucky. He was left an orphan at eight years of age, and was bound to Russell Fletcher, who took him to Overton county, Tenn., and from there to Sangamon county, Ill., arriving in the spring of 1832. He married Ellen Parmenter, who died, and he married Elizabeth Carter. They had eight children in Sangamon county—

LUCY J. married Christopher Wheelan, and live in Riverton.

REBECCA died, aged eighteen.

MARY E. married Stephen Huntsley, and live in Christian county.

MARTHA W., FRANCIS M., GEORGE H., CHARLES O. and *EDWARD*, reside with their parents, half a mile from Sherman.

CHERRY, BENJAMIN, was born Jan. 26, 1790, in Franklin county, Ga. When he was seventeen years old his parents moved to Overton county, Tenn. Benjamin was a soldier from Tennessee in the war of 1812. In the fall of 1819 he came to Sangamon county, and soon after went to work for Edward Clark, who came about the same time. Elizabeth Strickland was born May 12, 1799, near the sea coast, south of Charleston, S. C. Her parents moved to Tennessee, and from there to St. Clair county, Ill., thence to Sangamon county in 1819, and Elizabeth came in the spring of 1820. Benjamin Cherry and Elizabeth Strickland made arrangements to celebrate the 4th of July, but could not obtain the license from Edwardsville in time, and they were married July 11, 1820. They had seven children in Sangamon county, two of whom died young. Of the other five—

WYATT, born Nov. 9, 1821, married in Sangamon county to Susan Hall, have several children, and reside near Blue Mound, Macon county.

MARTHA, born in 1826, married William Allen, had seven children, moved to Missouri, and died near Carthage.

CLEMON died at twenty-three.

ALMYRA, born March 20, 1830, married David Huckleberry. See his name.

BENJAMIN, Jun., married Eliza Barnes. They had four children, and moved to Pike's Peak. Mr. Cherry died there. His widow and only living child, CHARLES, live in Springfield. He is employed at the watch factory.

Benjamin Cherry died in 1874, near Riverton.

CHILD, STEPHEN, was born June 12, 1802, in Waitsfield, Vt. His parents moved to Barnstown, Lower Canada, in 1806, and in 1815 to Hartland, Windham county, Vt., where they both died. In 1820 Stephen went to Potsdam, St. Lawrence county, N. Y., and engaged in teaching. He was there married, March 7, 1826, to Hannah Lyman, who was born Sept. 15, 1808, in Brookfield, Vt. They had two children in New York, and came to Sangamon county as part of a colony of fifty-two persons, arriving Oct. 26, 1833, in the village of Sangamo. They had three children in Sangamon county. Of their five children—

JOHN L., born March 23, 1827, in St. Lawrence county, N. Y., married in Sangamon county, Feb. 17, 1859, to Mary E. Anderson. They have two children, FRANKIE and CHARLEY, and reside near Farmingdale.

MARY L., born Sept. 27, 1831, in St. Lawrence county, N. Y., married in Sangamon county to George B. Seeley. See his name. They reside in Abilene, Kan.

MARTHA, born Dec. 8, 1833, in Sangamon county, married Thomas Frank Anderson. See his name.

STEPHEN, Jun., born April 14, 1848, in Sangamon county, resides with his mother, near Farmingdale.

HANNAH, born Nov. 29, 1850, died in her third year.

Stephen Child died Sept. 4th, 1873, and his widow resides near Farmingdale.

Mr. Child was a farmer and teacher all his life. He was an original abolitionist, and as an agent of the underground railroad, he assisted hundreds of colored people in their flight from bondage. He conducted a company of twenty-one at one time. It was his custom to go as far as he could travel in one night and return, but on some occasions he has gone as far sixty miles, and then left them in the hands of friends who would conduct them onward. The last time the writer of this, conversed with Mr. Child, he expressed special satisfaction that he had assisted so many human beings on their way to freedom, and gratitude that he had lived to see the day that there was not a slave in the United States of America.

CHURCHILL, GEORGE, was born about 1766, in Virginia. His parents died when he was quite young, and he went to Woodford county, Ky., where he was married to Sarah Arnold, who was born in that county about 1780. They had eleven children in Shelby county, Ky., and the family moved to Sangamon county, Ill., arriving in the fall of 1827, near what is now Mechanicsburg. Of their children—

MARY, married in Kentucky to William Threlkeld, brought up a large family, and never moved to Illinois. Their daughter SARAH J. is the wife of William P. McKinnie. See his name.

MARIETTA, born Jan. 31, 1829, in Shelby county, Ky., married there, Jan. 14, 1847, to Joseph H. Agee. They had two children born there, and in the fall of 1851 moved to Sangamon county, where seven children were born. Of their children: EDWIN H., born in Shelby county, Ky., resides with his mother. MARY B., born Jan. 29, 1851, in Kentucky, married in Sangamon county, Oct. 3, 1871, to Ambrose B. Cass, Jun. They live at East Lynn, Cass county, Mo. ALICE A. married Jan. 16, 1873, to Robert W. Jess, a native of Bellfast, Ireland. They live at Riverton. LIZZIE T., EMMA and J. ALVEY reside with their mother. The sixth, seventh and eighth children, viz: LUCY J., WILLIAM S. and CEPHAS L., all died under eight years. Joseph H. Agee died Sept. 25, 1865. The father and three children all died within nineteen days. Mrs. Marietta Agee and her family reside two miles east of Riverton.

LUCINDA, born in Kentucky, married there to William Crimm, and both died in Southern Illinois, leaving seven or eight children. The three eldest were WILLIAM, ABSALOM and MARTHA.

JOHN A., born March 6, 1800, in Shelby county, Ky., married there to Sarah Scoggin. They had three children, came to Sangamon county, and settled near Mechanicsburg, where they had six children. Of their children, JOEL, born July 19, 1823, in Kentucky, married in Sangamon county to Lucretia J. Bondurant. They had eleven living children. MARTHA A., MARY L., ELIZABETH J., JOHN T., THOMAS A., JOSEPH W., JESSE, EDGAR, HARVEY, ETHA G. and ARTHUR. Mr. C. and family moved to Kansas in 1865, and in 1875 returned to Illinois, and live in DeLand, Piatt county. WILLIAM, born April 4, 1825, in Kentucky, married in Sangamon county to Elizabeth Lemon. They reside in Monmouth, Polk county, Oregon. ANN, born Jan. 22, 1827, in Kentucky, died in Sangamon county in her eighteenth year. GEORGE, born August 15, 1829, in Sangamon county, went to Oregon, and there married Hannah E. Sherel. They have three children, and live in Linn county, Oregon. WILLOUGHBY, born Dec. 23, 1831, in Sangamon county, went, when a young man, to the Pacific coast, and lives in Oregon. SARAH E., born Jan. 4, 1834, in Sangamon county, resides with her sister, Mrs. Smith, in Illiopolis. JOHN, born Feb. 15, 1836, in Sangamon county, enlisted July 19, 1861, for three years, in Co. I, 41 Ill. Inf., re-enlisted as a veteran, Jan., 1864. He was promoted to Sergeant, July, 1863, and to 2d Lieut., Nov., 1864. Was with Sherman in his "march to the sea," and was honorably discharged, June, 1865. He was married Feb. 14, 1867, in Sangamon county, to Mary M. Graham. They have one living child, ANNA, and live three miles north of Illiopolis. LOUISA, born April 25, 1838, in Sangamon county, married April 10, 1860, to Reuben Smith, who was born Nov. 4, 1833, in Duchess county, N. Y. They have three living children, GEORGE, ADA and HERBERT, and live in Illiopolis. MARY, born Dec. 17, 1840, died in her eleventh year. Mrs. Sarah Churchill died Dec. 30, 1840, and John A. Churchill married July 3, 1842, to Mrs. Elizabeth Underwood, whose maiden name was Lemon. She was born March 29, 1808, in Georgetown, Ky. They had two children, JULIA, born July 12, 1843, in Sangamon county, lives with her mother. LEMON P. died in his sixth year. John A. Churchill died Feb. 4, 1845, and his widow and daughter reside in Mechanicsburg.

ALVAH, born in Kentucky, married there to Burnetta Samples, moved to Indiana, and from there to Sangamon county, in 1832, settling near Mechanicsburg. They had four children, and moved to Iowa; from there to Oregon in 1853, where he died.

LEWIS, born in Kentucky, married in Sangamon county to Mary A. Cooper. They had eleven children and moved to Iowa; from there, in 1853, to Oregon, with his brother Alva. He died Jan. 13, 1869, leaving a widow and children.

WILLOUGHBY, born Feb. 15, 1809, in Shelby county, Ky., married Oct. 6, 1834, in Sangamon county, Ill., to Elizabeth J. Humphreys. They had six children in Sangamon county, and in 1851 moved to the Pacific coast. Mrs. Churchill died at Dalles, foot of Cascade mountains, in Waco county, Oregon, and Mr. C. married in Oregon, August 11, 1852, to Matilda A. Price, who was born Jan. 12, 1828. They had six children. Of his children by the first marriage, GEORGE H., born May 13, 1837, in Sangamon county, married Catharine Reed, in Oregon. OWEN H., born June 16, 1845, in Sangamon county, Ill., is in Montana. DAVID H., born March 31, 1843, in Sangamon county, married July 23, 1875, to Minnie Lord. They live in Helena City, Montana Ter. MARY J., born Oct. 21, 1845, in Sangamon county, was married in Oregon to John M. Roach. They live in Clackamas county, Oregon. MARTHA A., born August 22, 1848, in Sangamon county, died April 18, 1864, in Oregon. Children of the second wife, all born in Oregon: OLIVER D., born May 19, 1853, JAMES E., born May 18, 1854, LAURA B., born May 8, 1856, near Harrisburg, was married June 18, 1874, to George Jordan. They live near Harrisburg, Oregon. THOMAS A., born July 27, 1857, and MINNIE D., born July 6, 1859, lives with her parents. Willoughby

Churchill and family reside near Harrisburg, Lynn county, Oregon.

ELIZABETH, born Sept. 11, 1811, in Shelby county, Ky., married in Sangamon county to Jesse Pickrell. *See his name.*

MARTHA, born July 16, 1815, in Shelby county, Ky., married in Sangamon county, June 16, 1833, to Griffin Fletcher, who was born Dec. 23, 1810, near Mt. Sterling, Montgomery county, Ky. They had ten living children. MARY A., born Sept. 20, 1836, married H. C. Stiver, Sept. 28, 1855, in Sangamon county. They have four living children, KATIE, NELLIE, CARRIE and CHARLES. Mr. Stiver moved to Texas in Dec., 1872. SARAH J., born Nov. 15, 1838, married Zachariah Pope, in 1854, in Sangamon county, and died May 3, 1857. RHODA E., born Jan. 4, 1841, married Levi S. Ridgeway, in Sangamon county, Feb. 16, 1857. They had four children, IRA H. and IDA S. (twins), CATHARINE E., ABBIE and LORA. Mr. Ridgeway died August 30, 1868, and Mrs. R. and family live near Decatur, Ill. DAVID C., born March 3, 1843, in Christian county, married in Sangamon county to Mary A. Garvey. *See sketch of the Garvey family.* JAMES L., born Nov. 3, 1845, is a grocer in Decatur. JOHN W., born Dec. 2, 1847, married May 10, 1869, to Emma Clevenger, in Abington, Knox county, Ill. They have three children, MAY D., THERON and STELLA, and live in Decatur, Ill. ABEL P., born Feb. 15, 1852, and MARTHA J., born May 24, 1854, live with their parents. Griffin Fletcher and wife reside in Decatur, Ill.

ELVIRA A., born Sept. 24, 1817, in Shelby county, Ky., was married Feb. 6, 1834, in Sangamon county, to John Garrett. They moved to the vicinity of Pittsfield, Pike county, Ill., in 1834, and had seven living children. BENJ. F., born in 1835, married in Pittsfield to Anna E. Adams, June, 1867, and live in Newton county, Kansas. MARY E., born in 1838, resides with her mother. LOUISA A., born in 1843, married S. Woolfolk. MARTHA A., born in 1846, lives with her mother. SARAH E., born in 1848, married July, 1872, to Robert Howard. They have one child, FLORENCE B., and live in St. Louis, Mo.

LOTHARIO, born in 1850, and ELIZA J., born in 1853, live with their mother in Pittsfield, Pike county, Ill. In 1866 Mr. Garrett sold out, with the intention of moving to Kansas. He left home alone with a load of goods, and was murdered in Bates county, Mo., in Nov., 1866.

DAVID B., born in 1821, in Kentucky, was killed by lightning in Sangamon county, May 7, 1842.

CULVIN S., born June 30, 1824, in Kentucky, married July 31, 1845, in Sangamon county, to Hester F. King. They had nine children; three died in infancy, and GEORGE W. died, aged ten years. HENRY H., born Jan. 14, 1847, married in 1873 to Lizzie Grubb, and resides near Baldwin City, Kansas. PERMELIA A., born June 5, 1849, married William Houston. *See his name.* FIELDING A., SALLIE and AMANDA P., reside with their parents, near German Prairie Station.

George Churchill died May 15, 1837, and Mrs. Sarah Churchill died Oct., 1847, and both were buried near German Prairie Station, Sangamon county, Ill.

CLARK, DAVID, born Aug. 28, 1776, in Essex county, N. J. Came to Kentucky in 1798, and was there married in 1800, to Rachel Rutter. They had two children; one died in infancy, and Mrs. Rachel Clark died in 1804. David Clark moved to Cincinnati, O., in 1805, and made brick for the first brick house built in that city. He returned to Somerset county, N. J., in the same year, and was married there in Feb., 1806, to Sallie Winans, who was born Oct. 25, 1788, in that county. They moved to Miami county, O., in 1809, and from there to Sangamon county, Ill., in 1829, settling on Sugar creek. After two years they moved to Wolf creek. They had six children, one of whom died in infancy. Of the other five—

Rev. *RICHARD W.*, born June 16, 1808, in Somerset county, N, J., was married in April, 1828, to Margaret Clark, a native of Fayette county, Ky. They have five children living. SALLIE A., born Jan. 11, 1831, in Sangamon county, was married in 1848 to Ezra Clark. They have six children, HATTIE A., LODORSKA J., PERMELIA A., DAVID M., IRENA and NELLIE, and live in Chesnut, Logan county, Ill. DAVID, born Jan. 2, 1834, in Sangamon county, is married, and resides in New Mexico. ELIZA, born Nov. 9, 1841, in McDonough county, was married in Logan county, Ill., to Jonas Shupe, May 13, 1858. He was a native of Ohio. They had one child, MARY E., who resides with her uncle, Dr. John Clark. Mr. Shupe died Jan. 13, 1865, and Mrs. Shupe was married Feb. 5, 1871, to John R. Ayers. They have one child, LENA, who resides with her parents in Mt. Pulaski. JOHN W., born Nov. 13, 1845, in Logan county, Ill., was married Dec. 28, 1874, in Chesnut, Logan county, to Emma Sterritt, a niece of Enoch Moore, of Springfield, recently deceased. Dr. John W. Clark is a practising physician at Milford, Iroquois county, Ill. MARY E., born Oct. 16, 1847, was married March 31, 1866, near Mt. Pulaski, to Benjamin Harding. They have four children, MAY, ELIZA, ELLIS and RICHARD, who reside with their parents near Mt. Pulaski. Rev. Richard W. Clark died Aug. 29, 1854, and his widow died Dec. 21, 1867, both in Logan county, Ill.

JOHN, born Nov. 25, 1810, in Miami county, O., studied medicine there. Came to Sangamon county with his father, remained one year, returned to Ohio, where he was married, Aug. 29, 1830, in Miami county, to Eliza Tremain, who was born May 24, 1810, in New York. They came to Sangamon county, and followed farming until 1842, when he moved to Mt. Pulaski and engaged in the practice of medicine. He was County Commissioner four years for Logan county, and Justice of the Peace seventeen years, during which time he married eighty-four couple. He has, since 1828, been a member of the M. E. church, and a trustee of the same, in Mt. Pulaski, from the time the church was organized at that place. Dr. John Clark and wife reside in Mt. Pulaski.

CARMAN W., born May 20, 1815, in Miami county, O., married March 29, 1838, in Sangamon county, to Harriet Crocker, step-daughter of David Riddle. She was born Aug. 2, 1817, in Lebanon, St. Clair county, Ill. They had seven children; one died in infancy. MARY W., born March 24, 1842, in Sangamon county, was married Oct. 17, 1866, to Alfred C. Wilson. They have four children, HARRIE, HARRIET H., CARMAN R. and ALFRED, and reside in Mt. Pulaski.

JOHN, born April 22, 1848, in Sangamon county, died July 29, 1866. DAVID T., born June 27, 1850, in Sangamon county, was married Jan. 27, 1876, to Lucy Powel. They reside in Mt. Pulaski. RICHARD H., born March 26, 1854, in Sangamon county, was married Dec. 22, 1875, to Mary E. Boggs. They reside in Mt. Pulaski. ALFRED R., born July 31, 1857, in Sangamon county, and MARION, born July 1, 1862, in Logan county, reside with their parents in Mt. Pulaski.

SALLY H., born Sept. 27, 1817, in Miami county, Ohio, was married Oct., 1834, to John Riddle, in Sangamon county. They have four children, all born in Sangamon county, ELIZA C., MARY E., FRANCIS A. and SALLIE W., and reside near Barclay, Sangamon county.

ELIZABETH, born Dec. 15, 1830, in Miami county, Ohio, was married Dec., 1847, to Alfred Gideon, who was born in Champaign county, Ohio. They have one child, DAVID C., born Nov. 27, 1847, was married Sept., 1868, to Sallie Row, a native of Ohio. David C. Gideon is a practicing physician at Watseka, Iroquois county, Ill.

David Clark was a local M. E. preacher for about forty years. His wife died Dec. 3, 1843, and he died Jan. 6, 1847, both on the farm near the present town of Barclay, Sangamon county, Ill.

CLARK, BARZILLA, and his wife, Nancy, came to what is now Salisbury township, Sangamon county, in 1821. They brought seven children, all of whom married and raised families. Their eldest daughter, Phebe, married John N. Campbell. See his name. Barzilla Clark died Sept. 23, 1840, and his widow died April 19, 1843, both in Sangamon county.

CLARK, ELISHA, was born in 1797, married in Indiana to Sarah Gard. They had three children in Indiana, and came to Sangamo, Sangamon county, in 1823. They had nine children in Illinois. Their daughter—

HUBERTY, born July 30, 1824, at Sangamo, Sangamon county, married E. George Batterton. See his name.

Mrs. Sarah Clark died in 1853, in Mason county, and Elisha Clark died in 1869, at Pekin, Ill.

CLARK, PHILIP, was born March 25, 1787, at Rye, England. He was married there to Elizabeth Gravett. They had five children, and Mrs. Clark died. Mr. Clark left his children there, and came to America in 1817, landing at Boston, Mass., and traveled by land and water to New Orleans, returned to England, and in company with his brother Edward, embarked at London in August, 1818, and landed at Baltimore in October following. They traveled on foot from Baltimore to Pittsburg, and from there to New Orleans by water. They returned the same way to the vicinity of Harmony, Ind., to visit the family of a relative by the name of Morris Burkbeck, who had emigrated from England a year or two before. He afterwards came to Illinois, and was Secretary of State under Gov. Coles. The Clark brothers went up the river to Shawneetown, and from there across the country to St. Louis. They recrossed the river into the American bottom and stopped with an Indian ranger, who told them about the Sangama country. They started for it, and arrived in November, 1819, on the Sangamon river, two miles north of Rochester. Philip Clark was married in 1823, in Indiana, to Martha Jessup, an English lady, who died without children, in Sangamon county. He married in Sangamon county to Polly Whitford, in 1835. Philip Clark had his five children sent from England. They embarked at London May 1, 1824, and were received in New York by an aunt on the 18th of June. The three daughters and one son arrived in Sangamon county in February, 1825. Of those five children—

MARY E., born in 1810, at Rye, Eng., arrived in Sangamon county February, 1825, married in 1832 to Samuel Hines. They had three children in Sangamon county, and moved to Iowa, where they had three children. They reside near Cox Creek Post Office, Clayton county, Iowa.

PHILIP, Jun., born Feb. 20, 1812, at Rye, Eng., embarked at London May 1, 1824, landed at New York city June 18th, was bound—by an aunt who came before them—apprentice in New York to a tailor, who treated him cruelly, and he ran away, went to Boston, obtained employment in a glass factory, saved some money, went by water to Philadelphia, walked from there to Wheeling, Va.; worked his way down the Ohio river, and up the Mississippi river to St. Louis, on a keel boat. At St. Louis he fell in with Elijah Iles and Richard Smith, both of whom knew his father, and he came with them to Springfield, arriving Oct. 15. 1824, to the surprise of his father. He was married May 19, 1836, to Christiana Campbell, on Richland creek. They had four children near Rochester, Sangamon county. He went to California in 1849, and returned in March, 1850, moved to Clinton in November of the same year, where three children were born. Of their seven children, MARY, born Dec. 18, 1839, married in Clinton, Jan. 19, 1857, to Robert Millard, have five children, and live in Clinton. JOHN G., born August 28, 1842, died in his twenty-second year. PHEBE, born March 1, 1847, married John Armstrong, and died July 5, 1868, in Clinton. SARAH F. lives with her parents. LOUIS P. died, aged four years. CHRISTIANA and MATTIE F. live with their parents, in Clinton, Ill.

MARGARET, born March 28, 1814, at Rye, England, married in Sangamon county, about 1834, to Daniel McClees. They had seven children in Sangamon county; four died in the same county, all grown, or nearly so. JOHN and HENRY were both Union soldiers. MARY J. married John Spence, who died of disease contracted in the army. She lives in Springfield. CHRISTIANA married Mr. Petty, and resides in Round Prairie, Sangamon county. CHARLES resides with his parents. Mr. McClees went to California in 1849, came home in 1853, returned, and his wife did not hear from him for fifteen years. They now reside at Port Angelos, Washington Territory.

SELINA, born July, 1816, in Rye, England, married in 1838, in Sangamon county, to John H. McMinany. She died in Fannin county, Texas.

HENRY R., born April, 1818, at Rye, England, married in Sangamon county, in 1842, to Jane Trotter. They had two children; both live in Sangamon county. Henry R. Clark resides near, Bolivar, Mo.

Philip Clark died in February, 1853, in Sangamon county. His widow married again, and resides in Missouri.

The object of the Clark brothers in coming to the country was to engage in the milling business. The site they selected was a favorable one, on the main Sangamon river, about two miles north of the present town of Rochester. The Legislature passed an act declaring that river navigable, and they abandoned the mill site. They went to a point on the South Fork, near where Edward Clark lived and died, and put a saw mill in operation in 1824, and a flouring mill in 1825. That was the first mill that did good work in this part of the country. Soon after they came to the country, Philip went to Lisle's hand mill, and remained three days and two nights to get two bushels of corn ground. They then bought a hand mill in St. Louis for their own use, but it kept about thirty families in bread for two years, until their own mill on South Fork was completed.

CLARK, EDWARD, was born Feb. 16, 1790, in the ancient town of Rye, Eng. It was the principal one of the three independent ports, which, together with the Cinque, or five ports, obtained charters granting special privileges from the British Sovereigns, in consequence of their having fitted out a fleet and conquered the Danish and Scandanavian freebooters, thus breaking up the system of piracy which had for years been devastating the English coasts. The office of Lord Warden of the Cinque ports, is one of the most ancient in the kingdom, reaching back to the time of Edward the Confessor, about the year 1050. Edward Clark's grandfathers on both sides were named Clark, but were no relation to each other. They were both sea captains, and his father, Henry Clark, was intended for the sea, but could never overcome the tendency to sea sickness, and engaged in other pursuits, chiefly mercantile and milling, to which the subject of this sketch was trained in early life. His brother Philip, having visited America in 1817, Edward sailed with him from London in August, 1818, and landed in October following. They arrived in what became Sangamon county in Nov., 1819, and located on the Sangamon river, about two miles north of the present town of Rochester. *For the route traveled, see his brother Philip's name.*

Edward Clark was married March 4, 1821, to Sarah Viney. Mr. Clark went to Edwardsville to obtain a license, and when he arrived there, learned that a law had been enacted by the legislature, in session at Vandalia, and approved by Gov. Bond, Jan. 30, 1821, providing for the organization of a new county, to be called Sangamon. The clerk declined to issue a license, and Mr. Clark insisted that as he was ready to marry he did not like to be delayed. The clerk told him that if he was determined to marry, he could go home, have the marriage ceremony solemnized, and after the county was organized, have it done again. The county was organized April 10, 1821, and after that a license was obtained and the marriage again solemnized by the same minister who officiated the first time, Rev. Rivers Cormack, of the M. E. Church. They had eight children, all in Sangamon county, namely—

ABRAHAM V., born April 9, 1822. He was never married, but went to California in 1849, and died Dec., 1850, at Sacramento City.

HENRY P., born Nov. 2, 1823. He was married Dec. 15, 1853, to Nancy T. Williams. They have four children, MARY J., SARAH V., EDWARD S., and WILLIAM T., the three eldest in Rochester, and the fourth in Oskaloosa, Iowa. Henry P. Clark lives one and a half miles southeast of Rochester.

MARY JANE, born Feb. 25, 1825, married Feb. 25, 1845, to James Richardson. They had three children. Mrs. R. died Sept. 6, 1857. Mr. Richardson is married again, and resides in Taylorville. Her youngest son, Abraham V. Richardson, lives at the homestead, near Rochester.

REBECCA S., born May 15, 1827, died unmarried, March 18, 1856.

GEORGE W., born Nov. 11, 1829, died Dec. 15, 1855.

EDMUND J. and *CHARLES A.*, twins, born Aug. 27, 1831.

CHARLES A., died Oct. 25, 1852, in Oregon.

EDMUND J., married Feb. 19, 1857, to Cassander Lovelace, who was born Sept. 9, 1838, in Shelby county. They have six living children, WILLIAM F., LOUISA J., REASON E., JASPER N., JOHN S. and ALVIN W., and live at the family homestead, two miles west of Rochester.

SARAH A., born Feb. 2, 1835, died Jan. 26, 1856.

Mrs. Sarah Clark died March 26, 1837, and Edward Clark was married Jan. 16, 1838, to Nancy Trotter. They had three children.

BENJAMIN F., born Oct. 15, 1838, enlisted July 25, 1862, in Co. I, 114th Ill. Inf., for three years. At the battle of Guntown, Miss., June 10, 1864, he brought on disease by excessive fatigue, and died March 1, 1865, in military hospital at Memphis, Tenn. His brother, Henry P., brought his remains home, and they were interred near Rochester.

WILLIAM T., born Nov. 16, 1842, enlisted Sept. 28, 1861, in Co. G, 10th Ill. Cav., for three years, re-enlisted as a veteran, served to the end of the rebellion, and was honorably discharged Nov., 1865, at San Antonio, Texas. William T. Clark lives in Oregon.

NANCY ANN, born March 16, 1845, and died Jan. 21, 1856. By looking back at dates it will be seen that four members of the family died from Dec. 15, 1855, to March 18, 1856. Disease, typhoid fever.

Mrs. Nancy Clark died Sept. 26, 1853, and Edward Clark died Jan. 10, 1875, both on the farm two miles west of Rochester, and within five miles of where he settled in 1819.

Wellington was in command of the district where Edward Clark lived when both were young men, and Mr. Clark knew him well. Mr. Clark witnessed the launching of the British ship, Victory, at the Chatham dock yards. It was on board that ship that Admiral Nelson was slain at the battle of Trafalgar, after promulgating the famous order which has become historic: "England expects every man to do his duty."

Edward Clark was a man of precise business habits, better suited to an older community than the one in which he spent the greater part of his long life. He was just in all his dealings, and was a model christian gentleman. He was a man of varied and extensive reading, and had accumulated a miscellaneous library from the standard works of the most distinguished authors in the English language.

CLARK, ORAMEL, was born August 11, 1792, in Lebanon, Connecticut, taken by his parents to Berkshire county, Mass., in 1797, and from there to Cooperstown, N. Y. He enlisted and served as a non-commissioned officer in the war of 1812, and moved to St. Lawrence county, N. Y., in 1817. He emigrated in 1818 to Kaskaskia, Ill., and in 1819 removed to where Athens, Menard county, now stands. He was the third man who settled on the north side of Sangamon river. In 1820 he returned on foot to visit his parents in New York. On returning to his home in Illinois, he married Jane C. Stewart, on Fancy creek, in Sangamon county. In 1821 he bought the preempted right to a farm from John Dixon (afterwards founder of Dixon, Ill.) on Fancy creek, ten miles from Springfield. He remained here until the death of his wife, in 1832, when he again visited his parents in New York, returning to Illinois in 1834. Of his five children—

MARIA died, aged four years, at Athens.

MARY J., born Nov. 5, 1824, in Sangamon county, was married March, 1842, to Abner Riddle. See his name.

RUSSELL W., born in 1827, in Sangamon county, died, aged twenty-one years. He was a medical student at the time.

WILLIAM A., born Jan. 4, 1829, on Fancy creek, Sangamon county, was apprenticed to the drug business in Springfield. Was a salesman from 1851 until 1853, when he emigrated to California, crossing the plains. He was married in Redwood City, Cal., Sept. 18, 1866, to Rebecca E. Teague, who was born July 1, 1849, in Springfield, Mo. They had two children, viz: GEO. W. and EDWARD O. The latter died June 16, 1875. William A. Clark and family reside at Redwood City, San Mateo county, California.

EDWARD O., born Dec. 3, 1831, in Sangamon county, married Feb. 14, 1855, in Waverly, Ill., to Virginia F. Harris, who was born March 8, 1835, in Morgan county, Ill. They have one child, ESTHER C., and reside near Carlinville.

Oramel Clark was married the second time, Oct. 28, 1836, to Judith W. Davis, of Elkhart, Ill. She was born August 12, 1802, in Union county, Ky. They moved to Springfield in 1838, and had five children, viz—

EMELINE, born August 20, 1838, in Sangamon county, was married in Springfield, March 23, 1863, to Col. N. Martin Curtis, who was born May 21, 1835, in

De Peyster, N. Y. He enlisted April, 1861, was mustered into the United States service May 15, 1861, as Captain of Co. G, 16th N. Y. Inf., and became Lieutenant Colonel of the 142d N. Y. Inf., Oct. 21, 1862, and Colonel Jan. 21, 1863; Brigadier General by brevet Oct. 27, 1864; Brigadier General, Jan. 15, 1865, and Brevet Major General. The last two promotions were for gallantry displayed in leading the troops in the capture of Fort Fisher, Jan. 15, 1865, where he lost his left eye. General Curtis was several times severely wounded. The Legislature of New York passed resolutions, April 5, 1865, thanking Gen. Curtis and the officers and men of his command (who were all New York troops), for their achievements on that occasion. Gen. Curtis was appointed, August 14, 1866, Collector of Customs for the District of Oswegatchie, and Special Agent Treasury Department March 4, 1867, which position he still holds. They have three children, EMMA P., MARY W. and FLORENCE R. Gen. Curtis is a breeder of fine stock, and resides on his farm near Ogdensburg, N. Y.

MARTHA and *SUSAN* (twins), born Sept. 23, 1840.

MARTHA married George W. Burge. They have two living children, GEO. C. and FRANK F., and reside at Ottawa, Kansas.

SUSAN is unmarried, and resides with her sister, Mrs. Burge.

CAROLINE J., born March 5, 1845, in Springfield, married Oct. 30, 1867, to John M. Amos. *See his name.*

Oramel Clark died Sept. 9, 1863, in Springfield, and his widow resides with her children.

CLAYTON, JOHN S., was born August 2, 1802, in Caldwell county, Ky. Elizabeth Clayton was born May, 1806, in the same county. They were there married in 1824, and had one child in Kentucky. The family moved to Morgan county, Ill., where one child was born, and moved back to Kentucky, where two children were born, and they again moved to Morgan county, Ill., in 1833 or '4, and after a few years spent there, moved to Sangamon county, in what is now Ball township, where they had seven children.

FRANKLIN JEFFERSON, born Feb. 13, 1827, in Caldwell county, Ky., married in Sangamon county to Elizabeth Scott. They have six children, RUTH JANE, GILBERT, AMANDA E., PERLEASY, EMMA and SHELTON L., and reside in Ball township, near Chatham.

ALEXANDER, born Sept. 16, 1829, in Morgan county, Ill., married in Sangamon county to Mary A. Marshall. They had two children, CHARLES E. and HENRY N., and Mrs. Mary A. Clayton died, and he married Theresa J. Penix. They have four children, MELISSA J., ADA M., MARY A. and JACOB B., and live in Ball township, four and a half miles southeast of Chatham.

MINERVA J., born in Kentucky, married in Sangamon county to John Ogden, who died, and she married William Smith, and lives near Moberly, Randolph county, Mo.

MARQUIS D., born March 16, 1831, in Kentucky, married in Sangamon county, August 29, 1860, to Susan A. Matthew. They had eight children, three of whom died young. The other five, CHARLES A., SARAH E., FRANKLIN L., THOMAS E. and MANFORD E. live with their parents, three miles north of Pawnee.

ELZIRA, born in Illinois, married William Easley, have six children, and live in Clark county, Mo.

MARY A., born in Illinois, married Simon T. Matthew. *See his name.*

GEORGE M. married Miss J. Patterson, who died, and he married Harriet E. Debow. They have one child, NETTIE FLORENCE, and live in Cotton Hill township, three miles north of Pawnee.

MARIETTA, born in Sangamon county, married George Lamb. *See his name.*

JOHN L., born in Sangamon county, married in 1873 to Mary Allen, and lives with his mother.

John S. Clayton died Sept. 7, 1861, and Mrs. Elizabeth Clayton resides in Ball township, four and a half miles southeast of Chatham.

CLAYTON, JOHN C., was born about 1808, in Caldwell county, Ky. He came to Sangamon county in 1829, with his cousin and brother-in-law, John S. Clayton. He was married at Alton to Ginsey Clack. He moved his family to

Champaign county in 1856, and died there the same year, leaving a widow and four children. His son Elias was a member of an Illinois regiment, and was killed in battle at Little Rock, Ark., in 1864. A daughter is married, and lives in Missouri.

The widow, with her son Hardin and another child, live near Urbana, Ill.

CLEMENTS, GEORGE, was born in Amherst county, Va.; was married to Lizzie Holliday, who was a native of Virginia also. They had six children in Virginia, and the family moved to Garrard county, Ky., and from there to Sangamon county, Ill., arriving early in 1830 in what is now Woodside township. Of the children—

WILLIAM, born Oct. 14, 1797, in Virginia, married in Kentucky and died, leaving a family there.

JOHN, born May 13, 1800, in Virginia, married in Kentucky to Elizabeth Turpin, came with his father to Sangamon county. They had three living children. HENRY D. married Eliza Skane, had two children, and she died. He lives in Sangamon county. LUCINDA married William Barger, and resides in Mechanicsburg. ELIZA married Isaiah Pryor, and live in Missouri.

THOMAS, born Nov. 22, 1802, in Amherst county, Va., married Sindicey Harris, August 2, 1822. They had eight children. AMERICA, born July 21, 1823, married John C. Cloyd. *See his name.* LOUISIANA, born July 16, 1826, married John A. Miller. *See his name.* JAMES A., born Nov. 18, 1828, in Ky., married Permelia Hatten, who was born in 1836, in Garrard county, Ky. They reside four miles southwest of Chatham. ELIZA A., born in Sangamon county, Oct. 22, 1832, resides with her sister, Mrs. Matthew Cloyd. FANNY, born Oct. 13, 1833, in Sangamon county, married Oct. 18, 1848, to Matthew Cloyd. *See his name.* GEO. W., born Oct. 14, 1835, died, aged ten years. SINDICEY J., born August 28, 1837, died March, 1854. THOMAS R., born May 6, 1839, married Sept. 4, 1861, to Elizabeth Ellison, who was born in Carthage, O. They have two children, ADA and JAMES H., and live in Chatham township. HENRY H., born Jan. 3, 1841, married Emily Sparks, has three children, and live near Topeka, Kansas. Mrs. Sindicey Clements died Feb. 21, 1842, and Thomas Clements married in 1844 to Mrs. Alcey Baucom, whose maiden name was Neville. Thomas Clements died March, 1855, and his widow resides with her daughter, Mrs. T. Gordon Cloyd,

SINDICEY married Henry Collier. They have one child, LOUISIANA, and live in Rochester.

ELIZA A., born March 29, 1811, in Amherst county, Va., married Samuel Cloyd. *See his name.*

FANNY, born July 17, 1808, married May 19, 1844, to John Levi. He died Dec. 23, 1872, and his widow lives in Rochester.

George Clements and his wife both died in Sangamon county.

CLIFTON, ELIAS, was born in Sussex county, Delaware, and married there to Sally Carlisle, a native of the same county. They had five children in that county, two of whom died young. The family moved, in 1802, to Fayette county, Ky., where one child died, and in 1816 they moved to Clarke county, Ind., and from there to Sangamon county, Ill., arriving Dec., 1834, in what is now Rochester township. Of their two children—

CLEMENT, born about 1794, in Delaware, married in Clarke county, Ind., to Nancy Martin. They came to Sangamon county a few years later than his father. Mrs. Clifton died in 1845. He went back to Indiana, and married Mrs. Susan Williams, whose maiden name was Huckleberry. They had one child, ELIAS, who died aged fifteen years. Mrs. Clifton died, and he married Melinda Alsop. She died in 1855, and he in 1857.

NANCY, born Oct. 31, 1800, in Sussex county, Delaware. She was married in Fayette county, Ky., April 27, 1816, to Uspshear D. Spicer. *See his name.* He died, and Mrs. Spicer married Adam Saftly. *See his name.*

Mrs. Sally Clifton died March 25, 1346, and Elias Clifton died Jan. 3, 1852, both in Sangamon county.

CLINE, JOHN, was born Jan. 2, 1798, in Frederick county, Va. His parents died when he was quite young, leaving four children. Their grandfather, George Sutherland, took them with him to Madison county, near London, Ohio, in 1802. In 1819 he prepared to visit the western country on horseback. Levi Cantrall was about moving to Illinois, and Mr. Cline engaged to drive his four-horse team, and they arrived in the American bottom in November. Mr. Cantrall purchased a supply of corn there, and moved to what became Sangamon county, arriving in Dec., 1819, in what is now Fancy Creek township. Mr. Cline drove the team, and arrived at the same time. He intended returning to Ohio in the spring, but when the time came he decided to raise a crop, and while thus engaged he was married, July 20, 1820, to Mrs. Lucy Scott, whose maiden name was England. He made arrangements to visit Ohio in fall of 1820, but his wife being sick, he deferred it, and has not yet made his visit. Mrs. Cline had one child by her first marriage—

ELIZA SCOTT, born Feb. 15, 1816. She is married, has three children, and lives in Kansas.

Mr. and Mrs. Cline had ten children in Sangamon county—

WILLIAM, born Oct. 8, 1821, married Sept. 6, 1842, to Eliza Canterberry. They had four children. MARIA L. married August 14, 1862, to Charles S. Jones, who was born July 19, 1844, in Ohio. He enlisted a few days before his marriage, in Co. C, 114th Ill. Inf., for three years. He was wounded June 10, 1864, at the battle of Tupelo, Miss., and was discharged on account of physical disability. Mr. and Mrs. Jones have one child, SCOTT, and live in the extreme southwest corner of Logan county, Post Office, Williamsville. JOHN N., born August 23, 1846, married July 29, 1867, to Dulcina E. Primm. They have one living child, NINIAN O., and live five and a half miles west of Williamsville. ASA M. married March 12, 1873, to Melissa McClelland, and live in Fancy creek township. WILLIAM F. lives with his father. Mrs. Eliza Cline died Sept. 7, 1871, and William Cline married in 1872, to Maria J. Purkins. They have one child, EDWARD E., and live in Menard county, near Cantrall.

GEORGE W., born April 8, 1823, married Elizabeth Primm, and died Aug. 14, 1845, about four months after marriage. His widow married Jacob Barnsback, and resides near Edwardsville.

MATILDA A., born May 3, 1825, married Andrew Lynch, had seven children, and he died, and she married David Jones. They have two children, and reside in Menard county.

ELIZABETH, born August 24, 1826, married James A. Turley, and he died Jan., 1852, leaving one child, ALMEDA, who married Joseph M. Smith, and resides near Cantrall. Mrs. Turley married George T. Sales. *See his name.*

JOHN, born August 30, 1828, married Jane Council, have six children, and live in Menard county.

DAVID, born June 17, 1830, married Jane Hornback, and both died, leaving three children.

ADALINE, born April 25, 1832, married William M. Blue. *See his name.*

STEPHEN E., born Nov. 1, 1834, died August 15, 1853.

JAMES, born July 17, 1837, married Eliza Hall, have four children, MARY E., IDA F., LUCY O. and HENRY A., and reside in Fancy creek township.

HENRY, born Oct. 8, 1839, married Mary Primm. They have three children, WILLIAM A., ALLEN C. and JENNIE, and live near Cantrall.

Mrs. Lucy Cline died June 4, 1875, and John Cline lives in Cantrall.

CLINKENBEARD, WM., was born Feb. 12, 1808, in Clarke county, Ky. He came to Sangamon county in 1825; remained one year, returned to Kentucky, and came back to Sangamon county in 1829. He was married April, 1835, to Lavina Elder. They had ten children in Sangamon county. The fourth, fifth and seventh died under six years. Of the other seven—

JULA A., born Sept. 15, 1836, married Edward L. Robinson, have three children, and live near Berry, Sangamon county.

WILLIAM H., born August 13, 1838, in Sangamon county, married August 14, 1864, to Ann J. Brachear. They have two children, HARVEY and LESLIE, and live near Pleasant Gap, Bates county, Missouri.

MARY, born in Sangamon county, married Henry Bryant, have five children, and live near Pleasant Gap, Mo.

THOMAS married Martha Robbins, and resides near Pleasant Gap, Mo.

JOSIAH, born March 12, 1852, resides in Buffalo, Sangamon county.

J. ALBERT and *LEVI F.* live with their parents.

William Clinkenbeard lived in Sangamon county until March, 1873, when he moved to Missouri, and resides near Pleasant Gap, Bates county.

CLOYD, DAVID, was born about 1766, in Botetourt county, Va. He was married there, moved to Culpepper county, and from there to Washington county, Ky., about 1815. He moved in company with his sons Thomas and Samuel, and his daughter Polly—who married Henry Lucas—to Sangamon county, arriving October, 1825, in what is now Curran township. David Cloyd died about 1839, and his widow in 1844 or '5, both in Sangamon county.

CLOYD, THOMAS, son of David, was born Jan. 14, 1798, in Botetourt county, Va., and went with his parents to Washington county, Ky., in 1815. He was married there April 27, 1820, to Ann Withrow. They had three children in Kentucky, and in 1824 moved to Fayette county, Ill., where they had one child, and from there to Sangamon county, arriving October, 1825, in what is now Curran township, north of Lick creek, where they had two children. Of their six children—

ANN CORDELIA, born June 29, 1820, in Washington county, Ky., married in Sangamon county to Rev. Charles D. Alsbury. *See his name.*

JOHN CALVIN, born Sept. 6, 1821, in Washington county, Ky. He was married in Sangamon county to America Clements. They had two children, one of whom died young. DICEY married James H. Jones, and lives in Henry county, Mo. Mrs. America Cloyd died, and J. C. Cloyd married September, 1848, to Sophia L. Lanterman. They have eight children. CHARLES married Elizabeth J. Branham, has one child, ELIZA M., and live in Curran township. ELEANOR married Asbury M. Branham. They have three children, WILLIAM C., CORD F. and a daughter, and live in Curran township. NANCY J., CORDELIA, WALLACE R., GORDON, AMANDA M. and JOHN C., Jun., live with their parents, three miles southeast of Curran.

NANCY, born Dec. 25, 1823, in Kentucky, married Jan. 2, 1840, to Robert Cummings. *See his name.*

MATTHEW, born Sept. 10, 1825, in Fayette county, Ill., married in Sangamon county, Oct. 18, 1848, to Fanny Clements. They have nine children. ROBERT T. lives with his parents. ELIZA J. married William F. Smith. *See his name.* WM. O. lives with his parents. JULIA F. married May 27, 1873, to Benjamin F. Caldwell. *See his name.* MATTHEW F., ANN M., HENRIETTA, ALICE and SAMUEL, live with their parents in Chatham township.

THOMAS GORDON, born June 7, 1827, in Sangamon county, married Sept. 27, 1849, to Priscilla J. Baucom, who was born Dec. 31, 1831, in Madison county. They have three children, THOMAS, JOHN C. and ANNIE E., and live near Chatham. Although Thomas G. Cloyd was but three and a half years old at the time, he remembers one incident connected with the "deep snow" of 1830-31. That was seeing his father drive a team over a stake and ridered fence, and it troubled him greatly, fearing that the team would go down through the snow and become stranded on the fence.

JOSEPH D., born Dec. 5, 1831, in Sangamon county, married Dec. 16, 1852, to Sarah M. Byers, who was born Oct. 13, 1833, in or near Shepherdstown, Va. They had nine children; one died young. MARY E., SARAH E., VIRGINIA B., JOSEPH D., Jun., THOMAS E., WILLIS, MARGARET F. and LAURA reside with their parents, half a mile north of Chatham.

Thomas Cloyd and wife now—June, 1873—reside near Woodside Station.

CLOYD, SAMUEL, brother to Thomas, was born Nov. 20, 1802, in Culpeper county, Va. He was taken by his parents to Washington county in 1815, and to Sangamon county in 1825. He was married May 1, 1832, in Sangamon county to Eliza Clements. They had but one child—

MARY A., born Oct. 15, 1832, on Lick creek, Sangamon county, married March, 1860, to John S. Highmore. She died Sept. 9, 1872, leaving two children, ELIZA A. and MARY E., who live with their father in Rochester. *See Bowling family.*

Samuel Cloyd died August 5, 1872, in Rochester, and his widow resides there.

COATS, RALPH J., born May 3, 1817, in Wyoming county, New York, came to Springfield Oct. 9, 1840. He was married in Livingston county, Michigan, May 14, 1845, to Amanda N. Wood, who was born in Wyoming county, New York, April 8, 1823. They returned to Springfield, Ill., where they had two children—

ABEL A., born August 4, 1846, in Springfield, enlisted May, 1864, in Co. E, 133d Ill. Inf., for one hundred days. He served full term and was honorably discharged with the regiment, Sept. 24, 1864. He was married in Springfield, Oct. 30, 1867, to Charlotte E. Gardner, who was born April 30, 1850, in Carrolton, Green county, Ill. They have four children, all born in Springfield. NINA B., RALPH W., CHARLES A. and MERWIN W. Abel A. Coats is in the grocery business, with his father, and resides in Springfield.

PERSIS E., born Jan. 6, 1849, in Springfield, was married there, Nov. 19, 1868, to Charles D. Timothy, who was born Jan. 3, 1842, in Franklin Grove, Lee county, Ill. They have three children living, CLARA I., WARREN A. and NETTIE B. Mr. Timothy enlisted Feb. 3, 1864, in Co. G, 75th Ill. Inf. On arriving at Springfield he was detached under Gen. Oakes in the mustering in and out department, and was honorably discharged March, 1866. He was elected a member of the Board of Supervisors for 1875, and resides two and a half miles north of Springfield.

Ralph J. Coates was elected Alderman of Springfield in 1857, for three years, was re-elected in 1860, 1864 and 1871. He is now, and has been in the grocery business in Springfield, Ill., for eighteen years, and resides there.

R. J. Coates' father was a soldier in the war of 1812, for four months. He died in Springfield, Ill., August 9, 1874, at the age of eighty-seven years.

COE, EBENEZER, was born August 25, 1812, in Loudon county, Va., and came to Sangamon county, Ill., with George M. Green, in 1839. He went back to Virginia in the fall of 1843, and was married in Loudon county, Sept. 17, 1844, to Jane Grubb, a native of that county. He returned to Sangamon county in 1851. Mrs. Coe died near Rochester, May 10, 1860. Mr. Coe was married March 26, 1861, in Loudon county, to Mrs. Julia A. Edwards, whose maiden name was Conard. They came soon after to Sangamon county, and Mrs. Coe died Dec. 22, 1869, leaving four children—

JOSEPH H., SAMUEL B., WILLIAM C. and MARY C.

Ebenezer Coe was married Dec. 13, 1870, in Decatur Ill., to Harriet Lanham, who was born July 25, 1830, in Sangamon county. They live one mile east of Rochester.

COLEMAN, MRS. ABIGAIL, whose maiden name was Robertson, was born in Surry county, N. C., and was married there to Theophilus Coleman, who was born in Virginia. They had four children in North Carolina. Mr. Coleman became a soldier in the war with England in 1812. He never returned, and his family never knew his fate. Mrs. Coleman, with her four children, moved in 1815 to Cumberland county, Ky., and to Sangamon county, Ill., arrived in the fall of 1820 on Richland creek, in what is now Salisbury township. Of her four children—

SARAH, born Jan. 6, 1801, in North Carolina, married in Kentucky to Joshua Crow, came with her mother to Sangamon county. They moved to Cass county, where she died many years ago, leaving seven children.

ELIZABETH, born May 19, 1804, in North Carolina, married John G. Purvines. See his name.

JANE, born Jan. 28, 1806, in North Carolina, married George K. Hamilton. See his name. He died, and she married Alexander C. Purvines. See his name.

JOHN R., born Feb. 29, 1808, in North Carolina, married Nancy Harris, had two children in Sangamon county, and moved to Crawford county, Mo., where they had four children, and Mrs. Coleman died. He married again, had four children, and is now a widower and resides in Missouri.

Mrs. Abigail Coleman was married in Sangamon county in 1824, to Robert Hamilton. They had two children in Sangamon county—

MAHALA married Mr. Rice, had one child, and Mr. Rice died. She married James Pease, had three children, and he died. Mrs. Mahala Pease resides near Cuba, Mo.

JAMES C. married in Missouri, enlisted in a Union regiment from that State, and died in the army.

Mrs. Abigail Hamilton died in Sangamon county, and Robert Hamilton died in Arkansas.

COLEMAN, JONATHAN B., was born Nov. 16, 1811, in Rutherford county, Tenn. When he was about seventeen years old he came to Sangamon county with his uncle, Charles K. Hutton, arriving in what is now Auburn township Oct. 15, 1827. He was married Nov. 10, 1835, to Mary Dodds. They had five living children, all born in Sangamon county, namely—

JAMES W., born Nov. 21, 1838, married Margaret Bowman, had two children, CHARLES U. and BELLE, and Mrs. C. died. Mr. Coleman married Elizabeth Mengle. They have two children, and live in Christian county.

JOSEPH E., born March 5, 1841, enlisted July 15, 1861, in Springfield, for three years, in what became Co. B, 11th Mo. Inf. He served full term and was honorably discharged Aug. 12, 1864. He married Lydia Dawson. They have one child, LETA, and live in Springfield. Mr. Coleman is a traveling salesman for a queensware house in St. Louis.

WILLIAM H. married Fanny B. Taylor, and lives in Ball township.

ELIZABETH A. and MARGARET E. live with their parents, near the Sugar creek Cumb. Presb. church, in Ball township.

COLEY, WILLIS, was born Feb. 14, 1792, near Ballston Springs, N. Y., and when he was a child his parents moved to Cazenovia, Madison county. Willis was there married in Feb., 1818, to Lucinda Chapin. His father owned some land in the military tract between the Illinois and Mississippi rivers. Soon after Willis was married his father sent him out to see it. He came on a raft down the Alleghany and Ohio rivers to Shawneetown, thence to St. Louis by keel boat. He went on foot to the military tract, and returned to Edwardsville July 4, 1819, he started from that place, on foot and alone, for his home in New York. At Terre Haute, Ind., he secured cooked food, and traveled two hundred miles to the Maumee river, without seeing any other human beings but Indians. He arrived at Cazenovia August 7, 1819. March 4, 1820, he started with his family, consisting of himself, wife and two children, accompanied by five or six other families. They moved by water to Shawneetown, Ill., where Mr. Coley lived three years. He then moved in a wagon drawn by two yoke of oxen, and in March, 1823, arrived in what is now Loami township, where they had three children. Of their five children—

ROBERT W., born in New York, married in Sangamon county to Rebecca A. Jarrett. She died Feb. 13, 1870, and Robert W. Coley died March, 1872. Their daughter LAVINA is the wife of John A. DeWitt, and lives in Springfield. Their son WILLIS lives in Loami.

CHARLOTTE, born August 15, 1819, in New York, married in Sangamon county to Reuben Moore, and moved to Texas in 1853. Reuben Moore died in 1863, leaving a widow and seven children. LUCINDA, ROBERT E., ELLEN and POLLY are married, and live in Texas. LAURA, their third child, married Lott Mason, and lives in Auburn, Sangamon county. EDGAR and WILLIE, the two youngest, live with their mother, near McKinney, Collin county, Texas.

HUBBARD S., born in Sangamon county, married March 4, 1852, to Susan Jacobs. They have two children, ANNIS and MAY, and live in Oswego, Labette county, Kansas.

JAMES M., born August 23, 1832, in Sangamon county, married Oct. 28, 1858, to Caroline Greenwood. She died six weeks after they were married. Mr. Coley married April 19, 1860, to America Gibson. They had two children, LEWIS B. and MARY F., the latter of whom died in her third year. J. M. Coley and wife live in Loami.

ANGELINE, born in Sangamon county, married Hugh Forrest, and both died.

Mrs. Lucinda Coley died at Loami, and Willis Coley was married Sept., 1851, to Mrs. Philena Jenkins, who was previously Mrs. Kidder, and whose maiden name was Sprague, a native of Windham county, Vt. After a residence of just half a century at Loami, Willis Coley moved, in 1873, to Oswego, Kansas.

COLBURN, PAUL, was born about 1761, in Hollis, Hillsboro county, New Hampshire. He was married in Massachusetts, to Mehetibel Ball, who was born about 1757. They had eleven children born in Sterling, Worcester county, Mass. In 1809 the family moved to the vicinity of Hebron, Grafton county, N. H., where they remained until Sept., 1815, when Paul Colburn and his wife, his son Isaac with his wife and two children, his son William and his wife, they having been married but a few days, and his unmarried daughter, Isabel, started from Hebron in wagons to seek a new home in Ohio, at that time the "far west." On reaching Olean, at the Alleghany river, they found the river too low to bring all their goods on boats, as they had intended. They sold their wagons and teams, put their remaining goods and their families on a raft, and started down the river, reaching Pittsburg on the evening of Dec. 24, 1815. Ice was forming in the river, and they were compelled to stop there for the winter. While they were in Pittsburg, Paul Colburn was joined by his son Ebenezer, who had been serving in the United States army in the war with England, then just ended. In the spring of 1816, Isaac and Ebenezer went up the Alleghany river and made a raft of logs suitable for making shingles, and partially loaded it with hoop poles. They expected to have gone down the Ohio river in June, but the whole season was one of unusual low water, and December arrived before they reached Pittsburg with their raft. The whole party went down on the raft to Marietta, O., where they engaged in farming and other pursuits. Ebenezer was married in Marietta, and in the spring of 1820 Paul Colburn and his wife, Isaac and his family, and Ebenezer and his wife, embarked on a raft, leaving William to close up the business at Marietta. They landed their raft at Louisville, Ky., and left Isaac there to work up and sell their lumber. The other members of the family continued down the river to Shawneetown; Paul Colburn, his wife and daughter remained there. Ebenezer and his wife went on to join some relatives of her's in Monroe county, Ill., about fifty miles south of St. Louis.

In August of that year Isaac Colburn and his wife died at Louisville within two days of each other, leaving six children among strangers, and on the first of November Mrs. Mehitibel Colburn died at Shawneetown. About the time of her death William Colburn embarked with his family on a boat at Marietta, floated down to Louisville, and took on board four of his brother Isaac's children, one having died, and another been placed in a good home. He then went to Shawneetown and joined his bereaved father and sister, arriving Dec. 24, 1820.

In March, 1821, Paul Colburn, his daughter Isabel, William Colburn, wife and three children, the four orphan children of Isaac Colburn, and a Mr. Harris, started in a wagon drawn by four oxen for Morgan county. They traveled through rain, mud and unbridged streams for about five weeks, which brought them to the south side of Lick creek, on what is now Loami township, where they found an empty cabin. From sheer weariness they decided to stop, and Mr. Harris, the owner of the wagon and oxen, went on to Morgan county.

Soon after their arrival Wm. Colburn gave a rifle gun for a crop of corn just planted, and in that way began to provide food. He secured a team and went after his brother Ebenezer, and brought him and his wife to the settlement, arriving in October, 1821.

Having succeeded in bringing so many of his descendants to the new country, and witnessed their struggles to gain a foothold and provide themselves with homes, Paul Colburn died Feb. 27, 1825, near the present town of Loami. Of his children who came to Sangamon county, we will notice each under separate heads, beginning with the daughters—

COLBURN, SALLY, born June 15, 1789, in Sterling, Mass., married there to Daniel Woodworth. They came some years after the first of the family arrived. They lived many years in Springfield, and both died in Sangamon county. Their daughter—

LOUISA H., married Gershom Dorrance. *See his name.*

SARAH, has been twice married, and lives in California.

An account is preserved of a ludicrous incident that transpired while Mr. Woodworth lived in Springfield. A rain storm came on suddenly and caught him away from home. He started on a run, with his head down, hat drawn over his eyes, and body bent forward. It so happened that Governor Ford found himself away from home in the same shower. Throwing himself in a similar attitude, he started on a run also; but there was this difference, they were running in opposite directions, and when both were at full speed, they came together with a square butt, like a couple of sheep. Each, on the spur of the moment, thought it was intentional on the part of the other, and each assumed a belligerent attitude, but before a blow was struck, both discovered that it was an accident, and with a hearty laugh, hurried on.

COLBURN, MARY, born Feb. 23, 1792, at Sterling, Mass., married Adna Phelps. *See his name.*

COLBURN, ISABEL, born Feb. 11, 1796, in Sterling, Mass., married in Sangamon county, to Adin E. Meacham. *See his name.*

COLBURN, ISAAC, born in Sterling, Mass., married in New Hampshire, and himself and wife died at Louisville, Ky., in 1821, leaving six children, one of whom died in infancy.

AZUBA remained in the vicinity of Louisville, and married a Mr. Summers.

ASA came to Sangamon county in 1832, went to Galena in 1836, and two or three years later was killed by a lead mine caving in on him.

LAVINA came to Sangamon county in 1836, married in Springfield to Jacob Nott, who died, and she married John Letterhose, and died in Loami.

LUCY, married in Sangamon county to Levi Sweet. He died, leaving her a widow with five children at Seyene, Dallas county, Texas.

COLBURN, WILLIAM, brother to Isaac, Abel and Ebenezer, was born June 3, 1793, at Sterling, Mass., married Aug. 15, 1815, at Hebron, N. H., to Achsa Phelps, who was born at that place July 9, 1796. They came to Sangamon county, Ill., arriving April 5, 1821, in what is now Loami township. They had three children before moving to Sangamon county, and eleven after, the youngest of whom died in infancy. Of the thirteen children—

CLARISSA, born Oct. 27, 1816, at Pittsburg, Pa., married in Sangamon county, Dec. 3, 1831, to William S. Walker. *See his name.*

ABIGAIL, born April 29, 1818, at Marietta, O., married April 9, 1835, to Lawrence Underwood. *See his name.*

FANNY, born Jan. 4, 1820, at Marietta, O., married in Sangamon county, Jan. 28, 1843, to David Phelps. *See his name.*

MEHETIBEL, born Dec. 5, 1821, in Sangamon county, married Dec. 16, 1838, to David Phelps. *See his name.*

SAMUEL PAUL, born Sept. 15, 1823, in Sangamon county, married Oct. 23, 1845, to Melinda Colburn, had one child that died in infancy, and Mrs. Colburn died Dec. 23, 1865, and he married Nov. 14, 1866, to Mrs. Isabel Lucas, whose maiden name was Colburn. They reside in Loami.

MARGARET P., born April 7, 1825, in Sangamon county, married Sept. 21, 1845, to Lewis Cotterman. They had two children, WILLIAM A. and FANNIE, and Mrs. Cotterman died Sept. 6, 1853. Her children reside with their father near Linden, Osage county, Kan.

ISAAC, born Feb. 22, 1827, in Sangamon county, married August 17, 1854, to Julia A. Ensley. They had three children. ACHSA E., born July 24, 1855, died in her eighth year. CHLOE E. and CHARLES E. live with their father. Mrs. Julia A. Colburn died Dec. 25, 1859, and Mr. C. married Sept. 20, 1863, to Mandana Phelps. They had three children, CORA A., CLARENCE E. and MARY O.; all died in infancy. Isaac Colburn and wife reside in Loami.

DANIEL W., born July 2, 1829, married Nov. 28, 1849, to Lucinda Huffmaster. They have eight children. SARAH married William Greer, has one child, and resides with her parents. FANNY married Christopher McLaughlin, who was born Feb. 10, 1846, in Montgomery county, Ky. They have two children, MINNIE and ANDREW, and reside at Loami. Mr. McLaughlin enlisted Feb. 22, 1864, in Co. A, 106th Ill. Inf., for three years; was honorably discharged at Springfield, August 1, 1865. SUSAN M. married Thomas Huggin, and resides in Curran. JAMES E., MARY M., WINFIELD S., DAVID L. and

LAURA A., reside with their parents, three miles south of Curran.

WILLIAM S., born Feb. 20, 1831, in Sangamon county, married July 8, 1853, in Fulton county, Ill., to Mary Ensley, who was born May 23, 1831, near Chillicothe, O. They had four children. MILLARD F. died in infancy. LINDA A., born March 11, 1856, married Dec. 26, 1872, to Lycurgus L. Smith, who was born June 20, 1849, at Mt. Pleasant O., and reside at Martin's Ferry, Belmont county, O. LUELLA R. and WILLIAM H. reside with their parents at Loami.

W. S. Colburn enlisted at Jacksonville, Ill., July 16, 1847, in Co. G, 16th United States Inf., for five years or during the war with Mexico, and was honorably discharged August, 1848, at Cincinnati, O. In the spring of 1850 he started for California, via the Isthmus of Panama. The vessel was bestormed and becalmed, so that he was on the Pacific ocean seven months from Panama to San Francisco. He has traveled in twenty-four States of the Union, and been on fourteen sea voyages. William S. Colburn enlisted June 27, 1864, in Co. F., 28th Ill. Inf., for three years; was honorably discharged August 2, 1865. He was detailed as clerk in the medical department soon after entering the army, was promoted to hospital steward, and served as such to the end of the rebellion.

EBENEZER, born April 9, 1833, in Sangamon county, married August 17, 1854, to Nancy A. Huffmaster. They had two children, ADNA P. and CLARISSA A., and Mrs. Colburn died August 10, 1859, and Mr. C. was married August 8, 1862, to Elizabeth Davis. They have five children, DANIEL W., HENRY W., ALPHA D., JULIA A. and INA A., and live in Loami.

LEVI O., born Nov. 13, 1835, in Sangamon county, enlisted July 13, 1862, in Co. F, 51st Ill. Inf., for three years. He was 1st Sergt., and as such, commanded the company part of the time. He was wounded in the arm at the battle of Chickamauga, served until June 27, 1865, when he was honorably discharged. He was married July 7, 1867, to Christiana Kinney. They have two children, BERTHA O. and WILLIAM E., and live at Loami.

DAVID P., born Oct. 5, 1837, in Sangamon county, enlisted August 9, 1861, in Co. B, 30th Ill. Inf., for three years, re-enlisted as a veteran, Jan. 1, 1864. He was appointed 2nd Sergt. at the organization of the regiment; promoted to 1st Sergt.; commissioned 1st Lieut., Jan. 20, 1865; commissioned Capt., May, 1865. Commanded the company from Oct. 4, 1864. He served until July 17, 1865, when he was honorably discharged. He was married April 12, 1866, to Tirzah Mengel. They have one child, LEONARD L., and reside at Loami.

JOHN T., born Nov. 23, 1840, married June 23, 1861, to Martha J. Back, who was born April 9, 1845, at Loami. They had four children. JAQUETTA and LILLIE died in infancy. MARY A. and MILLIE A. live with their parents in Loami.

William Colburn died June 10, 1869, at Loami, and Mrs. Achsa Colburn resides at Loami, on the same place settled by herself and husband in 1822, one year before the land was brought into market. William and his brother Ebenezer entered land together, and cultivated it for several years. About 1836 they built a steam saw and grist mill at the north side of Lick creek, and machinery for grinding was soon added. It was the first mill of the kind within a radius of ten or twelve miles, and around that mill the village of Loami grew up. They continued in that business for many years, three mills having burned on the same spot. They were not always the owners, but their families were always connected with such enterprises. The sons of Wm. Colburn are now—1874—the owners of a mill within one hundred yards of where the first mill was built. One mill has burned where the new one stands.

The hardships endured by them and their families would be difficult to relate. Mrs. Achsa Colburn, now seventy-eight years old, has an unlimited fund of reminiscences connected with their advent into the county, and the difficulties of raising a large family. A loom was an indispensible article where all were dependent on the work of their own hands for the entire clothing of themselves and families. Mrs. Colburn tried all the men in the settlement, those of her own family included, in order to find some person who could make a loom, but all declined to undertake it, some for want of skill, and all for want of tools. Mrs. C. then procured an axe, a hand saw, a drawing knife, an auger and a chisel, and went to work. She made with her own hands a loom, warping bars, winding blades, temples for the lateral stretching of the cloth, and for spools she used corn cobs with the pith pushed out. With these appliances she wove hundreds of yards of cloth, and made it up into garments for her family. This she did while caring for her family of fourteen children.

COLBURN, EBENEZER, brother to Abel, Isaac and William, was born Dec. 1, 1794, at Sterling, Mass., married in 1817, at Marietta, Ohio, to Julia Smith, who was born April 17, 1797, in Suffolk county, Long Island, N. Y. They came to Sangamon county and joined the other members of the family in Oct., 1822, in what is now Loami township. They had two children before their arrival, and five after coming to Sangamon county. Of the seven children—

ADNA P., born August 12, 1818, at Marietta, Ohio, married April 27, 1839, in Sangamon county, to Lodasca Sweet. They had three children, and Mrs. Colburn died, and A. P. Colburn was married July 28, 1844, to Macca M. Sowell. They had seven children, one of whom died in infancy. Of all his children: ALVA married Hannah VanPelt, and resides at Seneca, Nemaha county, Kan. URSULA, married Charles Jarrett. See his name. GILBERT, enlisted in 1862, in Co. I, 73d Ill. Inf., for three years. He was captured at the battle of Chickamauga, Sept. 19-20, 1863, and died in prison at Andersonville, Ga., July 1, 1864. THOMAS B. and WILLIAM R. enlisted Sept. 20, 1862, in Co. G, 16th Ill. Inf., for three years. They were captured while scouting near Dalton, Ga., May 22, 1864, and taken to Andersonville prison also. THOMAS B. died June 19, 1864, and WILLIAM R. died August 12, 1864. Thus the three brothers died in the same prison in less than two months. STEPHEN E., died in infancy. CHAS. C., born Nov. 22, 1849, married Miss Coverdale, and lives at Loami. JULIA J., born May 24, 1851, married Nelson Elmore. See his name. They live in Sangamon county. JAMES B. resides with his mother. Adna P. Colburn died Feb. 26, 1867, and his widow resides adjoining Loami on the west.

WILLIAM, born in Monroe county, Ill., married in Sangamon county to Eliza Porter; had four children, and Mrs. C. died, and Wm. C. married Mrs. Ellen Smith, whose maiden name was Clover. They have one child, and reside in Christian county, at Smith's mill, on the Sangamon river, near the line of Sangamon county.

CHARLOTTE, born Jan. 19, 1824, in Sangamon county, married Jonas Smith. See his name.

MARIA, born in Sangamon county, married Peyton Foster; has a family of children, and lives at Atchison, Kan.

MARY P., born in Sangamon county, married David Greening. See his name.

BURFITT G., born in Sangamon county, married to Lucy Large, have six children, and live in Cooper township.

ELLEN, married Ebenezer Colburn, Jun., and she died.

Mrs. Julia Colburn died, and Ebenezer Colburn, Sen., died April 12, 1864, both at Loami.

COLBURN, ABEL, was born Sept. 20, 1790, in Sterling, Mass., a brother to Isaac, William and Ebenezer. He was married in April, 1811, at Hebron, N. H., to Deborah Phelps, who was born at Hebron in July, 1794. Mr. Colburn was a soldier from that place in the war of 1812. They had nine children, all born at Hebron, and in 1839 Mr. Colburn came to Sangamon county, and afterwards brought his family. Of their children—

JOSEPH R., born August, 1812, married in Massachusetts, to Ruth Fowler, and moved to Springfield, Ill., in 1838. He aided in building the State House, then in course of construction. They had six children; two died under seven years. Of the other four, ABNER K. married in Minnesota to Phebe Walters, and resides in Portland, Oregon. IRA is married, and lives in Minnesota. CHARLES lives with Adna Phelps, near Springfield. FREMONT lives with his mother. Joseph R. Colburn died in December, 1870, and his widow resides at Preston, Minn.

ELVIRA M., born April 18, 1814, at Hebron, N. H., married at that place March 7, 1832, to Stephen F. Fowler. He died Jan. 21, 1845, at Quincy, Mass., and

Mrs. F. was married Oct. 8, 1845, at Troy, Wis., to Jeremiah D. Sanborn, who was born Feb. 7, 1818, at Franklin, N. H. Mrs. S. traveled across the American continent on wagons, except in crossing Lake Michigan, and spent five years in Nevada and California, and Mr. S. spent three years there. They reside at Loami.

ISABEL, born April 17, 1816, at Hebron, N. H., married Sept. 11, 1838, to Thomas Lucas, who was born June 19, 1811, at Romney, N. H. They had five children. GEORGE M. went from Loami to Springfield, and enlisted July, 1861, in what became Co. C, 11th Mo. Inf., for three years; was 1st Sergeant; re-enlisted as a veteran Jan. 1, 1864, and died of disease at Jefferson Barracks, Mo., Nov. 14, 1864. He was commissioned 1st Lieutenant, to date from August 18, 1864, but the commission did not reach the hospital until the day after his death. FRANCENA I. died at thirteen. EDWARD W. enlisted Nov. 20, 1861, for three years, in Co. B, 30th Ill. Inf.: re-enlisted as a veteran Jan. 1, 1864; was with "Sherman in his march to the sea;" served to the end of the rebellion, and honorably discharged July, 1865; was married October, 1866, to Mary A. Starr, has one child, VALLIE M., and resides at Loami. ISABELLA E. died at seven years. LUELLA A. married August, 1867, to James L. Mahard, and died March, 1873, leaving two children, MARY J. and GEORGE M. Thomas Lucas died March 4, 1851, at Loami. His widow married Samuel P. Colburn. *See his name.*

IRA C., born in 1818, married at Quincy, Mass., Sept. 4, 1838, to Cyrena Chard, a native of Pomfret, Conn., moved to Minnesota, and had three children. JOHN E. was a soldier in a Minnesota regiment, veteranized, served to the end of the rebellion, and lives in Minnesota. ROMANZA died at seven years.

ACHSA P., born Feb. 17, 1820, in Hebron, N. H., married August, 1838, at Quincy, Mass., to John P. Davis, who was born April 17, 1815, in Boston. They came to Sangamon county with her parents, and had three children. ELVIRA M. married Sanford Withrow. *See his name.* CHARLES W. died in infancy. LAURA E. married Josiah Jones. *See his name.* John P. Davis enlisted at Springfield, July 9, 1847, in Co. D, 4th Ill. Inf., for one year. He served as Sergeant of that company in the war with Mexico, until July 9, 1848, when he was honorably discharged. He raised Co. B, 30th Ill. Inf., entered the United States service as Captain of the same, August, 1861. His company re-enlisted as veterans, January, 1864. He was with Sherman in his "march to the sea," and was promoted to Major of the regiment while on the trip. He commanded the regiment several months, and was honorably discharged July 17, 1865. Now resides at Loami, Sangamon county, Ill.

LUTHER P., born September, 1823, married in New Hampshire to Lydia Whittaker, raised one daughter, and reside in Lebanon, N. H.

NATHAN P., born December, 1826, in Hebron, N. H., married in South Reading, Mass., to Mary J. Eames, had four children, moved in 1855 to Minnesota, was a member of the Convention that framed the State Constitution, and has served several terms in the State Legislature. He raised a cavalry company and fought the Indians in Minnesota in 1863. Was Paymaster at one time in the army, against the rebellion. He is a practicing attorney, and resides at Preston, Minn.

MELINDA, born Sept. 13, 1830, married Oct. 23, 1845, to Samuel P. Colburn. *See his name.*

EMELINE, born July, 1832, married in 1848 to William Huffmaster. *See his name.*

Abel Colburn died Oct. 21, 1851, at Springfield. His widow married Adam Barger. *See his name.* He died, and she resides with her son-in-law, Samuel P. Colburn, at Loami.

CONKLING, JAMES C., was born Oct. 13, 1816, in New York City. At the age of thirteen he entered the Academy at Morristown, N. J., and prepared for college. He entered Princeton in 1833, and graduated in 1835. He studied law in Morristown, N. J., about three years, and came to Springfield, Ill., arriving in Nov., 1838, and was admitted to the bar the following winter. James C. Conkling and Mercy A. Levering were married Sept. 21, 1841, in Baltimore, Md. She was the daughter of Judge Aaron R. Levering, of Georgetown, D. C., and was born in that city in Nov.,

1817. Mr. and Mrs. Conkling had five children—

CLINTON L., born Oct. 16, 1843, in Springfield, was educated at Yale college, New Haven, Conn., and graduated there in 1864. He entered into partnership with his father in 1866, as J. C. & C. L. Conkling, in the practice of law. He was married March 24, 1867, to Georgiana Burrell, a native of Brooklyn, N. Y. They have two children, GEORGIA and KATE, and reside in Springfield.

CHARLES, born in Springfield, resides with his parents.

JAMES, born Jan. 4, 1850, in Springfield, Ill., was married March 23, 1870, in Covington, Ky., to Fannie A. Lowry, who was born in Springfield, March 23, 1849. They have two children living, MAY and FANNIE. He is a member of the firm of Conkling, Slemmons, & Co., Springfield, Ill.

ANNIE V., born July 2, 1853, was married Nov. 25, 1875, to Nathan S. Wood. He is a banker in Lafayette, Ind., where they now reside.

ALICE resides with her parents.

Hon. James C. Conkling was elected Mayor of Springfield in 1845, being the sixth in that office. He was elected representative for Sangamon county in the State legislature in 1852, and again in 1866, when he drafted the original bill for the new State house, and was active in its passage. He is a member of the National Lincoln Monument Association, which has just erected a monument to the memory of Abraham Lincoln. He is the head of the firm of Conkling, Slemmons & Co. James C. Conkling, more than any other capitalist of Springfield, uses his wealth in extensive building enterprises, and for the encouragement of manufactures.

CONANT, SULLIVAN, was born Feb. 26, 1801, at Oakham, Worcester county, Mass. Lydia R. Heminway was was born November, 1803, in the same county. They were married Sept. 10, 1822, at Shutesbury, Mass., where they had three children, and moved to Amherst, where they had one child. They returned to Shutesbury, and from there started west, Nov. 2, 1830, traveling in wagons to Troy, N. Y., and from there to Rochester by canal, thence by wagon to Olean Point, where they embarked on a raft and floated to Pittsburg. There they took a steamboat down the Ohio, and up the Mississippi river to Chester, Randolph county, Ill., where the youngest child died. In January, 1831, Mr. Conant started with his family, in a sleigh, to visit some old friends near Carrollton, Greene county, Ill., going by Illinoistown, now East St. Louis. They continued their journey by Jacksonville to Springfield, arriving Feb. 18, 1831. When they left Chester the snow was about six inches deep, but when they arrived in Springfield it was on four feet of snow, being the height of the "deep snow." They had five children born in Springfield. Of their eight children—

ABIGAIL A., born July 5, 1823, at Shutesbury, Mass., was married in Springfield to William W. Lee, who was born August 20, 1822, in Delaware. They had four children. LAURA A., born Oct. 15, 1844, in Springfield, was married May 7, 1867, to John T. Capps, who was born Dec. 30, 1841, in Clarke county, Ky. They have two children, OLIVE and WILLIAM L. Mr. Capps was a student at Illinois College, Jacksonville, when the rebellion began. He enlisted August, 1861, in Co. B, 10th Ill. Inf., for three years; re-enlisted as a veteran January, 1864; was with Sherman in his "march to the sea;" served until July, 1865, when he was honorably discharged. He graduated Feb. 6, 1866, with the degree of Master of Accounts, at Eastman's National Business College, Poughkeepsie, N. Y. He is now of the firm of Dickerman & Co., Springfield Woolen Manufactory. LYDIA E., born March 23, 1847, in Springfield, was married Dec. 21, 1869, to S. O. Stockwell, a native of Auburn, N. Y. They have one child, CLARA L., and reside in Columbus, Ohio. THOMAS S., born Jan. 9, 1849, in Bloomington, Ill., was married in Springfield, May 29, 1872, to Mary J. Eaton. They have one child, ADDIE. T. S. Lee is engaged with his father-in-law in the grain business, and resides in Edinburg. EDWARD W., born March 9, 1853, in Taylorville. He was married in Springfield, Oct. 6, 1875, to Lou. H. Pasfield, adopted daughter of George Pasfield, Sen., and resides in Edinburg. Wm. W. Lee died July 12, 1870, and his widow resides in Springfield.

WILLIAM S., born Feb. 27, 1825, at

Shutesbury, Mass., was married in Springfield, Ill, to Mary Sykes. They had two children. JAMES was born in Petersburg, and is in business with his father. KATIE resides with her father. Mrs. Mary Conant died in Springfield, Feb. 12, 1864. Wm. S. Conant was married in Menard county to Eliza Kinkead, and reside in Petersburg, Ill. In 1844 W. S. Conant met with an accident from a falling derrick which slightly lamed him. A Mr. Brodie was killed by the same accident. They were raising a pole at a political meeting. Mr. Conant is extensively engaged in the furniture and undertaking business. He was the originator, and is now the owner, of Rose Hill cemetery, near Petersburg.

SUSAN E., born March 10, 1827, in Shutesbury, Mass., was married June 26, 1845, in Springfield, to George R. Connelly. *See his name.* He died, and she married Charles Dougherty. *See his name.*

LEVI J., born Oct. 25, 1831, in Springfield, was married there July 28, 1858, to Elizabeth Brodie. They had two children, JOHN B. and WILLIAM S. Mrs. Elizabeth Conant died Feb. 14, 1865, and L. J. Conant was married Mar. 1, 1875, at Vincennes, Ind., to Mrs. Sarah A. Baker, whose maiden name was Hargraves. She was born April 24, 1841, in Manchester, England. Mr. C. is in the grocery business, and resides in Springfield.

MARY A., born July 20, 1833, in Springfield, was married there to Cook S. Hampton. *See his name.*

PHINEAS H., born April 12, 1837, in Springfield, was married June 4, 1857, to Sarah J. Hobbs, who was born Dec. 1, 1838, in Jacksonville, Ill. They have three children, JULIA E., MINNIE L., and PEARL R., and reside in Springfield, Ill. P. H. Conant enlisted in Co. C, 124th Ill. Inf., for three years, and was mustered in as Corporal. Served until Feb. 6, 1864, when he was honorably discharged on account of physical disability. In the spring of 1866 he was appointed, by Mayor Dennis, deputy city marshal; served nearly three years. Was deputy sheriff under Shoup, and deputy U. S. collector under Harper. Sold goods at Illiopolis about three years, since which time he has been a commercial traveler

—28

for a Springfield grocery house, and lives in Springfield.

CAROLINE A., born Sept. 1, 1843, in Springfield, married Rev. Thomas M. Dillon, of the M. E. church. He is in the traveling connection, and resides (1874) in Martinsburg, Clarke county, Ill.

LYDIA J., born July 19, 1845, in Springfield, was married there, March 17, 1868, to George L. Dingle. G. L. Dingle was a soldier in an Illinois regiment, and did his part in aiding to suppress the rebellion. He is now deputy Postmaster at Santa Fe, New Mexico, and lives there. Mrs. Lydia R. Conant died May 30, 1867, and Sullivan Conant was married again. He resides in Springfield.

CONNELLY, JOHN, was born in 1794, in the District of Columbia. Ann Wetherell was born Feb. 20, 1800, in the District of Columbia, also. They were there married and had ten children. The family moved to Springfield, Ill., in 1837. Mr. Connelly was Register of the United States Land Office, in Springfield, during the administration of President Pierce, and part of the administration of President Buchanan. He also, at various times, filled a number of local offices. I have the history of but two of his children. His daughter—

MARY J., born in the District of Columbia, married in Springfield to John O. Rames. *See his name.* She died in 1854.

His second son—

GEORGE R., born Jan. 18, 1822, in the District of Columbia, was married in Springfield, Ill., Jan. 27, 1845, to Susan E. Conant. They had three living children, namely: JOHN L., born March 18, 1846, in Springfield, graduated at the Rush Medical College of Chicago. He was married Sept. 3, 1842, at Harristown, Ill., to Nannie Bedford. They had one child, MAGGIE P., who died young. Dr. J. L. Connelly resides at Harristown, Macon county, Ill., and is engaged in the practice of his profession there. GEORGE S., born Feb. 8, 1849, in Springfield, married Sept. 15, 1870, in his native city, to Mary Thomas, who was born Dec. 30, 1850, in Springfield, Ill. They have two children, ALICE MAY and LILLIE E. George S. Connelly resides in Springfield, and is engaged in merchandising. LILLIE E., born Sept. 2, 1851, in Springfield, married

Sept. 19, 1871, to Columbus M. Lloyd, who was born March 6, 1849, near Wabash, Wabash county, Ind. They live near Dawson, Sangamon county, Ill. George R. Connelly died of cholera, in Springfield, June 9, 1854. His widow married Charles Dougherty, Jun. See his name.

CONSTANT, JACOB, brother to John, who was the grandfather of Rezin H. He was also the brother of Isaac and Thomas, and was born about 1765, in Virginia. Eleanor Clinkenbeard was born about 1769, in Virginia, also. They were there married, and soon after moved on pack horses—that being the only way goods could be transported at that time through that mountainous country—to Fleming county, Ky. They had fourteen children in that county, and in 1814 moved to Clermont county, Ohio, where they had two children. The family moved to Sangamon county, Ill., arriving Oct. 26, 1826, in what is now Mechanicsburg township. Of their children—

ELIZABETH, born Nov. 17, 1790, in Fleming county, Ky., married there to Charles Morgan. See his name.

JOHN, born in Fleming county, Ky., went back from Ohio to Kentucky, and there married Margaret Wood. They came in company with his father to Sangamon county in 1826, where they had five children, and moved to Pike county, thence to northwest Missouri, where the living children now reside. The parents are both dead.

WILLIAM, born in Kentucky, went back from Ohio and married Rhoda Planck. They never came to Illinois, but he died, leaving one child, JOHN CONSTANT, who resides near Felicity, Clermont county, Ohio.

MARY, born in Kentucky, married in Ohio to Thomas Jones. They had ten children, and Mrs. Jones died. The living members of the family reside in and near Mt. Olivet, Clermont county, O.

ISAAC, born Nov. 17, 1794, in Fleming county, Ky., was married June 29, 1823, in Clarke county, Ky., to Nancy Peebles, who was born Sept. 13, 1794, in that county. They had two children in Kentucky, joined his parents in Clermont county, Ohio, and came with them to Sangamon county, Ill., arriving in the fall of 1826 in what is now Mechanicsburg township, where they had two children, and moved to what is now Logan county, where they had two children, and from there to Buffalo Hart grove, in Sangamon county, and had one child. They moved, in 1857, to Dawson. Of their children, RACHEL, born in Clarke county, Ky., March 29, 1824, married John Billington. See his name. JACOB, born August 17, 1826, in Clarke county, Ky., married in Sangamon county, May 16, 1850, to Lillias Wilson, who was born May 15, 1825, in Dumfriesshire, Scotland. They had seven children, three of whom died young, and HELEN MARY died Oct. 3, 1872, the very day she was thirteen years old. NANCY J., WILLIAM E. and JAMES H., live with their parents, adjoining Dawson on the east. MARGARET J., born July 15, 1829, in Sangamon county, married Oct. 26, 1850, to James Deavers. They have six children, and live near Mt. Pulaski. WILLIAM R., born April 13, 1832, in Sangamon county, married in 1852 to Jane Wilson, who was born in Dumfriesshire, Scotland. They had seven children in Sangamon county, and Mrs. Constant died May 7, 1864. Mr. C. was married in Dawson to Hattie Grabendich. They have two children, and live in Lawrence, Kansas. MARY A., born June 17, 1834, in Logan county, Ill., married Oct. 17, 1871, at Dawson, to Alfred Rape. See his name. SARAH E., born Dec. 17, 1836, in Logan county, married Sept. 14, 1856, to Horatio M. Van Winkle, who was born Feb. 1, 1834, in Shelby county, Ill. They have one child, LILLIAS E., and live in Dawson. Mr. Van Winkle enlisted August 15, 1862, in Co. C, 124th Ill. Inf., for three years; served full term exactly, and was honorably discharged August 15, 1865, at Chicago. MARTHA E., born April 19, 1840, in Sangamon county, married Dec. 6, 1869, to John S. Clinkenbeard, who was born Dec. 8, 1822, in Clarke county, Ky. They have two children, ISAAC and NANCY E., and live three miles southwest of Illiopolis. Mr. C. has two living children by a former wife, JOHN W. and MARY K. Isaac Constant died June 27, 1865, and his widow resides at Dawson.

HESTER, born in Kentucky, married in Clermont county, Ohio, to Josiah Johnson, had one child, and father and child died in Ohio. She came to Sangamon county, married John Rutherford, had four children, and the parents both died. Their son, JOHN T. Rutherford, was a soldier in an Illinois regiment, and died in the army. MARGARET married Matt. Noonan, and resides in Sangamon county. ALEXANDER is married and lives in Champaign county.

SARAH, born Dec. 27, 1799, in Kentucky, married James Carrico. See his name.

ELEANOR, born in 1803, in Kentucky, married Elijah T. Lanham. See his name.

JACOB, born Jan. 7, 1805, in Fleming county, Kentucky, married June 4, 1829, in Sangamon county, to Permelia Crocker. They had six children, two of whom died young. The other four, JAMES H. M., born March 4, 1830, married Catharine Blankenship, have four children. He was a soldier in a Sangamon county regiment. DAVID C., born Jan. 28, 1833, married in Texas to Annetta Snow. They are teaching among the Indians. THOMAS S., born July 2, 1835, married in Mt. Pulaski to Sarah Cass, daughter of Ninian Cass. MARY L., born Sept 25, 1839, married John Rinker; had one child, ANNETTA S. Mr. Rinker enlisted in 1861, in 30th Ill. Inf., and died near Vicksburg, in 1863. Mrs. Permelia Constant died Feb. 17, 1847, and Jacob Constant was married June 25, 1847, in St. Clair county, to Mrs. Celia Talbott, whose maiden name was Wakefield. They had four children. CHARLES A. married Sarah Horn, had one child, and live near Dawson. HARRIET E. and PERMELIA O., SARAH F. died at eleven years. Mrs. C. had two children by her first husband, THOMAS and MARY E. TALBOTT. The latter died in her fourteenth year. Jacob Constant and his wife reside one and a half miles southwest of Dawson.

BENJAMIN, born in Kentucky, married in Sangamon county to Matilda Lakin, had seven children, and Mr. Constant died in 1855. Two of his sons, JOHN W. and NORMAN A. were Union soldiers from Greene county, and both died in the army. His widow resides in Macoupin county.

JONATHAN, born Sept. 30, 1809, in Fleming county, Ky., came to Sangamon county in 1826, married May 19, 1836, to Mary Elder. They had five children, two of whom died young. Of the other three, GEORGE W., born June 7, 1837, married July 23, 1857, in Springfield, to Sarah Kent; have three living children, JOHN D., LYDIA F., NETTIE B.—the third child, IDA J., died in her fourth year. George W. Constant resides two and a half miles southwest of Illiopolis. JOHN W., born Sept. 22, 1839, married in Springfield, Jan. 30, 1865, to Clarissa G. Ingels. They have four children, MATTIE F., HARRY, MARY P. and WILLIE, and reside two and a half miles northeast of Illiopolis. SAMUEL W., born July, 1843, enlisted August 17, 1861, in Co. H, 30th Ill. Inf., for three years, was captured at the battle of Atlanta, Ga., July 22, 1864, was two months in Andersonville prison, exchanged Sept. 19, 1864, and honorably discharged on the 27th of the same month. He was married in Sangamon county, Dec. 24, 1867, to Mary J. Semple. They have one child, NELLIE D., and reside in Macon county, near Illiopolis. Mrs. Mary Constant died Sept., 1847, and Jonathan Constant was married Nov. 26, 1848, to Lavina Crocker. They had two children. MARY B., born Sept. 17, 1851, married June 6, 1872, to Squire Campbell, and died Nov. 19, 1872. LEWIS ALLEN, born Dec. 7, 1853, resides with his father. Mrs. Lavina Constant died August 26, 1858, and Jonathan Constant married Dec. 20, 1860, to Mrs. Sarah Ridgeway, whose maiden name was Bridges. They reside three miles northwest of Mechanicsburg.

MARGARET, married in Ohio to Greenbury Lanham, and had one child. The father and child died in Ohio. She died in Sangamon county.

NELSON, born in Clermont county, Ohio, married in Sangamon county to Elizabeth Walker. They have five children, and reside near Farmer City, DeWitt county, Ill.

Jacob Constant died Sept. 21, 1828, and Mrs. Eleanor Constant died Sept. 4, 1835, both in Mechanicsburg township, near where they settled in 1826.

CONSTANT, THOMAS, brother of Isaac, also of John, who was grandfather of Rezin H., was born Aug. 14, 1796, in Virginia. He was married June 17, 1796, in Kentucky, to Margery Edmonson. They had seven children in Kentucky, and moved to Xenia, Ohio. From there they moved to Sangamon county, Ill., arriving in the fall of 1820 in what is now Fancy creek township. Of all their children—

JOHN, born May 9, 1797, in Clarke county, Ky., married in Springfield, Ill., to Mary Latham, daughter of Judge Latham. They had four living children, and Mrs. Mary Constant died May 3, 1841. Mr. C. was married to Elizabeth Singleton. They had two children. Of the children by his first marriage, JAMES T. went to California, and died there. The other three were GARRETT, MARY and MARIA L. The children by the second marriage were JULIA and JOHN. Mr. Constant died, and his widow and children reside in Springfield.

ELIZABETH E., born June 14, 1799, in Clarke county, Ky., was married in Xenia, Ohio, to William F. Elkin. See his name.

ARCHIBALD E., born May 10, 1801, in Clarke county, Ky., married in Springfield, Ill., to Maria Latham, daughter of Judge Latham. They had five children; two died young. MARGERY is teaching in the Bettie Stuart Institute, in Springfield. MARY married Temple Elliott. See his name. KATIE resides among her friends. Mr. Constant came to Sangamon county in 1819, settling on Wolf creek; afterwards moved to Springfield, and purchased a quantity of land in what is now the Third ward, and known as Constant's addition. He was a Major in the Black Hawk war, from Sangamon county. He moved to Elkhart, Logan county, about 1863. Mrs. Maria Constant died there Nov. 13, 1868, and Archibald E. Constant died in Elkhart, Jan. 19, 1875.

WILLIAM, born May, 1803, in Clarke county, Ky. He was a physician, and was married in Sangamon county to Phœbe Johnson. She died, leaving three children. Dr. Constant was married in Jeffersonville, Ind., and had two children, KATIE and JOHN. Dr. William Constant died in 1865.

MARY, born June 22, 1805, in Clarke county, Ky., was married in Sangamon county, Ill., to Dr. Garrett Elkin. See his name.

NATHAN E., born April 8, 1807, in Clarke county, Ky., was married in Sangamon county to Sarah Dement. Mrs. Sarah Constant died, and he was married August 25, 1843, to Mary M. Stewart, daughter of James Stewart. See his name. They had three children. WILLIAM F. married Elizabeth A. Lake. They have one child, and reside two miles west of Williamsville. NATHAN E., Jun., enlisted August, 1862, for three years, in Co. G, 114th Ill. Vol. Inf. He was captured at the battle of Guntown, Miss., June 11, 1864, taken to Andersonville prison, where he remained three months. After that to several other prisons, to evade the Union army, then back to Andersonville. From there to Florida, and guarded in the woods until April 28, 1865, and released at the close of the rebellion. He had the usual experience of prisoners in the south. He and seven others cooked all their rations the first three months at Andersonville, in half a canteen. Sometimes he would give a day's rations for a chew of tobacco, and not a very large chew at that. He says words cannot describe the suffering that was endured by the Union soldiers in southern prisons. Robbery and murder prevailed among the prisoners until they found it necessary to organize a court and a regular jury, convicted six of their number and hung them. He says Wirz allowed them to go outside to hold the trial (of course guarding them), and furnished the lumber for the gallows. Mr. C. says that although ten years have elapsed since he was in that den of horrors, when he is not well the most dainty food smells to him like Andersonville prison rations. One blanket was all they were allowed for eight men. Nathan E. Constant, Jun., was married, after his return from the army, to Amanda Morton. They have three children, FANNIE E., WILLIAM and FRANK, and reside three miles west of Williamsville. Nathan E. Constant, Sen., died August 25, 1843, and his widow married Miletus W. Ellis. See his name.

ISAAC, born April 5, 1809, in Clarke county, Ky., was married in Sangamon county, Ill., Feb. 14, 1835, to Lucinda Merriman, daughter of Reuben Merriman, (now residing in Oregon). They had eight children. LAVINIA, born March 12, 1834, in Sangamon county, was married in Jackson county, Oregon,

April, 1854, to Dr. Jesse Robinson. They have four living children, EDWARD C., CHESTER L., THOMAS and MARY A., and reside in Oakland, Cal. WILLIAM T., born Nov. 2, 1836, in Sangamon county, Ill., was married in Oregon, April 3, 1862, to Jessie Bledsoe. He died August 4, 1867, leaving a widow and three children, ISAAC, WILLIAM T. and JULIA B., in Jackson county, Oregon. ELIZABETH M., born Jan. 2, 1839, in Sangamon county, married Jan. 1, 1856, in Jackson county, Oregon, to William T. Leever. They have seven living children, W. CONSTANT, LAVINIA, IDA, EDMONSON M., JULIAN D., THOMAS S. and ADA, and reside in Jackson county, Oregon. JULIA A., born Sept. 17, 1841, in Sangamon county, was married in Oregon, Dec. 5, 1861, to W. A. Owen. They have five living children, EUDORA, MINNIE, MABEL C., GLENN and WILLIAM, and all reside in Jacksonville, Oregon. MARGERY E., born Feb. 5, 1845, in Sangamon county, was married to Constantine Magruder, April 22, 1875. They reside at Central Point, Jackson county, Oregon. ELIZA A., born Oct. 20, 1851, in Sangamon county, Ill., died March 3, 1866, in Jackson county, Oregon. Isaac Constant was in the Black Hawk war from Sangamon county. He went to Oregon in 1849, took a claim under the homestead law, and returned to Illinois in 1850, disposed of his property, and with his family and some of his neighbors, emigrated to Oregon in 1852. They were among the first families who settled there. After they arrived, Mr. Constant had to go two hundred miles with pack animals, for provisions. The valley was teeming with Indians, but he lived to see them all pass away, and surrounded by a large circle of friends, he resides near Jacksonville, Jackson county, Oregon.

MARTHA, born August 23, 1811, in Xenia, Ohio, was married in Sangamon county, Ill., to William S. Stone. They had three children; one died in infancy. Of the other two, ELLEN, born in April, 1837, is unmarried. MARGERY, born March, 1838, was married in 1855 to Thomas Smith, of Independence, Mo. They have two living children. Mrs. Martha Stone died in St. Louis, Mo., in March, 1854. Mr. Stone died in Independence, Mo., in 1870.

ADALINE, born March 28, 1813, in Xenia, Ohio, was married in Sangamon county, Ill., March 25, 1835, to James D. Allen. Of their children, MARTHA, born Jan. 6, 1836, was married in Greensburg, Ky., Oct. 31, 1854, to George L. Harris. They have three children living, THOMAS A., BLANCHE and ADALINE. George L. Harris enlisted in the 6th Kansas Cav. Reg., and was killed July 29, 1864, at the battle of Fort Smith, Ark. Mrs. Harris was married March 21, 1873, in Shawnee, Kansas, to James Sharp. They reside in Shawnee. JULIA J., born Jan. 19, 1841, in Shawnee, Kansas, was married Dec. 10, 1856, in Independence, Mo., to Joseph F. Hagan. He was drowned in the Missouri river July 15, 1860. His widow married Wolf Bachrach, of Kansas City, August 9, 1865. They have one daughter living. Mrs. Julia Bachrach died in Kansas City, Mo., June 2, 1872. HATTIE, born August 19, 1844, died March 13, 1868. EMILY F., born Nov. 1, 1848, was married in Shawnee, Kansas, Jan. 27, 1875, to James T. Gillespie. They have one child, and reside in Shawnee. THOMAS, born Jan. 12, 1838, died July 21, 1845. Mr. and Mrs. Allen reside at Shawnee, Kansas, where they have lived for nineteen years.

MARGERY, born Nov. 24, 1814, in Xenia, Ohio, was married in Sangamon county to Josiah Francis. See his name.

LAVINIA, born Sept. 18, 1816, in Xenia, Ohio, was married in Sangamon county, Ill., April 2, 1839, to William Lavely. See his name.

EMILY, born Nov. 21, 1818, in Xenia, Ohio, was married in Sangamon county to N. B. Stone. They had six children; three died in infancy.

JULIA A., born Sept. 20, 1820, in Xenia, Ohio, was married in Sangamon county to Newton Francis. See his name.

Thomas Constant died Dec. 14, 1840, and Mrs. Margery Constant died March 1, 1842, both in Athens, Illinois.

CONSTANT, REZIN H., was born July 8, 1809, in Clarke county, Ky. His grandfather (John Constant) was shot in the thigh by an Indian while he was with a surveying party in Kentucky. He lived fifteen years after, but it finally caused his death. His son Jacob was the father of Rezin H. Neither this John nor Jacob ever came to Sangamon county. Rezin H. was married in his native county, July 27, 1830, to Abigail D. Constant. On the 9th of September following they started west with the family of his father-in-law—who was also his uncle, Isaac Constant—and arrived in Springfield Oct. 7, 1830, just in time to experience all the hardships connected with the "deep snow." R. H. Constant enlisted at Springfield, June 10, 1832, in Capt. Jesse Claywell's company, Col. James Collins' regiment, and Gen. James D. Henry's Brigade of Ill. Vol. Inf. He was commissioned Lieut., and was in the battle of Wisconsin, and commanded his company at the battle of Bad Axe, August 5, 1832, which terminated the Black Hawk war. Mr. Constant was one of the representatives of Sangamon county in the legislature of Illinois for 1846 and '47. They had eight children in Sangamon county, namely—

SARAH A., born Jan. 11, 1831, married in Sangamon county to Henry B. Grubb. They have five children, RICHARD, CATHARINE, ROBERT, GEORGE and HARLAND, and live in Springfield.

AMANDA, born Feb. 11, 1833, married Charles Dougherty. See his name. She died, leaving three children.

AMY, born Oct. 10, 1834, died in Sangamon county, July 25, 1852.

ALFRED S., born August 19, 1836, married in Sangamon county to Mary E. Wilson. They have four living children, JAMES R., FRANK, LUCIAN L. and HARRY W. Alfred S. Constant enlisted July 25, 1862, in Co. I, 114th Ill. Inf., for three years. Served until Jan. 16, 1863, when he was discharged on account of physical disability. He resides near Barclay.

ELIZABETH P., born March 15, 1839, married in Sangamon county to Ninian M. Taylor. See his name.

THOMAS S., born April 30, 1841, died in Sangamon county, March 26, 1857.

GEORGE M., born Jan. 31, 1844, enlisted at Springfield, June, 1862, for three months, in the 70th Ill. Vol. Inf. Served full time, and was honorably discharged with the regiment. He was married to Margaret E. Bates. They have two children, CRESSEY and PEARL, and reside at Mason City, Ill.

MARY C., born April 22, 1846, married in Sangamon county to David A. Taylor. See his name. They live near Gibson, Ford county.

Mrs. Abigail D. Constant died August 11, 1846, and Rezin H. Constant was married Sept. 27, 1847, to Mrs. Mary L. Harbert, whose maiden name was Halbert. They had three children—

CORDELIA F., born April 1, 1849, in Sangamon county, married there to Dr. Hamilton R. Riddle. See his name.

IRENA, born Sept. 7, 1851, in Sangamon county, married Dr. Isaac H. Taylor. See his name.

SABRA G., born April 5, 1853, in Sangamon county, married Feb. 21, 1872, to Russel O. Riddle. See his name.

Mrs. Mary L. Constant died May 18, 1863, and Rezin H. Constant resides in Clear Lake township, near Barclay.

CONSTANT, JOHN, born Sept. 13, 1781, in a fort or picketed station in Clarke county, Ky. He was married March 11, 1802, to Susan Edminston, who was born July 27, 1783. They had eleven children in Clarke county, Ky., three of whom died young, and the family moved in company with Robert Cass and family to Sangamon county, Ill., arriving Oct. 7, 1826, at Buffalo Hart Grove. Of their eight children—

MIRIAM, born Dec. 6, 1802, married in Kentucky, August 25, 1825, to Nathaniel Massey, and came with her parents to Sangamon county. They had one child, SUSAN, that died at fourteen years. Mrs. Massey married John Sinclair. See his name, with the Correll family.

JOHN W., born Oct. 29, 1804, in Clarke county, Ky., married there, Aug. 1, 1826, to Lucinda Cass, and moved to Sangamon county with his father in the fall of that year. They had four children: ARMINTA J., born August 6, 1827, in Sangamon county, married Horace B. Enos. See his name. JOHN T., born Feb. 13, 1830, married April 16, 1854, to Elizabeth C. Burns. They had six children, two of whom died under three years. MATTIE S., ROBERT F., EMMA M. and CORA K. reside with their parents at Buffalo Hart Station. ZACARIAH, born August 1, 1832, died Oct. 31, 1856. WM. R., born Sept. 26, 1833, enlisted

August, 1862, for three years, in Co. A., 73d Ill. Inf. He had two fingers shot from his right hand at the battle of Stone's river. Served to the end of the rebellion, and was honorably discharged with his regiment. He was married March 14, 1867, to Mary A. Perry. They have two children, and reside near Sabetha, Nemaha county, Kan. Mrs. Lucinda Constant died Feb. 23, 1836, and John W. Constant was married March 22, 1838, to Susan Grove. They had one child, ADAM H., born April 26, 1839, enlisted July 26, 1862, in Co. I, 114th Ill. Inf., for three years. Served full term, and was honorably discharged August 8, 1865. He was married August 26, 1862, (one month after he enlisted), to Mary F. Greening. They had three children. ULYSSES GRANT died young. ALFRED H. and GERSHOM K. live with their parents, three miles east of Buffalo Hart Station. John W. Constant died August 29, 1838, eight months before the birth of his son, Adam H. His widow resides with her son, Adam H.

JACOB D., born Oct. 15, 1807, in Clarke county, Ky., married April 4, 1832, in Sangamon county, to Sarah Correll. They had four living children. LOUISA J., born Feb. 18, 1833, married George McDaniel. See his name. MARY E., born August 8, 1834, died March 23, 1851. HARRIET L., born Dec. 31, 1835, died May 26, 1855. SUSAN, born June 20, 1837, married Augustus Bruce; had three children. HELEN died in her third year. ADELAIDE and WILLIAM reside with their parents, at Corinne, Box Elder county, Utah. Mrs. Sarah Constant died Feb. 8, 1842, and Jacob D. Constant married Hannah Garretson. They had two children. ANN E., born Sept. 20, 1844, married Eleazer Tuttle, have two children, and live in Atlanta. THOMAS, born Jan. 19, 1846, lives with Robert McDaniel. Jacob D. Constant died Oct. 19, 1846, and Mrs. Hannah Constant died Oct. 22, 1850, both in Buffalo Hart Grove.

MARGERY, born March 20, 1810, in Clarke county, Ky., married to Isaac Dawson, and died without children, Feb., 1845, in Sangamon county.

HARRIET L., born Dec. 22, 1811, in Clarke county, Ky., married in Sangamon county, Aug. 13, 1829, to Isaac L. Skinner. They had one child, SALLY, born Jan. 10, 1831, (in time of the "deep snow.") She went to Clark county, Ky., on a visit, and was there married, Feb. 6, 1851, to Henry Hall. They had two children. Mrs. Hall died May 29, 1860, at Kankakee. BELLE and ISAAC N. Hall reside with their father at Momence, Kankakee county, Ill. Isaac L. Skinner went to Kentucky to visit his father, and died there Aug. 26, 1831. His widow married in Sangamon county, Nov. 11, 1838, to James W. Langston. See his name.

THOMAS E., born Nov. 15, 1813, in Kentucky, died in Sangamon county Sept. 9, 1830.

WILLIAM A., born Jan. 29, 1816, in Clarke county, Ky., married in Sangamon county, March, 1842, to Mary A. Starr. They had seven children. JOHN E., born March 29, 1843, enlisted at Springfield, Ill., July 20, 1861, for three years, in what became Co. B, 11th Mo. Inf.; re-enlisted as a veteran in same company and regiment, Jan. 1, 1864, and was honorably discharged Jan. 15, 1866. He was married Jan. 15, 1871, to Hester F. King, have one child, EARL, and live near Buffalo Hart station. HARRISON CLAY, born Sept. 14, 1844, married Nov. 12, 1867, to Mary E. Enos. They have one child, CHARLES EDWARD, and reside one mile east of Buffalo Hart station. ALLEN S., born Aug. 7, 1846, enlisted May 3, 1864, in Co. I, 133d Ill. Inf., for one hundred days, and was drowned July, 1864, at Rock Island, while bathing in the Mississippi river. EMMA, born Aug. 12, 1848, ALICE, born Dec. 1, 1850, reside with their mother. HARVEY, born July 14, 1853, died Oct. 9, 1860. WILLIAM T., born Oct. 13, 1855, resides with his mother. William A. Constant died Aug. 15, 1855, and his widow married March, 1857, to Casper Byerline. They have two children, CHARLES F. and NOAH, and reside one mile east of Buffalo Hart station.

ELIZA J., born Oct. 23, 1821, died Oct. 19, 1837.

John Constant died Nov. 18, 1835, and his widow, Susan Constant, died March 18, 1864, both in Sangamon county.

CONSTANT, ISAAC, brother of Thomas, Abigail, John and Jacob. He was born April 3, 1789, in Clarke county, Ky.; was married July 4, 1811, in the same county, to Amy Dean. They had eight children in Kentucky, one of whom died there. The family moved to Sangamon county, Ill., arriving Oct. 7, 1830, in what is now Williams township. Of their seven children—

JOHN, born July 7, 1812, in Kentucky, died in Sangamon county Sept. 20, 1835.

REBECCA, born Aug. 21, 1813, in Kentucky, died in Sangamon county Nov. 18, 1832.

ABIGAIL D., born May 3, 1815, in Kentucky, married Rezin H. Constant. *See his name.*

MARY A., born Dec. 23, 1816, in Kentucky, married in Sangamon county to Miletus W. Ellis. *See his name.*

GEORGE W., born Oct. 23, 1818, in Clarke county, Ky., married in Sangamon county, Ill., Nov. 26, 1840, to Martha B. Stewart. They had three children in Sangamon county. WILLIAM S. married Parthenia Bates. They have one child, and live two miles northwest of Williamsville. JAMES H. married Mary Keagle. They have two living children, WILLIAM and LUCY, and live two and a half miles northwest of Williamsville. MARY A. married March 29, 1871, to James H. Groves, and reside two miles east of Williamsville. Mrs. Martha B. Constant died June 1, 1850. G. W. Constant was married Oct. 7, 1852, to Mary W. Stapleford. She was born in Milford, Kent county, Del., and came to Springfield Oct. 14, 1836, in company with her brother-in-law, Benjamin S. Clements, who was the first Mayor of Springfield. George W. Constant and wife reside at Williamsville.

AVERY G., born June 8, 1821, in Kentucky, married in Sangamon county to Louisa Fisher. They had six children. JULIA, the third child, married James Bates. *See his name.* ELLEN and ALBERT died young. CHARLES A. lives in Springfield. ISAAC F. and AVERY live with their mother. Avery G. Constant died March 6, 1858, and his widow resides at Williamsville.

SAMUEL D., born Feb. 21, 1823, died, aged six years, in Kentucky.

JAMES, born July 12, 1825, in Kentucky, died in Sangamon county March 2, 1842.

Isaac Constant died Dec. 25, 1854, and his widow died July 7, 1860, both in Williams township.

COOPER, AMBROSE, brother to Meredith, was born Dec. 18, 1796, in Botetourt county, Va., and taken by his parents to Smith county, Tenn., where he was married to Mary Kilbraith. They had two children in Tenn., and in 1821 moved to St. Clair county, Ill., where they had one child, and moved to Sangamon county in the fall of 1823, and settled two miles east of the present town of Sherman, where they had one child. Of their four children—

HUGH L., born in Tennessee, and married in Sangamon county, to Elizabeth Taylor. They moved to Iowa, where he died, leaving a widow and five children. One of them married and remained in Iowa. The mother and four children moved to Piatt county, Ill. Two of the sons married there, and moved to Kansas. The widow and two children live in Piatt county.

WILLIAM, born in Tennessee, raised in Sangamon county, went to California, and was married there to Sarah Ide. He came back to Sangamon county, and after a stay of some years, started on his return to California with his family. He died at sea, one day's sail from New Orleans, leaving a widow and two children. ANN E. is married and lives at Lebanon, Linn county, Oregon. ALICE and her mother reside at Red Bluff, Tehama county, Cal.

ANN, born in St. Clair county, married Samuel Yocom. *See his name.*

MEREDITH C., born May 29, 1824, in Sangamon county, married in 1846 to Frances A. Chapman. They have five children, and live in Williams township.

Mrs. Mary Cooper died Oct. 17, 1827. Ambrose Cooper was a soldier from Sangamon county in the Black Hawk war, and in 1831, and when the campaign was over he went to the Galena lead mines, remaining until the spring of 1832, where he enlisted in another campaign against the Indians, and was in the battles that finally subdued them. He returned to Sangamon county, and was married in April, 1836, to Eliza Wilson. They had seven children, four of whom died young.

STEPHEN L., born May 6, 1840, in Sangamon county, enlisted in Springfield, July 20, 1861, for three years, in what became Co. B, 11th Mo. Inf., served full term, and was honorably discharged Aug.

1, 1864. He was married Oct. 11, 1865, to Rebecca Summers, who was born Nov. 5, 1842, in Bracken county, Ky. They have two children, RUFUS and ALVEY, and live near Dawson.

HENRY, born Aug. 12, 1842, enlisted in Springfield July 20, 1861, in what became Co. B, 11th Mo. Inf., for three years; re-enlisted as a veteran January, 1864, and was honorably discharged Jan. 20, 1866, and resides with his parents.

DABNEY, born Sept. 2, 1846, lives with his parents.

Ambrose Cooper and wife are now (1874) both living one mile south of Barclay.

COOPER, MEDEDITH, born April 7, 1792, in Botetourt county, Va. His parents moved to Smith county, Tenn., when he was a young man. Polly Witcher was born July 21, 1794, in Cocke county, Tenn., and her parents moved to Smith county when she was but fifteen years of age. Meredith Cooper and Polly Witcher were there married, June 16, 1812. In September of that year Mr. Cooper enlisted for three months in a Tennessee regiment, and served four months against the Indians in Alabama, who were the allies of the British government, with whom we were then at war. Mr. and Mrs. Cooper had two children in Tennessee. In the spring of 1817 Mr. Cooper went to St. Clair county, Ill., raised a crop, and returning, brought his family in the fall of that year. The moving was done on two horses, as there were no wagon roads; and if there had been, they were unable to own a wagon. As a specimen of real life at that time, I give the statement of Mrs. Cooper, now quite aged, that she rode one horse, carried a child in her arms, and with a feather bed lashed to the saddle behind, wended her way, while her husband carried the other child, with all the household goods and farm implements he could put on the other horse. Three of their children were born in St. Clair county. The fame of the rich soil of the San-ga-ma country was known in St. Clair county, and Mr. and Mrs. Cooper resolved to emigrate thither. This time they put all their worldly goods and five children in an ox-cart, and arrived in the autumn of 1823 in what is now called Fancy Creek township, near the present town of Sherman, where they had seven children. Of all their children—

MARTHA, born Oct. 26, 1814, in Tennessee, married in Sangamon county to William Branson. See his name.

JAMES W., born Sept. 16, 1816, in Tennessee, was married in Sangamon county to Zarilda Taylor. They had four children. MELISSA married Charles Wood. They have one child, and live near Edinburg, Ill. PRISCILLA married James Wright. They have four children, and live near Riverton. JAS. M. married Ellen McGinnis. They have two children, and live three miles southeast of Williamsville. AMBROSE died Jan. 27, 1874, in Williams township. James W. Cooper went to Texas, hoping to improve his health, and died there in 1853. His widow died the next year in Sangamon county.

MINERVA, born Sept. 21, 1818, in St. Clair county, Ill., was married in Sangamon county to Jesse Yocom. See his name.

MARGARET J., born Sept. 1, 1820, in St. Clair county, was married in Sangamon county to George W. Yocom. See his name. Three of their children, NETTIE, CLARA and MINNIE, died in the winter of 1876.

MARY, born July 28, 1822, in St. Clair county, was married in Sangamon county, Ill., Jan. 30, 1851, to John Wilson, who was born Feb. 1, 1821, in Dumfriesshire, Scotland. They have three children, ANN, JAMES M. and THOMAS H., and reside one and a half miles east of Riverton.

NANCY, born May 7, 1825, in Sangamon county, married John Keagle. They have seven children. CHARLOTTE married Nathan Hussy. See his name. SIDNEY married Samuel Smith. She died, leaving one child, LETTIA, who married Silas Skinner and died. JOSEPH, SUSAN, HARLAN P. and HARRISA B., reside with their parents in Logan county, Ill.

REBECCA, born Aug. 11, 1827, in Sangamon county, married James Mills. She died Oct., 1871, in Sangamon county. James Mills died in the spring of 1874, in Moultrie county. Of their children: MARY F. married Samuel Harsh, and resides near Sullivan. LOUISA and

EMMA reside near Sullivan, Moultrie county, Ill.

AMBROSE, born Sept. 13, 1829, in Sangamon county, married Dorothy Keagle. They have five children, MARY J., JOHN M., AUGUSTA, GEORGE E. L. and JAMES W., and reside near Brownsville, Mo.

DAVID D., born August 10, 1831, in Sangamon county, married Juliet Withrow. They have seven children, SUSIE, JAMES A., DOUGLAS, LEE, AUGUSTA and EUGENE, and reside one and a half miles east of Sherman.

ROBERT, born July 8, 1834, in Sangamon county, was married Feb. 9, 1869, to Lavina Garner, who was born in Washington county, Indiana. They live near Sherman, Sangamon county, Ill.

MEREDITH, Jun., born Sept. 11, 1836, in Sangamon county, was married in March, 1873, to Mrs. Emma Jones, whose maiden name was Watson. They have one child, ANNA LEONORA, and reside in east St. Louis, Ill.

LOUIS I, born Feb. 3, 1839, in Sangamon county, was married Dec. 26, 1855, to Isaac M. Raynolds, who was born in Pike county, Ohio. They have five children, CHARLES M., JAMES A., POLLY E., EDWIN S. and BERTHA M., and reside one and a half miles east of Sherman. The place was for many years a trading post for the Indians, and from about 1832 to 1856 was the family homestead of the Coopers. Some of the younger members of the family remember a visit to their house by Abraham Lincoln on business. A large back log had just been put on. It was cut from the fork of a tree, and one limb projected quite a distance up the chimney. The children were greatly amused to witness Mr. Lincoln's interest in trying to determine how they brought it through the door and put it in the fireplace. Meredith Cooper, Sen., died Nov. 1, 1870, in Williams township, and his widow resides with their daughter, Mrs. Raynolds.

COOPER, JOHN, born in 1772, married in South Carolina, and seven of his children were born there. He moved with his family to Jefferson county, Tenn. Some of his children preceded him to Sangamon county. He came with his wife Elizabeth, and remaining children, about 1822, to what is now Cooper township. Nine daughters and three sons came to Sangamon county. The following are the names of the daughters, with the surnames of the men they married—

BETSY, Moffit; NANCY, Smith; MARY, Smith; LYDIA, Moore; RACHEL, Bragg; FANNY, Dickerson; LUCY, Mathews; EDITH, Saunders; and SUSANNAH, Keagle.

Mrs. Elizabeth Cooper died March 10, 1845, and John Cooper died April 10, 1846, both in Cooper township. Of their three sons—

COOPER, EPHRIAM, brother to Rev. John and Jacob Cooper. He was born about 1802, in Jefferson county, Tenn., came to Illinois when a young man, married, raised a family in Christian county, and died there Feb. 20, 1847.

COOPER, JOHN, was born June 3, 1794, in South Carolina, and was taken by his parents to Jefferson county, Tenn., where he was married to Susannah Peyton, had one child, JULIA G., and Mrs. Cooper died. Mr. Cooper was married in the same county to Susannah Giger, who was born Sept. 26, 1795, had two children in Tennessee, and moved to Sangamon county, Ill., arriving April 2, 1820, and settled two miles north of where Rochester now stands and one year later moved to what is now Cooper township, south of the Sangamon river. They had nine children in Sangamon county. Of all his children—

JULIA G., born Feb. 1, 1814, married in Sangamon county to John Welch. He died in 1840, leaving three children. JOHN C. died, aged seventeen. WILLIAM H. married Harriet Cooper. He enlisted in 1861 in Co. C, 27th Ill. Inf., for three years, re-enlisted as a veteran Jan. 1, 1864, and was severely wounded. He died January, 1870, and Mrs. Welch died later. They left two children. JAMES S. WELCH is a practicing physician at Sullivan, Moultrie county, Ill. Mrs. Julia G. Welch married Chesley Dickerson. They had one child. SUSANNAH married David Clark, and resides at Breckenridge. Chesley Dickerson died in 1846, and Mrs. Julia G. Dickerson married Daniel D. Johnson. *See his name.* They reside near Breckenridge.

Children of John Cooper by the second marriage—

MARY A., born Aug. 18, 1817, in Tennessee, married in Sangamon county to Lewis Churchill. *See his name.*

WILEY S., born July 30, 1819, in Tennessee, married in Sangamon county to Eliza Clawson, and live in Shelbyville.

LEWIS W., born Aug. 5, 1822, in Sangamon county, married to Elizabeth Todd. He died July 19, 1872.

BENJAMIN H., born Nov. 11, 1824, died Aug. 1, 1841, aged seventeen.

PATRICK, born June 29, 1826, in Sangamon county, married Elizabeth Firey, have four children, JOHN H., JACOB P., MARY E. and LAURA B., and reside near Edinburg, Christian county, Ill.

JAMES M., born Aug. 3, 1828, in Sangamon county, married April, 1851, to Mary A. Sutcliffe. They had three children, and all died under five years. Mrs. Cooper died Dec. 29, 1858. James M. Cooper was married Feb. 14, 1860, at Rochester, to Susan Stier, who was born May 19, 1833, in Harrison county, Va. They had four children, EMELINE F., IDA B., JAMES F. and MARY MAUD, and reside in Cooper township, five miles east of Rochester, on a part of the farm where his parents settled in 1821, and where Mr. Cooper was born.

MIVERVA J., born June 12, 1830, died in Sangamon county March 4, 1842.

SARAH A., born Nov. 2, 1832, in Sangamon county, married William T. Sudduth. *See his name.*

JOHN S., born Aug. 14, 1836, in Sangamon county, married to Minerva Ross, who was born in Ohio. They have three children, AMY, SARAH ELIZA and ANNIE, and reside at Shelbyville, Illinois.

GEORGE G., born June 8, 1839, in Sangamon county, died Nov. 10, 1842.

Mrs. Susannah Cooper died Sept. 21, 1859, and Rev. John Cooper died January, 1860, both in Cooper township. He was a local minister in the M. E. church, and preached almost as regularly as the ministers in the traveling connection. He solemnized the marriage of many couple among the early settlers. He was a justice of the peace and one of the county commissioners for many years, and when the township organization was affected his name was given to the township in which he lived as a mark of respect to his memory.

COOPER, JACOB, was born Dec. 18, 1800, in Jefferson county, Tenn., was married there to Anna Walden. One child was born in Tennessee, and they came to Sangamon county, Ill., with his brother, Rev. John Cooper, in 1819. Their second child was born in Sangamon county. One child died, and Mrs. Anna Cooper died Feb. 22, 1830. Jacob Cooper was married to Jane Kelly, daughter of William Kelly, of Springfield. They had five children. Of his children—

JOHN WESLEY was born Dec. 18, 1822, in Sangamon county; went to Missouri when grown, and married there to Anna Waldron. He died there, leaving a widow and two children.

Children of the second marriage were—

MELCINA A., born Nov. 22, 1830, in Sangamon county, married March 3, 1848, to Milton D. McCoy. *See his name.*

MELVINA C., born Aug. 27, 1832, in Sangamon county, married Dec. 27, 1849, to Benjamin F. Stokes. *See his name.* She died Sept. 15, 1850.

ELZIRAH C., born May 29, 1834, married Benjamin F. Stokes. *See his name.*

ALMARINDA, born June 26, 1836, married Joseph A. Waddell. They have six children, and reside in Rochester township.

WILLIAM JAMEISON, born Jan. 4, 1844, in Sangamon county, married Dec. 7, 1865, to Mattie S. West, of Rochester. They have two children, NORA BELL and MATTIE. Mrs. Mattie Cooper died April 25, 1873, and Wm. J. Cooper married Dec. 31, 1874, to Leonora O'Leary, of East St. Louis. W. J. Cooper resides two miles south of Rochester.

Jacob Cooper died Aug. 22, 1864, and Mrs. Jane Cooper died Aug. 24, 1864, both in Sangamon county, Ill.

COOK, ELI, was born Nov. 4, 1809, in Butler county, Ohio, and married there, April 7, 1829, to Sarah Jones, who was born Feb. 2, 1809, in Preble county, Ohio. They moved to Indiana, and from there to Effingham county, Ill., thence to Springfield, in 1837. Of their nine children, two died young, and of the other seven—

EMELINE, born March 7, 1832, in Indiana, was married in Springfield, July 4, 1850, to William Morgan. Their only child, FRANKLIN, is a printer, and lives in Springfield. She married for a second time, April 22, 1857, to John Fuller. They have one child, CLARENCE. Mrs. Emeline Fuller is now a widow, and lives in Springfield.

ADALINE, born Sept. 6, 1833, in Effingham county, Ill., was married in Springfield, Oct. 28, 1850, to George Fessenden, a native of Boston, Mass. They have three children. ASA, a telegraph operator, lives in Springfield, Ill. JULIA and ISABEL, the two latter reside with their mother, in Chicago.

ANGELINE, born Sept. 6, 1833, in Effingham county, Ill., was married in Springfield to James W. Watson. *See his name.*

H. FRANKLIN, born Sept. 14, 1836, in Butler county, Ohio, was married in Springfield, Dec. 23, 1858, to Lucinda Parker, adopted daughter of J. E. Roll. They had one living child, LEONARD, and Mrs. Lucinda Cook died Sept. 10, 1864. Mr. Cook was married in Springfield, Aug. 1, 1872, to Rebecca E. Baird, a native of New Jersey. H. Franklin Cook is a commercial traveler, with residence in Springfield.

MARY E., born May 20, 1833, in Sangamon county, was married in Springfield, Sept. 24, 1863, to Charles H. Edmands, who was born in Charlestown, Mass., Jan. 10, 1832. They had six children; four died young. FREDERICK D. and GEORGE A. reside with their parents, in Springfield, Ill. Hr. Edmands is a manufacturer and dealer in stoves and tinware.

JULIA R., born Dec. 16, 1839, in Springfield, was married Feb. 21, 1861, to James Gormley, of New Jersey. They have three children, DORA, MAY and AUSTIN, and live in Virginia City, Montana.

ELBRIDGE C., born June 29, 1841, in Springfield, is married, and lives in Cicero, Indiana.

Mr. Eli Cook was a hatter by trade, and followed that business in Springfield. He was Mayor of the city three terms, in 1846, '47 and '48. In 1849 he left for the Pacific coast, and died in Nevada City, California, March 25, 1853. His widow resides in Springfield.

CORRELL, LEVI, was born June 22, 1767, in New Jersey. When a young man he went to Kentucky, and was married Nov. 6, 1794, in Bath county, to Mary Hicklin. They had eleven children, four of whom died young. Of the other seven—

JOSEPH, born Oct. 8, 1795, died when a young man.

ELIZABETH, born Jan. 18, 1797, in Harrison county, Ky., married March 23, 1820, to Jonathan McDaniel. *See his name.*

HUGH, born July 6, 1804, in Harrison county, Ky. He was married May 2, 1826, in that county, to Mary Y. Sinclair. They had two children in Kentucky, and moved to Sangamon county, Ill., arriving in the fall of 1830 in what is now Mechanicsburg township, where they had four children. Of their six children, ELIZABETH, born May 9, 1827, in Kentucky, married in Sangamon county to Robert P. McDaniel. *See his name.* He died, and she married James H. McDaniel. *See his name.* CYRUS, born July 16, 1829, in Kentucky, came with his parents to Sangamon county, married at Concord, Morgan county, to Mary Brown. Cyrus Correll died Dec. 23, 1868, in Sangamon county, leaving one child, CORA, residing with her mother, who is the wife of Pierce Kiser, and lives in Mechanicsburg. CORDELIA, born Feb. 23, 1833, in Sangamon county, married Feb. 18, 1858, to John M. Carpenter, who was born March 26, 1829, in Butler county, O., and came to Sangamon county in 1850. They have three children, WINFORD H., DORA B. and MINNIE C., and reside three and a half miles northeast of Buffalo. DAVID, born March 29, 1836, in Sangamon county, is unmarried, and resides two and a half miles south of Dawson. STEPHEN, born May 12, 1838, in Sangamon county, married March 12, 1868, to Ann M. Semple, who was born Dec. 29, 1846, in Ireland. They have two children, WILLIE and MARY D., and reside two and a half miles south of Dawson, at the family homestead. MARY, born Sept. 7, 1840, in Sangamon county, married Mar., 1864, to Jesse Wheelin. Mr. Wheelin died Feb. 1, 1871, and Mrs. W. died Aug. 21, 1871. Their only living child, CYRUS E., born July

S, 1865, in Sangamon county, resides at the family homestead, two and a half miles south of Dawson. Hugh Correll died June 1, 1854, and his widow died Sept. 7, 1874, both where they settled in 1832, on the farm two and a half miles south of Dawson.

MARTHA, born March 13, 1806, in Kentucky, married Hugh McDonald. They had five children and moved to Texas, where Mr. McDonald and two sons, JAMES and THOMAS, and a daughter, MARTHA, died. Mrs. Martha McDonald returned, and died in Sangamon county. MARY E. married Mr. Grider, and lives in Decatur, Texas. SUSAN died at Quincy Ill., September, 1875. ANNA resides with her uncle, Thomas Correll.

THOMAS, born Jan. 18, 1808, in Harrison county, Ky. He was there married. Oct. 7, 1830, to Sally McDaniel. (She was born Aug. 28, 1811, in Clarke county, Ky.) They moved immediately after they were married to Sangamon county, Ill., arriving in the fall of 1830 in Mechanicsburg township, where they had eight children. Of their children, M. MARGARET, born July 13, 1832, married Edwin Tomlin. See his name. WILLIAM FLETCHER, born Oct. 16, 1833, married Feb. 25, 1868, to E. Fannie Purviance. They have two children, FRANK and KATE, and reside in Macon county, Ill., two and a half miles southeast of Illiopolis. D. SIMPSON, born Sept. 3, 1835, married Feb. 25, 1874, to Lizzie Peden, who was born Oct. 19, 1855, in Morgan county, O. They live two miles south of Illinois. WARNER H., born May 1, 1837, married Dec. 20, 1866, to Anna Simpson, who died in 1867, and he married March, 1871, to Lizzie St. Clair. They have three children, THOMAS, SAMUEL and ESSIE MAY, and live near Pleasant Plains, Ill. CORNELIUS, born May 19, 1839, married March 12, 1863, to Carrie A. Cass. She was born Dec., 1845, and was a daughter of William Riley Cass. They had two children, FLORA C. and VIRGIL, and Mrs. Correll died April 1, 1866. Mr. Correll was married Nov. 16, 1869, to Lidie N. Davies, in Philadelphia. She was born there May 30, 1843, of Scotch and English parents, and graduated in 1865 in one of the institutions of learning in her native city. They had three children, FANNY MARY, JESSIE NEWTON and HEBER WILBER; the latter died in infancy, and Mrs. Lidie N. Correll died March 23, 1874. Cornelius Correll is a graduate in the Law department of Michigan University, Ann Arbor. He is now a member of the firm of Correll & Co., druggists, Springfield. JOHN, born June 5, 1841, resides with his parents. LEVI S., born Aug. 14, 1843. He is a graduate of the Medical department of Ann Arbor University, Michigan. He is member of the firm of Correll & Co., composed of the brothers Cornelius, John and Levi S., druggists, Springfield. Levi S. was married July 8, 1874, in Springfield, to Lou Freeman. They reside in Springfield. FANNIE, born August 22, 1846, in Sangamon county, married Oct. 29, 1869, to Isaac Funk. They have two children, ARTHUR and MABEL; the latter died in infancy. They reside at Funk's Grove, near Shirley, McLean county. Thomas Correll and his wife reside within one mile of where they settled in 1830. It is two and a half miles southeast of Dawson.

Thomas Correll says that he raised a crop of corn in Kentucky, during the summer of 1830, and sold it for $75.00 He spent $5.00 in getting married, and brought the remaining $70.00 with him. He fed his father's stock during the winter of 1830 and '31, (being the winter of the "deep snow,") for which he received $30, making an even $100. With that money he came to Springfield and entered his first eighty acres of land. Having secured his land, he had not a cent of money to pay a hotel bill, and a man by the name of Constant hearing him relate his situation, kept him over night and trusted him for it. The ferryman at the Sangamon river took him over on the same terms, and that was the way he laid the foundation for his home. When they commenced keeping house they had neither a table nor chair. He made a shelf on the wall, and from that the first meal was taken standing. His wife's uncle, Henry McDaniel, was with them, and he praised her cooking, to keep her courage up. Mr. Correll, during the summer of 1831, rode eight miles to help David Riddle harvest his wheat, and returned home every night. He received sixty-two and a half cents per day for his labor. The first wheat he raised for himself he harvested with a reap hook, or sickle, tramped it out with horses, hauled it to St. Louis, one hundred miles, and sold it for fifty cents per bushel. As he accumulated some money, he bought fat hogs, and drove them to St. Louis. One year he made some money, and feeling liberal, he overpaid some of the men who helped him. The next year he lost all, and was thirty-seven and a half cents short in money to pay his hired help. One of those who had been overpaid by him the year before, would not suffer any reduction, and he had to raise the money in some other way. He thought that was not very encouraging, but his success in life since, makes the contrast very striking.

SUSANNAH, born Oct. 9, 1809, in Kentucky, married Jacob Morgan. See his name.

SARAH, born Dec. 31, 1811, in Kentucky, married Jacob Constant. See his name.

Mrs. Mary H. Correll died July 10, 1816, in Kentucky, and Levi Correll was married July 17, 1817, to Mrs. Elizabeth Sinclair, whose maiden name was Phillips. She was born July 27, 1807, in Northumberland county, Va. Her father died when she was quite young, and her mother, with her son and daughter, moved to Harrison county, Ky. Mr. and Mrs. Correll had two children in Kentucky, and moved to Sangamon county, Ill., arriving in the fall of 1830, in what is now Mechanicsburg township. Of their two children—

WILLIAM, born August 16, 1818, in Harrison county, Ky., was married in Sangamon county, Dec. 7, 1848, to Permelia A. Simpson. They had three children. CYRUS died in infancy. HENRY OWEN married Ada Elkin, and lives near Mechanicsburg. MARY EVA lives with her parents, three miles west of Mechanicsburg. William Correll says that himself and his half-brother, John Sinclair, broke forty acres of prairie in 1831, northeast of the old state house square, in Springfield. It included the land where Everybody's Mill, the jail, Opera House and Journal office now stand.

ELIZA, born Dec., 1821, in Kentucky, married in Sangamon county to Talbott Lyon. They had four children, and Mr. Lyon and all the children died. Mrs. Lyon married in Sangamon county to Gardner Bruce. They reside at Atchison, Kansas. Mrs. Elizabeth Correll has two children by her first husband, Mr. Sinclair.

MARY V. Sinclair, born July 27, 1807, in Northumberland county, Va., married Hugh Correll. See his name.

JOHN Sinclair, born in 1808, in Virginia, married in Sangamon county to Mrs. Miriam Massey, whose maiden name was Constant. They had several children, and the parents and all except two of the children are dead. Their daughter, Miriam, married Narcissus Rivaud, and reside at Kankakee. John Sinclair, Jun., went to South America, married a Spanish lady, and resides there.

Levi Correll died May 2, 1845, and Mrs. Elizabeth Correll died Nov. 10, 1852, both in Sangamon county.

COUNCIL, DAVID G., was born Jan. 15, 1817, in Montgomery county, Tenn. Came to what is now Christian county, Ill.; then to Sangamon county in the autumn of 1830. He came to Springfield in 1838, where he was married March 28, 1839, to Mary J. Donaldson, who was born in Kentucky in 1818. They had seven children, namely—

LOUISA, born May 14, 1841, was married Dec. 28, 1865, to Jacob S. Wright, who was born June 11, 1841, in Owen county, Ind. They have one child, CHARLIE. Jacob S. Wright came to Springfield in August, 1866. His father was a soldier in the war of 1812; was wounded in the head during an engagement with the Indians, and but for the interposition of Tecumseh would have been killed. He was made prisoner, taken to Sandusky, and retained there until exchanged. J. S. Wright enlisted at Lincoln, Ill., as a private, in Co. E, 7th Ill. Inf.; served three months, and re-enlisted in 1862 in Co. H, 106th Ill. Inf.; was at the siege and capture of Vicksburg, and in the expedition and capture of Little Rock, Ark.; served full time, and was honorably discharged in 1865, at Springfield, Ill., where he now lives.

WILLIAM M., born Feb. 8, 1843, in Springfield, was married Jan. 5, 1864, to Mary E. Huffman, who was born May 11, 1845, in Cincinnati, Ohio. Mrs. Mary E. Council died Sept. 2, 1871, leaving two children, MINNIE and ARTHUR, who reside with their father. William M.

Council was married June 9, 1875, in Springfield, to Jennie Barkley, who was born Sept. 1, 1841, in Lafayette, Christian county, Ky. W. M. Council lives in Springfield.

JAMES, born Feb. 9, 1845, in Springfield, Ill., was married there, April 30, 1860, to Alsinda A. Shawn, who was born Sept. 4, 1848, in Newark, Ohio. She is a niece of Judge Shawn, of Menard county. They have two children, FRANK A. and FLORENCE A. James Council is a contractor and builder, and resides in Springfield, Ill.

DAVID G., Jun., born Dec. 2, 1846, in Springfield, was married there, July 15, 1868, to Mrs. Jennie Kimble, whose maiden name was Richmond. She was born in 1846, in Painesville, O. They have one child, OLIVE L., and live in Springfield, Ill.

MARY E., born June 15, 1851, in Springfield, was married there, August 12, 1869, to Thomas D. Hirst, who was born June 7, 1836, in Loudon county Va. They have two children, EDDIE L. and HARRY E. T. D. Hirst is running a plaining mill in Clinton, Ill., and lives there.

MARTHA J., born August 2, 1853, and

JOHN T., born June 4, 1856, reside with their mother.

When D. G. Council came to Illinois, he left five sisters in Tennessee, whom he completely lost sight of. He accidentally heard that one sister had moved to Marion county, Ill. He visited her family, and after the close of the rebellion he visited his old home in Tennessee. He found his sisters still residing there with their families. Some of their sons had been in the Union army, and others had joined the rebels. One of his nephews from Christian county, Ill., was a prisioner at one time, and guarded by another nephew. (The boys were own cousins.) Two of those who went in the rebel army were killed or died in the service, and the remainder were doing well, and still resided in Tennessee. D. G. Council was the pioneer of stair building in Springfield, and foreman for Hannan & Ragsdale in their extensive contracts. He died in Springfield, Ill., August 28, 1875, and his widow resides in the city.

COUNCIL, WILLIAM, born Oct. 1, 1791, near Tarboro, Edgecomb county, N. C. He was a brother to Hardy Council. About 1800 the family moved to Tennessee, thence to Barren county, Ky., and from there to White county, Ill. William Council was there married, Nov., 1819, to Mary Graves, who was born June 15, 1802, in East Tennessee. They had one child, and moved to Sangamon county, arriving in the fall of 1821 north of Springfield, and kept a ferry on Sangamon river near where Carpenter's mill now stands. They had nine children in Sangamon county, namely—

GEORGE W., born Jan. 2, 1820, in White county, Ill., married Sept. 28, 1843, in Sangamon county, to Jane Mitts. They had eleven children, namely: WILLIAM C., born Oct. 26, 1844, enlisted August, 1862, in Co. C, 114th Ill. Inf., for three years, served full term, and was honorably discharged Aug. 3, 1865. He was married April 1, 1869, in Illiopolis, to Melissa A. Meredith, who was born June 25, 1849, in Orange county, Ind. She died April 29, 1873. He lives three miles west of Illiopolis. MARY A. married Charles Sweet, have two children, WILLIAM and ANNIE, and live in Topeka, Kan. JOHN M., born June 7, 1851, married Sept. 21, 1871, in Sangamon county, to Elizabeth E. Hay, born June 9, 1850, in Holmes county, O., have two children, FLORA BELLE and ROBERT ARTHUR, and live four miles west of Illiopolis. NELSON L., ELIZABETH, CHARLES F., HENRY N., FLORA M., EMMA E., GEORGE G. and ANNIE J., live with their parents, four miles west of Williamsville.

MARTHA A., born Jan. 30, 1822, in Sangamon county, married Stephen Yocom. *See his name.*

SARAH, born Nov. 23, 1826, in Sangamon county, resides with her brother, Hardy F. M.

NANCY J., born May 27, 1828, married John Cline. *See his name.*

ELIZABETH, born April 3, 1830, married Oliver P. Canterbury. *See his name.*

WILLIAM R., born March 30, 1832, married March 23, 1871, to Nancy E. Wigginton, and live in Menard county, three and a quarter miles northwest of Williamsville.

MARY G., born Feb. 26, 1834, married Dr. Henry Van Metre. See his name.

NELSON L., born Jan. 18, 1839, married Mary Lynch. They have seven children, and reside in Menard county, four miles northwest of Williamsville.

HARDY F. M., born Feb. 10, 1841, enlisted August, 1862, in Co. C, 114th Ill. Inf., for three years, served full term, and was honorably discharged Aug. 3, 1865. He was married Feb. 10, 1870, to Charity Ray, who was born in Ohio Jan. 22, 1850. They have one living child, OLIVER P., and reside at the homestead settled by his father in 1821. It is in Fancy Creek township, five miles west of Williamsville.

William Council died July 8, 1846, and his wife died Jan. 25, 1869, both in Sangamon county.

COUNCIL, HARDY, born Sept. 20, 1793, near Tarboro, N. C., was taken by his parents to Tennessee, thence to Barren county, Ky., and from there to White county, near Carmi, Ill. He was there married, in 1818, to Jane Hanna, who was born Feb. 25, 1795, in Kentucky. They moved on horseback the next year to Sangamon county, Ill., arriving in August, 1819, in what is now Fancy creek township, preceding his brother William two years. Mrs. Council carried a sack of wheat on the horse she rode, besides many household implements. Mr. Council carried all he could in the way of tools and other articles necessary for farming. He commenced improvements by building a camp or rough cabin. He was unable to obtain a plow, but being anxious to raise some wheat for a beginning, he took a grubbing hoe, or old fashioned mattock, and dug up about one acre and a half, near the junction between prairie and timber, and on the ground thus prepared, sowed the wheat brought by his wife, and raised a good crop. When the land was surveyed and brought into market, there was a line between his cabin and where he raised his crop of wheat. He could only enter one piece, and he chose that with the house on it. The land where the wheat grew was entered by another person, who never cultivated it, but allowed a growth of young cottonwood trees to start on it, which has made quite a grove, that can be seen for several miles; many of the trees are more than two feet in diameter each. Mr. Council and Robert McClelland came together, and they cut an ample supply of grass, and stacked it for their horses and cattle. They knew nothing of the danger of prairie fires, and before they were aware of the importance of protecting it, their hay was all burned. They kept their stock alive by cutting down elm trees, so that they could eat the buds. Mr. and Mrs. Council had seven sons born at that place, two of whom died in infancy. Of the other five—

JOHN H., born May 19, 1822, married Edna Lake. They have five children, JAMES H., CHARLES F., JOHN W. and GEORGE R., the two latter twins, and ANNA F., and reside near where his father settled in 1819, three miles west of Sherman.

WESLEY, born Nov. 21, 1824, was married April 14, 1853, to Martha A. Wigginton. They had twelve children, nine of whom died under thirteen years. the other three, JOHN, WILLIE and NELLIE reside with their parents in Williamsville.

WILLIAM F., born Jan. 21, 1828, married Rosanna England. They have seven children, MARY F., WILLIAM H., FLORA J., DAVID E., GEORGE A., NORA E. and U. S. GRANT, who reside with their parents in Menard county.

ROBERT, born March 23, 1831, married Ellen Cresee. They have three living children, JOHN W., MABEL and LILLIE M., and reside in Menard county, five miles northwest of Williamsville.

GEORGE W., born August 6, 1834, enlisted Oct. 25, 1862, in Co. B, 130th Ill. Inf., for three years, was transferred to Co. G, 1st New Orleans Vol. Inf., in which he was 2d Lieut. He served in that capacity nearly one year after the close of the war, and was honorably discharged. He was married March 24, 1868, to Olivia L. Miller, who was born Feb. 17, 1851, in West Liberty, O. They have two children, CLIFFORD and IDA E., and reside at the homestead settled by his parents in 1819, in Fancy creek township.

Mrs. Jane Council died March 30, 1863, and Hardy Council died July 26, 1873, both in Sangamon county, Ill.

COWGILL, WILLIAM M., was born near Lebanon, Warren county,

Ohio, and was married early in 1832, in Lebanon, to Clemantine Sayre, a native of the same county. They moved in the spring of that year to Springfield, Ill., and had five children, namely—

WILLIAM B., born March 29, 1833, in Springfield, and married in his native place May 16, 1855, to Margaret D. Sprigg, who was born Aug. 18, 1833, in Effingham county, Ill. They have three children, born in Springfield. WILLIAM C., born March 12, 1858; JOHN ALBERT, Jan. 17, 1860, and DUNCAN S., Oct. 6, 1868, all reside with their parents in Springfield. William B. Cowgill is a dealer in real estate.

CATHARINE L., born in Springfield, married June 30, 1852, to Daniel C. Brown. See his name.

ALBERT H., born in Springfield, married Mary L. Brown, and live in his native city.

MARY CLEMANTINE and CORNELIA SAYRE, reside in Springfield. The former is a teacher in the Bettie Stuart Institute.

William M. Cowgill was engaged in mercantile pursuits from 1832 to 1844, in Springfield, when he moved to Petersburg. Mrs. Clemantine S. Cowgill died in 1854, and William M. Cowgill died in 1862, both in Petersburg, Menard county, Ill.

COX, GEORGE, was born in South Carolina, came to Sangamon county with William and Joseph Drennan, in March, 1818, and died in November, 1819. His son, Jesse Cox, lives in Virden.

COX, SAMUEL, uncle to the Hampton brothers. He had two sons, Samuel and Sowell. Sowell owned the farm adjoining Mechanicsburg on the west. The house in which he lived was the only brick house between Decatur and Springfield. They came in 1825, and about 1838 moved to the vicinity of Palmyra, Mo.

CRAFTON, WILEY, was born Jan. 25, 1801, in Lunenburgh county, Va., went to Trimble county, Ky., where he was married in 1824 to Agnes Chalfant, who was born in that county about 1801. They had two children in Kentucky, and moved, early in 1831, to Vandalia, Ill., where they had one child, and the same year moved to Sangamon county, Illinois. They returned, in a short time, to Kentucky, then came back to Sangamon county, where they had four children. Of their children—

WILLIAM P., born May 25, 1826, in Trimble county, Ky., raised in Sangamon county, Illinois, married Nov. 28, 1855, in St. Louis, Mo., to Eliza C. Harrison. They have three children, PEYTON L., AGNES E., and WILLIAM P., and reside in Springfield. Wm. P. Crafton was elected Police Magistrate at the Springfield city election, April, 1876.

THOMAS T., born May 27, 1828, in Trimble county, Ky., raised in Sangamon county, married in Mt. Pleasant, Iowa, to Miss Dawson. They have two children, and reside in Atlantic, Cass county, Iowa.

MARY, born in 1831, at Vandalia, Ill., married Dr. J. L. Million, and resides in Springfield.

Wiley Crafton lives in Springfield.

CRAIG, WILLIAM, was born in 1790, in Fayette county, Ky. He was married April 20, 1821, near Stanford, Lincoln county, to Mary P. Swope, who was born there June 20, 1794. In 1827 they moved to Williamson county, near Franklin, Tenn., where they had five children. The family moved to Sangamon county, Ill., arriving in the spring of 1832 in what is now Island Grove township, south of Spring creek, where they had two children. Of their seven children—

ANDREW E., born Feb. 22, 1822, in Tennessee, died April 20, 1861, in Sangamon county.

WILLIAM, Jun., born Aug. 24, 1823, in Tennessee, enlisted Aug. 15, 1862, for three years, in Co. A, 106th Ill. Inf., served full term, and was honorably discharged Aug. 12, 1865.

MARGARET P., born Feb. 4, 1827, in Tennessee, is unmarried, and resides at the family homestead.

JAMES P., born May, 1829, in Tennessee, died in Sangamon county Oct. 19, 1852.

JOHN B., born Nov., 1830, in Tennessee, died in Sangamon county Jan. 30, 1858.

MARY M., born June 14, 1836, in Sangamon county, married Oct. 11, 1867, to Ammi C. Cheever, who was born Nov. 16, 1825, in Boston, Mass. They have two children, MARY A. and WILLIS C., and reside at the family homestead, in

Island Grove township, three miles north of Bates.

RICHARD B., born Aug. 1, 1837, in Sangamon county, resides at the family homestead.

William Craig died Oct. 2, 1847, and Mrs. Mary P. Craig died Dec. 25, 1871, both on the farm where they settled in 1832.

CRESSE, GEORGE, was born May 16, 1808, in Cape May county, N. J., came to Springfield, Ill., in Aug., 1839. In the spring of 1841 he returned to New Jersey, and was there married, Sept. 2, 1841, to Maria Marcy, who was born Feb. 17, 1823, near Hartford, Conn. He came with his bride back to Sangamon county, arriving Nov. 10, 1841. They moved to Menard county, and had four children. The family moved back to Sangamon county, near Pleasant Plains, in 1857, where they had one child. Of their five children—

ELLEN, born in Menard county, married Robert Council. See his name.

EDWARD M., CATHARINE L., (is a teacher,) MATTHEW W., and CORDELIA S. reside with their father.

Mrs. Maria Cresse died April 22, 1862, and George Cresse, with his two sons and two daughters, reside adjoining Sherman on the northwest.—1874.

CROOKER, G. W., was born July 29, 1814, in Cheshire county, N. H. He was married February, 1839, in Amherst, Mass., to Lois K. Thayer, who was born there in 1814. They moved to Sangamon county in company with his father-in-law, Asahel Thayer, arriving at Chatham May 19, 1839. They had ten children, five of whom died in infancy and childhood. Of the other five children—

EDWARD A., born March 3, 1840, in Sangamon county, was attending Illinois College, at Jacksonville, when he died, aged nineteen years.

WILLIAM B., born March 9, 1842, in Chatham, enlisted in Co. I, 73d Ill. Vol. Inf., was wounded at the battle of Perryville, and died at Taylorville, Ill., Aug. 11, 1865, aged twenty-three years.

SARAH T., born March 21, 1846, in Sangamon county, was married Sept. 1, 1864, to Dr. B. W. Fox, of Springfield. She died in Taylorville, May 15, 1869, leaving one child, LOIS F., who resides with her grand-parents in Taylorville Dr. B. W. Fox died June 20, 1875, at Quincy, Ill. His remains were buried at Taylorville.

GEORGE B., born Jan. 31, 1849, in Chatham, married Nannie Richardson. They have one child, EDWARD W., and reside at Taylorville.

ARTHUR H., born May 31, 1857, at Chatham, resides with his parents in Taylorville, to which place they moved from Chatham in 1867.

Mrs. Crooker gives a short account of the Chatham Ladies' Aid Society. It was organized Nov. 21, 1861, and disbanded early in '63. The society was small, but they made three large boxes of bedding and clothing suitable for tent and hospital, besides making up ten webs of domestic for the Springfield Soldiers' Aid Society.

CROW, ROBERT, was born in 1781, in Wythe county, Va. Margaret Kershner was born in 1787, in Augusta county, Va., where they were married, and soon after moved to Christian county, Ky. They had eight children there, and moved to Sangamon county, Ill., arriving in 1822, in what is now Auburn township. Of their children—

JANE married Philip Wineman, and died. See his name.

DAVID, born in Kentucky, never married, and lives with his sister, Mrs. Moore.

EDWARD, born in 1810, in Kentucky, died unmarried, in Sangamon county, July 28, 1868.

WILLIAM D., married July 17, 1846, to Julia A. Messick. They had seven children in Sangamon county. MARGARET E. married George E. Stoke, and resides in Ball township. WILLIAM T., JAMES G., ABRAHAM LINCOLN, CHARLES H., HERBERT A. and ADA M. Wm. D. Crow died April 27, 1869, and his widow and children reside at Crow's mill.

MARY, born in Kentucky, married Wm. McAllister, and had one child. All three died at the family homestead, near Crow's mill.

ELIZABETH, born in Kentucky, married in Sangamon county to Morrison M. Moore. See his name.

GRANDISON B., born in Chester county, Ky., was raised in Sangamon county, and went to Oregon in 1847, and in Sept., 1848, went to California, gold having been discovered there in June, 1848. After spending eighteen years there, he returned to Sangamon county, in 1866, and now resides at the family homestead, in Ball township.—1874.

FRANCES M., born in Kentucky, married in Sangamon county to George Armitage, and resides near Palmer City, Christian county.

Robert Crow died Sept., 1840, and his widow died Sept., 1851, both in Ball township.

CROW, WILLIAM, was born March 5, 1793, in Botetourt county, Va. Three brothers, John, Thomas and Andrew Crow, came from Ireland to America during the Revolutionary war. John was the father of him whose name heads this sketch. John Crow moved to Barren county, Ky., when William was a child. William Crow and Miriam Enyart were married in Cumberland county, Ky., and had one child. In 1819 they moved to Madison county, Ill., where he was ordained to preach the gospel by the recognized authorities of the Old School, or Regular Baptist, church. In the fall of 1820 he moved to what is now Salisbury, or Cartwright, township, in Sangamon county, north of Richland creek, where they had one child, and Mrs. Miriam Crow died, Aug. 7, 1823. William Crow was married in the fall of 1824, in Cumberland county, Ky., to Susan Hall. On his return to Sangamon county, he sold out and settled in what is now the southeast corner of Cass county, where two children were born. Of his four children—

JEROME E., born Sept. 2, 1817, in Cumberland county, Ky., was brought by his parents to Sangamon county, married in Cass county, June 19, 1844, to Eliza J. Brockman. They have five children, two of whom are married, and all live with and near their parents, in the vicinity of Humboldt, Richardson county, Neb.

REBECCA W., born June 9, 1821, in Sangamon county, and is believed to have been the first white child born on Richland creek. She was married Oct. 9, 1844, in Cass county, to Washington A. Mitchell, who was born Dec. 21, 1816, in Logan county, Ky. They have five children, WILLIAM I., CHARLES C., JOHN L., ALBERT J. and ANNAH E., and reside in the southeast corner of Cass county, one mile southwest of Ashland, Ill.

JOHN H., born March 14, 1826, in Cass county, married Sarah F. Dillon, of Sangamon county. They have three children, and reside in Tecumseh, Neb. See *Dillon family.*

MARY A., born Dec. 18, 1828, married August, 1848, in Cass county, to James L. Beggs. They have eight children, three of whom are married, and one of the married daughters resides in Chicago. Mr. and Mrs. Beggs reside in Ashland.

Mrs. Susan Crow died April 11, 1845, in Cass county, and Rev. William Crow died Aug. 22, 1865, at Brownsville, Neb. He preached from the time he came to Sangamon county until about 1860, a ministry of forty years. He was known to all Baptists throughout central Illinois.

CROUCH, DAVID, born Sept. 29, 1814, in Nicholas county, Ky., came to Sangamon county, Rochester township, in August, 1834. He was married March 29, 1835, to Mrs. Clara Ann Stafford, whose maiden name was Gregory. They had five children in Sangamon county—

PRUDA ANN, born Jan. 26, 1837, married March 18, 1858, to John S. Craig, have two children, EMMA L. and MARY L., and live near Morrisonville.

DELIA ANN, born Jan. 25, 1840, married in Sangamon county Jan. 8, 1857, to A. D. Young, born Feb. 28, 1837, in Shelby county, Ky. They have one child, JULIA D., born in Anderson county, Ky., and live one and a quarter miles south of Rochester.

JONATHAN G., born Jan. 18, 1843, married Nov. 26, 1867, to Margaret A. Bell. They have two children, FREDDIE and EDDIE R., and live two miles south of Rochester.

WILLIAM H., born Oct. 15, 1846, married March 16, 1872, to Emma Crouch. They live two miles west of Breckenridge.

KITTY A., born Oct. 11, 1851, married Henry George. They have one child, and reside four miles east of Pawnee.

David Crouch died Sept. 14, 1871, in Sangamon county, and his widow resides one and a quarter miles south of Rochester.

CROWL, JOSEPH, was born Sept. 3, 1794, in Shepherdstown, Va. He was a soldier from Maryland in the war of 1812, and was married Jan. 1, 1817, in Washington county, Md., to Mary A. Dillihunt, who was born Feb. 22, 1804, in Kent county, Md. They had ten children in Washington county, Md., three of whom died young. They moved to Sangamon county, Ill., arriving in the fall of 1834, at Springfield, and the next spring moved to what is now Cooper township, south of the Sangamon river, where they had five children. Of their twelve children—

MORDECAI, born July 20, 1820, in Maryland, married December, 1869, in Springfield, to Catharine E. Crowl, a native of Berkley county, Va. They reside four miles southeast of Pawnee, in Christian county.

UPTON, born Feb. 7, 1822, in Maryland, served one year from June, 1846, in the 4th Ill. Inf., under Col. E. D. Baker, in the Mexican war. He was married in 1850, in Sangamon county, to Sarah E. Taggart. They had one living child, MARY J., born April 22, 1858, married Feb. 10, 1874, in Springfield, to Eugene W. Renshaw, who was born June 25, 1851, in Decatur. He is a grandson of James, who was a brother to Samuel Renshaw. *See his name*. E. W. Renshaw lives one and a half miles northeast of Berry station. Upton Crowl died March 8, 1872, and his widow resides one and a half miles northeast of Berry, or Clarksville.

CORNELIA, born Oct. 18, 1823, in Maryland, married in Sangamon county, April 18, 1839, to Stephen Hussey. *See his name*.

MARY E., born Nov. 13, 1825, in Maryland, married in Sangamon county to William R. Ross. *See his name*.

JOSEPH F. and *JACOB J.* (twins), born Aug. 30, 1827, in Maryland; the latter died young.

JOSEPH F. was raised in Sangamon county, went with his sister (Mrs. Hussey) to Oregon, and was married May, 1853, in Yamhill county, to Julia A. Shortridge. They had nine living children. Eight of their children were born in Oregon. They reside near Nashville, Barton county, Mo.

ROBERT F., born July 5, 1829, in Maryland, died in Sangamon county, Aug. 14, 1843.

MIRANDA, born Oct. 18, 1831, in Maryland, married in Sangamon county to Isaac T. Darnall. *See his name*. He died, and she married, Feb. 11, 1873, to George W. Taylor, and live in Cooper township.

VAN BASSETT, born April 8, 1836, in Sangamon county, married in same county, Feb. 9, 1864, to Eliza Crowl. They have two children, and live in Christian county, four miles southeast of Pawnee.

VINTON, born June 12, 1838, in Sangamon county, died April 19, 1852.

HELEN, born May 26, 1840, in Sangamon county, married Dec. 24, 1863, to Thomas F. Morris, who was born Nov. 12, 1834, in Clarke county, O. They have two children, MARY LIDA and ISAAC C., and reside in Cooper township, three and a half miles southwest of Mechanicsburg.

MARIA A., born Feb. 14, 1843, in Sangamon county, married May 11, 1867, to Samuel Carper, who was born April 30, 1829, in Shepherdstown, Va. They have three children, JOSEPH W., JOHN B. and MORDECAI L., and reside at the family homestead where her parents settled in 1835, in Cooper township. It is one and a half miles north of Berry station, or Clarksville.

WILLIAM H., born April 14, 1845, in Sangamon county, married January, 1871, to Ella Miller. They have two children, and reside five miles southeast of Pawnee, in Christian county.

Joseph Crowl died Sept. 8, 1865, in Sangamon county, and his widow now (1874) resides on the farm where they settled in 1835. It is one and a half miles north of Berry station, or Clarksville.

CROSS, ALVIN, was born Oct., 1799, in Madison county, Ky. Margaret Forbes was born June 24, 1802, near Jonesboro, East Tenn. Her parents moved to Madison county, Ky., when she was three months old. In 1816 they moved to Humphreys county, Tenn. Alvin Cross went to that county, also, when he was a young man, and was there married, in Feb., 1818, to Margaret Forbes. They had four children in Tennessee, and moved to Johnson county, Ill., where they had one child, and from there to Sangamon county, arriving Jan., 1829, in what is now Auburn township, where they had seven children. Three of their children died young—

SQUIRE, born in Tennessee, married in Sangamon county to Mrs. Elizabeth Pike, whose maiden name was Baker. They have three children, and live at Medoc, Jasper county, Mo.

MARY A., born in Tennessee, married in Sangamon county, to Samuel Mitchell, and died.

RILEY and LAVINA, twins, were born in Tenn.

RILEY enlisted in an Illinois regiment, at Springfield, for the Mexican war, in 1846, died in the army, and was buried on the Rio Grande in 1847.

LAVINA, married in Sangamon county to Andrew Williams, and died.

JOEL McD., born in 1827 or '8, in Johnson county, Ill., raised in Sangamon county, went to California, married, has two children, and lives there.

REBECCA, born in Sangamon county, married John M. Jones, moved to Washington county, Iowa, and died there, leaving seven children. She had a twin mate that died in infancy.

F. MARION, born Dec. 14, 1838, in Sangamon county, married Nov. 16, 1870, to Emily A. Hayden. They have one child, WILLIAM F., and live in Cotton Hill township, four miles north of Pawnee.

LEROY, born in 1840, in Sangamon county, married Jan. 8, 1863, to Candace A. Campbell. They had four children, JOSEPH A. and MINNIE died young. CLARK FORBES and FRANCES BELL reside with their parents, in Ball township, four miles northwest of Pawnee. Leroy had a twin mate that died young.

ELIZABETH, born in Sangamon county, married Sept. 18, 1861, to Benjamin F. Davis, a native of Tazewell county, Ill. They have one living child, GEORGE W., and live two and a half miles southeast of Pawnee.

Alvin Cross died Feb., 1849, in Sangamon county, and Mrs. Margaret Cross resides with her daughter, Mrs. Davis.

CROWDER, PHILIP, was born May, 1759, near Petersburg, Va. He was married there to Susan Parish. They had five children born there. He then moved, in company with about forty families, to Greene county, Ky. They all moved on pack horses, and camped near each other every night, with armed men standing guard around them, for protection against the Indians. Mrs. Susan Crowder died in 1794 in Kentucky, and he was there married to Rachel Saunders. She had one child, and died there. Philip Crowder then married Sally Chandler. They had nine children, and moved to Sangamon county, Ill., arriving in Nov., 1830, and settled three and a half miles southwest of Springfield. Of all his children—

REUBEN, born in Virginia, was married to Nancy Michael, and came to Sangamon county in 1825, preceding his father. They had fifteen children; three died young. ELIJAH died, aged twenty-one. MARTHA was married in Kentucky to James Robinson, moved to Sangamon county, thence to Macon county. Mr. R. died, and his family reside in Missouri. ELIZABETH married Peter Christian. They had two children, and Mr. C. died. His widow married Andrew Lockwood, and both died. MARY, born November, 1813, in Green county, Ky., was married in Sangamon county Feb. 11, 1836, to Benjamin F. Dillard. See his name. MATHEW married Susan Schoolen. They live in Macon county, Mo. THOMAS M., born July 25, 1818, was married July 22, 1840, to Mary J. Dalby. They had seven children; three died young. SARAH A., born Jan. 12, 1842, was married Dec. 22, 1864, to Ole Nelson. They had three children, Mary J., Emma E. and Maggie M., and live near Springfield. HENRY, born June 19, 1844, was married June 8, 1871, to Margaret E. Williams. She died Oct. 3, 1871. He is a practicing physician. AGNES E., born April 6, 1847, was married April 13, 1865, to F. C. Arnold. They have two children, Fannie and Alice, and live near San Jose, Mason county, Ill. MARY A. born Sept. 3, 1850, was married Feb. 10, 1868, to Thomas W. Miller. They have one child, Anna M. DOUGLAS, WILLIAM A. and JAMES P., live with their parents. Thomas M. Crowder and family reside four miles west of Springfield. GREENBERRY married Sarah Scott, and both died, leaving two children, in Missouri. SUSAN married John Grabeal, who died, and she married Philip Meekum. They reside in Saline county, Mo.

RIAL M., born April 11, 1821, in Greene county, Ky., brought up in Sangamon county, was married in Missouri to Angeline Scott. They have seven children. Their daughter, LENORA, married Moses H. Moore. See his name. The other six children, WILLIAM A., MARY J., ISAAC M., ALZIRA M., LAURA A. and DAISY L., reside with their parents near McKinney, Collin county, Texas. JAMES married Margaret Martin, and died January, 1876, near New Boston, Mo. REUBEN, Jun., went, in 1847, to Washington Territory, married there, and his wife died. He resides near Olympia. AMANDA married John Martin. They had four children, and she died in Saline county, Mo. CATHARINE married Samuel Casebolt, and live near Miami, Saline county, Mo. Reuben Crowder died Sept. 8, 1835, near Springfield, and his widow married again. She is now a widow, and resides with the family of her son James, near New Boston, Macon county, Mo.

MARTHA, born about 1785, near Petersburg, Va., was married in March, 1805, in Green county, Ky., to Lewis Walker, a native of Virginia. They had some children in Kentucky, and came to Illinois in 1832, and brought up a large family, some of whom are living in Clark and Coles counties. Their sixth child, JUDIAH, born Dec. 7, 1820, in Green county, Ky., came with her parents to Clark county, Ill., in 1832, and was married there Dec. 3, 1840, to James C. Robinson, who was born Aug. 19, 1823, in Edgar county, Ill. They have eight children, all born in Clark county, and the family moved to Springfield in 1869. Of their children, NATHANIEL P., born Jan. 25, 1842, was married in Marshall county, Ill., to Miss Benedict. SERENA, born Nov., 1843, married R. S. Briscoe. JAMES P., born May 23, 1845, married Dora Shaw, a daughter of Judge Shaw, of Olney, Ill. J. P. Robinson is a lawyer, and resides in Olney. AMANDA, born April 12, 1848, lives with her parents. RICHARD M., born August 6, 1851, is a practicing lawyer in Denver, Col. JENNIE and JUDIAH M. live with their parents in Springfield. Hon. James C. Robinson studied law, and was admitted to the bar, in Marshall, Clarke county, Ill., in 1852 or '3. He was elected to Congress from that district in 1858-'60 and '62. He was the Democratic candidate for Governor in 1864, but his party being in the minority, he was, not unexpectedly, defeated. He represented in Congress the district in which Springfield is situated, in 1870 and '72. He is now a member of the law firm of Robinson, Knapp & Shutt, of Springfield.

SUSAN, born in Virginia, was married in Kentucky to Isaac Le Follett. They brought up a family in Kentucky, and both died there.

MATHEW, born in Virginia, married Elizabeth Scott. They had five or six children, and she died. He married Jane Laughlin. They had one child, and he died. His family reside in Oskaloosa, Iowa.

ELIZABETH, born May 31, 1790, in Virginia, married William Bradley. See his name.

HENRY, the only child by Philip Crowder's second marriage, was born in Green county, Ky., went to East Tennessee when a boy, and remained there.

MARY, born May 22, 1799, in Green county, Ky., and the eldest child by the third marriage, married Thomas Willian. See his name.

ABRAHAM, born in Kentucky, married and died without children.

JOHN C., born in Green county, Ky., was married there to Mary Laswell. They had two children there, and came to Sangamon county in 1826, preceding his father four years. Eight children were born in Sangamon county. Of their children, JAMES H., born Dec. 24, 1823, in Kentucky, was married in Sangamon county, April 10, 1849, to Mary A. Wright, who was born Nov. 7, 1831, in Adair county, Ky., and came to Sangamon county in 1839. They reside three and a half miles southwest of Springfield. SARAH J., born Dec. 12, 1825, in Kentucky, was married Jan., 1850, in Sangamon county, to E. J. Warren. They had seven children, and she died July 17, 1870. Two of her children, JOHN C. was drowned in 1874, THOMAS J. lives in Springfield. The other five reside with their father, near Mount Zion, Macon county, Ill. WILLIAM, born June 5, 1828, in Sangamon county, married Mary Wood. They had three children, and he died. NANCY, born Oct. 26, 1830, married John Harris, and died. MARY E., born April 24, 1833, died, aged seventeen years. THOMAS J., born May 28, 1835, was married June 24, 1856, to Elizabeth F. Wright, and she died Nov., 1872. He resides at Wautiska, Sanders county, Neb., and is a Methodist minister. FRANCES, born May 21, 1838, married Jesse Perkins. They have four children, and live in Williamsville. MARTHA A., born Sept. 25, 1840, married Theophilus Ludlam. They have five children, and live near Decatur. MATILDA, born April 28, 1843, died in her fourth year. CATHARINE A., born Oct. 27, 1845, married July 15, 1865, to Alexander H. Wright, and lives in Springfield. Mrs. Mary Crowder died, and J. C. Crowder married Ursula Albans. They had four children; one died in infancy. HENRY C., born April 21, 1855, died April 23, 1876. JOHN J. resides at Jacksonville. JOSEPH W. resides with his brother, James H. Mrs. Ursula Crowder died, and J. C. Crowder married Mrs. Elizabeth Cox. They had one child, LUELLA, and J. C. Crowder died April 10, 1863. His widow resides at Berlin.

WILLIAM, born Feb. 11, 1804, in Kentucky, was married there to Mary Fawcett. They had two children, born in Kentucky, and came to Sangamon county in company with his brother-in-law, Elisha Sanders, in the fall of 1829, where eight children were born. Of their children, ROBERT E. and JOHN, born in Kentucky, both married in Sangamon county, and died. MATILDA, born Dec. 9, 1831, in Sangamon county, was married Oct. 10, 1855, to John J. Warren, who was born Nov. 3, 1831, in Shelby county, Ill. They have seven living children, MARY A., WILLIAM C., THOMAS J., GEORGE B. MC., ANDREW J., ROBERT E. and ISAAC W. Two of the children are married, and reside east of Pawnee. Those that are living and single reside with their parents, near Pawnee. SARAH E. married Hiram White. JAMES M. died unmarried, aged twenty years. WILLIAM C. married Ruth Tilley, and resides in Palmer, Ill. AARON V. married Martha Ward, and lives in Christian county. ANGELINE and BENJAMIN F. died young. STAFFORD and JESSE W. reside with their parents, near Pana.

FANNIE married William White, in Kentucky, came to Sangamon county in 1830, and soon returned to Kentucky. CHANDLER, born in 1808, in Kentucky, married Lucinda Sanders. They had four children: JOHN married Catharine Stroude. They have three children, and live in Cotton Hill township. Chandler Crowder was drowned in 1839, while attempting to cross Sugar creek to reach his sick family. HORATIO, born in Kentucky, came to Sangamon county in 1829. He married Sallie Woozley. They had two children in Sangamon county. NATHAN W., born Nov. 4, 1833, was married Dec. 28, 1853, to Margaret Todd. They have four children, JOHN H., GEORGE A., HENRY M. and JAMES H., and reside in Pawnee. SARAH J., born Oct. 12, 1835, was married Jan. 28, 1853, to Seth Underwood, who was born June 16, 1829, near Sparta, White county, Tenn. They have seven children, JOHN H., SARAH F., AVERY C., THOMAS J., JEREMIAH, LEWIS ALFRED and WILLIE, and reside in Cotton Hill township, Sangamon county, Ill. Horatio Crowder died about 1835, and his widow married John M. Mathews. *See his name.* She died Dec. 28, 1850.

WASHINGTON, born July 9, 1813, in Green county, Ky., came with his father to Sangamon county in 1830. He was married Dec. 21, 1836, to Isabel Laughlin. They have seven children: JOHN F., (Dick), born Dec. 25, 1837, married April 12, 1860, to Jane E. Laswell. They had one child, ELMER E., who died in infancy, and Mrs. C. died May 7, 1863. Mr. C. was married Sept. 22, 1864, to Mary F. McMurry. They have three children, LUELLA B., GEORGIE M. and ESTELLA. Mrs. Mary F. Crowder died June 16, 1873, in Springfield. J. F. Crowder was married June 10, 1874, to Nannie Womack, have one child, CLINTON CARROLL, and live in Pawnee. MARY A. died in her eighth year. WILLIAM A., born April 16, 1843, married Nov. 30 1865, to Isabel W. Lanterman. They had four living children, HORACE A., CHARLES L., FRED and ETHEL, and live in Springfield. LUCELIA J. died July 19, 1862, in her eighteenth year. SADIE E. and CHARLES W. live with their parents. GEORGE L. died May 11, 1870, in his eleventh year. Washington Crowder and wife reside in Springfield, Ill. *See his account of the sudden change.*

ALBERT G., born Oct. 16, 1816, in Green county, Ky., came to Sangamon county with his parents in 1830. He was married Dec. 29, 1840, to Sarah A. Bartlett. They had two children born in Sangamon county. MARY J. married W. W. Lapham. They have two children, W. ALBERT and MINNIE F., and live at Decatur. FANNIE married John Jamison. He was born Sept. 24, 1834, in Glasgow, Scotland. They have three children, MARY F., SARAH and MARIA L. D. Mr. Jamison resides in Auburn. Albert G. Crowder died in 1847, and his widow died in 1848, both in Sangamon county.

Philip Crowder died February, 1844, and his widow died in September following, both in Sangamon county. Philip Crowder was a soldier in the revolution. An elder brother, who had a family, was drafted, and Philip volunteered in his place. It was not long before the close of the war—when he was about sixteen years of age. His son Washington remembers hearing him repeatedly state that he was at the siege of Yorktown, and witnessed the surrender of Cornwallis; that he saw the British commander hand his sword to Washington, and that they wept and embraced each other. Seeing Cornwallis so much affected, Washington said: "Never mind it; this is the fate of war."

CUTTER.—The origin of the family in the west was with Seth Cutter, who was born in Boston, Mass., about 1760. Family tradition makes him a descendant of a family who came over in the Mayflower in 1620. He was married in Boston to Mary Reed. In 1790 he joined a colony and decided to move west. One account says that his five eldest daughters rebelled, saying they would not go where they were in danger of being devoured by wild beasts or killed by Indians. Another account fails to mention that he had any daughters at the time, which leads to the inference that if such an incident took place, they were sisters, and not daughters. He had but one child (a son) in Massachusetts. The colony went under the protection of the United States army, commanded by Gen. Anthony Wayne, who established a military post where Cincinnati, O., now stands. Seth Cutter opened a farm which became part of the city. Portions of it are yet in possession of some of his descendants, while other portions, although leased soon after his death (about 1800), the title still remains in the family. Cutter street indicates the locality where he settled. He brought one child—Seth R., of whom we will yet speak more fully—and had three daughters, at what became Cincinnati. Martha, who is believed to have been the first white child born in Cincinnati, became the wife of Abraham Price. Susan married Samuel Foster, of Petersburg, Ky., and Mary married Abraham McFaren. Mrs. Mary Reed Cutter died, and Seth Cutter married Roxena Shingledecker. They had three children. Abigail married William Bernard, Abijah became a farmer in Hamilton county, and Lorena, born Dec. 9, 1805, married September, 1823, to Nicholas Goshorn. One of their sons, A. T. Goshorn, is now (May, 1876,) Superintendent General of the Centennial Exhibition at Philadelphia. Seth Cutter was killed in Cincinnati about 1800, by the caving in of a well. His son—

SETH R. CUTTER, born Jan. 1, 1785, in Boston, Mass., taken by his parents, in 1790, to Cincinnati, Ohio. After the death of his mother, and the second marriage of his father, he left home and went to Grainger county, Tenn., where he was married in June, 1806, to Elizabeth Easley, daughter of William Easley. In December, 1809, he returned with his family to Cincinnati, where he engaged in the provision trade, mostly in New Orleans and Cuba. He continued in that business about twenty years. They had six children in Cincinnati, and then moved to Sangamon county, Ill., arriving in July, 1828, in what is now Loami township, where they had three children. Of their nine children—

SARAH, born Aug. 24, 1812, in Cincinnati, O., married in Sangamon county to John Calhoun. *See his name.*

ABIGAIL, born Nov. 10, 1814, in Cincinnati, O., married in Sangamon county to Frederick Hawn. *See his name.*

ALBERT, born Jan. 16, 1817, in Cincinnati, O. He was a confirmed invalid, and died in Sangamon county Jan. 30, 1841.

SUSANNAH, born March 19, 1827,

in Cincinnati, O., married in Sangamon county to John C. Hall. *See his name.*

MARTHA A., born Sept. 10, 1821, in Cincinnati, O., married in Sangamon county, January, 1842, to Oliver Diefendorf. *See his name.* She died six weeks after marriage.

CAROLINE E., born Feb. 13, 1825, in Cincinnati, O., raised in Sangamon county, and married in her native city to Oliver Diefendorf. *See his name.*

WILLIAM F., born Oct. 8, 1828, in Sangamon county. He served from June, 1846, one year in the 4th Ill. Inf., under Col. E. D. Baker, in the war with Mexico. In 1848 he went to California, where he spent several years in mining, and died there of consumption.

JOHN W. and *ELIZA*, twins, born during the "deep snow," Jan. 11, 1831, in Sangamon county.

JOHN W. married in 1853 to Juliette Greening. They have five children: ALBERT lives with his parents. CAROLINE, born Jan., 1857, was married Jan., 1873, to James Mahanna, has one child, EDITH, and lives near Lake City, Ill. ANDREW, LAURA and OLIVER live with their parents. John W. Cutter and wife live near Lake City, Moultrie county, Ill.

ELIZA, married March 24, 1857, at Weston, Mo., to Samuel A. Graham, who was born July 19, 1825, at Charlotte, Mecklenburg county, N. C. They have five children, EVA B., MARGARET, OLIVER, MARY, MALCOLM E. and ISABEL, and reside in Springfield, Ill. Mr. Graham enlisted in Co. F, Georgia Battallion, Mounted Volunteers, in 1847, and served in the war with Mexico, until June, 1848, when he was honorably discharged, and came to Springfield, Ill. In 1863 he was elected to represent Loami township in the Sangamon county Board of Supervisors, and in Nov., 1867, was elected, for two years, Surveyor of Sangamon county.

Mrs. Elizabeth Cutter died Sept., 1835, in Sangamon county, and in May, 1836, Seth R. Cutter married Mary Prosser Wariner, who was born March 18, 1808, in Henrico county, Va. Her parents were married in Virginia. Her mother inherited some slaves, but refused to keep them, and to evade the influence of slavery, moved to this county. Mr. Wariner was an old school, or regular Baptist preacher, and preached in the vicinity of Loami many years. Mr. Cutter and wife had one child—

FRANCES A., born Feb. 12, 1837, in Sangamon county, married March 16, 1856, to Abner Bowen. *See his name.* Mrs. Bowen has some embroidery work done by her mother nearly half a century ago.

Mrs. Mary P. W. Cutter died Feb. 11, 1861, and Seth R. Cutter died Sept. 8, 1869, both at the homestead settled by him in 1828, in Loami township.

Mr. Cutter was engaged in pork packing in Cincinnati with Andrew Heredith. *See his name.* When they came west they built a steam flouring mill about two miles northwest of Loami. A village called Millville grew up around it. The mill, owners and village have all passed away.

CUMMINGS, THOMAS, was born about 1800, in Breckenridge county, Ky., married to Margaret Smith, came to Sangamon county, Ill., about the time his father-in-law (Thomas Smith) came, in 1822. They had eight children, namely—

MAHALA died unmarried, at thirty-five years of age, in Sangamon county.

REBECCA J. married John L. Smith. They had nineteen children, all except two of whom are living (1873). They had five sons who were Union soldiers in Illinois regiments. The parents and nearly all their living children live in Logan county, five miles northeast of Williamsville.

ROBERT, born Sept. 12, 1817, in Washington county, Ky., was brought to Sangamon county when he was about five years old, married Jan. 2, 1840, to Nancy Cloyd. They had six children. THOMAS N. married Sarah B. C. Harrison, have one living child, THOMAS O., and live in Woodside township. MARGARET A. died at two years old. AMANDA E. married Jacob Beam. *See his name.* MARY J. married Isaac M. Jones, and reside in Woodside township. JOSEPH R. and EMMA S. reside with their parents, one and a half miles northwest of Woodside station.

WESLEY E. married Melinda Owens, had two children, and the parents both died. Their children live in Macoupin county.

WILLIAM married Jane Owens. He died, leaving his widow and three children, in Litchfield, Ill.

JOHN T. married Melinda Richardson. She died, and he married Margaret Adams, has five children, and lives in Christian county. He is a traveling minister in the M. E. church.

ELIZABETH married John Kearley, had one child, and all died of cholera about 1850.

THOMAS H. married Mrs. Emma West, whose maiden name was Woods. She had two children by her first marriage, and they have three children, and live in Jersey county.

Thomas Cummings died September, 1846, and his widow died October, 1849, both in Sangamon county.

D

DARNEILLE, JOHN, was born June 8, 1791, in Bourbon county, Ky. He served fourteen months in the war of 1812-13, half the time as first Lieut., and was then promoted to Captain. Margaret Norton was born Oct. 25, 1793, in Bourbon county, also. They were married there, Feb. 20, 1814, and had three living children in Kentucky. The family moved to Sangamon county, Ill., arriving Nov., 1819, in what is now Chatham township, first at a place called Turkey Point, and in the spring of 1820, moved further up Lick creek, and made a permanent settlement five miles west of the present town of Chatham, where they had nine living children. Of their children—

MARTHA, born April 7, 1815, in Kentucky, married in Sangamon county to Thomas S. Hunter. See his name.

CATHARINE, born Aug. 2, 1817, in Bourbon county, Ky., married in Sangamon county to David Alexander. See his name.

BENJAMIN F., born Jan. 1, 1819, in Bourbon county, Ky., married in Sangamon county, Dec. 17, 1840, to Mary Jacobs, who was born Oct. 1, 1821, in Clarke county, Ky. They had eight living children in Sangamon county ELIZABETH married Samuel C. Sumpter, who was born in Sangamon county.

He enlisted July 20, 1861, at Springfield, for three years, in what became Co. C, 11th Mo. Inf.; reënlisted as a veteran, Jan., 1864, at LaGrange, Tenn., served until Jan. 15, 1866, when he was honorably discharged at St. Louis, Mo. Mr. and Mrs. Sumpter have three children, CORA, DORA and HOMER A., and reside five miles west of Chatham. MARGARET C. married James M. Greening. See his name. MARTHA J. married Lee R. Graham. See his name. MARIA F. married John Garvey. See his name. LORINDA J. married Feb., 1875, to Col. John Watson, and live in Auburn. EMMA S. married Dec., 1873, to William Vandoren. See his name. JULIA A. and BENJ. F., Jun., reside with their mother. Benjamin F. Darneille died Dec. 5, 1872, and his widow resides six miles west of Chatham.

Mrs. Darneille relates some incidents both instructive and amusing, of her early married life. She says that when herself and husband went to set up housekeeping, he had but ten dollars. Cooking stoves were not in fashion, but they bought pots, skillets, pans, spoons, knives and forks, etc., thus securing their outfit, and had some money left. Lamps and burning fluids were unknown, and for nearly ten years their only candlesticks were made by taking gourds and cutting off about half the bowl end, so that they would sit upright, and then cutting off the necks and inserting the candles. The first crop of oats Mr. Darnielle raised he hauled thirty bushels to Springfield, and gave the load even for eight yards of calico to make a dress for his wife.

THOMAS J., born Oct. 4, 1820, in Sangamon county, married Martha McGinnis. They had two living children in Sangamon county. JOHN D., born Nov. 29, 1848, married in Warsaw, Ky., to Jennie Brown, a native of that city, and resides there. They have two children, MELINDA and JAMES W. JAMES W., born in Sangamon county, Sept. 16, 1850, married Oct. 31, 1871, in Belvidere, Ill., to Belle Moulton, a native of Minneapolis, Minn. They have one child, MABEL, and reside in Chicago. Mrs. Martha Darnielle died, and Mr. D. married Mrs. America Gibson, whose maiden name was Forrest. Thos. J. Darnielle died Nov. 21, 1854, in Sangamon county. His widow married Jan. 13, 1859, to John R. Neal. See his name.

JAMES M., born Jan. 22, 1822, in Sangamon county, married Jan. 1, 1852, to Clarrissa Kinney. They have six children, CAROLINE K., MAGGIE H., JOHN H., FLORENCE E., CHAS. A. and JAMES M., Jun., reside with their parents, in Chatham, Sangamon county, Ill.

EMILY, born July 28, 1823, in Sangamon county, married Willis Webb. They had two children, and the whole family died.

LORINDA, born Jan. 31, 1825, in Sangamon county, married William McGinnis. See his name.

ELIZABETH, born Dec. 10, 1826, in Sangamon county, married Abraham Gish, had two children. Mrs. G. and one of the children died. The other child, BENJAMIN F., resides with his father, in Auburn township.

HENRY, died, aged fifteen years.

MARGARET, born Jan. 25, 1830, in Sangamon county, married James Hall. See his name.

HIRAM H., born May 16, 1833, died, aged twenty-one years.

JOHN W., born Feb. 3, 1836, in Sangamon county, married Melinda Drennan, had one child, and all died.

John Darneille died March 10, 1854, and his widow, Mrs. Margaret Darneille, died April 30, 1875, both on the farm where they settled in 1820.

John Darneille learned to write by firelight, and in the absence of paper, peeled buckeye bark from the trees, and when it became dry, did his writing on that, until he learned to keep accounts of all his business transactions. He acquired such fame as an accurate and legible penman, that he became the neghborhood letter writer. He was on the first grand jury that was ever empanneled in Sangamon county, May 7, 1821. They held their deliberations, some sitting on a pile of rails, and some on gopher hills out on the prairie, within the present limits of Springfield. He was elected as one of the Representatives of Sangamon county in the State Legislature of 1840, the first that ever assembled in Springfield.

DARNALL, AMELIA, whose maiden name was Yocom, sister to Jacob Yocom, was born October, 1793, near Lexington, Ky., and was married there, August, 1813, to Samuel Darnall. Seven children were born in Kentucky, and they moved to Indiana, where they had one child, and moved in 1829 to Funk's Grove, McLean county, Ill., where they had one child. Mr. Darnall died August, 1830. Mrs. D., with her nine children, moved to Sangamon county, Ill., arriving in the fall of 1830 in what is now Williams township. Of her children—

BENJAMIN F. died at twenty-one years of age.

EVELINE married Levi Smith, has eleven children, and live near Mt. Pleasant, Iowa.

SALLY died at sixteen years of age.

HARVEY, born August 10, 1821, in Bourbon county, Ky., married in Sangamon county to Agnes Simpson. They have eight children. MARY married Stephen Hussey, and live in Logan county. WINFIELD SCOTT, JAMES M., JOHN F., STEPHEN H., JESSE HARVEY B. and LILLIE E., live with their parents near Barclay.

NANCY J. married Franklin Yocom. See his name.

JAMES died at thirty-five years of age.

MELVINA married Thaddeus Evans, and died in Montgomery county, leaving six children.

ELIZABETH married David Bailey, has ten children, and live in Mason county.

REBECCA, born in Illinois, married March 6, 1866, to Oliver McGarvey, has one child, WILLIAM N., and she lives with her mother.

Mrs. Amelia Darnall resides (1874) one mile northeast of Barclay. She is more than eighty years old.

DARNALL, ISAAC T., born Oct. 17, 1809, in Montgomery county, Md., and came to Sangamon county in December, 1840, in Cooper township, south of the Sangamon river. He was married Dec. 14, 1852, to Miranda Crowl. They had five living children—

HILLERY W., JOSEPH E., BENJAMIN F., CHARLES A., and MARYLAND.

Isaac T. Darnall died Sept. 10, 1871. His children reside with their mother, who was married Feb. 11, 1873, to George W. Taylor. He was born Dec. 14, 1836, in Wayne county, Ind. They reside in Cooper township, three miles southwest of Mechanicsburg.

DAWSON, JOHN, was born Nov. 24, 1791, in Fairfax county, Va. His parents moved to Bracken county, Ky., in 1805. He enlisted in Bracken county in the war against England in 1812, and was wounded and captured at the battle of River Raisin. After being held as a prisoner in Canada by the Indians who had captured him, his friends paid a ransom for him, and he returned home. Cary Jones was born May 22, 1801, in Nicholas county, Ky. John Dawson and Cary Jones were married in Nicholas county, Oct. 9, 1817. They had one child in Nicholas county, and moved to Bracken county, where they had three children, and the family moved to Sangamon county, Ill., arriving Oct. 24, 1827, north of the Sangamon river, in Clear Lake township, where they had six children. Of their ten children—

NAPOLEON B., born June 10, 1820, is an invalid, and resides with his mother.

MARIA L., born July 22, 1822, in Bracken county, Ky., married in Sangamon county to George B. Merriman. See his name.

LUCY M., born March 7, 1825, in Bracken county, Ky., married in Sangamon county to Lindsay Ridgeway. See his name.

BERTRAND, born April 10, 1827, in Bracken county, Ky., is unmarried, and resides adjoining Dawson on the south. He is an extensive farmer and stock raiser.

MARTHA W., born Oct. 21, 1829, in Sangamon county, married Sept. 24, 1850, to James Vanvoris, of Pennsylvania. She died April 2, 1853, in Washington county, Pa.

MARY J., born Dec. 17, 1831, in Sangamon county, married John S. Merriman Nov. 9, 1848. See his name.

ISABEL, born Dec. 22, 1833, resides with her mother.

SARAH E., born July 31, 1837, in Sangamon county, resides with her mother.

JOHN, Jun., born March 22, 1840. He went to Cairo Ill., in 1862, and enlisted in the United States navy, served one year, and died at home Oct. 26, 1869.

DICK A., born April 3, 1842, in Sangamon county, died at eleven years of age.

John Dawson died Nov. 12, 1850, in Sangamon county. His widow resides on the farm where they settled in 1827. It is three miles southwest of Dawson.

Mr. Dawson was Captain of a company from Sangamon county in the Black Hawk war of 1831. He was elected to represent Sangamon county in the State Legislature of 1831 and '2. He was again elected in 1835, and continued, by re-election, to represent the county until 1840, and was consequently one of the "Long Nine" who secured the removal of the State capital to Springfield at the session of 1836-'7. [See article: "Long Nine."] Mr. C. was also a member of the convention that framed the State constitution of 1848. The ball received in his lungs at the battle of River Raisin was never extracted, and was the cause of his death.

DALLY, CRAWFORD, was born about 1795, in Pennsylvania, married in Virginia to Susan Sanders, and made their home in Washington county, Pa., until four children were born, and the family moved to Sangamon county, Ill., in the spring of 1835. Of their four children—

HESTER A., married three times, and died at Belleville, Ill.

MARY J., born Aug. 22, 1824, in Washington county, Pa., married in Sangamon county, to Thomas M. Crowder. See his name.

SUSAN M., born in 1826 in Pennsylvania, died in Sangamon county, aged twenty-four years.

AGNES E., born in Pennsylvania, married Andrew Armstrong, and died.

MILTON, born in 1831, in Pennsylvania, married in Sangamon county, to Nancy J. Sappington, had five children, moved to Missouri, and she died. He was a Union soldier in a Missouri regiment.

Mrs. Susan Dally died in 1835, and Crawford Dally died December, 1839, both in Sangamon county.

DAVENPORT, GEORGE, was born about 1781, in North Carolina, married, had one child, and his wife died there. When the child was three weeks old he carried it on horseback to Casey county, Ky. He was there married to Winney Clifton, a native of that county. They had two children, and moved to

Sangamon county, Ill., in the fall of 1819, and first camped where Springfield now stands, and three weeks later moved six miles west, at the north side of Spring creek, where seven children were born. Of his children—

THOMAS, born in North Carolina, raised in Sangamon county, married, and is living with his second wife near Independence, Mo.

WILLIAM, born in Kentucky, raised in Sangamon county, has his second wife, and resides near Mt. Pleasant, Iowa.

ELIZABETH, born in Kentucky, married Thomas Davis, has six children, and resides in Vernon county, Mo.

ALFRED S., born June 24, 1820, married Lucinda Tolley. They have seven children, JAMES, GEORGE, JOHN, ADOLPHUS, MARY, SOPHIA and NOAH, and reside two and a half miles northeast of Berlin.

MARY married Thomas Andrews, who died, leaving three children, and she married John Runnels, and he died, leaving a widow and two children, near Dallas, Texas.

NANCY married Jeremiah Kendall, had four children, and she died, leaving her family in Oregon.

URIAH L. was a soldier in the 4th Ill. Inf. under Col. E. D. Baker, and was wounded at the battle of Cerro Gordo, Mexico, and died eight or nine days later.

JOB C., born January 4, 1823, in Sangamon county, was married Dec. 4, 1845, to Alice J. Mosteller, who was born Nov. 29, 1830. They have five children, JOHN H., LAURA (the latter was married May 9, 1875, to William Sayre, and resides near Pleasant Plains), CHARLES M., NEWMAN and WILLIAM EDWARD. All the unmarried children live with their parents in Menard county, near Salisbury, Sangamon county.

ADOLPHUS died in 1850 in Chicago, aged about twenty-four years.

AMANDA married Allen Baker, and died in 1849.

RHODA married Thomas Ray. They have four children, and reside in Vernon county, Mo.

Mrs. Winney C. Davenport died Jan. 15, 1845, and George Davenport died Feb. 14, 1845, both in Sangamon county, eight miles west of Springfield.

DAVIDSON, SAMUEL, was born Oct. 19, 1821, in Morgan county, East Tenn. His parents moved, in 1826, to Macon county, Ill., and in 1828 to Macoupin county. Samuel spent most of his time in Sangamon county until 1840, and from that time he made his home in Ball township, where he was married May 9, 1850, to Amanda Nuckolls. They had nine children, one of whom, John D., died Nov. 26, 1869, in his seventh year. The other eight—

ANNIE E., GEORGE W., EMMA A., SAMUEL M., THOMAS J., AMANDA V., MIRIAM M. and CHARLES CARROLL reside with their parents, three and a half miles west of Pawnee.

DAVIES, JOHN, was born in Wales, and came to America when a young man. He was married in Adair county, Ky., to Catharine Antle. They had ten children in Kentucky, and Mr. Davies died there about 1810. His widow moved to Sangamon county about 1826, and settled near Salisbury. Of her children—

GEORGE married in Kentucky to Catharine Tolley, came to Sangamon county before his mother, and died in 1856. His widow and two children live in Kansas.

POLLY married in Kentucky to Richard Walker, came to Sangamon county in 1826, and died in 1870, leaving two children in Bond county.

MICHAEL, born in Kentucky, married twice in Sangamon county, leaving a widow and five children in Menard county.

HENRY, born Oct. 30, 1805, in Cumberland county, Ky., came to Salisbury, Sangamon county, in 1828. He was married there May 5, 1835, to Lucy McGlasson, who was born July 1, 1817, in Adair county, Ky. They had ten children in Sangamon county, namely: JULIA A. was killed by a falling chimney, at four years of age. ELIZABETH, born Jan. 30, 1839, married Ebenezer Colburn. See his name. MARY M., born July 2, 1841, married John Huffmaster. See his name. SALLIE A. died young. MARION, born Sept. 6, 1848, and ALONZO, born Jan. 2, 1852, live with their parents. EMILY J., born Sept. 5, 1854, lives with her sister, Mrs. Colburn. IRA JASPER, born May 25, 1857, and MATILDA, born Nov. 12, 1860, live with their parents. Henry Davies and wife now (1874) live in Loami.

NANCY married in Kentucky to Benjamin Ballenger, and died near Natchez, Miss.

WILLIAM, born in Kentucky, married Elizabeth Duncan, and both died, leaving two married children in Salisbury.

SALLY, born in Kentucky, married Thomas Miller, who died, leaving a widow and six children in Menard county.

JOHN, born July 23, 1815, in Kentucky, married in Sangamon county, November, 1834, to Polly Duncan. They have five children; two of them married, and all live in Salisbury.

MILTON, born in Kentucky in 1817, married Lucy A. McMurphy, have two children, and live in Salisbury.

Mrs. Catharine Davies died in 1846, in Salisbury.

DAVIS, AQUILLA, was born in 1756, in St. Mary's county, Maryland, and taken to Fauquier county, Va., when a youth. He was a soldier in the Revolution, and married in the latter county to Isabella Briggs. They had six children in Virginia, namely: Edward, William B., Alexander B., Thompson and Hezekiah, and a daughter Marion. They emigrated to Kentucky, where they had two children. In 1820 they moved to Illinois, settling first where Elkhart now is, which was then Sangamon county. Aquilla Davis laid out the town of Elkhart. In 1822 or '3 they moved to Fancy Creek, ten miles from Springfield. After several years Aquilla Davis and family returned to Elkhart. There are but three of their children living now, viz—

HEZEKIAH, born in Virginia, resides with his son in Tazewell county, Illinois.

BENJAMIN F., born in Kentucky, resides at Norwood, Franklin county, Kansas, and

JUDITH W., born August 12, 1802, in Union county, Ky., was married Oct. 28, 1836, to Oramel Clark. *See his name.*

Aquilla Davis died August 23, 1832, and Mrs. Davis died Jan. 23, 1833, both near Elkhart, Logan county, Ill.

DAVIS, JOHN, was born Oct. 15, 1809, in Baltimore county, Md. He was married there in May, 1829, to Mrs. Margaret Davis, whose maiden name was Gore. She was born Oct. 6, 1806, in the same county, and was married first in September, 1824, to Capt. Robert Davis, a soldier in the war of 1812. They had two children, and Capt. Davis died May, 1827.

John Davis and wife had two children in Maryland, and moved in 1832 to Preble county, O., where they had one child, and from there to Darke county, where one child was born. The family then moved to Sangamon county, Ill., arriving Feb., 1837, in what is now Gardner township, where they had three children. Of the two children of Mrs. Davis by her first marriage—

ELIZABETH, born Sept. 3, 1825, near Baltimore, Md., married in Sangamon county to Samuel H. Reid, Jun. *See his name.*

NANCY, born Aug. 6, 1827, near Baltimore, married in Sangamon county to Henry H. Foster. *See his name.*

Of the seven children by the second marriage—

ELLEN, born Dec. 12, 1830, in Maryland, married in Sangamon county Jan., 1855, to Joseph McCoy. They have one child, JOHN, born in Sangamon county, and reside in Missouri.

JAMES, born Jan. 23, 1832, in Maryland, brought up in Sangamon county, and went to California in October, 1853. The family have not received any reliable information from him since June 8, 1856, and have no hope that he is living.

MARTHA J., born March, 1834, in Preble county, O., and died in Sangamon county, November, 1848.

MARGARET, born in 1836, in Darke county, O., died in Sangamon county March 31, 1853.

SARAH, born September, 1840, in Sangamon county, married in the same county to James Bruce, has one child, ANNIE, and live near White Oak postoffice, Montgomery county, Ill.

JOHN, Jun., born Dec. 12, 1842, in Sangamon county, enlisted September, 1861, in Co. B, 10th Ill. Cav., for three years, and re-enlisted as a veteran December, 1863. He served until Jan. 5, 1866, when he was honorably discharged in Springfield, being the last man of the regiment. He was killed by lightning July 5, 1875, while attending to some stock on his father's farm, near Curran, Sangamon county.

DALLAS, born Oct. 4, 1846, in Sangamon county, married Dec. 31, 1868, to Louisa Smith. They have two children, MARY A. and THOMAS O., and live two miles east of Curran.

John Davis and wife reside two miles east of Curran, Sangamon county, Ill.

DAVIS, ISRAEL, was born Jan. 21, 1817, in Rutherford county, near Murfreesboro, Tenn. His parents died when he was about five years old. At the age of fourteen years he joined a family who was moving, and came with them to Green county, Ill., and from there to Sangamon county in 1834, and made his home in what is now Auburn township. He was married June 30, 1844, to Jane Kessler. They have five children—

CATHARINE married James Drennan, and lives in Auburn.

GEORGE lives in Auburn.

SUSAN married Joseph Rectric, and lives in Carlinville.

VIRGINIA and MARY live with their parents, in Auburn.

Mr. Davis was for many years employed at the depot of the Chicago and Alton railroad, at Auburn, and resides there.

DAVIS, RICHARD, was born April, 1800, in Kentucky. Elizabeth Neal, (sister to Mrs. Edward Williams. See his name.), was born about 1803, in Nelson county, Ky. They were married and had one child in Kentucky, and the family moved to Sangamon county, arriving before the deep snow of 1830–31, in Springfield. They had three children in Sangamon county. Of their four children—

GEORGE L., died unmarried in 1856.

DIANA, born July 16, 1832, in Springfield, married Nov. 8, 1855, to Philip Loeb, who was born Oct. 15, 1831, in Baden, Germany. They had three living children, PHILIP E., MARY C. and ARTHUR R. Philip Loeb died Sept. 17, 1866, in Springfield, and his widow and children live four and a half miles northwest of Springfield.

JOHN H., born Feb. 1836, is unmarried, and resides with his sister, Mrs. Loeb.

JAMES E. married Rosella La-grange. They have two children, and live in Springfield.

Mrs. Elizabeth Davis died March, 1850, and Richard Davis died April, 1865, both in Springfield.

DAWLEY, HARRISON, was born July 17, 1817, in Chatauqua county, N. Y., came to Springfield in March, 1839, and four or five years later went to Island Grove, where he was married, Oct. 26, 1847 to Jane Campbell, a daughter of Hugh Campbell. She was born March 11, 1826, in Tennesse, and raised on Richland creek. They had nine children; three died young, namely—

PATIENCE was killed in her third year, by a runaway horse belonging to Dr. J. M. Gibson.

MATILDA died in her third year, and

MAXWELL died in infancy.

CYNTHIA A., born Sept. 4, 1848, married Oct. 28, 1869, to M. F. Kibbey. They have three children, and live at El Paso, Sedgwick county, Kan.

JOHN H., WILLIAM E., EDWARD, JOSEPH C. and GEORGE T., live with their parents two miles south of Rochester.

DAY, GEORGE, was born Mar. 5, 1810, in Sheffield, Mass. His parents died when he was three years old, and he, with another brother and a sister, were taken by an aunt to Granby, Conn. He next lived with a half-sister, at Elbridge, N. Y. At fifteen years of age he went to Hartford, Conn., and engaged to travel in Ohio for a clock company. He sold clocks four years, returned to Hartford, and prosecuted the same business two years in Pennsylvania. Henrietta Shank was born March 19, 1816, at Hagerstown, Md. The family moved to Mercersburg, Pa., where her father died, and her mother married Jacob Divelbiss. See his name. The family moved to Ligonier, Pa. George Day and Henrietta Shank were married Feb. 20, 1834, had one child there, and moved to Illinois, arriving at Havana Oct. 29, 1837. They visited some friends who had left comfortable Pennsylvania houses, and were living in rail pens, covered with sod. Their bread was made from wheat ground without bolting. Mr. Day became a walking earthquake—having the chills and fever—but he was not happy, and determined to return to the Pennsylvania hills. His wife persuaded him to come to Springfield, where they arrived in Nov., 1837. When the grass and flowers appeared the next spring, he became reconciled, and has been well satisfied from that to the present time. They had seven living children in Sangamon county, namely—

SOPHIA H., born March 15, 1836, at Ligonier, Pa., married in Sangamon county, March 20, 1854, to David Ayers, who was born July 27, 1833, in Auglaize county, Ohio. Mr. Ayers died May 30, 1866, at Jacksonville, Ill. Mrs. Ayers resides with her parents.

HENRIETTA, born Feb. 16, 1840, in Springfield, married Dec. 7, 1865, to Joseph F. Boyd, who was born Jan. 4, 1837, in Hagerstown, Md. They have one child, GRACIE D., and live in Springfield.

WILLIAM, born Sept. 14, 1842, in Springfield, was married May 18, 1865, to Margaret E. Keyes. They have five children, EFFIE S., CATHARINE H., and CHARLES R., DAISY D. and MAGGIE M., and reside three miles north of Springfield.

ROBERT, born Jan. 30, 1845, enlisted April 27, 1864, for one hundred days, in Co. A, 133d Ill. Inf., served one hundred and forty-seven days, and was honorably discharged Sept. 24, 1864. He lives with his parents.

ELLIE M., born July 27, 1847,
JULIA C., born June 13, 1850, and
GEORGE E., born Jan. 12, 1854, live with their parents.

George Day and wife reside three miles northeast of Springfield.

DEARDORFF, ANTHONY, was born in 1786 in Pennsylvania. Elizabeth Powell was born in 1800, in Bedford county, Pa. They were married in 1818, in Franklin county, O., and had four children there. The family then moved to Sangamon county, Ill., arriving in the fall of 1823, in what is now Ball township, where they had six children. Of their ten children—

MARY, born in Ohio, married in Sangamon county to Morgan Matthew, who died, leaving a widow and three children in Missouri.

CATHARINE, born in Ohio, married in Sangamon county to John Kent. He died in the United States army at Vicksburg, in 1863. His widow and five children live in Missouri.

PETER, born in Ohio, married in Sangamon county to Nancy Williams. They had four children, and Mrs. D. died. Mr. D. and his children live in Iowa.

CHARLES P., born in Ohio, married in Sangamon county to Mrs. Sarah Rummerfield. They have five children, and live in Cass county, Ill.

REBECCA, born in Sangamon county, is unmarried, and lives in Ball township.

BARBARA, born in Sangamon county, married Joseph Beam. See his name.

ELIZABETH, born in Sangamon county, died at sixteen years old.

WILLIAM P., born in Sangamon county, married Catharine Parvin. He died, leaving a widow and two children in Cass county, Ill.

JOHN died at eighteen years of age.

SUSAN, born in Sangamon county, married Henry Shipman, and live in Adair county, Mo.

Anthony Deardorff died in 1834, and his widow married Simon Matthew. See his name. She died Oct. 21, 1850.

DEARDORFF, PETER, brother to Anthony, was born in Pennsylvania, married in Ohio to Hannah Brunk, came to Sangamon county in 1824 with George Brunk. They had four children. She died in 1874.

DELAY, JOHN, was born in Virginia, taken by his parents to Bath county, Ky., and was there married to Elizabeth Branch, a sister to Edward Branch. See his name. She was born Nov. 25, 1785, near Lynchburg, Va. They had eleven children in Bath county, and moved to Sangamon county, Ill., in 1829, and settled near Rochester. Of their children—

SARAH married in Kentucky to Thomas Baker. See his name.

JANE died in Kentucky, aged eighteen years.

JEMIMA died in Kentucky, aged sixteen years.

JUDITH, born March 8, 1809, in Kentucky, married in Sangamon county to Joseph Williams. See his name.

STEPHEN, born in Kentucky, married in Sangamon county, March 4, 1841, to Susan Baker, had nine children, and he died April 16, 1870. She lives in Cotton Hill township.

ELIZA, born April 19, 1813, in Bath county, Ky., married in Sangamon county to William Taft. *See his name.*

POLLY, born Jan. 5, 1820, in Bath county, Ky., married in Sangamon county to Samuel Torrence. *See his name.*

ELIZABETH, born in Bath county, Ky., married in Sangamon county to Samuel Keys. *See his name.*

GREENBERRY, born in Kentucky, died in Sangamon county, aged fifteen years.

ALVIN died in Kentucky, aged eight years.

John Delay died Dec. 23, 1850, and his widow died Oct. 3, 1869, both in Sangamon county.

DICKERSON, SAMUEL, was born about 1793, in Virginia. His parents moved to Pendleton county, Ky., when he was a boy, and his father engaged in salt-making at Grant's Lick. Susan Kane was born in 1800. They were married, and had six children in Kentucky. They moved to Logan county, Ill., in 1830, and in February, 1831, arrived in what is now Illiopolis township, five miles east of Mechanicsburg. Of their children—

HUGH W., born Oct. 25, 1811, in Pendleton county, Ky., married in Sangamon county, Aug. 7, 1833, to Catharine Greene. They had five children in Sangamon county. WILLIAM H., born July 11, 1834, enlisted in 1862 in Co. E, 116th Ill. Inf., for three years, married Sarah Enlow, has two children, and lives in Franklin county, Kan. ELIZA J. married John Taylor. *See his name.* ALEXANDER, born Oct. 12, 1844, enlisted August, 1862, in Co. B, 130th Ill. Inf., for three years. He was on duty at the capture of Vicksburg, though sick at the time, was sent to hospital at Memphis, where his father took charge of him in July, and started for home. He died on board a steamboat, Aug. 12, 1863. His remains were brought home and buried in Williams township. JOHN, born in Sangamon county, is publishing the Gazette, at Terre Haute, Ind. SAMUEL resides with his father. Mrs. Catharine Dickerson died in 1850, and H. W. Dickerson was married April 1, 1852, to Edna C. Rice. They had seven children, JOSIAH, AN-NA M. and ROBBY died under four years. MARY, CHARLES E., OLIVER P. and IDA BELL, the six living, reside with their parents near Barclay, in Williams township.

POLLY married William Hunter. *See his name.* Both died.

ARCHIBALD, born May 6, 1816, in Kentucky, married in Sangamon county to Celia Hunter. They had nine children. HARRIET married Michael Derry, and live near Bowling Green, Mo. JAMES R. enlisted July 19, 1861, in Co. I, 41st Ill. Inf., for three years, was wounded at the battle of Pittsburg Landing, April 6, 1862, was brought home and died on the fourteenth of the same month. SAMUEL, enlisted April, 1861, on the first call for 75,000 men, served three months, re-enlisted in 1862, in Co. I, 41st Ill. Inf., and served three years. He was married to Ellen Shinaman, have four children, and live near Mt. Auburn, Christian county, Illinois. LUCINDA, born November, 1845, married to Harry Blair, April, 1871, have one child, KATIE, and live near Illiopolis. AMANDA J., born Dec. 25, 1847, married John McGuffin, and reside in Illiopolis township. ZACHARY T., born Dec. 29, 1849, married Dec. 3, 1873, to Louisa S. Ream, and live in Illiopolis township. JOHN HENRY, born Sept. 2, 1852, ARCHIBALD, born Dec. 2, 1854, and ERASTUS, born Sept. 10, 1857, live with their mother. Archibald Dickerson was killed Sept. 2, 1865, at Harristown, Macon county, Ill., by an accident on the T., W & W. R. R. His widow resides three and a half miles southwest of Illiopolis.

MARTHA, born in Kentucky, married John Hunter, and both died, leaving a family in Christian county.

C. ALEXANDER, born April 11, 1827, in Campbell county, Ky., married April 12, 1848, to Melinda Ridgeway. She was born Jan. 26, 1831, in Sangamon county. They have eight children, HENRY CLAY, JOHN HARDIN, WILLIAM F., SAMUEL O., REUBEN J., SARAH J., ULYSSES GRANT and CHARLES, and reside in Illiopolis township, five miles east of Mechanicsburg, where his father settled in 1832.

AMELIA J. married Samuel Garretson. See his name.

Samuel Dickerson died in the fall of 1856, and his widow died in June, 1859, both in Illiopolis township.

DICKERSON, CHESLEY, a younger brother to Samuel, was born in Virginia, married in Gallatin county, Ky., to Betsy Lillard, and came to Sangamon county with his brother Samuel in 1831. They had four children. Their son—

WILLIAM, born in Sangamon county, enlisted July 19, 1861, in Co. I, 41st Ill. Inf., for three years, came home on sick furlough, and died March 30, 1862.

FRANCES, born in Sangamon county, married Philip Fredericks. They live near Ottawa, Kansas. Mr. F. was a soldier for three years in Co. I, 41st Ill. Inf.

ERASTUS, born in Sangamon county, married Lottie Enlow, and lives at Ottawa, Kansas.

MARIA, married and died.

Chesley Dickerson and wife both died in Sangamon county.

DICKSON, GEORGE, was born March 18, 1801, in Tennessee, came to Illinois with his parents, and was married Nov. 13, 1823, to Fanny Cooper, (sister to John Cooper, the father of James.) She was born July 16, 1804, in Tennessee. They had seven children—

MARY A., born Nov. 7, 1826, died Jan. 31, 1846.

SUSAN A., born Jan. 7, 1829, died Dec. 21, 1848.

ELIZABETH E., born April 10, 1831, died August 21, 1851.

JOHN C., born Dec. 26, 1836, married in 1869 to Ida Johnson. They have two children, and reside in Chatfield, Minn.

MELISSA N., born Feb. 10, 1838, married June 3, 1858, to George Flower, had two living children, and she married for a second time to James Prunk, have one child, and reside in Mechanicsburg.

THOMAS M., born May 18, 1841, was a soldier in an Illinois regiment, married in 1863, to Susan Lydic, in Christian county, have four children, and reside at Lamar, Barton county, Mo.

SARAH A., born Oct. 26, 1845, in Christian county, married Benjamin H. Giger. See his name.

George Dickson died Jan. 7, 1849, in Christian county, and his widow resides with her daughter, Mrs. Giger, in Mechanicsburg.

DIFENDORF, OLIVER, was born March 12, 1819, in Canajoharie, Montgomery county, New York, and came to Springfield, Ill., in November, 1840. He was married Jan., 1842, to Martha Ann Cutter. She died six weeks after their marriage. Mr. Diefendorf, about the time of the death of his wife, entered upon the duties of deputy clerk, at Springfield, in the circuit court of Sangamon county. He continued to discharge the duties of that position until June, 1846, when he volunteered in Co. D, 4th Ill. Inf., was commissioned 1st Lieut., and went into the Mexican war under Col. E. D. Baker. He was subsequently commissioned as 2d Lieut. in the 16th U. S. Inf., and served until the close of the war. He was married Oct., 1848, in Cincinnati, Ohio, to Caroline Cutter. They had three children, all of whom died in infancy. Aug. 23, 1850, they moved to Weston, Platt county, Mo. He was elected, Aug., 1851, for four years, clerk of the court of common pleas of that county. He was two years clerk in the office of the Surveyor-General of Kansas; was one of the thirty-two original proprietors of the city of Leavenworth, laid out in 1854. In 1856 he became a citizen of Kansas, and in the spring of 1857 a permanent resident of the city of Leavenworth. In Nov., 1867, he was elected clerk of Leavenworth county; re-elected in 1869, again in 1873 and in 1875. He is now—1876—in office, and resides in the city of Leavenworth.

DILLARD, WILLIAM, born April 16, 1786, in Virginia. Elizabeth Jacobs was born Oct. 14, 1791, in the same State. They had two children born there, and moved to Todd county, Ky., where four children were born, and the family moved to Sangamon county, Ill., arriving late in 1830, and settled three and a half miles west of Springfield. Of their children—

BENJAMIN F., born Aug. 10, 1810, in Virginia, married in Sangamon county, Feb. 11, 1836, to Mary Crowder. They had seven children, two of whom died young. EUSTACIA A., born Dec. 30, 1836, married June 6, 1861, to Edward Keyes. See his name. JOHN J., born Sept. 10, 1838, died Feb. 7, 1865. WILLIAM R., born Jan. 14, 1842, married Jan. 15, 1873, to Eliza J. Randall, who was born April 29, 1847, in Sangamon county. They live five miles northwest of Springfield. MARY E., born April 9, 1844, lives with her mother. RIAL MARTIN, born Jan. 22, 1847, married Feb. 9, 1871, to Lerne Kincaid, and live in Logan county, near Elkhart. B. F. Dillard died Sept. 5, 1868, near Elkhart, and his widow (in 1874) resides five miles southwest of Springfield, on the farm where they settled in 1837.

ADALINE, born March 17, 1813, married Lewis Tomlinson. See his name.

SARAH married James Hannah. They had two children, and he died. She and her children reside near Chester, Randolph county.

ELIZABETH married Henry Dye, and resides near Chester.

VIRGINIA married William Bradley, who died, leaving a widow and three children in DuQuoin.

MARIAN married James Hannah. They have two children, and reside in Perry county, Ill.

JOHN A. married Mary Hathaway, have four children, and reside near Chester, Randolph county.

Mrs. Elizabeth Dillard died Nov. 28, 1854, in Sangamon county, and William Dillard died Oct. 7, 1868, in Randolph county, Ill.

DILLON, JOSHUA, was born Oct. 4, 1806, in Fauquier county, Va. The grandfather of Mr. Dillon sprang from Quaker ancestors. He resided in Loudon county, Va., and was a soldier in the army that achieved American Independence. His son, Samuel, married in 1800 to Nancy Fletcher, and served his country in the war of 1812-15. Samuel Dillon and wife raised two children, Joshua, whose name heads this sketch, and Harriet. Joshua Dillon was married March 29, 1829, in Culpepper county, Va., to Elizabeth S. Jeffries, who was born there, August 10, 1808. They united in Virginia with the Regular Primitive Baptists in 1832-3, and still belong to that church. They moved to Sangamon county, Ill., arriving June 18, 1834, in what is now Fancy Creek township. They brought four children with them, and seven were born in Sangamon county. Of their children—

WILLIAM, born Jan. 31, 1830, in Fauquier county, Va., raised in Sangamon county, married in Macon county, April 14, 1853, to Mary E. Cantrill. They had ten children, FANNIE and ELLA MAY died young. WILLIAM S., LOUIS E., FRANK, GEORGE J., MARY E., ROBERT LEE and ANNIE SHEPHERD, twins, and PARTHENIA J., reside with their parents. Dr. William Dillon is a practicing physician, and resides at Payson, Adams county, Ill.

ROBERT, born June 29, 1831, in Culpepper county, Va., raised in Sangamon county, married March 16, 1858, in Decatur, Ill., to Maria F. Jennings, who was born Nov. 10, 1837, in New Jersey. Mr. Dillon enlisted in 1862, in Co. E, 41st Ill. Inf., and after four months service, he was honorably discharged on account of physical disability. In the spring of 1866 they moved to Nebraska, and from there in April, 1871, to Colorado; thence to New Mexico in 1873. They have six children, FRANCES H., JOSHUA L., RICHARD O., SARAH E., PARTHENIA A. and WILLIAM J., and reside near Trinidad, Colorado.

SARAH F., born July 27, 1832, in Culpepper county, Va., married in Sangamon county, Ill., Sept. 5, 1849, to John H. Crow. See his name. She died Jan. 19, 1855, leaving three children. HENRY L., the second child, died, aged twenty-two years. ELIZABETH H. was married Oct. 11, 1874, to Albert D. Harrison. They have one child, LOUIS ARTHUR, the first great-grand-child of Joshua Dillon. Mr. Harrison is a druggist in Tecumseh, Neb. ISAAC R. Crow resides with his father.

ANN ELIZABETH, born Oct. 7, 1833, in Culpepper county, Va., married in Sangamon county, Oct., 1853, to Reuben McDannold. They have seven children, JOHN L., PARTHENIA L., MARY A., WILLIAM R., THOMAS I., EMMA J. and EDDIE, and reside three miles west of Springfield, Ill.

HARRIET E., born March 20, 1836, in Sangamon county, died in her twelfth year.

MARY E., born Oct. 18, 1837, in Sangamon county, was married Oct. 23, 1852, to Eli Ulery, and died Dec. 5, 1864, at Mt. Zion, Macon county, Ill. Three only, of her seven children are living, DONNA I., PERLIE and ELI. They reside with their father.

THOMAS J., born July 15, 1839, died in his twelfth year.

PARTHENIA R., was born Nov. 1, 1841, in Sangamon county, married Mar. 23, 1862, in Macon county, to John H. Crow. They have two children, SARAH F. and LILLIE R., and reside in Tecumseh, Neb. *See his name.*

JOB A., born June 5, 1843, in Sangamon county. He enlisted for three years, in 1861, in Co. E, 41st Ill. Inf., was captured at Jackson, Miss., spent seventy-three days in a rebel prison at Belle Isle, and was honorably discharged at the expiration of his term of service. He was educated at Mt. Zion, Ill., graduated in 1867, at the Law school in Albany, N. Y. He was married in June, 1867, in Sangamon county, Ill., to Huldah J. Oder. They have one living child, JESSE P., and reside in Tecumseh, Neb. Job A. Dillon moved to Nebraska in 1868, was elected to the State Senate in 1872, and is a practicing lawyer in Tecumseh.

JOSEPH J., born Feb. 5, 1845, in Sangamon county, was married Jan. 26, 1869, to Sophia J. Irwin. They have one child, JOSHUA, and reside near Tecumseh, Neb.

AMANDA JANE, born July 6, 1847, in Sangamon county, Ill., educated at Mt. Zion, Ill., married May 30, 1865, in Springfield, Ill., to Dr. S. B. McGlumphery, who was born Aug. 27, 1831, in Washington county, Penn. He attended college at Waynesburg, Green county, Penn., and arrived in Decatur, Ill., Oct. 25, 1859. He graduated at Rush Medical College, Chicago, Ill., Jan. 27, 1864. He moved to Tecumseh, Neb., arriving April 20, 1872, and was appointed by the Governor assistant physician to the Nebraska Hospital for the Insane, Aug. 18, 1874. Dr. S. B. McGlumphery and wife have two living children, LENA B. and NELLIE S., and reside in Lincoln, Neb.

Joshua Dillon and wife reside near Tecumseh, Neb.

DIXON, JAMES M., was born Aug. 3, 1807, in Harrison county, Ky. He was married in that county, Jan. 23, 1827, to Joannah Bird, who was born Nov. 20, 1807. They had four children in Mason county, Ky., and moved to Sangamon county, Ill., in the fall of 1834, in what is now Mechanicsburg township, where they had two living children. Of their six children—

WILLIAM A., born Nov. 10, 1827, in Kentucky, died in Sangamon county, in his twenty-fifth year.

SARAH A., born Oct. 1, 1829, in Kentucky, raised in Sangamon county, married in Logan county to Abraham Copland. They had five children, and Mrs. C. died, Feb. 26, 1872, leaving her family near Mt. Pulaski.

JESSE D., born Oct. 10, 1831, in Kentucky, raised in Sangamon county, went to Oregon in 1849, married there to Louisa Milligan, has three living children, JOANNAH, RICHARD and JOHN, and lives at Lafayette, Yamhill county, Oregon.

LUCINDA, born Sept. 6, 1833, in Mason county, Ky., married in Sangamon county to James L. Barbre. *See his name.*

HESTER D., born Feb. 9, 1840, in Sangamon county, married Sept. 4, 1861, to Thomas Stoker, who was born Dec. 27, 1836, in Fairfield county, O. They had four children. DAVID A. died in infancy. JAMES A. died at six years of age. ARTHUR E. and ARMANELLA live with their parents in Buffalo.

RICHARD, born Feb. 29, 1844, in Sangamon county, married May 6, 1874, and lives near Mechanicsburg.

James M. Dixon died Dec. 19, 1843, near Mechanicsburg, and his widow married John C. Eckel. *See his name.*

DIXON, JOHN, was born Oct. 8, 1784, in the village of Rye, Westchester county, N. Y. After spending fifteen years as a merchant in New York city, he closed his business there and started, April 13, 1820, for the west. He came by the way of Pittsburg, Pa., and Shawneetown, Ill., passing over the site of the city of Springfield before there was any thought of a town rising there, and settled nine miles further north, in what is now Fancy creek township. Four years later he moved to Fort Clark, where Peoria now stands. At the end of six years he moved north, into the country owned by the Winnebago Indians, and April 11, 1830, bought a ferry on Rock river from a half-breed Indian. From that time it was known as Dixon's ferry.

As a village began to grow, it was abbreviated to Dixon, and has now grown to the city of Dixon, Lee county, Ill. This is merely a synopsis of a long and useful life. John Dixon is now (1876) in his ninety-second year. Of his family, I have no record. He lives in the city founded by himself, and bearing his own name.

DIXON, JOSEPH, was among the earliest settlers on Horse creek. He was the principal mover in establishing Zion chapel, in Cotton Hill township, to which he afterwards deeded five acres of land for church and cemetery purposes. His family are buried there, but he died in 1844 at the house of a daughter, near Franklin, Morgan county, Ill., and was buried there.

DIVELBISS, JACOB, was born March 29, 1797, in Franklin county, Pa. He was there married, Jan. 19, 1819, to Catharine Shank, who was born Dec. 3, 1791, in Washington county, Md. They had three living children born in Westmoreland county, Pa., and moved west, traveling from Pittsburg by water to Beardstown, Ill. Mr. Divelbiss and his son Noah walked from there to Springfield, the family following in a hack, and arriving may 1, 1838. Of their three children—

CATHARINE, born July 8, 1822, in Westmoreland county, Pa., was married there April, 1838, to Richard Hodge. *See his name.*

NOAH, born Nov. 28, 1824, in Westmoreland county, Pa., was married in Springfield, Aug. 8, 1848, to Cordelia Watson. They had five children. NOAH, Jun., born April 27, 1849, was killed by a railroad accident at Sag bridge, near Lemont, Cook county, Ill., July 17, 1873. ABBIE lives with her parents. CHARLES died in infancy. FREDDIE died in the eleventh year of his age. NELLIE lives with her parents. Noah Divelbiss came to Springfield with his father, and was deputy and acting clerk of the Supreme Court of Illinois from 1844 to 1848. He is now teller in the Marine and Fire Insurance Company's Bank, and resides in Springfield.

AMANDA, born Feb. 3, 1829, in Westmoreland county, Pa., was married in Springfield, Sept. 1, 1846, to Frank Hickox. He is a brother of Virgil, but came to Sangamon county too late to be classed as an early settler. Mr. and Mrs. Hickox had eight children, two of whom died young. ALICE, born June 23, 1847, was married May 26, 1864, to William Warner, and resides at Selma, Alabama. FRANK, born April 4, 1849, was married June 27, 1872, to Matilda C. Bailey, a native of Newport, Indiana. They live in Springfield, Ill. ELBERT W., born March 14, 1852, in Petersburg, was married in Springfield Jan. 10, 1875, to Kate Griffith, of St. Louis. They reside in Springfield. IDA MAY, born Nov. 9, 1854, was married in St. Louis, April 15, 1870, to William J. White. They have one child, MAGGIE, and reside in Springfield. NELLIE and her mother reside in Springfield with Mrs. Hickox's father.

Jacob Divelbiss was elected Assessor and Treasurer of Sangamon county in 1853, serving two years. He learned the wagon-maker's trade in his native county, and prosecuted the business in Springfield for many years. He made a hand in the shop a full half century. Mrs. Catharine Divelbiss died Aug. 18, 1875, and Jacob Divelbiss died suddenly Feb. 11, 1876.

DODDS, MRS. MARGARET, the mother of Joseph and Rev. Gilbert Dodds, was married three times. Her maiden name was Craig. She was born in South Carolina, and first married a Mr. Watson, who died, and she married a Mr. Kirkpatrick. He was a patriot soldier, who, while serving in the Revolutionary army, was captured, and died in the British prison on Sullivan Island, near Charleston. She lost two brothers in the Revolutionary army, also. The soldiers of the English army took all her provisions, and when she begged the officer in command to leave her sufficient corn and oats for seed, he replied with a volley of profanity, and told her she would have no use for it, as some loyal subject of the king would occupy her plantation. She remembered having seen Washington and his army, and Cornwallis with his army. After the death of Mr. Kirkpatrick, she married James Dodds. They had five sons and a daughter in Carolina, and in 1795 started to move their family to Kentucky. Before they passed out of Carolina the father and daughter sickened and died. Mrs. Dodds, with her five sons, moved on; but, on arriving at Red river,

Tennessee, decided to stop, and there remained two years, when they again moved on, and arrived in Caldwell county, Ky., in 1797 or '8. After her son Joseph came to Sangamon county, she came and spent two years with him, then returned to Kentucky. Twelve or fifteen years later she again came to Sangamon county, and spent her remaining days in the families of her sons Joseph and Rev. Gilbert Dodds. She died in Sangamon county, Jan. 17, 1846, in the ninety-seventh year of her age.

DODDS, JOSEPH, born May 28, 1785, in Abbeville District, South Carolina. He was taken by his mother to Caldwell county, Ky., in 1797 or '8. He was there married, May 3, 1810, to Mattie Drennan. They had three children in Kentucky, and in Oct., 1817, he accompanied his father-in-law, William Drennan, to Illinois. In November they stopped on Wood river, in Madison county, two miles north of Alton, and remained there until the next March, when the men and boys connected with four families started for Sugar creek, Sangamon county, piloted by William Moore, an Indian Ranger. They reached their destination on the first of March, 1818, stopping in what is now Ball township, northwest of Sugar creek. There had not been any survey made, but the spot selected by Mr. Dodds, and on which he built his cabin, is now section twenty-nine, town fourteen, range five west, and that of William Drennan is section thirty-two, same town and range. Mr. Dodds had been too busy with his crop to build anything better than a double rail pen for the protection of his family. One son was born in Madison county, and Mr. Dodds brought his family to their new home Nov. 3, 1818, where seven children were born. Of their eleven children—

WILLIAM D., born Sept. 18, 1811, in Caldwell county, Ky., was married Sept. 18, 1834, to Polly Eades, in Sangamon county. They moved, in 1835, to DesMoines county, Iowa, where they brought up fifteen children, namely: WILLIAM E., born Oct. 13, 1835, was married Jan. 6, 1857, to Deborah C. Maines, who was born Jan. 29, 1839, in Clermont county, Ohio. They had five living children: REBECCA S., born Nov. 4, 1837, was married Dec. 4, 1874, to Edwin G. Moran, who was born Oct. 22, 1854, in Kane county, Ill. They have one child, Ethel L., and reside near Bartlett, Fremont county, Iowa. SARAH L. and JOSEPH W., twins, JAMES H. and MARY E. The four latter live with their parents, near Bartlett, Fremont county, Iowa. JOHN H., born Nov. 27, 1838, was married Sept. 13, 1866, to Lucy Parrott. They have one living child, WILLIAM D., and reside near Danville, Iowa. JOSEPH R., born Jan. 1, 1841, was married Feb. 7, 1861, to Sarah E. Maines. They have four living children, MARY L., CARRIE B., LULU A. and CYRENE E., and live near Corning, Holt county, Mo. CYRENE E., born Oct. 22, 1842, was married March 19, 1861, to Henry Mathews. They have five children, HENRY L., HOWARD A., WARREN C., SAMUEL W. and MARY L., and live near Danville, DesMoines county, Iowa. JAMES H., born Sept. 9, 1844, died Jan. 21, 1863. REBECCA J., born August 25, 1846, was married March 9, 1861, to George W. Collis. They have one child, CHARLES L., and live near South Flint, Iowa. SAMUEL C., born July 28, 1848, was married Jan. 22, 1869, to Sarah Allison. They have two children, FREDDIE A. and MARY E., and live near Danville, Iowa. CHARLES W., born April 15, 1850, was married Dec. 2, 1874, to Sonora Parrott, and live near Greenwood, Polk county, Iowa. OLIVER E., born Mar. 25, 1852, was married to Lillie A. Clark, Oct. 20, 1875, and live near South Flint, Ia. MARTHA L., born Dec. 24, 1853, was married to James J. J. Redding, Feb. 22, 1869. They have two living children, WILLIAM D. and LAURA L., and live near Pleasant Grove, DesMoines county, Iowa. AILSEY, or ALICE E., born Jan. 11, 1856, married Jan. 15, 1874, to William F. GRIFFEL. They have one child, CLARA E., and live near South Flint, Iowa. MARGARET E., LAVINA V. V., AARON E. and FINIS E. live with their parents. William D. Dodds and wife reside near South Flint, DesMoines county, Iowa.

JOHN, born Jan. 26, 1814, in Caldwell county, Ky., was married March 10, 1836, in Sangamon county, Ill., to Rebecca King. They had four children: JOSEPH C. married Elizabeth Levi. They have three children, and live in

Pawnee township. MARY M. lives with her mother. JOHN H. was married Dec. 12, 1872, to Mary J. Funderburk, and lives in Auburn township. SAMUEL K. lives with his mother. John Dodds died Oct. 21, 1859, and his widow, Mrs. Rebecca Dodds, lives in Auburn township.

MARY, born Jan. 16, 1816, in Caldwell county, Ky., was married in Sangamon county to Jonathan B. Coleman. *See his name.*

J. WILSON, born May 28, 1818, near Alton, Madison county, Ill., was married Feb. 27, 1845, in Sangamon county, to Minerva J. Easley. They had fifteen children; three died young. BENJAMIN A. died July 30, 1873, aged twenty-seven years. PERNECIA E. was married to John W. Phelps. They have two children, and reside in Ball township. MARTHA J. was married April 6, 1873, to Thomas Black, Jun. *See his name.* MARY E., JAMES F. E., AMANDA C., WILLIAM D., EDWIN E. and FREDERICK B. (twins), EMMA A., JOHN G. and JOSEPH A.; the nine latter live with their mother. J. W. Dodds died March 8, 1875, and his family reside in Ball township, near the Cumberland Presbyterian church.

MARGARET, born July 2, 1820, in Sangamon county, was married Oct. 22, 1840, to James B. Easley. *See his name.*

SAMUEL, born June 3, 1822, in Sangamon county, died unmarried, aged forty-two years.

JOSEPH, born Sept. 5, 1824, in Sangamon county, was married March 30, 1847, to Elizabeth A. Holland. They have six living children, ISABELLA J., WILLIAM A., MARTHA E., JOSEPH N., ABNER L. and MARY E., who reside with their parents in Ball township, two hundred yards west of where his parents settled in 1818, and four miles southeast of Chatham, Sangamon county.

MARTHA A., born Nov. 22, 1826, in Sangamon county, was married April 16, 1846, to Strawther Eades. They have six children. EVA was married Oct. 24, 1867, to William M. White. They have one child, and reside in Bates county, Mo. MARY E. was married May 6, 1869, to W. E. Purcell. They have one child, and live in Auburn township, Sangamon county. REBECCA J. was married Nov. 16, 1871, to B. F. Peacock. They reside near Springfield. WILLIAM A., FINIS E. and MARTHA A., reside with their parents near Johnstown, Bates county, Mo.

FRANCIS EWING, born Jan. 27, 1829, in Sangamon county, was married Feb. 22, 1855, to Pauline K. Fletcher. They had four children. JOHN S. died, aged ten years. MARTHA F., VIRGINIA E. and HENRIETTA A., live with their parents. F. E. Dodds and family live near Pawnee, Sangamon county.

NANCY E., born Sept. 14, 1831, was married Oct. 30, 1856, to Chester F. Maltby, and died Oct. 7, 1870. C. F. Maltby resides in Virden.

ALEXANDER F., born July 27, 1834, was married Dec. 24, 1860, to Amelia R. Planck, and died Jan. 4, 1864, leaving a widow and one child, EVA M., in Springfield, Ill.

Mrs. Martha Dodds died Jan. 19, 1853, and Joseph Dodds died Jan. 21, 1868, both on the farm where they settled in 1818. Joseph Dodds became very much dissatisfied soon after coming to Sangamon county, and determined to return to Kentucky. He sold all the property he could spare to obtain money to defray the expense, and loaded his wagon; but his horses strayed away the night previous to the time he intended starting, and before he could find them his money was gone. He was thus compelled to remain. After becoming reconciled, he often expressed his thanks to those horses for running away.

DODDS, GILBERT, born June 6, 1793, in Spartanburg District, South Carolina, and was taken by his mother, first to Tennessee, and from there to Caldwell county, Ky. He was married Oct. 12, 1815, in Caldwell county, to Mary Clinton. Her father (James Clinton) was Captain of a company in the Revolution. Gilbert Dodds and wife had four children in Kentucky, and moved to Sangamon county, Ill., arriving in August, 1824, in what is now Ball township, and joined his brother Joseph, who came six years previous. They had eight children in Sangamon county, namely—

JAMES C., born Oct. 30, 1816, in Caldwell county, Ky., raised in Sangamon county, was married in Morgan county April 12, 1840, to Jane Boulware. They had six living children. JAMES W. enlisted for three years, Aug. 9, 1862, at Springfield, in Co. B, 114th Ill. Inf. He was a Sergeant, and commanded his company at the battle of Guntown, in June, and was killed in battle at Tupelo, Miss., July 15, 1864. A cenotaph at the Cumberland Presbyterian church, on Sugar creek, gives the above facts. PHILIP B. died, aged ten years. RICHARD N., born Nov. 25, 1851, is a druggist in Springfield. NANCY C. married William Mason. *See his name.* MARY was married August, 1874, to Henry Wyatt, at Franklin, Morgan county, Ill. FREDERICK C. lives with his sister, Mrs. Mason. Mrs. Jane Dodds died July, 1869, and James C. Dodds died April 12, 1872, both in Sangamon county.

NANCY J., born Jan. 30, 1819, in Caldwell county, Ky., was married Dec. 15, 1842, in Sangamon county, to John L. Drennan. *See his name.* He died July 22, 1853, and his widow married John B. Weber. *See his name.*

MINERVA, born Aug. 22, 1820, in Caldwell county, Ky., lost a limb by a fall from a horse in 1840, in Sangamon county, and has been an invalid since that time. She resides with her sister, Mrs. J. B. Weber.

FRANCIS N., born Oct. 8, 1822, in Caldwell county, Ky., and brought up in Sangamon county, was married Dec. 9, 1857, in Cass county, to Margaret Brady. They moved to Lykins county, Kan., where his wife died April 21, 1866, leaving one child, EMMA F., who resides with her grandmother Brady, in Virginia, Cass county, Ill. F. N. Dodds was married Nov. 6, 1867, to Mrs. Mary C. Pedig. They have four children, CHARLES E., MARY A., CORA B. and SARAH L., who live with their parents. F. N. Dodds was a soldier in the Mormon war of 1845, and the Mexican war of 1846 and '7, from Sangamon county. He was in a Union regiment from Kansas, and aided in suppressing the slaveholders' rebellion. They reside near Colona, Carroll county, Mo.

WILLIAM D., born July 3, 1825, in Sangamon county, was married to Angeline Corbey, in Sept., 1855. They have five children, HARRIET, ROSA, VIRGINIA, ALBERT and FREDERICK, and live at Chilicothe, Livingston county, Mo. W. D. Dodds is a minister, connected with the Cumberland Presbyterian church.

AMANDA E., born Dec. 22, 1827, in Sangamon county, was married Jan. 1, 1852, to Chester F. Maltby, who was born July 13, 1825, in New York. Mrs. Maltby died Dec. 21, 1852, in Petersburg, leaving one child, AMANDA E., who was married Jan. 16, 1873, to John G. Cheney, and resides near Auburn, Sangamon county.

JOHN H., born Feb. 14, 1830, in Sangamon county, was married July 3, 1855, to Ellen Goldsby. They had four children, JULIA A., JAMES E., GILBERT and CHARLES H. John H. Dodds died Sept. 7, 1873, near Petersburg, Menard county. His family reside four miles south of Petersburg.

ALFRED S., born May 20, 1832, in Sangamon county, studied medicine. He enlisted in Co. K, 133d Ill. Inf., in 1861, for three years, as a private, but acted as a surgeon. He served three years, and was honorably discharged Jan., 1865, at New Orleans. He was married Sept. 10, 1863, to Maggie Cunningham. They have four children, WILLIAM, HARRY, RALPH and FLORENCE. Dr. A. S. Dodds is a practicing physician at Bolckow, Andrew county, Mo.

THOMAS C., born Nov. 6, 1834, served sixteen months in Co. F, 28th Ill. Inf. He was honorably discharged Nov. 24, 1862, at LaGrange, Tenn., and was married Nov. 4, 1869, to Lauretta Colby. They have three living children, ELBERT C., EUNICE A. and MARY C., and reside six miles south of Petersburg, Menard county, Ill.

MARGARET A., born Oct. 8, 1837, died unmarried, Feb. 21, 1875, at the residence of her sister, Mrs. J. B. Weber.

MARY E., born Nov. 2, 1840, in Sangamon county, was married Jan. 16, 1868, to William Colby. They have three children, ALFRED I., LYDIA and ALICE, and reside near Annawan, Henry county, Ill.

IRA R., born Feb. 16, 1843, in Sangamon county, Ill., served three years and eight months in Co. F, 28th Ill. Inf., and was honorably discharged July, 1865, at New Orleans. He is unmarried, and resides near Hutchinson, Reno county, Kansas.—1875.

Rev. Gilbert Dodds became a minister in the Cumberland Presbyterian church in early life. He was for many years pastor of the Sugar creek church, and was always an active, energetic advocate of temperance. In 1847 he moved to Menard county, a few miles south of Petersburg. Mrs. Mary Dodds died July 9, 1866, and Rev. Gilbert Dodds died May 3, 1872, both near Petersburg.

DOHERTY, JAMES HILL, was born June 3, 1775, in Virginia. His father, Cornelius Doherty, was a native of Ireland, and emigrated to America about 1760, settling in Virginia. He was married there to Mary Hill. They had twelve children—six of each sex. The family moved to Kentucky the year after Daniel Boone, and lived in the fort known as Estell station, for seven years. The son, James Hill Doherty, was married in 1819 in Cumberland county, Ky., to Mary Foster, who was born in 1794, in South Carolina. They had two children in Kentucky, and moved to Sangamon county, Ill., arriving in the fall of 1824 on Richland creek, near where Pleasant Plains now stands. They had one child there, and Mrs. Mary Doherty and her second child—Elizabeth—died in the fall of 1824. In 1832 James H. Doherty left Sangamon county and moved to Missouri, thence to Arkansas, and in 1836 to Decatur county, Tenn., where he died July 22, 1852. Of his two children—

JOHN F. F., born Dec. 21, 1820, in Cumberland county, Ky., partially brought up in Sangamon county, Ill., continued with his father until 1842, when he left Tennessee for Texas. He returned two years after, and was married Oct. 22, 1844, in Decatur county, Tenn., to Elizabeth J. Maxwell, who was born Sept. 6, 1823, in Humphreys county, Tenn. They had one child born and died in Tennessee, and eight in Texas, namely: JAMES H., born June 29, 1848, in Rusk county, Texas, resides with his parents. MARIA L., born April 5, 1850, in Nacogdoches county, Texas, married Jan. 20, 1871, to James H. Hall, a native of Mississippi. They have one child, FANNIE J., born Jan. 20, 1874. Mr. and Mrs. Hall reside in Coryell county, Texas, near Rainey's Creek postoffice. WILLIAM J., born March 17, 1852, in Rusk county, Texas, resides with his parents. ROBERT R. P., born Oct. 26, 1853, and died Nov. 28, 1874. JOHN P., born April 7, 1856, CHARLES F., born Aug. 3, 1858, and SUSAN M., born Nov. 28, 1862—the three latter in Nacogdoches county—and SARAH E., born Sept. 14, 1867, in Limestone county, all reside with their parents. John F. F. Doherty and wife reside near Rainey's creek postoffice, Coryell county, Texas, and twenty-eight miles from Waco, the nearest express office.

MARY, born Sept. 18, 1824, in Sangamon county, was married there, Nov. 30, 1847, to Charles W. Smith, who was born Jan. 31, 1823, in Overton county, Tenn. They have five children, NANCY, MATHIAS M., ELIZABETH, JOHN D. and MARY, who reside with their parents in Macoupin county, ten miles northeast of Carlinville, Ill.

DOUGHERTY, CHARLES, was born Feb., 1792, near Derry, county Donegal, Ireland. In 1817 he came to America, landing first in Canada, and from there to New York. He was married about 1820, in Washington county, Pa., to Mrs. Susannah Gants. She had nine children by her first marriage. Mr. and Mrs. Dougherty moved to Wheeling, Va., where they had one child, and from there to Greenup county, Ky. In 1835 they moved to Coles county, Ill., and from there to Sangamon county, arriving in May, 1838, in what is now Riverton. Mrs. D. died there, March 5, 1852. Their only son—

CHARLES, Jun., born Oct. 10, 1822, in Wheeling, West Va., married Feb. 20, 1849, to Amanda Constant. She died March 1, 1858, leaving three sons, JAMES, REZIN and JOHN. Charles Dougherty, Jun., was married March 5, 1859, to Mrs. Susan E. Connelly, whose maiden name was Conant. They have three children, OMAR, ALLEN and LYDIA J., who live with their parents, one mile northwest of Dawson.

Charles Dougherty, Sen., resides with his son, Charles, Jun.—1874.

DONNER.—A family named Donner lived near Salem, Rowan county, N. C., in the latter part of the eighteenth century. The parents were German

—33

speaking, but it is not known whether they emigrated from Germany or were born in this country. They had three sons and three daughters, all born in North Carolina, and moved to Jessamine county, Ky., about 1811. They moved with their children to Decatur county, Ind., and in 1828 came to Sangamon county. Both died at a very advanced age, and were buried about three miles east of Springfield, near the Bennett school house. Of their children—

DONNER, LYDIA, born Dec., 1783, near Salem, Rowan county, N. C., accompanied her parents to Jessamine county, Ky., and was there married to James Walters. They had nine children in Kentucky, and in 1829 moved to Decatur county, Ind., where Mr. Walters died in June, 1830. Mrs. Walters moved to Sangamon county, arriving in Auburn township in 1839. *See Lydia Walters.*

DONNER, ELIZABETH, was married in Jessamine county, Ky., to William Walters. See the name of their son—

GREEN B. Walters.

DONNER, GEORGE, was born about 1786, in Rowan county, N. C., came with his parents to Jessamine county, Ky., and from there to Decatur county, Ind. He was there married and had five children. Mrs. Donner died there, and Mr. D., with his family, came to Sangamon county, Ill., in the autumn of 1828, settling about three miles northeast of Springfield. George Donner was married in Sangamon county to Mary Blue. They had two living children, and Mrs Mary Donner died in Sangamon county. Mr. Donner's five eldest children married in the latter county, and in 1838 he took his two children by the second marriage, and, in company with his son William and family, and his brother Jacob and family moved to Texas. They raised one crop fifty miles south of Houston. Not liking the country, they all returned in 1839, and George Donner moved on the farm he left. About two years afterwards he married Mrs. Tamsen Dozier, whose maiden name was Eustace. They had three children (all girls) born in Sangamon county. Of the five children of George Donner by his first marriage—

MARY, born in Indiana, was married in Sangamon county, Ill., to George Weaver. They had four children, and Mr. Weaver died, and she married Adam Harmon. They had two children, and Mr. H. died at Island Grove. The family live near Libertyville, Iowa.

WILLIAM, born May 3, 1812, in Decatur county, Ind., was married March, 1832, in Sangamon county, Ill., to Elizabeth Hunter, who was born May 1, 1819, in Gallatin county, Ky., and came to Sangamon county in the autumn of 1830. They had two children, and in 1838 moved to Texas with his father, where one child was born. He returned to Sangamon county in 1839, where two children were added to the family. Of their five children: JAMES W., born Jan. 7, 1834, in Sangamon county, was married April 20, 1857, to Elizabeth Snodgrass, who was born Feb. 6, 1837, in Harrison county, Indiana. They have six living children, GEORGE A., CHARLES F., NETTIE J., IRVING, ALBERT F. and DORA E., and live in Clear Lake township, one mile south of Riverton. James W. Donner enlisted August 8, 1862, in Co. H., 114th Ill. Inf., for three years. He was severely wounded by a musket ball, through the hip joint, at the battle of Guntown, Miss., June 10, 1864, was captured and taken to Mobile. After one month, sent to Cahawba, remained three months, thence to Macon, Georgia, and from there to the prison pens at Andersonville. As the close of the rebellion approached, all the prisoners who could travel on foot were removed, leaving about one hundred there. The prison was surrounded by artillery, bearing on the stockade. The rebel guards, in order to escape capture, cut down the wheels of the artillery, and fled before the Union forces. J. W. Donner, with others in like situation, was sent by Capt. Wirz to Thomasville by railroad, thence to the Union lines at Jacksonville, Florida, which was reached the latter part of April. They were sent by water to Hilton Head and Annapolis, Md. Then by railroad to Chicago and Springfield, reaching home July 10, 1865. He now draws a pension. SARAH E., born Sept. 27, 1836, was married July 27, 1855, to Gilbert Sponsler, who was born Sept. 18, 1833, in Dauphin county, Penn., came with his parents to Sangamon county in 1841, and settled in what is now Woodside township. They have four children:

WILLIAM A., GEORGE A., MARY F. and ALICE J., and reside in the Donner settlement, four miles east of Springfield. GEORGE T., born May 27, 1839, in Texas, enlisted at Springfield, August, 1862, in Co. G., 114th Ill. Inf., for three years, served full time, and was honorably discharged with the regiment at the close of the war. He was married March, 1868, to Sarah Scott, east of Springfield. They have three children, WILLIAM, NANCY M. and HARVY O., and reside near Latham, Logan county, Ill. RACHEL T., born May 7, 1842, was married Jan. 20, 1857, to Felix Carver. *See his name.* JOSEPH, born Sept. 30, 1845, enlisted, May 22, 1862, in Co. B, 68th Ill. Inf., for one hundred days, served four months, and was honorably discharged. He was married Nov. 22, 1868, to Mary L. Butler, who was born June 5, 1849. They have one child, LINNIE B., and reside with his mother, near Springfield, Ill. William Donner died July 22, 1867, within two miles of where his father settled in 1828. His widow, Mrs. Elizabeth Donner, resides four miles east of Springfield.

ELIZABETH, born in Indiana, was married in Sangamon county, Ill., to Absolom Harmon. They had six or seven children, and reside near Libertyville, Jefferson county, Iowa.

SUSANNAH, born in Indiana, was married in Sangamon county, Ill., to Daniel Blue. They had three children, and moved to Hancock county, Ill.

LYDIA, born in Indiana, was married in Sangamon county, Ill., to John Vancil. They had three or four children, and moved to Hancock county, Ill.

Of the children of George Donner's second marriage—

ELITHA CUMI, born in Sangamon county, Ill., lived through the disaster on the mountains, in 1846, and was married in California to Perry McCoon. He was killed by a runaway horse. His widow was married Dec. 8, 1853, to Benjamin W. Wilder. They have six children, and reside at Elk Grove, Sacramento county, California.

LEANNA C., born Dec. 5, 1834, near Springfield, Ill., lived through the disaster on the mountains 1846-7, was married in Sacramento City, Cal., Sept. 26, 1852, to John App. They had four children.

REBECCA, born Feb. 9, 1854, resides with her parents. LEONARD F. died in his sixth year, in San Francisco. JOHN Q. and LUCY E. reside with their parents near Jamestown, Tuolumne county, California.

Children of the third marriage—

FRANCES E., born July 4, 1840, in Sangamon county, Ill., lived through the disaster on the mountains, was educated at St. Dominic Catholic school, at Benicia, was married Nov. 24, 1858, in California, to William R. Wilder. They reside near Point of Timber, Contra Costa county, California.

GEORGIANA, born Dec. 3, 1841, near Springfield, Ill., lived through the disaster on the mountains, was educated at Benecia Catholic school, and married Nov. 4, 1863, to Washington A. Babcock, in California. They have three children, HENRY A., FRANK B. and EDITH M., and reside at Mountain View, Santa Clara county, California.

ELIZA P., born March 8, 1843, near Springfield, Ill., lived through the disaster on the mountains, was educated at St. Dominic Catholic school, at Benicia, Cal., was married in same State, Oct. 10, 1861, to Sherman O. Houghton, who was born April 10, 1828, in New York city. She is his second wife. He served in the 1st. regiment N. Y. Vol. Inf. through the Mexican war, was Mayor of San Jose, Cal., in 1855 and 1856, represented California in the 42d and 43d Congress. They have six children, ELIZA P., SHERMAN O., Jun., CLARA H., CHAS. D., FRANCIS F. and STANLEY W., all born in California except the last, who was born in Washington, D. C. Hon. S. O. Houghton and family reside in San Jose, Cal. He is a practicing lawyer.

George Donner was a good man. It is said by his former neighbors in Sangamon county, that it appeared to be a pleasure for him to do a kind act. For an account of the sad fate of himself and wife, see sketch of the Reed and Donner emigrant party.

DONNER, TOBIAS, born in 1788, near Salem, Rowan county, N. C., was a brother of George and Jacob, and the three sisters, Susannah, Lydia and Elizabeth. He moved with his father's family to Jessamine county, Ky., and was married there to Nancy Bettis, and moved to Decatur county, Ind. From there to he vicinity of Athens, Menard county, Ill., where they brought up a family.

DONNER, JACOB, was born about 1790, near Salem, Rowan county, N. C., accompanied the family to Jessamine county, Ky., thence to Decatur county, Ind., and from there (in 1828) to Sangamon county, Ill., where he was married to Mrs. Elizabeth Hook, whose maiden name was Blue, a sister of his brother George's second wife. She had two children by a former marriage, namely—

SOLOMON E. Hook, born Jan. 11, 1832, in Sangamon county, Ill., lived through the disaster on the mountains, and was married in California, Nov. 7, 1866, to Alice Roberts. They have three children, and reside in Winters, Yolo county, California.

WILLIAM Hook, born in 1834, in Sangamon county, Ill., lived through the disaster on the mountains, but on reaching food, arose in the night, ate too much, and died from the effects in 1847.

Of the five children of Jacob Donner and wife—

GEORGE, born August, 1837, near Springfield, Ill., lived through the disaster on the mountains, and was married in California, June 12, 1862, to Margaret J. Watson. They have six children. George Donner died February, 1875, and his family live at Sebastapol, Sonoma county, Cal.

MARY M., born March 18, 1839, near Springfield, Ill., experienced the hardships of the disasterous trip through the mountains in 1847, accompanied Mrs. Reed to California, and was married there to Sherman O. Houghton. Mrs. Mary Houghton died June 21, 1860, leaving one child, MARY M., who was born June 7, 1860, and resides with her father, in San Jose, Cal. See the name of Sherman O. Houghton, in connection with the family of George Donner.

ISAAC, born in 1841, in Sangamon county, LEWIS and SAMUEL, born in the same county, all three died from starvation and exposure in the California mountains during the winter of 1846 and '7.

For an account of the death of Jacob Donner and wife, see sketch of the Reed and Donner emigrant party.

DONNER, SUSANNAH, born about 1796, in Rowan county, N. C. She was married in Jessamine county, Ky., to Micajah Organ. See his name. They came to Sangamon county, Ill., in 1828, stopping east of Springfield, and moved in 1829 to what is now Auburn township.

DORRANCE, DANIEL, was born in 1768, in Hartford, Conn. He was married in 1799, in Seneca county, N. Y., to Margaret Gilland, a native of Pennsylvania. They had two children, and moved to Ontario county, where Mrs. Dorrance died, Nov. 30, 1812. Mr. D. there married Mrs. Mary Price, whose maiden name was Arnold. They had one child, and Mrs. Mary Dorrance died Sept. 10, 1815. Mr. D., with his three children, moved to Sangamon county, Ill., arriving June 8, 1822, in what is now Woodside township, and in the spring of 1823 moved to what is Loami township. Of his three children—

MARGARET, born March 30, 1800, in Seneca county, N. Y., married in Sangamon county to Henry Kinney, Jun. See his name.

GERSHOM, born Nov. 23, 1801, in Seneca county, N. Y., married in Sangamon county, Nov. 28, 1832, to Louisa H. Woodworth, who was born in 1814, in Massachusetts. They had nine children; three died in infancy, and DANIEL died at ten years. MARY L. married Nathan T. Underwood, have six children, and reside in Loami township. MARGARET E. married Benjamin Bane; had three children, CORA BELL, CARRIE and FREDDIE. Mr. Bane died Feb. 5, 1872. His widow and children reside one and a quarter miles east of Loami. JOHN J. resides in Christian county. LYDIA A., married George Collins and died, leaving one child, PHILIP. CLARISSA M., unmarried, and resides in Lincoln. Mrs. Louisa Dorrance died Feb. 1, 1855, and Gershom Dorrance resides one and a quarter miles east of Loami. He served in a lighthorse company from Springfield in 1831 and '2, in the Black Hawk war.

MARY A., born in 1814 or '15, in Ontario county, N. Y., married in Sangamon county in 1832, to David Lindsay. See his name.

Daniel Dorrance never married after coming to Illinois, and died Sept. 10, 1831, in Loami township. He was about seven years old when the battle of Lexington was fought, and he remembered having heard the firing of cannon at some of the battles that took place soon after. His father was a native Englishman, but was a surgeon in the revolutionary army, and lost his life in the service. A powder horn once owned by Dr. Dorrance is now in possession of his grandson, Gershom Dorrance, near Loami. It may have been picked up by him on some battle-field. It is carved with figures of men, trees, animals and other hieroglyphics, and the following inscription:

February 14, 1758.

Simon Hough's Horn, made at No. 4.

I Powder with my Brother Ball,
A Herow like, I conquer all:
Drumbs a Beeting, colours flying,
Trumpets sounding, men a Dying,
These are the bold Affects of

WAR.

DOUGLAS, MILTON, was born Sept. 25, 1816, in Greene county, Ky., and came to Island Grove, Sangamon county, in the fall of 1833. He was married Nov. 7, 1838, to Sarah A. Castleberry, who was born in 1820, in Lycoming county, Pa. They had three children, namely—

CHRISTINA, born in 1839, in Sangamon county, married John Clawson, have five children, and live near Beatrice, Neb.

WILLIAM J., born March 12, 1841, in Sangamon county, married Nov. 30, 1865, to Adaline Rawlings, who was born Jan. 12, 1841, in Lawrence county, Ill. They have four children, WILLIAM H., MILTON, ANNIE M. and GEORGE, and reside two and a half miles east of Berlin.

MARY E., born Sept. 19, 1843, married Jeremiah King. See his name.

Mrs. Sarah A. Douglas died Dec. 19, 1848, and Milton Douglas married Eliza Underwood, and she died in October, 1853. Mr. D. was again married Sept. 4, 1854, to Frances M. Rude, who was born March 20, 1833, in Morgan county, Ill. They had five living children, namely—

SARAH A., born Aug. 4, 1855, was married Aug. 10, 1871, to Joseph G. Cole. They have one child, LIZZIE, and reside in Shelby county, near Dalton City, Moultrie county.

CARRIE, MARGARET A., MARTHA E. and STEPHEN A., reside with their mother.

Milton Douglas died Sept. 15, 1869, and his widow resides two and a half miles east of Berlin.

DOUGLAS, SAMUEL, was born about 1767, in Loudon county, Va., married there to Amelia Johnson, a native of the same county. They moved to Adair county Ky., thence to Sangamon county, Ill., arriving in 1827, on Spring creek. They brought five children, namely—

THOMAS, born in Virginia, married in Sangamon county to Lucinda Hanks, moved to Iowa, thence to Oregon, have six children, and reside near Marysville, California.

SARAH, married in Kentucky, and remained there.

ELIZABETH died, aged twenty-five years.

MARGARET, married in Kentucky to William Hall. See his name.

JAMES, born March 12, 1809, in Loudon county, Va., came to Sangamon county, Ill., in 1827. He was married at the time of the "deep snow," Feb. 22, 1831, to Ellen Ralston. They had three children. THOMAS, born Dec. 16, 1832, was married Jan. 20, 1856, to Amanda Young. They have six living children, ISABELLA, ADALINE, LIONA, CHARLES, MILLIE J. and HATTIE MAY, and reside in Springfield. He is foreman in the T., W. and W. R. R. Company's shops. NATHAN, born August 4, 1835, was married in Feb., 1856, to Louisa Young. They have five children, ELLEN, JAMES M., MARY, ANN, and one other. Mrs. D. died in 1871, in Taylorville, and he married Nettie Phillips, at Elkhart. They have one child. Nathan Douglas is employed by the T., W. and W. R. R. Company, and resides at Bluff City, Ill. NANCY J., born Sept. 28, 1838, married Robert Stokes. They have five children, and reside near Edinburg, Ill. Mrs. Ellen Douglas died Sept., 1854, and James Douglas married Mrs. Nancy Keeling, whose maiden name was Dawson. She died.

JANE, born Dec. 6, 1817, in Adair county, Ky., was married in Sangamon county to Simmons Bradley. See his name.

Samuel Douglas died in 1830, in Sangamon county, and his widow died about 1857, near Mt. Pleasant, Iowa.

DOZIER, MRS. NANCY, born May, 1793, in Montgomery county, Ky., and married there to John Dozier. He died in 1829, leaving a widow and seven children. Mrs. Dozier, with part of her children, moved to Sangamon county, Ill., arriving in November, 1833, in what is now Woodside township, and the next spring moved to what is now Cotton Hill township. Of her seven children—

JAMES I., born Jan. 1, 1811, in Montgomery county, Ky., married Jan. 22, 1843, in Sangamon county, to Mary W. Armstrong. They had nine children. JANE, born Oct. 24, 1843, in Sangamon county, was married June 22, 1864, to George Dalbey, who was born in Pickaway county, O., Jan. 31, 1830. They have five children, GEORGE W., EDWIN J., CHARLES N., JAMES H. and SAMUEL. All live with their parents in Springfield. Mr. D. is trading in cattle in west Missouri. THOMAS. W., born April 14, 1845, married March 17, 1872, to Mary F. Greenawalt. They had one child, GEORGE A., and reside in Cotton Hill township, near Zion chapel. ZACHARIAH, JOHN, CAROLINE A., NANCY A., JAMES I., Jun., EDWARD S. and FRANK, reside with their parents on the farm where Mr. Dozier settled in 1834. It is between Horse and Brush creeks, in Cotton Hill township.

JANE, born February, 1814, in Kentucky, married there to J. Lenegar. She died in 1866 in Clarke county, Ill., leaving her husband and several children. Her son JOHN was a member of an Illinois regiment, and died at Jackson, Tenn., during the rebellion.

SUSAN, born in 1816, in Kentucky, married there to Bedford W. Higgins. See his name.

CAROLINE, born in 1818, in Kentucky, married in Sangamon county to Jackson Matthews, and both died in Sangamon county.

AMERICA, born in 1820, in Kentucky, married in Sangamon county to Joseph Mathews, and she died.

ANN, born in 1822, in Kentucky, married in Sangamon county to Daniel Keys, and reside near Pana. See his name.

JOHN, born March 5, 1830, in Montgomery county, Ky., married in Sangamon county, Jan. 7, 1855, to Susan Womack. They had five children; one died, aged four years. JAMES A., WILLIAM J., JESSE L. and NANCY E. reside with their parents, two miles west of Pawnee.

Mrs. Nancy Dozier was married in 1836 to Joseph Matthews, Sen. He died in 1844, and she died March 23, 1852, both in Sangamon county.

DRENNAN, WILLIAM, born April 9, 1768, in Pendleton District, South Carolina. Mary Thomas was born Jan. 13, 1771. They were married about 1790. Six of their children were born in that district, and they moved to Caldwell county, Ky., about 1803, where they had six children. In the fall of 1817 they moved to Illinois, first stopping on Wood river, about two miles from Alton, in Madison county. Their destination was the San-ga-ma country, but it was more economical to remain idle that winter than to move up, and thus incur the necessity of hauling provisions for themselves and stock. Early in 1818 William Drennan, his half brother, Joseph Drennan, his son-in-law, Joseph Dodds, and George Cox, left their families near Alton, and, with their teams, farming implements, provisions, and all the young men and boys belonging to the families who were able to assist in making a home, started, piloted by a white man named William Moore, who had belonged to a company that had been over the country before, in fighting the Indians. He was called an Indian Ranger. Arriving at Sugar creek, they took a day or two for exploring, and on March 10, 1818, drove to the spot on which William Drennan built his cabin and which proved to be section 32, town 14, range 5 west, when the government made its survey. It is on the northwest side of Sugar creek, and about twelve miles nearly due south of Springfield, and near where the Sugar creek Cumberland Presbyterian church now stands. Immediately after their arrival they built two cabins. One was occupied by George Cox alone. The other was occupied for the summer by William and Joseph Drennan and Joseph Dodds.

That was the one spoken of as belonging to William Drennan. As they had not the slightest idea of cultivating the prairie, these three men agreed to clear all the land they could in one body, and have a crop from it that year in common, with the understanding that before another year they were all to work together until an equal sized piece was cleared for the other two. They cleared the timber from about fifteen acres, fenced it, plowed as well as they could among the roots and stumps with a little short wooden mould-board plow, and planted it in corn and pumpkins. The soil in the timber was very light—so much so that in some places they would almost sink in over their shoes. In fencing this land, they inclosed about three-fourths of an acre of prairie. After they had plowed and planted their crop, one of the men suggested that it was quite a waste to have that under fence and nothing growing on it, and proposed that they break it up and plant something on it. In order to make sure work, they uncoupled one of their wagons, hitched four horses to the forward wheels, and fastened their wooden mould-board plow to the axle. They soon found this was a failure.

Try as they would, the plow would not enter the sod, and they reluctantly gave it up. While they were taking off the team and plow, one of the boys, full of fun and mischief, took up a hoe and began to shave the grass off, saying he could break the prairie with his hoe. That suggested an idea to one of the men, and he, also, took a hoe and began shaving the grass. It was the work of but a few minutes to remove the sod from a spot several feet in diameter. He then called one of the other men, and proposed that, as they were well advanced with their work, and there were seven or eight of them, and all had hoes, that they call all hands together, and shave the grass from the whole piece, plant something on it, and see what would be the result. The man spoken to first, laughed at the idea as ridiculous, but after studying a moment, he fell in with it, and the men and boys were all called up, and the grass shaved off, holes dug, and corn and pumpkin seed planted. They did not touch it any more; that killed the grass. The crop was fully twice as much in proportion to the area, as that planted among the stumps, and the next spring it broke up the nicest of any land they had ever seen. This taught them an important lesson, and caused them to make greater exertions to induce some one to invent a plow that would break the prairie. I have this account from the venerable William Drennan, who was one of the young men that assisted in doing the work, and who has lived in sight of the spot to the present time. Several years elapsed before a plow was invented that would do good work at breaking. In the mean time the early settlers continued clearing their land, that they might have it to cultivate, and were always uneasy for fear their timber would be exhausted.

There can be but little doubt that the same labor required to destroy the timber on one acre would have shaved the grass from two acres, with no better implements than a hoe. They could, by that means, have had better land to cultivate, twice the quantity of grain raised, and saved their timber, but the probability is they never thought of it. After the provisions they brought with them were exhausted, one of their number would return south, load a couple of horses with provisions, salt, and other indispensibles, in regular pack saddle style, and bring them to their new home. The distance was between sixty and seventy miles. They brought cows in the spring, and had plenty of milk. Wild honey was abundant, and Mr. Drennan told the writer that two of their number would cut down a hollow tree where bees had stored their wealth, and with a few hours work, would bring in from two to five gallons of honey. While they were doing this, others of their number would be looking for more bee trees, so that they always had four or five trees ahead, and knew just where to go when they needed more honey. For meat, they would hunt as the necessities required, some times one, and often all would hunt. In warm weather they would take venison, the breast of turkeys and geese, cut the meat into thin slices, sprinkle a small quantity of salt on it, and dry it on a frame work of sticks about three feet high, setting the frame in the sun, with a smouldering fire underneath. In this way the meat would soon be cured, and ready for use at any time. This they called jerked meat, a considerable supply of which could be kept on hand. Fresh meat, jerked meat, milk, honey and bread, constituted their bill of fare during the first summer. As trips were made back and forth, some of the younger sons of those who had families were brought to the new settlements. After the crops were cultivated, the men who had families returned to them, leaving the unmarried men and boys to take care of the property. The four men who came up in the spring, all brought their wives and children in the fall of that year. Mr. Cox arrived first, Joseph Drennan next, and, William Drennan, with his son-in-law, Joseph Dodds, came together, arriving Dec. 3, 1818. Of the twelve children of William Drennan, Sen.—

MATTIE, born in South Carolina, married in Kentucky to Joseph Dodds. *See his name.*

SAMUEL, born in South Carolina, married in Kentucky to Celia Greer, and died there, leaving a family.

WILLIAM, born Oct. 15, 1797, in Pendleton district, S. C., came to Kentucky, and from there to Sangamon county with his father, arriving March 10, 1818, in what is now Ball township. He was married May 30, 1822, in Sangamon county, to Margaret Anderson. They had twelve children, all born in Sangamon county, viz: JAMES A., born Aug. 6, 1828, married Dec. 8, 1853, to Rachel Cannon. They have six children, JANNETTA F., MARY E., ROBERT W., MINNIE W., IRA and FREDERICK, and reside in Ball township, five miles northeast of Auburn. SAMUEL, born Oct. 30, 1829, went to the Pacific coast in 1852, was married there May 28, 1868, to Louisa Fernald, who was born April 4, 1839, in North Berwick, Maine. They have three children, EDITH A., MABEL L., and DORA A., and reside in Santa Cruz, Santa Cruz county, Cal. JOHN T., born Jan. 13, 1832, enlisted August 9, 1862, at Chatham, in Co. I, 73d Ill. Inf., for three years. He was wounded at the battle of Chickamauga, Sept. 20, 1863, lay five days on the battlefield, before medical aid was given. He recovered, but is permanently disabled. He was discharged on account of physical disability, June 16, 1864, and resides with his parents in Ball township. WILLIAM, Jun., born March 7, 1833, was married Feb. 22, 1853, to Lucinda Cannon, and moved to Shelby county, Mo. They had four children, HENRY G., CHARLES W., DANIEL D. and MARGARET F. William Drennan enlisted in Co. F, 37th Mo. Inf., in 1862, to aid in suppressing the slaveholders' rebellion. A body of rebels, under the notorious Bill Anderson, lay in ambush until three companies of Union soldiers were in their power, when two companies were nearly annihilated, eighty men being slaughtered, it is believed, without an opportunity to surrender. It occurred near Centralia, Boone county, Mo., Sept. 27, 1864. William Drennan was among the slain. His widow and children reside near Shelbyville, Shelby county, Mo. MARTHA A., born April 25, 1835, married William Kenney. *See his name.* REBECCA, born May 3, 1837, married James Ewing, April 7, 1857. They have four children, ALICE M., CORA B., WILLIAM M. and JAMES E., and reside at Ivanhoe, Shelby county, Mo. MARGARET, born Jan. 30, 1839, resides with her parents. NANCY, born Nov. 29, 1840, married James M. Nuckolls. *See his name.* They had one child, LAURA M. She resides with her mother. Mrs. Nuckolls married James Bennington. They have one child, JOHN. Mr. Bennington and family reside five miles east of Auburn, in Pawnee township. ROBERT died, aged sixteen years. FRANCIS N., born July 5, 1845, married Sarah Graham. They have no children, and reside near Johnstown, Bates county, Mo. MARY E., born March 24, 1847, married Benjamin F. Fletcher. *See his name.* EMILY J., born May 18, 1851, married Charles I. Pulliam. *See his name.* William Drennan had his left hand amputated April 3, 1875, as the only way to save his life from the effects of a cancer. He and his wife are both living in view of the farm where he assisted his father in making improvements, March 10, 1818. There is no other man living in the county who was in it at that time. He is consequently, at this date—1876—beyond a doubt, *the oldest inhabitant of Sangamon county.*

RACHEL, born in South Carolina, married Alexander Ritchie, in Sangamon county, Ill. He died at Sulphur Springs, Hopkins county, Texas, where she now resides—1876.

THOMAS, born in South Carolina, was married in Sangamon county, to Eveline Moffitt. They had seven children. JAMES A. and REBECCA are unmarried and reside with their mother. MARY F. married James Bridges. See his name. THOMAS L. married Mary Knotts, and live in Ball township. John C. and MARTHA E. are unmarried and reside with their mother. Thomas Drennan died Sept. 13, 1848, and his widow resides in Ball township.

EZEKIEL N., born June 28, 1802, in South Carolina, was married June 16, 1825, in Sangamon county, Ill., to Mary Viney, who was born Dec. 26, 1807, in Kentucky, and came with her parents to Illinois, in 1817. E. N. Drennan and wife had ten living children in Sangamon county, Ill., and they moved to Adair county, Mo., in Sept. 1859. Of their ten children, WILLIAM S. V., born July 20, 1826, died unmarried, Aug., 1857, at Granby, Newton county. Mo. ALFRED D., born May 5, 1828, died unmarried, March 14, 1852, in Sangamon county, Ill. MINERVA J., born Jan. 29, 1830, in Sangamon county, was married there, August 29, 1848, to William Orr, who was born Feb. 18, 1820, in Ohio. They had three children in Sangamon county, and moved, in Sept., 1856, to Kirksville, Adair county, Mo., where one child was born. Of their children, EMMA F., born June 27, 1849, in Sangamon county, Ill., was married Nov. 18, 1868, to Oliver Ridgeway, of Sangamon county, Ill., have three children, *George, Charlotte* and *Arthur*, and live in Nodaway county, Mo. HENRIETTA E., born April 27, 1852, and ALFRED R., born March 18, 1855, both in Sangamon county, and MARY A., born Feb. 5, 1858, in Missouri, the three latter live with their parents. William Orr and wife reside near Troy Mills, Adair county, Mo. NEWTON L., born April 17, 1832, in Sangamon county, married in Adair county, Mo., Nov. 22, 1860, to Phebe Corbin. They had three children, WILLIAM L. THOMAS L. and ALFRED E. Mrs. Phebe Drennan died May 7, 1873, and he was married Sept. 10, 1874, to Martha L. Nevins, of Macoupin county, Ill. They reside near Troy Mills, Mo. SARAH C., born July 17, 1834, died unmarried in Adair county, Mo., June 16, 1872. REBECCA V., born June 30, 1836, was married Mar. 20, 1855, to Rufus Cavett, of Sangamon county, Ill. She died Oct., 1858, in Ringgold county, Iowa, leaving two children, MEDORA E. and JANE, who live with their father in Adair county, Mo. NANCY V., born Oct. 28, 1838, was married April, 1858, to Daniel M. Edwards, of Macoupin county, Ill. They have three children, LAURA A., GENERAL D. M. and MARY F., all born in Macoupin county, Ill., and they moved to Adair county, Mo., in Nov., 1866, where two children were born, NONIE V. and FREDERICK E. D. M. Edwards and family reside near Kirksville, Adair county, Mo. AMANDA K., born Nov. 30, 1840, in Sangamon county, Ill., was married Dec. 30, 1860, to Silas G. Phipps, of Adair county, Mo. They have eight children, SAMUEL E., OSCAR A., CHARLES E., EFFIE M., MINNIE R. MARY F., VAN, and D. GRANVEL, and reside in Randolph county, Mo. MARY L., born April 22, 1845, in Sangamon county, Ill., resides in Kansas City, Mo. THOMAS J., born Nov. 12, 1847, in Sangamon county, resides in Adair county, Mo. Mrs. Mary Drennan died Dec. 2, 1871, and Ezekial N. Drennan died Aug. 1, 1872, both in Adair county, Mo.

MARGARET, born in Kentucky, was married in Sangamon county, Ill., to John Ritchie. They moved to Henry county, Iowa, where he died, leaving a widow and five children near New London, Henry county, Iowa.

JOHN L., born Feb. 18, 1808, in Caldwell county, Ky., was married 1830, in Sangamon county, Ill., to Mary A. Alexander. They had three children. MARY J. married John Hazlett, and resides near Edinburg, Christian county, Ill. THOMAS H. married Mary McKinnie, and resides in Ball township. MELINDA J. married J. W. Darneille, and both died. Mrs. Mary A. Drennan died in 1842, and John L. Drennan was married Dec. 15, 1842, to Nancy J. Dodds. They had six children. GEORGE L., born Nov. 27, 1843, was married, Jan. 11, 1870, to Mary E. Ridgeway. She died Nov. 24, 1872, leaving one child, FRANK L., in Nodaway county, Mo., where he and his father reside. BENJAMIN F., born Feb. 15, 1845, married Anna E. Wheeler. They have three children, CHARLES F., FLORENCE M. and ADELLA, and reside in

Ball township, three miles southeast of Chatham. GILBERT C. is in the mercantile business with James A. Able and William R. Lockridge, in Pawnee. CHARLES lives at Pawnee. DAVID A. born Feb. 2, 1851, graduated at Rush Medical College, Chicago, Feb. 16, 1875, and is a practicing physician in Pawnee. ALFRED L. was married March 9, 1875, to Emma J. Christopher, and is farming near Pawnee. The four latter reside with their mother, at Pawnee, Sangamon county, Ill. John L. Drennan died July 22, 1853, and his widow married John B. Weber. *See his name*.

ELIZABETH, born in Kentucky, was married in Sangamon county, Ill., to Lewis Laughlin. They had five children, and reside near New London, Henry county, Iowa.

MARY ANA, born Oct. 11, 1811, in Caldwell county, Ky., was married in Sangamon county, Ill., Nov. 13, 1831, to Urban Alexander, who was born in Caldwell county, Ky., and his father, Joshua C. Alexander, emigrated to Sangamon county about 1820, settling on Richland creek. He served in the Black Hawk war, in the company of which Abraham Lincoln was Captain. Urban Alexander and wife had two children in Sangamon county, and moved to DesMoines county, Iowa, where two children were born. They returned to Sangamon county, had one child, and in the fall of 1844 they emigrated with several other families to Texas, and arrived in Fannin county, Texas, Dec. 5, of same year. One son was born there, and in 1851 they moved to Hopkins county, Texas. Of their children: REBECCA J., born Oct. 9, 1836, in Sangamon county, Ill., is unmarried, and resides near Black Jack Grove, Texas. JOHN S., born Aug. 21, 1838, in DesMoines county, Iowa, enlisted in 1861, in Co. K, 9th Regiment Texas Cavalry, under Brigadier-General L. S. Ross, of the Southern Confederacy. He was in many engagements, such as Corinth, Vicksburg, etc. At the close of the war he returned home, only to find his stock of hundreds of cattle all gone, save a few for family use. The homestead remained, and being brought up to believe that a man is never broke until his neck is, and knowing no such word as fail, J. S. Alexander began again. He was married Dec. 4, 1868, to Texanna Tallaferro. They have two children, CHARLES T. and HENRY B., and reside near Black Jack Grove, Hopkins county, Texas. Sarah A., born Sept. 2, 1840, in DesMoines county, Iowa, was married in Texas, March 14, 1860, to George D. Winniford. They had three children, NORVEL, SAMUEL and ROBERT LEE, who live with their mother. Mr. Winniford died in 1871, and the family reside near Black Jack Grove, Texas. MARTHA M., born Nov. 2, 1842, in Sangamon county, Ill., died August 11, 1855, near Black Jack Grove, Texas. THOMAS C., born in 1851, in Fannin county, Texas, enlisted in Gurley's Regiment Texas Cavalry, and operated principally in Louisiana, Arkansas and Indian Territory. He was married in the fall of 1866 to Martha Banta. They have five children, WILLIAM, JOHN, AMANDA, GEORGIA and WINFIELD S., and resied near Black Jack Grove, Texas. Urban Alexander died Dec. 20, 1853, from injuries received by being thrown from a wagon. Mrs. Mary A. Alexander died June 4, 1854, both near Black Jack Grove, Hopkins county, Texas.

REBECCA, born in Kentucky, was married in Sangamon county, Ill., to George Latimer, who died, and she married William Allison. They reside near Abingdon, Knox county, Ill.

DAVID, born July 3, 1816, in Caldwell county, Ky., was married Sept. 3, 1833, in Sangamon county, Ill., to Nancy Wilson, who was born April 6, 1816, in Morgan county, Tennessee. They emigrated to Texas in 1842. Of their children, ELIZABETH, born Nov. 3, 1835, in Sangamon county, was married Feb. 11, 1852, near Honey Grove, Texas, to S A Erwin. They had six children, MARY I., born June 26, 1853, near Honey Grove, was married there Sept. 8, 1871, to J. E. Breckeen, and reside in Honey Grove. JOHN E., born Oct. 18, 1855. M. M., born Dec. 31, 1858. WILLIAM J., born April 22, 1860. NANNIE A., born July 20, 1864, and EVA G., born Oct. 8, 1866, reside with their parents in Honey Grove, Fannin county, Texas. MARY, born June 5, 1837, in Sangamon county, Ill., was married, Sept. 3, 1860, near Honey Grove, to A. G. Stobaugh. They had four children, NANNIE E., MARTHA E., MARY A. and GUSSIE, who live with their father. Mrs. Mary Stobaugh died Nov. 15, 1869, in Honey Grove, and the family reside there. MARTHA, born March 12, 1840, in Sangamon county, Ill., was married Dec. 18, 1856, near Honey Grove, to Louis B. Chiles. They had nine children, JAMES E., NANCY J., the latter died in 1866, MARY E., LOUIS B., Jun., W. L., ELMO, MARTHA J., ROBERT and SAMUEL E., who reside with their parents, near Honey Grove, Fannin county, Texas. WILLIAM E., born Feb. 6, 1844, in Fannin county, was married Sept. 15, 1871, to Annie Tomlinson. They have two living children, J. E. and D. E., and live in Fannin county, near Honey Grove, Texas. ANN ISABELLA, born Feb. 21, 1858, in Fannin county, resides with her parents.

David Drennan and wife reside near Honey Grove, Fannin county, Texas. William Drennan, Sen., died Oct. 23, 1847, and his widow, Mrs. Mary Drennan died Oct. 2., 1856, both where they settled, in 1818, in Sangamon county, Ill. He in his eightieth year and she in her eighty-fifth year. William Drennan, Sen., was one of the three Commissioners who were appointed by the Governor of Illinois to locate the county seat of Sangamon county. The other two were Zachariah Peter and Rivers Cormack. They located it by driving a stake in the ground and calling it Springfield.

DRENNAN, JOSEPH, was born April 16, 1786, in Pendleton district, South Carolina. He was half brother to and much younger than Wm. Drennan, Sen. Joseph Drennan was married in South Carolina to Rebecca Evets, and had one child there. About 1807 the family moved to Caldwell county, Ky., where they had five children, and they moved to what is now Ball township, Sangamon county, Ill., coming himself in March 10, 1818, and bringing his family in Sept. of that year. They had three children. Of all his children—

ANDREW P., born Sept. 12, 1806, in Pendleton district, South Carolina, was married in Sangamon county to Ruth Smith, and had nine children. JOSEPH F., married Mary Watts, and both died, leaving seven children, in Logan county. ELIZABETH died at five years. MARY A., married John Byers, has three children, and reside in Virden. REBECCA J., married George Trimble.

See his name. JOHN, married Nancy Watts, has six children, and resides in Champaign county. Andrew J. married Hannah Watson, have four children, and resides in Champaign county. PETER C. married Margaret Smith, have six children, and reside in Champaign county. MARTHA married James A. Smith, has one child, GEORGE E., and resides in Chatham. RUTH F. is unmarried, and resides in Chatham. Mrs. Ruth Drennan died in 1851, and A. P. Drennan married Ruth Wright, and died April 6, 1874, in Chatham. His widow lives there.

JANE, born in Caldwell county, Ky., married in Sangamon county to John Smith. *See his name.*

WILLIAM G., born in Kentucky, married in Sangamon county to Sarah Jones, and both died.

RACHEL, born in Kentucky, married in Sangamon county, to James Mitts, and died, leaving two children in Ball township.

JOSEPH, Jun., born in Kentucky, was married in Sangamon county to Elizabeth Richardson, about 1833. They had two children, and he married Elizabeth Withrow. They had ten children. She died, and he married Sarah Purvis. They had six children, and he died in Macoupin county, Ill. Of his children: SMITH married Eliza J. Seaton, of Macoupin county. They have two children, and live in Ball township. ELIZA married N. W. Bates, had one child, and she died in Iowa. Of Joseph Drennan's other children I have no history. •

DAVID J., born May 3, 1816, in Caldwell county, Ky., was married in Sangamon county, Ill., to Sarah Hurley. They had nine children, three of whom died under seven years. Of the other six: JANE married Solomon Taylor and died. REBECCA married George Hilyard, and died, leaving seven children near Lewisburg, Wayne county, Iowa. AMANDA married Starkey D. Morrison. They have two children, CHARLES A. and DAVID J., and reside at Woodside Station. He is Postmaster there. NANCY married Levi Cassity. *See his name.* SARAH E. married Martin C. Bridges. *See his name.* JOSEPH H. married Mattie Forbes, and resides in Wood side township. Mrs. Sarah Drennan died March 3, 1869, and David J. Drennan resides two miles southeast of Woodside, and eight miles south of Springfield. David J. Drennan told the writer that one day he went out to kill a deer (if he could find one) during the "deep snow." He went without a gun, expecting to kill it with a knife, as they would break through the crust and stick fast in the snow. In going through the brush he broke through and went down until the snow was just under his arm pits. He was two or three hours in this position trying to extricate himself, and the perspiration and melting snow made his clothes as wet as though he had plunged into water. He got out of the brush far enough for the crust to bear him, and by the time he walked home his clothes were frozen. He was about thirteen years old when this happened, and says he was twelve years of age when he had his first pair of shoes; that he obtained them by cutting down an oak tree, peeling the bark off and taking it to Thomas Dawson's tannery, received leather in exchange for this bark, had it cut out in the rough, and took the leather to Robert Metcalfe to be made into shoes. He paid the shoemaker by picking the seed out of four pounds of cotton, which left one pound of cotton and three pounds of seed. The farmers raised cotton extensively then, each one having three or four acres, and not more of wheat or oats. Cotton was picked by hand, but afterwards Robert Pulliam built a cotton gin, made to run by a tread wheel and two oxen.

SAMUEL, born May 15, 1819, the first birth of the family in Sangamon county, was married Oct. 6, 1836, to Mary A. Baker, who was born Feb. 14, 1820, in Tennessee. They had six children. NANCY J. married Robert Penick, and died, leaving three children. ANDREW J. enlisted Sept., 1861, in Co. B, 10th Ill. Cav., for three years, re-enlisted as a veteran in Jan., 1864, served to the end of the rebellion, and was honorably discharged at San Antonio, Texas, in Nov., 1865. He was married to Martha H. Smith, have two living children, SAMUEL T. and REBECCA J., and reside in Curran township. EZEKIEL died at sixteen years of age. GEORGE W., MARY A. and LOUISA reside with their mother. Samuel Drennan died Jan. 11, 1855, and his widow resides three miles southeast of Curran.

EZEKIEL H., born Nov. 17, 1822, in Sangamon county, married Lavina Ray. They have five living children, and live in Auburn.

NANCY, born Jan. 7, 1825, in Sangamon county, married May 8, 1866, to John Harmon. See his name. She died Oct. 15, 1871.

Joseph Drennan died Oct. 22, 1865, and his widow Mrs. Rebecca Drennan died Dec. 7, 1866, both in Sangamon county.

DRESSER, REV. CHAS. D. D., was born Feb. 24, 1800, in Pomfret, Conn. He was a classmate of George D. Prentice, in Brown University, Providence, R. I., and graduated there in 1823. He then went to southeast Virginia and entered the family of Dr. Meade (afterward Bishop Meade), of Virginia, as tutor to his sons, and with him studied theology. He was ordained to the ministry in the Protestant Episcopal Church in 1829, and was married Nov. 8, 1832, in Dinwiddie county, near Petersburg, Va., to Louisa W. Withers, who was born there July 15, 1810. They had two living children in Virginia. Mr. Dresser came with his family to Springfield in April, 1838, where he became Rector of the Episcopal Parish. They had eight children in Springfield, four of whom died young. Of their six living children—

DAVID W., born Oct. 16, 1833, at Halifax Court House, Va., brought up in Springfield, graduated at Jubilee College, Robins' Nest, Peoria county, Ill., in 1851, and was there ordained to the ministry in 1855. Rev. D. W. Dresser was married Nov. 20, 1861, at Chesterfield, Ill., to Caroline Cundell, who was born there Jan. 4, 1841. He is now Rector of the Protestant Episcopal Parish at Carlinville, Ill.

THOMAS W., born Jan. 11, 1837, at Halifax C. H., Va., was brought up in Springfield. He graduated at Jubilee college in 1855, and at the Medical University of New York City in 1864. He was married in Springfield, Nov. 28, 1865, to Margaret Doremus. They have one child, CATHARINE. Dr. T. W. Dresser is a practicing physician and resides in Springfield, Illinois.

ELIZABETH, born Aug., 20, 1838, in Springfield, was married Dec. 31, 1873, to William P. Thayer. See his name.

EDMUND, born Sept. 2, 1843, in Springfield, spent several years as railroad telegraph operator, and is now master of transportation on the T. W. & W. R. R. He resides with his mother in Springfield, Illinois.

SAMUEL TREAT, born Sept. 6, 1846, in Springfield, spent several years as assistant clerk of the U. S. District Court in Springfield. Was, from Jan., 1875, to Jan., 1876, clerk in the office of Solicitor of the Treasury at Washington, D. C. He is now Deputy U. S. Marshal for the southern district of Illinois, and resides with his mother in Springfield.

VIRGINIA, born Oct. 12, 1852, in Springfield, resides with her mother.

Rev. Charles Dresser received the degree of Doctor of Divinity from St. Paul's college, Mo., in 1858, and was Rector of the Protestant Episcopal church in Springfield from 1838 to 1855. During that time, as the parish register shows, he solemnized the marriage of Abraham Lincoln and Mary Todd, Nov. 4, 1842. He was elected Professor of Divinity and Belles Letters in Jubilee College in 1855, and remained in that position for some time, when he returned to Springfield and died March 25, 1865. His widow resides at 818 West Edwards street, Springfield, Ill.

DUFF, ABRAHAM, was born May 15, 1777, in South Carolina. Virlinda Combs was born in South Carolina also, Aug. 6, 1781. Their parents moved on pack horses to the vicinity of Bowling Green, Ky. A. Duff and Verlinda Combs were married, and had nine children born there, and moved to St. Clair county, Ill., and from there moved in company with his son-in-law, John Sims; arrived April, 1819, on Spring creek, at a point six miles west of where Springfield now stands. Two children were born at the latter place. Of their eleven children—

ELIZABETH, born April 16, 1798, in Kentucky, married Elijah Putnam. Mr P. died, leaving his widow and child near Bloomfield, Iowa.

GEORGE, born Feb. 10, 1800, in Kentucky, married in Sangamon county, in 1822, to Jennie Archer. They had seven children in Sangamon county, and moved in 1839 to Newton county, Mo., where five children were born. MILTON, married Martha Lynn, and reside in Missouri. MISSONIAH, married John Powers in Missouri, came to Sangamon county and he died. She married again, is now a widow and resides in Missouri. WILLIAM, born Feb. 10, 1827, in Sangamon county, married April 7, 1853, to Mrs. Eley F. Archer, whose maiden name was Meacham. They have two children, JOHN G. and MINERVA A., and reside on the farm where his grandfather, Duff, settled in 1819. It is six miles west of Springfield. ABRAHAM, born in Sangamon county, raised in Missouri, but was living with his brother William, and enlisted in 1861 for three years, in Co. B, 10th Illinois Cavalry, and died at Quincy, Ill., Feb. 18, 1862, was buried at Old Salem, Sangamon county. GREENBERRY, born in Sangamon county, went from Missouri to California in 1853, and resides there. All the others reside in Missouri. Mrs. Jennie Duff died Feb., 1863, in Lincoln county, Mo., and George Duff resides in Newton county, Mo.

LUCINDA, born Nov. 14, 1801, in Kentucky, married John Sims. See his name.

MATILDA, born Aug. 5, 1804, in Kentucky, married Feb. 6, 1825, to Robert Archer. See his name.

COMBS, born July 4, 1807, in Kentucky, married in Sangamon county to Polly Hurley, have eleven children, and reside near Clinton, Ill.

COMELY, born July 8, 1809, in Kentucky, married Feb. 24, 1825, to John Morgan. See his name.

EFFY, born Aug. 24, 1811, in Kentucky, married Michael Archer. See his name.

MELISSA, born Aug. 28, 1813, in Kentucky, married John Henry, and moved to Missouri. Mr. H. died, leaving a widow and seven children.

GREENBERREY, born Aug. 10, 1815, in Kentucky, married in Sangamon county to Elizabeth Wilbourn. They have seven children, and reside near Mt. Auburn, Christian county.

MARY ANN, born Jan. 4, 1820, in Sangamon county, married John H. Robinson. See his name.

MARTHA A., born Aug. 4, 1821, in Sangamon county, married Thompson Smith, have three children, and reside at Clinton, DeWitt county.

Mrs. Verlinda Duff died Sept. 18, 1845, and Abraham Duff died Dec. 25, 1850, both in Sangamon county.

Mrs. Dorothy Combs, mother of Mrs. Duff, came to Sangamon county with her daughter, and died at her house Feb. 12, 1838, aged eighty-five years. Her husband, Bennett Combs, died in Virginia.

DUNCAN, MOSES, no relation to John, Rice, Marshall, etc. He was born in South Carolina, was a soldier in the war of 1812, was married in South Carolina, moved to Tennessee, had several children there, and the family moved to Sangamon county, Ill., arriving in 1826 or 1827, and settled on Spring creek.

HIRAM, JOHN, MARY, MARGARET and WILLIAM married in Tennessee, and came to Sangamon county with their father. MOSES, Jun., JOSEPH, DAVID and ARCHIBALD, the four latter unmarried, came with their parents also. JOSEPH and DAVID married in Sangamon county. In 1833 the whole family except two moved to Missouri. In 1835 the other two, WILLIAM and JOSEPH, went there also.

JOSEPH was a preacher in the M. E. church, and when the division took place he preferred remaining with the real Methodist Episcopal church, and returned to Sangamon county in 1844. In order to give his life in detail it may be said he was born May 21, 1808, in Franklin county, Tenn., came to Sangamon county in 1826 or 7, was a soldier in the Black Hawk war of 1831-2, and was married in Sangamon county, Oct. 18, 1832 to Nancy Lanterman. They had two living children, DAVID C., born Oct. 6, 1833, in Sangamon county, married Nov. 23, 1856 to Deborah Mills. They had four living children, SARAH B., DORA M., NANCY E., and MARY E., and reside in Williamsville. SOLOMON H., born June 6, 1835, died April 11, 1860. Rev. Joseph Duncan died May 10, 1854. His widow married Harrison Bishop. He died, and she resides with her son, David C. Duncan, in Williamsville. Rev. Joseph Duncan was a regular traveling preacher from the time he returned from Missouri until his death.

DUNCAN, RICE, was born Mar. 5, 1781, in North Carolina. He was brother to Marshal and John. When young his father's family moved to Cumberland county, Ky. He was there married to Barbara Antle. They had four children, and Mrs. D. died. He married Luranah Rutherford. They brought one child from Kentucky to St. Clair county, where they had five children, and moved to Morgan, and then to Sangamon county, arriving Oct., 1837, in what is now Salisbury. Of their children—

DELILAH, born Nov. 20, 1805, in Kentucky, married A. Buchanan, had twelve children, moved to Texas in 1845, and Mr. B. died soon after.

MATILDA, born Nov. 29, 1807, in Kentucky, married Levi Scott, had twelve children, Mr. S. died, and the family reside at Carthage, Ill.

WILLIAM T., born April 23, 1809, in Kentucky, married Clemantine French. They had six children, and he died. The family reside in Macoupin county.

SIDNEY S., born Dec. 18, 1810, in Kentucky, married in Sangamon county to Mary Rogers. They had three children. He was Judge of Morgan county court, and died Aug., 1872, in Jacksonville. His widow resides in Chicago

SUSANNAH, born July 13, 1816, in Kentucky, married Andrew P. Tannehill. They have six children, and live in Bates county, Mo.

NANCY, born Jan. 25, 1820, married Henry Antle. See his name.

SARAH B., born Feb. 21, 1823, married George Goodman, have seven children and live in Keokuk, Iowa.

BETSY J., born July 3, 1825, married William Dorrell, and live in Menard county.

ELLA A., born June 1, 1827, married Samuel Coleman, and both died, leaving one child, in Salisbury township.

AVARILLA, born Feb. 8, 1831, married Lemuel Miller, had two children, and died.

Mrs. Luranah Duncan, died May 29, 1862, and Rice Duncan died Oct. 7, 1863, both in Salisbury township.

DUNCAN, MARSHAL, was born in 1783 or 4, in North Carolina. He was brother to Rice and John. He went, when young, with his parents to Cumberland county, Kentucky. He left Kentucky with three children and came to Sangamon county, Ill., arrived in 1820 or 21 in Salisbury township. He was there married to Hannah Miller, a daughter of John Miller.

They had eight children. Of all his children—

JAMES T. and WILLIAM T. H., twins, born May 10, 1807, in Cumberland county, Ky.

JAMES T., married in Sangamon county, Aug. 27, 1829, to Mary Penny, who was born Dec. 6, 1809, in Pope county, Ill. They had nine living children, HESTER A., married John Gramlish, and resides in Salisbury township. FRANCIS M., born Dec. 30, 1852, married Martha J. Yoakum. They have eight children, CHARLES N., LAURA A., WM. R. and JAMES T., twins, JEANETTE A., GEORGE H., LOUISA E. and MARY L., and live in Salisbury township, northeast of Sangamon river. JANE, married John C. Berry, have six children, and live in DeWitt county. John W., died in Iowa in 1869, aged thirty-two years. FRANKLIN W., married Martha Irwin, have five children, and live in Menard county. JAMES T., Jun., married Olive Douglas, who died leaving one child; he and his child live in Salisbury township. SYLVESTER T., unmarried, resides at Salisbury. MATILDA, married James Potter, have four children, and live in Menard county. WILLIAM P., lives with his mother. James T. Duncan, died July 9, 1856, and his widow resides in Salisbury.

WILLIAM T. H., married in Sangamon county, in 1831, to Eve Miller. They had twelve children. MARION M., married Martha McMurphy, have five children, LUCY C., LAURA A., MARGARET N., OMER L., and LENA E., and live in Salisbury. POLLY A., married O. R. Baker. See his name. JAMES T., and SIMEON S., live with their mother. SARAH J., married Hamilton Combs, has four children, and live in Salisbury township. MARTHA, married Richard Gaines, and lives with her mother. MARGARET married Dr. A. F. Purvines. See his name. NANCY E., married Napoleon Connor, have two children, and live in Macoupin county. GEORGE W., is west. FARINDA, married Elisha Batterton. See his name. ALICE, married Turner Yoakum, and resides in Avoca, Iowa. THOMAS S., lives with his mother. William T. H. Duncan died Oct. 20, 1862, and his widow resides in Salisbury—1874.

MARSHAL T., born Dec. 27, 1809, in Cumberland county, Ky., married in Tennessee, Aug. 22, 1830, to Anna Sharp. They had three children, and Mrs. Duncan died in 1836 or 7, and Mr. Duncan, with his children, came soon after to Sangamon county. Of his children—WILLIAM T., born Sept. 19, 1832, in Tenn., raised in Sangamon county, and enlisted for three years, Aug. 13, 1862, in Co. B, 114 Ill. Inf., served until Aug. 3, 1865, when he was honorably discharged. He was married March 20, 1866, to Jane Grady. They have four children, MARY A., JASPER C., ANNA M., and WILLIAM H., and live seven miles northwest of Springfield. RACHEL M., born Aug. 11, 1834, in Tennessee, married in Sangamon county to Enos Campbell. See his name. MARY A., born Sept. 7, 1836, in Tennessee, married in Sangamon county to Solomon Penny, and died. Marshal T. Duncan died Aug. 23, 1840, in Sangamon county.

By the second marriage—

MINERVA, born Sept. 15, 1822, in Sangamon county, married John C. Irwin. See his name.

ARTAMESIA, born Nov. 30, 1828, in Sangamon county, married May 5, 1852, to Nathan Hartley, have six children, and live in Menard county. The remainder of the children are in Iowa and Kansas.

Marshall Duncan died in Sangamon county, in the fall of 1858, and his widow resides with her children in Iowa.

DUNCAN, JOHN, was born in 1789, in Cumberland county, Ky. He was married there to Sally Miller, and had six children there, and moved to Sangamon county, Ill., about 1827, in what is now Salisbury township, where they had six children. Three only of their children reside in Sangamon county.

POLLY married John Davies. See his name.

JOHN married Nancy Kane, have three children, and reside in Salisbury.

ARMINDA, born Feb. 14, 1828, in Sangamon county, married Jan. 8, 1849, to Frederick Luchsinger, who was born April 2, 1824, in Canton Glarus, Switzerland. They have six living children. HESTER A., married John Danenberger, and resides in Sangamon county. SARAH E. married Silas Danenberger, and resides in Salisbury township. JANE M.,

HARRIET E., JANETTA and ELIZA O. reside with their parents, near Salisbury.

Mrs. Sally Duncan died Nov., 1850, and John Duncan died in 1863, both near Salisbury.

DUNN, WILLIAM, an older brother to Elijah, was born in Fleming county, Ky., married there to Barbara Callerman, had five children, and moved to Sangamon county in 1829. Mr. Dunn died soon after, and a few years later his widow and children moved to Henry county, Ill.

DUNN, ELIJAH, was born about 1798, in Fleming county, Ky., and was married there to Eleanor Callerman, a native of the same county. She was a sister of D. K. Callerman. They had two children in Kentucky, and moved to Sangamon county, Ill., arriving in the fall of 1825, and settled two and one-half miles west of Springfield, and three years later they moved north of Spring creek. They had three children in Sangamon county. Of their children—

JOHN C., born Aug. 20, 1823, in Kentucky, raised in Sangamon county, went to Galena, engaged in lead mining, and died there about 1845, aged twenty-two years.

JAMES K., born June 21, 1825, in Fleming county, Ky., married in Sangamon county, March 15, 1869, to Bertha Kelly, who was born April 4, 1846. They had three children. CHARLES and ALFRED died in infancy, KATIE lives with her parents. J. K. Dunn resides on the farm where his father settled in 1828. It is four miles northwest of Springfield.

DANIEL A., born Jan. 8, 1828, in Sangamon county, married Eliza Ann Kelly. They had two living children, and Mrs. Dunn died March 15, 1871. Of her children—JOHN lives with his father, and OLIVER with his uncle, J. K. Dunn. D. A. Dunn resides four miles northwest of Springfield.

URIAH, born Nov. 13, 1833, in Sangamon county, died aged twenty years.

ELIZABETH, born Dec. 14, 1837, in Sangamon county, married Feb. 17, 1859, to Joel J. Manning, who was born in 1833 in Montreal, Canada, and came to Sangamon county in 1838. They had seven children. Their second, ELIJAH, died Aug. 24, 1873, aged 12 years. MARY E., FRANCES E., JAMES G., NORA M., IDA BELL, and a babe, reside with their parents four miles northwest of Springfield.

Mrs. Eleanor Dunn died about 1853, and Elijah Dunn died Aug. 7, 1866—both in Sangamon county.

DUNLAP, JOHN, was born May 15, 1785, probably in Pennsylvania, and went to Carter county, Tenn. Catharine Tipton was born Jan. 30, 1788, in Carter county, Tenn. They were married and had nine children there. The family moved to Sangamon county, Ill., arriving in the fall of 1828, in what is now Fancy creek township, where they had one child. Of their children—

ISAAC, born Jan. 2, 1806, in Tennessee, was married there to Mary H. Bowers, and came with his father to Sangamon county. They had twelve children. Isaac Dunlap died August 2, 1867, and his widow resides in Fancy Creek township.

MARGARET, born Jan. 2, 1808, married in Tennessee to Baptiste McNabb, came to Sangamon county with her father. They had four children, and he died. She married John McLoud. See his name.

SARAH, born March 9, 1810, married Samuel T. Boyd. He died, and she married Thomas Vandevender, who died, and she married Samuel T. Lacey, and resides in Logan county.

RUTH, born March 18, 1812, married in Tennessee to John E. Hedrick, came to Sangamon county with her father, and had ten children. The family are all in Missouri and Iowa.

TENNESSEE, born August 14, 1814, married Eliza Cutwright. He shot himself accidentally in 1840, in Logan county, leaving a wife and two children.

JAMES T., born Dec. 8, 1816, married Mary H. Brown. They had five children, and she died. He married Rosanna McCauley. They had six children. He was a soldier in the Mexican war from Sangamon county. He moved to Missouri, and was Captain of a Company in a Union Regiment, and was captured at the battle of Pittsburg Landing, was exchanged after seven months imprisonment, returned home, and served one term in the Missouri Legislature in 1863. He went again in the army, and was killed at the battle of Franklin, Tenn., in Dec., 1864, while acting as Captain of a Company.

SUSANNA, born April 15, 1819, married Benjamin F. Brown. *See his name.*

JOHN R., born in Carter county, Tenn., April 24, 1821, married in Sangamon county, Dec. 10, 1840, to Emily A. Brown. They had ten children. ALMYRA married Theodore Allen, have two children, and reside in Sullivan county, Mo. WILLIAM T. enlisted in Co. H, 36th Iowa Inf., in 1862, contracted chronic diarrhea in camp, was sent to hospital at Keokuk, brought home by his parents, and died July 3, 1863. JAMES A. married Zerilda Richards, had two children, and she died. He married Sarah E. Elliott, and resides in Fancy Creek township. ROBERT married Nellie Richards, and resides in Randolph county, Mo. ELIZA J. married George D. Power. *See his name.* FRANKLIN P. resides with his parents. MARY C. died, aged five years. JOHN R., Jun., CLARENCE P. and OLIVE L. reside with their parents, two and a half miles west of Sherman, Sangamon county, Ill.

MARY A., born Sept. 29, 1823, married Alexander Doake. He died and she married Jer. Falconer, who died, and she lives near Decatur.

EDNA M., born Jan. 13, 1831, married John Johnson, who died, and she married Robert T. Brown. *See his name.*

John Dunlap died Feb. 14, 1856, and his widow died May 26, 1857, both in Sangamon county.

DURBIN, JOSEPH, was born about 1776, in what afterwards became Madison county, Ky. He was married there to Elizabeth Logsdon, and they had twelve children in that county. He then moved his family to Sangamon county, Ill., arriving in 1829, and settled in what is now Pawnee township. Of his children—

EDWARD, SYLVESTER and MARGARET married in Kentucky, came to Sangamon county in 1828, and settled in what is now Cotton Hill township. In 1830 the whole family moved to that part of Montgomery which is now Christian county. His son—

CHRISTOPHER K., born in Kentucky in 1793, married there to Rachel Willis, and moved with his father to Sangamon and Christian county, Ill. They had thirteen children. Their fourth child, JAMES R., born June 18, 1820, in Madison county, Ky., remained with his father until April 10, 1842, when he was married to Ann Simpson. Their only living child, ANGELINE, married Thomas J. Gatton. He died April 20, 1867, leaving a widow and three children, Mary A., Andrew T., and James W. James R. Durbin died Dec. 1873, and his widow, his widowed daughter and her three children, reside near St. Bernard church in Ball township.

DUTTON, MATTHEW, was born April 5, 1778, in Windsor county, Vt. He spent his early life as a school teacher, and about 1818 entered the ministry in connection with the Congregational church. He never became a settled pastor, but all his ministerial work was done as an evangelist, several years of the time in Tennessee and some in Virginia. In 1832 he engaged in teaching and occasional preaching at Decatur, Ill. Elizabeth Williams was born March 22, 1791, in the town of Sharon, Litchfield county, Conn. She was married March 10, 1811, in northern New York, to David Carpenter. They had two children in the State of New York.

JOHN WILLIAM, born Mar. 4, 1811, went to sea at 16 years old. His second voyage was on board the ship Warrenton. The vessel was lost and not a soul on board saved.

THOMAS D., born March 8, 1813, married April, 1833, in Duchess county, N. Y., to Julia A. Wing. He died suddenly June 2, 1854, near Sullivan, Moultrie county, Ill., leaving a widow and six children.

David Carpenter died in New York, and his widow went to New York City and taught school until July, 1834, when she went to Decatur, Ill., to visit two of her brothers. Rev. Matthew Dutton and Mrs. Elizabeth Carpenter were married Nov. 15, 1834, in Decatur. They moved to Morgan county and a year later to Sangamon county, arriving at Mechanicsburg in July, 1838. Both being teachers, and in the absence of any school system, they built a school house and lived and taught in it for about twelve years. It was a frame building, plastered outside and in, and was almost snow white.' Nearly all who are now heads of families in the vicin-

—35

ity of Mechanicsburg received their education in that house.

Rev. Matthew Dutton died Feb. 21, 1857, and his widow (1874) in her eighty-fourth year resides in Mechanicsburg.

DRYER, JOHN, was born Dec. 13, 1783, in Great Barrington, Mass. He was married May 14, 1808, in New York, to Cynthia Stevens, who was born March 4, 1793, in Vermont. They had two children in New York, and in 1819 came to Sangamon county, Ill., settling six miles from where Springfield now stands, where they had one child, and moved to Springfield about 1825. Of their children—

LAVINIA M., born Dec. 22, 1812, in New York, married in Sangamon county June, 1830, to Hugh M. Armstrong. See his name.

ALMIRA, born April, 1815, in New York, married in Springfield, in 1836, to E. Geo. Johns.

JANE A., born Aug. 15, 1820, in Sangamon county, was married Sept., 1838, in Massachusetts, to William Cone, and reside three miles west of Springfield.

John Dryer was engaged in wool carding, and was the first man in the county to cultivate a nursery and introduce fruit trees. He died July 3, 1854, and his widow resides in Springfield now—1876—in her eighty-fourth year.

E

EARNEST, JACOB, born April 24, 1799, in South Carolina, was married there to Elizabeth Sims, who was born April 26, 1798. She was a sister of James and William Sims, one of whom was older and the other younger than herself. They moved to that part of Simpson which later became Logan county, Ky., where they had seven children. In 1817 the family moved to St. Clair county, Ill., where they had one child, and they moved to what became Sangamon county, Ill., arriving in the fall of 1819, on Spring Creek, in what is now Curran township, where one child was born. Of their nine children—

LAVINA, born Nov. 28, 1824, in Kentucky, was married in Sangamon county, Ill., to James McMurry. See his name. He died, leaving a widow and six children near Ione City, Ione Valley, California.

SARAH, born April 7, 1806, in Kentucky, was married Feb. 18, 1824, in Sangamon county, Ill., to John King. See his name.

WILLIAM, born August 18, 1807, in Kentucky, was married in Sangamon county, Ill., to Jane Parks. They had five children. Mr. Earnest and three of the children died near Northfield, Iowa. Mrs. Earnest died there, Dec. 7, 1870, and the children reside near Northfield.

ROBERT, born April 6, 1810, in Kentucky, was married in Sangamon county to Susan Kendall. They had one child, SUSAN A., born Jan. 25, 1831, married James Turner. See his name. He died and his widow married Henry B. Chambers. See his name. Robert Earnest died Sept. 22, 1831, and his widow married Joseph Ralston. See his name.

MAHALA, born Dec. 18, 1811, in Kentucky, was married in Sangamon county to James Parkinson. See his name.

GRIZELLA, born April 8, 1813, in Kentucky, was married in Sangamon county, Ill., to Martin L. C. Kendall. See his name. Mrs. Kendall and her two children died.

RACHEL, born March 5, 1816, in Kentucky, was married in Sangamon county, Ill., to Rezin D. Brown. See his name.

HENRIETTA, born April 3, 1818, in St. Clair county, Ill., was married in Sangamon county, March 22, 1838, to James V. Ingels. See his name.

SOPHIA, born April 2, 1820, in Sangamon county, married Amos W. Brown. See his name. Mrs. Brown died.

Mrs. Elizabeth Earnest died March 1, 1831, and Jacob Earnest married Rebecca Blunt. They had two children, and moved to Hancock county, Ill. Of their children—

ELIZABETH, born Sept. 29, 1833, in Sangamon county, was married July 29, 1852, to William Jones. They had eight children, JACOB H., FRANCIS M., MARY M., EMMA A., IANTHA B., IDA M., WILLIAM B. and LIBBIE. William Jones was drowned Jan. 1, 1869, while crossing the Mississippi river. Mrs. Elizabeth Jones was married Dec. 1, 1870, to William Isenberger.

They have two children, GEORGE W. and RACHEL, and reside near Appanoos, Hancock county, Ill.

JACOB H., born August 18, 1836, in Sangamon county, married in Hancock county, Feb. 19, 1860, to Elizabeth Riman, who was born May 16, 1836. They have five children, EDWARD M., HENRIETTA, LYDIA F., ALVIN P. and ZENA MAY, and reside near Appanoos, Hancock county, Ill.

Jacob Earnest died Sept. 29, 1842, and Mrs. Rebecca Earnest died March 8, 1858, both in Hancock county, Ill.

EARNEST, THOMAS, was born June 3, 1792, in South Carolina. His parents moved, when he was a boy, to Simpson county, Ky. In the Autumn of 1819 he came to Sangamon county and joined his brother Jacob, who had previously arrived with his family. Thomas Earnest commenced improvements south of Spring creek, eight miles west of Springfield, and entered land when it came into market. He was married Oct. 15, 1822, to Alletta Lanterman. They had twelve children in Sangamon county, two of whom died young.

SOPHIA J., born Aug. 24, 1823, was married Nov. 12, 1846, to Simon P. Rickard. See his name.

JOHN W., born Sept. 2, 1824, was married April 21, 1853, to Julia J. Woolley, of Green county, Ill. They have three children living, LEORA S., WILLIAM W., and CHARLES S., and reside in Macoupin county, near Greenfield, Green county, Ill.

PETER L., born Nov. 6, 1825, was married in Sangamon county, in 1849, to Elizabeth A. Thompson. They had ten children, five of whom are living, THOMAS H., WILLIAM H., MARY A., FRANK P., and JOSIAH T. P. L. Earnest is operating in the silver mines of San Juan, southwestern Colorado. His son, Thomas H., is now—1875—there attending to business. The family reside at Ottawa, Kansas. Peter L. Earnest is Postmaster in Ottawa.

SOPHRONIA, born Dec. 5, 1826, was married May 20, 1846, to Dr. Benjamin S. Robinson. See his name.

ALLETTA A., born March 5, 1828, married William Y. Kirk. They had one child, and Mr. Kirk died. His widow married Robert Watson of St. Louis.

They had one child, and reside near Millville, Ray county, Mo.

WILLIAM, born Nov. 21, 1829, in Sangamon county, enlisted Aug., 1862, for three years in Co. A, 106 Ill. Inf., and died of disease, July 17, 1863, near Vicksburg, Miss.

HENRIETTA M., born Jan. 10, 1831, married Henry W. Rickard. See his name.

JAMES L., born Oct. 18, 1832, in Sangamon county, died, March 5, 1848, away from home, in Calhoun county, Illinois.

ELIZA E. born Feb. 27, 1836, resides at the family homestead with her brother Thomas H.

THOMAS H., born April 24, 1837, was married Nov. 15, 1863, to Hannah H. Lyman. They had two children, CAROLINE B. and WILLIAM J., and Mrs. E. died May 19, 1872. T. H. Earnest resides eight miles west of Springfield, on the farm where his father settled in 1819.

Thomas Earnest died, Nov. 6, 1848, suddenly, while away from home, in Calhoun county. Mrs. Alletta Earnest died July 31, 1871, at the house of her daughter, Mrs. H. W. Rickard, caused by being thrown from a wagon.

EACHUS, ROBERT, was born Dec. 24, 1794, in Chester county, Pa., came to Springfield in the fall of 1840, and went on a farm he had purchased in what is now Curran township. The next spring he was joined by his sister Charlotte and his niece, Mary McPherson, who was born Oct. 25, 1819, in Chester county, Pa., and married in Sangamon county to James Short. See his name. Charlotte Eachus died Feb. 1, 1865, and Robert Eachus died Oct. 2, 1872, in Loami township.

EADES, WILLIAM, a native of Kentucky, married there, moved to Missouri, and from there to Sangamon county, Ill., arriving in the summer of 1825, in what is now Auburn township. His son—

STROTHER, married in Sangamon county to Martha A. Dodds. See the Dodds family sketch.

EARLY, DR. JACOB M., was born Feb. 22, 1806, in Virginia, came to Springfield, Ill., about 1831, was married near Springfield, to Catharine Rickard. Dr. Early was a practicing physician, and a local preacher in the M. E. church. In consequence of some political difficulty, he was shot and killed, March 11, 1838, in Springfield, by a merchant, Henry B. Truitt, who was son-in-law of William L. May, at that time member of Congress for this district. The difficulty was about appointments to office, all the parties interested being democrats. Dr. Early left two sons. His widow married Mr. Miles, and lives in Petersburg, Ill. *See history of the Rickard family.*

EASLEY, DANIEL, was born Oct. 18, 1773, in Stokes county, N. C. In 1791 he went to South Carolina, and in 1801 to Caldwell county, Ky. He was there married in 1805 to Mrs. Margaret Ritchie. They had five children in Kentucky, and came to Sangamon county, Ill., arriving in the spring of 1830 in what is now Ball township. Of his children—

WINIFRED, married Eddin Lewis. *See his name.*

JAMES B., born in Caldwell county, Ky., married Oct. 22, 1840, in Sangamon county, to Margaret Dodds. They had five children. Their son ROBERT HENRY married Fannie Easley, a distant relative, and resides in the southeast corner of Ball township. James B. Easley was a Justice of the Peace for many years. He died, and his widow married Warham Easley, and resides in Missouri.

BENJAMIN H., born in Kentucky, married in Sangamon county three times. He died, leaving a widow, who afterward married and died. His son WILEY married Sarah J. Phelps, a native of Kentucky. They had four children, MARTHA F., WILLIAM A., JAMES R. and FLORA A. Wiley Easley died, and his widow and children reside on the farm settled by their great-grandfather Easley in 1830. It is in Ball township.

SALLY, married Willis Shellhouse. *See his name.*

DANIEL W., born in Kentucky, died in Sangamon county at 12 years old.

Mrs. Margaret Easley died in Sangamon county.

Daniel Easley died at Auburn, Sangamon county, Feb. 13, 1874. If the date of his birth is correct, as given to the writer by the old gentleman himself about fifteen months before his death, he was 100 years, 3 months and 25 days old.

His recollection of events was quite distinct. He related incidents connected with the ascension of the first steamboat on the Ohio river, which he witnessed; also of the war of 1812. He united with the Cumberland Presbyterian church when he was eighty years of age.

EASTMAN, THOMAS, born Dec. 8, 1771, in Kingston, New Hampshire, was married in 1792, in Augusta, Me., to Sarah Cummings. They had nine children born in Maine. Mr. Eastman was captain of a cavalry company in the war of 1812, and was posted between the Kennebec and Penobscot rivers to carry dispatches back and forth. Maine being a district of Massachusetts, he represented that district in the Legislature of Massachusetts four or five times. When Maine became a State, he was elected one of its Senators. He was also a Judge of the Court of Sessions, in Waldo county, where he lived. Mrs. Sarah Eastman died Sept. 3, 1827, and Thomas Eastman was married Oct., 1828, in Boston, Mass., to Susan Frothingham, a native of that city. They had one child in Maine, and moved to Auburn, Ill., in 1836. Of his children only six came to Sangamon county, namely:

DAVID, born Oct. 20, 1794, was married Jan. 1, 1817, in Maine, to Salinda Wood, a native of Winthrop, in the same State. They had four children, and came to Auburn, Sangamon county, Ill., in 1836 or 7. Of their children, AUGUSTA, born in Maine, went from Sangamon county to California, and died there. LOUISA H., married Owen Maynard, and lives in Baltimore, Md. CHARLES H., died in Springfield, Ill., in 1849. GEORGE L., born May 5, 1833, in Maine, brought up in Sangamon county, went to California in 1852, and returned to Springfield in 1870, where he now lives. David Eastman died in 1844, at Auburn, and Mrs. Salinda Eastman died April 25, 1871, in Springfield.

ASA, born Sept. 12, 1802, in Winthrop, Maine, came in 1831 to Waverly, Morgan county, Ill., and laid out the town of Auburn, in Sangamon county, in 1835. He was married Sept. 21, 1837, in Waverly, to Susan E. Tanner, who was born Sept., 1820, in Warren county, Conn. They moved to Auburn in the fall of 1840, and to Springfield in the fall of 1841. Mr. and Mrs. Eastman had two children, ALLEN T., born Dec., 1839, in Waverly, died May, 1847, in Springfield. ANNIE S., born June 12, 1842, in Springfield, was married June, 1867, to James M. Johnson, a native of St. Louis. They have three living children, ALICE E., MARY SUSAN, and HERSCHEL ALLEN, and reside in St. Louis, Mo. Mrs. Susan Eastman died March, 1843, and Asa Eastman resides in Springfield, where he has been for many years largely identified with its business. He began as a partner with James L. Lamb in a flouring mill, and in 1865 he built the only grain elevator in the city, at a cost of about $75,000, and still owns it. He was the originator and one of the principal stockholders in the Leland Hotel, and was President of the Board of Directors when it was building.

ANN H., born Oct. 17, 1805, in Maine, lives with her brother Asa.

HANNAH M., born Aug. 29, 1813, in Maine, was married in Springfield, Ill., March 11, 1869, to Judge William Brown, of Jacksonville. He died April 25, 1871, in Jacksonville. His widow now resides with her brother Asa, in Springfield.

SAMUEL FRANK, the only child of Thomas Eastman by his second marriage, was born Oct. 12, 1830, in Palermo, Waldo county, Me., and came to Auburn, Ill., with his parents in 1836. Returned east and learned the trade of a machinist, at Manchester, N. H. He was married Oct. 5, 1853, at New Haven, Conn., to Mary A. Brown, who was born Oct. 1, 1831, in Bridgewater, Conn. They came in 1856 to Springfield, and have four children, HENRY F., FREDERICK A., CHARLES E., and S. FRANK, Jun., and reside in Springfield. Mr. S. F. Eastman is the proprietor of a machine shop, corner of Washington and Tenth streets, Springfield, Ill.

ECKEL, JOHN C., was born Nov. 27, 1793, in Baltimore, Md., went to Jefferson county, Tenn., was a soldier in the war of 1812, and was married in his native county, Nov. 19, 1819, to Mary Geiger, who was born June 11, 1797. They moved to Sangamon county, Ill., arriving June, 1821, in what is now Cooper township. They had seven children in Sangamon county.

SUSANNAH, born in 1824, married John North. See his name.

CHARLES E., married Martha Ridgeway.

WILLIAM H., married Jane E. Slater.

GEORGE, died in his sixteenth year.

JOHN C., Jun., born May 13, 1831, was married to Arminda Teal.

MARIA L., born Jan. 3, 1836, married Henry Colley. They had six children, and she died.

MARY, born May 4, 1838, was married Nov. 4, 1858, in Sangamon county, to Lafayette Wilmot, and moved to Kansas in 1859. In 1866 they moved to Oregon. Mr. W. was wounded nineteen times in fighting with Indians on the route. He is brother to Miles H. Wilmot, of Illiopolis.

Mrs. Mary Eckel died July 1, 1845, and John C. Eckel was married to Mrs. Joannah Dickson, whose maiden name was Bird. They had two living children.

EDGAR and JANE, twins, were born June 30, 1846. Edgar was married Jan. 13, 1868, to Elizabeth Parkes. They have two children, WILLIAM H. and MARY J., and live in Cooper township near Clarksville. JANE resides with her mother.

John C. Eckel died May 29, 1857, in Sangamon county, and his widow resides in Cooper township, two and one-half miles southwest of Mechanicsburg.

EBEY.—The origin of the family in America was with George Ebey, a native of Holland, who came to this country probably about 1750. On landing in Philadelphia he was sold for money to pay for his passage across the ocean. He was taken to Lancaster county, Pa., and after serving out his time, married and raised a family. He was a soldier in the Revolution, under Gen. Anthony Wayne, and was one of a number of soldiers called a "forlorn hope," at the storming of Stony Point. The assault was successful, but George Ebey was among the slain. His son—

GEORGE EBEY, married in Huntington county to Mary Ellabarger. They moved to Franklin county, O., in Dec. 1805. They had nine living children, and Mrs. Mary Ebey died March 15, 1815, in Ohio. Of their children—

MARY, married in Ohio to A. Hutchinson, and never came farther west.

ELIZABETH, born about 1792 in Pennsylvania, married in Franklin county, O., to Wm. Sells, and remained there.

JACOB, born in 1794 in Pennsylvania, married in Ohio to Sally Blue, and come in 1831 to what is now Cotton Hill township, Sangamon county; in 1840 moved to Adair county, Mo.; and in 1850 to Whitby's Island, Puget Sound; where Jacob Ebey and wife died a few years ago. Their son, ISAAC N., had gone there before his parents, and laid out the town of Port Townsend. He was killed by Indians, leaving a widow in Port Townsend. His sister, MARY Ebey, is now [1874] a widow Bozarth, and lives at Port Townsend.

HENRY, born in 1797 in Pennsylvania, came to Sangamon county in 1828. He died in 1858, leaving a widow and son in Fulton county.

BARBARA, born in Pennsylvania June 25, 1800, married in Franklin county, Ohio, to Rev. William Royal. *See his name.* He died, leaving a family at Salem, Oregon.

SUSAN, born Jan. 28, 1803, in Pennsylvania, married in Ohio to Daniel Hutchinson, and died, leaving three children.

JOHN N., born Sept. 10, 1805, in Huntington county, Pa., raised in Franklin county, Ohio, and came to Sangamon county Nov. 15, 1825, in what is now Woodside township. He was married May 28, 1826, to Mary Brunk, sister to George Brunk. They have ten living children, LEONIDAS C., MARIA J., GEORGE W., JOHN V., ELIZABETH E., HARRIET E., WILLIAM H., was killed at the battle of Belmont, Mo., Nov. 7, 1861. BARBARA A., ANGELINE B., and CHARLES B. Nearly all the living children are married. Mrs. Rebecca Ebey died June 2, 1873, and John N. Ebey resides at Whitehall, Greene county, Ill.

GEORGE, born Jan., 1811, in Ohio, came to Sangamon county in 1828, married in Ohio, in 1832, to Matilda Kirkpatrick. They had three sons in the Union army; one of them was killed in battle at Pittsburg Landing. George Ebey resides at Winchester, Scott county, Ill.

ROSANNA, born Jan. 28, 1813, in Ohio, came in 1828 to Sangamon county, and married David Beam. *See his name.*

George Ebey, Sen., came to Sangamon county in 1828, and died in 1848, at Winchester, Scott county, Ill.

EDWARDS, NINIAN W., born April 15, 1809, near Frankfort, Ky. His father, Hon. Ninian Edwards, was at the time Chief Justice of the Court of Appeals of Kentucky, and the same month in which this son was born Chief Justice Edwards was appointed Governor of Illinois Territory and moved with his family in June following to its capital, Kaskaskia. At the proper age Ninian W. was sent to Transylvania University, and graduated in the law department of that institution in 1833. Previous to his graduation he was married Feb. 16, 1832, in Lexington, Ky., to Elizabeth P. Todd, who was born Nov., 1813. Her father was Robert S. Todd, of Kentucky. *See sketch of the Todd family.* Mr. Edwards commenced the practice of law in 1832. In 1834 he was appointed by Gov. Jno. Reynolds, Attorney General of Illinois, the appointment being confirmed by the Legislature of 1834-5. The law requiring the Attorney General to reside at the capital, and Mr. Edwards not liking Vandalia as a place of residence, he resigned the office and moved to Springfield in 1835. They have four living children, namely—

JULIA COOK, born April 29, 1837, in Springfield, was married June 6, 1855, to Edward L. Baker, who was born June 3, 1829, in Kaskaskia, the ancient capital of Illinois. His father, Hon. David J. Baker, was a native of the State of New York, and came to Illinois in the year 1818. He became one of the prominent lawyers of the young State. E. L. Baker was educated at Shurtleff College, Upper Alton, and graduated in 1847. He read law with his father two years, after which he attended Harvard law school and was admitted to the bar in Springfield in 1855. He became part owner and editor of the *Illinois State Journal*, and in 1869 was appointed U. S. Assessor, remaining in that office until it was abolished. He was appointed Dec. 8, 1873, U. S. Consul to Buenos Ayres, Argentine Republic, South America. Edward L. Baker and wife have three children, EDWARD L., Jun., JULIA E. and WILLIS E., all born in Springfield. Edward L., Jun., is in Springfield. The two youngest are now [1876] with their parents in Buenos Ayres, South America.

ALBERT S., born Dec. 16, 1839, in Springfield, was married there June 3,

1863, to Josephine E. Remann, who was born April 28, 1842, in Vandalia, Ill. They have four children, GEORGIE, MARY E., NINIAN W. and ANNIE R. A. S. Edwards was in the commissary department during the rebellion. He and his family reside in Springfield, Ill.

ELIZABETH E., born Jan. 7, 1843, in Springfield, was married May 11, 1863, to Eugene C. Clover, son of Rev. Dr. Clover, at one time Rector of St. Paul's Episcopal church, Springfield, Ill. E. C. Clover was killed at the battle of Wichita, leaving a widow and two sons, LEWIS P. and LEGH K. Mrs. Clover and her two children reside with her parents in Springfield, Ill.

CHARLES, born July 6, 1846, in Springfield, was attending Yale College in the early part of the rebellion, and left there in the latter part of 1863 to fill a position in the commissary department of the U. S. army. After the war he was an instructor in Bryant & Stratton's commercial college in Springfield for a short time. Charles Edwards was married in Springfield Feb. 18, 1868, to Mary Hickox, daughter of Hon. Virgil Hickox. They have one child, FLORENCE, and reside in Springfield, Ill. Charles Edwards has been for ten years and is now connected with the *Illinois State Journal.*

Hon. Ninian W. Edwards was elected in 1836 one of the representatives of Sangamon county in the State Legislature. He was one of the seven representatives and two senators from Sangamon county who really secured the removal of the State capital from Vandalia to Springfield. See the article "*Long Nine.*" From 1836 to 1852 Mr. Edwards was in the State Legislature, either in the House or Senate. During that time he was a member of the convention that framed the State constitution of 1848. In 1854 he was appointed by the Governor, attorney before the board of commissioners to investigate the claims of canal contractors against the State, amounting to over $1,500,000. This was in the years 1852, '3 and '4. In 1854 Mr. Edwards was appointed by Gov. Matteson Superintendent of Public Instruction for the State of Illinois, and was afterward retained in office by the State Legislature until 1857. In the year 18— he drafted the law in regard to free schools, which was the first adopted in the State. He was appointed by President Lincoln U. S. Commissary in 1862.

Hon. N. W. Edwards has found time, aside from his multifarious official duties, to devote to literary pursuits. His history of Illinois, including the life and times of Gov. Edwards, written on the invitation of the Illinois State Historical Society, is in many respects a work of rare excellence, and is regarded as a standard on the subjects of which it treats.

EDWARDS, BENJAMIN S., came to Sangamon county later than his brother, Hon. Ninian W. He has filled many official positions with ability. He stands pre-eminent in his profession, and is a member of the law firm of Stuart, Edwards & Brown, Springfield Ill.

EDWARDS, ELCEY, born in Adair county, Ky., and came to Sangamon county with his brother J. Jordan, in 1837 or 8, married in Sangamon county to Emily Riggs. They had nine children.

JAMES A., born Sept. 10, 1840, married Lucinda Burton, have three living children, IDA MAY, BENJAMIN L., and EMMA, and reside five and one-half miles southwest of Loami.

ARCHY L., born Nov. 13, 1842, enlisted April, 1861, in Co. G, 7th Ill. Inf., on the first call for 75,000 men, served three months, and enlisted in Sept., 1861, for three years, in Co. B, 10th Ill. Cav., re-enlisted as a veteran Jan., 1864, and was honorably discharged Feb. 6, 1866. He resides with his brother, James A.

ALEXANDER H., married Sarah Conner, have two children, and reside in Audrain county, Mo.

MARTHA M., married John Adwell, who served as a Union soldier. They have five children, and reside in Ball township.

JANE, married John Hilderman, have one child, and reside in Ball township.

ALFRED, ROBERT, AMANDA and BETSY, reside with their parents, in Ball township.

EDWARDS, JAMES JORDAN, was born April 2, 1818, in Adair county, Ky., was taken by his father, Henry Edwards, in 1825, to the vicinity of Jacksonville, Ill. In 1837 or '8 he came to Sangamon county, and about the same time his brothers, Elcey and William, and their sister, America J., came. J. Jordan Edwards was married in Sangamon county to Virginia Jarrett. They had five children—

JAMES, born about 1843, enlisted in 1862, in Co. B, 10th Ill. Cav., for three years, and died near Rolla, Mo., March 8, 1863.

MARY, born Feb. 17, 1845, married Nov. 21, 1861, to William L. Drury, who was born Sept. 18, 1836. They had five children, MARY E. died at seven, and JAMES M. at three years of age. JOHN W., LAURA and CHARLES live with their parents, near Loami.

SARAH, born June 20, 1847, married Dec. 7, 1864, to Firman Price, who was born Sept. 1, 1839, in Monmouth county, N. J. He enlisted Aug. 14, 1861, at Springfield, for three years, in Co. A, 3d Ill. Cav., served more than full term, and was honorably discharged, Sept. 5, 1864. Mr. and Mrs. Price have four children, EDGAR N., MINNIE M., JOSEPH J. and FIRMAN L., and live in Loami township.

SIBYL married Martin Greer, have two children, and live in Missouri.

VIRGINIA married Blaney Pitts, had one child, and mother and child died.

Mrs. Virginia Edwards died April 5, 1852, and Mr. Edwards was married Oct. 1853, to Juliette Burton. They had six children—

HARRIET E., married Sept. 26, 1872, to James L. Mitchell, who was born March 17, 1850, in Morgan county. They live in Loami township.

EUNICE E., OSCAR F., STANLEY, CHARLES and OLLIE, live with their parents, three and a half miles southwest of Loami.

EDWARDS, WILLIAM, born Aug. 27, 1822, in Adair county, Ky., came to Sangamon county in 1837 or 8, with his brothers, J. Jordon & Elcey. He was married Oct. 18, 1840, to Mary Burton. They had ten children; five died under three years.

WILLIAM D., born July 9, 1844, in Sangamon county, enlisted Nov. 25, 1861, in Co. B, 10th Ill. Cav., for three years, served full term and was honorably discharged, married Sarah Masters, have two living children, and reside in Montgomery county.

JAMES A., died in 1863, aged eighteen.

HENRY N., ANDREW W., and MAGGIE, reside with their parents near Loami.

EDWARDS, AMERICA J., sister to J. Jordan, Elcey and William, was born in Morgan county, came to Sangamon county with her brothers, married Michael Morris, had four children, and he died near Knoxville, Iowa. She moved to Texas with her children.

EATON, JOHN, was born in 1791, in Bradford, Merrimack county, New Hampshire, and was married there in 1813 to Mary Cook, who was born at the same place in 1793. Mr. Eaton came to Springfield in June, 1838. The family came in 1840, and in 1841 moved to Petersburg, returning to Springfield in 1843. Of their children—

HIRAM G., born in 1814, in New Hampshire, came with the family to Springfield, married in 1850, at Fairfield, Iowa, and died about 1860, leaving a widow and three children, PAGE, BELLE and ALBERT, in Kansas.

MARY J., born in 1816, in Bradford, N. H., married in Springfield, Ill., to Francis Clinton, a native of Burlington, Vermont. They had two children in Springfield, LAURA married Maj. E. S. Johnson. See his name. MARY married Carl O. Wederkinch, and died April 10, 1875, in Colorado. Francis Clinton and wife both died in Springfield.

THOMAS S., born about 1818, in New Hampshire, came to Petersburg, Ill., in 1842, and died there in 1843.

PAGE, born Oct. 25, 1821, at Bradford, N. H., married May 25, 1852, in Springfield, Ill., to Margaret A. Lee, who was born August 12, 1832, in Delaware. They had six children, two of whom died under eight years. LELIA lives with her parents. KATE D., born June 8, 1855, married April 20, 1875, to Walter E. Powell, have one child, EMMA M., and live in Springfield. GRACE D. and WILLIE C. live with their parents in Springfield.

BENJAMIN C. married in New Hampshire, and remained there.

LOVENIA, born in 1825, at Bradford, N. H., married in Springfield to Thomas Lee, and died.

JOHN B., born Dec. 15, 1827, in Bradford, N. H., married in Sangamon county June 16, 1853, to Mary P. Jones, a native of Tennessee. They had ten children. SUSIE died young. MARY J., married Thomas Lee. *See his name with the Conant family.* WILLIAM W., ANTIONETTE and ANTHONY—twins—CHARLEY, JESSIE, MAY, GRIFFITH and DAISY; the eight latter live with their parents. J. B. Eaton lived in Springfield from 1839 to 1854, when he moved to Christian county, and came back to Springfield in 1866. He is now farming and grain dealing at Edinburg, but resides in Springfield.

LOUISA A., born in 1832, in Bradford, N. H., lived in Sangamon county, and died in 1850, at Beardstown, Ill.

SARAH M., born in Bradford, N. H., married in Sangamon county to Joseph Patterson, a native of Pennsylvania. They have seven children, and reside near Winchester, Scott county, Ill.

John Eaton was a soldier in the war of 1812. Later in life he was a carpenter and builder, and was erecting a mill at Naples, Ill., and died there in 1846. His widow died April, 1854, in Springfield, Illinois.

ELKIN, GARRETT, brother of William F., was born Dec. 31, 1797, in Clarke county, Ky. He studied medicine and graduated at Transylvania University, Lexington, Ky., came to Sangamon county in 1823, and practiced medicine in what is now Fancy creek township. He was married there, April 20, 1823, to Mary Constant, (*see Thomas Constant,*) and soon after moved to Springfield and practiced medicine there. They had six living children—

MARY A., born May 10, 1825, died June 17, 1843.

ADALINE C., born Sept. 28, 1827, in Springfield, was married May 22, 1851, to Dr. J. M. Major. They have two children, WILLIAM A. and CHARLES, and reside in Bloomington, Ill.

WILLIAM T., born Feb. 5, 1832, in Springfield, Ill., went to California with his father in 1850, and succeeded well for a time, but was obliged to return on account of an affection of the eyes. He is unmarried, and resides with his father.

HENRY, born Oct. 8, 1836, in Springfield, enlisted in the 33d Ill. Reg., in 1862, and served three years. Re-enlisted, and served to the close of the war. He died in Memphis, Tenn, in 1873.

—36

ROBERT, born Jan. 12, 1841, in Springfield, enlisted in a Cavalry Regiment in Colorado, and served to the close of the war. He resides in Omaha, Neb.

FRANCIS A., born March 22, 1843, died June 19, 1858.

Dr. Garrett Elkin was in the Black Hawk and Mormon wars, and was Sheriff of Sangamon county six years. He moved to Bloomington in 1844. Mrs. Mary Elkin died there Sept. 23, 1845. Dr. E. served as Captain of a company from Bloomington in the Mexican war—Col. E. D. Baker's regiment. He afterwards moved to the vicinity of Oskaloosa, Iowa, where he was married, Feb. 15, 1864, to Margaret J. Musgrove. They have six children, *GREENBURY G., FANNIE E., CHARLIE, CLARA E., LILLIE A.* and *WILLIS G.*

Dr. Garrett Elkin and family reside on a farm near Oscaloosa, Iowa.

ELKIN, WILLIAM F., was born April 13, 1792, in Clarke county, Ky. In 1811 he went to Xenia, O., and was there married Dec. 5, 1813, to Elizabeth Constant. She was born June 14, 1799, in Clarke county, Ky., also. They had four children in Ohio, and in 1820 moved to Brownsville, Ind., where they had three, and then moved to Sangamon county, Ill., arriving in December, 1825, in what is now Fancy Creek township, where they had six children, four of whom died under five years. Of the other nine—

ROBERT, born Dec. 17, 1814, in Ohio, died in Sangamon county, aged eighteen years.

THOMAS, born Sept. 16, 1816, in Xenia, O., raised in Sangamon county, married Feb. 28, 1843, in Jacksonville, Ill., to Harriet C. Church. She was born Feb. 19, 1820, in Lexington, Ky. They had three children, WILLIAM L., born June 3, 1844, in Sangamon county, enlisted Aug., 1862, for three years, in Co. G, 114 Ill. Inf., served full term and was honorably discharged in 1865. He studied law with Herndon & Zane in Springfield, went to Calvert, Tex., engaged in practice, and died there Oct. 29, 1873. WALLACE A., born April 5, 1846, in Sangamon county, and lives at Salt Lake City, Utah. LAURA F., born Jan. 5, 1850, in Springfield, married in St. Louis Aug. 7, 1872, to Edward Pew, a native of Kentucky. They have one child, EDWARD W., and live in St. Louis. Mrs. Harriet C. Elkin died Aug. 26, 1867. Thomas Elkin was married Dec. 4, 1873, in Springfield, to Mrs. Eva M. Smith, whose maiden name was Mealey. They reside in Springfield.

MARY A., born May 8, 1818, in Xenia, O., married in Sangamon county to Benjamin F. Pickrell. *See his name*. He died and she married Abner Riddle. *See his name*.

JOHN G., born March 28, 1820, in Xenia, O., married Oct. 24, 1843, in Springfield, Ill., to Eveline McNabb. They had four children, ALICE, born Feb. 20, 1845, married William A. Fullinwider. *See his name*. ADELAIDE, born Dec. 6, 1850, was married Dec. 3, 1875, in Mechanicsburg, Ill., to Henry O. Correll. *See his name*. LUCILLA, born July 6, 1853, in Mechanicsburg, married Samuel T. Fullinwider. *See his name*. ARTHUR, is attending Eureka College—May, 1876. John G. Elkin was a prosperous merchant for a period of fifteen years in Mechanicsburg. He died Aug. 27, 1867, in that place, and his widow resides there.

ZACHARIA E., born Nov., 1821, in Brownsville, Ind., raised in Sangamon county. He went overland in 1849 to Oregon, and from there to California and spent several years in mining. He went to Idaho in 1860, and was married Oct., 1873, to Mrs. Harriet Luckett, and resides in Idaho City, Boise county, Idaho.

GARRETT, born March 2, 1823, at Brownsville, Ind., raised in Sangamon county, married in Jacksonville, Ill., to Mrs. Martha Tegarden. They had eight children, and Mrs. Elkin died Oct. 24, 1872. He was married May 1, 1873, to Mrs. Matilda Conner, whose maiden name was Gibbons. They reside in Springfield.

ANDREW H., born Nov., 1825, in Indiana, died in Sangamon county, aged eighteen years.

MARGERY, born July 8, 1832, in Sangamon county, married July, 1852, in Springfield, to Edward A. Jones. They have three daughters, LUELLA, IDA and HATHAWAY, and reside near Decatur, Ill.

WILLIAM F., Jun., born Feb. 29, 1836, in Sangamon county, married Nov. 16, 1860, in Springfield, to Maria Louisa Harvey, who was born Oct. 13, 1839, in Springfield. They have seven living children, EMMA C., CHARLES H., ROBERT R., JOHN F., LEWIS P., ZACHARIA C. and CLARA B., and reside in Springfield.

William F. Elkin was one of the representatives of Sangamon county in the legislature of 1828 and '9 He raised a company in Springfield in 1831, and was Captain of it in the Black Hawk war of that year. He was again elected to represent the county in 1836 and 1838, for two years each time, and was consequently a member of the legislature that enacted the law for the removal of the capital from Vandalia to Springfield. *See the article: Long Nine.* His last labors in the legislature was at its first meeting in Springfield, in call session Dec. 9, 1839. In 1840 and '42 he was elected Sheriff of Sangamon county, for two years each. He was appointed Register of the U. S. Land Office at Springfield, in Sept., 1861, by his old "Long Nine" colleague, Abraham Lincoln. In 1867 he moved to Decatur, but held the office in Springfield until 1872, when he resigned. His wife died August 25, 1872, in Decatur, and W. F. Elkin resides near that city with his daughter, Mrs. Jones. He is in his eighty-fifth year.

ELDER, SAMUEL, born June 22, 1787, in North Carolina, or Sevier county, Tenn. Phebe Clinkenbeard was born Dec. 26, 1798, in Sevier county, Tenn. They were married March 20, 1813, in that county, and had three children there. They moved to Bourbon county, Ky, where one child was born, thence to Scott county, Ind., where they had five children. After seven years residence there, they returned to Bourbon county, Ky., where they had seven children, and the family moved to Sangamon county, Ill., arriving Nov. 27, 1834, in what is now Rochester township, where they had four children. Of their twenty children, five died in infancy.

LAVINA, born Feb. 12, 1815, in Tennessee, was married in Sangamon county to William Clinkenbeard. *See his name*.

HARRISON, born Feb. 29, 1816, died in his fourteenth year.

MARY B., born May 18, 1817, in Sevier county, Tenn., was married in Sangamon county, Ill., to Jonathan Constant. *See his name*.

JAMES, born Oct. 24, 1821, in Scott county, Ind., was married in Sangamon county, Ill., Feb. 27, 1844, to Harriet Walker. They had seven children. HIRAM died in infancy. SARAH J. died Sept. 14, 1859, in her fourteenth year, and WILLIAM W., the fifth child, died, aged three years. LYDIA E., born Oct. 5, 1849, was married Feb. 23, 1871, to Joseph F. Ellington, who was born Oct. 17, 1843, in Bath county, Ky. They have one child, JAMES A., and reside one mile north of Buffalo. MARY L., born Nov. 19, 1852, married Zachary T. Greening. See his name. FRANCES J., born Sept. 16, 1859, and HARRIET A., born July 4, 1867, reside with their parents, two miles north of Buffalo, Sangamon county, Ill.

RACHEL, born Dec. 8, 1822, in Indiana, died in Sangamon county, Nov., 1835.

SARAH, born March 4, 1825, in Scott county, Ind., was married in Sangamon county to Jotham S. Rogers. They had two children in Springfield. HANSON G. died, aged eight years. MARY L., born July 14, 1850, was married in Springfield, May 29, 1873, to John Hunter, who was born March 31, 1841, in Philadelphia. They reside in Washington, D. C. Jotham S. Rogers, died in Springfield, in 1851, and his widow married Isaac Lindsay. See his name. They have five children, and reside in Springfield.

JONATHAN, born July 24, 1826, in Bourbon county, Ky., was married in Sangamon county to Josephine Flagg. They had one child, IVA, who was married in Springfield, Ill., to Leonard Gardner, and have two children. Mrs. Josephine Elder died, and he married Sarah Wolvern. They have five children, and reside near Sullivan, Moultrie county, Illinois.

MERCY, born Jan. 7, 1829, in Bourbon county, Ky., was married in Sangamon county to Isaac Lindsay. See his name.

ISAAC, born March 12, 1830, in Bourbon county, Ky., was married Nov. 3, 1853, to Harriet Lanning, in Springfield. She was born March 6, 1835, in Auglaize county, Ohio. They have three living children, CHARLES A., EDWARD B. and ISAAC N., and live one and a half miles northeast of Lanesville, Sangamon county, Ill.

SAMUEL S., born May 5, 1831, in Bourbon county, Ky., was married in Springfield, Dec. 17, 1851, to Sarah A. Shives, who was born July 4, 1833, in Pennsylvania. They had two children, AUGUSTA J. married Dec. 17, 1875, to Lewis Allen Constant, son of Jonathan Constant. See his name. They live in Springfield. WILLIAM G. died in his third year. S. S. Elder has been for many years and is now engaged in the tin ware and stove business, and resides in Springfield, Ill.

ELIZABETH J., born May 30, 1832, in Kentucky, was married in Sangamon county, in 1850, to Ethan P. May. He was born June 12, 1829. They had thirteen children; two died young. MARY E., born March 15, 1851, married George Enlow, and lives in Rochester, Ill. GEORGE W., SARAH E., FANNIE A., MARTHA A., CHARLES, WILLIAM D., HARRIET J., EMMA L., SAMUEL L., AUGUSTA L. and FREDERICK T. The family reside in Rochester, Sangamon county, Ill.

SINAI ANN, born June 16, 1833, in Kentucky, was married in Sangamon county to Franklin Hoyt. They had one child, JAMES E., and Mr. Hoyt died. His widow married E. P. Walker. They had two children, SAMUEL M. and CHESTER, who reside with their mother. Mr. Walker enlisted and died in the army. His widow married William Hunter, who was born in Philadelphia. They have two children, DORA and WILLIE, who reside with their parents, in Jacksonville, Ill.

HARRIET, born August 15, 1835, in in Sangamon county, was married Jan. 11, 1855, to Levi F. Dyson, who was born Nov. 8, 1825, near Poolesville, Montgomery county, Md. They reside in Springfield. Mr. Dyson came to Springfield in Nov., 1841, and engaged in the stove and tinware business, which he continues to the present time.

DAVID L., born May 25, 1839, in Sangamon county, was married in Sullivan, Moultrie county, to Mary Berry. They have two children, JAMES and WILLIAM, and reside in Springfield, Illinois.

HANNAH R., born July 1, 1841, in Sangamon county, was the twentieth child. She was married Feb. 9, 1858, to George P. Sidener, who was born Dec. 5, 1833, in Bourbon county, Ky. They had seven children; two of whom died young. CHARLES LINCOLN, ADA A., JAMES GRANT, EDWARD B. and WILLIAM A., and reside two miles north of Rochester, Sangamon county, Illinois.

Samuel Elder died Oct. 24, 1846, and his widow resides with her daughter, Mrs. Dyson, in Springfield, Ill.

ELLIOTT, ANDREW, was born in 1792, in Rutherford county, N., C. He was there married to Zilpha Kelly. They had two children in North Carolina, and moved to Sangamon county, Ill., in company with his father-in-law, Wm. Kelly, arriving in the fall of 1819, and entered eighty acres of land in what is now the northwest corner of the city of Springfield, where they had seven children. Of their children—

ELIZABETH M., born Oct. 4, 1815, in North Carolina, married in Sangamon county to Caswell Stripling. Mrs. S. died, leaving one child. Mr. Stripling and his son FRANCIS reside near Nicolaus, Sutter county, Cal.

SARAH M., born Aug. 31, 1818, in North Carolina, married to Isaac Taylor. *See his name.*

J. WESLEY, born May 17, 1822, adjoining Springfield on the north, married, April 13, 1843, to Allissa or Alice Baldwin. They had ten children in Sangamon county—ROBERT, born Feb. 26, 1844, enlisted, Aug. 25, 1862, in Co. G, 114th Ill. Inf., for three years, served full term, and was honorably discharged Aug. 3, 1865, resides with his parents. JAMES H., born Aug. 22, 1845, resides with his parents. SARAH E., born Jan. 3, 1848, married James A. Dunlap. *See his name.* CATHARINE died in her fourth year. ZILPHA, died Nov. 20, 1864, aged fourteen. HARRIET, born June 30, 1852, married Abraham Langford, and resides six miles south of Springfield. ANDREW J., CALVIN and JOHN L., reside with their parents one and three-fourths miles northwest of Springfield, and within one mile of where J. W. Elliott was born.

THOMAS W., born Aug. 20, 1824, died in 1855, of cholera, in Springfield.

ANDREW H., born Nov. 22, 1828, married in 1852 to Matilda Tulley, had two children, and Mr. E. died Feb. 15, 1873, in Springfield. His widow resides in Mason City.

JAMES M., born April 22, 1835, married Louisa Rolls. He was accidentally shot while his wife was handing a gun to him, and died a week later, in Aug., 1861.

WILLIAM K., born March 13, 1838, married Martha Potts, and died May 2, 1865.

Mrs. Zilpha Elliott died March 2, 1842, and Andrew Elliott died Oct. 17, 1864, both at Springfield. Andrew Elliott was a soldier from North Carolina in 1812. He was a soldier from Sangamon county in the Winnebago war of 1827, in the Black Hawk war of 1831, and in the Mormon war of 1845. He kept the first hotel in Springfield. It was called the Buck Horn Tavern, and had a large pair of antlers for a sign. Andrew Elliott was the man who drove the Commissioners to see Sangamo town, when they were investigating the subject with the view of locating the county seat. He drove them through all the sloughs he could reach by a round-about way, and disgusted them before they reached the spot. They were thus induced to decide against Sangamo and in favor of Springfield.

ELLIOTT, JAMES, was born in 1798, near Richmond, Va. When a young man he emigrated to Woodford county, Ky., and was married near Frankfort, in 1827, to Mrs. Jane E. Plumer, whose maiden name was Taylor. She was born in Kentucky, in 1795. Her father was a distinguished Baptist minister (Rev. John Taylor). She is a sister of Mrs. Sallie Smith, and J. Wickliffe Taylor, of Bates, Sangamon county, Ill. Mr. and Mrs. Elliott had three children in Kentucky, and they moved to Sangamon county, Ill. arriving in May, 1835. They settled in what is now Cartwright township. Of their children—

JOHN J., born in 1828, in Franklin county, Ky., was brought up in Sangamon county, and died in Springfield, in 1861.

WILLIAM B., born in 1830, in Franklin county, Ky., brought up in Sangamon county, Ill., was married in 1857, in Jacksonport, Ark., to Ellen Tussell, who was born there. They had two children, TOM and MORMON. William B. Elliott died at Jacksonport, in 1864. His children live with their mother, who is married again, and resides in Jacksonport, Ark.

TEMPLE, born Dec. 9, 1835, in Franklin county, Ky., brought up in Sangamon county, was married Oct. 8, 1862, at Elkhart, Ill., to Mary Constant. They have five children, HALLIE, ARCHIE, RITA, HARRIE and GRIFFITH, and reside in Springfield. Temple Elliott was deputy Sheriff two years, from Nov., 1870, to Nov., 1872. He is now (June, 1876) connected with the State Register office.

James Elliot died June, 1856, in Sangamon county, and his widow resides with her son, Temple Elliott, in Springfield, Illinois.

ELLIOTT, MRS. SARAH, was born about 1791, in Maryland, and was taken by her parents to Harrison county, Ky. She was there married to Edward Elliott, a native of Pennsylvania. They had three children in Harrison county, and moved to Gallatin county where four children were born, and Mr. Elliott died, in 1829, near Warsaw, in that county. Mrs. Elliott, with her seven children, moved to Sangamon county, Ill., arriving in Oct., 1830, in what is now Mechanicsburg township. Of her children—

AMANDA, born in Kentucky, married, in Sangamon county, to Eleazer White, had six children, and died July, 1860, in Christian county.

OLIVER, born in Kentucky, raised in Sangamon county, married Mary Nellums, had three children, and he died Nov., 1873, at Moweaqua, Ill.

MILFORD, always called Milton, was born about 1818, in Kentucky, raised in Sangamon county, was with the Reed and Donner party, and starved to death in the mountains on the way to the Pacific coast, in the winter of 1846 and 7.

AMERICA, born Oct. 12, 1820, in Gallatin county, Ky., married in Sangamon county to James M. King. *See his name.*

MARY died, aged six years.

WILLIAM, born in Kentucky, married in Sangamon county to Elizabeth Miller. They have nine children, and reside near Mt. Auburn, Christian county.

REBECCA, born in Kentucky, married Thompson Kipper, have seven children, and live near Mt. Auburn.

Mrs. Sarah Elliott died Feb., 1857, near Mt. Auburn, Christian county, Ill.

ELLIS, HENRY, born Nov. 17, 1786, near Lexington, Ky. His father, John Ellis was born Jan. 29, 1749, and married Oct. 2, 1770, to Sarah Parrish, who was born April 20, 1757. They moved from Virginia to Kentucky. The family is of Welsh extraction. The father of John Ellis is said to have been with the second supply of emigrants from England to America. Martha Marshall Yates was born (after the death of her father) in Woodford county, Ky., Sept. 13, 1791, and was a sister of Henry Yates, Sen. *See his name.* Henry Ellis and Martha Yates were married Jan. 29, 1807, in Warsaw, Ky., and had ten children there, two of whom died in infancy. The family moved to Sangamon county, Ill., arriving in Sept., 1825, in Island Grove, two miles northeast of Berlin, where three children were born. Of their eleven children—

ABNER Y., born Nov. 30, 1807, at Warsaw, Ky., was married in Springfield, Ill., Jan. 26, 1832, to Ann M. Glascock, who was born Nov. 15, 1815. Their two children died in infancy, and Mrs. Ellis died Jan. 16, 1834. A. Y. Ellis was married June 8, 1837, at Paddock's Grove, Ill., to Virginia J. Richmond. Of their eight children born in Springfield, Ill.: VOLNEY R., born April 22, 1838, was married July 10, 1858, to Maria E. Smith. They are without family, and live in Quincy, Ill. ABNER Y., Jun., born June 1, 1840, was married Dec. 20, 1865, to Caroline L. H. Flagg, at Rochelle, Ogle county, Ill. She was born there, Nov., 1845. They have four children, RICHARD Y., ALFRED F., LUCY V. and WILLARD F. A. Y. Ellis, Jun., has been mailing clerk for seventeen years in the Springfield Postoffice, and resides in the city. JANE F., born July 10, 1842, in Springfield, is unmarried, and resides with her parents. ORVILLE P., born July 31, 1844, was married May 5, 1874, to Arabell S. Graves, at Bethalto, Madison county, Ill. They have one child, BESSIE, and reside at Bunker Hill, Ill. HENRY, born May 13, 1848, is a farmer, residing with his parents. JOHN CON-

DELL, born Jan. 30, 1851, is a telegraph operator at Alton, Ill. WILLARD F., born April 11, 1853, died Oct. 24, 1873. SALOME E., born Feb. 19 1857, lives with her parents. A. Y. Ellis, Sen., resides near Moro, Madison county, Ill. He was for several years Deputy Sheriff of Sangamon county, salesman in Gen. James D. Henry's store, and afterwards a merchant himself. He was elected Treasurer of Sangamon county in 1844, serving one term. Was Postmaster of Springfield, from 1849 to 1853, under Presidents Taylor and Fillmore. After a residence of forty years in Springfield, he moved in 1865 to Paddock's Grove, near Moro, Madison county, Ill., and resides there.

LAVINA, born Dec. 14, 1809, in Warsaw, Ky., was married there, Sept. 8, 1825, to Talbott Leonard, moved to the vicinity of Frankfort, where three children were born, and she died. Her children, JOHN W. and GEORGE H. are physicians in Tennessee. MARTHA married John Martin, and resides at New Liberty, Gallatin county, Ky.

WILLIAM H. H. born August 1, 1812, in Warsaw, Ky., married Mrs. Bashaba Smith, who died, leaving one child. He married Mrs. Nancy Dennison, whose maiden name was Hope. They had three children, and Mr. Ellis died Jan. 28, 1873, near Berlin.

MOLLY, born Dec. 12, 1814, in Warsaw, Ky., was married in Sangamon county, Nov. 4, 1840, to Elias Maxwell. They had one child, ABNER Y. He enlisted in 1861, in Co. D, 26th Ill. Inf. for three years, and died of disease contracted in the army, Dec. 24, 1864, at Berlin. Elias Maxwell died, and she married Andrew Scott. He died in 1860, and she in 1861.

LOUISA, born May 8, 1816, in Kentucky, was married May 18, 1835, in Berlin, Ill., to Thomas F. Foster. They brought up a family, and reside in Berlin.

ORMASINDA, born Feb. 17, 1818, in Kentucky, died Nov. 2, 1833, near Berlin.

MARTHA, born Sept. 12, 1822, in Warsaw, Ky., was married Oct. 4, 1842, in Sangamon county, to Oliver H. Rush. He died Jan. 5, 1855, leaving four children. MARY E. died, aged nineteen years. VIRGINIA married Morgan Belding, and lives at Corning, Adams county, Iowa. MARTHA married John Johnson, and lives at Worthington, Minn. ROBERT G., resides with his mother, in Berlin.

MILLICENT A., born April 7, 1824, in Kentucky, died Oct. 12, 1871, in Berlin.

JOEL H., born Jan. 16, 1828, in Sangamon county, was married May 8, 1852, to Caroline Harmon. They had one child, and mother and child died. He was married May 8, 1861, to Martha Simpson. They have two children, FLORENCE M. and DORA B., and reside in Berlin.

ROBERT, born April 27, 1830, in Sangamon county, was married Dec. 15, 1857, to Delia J. Pease. She died Aug. 2, 1872, leaving four children, GEORGE L., GREEK M., HENRY M. and GERTRUDE M. live with their father in Berlin.

RICHARD T., born Dec. 6, 1832, at Island Grove, enlisted August 11, 1861, in Co. D, 26th Ill. Inf., for three years. He was killed in a rifle pit at Atlanta, Ga., Aug. 8, 1864, within three days of the expiration of his term of service.

Henry Ellis, Sen., died June 13, 1854, in Berlin, and his widow resides there, in the eighty-fifth year of her age. [1876.]

ELLIS, LEVI D., born about 1791, in South Carolina. His father died before Levi D. was born. When the latter was thirteen years of age he accompanied some neighboring families to Tennessee, and stopped near Nashville, in that State. He hired out, bought some land with the proceeds, improved it and sent for his mother and the rest of the family. He learned the cabinet and carpenter's trades, in Nashville, and was married there, about 1811, to Cynthia Bradford, who was born in Fauquier county, Va., and was the only daughter of Captain William Bradford of that county. L. D. Ellis was drafted in the war of 1812, but hired a substitute, and was employed by the Government to stock guns. After the war they moved to the mouth of the Cumberland river, in Kentucky, and from there with two children to the vicinity of Belleville, Ill., thence, in 1817, to where Springfield now stands. Of their children—

WILLIAM, born Aug. 13, 1812, in Tennessee.

JAMES, born Aug. 13, 1814, in Kentucky.

DANIEL, born Aug. 25, 1816, in Illinois.

JACOB W., born July 20, 1818, in Sangamon county, Ill. (Until my attention was called to Jacob W. Ellis, it was thought Joseph E. McCoy was the first child born of white parents in the present limits of Sangamon county, but the date of Mr. Ellis' birth comes to me as a quotation from a record in the family Bible, and appears to be as much entitled to credence as any of the others.) He was married in Fulton county, Ill., June 21, 1838, to Sarah Kreider. Of their children—WILLIAM, born March 23, 1839, in Ellisville, Fulton county, Ill., enlisted in the 17th Reg. Ill. Vol. Inf., under Col. L. F. Ross, and died the next August at Ironton, Mo. MILLIE, born July 2, 1841, in Illinois, married Caleb Sullivan. He enlisted during the rebellion, and was with Sherman in his march to the sea. They have six children, WILLIAM, HARRY, WALTER, FREDERICK, BERTIE, and a babe. SARAH, married Abram Childers, in Fulton county, Ill. He served in the army. They have four children, MARY, ENORA, CORA and NELLIE. Mr. Childers resides in Lena Valley, Greenwood county, Kans. FLORENCE, married Thomas I. Tullis. They have one child, and live at Fairview, Fulton county, Ill. BIRD, born in 1853, is a farmer, and lives in Illinois. Mrs. Sarah Ellis died Aug. 20, 1857, in Prairie City, Ill., and Jacob W. Ellis was married Aug., 1858, in Fulton county, to Adelia Sanford. They have one child, FRANK, born March 4, 1861. J. W. Ellis is a carpenter. He moved to Kansas in the fall of 1870, and resides in Lena Valley, Greenwood county, Kansas.

FIELDING, born June 24, 1820, in Sangamon county, Ill.

JOSEPH, born Aug. 22, 1822, in Sangamon county.

JESSE, born Feb. 7, 1824, in Fulton county, Ill.

MARY, born March 12, 1826, in Fulton county, Ill.

Levi D. Ellis built a mill, with a brush dam, on Spring creek. He surveyed the first lots in Springfield, and moved to Fulton county, Ill., in 1823, where he built a mill on Spoon river, and laid out the town of Ellisville. Mrs. Cynthia Ellis died in the summer of 1846, and Levi D. Ellis died Aug. 7, 1857, both in Fulton county, Ill.

ELLIS, JACOB, brother of Levi D., came to Sangamon county later, and built a horse mill, cotton gin and blacksmith shop. He lived half a mile west of Levi, in Springfield, and moved to Fulton county the same year with his brother.

ELLIS, MILETUS W., born April 7, 1809, in Albemarle county, Va., and came to Sangamon county, Ill., arriving at Springfield, in Nov., 1830. He was married March 13, 1834, to Mary A. Constant. They had two living children.

MARTHA, married William Winn, and for a second husband married James Barr, and lives in Kansas.

JAMES C., married Matilda Newcomb, and resides at Hiram, Ohio.

Mrs. Mary A. Ellis died Sept. 4, 1846, and Miletus W. Ellis was married Nov. 7, 1847, to Mrs. Mary M. Constant, whose maiden name was Stewart. They had one child—

FANNIE W. She married George B. Jones. *See his name*.

Miletus W. Ellis died Aug. 28, 1872, and his widow resides at the homestead, three miles west of Williamsville. Mr. Ellis' father, mother, three brothers and three sisters, came to the county with him. All went to Bureau county.

ELMORE, HARDIN H., was born June 20, 1813, in Cumberland county, Ky., was taken by his parents to Adair county about 1827. From there he came to Sangamon county, arriving in Sept., 1834, in what is now Loami township. He was married April 6, 1836, to Sarah Forrest. They had three children, and Mrs. Elmore died April 6, 1844, within ten minutes of eight years from the time of her marriage. H. H. Elmore was married Oct. 20, 1847, to Sibyl Pirdy, who was born Nov. 26, 1823, in Kanawha county, W. Va. They have three children. Of all his children—

ELIZABETH J., born May 6, 1836, married Oct. 15, 1857, to R. R. Roberts. They have four children, LEWIS E., MARGARET, KATIE and ROBERT, and live in Sedan, Chautauqua county, Kansas.

SARAH A., born April 7, 1840, married Daniel Kinney. See his name.

AMERICA L., born March 28, 1844, married Charles King. They have five children, KATIE, THOMAS, FANNY, MARY E., and a babe, and reside near Sedan, Chautauqua county, Kansas.

By the second marriage—

NELSON F., born Aug. 29, 1847, enlisted in 1864 in Co. E, 133d Ill. Inf., for one hundred days, served full term, and was honorably discharged. He was married Sept. 22, 1868, to Julia J. Colburn. They have three children, FRANK, VIOLA, and a babe, and live five miles southwest of Chatham.

WILLIAM H. and JAMES B., live with their parents.

H. H. Elmore and wife reside in Loami.

ENOS, ABNER, was born July 20, 1791, near Utica, Oneida county, N. Y. He was in the American navy, under Commodore Perry, was in the naval battle on Lake Erie, Sept. 10, 1813, and was wounded by a boarding pike being thrust through him, by which he was fastened to the side of the ship until relieved by friends. He was captured a few months later, and the last six months of the war he spent in prison, at Montreal, Canada. He drew a pension to the end of his life. He went, in 1815, to Clark county, Ky., and was there married, August 6, 1817, to Anna Burns. They had six children, and she died Sept. 13, 1829, in Clark county, and he there married Anna Sudduth, June 9, 1830. She was born there Jan. 20, 1792. The family moved to Sangamon county, Ill., arriving Oct. 1, 1831, in Buffalo Hart Grove, where one child was born. Of his children—

AMARILDA, born Nov. 17, 1818, in Clark county, Ky., married in Sangamon county, Dec. 26, 1837, to Sylvester W. Ford. See his name.

JAMES, born July 10, 1820, in Clark county, Ky., married in Sangamon county, in 1847, to Phebe J. Goff. They have three children, and reside near Knobnoster, Johnson county, Mo.

HORACE B., born Jan. 17, 1822, in Clarke county, Ky., married in Sangamon county, April 3, 1844, to Arminta J. Constant. They had three children in Sangamon county. MARY E., born Dec. 20, 1845, married H. Clay Constant. See his name. JOHN R., born March 5, 1848, enlisted in Co. I, 114th Ill. Inf., March 8, 1865, for one year. He was transferred to Co. C, 58th Ill. Inf., July, 1865, served until March 7, 1866, when he was honorably discharged, at Montgomery, Alabama. He was married Oct. 28, 1874, in Sangamon county, to Jane F. Wilson, a daughter of Thomas Wilson. See Riddle family. They reside in Buffalo Hart township. ALFRED R., born Feb. 17, 1854, died aged six years. Mrs. Arminta J. Enos died Sept. 11, 1857, and H. B. Enos was married Nov. 10, 1858, in Erie county, New York, to Caroline C. Merrick, who was born Dec. 29, 1828, in Onandaga county, N. Y. They have one child, GERTIE J., born Sept. 30, 1860, and reside two and a half miles southeast of Buffalo Hart Station.

ROBERT B., born April 7, 1824, in Clark county, Ky., married in Sangamon county, August 27, 1865, to Mary F. Etter, who was born Oct. 13, 1844, in Lawrence county, Ind. They have one living child. GRACIE M. died in her third year. ARTHUR O. died in infancy. EDWARD LESLIE resides with his parents, two and three-quarter miles east of Buffalo Hart Station.

WILLIAM S., born Dec. 4, 1832, in Sangamon county, the only child by the second wife. He enlisted August 15, 1862, for three years, in Co. B, 130th Ill. Inf., and was wounded May 22, 1863, in five places, and again June 4, 1863, by a shot through the foot, all at the siege of Vicksburg. He recovered, and was captured April, 1864, in Gen. Bank's Red river expedition, was placed in a rebel stockade prison at camp Ford, near Tyler, Texas, remained in prison thirteen months and nineteen days, was released, went to New Orleans, St. Louis and Springfield, and was honorably discharged June 17, 1865. He was married Oct. 12, 1865, to Jane Dunn, who was born Jan. 29, 1847, in Yorkshire, England. They have two children, ANNIE and JANETTE, and reside two and a half miles east of Buffalo Hart Station.

Abner Enos died March 12, 1850, and Mrs. Anna S. Enos died Jan. 17, 1870, both in Buffalo Hart township.

ENOS, PASCAL P., born in 1770, at Windsor, Conn. Salome Paddock was born March 12, 1791, at Woodstock,

Windsor county, Vt. They were there married, Sept., 1815, moved to Cincinnati, Ohio, the same fall, and a year later to St. Charles, Mo., where one child was born. In the spring of 1817 they moved to St. Louis, where one child was born, and in the fall of 1821 moved to Madison county, six miles north of Edwardsville, Ill. While residing there, at the solicitation of the Vermont delegation in Congress, Mr. Enos was appointed by President Monroe Receiver in the land office then established at what was called Springfield District, although there was no town laid out. Mr. Enos arrived with his family in Sept., 1823. He opened the land office in a double log cabin, at what is now the northwest corner of Third and Jefferson streets. He soon after united with Elijah Iles, John Taylor and Thomas Cox, each entering a quarter section of land. They then laid out a town, and called it Calhoun; afterwards it was changed to Springfield. Mr. and Mrs. Enos had three children born in Springfield. Of their five children—

PASCAL P., Jun., born Nov. 28, 1816, at St. Charles, Mo., was married in Springfield, Ill., to Eliza J. Johnson. She died April 15, 1859, and he died Feb. 17, 1867, both in Springfield. They were without family. He served one term in the State Legislature, and was appointed United States Circuit Clerk by Judge McLean, and again by Judge Davis, and died in office.

ZIMRI A., born Sept. 29, 1821, in St. Louis, Mo., was married in Springfield, Ill., June 10, 1846, to Agnes D. Trotter, who was born in New York city Feb. 15, 1825. They have six children born in Springfield. PASCAL P., born April 6, 1847, resides in Kansas. GEORGE T., is a Civil Engineer, and resides at Toledo, Ohio. WILLIAM P., CATHARINE I., ALLEN Z., and LOUISA I., live with their parents. Z. A. Enos served two terms, of two years each, as County Surveyor of Sangamon county, and three terms as Alderman of Springfield. He and his family reside in Springfield. Ill.

MARTHA M., born April 26, 1824, in Springfield, died there Jan. 4, 1837.

SUSAN P., born Oct. 27, 1829, in Springfield, resides with her mother.

JULIA R., born Dec. 20, 1832, in Springfield, was married in 1860 to Ozias M. Hatch, who was born April 14, 1814, in Hillsborough, Hillsborough county, N. H. His father, Dr. Reuben Hatch, with his family, moved to Pike county, Ill., in 1835, and Ozias M. followed in 1836. He has been heard to say, in a jocular way, that he was born in New Hampshire, educated in Massachusetts, and graduated in Pike county, Ill. The latter, probably alluding to the fact that he was appointed, by Judge Samuel D. Lockwood, Clerk of the Circuit Court of Pike county, in 1841, for seven years. From 1847 to 1851, he was engaged in merchandising, in Griggsville. In 1851 he was elected to represent Pike county in the State Legislature for two years. In November, 1856, O. M. Hatch was elected, on the Republican ticket, Secretary of State, for Illinois, and re-elected in 1860, serving in all eight years. He was one of the original members of the National Lincoln Monument Association, temporarily organized April 24, 1865, and assuming a legal form on the 11th of May following. Mr. Hatch was elected Secretary of the Association Jan. 18, 1866, and holds the office to the present time—June, 1876. Mr. and Mrs. Hatch have three living children, OZIAS M., Jun., PASCAL E., and FRANK LOCKWOOD, and reside in Springfield, Illinois.

Pascal P. Enos held the office of Receiver of the Land Office at Springfield, under Presidents Monroe and John Quincy Adams. He was removed by President Jackson solely because they differed in politics—Mr. Enos being a Whig. He died April, 1832, in Springfield, and his widow now—June, 1876—in her eighty-sixth year, and the forty-fifth of her widowhood, resides in Springfield, Illinois.

ENGLAND, STEPHEN, born June 12, 1773, in Virginia. His parents moved to Bath county, Ky., when he was quite young. He was there married, about 1791, to Anna Harper, who was born Sept. 1, 1772, in Virginia. They had ten living children in Kentucky. The family moved, in March, 1813, to Madison county, Ohio, where they had two children. In the fall of 1818 the family moved to Madison county, Ill. The fol-

—37

lowing winter Stephen England, with two of his sons-in-law, came up to the San-ga-ma country to explore it. The nearest habitation to where Springfield now stands, was on the south bank of the Sangamon river, near where the C. and A. R. R. now crosses. They found a man named William Higgins living in a cabin there, which he had built in Jan., 1819. *See his name.* They remained over night with Mr. Higgins, and crossed to the north side of the river, each selecting a spot on which to make a home. In order to prevent others who might come after from choosing the same ground, they cut a few logs, laid them across each other in three piles, and each man cut his initials on a tree near by, as evidence that the land was claimed. That was near what was soon after called Higgins' creek, but is now called Cantrall's creek. They returned to their families, and early in March, 1819, Stephen England, his son David, his sons-in-law, Andrew Cline and Wyatt Cantrall, returned to their claims for the purpose of commencing improvements. The night after their arrival snow fell about one foot deep, and the weather was colder than it had been at any time during the winter. They commenced work, and Mr. England and his son soon had their house up, roofed, and the door and chimney place cut out. The other two men had their materials on the ground. By that time the melting snow warned them that they must cross the river at once, or they might be delayed several weeks. They returned to their families, and attempted to move them, but the ground was so soft from melting snow that their teams were unequal to the task of drawing the wagons with their heavy loads, and they again left their families. The same men returned, accompanied by two of the daughters of Mr. England. They then completed their houses, cleared land, planted their crops, and returned to Madison county for their families, bringing them to their new homes about the first of June, 1819. Of Mr. England's twelve children then living—

FANNIE, born Oct. 2, 1792, in Bath county, Ky, married Levi Cantrall. *See his name.*

SALLIE, born Nov. 2, 1794, in Bath county, Ky., married Wyatt Cantrall. *See his name.*

LUCY, born Feb. 13, 1797, in Bath county, Ky., crossed the Sangamon river with her father, April, 1819, and she is thought to be the fifth white woman that ever crossed the river, and the first to cook a meal on the north side. She was married afterwards to John Cline. *See his name.*

ANNA, born August 30, 1798, in Kentucky, was married to Andrew Cline. They had four children. The parents and two of the children died in Sangamon county. Of the other two: STEPHEN married for his third wife, Dorothy Wigginton. They have children, and reside near Elkhart, Logan county. PERRY married, has one child, and resides in Wisconsin.

POLLY J., born April 29, 1800, in Kentucky, married Evans E. Brittin. *See his name.*

SITHA, born April, 1802, in Kentucky, was married April 2, 1823, to George W. Anderson. They have seven children. The parents and five of the children died in Sangamon county, Ill. Of the other two: ELIZABETH married Andrew Ralph, and resides in Fancy Creek township. ELIZA married Charles Boker. He died, and she lives in Cantrall.

DAVID, born Nov. 25, 1804, in Bath county, Ky., was married Nov. 4, 1823, to Margaret Higgins. They had fourteen children, seven of each sex, all born in Sangamon county, Ill. LOUISA married Charles Turley, April 6, 1842. He was born Dec. 11, 1822, in Montgomery county, Ky. They have nine children: S. SANFORD married Jane McClelland. *See name of McClelland.* MAGGIE E. married R. C. Maxwell. They have two children, *Charles* and *Louisa*, and live near Lincoln, Logan county. AMANDA married John B. Taylor, of Williamsville, and resides there. DAVID married in Lincoln, and lives near there. SUSAN J. married Dr. McClelland of Williamsville, and resides there. JAMES P., MARSHALL, MEADE and INA M., live with their parents one and a half miles east of Williamsville, Sangamon county. EVELINE B. married James M. Mitts. *See his name.* JULIA A. married Thomas W. Lake. *See his name.* STEPHEN married Margaret Canterbury. They have three children, ASA, MARY and

WILLIAM L., and live in Menard county. ROSE ANN married William Council. *See his name.* WILLIAM B. married Martha Hall. They had three children. LAURA married Jeremiah Casey, and resides in Menard county. HETTIE and WILLIAM live with their mother. William B. England enlisted in 1862 for three years, in Co. K, 115th Ill. Inf. He was killed Sept. 20, 1863, at the battle of Chickamauga, Tenn. His widow married Thomas Swearingen, who served three years as a captain in the Union army. They reside at Athens, Menard county, Ill. CAROLINE married Jacob Beck, who was born Nov. 22, 1829, in Ross county, Ohio. They have six children, MARIETTA, CHARLES F., DAVID R., IDA M., MAGGIE and FREDERICK, and live near Williamsville. MARGARET married Asa Canterbury. *See his name.* They have eight children, and reside near Gibson City, Ford county, Ill. MARY A. married Milam Holland, who died, and she married James W. Mott. *See his name.* David A. enlisted for three years, Aug. 9, 1862, in Co. K, 115th Ill. Vol. Inf., served until June 1, 1865, when he was honorably discharged. He married Emma Mott. They have three children, HENRY W., ANNIE B. and LUCY, and live in Athens. JAMES M. and CHARLES F., twins. James M. married Mary A. Mott. He died, leaving a widow and one child, MARIA, in Athens. Charles F. married Rebecca Wood. They have six children, and reside in Illiopolis township. HENRY H. married Mary A. Price. They have three children, LURENA L., FLORA B. and WILLIAM H., and live near Cantrall. MILAM R. lives with his parents. David England remembers seeing Indians bury their dead by putting them in troughs and suspending them in trees, also building pens around them and leaving their bodies to decay. David England and his wife reside on the farm settled by his father in 1819, three miles west of Sherman.

ELIZABETH, born Nov. 12, 1805, in Kentucky, was married in Sangamon county, Jan. 24, 1822, to Hiram Wentworth. They died, leaving three children.

KEZIAH, born June 23, 1807, in Kentucky, was married in Sangamon county to Charles Smith. They had six children. The parents are dead, and the children live in California.

JOHN, born Jan. 15, 1811, in Bath county, Ky., was married in Sangamon county to Mary Smith. They had nine children. WILLIAM A. was married in 1868, to Olive Stanton, in Salem, Oregon. SARAH married William Trakes. ADELPHIA, born May 10, 1831, married Samuel Turley. They have eleven living children, and reside in Logan county. MATILDA A., born June 26, 1834, married W. H. Rankin. They have eight children, and live in Champaign county, Ill. ALBERT, born May 16, 1838. He served three years in the 2d Ill. Cav., and was honorably discharged. He is married, has four children, and resides in Monticello, Piatt county, Ill. MARY J. and MARION, twins, born March 15, 1840. Mary J. married A. Robinson, and live in Macon county, Ill. Marion married Catharine Grove, and live in Logan county. LUCY A., born July 23, 1842, married D. Thubert, and live in Macon county, Ill. ELIZABETH C., born Aug. 15, 1848, married Ezra McMasters. They reside in Elkhart, Logan county, Ill. JOHN C., born April 3, 1858, lives in Logan county. Mrs. Mary England died, and John England was married to Sarah Groves. They have one child, and reside at Mt. Pulaski. John England is a preacher in connection with the Christian church.

ADELPHIA, born May 15, 1813, in Ohio, was married in Sangamon county to Joseph I. Smith. They had three children. FRANCIS M. enlisted in 1861 for three years, in Co. C, 21st Ill. Inf., served full time, and was honorably discharged. He married Mary Young, and resides at Fort Madison, Iowa. ENOCH B. enlisted July, 1862, for three years, in Co. K, 106th Ill. Inf., served until the close of the rebellion, and was honorably discharged July, 1865. He married Louisa Stone. They have two children, and reside in Fremont county, Iowa. JULIA A. married James Rayburn. They have eight children, and live at Irish Grove, Menard county. Joseph I. Smith died Jan. 1, 1851, and his widow was married Dec. 20, 1855, to William B. Goodpasture. They have one child, JESSE F. Mr. Goodpasture was born in Overton county, Tenn.; came to Jacksonville, Ill., in 1829. The present Mrs. Goodpasture is his third wife. Two of his sons by a former marriage were soldiers in Co. K, 106th Ill. Inf. One of them lost his life in defense of his country in the Autumn of 1864. Mr. and Mrs. Goodpasture reside near Auburn.

JESSE, born Feb. 10, 1815, in Bath county, Ky., was married in Sangamon county, Ill., Dec. 31, 1833, to Mahala Smith. They have five children living; three died in infancy. AMERICA, born Oct. 16, 1834, was married March 10, 1853, to Isaac J. Sherman. They have three children, MARY J., MARTHA A. and MAHALA A., who live with their parents on Fancy Prairie. MARY, born May 4, 1837, was married March 20, 1856, to Cyrus B. Sherman. They have seven children, AMERICA E., MIRANDA J., WILLIAM H., EMELINE, IDA M., MARY A. and NOLA E., and live at Middletown, Ill. MIRANDA, born July 6, 1839, was married March 29, 1860, to William F. West. They had two living children, FRANK H. and IDA B., who live with their mother. Mr. West died March 30, 1863, and his widow married Absalom Miller, April 11, 1870. They have three living children, JOHN J., EDWARD and MYRA, and reside near Maryville, Nodoway county, Mo. PAREN, born May 20, 1841, was married Feb. 14, 1861, to Nancy M. Whittier, and reside near Lincoln, Neb. PERRY J., born Feb. 5, 1849, was married to Callie Hall, Oct. 10, 1872. They have two children, ARTHUR J. and ETHEL P., and live near Fancy Prairie, Menard county, Ill. Jesse England and wife reside near Fancy Prairie postoffice, Menard county, Ill.

Stephen England died Sept. 26, 1823, of a cancer in one of his ankles. He preached the gospel as long as he could stand, and delivered his last sermon sitting. His widow died June 1, 1841, both near where they settled in 1819, in what is now Fancy Creek township. Stephen England was a Baptist minister in Kentucky, and when he brought his family to the new settlement, the people having planted their crops, wished to have religious services, so Mr. England announced that he would preach at his own house late in June or early in July, 1819. Everybody in the entire settlement came. Two women walked five miles through the grass, which was almost as high as their heads. The husband of one of them walked and carried their babe. That was the first sermon ever preached north of the Sangamon river in this county, and probably in Central Illinois. Mr. England organized a church May 15, 1820, at his own house. There were eight members besides himself. The names of the persons constituting the church were Stephen England and Anna, his wife; Jechoniah Langston and Nancy, his wife; Levi Cantrall and Fannie, his wife; Mrs. Adelphia Wood, Mrs. Sarah Cantrall, the wife of Wyatt Cantrall, Mrs. Lucy Scott (daughter of Mr. England), afterwards Mrs. Cline. That was the first church organized in Sangamon county, and the organization has never been broken. It is now known as Antioch Christian church, and composed at present of about ninety members. It is occupying its third house of worship, which is a handsome wooden edifice situated within the limits of Cantrall, a town recently laid out. Elder Stephen England was pastor of the church until his death, in 1823. His son David united with the church about one year after his father's death. He was first elected deacon, then elder, and has continued in that office to the present time. Elder Stephen England solemnized the marriage of Philo Beers and Martha Stillman, Nov. 2, 1820, which was the first marriage in Sangamon county. *See Philo Beers*. This event occurred one and a half miles southwest of Williamsville. A couple came to Mr. England from Fort Clark, now Peoria, to avoid the trouble of going to Edwardsville for license. It was lawful to advertise their intentions for ten days, and then marry without license. That couple were married in the latter way.

ENYART, SILAS, was born June 21, 1788, in Hardin county, Ky. He was married Nov. 6, 1806, to Martha Duckworth, who was born June 7, 1789, in the same county. They had eight children born in Kentucky, one died in infancy, and the family moved to Sangamon county, Ill., arriving in the spring of 1834 in what is now Gardner township, six miles west of Springfield. Of their children—

ELIZABETH, born in Kentucky,

was married, in Sangamon county, to Zebulon Cantrill. *See his name.*

SARAH, born in Kentucky, was married in Sangamon county to Arthur B. McMurry. *See his name.*

POLLY, born in Kentucky, married in Sangamon county to Moses Laswell. *See his name.*

MATILDA, born in Kentucky, married in Sangamon county to William H. Talbott. *See his name.*

REBECCA J., born in Kentucky, married N. E. Bateman. They had six children, namely, MARY E., SARAH J., JAMES W., CHARLES N., EDWARD E. and EMMA E. Mrs. Bateman resides with her daughter, Mrs. Albert V. Arnold, in Springfield.

JAMES, died in 1844, aged twenty-one years.

WILLIAM, born June 25, 1825, in Hardin county, Ky., was married in Sangamon county, Ill., Jan. 13, 1852, to Sarah Elder. They had four children in Sangamon county. LUCY E. died in her third year. MINERVA, married James Merriweather. They have one child, ALLEN, and reside in Cotton Hill township. EMMA and EFFIE, reside with their parents two and one-half miles north of Pawnee, in Cotton Hill township. William Enyart left Springfield March 25, 1849, for the gold fields of California, with eight others, only three of whom returned. William Enyart was gone two years and three months, and made enough to buy himself a good home. During his absence he had an interview with James Baker. *See his name.*

Mrs. Martha Enyart died in 1835, and Silas Enyart died in 1837, both in Sangamon county, Ill.

EUSTACE, WILLIAM, born in Eastport, Me., settled in 1837 or 8 in what is now Talkington township, where Chas. T. Hoppin now resides. He was the first settler in the township. His daughter, Elizabeth, married John Barger. *See his name.*

EWELL, ISAAC L., was born April 29, 1819, in Barnett, Caledonia county, Vt., came to Springfield, Ill., in the fall of 1837, spent two years there as a miller, returned to Vermont, came back to Sangamon county, and was married Sept. 3, 1846, to Louisa E. Kelly. He moved to Peacham, Vt., in the spring of 1847, where they had one child, and returned to Sangamon county in 1850, where they had two children. Of their three children—

CHARLES W., born Feb. 7, 1848, in Peacham, Caledonia county, Vt., married in Sangamon county, Nov. 25, 1868, to Eliza J. Turner, have one child, MINNIE, and live in Curran township.

HORACE J., born Oct. 13, 1851, in Sangamon county, died May 23, 1863.

EUNICE M., born Nov. 24, 1857, in Sangamon county, and lives with her parents.

Isaac L. Ewell and wife reside two and a-half miles north of Curran.

F

FAGAN, WILLIAM, born in 1777, in North Carolina, was married there to Peninah Fruit, who was born Jan. 29, 1774, in the same State. They moved to Virginia, and from there to Christian county, Ky. In 1819 they emigrated, with four children, to southern Illinois, thence to Sangamon county, arriving in what is now Clear Lake township, in 1820. They moved next year to Buffalo Hart Grove, and from there to Springfield. In 1831 they settled on a farm three miles northwest of Springfield. Of their children—

ELIZABETH, born in 1801, in Virginia or Kentucky, died in Springfield, Ill., aged twenty-two years.

HANNAH, born in 1806, in Christian county, Ky., died aged about thirteen years.

JOHN, born May 17, 1809, in Christian county, Ky., was married April 15, 1830, in Springfield, Ill., to Mary Henry, who was born in 1812, in Ohio. They had nine children. ELIZABETH J., born Dec. 22, 1831, was married Oct. 15, 1851, to William C. Langston, she died Dec. 26, 1853, without children. CLARISSA and CLARINDA (twins), born Nov. 22, 1833. CLARISSA was married March, 1851, to Uriah C. Withrow, who was born Jan. 26, 1827. They had one son, W. A., who lives in Sangamon county, Ill. W. C. Withrow died Sept. 26, 1852, and Mrs. Withrow was married May, 1860, to Aaron Apgar. Mrs. Clarissa Apgar died Oct. 7, 1864, leaving one child, IDA BELLE, who lives in Sangamon county. CLARINDA was married April 16, 1861, to J. L. Robinette, who was born June 12, 1836, in Ohio. They moved to California in 1863, where Mrs. Robinette died June 13, 1864. GEORGE T., born Aug. 4, 1836, was married Sept. 3, 1857, to Rachel Hazlett, who was born Oct. 12, 1839, in Christian county. They have three living children, FRANKLIN, IRVING, and GEORGE, who reside with their parents in Christian county, Ill. SARAH F., born Oct. 28, 1838, was married Oct., 1855, to F. M. Montgomery. She died April 8, 1856. BRICE H., born Jan. 23, 1841, enlisted Feb., 1862, in Co. G, 10th Ill. Cav., served until after the capture of Little Rock, Ark., when he was taken sick and died in hospital there, Dec. 10, 1863. His body was brought home for interment. WILLIAM P., born May 18, 1843, died April 1, 1860. JAMES F., born Jan. 29, 1846, was married Aug. 29, 1870, to Eliza J. Buchannan, who was born Jan. 17, 1846. They moved to the southern part of Kansas, where Eliza J. Fagan died March 18, 1873. James Fagan returned to Sangamon county and lives with his father. CHARLES A., born March 12, 1849, died Aug. 20, 1872. Mrs. Mary Fagan died Aug. 14, 1850, and John Fagan was married April 14, 1852, to Mrs. Mary W. Norris, whose maiden name was Cole. They have two living children. MARY L., born Jan. 22, 1854, was married Feb. 15, 1871, to Jesse H. Potts, had one child, ADA BELL, who died young, and the family live in Christian county, Ill. BENJAMIN, born July 17, 1856, lives with his father. Mrs. Mary W. Fagan died Feb. 22, 1858, and John Fagan was married Dec. 20, 1860, in Logan county, Ohio, to Mary Williams, who was born April 17, 1826. They reside four miles northwest of Springfield, Ill.

GEORGE, born Feb. 19, 1814, in Christian county, Ky., was married in Sangamon county, Ill., Dec. 11, 1838, to Ruth Smith. They had six children. Of the three who lived to be grown— JOHN F., born Dec. 19, 1843, in Sangamon county, enlisted Jan. 18, 1862, for three years in Co. G, 10th Ill. Cav., re-enlisted as a veteran Jan. 18, 1864, served to the end of the rebellion, and was honorably discharged, at San Antonia, Texas, Nov., 1865. He was married in Sangamon county Sept. 2, 1868, to Mary E. Lightfoot. They have one child, HERBERT F., and reside three and one-half miles northwest of Springfield. GREEN B., born July 24, 1849, died April 10, 1866. WILLIAM G., born Jan. 22, 1852, lives with his parents. George Fagan and wife reside three miles northwest of Springfield, on the farm where his parents settled in 1830.

William Fagan died Nov. 24, 1843, and his widow died Sept. 27, 1846, both where they settled in 1830, three miles northwest of Springfield, Ill.

FAIRCHILD, MOSES, was born Aug., 1793, in Essex county, N. Y. He was married Nov. 9, 1817, at Shelbourn, Vt., to Adah Holabird, who was born there, in July, 1793. They had six living children in Essex county, New York, and the family moved to Sangamon county, Ill., arriving in the fall of 1833, at Rochester, where they had one child. Of their seven children—

HIRAM, born Oct. 10, 1819, in Essex county, N. Y., married in Springfield, Ill., Feb. 14, 1850, to Martha L. Beall. They had nine children in Sangamon county, six of whom died under four years. Of the other three, CHARLES H., born Oct. 27, 1850, HIRAM R., born Nov. 1, 1854, and WILLIAM P., born Oct. 29, 1856, all reside with their parents, three-quarters of a mile east of Clarksville, Sangamon county.

CHARLES, born Sept. 25, 1821, in Essex county, N. Y., married in Sangamon county, Jan. 31, 1848, to Lavina Sattley. They had eight living children, BELLE, MARY E., BENJAMIN S., ADAH E., CHARLES, ROBERT, RALPH S. and WINFIELD S. reside with their parents, one mile east of Rochester, on the farm where Moses Fairchild settled in 1833.

HENRY, born Sept. 20, 1823, in New York, raised in Sangamon county, married in Jacksonville to Jane Ragsdale. They had one child, HOMER LINCOLN, and Mrs. Jane F. died. Mr. F. married Nancy McKittrick. They have three children, and reside near Tower Hill, Shelby county, Ill.

MARY J., born May 27, 1826, in Essex county, N. Y., married in Sangamon county, March 24, 1852, to Joseph

E. Ross, who was born Oct. 13, 1823, in Clarke county, O., and came to Sangamon county, in 1841 or '2. They had four children, ADAH MAY and IDA F., the third and fourth, died young. JOHN HENRY and CHARLES OSCAR reside with their parents, two and a half miles north of Breckenridge.

DANIEL, born August 23, 1829, in New York, and died in Sangamon county, Dec. 8, 1846.

HYMAN, born Dec. 2, 1832, in New York, raised in Sangamon county, went to California in 1850 married there to Mrs. Mary J. Waddle, whose maiden name was Barker. They had twins, and Mrs. F. died. He was married in Sangamon county to Mrs. Susan Giger, whose maiden name was Benson. They have three children, and reside near Grafton, Yolo county, California.

MOSES, Jun., born July 9, 1835, in Sangamon county, died in his fourth year.

Moses Fairchild died in Sangamon county, and Mrs. Adah Fairchild resides with her daughter, Mrs. Ross.

FARQUAR, GEORGE, was born in 1794, in Uniontown, Penn. His father died, and his mother married Robert Ford, who was killed by Indians, leaving one son. Mrs. Ford with her two sons, George Farquar and Thomas Ford, came to Waterloo, Monroe county, Ill. Of the younger of the two half brothers, it is only necessary to say in this connection that Thomas Ford afterwards became Governor of Illinois. George Farquar was elected to represent Monroe county in the State legislature one term. He was appointed Jan. 15, 1825, by Gov. Coles, to the office of Secretary of State, and went to Vandalia in discharge of the duties of the office. He was married March 20, 1828, at Kaskaskia, to Ann Cranmer, a sister to Mrs. James L. Lamb. She was born in Cincinnati, Ohio, Dec. 25, 1806. Mr. Farquar resigned his office Dec. 31, 1828, and was appointed Jan. 23, 1829, by Gov. Edwards, Attorney General of Illinois. He resigned that office and moved to Springfield the same year, He afterwards represented Sangamon county in the State Senate, and was at one time Register of the United States Land Office in Springfield. Mr. and Mrs. Farquar had five children, four of whom died young, and one—

GEORGE M., born March 16, 1835, in Springfield, and died March 12, 1861.

Mr. George Farquar died Sept. 12, 1838, in Cincinnati. His widow married Antrim Campbell. *See his name.*

FAY MICHAEL.—See his name in connection with the Bradley family, in the Omissions.

FERGUSON, MRS. LUCY, was born about 1767 in Culpepper county, Va. Her maiden name was Pendleton. She was married there in 1791 to Benjamin Ferguson, who was also a native of Virginia. They had fifteen children born in Virginia, and Mr. F. died there. The mother, with five children, moved to Sangamon county, arriving in the fall of 1836, about three miles east of Rochester. Just before she left Virginia, Mrs. Ferguson was enumerating her descendants: there were seventy-five then. Of her five children who came west with her—

WILLIAM H., born February, 1798, married in Virginia in 1818 to Lucy Broadux. They came to Illinois with their mother. Mrs. Lucy Ferguson died in the fall of 1871, and Wm. H. died March, 1873, leaving four children, three of whom are now married.

LUCY C., born in Virginia, was married there in 1832 to Isaac Haines. He was a Methodist preacher. They came west with their mother. He died in 1838. She died in 1850, leaving two children, one of whom, WILLIAM C., married, and lives one mile south of Taylorville. LUCY A. married J. Clark, and resides opposite Cairo, in Missouri.

ELLEN, born in 1812, married in Sangamon county in 1838 to Daniel Johnson. They have one child, ELIAS, who married, and resides on the farm with his father, four miles east of Rochester. Mrs. Ellen Johnson died about 1841.

PHILIP C., born June, 1815, in Virginia, married there in 1836 to Mary Haines. They have five children living. They all reside in Kansas but one, EZEKIEL, who married a Miss Kelly, and lives near Taylorville. Philip C. Ferguson was a physician, and died from lockjaw in 1862. His widow resides near Wathena, Kan.

JAMES, born March 11, 1817, married in Sangamon county March 21, 1838, to Mary J. Young, who was born in 1824, in Trigg county, Ky. They have four children. MARTHA J., born Jan. 16, 1840, in Sangamon county, married Oct. 25, 1860, in Christian county, to Archibald Sattley. See his name. CLARA A., born April 24, 1842, married Feb. 15, 1862, in Christian county, to Charles E. Sattley. See his name. ALBERT L., born Jan. 31, 1849, and ADA M., reside with their father. James Ferguson came to Sangamon county with his mother, and engaged in farming; has been for twelve years justice of the peace at Stonington, and assisted in organizing the first Sunday school there, and has been superintendent ever since. Mrs. Mary J. Ferguson died Oct. 20, 1875.

Mrs. Lucy Ferguson died in the autumn of 1838, on the farm where they settled in 1836.

FIREY, JOSEPH, was born Oct. 2, 1789, in Washington county, Md. He was married there, Feb. 12, 1812, to Catharine Rouch, who was born Nov. 12, 1794, in the same county. They had two children, and Mrs. Catharine Firey died July 20, 1822. Joseph Firey was married June 29, 1824, to Magdalena Beard. They had four children, and Mrs. Magdalena Firey died in Maryland. Joseph Firey, with his two eldest sons, came to Springfield, Ill., Nov. 25, 1835, and a few days later moved to what is now Cooper township. He returned to Maryland the next year, and came back to Sangamon county with his younger children, in company with his brother Jacob, Wm. Mowry and Mrs. Troxell, with their families. Of his children—

HENRY, born March 25, 1815, in Washington county, Md., married in Sangamon county, Ill., May 21, 1840, to Minerva Lord. They had eight children. MARY E., born March 16, 1841, married Sept. 26, 1861, to George L. Hoasley, have one living child, WILLIAM. SARAH C., born August 4, 1843, married Jan. 20, 1869, to Benjamin R. English, have one living child, MARY A. ANN M., born March 6, 1846, married Oct. 20, 1864, to Sherman Yaukey, have two children, EDWIN H. and CLARA E. JOSEPH F., born Dec. 27, 1848, married Sept. 5, 1873, to Susan Thomson, and have two children, LILLIE and ELIZA. ALICE J., born July 4, 1851, married March 19, 1874, to William Daigh, and have one child, HENRY. LEWIS E., born July 12, 1854, ELIZA M., born March 2, 1857, and JOHN H., born Nov. 3, 1859. Henry Firey and family live near Grove City, Christian county, Ill.

LEWIS, born Jan. 6, 1817, in Washington county, Maryland, came to Sangamon county in 1835, is unmarried, and lives with his brother Henry, near Grove City, Ill.

By the second marriage—

CATHARINE, born May 16, 1825, in Maryland, married May 23, 1847, to George Ensminger, have eight children, CHARLOTTE, MARTHA, MARY A., SARAH M., WILLIAM, GEORGE, ARCHIBALD and LEWIS, and live near Grove City.

MARTHA ANN, born Sept. 22, 1826, in Maryland, married June 1, 1852, to Jefferson Singer. They had five children, WILLIAM, JOSEPH, LEWIS, ALFRED, JOHN and MARY. Mr. Singer died Feb., 1865. His widow and children live near Grove City.

JOHN L., born Oct. 16, 1829, in Maryland, married April 27, 1854, in Sangamon county, to Elizabeth Jones. He died Jan. 29, 1872, in Rochester, leaving a widow and one son, JAMES M.

MARY S., born July 8, 1832, in Washington county, Md., married Nov. 19, 1858, to John Troxell. See his name. She died Nov. 16, 1859, leaving one child, MARY.

Joseph Firey died August 25, 1862, near Mt. Auburn, Christian county, Ill.

FIREY, JACOB, was born April 14, 1791, in Washington county, Md., married there May 2, 1815, to Mary Houser, who was born June 3, 1796, in the same county. They had seven children, three of whom died under seven years. The family moved to Sangamon county, Ill., arriving in October, 1836, in what is now Cooper township, south of the Sangamon river, where his brother Joseph had preceded him the year before. Of their four children—

ISAAC H., born Feb. 2, 1820, in Washington county, Md., married in Springfield, Ill., Feb. 11, 1847, to Eliza Sattley. They have seven children. JACOB J., born Nov. 5, 1847, graduated March, 1869, at Bellevue Medical College, New York city. He was married June 29, 1869, at Ann Arbor, Mich., to Kate

Bessimer, who was born Aug. 18, 1850. They had two children, ALBERT and JOHN; the latter died young. Dr. J. J. Firey is a practicing physician, and resides in Taylorville, Ill. HATTIE E., born Nov. 4, 1849, was married June 10, 1875, to Ross M. Honck. ALBERT, WILLIAM H., SUSAN E., ISAAC E. and MARY E. The five latter live with their parents. Isaac H. Firey and family reside near Grove City, Christian county, Illinois.

SUSAN, born Oct. 23, 1822, in Washington county, Md., married in Sangamon county, Ill., to Peter Troxell. See his name.

ELIZABETH, born Feb. 26, 1824, in Washington county, Md., raised in Sangamon county, and married Patrick Cooper. See his name.

MARY ANN, born Oct. 26, 1825, in Maryland, married in Sangamon county to Samuel Prather. They had two children, who died young. Mr. Prather died Nov. 21, 1859, and Mrs. Mary A. Prather resides with her sister, Mrs. Cooper.

Mrs. Mary Firey died June 9, 1837, and Jacob Firey died May 18, 1853—she in Sangamon county, and he in Christian county, Illinois.

FISHER, JOHN B., was born Sept. 5, 1808, in Bourbon county, Ky. Nancy D. Webb was born May 23, 1809, in Nicholas county, Ky. They were married Sept. 10, 1829, in Nicholas county, and lived in Bourbon until five children were born. They moved to Sangamon county, Ill., arriving in the spring of 1839 in what is now Loami township, where eight children were born; two died under seven years—

NATHANIEL, born Nov. 10, 1830, in Kentucky, died in Sangamon county Feb. 10, 1847.

CHARLES W., born Jan. 10, 1833, in Kentucky, married in Sangamon county, Feb. 11, 1855, to Isabel A. Bowen; had five children. He went to Indiana, and enlisted in a regiment of that State for three years.

ELIZABETH A., born July 4, 1834, in Kentucky, married in Sangamon county Sept. 15, 1853, to William R. Harbour, have six children, and reside in Moultrie county, Ill.

SARAH J., born June 5, 1836, in Kentucky, married in Sangamon county
Feb. 23, 1854, to Daniel R. Williams, have five children, and live in DeWitt county.

JOHN W., born Dec. 11, 1838, in Bourbon county, Ky., enlisted in Sangamon county, Aug. 5, 1862, in Co. I, 73d Ill. Inf., for three years, was captured at Cassville, Ga., Sept. 24, 1864, was taken to Andersonville prison and remained until March 18, 1865, when he was paroled and exchanged. He had been reported hung, and given up by his friends as dead. He is yet an invalid from the effect of the cruel treatment in prison, and resides (April, 1874,) with his mother.

WILLIAM H., born Jan. 31, 1841, in Sangamon county, lives with his mother.

ISAAC N., born Aug. 21, 1842, enlisted Aug. 5, 1862, in Co. I, 73d Ill. Inf., for three years, served until he became disabled, and was transferred to the Veteran Reserve Corps, and was honorably discharged June 27, 1865, lingered until July 17, 1869, when he died at home.

LUCINDA M., HENRY C., HAMLET W. and ABNER R., live with their mother.

John B. Fisher enlisted August, 1861, in Co. B, 30th Ill. Inf., for three years. He was fifty-three years of age, but believed it to be his duty to enter the army. In the battle of Belmont, Mo., he became over-heated, from the effect of which he died at Cairo, Ill., Dec. 14, 1861. His widow resides two miles northwest of Loami.

FISHER, SAMUEL, was born Aug. 4, 1787, in Franklin county, Penn. His parents were Protestants, from Germany. Hannah Beaver was born Sept. 29, 1795, in the same county. Her father was a soldier in the revolution. Samuel Fisher and Hannah Beaver were married in their native county. They had thirteen children there and moved to Springfield, Ill., Nov. 13, 1840. Of their children—

ALEXANDER, born March 12, 1815, in Pennsylvania, was married Oct. 7, 1847, in Sangamon county, Ill., to Elizabeth Hershey. She died July 5, 1853, in Wabash county, Ill. Mr. Fisher was married in 1854, to Ann Elizabeth Field, who died July 11, 1858, and he was married April 18, 1859, to Mrs. Permelia Skinner. Alexander Fisher was elected Associate Judge of Logan county, in 1865, and resides in Mt. Pulaski, Ill.

—38

GEORGE, born April 30, 1816, in Pennsylvania, was married in Sangamon county, Ill., to Mary Hendricks. They reside near Belle Plain, Sumner county, Kansas.

SAMUEL B., was born Oct. 27, 1817, in Franklin county, Penn., was married Dec. 18, 1844, in Springfield, to Melvina Alvey. They had thirteen children in Springfield. EDMUND R., resides with his parents. SAMUEL A. is a salesman in a dry goods house in Cincinnati. FREDERICK F. was married in Jacksonville, Ill., May 7, 1876, to Lou Gorham. He is clerk in Coleman's store, and resides in Springfield. FANNIE resides with her parents. EMMA died Dec. 30, 1870, aged about sixteen years. IDA, BERTHA, KATE, MELVINA, IRVING, WILLIAM, ANNA W., and LAURA, reside with their parents. S. B. Fisher has been, since 1844, engaged in mercantile pursuits, and now resides in Springfield.

LOUISA, born March 4, 1819, in Pennsylvania, was married in Springfield to Avery Constant. See his name. They live in Williamsville.

WILLIAM, born Feb. 20, 1821, in Pennsylvania, was married July 3, 1856, in Athens, Ill., to Susannah Reed, who was born Dec. 5, 1832, in Franklin county, Penn. They have five children, HANNAH M., FRANK R., CARRIE B. and WILLIE C., the latter twins, and JULIA C. William Fisher has been since 1871 employed in the United States Revenue Department, and resides in Springfield.

CHARLES, born Dec. 24, 1822, in Quincy, Franklin county, Penn., came with his parents to Springfield, Nov. 13, 1840. He was married Oct. 22, 1850, to Sarah T. Moffitt, who was born in Springfield, a daughter of John B. Moffitt, one of the early settlers. They had two children. GEORGE T., born July 28, 1851, is a draftsman and architect and resides in Springfield. LILLIE resides with her father. Mrs. S. T. Fisher died Feb. 16, 1854. Charles Fisher is a carpenter and builder. He erected the First Presbyterian church, and superintended the wood work of the United States Court House. He resides in Springfield.

CAROLINE, born Sept. 16, 1824, in Franklin county, Penn., was married Feb. 17, 1848, in Springfield, Ill., to Phares A. Dorwin, who was born Sept. 10, 1820, in Champion, Jefferson county, N. Y. They had three living children, HENRY F., CHARLES G. and SHELBY C., all reside with their mother. Mr. Dorwin was engaged in the tin ware and stove business the greater part of his life, in Springfield, except during the rebellion, when he was in the Quartermaster's Department, stationed at one post all the time, in Kentucky. He died in Springfield, Feb. 17, 1870. His widow and three sons reside at 511 north sixth street.

SUSANNAH, born Sept. 3, 1826, in Pennsylvania, was married in Springfield, Ill., to Cyrus Culbertson. They reside at Sumner, Lawrence county, Ill.

MARY, born Dec. 14, 1828, in Pennsylvania, died in Springfield July 4, 1852.

HANNAH M., born May 14, 1831, in Pennsylvania, was married Dec. 12, 1855, in Springfield, to Shelby M. Cullom. They had two children, ELLA and CARRIE, both of whom are graduates of the Bettie Stuart Institute, and reside with their father. Mrs. Cullom died March 17, 1861, in Springfield, Ill.

KATE resides with her brother Charles.

JULIA, born March 28, 1835, in Franklin county, Penn., was married in Springfield, May 5, 1863, to Hon. Shelby M. Cullom. Mr. Cullom was born Nov. 22, 1829, in Wayne county, Ky., and taken by his parents to Tazewell county, Ill., in 1830. His father, R. N. Cullom, represented Tazewell county for several years in the State legislature—part of the time in the House, and a portion in the Senate. Shelby M. came to Springfield in 1854, and studied law in the office of Stuart & Edwards. He was admitted to practice in 1855, and soon after elected City Attorney of Springfield. In 1856 he was elected as one of the representatives of Sangamon county in the State Legislature, and again elected in 1860. On the assembling of the Legislature he was chosen Speaker of the House. In 1864 Mr. Cullom was elected to represent the Eighth district of Illinois in the United States Congress, and was elected for two successive terms. During that time he was Chairman of the Committee on Territories, and as such reported a bill, of which he was the author, for the suppression of polygamy in the territory of Utah, which became a law. He also secured the appropriations for the erection of the United States court house and postoffice in Springfield, at a cost of $320,000. In 1872 and 1874 he was elected to represent the county in the State Legislature. At the former term he was chosen Speaker of the House. Mr. Cullom is a practicing lawyer, is President of the State National Bank, and resides in Springfield.

At the Republican State Convention held in Springfield, May 24, 1876—the largest, most intelligent and most harmonious convention ever held in the State of Illinois—Hon. Shelby M. Cullom was unanimously nominated as the candidate of the party for Governor of the State. Although the writer does not claim to be a prophet, nor the son of a prophet, it is deemed safe to predict—June 1, '76—that unless death should intervene, he will be triumphantly elected in November, and inaugurated in January, 1877.

VICTORIA resides with her sister, Mrs. Cullom.

Samuel Fisher died May 11, 1856, and Mrs. Hannah Fisher died April 21, 1867, both in Springfield.

FLETCHER, JAMES, was born July 7, 1799, in Rockbridge county, Va., and was married there to Jane McElvain, a sister to Samuel McElvain. *See his name.* They moved to Adair county, Ky., in 1804 or '5, where they had eight children, and moved to Sangamon county, Ill., arriving Dec., 1828, in what is now Auburn township, where they had one child. Of their nine children—

JOB, born in Kentucky, married in Sangamon county to Nancy Chapin, moved to Galena, and from there to Williamstown, Chickasaw county, Iowa, where he lost his life from injuries inflicted by an enraged bull, in May, 1872. He left a widow and children residing there.

MARGARET, born in Kentucky, married in Sangamon county, Nov. 26, 1840, to Cary A. Patterson. They have two children. MARTHA A. married John D. Gates, and lives in Auburn township. MARGARET J. married O. F. Bettis. *See his name.* C. A. Patterson and wife live in Auburn township.

MARY died in Sangamon county in 1831.

JAMES W., born in Kentucky in 1816, and died in Sangamon county, July 6, 1864.

NATHAN, born in 1818, in Adair county, Ky., married in Sangamon county, Dec. 26, 1844, to Margaret J. Baxter. They have six children, MARY J., JAMES B., THOMAS A., MARTHA, HENRY and LUCRETIA—the two latter twins. Nathan Fletcher resides three miles southwest of Auburn.

ELIZABETH, born in Kentucky, married in Sangamon county to James H. Bettis. *See his name.*

JOHN R., born in Kentucky, married in Sangamon county to Margaret J. Kessler. He died August, 1870, leaving a widow and three children, four miles west of Auburn.

REBECCA J., born in Kentucky, married in Sangamon county to W. M. Essex, and lives in Macoupin county, Illinois.

NANCY, born in Sangamon county, married James R. Patterson. They had six children, and the whole family died in Auburn township.

James Fletcher and his wife both died in Sangamon county.

FLETCHER, JOHN, was born about 1774, in Rockbridge county, Va. Job Fletcher, whose name heads the following sketch, was a younger brother of his. John Fletcher was married in 1803, in Augusta county, Va., to Elizabeth McElvain, a native of Lancaster county, Penn., and sister of Samuel McElvain. *See his name.* Mr. and Mrs. Fletcher had three children in Virginia, and in 1806 emigrated to that part of Christian which became Todd county, Ky., where five children were born. They moved to Sangamon county, Ill., arriving in the spring of 1830 in what is now Ball township. The family, including his son Job, with his wife and child, consisted of eleven persons, and their first place of residence was a log cabin sixteen feet square, belonging to his brother Job, who had preceded him eleven years. Of their children—

JOB, Jun., or Capt. Job, as he was called in consequence of his military commission from the Governor of Kentucky, and to distinguish him from his uncle Job, only eight years older, and who was called Esq. Job. Job, Jun., was born Aug. 27, 1801, in Rockbridge county, Va., married Nov. 24, 1825, in Todd county, Ky., to Frances Brown, who was born in Kentucky, and moved, in connection with his father, to Sangamon county, arriving in the spring of 1830 in what is now Ball township, where they had six children. Of their eight children—MARY E., born Aug. 12, 1826, in Kentucky, married in Sangamon county to Jason N. McElvain. She died Aug. 3, 1875, near Nilwood, Ill. Mr. McElvain resides there. MARGARET F., born Oct. 25, 1828, died in her eleventh year. JOHN S., born April 28, 1830, died Jan. 11, 1854. WILLIAM D. died in his fourth year. PRESTON B., born March 4, 1834, married Sarah Wright. They have two living children, ELIZABETH and LLOYD, and reside near Butler, Bates county, Mo. PAULINE K., born Feb. 15, 1837, married Feb. 22, 1853, to Francis Ewing Dodds. *See his name.* They live six miles southeast of Auburn. BENJAMIN F., born Dec. 17, 1839, in Sangamon county. He enlisted Aug., 1862, for three years in Co. B, 114th Ill. Inf., and was captured at the battle of Guntown, Miss., June 10, 1864. He spent several months in Andersonville prison, and witnessed the breaking out of a spring, and confirms all that is said about it by Stephen Bell. *See his name.* Mr. Fletcher was released at the end of the rebellion, and honorably discharged April, 1865. He was married Feb. 28, 1867, to Mary E. Drennan. They have two children, CYRUS O. and MYRA F., and live at the homestead settled by his father in 1830, in Ball township, near Chatham. VIRGINIA A., born March 9, 1832, married March 20, 1860, to Charles G. Brown, who was born Oct. 4, 1829, in Jacksonville, Ill. They have two children, MARY C. and ROBERT F., and live in Pawnee township, six miles southeast of Auburn. Job Fletcher, Jun., and his wife celebrated their golden wedding Nov. 24, 1875, at the residence of their daughter and son-in-law Dodds. They reside part of the time at the homestead where they settled in 1830, and part of the time with their daughters and sons-in-law, Mr. F. E. Dodds and Mr. C. G. Brown. Capt. Job Fletcher at one time sold sixteen wagon loads of smoked hams and shoulders, in St. Louis, at $1.80 and $2.00 per one hundred pounds. It belonged to himself and Eddin Lewis. They hauled it ninety miles, and paid fifty cents per hundred for the hauling. At that time coffee sold for fifty cents per pound, sugar twenty-five cents, and calico fifty cents per yard; corn was worth six and a quarter cents per bushel, gathered, or four cents in the field. Capt. F. says the whole prairie country abounded with a kind of green headed fly, that was a great pest. In hot weather it was hazardous to attempt to drive a team over the prairie. From the Sugar creek timber to Carlinville, about thirty miles, was nearly always driven in the night. Instances are related of horses having been killed by exposure to those flies. As the country improved, the land drained, and the grass pastured down, the flies disappeared.

ANDREW, born in Kentucky, was killed by a falling tree in 1809, in his eighth year.

WILLIAM, born in Kentucky, died in Sangamon county Sept. 19, 1830, three days after the death of his father, in his twenty-third year.

JOHN, born Nov. 26, 1808, in Todd county, Ky., married in Sangamon county, Ill., Jan. 28, 1834, to Theresa Abell. They had one child in Sangamon county, and moved, in 1839, to McDonough county, Ill., where they had one child. LUCRETIA B., born Dec. 26, 1835, in Sangamon county, died in her sixth year. JAMES A., born Oct. 26, 1839, in McDonough county, and went with his father to Kansas in 1857. As wagon master in the employ of the government, he crossed the plains ten times during the rebellion. He was married in 1871 to Miss Murray, has two children, GRACE E. and WALTER W., and live near Mound City, Linn county, Kansas. Mrs. Theresa Fletcher died in McDonough county, Ill., late in 1839. John Fletcher was married in the same county, March 9, 1841, to Sarah Bullington, who was born Jan. 31, 1817, in Orange county, Ind. They had six children in McDonough county, and, in 1857, moved to Linn county, Kansas, where they had one child. Of their seven children: JOHN S., born May 3, 1843, in McDonough county, Ill., resides with his mother, near Mound City, Kan. WILLIAM C., born March 10, 1845, in

McDonough county, Ill., lives near Mound City, Kansas. LIZZIE J., born Jan. 22, 1848, in McDonough county, Ill., married in 1867, in Kansas, to Zalmon Kincaid, a native of Ohio. They have three children, RALPH, CHARLIE Z. and JOHN C., and live at Pleasanton, Linn county, Kansas. Mr. Kincaid is a merchant there. JOB H., born August 28, 1849, is engaged in farming and stock raising near Mound City, Kansas. ALBERT A., born Nov. 7, 1851, in McDonough county, Ill., raised in Kansas, and, in 1873, went to New York City, and is engaged in business at No. 60, Fulton street. ADALINE R., born Nov. 26, 1858, in Kansas, lives with her mother. John Fletcher died Jan. 8, 1864, near Mound City, Linn county, Kansas. His widow resides there. He spent several years as a school teacher, and was always interested in educational matters. He was a member of the Presbyterian church, and superintended a Sunday school. After his death his widow filled the latter position for several years.

MARGARET, born in 1811, in Todd county, Ky., married in Sangamon county, Ill., in 1833, to William Durley. He had previously been married to a Miss Mills, who died, leaving one child, Mildred M., born August 6, 1828, and who married George R. Laughton, in 1844, at Plattsville, Grant county, Wis. She died Jan. 8, 1864, leaving five children, George H., William R., Charles A., Adaline A. and Frank D., all of whom are living. William Durley died in 1835, and Mrs. Margaret Fletcher Durley died in 1836, leaving one child, ADELINE, who was born June 9, 1834, in Bloomington, Ill. She was married June 6, 1854, in Plattsville, Grant county, Wis., to Rufus A. Rice, who was born August 29, 1820, in Monmouth, Kennebec county, Maine. They have two children, FRANCIS ALLEN, born July 4, 1860, and EDWIN LEWIS, born Dec. 28, 1864, both in Chicago. Mr. and Mrs. Rice reside at No. 594, west Washington Street, Chicago, Ill.

REBECCA, born in Kentucky, married in Sangamon county to David C. Brown. He died Oct., 1872, and she resides in Virden.

ELIZABETH, born in Kentucky, died in Sangamon county, unmarried, in 1837.

JANE A. born in Kentucky, married Leroy M. Paden, and resides in Macoupin county, near Nilwood.

John Fletcher died Sept. 16, 1830, less than six months after bringing his family to the county. His widow survived him twenty-eight years, and died in the fall of 1858—he in Sangamon county, and she in Macoupin county.

FLETCHER, JOB, Sen., was born Nov. 11, 1793, in Rockbridge county, Va. His father died when he was an infant, and his mother moved with her elder son John, in the autumn of 1808, to Logan county, Ky., and the next spring to that part of Christian which was afterwards Todd county. Job remained in the family of his brother John, attending school and teaching. He served as a soldier six months in the war of 1812, and as such assisted in burying the dead after the battle of Tippecanoe, although he was not in the battle. Mary Kerchner was born May 25, 1789, in Augusta county, Va., and was taken by her parents to Todd county, Ky. Job Fletcher and Mary Kerchner were there married, Dec. 22, 1818. They had one child born in Kentucky, and moved to what became Sangamon county, Ill., arriving Nov. 11, 1819, in what is now Ball township, where they had six children. Of their children—

PERMELIA A., born Aug. 5, 1819, in Christian county, Ky., was married in 1844 to Eddin Lewis. See his name. He died, and she was married, Feb. 4, 1856, to Larkin Lewis. See his name.

JAMES H., born Jan. 22, 1821, in Sangamon county, died in his twentieth year.

JOHN, born April 11, 1822, in Sangamon county, went to Arkansas in 1853. He was married in 1854 to Mary Fletcher. He resided in Arkansas until after the battle of Prairie Grove, when they started for Illinois. Mrs. Fletcher died on the way, Dec. 27, 1862, leaving one child. Mr. Fletcher served his country in the 1st Ill. Cav., part of the time in the south and the remainder on the frontier against the Indians. He died in Bates county, Mo., April 10, 1874.

ELIZABETH, born Feb. 23, 1824, in Sangamon county, married Albert Stacy, a native of Montgomery county, Ill. They had three living children,

MARY L., PERMELIA V. and ALBERT E. Mr. Stacy died March 22, 1863, and his widow and three children resided on the farm settled by her father in 1819 until 1875, when she sold out and moved to the vicinity of Chanute, Neosho county, Kan.

JONAS L., born Sept. 1, 1826, in Sangamon county, was married April 22, 1851, to Amanda M. Short, of same county. They had three living children, EMILY J., JAMES J. and EDWARD. Mr. F. and family moved to Kansas Sept. 1, 1859, and settled on Big creek while the land still belonged to the Osage Indians. Their title was not extinguished until 1867. Jonas L. Fletcher was appointed county clerk at the organization of Neosho county, Nov. 4, 1864, served one and a half years, and was then elected for two years. Was admitted to the bar in 1867. In 1868 was elected probate judge of Neosho county for two years, and was re-elected in 1870 for two years. Judge Fletcher and family reside at Chanute, Neosho county, Kan.

ELIJAH I., born Dec. 4, 1827, in Sangamon county, died Sept. 5, 1846, in same county.

MARY died in her seventh year.

Mrs. Mary Fletcher died July 14, 1850, and Job Fletcher died Sept. 4, 1872, both within half a mile of where they settled in 1819, in Ball township, near Sugar creek Cumberland Presbyterian church. On the very night of his arrival in the settlement, Mr. Fletcher was called to write the will of George Cox, who came the year before with the Drennan and Dodds families. That was the first will from what is now Sangamon county ever put on record, and was registered at Edwardsville.

Mr. F. had to buy corn for bread and to feed his stock until he could raise a crop. The nearest point at which he found any for sale was three miles south of Edwardsville. Mr. Fletcher bought of Major Iles the first window glass ever sold in Springfield, and the first ever put in a window in Sangamon county. He also believed that he taught the first school in the county, in a log cabin built for that purpose, in 1820 or '21, south of Sugar creek. A Sunday school was organized near where he lived in 1825, by Rev. J. M. Peck, and Mr. F. taught in that school also. It was near where the Sugar creek Cumberland Presbyterian church now stands. William Drennan, Sen., was the first superintendent, and continued for about twenty years, as it became the Sunday school connected with that church. His grandson, John L. Drennan, is now the superintendent. Job Fletcher and John Taylor were appointed justices of the peace. The first in what is now Sangamon county. As such, Mr. Fletcher organized the first election precinct in the county. That was in 1819 or '20, when it was part of Madison county. The titles of the Indians to the lands were all extinguished before Mr. F. came into the county; but two and a half years of the time allowed them to hunt was unexpired, and the country was full of them. They, however, were all friendly. Mr. F. was present April 10, 1821, when the Commissioners, William Drennan, Sen., Zachariah Peter and Rivers Cormack, located the county seat. He saw the stake driven, marked Z and D, declared to be the county seat, and named Springfield. Job Fletcher was one of the representatives from Sangamon county at one session of the legislature in Vandalia. He was one of the Senators for the county at the session of 1836 and '7, which legislated for the removal of the State capital to Springfield, and was consequently one of the "Long Nine." He served one term in the Senate after the removal to Springfield.

FLETCHER, THOMAS P., was born in 1791, near Richmond, Va. His parents moved, when he was a boy, to Union county, Ky. He was there married to Marion Davis. They had six children in Kentucky, and moved to Sangamon county, Ill., arriving in 1828 in what is now Williams township, and in 1831 moved to Tazewell county, and from there to Logan county, in 1836. The mother died in 1845, and the father in 1865. Their children, Thomas J., Melinda, William D., Judith W., Rigdon S., Emily and James M., are married and live in different parts of the country. Two only are connected with old settlers families of Sangamon county.

ELIZABETH, born in Virginia, married Madison M. Merriman. *See his name.*

BENJAMIN F., born March 28, 1834, in Tazewell county, married Cordelia L. Merriman. They reside at the old homestead of her father, where he settled in 1829, two miles southwest of Williamsville. B. F. Fletcher enlisted Aug., 1862, in Co. B, 130th Ill. Inf., for three years, served full term, and was honorably discharged in 1865.

FLORVILLE, WILLIAM, was born about 1806, at Cape Haytien, West India. When the revolution commenced, in 1821 and 22, his god-mother took him to Baltimore, Md., and kept him in St. Mary's Convent until her death, when he was bound by the orphan's court to learn the trade of a barber. He then went to New Orleans, thence to St. Louis, and with others from St. Louis, on a hunting excursion, up the Mississippi, Illinois and Sangamon rivers, to New Salem, then in Sangamon county, arriving in the fall of 1831. It was late in the evening, and as he approached the village he fell in with a tall man, wearing a red flannel shirt and carrying an axe on his shoulder, just returning from his day's labor in the woods. They fell into an easy conversation and walked to a little grocery store together. The tall man was Abraham Lincoln, who soon learned that the stranger was a barber, nearly out of money and aiming to reach Springfield. That was enough to enlist the good will of Mr. Lincoln, who took him to his boarding house, told the people his business and situation. That opened the way for an evening's work among the boarders, and the next morning he started on his way rejoicing, and reached Springfield the second day. Mr. Florville was soon recognized by Dr. E. H. Merriman—See his sketch—with whom he was acquainted in Baltimore and St. Louis. Dr. M. proved his friendship in various ways. Mr. Florville spent some time in the employ of Gen. James D. Henry. He was married soon after his arrival to Phœbe Rountree, who was born Feb. 4, 1811, near Glasgow, Ky. They had five living children, namely:

SAMUEL H., born May, 1832, in Springfield, married Oct. 26, 1874, at Waverly, to Mary Belle Greene, who was born in 1849 in Morgan county. She died Nov. 23, 1875. S. H. Florville is a barber, and lives in Springfield.

ALSEEN, born Dec., 1833, in Springfield, married in 1851 to Mahlon Chaverous. They had two living children. JULIA C., born April 28, 1852, married April 27, 1871, to Clark Duncan, who was born Oct. 5, 1850, near Russelville, Ky. They have two children, ALSEEN and OTIS B., and live in Springfield. ADDIE lives with her mother. Mrs. Chaverous married Nov., 1863, to Richard Wright. They have three children, EDWARD, MARTIN and CLIFFORD, and live in Springfield.

SINEET, born Sept., 1837, in Springfield, married Gilbert Johnson. They had three children in Springfield. PHŒBE, born in 1855, married T. Adams, has one child, MABEL, and lives in Springfield. GILBERT, born Feb., 1857, and ANNIE, born in 1859, live with their mother. Gilbert Johnson died in 1858. Mrs. Sineet Johnson married Henry Scott. They had one child, ELIZA, and Mr. Scott enlisted in the army to suppress the rebellion, and was never heard of after. Mrs. Sineet Scott married March 1, 1865, to Jordan Richardson. They have four children, JAMES, WILLIAM, GEORGE and THOMAS. Mr. Richardson keeps a grocery store, and lives in Springfield.

VARVEEL, was born in 1839, in Springfield. In 1862 he went into the army under Maj. Gen. McClernand, was with him in all his campaigns, came home and died Oct. 2, 1864.

WILLIAM L., born March 10, 1840, in Springfield, married April 9, 1861, to Mary Jenkins. They have three living children, AQUILLA, URETTA and ELIZABETH, and live in Springfield.

William Florville died April 13, 1868, and Mrs. Phœbe Florville was married May 10, 1873, to Reuben Coleman, and resides in Springfield.

FLYNN, CATHARINE, was born May 14, 1828, in Dublin, Ireland, came with her parents to America when she was seven years old. They first made their home in Amherst, Mass., and then went to Philadelphia. From there she came with the family of Asahel Thayer to Sangamon county, arriving in Chatham May 14, 1839. She was married July 27, 1847, to Jacob Leonard, who was born June 17, 1822, in Stafford, Conn., and came to Chatham Sept. 14, 1844.

They had two children—

CHARLES F., died Jan. 27, 1854, aged two and a half years.

RICHARD F., died August 27, 1862, in his second year. Jacob Leonard and wife reside in Chatham. He is a retired farmer.

FOLEY, WILLIAM C., born June 16, 1808, in Prince William county, Va., and came to Springfield, Ill., arriving in the fall of 1838. He was married in Springfield, June 16, 1840, to Elizabeth E. Hutchinson. They had eight children, namely—

ANN V., born April 8, 1841, resides with her parents.

JOHN W., born May 18, 1843, in Springfield, married Sept. 18, 1864, to Marcia A. Purvines. They have three children, ARTHUR C., CORA MAY, and a babe, and live at Pleasant Plains, Illinois.

ADDISON F. died, aged seven years.

ELIZABETH C. and FLORA S. live with their parents.

ADELIA S. married A. B. Mars. He is a telegraph operator, and lives in Springfield.

WILLIAM C. and THOMAS E. live with their parents in Springfield.

FORD, DANIEL, was born Feb. 22, 1796, in New Jersey. His parents moved to Fayette county, Ky., when he was a boy. Mary Randolph was born in Fayette county, Ky., June 17, 1802. Daniel Ford and Mary Randolph were married there, May 11, 1820. Nine children were born in that county, and the family moved to Sangamon county, Ill., arriving in Nov., 1838, in what is now Ball township, where two children were born. Four of those born in Kentucky, and one in Sangamon county, died under four years of age. Of the other six—

WILLIAM R., born July 3, 1824, in Kentucky, married in Illinois, Nov. 6, 1849, to Minerva J. Scott. They have two children. SARAH E. married Charles M. Shepherd. See his name. WILLIAM P. resides with his parents, in Ball township, fifteen miles south of Springfield.

ANN E., born in Kentucky, May 10, 1816, married John Patterson. They have eight children: MARY R., the second child, married Robert Scott. See his name. WILLIAM V., the eldest child, JOHN R., AMANDA F., SAMUEL E., ROBERT D., IDA MAY and NENA F. reside with their parents, thirteen miles south of Springfield, on the George Lamb farm—1874.

AMANDA, born in Kentucky, married Josephus Parkinson. They had two children. IDA CORNELIA married Frank Shores, and resides in Chicago. KATE ELEANOR lives with her mother. Josephus Parkinson died May 11, 1866, and his widow resides in Chicago.

JOHN, born Jan. 13, 1834, in Kentucky, married Nov. 12, 1861, to Ara Holmes, who was born Jan. 31, 1843, in Brown county, Ohio. They have four children, ANNA L., CHARLES A., ALEX. E. and FREDDIE T., and live in Ball township—1874.

GEORGE W., born in Kentucky in 1837, died in Sangamon county, Feb. 12, 1858.

MARY, born in Sangamon county, married Thomas J. Scott. See his name.

Daniel Ford died May 21, 1852, in Sangamon county, and his widow died April 2, 1864, at Macomb, Ill.

FORD, THOMAS, was born in Fauquier county, Va. Mary Paine was born there also. They were married and had eleven children in that county. The family moved to Sangamon county, Ill., arriving in 1835 in what is now Fancy creek township, two miles northwest of Sherman. Of their eleven children—

JAMES G., born Sept. 22, 1801, came to Sangamon county with his father. He never married, and resides near Linden, Johnson county, Wis.

JOSEPH W., born in Virginia, died unmarried.

SAMUEL, born in Virginia, married Jane Evans, had one child, and all died in Sangamon county.

SARAH, born and married in Virginia to Patrick Welch, had two children, and Mr. W. died in Virginia. She and her two sons came to Sangamon county with her father. JOHN went to Missouri, married there, enlisted in the Union army, and died at Memphis, Tenn., in 1862 or '3. JAMES married Miss Beck, and lives near Elkhart. Mrs. Welch married Sanford Cherry, and resides near Elkhart, Ill.

DANIEL, born in Virginia, came to

Sangamon county with his parents, is unmarried, and resides near Linden, Wis.

ELIZA, born in Virginia, married in Sangamon county to Sanford Cherry. They had four children, and she died in Sangamon county. Mr. Cherry married her sister, Mrs. Welch. They reside near Elkhart, Ill.

MARY, born in Virginia, married in Sangamon county to William Glascock. They have three children, and reside near Linden, Wisconsin.

SYLVESTER W., born Nov. 27, 1813, in Fauquier county, Va., married Dec. 26, 1837, to Amarilla Enos, in Sangamon county. They had seven children in Sangamon county. MARY C., born Jan. 24, 1839, died in her fifth year. ABNER T., born Oct. 4, 1840, enlisted August, 1862, in Co. I, 114th Ill. Inf., for three years, served full term, and was honorably discharged in 1865, married October, 1874, to Rebecca McGinnis, near Williamsville. SARAH E., born July 12, 1842, married Daniel Pottle. See his name. WILLIAM H., born Sept. 22, 1845, enlisted July 20, 1861, at Springfield, in what became Co. B, 11th Mo. Inf., and was drowned Sept. 2, 1861, while bathing in the Mississippi river near Cape Girardeau, Mo. SYLVESTER W., Jun., born Sept. 3, 1847, enlisted January, 1865, for one year, in Co. I, 114th Ill. Inf., served until the spring of 1866, and was honorably discharged. AMARILLA, born Nov. 28, 1850, and ARMINTA, born March 29, 1853, are unmarried, and reside with their mother. Sylvester Ford died July 10, 1866, and his widow resides three miles southeast of Buffalo Hart station.

WILLIAM, born in Virginia, came to Sangamon county with his parents, married in Wisconsin, and moved to California.

THOMAS, Jun., born in Virginia, raised in Sangamon county, married in Wisconsin to Mary Perry, and live near Linden.

FRANCIS, born in Virginia, came to Sangamon county with his parents, married to Frances Adams in Wisconsin, and resides near Linden.

Thomas Ford and the younger members of the family moved to Johnson county, Wisconsin, near Linden, in 1849. He and his wife both died there.

—39

FORDEN, JOHN, born Jan. 12, 1798, near Elkton, Md. His parents moved to Bourbon county, Ky., when he was quite young. He was married April 22, 1824, in Clarke county, to Emeline Sidener, who was born Nov. 10, 1808, in that county. They made their home in Bourbon county until four children were born, and moved to Sangamon county, Ill., arriving in the spring of 1831, and settled five miles east of Springfield. Of their children—

JAMES W., born March 27, 1825, in Bourbon county, Ky., died in Sangamon county Aug. 23, 1851.

SARAH A., born Jan. 9, 1827, in Kentucky, married in Sangamon county to William S. Currey. She died September, 1854.

GEORGE W., born Jan. 11, 1829, in Bourbon county, Ky., married in Sangamon county Feb. 15, 1855, to Permelia J. Rucker. They have six living children, MARY E., CHARLES T., GEORGE E. JOHN W., LAURA and JAMES R., reside with their parents three-quarters of a mile northeast of Sangamon station.

JOHN M., born Jan. 28, 1831, in Bourbon county, Ky., married in Sangamon county Feb. 13, 1855, to Eliza Wright. They have one living child, ALICE. Mr. Forden is a merchant, and resides in Springfield.

Mrs. Emeline Forden died June 29, 1834, and John Forden died Dec. 1, 1849, both in Sangamon county.

FORREST, DENNIS, was born Oct. 25, 1784, in North Carolina. He was married June 13, 1811, in Nicholas county, Ky., to Elizabeth McClintock, who was born Feb. 17, 1790, in Pennsylvania. They had eight children, all born in Nicholas county, Ky., and the family moved to Sangamon county, Ill., arriving in the fall of 1835 in what is now Chatham township. Of their children—

JANE M., born June 20, 1812, in Kentucky, was married there to John T. Webb, and came with her parents to Sangamon county. They had four children, and moved to Macomb, where Mrs. Webb died, September, 1866. Two children died also. DENNIS and PERMELIA live with their father at Macomb, Ill.

SARAH T., born March 20, 1815, married H. H. Elmore. See his name.

ELIZA, born June 20, 1817, married L. P. Matthews. *See his name.* She died in June, 1866, leaving three children.

JAMES A., born in Nicholas county, Ky., is living with his third wife. He has three children. ISABEL married a Mr. Davis. The other two are ANGELINE and JAMES, Jun. J. A. Forrest resides in Nodaway county, Mo.

ARTAMESIA, born March 2, 1821, in Kentucky, married William Carter. She died, leaving one son, FRANKLIN, in St. Joseph, Mo.

AMERICA, born Oct. 11, 1823, in Kentucky, married in Sangamon county, March, 1842, to William Gibson. They had two children. WILLIAM D. died Aug. 14, 1847. LIZZIE J. died Aug. 22, 1866, in her eighteenth year. Mr. Gibson died Dec. 26, 1849. His widow married Sept. 5, 1855, to Thomas J. Darneille, who died Nov. 21st of the same year. She was married Jan. 13, 1859, to John A. Neal. *See his name.*

MARGARET L., born June 25, 1826, was married June 15, 1845, to James E. Gibson. *See his name.*

HUGH M., born Dec. 6, 1831, married Angeline Cooley. She died, and he married Ann Greenwood, and he died.

Dennis Forrest died July 29, 1855, and his widow, Elizabeth Forrest, died Aug. 23, 1873, in Chatham.

FORTUNE, BENJAMIN, was born March 16, 1810, in Nelson county, Va. His parents moved in 1827, to Anderson county, Ky. He was married Nov. 24, 1830, in the adjoining county of Shelby, to Mary A. Bullard. They had one child, and moved to Sangamon county, Ill., arriving April 2, 1832, in what is now Illiopolis township, four miles east of Mechanicsburg, where they had two living children. Of their three children—

ELIZABETH A., born August 28, 1831, in Shelby county, Ky., married Oct. 2, 1851, in Sangamon county to Riley Wilkins, who was born Feb. 14, 1820, in Pickaway county, Ohio. They have two living children, MARY A. and WILLIAM B., and reside in Mechanicsburg.

THOMAS W., born July 20, 1836, in Sangamon county, enlisted June 3, 1862, for three years, in Co. A, 73d Ill. Inf. He was elected Ord. Sergt. at the organization of the company, promoted to 2d Lieut. Jan. 1, 1863, and 1st Lieut., Aug. 14, 1863. Becoming physically unable to discharge the duties of his office, he resigned Aug. 11, 1864. He was married in Mechanicsburg, June 17, 1866, to Martha J. Young, who was born July 3, 1840, in Frederick county, Md. They have three children, IDA MAY, NORMAN and THOMAS B., and reside near Mechanicsburg.

ELIZA J., born Aug. 7, 1838, in Sangamon county, married June, 1862, to James W. Craig. She died Feb. 23, 1871, leaving four children, CARRIE L., MABEL B., CHARLES A. and LAURA. They live with their father, who is married a second time, and resides near Jacksonville, Ill.

Mrs. Mary A. Fortune died April 8, 1841, and Benj. Fortune was married Oct. 25, 1844, to Mrs. Eliza Little, whose maiden name was Morgan. They had two living children—

JENNETTA W., born Oct. 17, 1843, in Sangamon county, married Jan. 10, 1860, to George W. Wantling, who was born Dec. 11, 1842, in Fairfield county, Ohio, and came to Sangamon county in 1854. They had three living children, FANNIE F., HATTIE and GEORGE O. reside with their parents, four miles southeast of Mechanicsburg.

ANNIE H., born Oct. 10, 1851, in Sangamon county, married Nov. 24, 1870, to William E. Barnes, who was born Oct. 27, 1848, in Chillicothe, Ohio. They have three children, BENJAMIN, OTIS and OMO, (the two latter twins,) and live in Mechanicsburg.

Mrs. Elizabeth Fortune died March 13, 1868, and Benjamin Fortune resides in Mechanicsburg.

FORTUNE, THOMAS E., brother to Benjamin, was born Feb. 11, 1791, in Nelson county, Va., married Miss Wright. They had one child, and Mrs. F. died there. Mr. Fortune and his only child went with his father to Anderson county, Ky. He moved to Sangamon county, Ill., arriving, in 1834, at Mechanicsburg. His daughter—

ELIZABETH J. B., born Sept. 12, 1813, in Nelson county, Va., married in 1831 in Anderson county, Ky., to Samuel Butts. They had one child born in Ky., and came with her father to Mechanicsburg, in 1834, where they had two children, and Mr. Butts died. His widow married Dec. 18, 1853, in Mechanicsburg, to Barnabas Barrows. They have one child. Of her four children, JULIA F. BUTTS, born Dec. 8, 1832, in Ky., married in Mechanicsburg to Isaac Allen, have four children, and live in Jacksonville. ANN E. BUTTS, born Jan. 8, 1837, in Mechanicsburg, married March 14, 1866, to Joseph Barrows, have three children, and reside near Jacksonville. THOMAS S. BUTTS, born Sept. 20, 1840, in Mechanicsburg, was last heard from, in 1872, at Montana City. CHARLES BARROWS resides with his parents near Jacksonville.

Thomas E. Fortune was in the mercantile business, in Mechanicsburg, for many years, and left there about the close of the rebellion. He resides with his granddaughter, Ann E. Barrows, near Jacksonville.

FOSTER, CONSTANTINE, born Oct. 18, 1792, in Cape May county, N. J., was married in Cumberland county, N. J., to Margaret Sayre, who was born in same county Feb. 25, 1800. They had five living children in Cape May county. The family moved in 1832 to Dayton, O., thence to Sangamon county, Ill., arriving in the autumn of 1833 in what is now Cartwright township, and two years later moved into what is now Gardner township. One child was born in Sangamon county. Of their six children—

ELIZA L., born May 13, 1820, in New Jersey, was married June 22, 1837, in Sangamon county, to F. Ewing Berry. He died four months after marriage. A daughter, FRANCES E., born June 4, 1838, in Sangamon county, was married Aug. 27, 1857, to Henry F. Lyon. He died April 25, 1858, and a daughter, IDA, born Sept. 14, 1858, died in infancy. Mrs. Frances Lyon was married April 21, 1862, by the Rev. Peter Cartwright, to Rev. B. F. Lodge, of the M. E. church, who was born Dec. 26, 1834, in Reading, Hamilton county, Ohio. Rev. B. F. Lodge was a member of the Illinois Conference, M. E. church, for nine years during that time, traveling the Sangamon and Chatham circuits. He located at his own request, and began farming in 1866. They have four living children, CHARLES A., JULIA E., FRANK BERRY and FANNIE MAY, and reside near Lodge, Piatt county, Ill. Mrs. Eliza L. Berry was married June 2, 1840, at the residence of her father, to Charles W. Hunt, who was born May 25, 1805, in Blount county, Tenn. An incident connected with their marriage will be appropriate here. Delegations from Cass, Schuyler and McDonough counties, with music and banners, were on their way to the great Harrison, or Whig, convention at Springfield, and passed Mr. Constantine Foster's residence just as the guests had seated themselves at the dinner table. The delegations halted and gave them a serenade. All rose from the table except two Democrats, who refused to leave their dinners to see a Whig delegation to what proved to be the greatest political gathering in the State that year. Mr. and Mrs. Hunt had nine children. Of those, eight lived to maturity, namely: HARRIET J., JOHN B., J. ELBRIDGE (the latter died Nov. 23, 1875), CATHARINE L., CHARLES R., JOSEPH F. (the latter died Feb. 11, 1776), WILLIAM B. and ESTHER L., were all born near Burlington, Iowa, where the family now reside.

CATHARINE, born June 7, 1833, in New Jersey, was married Nov. 28, 1839, in Sangamon county, Ill., to John C. Bone. They had one child, and mother and child died. Mr. Bone resides in Chicago, Ill.

JOHN S., born May 1, 1825, in Cape May county, N. J., was married in Sangamon county, Ill., May 27, 1847, to Eliza A' Carson, who was born June 17, 1831, in Cape May county also. They are without children, but brought up an adopted daughter—Elizabeth Nottingham—who married Alexander Higgins. See his name. They adopted another daughter—Minnie Virden—who lives with them. John S. Foster was a licensed preacher in the M. E. church for several years, and, at his own request, his license was discontinued in 1874. He resides in Springfield, Ill.

JACOB, born June 18, 1829, in New Jersey, was married April 6, 1853, in Sangamon county, to Roxanna Bates. They have six living children: CHARLES F., ELLA C. (the latter graduated at the Bettie Stuart Institute, June 10, 1874. She was married Aug. 23, 1874, to William W. Crane, M. D. They have one child, LINA C., and reside in Cincinnati, Ohio.) OLIVER C., EUGENE E., BUCK-

MAN B. and ELIZA K. Jacob Foster and family reside in Springfield, Ill.

JOSEPH R., born June 28, 1831, in New Jersey, was married Feb. 22, 1854, in Sangamon county, to Harriet E. Lyon. She died in November of the same year, and he married Jane Mathis. They have five children, HARRIET J., LUELLA M., IDA, MAGGIE and BERTHA, and reside in Springfield.

MARY J., born Jan. 1, 1834, in Sangamon county, married John Epler, and died.

Constantine Foster died Sept. 29, 1865, and Mrs. Margaret Foster died April 9, 1867, both in Sangamon county, and are buried at Pleasant Plains.

FOSTER, GEORGE, was born in Clarke county, Ky., and married there to Sarah Miller, a native of the same county. They had three children in Kentucky, and moved to Sangamon county, Ill., in what is now Loami township, in 1826, where they had five children. Of their eight children—

WILLIAM, born March 15, 1823, in Clarke county, Ky., married in Sangamon county, in Sept., 1848, to Elizabeth J. Shutt. They have nine children, GEORGE R., WILLIAM P., JACOB F., SARAH E., JOHN D., LEONARD G., MARIAN E., EVA J., and CHARLES H., reside with their parents four and one-half miles northwest of Auburn.

ELIZABETH, born in Kentucky, married in Sangamon county to William Roach, and reside at Ft. Scott, Kansas.

PEYTON, born in Kentucky, married in Sangamon county to Mary J. Foster. They have two children, and live in Henry county, Mo.

POLLY, born in Sangamon county, and married George Organ. *See his name.*

LEONARD, born in Sangamon county, married Elvira Gates, has several children, and reside in Auburn township.

SARAH, born in Sangamon county, married Alexander Orr. *See his name.*

MATILDA, born in Sangamon county, married Micajah Cudaway, and reside in Henry county, Mo.

JOHN, born in Sangamon county, married Fanny Bogy. She died in Kansas, and he married Fanny Wright. They have two children, and live in Sangamon county, near Virden, Ill.

George Foster died in Auburn township, Sangamon county.

FOSTER, PEYTON, was born about 1799, near Winchester, Scott county, Ky., and was married there to Polly Daniels, a native of the same county. They had six children in Kentucky, and moved to Sangamon county, Ill., with his brother George, arriving in the year 1826, and settled in what is now Loami township, where four children were born. Of their nine children—

JEANETTE, born in Kentucky, married Edward Greenwood. *See his name.*

WILLIAM H., born in Kentucky, married Margaret Greenwood, and she died in Nebraska, on the road to the Pacific. He and his children live in California.

GEORGE W., born in Kentucky, married in Sangamon county to Lucille Short. She had four children and died. He married again, and resides in Louisiana, Mo.

JOHN D., born in Scott county, Ky., married in Sangamon county to Eunice Miller. They had seven children. GEORGE W. served as Quartermaster Sergeant in the 22d Mo. Inf., of which his father was Colonel. He was afterwards Orderly Sergeant in Co. E, 39th Mo. Inf. He married Mary M. Scott, has five children, EMMA D., WILLIAM F., ADA, JOHN D. and DORA B., and reside in Loami township. EMILY M. married Joseph P. Ringo, in Adair county, Mo., has six children, and resides in Oregon. PEYTON F. married Martha Dunn, and has two children. LUCINA is married, and resides in Adair county, Missouri. LEONORA P. married William Canham. They have two children, WILLIAM E. and JENNIE, and live in Chatham township. JAMES H. B. lives in Chatham township. Mrs. Eunice Foster resides with her daughter, Mrs. Canham. John D. Foster is married to a second wife, has one child, and is a practicing attorney at Commerce, Scott county, Mo. He served one year—from 1846 to 1847—in the 4th Ill. Inf., under Col. E. D. Baker, in the Mexican war. He was Colonel of the 22d Mo. Inf. in the war to suppress the rebellion.

PEYTON, born in Kentucky, married in Sangamon county to Maria Colburn. They have five children, and reside in Kansas.

POLLY, born in Kentucky, married in Sangamon county to Alfred C. Campbell. See his name.

JAMES was accidentally killed in infancy.

HIRAM B., born in Sangamon county, married Martha Ferguson, have two children, and reside in Macon county, Mo.

JAMES M., born in Sangamon county, married and died.

Mrs. Polly Foster died January, 1872, and Peyton Foster died Sept. 7, 1872, both in Missouri.

FOSTER, IVINS, was born Nov. 23, 1794, in Harrison county, Ky. Margaret McKee was born Jan. 24, 1796, in the same county. They were there married, Feb. 26, 1819, and had three children in Harrison county, and then moved to Gallatin county, where one child was born. They then moved to Sangamon county, Ill., arriving in Nov., 1829, in what is now Curran township, north of Lick creek, where four children were born. Three of their children died under five years. Of the other five—

WILLIAM D., born Jan. 24, 1820, in Harrison county, Ky., was brought by his parents to Sangamon county. He studied medicine three years in Springfield, and attended one course of lectures in St. Louis. In consequence of impaired health, he was advised by the Faculty to take a sea voyage. In June, 1843, he embarked for Europe, visiting England, he went to Scotland intending to complete his education there. While visiting a hospital, in pursuit of knowledge, he contracted small pox, and would have been kindly cared for at the residence of a friend, where he was taken sick, but he preferred being removed to the Royal Infirmary, of Edinburg, where he died Dec. 29, 1843.

MARY J., born Dec. 8, 1821, in Kentucky, married in Sangamon county April 1, 1847, to Samuel W. Dunn. He was born Oct. 6, 1821, in Harrison county, Ky., and came to Sangamon county in 1844. They had eight children, six of whom died under five years. The others, NARCISSA and WILLIAM SHERMAN, reside with their parents in Curran township.

JOEL S., born March 15, 1824, in Kentucky, died in Sangamon county aged twenty-three years.

SAMUEL L., born June 29, 1830, in Sangamon county, married Dec. 27, 1855, to Lydia Lee, who was born Feb. 14, 1834, in Dover, Del. They have four living children, namely: MARY A., LOUIS K., ROBERT and MARGARET B., and live near the family homestead in Curran township.

JOHN W., born Jan. 29, 1833, in Sangamon county, unmarried, and lives with his mother.

Ivins Foster died Jan. 4, 1866, and his widow now—1874—resides one and one-half miles southeast of Curran, where they settled in 1829.

FOSTER, MEREDITH, was born Nov. 14, 1790, in Louisa county, Va., and was married in Culpepper county, Feb. 10, 1820, to Margaret Boyer, who was born March 9, 1797, in Culpepper county, Va. They had six children in Virginia, and the family moved to Sangamon county, Ill., arriving in the fall of 1835, lived several days in camp about four miles west of Springfield, and then moved on a farm near by. They had four children in Sangamon county, one of whom died young. Of their nine children—

WILLIAM B., born April 9, 1822, in Page county, Va., came with his parents to Sangamon county in 1835; went in 1849 to California. He was married there to Emma Creamer. They had three children, MAGGIE, IDA and WILLIE, and Mrs. Foster died. Mr. Foster married again, and resides at Richmond, Sacramento county, Cal.

HENRY H., born Sept. 4, 1824, in Page county, Va. He was married in Sangamon county Dec. 2, 1847, to Nancy Davis. See sketch of John Davis. They have one child, ROBERT MEREDITH, and reside in Curran township, near Chatham.

JOHN E., born July 24, 1826, in Page county, Va. He enlisted at Springfield, Ill., in 1846, in Co. A, 4th Ill. Inf., and served under Col. E. D. Baker through the Mexican war. He died on his way home, June 13, 1847, at Virginia, Cass county, Ill.

ABNER M., born Jan. 25, 1828, in Page county, Va., married in Sangamon county, December, 1863, to Mrs. Hatch, who was formerly Mrs. Murphy, and whose maiden name was Lawton. She is a native of Lincoln, Penobscot county, Maine. They reside two miles east of Loami.

MARY J., born Nov. 21, 1830, in Page county, Va., married in Sangamon county to James Lockridge. *See his name.* They had ten children, four of whom died young. Of the six, CHARLES M., MARY M., SARAH I., LULA A., LENORA and EVA, reside with their parents.

CATHARINE A., born April 20, 1834, in Page county, Va., married in Sangamon county to James Young. They have eight children, ABNER, MAGGIE, JAMES, EUGENE, NANCY, FRANK, ALBERT and ETTA, and reside near Curran.

ROBERT F., born Jan. 3, 1837, in Sangamon county, Ill., and lives with his sister, Mrs. Grissom, near Chatham.

CHARLES N., born Dec. 3, 1838, in Sangamon county, and was killed July 5, 1868, by an accident on the Chicago & Alton railroad.

MARGARET E., born Dec. 28, 1842, in Sangamon county, married Nov. 19, 1861, to Thomas Grissom, who was born Feb. 8, 1841, in Sangamon county, Ill. They have three children, AGNES, IDA and EDWARD, and reside three miles northwest of Chatham.

Mrs. Margaret Foster died Dec. 13, 1866, and Meredith Foster died Aug. 31, 1867, both in Sangamon county.

FOUTCH, JOHN, was born May, 1776, in Loudon county, Va. Three brothers by the name of Fouche came from France and settled in Loudon county, Va., before the American revolution. Two of them were soldiers in that war, and one of them was Abraham, the father of John, whose name heads this sketch. John Foutch went to Fayette county, Ky., when he was a young man, and was there married, in 1796, to Nancy A. Wherrett, who was born March 8, 1778, in St. Mary's county, Md. They had five children born in Fayette county, near Lexington, and the family moved to Dearborn county, near Harrison, Indiana, where they had four children, and moved to Franklin county, where one child was born, thence to Sangamon county, Ill., arriving in the fall of 1825 at the south side of Richland creek, east of where Pleasant Plains now stands, and in the spring of 1826 moved to Island Grove, Sangamon county. Of their ten children—

ABRAHAM, born April 1, 1797, in Fayette county, Ky., was married in 1820, in Franklin county, Ind., to Elizabeth Vansickle, and came to Sangamon county in 1825. He brought one child from Ind., and had seven children in Sangamon county. In 1849 they moved to Polk county, near DesMoines, Iowa, and from there, in 1870, to Elmore, near Brownsville, Neb., where they now reside. Abraham Foutch was justice of the peace for many years in Sangamon county. He was one of the three Commissioners of Sangamon county at the time the State House (now used as a Court House) was built.

THOMAS, born Nov. 25, 1799, in Fayette county, Ky., was married Dec. 21, 1820, in Fayette county, Ind., to Sarah Wherrett, who was born Nov. 20, 1800, in Fayette county, Ky. Her parents moved to Jessamine county, and from there to Fayette county. Mr. and Mrs. Foutch had two children in Indiana, and moved to Sangamon county, Ill., in 1825, where they had four children. ELIZABETH A., born Nov. 21, 1821, in Indiana, was married in Sangamon county, Ill., Dec. 5, 1839, to Thomas Pollock. *See his name.* NANCY, born Jan. 23, 1824, in Indiana, was married in Sangamon county, Jan. 2, 1842, to J. D. Bevan. *See his name.* JOHN, born Sept. 6, 1826, in Sangamon county, was married April 12, 1849, to Martha M. Smith. They had nine children. SARAH M., married F. P. Gillespie, have three children, *Mattie M., Guy E.,* and *William E.*, and reside one-half mile south of New Berlin. THOMAS, the second, and ELLA M., the sixth child, both died under three years. The other six, HATTIE S., JOHN W., CARRIE M., LIZZIE D., EDWARD L. and GEORGE T., reside with their parents in New Berlin. Mr. John Foutch resides within two miles of his birthplace and has done so all his life, with the exception of one year. CAROLINE, born March 8, 1829, in Sangamon county, was married there April 8, 1847, to Thomas A. Kerlin. They had one living child, LIZZIE A. She lives with her grandfather Foutch. Mrs. Kerlin died Dec. 31, 1854.

Mr. Kerlin is married again, and lives near Bedford, Mo. WILLIAM W., born Sept. 4, 1834, in Macoupin county, was a graduate of Shurtleff College, Upper Alton, and enlisted Aug. 17, 1861, for three years in Co. D, 26th Ill. Inf. At the organization of the company he was elected and commissioned First Lieutenant. He was taken sick while with his regiment, at Quincy, Ill., came home and died of typhoid fever Sept. 25, 1861. HUGH, born Dec. 19, 1836, in Sangamon county, was married Sept. 2, 1858, to Mary Wykoff. They have one child, WILLIAM W., and live at Decatur. Thomas Foutch and wife reside in Island Grove township, three and a-half miles west of Berlin.

HUGH, born March 12, 1802, in Kentucky, was married in Sangamon county, December, 1827, to Nancy Rhea. They had nine children, and he died December, 1845, in Fulton county. His widow married William Meeker, and resides in Iowa.

ELIZABETH, born August, 1804, in Kentucky, was married September, 1824, to Samuel Blair. They had twelve children. The parents died at Montezuma, Pike county, Ill. Two of their children, THEOPHILUS and NANCY A., are married, and reside near Montezuma, Ill.

JOHN, born Oct. 25, 1805, in Kentucky, was married in Sangamon county in 1827, to Jehoida Rhea. They had four children, and she died. He married Letitia Farris. They have nine children, and reside in Fulton county, five miles west of Havana.

SUSAN, born June 10, 1809, in Dearborn county, Ind., was married Dec. 11, 1828, to William Rhea. *See his name.*

DOROTHY, born April, 1811, in Dearborn county, Ind., was married in Sangamon county, December, 1830, to Samuel Peebler. They have had six children. The parents both died in 1842, on the same day, and were buried in one coffin, at Fairfield, Iowa.

MARY A., born Dec. 25, 1812, in Dearborn county, Ind., was married in Sangamon county Dec. 11, 1828, to Henry Harmon. *See his name.*

SIRON, born May 10, 1815, in Dearborn county, Ind., was married in Sangamon county, February, 1837, to Anthony H. Shull. *See his name.*

WILLIAM, born Jan. 8, 1818, in Indiana, died in Sangamon county, Oct., 1831.

Mrs. Nancy A. Foutch died March 12, 1845, and John Foutch married Celia Harmon. He died Sept. 15, 1848, and Mrs. Celia Foutch died in 1851, all in Sangamon county.

FOWKES, WILLIAM L., was born Jan. 17, 1793, in Loudon county, Va. He was married there, July 20, 1813, to Mrs. Margaret D. Saunders, whose maiden name was Saunders. She was born March 1, 1788, in the same county. She had three sons by her first marriage. *See names of Presley, Asbury, John and Cyrus G. Saunders.* Mr. and Mrs. Fowkes had two children in Loudon county, Va., and Mr. Fowkes served a term in the war of 1812, about the time of his marriage. They moved, in the spring of 1817, to Warren county, Ky., where they had four children, and moved to Sangamon county, Ill., arriving in Oct., 1826, and settled three miles west of Springfield, where one child was born. Mr. Fowkes taught school there in a house built of round logs, with the earth for a floor, oiled paper for window lights, and a fire place as wide as one end of the house. That house was built in 1827. In the spring of 1831 Mr. F. moved to German Prairie, four miles northeast of Springfield. Of their seven children—

ROBERT H. S., born May 2, 1814, in Loudon county, Va., married in Sangamon county, Jan. 21, 1841, to Mary G. Pettus. They had four children. JOHN T. married Sarah O. Hulbert, and reside near Grove City, Christian county. ALBERT married Adaline Barnes, and resides at Topeka, Kan. GEORGE W. enlisted in 1862, for three years, in Co. I, 41st Ill. Inf., and was killed at the battle of Jackson, Miss., July, 1863. ELIZABETH A. resides with her father. Mrs. Mary G. Fowkes died Feb. 26, 1852, and R. H. S. Fowkes was married Oct., 1852, to Mrs. Harriet Fuller, whose maiden name was Pettus. They have four children: JAMES H., MARY E., WILLIAM E. and NEWTON C., and reside near Mt. Auburn, Christian county.

ELIZABETH M., born Feb. 26, 1816, in Loudon county, Va., resides with her brother, William H., near Springfield.

HARRIET L., born April 8, 1818, in Kentucky, married in Sangamon county, June, 1841, to Simon D. Etzroth, who died in 1845, and she married James Clark, in March, 1848. They had two children. JOANNA married John Copper, and resides near Mt. Pulaski or Lincoln. HARRIET J. is married. Mrs. Clark died Jan., 1852.

WILLIAM H., born April 17, 1820, in Warren county, Ky., married in Sangamon county, Nov. 28, 1843, to Mary Riddle, who was born May 13, 1819. They had seven living children. LILLIE E. died, aged seven years. MARGARET E., MARY L., GEORGE F., SARAH A., WILLIAM D. and MARTHA J. reside with their parents, adjoining Springfield on the west. William H. Fowkes enlisted in 1861, in Co. F, 4th Iowa Inf., served nine months, and was honorably discharged on account of physical disability.

LOUISA M., born Aug. 1, 1822, in Kentucky, married in Sangamon county to Henry J. King, Nov. 5, 1840. They had four children, and live near Timber Creek Postoffice, Marshall county, Iowa.

JOSEPH F., born Oct. 8, 1824, in Kentucky, married in Sangamon county to Jane Curry. Both died; Mr. Fowkes, Jan. 6, 1866. Three of their children live at Topeka, Kan. MARY J. lives in Christian county.

MARGARET S., born March 23, 1827, in Sangamon county, died in her eighth year.

Wm. L. Fowkes died Nov. 26, 1864, and his widow died Nov. 20, 1873, both in Christian county.

FOWLER, MASON, was born about 1766 in Virginia. He was married and had five children in that State, and the family moved to the vicinity of Nashville, Tenn., where they had seven children. They moved from there to Southern Illinois in 1816, and in the spring of 1820 Mr. Fowler, with his two sons, Edward and John and a young man by the name of Frederick Wise, came to what is now Cotton Hill township, Sangamon county. They raised a crop, built a house that summer, returned south and brought Mr. Fowler's family to their new home on Horse creek in the fall of that year. Of their children—

EDWARD and JOHN, born in Virginia, married in Sangamon county to two sisters by the name of Hale, and moved to Wisconsin near Galena. The two brothers and ten other citizens, including an Indian agent and interpreter, were riding over the country without suspecting danger. They were attacked by Indians and eleven of them killed. One only escaped—a man by the name of Pierce Holly, who had the fleetest horse, and that alone saved his life. The widows of the Fowler brothers married again, and continued to reside in that region of country.

ELIZABETH, born in Virginia, married in Sangamon county to Mr. Pierce. They both died, leaving three sons, who were raised by William Southwick and Joseph Enslee, in Sangamon county.

ANN, born in Virginia, married in Sangamon county to Dr. Samuel D. Slater. She died in 1832 or '3, leaving two children.

REBECCA, born in Virginia, married in Sangamon county to Frederick Wise. See his name.

TABITHA, born in Tennessee, married in Sangamon county to a Mr. Hale.

THOMAS, born in Tennessee, came to Sangamon county with his parents, and after the death of his brothers Edward and John, left home with the avowed purpose of avenging their death. After an absence of ten years with the Indians, he visited his friends in Sangamon county, went again to the Indians, and was never heard of after.

NANCY, born in Tennessee, married in Sangamon county, to Wm. Kirkpatrick. She died in Sangamon county, leaving five children.

WILLIAM, born in Tennessee, married in Sangamon county, in 1834, to Polly Durbin, and moved, in 1842, to Dubuque county, Iowa.

Mrs. Prudence Fowler died about 1823, in Sangamon county, and Mason Fowler married Mrs. Anna M. Seeley, whose maiden name was Slater. They had two children—

ELIZA A., born in Sangamon county, married to a Mr. Clarke. They live in Iowa.

MILTON E., born in Sangamon county, went to Iowa, married there, returned to Sangamon county, inherited his father's homestead by will, and died there, Sept. 5, 1867.

Mason Fowler died March, 1844, and Mrs. Anna M. Fowler died about 1853, both in Sangamon county.

FOWLER, THOMAS, was born about 1800, in Lincolnshire, England, and was married there to Millicent Bowis, who was born about 1803, in the same shire. Six children were born in England, and the family embarked at Liverpool, May 15, 1835, and landed in New York after a voyage of nine weeks. They came to Sangamon county in the latter part of July, 1835, and settled in Loami township, where three children were born. Of all the children—

MILLICENT, born in England, married in Sangamon county to William Jarrett. *See his name.*

THOMAS, born in England, died in Sangamon county, at twenty-one years of age.

JOHN B., born June 10, 1827, in Lincolnshire, England, married in Sangamon county, Jan. 23, 1849, to Sarah A. Greening. They have seven children, AFFYLINE, THOMAS, ABIGAIL, JOHN, JAMES, WILLIAM and GEORGE, and reside six miles southwest of Chatham.

ROBERT, born in England, married in Sangamon county to Minerva Bilyeu, have eleven children, and live in Crawford county, Kansas.

JANE, born in England, married in Sangamon county to Willis R. Webb, who died, and she married Young Hudson. *See his name.*

ELIZABETH, born Dec., 1833, in England, married in Sangamon county, May 11, 1854, to William M. Gibson. *See his name.*

MARY, born in Sangamon county, married to Thomas N. Park. *See his name.*

FANNY, born in Sangamon county, married Charles Strong, have one child, and live in Crawford county, Kansas.

GEORGE W., born in Sangamon county, married Mary Brown, and live in Crawford county, Kansas.

Thomas Fowler died July 7, 1867, and his widow resides with her daughter, Mrs. Jarrett—1874.

FRANCIS.—The records of this family date back in Connecticut as far as 1632, but the immediate ancestor of *that family* who came to Springfield, Ill., was Simeon Francis, Sen., who was married May 24, 1793, in Connecticut, to Mary A. Adams. They were both natives of that State. Mrs. Francis died Sept. 18, 1822, and Mr. Francis died Sept. 7, 1823, both in their native State, leaving nine children, (seven sons and two daughters), who assembled at the family homestead in Wethersfield, Conn., in the spring of 1829, and decided to sell the property and seek homes in the west. The eldest brother—

FRANCIS, CHARLES, was born March 19, 1794, in Wethersfield, Conn.; married Elizabeth Haskell there. He did not unite with the others on the point of destination, but emigrated to Cherry Valley, then in Madison, now in Otsego county, N. Y. Afterwards he moved to Ohio, and in the autumn of 1834 started for Chicago. At that time emigrants traveled with wagons, camping wherever night overtook them. By the time he reached Laporte, Ind., winter set in with great severity. After leaving that village they met a party returning from Chicago, who represented that there were no provisions in that settlement, nor work of any kind progressing. This news turned him back, and, reaching Laporte, he remained there until the following spring, when he settled in what was known as the Galena woods, near Laporte. Charles Francis and wife had seven children—

MARY A. died in Wethersfield, Conn., Aug. 19, 1826.

JOSEPH H., born Sept. 23, 1821, in Wethersfield, Conn., was married March 4, 1849, in Laporte county, Ind., to Catharine Martin. They have two children, MARY E., born Jan. 7, 1850, was married Oct. 13, 1872, to Ralph W. Marshall, who was born in Will county, Ill., June 1, 1843. He was 1st Lieut. in Co. A, 20th Ill. Reg. Vol. Inf. They have three children, MARY E., FRANCES R. and JOSEPH R., and reside in Joliet, Ill. FRANCIS G., born March 10, 1852, resides with his parents, in Laporte county, Ind.

LUKE, born May 16, 1823, in Wethersfield, Conn., was married June 5, 1848, to Betsy A. Marshall, in Galena town, Laporte county, Ind. They are without family, and reside in Laporte.

SIMEON, born April 23, 1827, in Wethersfield, Conn., was married in Indiana, May 12, 1859, to Mary E. Martin, of Laporte county. They have two children, CHARLES W. and JESSIE G., and reside at Three Oaks, Mich.

W. WALLACE, born Dec. 17, 1828, in Wethersfield, Conn., was married March 29, 1851, in Indiana, to Ann M. Martin. They had six children. SARAH B., born June 10, 1852, married A. J. Holman. They had two children, FREDERICK and CATHARINE. Mrs. Sarah B. Holman died Dec. 17, 1873. FREDERICK, born June 9, 1854, resides at Austin, Nevada Territory. MARY A., CHARLES W., HULDAH A. and JOSEPH F., live with their father. Mrs. Ann M. Francis died Sept. 29, 1869, and W. W. Francis was married Feb. 20, 1871, to Mary E. Plimpton, of New Buffalo, Berrien county, Mich. They have one child, DWIGHT P., and reside at Rolling Prairie, Laporte county, Ind.

CHARLES, Jun., born April 4, 1831, in Madison county, N. Y., married Minerva Weed, Nov. 9, 1856. Mrs. Minerva Francis died April 11, 1865, and Charles F. Francis was married June 1, 1869, to Miss R. B. Hollingsworth, of Porter county, Ind. They have one child, MARY E., and reside at Three Oaks, Mich.

EDWIN, born August, 1833, in Madison county, N. Y., died in Laporte, Ind., October, 1839.

Mrs. Elizabeth Francis died in 1856, and Charles Francis died in 1870, both in Laporte, Ind., leaving their children in good circumstances.

The eight Francis brothers and sisters who left Connecticut for Illinois, embarked on the sloop Falcon, at Hartford, Conn., Sept. 17, 1829. Their journey was down the Connecticut river and across Long Island sound to New York city; up the Hudson river to Albany, thence to Buffalo by canal, and from Buffalo to Lower Sandusky, in a sailing vessel, on the lake. From there to Cincinnati by wagons. Many hardships were experienced in traveling through Ohio, with poor accommodations, bad roads, and oftentimes want of provisions. At one place where they stopped over night, they had to appease their hunger with honey, corn bread and fresh pork. After this meal they were ill for several days. At Cincinnati they took steamer down the Ohio and up the Mississippi river to St. Louis, where they arrived Dec. 3, 1829, having escaped the wreck of one steamer on the way, and traveled every day but one Sunday for seventy-seven days, to accomplish a journey which can now be made in half as many hours. They remained together in St. Louis until the summer of 1831, when Josiah came to Springfield and issued a prospectus for the Sangamo Journal, soliciting subscriptions to the same. Simeon and J. Newton came later, and the first number of the Journal was issued Nov. 10, 1831. Of the six brothers and two sisters who arrived in St. Louis—

FRANCIS, SIMEON, was born May 14, 1796, in Wethersfield, Conn., served an apprenticeship in a printing office in New Haven, Conn. After which he formed a partnership, under the name of Clapp & Francis, and published a paper in New London, Conn., in 1824. He was married in the latter place, sold out, and moved to Buffalo, N. Y., where he published the Buffalo Emporium, under the firm name of Lazwell & Francis. They being Free Masons, and the Morgan excitement breaking out at the time caused a suspension of the paper and closing the business of the firm early in 1828. He came to Springfield, Ill., in 1831. Simeon Francis and wife were without family, but brought up Ann Douglas, a niece of Mrs. Francis, who returned to New York in 1836, married Capt. George Barrell, and resides in Springfield, Ill. Simeon Francis, in connection with his brothers Josiah, Allen and J. Newton, published the "Sangamo Journal" through all its changes to the present daily and weekly "State Journal." In 1840 President Harrison appointed Simeon Francis, Indian Agent for Oregon, but after making all necessary preparation for his trip there he resigned. He and his brother Allen sold their interest in the State Journal, June, 1856, to Baker & Bailhache. Simeon then engaged in mercantile business, under the firm name of Francis & Barrell. He was for several years Secretary of the State Agricultural Society. In 1859 he closed his business in Springfield, and moved to Portland, Oregon. He edited the Oregon Farmer, and was President of the Oregon

State Agricultural Society. In 1861 President Lincoln appointed him Paymaster in United States army, with residence at Ft. Vancouver, Washington Territory. In 1870 he was retired on half pay, and returned to Portland, Oregon, where he died, Oct. 25, 1872. His widow resides there—1876.

FRANCIS, MARY A., sister of Simeon, Josiah, Allen, Charles, Calvin, Edwin and Huldah, was born Aug. 9, 1798, remained with her brother Edwin, in St. Louis, until his death, when she came to Springfield, Ill., in June, 1834. She died unmarried, at the residence of her brother Simeon, Oct. 17, 1834.

FRANCIS, CALVIN, born June 12, 1802, in Wethersfield, Conn., was married Oct. 21, 1823, to Abigail D. Francis, of his native place. They had several children, all of whom died except two. Calvin Francis and family came with his brothers and sisters to St. Louis, remained there until Sept. 8, 1836, when he moved to Wesley city, Tazewell county, Ill., and in 1837 to Athens, in what was then Sangamon county. In 1853 he moved to Springfield, and was for several years connected with the Journal office.

Of his children—

JEANETTE, born in Wethersfield, Conn., was married Jan., 1844, to Abner B. Hall. They have three children, IDA F., ABBIE J. and CALVIN, and reside in Athens, Menard county, Ill.

MARY F., born in Buffalo, N. Y., was married Dec., 1848, to B. C. Whitney. They have three children, CHARLES F., JOHN C. and GRACE M., and reside in Athens.

Calvin Francis moved from Springfield to Chatham, Ill., in 1863. Mrs. Abigail D. Francis died there, Oct. 23, 1865. He resides with his children in Athens, Menard county, Ill.

FRANCIS, JOSIAH, born Jan. 17, 1804, at Wethersfield, Conn. He was the first of the family who came to Springfield, Ill., arriving in the summer of 1831, and at once took measures to establish the *Sangamo Journal*, and issued the first number Nov. 10, 1831. He severed his connection with the *Journal*, in 1835, and was married the same year to Margery Constant, near Athens, Ill., and in 1836 engaged in mercantile pursuits in Athens. While there, he represented Sangamon county in the State Legislature, in 1840. A few years later he returned to Springfield, and was elected Sheriff of Sangamon county, and still later Mayor of Springfield. He was Quartermaster-General of Illinois, under Gov. Yates, and resigned a short time before the rebellion commenced. Josiah Francis and wife had four children, viz:

THOMAS N., born Jan. 8, 1837, at Athens, Ill., learned the printing business in the *Journal* office, enlisted in the *first company and regiment* raised in Illinois for the suppression of the rebellion, viz., Co. I, 7th Ill. Vol. Inf., for three months. At the expiration of that time he re-enlisted in same company and regiment for three years, was chosen 2d Lieutenant of his company, and promoted at the battle of Ft. Donnelson to 1st Lieutenant and Adjutant of his regiment. He was wounded at the battle of Corinth, Miss., Oct. 4, 1862, and resigned the following November. He was married in St. Joseph, Mo., to Amelia E. Hancock, a native of Pennsylvania. They have one child, MARGERY, and reside at 96, west Adams street, Chicago, Ill.

JULIA J., born Dec. 25, 1839, in Athens, was married Feb. 13, 1866, at Independence, Mo., to Hobart T. Ives, who was born Aug. 2, 1839, in Litchfield, Conn. They returned to Springfield, and have two children, FRANCIS S. and MATTIE J., and reside in Springfield. Mr. Ives served two years as county collector. He also served as Alderman in the Springfield city council.

ANNA E., born March 31, 1842, in Springfield, was married Oct. 10, 1866, in Springfield, to Dr. John E. Hanback, who was born Sept. 24, 1834, at Winchester, Ill., graduated at Illinois College, Jacksonville, in 1868, studied medicine in Rush Medical College, Chicago. They have two children living, GERTRUDE A. and CARRIE B. Dr. Hanback was city physician of Springfield for 1874. They reside at Winchester, Scott county, Ill.

CHARLES S., born Feb. 21, 1845, in Springfield, was married in 1868 to Lydia Newell. She died June 21, 1870. He was married May 23, 1873, in Chicago, to Eunice E. Teachoute. They have one child, CHARLES S., Jun., and reside at Three Oaks, Michigan.

Mrs. Margery Francis died Dec. 17, 1846, and Josiah Francis was married in March, 1848, to Jeanette Hicks, in Menard county. They had three children—

EDWIN G. died May 24, 1875, in Springfield, Ill.

MARY A., born in Springfield, Ill., resides with her sister, Mrs. Ives.

JEANETTE, born in Springfield, Ill., resides there with Mrs. Young.

Mrs. Jeanette Francis died Dec., 1861, and Josiah Francis died Oct. 8, 1867, both in Springfield.

FRANCIS, EDWIN, was born Oct. 9, 1807, in Wetherfield, Conn., died of cholera in St. Louis, Mo., June 4, 1834.

FRANCIS, HULDAH, born May 10, 1811, in Wethersfield, Conn., came to Springfield June, 1834, and was married in 1837 to Joseph Williams. *See his name.*

FRANCIS, ALLEN, born April 12, 1815, in Wethersfield, Conn., resided in St. Louis until the death of his brother Edwin, in 1834, when, with his two sisters, he came to Springfield, Ill. Worked in the *Journal* office, and subsequently became a partner in the same. He was married Dec. 25, 1838, in Springfield, to Cecilia B. Duncan, of Glasgow, Scotland, and sister of David Duncan, who was drowned in attempting to cross the Sangamon river on horseback, in 1837. They had six living children, namely—

CECILIA J., born in Springfield, married in Oregon to Hermon Hofferkamp, and now resides in Washington Territory.

MARIETTA, born in Springfield, Illinois, married in Victoria, Vancouver's Island, to David A. Edgar, of Staten Island, N. Y.

HULDAH G., born in Springfield, Ill., married Byron Z. Holmes, of Portland, Oregon, and resides there.

ELIZA E., born in Springfield, Ill., married William T. Gilliham, of Portland, Oregon.

ALLEN, BUNN, born in 1849, in Springfield, accompanied his father to the Pacific coast. Subsequently became agent for a fur company in San Francisco, was stationed at Fort Constantine, in Alaska, and never saw a white woman or heard his native language for over eighteen months. He is now interested in a quartz mine in that territory, which he discovered in the autumn of 1874.

EDWIN H., born in 1851, in Springfield, went to Alaska soon after it was purchased of Russia by the United States, was appointed deputy collector at Sitka, and clerk of the city council. He has seen much of frontier life, is master of the Russian language, and many of the Indian languages, and reside at Sitka, Alaska.

Allen Francis was for several years a member of the city council of Springfield, Ill., from the first ward. He erected the *Journal* buildings, and a brick dwelling on the corner of Sixth and Carpenter streets. In Oct., 1861, President Lincoln appointed him consul at Victoria, Vancouver's Island. He left for that point February, 1862, and resigned in 1871. He, with his two sons, engaged in the fur trade with the Indians, on the north Pacific coast. He resides in Victoria, Vancouver's Island.

FRANCIS, J. NEWTON, born June 6, 1817, in Connecticut, came to Springfield with his brother Simeon in 1831, and was married in Springfield to Julia A. Constant. Mr. F. was connected with the *State Journal* until Nov., 1843, when he accidently shot himself while returning from a hunting excursion, near Monticello, Piatt county, Ill., leaving a widow and one child—

JANE N., who was married in 1862, at Little Rock, Ark., to Isaac Treadway, and lives in St. Louis, Mo.

Mrs. Julia A. Francis married R. V. Kenedy. They have two children, and reside in Chicago. This ends the history of the Francis brothers and sisters who came from Connecticut.

FRANCIS, CHARLES B., was born Oct. 30, 1799, in Pittsfield, Mass., and was there married to Roxanna Goodrich. They had two living children, and moved to Springfield, Ill., in 1835. He was for several years engaged in the manufacture of cabinet furniture with his brother Josiah. They were distant relatives of Simeon Francis and his brothers, founders of the *Illinois State Journal*. Charles B. Francis united with others in building, under contract, fifteen miles of the Northern Cross railroad—now Toledo,

Wabash & Western railroad—from New Berlin to Springfield. Of his children—

MARIETTA, born Nov. 29, 1826, in Pittsfield, Mass., was married Feb. 11, 1846, in Springfield, Ill., to James L. Riggs. They have one daughter, ALICE, born July 16, 1853, was married in Peoria, Ill., to Alexander G. Tyng, Jun. Mr. Riggs died June 30, 1859, in Brimfield, Ill., and his widow and daughter reside in Peoria.

JANE A., born Oct. 23, 1830, in Pittsfield, Mass., was brought up in Springfield, Ill., and married Dec. 11, 1851, at Brimfield, Ill., to Robert A. Smith. They have seven children, and reside in Peoria, Ill.

Charles B. Francis died Oct. 10, 1843, in Jacksonville, Ill., while in attendance at the Illinois Baptist Convention. Mrs. Roxanna Francis, after living a widow twenty-nine years, was married in Pittsfield, Mass., Oct. 7, 1872, to Jirah Stearns, and resides in Newberry, N. J.

FRANCIS, JOSIAH, was born Sept. 24, 1801, in Pittsfield, Berkshire county, Mass. He was married Dec. 2, 1824, in Pittsfield, to Fidelia Clark, who was born Jan. 11, 1803, in Westhampton, Hampshire county, Mass. In 1825 they moved to Palmyra, Wayne county, N. Y., where they had two living children. They moved to Springfield, Ill., arriving June 30, 1836, and had one child in Springfield. Mr. Francis engaged in the manufacture of cabinet furniture, in connection with his brother Charles B., and continued in that business until 1852, when he engaged in farming, four miles northeast of Springfield, near what is now German Prairie station. Of his children—

LUCIUS C., born Dec. 26, 1828, at Palmyra, Wayne county, N. Y., married Aug. 23, 1860, in Springfield, Ill., to Clara Pierson. She died Nov. 14, 1864. Mr. Francis was married Dec. 23, 1873, in Atlanta, Ill., to Mrs. Susan Leonard, whose maiden name was Keigwin. She was born March 21, 1840, in Springfield. They reside half a mile west of German Prairie station, but their postoffice is Springfield, Ill.

JAMES S., born Jan. 15, 1831, in Palmyra, Wayne county, N. Y., resides with his father.

MARIA E., born Oct. 23, 1837, in Springfield, Ill., and lives with her father.

Mrs. Fidelia Francis died Oct. 21, 1874, in Sangamon county, and Josiah Francis resides near German Prairie station, with his postoffice at Springfield, Ill.

FRAZEE, HENRY S., born April 16, 1811, in Monmouth county, N. J. His mother died when he was an infant, and his father when he was nine years old. Henry S. Frazee and Sarah Van Patten were married Nov. 5, 1836, in Somerset county, N. J. They moved in company with her father to Sangamon county, Ill., arriving Aug. 9, 1838, at Springfield. They had four children in Sangamon county, namely—

CORNELIA A., born Oct. 24, 1839, in Sangamon county, married Dec. 25, 1863, to Lewis Large. He enlisted Sept. 21, 1861, for three years, in Co. A, 10th Ill. Cav., served until April 16, 1862, when he was discharged on account of physical disability. He died March 25, 1864, just three months after marriage. Mrs. Cornelia A. Large was married Dec. 31, 1868, to Seth W. Wickham. They have one child, MINNIE L., and reside one mile south of Farmingdale.

HANNAH, born Nov. 8, 1842, married March 10, 1864, to Richard G. Large. He enlisted Sept. 21, 1861, in Co. A, 10th Ill. Cav., for three years; re-enlisted as a veteran January, 1864, served to the end of the rebellion, and was honorably discharged November, 1865, at San Antonio, Texas. They had three children. ROSE B., the youngest, died in infancy. HENRY GRANT and EDWARD F. live with their parents, near Fredonia, Wilson county, Kansas.

ELIZABETH, born August 11, 1845, is a teacher, and resides with her parents.

MARGARET, born Dec. 6, 1849, married Jan. 3, 1869, to Edward M. Beach. See his name.

Henry S. Frazee and wife resides one and a half miles south of Farmingdale—1874.

FULLINWIDER, HENRY, was born in 1799, near Hagerstown, Md., and was taken when quite young to Shelby county, Ky. This family, with others, soon after assembled in a block house for protection. The men all being out, Indians attacked the fortifications, and killed an elder brother of Henry, a lad who was aiming to enter the fort. A hole was dug under the timbers from the inside, and his body drawn in, to prevent its falling into the hands of the Indians. This circumstance made an impression on the mind of Henry that was never effaced. Harriet Neal was born in 1789, in Fauquier county, Va., and was taken when quite young to Kentucky. Henry Fullinwider and Harriet Neal were married. They had thirteen children, all born in Shelby county, Ky., four of whom died young. In the fall of 1833 Mr. Fullinwider visited Sangamon county, and purchased a farm adjoining Mechanicsburg on the east. He returned to Kentucky for his family, and died there July 21, 1834. The family moved to the home thus provided, arriving at Mechanicsburg in the fall of 1834. Of their nine children—

LUCINDA N., born Dec. 27, 1809, in Shelby county, Ky., married in Kentucy, March 8, 1832, to Richard Bird. See his name.

SAMUEL N., born Feb. 17, 1811, in Shelby county, Ky., married Matilda Hathaway. They had three children, and Mrs. F. died in Sangamon county from injuries received while riding in a wagon. Two of their children are dead. HARRIET married Lee Phillips, and resides at Fremont, Neb. Samuel N. Fullinwider married in Chatham to Mary Thornton. They reside at Fremont, Dodge county, Neb.

ELIZABETH G., born March 8, 1812, in Kentucky, married there, Feb. 10, 1832, to Talbott Lyon. They had three children: HARRIET H. married Joseph Foster, and died. See his name. Mrs. Elizabeth G. Lyon died, and Mr. Lyon married Eliza Correll, and he died. See Correll.

JACOB N., born June 5, 1814, in Shelby county, Ky., married in Sangamon county, March 23, 1837, to Sarah A. Ballard. They had eleven children, three of whom, MARY E., ANN E. and JOHN W., died under four years. Of the other eight. ELIZABETH J., born March 8, 1838, married David S. Hall. See his name. WILLIAM A., born Nov. 20, 1842, in Mechanicsburg, was married there, March 4, 1875, to Alice Elkin, and resides near Mechanicsburg. HARRIET N., born Sept. 11, 1845, near Mechanicsburg, was married there to Edward W. Bennett. See his name. HENRY T., born March 1, 1846, was married Dec. 28, 1871, to Sarah C. Lindsly, who was born June 13, 1849, in Christian county, Ill. They had one child, CHARLES W., who died in infancy. Mr. and Mrs. F. reside three miles northeast of Mechanicsburg. MARCUS L., born June 13, 1849, in Mechanicsburg, graduated in 1871, at the Wesleyan University, Bloomington, Ill., and graduated in medicine Jan., 1874, at Rush Medical College, Chicago, Ill. He was married May 11, 1876, in Bloomington, Ill., to Clara F. Munsell, and resides in Mechanicsburg. Dr. Fullinwider is practicing his profession there. SAMUEL T., born June 21, 1851, in Mechanicsburg, graduated June 17, 1874, at Wesleyan University, Bloomington, Ill., and was married in Mechanicsburg, May 27, 1875, to Lucilla Elkin. They reside near Mechanicsburg. JACOB T., born Nov. 24, 1853, and OWEN H., born August 19, 1856. The two latter live with their parents. Jacob N. Fullinwider resides on the farm where the family settled in 1834, adjoining Mechanicsburg on the east, and is one of the most extensive farmers and stock raisers in Sangamon county.

NANCY N., born July 3, 1818, in Shelby county, Ky., married in Sangamon county, Nov. 23, 1837, to Rev. Arnold Bowman, of the M. E. church. They had seven children. LAVINIA married Capt. Theodore True, of the U. S. Army, and resides—1876—at Fort Bridger, Wyoming Territory. HARRIET F., born in October, 1844, resides with her mother. JOHN was killed, aged about twenty years, in Sangamon county, while hauling logs. JENNIE married Lewis P. Butler, a practicing lawyer at Murphysboro, Ill. MATILDA married Dr. Josiah Richardson, and resides in Louisville, Ky. They have one child, RICHARD H., born Oct. 13, 1860, in Springfield, Ill. HOWARD lives with his mother. Rev. Mr. Bowman was a preacher in the M. E. church twenty-eight years, and died Oct. 3, 1865, near Mechanicsburg. His widow resides at Mattoon, Ill.

SOLOMON N., born in 1820, in Shelby county, Ky., married in Sangamon county to Elizabeth Little. They had three children, HENRY, HARRIET and

ELIZABETH. Mrs. Elizabeth Fullinwider died, and S. N. Fullinwider married Amanda Fox. They had two children. Mr. F. enlisted in the army to suppress the rebellion, and died Jan. 10, 1864, at home on sick furlough. His widow married Marion Smith, and resides one mile east of Buffalo.

SIMON P., born May 14, 1826, in Shelby county, Ky., was married Aug. 22, 1848, in Sangamon county, Ill., to Louisa C. Hesser. They have five living children. EDWIN R., born July 2, 1840, enlisted at Cincinnati, O., March 10, 1865, in Co. K, 81st Reg. Ohio Inf., for one year or during the war, and was honorably discharged July 13, 1865, at Louisville, Ky. He was married Nov. 3, 1870, in Mechanicsburg, Ill., to Flora Gore. They have three children, SIMON P., ESTELLA J. and EDWIN E., and live near Wheatfield postoffice, Sangamon county, Ill. HENRY N., born May 14, 1851, lives with his parents. G. SAMUEL born Dec. 22, 1852, is a clerk in Springfield. KATIE L. and RICHARD S. reside with their parents, one-half mile east of Lanesville, Sangamon county, Ill. Their postoffice is Wheatfield.

MARCUS L., born June 29, 1829, in Kentucky, married in Mechanicsburg to Sarah Fairbanks. They had two children, GEORGE and CALVIN, and Mrs. F. died. He married Maria Ely, and had two children, LINCOLN and GUY. Mrs. Maria Fullinwider died. Mr. Fullinwider married a third time early in 1876, and lives at Fairmount, Vermilion county, Ill.

JOHN H., born Sept. 17, 1831, in Shelby county, Ky., married in Sangamon county Sept. 20, 1855, to Isabel Hall. They have four living children, HARRIET J., JOHN GRANT, HENRY A. and NANNIE BELLE, and reside adjoining Buffalo on the east.

Henry Fullinwider died in Kentucky, July 21, 1834, and Mrs. Harriet Fullinwider died Jan. 31, 1867, in Sangamon county.

FUNDERBURK, HENRY, was born Feb. 18, 1773, in Orange district, S. C. Polly Rape was born in February, 1786, in the same district. They were married and had two children. They then moved to Dickson county, Tenn., where four children were born, and then to St. Clair county, Ill., in 1816. From St. Clair county they moved to what became Sangamon county, arriving in the spring of 1817 or '18 west of Horse creek, near where Daniel G. Jones now resides, in Cotton Hill township. Mr. F. moved in company with William Nelson. They both built cabins and raised crops the year they came. Mr. F. had seven children born in Sangamon county, making a total of thirteen. Of their children—

POLLY, born Dec. 14, 1803, in South Carolina, came with her parents to what is now Sangamon county, in the spring of 1817 or '18, married Elijah Hinkle, who died, and she married William Chambers, and he died, and she married John Bowman, and resides near Taylorville. She had no children. She could have given me definite information whether the family came in 1817 or 18, but I could not obtain any information from herself or her brother James.

ELIZABETH, born Jan. 31, 1806, in South Carolina, came to Sangamon county with her parents in the spring of 1817 or '18, married Thomas Hanks. They have eleven children, and reside near Whitehall, Greene county.

JACOB, born Nov. 9, 1808, in Tennessee, married in Sangamon county to Ruth Sampson. They have ten children, and live in Vernon county, Mo.

JAMES, born Dec. 14, 1810, in Tennessee, married in Sangamon county to Nancy Nelson. They have six children, and live near Taylorville.

HENRY, born Feb. 14, 1813, in Tennessee, married in Sangamon county Nov. 5, 1835, to Jane Snodgrass. They have eight children. E. JANE, born May 6, 1838, married John Durbin, have five children, and live near Conesville, Muscatine county, Iowa. JOHN S., born April 14, 1840, died April 8, 1842. CARTER, born August 14, 1857, married Alice Wenicke, and live near D. G. Jones, in Cotton Hill township. POLLY, born Jan. 15, 1846, lives with her parents. LEWIS, born June 12, 1851, married Mary Hinkle, and live in Christian county, east of Pawnee. COOPER, born Jan. 8, 1851, resides east of Pawnee. NANCY, born July 17, 1853, and JAMES H., born Sept. 9, 1857, live with their parents in Cotton Hill township.

MILLY, born March 17, 1815, in Tennessee, married in Sangamon county to Abishai Rape. They both died, leaving a daughter, who married George Morgan, and lives in Christian county.

SALLY, born April 8, 1819, in Sangamon county, married Henry Dixon. They had eight children, and Mr. D. died. The family live near Taylorville.

RAPE, born Feb. 10, 1821, in Sangamon county, married Amanda Jones. She had one child, ALEXANDER. He married Harriet A. Levi, who died, and he married Salena Morrow, and lives in Christian county. Mrs. Amanda F. died, and Mr. F. married Mary Sanders, and she died. He then married Caroline Armstrong. They had eight children, MARY J., ABEL, GEORGE W., AMANDA, ALBERT C., MELVIN, EDWARD L., and MILES, and reside in Ball township.

MARTHA, born June 3, 1826, in Sangamon county, married John H. Sanders. See his name.

NANCY, born April 1, 1828, in Sangamon county, married James White. He died, leaving a widow and seven children, at Taylorville.

ELIZA, born Aug. 2, 1830, in Sangamon county, married Robert E. Sanders. See his name.

ORLENA, born Oct. 21, 1832, in Sangamon county, married William Crowder, who died, and she married Benj. Howard, have four children, and live near Taylorville.

Mrs. Polly Funderburk died Aug. 1, 1841, and Henry Funderburk died Aug. 14, 1843, both near where they settled in 1818, in Cotton Hill township.

FUNDERBURK, DAVID, born Jan. 9, 1795, in Orange District, S. C., was bound apprentice to a hatter, but instead of teaching him how to make hats, his master put him to work in the fields with the negroes and otherwise treated him harshly, so he ran away and enlisted in the 3d U. S. Rifle Reg. for five years, from Aug. 15, 1814. It was so near the close of the war with England that he was not in any battle. His five years were spent in garrison duty on the frontier, and was at Ft. Osage, on the Missouri river, near the present line between Missouri and Kansas, when his term of enlistment expired, Aug. 15, 1819. He, with eight other discharged soldiers, fastened two canoes together, with a platform over them, and all left for St. Louis with their knapsacks. Mr. F. says that they were somewhat crowded, and on the way down he *stole* a canoe, and taking a comrade left the other seven who began drinking and ran their craft on a sawyer, which upset it, and they lost everything except what they had on their persons, but the men clung to the sunken log, and but for the stolen canoe they must all have drowned. Mr. F. and his comrade took them all safely to shore. He has always, in his quaint way, insisted that that was "providential stealing." On arriving at St. Louis, he learned that his uncle, Henry Funderburk, had moved into the Sangamo country, and he determined to visit him. He found his uncle on the 31st of Aug., 1819, in what is now Cotton Hill township, between Brush and Horse creeks, and went to work to supply himself with clothing, in place of that which was lost on the river. David Funderburk was married in March, 1821, to Hannah Hinkle. They had eight living children, all born in Sangamon county. Of their eight children—

SARAH, born April 2, 1822, married Henry Voyles. They have eleven children, and live in Madison county, near Staunton, Macoupin county.

MARY J., born March 18, 1827, married Thomas Funderburk. They have five children, and live near Staunton, Macoupin county, Ill.

JOHN S., born March 16, 1831, married Mrs. Eliza J. Voyles, whose maiden name was Davis. They have six children, EDWARD E., MARY E., JOSEPH E., WILLIAM A., MARTHA and VELMA, and live in Madison county, near Staunton, Macoupin county, Ill.

PHEBE, born in Sangamon county, is married, and resides there.

ALFRED N., born Sept. 27, 1837, married Emily Ward. They have three children, WILLIAM B., THOMAS L. and BENJAMIN A., and reside in Cotton Hill township.

DAVID, Jun., born Dec. 22, 1839, enlisted at Springfield in 1861, for three years, in what became Co. B, 11th Mo. Inf., served full time, and was honorably discharged in 1864. He was married to Sarah A. Terry. They have four children, MINNIE L., ADDIE L., MARY

A. and a babe—1873—and reside at the homestead settled by his parents in 1821, in Cotton Hill township.

WILLIAM F., born Nov. 22, 1842, enlisted in August, 1862, in Co. —, 114th Ill. Inf., for three years. He was wounded and captured at the battle of Guntown, Miss., June 10, 1864; one arm was amputated by a rebel surgeon. He was held a prisoner until the close of the rebellion. Is unmarried, and resides in Christian county.

THOMAS J., born May 6, 1845, married Angeline N. Carlton. They have four children, NELLIE VIOLA, JESSIE MAY, HANNAH E. and WILLIAM, and reside near the family homestead in Cotton Hill township, Sangamon county.

Mrs. Hannah Funderburk died Sept. 22, 1873, after nearly fifty-three years of wedded life. David Funderburk resides with his children part of the time, near Staunton, and part in Sangamon county, Illinois.

G

GAINES, RICHARD, was born Nov. 8, 1777, in Charlotte county, Va. Amy C. Green was born Feb. 3, 1782, in the same county. They were married and had three children, and moved to Barren county, Ky., about 1807, where they had three children, and the family moved to Christian county, where one child was born, and then moved to Sangamon county, Ill., arriving in November, 1825, in what is now Cartwright township, and settled about one mile north of where Pleasant Plains now stands. Of the seven children—

ROBERT G., born June 20, 1801, in Virginia, married June 26, 1823, to Hannah Quaite. They had nine daughters and one son, and Mrs. Gaines died April 27, 1843. Mr. Gaines is living with his third wife, in Missouri.

MILDRED, born Oct. 4, 1802, in Virginia, married Feb. 22, 1823, to Samuel Black. See his name.

RICHARD F., born March 18, 1806, married in Sangamon county to Mary Black. They have five children, and live five miles north of Jacksonville.

JOHN, born April 20, 1808, in Kentucky, married Feb. 25, 1836, in Sangamon county, to Sarah Renshaw, had six children, and Mrs. Gaines died. Mr. Gaines lives with his brother-in-law, William Batterton.

COLEMAN, born Dec. 28, 1809, in Kentucky, married in Sangamon county Nov. 17, 1831, to Susan Batterton. They had one son, JOHN ST. CLAIR, who died, aged seventeen years. Mrs. Gaines died in 1833, and Mr. G. was married Oct. 9, 1834, to Priscilla McDonald, and lives at Lincoln, Ill.

ELIZA, born Dec. 4, 1811, married Jan. 1, 1833, to William Batterton. See his name.

ABRAHAM CLAY, born June 1, 1814, in Kentucky, married in Sangamon county Nov. 21, 1839, to Mary Sackett. They had eight children, and Mrs. G. died May 9, 1863, and he was married Sept. 15, 1864, to Mrs. Sarah J. Newell, whose maiden name was Mills. They have two children, and live near Odell, Ill.

Richard Gaines was a local preacher in the M. E. church for twenty-five or thirty years. He died Jan. 7, 1845, and Mrs. Amy C. Gaines died Aug. 19, 1871, both in Sangamon county.

GARDNER, JOHN, was born June 21, 1805, in that part of Gallatin that is now Trimble county, Ky. Mary C. Duncan was born March 27, 1810, in the same county. They were married there June 13, 1830. They had one child in Kentucky, and moved to Sangamon county, Ill., arriving April 17, 1833, two miles west of Springfield, and early in 1834 moved to what is now Gardner township, two miles north of Farmingdale. They had eight children in Sangamon county. Of their children—

HIRAM E., born April 28, 1831, in Trimble county, Ky., opposite the city of Madison, Ind. He was raised in Sangamon county, and married June 17, 1857, in St. Louis, Mo., to Louisa R. Brown. They had one child, EDWIN B., born Sept. 27, 1858, and died July 13, 1873. Mrs. Louisa R. Gardner died July 23, 1859, and Hiram E. Gardner was married Feb. 8, 1865, in Sangamon county, to Harriet E. Bradford. They have three children, LOUISA B., HARRIET M. and HARRY B., and reside in Gardner township, one mile northwest of Bradfordton.

Hiram E. Gardner has represented Gardner township in the Sangamon county Board of Supervisors for several years, and is one of the most extensive farmers in the county.

SARAH A., born Oct. 15, 1833, in Sangamon county, lives with her mother.

NANNIE C., born Sept. 12, 1836, in Sangamon county, died April 10, 1857.

JOHN P., born July 5, 1839, in Sangamon county, married Sept. 7, 1869, to Susan L. Kendall. They had one child that died in infancy, and Mrs. Gardner died June 30, 1871. John P. Gardner was married November, 1874, to Lou. Gibson, and lives in Curran township, five miles west of Springfield.

CRANMER died Aug. 3, 1843, aged two years.

JAMES, born March 27, 1844, in Sangamon county, lives with his mother.

MARY E., born April 3, 1847, in Sangamon county, lives with her mother.

LUCY M., born June 19, 1851, in Sangamon county, married Feb. 24, 1869, to William Hurt, a native of Kentucky. They have two children, and reside two miles southeast of Pleasant Plains.

WILLIAM P., born June 13, 1854, lives with his mother.

John Gardner died Feb. 11, 1868, and his widow, Mrs. Mary C. Gardner, resides two miles north of Farmingdale, where they settled in 1834.

John Gardner was one of the commissioners who divided Sangamon county into townships, and the township where the family reside bears the family name, in honor of his memory.

GARDNER, HIRAM K., was born June 5, 1803, in Trimble county, Ky., and was married there May 29, 1827, to Eliza Morris. He moved in company with his brother John to Sangamon county in April, 1833. He now—1876—lives in Gardner township.

John Gardner was born March 15, 1772, and his wife, Nancy, was born Jan. 12, 1773, both in Virginia. They were the parents of Hiram K. and John Gardner.

GARD, EPHRAIM, was born March, 1776, in Union county, Penn., and was married there to Susannah Sutton, a native of the same county. They moved to Butler county, Ohio, where they had twelve children. Mr. Gard was captain of a company from that county, in the war of 1812. He moved in 1826 to Fayette county, Ind., and from there to Sangamon county, Ill., arriving in the fall of 1839, where Pleasant Plains now stands. Of their children—

KEZIAH, born in 1801, in Ohio, married there to John McDowell, and came to Sangamon county a year later than her parents. They moved about 1845 to Menard county, where they both died, leaving several children.

MARIA, born in 1803, in Ohio, married Abijah Stout, who died in California, leaving a widow and nine children in Butler county, Ohio.

REBECCA, born in 1805, married in Ohio to Joseph Hamilton, moved to Fayette county, Indiana, thence to Little Rock, Arkansas.

JACOB, born Sept. 23, 1806, in Butler county, Ohio, married there, March 10, 1835, to Jane Campbell, had one child in Ohio, and moved to Fayette county, Ind., in 1827, where they had three, and moved to Sangamon county, Ill., arriving Nov., 1834, in what is now Gardner township, where they had five children. Of their nine children—MORRIS, born Aug. 24, 1827, in Ohio, married Rhoda Jackson, had three children, and died in Gardner township. His widow married James Sherwood, and lives at Cuba, Fulton county, Ill. DEMARIS, born Jan. 27, 1829, in Indiana, married Feb. 22, 1849, to Berry D. Stone. They had two children. ELIZA J., married June 22, 1869, to Daniel Diehl, who was born Oct. 5, 1834, in Berks county, Penn. They have three children, Ora Etta, John H., and Allie Demaris, and live at Cross Plains Postoffice. JOHN B., lives with his grandfather Gard. B. D. Stone died, and his widow married, Nov. 22, 1853, to James M. Pelham. See his name. SUSANNAH, born Nov. 11, 1831, married, Feb. 22, 1849, to Butler Stone, and he died, leaving one child, ALICE S., who married Wm. C. Price, have two children, Nora and Henry, and live in Umatilla Oregon. Mrs. S. Stone married Jacob C. Lacy. See his name. ABIGAIL M., born June 27, 1834, married Lewis Nelson, who died, leaving a widow and six children in DeWitt county. EPHRAIM H., born June 27, 1838, married Mary E. Garrett. They have four living children, WILLIAM

C., CHARLES D., HENRY and MARY ELLEN, and live near Cross Plains Postoffice. RACHEL E., born Jan. 27, 1840, married Alfred Ross. *See his name.* JOHN L., born March 18, 1841, married May 17, 1860, to Sarah E. Miller. They have four children, OPHELIA, LUELLA, OLIVER and WILLIAM M., and live two and one-half miles southeast of Salisbury. Jacob Gard and his wife reside three miles south of Salisbury, in Gardner township.

JAMES L., born Oct. 22, 1808, married Oct. 30, 1829, in Indiana, to Sarah Sutton, moved to Sangamon county, Ill., arriving Sept. 21, 1839, where Pleasant Plains now stands. They brought five children, and had five in Sangamon county. MARTIN V., born Oct. 22, 1831, married Elizabeth Jackson, Feb. 22, 1849. They had five children. The parents and two of the children died. BENJAMIN B., born June 29, 1833, married Mary Shrader, and resides in Cass county, Mo., near State Line. LUCINDA, born April 13, 1835, married Ephraim Jackson, have two living children, *Buchanan* and *Adam*, and live two miles east of Salisbury. SAMUEL S., born Jan. 8, 1836, married Esther Jackson, and live in Menard county. JEREMIAH, born June 22, 1838, married Sarah E. Oliver. He enlisted for three years, Aug., 1862, in Co. F, 78th Ill. Inf., was in many of the greatest battles, and went with Sherman in his "march to the sea." He was honorably discharged, in June, 1865, and was accidentally killed in a well, July 11, 1866, near Hickory Ridge, Hancock county, Ill. ANN M., married Newton Goodman. He died, leaving a widow and four children in Menard county. THOMAS V., married Sarrilda Pryor, have five children, and live in Menard county. ALCEMENA married S. T. Lewis, who died, and she married George Neale, and lives in Cass county, Mo. MARY J., married George R. Ward, and lives in Menard county, one mile north of Salisbury. ELIZA A. married Samuel Hibbs, and lives in Menard county. James L. Gard and wife reside three miles south of Athens, in Menard county.

JOHN S., married Mary Ellis, and died, leaving a widow and children in Indiana.

HARRISON, born in Ohio, married in Indiana to Serena Cook, came to Sangamon county in 1838, and resides near Florence, Morgan county, Mo.

JEREMIAH, married in Indiana to Dicey A. Smith, moved to Little Rock, Ark., and died there.

EPHRIAM, Jun., born in Ohio, came to Sangamon county with his father, married, in Morgan county, to Pauline Parr and died, leaving a widow and children in Morgan county.

LUCINDA, born Jan. 7, 1821, in Ohio, married, in 1854, in Sangamon county, to Solomon Miller. She had one daughter, RHODA, who married Henry Grady, had four children, EMMA J., ALMEDA, ANNETTA and LUCY. Mr. Grady died, Nov. 14, 1871, and his family live near Cross Plains Postoffice. Solomon Miller died. *See his name.* His widow resides in Gardner township.

DAVID, born in Ohio, married in Indiana to Lydia Hockenberry, came to Sangamon county, in 1839. They had three children. David Gard and his son ALBERT, aged five years, were killed by lightning, June 21, 1850, near Salisbury. They had taken refuge under a tree during a shower of rain.

Mrs. Susannah Gard died, Aug. 10 1851, and Ephraim Gard died Nov. 21, 1863, both in Gardner township.

GARRETSON, SAMUEL, was born Dec. 7, 1785, in York county, Pa. Ann Pierce was born April 1, 1786, in Chester county, Pa. They were married Oct. 26, 1808, in Newbury township, York county, Pa., according to Friends' ceremony, in open meeting. They had one child in York county, and in 1810 moved to Anne Arundel county, Md., where they had nine children. Mrs. Ann Garretson died April 30, 1827, in Maryland. Mr. G. was married March, 1834, at Newbury, Pa., by Friends' ceremony, to Hannah Cadwallader. His four eldest children remained east, but Mr. G., with his six youngest, moved to Sangamon county, Ill., arriving May 22, 1837, in Fork Prairie, near Rochester. Of the six children—

VINCENT, born Dec. 11, 1815, in Anne Arundel county, Md., married in Sangamon county, March 31, 1846, to Elizabeth T. Barrickman, a native of Clark county, Ind. They had one child,

FRANCES, that died in infancy, and Mrs. G. died March 18, 1857. Vincent Garretson was married March 11, 1858, in Baltimore, Md., to Sarah A. Miller, who was born Dec. 16, 1815, in Anne Arundel county, Md. They had three children in Sangamon county; all died young. Mr. and Mrs. Garretson reside four miles southwest of Illiopolis.

HANNAH R., born April, 1817, in Maryland, married Feb. 22, 1843, in Sangamon county, to Jacob D. Constant. *See his name.* She died Oct. 22, 1850.

THOMAS P., born Sept., 1818, in Maryland, came to Sangamon county in 1839, married in Menard county, to Martha M. Harrison. She died in Springfield, and he married Phœbe Campbell. They have seven children, and live near Lincoln, Ill.

ELI, born May 5, 1820, in Maryland, died in Sangamon county, Sept. 14, 1838.

JOHN, born in 1821, in Maryland, married in Sangamon county to Harriet Sherman. He died August 26, 1843, near Rochester. His widow married Mr. Cotton, and lives at Elkhart.

SAMUEL, Jun., born Dec. 4, 1823, in Anne Arundel county, Md., married in Sangamon county, Nov. 7, 1848, to Amelia J. Dickerson, who was born Feb. 25, 1828, in Kentucky. They had six children. JAMES T., the eldest, died in his thirteenth year. HARRIET, the youngest, died in infancy. SUSAN ANN, born Dec. 7, 1854, CHARLES V., born July 15, 1856, ARCHIBALD F., born June 22, 1858, MARY M., born Sept. 9, 1860, live with their parents, three miles northeast of Rochester.

Mrs. Hannah Garretson died Sept. 26, 1838, and Samuel Garretson, Sen., died May 1, 1847, both in Sangamon county.

GARLAND, NICHOLAS AUSTIN, born Feb. 23, 1806, in Albemarle county, Va., was married July 16, 1827, at Liberty, Bedford county, Va., to Mary C. M. Phillips, who was born there, May 2, 1810. They had one child there, and in 1829 moved to the vicinity of where Carondelet, Mo., now stands. In moving, he went across the country with a six horse team, taking with him seven or eight slaves that he had inherited from his father's estate. That was about all the property he had, but soon after his arrival in Missouri, he resolved that he could not conscientiously hold slaves, and determined to extricate himself from the uncongenial position. He hired them out for a few years, with a proviso for each to be free at a given time, and retained them all under his control until the last one was liberated. He still farther manifested his aversion to slavery by moving his family to Illinois, arriving in Springfield in 1832. In 1837 Mr. Garland left the city and settled in what is now Cotton Hill township, in section thirty-two, town fourteen, range four west, where he built a horse mill in 1838, and ran a turning lathe in connection with it, doing general cabinet work. He afterwards sold this farm and entered a tract one mile east, in section thirty-three. N. A. Garland and wife had one child in Missouri and six in Sangamon county. Of their eight children—

SAMUEL R., born in Virginia, died in Springfield, Ill., in his seventh year.

LUCY P., born Dec. 13, 1831, in St. Louis county, Mo., brought up in Springfield, Ill., was married August, 1856, in Sullivan, Moultrie county, Ill., to Charles L. Roane. They have five children, MARY, LUCY, SARAH, CHARLES and FANNIE, and reside at Sullivan, Moultrie county, Ill.

AUSTIN M., born Oct. 29, 1833, in Springfield, was married Nov. 10, 1859, near Chatham, to Sarah E. Hoppin, who was born June 17, 1838, in Madison county, N. Y., and came with her father, F. B. Hoppin, to Sangamon county in 1852. They have four children, MARY H., LUCY H., GERTRUDE G. and FRANK H. Austin M. Garland learned the printing business in the *State Register* office. He was a member of the firm of Garland & Jones in publishing a campaign paper in 1858, called the *Illinois American*. That paper was merged into the *Daily Independent* by Garland & Wheler, in the fall of 1859. Garland sold his interest in the paper the following summer, and engaged in farming from Jan., 1860, to Jan., 1871, when he returned to Springfield. He was elected Secretary of the State Agricultural Society in 1870, and continued in that position, by re-election, annually, four years, ending in the winter of 1874-5.

JAMES M., born Sept. 26, 1835, in Springfield, was married there, Feb. 24,

58, to Mary E. Hawley. They have seven living children, CHARLES HAW-LEY, CORA BELL, MARY E., JOHN AUSTIN, ALICE M., JOSIE and EDWARD M. Mr. Garland has been for several years and is now a merchant of Springfield, Ill., where he and his family reside.

ELIZABETH A., born Sept. 19, 1837, in Springfield, was married at Sullivan, Moultrie county, Ill., Oct. 6, 1873, to Kemper Campbell. They have one child, HATTIE, and reside at Lovington, Moultrie county, Ill.

ELLEN D., born Sept. 16, 1839, in Springfield, Ill., was married Sept. 15, 1857, to Andrew J. Lynn, who was killed at the battle of Stone's river, Tennessee, leaving two children, ANDREW J. and ANNIE, who live with their mother. Mrs. Lynn was married Sept. 26, 1865, to Thomas M. Bushfield, of Sullivan. They have one living child, CHARLES, and reside in Sullivan, Moultrie county, Ill.

MARY F., born Nov., 1841, in Springfield, Ill., married Daniel W. Rawlins, of Jacksonville, Ill. They have two living children, DANIEL WESTERVELT and ELEANOR GARLAND, and reside in Liberty, Bedford county, Va.

Mrs. Mary C. M. Garland died August 6, 1844, and N. A. Garland was married March 22, 1849, to Mrs. Rhoda G. Stringfield, whose maiden name was Jack. She died Feb. 22, 1852, and N. A. Garland was married July 28, 1853, to Mrs. Lucy S. McDaniel, whose maiden name was Burr, sister of Hon. A. G. Burr, of Green county, Ill. They had five living children—

WILLIAM B., born in Springfield, Ill., resides in Denver, Colorado.

ALBERT E., PAULINA C., AGNES and LAURA, live with their mother.

Nicholas A. Garland died Jan. 4, 1874, and Mrs. Garland and family reside in Springfield, Ill.

GARVEY, SAMUEL, was born Aug. 31, 1794, in Culpepper county, Va. His father, Job Garvey, was born in Scotland, and brought to America when he was quite young. His parents both dying early, he was bound to a man who proved to be a cruel master. Determined to escape the hard servitude, and partly from patriotic motives, he enlisted as a soldier in the revolutionary army, and served the whole seven years. When Samuel was about one year old his parents moved to Woodford county, Ky., and four or five years later moved to Franklin county, about eighteen miles south of Frankfort. Samuel volunteered in a regiment of dragoons at Frankfort, under Col. Dick Johnson, and was in the battle of the river Thames, in Canada, in which Col. Johnson is reputed to have killed the Indian chief Tecumseh. After his return the family moved to that part of Gallatin which is now Owen county, Ky. Samuel Garvey was there married, Dec. 26, 1816, to Maria Elliston, who was born July 25, 1800, in Franklin county. They lived in Owen county for some time, then, with a family of seven children, moved to Sangamon county, Ill., arriving in the fall of 1830, in the vicinity of what became Mechanicsburg, where they had five living children. Of their twelve children—

SCOTT, born Nov. 12, 1817, in Kentucky, died in Sangamon county in the twenty-first year of his age.

LEMUEL, born Sept. 11, 1819, in Kentucky, died in Sangamon county in his twenty-sixth year.

MARY A., born Aug. 11, 1823, in Kentucky, married William H. Hampton. See his name.

SAMUEL, Jun., born Aug. 27, 1825, in Owen county, Ky., married in Sangamon county, July 31, 1849, to Sarah A. Gideon. She was born Jan. 13, 1828, in Champaign county, Ohio, and came to Sangamon county in 1846. They had five children. MARY A., born May 21, 1850, married Sept. 9, 1869, to David C. Fletcher. They have three children, NEVADA, CORINNA and LENORA, and reside in Illiopolis township, three miles east of Mechanicsburg. D. C. Fletcher was born May 3, 1843, in Christian county. He enlisted Aug. 6, 1862, for three years, in Co. A, 73d Ill. Inf., was wounded at the battle of Stone's river, Tenn., also at Adairsville, Ga.; served to the end of the rebellion, and was honorably discharged in June, 1865. ANN M., born Aug. 23, 1852, CATHARINE J., born Oct. 16, 1854, and HENRY C., born Aug. 13, 1863, reside with their parents. ANDREW S. died Dec. 6, 1871, aged four years. Samuel Garvey, Jun., resides two and a half miles east of Mechanicsburg.

ELIZABETH A. and *NANCY C.,* twins, born March 1, 1827, in Kentucky.

ELIZABETH A. married in Sangamon county to John P. Jack, and resides at Edina, Knox county, Mo.

NANCY C. married John S. Hampton. *See his name.*

WILLIAM F., born Aug. 22, 1829, in Owen county, Ky., married in Springfield, Feb. 2, 1854, to Elizabeth A. Williams, who was born Nov. 29, 1829, in Montgomery county, Md. They had six children. Their second, THOMAS E., died, aged eight years. The fourth, EMMA J., died, aged two years. HORACE O., CLARA, WILLIAM H. and SAMUEL, reside with their parents, one and a quarter miles southwest of Illiopolis.

JANE, born March 25, 1831, in Sangamon county, married Nov. 5, 1872, to Josiah T. Peden, a native of Pennsylvania, and resides at Illiopolis.

JEREMIAH C. died, aged six years, and

EMILY died, aged four years.

JOHN, born June 29, 1839, in Sangamon county, married Oct. 12, 1869, to Maria F. Darneille. They had four children. OWEN and OLIN died in infancy. MINNIE F. and BERTHA live with their parents at the homestead of his father, one and a half miles east of Mechanicsburg.

HENRY C., born July 15, 1844, died April 26, 1864.

Mrs. Maria Garvey died Jan. 17, 1871, and Samuel Garvey, Sen., resides one and a half miles east of Mechanicsburg, and within that distance of where he settled in 1830, just before the "deep snow."

GATES, MICHAEL, born Jan. 30, 1776, in Lancaster county, Penn. His parents moved to the vicinity of Salisbury, North Carolina, when he was three years old. He was married there to Catharine Groves. They moved to Muhlenburg county, Ky., where seven children were born, and the family moved to Sangamon county, Ill., arriving in the fall of 1830—except Andrew and Mary, the two eldest children, who arrived May 31, 1831, in what is now Auburn township. Of their seven children—

MARY A., born October, 1805, in Kentucky, was married in Sangamon county, Ill., to Simeon Vancil. *See his name.* She died March 6, 1873.

ANDREW, born Jan. 17, 1807, in Muhlenburg county, Ky., was married in Sangamon county to Lucinda Wood. They had twelve children, six of whom died young. Of the other six, CATHARINE A. married H. B. Organ. *See his name.* ANDREW J. Jun., married Miriam Davis, and live in Auburn township. MARY E. married Jerome Baldwin, and live in Macoupin county, Ill. LEANDER A. is a teacher, and lives with his parents. LUCINDA E. was married Feb. 20, 1873, to A. J. Lentz, and resides in Sangamon county, near Virden. SARAH F. lives with her parents. Andrew Gates and wife reside five miles southwest of Auburn.

PETER, born Sept. 21, 1808, in Kentucky, came to Sangamon county, Ill., in Oct. 1829, and was married there to Christiana Dukes, who died March 24, 1848, and he married Sarah A. Wood, October, 1848, in Macoupin county, Ill. They had eleven children; six died young. WILLIAM F., born Oct. 14, 1849, was married Oct. 13, 1872, to Maggie Shanklin, in Macoupin county, and resides in Auburn township. JOHN M., born Sept. 2, 1852, died Nov. 24, 1872. GEORGE W., PETER M. and JAMES E., reside with their parents near Virden.

ELIZABETH, born Jan. 21, 1821, in Kentucky, was married there to Isham Gibson. He died in 1875, and Mrs. Gibson resides in Missouri.

CATHARINE, born August, 1811, in Kentucky, was married in Sangamon county, Ill., to Hardy Gatlin, and died March, 1852.

MARGARET, born February, 1813, in Kentucky, was married in Sangamon county, Ill., to Samuel Davidson, and died in 1861.

FANNY, born October, 1815, in Kentucky, was married in Sangamon county to Joseph Poley. *See his name.*

Michael Gates died in 1848, and his wife died in 1849, both in Sangamon county, Ill.

GATTON, MRS. RUTH, was born in 1775. Her husband, Thomas Gatton, died in 1828, in Grayson county, Ky. Mrs. Gatton with her daughters, Maria and Eliza, came to Sangamon county, under the care of her son Josephus, who had returned to Kentucky to be present at the death of his father. Of her children who came to Sangamon county—

JOHN A., born March 11, 1797, in Washington county, Ky., was married in Grayson county to Anna Newton. They had two children in Kentucky, and moved to Sangamon county, Ill., arriving Oct. 16, 1827, in what is now Ball township, where five children were born. Of their seven children—MONICA, born in Kentucky, was married in Sangamon county to Benjamin Burtle. *See his name.* THOMAS O., born Feb. 17, 1826, in Grayson county, Ky., was married in Sangamon county, Dec. 26, 1850, to Melinda Harper. They had eleven children, six of whom died young. Of the five living—ROSETTA, STEPHEN A. D., and MARY J., were born in Sangamon county, Ill. RUTH J. and MARTHA F. were born in Kansas. T. O. Gatton resides near Osage Mission, Neosho county, Kansas. JOSEPHUS, born in Sangamon county, married Mary E. Harper. They had one child, and Mrs. Mary E. Gatton died. Josephus Gatton married Rebecca McNeely. They live in Cotton Hill township. RUTH A. married Robert Gatton, and lives in Auburn, Sangamon county, Ill. JOHN W. lives in Ball township. SARAH E. married James H. Burtle. *See his name.* She died. THERESA lives with James H. Burtle. John A. Gatton died in Feb., 1847, and Mrs. Anna Gatton died Oct., 1865, both in Ball township, and are buried near St. Bernard Catholic church, Sangamon county, Ill.

THOMAS, born October, 1804, in Washington county, Ky., was married in Grayson county, Ky., to Martina Thompson, and came to Sangamon county in 1828. A few years later he went to Galena and engaged in lead mining. He moved to Dubuque, thence to DeWitt, Clinton county, Iowa, where the parents both died, leaving three children.

JOSEPHUS, born Sept. 13, 1806, in Washington county, Ky., was taken by his parents, in 1813, to Grayson county, Ky. From there he came to Sangamon county, arriving Oct. 16, 1827, in what is now Ball township. He returned to Kentucky at the time of his father's death. He experienced all the hardships of the deep snow of 1830 and '31. For several weeks the family lived on bread made of corn that was beaten with a pestle until fine enough, then sifted through a deer skin which was stretched over a hoop and burned full of holes with a hot iron. He says the happiest time of his life was when he was able to go to mill and obtain two sacks of corn meal. When the Black Hawk war broke out he did not wish to go, but his mother said her brothers were soldiers in the Revolution, and she wished him to go and never return with a wound in his back. He enlisted in a Sangamon county company, did his duty, and returned in safety. Josephus Gatton was married in Sangamon county, July 24, 1834, to Mary Burtle. They had five living children. RUTH E., born April 16, 1835, was married in 1859 to James A. Able. They have five children, JOSEPH, MARY E., WILLIAM, EMMA and CHARLES, and reside one and a half miles southwest of Pawnee. SARAH E., born May 25, 1837, married John W. Bell. *See his name.* THOMAS J., born Aug. 23, 1838, married Angeline Durbin. He died April 20, 1867, leaving a widow and three children near St. Bernard's church, Sangamon county, Ill. MARY M., born Feb. 13, 1840, married Nathan J. Durbin. They have six children, and reside in Cotton Hill township. WILLIAM W., born Aug. 19, 1841, lives with his father. Mrs. Mary Gatton died May 5, 1843, and Josephus Gatton was married Jan. 29, 1844, to Eveline Husband. They had six children. J. NEWTON, born Oct. 21, 1844, was married Dec. 15, 1859, to Georgetta C. Mourer. They have two children, GEORGIA and FRANKIE, and reside six miles south of Springfield. ELIZA J., born Feb. 1, 1847, was married Oct. 5, 1870, to John L. Bliss, who was born in Bath county, Ky., Aug. 20, 1846. They have one child, LUELLA, and live seven miles south of Springfield. JAMES H., JOSEPHUS M., SUSAN E. and WATSON T., live with their mother. Josephus Gatton died March 25, 1876, and was buried at Oak Ridge cemetery, Springfield. His widow and children reside six miles south of Springfield.

MARIA, born March 13, 1811, in Kentucky, married James Miller, who died, and she married Joseph Burtle. *See his name.*

ELIZA E., born May 17, 1813, in Kentucky, married James Burtle. See his name.

Mrs. Ruth Gatton died October, 1832, near St. Bernard's church, Sangamon county, Ill.

GEORGE, EDWARD, born about 1809, in Fauquier county, Va., went to Bath county, Ky., about 1815, and came to Sangamon county in the fall of 1833. He was married to Catharine Whaley. They had nine children. She and three of the children died near the same time. He married Mary Martin, and she died. He then married Mrs. Lucinda Jones, whose maiden name was Pike. They have five children. He died in 1875. His widow and children live near Rochester.

GEORGE, WILLIAM, was born in Cabell county, West Va., came with his family to Sangamon county, in 1829 or 30, and settled in what is now Loami township. His sons—
JOHN, WILLIAM and *FRANCIS*, all have families, and reside near Edinburg, Christian county, Ill.

GELLING, JOHN, was born Nov. 13, 1805, in the city of Douglas, Isle of Man, and came to America in 1830. He landed at New York, and went to the vicinity of Morristown, N. J. Hannah Monson was born in 1797, near Morristown, N. J. She was of an old French family that was among the earliest settlers of New Jersey. John Gelling and Hannah Monson were married June 23, 1833, near Morristown. They moved in 1838 to Vevay, Switzerland county, Ind. Mr. Gelling, his wife, and a girl living in the family, started from Vevay in a wagon, and drove through Indianapolis to Springfield, arriving in October, 1839. Since that time he has resided four years in Morgan county. With that exception, he has been in Sangamon county to the present time. They never had any children. Mrs. Hannah Gelling died Dec. 30, 1872, and John Gelling resides two and a half miles south of Dawson.

Miss Ellen C. Gelling, sister to John Gelling, resides with him. She was born on the Isle of Man, and came to Sangamon county in 1852.

Robert Gelling, brother to John and Ellen C., born in 1809 on the Isle of Man, and married there, came to Sangamon county in 1855. He has two sons and two daughters, and resides two miles south of Dawson.

GIBSON, WILLIAM, was born about 1780, near Staunton, Va., and was taken by his parents, at six or seven years of age, to Fayette county, Ky. He was married in Boone county, in 1809, to Mary Holman. She was born July 29, 1789, in Woodford county. Her father, Edward Holman, and Jesse Holman—for many years Judge of the Supreme Court of Indiana—were brothers. She was consequently a cousin to Hon. Wm. S. Holman, of the Fifth Congressional District of Indiana. Mr. and Mrs. Gibson had six children, near Lexington, Fayette county, Ky., and moved to Sangamon county, Ill., arriving Nov. 1, 1829, and settled in what is now the northwest corner of Chatham township. Of their children—

DAVID E., born April 16, 1811, in Fayette county, Ky., married in Sangamon county, April 14, 1831, to Mary Greenwood. They had five children: MARY A., born Feb. 12, 1832, married May 12, 1855, to John C. Cresswell, who was born Feb. 21, 1832, in Jersey county. They have four living children, ALICE D., DAVID E., LIZZIE and LAURA, and live five miles south of Loami. WILLIAM M., born Jan. 1, 1834, married May 11, 1854, to Elizabeth Fowler, who was born Dec., 1833, in Lincolnshire, England. They have five children: MARY, JOANNA, DAVID E., THOMAS and WILLIAM M., Jun. JOHN T., born March 5, 1836, married March 7, 1861, to Millicent Jarrett. They have four children, MARGARET L., ARTAMESIA, WILLIAM E. and JOSEPH F., and live five miles south of Loami. AMERICA, born Sept. 6, 1838, married James M. Coley. *See his name.* ELIZABETH, born Jan. 12, 1841, married Henry A. Weber. They had five children; all of them died under three years, and Mr. W. died Sept. 2, 1872, at White Oak, Montgomery county. Mrs. Weber resides with her father. Mrs. Mary Gibson died March 24, 1842, and David E. Gibson was married June 25, 1851, to to Julia A. Hall. They had five children. JANE died, aged four years. SUSAN, ILLINIA, HARRIET and DAVID E., Jun., reside with their parents, five miles south of Loami. David E. Gibson started to Jacksonville, about twenty-five miles distant, when there was but little improvement on the prairie. A snow storm set in soon after he started, and as night approached and he thought himself almost at the end of his journey, he discovered that he was only one and a half miles from home. He had been riding around a circle all day.

David E. Gibson remembers that in 1832 seed corn was so scarce that his father sent him to St. Clair county for some. He paid $1.00 per bushel, and shelled it himself. Settlements were so far apart that no food could be obtained. With two small scraps of bread—one from corn meal, the other from shorts—a drink of buttermilk and some wild onions, he traveled seventy-five miles, to reach home.

WM. HOLMAN, was born March 16, 1816, in Kentucky, was married March 3, 1841, in Sangamon county to America Forrest. They had one child, ELIZABETH, who died, aged eighteen years. W. H. Gibson died Dec. 26, 1849. His widow married Thomas J. Darneille. *See his name.*

ABIGAIL, born Jan., 1822, in Kentucky, married James M. Brown, in Sangamon county. They had two living children, and moved to California. He was murdered and robbed there of $3,000 in gold, Oct., 1870. His family moved from California to Nevada, thence to Oswego, Kansas. Of their children—ELIZABETH, married, and JAMES lives with his mother. *See name of Joshua Brown and his son, James M.*

JAMES E., born May 16, 1823, in Kentucky, married, June 5, 1845, in Sangamon county, to Margaret L. Forrest. He died, Jan. 13, 1873. in Chatham. His widow resides at Pioneer, Williams county, Ohio.

MARY, born in 1825, in Kentucky, married in Sangamon county, Ill., to Charles R. Campbell. *See his name.* They have two children, WILBUR and ABIGAIL.

JOHN A., born in 1827, in Kentucky, brought up in Sangamon county, went to California, in 1851, last heard from in 1865.

William Gibson died, Oct. 5, 1838, and his widow died, Sept., 1869, both in Sangamon county.

GIBSON, JAMES M., brother to Preston H., born May 19, 1812, in Gal-

latin county, Ky., eight miles above Warsaw. He came to Sangamon county about 1829, and was married April 14, 1832, to Sally Greenwood. They had eight living children—

NANCY J., born March 21, 1833, married James E. Campbell, who was born Oct. 22, 1821, at Delphi, Ross county, Ohio. They have eight children, MARY A., GEORGE W., PERMELIA C., MARGARET R., THEODORE M., COMMODORE P., EMMA F. and ALLEN EVA, and reside three miles southwest of Curran.

JOHN W., born Nov. 18, 1834, in Sangamon county, went to California in 1859, and lives at Saratoga, Santa Clara county.

SAMUEL P., born Feb. 10, 1836, in Sangamon county, married Sarah Van Doren. They have three living children, EMMA, PETER and WILLIAM, and live in Piatt county.

THOMAS B., born Sept. 8, 1838, married March 1, 1864, to Sophia A. McComas, have three children, LONA M., ARCHIE C. and NELLIE E., and live five miles west of Chatham.

PRESTON H., born July 19, 1840, in Sangamon county, married Mary E. Sommers, have one child, HELEN, and live at Brownsville, Neb.

MARGARET R., born Feb. 10, 1842, in Sangamon county, married G. W. Campbell. They have three living children, EUGENE, ROBERT and JAMES L., and live in Piatt county, Ill.

MARTHA A., born Jan. 7, 1844, married Dec. 30, 1869, to James Kinter, who was born Dec. 23, 1846, in Jefferson county, Pa. She died May 24, 1873, in Curran township.

DAVID W., born June 6, 1848, resides in Curran township.

Mrs. Sally Gibson died May 12, 1853, and J. M. Gibson was married Sept. 7, 1854, to Cynthia McComas. They had five children—

VAN OSCAR, GARRETT M., CHARLES L., ETTA F. and JAMES L., all live with their mother.

James M. Gibson died May 12, 1865, and his widow, Mrs. Cynthia Gibson, resides two miles south of Curran.

GIBSON, PRESTON H., was born Sept. 28, 1810, in that part of Boone which is now Gallatin county, Ky., eight miles above Warsaw. He was married in that county May 14, 1835, to Ann Finley. She was born Dec. 26, 1811, in the city of Philadelphia. When she was an infant her parents moved to Cincinnati, Ohio, where they both died when she was quite young. She was adopted by her aunt, Mrs. Robinson, and taken to Gallatin county, Ky., at sixteen years of age. Mr. and Mrs. Gibson moved immediately after they were married to Sangamon county, Ill., arriving June 10, 1835, in what is now Curran township, north of Lick creek. They had four children in Sangamon county—

JOHN E., born Jan. 28, 1838, married Feb. 7, 1861, to Sarah McGinnis, and had one child. It died on the 12th, and the mother on the 28th, of March, 1865. John E. Gibson lives with his mother, but spends much of his time at his farm in Nodaway county, Mo.

NANCY A., born Jan. 26, 1840, married, Oct., 1864, to William H. Trimble. See his name.

JAMES W., born Sept. 20, 1842, is unmarried, and resides with his mother.

HAMPTON, born Nov. 12, 1844, married Oct. 25, 1866, to Susan A. Patteson, have three children, JEAN W., PRESTON A. and JOHN E., and lives near the family homestead in Curran township.

Preston H. Gibson died Sept. 8, 1863, and his widow, Mrs. Ann Gibson, resides on the farm settled by herself and husband in 1835. It is in Curran township, north of Lick creek.

GIBSON, JAMES H., was born Sept., 1809, in Gallatin county, near Warsaw, Ky. He came to Berlin, Sangamon county, in 1840, and practiced medicine there more than thirty years. He died near Berlin, Nov. 22, 1873, leaving a widow, and a daughter who is married, and has two children.

GIGER, GEORGE, was born June 9, 1748, and was married in Greenbrier county, Va., to Mrs. Anna Auts, whose maiden name was Creek. She was born Nov. 19, 1765. He died in Tennessee, and she came to Sangamon county with her children, sketches of whose lives are found below. She died, Oct. 12, 1837.

GIGER, SUSANNAH, born Sept. 26, 1795, in Jefferson county, Tenn., and was there married to John Cooper. See his name.

GIGER, MARY, was born June 11, 1797, in Jefferson county, Tenn., and was married there to John Eckel. See his name.

GIGER, HENRY, was born May 14, 1799, in Jefferson county, Tenn. Nancy Todd was born May 7, 1798, in Cocke county, Tenn. They were married March 11, 1819, in Jefferson county, and moved, in company with their brother-in-law, John Cooper, to Sangamon county, Ill., arriving April 2, 1820, at a point two miles north of Rochester, and one year later moved into what is now Cooper township, where they had five living children, namely—

ANNA, born April 4, 1821, married April 3, 1836, to James Wilson. They had one child, NANCY A., born Jan. 28, 1837, married March 9, 1858, to Harrison Furrow. They had six children, GEORGE LINCOLN, MARY, LAURA B., EDWARD, ANNA and WILLIAM, and live in Christian county, seven miles east of Rochester. James Wilson died Sept. 12, 1839, and his widow married in October, 1843, to Edward Jones, who died May 3, 1867, and she married April 17, 1873, to Peter Gore. They live in Mechanicsburg.

ALEXANDER T., born June 23, 1824, married Dec. 15, 1845, to Mary J. McCoy, had eight children; three died young. JAMES H., ADDISON, OTTO, ADELIA and ELBRIDGE, live with their parents, in Mitchell county, near Cawker City, Kan.

BENJAMIN A., born Jan. 8, 1827, married Nov. 30, 1848, to Mary A. V. Kirke. She died May 10, 1853. Mr. Giger was married Oct. 26, 1853, to Margaret J. Kirke. They had three children. IDA L. died, aged four years. WILLIAM E. and H. DOUGLAS, live with their father. Mrs. M. J. Giger died May 19, 1869, and he was married March 1, 1870, to Mary E. Johnson, who was born May 14, 1845, in Springfield. They had one child, NOLA B., who died young. B. A. Giger and wife live in Sand Prairie, Cooper township, where his parents settled in 1822. It is five miles east of Rochester. Mr. G. is serving his second term as justice of the peace—1874.

ADDISON, born Jan. 1, 1829, married January, 1862, to Susan Benson, had one child, and Mr. Giger died Jan. 15, 1864. His widow married and went to California, where his son FRANKLIN died.

MARTHA D., born Jan. 30, 1831, married July 26, 1848, to John L. Green. They had two children, and Mr. G. and both children died. Mrs. G. married Lewis J. Eyman, who enlisted in Macon county Sept. 2, 1862, in Co. E, 116th Ill. Inf., for three years, was commissioned Capt. Sept. 6, 1862, and was killed in battle at Arkansas Post, July 11, 1863. His widow and two sons, HENRY A. and EDWARD O., reside temporarily—1874 —at Eureka, Ill., for educational purposes. Their home is at Mechanicsburg.

Henry Giger died Nov. 21, 1844, on the farm where he settled in 1822. His widow resides in Mechanicsburg.

GIGER, BENJAMIN, was born July 25, 1803, in Jefferson county, Tenn. He came to Sangamon county on a visit in 1828, returned to Tennessee, and moved, in company with his widowed mother and his brother-in-law, John North, arriving April 12, 1829, in what is now Cooper township. Benjamin Giger was married in Sangamon county, Nov. 18, 1832, to Susanna Todd, who was born Dec. 20, 1808, in his native county. They had three living children in Sangamon county, namely—

LETITIA A., born Sept. 15, 1836, in Sangamon county, married Jan. 27, 1853, to Aaron H. Martin, who was born Dec. 4, 1825, in Clarke county, Ind. They had five children, ALBERT T., SUSAN A., MARY L., FLORA L. and JENNIE I., and live in Mechanicsburg.

HENRY, born June 28, 1840, in Sangamon county, married Feb., 1863, to Mary J. Kirk. They have two children, ALBERT O. and LAURA B., and live near Norborne, Corroll county, Mo.

BENJAMIN H., born June 30, 1846, in Sangamon county, married April 6, 1865, to Sarah A. Dickson. They had three children: SUSANNA, the youngest, died in her fourth year. ALVIN C. and MATTIE T. reside with their parents in Mechanicsburg.

Benjamin Giger had natural talents for inventing useful machinery. It is believed by his descendents that it was from some machinery of his inventing that the original ideas embodied in the McCormick reaper were obtained. He did invent and construct many ingenious and useful implements. He would often study for days at a time, sometimes quitting his work in the daytime, would go to bed, cover up head and ears, and continue in the deepest study. When a plan or design was fully matured, he would leave his work, or arise from bed, as the case might be, and write, without stopping to eat or sleep, until his thoughts were transferred to paper. He invented a machine for heading grain; also some plows and other agricultural implements, and was on his way to Washington with his models, for the purpose of obtaining patents. He was taken sick on board a steamer ascending the Ohio river, and died at Brownsville, Pa., June 23, 1850. His widow died Nov. 28, 1858, in Sangamon county.

GIGER, ANNA, born Nov. 4, 1807, in Jefferson county, Tenn., married there to John North. See his name.

GLASCOCK, DANIEL M., was born May 11, 1795, in Loudon county, Va. Three brothers by the name of Glascock came from France, with LaFayette, and fought in the revolutionary army until Independence was acknowledged by England. They all remained, married and raised families on James river, Va. One of them had a son James, and it is his son, Daniel M., whose name heads this sketch. Mary E. Lake was born Sept. 20, 1798, in Loudon county, Va. Daniel M. Glascock and Mary E. Lake were there married, Aug. 18, 1818. They made their home in Fauquier county, until seven children were born, and then moved to Sangamon county, Ill., arriving in the fall of 1833, in what is now Fancy Creek township, where they had three children. Of their ten children—

LUCINDA C., born Aug. 12, 1819, in Fauquier county, Va., married in Sangamon county, Sept. 19, 1837, to Elisha Primm. See his name.

BAYLIS K., died in Virginia, June 4, 1832, aged eleven years.

MARY E., born Oct. 30, 1823, in Virginia, married in Sangamon county to Elijah S. Primm. See his name.

MARGARET E., born July 16, 1826, in Virginia, married in Sangamon county to Martin L. Bishop. They have five children, and live in McLean county, Illinois.

JAMES B., born Nov. 11, 1828, in Fauquier county, Va., raised in Sangamon county, married, Aug. 31, 1850, to Sarah M. Stone, who was born Aug. 4, 1831, in Menard county. They have four living children, WILLIAM M., MARY E., MARGARET A., and EMMA E., and reside in Menard county, two and one-half miles north of Cantrall.

THOMAS, born Feb. 24, 1831, in Fauquier county, Va., married in Sangamon county to Mary J. Brittin. She died Feb. 1, 1859. Thomas Glascock was married, Aug. 28, 1860, to Mrs. Eliza F. Brittin, whose maiden name was Mallory. They have three living children, LIZZIE FLORENCE, WILLIAM O., and NETTIE A., and reside in Fancy Creek township, four miles northwest of Sherman. Thomas Glascock served several years as a member of the Board of Supervisors of Sangamon county.

DANIEL, died May 15, 1848, aged thirteen years.

ELIAS L., born Oct. 24, 1837, in Sangamon county, married Emeline Miller. They had three children, and she died. Mr. G. married Margaret King, and live in Butler county, Kansas.

EZEKIEL F., born Feb. 5, 1840, in Sangamon county, married Mary Hurt, who was born Feb. 6, 1844, in Menard county. They had four children. LYDIA A., the second child, died in her third year. MARGARET E., MARY L., and EMMA E., reside with their parents three miles southwest of Cantrall.—1874.

Daniel M. Glascock died March 4, 1840, and his widow died April 4, 1840, both in Sangamon county.

GOODELL, CALVIN, born Nov. 5, 1783, in Connecticut, was married in New York to Martha Coley, who was born Feb. 14, 1789. They had six children in New York, and moved to Sangamon county, Ill., arriving in 1824, in what is now Loami township, where five children were born. Of their children—

CHLOE, born May 11, 1809, in New York, was married in Illinois to Philip Aylesworth. She died, leaving four children.

HARRISON, born April 9, 1811, in New York, was married in Sangamon county to Mary Taylor. They have seven children, and live in Woodford county, Ill.

PHYLATTA, born March 13, 1813, in Madison county, N. Y., married Johnson Harding, had three children, and Mr. Harding died, and she married George Beach, who was born in 1810, in Maryland. They had eight children, three of whom died under ten years. Of the other five: LAFAYETTE, born Nov. 5, 1842, married May 29, 1862, to Catharine Alexander, have one child, CHARLES D., and live five miles west of Chatham. MARY, born Oct. 19, 1839, married June 2, 1860, to Josiah S. Kirk, who was born Dec. 7, 1834, in Washington county, Va. They have three children, MARY J., GEORGE A. and MARTIN F., and live in Loami. JOSEPH, born Feb. 8, 1852, OSCAR F., born Oct. 13, 1854, and JULIA A., live with their parents. George Beach and wife reside in Loami.

SCHUYLER, born July 18, 1815, married Melinda Sowell, have eleven children, and live in Miami county, Kan. See Sowell family.

WILLIS, born Sept. 1, 1817, in New York, married in Sangamon county to Sally Sowell. They had one child, ALICE, and he died. See Sowell family.

JOSEPH, born Jan. 5, 1820, in New York, married in Sangamon county, moved to California, and died there, leaving a widow and two children.

WILLIAM, born Sept. 21, 1822, married to Mrs. Sally Goodell, whose maiden name was Sowell, and lives in Missouri.

MARY A., born Dec. 3, 1824, in Sangamon county, married Martin Thurber. They had six children, and Mr. T. died. The widow and children live in Hancock county, Ill.

CALVIN, Jun., born April 13, 1827, in Sangamon county, was a soldier in an Illinois regiment, and died in the army.

ADALINE, born Dec. 30, 1829, in Sangamon county, married Herman Burt, had five children. He died in Indiana. She resides in Madison, Wis.

NEWTON M., born in 1840, in Sangamon county, married, has three children, and lives in Menard county.

Mrs. Martha Goodell died Sept. 13, 1852, and Calvin Goodell died March 10, 1863, both at Loami.

Mr. Goodell was always engaged in milling. He built a mill on a small stream one mile east of Loami. Cultivation soon drained the country and cut off his supply of water. True to his Yankee origin, he then put horses inside the wheel, and ran it on the principle of a squirrel cage.

GOODAN, LEVI W., was born in Pennsylvania, taken by his parents to Bath county, Ky., was a soldier from that county in the war of 1812, and after the war was married in that county to Garner Crouch. They came to Sangamon county in 1820 or '21, and settled at what is now Sangamon station, where they had two children, and Mrs. Goodan died there. Of their children—

WILLIAM died in Springfield.

DAVID married in Springfield to Catharine VanNostrand, and died, leaving a widow and children near Pana.

Levi W. Goodan died near Pana, also.

GOODAN, ELEANOR, sister to Levi W., married Andrew Jones. See his name.

GOLD, HEZEKIAH S., was born June 6, 1807, at Cornwall, Litchfield county, Conn. He married Sept. 6, 1836, to Chloe A. Peet, who was born April 26, 1812, in the town of Warren, in the same county. They had one child there, and moved to Waverly, Ill., in the fall of 1839. In the summer of 1840 he bought land and built a house three and a half miles east of Waverly, in what is now Talkington township, Sangamon county, where they had two children. Of their three children—

HENRY M., born July 25, 1837, in Litchfield county, Conn., raised in Sangamon county, enlisted in 1861 for three years, in Co. I, 14th Ill. Inf. He was accidentally wounded September, 1861, and died Nov. 7, 1861, in the court house hospital at Rolla, Mo.

MYRON S., born Dec. 1, 1842, in Sangamon county, enlisted in 1862 for three years, in Co. G, 101st Ill. Inf. He was discharged on account of physical disability late in 1862, and lives in Talkington township, near Waverly.

ETHEL EDWARD, born Feb. 1, 1847, in Sangamon county, lives in New York city. He is—1874—superintendent of the Gold Heating company, manufacturers of sanitary heaters, 105 Beekman street.

Mrs. Chloe A. Gold died Sept. 3, 1857, in Talkington township. Hezekiah S. Gold enlisted Oct. 15, 1861, in the fifty-sixth year of his age, at Springfield, in Co. K, 2nd Reg. Ill. Light Art,, for three years, served more than full term, and was honorably discharged Dec. 30, 1864, and now resides on the farm where he settled in 1840, being the second settler in what is now Talkington township, William Eustace being the first.

GRAGG, MRS. MARTHA, whose maiden name was Runnels, was born in Albermarle county, Va., and taken by her parents, when she was quite young, to Montgomery county, Ky., where she was married to John Gragg. They moved to Nicholas county, where Mr. Gragg died, leaving a widow and three children, who returned to her friends in Montgomery county, Ky., where the eldest—

JESSE, died, aged eighteen years.

Mrs. Gragg and her two children moved to Sangamon county, Ill., arriving in the fall of 1838, near Mechanicsburg. Of the two children—

MARGARET, born Nov. 13, 1814, in Nicholas county, Ky., was married in Sangamon county to Elder John L. Wilson. See his name.

WILLIAM, born June 10, 1818, in Nicholas county, Ky., came to Sangamon county in 1838, and was married March 26, 1844, to Sophia McBride. They had four living children in Sangamon county, namely: THOMAS J., born Jan. 1, 1845, was married Jan. 20, 1870, in Sangamon county, to Lucinda Fry, who was born Nov. 6, 1850, in Shelby county, Ky. They have one living child, CLARA, and live five miles southeast of Mechanicsburg. JOHN H., born Aug. 17, 1847, was married May 31, 1871, to Matilda D. Blair, who was born Sept. 22, 1851, near Moro, Madison county, Ill. They have one child, WILLIAM B., and live four and a-half miles east of Mechanicsburg. WILLIAM, Jun., born June 10, 1851, was married, Feb. 8, 1876, at the house of Vincent Garretson, to Fanny Hissey, and live near Mechanicsburg. HARVEY, born Jan. 21, 1853, lives at the homestead. Mrs. Sophia Gragg died Dec. 26, 1872, and William Gragg died July 30,

1875, five miles southeast of Mechanicsburg, in Illiopolis township.

Mrs. Martha Gragg died Aug. 31, 1843, in Sangamon county.

GRAHAM, ROBERT, was born about 1794, in Washington county, Penn. Sarah Mitchell was born in 1797, in the same county. They were married, Jan. 24, 1819, and had three children in Penn. The family moved, in 1834, to Richland county, Ohio, where two children were born, and then moved to Sangamon county, Ill., arriving, Nov., 1838, in what is now Woodside township. Of their five children—

JOHN L., born March 8, 1821, married in Sangamon county, in 1844, to Mary Johnson. They have eight children, and live in Bates county, Mo.

WILLIAM M., born Jan 5, 1830, in Penn., married in Sangamon county to Rebecca Trumbo. She had one child, REBECCA, who married Mitchel Lawson. Mrs. Graham died, and Mr. G. was married, Aug. 26, 1857, to Lucy Marsh. They have three children, WILLIAM M., LYDIA C., and CORDELIA, and live in Springfield.

ROBERT S., born Sept. 24, 1833, married Nov. 21, 1856, to Adaline B. Megredy. They have five children, MARY A., WILLIAM P., JOHN C., SARAH E., and NELLIE G., and live in Christian county, near Pawnee.

GEORGE W., born May 5, 1835, married Ellen S. Shutt. They have two children, and live in Fayette county.

THOMAS P., born March 2, 1837, in Ohio, died in Sangamon county, aged twenty years.

Robert Graham died Nov. 1, 1840, in Sangamon county. His widow married Charles Rice. He died June 7, 1862, and she lives with her Graham children.

GRAHAM, NATHANIEL, was born in Pennsylvania. When a young man he went to Columbus, Ohio, and a few years later to Fleming county, Ky., where he was married to Sarah Harbor. They had eight children in Fleming county, and the family moved to Springfield, Ill., arriving in the fall of 1826. In the spring of 1827 they moved three and a half miles east of Springfield, between Sugar creek and the South fork of Sangamon river. Of their eight children—

NANCY, born in Fleming county, Ky., married in Sangamon county to James Woods. They had ten children, two of whom lived to be married, but all are dead. Mr. and Mrs. Woods live at Darlington, Lafayette county, Wis.

WILLIAM, born in 1808, in Fleming county, Ky., married in Sangamon county to Elizabeth Trotter. They had four living children. JAMES lives in Springfield. HESTER married David Carver, and lives in Springfield. CHARLES married Jane Hart, and lives in Springfield. William Graham and wife are both dead.

SARAH, born in Kentucky, raised in Sangamon county, married in Lafayette county, Wis., to John Woods.

THOMAS, *KEZIAH* and *HESTER*, all died.

MARY, born Jan. 3, 1818, in Kentucky, married Dec. 22, 1840, to Turner Lloyd. They have six children, and live in Springfield.

JOSHUA, born Jan. 6, 1821, in Fleming county, Ky., married Sept. 25, 1848, in Sangamon county, to Elizabeth A. Branch. They had eight children, five of whom died under two years. NANCY ELIZA, GEORGE E. and REBECCA E., reside with their parents near Sangamon station, on the farm where his parents settled in 1827.

Nathaniel Graham and his wife both died in Sangamon county, on the farm where they settled in 1827.

GRANT, JAMES, was born in Rutherford county, N. C. He was there married to Sarah Elliott, sister to Andrew Elliott. They had two children in North Carolina, and moved to Sangamon county, arriving in the fall of 1834, near Springfield, where two children were born. Of their four children—

WILLIAM, born in North Carolina, raised in Sangamon county, and married Mrs. Sarah Gibbons. They have children, and live at Greenview, Menard county.

MYRA, born in North Carolina, raised in Sangamon county, was a deaf mute, and died at the Institution for the Deaf and Dumb, at Jacksonville.

JOHN A., born in Sangamon county, is unmarried, and lives at 439 north Fourth street, Springfield.

JAMES, Jun., is married, and lives at 439 north Fourth street.

James Grant and his wife both died in Sangamon county.

GREENWOOD, JOHN, was born in Virginia. His parents moved to Warren county, Ky., when he was quite young. He was a fellow student with Judge S. T. Logan, at Glasgow, Ky., and intended making the law his profession, but abandoned it. He was married in Barren county, Ky., to Tryphena Garrison, and had two living children there. The family moved to Sangamon county, Ill., arriving in the fall of 1831, in what is now Fancy Creek township. In the spring of 1832 they moved to Fort Clark, now Peoria, where Mrs. Greenwood died, May 26, 1832. Mr. G. returned with his two children to Sangamon county, and was married Nov. 20, 1832, to Mary Sale. They had one child there, and the family, except the eldest son, moved to Bush's ferry, on Rock river, in Lee county, Ill., where Mr. Greenwood was accidentally killed while raising a house for himself. His widow and children returned to Sangamon county, and she was three times married. She and all her husbands are dead. Of Mr. Greenwood's three children—

BASIL, born Sept. 29, 1819, in Barren county, near Glasgow, Ky., married Nov. 15, 1849, near Pleasant Plains, Sangamon county, to Eliza A. Townsend, who was born May 29, 1823, in Cape May county, N. J., and came with her parents to Sangamon county in 1841. Basil Greenwood and wife had five children: TRYPHENA A., born Sept. 27, 1850, in Sangamon county, was married April 28, 1870, to Charles Whitmer. They have one living child, NELLIE MAY, and live in Taylorville, Ill. PARTHENIA J. died in Springfield, aged five years. JOHN R., born Oct. 13, 1854. SARAH M., born Dec. 11, 1856, live with their parents. JULIA A., born July 8, 1859, in Sangamon county, was married Sept. 19, 1875, to Asa H. Culver, formerly of Ohio. They live in Edinburg, Ill. Dr. Basil Greenwood and family reside in Edinburg, Christian county, Ill., where he is engaged in the practice of his profession. He was isolated from his relatives by the death of his mother, and fared exceedingly hard. When a boy he walked and led an ox from Illinois to Philadelphia for a drover, who failed there and left the boy without a cent of money, to work his way back as best he could. He apprenticed himself and learned the trade of a carpenter in Springfield. After spending twelve years without knowing where a single relative was, he accidentally met his brother John, and after a long interview, became satisfied that they were brothers, and for the first time learned that his father was dead. From the business of a carpenter he went to dealing in drugs and medicines, and then studied medicine. For the last twelve years he has been engaged in practicing his profession.

JOHN, Jun., born April 2, 1829, near Glasgow, Ky. He had both his hands seriously crippled when he was a child. He enlisted at Springfield, in May, 1846, in Co. I, 4th Ill. Inf., and served thirteen months in the Mexican war; was honorably discharged, and received one hundred and sixty acres of land. He was married in Springfield, August 7, 1854, to Emily Blakely, who was born Sept. 30, 1836, in Cincinnati, Ohio. They have three living children, ANNIE G., MINERVA A. and JOHN W., and reside at Williamsville. By the second wife—

WILLIAM C., born August 24, 1833, in Sangamon county, married near Galena to Elizabeth Keithley. They have one living child, CHARLES E., and reside at 522 south Ninth street, Springfield, Illinois.

GREENWOOD, WILLIAM, was born about 1772, near Petersburg, Va. He was there married to Ruth Brooks, and moved to Cabell county, W. Va., where eight children were born. They moved to Sangamon county, Ill., arriving in Oct., 1824, in what is now Curran township. Of all their children—

ELIZABETH, born in 1804, in Va., was married in Sangamon county, Ill., to Montague A. Morris, and for a second husband married George Hilyard. She died without children, in Pike county, Illinois.

THOMAS, born Jan. 5, 1806, in West Virginia, was married in Sangamon county, Ill., to Ann Lindley. They had eleven children, two of whom died under ten years of age. Of the other nine— ELIZA, married John Mullen, had two children, and she and one of the children died. The other child, HENRY, lives in Decatur, Ill. SIMON L., born Aug. 27, 1827, was married, Jan. 16, 1853, to Elizabeth Myers. She died, Dec. 30, 1871, leaving four children, JOHN T., ANN M., BYRON S. and GEORGE W. Simon L. Greenwood died, June, 1874, in LaFayette county, Mo. MARY died in her eighteenth year. RUTH A., born Feb. 27, 1832, was married, Aug. 30, 1855, to Hugh M. Forrest, who died Jan. 7, 1857, and she was married, Jan. 20, 1859, to David E. McGinnis. See his name. WILLIAM B., born Aug. 28, 1836, married Anna Young. They had three children, and he enlisted in Co. I, 33d Ill. Inf., for three years. He was discharged on account of physical disability, and died of disease, at Pilot Knob, Mo., in 1864. SARAH M. married Robert McCartney. They have four children, and reside in Jacksonville, Ill. CAROLINE married James M. Coley. See his name. She died six weeks after marriage. SUSAN married Newton Harlan, have three children, and live in Nebraska. THOMAS, Jun., born Nov. 14, 1845, enlisted in Co. I, 73d Ill. Inf., and died at Nashville, Tenn., Jan. 17, 1863. Mrs. Ann Greenwood died, Oct. 11, 1848, and Thomas Greenwood died, Nov. 7, 1868, both in Sangamon county, Ill.

ANN, born in 1808, in West Virginia, was married in Sangamon county, Ill., to Calvert J. Morris. They moved to Missouri, and both died there, leaving three children.

JOHN, born Jan. 3, 1810, in Cabell county, W. Va., was married in Sangamon county, Oct. 20, 1832, to Eliza Miller. They had three living children. JAMES W., born Feb. 2, 1834, was married, Dec. 18, 1856, to Margaret Baker, who was born Oct. 27, 1834. They had five children—JOHN W. died in his tenth year. HARRIET C. died in her third year. NANCY J., JAMES W. and THOMAS SHERIDAN. The three latter live with their parents in Loami township. LEAH M. was married, Jan. 25, 1855, to Fielding M. Neal. See his name. RUTH J. was married, Jan. 3, 1855, to Joel L. Franklin. They have three children, MARY E., JULIA B. and EMILY A., and live near Tolono, Champaign county, Ill. Mrs. Eliza Greenwood died, Feb. 10, 1841, and John Greenwood was married, March 10, 1842, to Emily Miller, who died April 21, 1866. John Greenwood resides five miles west of Chatham.

POLLY, born Jan. 8, 1812, in West Virginia, was married in Sangamon county, Ill., to David E. Gibson. See his name.

SALLY, born in West Virginia, was married in Sangamon county, Ill., to James M. Gibson. See his name.

EDMUND was born Jan. 8, 1814, in Cabell county, West Virginia, and at ten years of age was brought by his parents to Sangamon county, Ill. He was married Aug. 11, 1835, in Springfield, to Jeanette Foster. They had four children in Sangamon county, and in the fall of 1852, moved to Adair county, Mo., where they had one child. Of their children, JAMES M., born Nov. 15, 1836, in Sangamon county, Ill. He first attended school at the McGinnis school house, on Lick creek, and at the public school in Loami. He was always noted for his love of fun, and the facility with which he learned all his lessons, generally "working the sums" for all the boys in school. At the age of sixteen—the very time his facilities for education should have been increased—the family moved to Missouri, and the next four years was spent on the farm without entering school; but his ardor for learning could not thus be quenched. He managed to buy an old algebra, geometry, Latin grammar and Butler's Analogy, and studied them of nights, rainy days and Sundays, until their contents were mastered. In the winter of 1855 he taught the first public school ever held in the township where his father now lives, receiving fifteen dollars per month for his services. The next winter he attended school at Kirksville, Mo. He continued laboring on the farm until September, 1857, when he entered the seminary at Canton, Mo., taking in one year the entire course with the exception of Greek, passing examinations in twenty branches; but nature rebelled against such overwork, and he was not able to graduate, although his oration was ready for delivery. For a year books were thrown aside. From 1859 to 1866 his winters were spent in teaching, and the remainder of each year in farming. In August, 1867, he accepted the chair of Mathematics, Astronomy,

Mechanical Philosophy and Logic, in the North Missouri State Normal School, at Kirksville. He filled that position until June, 1870, when he was elected to the same position in Mt. Pleasant College, Huntsville, Mo. In December following he was re-elected, and accepted his former position in the State Normal School, at Kirksville, Mo., which he held until June, 1874. At the latter date Prof. Greenwood was elected out of seventeen applicants to the position of Superintendent of the Kansas City public schools. After that he was elected Principal of the South Missouri State Normal School, at Warrensburg, also of the Northwest Normal School, at Oregon, Holt county, Mo., both of which he declined, justly regarding his present connection with the Kansas City schools as the second educational position in the State. For the last ten years he has done as much to popularize and defend the cause of education as any man in the State, having delivered upwards of five hundred public addresses to Missouri audiences on educational topics, besides having written extensively on similar subjects for the leading Journals of the State. He has been and is now an untiring student, not only of the ablest American authors in his favorite department, but also of the best English, French and German writers on the more advanced Mathematics. His mathematical library is said to be the best collection in Missouri. The State University of Missouri, as a slight recognition of his services, conferred upon Prof. Greenwood the degree of Master of Arts. It will thus be seen that what appeared to be the crushing out of his aspirations for education, by removing him from all schools, was only placing him on missionary ground, where he could see the imperative needs of the growing State, and educate himself for the great work before him. I imagine that the early settlers of Sangamon county will take special pleasure in perusing this brief sketch of the trials and triumphs of a son of one of their own families. JAMES M. Greenwood was married Nov. 1, 1859, in Carroll county, Mo., to Amanda A. McDaniel. They have three children ADA M, HERVEY V. and NETTIE E., and reside in Kansas City, Mo. RUTH E., born April 5, 1838, in Sangamon county, married March 26, 1857, in Adair county, Mo., to James J. Hatfield, and have three children, EDMUND E., NETTIE and JAMES P. Mr. and Mrs. Hatfield live near Brunswick, Chariton county, Mo. PEYTON F., born Feb. 12, 1840, in Sangamon county, attended district school with his brother, James M., in his native county, and private schools in Kirksville, Mo. He also spent one year in the Baptist College at Lagrange, Mo. He was married Sept., 1861, to Frances M. Foster, who died in six weeks after marriage. In April, 1864, he married Julia Bryan, and has three children, EVA, SAMUEL E. and GRACE. Peyton F. Greenwood is a practicing lawyer, and resides in Kirksville, Mo. SARAH E., born Oct., 1852, in Sangamon county, and POLLY, born May 5, 1854, in Adair county, Mo., live with their parents. Edmund Greenwood and wife reside near Brashear, Adair county, Mo. The business habits of Mr. Greenwood are somewhat remarkable. He was never sued, nor never sued another, and for nearly thirty years has not given a note or any evidence of indebtedness. His son, Prof. James M., never gave but one note, and paid that within two weeks. Their motto is, "If you can't pay, don't buy."

MARGARET, born in West Virginia, was married in Sangamon county, Ill., to William H. Foster. *See his name.*

WILLIAM V., born April 18, 1826, in Sangamon county, was married there, Dec. 4, 1845, to Barbara A. Starr. They have two children. CHRISTOPHER C. enlisted Dec., 1863, in Co. B, 10th Ill. Cav., served until the close of the rebellion, and was honorably discharged, in Nov., 1865, at Galveston, Texas. He was married Dec. 21, 1875, at Chatham, Ill., to Zula Hillerman, and lives in Chatham. GEORGE W. enlisted, Dec., 1863, in the same company and regiment with his brother, and was honorably discharged, on account of physical disability, in 1865. He was married, Dec. 16, 1875, to Emma A. Baker, and lives in Chatham. William V. Greenwood enlisted in Co. I, 73d Reg. Ill. Inf., in July, 1862, for three years, was appointed first Duty Sergeant, served until Dec., 1863, when he was discharged on account of physical disability. He resides in Chatham, Sangamon county, Ill.

Mrs. Ruth Greenwood died July 6, 1837, and William Greenwood died Aug. 16, 1855, both in Sangamon county, Ill.

GREENING, THOMAS A., was born Nov. 19, 1796, in Fauquier county, Va. His parents, Reuben Greening and Sarah Allen, were born and married in that county. In 1804 they moved to the vicinity of Cumberland Gap, Claiborne county, Tenn., and in 1808 moved to Clarke county, Ky., where they spent the remainder of their lives. Thomas A. was a soldier from that county in the war of 1812. He was married there, in 1816, to Elizabeth Dawson. She was born Jan. 1, 1789. They had six children in Kentucky, moved to Montgomery county, Mo., and from there to Sangamon county, Ill., arriving in the fall of 1830, at Buffalo Hart Grove, where they spent the winter of the "deep snow." In the spring of 1831 they moved to what is now Loami township, where they had four living children. Of their children—

ELIZA A., born in Clark county, Ky., married to John A. Neal. See his name.

THOMAS, born in Kentucky, married in Sangamon county, to Dicey Bilyeu, and both died.

DAVID, born Sept. 20, 1822, in Clark county, Ky., married in Sangamon county, Dec. 6, 1842, to Mary P. Colburn, who was born March 25, 1827. They have seven children. JAMES enlisted in 1861, in Co. —, 30th Ill. Inf., for three years; re-enlisted as a veteran, Jan. 1, 1864, served to the end of the rebellion and was honorably discharged, July 17, 1865. He was married to Florence Skinner, and has five children, DAVID O., ANNIE E., WILLIAM T., JAMES O. and MINNIE O., and live in Chatham township. MARIA E. married Charles T. Dodd, has one child, WARREN L., and lives in Loami township. ZACHARY T., NOAH L., GEORGE W., WILLIAM D. and ULYSSES TECUMSEH live with their parents in Loami township, north of Lick creek. David Greening remembers that during the winter of the "deep snow" the deer would assemble in the rush flats in Buffalo Hart Grove, beat the snow down, and secure sufficient food to sustain life. He saw twenty-five or thirty deer in an open space with the snow banked up fifteen or twenty feet around them. It had drifted in that form. The crust was of sufficient strength to bear a man, and they could walk to the brink and look down. Dogs that ventured in were soon killed, and even wolves fared no better, except that some of them burrowed out, in order to escape from the enraged deer.

AMANDA died at eleven years of age.

ABIGAIL, born in Kentucky, married in Sangamon county to A. J. Sweet, had three children, and Mr. Sweet died. She married Levi Church, has four children, and resides at Waverly.

SARAH A., born in Clark county, Ky., married in Sangamon county to John B. Fowler. See his name.

ELIZABETH, born Oct. 17, 1830, in Sangamon county, married John H. Miller. See his name.

JOHN W., born Sept. 17, 1833, in Sangamon county, married Mahala A. Neal, and have two children. CHARLES W. lives with his parents. CAROLINE married George W. Neal. See his name. John W. Greening enlisted August 9, 1862, in Co. B, 30th Ill. Inf., for three years, was forty-seven days under fire at the siege of Vicksburg, was with Sherman in his march to the sea, served full term, and was honorably discharged at Springfield, June, 1865, and resides in Chatham township.

JULIETTE married John Cutter. See his name.

JAMES M., born Dec. 14, 1839, in Sangamon county, married March 5, 1863, to Margaret C. Darneille. They have four children, MARY E., JAMES F., EMMA MAY, HARVEY E. and LAURA EDITH, and live at the homestead settled by his parents in 1831. It is in Loami township.

Thomas A. Greening died May 4, 1855, and his widow died Jan. 31, 1872, in her eighty-fourth year.

Thomas A. Greening kept a store for several years where his son, James M., now lives. His goods were all hauled from St. Louis and Alton. He would send teams down loaded with produce, which was exchanged for goods and hauled back. There was no competition nearer than Springfield.

GREENING, JOHN F., brother to Thomas A., was born Nov. 20, 1806, in Powell's Valley, near Cumberland Gap, Claiborne county, Tenn. His parents moved, in 1808, to Clark county, Ky. He was married in Bracken county, May 26, 1831, to Elizabeth G. Rose, who was born Sept. 6, 1814, in that county. They had one child in Kentucky, and moved, in the fall of 1834, to Hamilton county, Ind., where they had one living child, and the family moved to Sangamon county, Ill., arriving Oct., 1839, on German Prairie, northeast of Springfield, where they had two children, and in Feb., 1844, moved to Buffalo Hart Grove, where they had four children. Of their eight children—

URSULA L., born May 4, 1832, in Kentucky, married Sept. 30, 1856, in Sangamon county, to Thomas F. Burns. *See his name.*

SARAH E., born July, 4, 1838, in Indiana, died Dec. 29, 1861, at Buffalo Hart Grove.

GERSHOM K., born May 31, 1841, near Springfield, enlisted July 25, 1862, in Co. I, 114th Ill. Inf., for three years, served full term, and was honorably discharged Aug. 8, 1865, was forty-seven days under fire at the siege and capture of Vicksburg, was with Gen. Thomas at the battle of Nashville, and was at the siege and capture of Mobile, and now—1874—lives with his brother Zachary T.

MARY F., born Jan. 8, 1844, married Adam H. Constant. *See his name.*

ZACHARY T., born Aug. 3, 1846, in Sangamon county, married Dec. 27, 1871, to Mary Elder. They have one child, GEORGIE, and live two miles south of Buffalo Hart station.

WINFIELD S., born March 27, 1849, in Sangamon county, lives with his brother Zachary T.

ISADORE A., born May 22, 1852, and

JOHN F., Jun., born July 29, 1857, live with their parents.

John F. Greening and his wife are both living—1874—and reside one and one-half miles east of Buffalo Hart station, Sangamon county.

GREENAWALT, JACOB, was born Oct. 27, 1804, in Hardin county, Ky. Mary Bradley was born Aug. 4, 1810, in Larue county, Ky. They were there married, Jan. 29, 1827, and had two children in Kentucky, and moved to Sangamon county, Ill., arriving Oct., 1830, in what is now Ball township, and the next year moved to Putnam county. The Black Hawk Indian war breaking out, he returned to Sangamon county. After the capture of Black Hawk, he went back to Putnam, but sold out there, and returned to Sangamon in 1836. They had six children in Illinois. Of their children—

FRANCIS M., born Jan. 11, 1828, in Kentucky, married in Sangamon county to Louisa Proctor. They have seven children, and live in Edinburg.

JOHN W., born July 23, 1830, married in Sangamon county to Elizabeth A. McAtee. They have four children, JAMES H., SMITH, JOHN T. and LUNETTA F., and live in Cotton Hill township, four and one-half miles north of Pawnee.

GEORGE W., born Feb. 24, 1833, in Sangamon county, married Lemira Holoway, and live at Raymond, Montgomery county, Ill.

SARAH E., born Feb. 24, 1836, in Illinois, married in Sangamon county to Wm. A. Penn, moved to Texas in 1853, and he was killed at the battle of Pea Ridge. His widow married Mr. McCann, and lives in Texas.

WM. JASPER, born Oct. 14, 1839, in Sangamon county, married Mrs. Elizabeth Hayden, whose maiden name was Vancil. He died, leaving a widow and one child. The widow married Absolom Scott, who died, and she lives in Piatt county with her children.

JAMES N., died July 8, 1861, in his eighteenth year.

MARY F., born July 19, 1853, in Sangamon county, married Thomas Wm. Dozier. *See his name.*

Jacob Greenawalt died Feb. 24, 1863, in Cotton Hill township. Mrs. Mary Greenawalt married Michael Fay, and live in Cotton Hill township. *See Bradley family in the Omissions.*

GREENAWALT, THOMAS B., was born in 1816 or '17, in Hardin county, Ky., and came with his brother Jacob to Sangamon county, in 1830. David B. and Lewis B. are younger brothers to Thomas B. and Jacob, but have not been in the county sufficient time to be included as "early settlers." Thomas B. married in Sangamon county to Mary E. Gatton. They had four living children in Sangamon county, namely:

WILLIAM R., born July 25, 1841, married Mary E. Burtle. They have five children, THOMAS B., JAMES F., MINNIE E., LAURA R., and JOHN E., and live two miles southeast of Pawnee.

SARAH A. died at twelve years of age.

MARY J., married G. J. Boll. See his name.

JAMES R., lives with his brother Wm. R.

Thomas B. Greenawalt died Jan., 1848, and his widow died July, 1849, both in Ball township.

GREENSLATE, JOHN, was born Nov. 18, 1801, near Lexington, Ky., and raised in Greenup county. He was married June 8, 1826, in Portsmouth, O., to Sarah M. Oliver, who was born Feb. 18, 1808, in Lewis county, Ky. They made their home in Greenup county until they had four children, and moved to Louisville, Ky., thence to Alton, Ill., and from there to Sangamon county, arriving in May, 1836, four miles northeast of Springfield, where four children were born; two died, each in their eighth year. Of the other six children—

GEORGE, born Sept. 8, 1827, in Greenup county, brought up in Sangamon county, and married in Logan county to Mary J. Iden. They had four children, and he enlisted in 1862, for three years, in the 116th Ill. Inf., at Lincoln, and died at Jackson, Tenn., Dec. 8, 1862. His widow married James Broughton, and lives near Mt. Pulaski.

LUCINDA M., born June 12, 1830, in Kentucky, married in Sangamon county to Jackson Kelly, had two children, and Mr. K. died. She then married John Napier, and lives near Camp Butler.

MARY J., born April 17, 1832, in Kentucky, married William Scroggins, had three children, and Mr. S. died. She married Benj. Baker, has five children, and lives in Logan county.

SILAS M., born in Kentucky, died in Sangamon county in his eighteenth year.

SARAH E., born and died in Sangamon county, in her twenty-first year.

JAMES C., born April 11, 1842, in Sangamon county, enlisted in 1861, for three years, in the 32d Ill. Inf., at Springfield, and was killed in battle, April 6, 1862, at Pitsburg Landing, Tenn.

John Greenslate died June 26, 1845, in Sangamon county, and his widow married William Bedinger. See his name.

GREEN, GEORGE M., born Dec. 25, 1809, in Prince William county, Va. He was married Dec. 26, 1833, in Loudon county, to Mary Miller. They had two children, and moved to Sangamon county, Ill., arriving Oct. 2, 1839, near Mechanicsburg, and May 9, 1840, moved south of the Sangamon river into what is now Rochester township, where two children were born. Of their four children—

ANN N., born Sept. 16, 1836, in Loudon county, Va., married Feb. 21, 1856, in Sangamon county, to William H. Rhodes. She died, Sept. 17, 1870, leaving six children, JOHN D., CHARLES W., GEORGE W., MINNIE V., HARRIET E. and MARY O. They live with their father near Rochester.

MARGARET J., born May 10, 1839, in Loudon county, Va., married in Sangamon county to Robert H. Sattley. See his name.

CHARLES F., born June 4, 1842, in Sangamon county, died July 7, 1861.

GEORGE H., born March 5, 1844, in Sangamon county, married in the same county, Dec. 24, 1869, to Catharine Hughes. They have two children, and reside near Coon Creek Postoffice, Barton county, Mo.

Mrs. Mary Green died Aug. 3, 1848, in her native county of Loudon, where she had gone hoping to improve her health. George M. Green was married Jan. 3, 1849, in Sangamon county, to Harriet Sattley. They have eight children—

EMILY F., EDWARD F., JOHN W., MARY E., IDA E., ROBERT W., LEWIS M., and JESSIE L.

George M. Greene and family reside two miles southeast of Rochester.

Mrs. Margaret Green, mother of George M., John, James and William, came to Sangamon county, with her four sons, in the fall of 1839. Her husband, Rolla Green, and her second son, Summer, having died in Virginia. She died in Sangamon county, at the house of her son George M.

GREEN, JOHN, born in Loudon county, Va., came to Sangamon county in 1839, with his mother and brothers, and after a few years stay went to the Wis-cousin lead mines, thence to the northern pineries, and from there to California, in 1854. He now—1874—lives near Merced, California.

GREEN, JAMES, was born Oct. 9, 1830, in Loudon county, Va., and brought by his mother to Sangamon county, in 1839. He was married in Sangamon county, Feb. 18, 1858, to Caroline Horning, who was born Oct. 29, 1836, in Baden, Germany, and came to Sangamon county in 1857. They have five children in Sangamon county, namely—
MARGARET C., EMILY F., GEORGE W., BERTHA and JOHN F., and reside in Sand Prairie, Cooper township, five miles east of Rochester.

GREEN, WILLIAM, born in Loudon county, Va., was brought by his mother to Sangamon county, in 1839, is unmarried, and lives east of Rochester.

GREEN, GEORGE, was born about 1800, in Lexington, Ky. He was married in Kentucky to Nancy Danley, and had three children there. They moved to Sangamon county, Ill., about 1830, and settled in what is now Clear Lake township, where they had four living children. Of their seven children—
ELIZABETH, born in Kentucky, came with her parents to Sangamon county, went to Missouri on a visit, and was there married to William Lee, and died there, leaving several children.
VIRGINIA died at sixteen years of age.
DANIEL M., born in Kentucky, died in Sangamon county, Oct. 27, 1861, unmarried.
MELINDA A., born in Sangamon county, married Cyrus Spousler. She died Sept. 9, 1860, in Sangamon county, leaving one child, ALICE, who resides with her father, in Iowa.
GEORGE W., born in Sangamon county, married Lydia Turner, in Macon county. Mr. Green died March 5, 1874, leaving a widow and ten children at Harristown. G. W. Green was a soldier in the 10th Ill. Cav.
MARY S., born Oct. 6, 1839, in Sangamon county, married Sept. 2, 1860, at the residence of Rev. Albert Hale, in Springfield, to Henry P. Hankins, who was born Oct. 31, 1831, in Mercer county, N. J. They had four children. AMELIA T. and IDA MAY died in infancy.

HENRY T. died Nov. 4, 1871, in his ninth year. IRVIN T. resides with his parents at Illiopolis. Mr. Hankins is a manufacturer of and dealer in cabinet furniture.
Mrs. Nancy Green died Oct. 9, 1839, and George Green died Nov. 17, 1862, both in Sangamon county. George Green was a soldier in the Black Hawk war.

GREEN, JOSIAH, was born in 1800, in South Carolina. Rebecca Long was born in South Carolina also. The father of each of them were Baptist preachers. Josiah Green and Rebecca Long were married in Kentucky. They had six children there, and the family moved to Sangamon county, arriving in 1828, in what is now Mechanicsburg township, where five children were born. Of their ten children—
CATHARINE E., born in Kentucky, married in Sangamon county, in her fifteenth year, to Hugh Dickerson. See his name.
JOHN L., born in Kentucky, married in Sangamon county, July 28, 1848, to Martha D. Giger. He was a traveling preacher in the M. E. Church for seven years, and died Feb., 1850. His widow married Lewis Eyman. See Giger family.
WILLIAM H., born in Kentucky, married in Sangamon county to Sarah E. Burch. They have one living child, LULU, and reside at Kearney Junction, Nebraska.
ELIZA A., born in Kentucky, married in Sangamon county to Robert T. Penn, have ten children, and live near Frankfort, Ky.
LEANDER, born in Kentucky, married in Sangamon county, Nov. 5, 1852, to Mary E. Baker. They have two living children. Mr. Green served three years as Lieutenant and Quartermaster in the 41st Ill. Inf., and now resides at Medoc, Missouri.
SOWEL M., born in Sangamon county, spent several years in California, returned, and was married in Sangamon county to Eliza Keller. She died June 11, 1864, leaving one child. Mr. Green was married in 1867 to Mary Powell. They have three children, and live in Sullivan, Moultrie county.

SAMUEL, born in Sangamon county, married Mary McIntyre, have six children, and live in Gainesville, Texas.

MARTHA A., born August 9, 1835, in Sangamon county, married at Mechanicsburg, Jan. 9, 1856, to Samuel K. Skeen, who was born Dec. 31, 1828, in Rockbridge county, Va. They have four children, namely: ARABELLA, born Feb. 24, 1857, married Dec. 28, 1873, to Samuel Hearing, a native of Reading, Pennsylvania. They live in Springfield. ELLA M., ROLVIN B. and JENNIE MAUD reside with their parents, at Illiopolis. Mr. Skeen is Station and Express Agent of the T., W. and W. R. R. at that place.

FRANCIS M., born May, 1839, in Sangamon county, married in Moultrie county to Caroline Steutsman, and she died in 1860. He enlisted in 1861 in the 7th Ill. Inf., for three years; served full term. He then raised Co. I, 41st Ill. Inf., was commissioned 1st Lieutenant, and promoted to Captain. Served to the end of the rebellion, and was honorably discharged. He was married Sept., 1865, in Smithland, Ky., to Hannah Richardson. They have four children, and his family reside near Hutchison, Kan.

ELIZABETH, born May 28, 1841, in Sangamon county, married Mr. Snyder, and died six months after marriage, at Sullivan, Ill.

Mrs. Rebecca Green died Aug. 11, and Mr. Green married March, 1848, to Mrs. Eliza Smith, whose maiden name was Burch. She died, and Josiah Green died August 11, 1855, all in Sangamon county.

GREGORY, GEORGE, was born Jan. 7, 1808, at Ripley, Derbyshire, England. Sarah Knowles was born Sept. 15, 1810, at Brackenfield, and they were married, June 6, 1830, at Matlack, all in Derbyshire. They had one child at Brackenfield, and Mr. Gregory came to America alone, landing at Philadelphia, in March, 1832. After about fourteen months spent in building steam engines, he returned to England, to learn that his family had already sailed for America. He came back at once to Philadelphia. They had two children in Chester county, Penn., and came to Sangamon county, Ill., arriving late in the fall of 1836, at Springfield, where they had one living child, and the family moved to a farm he had previously purchased, five miles west of Springfield, and north of Spring creek, where they had six living children. Of the ten children—

GEORGE, Jun., born Feb. 2, 1832, at Breckenfield, Derbyshire, England, was killed Jan. 1, 1842, by a horse running away with him while he was riding from Springfield to the farm.

ISAAC, born Nov. 6, 1834, in Pennsylvania, was married in Sangamon county, in 1856, to Susan Ray. They had four children, SAMUEL, ISAAC and THOMAS, twins, and ALBERT. Mrs. Susan Gregory died, and Isaac Gregory married Delia V. Moore. They have one child, FANNIE, and live near Macon, Macon county, Ill.

SAMUEL, born Sept. 30, 1836, in Pennsylvania, married in Sangamon county to Harriet Wardaugh. They had two children, and Mrs. Harriet G. died. Mr. Gregory was killed, Jan. 11, 1868, by being thrown from a horse, in Macon county. His two children, SARAH and EMMA, live with their grandfather Gregory.

JACOB, born Sept. 23, 1838, in Springfield, Ill., married Laura Stone. They have two children, MARY and GEORGE, and live near Macon.

BENJAMIN, born Jan. 12, 1842, the first on Spring creek, died in his fifth year.

ELIZABETH, born Jan. 25, 1844, in Sangamon county, married April 26, 1862, to William Day, a native of Louisiana. They have three children, EDWARD, ORLAND and SUSAN, and live with her parents.

MARY, born April 25, 1848, in Sangamon county, married Benjamin Wallace. They have two children, GRACIE and STELLA, and live in Keokuk, Iowa.

EMMA, born April 13, 1852,

ELIZA, born Jan. 6, 1854,

GEORGE, Jun., born Dec. 28, 1856, live with their parents.

George Gregory commenced work in Philadelphia, in the machine shops belonging to the State of Pennsylvania, in connection with the first railroad built in that State, which is now the Pennsylvania Central Railroad. He assisted to remove the first five locomotives that came from England, from the ships, and put them to work on the road in 1832. The people were afraid of the engines, and when the first eighty-two miles were built, from Philadelphia to Columbia, the passenger trains were run by horses; locomotives being used to draw the freight trains only. Parties interested in stage lines, taking advantage of the general distrust, caused placards to be published, with cuts representing the blowing up of locomotives, with the air full of legs and arms of human beings. Mr. Gregory remembers that a *stage* overturned, and *killed* four passengers, between Lancaster and Harrisburg. They were members of the Legislature, and their bodies were put on board a freight train, at Lancaster, and taken back to Philadelphia for interment. Mr. Gregory grimly remarked that they were the first *passengers* ever drawn by a locomotive over that road.

After working three years in connection with that road, rather than submit to a reduction of his wages, from $80 per month, Mr. Gregory came to Springfield, in 1836, and engaged in blacksmithing on his own account, running six fires. He was afterwards induced to take charge of the engines on the Northern Cross, now part of the Toledo, Wabash & Western railroad. He ran the road for about three years, and in the capacity of engineer, with T. M. Averitt as fireman, ran a locomotive from Jacksonville to Springfield, arriving Feb. 15, 1842, *being the first railroad engine that ever entered the Capitol of the State of Illinois.* Mr. Gregory long since abandoned railroading, and has for many years been a successful farmer. He resides five miles west of Springfield.

GREGORY, JAMES, was born about 1784, in New York City, and was married to Mrs. Abigail Johnson, whose maiden name was Carter. She had six children by her first husband. *JOEL JOHNSON*, of the Revere House in Springfield, is the only one of them that ever came to Sangamon county. *See his name.* Mr. and Mrs. Gregory had four children in New York, and in 1819 or 20, moved to Gallatin county, Ill., and from there to Sangamon county, arriving Dec. 31, 1824, in what is now Rochester township. Of their four children—

DELIA ANN, born Sept., 1808, in New York, married in Gallatin county to Nelson Alley. They moved to Sangamon county in 1829, had five children, and moved to Monmouth, Ill., where Mr. Alley died. The widow and children reside there.

CLARA ANN, born April 2, 1810, in New York, married in Sangamon county to Henry C. Stafford. *See his name.* He died, and she married David Crouch. *See his name.*

WILLIAM, born Oct. 12, 1812, in New York, married in 1837, in Sangamon county, to Martha Asbury, had four children, and he died March 8, 1855, near Rochester. His family moved to Missouri.

JAMES, Jun., born Sept., 1817, in New York died in Sangamon county, March 4, 1834.

James Gregory died May, 1834, and Mrs. Abigail Gregory died Dec. 25, 1847, both in Rochester township.

GROESBECK, CORNELIUS, was born March 1, 1817, in Rensselaer county, N. Y. He was there married, Feb. 14, 1838, to Rebecca Brown, who was born Jan. 13, 1817, in New York also. They moved to Springfield, Ill., arriving Oct. 25, 1839, had three living children in Springfield, namely:

HARRIET, born Sept. 18, 1840,

IDA, born in 1853, and

MARY, born in 1862, all live with their parents in Springfield.

Mr. Groesbeck has three brothers who were early settlers in Sangamon county. Nicholas and Stephen live in Utah City, Utah Territory, and Jacob lives in Missouri.

GROVE, JOHN R., was born August 28, 1805, in Montgomery county, Ky. Maria L. Grooms was born Feb. 11, 1812, in the same county. They were married in Mt. Sterling, Ky., Feb. 14, 1832, and had two children in Bath county. The family moved to Sangamon county, Ill., arriving late in 1835, in what is now the northeast corner of Chatham township, where they had two children. Of their four children—

ELIZABETH C., born July 15, 1833, in Bath county, Ky., married in Sangamon county to Andrew T. Thompson. *See his name.*

SARAH E., born Jan. 11, 1835, in Bath county, Ky., married in Sangamon county to William O. Jones. They had five children: CHARLES L., FREDERICK O., MARIA L., ALBERT

HALE and EDNA G. Mr. Jones died Dec., 1873, near Decatur, and his family reside there.—1874.

LOUISA J., born April 17, 1837, in Sangamon county, married about 1860, in Decatur, to Noah Matkin. They had two children, OTTO and JOHN. Mr. Matkin died in 1868, and his family reside in Greencastle, Ind.

MARIA E., born Jan. 15, 1843, in Sangamon county, died Nov. 26, 1858, in Jacksonville, Ill., while attending school there.

Mrs. Maria L. Grove died Nov. 7, 1844, and Mr. Grove was married Sept. 21, 1846, to Priscilla M. Thompson. They had one child—

JOHN H., born Dec. 5, 1847, and died Dec. 18, 1862.

John R. Grove died Sept. 20, 1849, in Mechanicsburg. His widow married Rev. Joseph M. Grout. *See sketch of the Thompson family.*

GROVE, HENRY, born Oct. 20, 1784, at Ephrata, Lancaster county, Penn. His father, Jacob Grove, moved to Dauphin county, Penn., nine miles east of Harrisburg, about the year 1800. The ancestors of this family came from Germany and settled at Ephrata, Lancaster county, Penn., about 1725. They spelled their name Graff, and were seventh day Baptists. As early as 1728, there was a church of that order established at the aforesaid place, as the church records still show. There are deeds of land at Ephrata, bought by Abraham Graff, dated 1760. He had five children, and died in Lancaster county in 1788. His son Jacob, born in 1751, wrote his name Groff, and there are many of his descendants still living in Lancaster county, Penn., who adhere to that spelling. He married Nancy Kneisley, of Ephrata, about 1780. They had sixteen children, one of whom was Henry, the subject of this sketch. He spelled his name Grove, and the change to Groves has since been made. Henry Grove was married in Hummelstown, Dauphin county, Penn., June 7, 1808, to Eve Hammaker, who was born Jan. 9, 1791, in that county. They had twelve living children there. He and his family moved to Springfield, Ill., arriving Nov. 1, 1836, and in March, 1837, moved into what is now Williams township. Of their twelve children—

ADAM, born March 16, 1809, in Pennsylvania, was married at Xenia, Ohio, to Sarah A. T. Horn, and came to Springfield, Ill., in 1830, preceding his father six years. They had seven children, and Mr. G. died at Athens, Ill., in 1851. His widow married John England. *See his name.* One only of Adam Groves' children reside in Sangamon county, viz— JOHN H., born in 1837, in Springfield, is unmarried, and resides at Williamsville.

JACOB, born in 1811, in Pennsylvania, was married about 1817, in Harrisburg, Penn., to Barbara Phillips. They came to Sangamon county, where they had one living child, LYDIA A. She married Robert McClelland, Jun. *See his name.* Jacob Groves died about April, 1865, and his widow died in the autumn of 1870.

SUSAN, born July 28, 1815, near Harrisburg, was married Dec., 1838, in Sangamon county, to John W. Constant. *See his name.*

JOHN, born Feb. 27, 1817, in Dauphin county, Penn., was married Nov. 9, 1865, at Williamsville, to Pauline Keck, who was born in 1843. They have two children, HENRY C. and BARBARA C., and live at Elkhart, Logan county, Ill.

HENRY, born in 1819, in Pennsylvania, married Feb., 1844, to Sarah Fleming, of Scott county, Ill., and died in June, 1844, leaving a widow without children.

ELIZA, born Dec. 27, 1820, in Pennsylvania, was married Dec. 23, 1847, in Sangamon county, to Andrew Lester. Mr. Lester died in 1859, and his widow died in 1866, both in Williamsville.

GEORGE, born Sept. 22, 1822, in Hummelstown, Penn., was married Nov. 26, 1844, in Fancy Creek township, Sangamon county, to Jane Brown, who was born April 29, 1826. They had six living children: JAMES H., born Oct. 8, 1847, was married March, 1871, in Williamsville, to Mary A. Constant, daughter of G. W. Constant. *See his name.* They have one child, FRANK, and live near Williamsville. JOHN W., born June 13, 1849, was married in Williamsville, Dec. 24, 1875, to Isabel J. Shick. They live in Chicago. GEORGE A., born April 19, 1851, lives in Williamsville, Ill. ISAAC F., MARY E. and EDWIN L. reside with their parents, in Chicago, Ill.

NANCY, born Dec. 25, 1824, in Dauphin county, Penn., was married in Sangamon county, Ill., in 1844, to Shelby Starr. See his name.

SARAH, born Jan. 1, 1828, in Penn., was married in Sangamon county, Aug. 12, 1849, to James Lester. They had ten living children—HENRIETTA, MATTIE, the latter was married, in 1872, to Edward Vanmeter. See his name. BARBARA A., ANDREW J., GEORGE W., CLARA B., LYDIA A., JAMES N., WALTER S. and ELMER G. James Lester and family reside one mile northeast of Williamsville.

ISAAC, born Jan. 25, 1830, at Harrisburg, Penn., was married June 5, 1851, in Sangamon county, to Lucinda Alexander, daughter of Henry Alexander. They had six children, three of whom died young. SUSANNAH, born May 31, 1854, was married Feb., 1872, in Williamsville, to John McClelland. They have two living children, and reside near Williamsville. HENRY A. and ISAAC N. live with their parents, at Chicago, Illinois.

AFFINDA, born July 28, 1833, in Pennsylvania, was married Oct., 1861, in Sangamon county, to Alanson Albright. They have seven children, SUSAN, GEORGE, CHARLES, CATHARINE, FREDERICK, AARON and MARY, and live near Roseville, Vermilion county, Ill.

RACHEL C., born July 28, 1835, in Pennsylvania, was married in Sangamon county to James H. Taylor. See his name.

Mrs. Eve Groves died Nov. 6, 1862, and Henry Groves died Jan. 7, 1863, both in Sangamon county, Ill., near Williamsville.

GRUBB, SAMUEL, was born July 23, 1819, in Loudon county, Va. He went to Catawba, Clarke county, Ohio, in 1838, and to Sangamon county Ill., in the fall of 1839. After one or two visits back to Virginia, and three years spent in California, Samuel Grubb was married Nov. 19, 1853, in Rochester, to Adaline E. Lock. They have eight living children— SAMUEL C., JESSIE A., RACHEL J., ALBERT C., WILLIAM O., OSCAR B., CROMARTIE J. and JOHN TRACY, and reside two miles northeast of Rochester.

GRUBB, SAMUEL, born May 16, 1794, in Chester county, Penn., married in Perry county, Penn., to Ann Rogers, who was born about 1798 in the same State. They had six living children there, and moved to Madison county, Ill., in 1836, and to Springfield, May 10, 1838. Of their children—

HENRY B., born July 31, 1820, was married in Sangamon county, July 3, 1850, to Sarah A. Constant, daughter of Rezin H. Constant. They had six living children: WILLIAM R., AMANDA P., ROBERT, GEORGE and HARLAN R. H. B. Grubb is a bridge builder, and resides in Springfield.

JANE, born Dec. 17, 1821, was married in Springfield to William C. Beam, in August, 1849. They live in Springfield.

RICHARD R., born Jan. 31, 1824, was married in Springfield, May 13, 1852, to Catharine Hawker. She died Dec. 2, 1852, and he was married May 8, 1854, in Sangamon county, to Matilda Rusk, a daughter of Benj. F. Rusk. Richard R. Grubb died Jan. 28, 1862, and his widow died March 30, 1871, leaving one child, MARGARET J., who lives with her aunt, Jane Beam.

SAMUEL and WILLIAM, twins, born March 18, 1827.

SAMUEL, was married April 27, 1855, in Springfield, to Elizabeth Drennan. They had two living children, namely: SAMUEL, is a clerk in the Postoffice in Springfield. FLORA lives with her mother. Samuel Grubb died Dec. 3, 1873, and his widow and children reside in Springfield, Ill.

WILLIAM Grubb, the other twin, died in May, 1857.

MARY A., born April 16, 1834, was married about 1854, in Springfield, to Willis H. Whitehurst, a native of Kentucky. They had one child, WILLIAM H., who is a railroader, and lives in Rock Island.

Mrs. Ann Grubb died July 14, 1873, in Springfield, Ill. Samuel Grubb was a Fife Major in the war of 1812. He built many bridges in Sangamon and adjoining counties, and had the reputation of being a skillful workman. He died August 26, 1875, in Springfield, Illinois.

—44

EXPLANATION:—For the convenience of those consulting this volume, the explanation is again inserted, by which it may be known what generation of a family any person belongs to, by the kind of type used in printing his or her name. Original early settlers or heads of families are in LARGE LETTERS; second generation, *ITALIC CAPITALS*; third, in CAPITALS; fourth, in SMALL CAPITALS; fifth, in *Italics*.

H

HAINES, CHRISTOPHER, was born July 4, 1795, in Russell county, Va. His parents soon after moved to Allen county, Ky. He was married in that county, Oct. 12, 1815, to Myrah Gatewood, who was born June 9, 1797, in Alabama, and partly raised in Georgia. They had two children in Allen, and moved to Barren county, where five children were born, thence to Sangamon county, Ill., arriving Oct. 22, 1829, in what is now Cotton Hill township, where they had three children. Of their ten children—

NANCY W., born Aug. 11, 1816, in Allen county, Ky., was married in Sangamon county, Ill., to Samuel D. Snodgrass. See his name.

JOHN G., born Jan. 5, 1818, in Allen county, Ky., was married in Springfield, Feb. 20, 1840, to Mary A. Palmer, who was born March 5, 1820, in East St. Louis. Her parents came from Oswego, N. Y. She was educated at Rock Spring Seminary, Ill., and came to Springfield in Jan., 1835. They had eight children, five of whom died under five years of age. HESTER A., born July 29, 1841, was married May 22, 1859, to A. J. Maxfield, who was born July 29, 1837, at Cambridge, Ohio. They have two living children, WILLIAM O. and VIRGINIA T., and live in Cotton Hill township. DOCIA C., born April 15, 1843, was married Oct. 6, 1866, to John R. Moore. She died Jan. 8, 1873. MARTHA J., born Jan. 15, 1854, was married June 12, 1873, to A. B. Allen, and live at Roodhouse. Mrs. Mary A. Haines died Jan. 31, 1874, and John G. Haines was married, Sept. 7, 1874, to Eliza P. Criteser. They have one child, WINFORD I. J. G. Haines enlisted in Springfield, Ill., April, 1861, in the 7th Ill. Inf., for three months, and was discharged at Paducah, Ky., re-enlisted in 2nd Ill. Art., served one year and one day. He and his family live in Cotton Hill township, ten miles southeast of Springfield. He has served eight years as Justice of the peace.

SAMUEL, born July 5, 1820, in Barren county, Ky., was married in Sangamon county, Ill., May 10, 1842, to Mrs. Matilda J. Stout, whose maiden name was William. They had six children; two died in infancy. THOMAS M. died August 28, 1868, in the twentieth year of his age. He was a member of the High school in Springfield at the time. SAMUEL G. died in his fifth year. MARY P. and SARAH V. reside with their parents, in Springfield, Illinois.

MARIA, born Sept. 2, 1822, in Barren county, Ky., was married Jan. 8, 1840, in Sangamon county, Ill., to Eri Darwin. She died May 4, 1841, leaving one child, LAURA, who has been twice married, and is now the wife of James Masterson. They live in Washington Territory, and have four children.

FLETCHER born Nov. 5, 1824, in Barren county, Ky., was a soldier in the Mexican war from Sangamon county, under Col. E. D. Baker. He married Lucinda J. Hatler, who died, leaving one child, JAMES WM., who married Susan Kessler, and lives in Taylorville. Mr. F. Haines married Lydia Anderson. They have five children, MILLARD F., ELIZABETH, MARY J., EDITH and SHERMAN, and live near Taylorville.

JAMES M., born Nov. 23, 1826, in Barren county, Ky., brought up in Sangamon county, was married May 24, 1853, in Christian county, Ill., to Mira O. Ricks, who was born Oct. 31, 1835, in Trigg county, Ky. They had six living children in Sangamon county, Ill. ALICE E., BENETTIE L., MARGARET E., ULYSSES G., IDA M. and ARTHUR G. reside with their parents, at the homestead settled by Mr. Haines' parents in 1830, in Cotton Hill township, at the junction of Horse creek and the South Fork timber, ten miles southeast of Springfield, near New City, Ill.

DOCIA, born June, 1829, in Barren county, Ky., was married in Sangamon county, Ill., to John B. Ricks, who was born Nov. 14, 1831, in Trigg county, Ky.

They have five children: JAMES B., born Dec. 25, 1852, was married Dec. 23, 1872, in Bloomington, to Pammie L. Geltmacher. They have one child, and live in Taylorville. He is a lawyer, and engaged in practice there. HENRIETTA L., LAURA B., MARGARET E. and QUINTUS A. reside with their parents in Taylorville. John B. Ricks has served one term or more as sheriff of Christian county, was a representative of that county in the legislature of 1867, and aided in enacting the law for building the present State House, and is now—1876—clerk of the circuit court of Christian county.

FRANCIS A., born March 22, 1832, in Sangamon county, went to Oregon in 1852, returned in 1859, and was married, Jan. 17, 1859, at Princeton, Bureau county, Ill., to Zerilda A. Britt, and now—1876—live at New City, Sangamon county, Ill.

BENJAMIN K., born Aug. 20, 1834, in Sangamon county, enlisted April 18, 1861, for three months, in Co. G, 7th Ill. Inf., served until July 25, 1861, enlisted in the 2d Ill. Art., for three years, served full term, re-enlisted as a veteran, and served to the end of the rebellion, in 1865, when he was honorably discharged. He was married, June 9, 1873, to Nancy J. Haines, and lives near Palmer, Christian county.

WILLIAM F., born Oct. 23, 1839, in Sangamon county, was married, May 17, 1858, to Burrilla Ashford, who was born March 8, 1840, in Allen county, Ky. Mr. Haines enlisted April 18, 1861, in Co. G, 7th Ill. Inf., for three months, served until July 5, 1861, when he was discharged for physical disability. Mr. and Mrs. Haines had three children, THOMAS E., the eldest, died in his fourth year. LENA L., the youngest, died in infancy. ETTA FRANCES, born Aug. 24, 1864, lives with her parents in Springfield, Ill.

Christopher Haines died March 29, 1850, and Mrs. Myrah Haines died Nov. 11, 1859, both on the farm where they settled in 1830.

HALBERT, DR. JAMES, was born Aug. 19, 1785, in Essex county, near Port Royal, Va. Nancy Reynolds was born in the same county, and they were married there Dec. 24, 1816. They had six children and moved to Ross county, near Chillicothe, Ohio, about 1831, where one child was born. Mrs. Nancy Halbert died there in Nov., 1834. The family moved to Sangamon county, Ill., arriving at Springfield in the fall of 1839, and a few weeks later settled in what is now Clear Lake township. Of their eight children—

MARY L., born Nov. 15, 1817, in Essex county, Va., married March 31, 1836, in Ohio, to Eli Harbert, who was born Aug. 11, 1811, and moved at once to the vicinity of West Point, Tippecanoe county, Ind., where two children were born, and Mr. Harbert died there Nov. 29, 1839. The widow came with her two children to the house of her father, in Sangamon county, in Jan., 1840, where one child was born. Of her three children—SAMUEL M., born May 31, 1837, near West Point, Tippecanoe county, Ind., married in Sangamon county, Dec. 25, 1862, to Serilda Miller, who was born Feb. 14, 1844, in Sangamon county. They have two living children, JOHN and ANNA, and live four miles northwest of Illiopolis. NANCY R., born Sept. 11, 1838, near West Point, Tippecanoe county, Ind., married in Sangamon county, Sept. 14, 1858, to Amariah D. Gilbert, who was born April 10, 1828, in Portage county, Ohio. They have three children, ELI J., OLLIE M. and FANNIE J. Mr. Gilbert was appointed, April 1, 1869, Postmaster at Illiopolis, and continues to hold the office—1876. ELI C., born Feb. 3, 1840, in Sangamon county, after the death of his father. He enlisted July 25, 1862, in Co. I, 114th Ill. Inf., was captured after the battle of Guntown, Miss., June, 1864, and spent six months in Andersonville prison. After that he was in other prisons, and was honorably discharged Aug. 3, 1865. He was married in Sangamon county, Sept. 21, 1870, to Mary E. Griggs, who was born March 11, 1849, at Leroy, Ill. They have two children, MINNIE PEARL and HENRY OTIS, and live four miles northwest of Illiopolis. Mrs. Mary Harbert was married in Sangamon county to Rezin H. Constant. See his name. She died May 18, 1863.

SALLY, born Jan. 23, 1820, in Virginia, married in Sangamon county to James S. Taylor. See his name.

SIDNEY R., born Feb. 3, 1822, in

Virginia, married in Sangamon county to John C. Woltz. *See his name.*

FANNY, born June 22, 1825, in Virginia, married in Sangamon county to Thomas L. Simpson. *See his name.*

KITTY, born Nov. 19, 1827, in Virginia, married in Sangamon county to Ninian R. Taylor. *See his name.*

ALEXANDER S., born June 15, 1830, in Essex county, Va., came with his father to Sangamon county, was educated at Illinois College, in Jacksonville, graduated at Jefferson Medical College, N. Y., and was married, May 8, 1855, to Mary E. Latham, Dr. A. S. Halbert died Feb. 11, 1859, leaving one child, KATIE TODD. His widow and child reside with her mother on seventh street, Springfield.

MARGARET J., born Sept. 13, 1833, in Ohio, married in Sangamon county to Isaac J. Taylor. *See his name.*

Dr. James Halbert died Nov. 5, 1858, in Sangamon county. He was a regularly ordained minister in the Baptist church. Dr. Halbert was among the first to introduce sheep raising into Sangamon county, and was *the first* in Clear Lake township. He was a man of great energy, strong intellectual abilities, and great originality of mind.

HALE, ALBERT, was born Nov. 29, 1799, in Glastenbury, Hartford county, Conn. At the age of fourteen years he became a clerk in a store in Wethersfield, Conn., remaining eight years. During that time he embraced religion. He attended Yale College, and graduated there in 1827, and then commenced studying for the ministry. He next became an agent of the American Tract Society, spending one and a half years in South Carolina, Florida and Georgia, part of the time in Sunday school work among the "Sand hills" of the latter State. He returned to Yale, was licensed and ordained to preach in 1830, by the New Havan Association East—Congregational. After preaching a few months in the vicinity of Boston, making his home in the family of Rev. Dr. Lyman Beecher, he came west, landing at Shawneetown, Ill., Nov. 11, 1831, remained there a few weeks, and went to Greenville, Bond county, and made his home in the McCord settlement, where he labored half the time and spent the other half traveling over the State, doing the work of an evangelist, for about eight years. During that time he visited Springfield a few times. He received a call from the Second Presbyterian Church, to become its pastor, and accepting the call, he came and entered upon its duties in 1839. Rev. Albert Hale was married April, 1839, at what is now Godfrey, Madison county, Ill., to Abiah Chapin, a teacher in Monticello Female Seminary at that place. They had three children, all born in Springfield.

CATHARINE and
SOPHIA reside with their father.

ALBERT F., born Oct. 2, 1844, in Springfield, graduated at Yale College in 1866, studied theology, and was licensed and ordained to preach by Springfield Presbytery in 1871.

Mrs. Abiah Hale died Jan., 1865, in Springfield. Rev. Albert Hale was pastor of the Second Presbyterian Church in Springfield for twenty-seven years, until 1866, when, in consequence of the infirmities of age, he resigned. He continues to preach, both in city and county, as his strength will permit, and resides in Springfield.

HALL, DAVID, was born Dec. 25, 1799, in Shelby county, near Shelbyville, Ky. David Hall and Juliet Owen were there married, Dec. 23, 1823. They had six children in Shelby county, and moved to Sangamon county, Ill., arriving Sept. 23, 1834, at Mechanicsburg, and soon after settled about four miles further west, in the same township, where five children were born. Of their eleven children—

GEORGE M., born Oct. 10, 1824, in Kentucky, died in Mechanicsburg, Oct. 26, 1852.

MARY M., born Dec. 31, 1825, in Kentucky, married Sept. 18, 1845, in Sangamon county, to Wesley Hathaway. *See his name.*

OWEN, born Jan. 11, 1828, in Kentucky, died Nov. 6, 1847, in Sangamon county.

DAVID S., born Jan. 9, 1830, in Kentucky, married in Sangamon county, March 15, 1855, to Elizabeth J. Fullinwider. They had five children. The second, ADA G., died in her second year GEORGIA E., CHARLIE B., ED

WIN P. and JACOB F. live with their parents in Mechanicsburg.

WILLIAM, born Dec. 22, 1831, in Kentucky, married Sept. 30, 1856, in Sangamon county, to Sarah A. Mantle. They had one child, EVA MAY, who died at seven years of age. Mrs. Sarah A. Hall died in March, 1863, and William Hall was married June 13, 1871, in Shelby county, Ky., to Fannie Saunders, a native of that county. He is a merchant in Mechanicsburg, and resides there.

ALLEN, born Oct. 31, 1833, in Shelby county, Ky., married in Sangamon county, March 13, 1862, to Rachel A. Mantle, who was born Nov. 3, 1838, in Fayette county, Ohio. They have one child, CARRIE MAY, and reside in Mechanicsburg. Mr. Hall is a merchant there.

ISABEL, born Feb. 22, 1836, in Sangamon county, married John H. Fullinwider. See his name.

PRESTON, born Feb. 7, 1838, in Sangamon county, married March 12, 1867, at Mt. Sterling, Ky., to Sarah L. Davis, who was born there, August 28, 1840. They had four children, OWEN D., ELIZA E., HARRISON P. and ARVIL C. Mrs. Sarah L. Hall died in 1875, and Preston Hall lives near Mechanicsburg.

HENRY H., born Dec. 13, 1840, in Sangamon county, studied at the Hahnemann Medical College, Chicago, and is a practicing physician at Pana.—1874.

HATTIE E., born April 12, 1844, in Sangamon county, married May 10, 1870, to John C. O'Conner. They had one child that died in infancy in 1872. J. C. O'Conner was born Feb. 16, 1845, at Fredonia, Licking county, Ohio. He enlisted August 4, 1862, for three years, in Co. C, 124th Ill. Inf., at Camp Butler. In August, 1863, he was detailed to take charge of the regimental medical stores, and was detailed in April, 1865, as Medical dispenser for Post Hospital, at Montgomery, Ala. He was mustered out with his regiment at Chicago, in Sept., 1865. He studied medicine at Ann Arbor, Mich., in 1867 and '8, and is now a druggist at Buffalo.

EVELINE O., born April 18, 1845, died August 28, 1849.

David Hall died April 25, 1864, in Mechanicsburg, and his widow, Mrs. Juliet Hall, resides with her daughter, Mrs. O'Conner, at Buffalo, Sangamon county, Illinois.

HALL, BENJ. LOGAN, brother to David Hall, was born Jan. 6, 1806, in Shelby county, Ky. He was there married Jan. 6, 1831, to Eveline Pickrell. They had one child in Kentucky, and moved to Sangamon county, Ill., arriving in Sept., 1833, in what is now Mechanicsburg township, where ten children were born, three died young. Of their eight children—

OLIVER P., born March 11, 1832, in Shelby county, Ky., married in Sangamon county, Jan. 24, 1855, to Susan M. Short, who was born Oct. 14, 1833, in Pickaway county, Ohio, and came to Sangamon county in 1846. They had six children. HARVEY E., the second child, born Oct. 7, 1857, died March 12, 1864. The other five, WILLIAM L., LEWIS B., J. LESLIE, RENA and OSCAR E., live with their parents, one and one-half miles north of Mechanicsburg.

GEORGE W., born Feb. 19, 1836, in Sangamon county, married Jan. 14, 1859, to Eliza G. Hammitt. They had three children, and Mrs. Hall died Nov. 10, 1869. The children, MATTIE B., VIRGINIA M. and ELIZA L., live with their aunt, Mrs. Rev. H. Buck, in Decatur. Geo. W. Hall was married, Aug. 16, 1870, to Laura McNeill, in Mechanicsburg, and in August following, moved to Ottawa, Kansas, where Mr. Hall died Jan. 15, 1872. His widow lives in Mechanicsburg.

MARIA B, born June 18, 1838, married Nov. 16, 1865, to David H. Hall, who was born Jan. 19, 1828, in Shelby county, Ky. They had five children; three died young. EVELYN and FLORENCE, twins, live with their parents in Woodside township, four miles southwest of Springfield.

FRANKLIN, born Aug. 10, 1840, married Sept. 13, 1864, to Cecelia Hanks, in Sangamon county. They had one child, and Mrs. Hall died March 23, 1866. F. Hall and Elizabeth Hanks—sister to his first wife—were married Sept. 18, 1867, in Decatur. They have two children, and live in Taylorville.

WILLIAM T., born Dec. 21, 1841, in Sangamon county, married Jan. 9, 1872, in Jacksonville, Ill., to Florence M. Winn. They live at Salina, Kansas.

HARDIN O., born April 2, 1849, married Oct. 18, 1870, near Mexico, Mo., to Irene Lucky. They have one child, ROBERT L., and live three miles northwest of Mechanicsburg.

MARY L., born Sept. 29, 1851, died Feb. 28, 1866.

EVA F., born July 14, 1855, died Sept. 26, 1867.

BENJAMIN L., Jun. born Sept. 11, 1858, lives with his parents.

Benj. Logan Hall and wife reside in Buffalo, Sangamon county, Ill.

HALL, MRS. ELIZABETH, whose maiden name was Foster, was born in Bedford county, Va., and married there to John Hall. They had five children in Va., and moved to Adair county, Ky., where four children were born, and Mr. Hall died there. His widow and children moved to Sangamon county, Ill., arriving in the fall of 1830, north of Spring creek, and six miles west of Springfield. Mrs. Hall was married there to Samuel Willis, and in 1844 or '5, moved to DeWitt county, where Mr. Willis died. She now lives with her son,

CASWELL HALL, near Leroy, McLean county, Ill. Her son—

JOEL HALL, born Feb. 19, 1821, in Adair county, Ky., came with his mother to Sangamon county in 1830. In 1841 he went to DeWitt county, and was there married to Martha Banta. They moved to Missouri, in 1856, have nine living children, and reside in Eagleville, Harrison county, Mo. Her daughter married Trulove Sparks. See his name.

HALL, MRS. HANNAH, whose maiden name was Cunningham, was born in 1798, in Pendleton county, Va. She was married Nov. 3, 1814, in that county, to Dr. Samuel B. Hall, and they had eight children in Virginia. Dr. Hall died Oct. 16, 1827, and Mrs. Hall, with her children, moved to Sangamon county, Ill, arriving Nov. 20, 1833, in what is now Chatham township, and the next year moved to what is now Loami township. Of her children—

JOHN C., born Feb. 17, 1816, in Virginia, married in Sangamon county, Feb. 20, 1840, to Susan Cutter. They had six living children. ELIZABETH married John W. Joy, who enlisted in Co. I, 73d Ill. Inf, for three years, was discharged on account of physical disability, and died in 1863. Mrs. Joy married John Brigham, has three children, and lives in Travis county, near Onion creek Postoffice, Texas. Mr. Brigham was a Union soldier also. JOHN C., Jun., enlisted in Co. B, 30th Ill. Inf., March 28, 1864, for three years, and was discharged July 14, 1865, at Springfield, Ill. He married Catharine Williamson. They have three children, and live near Onion creek, Texas. SETH R. served six months in the Union army, and now lives in Texas. SARAH C. married Newton Young, and lives near Loami. ADA D. and VIRGINIA D. reside with their parents, near Onion creek Postoffice, Travis county, Texas.

ELIZABETH M., born Oct. 11, 1817, in Virginia, was married Jan. 15, 1838, in Sangamon county, to Harness A. Trumbo. See his name.

WILLIAM C., born May 30, 1819, in Virginia, was married in Sangamon county, April 26, 1849, to Leah Priddy. They had two children, and the parents both died. Their son, SAMUEL B., born Jan. 26, 1850, and LEE, born Oct. 25, 1851, live in Loami township.

JAMES A., born Jan. 23, 1821, in Virginia, was married in Sangamon county, Ill., to Elizabeth McGinnis. They had two children, and mother and children died. Mr. Hall was married Dec. 16, 1852, to Margaret Darneille. They had eight children. ELIZABETH and VIRGINIA died under seven years. JEFFERSON died, aged eight years. The other five, LAURA, HANNAH, JOSEPH, JOHN and JAMES, live with their parents, one half mile east of Loami.

REBECCA A., born Oct. 7, 1822, married James Megredy. See his name.

SAMUEL B., born July 18, 1824, in Virginia, brought up in Sangamon county, Ill., went to California in 1849, returned to Sangamon county in 1874, is unmarried, and lives near Loami.

GEORGE W., born June 18, 1826, in Virginia, died in Sangamon county, unmarried, April 17, 1873.

JOSEPH, born March 19, 1828, in Virginia, raised in Sangamon county, went to California in 1850, is unmarried, and resides near Loami.

Mrs. Hannah Hall was married May 1, 1835, to Adam Trumbo. *See his name.* He died, and she died at the house of her son, James A. Hall, Jan. 30, 1872.

John Cunningham, the father of Mrs. Hannah Hall, was a native of Hardy county, Va. He came with Mrs. Hall, in 1833, to Sangamon county, and died a few years later, near Loami.

HALL, HENRY, was born in 1774, near Hagerstown, Md., and married in Loudon county, Va., to Sally Harper, who was born about 1783. They had five children in Pittsylvania county, Va., and in 1816, the family moved to Martin county, Ind., where three children were born, thence to Sangamon county, Ill., arriving Oct., 1828, in what is now Loami township. Of their eight children—

NANCY, born in 1801, in Virginia, married William Taylor, and had five children—GEORGE W., married Lucinda Turpin, have five children, and live in Christian county, Ill. LOUISA married Wm. Hays, have four children, and live in Shelby county, near Mowequa. SALLY JANE married Peter Workman. *See his name.* NANCY married Jacob Workman. *See his name.* MARY married Ezekiel Preston, have five children, and live in Mowequa, Ill. Wm. Taylor died Aug., 1830, and his widow married David Hays, had four children, and live in Christian county, near Mowequa.

AARON, born Dec. 25, 1802, in Virginia, married Feb. 10, 1825, to Nancy Hays, in Indiana, had two children there, and came with his father to Sangamon county, in 1828, where they had eight children. Of their children—PRISCILLA A., born Sept. 21, 1825; married Henry Jacobs. *See his name.* ELIZA J., born Sept. 20, 1827, married William Hays. Mr. and Mrs. Hays died, leaving three children. JEANETTE died, aged fourteen years. ELIZA JANE married Charles I. Turpin, Jun. *See his name.* CAROLINE F. married Dennis Turpin. *See his name.* ELIZABETH D. married George Jacobs, and both died, in Christian county. HENRY W., WILLIAM and ALFRED T., died under four years. AARON, Jun., born Aug. 25, 1837, in Sangamon county, married Rebecca Turpin, had five children—ELMER E. died young. CHARLES D., THOMPSON A., JAMES M. and JOSEPH E., live with their parents near Loami. NANCY married Asa Turney, and lives in Morgan county. JOHN died at two, and SUSAN at eleven years old. Aaron Hall died Dec. 13, 1851. His widow married, July 6, 1852, to Wm. L. Dodd, and live three and one-half miles south of Loami.

THOMAS, born in Virginia, died in Indiana, aged fifteen years.

WASHINGTON, born May 8, 1809, in Pittsylvania county, Va., married in Sangamon county, Nov. 6, 1831 to Susannah H. Wyckoff. They had nine living children in Sangamon county. JULIA A., born April 23, 1833, married David E. Gibson. *See his name.* THOMAS M. died in his tenth year. JAMES WARREN, born Oct. 16, 1836, married Nov. 22, 1868, to Mary A. Dodd, who was born Dec. 13, 1842, in Bradley county, Tenn. They live four miles south of Loami. MARY J., born March 27, 1838, married Thomas Baker. *See his name.* SUSANNAH H. and JOHN W., twins, born Aug. 16, 1841. SUSANNAH H. married, Jan 22, 1858, to Thomas Cosser, a native of England. He went from Sangamon county to Navarro county, Texas, in Feb., 1860, and Mrs. Cosser went in September following. Mr. Cosser went into partnership with Maj. H. P. Darling, in the business of wool growing. Whilst engaged in sheep shearing, at Laredo, near Ft. McIntosh, Webb county, Tex., in April, 1866, Mr. Cosser, a Mr. Smith and a negro boy were killed by Indians, who made a raid on them and were gone before the soldiers in the fort were aware of their presence. Mr. Darling was killed at the same time, but some miles away. Mrs. Cosser, Mrs. Smith, and a daughter of Maj. Darling, buried the bodies with their own hands. Mrs. Cosser returned to Sangamon county, and was married to Thomas Baker. *See his name.* JOHN W. enlisted in 1862, for three years, in Co. I, 73d Ill. Inf., served full time and was honorably discharged. He was married in Oct., 1873, to Nancy J. Watts. They have one child, FRANK W., and live at Charleston, Ill. ALBERT T. died in his ninth year. CYRUS, born Jan. 5, 1856, and DAVID W., born Feb. 12, 1857, live with their father. Mrs. Susannah H. Hall died March 10, 1867, and Washington Hall resides three and one-half miles south of Loami, on the farm where he settled in 1832. He was the administrator of the estate of his brother-in-law, Wm. Taylor, in 1830. From that time to 1867 he administered on the estates of at least fifty of his deceased neighbors. He filled many local offices, and during the great rebellion, he three times enrolled the names of those subject to military duty in the townships of Talkington and Loami, for the United States Government.

THOMPSON, born Aug. 19, 1811, in Pittsylvania county, Va., married in Sangamon county, Jan. 17, 1839, to Eveline Jacobs. They had eight children, three died young. Of the other five—
WILLIAM T., born Sept. 7, 1841, in Sangamon county, married Nov. 7, 1869, to Jennie Lowry, who was born May 3, 1849, in county Down, Ireland. They have two children, EVA A. and SAMUEL E., and reside four and one-half miles south of Loami. SARAH A. married Wm. G. Miller. See his name. AMANDA married James M. Joy, had two children, WARREN, died in infancy, and IDA E. lives with her parents in Loami township. MARY E. and GEORGE T. live with their parents, three and one-half miles south of Loami.

SALLY A., born in 1821, in Indiana, married in Sangamon county to Andrew Hays, have eight children, and live in Christian county, near Mowequa.

HENRY, Jun., born in 1823, in Indiana, married in Sangamon county to Emeline Wyckoff, had six children, and Mrs. Hall died. Mr. Hall married Margaret McNeely, had three children, and he died in Loami township.

EMILY, born in 1828, in Indiana, married in Sangamon county to James Dobson. She died April 28, 1852.

Henry Hall died Dec. 24, 1846, and his widow died Oct. 22, 1860, both in Loami township.

HAGGARD, HARMON, was born July 13, 1799, near Boonesboro, Clark county, Ky. Sally B. Steele was born May 26, 1804, in the same county. Their parents moved to Christian county, in the same State, where they were married, Nov. 25, 1822, and had two children there. They moved to Sangamon county, arriving in 1830, in what is now Gardner township, where they had four children. Of their six children—

ELIZABETH, born August 6, 1825, married Daniel Whitehead, and died near Joliet, leaving two children.

ZARELDA, born April 12, 1828, in Christian county, Ky., married in Sangamon county, to William P. Hazlitt. See his name.

ROBERT, born August 26, 1833, in Sangamon county, married Elizabeth Ray. See Ray family. She died, and he married again and lives near Labette, Kansas.

MARTIN, born Jan. 2, 1836, married Catharine Tigar, who died, and he lives near Labette, Kansas.

SALLY, born March 14, 1841, married E. J. Robinson, and lives in Labette county, Kansas.

HARMON, Jun., born May 12, 1846.

Mrs. Sally B. Haggard died Sept. 3, 1852, and Harmon Haggard married Mrs. Sarah Humphrey, whose maiden name was Worley. He died August 28, 1874, near where he settled in 1830.

HAM, HEZEKIAH, was born Oct. 1, 1807, in Nicholas county, near Carlisle, Ky. He came to Sangamon county, Ill., in the fall of 1831, and was married Dec. 22, 1837, to Mary A. Arnold. They had six living children in Sangamon county, namely—

MARY J., married March 25, 1858, to Henry T. Zeigler.

JOSEPH C. enlisted in Co. G, 14th Ill. Inf., in 1861, for three years. He was mortally wounded at the battle of Pittsburg Landing, April 6, 1862, and died the next day on the battlefield.

SARAH E., married James Steele, has five children, and lives in Menard county.

JOHN W., born Jan. 8, 1846. He enlisted Dec. 15, 1863, in Co. G., 114th Ill. Inf., for three years, served until March 7, 1865, when he was discharged on account of physical disability. He was married August 29, 1867, to Rebecca Yocom. They had two children. CHARLES E. died in his third year. WILLIAM T. lives with his mother, two miles northwest of Dawson. John Ham died in the spring of 1875.

WILLIAM T., born Dec. 5, 1847, married Jan. 16, 1872, to Alice A. Smith. They have one child, LEWIS, and live near Belle Plain, Sumner county, Kansas.

LAURA F., born Dec. 17, 1852, married John B. Jones, have one child, HARRY, and live in Logan county, near Buffalo Hart Postoffice.

Hezekiah Ham died April 21, 1859, in Sangamon county, and his widow, Mrs. Mary A. Ham, resides with her daughter, Mrs. Jones.

HAMILTON, GEORGE KNOX, was born August 17, 1798, in Davidson county, Tenn. He came, in company with his father, four brothers and two sisters, to Sangamon county, arriving in the fall of 1819, and settled near what is now Bradford Station. He was married March 5, 1823, to Jane Colman. they had three children, namely—

ROBERT F., born Nov. 15, 1824, in Sangamon county, married Oct. 28, 1847, to Tabitha J. Purvines. They had ten children; two died in infancy. FRANCES A. married Abraham Weir. They have two children, NELLIE T. and FRANK MILTON, and reside one mile east of Pleasant Plains. MARY J. married Andrew Zane. See his name. MARTHA E. married Samuel Ayers. SYLVIA H. died April 3, 1876, in her twenty-second year. CLARA M., WILLIAM L., CORDIA A. and KATIE C. reside with their parents, one and a quarter miles northeast of Pleasant Plains. Mr. Robert F. Hamilton has in his possession documents showing that the Richland Primitive Baptist Church was organized Sept. 16, 1820, by Robert Brayle, moderator, and Simon Lindley, clerk. It was the second church of any kind organized in Sangamon county; the first having been effected May 15, 1820, by Elder Stephen England. See his name.

MARTHA M., born March 28, 1827, in Sangamon county, married Azro Emery, in Crawford county, Mo., had two children, and died. Her husband and children reside in Missouri.

GEORGE K., Jun., born April 11, 1829, after the death of his father, raised in Sangamon county, married in Crawford county, Mo., to Nancy Anderson. They had three living children, and both died in Cartwright township. Of the children—WILLIAM F. is a clerk in Springfield. ELLA J. and THEODOSIA B. live with their grandmother Purvines.

George Knox Hamilton died Oct. 14, 1828, in Sangamon county, and his widow married Alexander C. Purvines. See his name.

Robert Hamilton, the father of G. K. Hamilton, was born in North Carolina, married in Tennessee, moved to Pope county, Ill., and was one of the early representatives of that county in the State Legislature, came to Sangamon county in 1819, moved to Arkansas a few years later, and died there in 1833 or '4. His sons and daughters, all except Geo. Knox, left Sangamon county many years ago. Some went to Missouri, and three of them from there to Oregon, where two of them have families, and now reside.

HAMILTON, WILLIAM S., born in New York—a son of Alexander Hamilton, the distinguised Statesman who was slain by Aaron Burr—came to Springfield when it was regarded as the temporary county seat. He was elected one of the representatives of the county in the State Legislature of 1823-4. He was an advocate of the movement to make Sangamo the county seat. After that he went to Galena and engaged in lead mining. On the discovery of gold in California, he went there, and died.

HAMLIN, HENRY N., was born Jan. 30, 1816, in Oneida county, N. Y. He came to Sangamon county in the Spring of 1837, to assist his uncle, Asa Hamlin, who had a contract to build several miles of the Northern Cross—now T., W. & W. R. R. His uncle died in the fall of that year, leaving his contract unfinished. Henry N. had loaned him all his savings from several years school teaching. He not only lost that, but his wages while he was with his uncle, also. On realizing the situation, he went to Morgan county, near Franklin, and resumed his profession as a teacher. He was there married, Dec. 30, 1838, to Eveline Scott. In March, 1839, they moved to Sangamon county, in what is now Chatham township. He engaged in farming, and taught school in the winter. In the spring of 1840 he returned to Morgan county, and remained there until 1847, when he came back to Sangamon county. They had five children—

MARY ANTIONETTE, born Oct. 3, 1839, in Sangamon county, married Dec. 29, 1859, to James N. Puntenney.

—45

They have five children, CHARLES SUMNER, LIZZIE ETTA, MINNIE ETHEL, SARAH EVELINE and a daughter, and live near Butler, Montgomery county, Illinois.

DWIGHT MONSON, born Oct. 23, 1843, in Morgan county, enlisted at Springfield, August, 1862, for three years, in Co. D, 126th Ill. Inf., served to the end of the rebellion, and was honorably discharged in 1865. He was married Jan. 23, 1872, to Anna Chambers, who was born Dec. 6, 1850, near Madison, Ind. They have two children, HENRY NOBLE and CHARLES CARROLL, and live in Springfield.

ERASTUS EMMONS, born July 9, 1845, in Morgan county, raised in Sangamon county, and lives at Centralia, Nemaha county, Kansas.—1874.

FRANCIS L., born June 8, 1848, in Sangamon county, lives with his mother.

LAURA H., born April 10, 1851, in Sangamon county, married Dec. 26, 1871, to Samuel L. Ridgeway, and lives in Atchison county, Mo.

Henry N. Hamlin died July 30, 1853, in Sangamon county, and his widow resides near the centre of Ball township, four and a half miles southeast of Chatham.

H. N. Hamlin was an ordained minister in the M. E. Church, but never entered into the traveling connection. Emmans Hamlin, of Mason & Hamlin, Organ Manufacturers, Boston, and W. Hamlin, manufacturer of the George Wood organ, at Cambridge, Mass., are brothers of Henry N.

HAMMOND, CHARLES, was born about 1767, in Virginia, near where the river Rappahannock empties into Chesapeake Bay. He was there married to Nancy Carter, and had two children. About 1795 they moved to Woodford county, Ky., where twelve children were born. Their fourteen children grew to be men and women. Two died unmarried, and nine of them married in Kentucky, and remained there. One son moved to Sangamon county in 1825, and a son and daughter came with the parents, arriving Sept. 26, 1839, in Island Grove township. Of the three children who came to this county—

JOHN, born in Woodford county, Ky., married there to Nancy Smith, and moved to Sangamon county, Ill., arriving about 1825 in what is now Island Grove township, where they had four living children. FLORINDA married William Fink, and lives in Macoupin county. EMILY married Wilson Moore, has one child, and lives in New Berlin. LUCINDA married Jacob Bartley, and lives in Piatt county. JOHN A. married Miss Hudson, and lives in Piatt county. John Hammond moved, in 1866, to the vicinity of Cerro Gordo, Piatt county, Ill.

EMILY, born in Kentucky, married John Ryan, had one child, and Mr. Ryan died in Dubuque, Iowa. His widow married William Thorpe, and lives at Kingston, Peoria county, Ill.

WILLIAM, born June 1, 1816, in Woodford county, Ky., married March 6, 1842, in Sangamon county, to Emeline Underwood. They had three children— ARTHUR C. enlisted, Aug. 9, 1861, in Co. B, 30th Ill. Inf., for three years, re-enlisted as a veteran, Jan., 1864, served until July 27, 1865, and was honorably discharged at Springfield. He was musician during the whole time; was with Sherman in his "March to the Sea." He lives in Loami. MARY H. married Oct. 1, 1865, to James C. Thralls, who was born Dec. 1, 1843, in Vigo county, Ind. He enlisted, in 1861, in Co. B, 21st Mo. Inf., for three months, enlisted Sept. 1, 1861, in Co. B, 3d Mo. Cav., for three years, served until Feb., 1864, when he was honorably discharged, at St. Louis. Mr. and Mrs. Thralls have three children, OWEN P., FRED C. and ARTHUR, and live in Loami—1874. William Hammond and wife live in Loami—1874.

Charles Hammond moved from Island Grove to Jacksonville, Ill., in March, 1843, and died there, July 4, 1843. His widow died Sept., 1845, at Island Grove.

HARBUR, LEVI, was born Nov. 21, 1797, in Garrard county, Ky. When he was a child his parents moved to Christian county, in the same State. He was there married, June 29, 1817, to Eleanor Ashley, and moved to Madison county, Ill., in Sept. following, accompanied by his wife and his brother Samuel. He left his brother in Madison county, and with his wife went to the southern part of Missouri, remaining one and a half years, and had one child there. He returned to Madison county, where Mrs.

Eleanor Harbur died, Sept. 10, 1819. Leaving his child in the care of a friend, he came to what is now Sangamon county, one and a quarter miles east of the town of Loami. He went eighty miles to Edwardsville, obtained a license, returned to the San-ga-ma country, and was married March 25, 1820, to Mary Sawyers. They had ten living children in Sangamon county. Of his children—

WILLIS, born April 24, 1818, in Southern Missouri, was married in Sangamon county to Elizabeth Darneille. They have five children, and live in Scotland county, Mo.

By the second wife—

DELILAH, born March 9, 1821, married Benjamin Wyckoff, had one child, and Mr. W. died, and she married Peter Ellicott. They have two living children, and live in Scotland county, Mo.

ELIZABETH, born Sept. 13, 1822, married Joseph Farrer, who died, leaving two children, and she married Lorenzo Garner, had several children, and she died near Warsaw, Ill.

REBECCA, born April 2, 1825, married Elza Boyer, had one child, and she and her husband both died.

MARY, born Jan. 8, 1827, married Turner Underwood. See his name. He died and she married Mr. Thompson, and resides at Hamburg, Fremont county, Iowa.

SAMUEL E., born Sept. 10, 1830, married Lucinda Thurman. They have seven children, and live in Greene county, Mo.

WILLIAM R., born Sept. 19, 1832, married Elizabeth Fisher, have six children, and live in Moultrie county, Ill.

NANCY JANE, born Sept. 6, 1835, married Robert Gray, had three children, and Mr. Gray died, and the widow married Miles Meacham, and lives in Warren county, Ill.

MARION D., born Sept. 21, 1842, married Martha Meacham. She died, leaving one child, and he married Sarah Meacham. They have one child, and live in Warren county, Ill.

SARAH A., born Feb. 16, 1845, married Martin Landgrebe, have four children, and live in Moultrie county, Ill.

LEVI M., born August 5, 1848, lives with his father.—1873.

Mrs. Mary Harbur died Sept. 8, 1857, and Levi Harbur was married Oct. 1, 1861, to Frances Young. They have two living children—

ELISHA Y. and

ORA ELLEN, live with their parents on the farm where Mr. H. settled in 1827. It is three miles south of New Berlin.

Levi Harbur says that the snow of 1830–31 was three feet four inches on an average, and that he resolved if it ever went off, Illinois would not hold him long. The snow went off, but he did not. I have measured a stump near where Mr. H. resides. It is white oak, eight feet high and two feet in diameter at the top. Mr. Harbur says he cut it not more than two feet above the snow, so that the snow must have been six feet deep at that place, but that was drifted. It will be seen that the two brothers spell the family name differently; each claim to be right.

HARBOUR, SAMUEL, was born Sept. 24, 1799, in Garrard county, Ky., and was taken by his parents, in infancy, to Christian county. In 1817 he accompanied his brother Levi to Madison county, Ill., and from there he came to what is now Chatham township, Sangamon county, arriving Oct., 1819. He was married March, 1823, to Elizabeth Briscoe. They had one child—

ELIZABETH, born Jan. 26, 1824, married James McBride. They had five children, and she died, April 5, 1854, leaving her family in Brown county, Ill.

Mrs. Elizabeth Harbour died Feb., 1824, and Samuel Harbour and Elizabeth Lindley were married July 28, 1826. They had nine children—

LEVI, born March 11, 1827, married Jan. 27, 1847, to Cynthia Bilyen. They have ten children—ANNA married Samuel Workman. See his name. SAMUEL married Mary Workman, have two children, PETER and LEVI, and live in Loami township. PETER married Sally Workman, and live in Loami township. MARY J. married John Brewer, have one child, JESSE, and live in Chatham township. NANCY married Jacob Workman, have one child, and live in Loami township. ELIZABETH, DICEY, SALLY, LEVI, Jun., and JOHN

W., reside with their parents, two miles south of Loami.

WILLIS, born Oct. 17, 1828, married Oct. 14, 1858, to Matilda L. White. They have five living children, ELIZABETH, JOHN W., MARTHA J., WILLIS, Jun., and BENJAMIN F., and reside five miles southwest of Chatham.

ANNA, born July 6, 1830, married Jacob Workman. See his name.

ELISHA, born March 4, 1832, married Manvilla Shelton. They had six children, and Mrs. Harbour died, and he married Tabitha Ribble, and lives in Macoupin county.

JOSEPH, born Dec. 13, 1833, in Sangamon county, married March 15, 1860, to Rachel L. White, who was born Nov. 10, 1842, in Lafayette county, Wis. They had nine children, three of whom died under three years of age. Of the other six—EMMA J., RACHEL A., GEORGE B., MATILDA E., CHARLES M. and DAVID F., reside with their parents, five miles west of Chatham.

LAVINA J., born Dec. 11, 1835, married Oct. 19, 1856, to Jasper Harbour. Mr. H. died Nov. 25, 1869, in Barton county, Mo., leaving a widow and three children, who live in Chatham township.

NANCY D., born Feb. 26, 1839, lives with her mother.

SAMUEL, Jun., born Dec. 10, 1841, died Jan. 23, 1865.

Samuel Harbour died in 1874, and his widow resides on the farm where they settled, in 1829. It is five miles west of Chatham.

HARDIN, ASA, born Nov. 22, 1785, in Adair county, Ky., was married there, Feb. 4, 1813, to Elizabeth Taylor, who was born Feb. 29, 1790, in Orange county, Va. They had ten children in Kentucky, and moved to Morgan county, Ill., and two years later to Sangamon county, Ill., arriving in the fall of 1832, at Island Grove. Of their children—

JAMES T., born Dec. 3, 1813, in Adair county, Ky., came to Sangamon county, with his parents, and was married May 1, 1843, in Iowa, to Mary A. Pitzer. She died, leaving two children—OLIVIA died young. BEN is a teacher, and lives with his uncle, William Stitt, in Sangamon county. James T. Hardin went to California, and was drowned by the upsetting of a skiff on Feather river Nov. 3, 1849.

NANCY J., born April 29, 1815, in Adair county, Ky., was married in Sangamon county, Ill., to George Crane. They have five children, and live at Fairfield, Iowa.

SARAH F., born Nov. 25, 1816, in Kentucky, was married in Sangamon county, Ill., Aug. 14, 1834, to Greenbury Rucker. They had two children. MYRA married James Phillips. They have two children, and live at Centre Ridge, Woodson county, Kansas. MARY lives with her uncle, William Stitt. Mr. Rucker died in 1846, and Mrs. R. died in 1854; he in Morgan county, and she in Sangamon county, Ill.

STEPHEN, born March 25, 1818, in Kentucky, was married in Sangamon county, Dec. 25, 1844, to Elizabeth C. Parker. They had five children. ALICE died, aged seventeen. VIRGINIA died in her twentieth year. JULIETTE and CLARA live with their uncle and aunt Stitt. CHARLES is a member of Co. G, 1st United States Dragoons now—1873—and stationed in California.

MARY, born July 5, 1819, in Kentucky, was married in Sangamon county to John R. Reagor, who died, leaving four children. Mrs. Mary Reagor married M. D. Archibald. They had two children, and she died in Iowa.

JOHN J., born Nov. 25, 1820, in Adair county, Ky., was married in Sangamon county, Sept. 12, 1855, to Mrs. Frances C. Butler, whose maiden name was Brown. They have one living child, J. DICK. Mr. Hardin was elected city assessor and collector of Springfield, in 1864, elected clerk of Sangamon county, in Nov., 1873, and resides in Springfield.

EVAN T., born Dec. 23, 1822, in Kentucky, brought up in Sangamon county, was married there Jan. 29, 1852, to Lentha A. Boynton. They have seven children. Evan T. Hardin and family live near Calhoun, Harrison county, Iowa.

ELIZABETH, born Sept 5, 1824, in Adair county, Ky., was married in Sangamon county, Ill., to William Stitt. See his name.

WILLIAM, born Nov. 25, 1827, in Kentucky, was brought up in Sangamon county, Ill., and enlisted in June, 1846, in Co. A, of the 4th Ill. Inf., under Col. E. D. Baker, and died in Mexico, Oct. 30, 1846.

ALBERT, born Sept. 17, 1830, in Adair county, Ky., brought up in Sangamon county, enlisted in 186–, in Co. C, —— Ill. Inf., for three years, and died at Bowling Green, Ky.

Asa Harding died Aug. 22, 1847, and Mrs. Elizabeth Harding died Feb., 1854, both in Sangamon county, Ill.

HARMON, MRS. CATHARINE, whose maiden name was Sears, was born about 1755, in North Carolina. She was married to George W. Harmon, and had three children in North Carolina. They moved to Simpson county, Ky., where they had six children. Mr. Harmon died there about 1825. Mrs. Harmon, with eight of her children, moved to Sangamon county, Ill., arriving in the fall of 1827, in Island Grove. One of her children married in Kentucky and came later.

ADAM, born in 1780, in North Carolina, came to Sangamon county in 1847 or '8, and married Mrs. Polly Weaver, whose maiden name was Donner, daughter of George Donner. *See his name.* They had two children, and he died in 1853. His family moved to the vicinity of Fairfield, Iowa.

JACOB, born in North Carolina, married in Kentucky, to Esther Imler, came to Sangamon county, had three sons, and moved to Fairfield, Iowa, where Mr. H. died. His sons went to Lone Tree, Oregon, and reside there.

FRANCES, born in North Carolina, married in Kentucky to David Charlock, came to Sangamon county in 1827, and had four children. Their eldest and youngest sons went to Mason county, and died there. ABSOLOM P., born Jan. 1, 1829, in Sangamon county, married Jane Foster, have eight children, MARY F., JOHN W., SARAH L., ROXANA, MARIA, MARTHA, MINNIE and ROSABEL, and live near Berlin. Absolom P. Charlock enlisted Aug., 1862, in Co. A., 106th Ill. Inf., for three years, served full term, and was honorably discharged. ELIZABETH, born April, 1830, married James Walker, and lives in Berlin. David Charlock died in 1842, and his widow resides in Berlin.—1875.

MARY, born in Kentucky, married in Island Grove to Jacob Sears, and she died in 1849, in Sangamon county. He went, in 1855, to Missouri, and was then nearly one hundred years old.

ABSOLOM S., born in Kentucky, married in Sangamon county to Elizabeth Donner, daughter of George Donner. They had eight children in Sangamon county, and Mrs. H. died May 16, 1850. The family moved to Libertyville, Iowa, where Mr. Harmon died, April, 1871.

CELIA, born Sept., 1818, in Kentucky, married in Sangamon county to John Foutch, Sen. *See his name.*

HENRY M., born May 4, 1805, in Simpson county, Ky., married Dec. 11, 1828, in Island Grove, to Mary A. Foutch. They had eight living children in Sangamon county. CAROLINE, born Dec. 20, 1829, married June 4, 1852, to Joel Ellis. *See his name.* GEORGE W., born Oct. 11, 1831, married Dec. 30, 1858, to Nannie H. Taylor, who died Sept. 23, 1860. He enlisted August, 1862, in Co. A., 106th Ill. Inf., for three years, was commissioned 1st Lieutenant at the organization of the company, promoted to Captain, April, 1863, and resigned in Oct., 1864, after which he spent four years in the gold diggings of Montana. He was married Dec. 31, 1871, to Mrs. Almira E. J. Melvin, whose maiden name was James. She was born Jan. 29, 1842, in Rockbridge county, Va. G. W. Harmon and wife reside in Berlin. CATHARINE, born Dec. 27, 1833, married Dec. 25, 1866, to John W. Bucher, have four children, and live in Island Grove. JOHN W., born Dec. 23, 1835, married March 23, 1862, to Isadora Montague. They have three children, and live near Riverton, Fremont county, Iowa. THOMAS W., born March 14, 1838, enlisted Aug., 1861, in Co. D, 26th Ill. Inf., for three years, was wounded at Mission Ridge in 1863, and died from its effects, May 16, 1864, at Camp Butler. NANCY A., born Dec. 26, 1840, married Dec. 25, 1860, to Anthony A. Rhodes, had one child, and she died Dec. 14, 1868. HENRY H., born Nov. 1, 1844, married Dec. 26, 1870, to Millie Garrard, have one child, and live at Marysville, Kan. FRANKLIN P., born Nov. 21, 1852, lives with his mother. Henry M. Harmon died August 1, 1871, and his widow resides in Berlin.

MARGARET, born in Kentucky, married to Govert Fleharty. They have five children, and live near Oxford, Henry county, Ill.

CATHARINE, born in Kentucky, married David Weger. They had five children; two died. She resides in Iowa.

Mrs. Catharine Harmon moved to Iowa in 1854, and died near Libertyville, Jefferson county, in the summer of 1860, aged about one hundred and five years.

HARNSBERGER, JACOB, was born in 1781, in Rockingham county, Va., and was there married to Catharine Harnsberger. They had two children in Virginia, and moved to Clarke county, Ohio, where seven children were born, and from there to Clinton county, Ind., where one child was born, and Mrs. Harnsberger and one child died there. The eldest son went to Wisconsin, married, had one child, and died there. Two sons and three daughters remained in Indiana. Mr. Harnsberger and three sons came to Sangamon county, arriving Aug. 29, 1839, in what is now Cartwright township. Of the three sons—

HENRY M., born Feb. 2, 1823, in Clarke county, Ohio, married Feb. 18, 1846, in Sangamon county, to Melinda A. Harrison. They had four children—JOHN J. married Nancy C. Campbell, has one child, CARRIE, and lives in Menard county, near Pleasant Plains. G. LEONARD, S. AMANDA C. and M. A. VIRGINIA, live with their parents. Henry M. Harnsberger and wife reside three and one-half miles northeast of Pleasant Plains—1873.

GEORGE G., born in 1825, in Ohio, and married Mary Scott. They have four living children, and reside six miles northeast of Decatur.

JACOB S., born in 1829, married Sarah Starr, have three children, and reside near Tionus, Bibb county, Ala.

Jacob Harnsberger died Sept., 1847, in Montgomery county, Ala.

HARRISON, EKEKIEL, was born Oct. 6, 1752, in Rockingham county, Va. Sarah Bryan was born July 31, 1753, in the same county. They were there married in 1775, and had nine children in Virginia. The family emigrated, about 1816, to Christian county, near Hopkinsville, Ky. Mr. H., with his wife, three sons and one daughter, moved to Sangamon county, Ill., arriving Nov. 4, 1822, north of Richland creek, in what is now Cartwright township. Of the four children—

JESSE, born May 24, 1777, married in Virginia to Rachel Harrison, moved to Christian county, Ky., and from there to Sangamon county, and after a stay of but two years, moved to Missouri. His first wife died in Missouri. He married again, had five children, and died on the evening of Dec. 31, 1872, at Mexico, Audrain county, Mo.

REUBEN, born June 12, 1779, in Rockingham county, Va., married there, May 16, 1804, to Parthenia Harrison. She had one child, and died in Virginia. Mr. H. was married Nov. 29, 1810, to Barbara A. Harnsberger. They had three children, and moved, in 1818, to Christian county, Ky., where one child was born, and came to Sangamon county, Ill., in company with his father, arriving Nov. 4, 1822, on Richland creek. Of his five children: LEONARD C., the only child by the first wife, was born Feb. 1, 1805, in Virginia, entered the ministry in the M. E. Church at eighteen years of age, was married in South Carolina, moved to Summerfield, Alabama, and died there in 1867, leaving a widow and eight children. Of the children by the second wife, GEORGE M., born March 20, 1813, in Virginia, came to Sangamon county with his parents in 1822. He studied medicine in Springfield under Dr. Jacob M. Early, rode on horseback to Virginia, sold his horse there and went by stage to Philadelphia, and graduated in April, 1840, at Rush Medical College. He was the second graduate in any medical college, from Sangamon county, Dow Matheny being the first. Dr. George M. Harrison was married May 28, 1840, near Harrisburg, Rockingham county, Va., to Maria B. C. J. Houston. They came at once to Sangamon county, and he engaged in practice on Richland creek, where they had three living children, namely: ANN AMANTHA, born August 13, 1841, in Sangamon county, Ill., was married June 7, 1866, in Virginia, to Frank W. Elliott. They have three children, *Irene H., Charles E.* and *William H.*, and live in

Cartwright township. REUBEN H., born Nov. 9, 1842, in Sangamon county, enlisted in 1862, for three years, in the 114th Reg. Ill. Inf., served full time, and was honorably discharged in 1865. He was married in the spring of 1875, in Nebraska, to Mary J. Hendrickson, and resides on land received for his services in the army, situated near York Center, York county, Nebraska. SARAH B. C., born May 8, 1844, married Thomas Cummings. *See his name.* Mrs. B. C. J. Harrison, died Jan. 11, 1845, and Dr. G. M. Harrison was married Nov. 25, 1847, to Mary A. Megredy. They had nine living children: EMMA E., born April 27, 1849, was married March 28, 1872, in Sangamon county, to Philip Oscar Hodgen, who was born Nov. 19, 1845, near Burlington, Iowa. They have two children, *William O.* and *Clara M.*, and reside in Petersburg, Menard county, Ill. M. JENNIE, born May 22, 1850, was married Dec. 26, 1872, to George S. Beekman. They have one child, *Harry J.*, and live in Tallula, Menard county, Ill. JULIA S. was married Jan. 1, 1874, in Sangamon county, to William E. Beekman. They had one child, *Edward J.*, and Mrs. Julia S. Beekman died June 18, 1875. ANNIE, MELINDA, JOHN R., WILLIAM H., MARY R. and HENRIETTA live with their mother. Dr. George M. Harrison died Sept. 1, 1873. He had been to the house of a neighbor on business, and was returning late in the evening. His horse arriving at home without a rider, search was instituted, and his body found at the crossing of a sharp ravine, where it was thought the horse had tripped and thrown him over its head. His widow resides on the farm where he commenced practice in 1840. It is north of Richland creek, and two and a half miles west of Salisbury. JOHN H., born April 6, 1815, in Rockbridge county, Va., raised in Sangamon county, and married in Menard county, May 17, 1843, to Sarah A. Conover, who was born March 15, 1825, near Princeton, N. J. They had eight living children. PARTHENIA E. F., died Feb. 2, 1862, in her seventeenth year. CHARLES D. lives in Kansas. SUE, SAM. B., GEORGE R., HOAT and VANNIE live with their parents. John H. Harrison resides on the farm where his grandfather Harrison settled in 1822. From that to the present time (1873) his home has been on the same spot, included within an area of four rods square. SARAH U., born Dec. 20, 1817, in Kentucky, married Feb. 14, 1849, to Daniel Megredy, and died July 4, 1849, less than five months after marriage. MELINDA A., born March 20, 1820, in Christian county, Ky., married in Sangamon county to Henry M. Harnsberger. *See his name.* Mrs. Barbara A. H. died Aug. 23, 1842, in Sangamon county, and her husband, Reuben Harrison died May 3, 1852, at Summerfield, near Selma, Alabama.

EZEKIEL B., born July 19, 1786, in Virginia, married Ann Bell. They had six children in Kentucky. One, a twin, died when they were moving to Illinois, and they had four children in Sangamon county. Their son, MILTON B., married Mrs. Martha Sutton, whose maiden name was Hunter. They have one child, MARTHA H. ANABEL, and reside in Petersburg. LUCINDA P. married Enoch Megredy. *See his name.* Mrs. Ann H. died, and Ezekiel B. Harrison married Elizabeth Stewart, and he died in June, 1851, at Petersburg.

LUCINDA B., born March 13, 1792, in Virginia, married in Sangamon county to Rev. Theophilus Sweet. *See his name.* She died August 20, 1873, at the house of her nephew, J. H. Harrison.

Ezekiel Harrison died about 1835, and Mrs. Sarah Harrison died June 6, 1845, both in Sangamon county.

HARRISON, FIELDING, was born about 1777, in Rockingham county, Va. Anna Quinn was born about 1779, in Culpepper county, Va. They were married in Culpepper, and made their home in Rockingham county, until they had one child. They moved about 1805 to Christian county, Ky., where they had five children, and from there moved to Sangamon county, Ill., arriving Nov. 1822, at the north side of Richland creek, in what is now Salisbury township. Of their six children—

PEYTON L., born Sept. 7, 1804, in Rockingham county, Va., married Nov. 13, 1827, in St. Louis, Mo., to Eliza B. Cartwright, both of Sangamon county. They had nine children in Sangamon county. FRANCES A., born Nov. 27, 1828, married William H. Purvines. *See his name.* WEALTHY M. J., married

Nathan S. Purvines. *See his name.* SARAH M. married, Feb. 22, 1854, to Amos Ely, a native of Philadelphia. They had two children. HARRY died, aged six years. ALBERT lives with his parents in Chicago. P. QUINN, born May 20, 1837, married June 4, 1867, to Emeline L. Lamothe, who was born Dec. 12, 1843, in Alton. They have one child, LUELLA, and live two miles east of Pleasant Plains. CATHARINE married William P. Crafton. *See his name.* PETER L. married Elizabeth F. Cartwright. They have two children, and live near Pleasant Plains. EMILY W. married Benjamin Berry, of Morgan county, Ill. They have one child, WILLIAM PEYTON, and live at Pleasant Plains. CAROLINE A. married Josiah W. Owen, and live five miles west of Pleasant Plains. VICTORIA M. married Dr. James T. Logan. They have one child, EVA MAY, and live at Tolona, Ill. Peyton L. Harrison remembers seeing sixteen hundred Pottawattomie Indians camped about one mile north of where he now lives. They were about leaving the country, in the winter of 1823 or '4. While the Indians were there he fired into a herd of deer and killed one. Some of the Indians saw him, and he feared they would take his game, but his fears were soon dispelled by their expressing admiration for the young hunter, in saying boy! boy! then pointing to the deer they said, buck! buck! Peyton L. Harrison and wife reside one mile west of Pleasant Plains.

JOHN F., born Feb. 5, 1807, in Christian county, Ky.—the day was long known as the cold Friday—He married Parthenia Harrison (a sister to Milton B. Harrison of Petersburg.) They had six children, and live in Petersburg.

PEACHY A., born Nov. 19, 1809, in Kentucky, married in Sangamon county to Robert Harrison. They had nine children. Of their children—FIELDING T. lives in Alton. CASTLE R. lives in Jacksonville. JOHN H. lives in Taylorville, Ill. SIMEON B lives at Morrisonville, Ill. JAMES married and lives in Kansas. Robert Harrison died in 1855 or '6, and Mrs. Peachy A. Harrison died in 1866, both in Alton.

MARY E., born June 5, 1811, in Kentucky, married in Sangamon county to Irwin Randall. They have seven children, and live in Edwardsville.

SIMEON Q., born Sept. 27, 1816, in that part of Christian which is now Trigg county, Ky., married in Sangamon county to Mary A. Renshaw. They had five living children. ROBERT P. married Almeda J. Bone. ANNIE Q., born May 26, 1848, married, Jan. 19, 1870, to Dr. Joseph B. Cloud (son of Rev. Newton Cloud, of Jacksonville, Illinois.) He died Dec. 31, 1872, in Pleasant Plains. Mrs. Cloud lives with her father—1873—JENNIE E., born Dec. 19, 1850, married Dec. 24, 1868, to Frank Cassell. They have one child, S. QUINN, and live in Pekin. Mr. Cassell is a practicing lawyer. MARY R., IDA V. and SUE A., reside with their parents, two miles northeast of Richland station, Sangamon county.

MARTHA J., born Jan. 31, 1820, in Kentucky, married in Sangamon county to James Harrison. They had four children. James Harrison died July 8, 1873, near Shullsburg, Wis., and his widow resides there. Their son, Dr. W. H. Harrison, lives at Warren, Ill.—1873.

Fielding Harrison died June 11, 1829, and his widow died Aug., 1835, he in Sangamon county, and she in Alton, Illinois.

HARROWER, WILLIAM, born Aug. 20, 1808, in Stirling, Scotland. In 1833 he came to New York city, and returned to Scotland in about three years, and came back in company with a number of Scotch people; his future wife being of the party. He was married, May 9, 1838, in New York city, by Dr. Brownlee, to Janette Blacklock, who was born June 18, 1809, in Lockerbie, Scotland. They at once moved to Springfield, Ill., arriving in the fall of 1838, where they had four children.

DAVID W., born Sept. 29, 1839, lives with his mother.

JAMES, born Jan. 22, 1841, died March 6, 1871, in Springfield, Ill.

AGNES, born June 2, 1842, in Springfield, was married Oct. 12, 1864, to James B. Smith, son of Rev. James Smith, D. D. J. B. Smith was born June 3, 1840, in Nashville, Tenn., graduated at Cincinnati Medical College, in 1865, and practiced medicine in Cerro Gordo and Dawson, Ill. Dr. J. B. Smith and wife had four children, BRAINARD HAR-

ROWER, NETTIE E., ANNIE F., and JAMES B. L. Dr. J. B. Smith died Dec. 30, 1869, in Springfield. Mrs. Agnes Smith and children reside with her mother.

ANN JANET, born July 17, 1844, died June 7, 1851, in Springfield, Ill.

William Harrower died July 27, 1869, in Springfield. His widow resides on east Monroe street, Springfield, Ill. Mr. Harrower was a stone mason, and worked on the Capitol which he found in course of construction by the State of Illinois. He completed it by building the porticos. He was an earnest, consistent member of the Presbyterian church, and as such won the esteem of the community generally. He served several years as a member of the city council of Springfield.

HARGIS, THOMAS, was born in 1775, in West Virginia, and was married there about 1800 to Susan Riley. She was born in 1782. They had two children in Virginia, and moved to Cumberland county, Ky., where they had eight children, and then moved to Sangamon county, Ill., arriving in the fall of 1830 in what is now Fancy creek township. Of their ten children—

NANCY married James McDaniel, and died, leaving four children, who live with their father at West Point, Iowa.

ELIZABETH married Spencer Stone, had nine children, and Mr. S. died. Two of their children—JEFFERSON married Sarah Moran, and lives one mile east of Athens. SARAH married James B. Glascock. *See his name*. Mrs. Stone lives at Wapella, Ill.

JOHN C. died in Kentucky, at twenty-five years old.

SARAH married Jeremiah Dooley, moved to Galena, and she died, leaving three children there.

DORCAS married Jefferson Smith, moved to Wisconsin and died, leaving two children there.

WILLIAM married Nancy Strode. They had nine children, and moved to Doniphan county, Kan., in 1857, and he died there. One son, THOMAS J., was living in Sangamon county in 1862, and enlisted in Co. K, 115th Ill. Inf., for three years. He was wounded at the battle of Chicamauga, and discharged on account of physical disability. He was married, while a soldier, to Harriet Judd, and resides three miles east of Springfield. The family of William Hargis live near Troy, Kansas.

THOMAS married Druzilla Shepherd. He died, leaving a widow and four children, in Fulton county, Ill.

ALVA W. was killed in Kentucky by a cotton gin, at seven years of age.

MINERVA J. married John Smith, have nine children, and live in Fulton county, Ill.

AMANDA married Alonzo McCauley, have five children, and live in Fulton county.

SUSAN B. married James B. Strode. *See his name*.

Thomas Hargis established a pottery soon after he came into the county. He was a local preacher in the M. E. church in Kentucky, and joined the traveling connection in Illinois. He was in charge of a circuit at the time of his death, which took place in Fulton county in June, 1850. His widow died there in 1860.

HARPER, JAMES, was born Jan. 3, 1801, in Tennessee. He was married there to Elizabeth Cochran, who was born Oct. 7, 1801. They had five children in Tennessee, and moved to Sangamon county, Ill., arriving June 10, 1831, where they had three children. Of their children—

LOUISA, born Sept. 29, 1821, in Tennessee, was married in Sangamon county to Allison Lucas.

MARTHA, born May 15, 1823, in Tennessee, and died in Sangamon county, Illinois.

WILLIAM, born Oct. 1, 1825, in Tennessee, married in Sangamon county to Lucretia Penick, and live in Christian county, Ill.

LAFAYETTE, born Aug. 9, 1827, in Tennessee, raised in Sangamon county, was a soldier, from Galena, in the Mexican war, married, Sept. 18, 1847, to Martha J. Smith, have eight children, and live near Osage Mission, Kansas.

ELIZABETH J., born March 10, 1831, in Tennessee, married in Sangamon county to Zacharia Burtle. *See his name*.

MELINDA, born April 17, 1833, in Sangamon county, married Thomas O. Gatton. *See his name*.

FRANCIS M., born July 16, 1835, in Sangamon county, married Bell Deboe, and live in Cotton Hill township, Post-office, Pawnee.

MARY E., born April 16, 1839, in Sangamon county, married Josephus Gatton, Jun. See his name.

James and Elizabeth Harper both died in Sangamon county, and were buried at St. Bernard Catholic church.

HARLAN, JOHN C., was born April 18, 1815, in Cecil county, Md.; came to what is now Ball township, Sangamon county, April 2, 1839. He remained one year, returned to Maryland, came to Sangamon county the second time, traveling all the way in a wagon, and most of the time alone. He was married in Ball township, east of Chatham, July 11, 1843, to Lydia A. White, who was born Sept. 3, 1825. They moved to the vicinity of Waverly, Morgan county, and had nine living children there. Of their children—

LOUIS E., born April 13, 1844, married Dec. 25, 1872, in Shelby county, Ill., to Susan Humphreys, and resides near Buckley, Ill.

JOHN C. and WILLIAM P., twins, born Jan. 2, 1848, reside with their parents.

JOANNA, born Oct. 21, 1850, married William R. Megredy, Oct. 8, 1872. See his name.

SARAH A., born Sept. 24, 1852, GEORGE F., born Sept. 20, 1856, CHARLES O., born Sept. 17, 1858, MARY L., born March 11, 1861, and ELMER E., born July 11, 1863, all reside with their parents.

John C. Harlan moved in March, 1868, to the vicinity of Buckley, Iroquois county, Ill., and now—1876—resides there.

HARLAN, SILAS, was born Jan. 5, 1781, in Berkley county, Va. He went to Christian county, Ky., and came to Sangamon county, Ill., arriving in 1827. He entered about one thousand acres of land, and improved a farm, three and a half miles south of Chatham. Elizabeth Messick was born March 26, 1809, in Rockingham county, Va., and her father moved the next year to Christian county, Ky. In 1827 Elizabeth came to Sangamon county with the family of John French. Silas Harlan and Elizabeth Messick were married Sept. 10, 1829, and had nine children in Chatham township, some of whom died young. Of their children—

GEORGE W., born in 1830, died unmarried in 1860.

MARY J. married Hugh Aldrich, and died in 1863, leaving four children.

SARAH E. married Francis M. Cook, and lives near the old homestead.

SILAS, Jun., died in 1860, aged twenty-three years.

RACHEL, born in 1839, in Sangamon county, and married James Irwin. He enlisted July, 1862, for three years, in the Springfield Light Artillery, was promoted, June 28, 1864, to Second Lieutenant; and Oct. 4, 1864, to First Lieutenant. He served until the end of the rebellion, and was mustered out with the battery at Springfield, Ill., June 30, 1865. Mr. Irwin is a farmer, and resides three miles south of Chatham.

Silas Harlan died Nov. 9, 1844, and his widow married Sept. 8, 1846, to George Roberts, who was born Oct. 2, 1818, in Jefferson county, N. Y. They had six children in Sangamon county, namely—

ERASTUS enlisted in 1861 in Co. B, 10th Ill. Cav., was wounded at the battle of Little Rock, Ark., Sept. 10, 1863, came home and died Dec. 1, 1863.

NORA, born Aug. 2, 1849, married in 1866 to William H. Beardon, and lives in Chatham township.

MINERVA C. married Asa Brewer, and lives in Loami township.

George Roberts enlisted Sept. 21, 1861, for three years, in Co. B, 10th Ill. Cav., re-enlisted as a veteran Jan. 1, 1864, and was honorably discharged with the regiment at San Antonio, Texas, Nov. 22, 1865. He was appointed train master April 1, 1862, and was company farrier during the whole term of his second enlistment. Mr. Roberts resides three miles south of Chatham.

HARRIS, JOB F., was born Sept. 19, 1798, in Rockbridge county, Va., and was taken by his parents to Barren county, Ky., in 1806. He was apprenticed to learn the business of cabinet making, and moved to St. Louis, in 1816. Business being dull, his master released him, and he spent some time on the lower Mississippi, and went from New Orleans to the Rocky mountains, with a company of trappers, returning in the fall of 1818. In the fall of 1822 he came to Sangamon county, in what is now Ball township. In 1827 he enlisted in a Sangamon county company to fight the Winnebago Indians, but the campaign ended without fighting. Job F. Harris was married, May 24, 1844, to Mrs. Mary Phillips. They had two children—

ELIZABETH B. and JOHN M.

Mr. Harris died July 29, 1866. His widow and children live two and a half miles northeast of Auburn.

Mr. Harris voted for Abraham Lincoln every time he was a candidate for any office, from Captain of a military company to President of the United States for the second time.

HARVEY, ABNER, was born April 13, 1804, in Adair county, Ky. Eliza A. Davis was born May 9, 1809, in Kentucky. They were married, had one child in Kentucky, and moved to what is now Irish Grove, Menard county, and from there to what is now Gardner township, Sangamon county, arriving in the spring of 1831, where five children were born. Of all their children—

THERESA, born July 18, 1829, in Kentucky, died in Sangamon county, aged twenty-two years.

JOHN F., born Dec. 10, 1831, in Sangamon county, married at Irish Grove, Nov. 11, 1857, to Lydia J. Stone, who was born there, July 25, 1835. They have five living children: MAUD O., HALLECK, AGNES, WILLIE and CORA, and reside in Urbana, Illinois.

ALFRED C., born Jan. 7, 1834, died aged seventeen years.

ELIZABETH J., born Oct. 15, 1835, in Sangamon county, married Dec. 19, 1856, to Sylvester M. Bailey, who was born Oct. 19, 1834, in Fairfield county, Ohio. They had seven children. MARION E. died in his second year. EVA MAY died in her ninth year. WALTER H., THERESA A., WILLIAM A., SARAH L. and MAUD E. The five latter reside with their parents. S. M. Bailey enlisted August, 1862, for three years, in Co. K, 115th Ill. Inf., was commissioned 1st Lieutenant at the organization of the company, and acted as Captain, but never was mustered, as he was soon after wounded at the battle of Chickamauga, Sept. 20, 1863, while in command of his company. He has since served three years as a member of the Sangamon county Board of Supervisors for Salisbury township, and now resides near Sylvandale, Labette county, Kansas.

OLIVER G., born July 20, 1838, in Sangamon county, married Josephine Reeves. They have three children, LILLIAN, FRANKLIN C. and PAUL CLIFFORD, and reside at Cantrall, Sangamon county.

MARY, born August 30, 1840, and died aged two years.

Abner Harvey died about 1840, and his widow died soon after, both in Sangamon county.

HARVEY, WILLIAM, was born in Harrisburg, Pa., and when a young man went to Washington county, Md. He was there married, in 1829, to Eliza Rice, who was born Nov. 9, 1804, in Chambersburg, Pa. They had three children in Maryland, and came to Sangamon county, Ill., arriving in Nov., 1835, at Springfield, where they had two children. Of their five children—

CHARLES C., born June, 1831, in Maryland, raised in Springfield, went to California, in 1849, and died there in 1853.

MARY J., born April 11, 1833, in Williamsport, Washington county, Md., married in Springfield, March 9, 1853, to William Stadden, who was born March 9, 1826, in Licking county, Ohio. They had six living children. CLARA M. died, aged seven years. WILLIAM H. and RICHARD M. live near Sanford, Orange county, Fla., engaged in the cultivation of oranges and lemons. GEORGE B., EDWIN L. and EVA DELL, live with their mother. William Stadden died Oct. 23, 1873, and his widow resides in Springfield.

Mr. Stadden was for twenty-five years connected with the Auditor's department of the State of Illinois. After that he was for several years Superintendent of Insurance, and died in office.

WILLIAM R., born Oct., 1835, in Williamsport, Md., and raised in Springfield. At the beginning of the rebellion he went to New Mexico, went with a frontier regiment of the Union army, and was never heard of after.

SAMUEL S., born Oct., 1837, in Springfield, and raised there. He was married at Montgomery, Alabama, and resides at Pensacola, Florida.

MARIA L., born Oct. 13, 1839, in Springfield, married William F. Elkin, Jun. *See his name.*

William Harvey was elected Sheriff of Sangamon county, in 1846, serving one term. He died Sept., 1854, and Mrs. Eliza Harvey died Sept., 1870, both in Springfield.

HATHAWAY, WESLEY, was born Dec. 2, 1814, in Boone county, Ky. His parents moved to Montgomery county when he was about twelve years old. He came to Illinois in May, 1831, first stopping at Jacksonville. Mr. Hathaway returned to Kentucky in 1832, and remained two years at Sharpsburg and Mt. Sterling as a clerk. He came back to Morgan county, Ill., in 1834, and in 1835 went to the Job settlement in McDonough county, and engaged in merchandising as a partner of Dr. George B. Rogers, with whom he came to the State in 1831. He closed his business there, and came to Mechanicsburg, Sangamon county, in 1838, and first engaged in teaching. A year or two later he commenced merchandising with B. Logan Hall. Wesley Hathaway and Mary M. Hall were married Sept. 18, 1845, in Sangamon county, where they had seven children, namely—

ALICE O., born Dec. 30, 1847, married May 9, 1872, to Joseph H. Grubb, who was born Nov. 21, 1848, in Perry county, Pa. He enlisted at Springfield for one year, March 2, 1865, in Co. I, 114th Ill. Inf., served in that regiment until it was mustered out in July, 1865, when he was transferred to Co. D, 58th Ill. Inf., served full term, and was honorably discharged March 2, 1866. Mr. and Mrs. Grubb live at Illiopolis.

JULIET, born Aug. 22, 1849, died in her sixth year.

WALTER A., LUELLA B., DAVID L., MARY AUGUSTUS and *ANNA MAY*, live with their parents in Buffalo, Sangamon county, Ill. Mr. Hathaway is a merchant there.

HATLER, JAMES, was born March 23, 1800, probably in Tennessee, and taken by his parents to Allen county, Ky. He was there married to Nancy Dean, Jan. 30, 1823. She was born in that county. They had five children, and came to Sangamon county, Ill., arriving in the fall of 1834, in what is now Cotton Hill township. The next year three members of the family died, including both parents, namely: Mrs. Nancy Hatler died July 9, 1835; their daughter, Rebecca, died July 14, aged eleven years; and James Hatler died Sept. 4, 1835. That broke up the family, and the four children were taken to Greene county, and raised by their grandfather and uncle. Of the children—

GRANVILLE, born Sept. 14, 1825, in Allen county, Ky., married Oct. 22, 1846, in Greene county, Ill., to Sarah Finley, who was born in that county, Nov. 17, 1828. They have nine children; one born in Greene county, and eight in Sangamon, namely: JAMES H., born Jan. 17, 1848, in Greene county, married, Nov. 16, 1871, to Salome Bomhoff, who was born in Sangamon county, Nov. 30, 1851. They reside in Cotton Hill township. The third child, NANCY J., born Oct. 22, 1851, married Silvan Williams. *See his name.* The other seven children, LEWIS J., JOHN H., MARY E., ROSA M., EMMA J., EFFIE and RUFUS CARROLL, live with their parents, in Cotton Hill township. Granville Hatler owns and lives on the farm purchased by his father on coming to the county in 1834.

GILBERT, born Jan. 20, 1828, in Allen county, Ky., married in Greene county, Ill., to Delilah Finley. He died April 13, 1872, leaving a widow and five children—SARAH J., JOSEPHINE, NANCY E., ALBERT and DAISEY. The family live in Cotton Hill township.

LUCINDA J., born April 14, 1830, married Fletcher Haines. *See his name.*

FRANCIS M., born Feb. 28, 1833, in Allen county, Ky., married in Greene county, Ill., to Sarah Overbey, have three children, and reside near Athensville, Greene county, Ill.

HAWLEY, ELIPHALET, was born Dec. 17, 1782, either in New York or one of the New England States. He was married Aug. 24, 1815, in Albany, N. Y., to Elizabeth McMurdy, who was born there Feb. 26, 1797, of Scotch ancestors. Mr. and Mrs. Hawley had two living children in Albany. In September, 1821, they left for the west, the family traveling in a carriage, and hauling their household goods in wagons. When they arrived at Olean Point, on the Alleghany river, they transferred their goods to a raft and floated down to Pittsburg, where they remained until the next spring. One child was born there. Mr. Hawley and Mr. Wheelock united in purchasing a boat, in which their two families descended the Ohio river to Shawneetown, arriving in April, 1822. Mr. Wheelock settled in Atlas, Pike county, and Mr. Hawley came to Sangamon county, arriving in April or May, 1822, in what is now Fancy Creek township, in the same carriage, and drawn by the same horses, they started with. Mr. Hawley had soldiers' claims, and located them in the military reservation west of the Illinois river, and began improving a farm on Spoon river, in Fulton county, five miles northwest of the present town of Havana. He was returning to his family on horseback, and, in attempting to swim his horse across Salt creek, in Mason county, was drowned, June 21, 1822. The horse came home, and upon search being made, the body was found a week later and interred. It was afterwards moved to Indian Point, in Menard county. The widow and children removed to Springfield the next winter. William S. H. Hamilton (*See his name*) was then a practicing lawyer in Springfield. The court appointed him guardian of the three orphan children. James Adams (*See his name*) was appointed administrator of the estate. Of the three children—

ELIPHALET B., born May 30, 1816, in Albany, N. Y., raised in Sangamon county, and married in Springfield, July 12, 1838, to Mary D. Sayre, who was born June 26, 1815, in Lebanon, O. They had four living children in Springfield, namely: MARY E., born July 19, 1839, in Springfield, married James M. Garland. *See his name*. ISABELLA G., born July 21, 1843, in Springfield, married Aug. 4, 1862, to George M. Brinkerhoff, who was born Aug. 20, 1839, in Gettysburg, Penn., graduated at Pennsylvania College in the class of 1859, and soon after came to Springfield. Mr. and Mrs. Brinkerhoff have four children, JOHN H., MARIAN B., GEORGE M., jun., and MARIA C., and reside in Springfield. Mr. Brinkerhoff is Secretary of the Springfield Iron Company, and one of its stockholders. MARIA D., born June 22, 1848, in Springfield, married in her native city, July 10, 1872, to Edward B. Springer, who was born July 15, 1847, in New York city. They have one child, GEORGE HAWLEY. Mr. Springer is connected with the firm of Keith Brothers, merchants of Chicago, and resides in that city. BENJAMIN died Sept. 9, 1864, aged twelve years. Eliphalet B. Hawley, when quite young, entered a dry goods store in Springfield as clerk, and thus qualified himself for mercantile pursuits. He was in that business about thirty years, the greater part of the time on his own account. He retired a few years ago, but still resides in Springfield. He has for many years been a Ruling Elder in the Second Presbyterian church of this city.

ISAAC A., born Nov. 26, 1819, in Albany, N. Y., brought up in Sangamon county, married in Springfield April 30, 1851, to A. Eliza McCauley, who was born Jan. 13, 1828, in Washington county, Penn. They have one daughter, ADDIE E., living with her parents in Springfield. Isaac A. Hawley commenced as a clerk, and from 1837 to 1857 was a dry goods merchant in the same building, southwest corner of Adams and Sixth streets. In 1864 he was elected Treasurer of Sangamon county, serving two years. He is now —1876— engaged in the insurance business.

ISABELLA G., born Nov. 28, 1821, in Pittsburg, Penn., brought up in Springfield and educated in Monticello Female Seminary, at Godfrey, Ill. She made teaching her profession until her health failed. She died April 15, 1845, in Schuyler county, Ill.

Mrs. Elizabeth Hawley was married Aug. 9, 1823, in Springfield, to John Moore. *See his name*.

HAWN, FREDERICK, was born June 5, 1810, at Indian Castle, now Danube, Herkimer county, New York. His ancestors were of German origin; his grandfather, Conradt Hahn, was born in the kingdom of Bavaria, and married there to a Miss Windacre. They emigrated to America about 1765, and settled in Canajoharie, Tryon county, now Montgomery county, New York. Mrs. Hahn died in 1775. Conradt Hahn was a soldier in the Revolutionary army, and was killed in battle at Oriskany, Oneida county, New York, leaving four children. The eldest, Conrad, married Catharine Young. Frederick, whose name heads this sketch, is their son. By assimilation with the

English language the name was changed from Hahn to Hawn. Frederick Hawn studied civil engineering, and was thus employed on the first railroads constructed in the States of New York and Pennsylvania. He came to Sangamon county, Ill., arriving in Oct., 1835, where he was married, Nov. 9, 1837, to Abigail Cutter. See *Cutter family*. Mr. and Mrs. Hawn had two children in Sangamon county, and in 1843 moved to Weston, Platte county, Missouri, where they had one child. Of their children—

MARIA G., born Sept. 9, 1838, in Springfield, Ill., was married in Weston, Missouri, Nov. 4, 1857, to Joseph C. Hemingray, a native of Pittsburg, Penn. They have two children, REUBEN PHELPS and LILEON KERR, and reside in Leavenworth, Kansas. Mr. Hemingray is a practicing lawyer.

MARTHA, born Feb. 17, 1842, in Sangamon county, Ill., was married June 21, 1875, in Leavenworth, Kansas, to Charles H. Lamar, a native of Tennessee. They live near Weston, Platt county, Missouri. Mr. Lamar is a farmer. Mrs. Hemingray and Mrs. Lamar have for many years been active members of the Protestant Episcopal Church in Leavenworth.

LAURENS, born Sept. 4, 1847, at Weston, Missouri, graduated at Cornell University, Ithica, New York, in the class of 1875. He is now—1876—studying law in Leavenworth, Kansas.

Frederick Hawn was professionally engaged in the earlier public improvements of Illinois. After his removal to Missouri he was the civil engineer in the construction of the Hanibal & St. Joseph Railroad, and in the geological survey of the State of Missouri. In 1860 he moved to Leavenworth, Kansas, and was connected with the survey of the United States lands, and later was engaged in the geological survey of the State of Kansas. He has written extensively on the natural resources of the latter State, and climate of the west. Frederick Hawn and family reside in the city of Leavenworth, Kansas.

HAZLETT, ROBERT, was born Dec. 20, 1799, in Stokes county, N. C. Rebecca Daigh was born Dec. 12, 1802, in Bath county, Va. They were married March 29, 1820, in Virginia, had three children there, and moved to Sangamon county, Ill., arriving in the fall of 1828, at Springfield. In the spring of 1831 they moved to what is now Cooper township, where they had three children. Of the six children—

WILLIAM P., born Nov. 29, 1821, in Bath county, Va., married in Sangamon county, Oct. 19, 1843, to Zerilda Haggard. They had ten children, three of whom died under three years. Of the other seven—SARAH R. married Dec. 24, 1863, to Brice A. Patton, has three children, and lives in Lawrence county, Mo. ROBERT H., born July 6, 1847, is a graduate of the Law School of the University of Michigan, at Ann Arbor. He resides in Springfield, and is one of the law firm of Hazlett & Kane. ELIZABETH A. married Feb. 23, 1870, to Henry Spengler. They have one child, LOURETTA n., and live two miles southeast of Farmingdale. WILLIAM J., MARTIN M., CHARLES E. and AMELIA B., reside with their parents, three-quarters of a mile east of Bradfordton.

JOHN A., born Feb. 9, 1823, in Mason county, Va., was married in Sangamon county, Ill., to Mary J. Dreman. They have nine living children, and live five miles north of Edinburg, Ill.

ELIZA J. married Isaac Troxell. They had two children, WILLIAM E. and GEORGE L., and Mrs. Troxell died.

ELIZABETH A., born Feb. 14, 1828, in Sangamon county, was married, Feb. 13, 1851, to Henry W. Neeley. They had one child, and moved to Grimes county, near Anderson, Texas, in 1852, where they had five living children. JOSEPH W., born in Sangamon county, married Sept. 8, 1870, to Frances C. Criger, and live near Anderson, Texas. REBECCA L., born in Texas, married Nov. 30, 1871, to Daniel McMahon, and live near Anderson, Texas. GEORGE L., ELIZA A. and ADA E., live with their mother. H. W. Neeley died July 3, 1871, near Anderson, Texas, and his widow and child reside there.

CHARLES F., born Feb. 29, 1832, in Sangamon county, went to California in the spring of 1853, and reside at Tehama, Tehama county, Cal.

REBECCA V., born May 29, 1833, married Ephraim Nelms, had two childen, and Mr. N. died. She married John M. Abel, have four children, and live near Niantic.

Robert Hazlett died Aug. 15, 1835, and his widow married Joseph Firey, of Christian county. They had two children; both died young. Mr. Firey died, and his widow resides near her son, John A. Hazlett, in Christian county.

HEDGES, JOSIAH, born about 1788, in Maryland, and was taken to Virginia, and from there to Grayson county, Ky., when he was about twelve years old. Anna Brown was born Dec. 25, 1798, in Davis county, Ky. Josiah Hedges and Anna Brown were there married and made Grayson county their home until they had three children, and then moved to Sangamon county, Ill., arriving in the fall of 1826, at the north side of Island Grove, two and a half miles northwest of the present town of Berlin, where two children were born. Of their five children—

LUCINDA, born in Kentucky, married in Sangamon county to Henry Hawkins. They have nine children, and live near Beatrice, Gates county, Nebraska.

LEAH, born in Kentucky, died in Sangamon county, Sept. 25, 1842, aged about twenty-four years.

MARINDA, born in 1820, in Kentucky, married William D. Chilton, and live near Berlin.

CALEB, born July 4, 1828, in Sangamon county, married Jan. 11, 1866, to Theresa Dunlap, who was born May 30, 1841, in Knox county, Ky. They have three children, HARDIN W., LOGAN H. and DORA BELL. Caleb Hedges lives on the farm settled by his father in 1826, and where he was born. It is two and a half miles northwest of Berlin.

ELIZABETH A., born April 4, 1833, in Sangamon county, married Nov. 18, 1863, to George W. Dunlap. He was born March 29, 1829, in Knox county, Ky. They have four children, IRVIN T., SARAH A., WILLIE H. and GEORGE A., and live north of Island Grove, and two and a half miles northwest of Berlin.

Mrs. Anna Hedges died June 9, 1872, and Josiah Hedges died August 29, 1872, both on the farm where they settled on coming to the county in 1826.

Mr. Hedges moved from Kentucky with an ox team. One of his oxen was trained to work in shafts. He made a light wagon all of wood, and with that ox did all his marketing after coming to the country. When he came he brought money to enter forty acres of land. By industry and economy he became the owner of nine hundred acres of the richest land in the county.

HEDRICK, CHARLES. See family sketch in Omissions.

HELM, MEREDITH, was born March 2, 1802, at Williamsport, Md. His father died when he was quite young, leaving ample means for his education. After graduating in his literary studies, he attended the Baltimore Medical College, graduated there also, and entered on the practice of medicine in his native town. Elizabeth Orendorff was born in 1805. Her mother died when she was quite young, and she was raised by an aunt who is yet living (1873) near Hagerstown, aged more than one hundred years. Dr. M. Helm and E. Orendorff were married in 1824. They had two living children in Maryland. Dr. Helm traveled on horseback in the summer of 1833, visited Springfield, and returning to Maryland, brought out his family in the summer of 1834. He bought land and tried farming near Rochester, but soon abandoned it, returned to Springfield and practiced medicine to the end of his life. They had two living children in Sangamon county. Of their four children—

THOMAS M., born Jan. 22, 1829, in Williamsport, Md., studied medicine under his father in Springfield, and attended lectures in Chicago during the winter of 1849 and '50. He also attended lectures in the winter of 1852 and '3, at the University of St. Louis, where he graduated. Since that time he has been engaged in practice. Dr. Thomas M. Helm was married March 12, 1857, to Henrietta B. Jones. They have two living children, CHARLES W. and LULU, and reside at Williamsville.

DAVID, born Feb. 22, 1832, in Maryland, qualified himself for, and engaged in, the practice of medicine in Springfield. He was soon after thrown from a sulkey by a fractious horse, which caused his death, in August, 1857.

WILLIAM McK., born in 1836 in Sangamon county. At sixteen years of age he went to California, and was with the Walker (Nicaragua) expedition. Returning home he studied medicine, graduated at the McDowel Medical College of St. Louis, and is now a practicing physician. Dr. William McK. Helm married Harriet Wilson. They have four children, and reside at Mt. Auburn, Christian county.

HENRY, born in Springfield, and lives there.

Dr. Meredith Helm died March 9, 1866, and his widow died Jan. 14, 1870, both in Springfield.

HENDRIX, ANTHONY, was born Dec. 19, 1789, in Fleming county, Ky., and married there to Nancy Dean, who was born in Clark county. They had six children in Kentucky, and the family moved to Sangamon county, Ill., arriving in the fall of 1830, first in Williams and then in Clear Lake township, where four children were born. Of their ten children—

SUSAN, born in Fleming county, Ky., married Simeon Taylor. See his name.

REBECCA, born in Kentucky, married Philip Smith. See his name.

AMY, born in Fleming county, Ky., married in Sangamon county to Charles Kinnaman. She had three children, and died in Clear Lake township. Her son, ANTHONY W., married Emily Blue, and lives in Logan county. ANDREW J. married Miss Hendrix, and lives in Clayton. CELIA J. is unmarried and resides in Williamsville.

SAMUEL W., born March 29, 1822, in Fleming county, Ky., married in Sangamon county to Mary E. Neville, Jan. 28, 1845. They had seven living children. HIRAM A. married Nancy Blue, have four children, and live in Logan county. CYNTHIA A. married Henry Marshall, have four children, and live near Barclay. MARY E. married Felix Jones, and lives near Barclay. IRENA C. and HERSCHEL V. live with their mother. Samuel W. Hendrix died Feb. 13, 1874, and his widow lives at Barclay.

SALLY A., born in Kentucky, married in Sangamon county to Benjamin Kinnaman, have two children, and live in Clayton, Ill.

ELIZABETH, born in Kentucky, married in Sangamon county to John Smith. They had three children, namely: SUSAN married William Smith, had one child, and died. ALICE A. married William T. Ham. See his name. JENNIE married George Strawn, and lives in Williamsville. John Smith died, and his widow married Stephen King. See his name.

NANCY A. married Jesse Alexander. See his name.

MARY married George Fisher, have six children, and live in Kansas.

ELIZA married Hiram Alexander. See his name.

JOHN, born in Sangamon county, Sept. 19, 1835, married Caroline Taylor. They have three children, EMILY F., NANCY A. and MARY J., and live in Illiopolis township.

Mrs. Nancy Hendrix died August 29, 1839, and Mr. H. married Catharine Wickoff. She died May, 1866, and Anthony Hendrix died Dec. 6, 1866.

HENKLE, JUSTUS, was born about 1775, in Virginia. Elizabeth Judy was born about 1778, in Randolph county, Va. They were married in Randolph county, and had eleven children in Virginia, and moved from there to Belleville, Ill., in the fall of 1817. They moved from there to the San-ga-ma country, arriving about the middle of March, 1818, at the west side of Horse creek, in what is now Pawnee township, about one mile north of Pawnee. Mr. Henkle made improvements there, and entered the land when it came into market. Of their children born in Virginia—

MARTIN married in Sangamon county to Martha Bagby; both died without children.

SARAH, married twice, is now a widow, and resides with her only daughter, who is the wife of James Card, and lives in Taylorville.

CATHARINE died unmarried, in Sangamon county, aged sixty-two years.

ELIJAH married Polly Funderburk. They never had any children, but adopted and raised Marshall Henkle, who lives in Christian county. Elijah Henkle died there.

LEVI married Nancy Vandever. She had one child, and died, and he married Harriet McWilliams. They had two children, and Mr. Henkle died.

HANNAH, born in Virginia, married in Sangamon county to David Funderburk. *See his name.*

ELIZABETH married Garret DeMor, and died, leaving one child.

ABIGAIL died, aged thirty-two years.

JESSE married Nancy Johnson, and had four children. He and all except one of his children are dead.

DELILAH died, aged eighteen years.

JACOB, born July 25, 1812, in Randolph county, Va., served three months in the Black Hawk war, from March, 1831. He was married in Sangamon county, Nov. 20, 1836, to Nancy Hatchett. They have ten children, all born in Sangamon county. DICEY E. married Samuel N. Galloway, April 14, 1853. He was born Oct. 28, 1821, in Bath county, Ky. They have one child, JAMES ALPHEUS, and live in Cotton Hill township, Sangamon county, Ill. JOHN Y. married Dulcina Lockridge. They have one child, ADA. DIANA F., born April 23, 1842, was married April 7, 1863, to Michael Baker, who was born Sept., 1830, in Prussia. They have one child, GEORGE C., and live three-fourth of a mile south of Pawnee. MARTIN V., born Aug. 12, 1844, married March 13, 1867, to Sarah E. Hoover, who was born in Christian county, Aug. 22, 1849. They have two children, CHARLES M. and NANCY I., and live near Pawnee. SARAH J., born April, 1847, married Aug. 15, 1869, to Charles H. Willison, who was born Dec. 15, 1830, in county Tyrone, Ireland. He had previously married Sarah O'Neal. *See Samuel O'Neal.* They had one child, LAURA BELL, and live one mile east of Pawnee. ELVIRA, HARRISON H., MARY A., AMANDA and LAURA A., reside with their parents, two miles north of Pawnee. Jacob Henkle remembers that when his father moved from St. Clair county, it was with the following named families: John Neeley, from Tennessee; Henry Funderburk, of South Carolina; Joseph Dixon, of St. Clair county; Robert Davis and a Mr. Short, both from the south, numbering in all fifty-three persons. They were the first settlers in that part of the country, and they kept as close together as possible for protection against the Indians. They were Kickapoos and Pottowattamies, and were friendly with the whites; but it was not pleasant to be alone and know that you were in their power.

Mrs. Elizabeth Henkle died in 1836, and Justus Henkle died in 1842, near where they settled in 1818.

HENKLE, JASON C., was born Oct. 10, 1820, in Pendleton county, Va., and came to Springfield July 8, 1838. He was married April 16, 1849, in Clarksville, Mo., to Kate Travis, who was born Nov. 25, 1825, in Calhoun county, Ill. They had nine living children in Springfield—

ANNA T., born March 20, 1850, died Jan. 1, 1873.

ELLA died in her twelfth year.

CLINTON M. died in his fourth year.

VIRGINIA died in her twenty-second year.

GEORGE E., CHARLES C., EMMA, IRVING and *JESSE C.*, live with their father.

Mrs. Kate Henkle died Jan. 26, 1871, and Jason C. Henkle resides in Springfield. He has been for many years in the mercantile business, and is now a member of the firm of Woods & Henkle. For ten years he has been a director of the First National Bank of Springfield.

HENRY, JAMES D., was a native of Pennsylvania, but the exact date and place of his birth is not known. His earlier years being devoted to manual labor, he was barely able to read and write when he arrived at the age of manhood. In 1823 he came to Edwardsville, Ill., where he labored as a mechanic during the day, and at night attended school. He next engaged in merchandising there, and moved to Springfield in 1826, where he continued in the same business, and was soon after elected Sheriff of Sangamon county. While discharging his duties as Sheriff, the Winnebago war of 1827 came on. A battalion of four companies was raised, and under command of Col. Tom M. Neale, with Sheriff Henry as Adjutant, started in pursuit of the savages. Six of the leaders gave themselves up, and thus ended the campaign.

When the Black Hawk war began in 1831, Adjutant Henry was appointed to command the first of the two battalions from Sangamon county. The Indians re-

—47

treated before the soldiers across the Mississippi river, and the chiefs returned and made a treaty of peace June 30, 1831. In the spring of 1832, when the chief Black Hawk again commenced hostilities, Col. Henry was once more appointed to command a batallion; but before meeting the enemy, the term of enlistment of the whole eighteen hundred men in the field expired. A regiment was immediately organized of those among the disbanded forces who were willing to volunteer for the purpose of holding the savages in check while more permanent forces could be raised. Col. Henry acted as Lieutenant-Colonel of this temporary organization. Three thousand two hundred men were raised, and Lieut.-Col. Henry was appointed General of the third brigade of twelve hundred men. Gen. Henry commanded in the battle of Wisconsin, July 21st, and the battle of Bad Axe, Aug. 2, 1832, winning both battles, which terminated the war. (See account of the Winnebago and Black Hawk wars, pages 53 and 54.) He had achieved these victories against not only the wishes, but machinations, of the officers of the regular army.

On his return from the scene of conflict, the citizens of Springfield gave him a public reception in recognition of his services; but owing to his extreme sensitiveness in presence of the ladies, he never entered the apartment presided over by them. The exposures and hardships of the campaign brought on disease of the lungs, and he went south, hoping by spending the following winter in a warm climate to avert its effects; but it was too late. He died March 4, 1834, in New Orleans. Such was his singular modesty, that those in whose hands he fell for the closing scenes of his life, did not know until after his death that he was General Henry, the hero of the Black Hawk war. Gov. Ford, in his History of Illinois, speaks of Gen. Henry as the idol of the people, and says: "If he had lived he would have been elected Governor of the State in 1834 by more than twenty thousand majority; and this would have been done against his own will, by the spontaneous action of the people."

HENTON, WILLIAM, was born Oct. 22, 1807, in Green county, Ky., taken by his parents to Washington county, Indiana, and from there to Bond county, Illinois, in 1818. In 1828 he came to Sangamon county, and was married Aug. 16, 1832, to Pauline Short. They had seven living children in Sangamon county, namely—

JAMES J., born Sept. 30, 1835, married Janetie Barger, who died Nov. 21, 1864, leaving four children. Mr. Henton is married again, and lives near Linden, Kan.

MARY E., born Dec. 31, 1838, died March 4, 1859.

CATHARINE A., born Feb. 19, 1840, in Sangamon county, is unmarried and lives—1873—at the old homestead of her grandfather, Caleb Short. It is two and a half miles north of Curran.

THOMAS H., born Aug. 6, 1841, lives with his sister Catharine.

JOHN R., born Feb. 18, 1843, married Vinley A. Patterson, has two children, and lives near Linden, Osage county, Kansas.

ELIZABETH A., born Aug. 6, 1845, lives with her sister Catharine.

CHARLES G., born June 6, 1847, married Rebecca Taylor, has three children, and lives two and a half miles north of Curran.

William Henton died Nov. 1, 1848, and Mrs. Pauline Henton died Oct. 24, 1853, both in Sangamon county.

HENTON, ALLIE M., was born June 16, 1814, in Shelby county, Ky., came to Springfield in the fall of 1829, and lived in the family of her uncle, Andrew Laswell, until the marriage of her brother William, in whose family she lived until she was married to Daniel K. Callerman. See his name.

HENSLEY, SIMON, was born Feb. 26, 1785, in Washington county, Va. He was married Feb. 2, 1820, near Dayton, Montgomery county, Ohio, to Mary Arnold, who was born Aug. 24, 1792, in Ohio. They had two children in Ohio, and moved to Sangamon county, Ill., arriving in the fall of 1823, in what is now Island Grove township, north of Spring creek, where two children were born. Of their four children—

JOHN, born Jan. 20, 1821, in Ohio, married in Sangamon county, Thursday, between Christmas and New Year, Dec., 1861, to Leanah Lynch. She was born Jan. 12, 1841, in Pickaway county, Ohio. They had six children—MARY and

JAMES died young. KATIE, WILLIAM, SAMUEL and HARRY, live with their parents, in Cartwright township, four miles east of Berlin.

SAMUEL, born June 16, 1822, in Ohio, is unmarried, and lives with his brother John.

JAMES, born Jan. 2, 1824, in Sangamon county, died Aug. 18, 1831.

GEORGE, born Dec. 13, 1825, in Sangamon county, married, in 1857, to Calista Huber, a native of Ohio. They have three children, MARY J., HORACE and BELLE, and live near Topeka, Kansas.

Simon Hensley died Aug. 12, 1826, in Sangamon county, and his widow married Aug. 22, 1827, to Josiah Kirkpatrick. They had two children—

JACOB KIRKPATRICK, born Oct. 5, 1828, in Sangamon county, married Huldah Atkinson. They have three children, HENRY, WILLIAM and MARY, and live—1873—near Roseville, Warren county, Ill.

MARY A. KIRKPATRICK, born Aug. 19, 1831, in Sangamon county, married Dr. Remer Sanders. They have two children, MARINDA and CLARA, and reside near Avon, Fulton county, Ill. Dr. Sanders is a practicing physician, now—1873—on a tour to Europe.

Mrs. Mary A. Kirkpatrick died, in 1857, and Josiah Kirkpatrick died March 18, 1872, both in Warren county, Ill.

HENWOOD, BERRYMAN, was born July 11, 1821, in Cabell county, West Va. He came to Sangamon county, stopping with his uncle, Berryman Knight, near Chatham. He was married to Sarah Jordan. They had three children in Sangamon county—

MARGARET E, born Jan. 18, 1843, in Sangamon county, married Aug. 15, 1856, to John McLaughlin. They had two children, ELIZABETH A. and JOHN B., and Mr. McLaughlin died Nov. 28, 1861, in Arkansas, and his widow married George W. Saunders. See his name.

MARTHA A., born March, 1844, and SARAH I., born in 1846, are both married, and live in Missouri.

Mrs. Sarah Henwood died, and he was married twice after, and lives in Osceola, Arkansas.

HERMON, DAVID H., was born Jan. 12, 1805, in Wilkes county, North Carolina. His grandfather was German and his grandmother English. Sally Mitts was born Feb. 11, 1811, in Grant county, Ky. They were married in that county, August 27, 1827, had one living child there, and moved to Sangamon county, Illinois, arriving Oct. 26, 1830, in what is now Ball township. They lived in a cabin one mile west of Sugar Creek timber, and spent the winter of the "deep snow" there. But one other family lived away from the timber. The recollection of Mr. Hermon is that rain fell for a day or two until the earth was saturated. The day before Christmas the rain turned to snow, and by night it was about six inches deep. Snow continued to fall almost every day for six weeks. Feb. 11, 1831, was the first time he saw the sun, and then it was partially eclipsed. He burned all the rails and loose timber of every kind near his house, and it was all he could do to keep himself and family from freezing. Mr. and Mrs. Hermon had four children in Sangamon county. Of their children—

MARY A., born August 26, 1829, in Kentucky, was married in Sangamon county to Green Ray. They had three living children, GEORGE R., REZIN L. and DAVID. Mr. Ray died, and Mrs. Ray was married June 28, 1855, to T. Stopperun. They had two children, FREDERICK and LIZZIE. Mr. Stopperun died, and his widow married Thomas McCallum. They live in Chicago.

JOHN H., born Nov. 12, 1831, in Sangamon county, was married May 8, 1856, to Nancy Drennan, who died, and he was married Oct. 15, 1872, to Mrs. Gracie Smith, whose maiden name was Levi. They have one child, FLORENCE M., and live in Chatham.

PRYOR J., born Dec. 22, 1833, in Sangamon county, near Chatham. He attended the district school until he was twenty years of age, after that the Springfield University one winter, and spent much of his time in teaching until May 1, 1855, when he entered the office of Dr J. N. Wright, of Chatham. He graduated at Rush Medical College, Chicago, Jan. 21, 1863, and was married to Eliza A. Neale, April 15, 1863. They have four living children, FRANCIS E., JULIA A., HARRIET L. and FLORENCE M. Dr. P. J. Hermon is a practicing physician, and resides in Raymond, Montgomery county, Ill.

DAVID C., born April 24, 1838, in Sangamon county, was married April 4, 1861, to Lousetta Shidy. They have two living children, EMMA F. and MILDRED L., and live in Chatham.

GEORGE W., born May 17, 1840, in Sangamon county, was married Feb. 26, 1863, to Sarah Childers. They have four children, NORA E., EMMA D., AUGUSTA M. and LENA P., and live near Raymond, Ill.

WILLIAM, born Nov. 20, 1842, near Chatham, was married Nov. 17, 1875, to Emma Mitts.

JAMES D., born Nov. 13, 1844, died Nov. 7, 1865.

SARAH E., born April 28, 1849, was married Sept., 1865, to John Mitts. They have two children, NORA and CORA L., and live near Chatham.

JOSEPHINE, born Sept. 2, 1853, and died Jan. 3, 1860, in Sangamon county.

David H. Hermon and wife reside two miles east of Chatham, near where they settled in 1830.

HERRIN, JAMES, was born April 6, 1802, in Harrison county, Ky., was married in that county Aug. 1, 1833, to Mary A. McDaniel, and soon after started, in company with her parents, to Sangamon county, Ill., arriving Nov. 14, 1833, in what is now Clear Lake township, east of the Sangamon river. They had four children, all born in Sangamon county, namely—

DAVID C., born May 25, 1834, married May 22, 1862, to Sarah J. North. They have five children, ROBERT E., JAMES W., GEORGE E., DAVID A. and JESSE LEE, and reside three quarters of a mile northwest of Lanesville, Wheatfield Postoffice, Sangamon county, Illinois.

WILLIAM F., born Nov. 18, 1836, married Sept. 10, 1863, to Mary A. North. They have four children, BELLE N., JAMES E., CHARLES F. and BURT A., and reside one and a half miles east of Buffalo, Sangamon county, Illinois.

HARRIET F., born Jan. 6, 1838, married in 1860 to Robert Hewitt, who was born in New Jersey. They have three children, MARY FRANCES, IMLA and JOHN E., and reside in Menard county, one and a half miles north of Ashland, Cass county, Illinois.

JOHN A., born Aug. 4, 1841, died at fifteen years old.

Mrs. Mary A. Herrin died March 25, 1868, in Clear Lake township, on the farm where they settled in 1835. James Herrin resides with his son, William F., near Buffalo, Sangamon county, Illinois.

HERNDON, ARCHER G., born Feb. 13, 1795, in Culpepper county, Va., went to Greensburg, Green county, Ky., when he was about ten years old, and was there married, in 1816, to Mrs. Rebecca Johnson, whose maiden name was Day. Her father was a revolutionary soldier. Mr. and Mrs. Herndon had one child in Kentucky, and they moved to Troy, Madison county, Ill., where one child was born; from there they moved to Sangamon county, Ill., arriving in the spring of 1821, settling on what is now German Prairie, five miles northeast of Springfield, where two children were born. Of their four children—

WILLIAM H., born Dec. 25, 1818, in Green county, Ky., was married in Sangamon county, March 26, 1840, to Mary J. Maxey, who was born July 27, 1822. They had six children. JAMES N., born April 26, 1841, in Springfield, Ill., married Mary Dunlap, and lives in Fancy creek township. ANNIE M., born April 9, 1843, in Springfield, was married June 26, 1863, in her native place, to Frank Fleury, who was born Sept. 28, 1840, in Meadville, Penn. They have one child, ANNIE MAY. Mr. Fleury was city clerk during 1868, '69, '70 and '71. He is now engaged in the drug business, in Springfield, where he resides. BEVERLY P., born Dec. 30, 1845, lives in Colorado. ELIZABETH R., born Nov. 11, 1849, married, Aug. 27, 1867, to James S. Cooper, who was born July 16, 1842, in Belleville, St. Clair county, Ill. They live in Springfield, Ill. LEIGH W., born Oct. 22, 1852, lives with his father. MARY N. lives with her sister, Mrs. Fleury. Mrs. Mary J. Herndon died Aug. 18, 1860, and W. H. Herndon was married July 31, 1861, to Anna Miles, who was born March 1, 1836. They have two children, NINA BELLE and WIL-

LIAM M., and live in Fancy Creek township, six miles north of Springfield, Illinois. Wm. H. Herndon was for many years a practicing attorney in Springfield, Ill., and was the law partner of Abraham Lincoln, from 1848 to the death of Mr. Lincoln.

ELLIOTT B., born Aug. 1, 1820, at Troy, Madison county, Ill., has practiced law in Springfield since 1842. He was city attorney during 1854 and '5, and county attorney in 1856. He was United States District Attorney, under President Buchanan, and was corporation counsel during 1874 and '5. E. B. Herndon was married, Sept. 30, 1875, to Mrs. Jerusha Lee, whose maiden name was Palmer. She was born April 16, 1833, in Ogdensburg, St. Lawrence county, N. Y. Mr. Herndon is a practicing lawyer, and resides in Springfield, Ill.

ARCHER G., Jun., born Nov. 29, 1825, in Sangamon county, Ill., was married in DeWitt county, Oct. 15, 1846, to Roanna R. Robbins, who was born April 17, 1829, in Campbell county, Ky. They had eleven children, three of whom died under two years. Of the other eight—WILLIAM FRANCIS, born April 9, 1848, was married Sept. 14, 1871, to Mary H. Bryant, who was born Sept. 21, 1852. They have one child, EDGAR BRYANT, and live in Springfield, Illinois. NONA R. died Jan. 17, 1876, from burns, caused by the explosion of a lamp. LOAMI D., ELLIOTT G., RODELIA A., MOLLIE E., ROMEPEER R. and ELMA R.; the six latter live with their parents. Archer G. Herndon, Jun., and family, reside near the southeast corner of Rochester township.

NATHANIEL F., born in 1827, in Sangamon county, Ill., died there, in 1834.

Archer G. Herndon, Sen., was engaged in mercantile pursuits, from 1825 to 1836, in Springfield, and during that time erected the first regular tavern in town. He was one of the "Long Nine" who were instrumental in having the capital removed from Vandalia to Springfield, having been elected State Senator in 1836. He was receiver of public moneys, from 1842 to 1849, in the Land Office, in Springfield. A. G. Herndon, Sen., died Jan. 3, 1867, and Mrs. Rebecca Herndon died Aug. 19, 1875, both in Springfield, Illinois.

HESSER, SAMUEL L., born June 2, 1797, in Winchester, Va. He was married May 31, 1821, to Sarah Fry. They had one child, viz—

MARY A., born in Virginia, married Edward Huffman. They have one child, SALLIE P., and reside in Winchester, West Va.

Mrs. Sarah Hesser died Jan. 15, 1825 and Samuel L. Hesser was married Sept. 12, 1826, to Ann Maria Slagle, in Hagerstown, Md. She was born in that city Oct. 4, 1803, and brought up in Winchester, Va. They had five children in Berryville, Frederick county, Va., and the family moved to Sangamon county, Ill., arriving at Springfield June 6, 1836, where they had four living children. Of their nine children—

LOUISA C., born June 26, 1827, in Berryville, Va., married in Mechanicsburg, Ill., Aug. 22, 1848, to Simon P. Fullinwider. See his name.

ANN M., born Oct. 16, 1828, in Virginia, married in Sangamon county to Jefferson McBride. See his name.

EDMONIA E., born May 31, 1831, in Virginia, married in Sangamon county Feb. 4, 1852, to Dial Davis. She died July 4, 1861, leaving six children—FRANKLIN P., SALLIE M., CHARLES E., HENRY S., DIAL W.—the latter died Nov. 25, 1875—and CARRIE E. The five living children reside with their father at Mt. Auburn, Christian county, Ill.

GEORGE W., born Sept. 30, 1833, in Berryville, Va., married in Sangamon county May 15, 1860, to Caroline Morgan. They have five children, BYRON B., JESSE M., HOMER H., ARTHUR A. and CLARA B., and reside two miles northeast of Wheatfield postoffice, Lanesville, Sangamon county, Ill.

JOHN L., born March 16, 1835, in Virginia, brought up in Sangamon county, enlisted Aug. 7, 1862, at Camp Butler, for three years, in Co. A, 73d Ill. Inf. He went in as 1st Corporal; promoted to 5th Sergeant Oct. 25, 1862; promoted to Orderly Sergeant Jan. 8th, and 2d Lieutenant Sept. 17, 1863. He never had a day's sickness or missed a march or battle while in the service, except when he was in prison. He was captured at the battle of Chicamauga, Sept. 20, 1863, and was in different rebel prisons nineteen months, principally at Andersonville. Mr. Hesser says the battlefield was pleasant compared with the gloomy prisons, where starvation, filth, vermin and disease prevailed. He expresses his gratitude that through the whole eighteen months he had one friend who was ever faithful and true, John W. North, of the same company and regiment. See his name. Mr. Hesser says that by the aid of each other and the will of God, they escaped with their lives. It was not death they dreaded so much as the "thought of staying with those south-down sons of sin, dead or alive." He served full time, and was honorably discharged at the close of the rebellion. He was married in Sangamon county, Ill., to Mary J. Crumley. They have one child, SARAH M., and reside two miles east of Riverton, Sangamon county, Illinois.

HENRIETTA C., born Nov. 6, 1836, in Springfield, married Oct. 18, 1859, in Sangamon county to Samuel Pheasant, who was born Nov. 24, 1819, in Washington county, Md. Came to Sangamon county in 1857. They had four children. DANIEL Z. died, aged eight years. HENRIETTA M., WILLIAM L. and SAMUEL E., died under two years. Mr. and Mrs. Pheasant reside one mile south of Buffalo, Sangamon county.

JACOB A., born Nov. 12, 1838, in Springfield, went to Texas in 1859, and there married Maggie Marchbanks. They have one living child, CHARLES, and reside at Corsicana, Nevarro county, Texas.

CORNELIUS N., born Nov. 17, 1843, in Springfield, died, aged seven years.

CHARLES S., born Sept. 3, 1845, in Springfield, married April 1, 1873, in Nebraska, to Fannie Stillwell, and reside near York, York county, Neb.

Samuel L. Hesser was one of the eight men who organized the first Masonic Lodge in Springfield. He died Oct. 15, 1871, at Buffalo, Sangamon county, and his widow resides there.

HESSER, ARMSTEAD N., younger brother to Samuel L., came to Springfield in 1837, raised a family of several children, and himself and wife both died in 1847. Their daughter—

M. ADDIE, married Richard C. Bird. See his name.

HICKMAN, WILLIAM, born Sept. 1, 1790, near Winchester, West Virginia, went to Shelby county, Ky., in 1812, and his father's family moved there the same year. He was married there in 1813, to Mary M. Cardwell, who was born March 18, 1795, in Virginia. They had seven children in Shelby county, and moved to Sangamon county, Ill., arriving Nov. 8, 1833, at Springfield, and in the spring of 1834 settled near Mechanicsburg, where one child was born. Of their children—

GEORGE T., born Nov. 8, 1814, in Shelby county, Ky., was married in Sangamon county, Ill., April 7, 1842, to Elizabeth Lyon, who was born Dec. 21, 1823, in Shelby county, Ky. They had seven children in Sangamon county. WILLAM H., born Sept. 15, 1843, enlisted August 5, 1862, in Co. B, 30th Ill. Inf., for three years. He was taken sick in going to the field of conflict, and died Jan. 17, 1863, in military hospital, Memphis, Tennessee. JAMES F. married Sophia C. Burns, and lives in Menard county, near Buffalo Hart, Sangamon county, Ill. MARY E., RICHARD O., CALVIN WESLEY, HENRIETTA and THOMAS C. reside with their parents, five miles southeast of Williamsville.

WILLIAM A., born Oct. 26, 1816, in Shelby county, Ky., was married in Nelson county, Ky., to Burnett Barber, who died, leaving two children. W. A. Hickman married Sue Elsuit. They have one child. William A. Hickman is a practicing physician, and resides at Owensboro, Ky.

JAMES F., born Feb. 14, 1819, in Shelby county, Ky., was married in Sangamon county, Ill., Nov. 3, 1863, to Sarah E. Bice. They had four children, WILLIAM and ARTHUR, the first and fourth, died under two years. MARY IRENE and GEORGE THOMAS live with their parents, one and a half miles north of Barclay, at the Bice family homestead.

JOHN F., born April 8, 1821, in Shelby county, Ky., was married at Harrodsburg, Ky., to Sally Curry. She had one child, and died, and he married Emma Wilson. He is a practicing physician at Bardstown, Ky.

MARY A. E., born May 19, 1823, in Kentucky, was married in Sangamon county to Harrison D. Lyon. See his name.

JULIET A., born March 26, 1825, in Kentucky, was married in Sangamon county, Ill., to H. C. Linsley. They have seven children, and live near Grove City, Christian county, Ill.

RICHARD O., born Nov. 1, 1831, in Shelby county, Ky., brought up in Sangamon county, Ill., was married there, August 8, 1872, to Maggie Perill. They have one child. He was, in 1873, Treasurer of Montana Territory, and resides at Virginia City.

SUSAN E., born April 26, 1834, near Mechanicsburg, Sangamon county, Ill., was married there, June, 1859, to Ambrose J. Sell, who was born Dec., 1827, in Hanover, York county, Penn., and came to Springfield in May, 1851. Mr. and Mrs. Sell have one child, EDWIN A., and reside in Springfield, Ill. Mr. Sell is a grocer on north Fifth street.

Mrs. Mary M. Hickman died July 17, 1835, and Mr. Hickman was married Oct. 11, 1837, to Mary Ann Lemon. Their only living child—

EUCLID L., born May 4, 1840, in Sangamon county, is unmarried, and lives near Barclay, Sangamon county, Ill.

Mrs. Mary Ann Hickman died Jan. 19, 1843, and William Hickman was married Feb. 14, 1845 to Mrs. Elizabeth Burrell, whose maiden name was Short. William Hickman died Jan. 15, 1874, in Springfield, Ill., in his eighty-fourth year. His widow resides on north Seventh street, Springfield, Ill.

HICXOX, ADDISON, was born May, 1798, in Middlebury, Conn., was a brother to Horace and Virgil. He was married Nov. 10, 1823, in Jefferson county, N. Y., to Rhoda Stanley, who was born March 10, 1803, in that county. They had three living children in New York, and moved to Springfield, Ill., in 1836, and had three children in and near Springfield. Of their six children—

HARRIET M., born March 18, 1826, in Jefferson county, N. Y., married in Springfield, Ill., Jan. 1, 1857, to Benjamin F. Haines, who was born March 19, 1824, in Xenia, Ohio, raised in Bloomington, Ill., came to Springfield in 1863 or '4, and was engaged in milling until 1873, when he moved to Florida, and engaged in the culture of oranges and lemons. Mr. and Mrs. Haines now reside at Spring Garden, Florida.

EATON R., born Nov. 1, 1827, in Jefferson county, N. Y., and raised in Springfield, Ill. In 1851, Mr. Hickox went to California, returning in 1857, he soon after engaged in mercantile business, in Atlanta, Ill., where he was married, Aug. 7, 1858, to Sallie B. Mahew, a native of New Jersey. They had three children, ADDISON, RAY and HUGH, and Mrs. Hickox died Dec. 1, 1863. Mr. Hickox was married, Sept. 7, 1864, to Hannah L. Mahew, in Atlanta, and soon after moved to Springfield, where they had one living child, ANNA B., and reside in Springfield. At one time Mr. Hickox was engaged in the milling business with his father. He is now in the grain trade, in connection with the Springfield Elevator. While in Atlanta, he was Postmaster.

ADA A., born Sept. 3, 1830, in Jefferson county, N. Y., married in Springfield, May 1, 1854, to William H. Ames, of St. Louis. Mrs. Ames died Feb. 4, 1855, in Springfield.

MARTIN, born Sept. 14, 1837, in Springfield, married Jan. 25, 1859, in Atlanta, Ill., to Mary James, a native of Ohio. They had one son, L. JAMES, and Mrs. Hickox died April 28, 1863. Mr. Hickox and his son reside in Springfield. He is proprietor of the Excelsior flouring mills.

SILAS W., born Aug. 12, 1840, in Sangamon county, enlisted on the first call for 75,000 men, in April, 1861, in Co. I, 7th Ill. Inf., served three months, and was honorably discharged. Enlisted in 1862, in Co. M, 10th Ill. Cav., for three years. He was captured at Clarks Mills, southeast Missouri, in 1863, forced to take an oath not to go into the service again. Silas W. Hickox was married, June 15, 1864, to Susan F. Keyes. They have three children, WALTER, ELLA and CLARA, and reside in Springfield, Ill. S. W. Hickox is a member of the firm of Leggott & Hickox, in the stove and tinware trade.

DOUGLAS, born March 10, 1846, in Springfield, Ill., was married, Sept. 5,

1867, to Martha Jane Keyes. They have four children, FLORENCE MAY, REED KEYES, HENRIETTA M. and GEORGE L., and reside in Springfield, Illinois.

Addison Hickox went to St. Augustine, Fla., for the benefit of his health, and died there Jan. 10, 1872. His remains were brought to Springfield, and interred in Oak Ridge Cemetery. His widow, Mrs. Rhoda Hickox, resides in Springfield.

HICKOX, HORACE, brother to Virgil and Addison, was born Oct. 18, 1795, in Middlebury, New Haven county, Conn. He was married in 1817, at Rutland, Jefferson county, N. Y., to Eliza Stanley, who was born Oct. 28, 1799, at Augusta, Oneida county, N. Y. They had five children, three of whom died young. The family moved to Springfield, Ill., arriving early in 1836. Of their two children—

VOLNEY, born Nov. 1, 1835, in Rutland, N. Y., brought up in Springfield, prepared for college by Prof. Beaumont Parks, graduated at Yale College in the class of 1857, and admitted to the practice of law in 1858 at the bar of St. Louis, Mo. Early in the war of the rebellion he was appointed additional aid-de-camp on Gen. McClellan's staff; was mustered out in the spring of 1862. He was re-appointed, with the rank of Captain, on Gen. Fremont's staff, and soon after assigned to duty on Gen. Hunter's staff, and was honorably mustered out in January, 1864. From the spring of 1865 to 1866, he was an army correspondent of the Cincinnati *Commercial*. In the fall of 1866 he went to New York, and was sent to the City of Mexico as correspondent of the New York *Tribune*, returning from there in 1867. Volney Hickox was married Oct. 1, 1873, at Batavia, Illinois, to Cassandra Browning Moore, who was born at that place, Sept. 9, 1849. They have one child, HART, and reside in Springfield. Mr. Hickox is a practical stenographer.

LELIA, born March 11, 1838, in Springfield, married in her native city in 1860 to John Hunter, an attorney of Cincinnati. She died December, 1871, in Springfield.

Mr. Horace Hickox was engaged in milling, in connection with his brother Addison, for many years. Mr. and Mrs. Hickox reside in Springfield.

HICKOX, VIRGIL, was born July 12, 1806, in Jefferson county, New York, his parents having moved there in 1803, from New Haven county, Connecticut. He received a common school education in his native county, and started, August 25, 1828, for the southwest. After a wearisome journey of two months by wagon, he arrived in St. Louis, at that time a city of but 5,500 inhabitants. In one hour after his arrival he was engaged to work as a journeyman carpenter, at one dollar per day. From that time he was busily employed until 1833, when he went to the Galena lead mines, where he spent one year. He then came to Springfield, Ill., and opened a store, May 5, 1834, and continued in the mercantile business nearly nineteen years. In 1851 he united with other business men in organizing a company to build a railroad from Alton to Springfield, and continued in the directory until the road was constructed to Joliet, and had charge of the right of way in constructing that much of the present Chicago and St. Louis railroad. From him emanated the law regarding the assessment and taxation of railroad property, which was in force from 1855 to 1872. He withdrew from active connection with the road in May, 1874. In May, 1869, he was appointed by Gov. Palmer to the office of Canal Commissioner, serving two terms of two years each. He was a director of the old State Bank of Illinois, in 1839-40-41. In January, 1874, he became President of the Springfield Savings Bank, and as such continues to manage its business to the present time. He has always been a Democrat in politics, and acted as Chairman of the Democratic State Committee for nearly twenty years. In that capacity he received and still holds the last letter ever dictated by his lifelong personal and political friend, Hon. Stephen A. Douglas, that of May 10, 1861, in which he declared there could be but two parties, that of patriots and traitors, and advised his political friends to lay aside every feeling that would impede united action for the preservation of the Union. Mr. Hickox has some peculiar views with regard to government. He believes that the United States should not own any property except what is necessary for forts and arsenals, and for the transaction of business at the seat of government. He also holds that the whole postal system should be abolished, and that the laws of trade should regulate the transportation of what is called mail matter in the same manner as such laws regulate all other transportation. He thinks that if men and women were as careful to obey the scripture injunction, "six days shalt thou labor," as they are to rest on the seventh, there would be less suffering from want.

In Oct., 1839, Mr. Hickox was married in Springfield to Miss Catharine Cabanis, a native of Kentucky. She died Sept. 25, 1875, leaving three sons and three daughters. Mr. Hickox resides in Springfield, in the same house he brought his young wife to, nearly thirty-seven years ago.

HIGGINS, WILLIAM, was born Sept. 7, 1770, in Virginia. His parents moved to Fayette county, Ky., when he was a young man. He was married there to a Miss Young, who died, and he was married March 2, 1804, in Boone county, Ky., to Mary Moschy, who was born July 10, 1781, in North Carolina. They had twelve living children in Fayette county, Ky., and the family moved to Sangamon county, Ill., arriving Oct. 1, 1830, in what is now Woodside township, seven miles south of Springfield. Of their twelve children—
DRUCILLA W., born Jan. 1, 1805, in Kentucky, died in Sangamon county in 1836 or 1837.
BEDFORD, W., born May 6, 1806, in Kentucky; came to Sangamon county with his parents; went back to Kentucky and married Susan Dozier. They had one living child, ROBERT, born Nov. 22, 1835, in Montgomery county, Kentucky; married in Sangamon county Oct. 3, 1860, to Lydia Stair. They have five living children, CHARLES W., FRANK H., ELMER E., DORA B., and CATALINA, and reside in Pawnee. Mrs. Susan Higgins died, and B. W. Higgins was married July 27, 1841, to Mary A. Norris. Of their seven children, ELLEN married John L. Parker, and lives in Cotton Hill township. WILLIAM A. enlisted Aug., 1862, in Co. E, 114th Illinois Infantry; served until Feb., 1865, when he was discharged on account of physical disability, and now draws a pension. He was married Dec. 16, 1873, to Sarah Durrell, and lives in Palmer. MARTHA S. married John Lockwood, and lives near Oconee. JOEL T., ANNA, BENJAMIN H., and EMMA F. live with their parents in Cotton Hill township.
ELIZABETH, born in Kentucky, married in Sangamon county to James M. Haley, and died, leaving one child, ELEANOR, who married Joseph Lockridge. See his name.
ROBERT O., born July 4, 1811, in Fayette county, Kentucky; was serving an apprenticeship when his parents came to Sangamon county, and he arrived in 1832. He was married in Franklin, Missouri, to Camilla A. Donaldson, a native of Baltimore, Maryland. They had one child in Missouri, and then moved back to Sangamon county, where they had six living children. EDWIN L., born March 24, 1840, at Booneville, Missouri, and brought up in Sangamon county; enlisted April 24, 1861, in Company I, 7th Illinois Infantry, for three months; served full term, and was honorably discharged. He enlisted Aug. 21, 1861, for three years in Company K, 33d Illinois Infantry-Normal. He was wounded June 18, 1863, at the siege of Vicksburg. The wound was a remarkable one. A musket ball entered his face below and forward of the right ear, passed over the roof of the mouth, and came out of the left eye. He recovered without totally losing the sight of that eye. He re-enlisted Jan. 1, 1864, as a veteran in the same company and regiment. He was promoted through all grades from private, and was commissioned as Captain Nov. 16, 1864, and served to the end of the rebellion, and was honorably discharged Dec. 7, 1865. He was appointed by Gov. Palmer, March 24, 1869, Assistant Adjutant General, and was appointed by Gov. Beveridge, Jan. 20, 1873, Adjutant General of the State of Illinois, which he held two years. Gen. E. L. Higgins was married Sept. 7, 1870, to Mrs. Mary J. Hoskins, whose maiden name was Huntington. She was born July 30, 1847, at Geneva, New York. She had one child, Charles H. Hoskins who died July 26, 1874, in his sixth year. Mr. and Mrs. Higgins have one living child, FLORA BELLE, and reside in

—48

Springfield. ALEXANDER D., born Dec. 21, 1844, in Sangamon county, Ill., enlisted August 15, 1862, in Co. G, 114th Ill. Inf., served three years, and was honorably discharged, August, 1865. He was married in Springfield, Nov. 29, 1872, to Lizzie Nottingham. They have one living child, RALPH, and live in Springfield. JULIA E. and ROBERT ALONZO live with their parents. EMMA married Justus Graves, and lives at Evanston, Ill. FRANK and WALTER L. live with their parents. Robert O. Higgins and wife reside in Springfield, Illinois.

URMANET, born in Kentucky, died in Sangamon county, aged thirty-one years.

WILLIAM E., born in Kentucky, went from Sangamon county to Missouri, and from there, in 1849, to California. He was on his way home, and died on shipboard, on the Pacific ocean in 1851.

SINAI MELVINA, born in Kentucky, married in Sangamon county to Thomas J. Haley. They had two children. BENJAMIN H., born in Sangamon county, enlisted May 29, 1861, in Co. A., 3d Ill. Cav., served full term, and was honorably discharged Sept. 5, 1864. He is married, and lives at Palmer, Ill. EDWARD enlisted May 10, 1861, in Co. A, 3d Ill. Cav., for three years, served until May 11, 1864, when he was discharged on account of physical disability, and died, in 1865, at Woodside. T. J. Haley and wife live at Palmer, Christian county, Illinois.

JOEL V., born Oct. 8, 1817, in Fayette county, Ky., came to Sangamon county in 1830, and was married June 16, 1850, to Margaret B. Womack, who was born Nov. 13, 1822, in Butler county, Ky. They had eight living children in Sangamon county, JAMES N., GEORGE B., SINAI M., JOEL E., MARY A., ANNIE E., JOHN A. and IDA L., live with their parents on the farm where Mr. Higgins father settled in 1830. The house in which he lives was built by his father in 1831, entirely of black walnut lumber; the frame, doors, door and window casings, sash, weather boarding, shingles, and everything else. It is two stories high, two rooms long, and stands seven miles south of Springfield.

THOMAS W., born March 2, 1819, in Kentucky, married in Sangamon county to Mary Husband, have five children, and live in Bates county, Missouri.

ALONZO, born in 1822, in Kentucky, died in Sangamon county, in 1844.

CAROLINE, born July 31, 1823, in Kentucky, married in Sangamon county, June 24, 1847, to Thomas A. Rogers, who was born June 16, 1822, in Kentucky. They have seven children—ALONZO H., born Aug, 6, 1848, married Eliza Adams, and reside in Cotton Hill township. The other six moved with their parents, in 1873, to the vicinity of Gerard, Crawford county, Kansas.

BENJAMIN died, aged ten years. William Higgins died Aug. 7, 1840, and his widow died Dec. 7, 1866, both on the farm where they settled in 1830.

HIGGINS, WILLIAM, was born April 12, 1774, in Barren county, Ky. He was married to Elizabeth Downing. She had one child, and died, and he was married, March 6, 1800, to Rosanna Megery, who was born Dec. 18, 1778, in the same county. She had five children, and died there. In 1817 Mr. Higgins moved his family to St. Clair county, Ill., and was there married to Rosanna Duncan. He started with his family, in the fall of 1818, to the San-ga-ma country. They stopped, on Sugar creek, with the Drennan's, until Jan. or Feb., 1819, when they moved about fifteen miles north, and built a cabin on the south side of the Sangamon river, above where the Chicago & Alton railroad now crosses. While he was living in camp, before his cabin was completed, himself and wife crossed to the north side of the river on horseback. They were belated, and spent one night in the river bottom, near the mouth of Fancy creek. A few days later Mr. Higgins went to the north side alone, found five bee trees, and killed a panther, which measured nine feet from tip to tip. He went over soon after, accompanied by his wife and two daughters, one of whom is now—1876—the wife of David England. These three are believed to have been the first white women who ever crossed to the north of the river, in what is now Sangamon county. Stephen England and his two sons-in-law came on their exploring expedition, and stopped with Mr. Higgins who accompanied them to the north side, and led the way to the vicinity of where Cantrall now stands, and all four selected sites for improvement. The creek was for several years called, in honor of his having first visited the locality, Higgins creek; since changed to Cantrall's creek. Soon after this, a Mr. Chapman, son-in-law of Judge Latham, crossed the river and built a cabin on the north side, between where the Chicago & Alton and Gilman, Clinton & Springfield railroads now cross. His wife is thought to have been the fourth white woman on that side of the river. Mr. Chapman established a canoe ferry there, which for three years was the only chance for crossing the river. Persons could be taken over safe and dry, animals could swim, and wagons were taken to pieces, and with their loads were carried over, piece by piece. About three years later a boat was first used for a ferry. The latter part of April, 1819, Stephen England, his two sons-in-law, his son David, and two of his daughters crossed over and finished building their houses and planting their crops. Those two daughters of Mr. England were the fifth and sixth women north of the river. One of them, Lucy, was the wife of John Chine. This account was given to me by David England and his wife, who was Margaret Higgins. Of the five children of Wm. Higgins, by his second wife—

CATHARINE, born May 12, 1801, in Kentucky, married Wm. Bradbury in St. Clair county, and both died there, leaving four children.

MARGARET, born Sept. 6, 1804, in Barren county, Ky., married David England. *See his name.*

LOUISIANA, born Nov. 16, 1806, in Kentucky, married in Sangamon county to George Harper, raised a family, and lives in Oregon.

INDIANA, born March 24, 1809, in Kentucky, married Wm. Crane, in Sangamon county. She died, leaving one child, JOSEPH A. CRANE, who is now a practicing attorney, in Freeport, Illinois.

WILLIAM H., born Feb. 25, 1813, in Kentucky, married Priscilla Kearney, have five children, and live in Cedar county, Missouri.

ROSANNA, born Dec. 16, 1816, in Kentucky, married in Sangamon county to Milton Claypool. He died, leaving a widow and eleven children, in JoDaviess county, Illinois.

William Higgins built a boat, and in 1823 took his goods down the Sangamon, and up the Illinois rivers to a point near Lewiston, and after that built a mill near Canton, Ill. He moved from there to the northern part of the State, where he and his third wife died, leaving four children.

HILL, WILLIAM R., was born August 7, 1820, in Jessamine county, Ky. His father, John H. Hill, came with his family to Sangamon county, in Auburn township, Oct. 15, 1836. In 1837 they moved to Christian county. William R. went with the family, and returned to Auburn township when he was about twenty-one years of age. He was there married, Oct. 6, 1858, to Jennie Mason. They have four children—
MARTHA E., FANNY M., WILLIAM M. and *JENNIE M.*, and reside one mile northeast of Auburn.

HILDRETH, HARVEY. *See his name in connection with the "sudden change," page 65.*

HILLMAN, OLIVER, born May 10, 1785, in Philadelphia, was married July 23, 1807, in that city, to Rachel Smith. They had six children in Philadelphia and New Jersey, and moved with a part of their family to Springfield, Ill., arriving in April, 1839. Of their children—

RICHARD S., born July 7, 1808, in New Jersey, was married Aug. 11, 1831, in Philadelphia, to Margaret Knorr. They had four children there, two of whom died under three years of age. The family moved to Springfield, Ill., in 1840, where two children were born. In 1846 or '7 Mr. Hillman moved to St. Louis, where twins were born, one of whom died young. Of their five living children: MARY C., born July, 1833, in Philadelphia, was married in Sangamon county, Ill., to Joseph P. Hesser. They have five children, and live in Bloomington, Illinois. RACHEL S., born Sept. 30, 1835, in Philadelphia, was married Oct. 18, 1855, in Springfield, Ill., to Daniel P. Hopping, who was born Feb. 21, 1832, in Morris county, New Jersey. They have five children, JOSEPH F., MARY E., WILLIAM P., HERBERT P. and SAMUEL M., and reside in Springfield. D. P. Hopping is a contractor and builder.

He, in connection with Mr. Henry Ridgely, established a planing mill in 1867. It was the first of the kind in Springfield. ELMIRA J., born March 11, 1841, in Springfield, Ill., was married in 1863 to William Wyatt. They live in Jacksonville, Ill. ANN E., born Sept. 7, 1845, in Springfield, Ill., married Lewis A. Wood. *See his name.* MARGARET, born April 3, 1848, in St. Louis. (Her twin mate, Richard, died in his third year.) She was married Jan. 22, 1868, to Francis C. Fessenden. They have four living children, FRANCIS E., Jun., BIRDIE L., GEORGIE and RICHARD P. Mr. Fessenden is a stairbuilder, and resides in Springfield, Ill.

Mrs. Margaret Hillman died May 23, 1848, in St. Louis. Richard S. Hillman was married Feb. 8, 1849, in that city, to Mrs. Eliza J. Vinton, whose maiden name was Bell. She died without children, Feb. 15, 1852, at Campbellsville, Ky. R. S. Hillman brought his family back to Springfield, Ill., in 1853, and was there married, Dec. 14, 1854, to Ann J. Williamson. They had two living children, RICHARD and MARY JANE live with their mother. Richard S. Hillman died May 31, 1862, in Springfield, and his widow married Samuel Yocom. *See his name.*

JOHN S., born Nov. 29, 1809, in Philadelphia. He was married three times, and all his wives and three children died there. He came to Sangamon county, Ill., in 1839 or '40, and was married in the same county to Mrs. Sarah A. Unclesbee, whose maiden name was Poffenberger. They had eleven children, three of whom died under six years. Of the other eight, RICHARD, born Sept. 26, 1843, married Dec. 29, 1874, to Elizabeth J. Rape. They have one child, EARNEST S., and live in Cotton Hill township. MARGARET A., born March 7, 1848, was married May 8, 1867, to William T. Johnson. They have two children, and live in Springfield. He is engineer at the new State house. RACHEL E., born April 20, 1849, was married March 7, 1871, to Isaac Fisher. They have one child, JESSIE, and live near Mt. Pulaski. GEORGE H. lives with his mother. WILLIAM A. married Dec. 15, 1875, to Flora E. Cooper, and lives near Williamsville. DANIEL R., MARY E., SARAH J.,

JOHN L. and LIZZIE, the six unmarried, live with their mother. John S. Hillman died March 22, 1872, and his widow resides in Cotton Hill township, near New City Post-office.

ALLEN, born Sept. 3, 1811, in Philadelphia, was married there and had two children. He moved to Sangamon county, Ill., and died there. His family returned to Philadelphia.

MARY, born August 29, 1813, in Philadelphia, was married there to John Unsworth. Their son, WILLIAM, lives with his third wife in Springfield, Ill.

MARGARET, born Jan. 28, 1816, in Philadelphia, was married there to John Hardin, and never came west.

FRANCIS, born Oct. 8, 1817, in Philadelphia, died in Springfield, Ill.

Mrs. Rachel Hillman died March 21, 1842, in Springfield, Ill. Oliver Hillman married Mrs. Mary A. Short, and he died March 11, 1856, in Sangamon county.

HINMAN, JOHN B., was born Sept. 12, 1804, in Madison county, N. Y., came to Sangamon county, Ill., with his uncle, Henry Kinney, Sen., arriving May 6, 1822, in what is now Loami township. He was married Dec. 25, 1824, to Jane Smith, who was born Dec. 11, 1802, on Long Island, N. Y., and came to Sangamon county in Sept., 1822, with her sister, Mrs. Julia Colburn. They had eight children in Sangamon county—

EMILY, born March 3, 1826, married, Feb. 5, 1846, to George Dill, who was born June 2, 1825, in Preble county, Ohio. They had eight children—EMMA C. died in her sixth year. HENRY H. married Alice Wilson, have one son, and live in Curran township. SARAH J. married Martin Shelton. *See his name.* JOHN B., AMOS S., SUSAN A., JULIA M. and GEORGE W., live with their parents, in Chatham township.

LOLA A., born Aug. 15, 1827, married Joseph Sweet, have seven children, and live in Chatham.

DICEY, born Dec. 1, 1829, married Samuel Dill, and live in Girard, Illinois.

NANCY, born Jan. 25, 1832, married Abraham Dill, had five children; one was killed by a runaway team. The other four live with their parents, east of Auburn.

JULIA A., married Joshua Henderson, had two children, and mother and both children are dead.

JOHN B., Jun., died, at ten years of age.

SMITH J. married Jan. 1, 1859, to Melvina Catlett, who was born in Garrard county, Ky., have four children, and live in Chatham township.

CALVIN A., married Laura A. Emmons, of Preble county, Ohio, have two children, and live one mile east of Loami.

John B. Hinman and his wife reside one mile east of Loami, where they settled in 1832.

Mrs. Lola Hinman, the mother of John B., came to Sangamon county with him, in May, 1822, and died in September of the same year.

HINSLEY, ALFRED, was born in 1792, in North Carolina. He was there married, in 1819, to Lucy Elkin, who was born April, 1803. They had two children in North Carolina, and moved to Jones county, Ga., where two children were born, from there to Smith county, Tenn., where one child was born. The family moved to White county, Ill., and from there to Sangamon county, arriving Nov., 1834, at old Salem, and in 1836 moved to what is now Gardner township, where they had one living child. Of their children—

CAROLINE, born in 1810, in North Carolina, died in Illinois, unmarried, in 1857.

JANE, born in North Carolina, married in Illinois to Alfred Wagoner. They have five children, and live in Petersburg.

MARTHA, born in Georgia, married in Illinois to James S. Carter, have four children, and live in Petersburg.

ALFRED N., born Dec. 27, 1826, in Jones county, Ga., married in Sangamon county, July 23, 1851, to Margaret A. Lemmon. They have three children, SUSAN A., MILDRED L. and ULICK P., and live at Salisbury.

LECY, born in Smith county, Tenn., married in Illinois to James Bryant, have four children, and live in Petersburg.

JAMES F., born in Sangamon county, has been twice married, and lives in Petersburg.

MARY, born Jan. 11, 1840, in Menard county, married S. Spear, and lives in Bates county, Missouri.

SARAH, born Dec. 3, 1842, in Menard county, was killed March 7, 1868, at Greenview, Ill., by an accident on the Jacksonville branch of the Chicago & Alton railroad.

Alfred Hinsley died Oct. 13, 1844, and his widow resides in Petersburg.

HOAG, WILLIAM C., was born Aug. 8, 1816, at Oxford, Butler county, Ohio. He came to Sangamon county, Ill., arriving at Springfield, Aug., 1836, and was married at Salisbury, Feb. 16, 1837, to Melinda Miller. They had seven living children—

JANE died at sixteen years old.

ALONZO, at fourteen, and

FLORILLA at three years old.

BARILA born Dec. 18, 1844, married Thomas C. Yoakum. See his name.

SOLOMON M., born Dec. 31, 1846, married Ida Carman, have one child, NORMAN, and live in Salisbury.

WINFREY V., born July 3, 1851, and

FRANKLIN T., born Nov. 5, 1857; the two latter live with their parents.

William C. Hoag and wife are both living—1874—in Salisbury, Sangamon county, Illinois.

HODGE, RICHARD, born May 19, 1819, in Smithfield, Jefferson county, Virginia, was married April, 1838, to Catharine Divelbiss, in Westmoreland county, Penn. They moved to Springfield in the fall of 1839, and had five living children—

JACOB, born Oct., 1840, was married March 19, 1863, to Elizabeth J. Dennis, who was born June 7, 1844, in Springfield. They have five children, MINNIE, MARGARET, LIZZIE, ABBIE and SALLIE, and live in Springfield. Jacob Hodge is a wagon manufacturer.

NOAH, born Feb. 6, 1842, in Springfield, Ill., was married in Jackson, Mississippi, to Miss D. L. O. Johnson. She died Aug. 10, 1874, leaving two children, EDGAR O. and D. L. O., who live with their father. Noah Hodge was Circuit Clerk of Hinds county, Miss., from Sept. 12, 1869, to Jan. 4, 1876. He moved to Akron, Ohio, and was married there, May 16, 1876, to Sarah W. Ashmun. Mr. Hodge is a practicing lawyer, and resides at Akron.

RICHARD, Jun., born June 25, 1846, was married in Springfield, Ill., Oct. 21, 1872, to Sallie Pierce. He is a wagonmaker, and lives in Springfield.

GEORGE W., born Feb. 22, 1849, lives near Springfield, Illinois.

KATE, born Oct. 10, 1851, was married Feb. 8, 1871, in Springfield, Ill., to Jonas F. Stover, who was born May 12, 1846, in Northampton county, Pennsylvania. They have two children, ELSIE E. and NELLIE E., and live in Akron, Ohio.

Richard Hodge died May 30, 1852, on his way to California. It was his second trip there. Mrs. Catharine Hodge lives with her son, Noah, in Akron, Ohio.

HODGERSON, JOHN, was born in Ireland, and brought to America at ten years old. He was married in Greenbrier county, Va., to Betsy Martin, moved to Cabell county, and from there to Sangamon county, Ill., bringing seven children, and settled five miles west of Loami, where two children were born. Mr. Hodgerson died, about 1843, and his widow in 1850 or '51. Their daughter—

REBECCA, married John C. Buchanan. They had seven children. Mr. Buchanan and five of the children died. Mrs. Rebecca Buchanan lives five miles southwest of Springfield.

HOFFMAN, MOSES, was born Nov. 24, 1798, in Greenbrier county, Va. His parents moved to Clark county, Ohio, when he was a boy. He was married there, Dec. 2, 1823, to Mrs. Rhoda Winn, whose maiden name was Turman. She was born Feb. 14, 1806, near Springfield, Ohio. They had three children there, and moved to Sangamon county, Ill., arriving Nov., 1829, in what is now Fancy Creek township, where they had three living children. Of their six children—

MARY A., born Dec. 10, 1824, in Ohio, was married in Sangamon county, Sept. 12, 1844, to James W. Dunn. They had seven living children, namely: ALWILDA, RICHARD M., HENRY C., IDA, MARGARET, JAMES W. and MARY, and live near Corvallis, Benton county, Oregon.

MARGARET, born Jan. 2, 1827, in Ohio, was married, April 10, 1845, in Sangamon county, Ill., to James H. Thaxton. See his name.

LEWIS F., born Sept. 21, 1828, in Champaign county, Ohio, was married, Jan. 17, 1861, in Sangamon county, to Hannah A. Gamble, a native of Holmes county, Ohio. They had two living children, LORA and ELMER G., and live at the homestead settled by Mr. Hoffman's parents in 1829; it is six miles north of Springfield.

AMANDA, born Dec. 20, 1832, in Sangamon county, was married, Jan. 1, 1850, to John B. Huffman. They have eight children, and reside near Winterset, Iowa.

LUCINDA, born Oct. 3, 1835, in Sangamon county, was married, May 23, 1852, to John L. B. Dunlap. They had four children—CATHARINE married James H. Blue. See his name. CHARLES F., FLORENCE and ELIZA. J. L. B. Dunlap died, June, 1863. His widow and children live two miles north of Cantrall. See his name.

CLARISSA, born Aug. 20, 1840, in Sangamon county, was married, March 11, 1858, to Willard R. Shepherd. They had three children; one died in infancy. JENNIE H. and JULIA G. reside with their parents, in Menard county, sixteen miles north of Springfield.

Moses Hoffman was a soldier in the Black Hawk war. He died in Sangamon county, June 3, 1842. His widow was married, Feb. 6, 1847, to Solomon Wood. They have one child—

SOLOMON S., was born Feb. 23, 1848, was married April 8, 1868, to Mary J. Wolf, who was born Jan. 8, 1850, near Mansfield, Ohio. They have two children, JOHN W. and CHARLES O., and live one mile south of Sherman. Solomon Wood died April 18, 1848, in Logan county, and his widow resides with her son, Lewis F. Hoffman.

Mrs. Wood remembers that her first husband measured the snow of 1830 and '31, and it was full four feet on a level; she also remembers the steamboat, Talisman, that came up the Sangamon river to Bogues' Mill, or Portland, as it was sometimes called. It was on the south bank of the Sangamon river, about half way between the Chicago & Alton and Gilman, Clinton & Springfield railroad bridges.

HOLLAND, TURNER, was born July 17, 1806, in Maryland, and was taken by his parents to Bath county, Ky. When a young man he went to Maysville and learned the tanning business, and then came to Springfield, Ill., arriving in August, 1831. He was sick several weeks, and when he became convalescent was introduced to Levi Cantrall, who he was told, had a tannery in connection with his farm in Fancy Creek township. He engaged to work for Mr. Cantrall, and in Feb., 1832, was married to his daughter, Nancy Cantrall. They had eight living children in Sangamon county, namely—

AMANDA, born May 30, 1833, married Elias B. French. She had one child, and died April 3, 1854.

FANNY, born Dec. 5, 1835, married Oct. 8, 1854, to Thomas R. Claypool. He was born Feb. 19, 1826, in Champaign county, Ohio, came with his parents to what was then Sangamon, but now Menard county, in 1827. They have five living children, IDA M., CLARA B., LEVI B., CHLOE L. and FREDDIE D. Thomas R. Claypool lives adjoining Cantrall on the north.

MILAM A., born July 19, 1837, married Mary A. England. He died in Feb. 1857, about one month after marriage.

FRANCIS M., born March 2, 1839, died in March, 1857.

WILLIAM H. H., born Oct. 28, 1840, enlisted August 12, 1862, for three years, in Co. C, 114th Ill. Inf. He was captured at the battle of Guntown, June, 1864, and spent nine months in prison—at Andersonville three months, Charleston six weeks, and the remainder of the time at Florence, S. C. He served his full term, and was honorably discharged July 1, 1865; was married Feb. 12, 1867, to Ruth A. Canterbury. They have two children, ALBERT C. and CHARLES T., and live near Cantrall.

BENJAMIN F., born July 8, 1842, married Dec. 28, 1865, to Margaret Hunt, who was born Sept. 30, 1843, in Clarke county, Ohio. They have two children, and live near Cantrall.

LUCINDA, born Feb. 17, 1844, married March 1, 1866, to James I. Wood. They had one child, JAMES I., Jun. Mr. Wood died July 2, 1870. His widow lives near Cantrall.

PRISCILLA, born March 17, 1846, married to William Hurt. They have three children, and live at Elkhart.

Mrs. Nancy Holland died, and Turner Holland was married in March, 1852, to Mrs. Hannah Lloyd, whose maiden name was Whitney. They had four living children in Sangamon county.

NANCY M. lives with her brother, B. F. Holland.

ELIZA J., lives with her sister, Mrs. Wood.

ROZETTA lives with her sister, Mrs. Hurt.

ABIGAIL lives with her brother, Wm. H. H. Holland.

Turner Holland died March 6, 1866, and his widow died March 11, 1866, both at Athens, Ill., to which place they had moved a short time before.

HOLLENBACK, ANDREW F., born Jan. 14, 1807, in Great Barrington, Berkshire county, Mass. He came to Sangamon county, Ill., arriving Nov. 11, 1830, at Rochester, but a few days before the "deep snow," and remembers that Archibald Sattley and himself gathered corn during the whole winter, and fed sixty head of cattle and fifteen horses. They kept a wagon road open through the fields, and each would take a basket and bring the corn to the wagon. He thinks the snow was from four to four and one-half feet deep. He was married in Rochester, Dec. 30, 1838, to Juliann E. St. Clair, who was born Oct. 9, 1818, in Vermont. They had three children; two died in infancy. Their son—

RANSOM A., died at Buffalo, Dec. 21, 1867, in his twenty-fifth year.

Mrs. Hollenback died Aug. 29, 1873. Mr. Hollenback was appointed Postmaster at Buffalo, in April, 1870, and holds the office to the present time. A. F. Hollenback was married Feb. 3, 1875, in Joliet, Ill., to Mrs. Mary A. Ledyard, whose maiden name was Carpenter. She was born Dec. 18, 1818, in Barre, Orleans county, New York. She has a son, George R. Ledyard, who lives with them, at Buffalo, Sangamon county, Ill.

HOPPIN, FRANKLIN B., brother to Daniel and Charles T., was born May 18, 1815, in Madison county, N. Y., married there to Sarah McConnell, and had two children there. He moved to Sangamon county, and settled near his brothers, Charles T. and Daniel, adjoining Chatham on the southwest. Of his children—

SARAH, born in New York, married in Sangamon county to A. M. Garland. See his name.

FRANKLIN S., born in New York, raised in Sangamon county, married Sarah Pierce, and lives in Louisiana.

F. B. Hoppin died June, 1866, and was buried in Oak Ridge Cemetery, Springfield. His widow resides with her daughter, Mrs. Garland, in Springfield.

The three Hoppin brothers and the McConnell brothers were among the earliest wool growers in Sangamon county. They prosecuted the business very extensively, from about 1840 until the close of the rebellion in 1865, when the business declined for a time.

HOPPIN, CHARLES T., born June 8, 1817, in Madison county, N. Y., was married there to Eliza McConnell. They had one child and moved to Sangamon county, Ill., and settled near Chatham, where his brother Daniel then lived. They had two children in Sangamon county. Of their three children—

SARAH L., born in Madison county, New York, married in Sangamon county, Ill., to E. F. Richmond. They have two children, CALISTA and CHARLES S., and live in Davenport, Iowa. Mr. Richmond is a lawyer in practice there.

MARY E., born in Sangamon county, married Allen E. Parmenter, and died March, 1870, in Sangamon county. Mr. Parmenter was born Dec. 30, 1842, in Madison county, New York. See his name in connection with the family of Daniel Hoppin.

CHARLES C., born in Sangamon county, lives with his father.

Mrs. Eliza Hoppin died in Oct., 1852, in Talkington township, and Charles T. Hoppin was married Feb., 1855, in Madison county, N. Y., to Phinetta G. Parmenter. They have seven children born in Sangamon county, GEORGE L., NETTIE A., KATE L., FLORENCE M., FREDDIE P., ANNIE E. and CARRIE P., and reside in Talkington township, seven miles west of Auburn.

HOPPIN, DANIEL, was born Sept. 16, 1819, in Madison county, N. Y. He visited Sangamon county, in company with his father, in 1839, and bought land near Chatham. In the fall of 1840 he came out with a flock of five hundred sheep for himself, and about two hundred for Edward F. McConnell. He was one of the earliest and most extensive wool growers in the county, and continued it for many years. Daniel Hoppin and Cordelia Bradley were married, March, 1848, at Chatham. They had three living children—

ANNA E. married Allen E. Parmenter. She died in 1875, in Talkington township. See his name in connection with the family of Charles T. Hoppin.

GEORGE B., and

CHESTER F. live with their parents.

Daniel Hoppin and wife reside near Pocahontas, Bond county, Ill.—1874.

HAUGHTON, ALVIN. See family sketch in Omissions.

HOUSTON, JOHN, born May 1, 1770, in Rockingham county, Virginia, was married April 23, 1807, in Augusta county, Va., to Mrs. Jane Curry, whose maiden name was Curry. She was born June 29, 1776, in Augusta county, and had one child by her first marriage—

ELIZABETH CURRY, born Mar. 31, 1801, in Augusta county, Va., was married there to James Curry, Feb. 17, 1817. They had three children in Virginia, and moved to Rush county, Ind., where two children were born, thence to Sangamon county, Ill., arriving in 1841. Of their five children: ROBERT J., born Nov. 9, 1818, in Virginia, was married March 27, 1839, in Indiana, to Mary Bracken. They had seven children: SARAH J. married David Myers, who died, leaving three children, and she married Wesley Sparks. They have two children, and live near Dawson. AMERICA, died in 1862, aged nineteen years. WILLIAM, born Dec. 25, 1845, lives in Berlin. GEORGE B., THOMAS J., ROBERT W. and JOHN W. reside at the homestead. Mrs. Mary Curry died Jan. 24, 1869, and R. J. Curry was married August 8, 1869, to Sarah French, a native of Onondaga county, New York. They had two children, ESTELLA and COQUILLA. Robert J. Curry died Feb. 23, 1874, suddenly, while waiting at German Prairie station for a train to Springfield. Mrs. Sarah Curry was married August 14, 1875, at

Barclay, to George Whitesides, and reside five miles northeast of Springfield. John Houston and wife had three living children. They moved to Sangamon county, Ill., arriving Nov. 14, 1828, and on the twenty-eighth of the same month moved to German Prairie, five miles east of Springfield. Their eldest child—
JAMES M. died, aged fourteen years.
MARY, born Oct. 19, 1809, in Augusta county, Va., married in Sangamon county to David Newsome. *See his name.*
SAMUEL, born Feb. 23, 1813, in Augusta county, Va., was married in Sangamon county, Ill., Nov. 7, 1833, to Lucretia Rudder, who was born Sept. 6, 1816, in Bath county, Ky., and came to Sangamon county in the fall of 1830, with her grandfather, Andrew Cartmell. They had ten living children—NANCY J. married Jonathan T. Payne, and died April 8, 1852. MILETUS C. married Eliza W. Miller. JOHN A. enlisted in 1862, for three years, in Co. I, 114th Ill. Inf., was at home on sick furlough, and died May 27, 1865. WILLIAM T. enlisted in 1862, for three years, in Co. G, 114th Ill. Inf., served full time, and was honorably discharged in 1865. He was married in Sangamon county, Sept., 1866, to Permelia Churchill. They have one child, WILLIAM F., and live at Edinburg, Ill. CHARLES G. was married in San Francisco, Cal., to Maggie E. Hall. They have three children, and reside in Baltimore, Md. JAMES W. married Frances Nave. They have one child, and live in Springfield, Ill. ANNA M. married Alexander Dixon. They have one child, and live five miles east of Springfield. F. EDWARD, GEORGE S. and VIRGIL T., live with their parents. Samuel Houston and wife reside near German Prairie station, on the farm where his father settled in 1828.

John Houston died Jan. 31, 1841, and his widow died Oct. 18, 1852, on the farm where they settled in 1828.

HUDSON, JOHN, was born April 25, 1794, in Mecklenberg county, Virginia, and taken by his parents to Cabell county, West Va. John Hudson was a soldier from that county, serving from Sept., 1813, to April, 1814. He was married in Cabell county, Oct. 8, 1814, to Margaret McCray, who was born April 7, 1803, in Rockingham county, Virginia. They had three children in Cabell county, and moved to Sangamon county, Ill., arriving in the autumn of 1826, in what is now Loami township, where they had eight children. Of their children—
YOUNG M., born Sept. 22, 1819, in Cabell county, W. Va., was married in Sangamon county, Ill., Oct. 5, 1843, to Minerva L. Meacham. They had one living child, ELSA JANE, who married Daniel Staley, Jun. *See his name.* Mrs. M. L. Hudson died Sept. 2, 1851, and Y. M. Hudson was married, Feb. 2, 1853, to Mrs. Jane Webb, whose maiden name was Fowler. They reside in New Berlin.
JANE C., born Aug. 3, 1821, in Cabell county, W. Va., married in Sangamon county to Wm. Hodgerson. They have eight children, and live five miles south of Waverly.
WILLIAM E., born Dec. 31, 1824, in Cabell county, W. Va., married in Sangamon county to Harriet Nipper, who died Aug. 31, 1851. Mr. H. married Mary Lacey. They have three children, MARY M., ELLIE K. and LUCINDA A., and live three and one-half miles west of Loami.
RACHEL S., born Feb. 22, 1830, married Willis Meacham. *See his name.*
JOHN M., born Jan. 4, 1833, married March 29, 1860, to Sarah J. Campbell, have one living child, LUCY E., and live three and one-half miles south of New Berlin.
GEORGE W., born Jan. 30, 1836, married Nancy H. Park, and he died, without children. She married James L. Short.
ANDREW J., born Jan. 23, 1839, married Feb. 20, 1862, to Mary M. Smelters. She was born Aug. 28, 1840, in Ohio. They live three and one-half miles south of New Berlin, in Loami township.
FRANCIS M., born Nov. 14, 1842, in Sangamon county. He enlisted April 16, 1861, (the first man to enlist in Loami township) in Co. G, 7th Ill. Inf., on the first call for 75,000 men; served full term, and was honorably discharged. He was elected Coroner of Sangamon county, in 1864. He lives with his father near Loami.

—49

SARAH E., born Feb. 9, 1845, married Thomas N. Park. *See his name.*

Mrs. Margaret Hudson died Oct. 2, 1854, and John Hudson was married June 21, 1855, to Mrs. Grezelle McNew, whose maiden name was Park. They reside now—1873—in Loami township, three and one-half miles west of Loami, and the same distance south of New Berlin.

Mr. John Hudson says that his father and the father Bishop, Thomas A. Morris, lived neighbors, in Cabell county, W. Va. When Thomas A. was a young man, he was a deputy under his brother Edward, who was clerk of Cabell county. While in the office, at Guyandotte, the county seat, Thomas A. attended a Methodist camp meeting there, and was converted. He visited his father soon after and told him he felt it to be his duty to preach the gospel. His father then proposed to give out an appointment for his son in two weeks from that time, with the promise that if he (the father) thought the son could preach, he would tell him so. The appointment was filled, the father listened very attentively, and at the close said to his son: "Well, Tommy, I think that if you don't get the big head, you will make a preacher." That was thought to be an evidence of remarkable liberality on the part of the old gentleman, in view of the fact that he belonged to the anti-mission or predestinarian Baptists.

Mr. Hudson heard that effort of the boy, and the criticisms of the father, and has been familiar with the history of the young preacher through all his progress to the present superannated Bishop Morris.—1873. Two brothers of Bishop Morris were early settlers in Sangamon county. *See their names.*

HUDSON, JOHN, was born Dec. 25, 1799, on Roanoke river, Virginia. He was taken by his parents to Wilson county, and from there to Rutherford county, Tenn. Nancy Pitts was born April 4, 1805, in Wayne county, N. C. Her father died there, and her mother, with seven children, moved to Rutherford county, Tenn., in the fall of 1815. John Hudson and Nancy Pitts were married in that county, near the junction of east and west Stone's river, Sept. 30, 1824, had two children there, and moved to Sangamon county, Ill., arriving in the fall of 1829, about two miles east of Loami, where five children were born. Of their children—

LOUISA E., born July 20, 1825, in Tennessee, married in Sangamon county to William Herrold, had one child, SARAH J., who married August 2, 1870, to Benjamin Card, a native of England. They have one child, WILLIAM H., and live in St. Louis, Mo. Mr. Herrold died, and she married Homer E. Starks. She died, leaving four children. NANCY A. lives with her aunt Edwards. LOUISA M. lives with her grandmother Hudson. JULIA A. and ELLEN T. live with their father, who is married, and resides in Kansas. He served in an Illinois regiment, and was with Sherman in his "march to the sea."

ROBERT W., born April 4, 1828, in Tennessee, died in Sangamon county, July 6, 1849.

CAROLINE, born Feb. 13, 1830, in Sangamon county, married David Edwards. They have three children. NANCY E. married John W. Smith; have three children, MARK C., NELLIE C. and KATIE A., and live in Curran township. VAN GOLTRA and JANE M. M. reside with their parents in Chatham township.

AMERICA A., born Feb. 15, 1832, married Henry R. Burton, and had nine children. MARY F. married William Bell, and died, leaving two children. H. R. Burton enlisted in Dec., 1863, for three years, in Co. H, 10th Ill. Cav., served to the end of the rebellion, and was honorably discharged. He died March 28, 1872, in Brown county. His widow married John Bell, and lives in Chatham.

JOHN H., born Jan. 7, 1836, in Sangamon county, married March 4, 1855, to Elizabeth McLaughlin. She died Jan. 10, 1856, and he was married April 12, 1868, to Charlotte E. Smith, in Milford, Wis. She was born in Fulton county, N. Y., Oct. 26, 1842. They live in Talkington township, eight miles west of Auburn—1873.

WILLIAM V., born April 8, 1838, in Sangamon county, and lives with his brother, John H.

BLANEY L., born Oct. 11, 1841, died Oct. 6, 1864.

John Hudson died Oct. 24, 1844, in Sangamon county, and his widow lives with her sons, John H. and William V.

Benjamin Hudson, the father of John Hudson, with his wife, two sons, William and Richard, and his daughter, Susan, came to Sangamon county in 1827. In the fall of 1839 they all moved to Washington county, Iowa.

Mrs. Nancy Pitts, the mother of Mrs. Nancy Hudson and Blaney Pitts, the youngest brother of Mrs. H., came with herself and husband to Sangamon county, and both went to St. Clair county, where the mother died. Blaney Pitts has been twice married, and lives in Marion county.

Mrs. Hudson vividly remembers the privations she endured on coming to the country. The first year they all shook with ague. The next year the "deep snow" came. Their cabin was built with the door outside. One morning they got up and could not open it; the snow was drifted higher that the door. By loud calls they attracted the attention of her father-in-law, who came and shoveled the snow away, and relieved them from their imprisonment. They were for a long time without tea, coffee or sugar, and had to substitute hominy for bread. She thought that if she could only get out of Illinois she would never want anything more, but would be happy the remainder of her mortal life. Four years later herself and husband visited Tennessee. The hills seemed higher—she thought the stone on the land had increased ten fold, and the soil was a deeper red than ever before. Her chief desire was to return to Illinois, and she has always been satisfied since that time.

Mrs. Hudson, describing a visit to St. Clair county to see her mother, says they traveled in a one-horse carriage over country where it yielded at least forty bushels of green flies to the acre. It was all they could do to save the life of their horse by wrapping it up with bed clothing. After that they laid up in daylight and traveled at night.

HUCKLEBERRY, HENRY, was born about 1779, in Pennsylvania. His parents had just emigrated from Baden, Germany, and soon after his birth they moved to Kentucky, a short distance above Louisville. A few years later, while returning from school, his youngest brother was captured by Indians. The father pursued them, and when about to rescue his boy, an Indian sunk a tomahawk in the boy's head, and threw him from the canoe into the Ohio river. It was near the mouth of a small stream that is called Huckleberry creek to the present time. The family soon after moved to Clark county, Ind. Henry was married there to Susan Wigal. She was born in 1792, in Virginia, and taken by her parents to Clark county. They had ten children in that county, and the family moved to Sangamon county, Ill., arriving in Oct., 1833, and settled in what is now Mechanicsburg township, where they had one child. Of their children—

ANNA, born Nov. 15, 1807, in Indiana; married there to Wm. B. Johnson. See his name.

ELIZABETH, born Feb. 21, 1810, in Indiana; married there to Blakely Smith. They had two living children, and Mr. Smith died Aug., 1847, at Carlington, Louisiana, while traveling on business. His widow married March 18, 1851, in Sangamon county, to John Langley. They had one child. Of her three children, ANGELINE SMITH married Silas Igo, have seven children, and live in Christian county. HENRY J. SMITH married Aug. 27, 1859, to Nancy A. Martin. They have three living children, ELIZA A., LAURA J., and BENJAMIN F., and live near Mechanicsburg. LAURA B. LANGLEY married Henry Frampton, have two children, and live near Mechanicsburg. John Langley and wife live four miles south of Dawson, Sangamon county.

JONATHAN, born Feb. 5, 1814, in Clark county, Ind., married in Sangamon county April, 1841, to Luann McDaniel. They had five children. MARY E. died Sept. 22, 1873, in her 30th year. MARIA, born June 20, 1846, married James H. McDaniel (son of Jeptha). Mr. McDaniel died Aug. 14, 1870, leaving two children. His widow and children, ALBERT and LESLIE, live with her father. CAROLINE lives with her father. JAMES H. married Lavica Lenville, and lives near Illiopolis. ANN E. lives with her aunt, Mrs. North. Mrs. Luann Huckleberry died Jan. 2, 1855, and Jonathan Huckleberry lives two miles southeast of Illiopolis—1874.

ELIZA, born July 19, 1816, married Wm. Laughrey; had two children, and all the family died.

DAVID, born Nov. 5, 1818, in Clarke county, Ind., married Nov. 19, 1848, in Sangamon county, to Almyra Cherry. They have five living children, namely: WILLIAM H., BENJAMIN F., OWEN O., ORAH A., and CHARLES L., and live three miles south of Riverton, Sangamon county.

JOHN W., born Sept. 2, 1822, in Ind. He enlisted in Sangamon county in Co. D, 4th Ill. Inf., and served from 1846 to 1847, in the war with Mexico. He was married Jan. 12, 1851, to Barbara S. Derry, who was born March 1, 1834, in Loudon county, Va. They had six children; three died under five years. ALICE E. married Absalom J. Barracks, have four children, and live near Illiopolis. ALONZO E. and IDA MAY live with their parents, three miles south of Dawson, Sangamon county. John W. Huckleberry enlisted Aug. 6, 1862, for three years, in Co. A, 73d Ill. Inf. He was captured at Stone's River Jan. 1, 1863; was paroled at Richmond, Va., and exchanged at St. Louis; served in the Invalid Corps the rest of his term, and was honorably discharged in 1865.

CHRISTIANA, born Feb. 4, 1824, in Indiana; married in Sangamon county Nov. 28, 1850, to John R. Williams, who was born July 30, 1824, in Dearborn county, Ind. They have six children, JOHN H., FLORENCE A., GEORGE L., EDGAR H., LUCIUS A., and MELISSA B., and live three miles south of Dawson. John R. Williams served one year, from June, 1846, in Co. D, 4th Ill. Inf, in the war with Mexico.

ELI L., born April 7, 1829, in Ind., married in Sangamon county Dec. 14, 1856, to Emily H. Derry, who was born Aug. 26, 1840, in Loudon county, Va. They have seven children; three died under five years. The other four, MARY M., SAMUEL L., HATTIE MAY and NORA, live with their parents at Illiopolis. E. L. Huckleberry enlisted Aug. 6, 1862, in Co. A, 73d Ill. Inf, for three years; served until Jan. 23, 1863, when he was discharged on account of physical disability.

AMERICA, born April 14, 1832, in Ind., married Nathan Potts; have two living children, and live near Taylorville.

SUSAN, born March 11, 1835, in Sangamon county, died at seventeen years of age.

Henry Huckleberry died March 13, 1859, and his widow died Dec. 31, 1868, both near where they settled in 1833, in the vicinity of Mechanicsburg. Henry Huckleberry was a soldier in the war of 1812. He fought at the battle of Tippecanoe, and it is well attested that he killed the last Indian that was slain at that battle.

HUFFMASTER, WM., was born about 1800, either in Germany or immediately after the arrival of his mother in Virginia, his father having died in Germany. The widow married a man named Sawyers, had two children, and he died, and she married Henry Brown, and moved from St. Clair to Sangamon county, as early as March, 1819, and settled at the north side of Lick creek, in Loami township. William had a sister, Lucinda. They came with Mr. Brown, their stepfather, to Lick creek, and while he went back after another load of goods, Huffmaster cut logs, built a cabin, and had it ready for the family when Mr. Brown returned. He had also made a trough, placed it in the cabin, cut down bee trees, and filled the trough with honey. When John Campbell came and settled at the south side of Lick creek, he thought himself the first settler, but hearing the sound of an axe, he went over and found that Huffmaster had been there before him. After more settlers came in, Huffmaster was in the woods with Samuel Harbour, and they found a panther up a tree. Harbour went for a gun, and the panther came down. Huffmaster urged on the dogs, and securing a large club, went to their assistance, and when Harbour returned, to his surprise, found the panther stretched out dead with Huffmaster and the dogs standing around it. Huffmaster's powers of endurance were remarkable. It is well attested that he split 700 rails in one day. He was married, about 1821, to Clarissa Smith, who was born in Kentucky, and came with her parents to Sangamon county, about 1820. They had eleven children—

SARAH, born Sept. 4, 1823, married in 1844 to Asa Morris. They have several children, and live in Missouri. Their son, Mayhew Morris, lives near Loami.

ELIZABETH, born Nov. 8, 1824, married Brice R. Weir, had two children, and she died. Their daughter, SUSAN, married Jesse Dodd, and lives in Chatham township. JANE married Lawrence Underwood, and lives in Loami township.

EDMUND, born April 26, 1827, married Elizabeth Colburn, and for a second wife married Susan Parker, and lives in California.

WILLIAM, Jun., born Dec. 9, 1829, married in 1848 to Emeline Colburn, and had two children. IRA W. lives at Loami. PAUL E. is a member of Co. B, 16th U. S. Inf.—1873. Mrs. Emeline Huffmaster died in 1854, and he married Achsa Underwood, have several children, and reside near Owanaco, Christian county, Illinois.

DAVID, born Feb. 17, 1831, married Adelia Parker, had one child, and Mrs. Huffmaster died in Sangamon county. Mr. H. started to California overland, in 1856, and lost his life in a singular manner. He was playing with a favorite dog, while holding a gun in his hand. The dog struck the hammer and the gun went off, lodging the charge in the shoulder of Mr. H., causing his death in a few days. His daughter, LYDIA, is now in California—1873.

LUCINDA, born June 15, 1832, married Daniel W. Colburn. *See his name.*

MARY, born June 12, 1834, married James Davis, had two children, and she died. Her sons, ADIN and SIDNEY, live in Loami.

JOHN, born May 21, 1836, married, Jan. 4, 1866, to Mary Davis. They have four children, FRANK, EZRA, WALTER and LUCY, and live near Loami.

NANCY A., born May 26, 1838, married Ebenezer Colburn. *See his name.*

ROBERT, born Nov. 31, 1842, lives in Loami.

DANIEL, born Nov. 21, 1844, enlisted in 1861, in Co. C, 11th Mo. Inf., for three years, and died in the army, March 8, 1862.

William Huffmaster died Oct. 19, 1861, and his widow died Sept. 23, 1866, both at Loami.

HUGHES, CHARLES F., was born July 9, 1807, in Baltimore, Md. His father, John Emanuel Hughes, was born March 13, 1767, in Montpellier, France, and married in Baltimore, Md., U. S. A., Oct. 7, 1806, to Juliana S. B. Wiesenthal, who was born in Baltimore, Jan. 12, 1785. Her father was physician to Frederick the Great, of Prussia. Charles F., the subject of this sketch, graduated at St. Mary's College, Emmettsburg, Md., at the age of twenty; studied medicine under Dr. Edrington, in Baltimore, and graduated three years later at Maryland Medical College, Baltimore. His health being impaired, he took a sea voyage, immediately after graduating. On their arrival at Guatemala, Central America, they were surprised by the negroes, who were in successful insurrection. They killed all the officers, crew and passengers, except Dr. Hughes and another physician, whose lives they spared solely because they were "medicine men." For seven years he practiced his profession among those savages, watching for an opportunity to escape. He was always under surveillance when vessels were in port. Finally, while discharging his duties in a hospital near the landing, he saw an American vessel approaching, and secreted himself among some barrels until the way was clear, when he reached the vessel and returned to his native land. He was married, Sept. 3, 1835, to Sarah J. Chambers, who was born in 1812, in Chestertown, Maryland. She was the daughter of Gen. Campbell Chambers, an officer of the war of 1812. He was born April 2, 1783, and married Jan. 18, 1807, to Sarah J. Clarkson, who was born Oct. 18, 1787, in Kent county, Md. Dr. Hughes came to Springfield in 1836, and engaged in the drug business for a short time. For two years he practiced medicine in the different small towns of the county, then resumed the drug business in Springfield. Dr. Hughes and wife had six children, two of whom died young. Of the four living children—

ANNA C., born July 23, 1836, in Baltimore, was married Oct. 31, 1861, in Springfield, Ill., to Charles W. Salisch. *See his name in connection with the Capps family.*

MARY E., born Oct. 14, 1838, in Sangamon county, was married Feb. 4, 1861, in Springfield, to Herman H. Abrams, who was born in 1837, in Springfield.

They have four living children, NINA, JOHN, VICTOR and FREDERICK. Mrs. Abrams died Oct. 8, 1874, at Cameron Junction, Missouri, and is buried at Palmyra, Mo. Mr. Abrams and his children reside at the former place.

JOHN C., born Jan. 10, 1841, in Mt. Auburn, Christian county, Illinois, enlisted August 15, 1862, in Co. B, 114th Ill. Inf., and was appointed Corporal. He was at the siege and capture of Vicksburg, and in the battle of Jackson, Miss., and was discharged on account of physical disability, Sept. 18, 1863. John C. Hughes was married Feb. 14, 1865, in Springfield, Ill., to Sarah C. Henry, who was born Dec. 19, 1845, near Pleasant Plains, Sangamon county. They have four living children, BERTHA B., OLIVE I., S. LUCRETIA and KATE. Mr. Hughes has been employed in the book room of the *State Journal* Company for sixteen years—except the time spent in the army—the last six years as Superintendent of the State printing, is so engaged at the present time—1876—and resides in Springfield.

JULIANA B., born Sept. 4, 1843, in Rochester, Sangamon county, Ill., was married March 20, 1865, in Palmyra, Missouri, to Oliver T. Prickett, who was born Feb. 26, 1845, in Fairmont, Virginia. They have two children, RALPH and GUY, and reside at Carbondale, Ill.

Dr. Charles F. Hughes was one of the founders of the Episcopal church in Springfield, and was treasurer of the same several years. He died Sept. 2, 1850, and Mrs. Hughes died May 20, 1871—both in Springfield.

Dr. Hughes was the eldest of three brothers and two sisters, all natives of Baltimore, Md. Andrew W. came to Springfield in 1836, and after a stay of a year or two, returned east and died in 1875, in Washington, D. C. John T. was a Surgeon in the U. S. army, stationed at Jefferson Barracks, Mo. He died in the Island of St. Thomas, in 1848. Maria E. was married in Baltimore to Henry Reigart, and resides there. Sophia J. came to Springfield in 1840, and married Mr. Biersted in 1858. He died in 1860, in Carrollton, Ill., and she resides in Baltimore. Mrs. Juliana S. B. Hughes, mother of the above named, came to Springfield with her daughter, Sophia J., in 1840, and died here in 1848.

HUGGINS, JOHN, was born about 1788, in New York, and raised in Greenbrier county, Va., and went to Gallia county, Ohio, when he was a young man. Jane Hazlitt was born about 1797, in Stokes county, N. C., and was taken to Gallia county, Ohio, when she was quite young. They were married, had seven children, and moved to Virginia, where one child was born; thence to Carter county, Ky., where one child was born, and to Sangamon county, Ill., arriving in the fall of 1840, in what is now Loami township. Of their children—

HANNAH, born in Ohio, June 5, 1818, married in Sangamon county to James Short, and had two children. Mr. Short went to California, was on his way home, and is believed to have been lost on the ship Central America, about 1855. His widow died July 7, 1871. Their daughter, FANNIE, married Peter Workman. *See his name.* His wife and two children live with their grandmother Huggins. JAMES A. SHORT lives with his grandmother Huggins, also—1874.

CHARLES, born April 30, 1820; died, aged 23.

JOHN T., born April 16, 1822, married Mrs. Lucy Runyon; has two children, and lives near Bethany, Harrison county, Missouri.

ELIZABETH, born April 22, 1824, lives with her mother.

SARAH, born June 18, 1826, in Ohio; married Jan. 20, 1852, in Sangamon county, to Ethan A. Bell, who was born July 25, 1829, in Madison county, Ill. They have three children, SUSAN J., MARTHA E., and THOMAS B., and reside three and one-half miles west of Loami.

MARTHA, born Aug. 4, 1828; lives with her mother.

FRANCES M., born July 22, 1831, married Daniel Whitehead; have eight children and reside near Edinburg, Illinois.

PHEBE, born Jan. 22, 1833, in Virginia, married James Lindsay, who died, leaving a widow and five children, in Davis county, Missouri.

JUNIOR, born June 3, 1837, in Carter county, Ky., married in Sangamon county to Lavina Bartlett; had two children, and live near Edinburg, Illinois.

John Huggins died Sept. 19, 1845, and his widow lives half a mile west of Loami, Illinois.

HUMHPREYS, OWEN, was born May 27, 1769, near Humphreysville, now Bryn Mawr, Montgomery county, Penn. His parents moved to Fleming county, Ky., when he was quite young. Mrs. Isabel Keith, whose maiden name was Lee, was born Sept. 7, 1771, but whether it was in Virginia or Kentucky is not known. Owen Humphreys and Mrs. Isabel Keith were married in Fleming county, Ky. They had seven children born in Fleming and Bath counties, and Mrs. Isabel Humphreys died April 12, 1823, in Bath county. Owen Humphreys, with some of his children, came to Sangamon county, Ill., arriving in the fall of 1828 or 1829, and settled three and a half miles southeast of Springfield, and west of Sugar creek. Of his seven children—

THOMAS L., born Jan. 24, 1799, in Fleming county, Ky., married in Bath county, to Sally Foster. They had four living children in Fleming county, and moved to Bath county, where one child was born, and then moved to Sangamon county, Ill., arriving in the spring of 1830, three and a half miles southeast of Springfield. Mr. Humphreys being sick that summer, they returned to Bath county, Ky., and came back to Sangamon county in 1844, settling at the same place he occupied in 1830. Some of his children died young, and he brought but three with him to Sangamon county the second time, viz: MARY, born June 6, 1824, near Flemingsburg, Ky.; married March, 1847, in Sangamon county, to George W. Williams, who was born Oct. 27, 1822, at Columbus, Ohio. He is a descendant of Roger Williams, of Rhode Island. Mr. and Mrs. Williams had five children, three of whom died in infancy. LLEWELLYN died in her ninth year. MARY T., born Jan. 1, 1848, in Sangamon county, was married Dec. 28, 1865, to Charles E. Payne. They had four children, all of whom died under four years. Mr. and Mrs. Payne live five miles southwest of Edinburg. Mr. and Mrs. Williams reside five and a half miles southwest of Edinburg, Christian county, Ill. MINERVA, born June 12, 1828, in Fleming county, Ky., died Oct., 1854, in Christian county, Ill. CHARLES, born Dec. 8, 1830, in Bath county, Ky.; came with his parents to Sangamon county; enlisted Aug. 5, 1861, in Co. C, 2d Ill. Light Artillery, for three years. After serving two and a half years, he was commissioned Lieutenant of Co. C, 8th U. S. Colored Artillery, and served eleven months. Charles Humphreys was married March 23, 1865, near Virden, Ill., to Julia Goodrich. They have three children, CHARLES, NELLIE and HATTIE. He is a merchant in Virden, and resides there. Mrs. Sally Humphreys died March 18, 1852, and Thomas Humphreys died Aug., 1855, both in Christian county, Illinois.

CHARLES F., born June 18, 1801, in Fleming county, Ky.; never married. He superintended an establishment for producing iron from the ore, in Greenup county, Ky., until his health failed, when he came to Sangamon county, and died at his father's house, Feb. 9, 1831.

ALEXANDER, B. V., born Nov. 27, 1803, in Fleming county, Ky., married Oct., 1827, in Bath county, to Nancy R. Whitecraft. They moved, in a few weeks, to Springfield, Ill., arriving Dec., 1827. They had one child born in Springfield, and in 1829 moved to Sugar creek timber, three and a half miles southeast of Springfield, where six children were born. Of their children—JOHN O., born July 18, 1828, in Springfield, is unmarried, and resides seven miles southwest of Edinburg. BENJAMIN F., born Sept. 10, 1830, in Sangamon county, married Oct. 11, 1866, in Christian county, to Mrs. Mary J. Martin, whose maiden name was Wood. She was born Jan. 13, 1812, in Montgomery county, Ky. They had one child, and B. F. Humphreys died Nov 30, 1870. His widow and daughter, IDA, resides at Edinburg, Ill. CHARLES F., born Feb. 3, 1833, in Sangamon county, enlisted Aug. 5, 1861, in Co. C, 2d Ill. Light Art. He was promoted through all the grades to First Lieutenant. Served exactly four years, and was honorably discharged at Springfield, Ill., Aug. 5, 1865. He was married Jan. 19, 1875, to Jane A. Williams, and reside one-half mile southeast of Rochester, Sangamon county, Ill. DAVID C. died in his second year. THOMAS E., born Sept. 29, 1838, in Sangamon county, enlisted Aug. 15, 1862, in Co. E, 114th Ill. Inf., for three years. He was color bearer of his regiment, and was wounded

Dec. 16, 1864, the second day of the battle of Nashville; recovered, served his full time, and was honorably discharged at the close of the rebellion. He died at the family homestead, in Christian county, Ill., Dec. 26, 1868. MARY M. J., born Feb. 29, 1840, in Sangamon county, Ill., was married March 3, 1875, to Dr. J. Henry Dickerson, who graduated Feb. 23, 1870, at the Philadelphia University of Medicine and Surgery. Dr. Dickerson and wife reside ten miles northwest of Taylorville, Christian county. *See Dr. Dickerson's name in connection with the name of his grandfather, Robert Bell.* JOSEPH A., born Jan. 2, 1843, is unmarried, and resides at the family homestead. Alexander B. V. Humphreys was engaged in blacksmithing while he lived in Springfield; but the business of his life was farming, in which he was eminently successful. In March, 1850, he moved with his family to Christian county, seven miles southwest of Edinburg, where Mrs. Nancy R. H. died Feb. 28, 1862, and A. B. V. Humphreys died Oct. 8, 1865.

MARY A., born Jan. 17, 1807, in Fleming county, Ky., married in Sangamon county to Philetus G. Pierce. They had five children in Sangamon county. ISABEL died young. The family moved in 1851, to the vicinity of Roseburg, Douglas county, Oregon, where Mr. Pierce died, in 1858 or '9, and Mrs. Pierce died Jan., 1872. Their four children, JOHN D., ELIZABETH, CAROLINE and OWEN reside in Oregon.

JOHN D., born Oct. 2, 1809, in Bath county, Ky., married Nov. 8, 1832, in Sangamon county, to Mary McKinnie. They had two children. MIRANDA, born August 1, 1833, died in her third year. DAVID, born Dec. 4, 1834, in Sangamon county, married June 9, 1857, to Mary A. Chapman, who was born March 2, 1835, in Devonshire, England. They have three children, JOHN J., MARY A. and MINNIE E., and reside at Farmingdale, Sangamon county, Illinois. He is station agent and postmaster there. John D. Humphreys died in July, 1835, three and a half miles southeast of Springfield, and his widow married John Branson. *See his name.*

ELIZABETH, born Feb. 11, 1812, in Bath county, Ky., married in Sangamon county to Willoughby Churchill. *See his name.* They had four children, and started, in 1850, to Oregon. Mrs. C. died at the Dalles, a narrow gorge in Columbia river. The family reside near Harrisburg, Linn county, Oregon.

DAVID, born Feb. 4, 1819, in Kentucky, died in Sangamon county, Sept. 6, 1834.

Owen Humphreys died Jan., 1846, in Sangamon county, near Mechanicsburg.

HUNTER, JAMES, was born August 14, 1778, in Loudon county, Va., and went, when a young man, to Gallatin county, Ky. He was there married to Rachel Scott, who was born Oct. 17, 1783, in Virginia. They had nine children in Gallatin county, and moved to Sangamon county, Ill., arriving Dec., 1828, in what is now Illiopolis township. Of their children—

WILLIAM, born Feb. 17, 1807, in Kentucky, married in Sangamon county to Polly Dickerson. They both died, leaving a large family near Mt. Auburn, Christian county.

ELIZABETH, born May 1, 1809, in Gallatin county, Ky., married in Sangamon county to William Donner. *See his name.*

JOHN, born Aug. 8, 1811, in Gallatin county, Ky., married in Sangamon county to Martha Dickerson, who was born Sept. 25, 1811. They had six children—MARY J., born May 18, 1840, married Harrison P. Hampton. *See his name.* HUGH L., born Oct. 1, 1841, enlisted July 19, 1861, for three years, in Co. I, 31st Ill. Inf., served full term, and was honorably discharged, Aug. 20, 1864, was married, March 30, 1865, in Sangamon county, to Rose Ann Ream, and lives three and one-half miles southwest of Illiopolis. RACHEL F., born Feb. 9, 1843, married Nov. 14, 1861, to James Lee, who was born Nov. 16, 1838, in Gallipolis, Ohio. They had five children—HARRIET A. died in infancy. WM. GRANT, FLORENCE, LAURA V. and ALLIE live with their parents, three miles southwest of Illiopolis. SARAH E., born July 4, 1845, married Thomas Sidener, have two children, and live near Rochester. THOMAS S., born Sept. 18, 1847, and ARCHER SCOTT, born Sept. 28, 1852, live in Illiopolis township. Mrs. Martha Hunter died Aug., 1854, and John Hunter died Dec. 22, 1856.

JAMES, Jun., born Feb. 14, 1814, in Gallatin county, Ky., was brought by his parents to Sangamon county, in 1828, and was married in Macon county to Lucinda Warnick. They had one child—SARAH L., born Dec. 25, 1839, married, April 18, 1861, in Springfield, to Sylvanus Dake, who was born Feb. 26, 1834, in Cattaraugus county, N. Y. They had three children—JULIA ANNA died in her second year. CORNELIA F. and OSCAR H., live with their parents in Illiopolis. Mrs. Lucinda Hunter died Dec. 31, 1839, and Mr. Hunter married Rebecca Newell. They had two children, WILLIAM and MARGARET A. They live in Iowa. James Hunter died in 1845. His widow married a Mr. Peeds.

CELIA, born Feb. 29, 1816, in Gallatin county, Ky., married in Sangamon county to Archibald Dickerson. *See his name.*

SALLY, born in 1818, in Kentucky, raised in Sangamon county, married in Macon county to Joseph Hanks, and had four children. RACHEL married Oct. 26, 1857, to Elijah Gathard, have six children, and live seven miles east of Springfield. MARGARET married Dr. Frank Hall, and died. CELIA married Dr. Frank Hall. *See his name.* Mr. and Mrs. Hanks died in Macon county.

MARGARET J., born Dec. 26, 1819, in Kentucky, married in Sangamon county to Wm. Freeman, had three children, and the parents died in Macon county.

RACHEL, born April 26, 1822, in Kentucky, raised in Sangamon county, married Lewis Freeman, had three children, and Mrs. F. died in Macon county. Mr. F. moved to Iowa City, Iowa.

THOMAS, born Sept. 14, 1824, in Kentucky, died in Sangamon county, at about twenty years of age.

Mrs. Rachel Hunter died April 18, 1865, and James Hunter died April 22, 1867, both in Illiopolis township, near where they settled in 1828.

HUNTER, THOMAS S., was born Feb. 8, 1814, in Hardin county, Ky. His father died in 1818, his mother married Wm. Y. Singleton, and the family came to Sangamon county Ill., in the spring of 1837. Mrs. Singleton died in

—50

1855. Thomas S. Hunter was married June 13, 1844, to Martha Darneille. They had three children, namely—

MARTHA R., married James W. Barger. *See his name.*

JAMES W. and *ROBERT S.*, live with their parents, five miles west of Chatham.

Of the three sisters—

HUNTER, ELIZA, married James Lampton, and died, leaving three children in Mason county.

HUNTER, MARY M., married G. R. Vigus, who died, leaving a widow and one son near Ottawa, Kansas.

HUNTER, REBECCA H., married Absolom D. McGraw. *See his name.*

HURST, CHARLES R., was born Sept. 20, 1811, in Philadelphia, Pa. He came to Springfield in March, 1834, and first engaged as clerk with Bell & Tinsley, dry goods merchants, on Jefferson street, between Second and Third, where the Springfield Manufacturing Company's works now stand. He bought out the dry goods business of Joshua F. Speed, and has been in the mercantile business to the present time; now as one of the firm of Hurst & Ruth. Charles R. Hurst was married in Springfield to Ann Taylor, a daughter of Col. John Taylor. They had six living children, all in Springfield—

JENNIE E. and *ANNA W.* reside with their parents.

GEORGIA S. was married April, 1874, to Maurice Starne, a son of Hon. Alexander Starne, and resides in Springfield.

CHARLES H., *EDWARD S.* and *HUIZINGA M.* reside with their parents in Springfield.

Mr. Hurst served the city of Springfield as alderman eight years. He was chairman of the committee on finance during the whole of that time. He also served three years as Waterworks Commissioner.

HUSBAND, HARMON, was born April 10, 1791, in North Carolina, and taken by his parents to Christian county, Ky. Sarah Pyles was born Nov. 12, 1790, in South Carolina. Her parents moved about 1795, to the vicinity of Mt. Sterling, Ky., and three or four years later moved to Christian county. Harmon Husband and Sarah Pyles were there married in 1811, and had five children in that county. The family moved to Sangamon county, Ill., arriving in Oct., 1820, and settled three miles east of the present town of Auburn, where seven children were born. Of their children—

EVELINE, born April 1, 1814, in Christian county, Ky., married Josephus Galton. See his name.

ELIZABETH, born about 1816, in Kentucky, married Thomas Mason. See his name. She died Dec. 23, 1850, leaving four children.

MARY A., born in Kentucky, married Thomas J. Higgins. See his name.

JANE, born in Kentucky, is unmarried, and lives at the family homestead.

MARTHA, married Wm. M. Snow, and died March 8, 1856, in Carlinville, leaving one child, ENOCH W. SNOW. He lives at the Husband family homestead.

SUSAN died in 1850, aged twenty-eight years.

JAMES E. D. is unmarried, and lives at the family homestead.

JOHN Q. A., born Feb. 19, 1828, in Sangamon county, married Jan. 7, 1864, to Ann E. Barrow. They have three children, EFFIE A., MINNIE A. and CLARLES H., and live six miles south of Springfield.

SARAH R., and

WILLIAM H., twins, born in Sangamon county, are both unmarried, and live at the family homestead.

EMILY, born in Sangamon county, married Lockwood M. Todd. See his name. They live in Virginia City, Montana Ter.

Harmon Husband died Feb. 15, 1848, and Mrs. Sarah Husband resides—1874—on the farm where they settled in 1820. It is three miles east of Auburn, Sangamon county, Illinois.

HUSTON, MARTHA, was born May 4, 1819, in Cumberland county, Penn. She came to Chatham, May 14, 1839, on a visit to her sister, Mrs. Wm. P. Thayer, and was married in Chatham, Sept. 28, 1843, to Henry Thayer, who was born July 1, 1812, in Boston, Mass., and came to Sangamon county, in April, 1841. They had eight children—

JOSEPH L., died at two years of age.

HENRY, died in his thirteenth year.

Of the other six Thayer children—

ELLEN M., born June 29, 1844, married, Aug. 25, 1864, to Thomas McElwain. They have one living child, ANNA ROSA, and live in Chatham.

OLIVE J., E. RUGGLES, CHARLES M., ANNA C. and EMMA A., reside with their parents in Chatham—1874.

HUSSEY, NATHAN, was born Sept. 20, 1785, in York county, Penn.; went to Washington county, Va., when a young man. Mary Stewart was born in the latter county Oct. 1, 1785. They were there married in 1803, and soon moved to Green county, Ohio, about fourteen miles southeast of Xenia. Seven of their children were born there, and the family moved to Sangamon county, Ill., arriving May 10, 1819, in what is now Fancy Creek township, where two children were born. Of their nine children—

CHRISTOPHER and MARY, twins, were born March, 1805, in Ohio.

CHRISTOPHER was married Sept. 12, 1828, in Sangamon county, to Elizabeth Primm, and died Sept. 16, 1830, leaving a widow without children.

MARY was married Feb. 27, 1829, to Joseph R. Young. They had three living children in Sangamon county. In 1850 they moved overland to Oregon, with their three children. DAVID died on the summit of the Rocky mountains. MARGARET died soon after their arrival in Oregon. Mr. Young died there in 1855, from the effects of a gun-shot wound, received in the Black Hawk war as a soldier from Sangamon county. His only son, STEPHEN, is married, and practicing medicine at or near McMinville, Oregon. Mrs. Mary Young still resides on her farm near McMinville, Yamhill county, Oregon.

WILLIAM S., born Nov. 2, 1809, in Green county, Ohio, was married Dec. 18, 1834, in Sangamon county, Ill., to Sarah Yocum. They had seven children, all born in Sangamon county, and in 1851 moved overland to Oregon. Of their seven children—NATHAN, born in 1835, married Charlotte Keagle. They have four living children, HENRY C.,

MATTIE R., ANNIE L. and SARAH A., who reside with their parents, three miles south of Williamsville. JACOB Y., born in 1836, in Sangamon county, Ill., enlisted Sept., 1861, in Co. A, 32d Ill. Inf., for three years; was wounded in the battle of Pittsburgh Landing, April, 1862, and was discharged on account of physical disability Sept., 1862. He now draws a pension. He married Sarah Yocum. They have two children, WILLIAM M. and CHARLES H. Jacob Y. Hussey is station agent at Barclay, and resides on a farm near that place. HENRY CLAY, born Feb. 13, 1838, enlisted Sept., 1861, in Co. A, 32d Ill. Inf., for three years, and died of typhoid fever, near Pittsburgh Landing, May, 1862. MARY J., born in Sangamon county, April 15, 1839, was married in 1856, in Oregon, to Alfred F. Thompson, who was born in McMinn county, Tenn. They have six living children, WILLIAM H., JOHN W., MARY E., ROBERT E. and LULA B., and reside two miles northeast of Barclay. WILLIAM F., born Sept. 3, 1841, enlisted Oct. 3, 1864, in Co. B, 30th Ill. Inf. In Feb., 1865, that regiment was merged into another, and he became a member of Co. A, 77th Ill. Inf. He was honorably discharged Aug. 31, 1865, and was married Feb. 14, 1866, to Alice C. Irwin. They have two living children, ALICE M. and WILLIAM H., who reside with their parents in Williamsville, Sangamon county, Ill. STEPHEN, born Nov. 28, 1842, enlisted in the same company and regiment with his brother, William H., and was honorably discharged at the same time. He married Mary Darnall. They have three living children, who reside with their parents at Lawndale, Illinois. MARIA E., the youngest child, lost her life in Oregon, in 1860, by her clothes accidentally taking fire while attending a sick friend. Her father's hands were so badly burned in his efforts to extinguish the fire that it made him a cripple for life. Mrs. Sarah Hussey died in 1852, and William S. Hussey was married in Oregon, May, 1855, to Mrs. Jemima Gilbreath, whose maiden name was Thompson, a native of Tennessee. They had two living children in Oregon, and in 1864, Mr. Hussey returned with his family to Sangamon county, Ill. Of their two children—JOSEPHINE C. was married in 1872, to Richard W. Barger. They have one child, SARAH, and R. W. Barger is a practicing attorney-at-law, and resides in Des Moines, Ia. CHARLES A. lives with his parents. Mrs. Jemima Hussey had two children by a former marriage. SARAH C. died in 1865. WILLIAM C. Gilbreath graduated June 18, 1875, at the Wesleyan University, at Bloomington, Ill. He was married, Aug. 6, 1875, to Lillie D. Lyon, of Pontiac. He is now a merchant in Williamsville. W. S. Hussey was elected Justice of the Peace, in 1858, in Oregon, which office he held until his return to Illinois, when he was elected a member of the Board of Supervisors of Sangamon county, twice, and tendered the office the third time, but declined. *William S. Hussey* and wife reside in Williamsville, Sangamon county, Illinois.

NANCY A., born March 29, 1811, in Ohio, was married in Sangamon county, to Abraham D. VanMeter. *See his name.*

SOPHIA, born July 18, 1813, in Ohio, was married in Sangamon county, Ill., to James Brown, and moved to Oregon in 1850. They have seven children, and reside in McMinnville, Yamhill county, Oregon.

NATHAN, born Dec. 14, 1815, in Ohio, was married in Sangamon county to Sarah Burton. They had five children in Sangamon county, and in 1845 moved to Oregon, where their family was increased to eight children. The mother and three children died, and the father and five children reside near Fort Haskins, Oregon.

STEPHEN, born Oct. 16, 1818, in Ohio, was married in Sangamon county, Ill., to Cornelia Crowl. They had five children in Sangamon county, and moved to Oregon, in 1850, where others were born. Mrs. H. and four of their children died there. One of the living children, ELIZABETH, is married to James Peterson, and resides in Portland, Oregon. The other three, with their father, moved to California, where he died.

MARGARET, born April 5, 1821, in Sangamon county, married Henry Bird. *See his name.*

ELIZABETH S., born Aug. 1, 1823, in Sangamon county, married William Lynch. They have two sons, and reside in Fairfield, Iowa.

Mrs. Mary S. Hussey died in Sangamon county June 30, 1841, and Nathan Hussey accompanied two of his children to Oregon, and died there Oct. 29, 1857.

HAMPTON, JAMES P., was born April 17, 1787, in the vicinity of Hampton Roads, Va. In 1790 his parents crossed the Alleghany mountains, and embarking in boats, at Pittsburg, went down the Ohio river. Some families had been massacred a short time before, at Limestone, now Marysville. The Hamptons and their friends intended landing at the same point, but were convinced by the movements of the savages on shore that it would not be safe. They landed further down, and thus saved their lives, but the Indians captured one of their boats with all their stores. Mr. Hampton settled in what became Franklin county, Ky. James P. was a soldier from that county, in the war of 1812-'13, under Gen. Harrison. He was married in 1818, in the adjoining county of Woodford, to Sarah Poindexter, who was born in that county, March 24, 1800. They made their home in Franklin county, four miles from Frankfort, until they had five living children. The family moved to Sangamon county, Ill., arriving Oct., 1829, in what is now Illiopolis township, where they had two living children. Of their seven children—

WILLIAM H., born July 17, 1821, in Franklin county, Ky., married April 20, 1843, in Sangamon county, to Mary A. Garvey. They had ten children in Sangamon county—EMILY J., ANNIE M., JAMES W., SURRILDA E., FRANKLIN P., HATTIE; LOUISA died in her eighth year; LAURA, NANCY and ELBIE, the nine living, reside with their parents in Illiopolis township, two miles east of Mechanicsburg.

JAMES M., born about 1823, in Kentucky, died in Sangamon county, July 17, 1845.

JOHN S., born Aug. 29, 1824, in Frankfort, Ky., married in Sangamon county, April 29, 1847, to Nancy C. Garvey. They had eight children born in Sangamon county; one died in infancy. MARY E., born Sept. 6, 1848, married March 26, 1872, to John S. Ford, have one child, HORACE N., and live three miles east of Mechanicsburg, in Illiopolis township. ELIZA F., SUSAN B. and SARAH, live with their parents. CHARLES LINCOLN was drowned while bathing, July 27, 1875. ELEANOR and ARTHUR E. reside with their parents. John S. Hampton had one foot amputated in June, 1875. He has acted as a Justice of the peace many years, and part of the time was engaged in merchandizing. He now—1876—resides in Illiopolis, Illinois.

MARTHA J., born Nov. 23, 1826, in Kentucky, is unmarried, and lives in Illiopolis.

MARY A., born Aug. 29, 1828, in Franklin county, Ky., married in Sangamon county, Aug. 7, 1862, to Simon P. Williams, who was born Sept. 17, 1825, in Tuscarawas county, Ohio. They had two children, ROLLIN E. and RENA A., and Mrs. W. died July 19, 1873. Mr. Williams and his children live in Illiopolis.

PRESTON B., born Jan. 28, 1831—during the "deep snow"—in Sangamon county, married in Mechanicsburg, March 5, 1857, to Dorothy Rankin, who was born March 25, 1832, in York county, Maine, raised in New Hampshire, and came to Mechanicsburg, April, 1855. They have five children, SHERIDAN, ABRAHAM LINCOLN, JOHN LOGAN, FLORA MAY and JAMES GRANT. Preston B. Hampton enlisted Aug. 4, 1862, for three years, in Co. A, 73d Ill. Inf., served until April 18, 1863, when he was discharged on account of physical disability. He resides in Illiopolis township, five miles east of Mechanicsburg, on the farm where his parents settled in 1829, and where he was born.

HARRISON P., born April 2, 1840, in Sangamon county, enlisted Aug. 4, 1862, for three years, in Co. A, 73d Ill. Inf., served to the end of the rebellion, and was honorably discharged with the regiment, June 24, 1865. He was married March 14, 1867, to Mary J. Hunter. They have two children, EBER and CALLIE, and live in Illiopolis.

James P. Hampton died Dec. 15, 1853, and his widow died Jan. 14, 1858, both near Illiopolis, Sangamon county, Illinois.

HAMPTON, SAMUEL C., brother to James P., was born about 1791, in Franklin county, Ky. He was there married, in 1819, to Catharine Johnson, a native of Virginia. They had four children in Frankfort, Franklin county, Ky. The eldest, J. Henry, died there. Mr. Hampton moved with his family to Sangamon county, Ill., arriving in the fall of 1830, in what is now Mechanicsburg township, where they had one child. Of their four children—

JAMES W., born Oct. 4, 1823, in Frankfort, Ky., married in Springfield to Elizabeth Johnson. They had three children, two of whom died young. JOHN T. is married, and resides in Decatur, Ill. Mrs. Elizabeth Hampton died, and James W. Hampton married Ada Baker. They had three living children, FRANK, NETTIE and CHARLES R. James W. Hampton died Oct. 25, 1875, in Springfield, Ill. His widow and children live at 817 South Fourth street.

ELIZABETH, born in 1825, in Kentucky, married in Sangamon county in 1842 to Isaac Hart. They had five children, and in 1860 moved to, and are now living at, Ottumwa, Iowa.

SETH COOK, born April 18, 1828, in Frankfort, Ky., was married Sept. 8, 1853, in Springfield, to Mary A. Conant. They had seven children—SETH COOK, Jun., the eldest, and EMERY E., the youngest, died under five years. The other five, HARRY L., LYDIA C., ALBERT S., RUTH M., and RUFUS C. live with their parents. Mr. Hampton has been, from his boyhood, engaged in merchandizing, and is now in that business in Springfield—1876.

CHARLES B., born March, 1830, in Sangamon county, died March 1, 1874, in Springfield, leaving neither wife nor children.

Samuel C. Hampton died about 1839, and Mrs. Catharine Hampton died Jan. 19, 1859, both in Sangamon county, Illinois.

I

ILES, ELIJAH, was born Mar. 28, 1796, in what was then Fayette county, Ky., about sixty miles east of Lexington. His grandfather was an Englishman, and his grandmother Welch. Thomas Iles, the father of Elijah Iles, was born in Chester county, Pa., in 1765, emigrated to Kentucky about the year 1790, married Elizabeth Crockett, a relative of David Crockett. Their five children were Mary, Elijah, William, Washington and Elizabeth. The latter was eight days old when the mother died. Elijah, the subject of this sketch, attended school for two winters, where reading, writing and arithmetic were the highest branches taught. He became proficient in these studies, and taught school himself two winters. His father then gave him $300 with which he bought one hundred head of yearling cattle. These he herded among the mountains in the eastern part of Kentucky, about twenty miles outside of civilization, on the Little Sandy river. Here he camped, his only companions being his horse, dog, gun, milk cow and the cattle. These last he shifted from one valley to another, wintering the cattle without grain, and they would be in tolerable condition in the spring. His meals generally consisted of a stew made of bear meat, venison, turkey, and a piece of fat bacon. He baked his corn bread on a johnny-cake board or in the ashes. This, together with sweet milk (not skimmed) and honey, he thought good living, and although alone, enjoyed life. Sometimes the young men from Lexington and Paris would join him for a hunt, always bringing *good whisky* and other refreshments. He sold his cattle, in three years, for about ten dollars a head, realizing a large sum of money for that time, and with this left for Missouri, on horseback, arriving at St. Louis in 1818, which was only a French village of 2,500 inhabitants. From there he went to Old Franklin, Mo., opposite where Brownsville now stands. Here he engaged as clerk in a store, and acted as land agent for eastern capitalists. He remained there three years, investing his money in lands. In 1821 he visited Kentucky; returning, he passed through central Illinois. There were no roads then, and his only guide from Vincennes to Vandalia, and from the latter place to the Sangamon valley, was the surveyors stakes. He was so much pleased with what is now Sangamon county that he determined to locate here, and returned to Missouri to sell some of his land and collect some money. Proceeding to Illinois, on horseback, he crossed the Mississippi river at the present town of Louisiana, swam his horse across the mouth of the Illinois river, rode from there to Carrolton, thence to Diamond Grove, near where Jacksonville now stands. There he found a settlement. From there he proceeded by way of Island Grove to the head of Spring creek, and thence to Springfield, arriving in June, 1821, just after it had been made the temporary county seat of Sangamon county, which embraced all of Illinois north of Greene and Madison counties. The inhabitants of Springfield consisted of the families of Charles R. Matheny, John and William Kelly, Andrew Elliott, Levi D. and Jacob Ellis, Lanterman, Little and Lindsay. Mr. Iles boarded with John Kelly about a year. He describes it as being the best boarding house he ever had, before or since. Two of Mr. Kelley's brothers were hunters, and the table was well supplied with venison, wild turkey, prairie chickens, squirrels and fresh fish. The bread was the old fashioned hoe cake, with plenty of milk and honey. Soon after domiciling himself at Mr. Kelly's, Mr. Iles concluded to visit some friends north of the Sangamon river. Arriving at the stream he found the banks full, and a horn left on the south side, opposite the ferry, to be blown by persons desiring to cross. Mr. Iles blew this horn, at intervals, for several hours, but failed to attract the attention of the ferryman. Despairing of crossing for that day, he returned to Springfield that night, and the next day started again, with the same result. He returned the second night to Springfield, and the third day, by loud and continuous blowing, he succeeded in crossing and visiting his friends. On returning, Mr. Iles contracted for the building of a log store, sixteen feet square, with a shed attached, and set out on horseback for St. Louis, to buy goods. He remained four weeks, and bought fifteen hundred dollars worth of merchandise, consisting of wrought iron, pot metal, dry goods and groceries. Mr. Iles loaded these on a keel boat, which was towed up the Mississippi by six men having a rope, which they pulled from the shore. He found but one house at Alton, one at the mouth of the Illinois river, and an empty cabin, built by Mr. Beard, where Beardstown now stands. Here he was landed with his goods, and the men returned with their boat, leaving Mr. Iles alone on the bank in a wilderness. He paid seventy-five dollars freight to Beardstown. After a month's delay, he succeeded in bringing all his goods to Springfield, and opened the first store in town, July, 1821. The Indians were about as numerous as the whites, and his sales were about equal. Everyone seemed honest, and he often left his store open. The Indians paid him in furs and undressed deerskins. The whites in silver coin, homemade jeans, and cotton and linen cloth, beeswax, honey, butter, etc. His trips to St. Louis were made on horseback. Silver was the only currency. This he carried in saddlebags, thrown over the saddle, and when he stopped at a house on the way, took them in, dropping them behind the door of the room he entered, without fear of their being molested. Indeed, any one traveling with money in those days rather made a show of it, to impress the early settlers *with their importance.* When Mr. Iles' first stock was reduced, he locked the store, leaving the key with Mr. Matheny, and left for St. Louis, in perfect confidence that all would be safe; but on his return found the store had been robbed of nearly everything. About a month afterwards he heard of a man by the name of Cotteral, who had been living with two families by the name of Percifield, on the bluffs, not far from where Naples now stands, traveling with a two-horse wagon, and peddling such goods as were stolen from him. Mr. Iles took an officer and searched the Percifields, finding goods like his, but could not identify them, as the marks were removed, so he abandoned the search. Several persons were robbed about this time, and his searching the Percifields led to the belief that they were the thieves, and a regulating company, headed by Murray McConnell, drove them from the country. Mr. Iles heard afterwards that one was hung and the other sent to the penitentiary. Aside from this, Mr. Iles believes no country was ever settled by a more honest and industrious people. He invested in land as soon as it came into market, and among his entries was the southwest quarter of section twenty-seven, town sixteen north, range five west, being the northeast part of the present city of Springfield. This entry was made in 1823, at one dollar and a quarter per acre. P. P. Enos, D. P. Cook and Thomas Cox entered the other three-quarters of the section joining his on the southwest corner. This is near the intersection of Washington and Second streets. These four laid off the original town plat, the title being, by agreement, in the names of P. P. Enos and Elijah Iles. The legislature of 1825, then meeting in Vandalia, appointed three Commissioners to locate the county seat of Sangamon. The competing points were Springfield, Sangamo, about seven miles northwest, on the Sangamon river; a point near the mouth of Spring creek, and one on Prairie creek, near Salisbury. The Commissioners had visited, on horseback, all the competing points except Springfield and the one near the mouth of Spring creek. A strong opposition had sprung up between the two latter points, owing to the efforts of a land company, which had bought up the Spring creek site for a speculation. But Messrs. Enos and Iles were too shrewd for them, and they employed Andrew Elliott to pilot the Commissioners to the Spring creek site. He was, of course, a Springfield man, so he concluded to take them the longest and roughest route he knew of. There were neither bridges or roads, so he had it all his own way, and they swam several creeks, waded through marshes and almost impenetrable thickets, but finally arrived at the place, and pronounced it a fine site for a city, but suggested that the people who were to fill it might never find it. And they directed Mr. Elliott to take them by a more direct route, but the return route was even more perilous than the other. By this time the Commissioners were convinced that the Spring creek site was inaccessable, and, on a promise from Messrs. Enos and Iles that they would give the county forty-five acres of land, and what was of more consequence to the Commissioners, namely, cashing their warrants issued at a dollar a day for their services, they decided to locate the county seat permanently at Springfield. This forty-five acres include the old State house square. A court house was built on Jefferson street, between First and Second, of rough logs, and the space between them filled with black mud. It consisted of one room, thirty feet square, without a floor, a small platform was erected for the Judge, and the jury on retiring had all out-doors for their deliberations. When court was not in session, which was the greater part of the time, the room was used as a refuge for emigrants until more permanent quarters could be provided. In 1826, Elijah Iles was elected a State Senator, and again in 1830.

In 1827, the Winnebago Indians became troublesome. Troops were called for, and Mr. Iles was elected Major of the regiment commanded by Col. Tom M. Neal. On arriving at Galena, they found the Indians suing for peace; a treaty was made, and the troops disbanded. This was the Winnebago war. The Black Hawk war occurred in 1831, and a regiment was raised in this part of the State. Major Iles was a private in one of the companies from Springfield. *See sketch of the Black Hawk war, page 54.* In this expedition were—Gen. Stillman, commanding; Zachary Taylor, afterwards President; Lieut. Jeff. Davis, afterwards President of the Confederacy; Abraham Lincoln, Hon. John T. Stuart, Gen. Harney, William S. Hamilton, son of Alexander Hamilton; Lieut. Robert Anderson, of Fort Sumter fame; Major Fry, and many others, who afterwards became distinguished. They had some skirmishes with the Indians, and were discharged. Volunteers were called for to protect the frontier, until new recruits could be brought forward. A battalion was formed, and Mr. Iles was elected Captain of a company. He insists that he was the least qualified of any of them for the office, and he was chosen because the aspiring members were envious of each other. But it is more than probable that his qualifications were as good as any of them. The title of Major still clings to Mr. Iles, and has become almost part of his name. In 1838 and '9, he built the American House (now the Central Hotel), located on the southeast corner of Sixth and Adams streets. This was the largest hotel at the time in Illinois, and created a greater sensation while building than the Leland, which was built in 1866, at a cost of $350,000.

In the early settlement of Illinois, Major Iles invested largely in land, that became valuable in after years, placing him in independent circumstances. He has reached a ripe old age, and enjoys the respect and confidence of ALL WHO KNOW HIM. He was a member of the committee to secure the removal of the State capital from Vandalia to Springfield.

In 1824 Elijah Iles was married, in Springfield, to Melinda Benjamin, a native of Lima, Livingston county, N. Y. They had two children, namely:

LOUISA ELIZABETH, born in 1825, in Springfield, married in 1856, to T. J. Carter. Mrs. Carter died in 1857, without children. Mr. Carter was born Sept. 15, 1817, at Wilmington, Middlesex county, Mass.; his ancestors were among the earliest settlers of New England. Rev. Thomas Carter was educated at Exeter, England, emigrated to Boston, in 1630, and finally settled in Charlestown, then a portion of the town where T. J. Carter was born. It was from him that the Carter family in America descended. One of the fifth or sixth generation from Rev. Thos. Carter was Timothy Carter, who married Sabra Jaquess. They were the parents of Thos. J. Carter. The first fifteen years of his life was spent with his parents on a large dairy farm, and attending a district school. In 1832 he entered Phillip's Academy, at Andover, Mass. Failing health, caused by too close application to study, caused him to abandon a collegiate course, and devote himself to civil engineering. His earliest labors in this profession were in connection with some of the most distinguished civil engineers of his time, who were in charge of the public works then in progress in the eastern part of the United States and in Canada. In 1850 Mr. Carter was solicited by Boston capitalists to accompany them on a western tour. During that trip they devised plans out of which grew the great lake railroad route, connecting Boston with Chicago and the west. In 1852 Mr. Carter was appointed Vice President and General Superintendent of Engineers for the construction of the Wabash line from Toledo to St. Louis. He was engaged on this work four years, with residence in Springfield.

During that time he was married, and so soon lost his wife. In 1857 he left for Kansas, and in 1859 for Texas, where he built a short railroad. He obtained a charter from the State of Kansas for a railroad from the Missouri river to the Pacific, now known as the Kansas Pacific route, and commenced building it in 1863.

In that year he was appointed by President Lincoln, U. S. Government Director for the Union Pacific Railroad, the duties of which he discharged for five years. In 1868 he was requested to report on a branch road from the Union Pacific to the Colorado mines, which was the origin of the narrow guage system in that section of the country. In 1869 Mr. Carter visited portions of Europe, intending a more extended tour at some future time, which he took in 1875, accompanied by his bride, formerly Miss Allie S. Hoge, of Brooklyn, N. Y. They spent six months in visiting Great Britain, France, Germany, Belgium, Austria, Italy, Egypt, Palestine, Turkey and Greece. The title of Colonel was confered on Mr. Carter in civil life, as a compliment for the aid he rendered during the canvass and election of the first Whig Governor of New Hampshire. He has worn it to the present time. He is now, while this is in press, on a visit to the Centennial Exhibition.—June, 1876.

IRA THOMAS, born in 1830, in Springfield, resides with his father, Major Iles, who is now in his eighty-first year. While Springfield continues to be his home, he spends much of his time traveling, and with relatives in other parts of the country.

ILES, WASHINGTON, was born July 18, 1800, in Bath county, Ky. At eighteen years of age, he visited Illinois on business for another man, traveled over the country along the Sangama river, and found that the land was very rich. A wealthy man from Kentucky had brought out a drove of horses, sold them on credit, and when the money was due, came to collect it, but found his customers unprepared to pay. It was then lawful to imprison men for debt, and he threatened to collect his money in that way. His creditors combined and convinced him that it would not be very pleasant to attempt it, and he left the country in haste. On reaching home he offered Mr. Iles one-half the amount of the claims if he would collect them. The offer was accepted. He found the men were honest, and by kind treatment he succeeded in collecting every dollar. Mr. Iles returned to Kentucky, and was married in Flemingsburg, May 21, 1822, to Ann Foster, who was born there Dec. 3, 1804. They lived near Owensville, Bath county, Ky., for some time, and then, with two children, moved to Sangamon county, Illinois, arriving at Springfield in the year 1825. Nine children were born in Sangamon county. Of their children—

MARTHA H., born June 14, 1823, in Kentucky, died Aug. 26, 1827, in Sangamon county, Illinois.

MARY E., born Aug. 4, 1825, in Bath county, Ky., was married in Sangamon county to Jacob G. Loose. See his name.

CORDELIA M., born May 25, 1827, in Sangamon county, Ill., married Obed Lewis. See his name.

MELINDA A., born April 23, 1829, in Sangamon county, married Joseph B. Pirkins. See his name.

ANN E., born May 27, 1831, in Sangamon county, was married there to William H. Bourne. They have five children, namely: CARRIE, ANNIE, KITTIE, VIRGINIA and BENJAMIN. W. H. Bourne and family till recently lived near Sharpsburg, Bath county, Ky. Removed in 1876 to Springfield, Illinois, and reside one mile south.

WASHINGTON T., born April 6, 1833, in Springfield, Ill., was married in Bath county, Ky., Dec. 6, 1864, to Emily Jones, who was born in that county April 4, 1844. They have three children—JULIA J., LINNA L., and BENJAMIN, and live four and one-half miles southeast of Springfield.

NANCY V., born July 23, 1835, in Sangamon county, was married there Nov. 1856, to Norman M. Broadwell, who was born Aug. 1, 1825, in Morgan county, Ill. Of their seven children—Two died young. ANNA, LOUIE, LUCY, STUART and VIRGINIA live with their parents in Springfield. N. M. Broadwell served one term in the State Legislature of Illinois. In the spring of 1862, he was elected County Judge, Illinois, to fill the vacancy caused by the death of Judge William D. Power, and served until Dec., 1865. He was mayor of the city in 1867, and again in 1869, and is a practicing attorney in Springfield.

ELIJAH F., born Feb. 18, 1838, in Springfield, was married, Oct. 6, 1863, in Lincoln county, Mo., to Mildred Steele, who was born in that county, Feb. 16, 1844. They have four children born in Sangamon county, LEWIS W., DAVID S., ELIJAH F., jun., FRANK B. and a boy, and live two and one-fourth miles south of Springfield, Illinois.

EDWARD, born Oct. 1, 1841, in Sangamon county, is an extensive importer and breeder of thoroughbred cattle. He is unmarried, and resides two miles south of Springfield, on the farm where his father settled in 1826.

JULIA E., born Feb. 9, 1843, died in 1857.

MARIA, born Nov. 11, 1845, died in her third year.

Mrs. Ann Iles died Aug. 25, 1866, and Washington Iles died July 4, 1871, both near Springfield, Illinois.

Washington Iles was a soldier in the Winnebago and Black Hawk wars. He aided in bringing the steamboat, Talisman, up the Sangamon river, opposite Springfield—the only steamboat that ever ascended that stream so high.

INGELS, JAMES V., was born April 5, 1815, in Fayette county, Ky. His father, Thomas Ingels, was born April 20, 1789, in Penn., was taken by his parents to Bourbon county, Ky., and was married in Fayette county to Judith Haley. They had six children, and moved to Jacksonville, Ill., thence to that part of Schuyler which is now Brown county, where they had three children, and Mrs. Judith Ingels died. Thomas Ingels married again, his wife died, and he moved, with part of his children, to Gentry county, Mo., and died there. Two of his sons came to Sangamon county, James V. and John. The former, whose name heads this sketch, came in Oct., 1837, and was married March 22, 1838, to Henrietta Earnest. They had four living children, namely—

SARAH J., born Feb. 13, 1840, married Jan. 31, 1867, to Charles W. Hall. They live in Piatt county, near Weldon, DeWitt county.

JACOB E., born June 25, 1841, in Sangamon county, went to Idaho Territory in 1862, married there July 14, 1867, to Augusta Thompson; moved to California, where she died. He returned to Sangamon county, and was married Jan. 25, 1871, to Salome O. Turner. They have two children, EDWARD E. and

—51

JAMES T., and live six miles west of Springfield, Illinois.

S. *GERARD*, born Aug. 22, 1848, and

HENRIETTA E., born Feb. 14, 1858, live with their parents.

James V. Ingels resides in Island Grove township, four miles east of Berlin —1874.

INGELS, JOHN, was born Sept. 2, 1819, in Fayette county, Ky. He is a brother of James V. John Ingels was married in Sangamon county, March 14, 1843, to Elizabeth King. They have eight children born in Sangamon county, namely—

JOHN T., born Sept. 12, 1845, married Dec. 29, 1870, to Martha J. Morrison, a daughter of John B. Morrison. She was born March 5, 1852, in Island Grove township. They reside near Berlin.

MARIA A., born Nov. 1, 1847, lives with her parents.

CHARLES K., born June 3, 1850, married, Nov. 5, 1873, to Nannie Reed, daughter of Calvin Reed. They live near Berlin, Sangamon county, Illinois.

SOPHIA F., born May 7, 1852, married Nov. 6, 1873, to John Bates, and live near Virginia, Cass county, Ill.

JOANNA B., born Nov. 1, 1856.

WILLIAM W., born Jan. 27, 1859.

JAMES V., Jun., born May 31, 1863, and

ELIZABETH, born July 14, 1865; the four latter reside with their parents, near Berlin, Sangamon county, Illinois.

INNIS, ALEXANDER, was born Nov. 26, 1780, in Bellarona, county Down, Ireland. Ann Wilson was born March 16, 1794, in Drumlee, in the same county. They were married in Drumlee, in Aug., 1812, had one child, and emigrated to America, settling in St. Lawrence county, New York, in 1826. Their only child—

ELIZABETH, born Dec. 13, 1813, in Backaderry, county Down, Ireland, married in St. Lawrence county, New York, to Charles Watts. *See his name.*

Mr. and Mrs. Innis moved from New York to Sangamon county, Ill., arriving in the spring of 1835 at the house of their daughter, Mrs. Charles Watts. They purchased a farm one mile southwest of the present Farmingdale station. Alexander Innis died Nov. 27, 1854, and his widow died Sept. 16, 1869, both in Gardner township, Sangamon county, Illinois.

IRWIN, SAMUEL L., born June 6, 1779, in Cabarras county, N. C. Rachel Hudson was born Oct. 15, 1785, in Rockingham county, Va. She was taken by an uncle to Cabarras county, N. C., where she was married Sept. 23, 1802, to Samuel L. Irwin. They had ten living children born in North Carolina, and in the fall of 1818 the family moved to that part of Tennessee then called the Cherokee purchase, where one child was born. The family moved to what became Sangamon county, Ill., arriving April 20, 1820, and first pitched their tents in what is now the northeast part of Pleasant Plains. After a few months' stay, they moved about two miles down Richland creek, at the south side, where four children were born. Of their fifteen children—

HANNAH, born July 11, 1803, in North Carolina, married in Sangamon county to William Miller. They had eight children; three died young. Four of the living are married, namely: FRANCIS, VIRGIL, JANE and SARAH. Hugh is unmarried, and lives with his mother. Mr. Miller died in Feb., 1870, and his widow resides in Morgan county.

MARY, born Jan. 10, 1805, in North Carolina, married in Sangamon county to Samuel Purvines. *See his name.*

JANE, born June 26, 1806, in North Carolina, died in Sangamon county Jan. 15, 1832.

DEBORAH, born Nov. 7, 1807, in North Carolina, married in Sangamon county to Miles Stevenson. *See his name.*

WILLIAM C., born Feb. 7, 1809, in North Carolina, married in Sangamon county to Matilda Plunkett. They had eight children. NANCY J., born Sept. 13, 1833, married Daniel Penny, and died Jan. 19, 1863. CHRISTOPHER C., born Sept. 4, 1835, married Jan. 25, 1858, to Lucinda C. Capps, who was born April 1, 1841, in Hardin county, Ky. They have three living children, WILLIAM C., ELMER E. and EVA MAY, and live two miles east of Pleasant Plains. MARTHA married Elder C. C. Purvines. *See his name.* RUFUS R. and ELIZABETH

J. live with their mother. SAMUEL G., born Feb. 20, 1844, enlisted in 1862 for three years, in Co. F, 114th Ill. Inf. He was captured June 10, 1864, at the battle of Guntown; was starved three months in Andersonville prison pens; escaped; served to the end of the rebellion, and was honorably discharged in 1865. He was married Aug. 27, 1867, to Martha C. Davis, who was born Nov. 19, 1848. They have three children, OLLA B., MARY J., and SUSIE E., and live near Bates, Sangamon county, Ill. JULIUS H., born March 28, 1846, enlisted Feb. 6, 1865, in Co. A, 152d Ill. Inf., served to the end of the rebellion, and was honorably discharged Sept. 11, 1865; married Feb. 27, 1870, at Mount Pleasant, Iowa, to Harriet I. Cassiday, who was born in Jefferson county, Iowa. Her mother was a daughter of Shadrach Scott, brother of Dallas Scott. They live three miles northeast of Pleasant Plains. JAMES M. and William H. live with their mother. William C. Irwin died in 1852, and his widow resides in Menard county, eight miles north of Pleasant Plains.

NANCY, born Oct. 2, 1810, died in 1824.

HUGH B., born Aug. 30, 1812, in North Carolina, married in 1836 in Sangamon county, to Priscilla Kyle. They had five children, and he died Oct. 18, 1852, and his widow resides in Menard county. THOMAS, the eldest, and CHARLES, the youngest, live in Missouri. Their son, HENRY, was a soldier in Co. F, 114th Ill. Inf., from Aug., 1862, to the end of the rebellion. He was married, had one child, and his wife died Oct., 1873. He resides in Menard county, and is married again. JANE is dead, and CYNTHIA lives in Menard county, Illinois.

ALEXANDER B., born Feb. 7, 1814, in Cabarras county, N. C., married in Sangamon county Oct. 18, 1838, to Cynthelia Broadwell. They had four living children. AMOS D., born Oct. 12, 1839, married Rebecca J. Plunkett; have two children, ROBERT A. and ADOLPHUS J., and live at Pleasant Plains. JOHN B., born March 27, 1841, enlisted Sept., 1861, for three years, in Co. C, 64th Ill. Inf. He was wounded Oct. 4, 1862, at the battle of Corinth, Miss., and died of his wounds at Jackson, Tenn., March 20, 1863. BETSY J., born April 1, 1843, married William Huber; have one child, and live near Medina, Jefferson county, Kansas. SAMUEL P., born Feb. 22, 1845, enlisted Jan., 1862, in Co. C, 64th Ill. Inf., for three years. He was wounded in June, 1864, at Kennesaw mountain, Ga., by a musket ball entering the left side of his face and coming out of the back of his neck. He recovered, and went with Sherman in his "march to the sea;" served to the end of his term, and was honorably discharged. He was married Feb. 21, 1867, to Almeda Howard, who was born in St. Lawrence county, N. Y. They have three children, JOHN A., SAMUEL and CYNTHELIA, and live three miles east of Pleasant Plains. Mrs. Cynthelia Irwin died Aug. 10, 1847, and Alexander B. Irwin was married Feb. 28, 1855, to Mrs. Jane S. Seaman, whose maiden name was Broadwell. They have four children, namely: JAMES H., ARABEL A., RACHEL A., and MAGGIE S., and reside in Cartwright township, two miles east of Pleasant Plains. Mr. Irwin has served a number of years as a Justice of the Peace, also as a member of the Board of Supervisors of Sangamon county. On the seventh day of Feb., 1874, Alex. B. Irwin gave a festival commemorating the sixtieth anniversary of his birth. The invitations were to relations, only, with, perhaps, the single exception of the writer of this sketch and his wife, which they were very reluctantly compelled to decline. There were *two hundred and sixty-four* guests present. By way of recognizing the fact that they were all descendants of a family of the earliest settlers in the county, no meat except that of wild game was served—buffalo and venison, from the western plains, and wild turkeys from Wisconsin, with prairie chickens, quails, etc., taken nearer home. Four States were represented by the different branches of the family, and if all had been present it would have included half a dozen more States. The host was not in good health at the time, but still enjoyed the company of so many of his relatives. He was the recipient of a number of presents; among others, a fine gold-headed cane, and a beautiful silver watch, the two latter accompanied by some cheering words from a niece, appropriate to the occasion.

RACHEL, born March 26, 1816, died in 1852.

MATILDA B., born Feb. 13, 1818, married William Conner, and lives in Cartwright township.

ROBERT T., born March 7, 1820, in that part of Tennessee then called the Cherokee purchase, married in Sangamon county Jan. 14, 1847, to Mary E. Day, who was born March 20, 1820, at Ogdensburg, N. Y. They had twins. SOPHIA J. married Joseph J. Dillon. *See his name.* FRANCES MARIA married Peter S. Cartwright. *See his name.* Robert T. Irwin resides near Pleasant Plains, in Sangamon county, Illinois.

BENJAMIN F., born May 18, 1822, in Sangamon county, married Oct. 11, 1844, to Jane Combs, of Menard county. They had one child, MARY T., born March 28, 1846, married Aug. 5, 1869, to John W. Whitcomb, who was born Dec. 6, 1842, in Owen county, Ky.; went to Missouri in 1859, and when the rebellion broke out, he entered the enrolled State militia (loyal); served nine months; came to Sangamon county in June, 1863, and enlisted in Feb., 1864, for three years, in Co. C, 64th Ill. Inf. He was with Sherman on his "march to the sea;" was in North Carolina when the rebellion ended, and was present at the great review in Washington, D. C., in May, 1865; was honorably discharged at Chicago July 18, 1865. Mr. and Mrs. Whitcomb have two children, LIZZIE ETHEL and CHARLES FRANKLIN. They live one and one-half miles south of Farmingdale, in Sangamon county. Mrs. Jane Irwin died March 7, 1848, in Sangamon county, and B. F. Irwin was married Jan. 16, 1870, at Mount Florence, Kansas, to Mattie Huber. Her mother resides there. They had two children. ETHEL died in infancy, and EDWARD F. lives with his parents, at Pleasant Plains, Illinois. B. F. Irwin has served several years as Justice of the Peace and Police Magristrate.

JULIUS H., born July 22, 1824, in Sangamon county, married Oct. 24, 1851, to Sarah Kyle; had six living children, SAMUEL W., MARY L., ARMINTA A., EMMA D., CHARLES H., and BENJAMIN F. Mrs. Sarah Irwin died Nov. 24, 1873, and Julius H. Irwin died Oct. 5, 1875. Their children reside at the homestead, one mile southeast of Pleasant Plains.

JAMES C., born May 6, 1827, married March 18, 1862, to Jane Howard, who was born Nov. 29, 1839, in St. Lawrence county, N. Y. They have four living children, LIMIE E., ROBERT H., FRANCES M. and KATE B., and reside two miles southeast of Pleasant Plains.

JOHN M., born April 24, 1829, in Sangamon county, married March 15, 1859, to Sarah May, who was born April 6, 1831, at Circleville, Ohio. They had two children, ABRAHAM L., and MARY M., and Mrs. Irwin died Oct. 8, 1864. He was married May 16, 1867, to Ann Williams, who was born Jan. 30, 1841, in St. Lawrence county, N. Y. They have two children, LULU M. and ALBERT W., and reside at Pleasant Plains.

Samuel L. Irwin died March 1, 1845, and his widow died July 6, 1867, both on the farm where they settled in 1820. Samuel L. Irwin was, at the time of his death, in his sixty-seventh year, and his widow, at her death, was in her eighty-third year.

IRWIN, WILLIAM, was born March 31, 1789, in Cabarras county, N. C. He was cousin to Samuel L. Irwin. Robert Irwin, the father of William, was killed by a runaway team, about the time of the war of 1812. There is a tradition in the family that the original name was Erwin. William Irwin was married, Oct. 2, 1811, in his native county, to Margaret Purviance. They had five children born in North Carolina, one died in infancy, and Mr. Irwin, with his wife and son, came to Sangamon county, Ill., arriving in the fall of 1827 on Richland creek, in what is now Cartwright township. He returned to North Carolina the next spring, and brought out the remainder of the family, arriving in the fall of 1828. They traveled in wagons, and were seven weeks on the road. Three children were born in Sangamon county. Of their children—

ROBERT S., born Nov. 14, 1813, in Cabarras county, N. C., was married in Sangamon county, Jan. 19, 1837, to Cynthia Duncan, who was born Aug. 18, 1818, in Adair county, Ky. They had ten children—SANFORD, JAMES S.,

MARY and ROBERT died under twelve years. WILLIAM F., born Oct. 21, 1837, was married, May 23, 1872, to Ellen J. Williams. They have one child, WARREN H., and reside in Salisbury township, near the Iron Bridge. MARTHA J., born Dec. 15, 1839, was married, Jan. 14, 1864, to Franklin W. Duncan. They have four children living, MARY M., JASPER N., CYNTHIA and GREEN, and live in Menard county, Ill. GREEN P. died Sept. 4, 1871, aged twenty-six years. OSCAR; HARVEY D. was married Dec. 31, 1874, to Mary E. Wells. They have one child, ADA R., and live in Salisbury township. CHARLES CARROLL. The two unmarried sons reside at the homestead. Mrs. Cynthia Irwin died April 6, 1872, and Robert S. Irwin died May 3, 1874, both in Salisbury township, east of the Sangamon river, and near the Iron Bridge.

JOHN C., born June 16, 1816, in North Carolina, was married, June 12, 1842, in Sangamon county, to Minerva Duncan. They have eight children, EWIN, VIRGINIA and HARRIET died under four years. AUSTIN F., born Aug. 12, 1845, married Ann Brown, and live near Ft. Scott, Kansas. TARLETON, SILAS, JANE, CHARLES and LUELLA reside with their parents, two miles northwest of Salisbury, in Sangamon county.

WILLIAM F., born March 12, 1820, in North Carolina, was married in Sangamon county, Jan. 23, 1851, to Matilda D. Campbell. They have one child, MARY E., and reside in Menard county, two and one-half miles northwest of Salisbury.

JANE E., born July 6, 1822, in North Carolina, married John B. Gum, in Sangamon county, Ill. They have five children, and live seven miles west of Petersburg, Menard county.

SAMUEL I., Jun., born Jan. 25, 1825, married Matilda Green, and live in Lincoln, Ill.

JAMES H., born Nov. 9, 1828, married and lives in Logan county, Illinois.

NANCY, born Nov. 15, 1831, married Enoch Wiseman, who died, and she married Abraham Wiseman, and lives in Delavan.

WARREN I., born June 16, 1834, married Mary Shively, who died. He married Eliza Wiseman, and lives in Logan county.

Mrs. Margaret Irwin died Oct. 25, 1852, and William Irwin died June 13, 1871, and both were buried at the Baptist church, in Cartwright township, where they settled in 1828.

IRWIN, JOHN, was born Jan. 20, 1804, in Williamsport, now Monongahela, Washington county, Penn. He came west, stopping a short time in St. Louis, and joined his brother Robert in Springfield, Ill., in 1838. He remained a few years, returned to his native place, and was married there, Jan. 31, 1844, to Margaret Jack Guthrie, who was born May 23, 1820, at Greensburgh, Westmoreland county, in the same State. They came at once to Springfield. Mr. Irwin was for several years in business as a dry goods merchant, first with his brother Robert and Col. John Williams. Then the Irwin brothers bought out the interest of Col. Williams, and a few years later, when Robert became connected with the Marine and Fire Insurance Bank, John continued in the mercantile business alone, and still later admitted as a partner, Walter Davis. In consequence of declining health, Mr. Irwin retired from business about 1857. Mr. and Mrs. Irwin had three children in Springfield—

WILLIAM is married, and lives in Colorado.

HETTY W. resides in Springfield, Illinois.

MARGARET, born Jan. 2, 1850, in Springfield, married Nov. 22, 1871, to Cleveland J. Salter, who was born Oct. 12, 1845, in Waverly, Morgan county, Ill. They have one child, CLEVELAND I., and reside in Springfield. Mr. Salter is in the mercantile business with his father, J. D. B. Salter.

Mrs. Margaret J. Irwin died June 14, 1850, and John Irwin died May 21, 1859, both in Springfield, Illinois.

IRWIN, ROBERT, was born Nov. 7, 1808, in Monongahela City, Pa. He came west when a young man, and was married in St. Louis, Mo., May 30, 1833, to Clara C. Doyle, who was born in Philadelphia, Pa., March 9, 1815. Mr. and Mrs. Irwin left St. Louis, crossing the Mississippi river on the ice when it was in motion, jumping the open space between the ice and the shore. They came by stage, stopping two nights on the way, and arrived in Springfield in January, 1834. They had five children in Springfield, two of whom died young—

ELIZA J., born Feb. 7, 1834, in Springfield, was married there, August 11, 1859, to William H. Marston, who was born August 19, 1832, in Deerfield, New Hampshire. He went to New York in 1851, and came to Springfield first in 1853, spending part of each year in the latter city, until 1861. Mrs. Marston died Feb. 25, 1868, in New York, leaving three children, ROBERT I., LAURA and ELLA, who live with their father. After the death of his wife, Mr. Marston spent part of 1870 and '71 in London, England. He is now engaged in business at No. 36, Broad street, and resides at No. 110, West Forty-fourth street, New York City.

SARAH ELLA, born March 9, 1839, was married Oct. 5, 1865, in Springfield, Illinois, to Charles D. Chase a native of New Hampshire. They have one living child, a daughter, and reside in Deerfield, New Hampshire.

ROBERT T., born Oct. 30, 1844, is unmarried, and resides in his native city.

Robert Irwin formed a partnership with John Williams, as dry goods merchants, soon after he came to Springfield. His brother John was admitted to the firm, and still later the Irwin brothers transacted business alone, until Robert became connected with the Fire and Marine Insurance Co. Bank, first as Secretary, then as Cashier. He continued in the latter position until his death, March 8, 1865. His widow resides in Springfield, Illinois.

J

JAYNE, GERSHOM, born Oct. 15, 1791, in Orange county, New York, received his diploma from the New York medical authorities, and came west, locating, in 1820, at what became Springfield, Illinois, being the first practicing physician that settled in the place. He was married in 1822, to Sibyl Slater. They had four children—

JULIA M., born in June, 1824, in Springfield, was married there, June 1, 1843, to Hon. Lyman Trumbull, a native of Colchester, Conn. He was, at the time, Secretary of State for Illinois. In 1848 he became one of the Supreme Court Judges of Illinois. In 1854 he was elected representative in Congress, and elected in January, 1855, as one of the two United States Senators from Illinois. He was twice re-elected, serving, in all, eighteen years, ending in 1873. Mr. and Mrs. Trumbull had six children. Three only are living, WALTER, PERRY and HENRY. Mrs. Julia M. Trumbull died in August, 1868, in Washington, D. C. Hon. Lyman Trumbull resides in Chicago Illinois.

WILLIAM, born Oct. 8, 1826, in Springfield, was educated at Illinois College, Jacksonville, studied medicine with his father in Springfield, and graduated in the medical department of Missouri State University in 1849. Dr. William Jayne was married Oct. 17, 1850, in Jacksonville, Ill., to Julia E. Witherbee, who was born in 1830, in Vermont. They had six children, four of whom died young. Of their two living children, WILLIAM S., born Oct. 18, 1851, in Springfield, Illinois, was married in his native city, Nov. 18, 1875, to Margaret E. Palmer, daughter of Ex-Governor John M. Palmer. She was born March 20, 1854, in Carlinville, Ill. William S. Jayne is connected with the office of the Auditor of State, and resides in Springfield, Ill. LIZZIE, born July 10, 1855, in Springfield, resides with her parents. Dr. William Jayne, in addition to his professional duties, has found time to engage in politics. He was elected, in 1859, Mayor of Springfield. In 1860 was elected State Senator for one term of four years, and resigned, in 1861, to accept an appointment by President Lincoln, of Territorial Governor of Dakota. In April, 1876, he was again elected Mayor of Springfield, and is consequently the Centennial Mayor of the Capital city. Dr. Wm. Jayne still continues the practice of medicine, and resides in Springfield, Illinois. As this goes to press—June, 1876—he is on a visit to the great American Centennial Exposition, at Philadelphia.

HENRY, born June 8, 1837, in Springfield, enlisted as a private in Co. I, 7th Ill. Inf., for three months, re-enlisted in the 7th Ill. Cav., was hospital steward, and afterwards commissioned Lieutenant of Co. K, by Gov. Yates. He was appointed, by President Lincoln, aid-de-camp, with the rank of Captain in the fifteenth army corps, and in that capacity served until the close of the rebellion, when he was appointed, by President Johnson, Lieutenant in the United States Cavalry, but did not accept. Henry Jayne attended medical lectures at Ann Arbor, Michigan, University, in 1865, and located in Taylorville in 1866, for the practice of medicine. He was married Sept. 8, 1868, to Jennie Cheney, daughter of Thomas Cheney. *See name of Archibald Sattley.* Dr. Henry Jayne is engaged in the drug business in Taylorville, and resides there.

MARY ELLEN, born Nov., 1842, in Springfield, resides with her mother.

Dr. Gershom Jayne was one of the first Commissioners of the Illinois and Michigan canal, appointed in 1830 and '31. When he located in Springfield there was not another physician so far north in the State. He practiced forty-seven years, and died April 17, 1867, in Springfield, and his widow resides there.

JACOBS, DANIEL, was born May 27, 1795, near Winchester, Clark county, Ky. Charlotte Webb, was born April 19, 1797, in Jessamine or Clark county, Ky. Her father, Adin Webb, was a soldier from Clark county, in the war of 1812, and died somewhere in the northern lake region. Daniel Jacobs and Charlotte Webb were married, Jan. 30, 1819, in Clark county. They had four children in Kentucky, and moved to Sangamon county, Ill., arriving Nov 7, 1825, in what is now Loami township, where seven children were born. Of their eleven children—

HENRY W., born March 5, 1820, in Kentucky, married in Sangamon county, July, 1846, to Priscilla A. Hall. They had eight living children; and AARON died, aged nineteen years. Mr. Jacobs lives in Graysonville, Missouri.

MARY, born Oct. 1, 1821, in Kentucky, married in Sangamon county, Dec. 17, 1840, to Benjamin F. Darneille. *See his name.*

AMANDA, born April 19, 1823, in Kentucky, married in Sangamon county to John T. Wyckoff. She had one child, and died.

ELIZABETH, born Feb. 17, 1825, in Kentucky, married in Sangamon county to L. P. Bradley. They have nine living children, and reside two miles west of Girard, Illinois.

MARTHA, born April 2, 1827, in Sangamon county, married, July 16, 1850, to James L. Foster, who was born Jan. 8, 1822, in Boone county, Ky., and came to Sangamon county in 1848. They had eight children—LIZZIE and MARTHA W. died, aged four years each. ELLEN, born May 25, 1851, married Feb. 18, 1874, to Luther Rigg, and live in New Berlin township. GEORGE W., JAMES A., HUBBARD C., SUSAN and CHARLES reside with their parents, one and one-fourth miles west of Loami.

JAMES A., born Aug. 4, 1829, in Sangamon county, married Oct. 11, 1855, to Mary E. Neal. They had five children—LIZZIE, the third child, died Feb. 24, 1865, aged five years. AMANDA, HENRY C., CHARLOTTE and ALPHEUS live with their parents, at the homestead where Mr. Jacobs' parents settled in 1825, and where he was born. It is two miles southeast of Loami.

SUSAN, born Nov. 20, 1831, in Sangamon county, married, March 4, 1852, to Hubbard S. Coley. *See his name.*

ISABEL, born Jan. 30, 1834, in Sangamon county, married Stephen Staley. *See his name.*

CHARLOTTE, born Jan. 22, 1836, in Sangamon county, married W. Washington McGinnis. *See his name.*

KATE, born Feb. 16, 1838, married Greenberry McGinnis. *See his name.*

ANNIS, born Oct. 10, 1840, in Sangamon county, married Feb. 10, 1859, to James E. Dodd, have five children, and live five miles west of Auburn.

Daniel Jacobs died Oct. 5, 1853, and his widow resides—1874—at the homestead settled by them in 1825, two miles southeast of Loami.

JACOBS, GEORGE, was born in 1793, in Clarke county, Ky. He was married there to Nancy Haney. They had five children, and moved to Sangamon county, Ill., with his brother Daniel, arriving Nov. 7, 1825, in what is now Loami township, where five children were born; about 1839 the family moved to Christian county, where one child was born. The only representative of the family in Sangamon county is—

EVELINE, born Oct. 12, 1819, in Clark county, Ky., married Thompson Hall. *See his name.*

SARAH married Willis Vaden, have two children, and live in Shelby county.

JAMES married Elizabeth Atterbury. She died, leaving two children, and he married Belle Covington, and live in Macon county.

The other children are all dead.

George Jacobs died Jan. 1, 1845, and his widow died Jan. 16, 1857, both in Christian county, Ill.

JAMES, ABRAHAM, was born in 1792 in Pennsylvania. He was married in Nicholas county, Ky., to Jane Beatty. They had five children in Kentucky, and moved to Sangamon county, Ill., arriving in the fall of 1829 in Rochester township. Of their five children—

WILLIAM, born in 1812, in Kentucky, came with his parents to Sangamon county, and died, unmarried, in Missouri in 1858.

MARY J., born in 1814, in Kentucky, married in Sangamon county to William Herbert. They have four children, and live in Orangeville, Stephenson county, Illinois.

RACHEL, born in Kentucky, married in Sangamon county to William Coe; have three children, and live in Cotton Hill township.

ELLEN, born in 1826, in Kentucky, raised in Sangamon county, married in Missouri to Richard Opie; have four children, and live near High Point, Moniteau county, Missouri.

JAMES A., born Jan. 28, 1828, in Nicholas county, Ky., married in Sangamon county, August 28, 1856, to Amanda Bashaw. They have six children, MAHLON F., ISABEL J., HANNAH L., ARMINDA E., IRA H. and IRENE A., and reside in Clear Lake township, seven miles due east of Springfield.

Abraham James moved to Stephenson county, Illinois, in 1846, and Mrs. James died there. He moved to Missouri, married; had two children, and he died June, 1867, in Moniteau county, Mo.

JACK, ROBERT, was born Nov. 9, 1778, in Virginia. His parents moved to Kentucky when he was a boy. He was married there to Nancy Fleming, who was born Nov. 25, 1786, in Pennsylvania. They had five children in Kentucky, and the family moved to Sangamon county, Ill., arriving in 1825 or '6, near Old Berlin. Of their children—

JAMES died at fourteen or fifteen years of age.

MARGARET married Elias Jefferies. *See his name.*

RHODA G., born June 30, 1813, married Nov. 21, 1833, to John W. Stringfield. He died Dec. 6, 1847, and she was married March 22, 1849, to Nicholas A. Garland. *See his name.*

MARIA, born in 1815, married about 1833 to Robert Patton. They moved to Lawrence county, Mo., had five children, and returned to Sangamon county during the war, and Mr. Patton died here in 1863. His family live in Missouri.

JOHN D. died at eight or ten years of age.

Robert Jack died about the spring of 1834, and his widow died January, 1863, both in Sangamon county.

JARRETT, JONATHAN, was born July 23, 1778, in Kanawha county, West Virginia. He was married there to Sarah Anderson. They had six children, and Mrs. Jarrett died Oct. 28, 1812. Mr. Jarrett married Jan. 1, 1814, to Rebecca Wilson. They had six children in West Virginia, and moved to Sangamon county, Ill., arriving Nov., 1826, and settled one and one-half miles south of the present town of Loami, where two children were born. Of his fourteen children—

MORDECAI, born Dec. 21, 1803, in West Virginia, was a soldier in the Black Hawk war, and died, unmarried, in Sangamon county Feb. 5, 1856.

LEAH, born Feb. 27, 1805, in West Virginia, married there to Achilles Morris. *See his name.* He was Captain of a company, and died in 1847, in Mexico. His widow married L. Samples. He died in Sangamon county, and she moved to Missouri with her children, and died there in 1871.

DAVIS, born Dec. 11, 1806, in Virginia, enlisted in Sangamon county under his brother-in-law, Capt. Morris, and died near Carlinville, just as the company had started for the Mexican war in 1846.

NANCY, born Jan. 15, 1808, in West Virginia, married there to Joshua Morris. They moved to Ray county, Mo., and both died, leaving six children.

SANGAMON COUNTY.

MARY, born Sept. 11, 1809, in West Virginia, married in Sangamon county to Peter Morris, moved to Ray county, Mo., where he died. She married Charles Shrewsbury, had three children, and she died.

MARGARET, born Feb. 15, 1810, in West Virginia, married in Sangamon county to Rowan Morris; had eight children, and moved to Dallas county, Texas.

By the second marriage—

WILLIAM, born Oct. 17, 1814, in West Virginia, married in Sangamon county, Aug. 12, 1841, to Milicent Fowler. They had three children—THOMAS, born July 27, 1842, in Sangamon county, married Nov. 7, 1868, to Florence Lowery, had three children—ROSANNA died in infancy. ABNER W. and THOMAS L. live with their parents, five miles south of Loami. MILICENT, born Feb. 5, 1845, married John T. Gibson. *See his name.* JONATHAN died in his third year. William Jarrett and wife reside five miles south of Loami, Sangamon county, Illinois.

SARAH, born Feb. 24, 1817, in West Virginia, married in Sangamon county, Aug. 11, 1836, to Charles J. Turpin. *See his name.*

JONATHAN, Jun., born Aug. 1, 1818, in West Virginia, married in Sangamon county to Emily Meacham. She died, leaving one child, SARAH A., who married Cyrus W. Baker. *See his name.* Jonathan Jarrett, Jun., married Sarah J. Baker. They had seven children—ARMINDA J. married Thomas Westfall, have one child, and live in Ottawa, Kansas. MARGARET married, Sept. 22, 1871, to Charles Dood, and live in Talkington township. PAULINE lives near Loami. MARY JOSEPHINE married, April 5, 1876, to Wm. Abner Knight. *See her name.* EMMA, JAMES M. and CHARLOTTE MAY live near Loami. Jonathan Jarrett, Jun., died Dec. 4, 1863, and his widow died Feb. 15, 1876. Their unmarried children live near Loami, on the farm settled by his father in 1826.

REBECCA A., born July 16, 1822, in Virginia, married in Sangamon county to Robert Coley. *See his name.*

SIBYL, born May 8, 1825, in Virginia, married in Sangamon county to Charles Priddy. They had six children, and she died in Loami township. The children live with their father in Missouri.

PETER L., born Dec. 20, 1830, in Sangamon county, married, Dec. 13, 1849, to Mary M. Meacham. Both died, leaving one child, LEWIS L., who lives with his uncle, William Jarrett.

CHARLES, born July 26, 1832, in Sangamon county, married Ursula Colburn. They have four children, REBECCA, LILLIE MAY, LAURA and ALVA, and live four miles south of Loami.

Jonathan Jarrett, Sen., died Apr. 28, 1834, and Mrs. Rebecca Jarrett died Dec. 11, 1863, both in Loami township. He owned slaves in Virginia, and brought two of them with him to Sangamon county. Others followed, and they were all content to work as they had done in slavery—some of them even better. One of them was a tanner, and by his aid Mr. Jarrett carried on tanning for many years.

JARRETT, WILLIAM B., born March 11, 1814, in Kanawha county, Va.; was second cousin to Jonathan Jarrett, Sen. He came to Sangamon county, Ill., arriving in 1828, with his sister, Mrs. Elizabeth Swan, who afterwards returned to West Virginia. Wm. B. Jarret was married, Aug. 16, 1838, in Morgan county, where Waverly now stands, to Jane Huggins, who was born Dec. 26, 1816, in Gallia county, Ohio, and came to Sangamon county with her mother and step-father, Charles Alsbury, arriving at Springfield in 1825. Wm. B. Jarrett and wife had nine children—

ELI, born June 4, 1839, in Sangamon county, married Sarah Robinson, have two children, and live in Christian county.

IRVIN, born Sept. 25, 1840, married Joanna Wheeler, have four children, MARY J., NANCY, SARAH and JOANNA, and live five miles west of Loami.

LEAH, born Aug. 18, 1842, married John H. Meacham. *See his name.*

GEORGE R., born Aug. 28, 1844, married, Feb. 22, 1867, to Elizabeth Buchanan, have one living child, WILLIAM W., and live four miles west of Loami.

NANCY J. born Nov. 7, 1846, in Sangamon county, married Robert Hug-

—52

gins. He served in an Ohio regiment in suppressing the rebellion. They have three children, and live at Osage Mission, Kansas.

HARRIET A., born Jan. 25, 1848, in Sangamon county, married, Sept. 22, 1870, to James A. Hill, who was born May 8, 1838, in Greene county, Ill. They had two children—ANDREW J. died in his second year. MARY A. lives with her parents, four miles west of Loami. James A. Hill was five years in Co. G, Third Arkansas Infantry, Confederate army.

WILLIAM W.,
JOHN H., and
STEPHEN A. D. live with their parents.

Wm. B. Jarrett and wife reside five miles west of Loami, Sangamon county, Illinois.

JEFFERIES, ELIAS, was born March, 1800, in Ross county, Ohio. His ancestors were from Hardy county, Va. Elias was married March 11, 1824, to Rachel Johnstone. She was born in the same county in 1805. Her ancestors were from Monroe county, Va. Mr. and Mrs. Jefferies had one child in Ohio, and moved to Springfield, Ill., arriving in the fall of 1826, where they had one child. Of the two children—

GEORGE J., born May 13, 1826, in Ohio, raised in Sangamon county, and died in Ohio, in his nineteenth year.

NIREM A., born Aug. 2, 1828, in Springfield, raised in Ohio, married in 1861 to Ruth J. Weese, in Sangamon county. They had four living children, and Mrs. Jefferies died June 4, 1872. Mr. Jefferies married in 1874 to Miss Weese, and, with his four children, JOHN, HENRY C., LAURA L. and GEORGE, live four miles north of Springfield.

Mrs. Rachel Jefferies died Dec. 3, 1830, and Elias Jefferies was married to Margaret Jack. They had four children, three of whom died under five years of age.

ROBERT J., born April 27, 1836, married April 30, 1857, to Mary Weese. Mr. Jefferies has served four years as Justice of the Peace, and is now—1874—in his second term. He has no children, and lives in Fancy creek township, eight miles north of Springfield.

Mrs. Margaret Jefferies died in the fall of 1838, and Elias Jefferies died in the spring of 1840, both in Springfield township, Sangamon county, Illinois.

JOHNSON, ANDREW, was born in Dumfrieshire, Scotland, and came to America when he was a young man, and to Sangamon county as early as 1826 or '7. He was a millwright, and built a mill on the South Fork of Sangamon river for Edward Clark. Andrew Johnson was married about 1827 to Mrs. Mary Barker, whose maiden name was Williams. They had three sons, namely—

JOHN, born Oct. 23, 1828, in Sangamon county, married March 1, 1849, to Phœbe E. Bell. They had five living children. ISAIAH B., born May 9, 1851, married April 27, 1871, to Annie Lovelace. They have one child, ELIZABETH, and live two and one-half miles south of Rochester. LAURA J., born Feb. 14, 1854, married Dec. 30, 1869, to Henry R. Hedrick. They have two children, and live two miles west of Clarksville. ROBERT SUMNER died, aged four years. JOHN A., born March 1, 1861, and MINNIE S., born Sept. 17, 1866. The two latter live with their father. Mrs. Phœbe E. Johnson died Feb. 17, 1871, and John Johnson was married June 13, 1873, to Theresa Taff, who was born Oct. 21, 1846, near Mechanicsburg. They reside two miles south of Rochester.

SAMUEL, born Sept. 18, 1831, in Sangamon county, married Sept. 22, 1852, to Lavina J. Baker; had one child, JANETTA F., born Sept. 5, 1854, married Dec. 14, 1871, to Joseph Sharp, and live in Cotton Hill township. Mrs. Lavina J. Johnson died March 24, 1856, and Samuel Johnson was married Aug. 26, 1856, to Louisa Taff, who was born July 4, 1839, near Athens, Menard county, Illinois. They have eight children, MARIETTA, THERESA A., JAMES E., IDA F., FLORA A., MARTHA C., ARTHUR and IRO, and reside three-quarters of a mile southwest of Clarksville, Berry Postoffice.

ANDREW, Jun., born in 1833, and died, aged twelve or thirteen years.

Andrew Johnson died in Sangamon county, and his widow married Greenberry Baker. See his name.

JOHNSON, JOHN, was born about 1795, in Cazenovia, Madison county, N. Y. He was married to Elizabeth Coley, had three children in New York, and moved, in company with her brother, Willis Coley, to Shawneetown, Illinois, and came to Sangamon county in 1825, where they had one child. Of their four children—

EMELINE, born in New York, married in Sangamon county, in 1836, to Rev. Peter Wallace. She died in 1862, at Sidney, Champaign county, leaving four children, who live with their father, who is married again, and is presiding Elder at Quincy, Illinois.—1874.

LUCINA, born in New York, married in Sangamon county to James Langford, and lives in St. Louis, Mo.

JAMES, born in New York, married in 1838 to Margaret Cheney. He died, and his widow married, and lives in San Francisco.

FRANCIS M., born Oct. 11, 1830, in Sangamon county, married in 1851 to Columbia Withrow. They had five children in Sangamon county. OSCAR, born July 5, 1852, married July 4, 1872, to Mary A. Sanborn. They have one child, LOUIE GLENN, and live in Loami. FLORA B., CHARLES L., NELLIE and HARRIET E. live with their parents at Onarga, Iroquois county, Illinois.

John Johnson died Sept. 15, 1870, and his widow lives with her son, F. Marion Johnson, at Onarga, Illinois.

JOHNSON, ELIAS, was born in Delaware, and went to Fayette county, Ky., when a young man. He was there married to Margery Martin, a native of Delaware also. They had four children in Kentucky, and moved to Clark county, Ind., where six children were born, and in 1830 the family moved to Sangamon county, Ill., and settled in what is now Cooper township. Of their children—

AARON, married in Indiana, moved to Texas, had four children, came to Sangamon county on a visit, and died in 1851 in Cooper township.

JOHN, born about 1805 in Casey county, Ky., went back from Indiana, and was married near Lexington to Elizabeth Martin; came to Sangamon county; his wife died. He married again, and died in 1866 in Sangamon county, leaving children by both marriages.

DANIEL, born Aug. 1, 1807, in Casey county, Ky., married in Sangamon county, in 1838, to Mary E. Ferguson. They had two children—one died young. ELIAS J., born April 10, 1841, in Sangamon county, enlisted Aug., 1862, for three years, in Co. E, 114th Ill. Inf., served full term, and was honorably discharged. He was married, Jan., 1869, to Mary M. Boyce, and lives near Breckenridge. Mrs. Mary E. Johnson died in Aug., 1845, and Daniel Johnson was married, April, 1846, to Sarah Young, who died in Sept., 1846. Daniel Johnson was married in Jan., 1851, to Mrs. Julia G. Dickerson, who had previously been Mrs. Welch, and whose maiden name was Cooper. They had four children; all died under seven years. They reside in Breckenridge, Sangamon county, Illinois.

WILLIAM B., born in 1809, in Casey county, Ky., came with his parents to Sangamon county, returned to Clark county, Ind., and was married there, in 1831, to Anna Huckleberry. They had six children in Sangamon county. TODD S. is married, and is a traveling preacher in the M. E. Church, and resides at Oconee, Ill.—1874. SARAH lives with her mother. EARLY S., MELVILLE C. and ASBURY C., have families, and live near Monticello, Ill. NORMAN A. lives with his mother. Wm. B. Johnson was a local preacher in the M. E. Church. He died in 1870, and his widow resides at Monticello, Piatt county, Ill.—1874.

JAMES, born in Clark county, Ind., united with the M. E. Church, in Springfield, went to Texas, about 1850, and became a traveling preacher, and Presiding Elder in the M. E. Church, South; married there, and resides at Huntsville, Walker county, Texas—1874.

ELISHA, born July 16, 1814, in Clark county, Ind., married Sarah A. Hutchins, had three children in Sangamon county, and in the fall of 1847 moved to Arkansas, where they had three children—COLBERT R., born Jan. 28, 1843, in Sangamon county, married in Texas, and died there, leaving a widow and two children. MARY, born May 14, 1845, in Springfield, married Benj. A. Giger. See his name. ELIZABETH, born April 13, 1847, in Sangamon county, married in Springfield, Sept. 19, 1869, to John W. Corby, and lives in Springfield. MAR-

GERY, born and died in Arkansas, aged fourteen. JAMES H., born April 25, 1854, in Arkansas, lives with his sister, Mrs. Giger. NANCY I. died, aged seven years. Mrs. S. A. Johnson died in 1857, in Arkansas. Elisha Johnson was married to Mrs. Jane L. Creger, moved back to Sangamon county in 1865, and died Dec., 1866, in Cooper township, leaving a widow and one child, who soon returned to Arkansas.

ZACHARIAH, born in 1816, in Indiana, married in Sangamon county to Delilah Todd, and had three children—SARAH A. and MARY E., twins, born Aug. 29, 1848. SARAH A. married Joseph Bardwell, and live near Breckenridge. MARY E. married Hosea B. Ross, and live near Rochester. JAMES F., born June 11, 1850, married Fannie Rhodes, and lives near Breckenridge. Z. Johnson died about 1855, and his widow married Joseph Johnson. *See his name.*

JOSEPH, born in Indiana, married in Sangamon county to Mrs. Delilah Johnson, whose maiden name was Todd. They had three children, and she died in 1866. He married Amanda J. Frazee. Joseph Johnson died in Cooper township, and his widow and one child live at Macon, Macon county, Illinois.

ELIAS H., born about 1830, in Indiana, died unmarried, in 1860.

ELIZABETH, and

SARAH A., born in Indiana, and died in Sangamon county, the former at twenty, and the latter aged four years.

Elias Johnson and Mrs. Margery Johnson both died in Cooper township, Sangamon county.

JOHNSON, JOEL, was born May 21, 1806, in Berkshire county, Mass. His father died when he was five months old. His mother married a Mr. Gregory, and when Joel was five years of age she left him with an uncle, and moved to Sangamon county, Ill. *See the name of Gregory.* Joel Johnson saw his mother no more for twenty-one years. He left Massachusetts and first visited an elder brother in Salem, Columbiana county, Ohio. He then traveled by steamboat down the Ohio and up the Mississippi rivers, to St. Louis, and from there to Sangamon county, to visit his mother, arriving in July, 1832. He was returning to his brother in Ohio, and had reached St. Louis, when he discovered that he had only five dollars. That would pay for a deck passage on a steamboat, but he lacked a single dollar to buy food for the trip; and for want of that the whole course of his life was changed. He found work in St. Louis at his trade as a boot and shoe maker. But when he had saved fourteen dollars, there was no farther employment for him. By this time he abandoned the idea of returning to Ohio, because he had heard so much said in favor of Ill. With his fourteen dollars he procured leather and other materials, and left for Edwardsville, Ill., where he opened a shop and went to work. He had a severe fit of sickness during the winter of 1832 and '33. In April, 1833, he moved to Springfield, coming with Alexander B. Irwin, who was hauling goods from St. Louis. Mr. Irwin only charged him fifty cents for bringing himself and goods. Joel Johnson was married in February, 1834, at Carlinville, Ill., to Eliza Newman, who was born in 1815, in Madison county, Ill. They had five children, two of whom died under three years—

CHARLES, born in Springfield, died aged twenty-one years.

EDWARD S., born Aug. 9, 1843, in Springfield. Served a four years' apprenticeship at the printing business, and was engaged with his father in the boot, shoe and leather business when the rebellion broke out. He enlisted at the first call for 75,000 men, April, 1861, in Co. I, 7th Ill. Vol. Inf., for three months; was appointed first sergeant, and served as such full time. He re-enlisted July 24, 1861, for three years, in the same company and regiment, at Mound City, Ill. Sergeant Johnson remained there in charge of the property, while the company returned home on furlough. At the election of officers in Springfield, although absent, he was elected First Lieutenant, and served as such until Feb. 15, 1862, when he was promoted to Captain, to fill the vacancy caused by the death of Capt. Noah E. Mendell, who was killed at Fort Donelson two days before. Capt. Johnson commanded his company until Dec. 22, 1863, when he re-enlisted with his company, as a veteran. He continued in command until April 22, 1864, when he was promoted to Major of the regiment. Major Johnson was appointed by Gen. John M. Corse, September 30, 1864, Post Commandant at Rome, Ga., and served as such until the movement of the grand army on Sherman's "march to the sea," in November following. He then returned to his regiment, and served with it until all were mustered out, July 25, 1865. He participated in the battles of Fort Henry, Fort Donelson, Pittsburg Landing, siege and capture of Corinth, Florence, Savannah, Bentonville, besides innumerable skirmishes. Major E. S. Johnson was engaged in business in Springfield from the close of the rebellion for more than two years. In consequence of impaired health, and for observation, he planned a European tour, and in company with Dr. Rufus S. Lord, left Springfield March 30, 1868. They went by steamer from New York to Liverpool, thence to London, and from there to Paris. Thence to Nice on the Mediterranean; entered Italy at Genoa, thence to Pisa, Leghorn and Naples. They visited Herculaneum, Pompei, Vesuvius, etc. From Naples to Rome, Florence and Verona. In Austria, they visited Trieste and Vienna, thence to Dresden in Prussia. From there to Berlin, Pottsdam, Cologne, down the Rhine to Coblentz and Mayence, where they left the Rhine, and visited Baden-Baden, Heidelberg and Strasbourg, entered Switzerland at Basle, thence to Berne, Luzerne, Mount Rigi, Martigny, and by the mountain pass Tete Noir to Chamounix, in the midst of the mountain region, including Mont Blanc. Thence to Geneva, by Diligence, and from there to Paris, where he met Dr. Lord, whom he had previously left at Strasbourg. They proceeded to London, thence to Edinburg, Scotland, and back to Liverpool, where they took steamer for New York. From the latter city they proceeded to Saratoga, Ticonderoga, on Lake George, Plattsburg, Ogdensburg, Prescott, Montreal, Quebec, Toronto, Niagara Falls, Buffalo and Sarnia, where they took steamer on the lakes for Chicago, reaching Springfield early in September.

Edward S. Johnson was married, Aug. 10, 1869, in Springfield, to Laura I. Clinton, who was born Oct. 21, 1848, in Springfield, also. They have one child,

EDWARD RUSSELL, born May 9, 1875, and reside in Springfield, Illinois.

JOHN W., born April 15, 1845, in Springfield, enlisted Dec., 1863, for three years, in Co. I, 7th Ill. Inf. He was killed, Oct. 4, 1864, at the battle of Allatoona Pass, Ga.

Mrs. Eliza Johnson died, and Joel Johnson was married, Jan. 3, 1852, to Mrs. Elizabeth T. Campbell.

Joel Johnson engaged in the boot and shoe business, on coming to Springfield, in 1833, and in 1835 opened a hotel. He has been in that business forty-one years, and is the oldest hotel keeper in central Illinois, if not the oldest in the State, and is now the proprietor of the Revere House.

JOHNSON, LUE, was born about 1786, at Middlebury, Vermont. A short time before his birth, his father had a difficulty with an Indian of the St. Regis tribe, who were on friendly terms with the whites. In a scuffle the Indian threw Mr. Johnson, and was about to take his life, when a chief of the same tribe came to his rescue, and killed the Indian, in order to save the life of his white friend. The name of that chief was Lue—pronounced Lu-e, and Mr. Johnson named his first born son for the dusky friend who saved his life. The father of Lue Johnson died when he was five years old, and his mother married Orson Douglas, an uncle to Stephen A. Douglas. Lue Johnson was married in Ferrisburg, Vt., to Betsy Benham, who was born in 1787, in Cheshire, New Haven county, Ct. They had seven children in Vermont, and moved in 1829 to Pontiac, Michigan, where Mrs. Johnson died in 1833. Lue Johnson moved to Sangamon county, Ill., arriving in the spring of 1836, near Rochester. Of his seven children—

HENRY, born June 30, 1816, at Burlington, Vt., went with his parents to Michigan, and preceded his father to Sangamon county, arriving Oct. 7, 1832, at Rochester. He left Michigan by stage. The stage broke down in Indiana, fifty miles from Chicago. He enjoyed the hospitality of an Indian wigwam one night, walked to Chicago, which then consisted of a fort, a few huts, and 1,000 Pottowattomie Indians. He did not think the place worth stopping at, and came on to Sangamon county. Henry Johnson was married Nov. 8, 1838, near Rochester, to Joanna Twist. They had nine children in Sangamon county. CALVIN C., born Jan. 14, 1840, married in Sangamon county to Amelia St. Clair. They have one child, EMMA FAY, and live at the Union Stock-Yards, Chicago. MARY N., born March 9, 1842, married in 1868 to William Lowe. They have two children, and live near Edinburg, Christian county. ELIZABETH A. and ORSON D., twins, born Aug. 3, 1844. ELIZABETH A. married William Shipley. They have one child, ALBERT R., and live in Springfield. ORSON D. enlisted Aug. 4, 1862, for three years, in Co. I, 114th Ill. Inf., and died at Memphis, Tenn., Jan., 1864. His remains were brought home, and buried west of Rochester. LAURA R., born Sept. 19, 1853, HENRY F., born Nov. 25, 1857, CHARLES A., born Aug. 25, 1859, and FLORA E., born Sept. 6, 1861, reside with their parents, three miles northeast of Rochester, Sangamon county, Ill. Henry Johnson served from 1867 to 1872 in the Sangamon county Board of Supervisors. He displayed such splendid horsemanship at the Sangamon county Fair, in a contest not mentioned in the programme, Sept., 1875, that he was presented with a fine gold-headed cane, purchased by an impromptu collection from the spectators.

MARY A., born July, 1830, in Vermont, was married in Springfield, Ill., to William Cole. They had one child, FLORA, born in 1851, in Springfield, married Abner Thompson. They have two children, and live in Decatur. Mr. and Mrs. Cole died in Iowa.

ANN ELIZABETH, born in 1825, in Vermont, was married in Springfield, Ill., to Peter Fields, who died in 1852. She married Alexander Fisher. See his name.

ORSON D., born in 1827 in Vermont, married in Rochester to Lydia Eggleston. They have four children, two of whom are married, and live in Mt. Pulaski, Logan county, Ill.

FLORA A., born in 1829 in Vermont, died in 1845 in Springfield.

LUE, Jun., born in 1831 in Vermont, and died in 1837 near Rochester.

Lue Johnson, Sen., died Sept., 1838, near Rochester, Ill.

JOHNSON, LEWIS, was born Jan. 16, 1812, in Somerset county, Penn. He came to Springfield July 8, 1838. He was married to Martha J. VanDoren. They had one child, MARTHA J., and Mrs. Johnson died July, 1845, in Somerset county, Penn., while on a visit to his parents. Lewis Johnson married in 1854, to Mrs. Margaret W. Thompson, whose maiden name was VanDoren. They had four children. LEWIS W. died at six years. GEORGE W. died in his fourth year. MARGARET E. and GEORGIE E. reside with their parents in Chatham, Sangamon county, Illinois.—74.

JONES, ALEXANDER, brother to Robert, William and Thomas. He was born in 1786, in Orange county, N. C. His parents moved, when he was a child, to Madison county, Ky., and from there to Pulaski county, in the same state. Susan Woozley was born in 1788, in Halifax county, Va., and taken when young to Pulaski county, Ky. Alexander Jones and Susan Woozley were married in Pulaski county about 1808. They had one child in that county, and moved to Bedford county, Tenn., where one child was born, and then moved to that part of Barren which has since became Hart county, Ky., where three children were born. In 1821 they moved to Wayne county, Ill., where they had two children, and then moved to Sangamon county, arriving Oct. 9, 1827, in what is now Ball township, where one child was born. Of their eight children—

THOMAS W., born in Pulaski county, Ky., married in Sangamon county to America Pittman, moved to Missouri, and died there in 1853, leaving a widow and children. T. W. Jones was a soldier in the Black Hawk war. He was also Capt. of a company from Sangamon county in the Mexican war. His company was in several battles, but every man lived to return except one, who sickened and died.

JAMES B., born in Bedford county, Tenn., raised in Sangamon county, married three times, and died in Missouri in 1853.

ROBERT W., born in 1814, in Hart county, Ky., died in Sangamon county in 1833.

JOSHUA W., born Sept. 9, 1817, in Hart county, Ky., married in Sangamon county to Polly Ann Wills. They had seven living children, viz: ADOLPH W., born July 19, 1846, was a soldier in the

143d Ind. Inf.; residence not known. LAURA J., born Oct. 25, 1847, married Jan. 20. 1869, to J. W. Renn, who was born Oct. 15, 1847, in Sangamon county. They have three children, JESSIE A., LAURA S. and EDNA, and live half a mile east of Woodside, Sangamon county. WILLIS A., WILEY E., AMERICUS V., JAMES A. and HORATIO S. live with their father. Mrs. Polly A. Jones died Apr. 8, 1867, and J. W. Jones married Sept. 3, 1869, to Mary E. Dryer of McLean county, and have two children, LUELLA and JUNETTIE. Joshua W. Jones resides in Ball township, adjoining the farm where his father settled in 1827. It is three miles east of Chatham. He studied medicine, and practiced it eight years, but now confines his business to farming.

MOSES A., born July 31, 1820, in Hart county, Ky., married in Sangamon county, Jan. 18, 1846, to Nancy Armstrong, who was born in Virginia, Feb. 16, 1824. They had eleven children. SUSAN J. and MARY E. died, each in their second year. The other nine: CAROLINE A. married William D. Patton. *See his name.* ELIZABETH A., and THOMAS A. live with their parents, JAMES B. is a druggist, and lives in Springfield, ROBERT W., JOHN M., ANDREW J., ELIZA B. and CHARLOTTE F. reside with their parents in Ball township, ten miles due south of Springfield.

BURRELL T., born in Wayne county, Illinois, raised in Sangamon county, married in Missouri to Charlotte Williams, moved to Clinton, DeWitt county, Ill., and died in 1864, leaving a widow and two children. They now live in California. He practiced law in Missouri, and edited a paper in Clinton, Illinois.

AMANDA J., born in Wayne county, married Rape Funderburk. *See his name.*

SUSAN D., born in Sangamon county, married in Missouri to Caswell Williams, and died there in 1847.

Mrs. Susan Jones died Jan. 20, and Alexander Jones died Oct. 20, 1844, and both are buried in Ball township.

JONES, ROBERT, born Sept. 25, 1790, in Orange county, North Carolina, was a brother of Alexander, William and Thomas. When he was a child his parents moved to Madison county, Ky., and from there to Pulaski county, same State, where his father died, and all the family moved to Bedford county, Tenn. He went from that county as a soldier in the 4th Tenn. Reg. during the war of 1812, and was in a battle against the Indians on the Talladega river, Alabama, in which Gen. Jackson was in immediate command. Robert Jones served three months and fourteen days. He went from Tennessee to Hart county, Ky., where he was married about 1816 to Tabitha Lard, who was born June 18, 1795. She was a sister of John Lard. Mr. and Mrs. Jones had one child in Kentucky, and moved to Wayne county, Ill., where four children were born; thence to Sangamon county, Ill., arriving May 13, 1828, in what is now Ball township, where they had three children. Of all their children—

MAHALA, born Nov. 9, 1818, in Hart county, Ky., died Aug. 7, 1838, in Sangamon county, Illinois.

ALEXANDER J., born Jan. 9, 1820, in Wayne county, Ill., brought up in Sangamon county, was married June 26, 1871, in Christian county, Ill., to Cassandra E. Hunt. Mrs. C. E. Jones died May 5, 1875, leaving one child, MELISSA A., who lives with her father in Ball township, Sangamon county, Illinois.

JOAB, born Aug. 27, 1823, in Wayne county, Ill., died Aug. 30, 1844, in Sangamon county.

JOHN G., born July 21, 1825, in Wayne county, died Sept. 2, 1838, in Sangamon county.

MADISON, born Aug. 7, 1827, in Wayne county, Ill., died Feb. 16, 1849, in Sangamon county.

DRURY, born June 12, 1830, in Sangamon county, was married there July 11, 1850, to Amanda M. Porterfield. They had three children. JAMES M. lives with his father. ROBERT P. died, aged seven years. MINERVA J. died in infancy. Mrs. A. M. Jones died Apr. 22, 1855, and Drury Jones was married Sept. 11, 1856, to Susannah Meredith. They had seven children. SARAH M. A. died in infancy. AMANDA J. was married Oct. 1, 1874, to Charles R. McClure, and lives near Pawnee, Sangamon county, Ill. The other five, CHARLES C. L., DAVIS A. W., WILLIAM A. E., FRANCIS M. J. and MARY E. T. M., live with their parents, in Ball township, Sangamon county, Illinois.

CALVIN, born Aug. 22, 1832, in Sangamon county, died, unmarried, Dec. 15, 1855.

ROBERT WILEY, born May 17, 1838, in Sangamon county, died Dec. 12, 1815.

Mrs. Tabitha Jones died Sept. 22, 1861, and Robert Jones died May 16, 1874, both in Ball township. He was in his eighty-fourth year.

JONES, WILLIAM, was born about 1793, in Orange county, N. C. He was married in Wayne county, Ill., in 1824, to Lucinda Gore, had three children in that county, and the family moved to Sangamon county with his brothers, Alexander and Robert, in 1827 or '8 and settled in Ball township, where eight children were born. Of all the children—

MARGARET, born March 28, 1825, married Elijah Wall, who died, and she married Smith McAtee, and had two children—JANE McATEE is unmarried and lives in Cotton Hill township. MARY McATEE married Henry B. Rose, and lives near Independence, Kansas. Smith McAtee died, and she married Felix Stovall, and he died.

MARY, born Sept. 16, 1826, in Wayne county, married Richard Wall. See his name.

SARAH, born Jan. 30, 1827, married Johnson Wall, and she died.

JAMES, born Nov. 5, 1828, in Sangamon county, was a member of an Illinois regiment, and died in Mexico, in time of the war in 1846 or '7.

ELIZABETH married Logan Lightfoot, as her third husband, and lives in Davis county, Iowa.

DELILAH married to Wm. Callaway in Marysville, California.

ANDREW J., born in 1835, in Sangamon county, served three years in the Union army, married Elizabeth Lard, and lives near Independence, Kansas.

SUSAN, born Feb. 21, 1837, in Sangamon county, married, Jan. 8, 1853, to David B. Greenawalt, who was born June 30, 1819, in Hardin county, Ky. They have three children, MARY M., DAVID M. and IVEY D., and live two miles north of Pawnee.

ROBERT A., born in 1839, in Sangamon county, served in the Union army, married Sarah J. Keys, and live near Independence, Kansas.

NEWTON C., born in Sangamon county, served three years in the Union army, married, and lives near Grafton, Kansas.

Mrs. Lucinda Jones died May 19, 1843, and Wm. Jones died April 2, 1844, both in Sangamon county.

JONES, THOMAS, brother to Alexander, Robert and William, was born in Pulaski county, Ky., about 1800, married in Wayne county, Ill., to Zilpha Green, came to Sangamon county in 1828, bringing three children, and had seven children in Sangamon county. Of the ten children—

ABIGAIL, born in Wayne county, married Richard Kelly, who died, and she married Benj. Howard, and she died in Christian county, leaving one child.

MARY A. married Dempsey Tucker, and had four children. Mr. Tucker and one child died. The widow married James Davidson, and she died.

PIERCE, born in 1827, in Wayne county, Ill., married in Sangamon county to Elizabeth Enochs, and live in Iowa.

SALLY, born in 1829, in Sangamon county, married Eli Davidson.

FIELDING, born in Sangamon county, was twice married, and lives in Iowa.

EMERINE, born in Sangamon county, married James Enochs, and live in Iowa.

GREEN, born in Sangamon county, married Susan Smith, and lives in Ball township.

MAHALA, born in Sangamon county, married Wm. Fry, who was killed on the road south of Springfield, leaving four children. The widow and children live near Edinburg, Christian county, Illinois.

ALEXANDER, born in Sangamon county, married to Mrs. Mary A. Pugh, and live near Edinburg, Christian county.

Mrs. Zilpha Jones died in 1850, and Thomas Jones married Polly Kelly, and he died about 1855—both in Sangamon county.

JONES, WILLIAM, Jun., was born about 1808, in Kentucky. His father, James Jones, was a brother to Alexander,

Robert, Thomas and William. William, Jun., came to Sangamon county, when a boy, with his uncle, Robert Jones. He was married in 1831 to Martha A. Lillard, who was born July 24, 1815, in Rockingham county, N. C., and came to Sangamon county in 1829. They had seven living children—

TEMPERANCE, born August 25, 1832, married April 8, 1852, to A. C. Campbell.

SARAH E., born Dec. 24, 1834, married in 1854 to W. C. Enix. They have three living children, and live near Moravia, Monroe county, Iowa.

TABITHA A, born Nov. 6, 1837, married Alexander Elliott, August, 1853, have five living children, and live near Palmer, Christian county.

ROBERT A., born April 14, 1840, married March, 1862, to Rachel A. Sears, have three living children, and reside at Palmer, Illinois.

JAMES T., born July 10, 1845, in Sangamon county, is married and living in Washington Territory.

WILLIAM C., born April 28, 1848, in Sangamon county, married Burnetta Hill, who died, and he married Alice M. Shadrick, and lives in Palmer, Christian county, Illinois.

NANCY J., born Jan. 10, 1851, married James P. Lawley. See his name.

William Jones, Jun., died in 1858, in Sangamon county, and his widow, Mrs. Martha A. Jones resides near Palmer, Christian county, Illinois.

JONES, ANDREW, was born Jan. 10, 1783, in Culpepper county, Va. His parents died when he was quite young, and about 1808 he went to Bath county, Ky., and was there married, in 1812, to Eleanor Goodan, who was born March 16, 1793, in Pennsylvania, and was taken by her parents to Kentucky when she was young. They had five children in Bath county, and the family moved to Sangamon county, Ill., arriving in the fall of 1825, on Round Prairie, where one child was born. Of their six children—

RACHEL, born Sept. 8, 1814, in Bath county, Ky., was married in Sangamon county to George W. Poffenberger. See his name.

LEVI W., born April 26, 1817, in Bath county, Ky., was married in Sangamon county, Feb. 23, 1837, to Grace McClees, who was born Feb. 22, 1817, in Bath county, Ky. They have three children. EMILY, born Nov. 28, 1837, married William Beadle. They have two children, ELIZA E. and WILLIAM A., and live in Springfield, ELIZABETH E., born Oct. 29, 1842, married William Underwood. They have three children, JOSEPH, CLARA and ETTIE F., and live near Santa Fe, Missouri. LEVI W., Jun., born Dec. 22, 1848, lives with his parents, one and a half miles west of Rochester, Sangamon county, Illinois.

ELIZA, born Sept. 12, 1819, in Bath county, Ky., was married in Sangamon county, Ill., to Samuel Miller. See his name.

DANIEL G., born Nov. 15, 1822, in Bath county, Ky., was married in 1849, in Sangamon county, to Amanda J. Brunk. She died Sept. 28, 1865, leaving two children. LAURA, born Feb. 3, 1852, died Jan. 18, 1870. GEORGE A., born May 31, 1860, lives with his father. Daniel G. Jones was married May, 1869, to Mary F. Rickard. They have two children, MARY R. and HELEN, and live fourteen miles south of Springfield, in Cotton Hill township.

EVELINE, born May 1, 1825, in Bath county, Ky., was married in Sangamon county, Ill., to Joseph E. McCoy. See his name.

JOHN A., born Oct. 4, 1829, in Sangamon county, was married there to Louisa Smith. They have four children, ARTHUR E., EVA E., GEORGE A. and LOUELLA, and live in Clinton, DeWitt county, Illinois.

Andrew Jones died Oct. 20, 1854, and Mrs. Eleanor Jones died March 8, 1859, both in Sangamon county, Illinois.

JONES, REUBEN, brother of Andrew and Levi, was born in Virginia, and married in Fleming county, Ky., to Jennie Bracken. They had four children in Kentucky, and moved to Sangamon county, Ill., in 1824, where Mrs. Jennie Jones died. Reuben Jones married again and moved to McLean county, Illinois. He died in southeastern Illinois.

JONES, LEVI, brother of Andrew and Reuben was born in Virginia, and married in Fleming county, Ky., to Fanny Shackleford. They had three children there, and came to Sangamon county in 1824. The parents settled on German Prairie, northeast of Springfield. Their three children married and moved to Iowa.

JONES, EMANUEL, was born Jan. 1, 1818, in Fleming county, Ky. His parents moved in 1828 to Kaskaskia, Ill. He came in 1836 to Sangamon county, to join his two brothers, and was married early in 1837 to Eliza Shane. They had seven children, namely—

JOSIAH, born May 5, 1838, enlisted July 20, 1861, at Springfield, in what became Co. C, 11th Mo. Inf., for three years. He was wounded May 22, 1863, in one knee and one hand, at the assault on the rebel fortifications at Vicksburg. After recovering, he was transferred to the Vet. Res. Corps, and was detailed as a ward master and steward in the military hospital at Keokuk, Iowa, served full term, and was honorably discharged Aug. 5, 1864. He was married March 17, 1868, at Loami, to Laura E. Davis, and had three children. CARRIE, died in infancy. HARRY and ALICE live with their parents at Loami.

CATHARINE, born 1841, married George Brewer, and lives in Macon county.

JOHN, born 1844, enlisted in 1862 in Co. I, 63d Ill. Inf., for three years, and died at Columbus, Ky., in 1863.

CYNTHIA, married Alexander Scott, and lives in Macon county.

WILLIAM lives at Decatur.

THOMAS and

MARTHA live with their mother.

Emanuel Jones moved from Loami to Macon ocunty in 1854, and died there Aug. 9, 1858. His widow, Mrs. Eliza Jones, and two youngest children, live in Shawneetown, Illinois.

JONES, JAMES, elder brother to Emanuel and John, was born in Fleming county, Ky., was taken by his parents to Kaskaskia, Ill., in 1828, and came to Sangamon county in 1831. He was married in Sangamon county to Jane Snyder; raised a family, moved to Macon county, and now resides near Decatur.

JONES, JOHN, eldest brother to James and Emanuel, was born in Fleming county, Ky., went to Kaskaskia, Ill., in 1828, from there to Sangamon county, with his brother James, in 1831, was married in Sangamon county, at fifty-five years of age, to Emeline Shane, and both died without children.

JONES, ENOCH, was born in Maryland, came to Sangamon county among the earliest settlers, and located in Island Grove. He brought a wife and seven children. Six of his children were by a former wife, who had been a widow, Halliday, with four children. Her daughter, Sarah Halliday, married Starling Willis. See his name. The whole family moved to Knox county, where the parents died.

JONES, HENRY, was born August 25, 1793, in Caroline county, Va. He was a soldier in the war of 1812. Mary F. Chiles was born Nov. 11, 1801, in the same county, and they were married there, Jan. 9, 1819. They had six children in Virginia, and moved to Todd county, Ky., where two children were born. The family then moved to Sangamon county, Ill., arriving in the fall of 1834, in what is now Springfield township, south of Sangamon river. Of their children—

SARAH A. M., born Oct. 16, 1819, in Virginia, married in Sangamon county to Thomas McKinnie. See his name.

WILLIAM B., born July 4, 1821, in Virginia, married Jan. 31, 1843, to Elizabeth A. McKinnie, and live five miles west of Springfield.

HENRY H., born Sept. 17, 1822, died August 25, 1835.

MARY W., born Feb. 15, 1824, lives with her mother.

JOSEPH W. and RICHARD J., twins, born Sept. 14, 1825, in Virginia.

RICHARD J. married Melinda Browning, have three children, and live in Springfield. He is a cabinet maker.

JOSEPH W., married Lucy Ransdell, have five children, RICHARD N., JOHN H., ELIJAH ARTHUR, WILLIAM E. and GEORGE E., and live in the northwest corner of Springfield township.

ELEANOR L., born June 30, 1829, in Kentucky, married Sept. 8, 1853, in Sangamon county, to Levi Bowker, who was born April 27, 1823, in Cape May county, N. J. They have seven children, WILLIAM H., JOHN L., EDMUND F., MARY E., THOMAS E., JAMES M. and ALBERT CHILES, and reside five miles northwest of Springfield.

JONATHAN E., born July 21, 1833, in Kentucky, married Nov. 29, 1866, to Martha E. Marshall, who was born Sept. 12, 1842, at Columbus, Ohio. They had two children, JENNIE B., the youngest, died in infancy. CHARLES HENRY lives with his parents, five and a half miles northwest of Springfield.

Henry Jones died Jan. 1, 1848, and his widow resides in the northwest corner of Springfield township, six miles from Springfield, Illinois.

JONES, STROTHER G., was born Dec. 18, 1813, in Lincoln county, Ky., and was taken by his parents in 1818 to Shelby county. His grandfather, Josiah Jones, was born in Wales, and was married there. His wife was of Scotch descent. They emigrated to America before the Revolution. Strother G. says they were both sold to pay for their passage across the ocean; that they were both in the battle of Bunker Hill, and that his grandmother received a wound in the breast. They afterwards settled in Rappahannock county, Va., and raised a family. Four of their sons emigrated to Kentucky. One of them, Josiah, walked the whole distance, without shoes or hat. His entire wardrobe consisted of a single garment, a sack made of tow linen, and fastened by a draw-string around the neck. He was married in Mercer county to Nancy Finley, a daughter of Col. Obadiah Finley. Mrs. Finley's maiden name was Gaines. She was a sister to the mother of President Harrison. There is a family tradition, that in the early troubles with the savages, in Kentucky, Mrs. Finley slew four Indians. Strother G. Jones was married July 10, 1834, in Mercer county, Ky., to Lucy Newton, who was born in that county March 5, 1817. They embarked at Louisville, on a steamboat, and came by the Ohio, Mississippi and Illinois rivers to Beardstown, and from there by wagon road, stopping at the house of John B. Broadwell, at a place then called Clayville, one mile south of the present town of Pleasant Plains, arriving in Springfield March 16, 1836. They had four living children in Springfield, namely—

ELIZABETH A., born June 12, 1836, in Springfield, married, Sept. 4, 1853, to Nimrod Nooe. They have eight children, and live near Mattoon.

MARY E., born Sept. 2, 1839, in Springfield, married Daniel Pottle. See his name.

JAMES W., born July 15, 1846, in Springfield. He enlisted June 28, 1862, in Co. F, 70th Ill. Inf., for three months; served until Oct. 23, 1862, when he was honorably discharged. He enlisted in the 11th Mo. Inf., but was taken out by his father because he was under age. He was married, Oct. 12, 1865, to Sidney E. Taylor. They have two children, MAGGIE and WILLIAM A., and live one and one-half miles northwest of Dawson.

LUCY E., born Aug. 30, 1850, in Springfield, married to Wm. A. Burns. See his name.

Strother G. Jones married, June 14, 1865, in Logan county, for his second wife, Lucy E. Cass. They have four children—

MORRIS A., born at Morris, Grundy county, Illinois.

SHIRLEY A., EARNEST, STROTHER J. and JESSIE MAY; the three latter born in Sangamon county, and all four live with their parents, at Dawson.

S. G. Jones was City Marshal of Springfield, under Mayor John Calhoun. He was justice of the peace and Postmaster at the same time, in Dawson. He took an active part in organizing the Old Settlers' Society, and was President of the same for two years—1868 and '9—and vice-President and acting-President the year after.

JONES, THOMAS, was born August 31, 1770, his descendents think in Virginia, and that he emigrated to Kentucky when a young man. He was married in Bourbon county, Ky., August 20, 1799, to Polly Bryan, a daughter of the founder of Bryan's Station. They had eight children in Kentucky, four of whom died there. Mr. Jones came to Springfield in the spring of 1834, and purchased a farm adjoining Springfield on the north. He built a house on the land which is now part of the residence of Judge S. T. Logan. He returned to Kentucky for his family, and found his wife sick. She died soon after, and Mr. Jones moved, with three of his children, to Springfield, arriving in Nov., 1834. Of those three children—

SARAH, born Jan. 21, 1811, in Kentucky, was married there to N. G. Baldock. He died in Kentucky, and she came with her father to Sangamon county, where she was married in March, 1837, to Thomas P. Smith. They moved to Missouri, and both died there, leaving four children, namely: MARY, THOMAS, AFFIA and JULIA—the latter dead. Mary returned to Illinois, where she married, and now resides in Menard county, Illinois.

WILLIAM T., born May 8, 1817, in Bourbon county, Ky., was married in Sangamon county, Ill., April 12, 1840, to Lavina J. Merriman. They have two children born in Sangamon county. HENRIETTA B. married Dr. Thomas M. Helm. *See his name.* GEORGE B. married Frances W. Ellis. They have three children, WILLIAM, ALLIE and BELLE, and live with his parents, two and one-quarter miles west of Williamsville.

THOMAS N. died, unmarried, Jan., 1838, in Sangamon county, Illinois.

Thomas Jones died Oct. 23, 1841, about three miles west of Williamsville, Sangamon county.

JUDD, EZEKIEL, was born Feb. 14, 1797, in Mason county, Ky., and was taken by his parents to Clermont county, Ohio. He was married in the adjoining county of Brown, to Delilah Lakin. They had two children in Brown county, and moved with his brother, Corban, to Sangamon county, Ill., arriving in the fall of 1825 in what is now Clear Lake township, where they had several children. After a residence of nearly a quarter of a century in the county, he moved, about 1850, to Winchester, Scott county, Ill., where Mrs. Delilah Judd died. Ezeziel Judd and his four living children reside in Jackson, Michigan.

JUDD, REZIN, was born Dec. 26, 1798, in Mason county, Ky., and taken when a child to Clermont county, Ohio. He was married, in the adjoining county of Brown, Jan. 3, 1822, to Eve Shinkle, who was born in that county Dec. 2, 1804. They had two children, and moved to Sangamon county, Ill., arriving in the fall of 1826, in what is now Clear Lake township, where his brothers, Ezekiel and Corban, had settled the year before. They had eight children in Sangamon county—

ALBERT J. and *MARY I.* died, each in their fourth year.

ELIZA A., born Oct. 18, 1822, in Brown county, Ohio, married in Sangamon county to Thomas A. Magee. They had six living children. Mr. Magee died, in 1863, and his widow lives five miles south of Mechanicsburg, in Christian county, Illinois.

NELSON S., born Oct. 22, 1825, in Brown county, Ohio, married in Sangamon county, Nov. 15, 1849, to Susan Miller, who was born April 20, 1831, in Champaign county, Ohio. They have six living children, ELIZA J., SARAH E., GEORGE W., MARY M., ANNA E. and EMMA A., and live three miles southwest of Dawson, Sangamon county, Illinois.

JOHN A., born Sept. 6, 1830, in Sangamon county, died Oct. 7, 1848.

ARMINDA E., born April 17, 1833, in Sangamon county, married John H. Shankland. They have three children, and live in Riverton.

WILLIAM W., born Aug. 19, 1836, in Sangamon county. He served three months in Co. F, 70th Ill. Inf.; and enlisted in May, 1864, for one hundred days, in Co. I, 133d Ill. Inf., served full term, and was honorably discharged. He is Postmaster, at Dawson, and lives with his mother—1874.

MARGARET E., born Feb. 13, 1839, in Sangamon county, married, May 30, 1871, to Robert Alls. He was born Dec. 2, 1833, in Montgomery county, Va., was married in Clinton county, Illinois, to Mary M. Potts, who died, leaving one child, REBECCA V. He was married in Sangamon county, Feb. 11, 1867, to Mrs. Maria L. Grabenlich, whose maiden name was Morgan. *See Morgan's name.* She died, leaving one child, CHARLES A., and he married M. E. Judd. They have one child, REZIN A., and live near Dawson, Illinois.

MARQUIS L., born Dec. 23, 1841, in Sangamon county, enlisted in 1862, for three years, in Co. F, 70th Ill. Inf.; served full term, and was honorably discharged. He lives in Dawson.

REZIN A. V., born Dec. 16, 1846, in Sangamon county, and lives with his mother.

Rezin Judd died, July 7, 1873, and his widow resides with her three sons, in Dawson, Sangamon county, Illinois.

JUDD, CORBAN C., born Nov. 16, 1800, in Marion county, Ky., was married in Brown county, Ohio, March 7, 1824, to Nancy Lakin. She was a twin sister of his brother Ezekiel's wife, with whom they moved to Sangamon county, Ill., in the autumn of 1825. They had eight children—

MILTON Y., born June 18, 1825, in Ohio, was married in Sangamon county, about 1850, to Rebecca Miller. They had four children, MARY, NATHAN, ELIZABETH and SARILDA. Milton Y. Judd enlisted in Cincinnati, Ohio, for the Mexican war, served his term, and died, Nov. 5, 1872, in Minneapolis, Minnesota. His widow and children live in Champaign county, Ohio.

ADDISON E., a twin brother of *MILTON Y.*, died near Mechanicsburg, Sangamon county, February 22, 1844.

MARIA L. died in infancy.

WILLIAM D., born June 8, 1830, in Sangamon county, was married, about 1852, to Charlotte McCord, of Mt. Pleasant, Ill. He served three years in the Federal army, and died at Dewitt, Ohio, leaving four children—ADA J. and D. WILLIS, who live with J. S. Judd, in Whitehall, and MAMIE and BELLE, who are married, and live in St. Louis, Missouri.

CAROLINE M., a twin sister of *WILLIAM D.*, was married to James McFarland, in 1849, at Carrolton, Ill. He died, in 1858, leaving a widow and two daughters, DORA and BELL. Mrs. Caroline M. McFarland married John J. Bell, who died Jan. 1, 1875, leaving a widow and three children, JAMES, DAVID and LEMPE, who live near Berdan, Greene county, Illinois.

JOHN S., born April 30, 1835, in Platte Valley, Grant county, Wisconsin, accompanied his father and family to Whitehall, Ill., arriving in June, 1847. He was married there, Oct. 20, 1858, to Sarah E. Culver, of Whitehall, daughter of Rev. S. H. Culver, D. D. She died without issue, Feb. 4, 1862. John S. Judd enlisted June, 1862, as first Lieutenant, in Co. I, 91st Ill. Inf., returned home in 1865, and was married, Jan., 1866, to Melissa J. Culver. She died April 29, 1869, without issue. J. S. Judd was married, June 20, 1870, to Melissa A. McCallister, of Whitehall. They have three children NORMAN W., HERMAM S. and CORBAN E. John S. Judd has been a leading merchant of Whitehall, Greene county, Ill., since 1858.

MELINDA A., born about 1837, married Rev. John C. Wood, of Bunker Hill, Ill., in 1854 or '5. They have five children, and live at Bunker Hill, Macoupin county, Illinois.

WATSON W., born about 1840, enlisted in 1861, and died in service Jan. 13, 1862, at Laclede Hotel, St. Louis, Missouri.

MARY E., was born about 1842, and died in 1853, at Waterloo, Iowa.

Corban C. Judd served as a soldier two terms, from Sangamon county, in the Black Hawk war. He served in the Mexican war, under Gen. Scott, and died at Pueblo, Mexico, Dec. 17, 1847. His widow, Mrs. Nancy Judd died April 26, 1851. John S. Judd writes to the author that the four youngest children of Corban C. Judd were given a kind home by J. S. Hackney, one of the noblest sons of Illinois, formerly of Logan county.

K

KANE, ANDREW J., was born Feb. 11, 1818, in Guilford county, North Carolina. His father died when he was an infant, and his mother, with her three children moved to Greene county, Ind., in 1830. Andrew J., when approaching manhood, went to Indianapolis, where he remained several years, learning the trade of a carpenter. Mr. Kane next traveled by the way of Michigan City to Chicago. That place was such a miserable quagmire, he did not think it worth stopping at, and started for Springfield. He stopped one night at Irish grove, in Menard county, paid his last cent for lodging, and left without breakfast and without letting the family where he stopped know that it was because he had no money. When within five or six miles of his destination, his hunger prompted him to stop and ask for something to eat, stating that he had no money. Breakfast was readily prepared, and enjoyed with a keen relish. He came on toward Springfield, and found men building a bridge across the Sangamon river, where Carpenter's mill now stands. He obtained employment there, and when he received his first pay, he walked back to the house where he had been supplied with breakfast, and handed the man a twenty-five cent piece, and told him what it was for. The old gentleman turned to his wife, handed her the money, and said: "There, mammy, give him back a bit"—meaning a twelve and one-half cent piece. Mr. K. refused to take any change. The host was Nathan Hussey, whose name heads a sketch in this volume. Mr. Kane's arrival was in July, 1839. He was married May 13, 1847, to Caroline M. Beers. They had seven living children—*MATTIE E., CHARLES P., JULIA E., HENRY B., EUGENE S., CAMPBELL N.,* and *BELLE C.,* all live with their parents. Charles P. is a practicing attorney, of the firm of Kane & Hazlett, Springfield. Henry B. is one of the letter-carriers employed by the United States government.

Andrew J. Kane and wife reside in Springfield. He was ordained to preach the gospel in 1842, in connection with the Christian church, and has continued preaching to the present time—June, 1876.

KEAGLE, JOHN, was born July 14, 1794, near Harrisburg, Pa. He was married there to Mary A. Parker. They had two children in Pennsylvania, and moved to Ross county, Ohio, where they had six living children, and moved to Sangamon county, Ill., arriving in 1835, in what is now Fancy Creek township. Of their eight children—

JOHN, Jun., born in Pennsylvania, married in Sangamon county to Adaline Cooper. They have six children. Their daughter CHARLOTTE married Nathan Hussey. *See his name.* John Keagle and family live in Logan county, Illinois.

JOSEPH, born Sept. 8, 1818, in Pennsylvania, married in Sangamon county, in 1842, to Angeline Hall. They raised six children, and Mr. Keagle died in 1871. His widow lives near Barclay, Illinois.

MARY married Robert Stringfield, have three children, and live in Williamsville.

SAMUEL, married Christiana Farris, and lives in Fancy Creek township.

DOROTHY married Ambrose Cooper. *See his name.*

LETITIA married James C. King, and lives in Logan county.

HARRISON lives in Logan county, Illinois.

Mrs. Mary Keagle died August, 1851, and John Keagle died June, 1872, both in Sangamon county, Ill.

KEEDY, JOHN A., was born in Pennsylvania, in the year 1800, was married in Maryland about 1830, to Susan Wolgamot, who was born in 1800, in Washington county, Md. Two children were born in Maryland. The family moved to Springfield, Ill., in 1838, coming all the way in wagons. They brought with them the first carriage ever used in Sangamon county. They had one child in Springfield. Of the three children—

MARGARET, was born July 4, 1832, and was married in Springfield Sept. 19, 1855, to Amzi McWilliams, a native of Ohio, a lawyer by profession, and who was at one time State's Attorney for this circuit. They had one living child, FREDERICK V., born August 7, 1856, now attending school at Litchfield, Ill., and living with his uncle, Maj. Robt. McWilliams.

JOHN D., born July 15, 1832, in Washington county, Md., married in Springfield, Jan. 18, 1855, to Charlotte Opdycke, a daughter of Stacy B. Opdycke. *See his name.* She was born in Chester, Ill., March 19, 1835. They had five living children, viz: STACY B. died at eight years of age. SUSAN, CHARLOTTE, JOHN D., Jun., and HANNAH live with their parents. John D. Keedy was several years Deputy Sheriff, is now serving his second term as Justice of the Peace in Springfield, where he resides.—1876.

WILLIAM, born about 1839, in Sangamon county. He left home some time in 1863, in declining health. The family received one letter from him, from New York City, since which time they have heard nothing from him, but suppose that he is dead.

Mr. John A. Keedy was alderman one term in 1846, and was for a while merchandising with Tinsley & Co. He died Sept. 27, 1854. His widow is still living in Springfield, Illinois.

KEIGWIN, STERRY S., born Oct. 11, 1803, in Windham county, Connecticut. Susannah Morse was born Feb. 14, 1811, in Sutton, Massachusetts. They were married May 23, 1833, in Millberry, Mass., and made their home there until they had one child, and then moved to Illinois, first stopping in McLean county, and then moved to Springfield in May, 1838, where one child was born. Of their two children—

CORNELIA M., born July 10, 1835, at Millberry, Mass., married in Springfield, Ill., to F. A. Moore, and died Sept. 13, 1856, at LaCrosse, Wisconsin.

SUSAN K., born March 21, 1840, in Springfield, Ill., married June 11, 1868, in Atlanta, Ill., to John P. Leonard. He died at the latter place March 16, 1872. Mrs. Susan K. Leonard was married Dec. 23, 1873, to Lucius C. Francis. See his name.

Sterry S. Keigwin moved from Springfield, in 1858, to Washington county, Mo., and in 1861 to Atlanta, Ill., where he now resides.

KELLY, HENRY, was born about 1742. The place of his birth is not certainly known to his descendants. He was married, and had five sons and two daughters, all born in Rutherford county, North Carolina, namely: *JOHN, ELISHA, ELIJAH, WILLIAM* and *GEORGE W*. The daughter, *ELEANOR*, married in North Carolina to Joseph Reavis. *SALLY* married a Mr. Greenawalt. Two of the sons, John and Elisha, preceded their father to Sangamon county. Henry Kelly owned slaves, but none of the sons, except George, would have them; so he freed the slaves, and gave land to his sons, instead. The daughters had three slaves, each; and, after tarrying less than thirty days in Sangamon county, moved on to Missouri. Henry Kelly died in June, 1832, and was buried about two miles north of Curran. He was about ninety years old. His widow moved several years later to the vicinity of Bolivar, Polk county, Mo., and died there about 1840. The following sketches are headed with the names of the five sons.

KELLY, JOHN, was born about 1783, in Rutherford county, North Carolina. He was there married to Mary Whitesides, had five children there, and moved to Illinois in the fall of 1818, first stopping on Macoupin creek. In the spring of 1819 he moved to what is now Springfield, and built the cabin in which the first court of Sangamon county was held, in May, 1821. It stood at what is now the northwest corner of Second and Jefferson streets. It was the first building of any kind erected within the city limits of Springfield. In September or October of that year Mrs. Kelly died. Mr. Kelly had business unsettled in North Carolina, and returned for that purpose. While there he was married, in the fall of 1821, to Margaret Waldrup, and brought her at once to his new home. She never had any children. Of his five children—

JONATHAN, born Sept. 19, 1808, in Rutherford county, N. C., married Sept. 8, 1831, in Fayette county, Ill., to Sarah Cook, who was born Dec. 3, 1812, in Tennessee. They had eight children in Sangamon county, namely: WILLIAM W., born Feb. 11, 1833, married Mrs. Almeda McMurray, whose maiden name was Davis. She had two children by her first marriage, and they have two, THOMAS J. and SARAH E., and live with his mother, near Curran. MARY F., born June 10, 1834, married Wm. B. Cobb. They had eight children. Mr. Cobb and two of the children died. The widow and six children live in Gardner township. JOHN C., born March 27, 1837, married Emily J. Kellums, had four children, CASSIUS K., IDA B., MARY E. and LYDIA A., and Mrs. Kelly died, and he married Mary J. Woods; have two children, EMMA L. and JOHN H., and live in Hancock county, Ill. ELIZABETH A., born Oct. 5, 1839, married Oct. 10, 1872, to Charles A. Jackson, of New York, and live in Nebraska. HARRIET L., born Jan. 20, 1842, married William D. Kelly. See his name. BENJAMIN F., born April 12, 1848, married Margery S. Hibbs, of Mason county, and live two miles north of Curran. MELISSA E. died in infancy. SARAH ELLEN lives with her mother. Jonathan Kelly died June 23, 1873, and his widow resides one and three-quarter miles north of Curran.—1874.

SARAH married Ewell Rigg. See his name. She died July 16, 1854.

ELIZABETH married Henry Robertson, and had thirteen children. Mr. R. and seven children died. The widow lives two and a half miles east of Loami.

WILLIAM R. married Florella M. Alford, have six children, and live near Edinburg, Ill.

MARY M. married William S. McGinnis. See his name. Their son, JOHN, married Sarah F. Vestal, in Missouri, and lives in Loami township.

John Kelly died about 1823, in Springfield, and was buried north of Hutchison cemetery, where his first cabin was built. His widow married Zachariah Peter. See his name.

KELLY, ELISHA, born March 13, 1787, in Rutherford county, North Carolina. He came to Macoupin county, Ill., about 1817, and remained there for two years, spending most of his time in hunting. He is the old bachelor spoken of on page thirty-two. His selecting the place for a hunting ground and inducing others to come, was the beginning of Springfield. The parties caused to come were his father, Henry Kelly, and his three brothers, William, John and Elisha. The younger brother, George, came a few years later, at the same time the sisters halted here on their way to Missouri, where they went because they could not keep their slaves in Illinois. Elisha Kelly abandoned his bachelor life, and was married in Sangamon county Feb. 24, 1823, to Nancy Sims, who was born Sept. 27, 1803, in Sparklenberg county, S. C. She was a sister of John Sims. They had six children in Sangamon county, namely—

JOHN R., born Dec. 24, 1823, married Sarah Yeaman, and had three children, and the family moved to Texas. *CHARLES* died there at twenty-one years. *CAROLINE* married, and lives in Dallas county, Texas. *ANNA* lives with her sister, Caroline. The parents both died in Texas. Mr. Kelly tried to reach the Union lines, but was forced into the rebel army, contracted disease, and went home and died.

LOUISA E., born Dec. 24, 1824, married Sept. 3, 1846, to Isaac L. Ewell. See his name.

MARTHA, born Aug. 27, 1836, married Thomas Desper; had several children, and live in Missouri.

ELMIRA, married James Wilson, and died in Texas, leaving several children. Mr. Wilson married again, and lives in Sangamon county.

WILLIAM D., married Harriet, daughter of Jonathan Kelly. He died, and she married Erastus Canfield; has two children, and live near Plymouth, Hancock county, Illinois.

ZILPAH M. is living with her third husband in Texas.

Mrs. Nancy Kelly died Jan. 27, 1855, and Elisha Kelly died April 6, 1874, both in Curran township, Sangamon county.

KELLY, WILLIAM, was born in Rutherford county, North Carolina; married there to Dicey Ann Cook; came to Sangamon county in company with his son-in-law, Andrew Elliott, in the fall of 1819. They had children, and some live in North Carolina, and some in Sangamon county. Of their children—

ZILPAH, born March 12, 1797, in North Carolina, married there to Andrew Elliott. See his name.

ZILLA, married John Holt.

EMMA LEECA married Lucien Berry.

JANE married Jacob Cooper. See his name.

ALZIRA married Benjamin Cook.

ALTA married William McGinnis, who died, and she married John Fullerton, and resides at Carthage, Jasper county, Missouri.

CLEMANTINE married Nathan Ralstow.

William Kelly and wife moved to Jasper county, Mo., in 1836, and both died there, near Carthage.

KELLY, ELIJAH, born in Rutherford county, North Carolina, married there to Esther Cook, came to Sangamon county in 1821 or '2. They had seven children. Elisha Kelly died in Sangamon county about 1832. His widow and children moved to Missouri.

KELLY, GEORGE, born in Rutherford county, North Carolina, came to Sangamon county about 1821; married Elizabeth Orendorff; moved about 1836 to the vicinity of Bolivar, Polk county, Mo.; raised a family of eight children, and Mr. Kelly and his wife both died there.

KENT, JOSIAH P., was born Nov. 28, 1804, near Bainbridge, Ross county, Ohio. Clarissa Poole was born Nov. 19, 1816, in the same county, near Chillicothe. They were there married Aug. 2, 1836, and came to Sangamon county, arriving in November of that year, in what is now Illiopolis township. They had two children—

ADALINE, born Aug. 7, 1837, in Sangamon county, married Nov. 8, 1854, to Charles M. Turner, who was born Dec. 2, 1820, in Juniata county, Pa., and came to Sangamon county in 1847, to visit his sister, Mrs. S. G. Nesbitt. Mr. and Mrs. Turner had seven children, three of whom died under two years. ELIZA A., MARY E., CHARLES A. and LAURA BELLE reside with their parents in Illiopolis.

JAMES T., born August 8, 1842, in Sangamon county. He served nine months in the U. S. Navy in the war to suppress the rebellion, and was married Sept. 6, 1869, in Sangamon county, to Jennie Dorrell. They have two children, HORACE G. and GEORGE, and reside at Washington Heights, office 202, LaSalle street, Chicago, Illinois.—1874.

Josiah P. Kent died July 26, 1856, in Illiopolis township. Mrs. Clarissa Kent was married March 17, 1861, to Albert Booth. He died March 1, 1873, in Springfield, Illinois, and his widow resides there.

KENT, JESSE H., born in 1809, near Bainbridge, Ross county, Ohio. He was married in 1838, in Christian county, to Lydia A. Walker, but soon after made their home in the eastern part of Sangamon county, Ill., where one child was born, and they moved to Springfield, where they had four children. William and John T. died young. Of the other three children—

SARAH E., born June 25, 1840, near Mechanicsburg, married George W. Constant. *See his name.*

JAMES H., born in Springfield, enlisted in 1861, in Company I, 7th Ill. Inf. for three years, was wounded in 1864, and discharged on account of physical disability, married Jane Howard, and she died.

JOSIAH P., born in Springfield, married Lou Rogers, and lives with his father, near Savannah, Mo.

Jesse H. Kent lived in Springfield until 1874, when he moved to the vicinity of Savannah, Mo., where he now resides.

KENNEY, MATTHEW P., was born Sept. 3, 1808, in Christian county, Kentucky. He came to Sangamon county, Ill., in 1827, and was married Jan. 6, 1829, to Amanda Viney. They had seven living children in Sangamon county, namely:

JAMES T. married Mary Crane, and lives in Auburn township.

JOHN N. married Amanda Wallace, and lives one and a quarter miles south of Auburn, Sangamon county, Illinois.

WILLIAM married Martha A. Drennan, and live in Bates county, Missouri.

REBECCA married Elias Tusker, have three children, and reside three and a half miles east of Auburn, Sangamon county, Illinois.

MATTHEW S.,
NINIAN E. and
ABRAHAM V. live with their mother.

Matthew P. Kenney died Dec. 13, 1851, and his widow resides—1873—on the farm where they settled in 1829. It is three miles east of Auburn, Sangamon county, Illinois.

KESSLER, ADAM, was born Oct. 22, 1807, in Baden, near Heidelburg, Germany. May 10, 1839, he embarked for America, and spent the whole summer on the Atlantic ocean, arriving in the fall. He went to Ohio, and found employment in constructing one of the canals of that State. He went from there to St. Louis, Mo., and in the fall of 1840 arrived in Springfield. His parents came to this country in 1842, and died in Springfield. Adam Kessler was married, Feb., 1849, to Catherine Weis, who was born in Baden, Germany, also. They had four children—

ELIZABETH, born in Springfield, married, Jan. 27, 1870, to John C. Schuler, who was born July 22, 1846, in Doirwangen, Germany. They have four children, CATHARINE, JOHN, CONRAD and MARY, and live in Springfield.

—54

GEORGE, JOHN and MARY, all reside in Sangamon county. Mrs. Catharine Kessler died in 1859, and Mr. Kessler was married, Nov., 1859, to Mrs. Mary Giesler, whose maiden name was Hes. They have six children—
CHRISTINA, ADAM, BARBARA, EMMA, MARY and FREDERICK, and reside in Springfield.

Mr. Kessler was for many years engaged in horticulture and market gardening, by which he has acquired a competence. In the summer of 1870 he visited Germany, returning in the fall of that year.

KESSLER, BENJAMIN, was born Dec. 28, 1803, in Botetourt county, Va., came to Sangamon county in 1827, raised a family, and lives in Auburn.

KEYS, ISAAC, was born Jan. 11, 1790, in Fayette county, Kentucky, and when a young man went to Pickaway county, Ohio. Elizabeth Hess was born about 1795 in Virginia, and was taken by her parents, when she was a child, to Pickaway county, Ohio. Isaac Keys and Elizabeth Hess were married, and had three children in that county. They moved to what became Sangamon county, Ill., arriving in 1819, in what is now the southwest corner of Rochester township, where they had five children. Of their eight children—

MARY, born in Pickaway county, Ohio, married in Sangamon county to Timothy Shoup. See his name.

SAMUEL, born in Pickaway county, Ohio, married in Sangamon county to Elizabeth Delay. They had six living children. HENRY, born in 1845, went to Washington Territory in 1871; has not been heard from since 1872. MARY married John Poffenberger, and died in 1870. LORENZO D., born Aug. 10, 1862, died, aged thirteen years. JULIA A., FLORENCE G. and WINNIE live with their parents. Samuel Keys and wife live in the southwest corner of Rochester township, Sangamon county, on the farm where his father settled in 1819.

DANIEL, born in 1817, in Ross county, Ohio, married in Sangamon county, Ill., Jan. 3, 1844, to Sarah J. Armstrong, who died, Sept. 28, 1844, leaving one child, SARAH J. She married Robert A. Jones. See his name. They live near Independence, Montgomery county, Kansas. Daniel Keys married, May 7, 1845, to Nancy A. Dozier, who was born Sept. 26, 1823, in Montgomery county, Ky. They had eight children in Sangamon county, and in 1860 moved to Christian county, where they had two children. Of their children—JAMES A., and ISAAC W. live with their parents. NANCY A. died young. MIRANDA A., born Jan. 28, 1852, married, in 1871, to Sylvester Miller, and live in Christian county, Illinois. JOHN, CHARLES, EDWIN S., JESSIE F., MARY J. and HATTIE M. All the unmarried children live with their parents, one and one-half miles northwest of Pana, Christian county, Illinois.

ISAAC, Jun., born Jan. 16, 1825, in Sangamon county, married, February 14, 1852, near Rochester, to Almira J. Neal. They had three children. EDWARD D. is bookkeeper in the Fire and Marine Insurance Bank, and lives with his parents. ANNIE E. lives with her parents also. NELLIE I died Sept. 5, 1875, aged eighteen years. Isaac Keys was Deputy United States Marshal in the southern district of Illinois, from 1857 to 1862, when he was appointed by President Lincoln, Provost Marshal for the eighth congressional district of Illinois, and served until Sept., 1865, all that time without the slightest complaint of irregularity. He was one of the original proprietors of the Fifth street horse railroad, and superintended the construction of the same. After that, he was interested in the Barclay coal mine, and superintended that. He now resides in Springfield.

JAMES, born April 11, 1828, in Sangamon county, married Jan. 1, 1863, to Nannie Gardner, daughter of Hiram K. Gardner. She was born Feb. 6, 1835, in Trimble county, Ky. Mr. and Mrs. Keys have one daughter, IDA, born Oct. 21, 1863. Mr. Keys is a dealer in real estate, and lives in Springfield, Illinois.

CLARISSA, born in Sangamon county, married Allen Miller; has seven children, and lives in Springfield.

ELIZA A., born April 3, 1832, in Sangamon county, married May 16, 1852, to Jasper Newton Inslee. They had five children. ANN E. died in her second year,

EMMA J., MARY L., MELISSA and JOSEPH W. live with their parents in Cotton Hill township, Sangamon county, Illinois.

MARINDA, born in Sangamon county, married Marion Goldsby; has a family of children, and live in Cass county, Missouri.

Mrs. Elizabeth Keys died in May, 1847, and Isaac Keys, Sen., died May 2, 1848, both on the farm where they settled when they came to the county in 1819.

KEYES, HUMPHREY, was born in 1763, at Keyes' Ferry, Jefferson county, Va. It is on the Shenandoah river, six miles from the junction with the Potomac. He was married in Loudon county to a Miss Struder. They had five children, and Mrs. Keyes died. Humphrey Keyes was married in Monroe county, Va., to Sarah Hanley, who was born in that county in 1776. They had six children in Monroe county, and moved to Sangamon county, Ill., arriving at Springfield, Nov. 10, 1830. Of his children by the first marriage—

ISAAC, born and married in Virginia, died in the Wabash Valley, Indiana, leaving a widow and four children. She married Mr. McCullough, and lives in Edgar county, Illinois.

JOSEPH, born and married in Virginia, brought up a family there.

LUCRETIA, born in Virginia, was married there to Joseph Fawcett, and both died in St. Charles, Missouri, leaving five children.

THOMAS, born and married in Virginia, died in Bond county, Ill., without family.

PHOEBE, born in Virginia, was married there to Joseph Bywater. They brought up a family in Rockingham county, Virginia.

The children of Mr. Keyes by the second marriage are—

GERSHOM, born Feb. 16, 1804, in Monroe county, Virginia, one hundred and eighty miles south of Richmond, was married in that county, June 17, 1830, to Amanda Nichols, and came to Sangamon county with his parents in 1830. They had one child, and Mrs. Keyes died, Sept. 23, 1832. Her son, ISAAC P., died, aged twelve years. Mr. G. Keyes was married June 12, 1836, in Springfield, Ill., to Matilda Matheny. They had two children. DOW, born May 11, 1837, in Springfield, Ill., was married Dec. 5, 1872, near Springfield, to Elizabeth H. Wilson, who was born in St. Lawrence county, New York. They reside at Pana, Illinois. C. HUMPHREY, born Feb. 4, 1840, in Springfield, Illinois, enlisted in 1861, in Co. B, 33d Ill. Inf., was wounded at Mobile, and came home in 1865, where he was honorably discharged. He went to Kansas in the summer of 1866, and was there married in May, 1867, to Mary Smith, who was born in Sangamon county, Ill. She was a daughter of Colby Smith, of Cotton Hill township. She died in 1869. C. Humphrey Keyes was married in August, 1871, to Hattie Burt. They have one child, GERTIE, and live near Xenia, Bourbon county, Kansas. Mrs. Matilda Keyes died, Sept. 18, 1840, and Gershom Keyes was married, June 8, 1843, in Springfield, Illinois, to Priscilla Norris. They had ten children near Springfield. ELLA, the sixth child, died, aged nine years. MARY A. lives with her parents. JAMES, born April 29, 1845, was married July 3, 1872, in Pana, to Nellie Elmore, and lives in Carlinville. ROBERT C., born July 15, 1848, lives in Springfield with Henson Robinson. ARNOLD R. lives with his parents. MAGGIE, born July 3, 1851, was married June 25, 1874, to Samuel R. Ray, have one child, GERSHOM, and live in Shelby county, postoffice, Pana. NOAH G., GEORGE B., VIRGINIA N. and S. ROBERTA. The four latter live with their parents. Gershom Keyes and family moved, in 1870, to a farm four miles north of Pana, Illinois, where they now reside—1876.

JAMES W., born Nov. 1, 1805, in Monroe county, Va., was married Jan. 9, 1827, in Botetourt county, Va., to Lydia Spickard, who was born June 17, 1807, in same county. They had two children born and died there, and moved to Springfield, Ill., arriving April, 1831. They had nine children in Springfield; one died in infancy. Of their eight children—CHARLES A., born Dec. 4, 1831, in Springfield, graduated at Illinois College, in 1854, was admitted to the bar in 1856, and was city attorney during 1857 and '58. Charles A. Keyes was married in Xenia, Ohio, to Elizabeth Lanman. They have two living children, LILLIAN and MARY E.

C. A. Keyes represented Sangamon county in the State Legislature of Illinois, in 1862. He was appointed Master in Chancery of Sangamon county, by Judge E. Y. Rice, in 1867, re-appointed by Judge B. S. Edwards, and again by Judge John A. McClernand. He held the position until May, 1875, and with his family resides in Springfield. MARY C., born Aug. 1, 1833, in Springfield, was married Jan. 11, 1864, to William H. VanDoren. They had three children—VIRGINIA E. died, aged three years. SUSAN F. and JAMES K. live with their parents, in Springfield, Ill. EDWARD L., born Aug. 26, 1835, married Ann Dillard. They had four children, CORA, OSCAR, ANNIE and MARCUS, who live with their father. Mrs. Ann Keyes died in the summer of 1874, and E. L. Keyes and family live four miles north of Springfield, Ill. HENRIETTA M., born July 29, 1839, in Springfield, Ill., was married, May 8, 1861, to Henson Robinson, who was born March 15, 1839, in Xenia, Ohio, where he learned the tinning business, and came to Springfield, Ill., July 1, 1858. They have three living children, LYDIA M., MARGARET H. and CHARLES H., who live with their parents. Henson Robinson is now, and has been for fourteen years, engaged in the tinware and stove business in Springfield. His father, John Robinson, came to Illinois, and bought land in Sangamon county, in 1838. He returned to Ohio for his family, but before they were ready to start he died, in 1842, in Xenia, Ohio. THOMAS R., (twin to Henrietta M., is unmarried, and lives with his parents. SUSAN F., born Nov. 1, 1841, in Springfield, married Silas W. Hickox. *See his name.* MARGARET E., born July 17, 1846, married William Day. *See his name.* MARTHA J. born Sept. 6, 1848, married Douglas Hickox. *See his name.* James W. Keyes was Postmaster in Springfield seven months, under President Van Buren, and again during the administration of President Buchanan. He was Justice of the Peace fourteen years. Mr. Keyes and family reside four miles northwest of Springfield, Illinois.

ALEXANDER, born in 1811, in Virginia, died in Springfield, in 1831.

MARGARET W., born March 31, 1814, in Union, Monroe county, Va., was married in Sangamon county, Ill., to L. C. Backenstoe. They had one child, VIRGINIA E. Mr. Backenstoe died, in 1833, and his widow married James F. Reed. *See his name.*

ELIZABETH, born in 1816, in Virginia, died, in 1832, in Sangamon county, Illinois.

ROBERT CADEN, born in 1818, in Monroe county, Va., came to Sangamon county with his parents, in 1830, went, in 1845, to California, with a drove of cattle belonging to other parties, from there to Oregon, and returned to California, where he met his sister, Mrs. Reed, July 4, 1847, at the house of Capt. Yontz, where a party had assembled to celebrate the national anniversary. R. C. Keyes brought eighty-one Americans with him, and found one hundred and twenty-seven others on the ground. They united in what is believed to have been the first celebration of the fourth of July on the Pacific coast. Capt. Yontz furnished all the provisions, and the ladies present made a flag by sacrificing their underclothing. Mr. Keyes was fourteen years superintendent of the Almaden quicksilver mines in California. Robert C. Keyes was married about 1853, in California, to Mrs. Roberts, of Australia, but of English birth and parentage. She was the widow of an Episcopal clergyman, who was married in Australia, and died soon after coming to California. Mr. and Mrs. R. C. Keyes had three children, and he died Sept. 14, 1865. His widow and children reside in San Jose, California.

Humphrey Keyes died Oct. 11, 1833, near Springfield, Ill., and his widow, Mrs. Sarah Keyes, died May 29, 1846, four miles above the mouth of Blue river, and near where Manhatten, Kansas, now stands. She was on her way to California with her daughter, Mrs. Reed. *See Reed and Donner party.*

KING, JEREMIAH, was born Sept. 10, 1808, in Kentucky. His father was a soldier in the war of 1812. His mother died during the war, and his father was wounded, from the effects of which he died on his way home. Jeremiah was taken to Xenia, Ohio, where he was apprenticed to the tanning business. He came to Sangamon county in 1827, and was married Aug. 21, 1828, to Julia A. Brown. They had ten children, four of whom died in infancy. Of the other six—

MARTHA A., born May 9, 1831, married James L. Plunkett. See his name.

JACOB, born Dec. 15, 1832, married Elizabeth Carson, and resides near Lamor Station, Nodaway county, Mo.

ELIZA J., born Jan. 12, 1835, married William C. Langston. See his name.

MARY E., born Oct. 4, 1841, married Beatty J. Strode. See his name.

MARGARET L., born Dec. 9, 1845, married Elias Glascock. See his name. They reside in Menard county, Illinois.

LEVI T., born Jan. 24, 1848, was married Oct. 8, 1871, to Mary E. Rhodes. They have one child, MAGGIE M., and live with his mother, seven miles north of Springfield.

Jeremiah King died Dec. 21, 1869, and his widow resides in Fancy Creek township, seven miles north of Springfield.

KING, JOHN, was born Jan. 22, 1804, in Kentucky. He was a brother to Jeremiah King, came to Sangamon county about 1821, and was married Feb. 18, 1824, to Sarah Earnest. They had ten children, three of whom died in infancy. Of the other seven—

WILLIAM E., born June 12, 1826, married Almyra Bradley. He died Feb. 16, 1856, leaving a widow and two children. She married Henry Morgan. See his name. He died, and she resides near Fredonia, Kansas.

ELIZABETH, born Feb. 1, 1828, in Sangamon county, married March 14, 1843, to John Ingels. See his name.

JEREMIAH, born Sept. 19, 1830, married Aug. 29, 1862, to Mary E. Douglas, who was born Sept. 19, 1843, in Sangamon county. They have six children, IDA, SARAH, ANNIS, ELIZABETH, EDWARD and MARY, and reside two and one-half miles west of Curran.

JOHN E., born Dec. 21, 1832, married Nancy Campbell; have four children, and live near Fredonia, Kansas.

CHARLES W., born July 6, 1835, married Oct. 3, 1872, to Virginia Beach, and live with his mother.

SARAH C., born May 12, 1836, married Daniel H. Brundage; have six children, and reside in Iola, Allen county, Kansas.

MARTHA F., born March 18, 1839, married Feb. 14, 1860, to Jacob J. Ingels, who was born Aug. 25, 1834, in Bourbon county, Ky. They had three children. The two youngest died in infancy. Mrs. Ingels died May 23, 1866. LIZZIE, born Sept. 14, 1861, is the eldest child, and the only member of the family living, resides with her grandmother King.

John King died Dec. 29, 1838, and his widow resides four miles northwest of Curran, Sangamon county.

KING, TURNER R., born Jan. 12, 1812, at Sutton, Worcester county, Mass., came to Springfield, Ill., arriving Dec., 1840, remained until 1842, and went to Missouri. From there, in 1844, he went to Pekin, Ill., and in June, 1849, he returned to Springfield, Ill. President Taylor appointed him Register of the Land Office. He retained the position during that administration. In 1854 he was elected, unsolicited by himself, Police Magistrate, and served one year. In the autumn of 1862 was appointed United States Collector for the eighth Congressional District, by President Lincoln, and held the office until 1865. In 1868 he moved to his farm, near McLean station, McLean county, Ill., where he now resides. He never married.

KING, WILLIAM B., was born April 23, 1783, in Fauquier county, Va., and when a young man went to east Tennessee. Anna R. Greening—a sister to Thomas A. and John F. Greening—was born July 5, 1788, in Fauquier county, Va., and taken by her parents to east Tennessee. William B. King and Anna R. Greening were there married about 1807, and at once moved to Fayette county, Ky., and from there to Clark county, Ky., where they had four children; and the family moved to Bracken county, Ky., about 1815, where seven children were born, and all the family, except the eldest son, moved to Sangamon county, Illinois, arriving Oct., 1830, and settled three miles east of Springfield, where one child was born. Arriving so late in the season gave but little opportunity to prepare for winter. They built a log cabin, roofed it with clap-boards, and cut out a place for a door and a chimney; but the snow come on before they could build a chimney, make a door, or chink and daub the cracks. They spent the winter with the cabin in that condition. Thirty-one snows fell that winter, making the "deep snow." Of their thirteen children—

THOMAS A., born April 22, 1809, in Clark county, Ky., married Nov. 11, 1830, in Bracken county, to Ann Mann, and came to Sangamon county, arriving Oct., 1831, and settled three miles east of Springfield. They had twelve children in Sangamon county; five died young. ELIZABETH, born April 16, 1832, married Anderson Todd; have ten children, and live in Illiopolis township. WILLIAM, born Nov. 21, 1835, died Jan. 23, 1862. MELVIN, born Oct. 6, 1839, enlisted July, 1862, for three years, in Co. I, 114 Ill. Inf. Served full term, and was honorably discharged Aug., 1865. He was married in Sangamon county Nov. 12, 1867, to Artamesia M. Kipps, who was born July 2, 1850, in Cobb county, Georgia. They have two children, ANNIE A. and LINNIE J., and live half a mile east of Riverton. URIAH, born Aug. 20, 1842, enlisted at Chicago, June 17, 1861, in Co. E, 24th Ill. Inf., for three years. He was wounded at the battle of Chickamauga, Sept. 19, 1863, and captured the next day, and after enduring the horrors of nearly all the famous rebel prisons, at Richmond, Danville, Andersonville, Savannah, Millen, Thomasville, and back to Andersonville, was released March 20, 1865, and returned, via Vicksburg and St. Louis, to Springfield, and was honorably discharged June 7, 1865, being within ten days of one year over time. Uriah King was married Oct. 1, 1868, to Melvina Bailey, who was born March 17, 1850, in Sangamon county. They have two children, JULIA BELLE and MANETTA, and live one and one-quarter miles east of Riverton. JOHN H., born June 28, 1848, lives with his parents. JULIA A., born Dec. 6, 1851, married Dec. 11, 1872, to John G. Turney, who was born July 27, 1844, in Northumberland county, Canada West. They live one mile east of Riverton. THOMAS A., Jun., born July 29, 1855, lives with his parents. Thomas A. King and wife reside where they settled in 1831. It is one mile east of Riverton, Sangamon county, Illinois.

REUBEN, born Jan., 1811, in Clark county, Ky., came with his parents to Sangamon county in 1830, and was a soldier in the Black Hawk war in 1831-32. He was married to Susan Howell. They raised a large family in McLean county, and moved to Iowa, where Mrs. Susan King died, and he married a second time. When the rebellion commenced, he enlisted in the 12th Iowa Inf., at fifty-two years of age, and was killed at the battle of Pittsburg Landing, April 6, 1862. His son, THOMAS, enlisted in 1862 in Co. I, 114th Ill. Inf. Served to the end of the rebellion, and was honorably discharged. He died in McLean county in 1874. JAMES enlisted in the 10th Mo. Cav., and was never heard of after the Price raid of 1862 in Missouri. ISABEL married George Arnold, and lives in McLean county, ten miles east of Lexington. She is the only living member of Reuben King's family.

ELIZABETH, born March 2, 1813, in Kentucky, married in Sangamon county to Uriah Mann. *See his name.*

JAMES M., born Jan. 30, 1815, in Clark county, Ky. He went to the Wisconsin lead mines, in 1834, and worked for three and one-half years at smelting lead for William S. Hamilton, son of Alexander Hamilton, who was killed by Aaron Burr. He married, Nov. 14, 1839, in Sangamon county, to America Elliott. They had nine children; three died young. CLIFTON H., born Sept. 18, 1840, enlisted July, 1861, at Springfield, in what became Co. B, 11th Mo. Inf., served three years, and was honorably discharged, at St. Louis. He was married, March 7, 1865, to Alida Yocom, had one child, ALIDA, and Mrs. King died March 27, 1866. He was married Dec. 12, 1867, in Sangamon county, to Martha Wilson. They have three children, ARTHUR W., LUELLA and MARGARET, and live in Murray county, near Worthington, Noble county, Minn. CLARISSA A., born Jan. 6, 1843, died Oct. 12, 1863. HESTER F., born July 3, 1845, married John E. Constant. *See his name.* WILLIAM T., born June 30, 1849, married Sept. 25, 1873, at Petersburg, to Mary F. McCrea, and live three-quarters of a mile east of Barclay. MARY F., born May 26, 1853, and RUFUS H., born Dec. 25, 1855, live with their parents, three-quarters of a mile east of Barclay.

WILLIAM G., born in 1817, in Bracken county, Ky., raised in Sangamon county, married in New Orleans to Sarah R. Tonguelet, had two children, went to California in 1849, and died there in 1871.

HENRY J., born in 1819, in Bracken county, Ky., married in Sangamon county, in 1840, to Louisa Fowkes. They had six children, and moved to the vicinity of Marshalltown, Iowa. His son, WILLIAM, enlisted in an Iowa regiment, and died at New Madrid, Missouri.

SARAH, born in 1821, in Bracken county, Ky., married in Sangamon county to Nathaniel B. Neal. See his name. He died, and she married Hudson Lanham, and had four children. ROSA married John Brautner, and resides in Springfield. Mrs. and Mrs. Lanham died at Riverton.

STEPHEN, born in 1823, in Bracken county, Ky., married in Sangamon county to Mrs. Elizabeth Smith, whose maiden name was Hendrix. They had seven children: ALBERT died, aged fourteen years. NELLIE, LINCOLN, CHARLES, WILLIE, KATIE and EDDIE, and reside four miles southeast of Williamsville.

HESTER F., born Jan. 21, 1825, in Bracken county, Ky., married in Sangamon county to Culvin S. Churchill. See his name.

ANNA R., born August 21, 1826, in Bracken county, Ky., married in Sangamon county, Nov. 10, 1843, to Christopher Mann. See his name.

FIELDING A., born Nov. 14, 1828, in Bracken county, Ky., raised in Sangamon county, went around Cape Horn to California in 1849, enlisted and fought Indians there three years during the rebellion, is unmarried, and resides at You Bet, Nevada county, California.

JOHN F., born Dec. 12, 1831, in Sangamon county, married Oct. 18, 1860, also in Sangamon county, to Mary J. Threlkeld. She was born Jan. 5, 1838, in Bracken county, Ky. They have seven children, ELMA E., JOHN L., JESSIE V., CHARLES W., THOMAS M., HENRY O., and TILLIE M., and reside two miles southeast of Riverton, Sangamon county. John F. King was commissioned as Justice of the Peace in 1858, and served until he enlisted, July 18, 1862, in what became Co. I, 114th Ill. Inf. He recruited the company, and was elected Captain, but was not commissioned, but when the regiment was organized he was elected and commissioned, Sept. 18, 1862, as Lieutenant Colonel. He was commissioned August 23, 1864, as Colonel, but never mustered, because the regiment was then reduced to a minimum. He resigned Dec. 9, 1864. Col. King was commissioned, in 1866, as assistant assessor in charge of distilleries. Commissioned as gauger in 1867, and in 1869 as U. S. Storekeeper, all in the eighth district of Illinois. He served three years as Secretary of the Old Settlers' Society.

William B. King died Oct. 19, 1863, and Mrs. Ann R. King died March 27, 1873, both in Sangamon county, Illinois.

KILGOUR, JAMES W., was born Dec. 14, 1823, near Chillicothe, Ohio. His father died when he was quite young, and his mother married William V. Brown. They had one son, who died at seven years of age. The family moved to Sangamon county, Ill., arriving in the fall of 1832 in what is now Fancy Creek township. Mrs. Brown died, April 17, 1857, and William V. Brown died in 1871.

James W. Kilgour was married, Aug. 10, 1846, to Hannah H. Alexander. They had four children, namely—

WILLIAM J. died, at ten years of age.

MARY E., aged eight, and

GEORGE, in infancy.

SARAH ANN, born Sept. 23, 1851, married Sept. 29, 1870, to B. F. Larkin, and live in Logan county, two and one-half miles west of Williamsville, Illinois.

Mrs. H. H. Kilgour died, March 12, 1855, and J. W. Kilgour was married, Dec. 5, 1855, to Nancy E. Tipton, who was born March 17, 1824, in Carter county, Tenn. They have one child—

ISAAC F., born Oct. 17, 1856, and lives with his parents.

James W. Kilgour enlisted Feb. 17, 1863, in Co. G, 7th Ill. Inf., for three years, served until July 17, 1865, when he was honorably discharged with the regiment. He resides at Sherman, Sangamon county, Illinois—1874.

KINNEY, HENRY, was born March 1, 1774, in Woodstock, Connecticut. In 1795 he went to Cazenovia, N. Y., and from there to Clinton, Oneida county, in the same State, and was there married, March 4, 1798, to Dicey Pond. She was born Sept. 4, 1778, in Hartford, Conn. They lived at Cazenovia, Madison county, N. Y., until they had three children, and moved to Sangamon county, Ill., arriving May 6, 1822, in what is now Loami township. Of their three children—

HENRY, Jun., born Aug. 4, 1807, in New York, married in Sangamon county, Oct. 23, 1828, to Margaret Dorrance. They had five children in Sangamon county, namely—DANIEL married Annis Elmore. They have two children, HENRY H. and EDITH C., and live one and one-quarter miles east of Loami. CLARISSA, born April 9, 1831, married James M. Darneille. See his name. CAROLINE died, March 6, 1853, in her twenty-first year. ELIZA J., born Oct. 9, 1834, married, Nov. 30, 1854, to John R. Shelton. See his name. REBECCA married David M. Vanderen. See his name. Henry Kinney, Jun., and his wife reside in Chatham. He was a soldier in the Black Hawk war, in 1831, in a cavalry company, under Capt. Jonathan Saunders.

MAJOR, born Jan. 2, 1810, in New York, married, Nov. 15, 1834, to Melissa S. Pond, who was born March 12, 1819, at Meadville, Penn. Her father, Martin T. Pond, moved to Logan county, Illinois, before the "deep snow," and was living there when his daughter Melissa was married. He moved to Concord, Morgan county, and died there, Feb. 2, 1864. Major Kinney and wife had five children in Sangamon county, namely—DICEY, born Nov. 25, 1840, married, March 29, 1860, to Wm. D. Farrar, have three children, FRANK D, ALLICE G. and STELLA K., and live in Osage county, Kan. AMANDA, born Aug., 1842, married, in 1862, to James N. Moore. She died, Nov. 7, 1864, leaving one son, HERBERT D., who lives with his father, near Virginia, Cass county, Ill. HENRY, born Nov. 21, 1844, married, April 9, 1868, to Anna F. Hesser, who was born June 3, 1845, near Palmyra, Mo. They have two children, WILLYS H. and EUGENE E., and live near Loami. JULIUS M. died March 4, 1864, in his sixteenth year. ALICE, born July 18, 1851, lives with her parents. Major Kinney and wife reside near Concord, Morgan county—1874. He was a soldier in a Light Horse company in the Black Hawk war.

JOHN, born Sept. 2, 1813, in New York, married in Sangamon county, Nov. 3, 1836, to Asenath Sweet. They have two children, both married. Mr. and Mrs. Kinney live at Linden, Osage county, Kansas.

Mrs. Dicey Kinney died, Sept. 15, 1850, and Henry Kinney, Sen., died March 18, 1859, both in Loami township. He was a member of the Baptist church sixty-seven years, and a deacon the greater part of that time.

KIRK, WILLIAM B., was born Jan. 18, 1787, in Virginia; was married there Aug. 31, 1809, to Mary Young, a native of Virginia also; and moved to Bath county, Ky., where they had seven children. They moved to Sangamon county, Ill., arriving Nov., 1836, in what is now Cartwright township. Of their children—

RACHEL B. married S. A. Craig, and remained in Kentucky.

JOHN A., born Oct. 17, 1812, in Kentucky, married in Sangamon county to Julia W. Cunnin, who died, and he married in Kentucky to Isabel Frazier, who died in Menard county, leaving one child, MARY J. She married Henry Giger. See his name. J. A. Kirk married Sarah Ferguson, who died, leaving one child, JOSIAH B. He enlisted in an Illinois regiment, and died of disease near Memphis, Tenn., in March, 1863. J. A. Kirk died in Cooper township, Jan., 1861.

WILLIAM Y., born Feb. 21, 1815, in Kentucky, married in Sangamon county to Alletta A. Earnest. They had one child, JULIA F., married and lives in Missouri. Mr. K. died in Sangamon county in 1852. His widow married a Mr. Watson, and lives in Missouri.

MARY A. V., born April 15, 1820, in Bath county, Ky., married in Sangamon county to Benjamin A. Giger. See his name.

ANDREW ST. CLAIR, born April 13, 1822, in Bath county, Ky., raised in Sangamon county, was farming there, and in February, 1861, left home unexpectedly, and the first heard of him at the end of two years, he was in the Union army. Served three and a half years, and was honorably discharged. He resides four miles north of Athens, Illinois.

MARGARET J., born Oct. 6, 1824, in Bath county, Ky., married in Sangamon county to Benjamin A. Giger. See his name.

AGNES S., born Sept. 11, 1827, in Kentucky, died unmarried in Sangamon county, Oct. 29, 1866.

William B. Kirk died April 12, 1847, and his widow died March 22, 1848, both at Mechanicsburg, Sangamon county, Illinois.

KNIGHT, MRS. ELIZABETH, whose maiden name was Bowen, sister to Zaza Bowen, was born Jan. 1, 1796, in Guilford county, N. C. She was married in that county to Abner Knight. They had two children there, and she and her husband, in company with her widowed mother and family, moved to Cabell county, West Va., where Mr. and Mrs. Knight had six children. Abner Knight died there, Dec. 17, 1838. Mrs. Knight, with six of her children, moved to Sangamon county, Ill., arriving April, 1839, in what is now Loami township. Of all her children—

EZEKIEL, born in North Carolina, left home in Virginia about the time the family came west. He went down the Mississippi river, and has never been heard of by the family since.

MINERVA, born Aug. 21, 1817, in North Carolina, married, May 26, 1837, in West Virginia, to Wm. F. Joy. They had seven living children in West Virginia, and came to Sangamon county in 1857, where one child was born. Of the eight children—JOHN W. married Elizabeth Hall. Mr. Joy enlisted, Aug., 1862, in Co. I, 73d Ill. Inf., for three years, was wounded at the battle of Perryville, brought home, and died. JAMES M. enlisted in Aug., 1862, in Co. I, 73d Ill. Inf., for three years. He was captured at the battle of Chickamauga. He was five weeks in Libby prison, at Richmond, five months at Danville, eleven months in Andersonville, with its usual bill of fare. He was released from that place, March 27, 1865, and honorably discharged, June 17, 1865. He married Amanda Hall, has one child, and lives in Loami township. WILLIAM E. enlisted Aug., 1862, in Co. I, 73d Ill. Inf., for three years, was wounded at the battle of Perryville, Ky.,

—55

and discharged on account of physical disability. He married Celestine Cook, has two children, LETTIE MAY and WILLIE, and lives in Loami. JOSEPH O. enlisted Aug., 1862, for three years, in Co. I, 73d Ill. Inf., was wounded at the battle of Mission Ridge, Nov. 24, 1863, recovered, served full term, and was honorably discharged, June 24, 1865, at Springfield. He was married to Jane Baker. They have three children, and live near Loami. MARY E. married John D. Nevins, had two children, NELLIE and JOSEPH O., and Mr. Nevins died. His widow and child live with her mother. BUENA V. enlisted in 1863, for three years, in Co. I, 16th Ill. Cav., He was captured, and first put in Libby prison, was one winter at Belle Isle, taken thence to Andersonville, where he died, July 5, 1864. WIRT W., and ZAZA B., live with their mother. Wm. F. Joy died, March 17, 1873, and his widow resides two and one-half miles southwest of Loami, Sangamon county.

NANCY L., born Feb. 2, 1821, married Michael Cassity.

JAMES M., born Oct. 8, 1823, in West Virginia, married, Sept. 17, 1850, in Sangamon county, to Rachel Tilley. They have ten children—ZAZA B. lives near Loami. WILLIAM A. was married, April 5, 1876, to Mary Josephine Jarret, and live near Loami. LEROY G., JOHN M., SUSANNA, MARY A., LIZZIE M., JAMES M., NANCY J. and LYDIA; the seven latter live with their parents, one and one-half miles west of Loami, Sangamon county, Illinois.

SUSANNA, born in 1825, in Virginia, married Wm. Boyd, and died, leaving five children in Indiana.

ZAZA D., born in Virginia, died in Sangamon county, at twenty-six years of age.

ABNER W., born May 18, 1832, in Virginia, married in Sangamon county, Oct. 11, 1858, to Hepsey Nipper, who died, leaving one child, ALICE. Mr. Knight was married, Oct. 17, 1872, to Catharine R. Langston, who was born Aug. 17, 1851, in Mason county. They live near Mason City, Illinois.

WILLIAM, born in West Virginia, died in Sangamon county, aged twenty-two years.

Mrs. Elizabeth Knight resides with her son, James M., in Loami township—1874.

KNOTTS, THOMAS, was born in Lee county, Virginia, and was married there to Ella Young. They moved to Washington county, Ind., and from there to Sangamon county, Ill., arriving in the spring of 1819, in what is now Ball township. They had ten children, four of whom, or their descendants, live in Ball township, namely—

LUCY married Martin G. Pulliam. See his name.

ALBION, born April 1, 1814, was married April 16, 1835, in Sangamon county, to Linna Davidson, who was born Dec. 23, 1819. They had seven children in Sangamon county. THOMAS, born Nov., 1837, married Cassandra Peddecord, a native of Ohio county, Ky., and daughter of Jonathan Peddecord, now of Ball township. Thomas Knotts and wife had two children, CORDELIA E. and THOMAS. Mr. Knotts died Dec. 26, 1870, and his widow and children live in Ball township. JOHN, unmarried, and lives with his father. ELLA married George S. Pulliam. See his name. SAMUEL was born a cripple, in 1845, lives with his father. ELIZABETH married Joseph Dragoo, and lives in Ball township. JOSEPH O. married Martha Brawner, and lives in Pawnee township. WILLIAM J. lives with his father. Mrs. Linna Knotts died, and Albion Knotts was married March 2, 1854, to Mary J. Peddecord. They have four children, CHARLES W., ALBERT, HENRY J. and EDDIE, all live with their parents on the farm where their grandfather Knotts settled in 1819. It is in Ball township, two and a half miles southeast of Chatham.

THOMAS, Jun., married in Sangamon county to Elizabeth Brawner. They have six children, and live two and a half miles southeast of Chatham.

RUTH married Henry Shoup. See his name.

AMELIA married Mr. Withrow, and lives in Macoupin county, Illinois.

DANIEL married Martha Keagle. She lives in Springfield.

ETTA married John M. Taylor, and lives in Iowa.

Thomas Knotts, Sen., died within one year after bringing his family into the new country.

KNOX, THOMAS J., was born in 1802, at Wheeling, Va. He went to Kentucky when a boy, and came to Sangamon county in 1820, stopping in what is now Clear Lake township. He was commissioned 2d Lieutenant of 25th Ill. Militia by Gov. Edwards, March 4, 1830, and served in the Black Hawk war. He was married in 1830 to Mrs. Mary Myers, whose maiden name was Danley. She had four children by her first marriage. Her son, Samuel Myers, lives north of Riverton, Illinois.

Mr. and Mrs. Knox had six children in Sangamon county, namely—

RUTH M., married Lewis Allen, had one child, and lives near Carthage, Missouri.

MARGARET J., married John Hawker, have five children, and lives in Pana.

CARY J. married Peter Mann. See his name.

NANCY A. married Charles Parker. They had one child. Mr. Parker enlisted August, 1862, for three years, in Co. C, 114th Ill. Inf., was wounded and captured June 10, 1864, at Guntown, Miss. He died from the effects of privation in Andersonville prison. His widow married Charles Cruser, has two children, and lives near Carthage, Mo.

JAMES M., born in Sangamon county, enlisted August, 1862, for three years, in Co. I, 114th Ill. Inf. He was transferred to the quartermaster's department, served his full term, and was honorably discharged in 1865. He was married in 1867, in Sangamon county, to Elizabeth Johnson. They have two children, and live near Danvers, McLean county.

MARY ALICE A., born May 7, 1843, married Dec. 24, 1867, to William Richardson, who was born May 11, 1840, in New Haven, Conn. They have two children, GERTRUDE and JANET, and live two miles east of Riverton.

Thomas J. Knox died Dec. 8, 1857, and his widow was killed by a team backing off an embankment in Clear Lake township, August 15, 1861.

L

LAMB, GEORGE, was born Dec., 1789, near Hagerstown, Maryland, and when quite young went to Mt. Pleasant, Westmoreland county, Pennsylvania, where he learned the business of saddle and harness-making. He was married at Mt. Pleasant May 24, 1820, to Eliza H. Hubbs, who was born in that place in 1794. She was the daughter of Dr. Charles Hubbs, who, although a member of the Society of Friends, was a surgeon in the American army, near the close of the Revolution. Later in life, Dr. Hubbs became a preacher in the Baptist church. George Lamb's ancestors were members of the Society of Friends also. Mr. and Mrs. Lamb had three children in Pennsylvania, and moved to Kaskaskia, Randolph county, Ill., in the spring of 1830, where two children were born. One died in infancy. Mrs. Eliza H. Lamb died Aug. 15, 1834, in Chester, Ill., and in June, 1836, George Lamb moved to Springfield. Of his four children—

CHARLES H., born May 19, 1822, at Brownsville, Fayette county, Penn., accompanied his parents to Illinois, and came to Springfield in 1832, preceding his father, to attend school. He remained one year, and returned to his parents, who had moved from Kaskaskia to Chester, Ill. He afterwards learned the printing business, in the *Sangamo Journal* in Springfield, with Simeon Francis & Co. In 1841, Charles H. Lamb started the *Rock River Register*, at Grande de Tour, Ogle county, Ill., but sold out the following spring. He was afterwards, with his uncle, James L. Lamb, in the pork packing business. He is unmarried, and resides on his farm, near Pawnee, in Ball township, Sangamon county, Illinois.

MARY ELIZA, born Oct. 6, 1824, near Mt. Pleasant, Penn., died Aug. 23, 1834, at Chester, Illinois.

WILLIAM H., born Nov. 14, 1826, in Pennsylvania, died Oct. 1, 1834, at Chester, Illinois.

SUSAN M., born Sept. 3, 1830, in Kaskaskia, Ill., was brought up by her aunt, Hannah G. Mather, and married in Springfield, Ill., Nov. 14, 1855, to Dr. C. Perry Slater, who died at Springfield March 12, 1858, leaving two children. JULIA died in infancy. HANNAH M., born Sept. 10, 1856, in Springfield, lives with her mother in Chicago. Mrs. Susan M. Slater was married Nov. 9, 1870, to James H. Roberts. *See his name.*

George Lamb was married March 28, 1840, in Springfield, to Mrs. Lucinda Crowder, whose maiden name was Sanders, a native of Kentucky. They had three children—

JAMES T., born May 23, 1841, in Sangamon county, was married Dec. 5, 1867, to Mary Weber. They had four children, CHARLES W., who died Sept. 8, 1875; EMILY O., GEORGE CARROLL and JOSEPH F., and live in Ball township, four miles northwest of Pawnee, Sangamon county, Illinois.

GEORGE G., born Aug. 16, 1845, in Sangamon county, was married there Feb., 1869, to Marietta Clayton. They have three children, JAMES, ESTELLA and CHARLES, and live in Cotton Hill township, three and a half miles north of Pawnee.

MARY E., born Oct. 11, 1848, in Sangamon county, was married there Nov. 14, 1867, to William O. Matthews. *See his name.* They have two children, IDA M. and FANNIE A., and live in Cotton Hill township, three and a half miles north of Pawnee, Sangamon county, Illinois.

George Lamb died Aug. 26, 1867, and Mrs. Lucinda Lamb died Jan. 18, 1872, both in Sangamon county, Illinois.

LAMB, JAMES L., brother to George Lamb, was born Nov. 7, 1800, at Connellsville, Fayette county, Penn. His father, George Lamb, died while he was quite young, leaving six children to be cared for by the widowed mother. The family were members of the "Society of Friends." James early desired to assist his mother in bringing up the family, and at twelve years of age went to Cincinnati, making his trip on horseback, and engaged as clerk with Hugh Glenn, a relative of the family, and a prominent merchant of that city. In 1820 J. L. Lamb removed to Kaskaskia, Ill., where he engaged in mercantile pursuits and pork packing, in company with Col. Thos. Mather and S. B. Opdycke, at that place and at Chester, Ill. This firm packed and shipped the first barrel of pork ever sent to New Orleans from Illinois. J. L. Lamb was married, Jan. 13, 1824, at Cincinnati, Ohio, to Susan H. Cranmer, daughter of Dr. Cranmer of that city. She was born there, Aug. 13, 1803. They moved to Springfield, Ill., in 1831, and in moving his effects it was necessary to charter a boat at St. Louis, and take it up the Kaskaskia river to the village. This was the only instance of a steam boat ascending that stream. The goods were landed at Beardstown, and transported to Springfield in wagons. Mr. and Mrs. J. L. Lamb had seven children; two died young. Of the other five—

JOHN C., born June 16, 1825, in Kaskaskia, was married in Goshen, N. Y., Dec., 1868, to Anna Pougher, a native of England. J. C. Lamb was engaged with his father in pork packing, and is now the proprietor of the Ætna foundry and machine works, in Springfield, Illinois.

SUSAN A., born April 3, 1828, in Kaskaskia, was married in Springfield, Oct. 20, 1847, to John Cook, who was born June 12, 1826, in Belleville, Ill. Mr. and Mrs Cook had seven children, four of whom died in infancy. JAMES L., JOHN C. and WILLIAM J. live with their parents. John Cook was the only son of Hon. Daniel P. Cook, one of the early congressmen from Illinois, who married a daughter of Gov. Ninian Edwards. She died when the subject of this sketch was quite young, and he was brought up by his grandfather, Gov. Edwards. He was under the instruction of Rev. John F. Brooks (then of Belleville, but now of Springfield), from 1831 to 1840, and entered Illinois College, at Jacksonville, in 1841. He was obliged to abandon his studies the next year, from a temporary loss of sight, and afterwards attempted to finish his education at Kemper College, St. Louis, Mo., but failed from defective sight; and clerked in a commission house in the latter city for three years. Jan. 8, 1846, he formed a partnership with Hawley & Edwards, in Springfield, Ill., in the dry goods business. In 1854 John Cook was elected Mayor of Springfield, and in 1856 Sheriff of Sangamon county. At the expiration of his term, Gov. W. H. Bissell appointed him Quartermaster General of Illinois, and in 1858 he organized an independent military company, called the Springfield Zouave Grays, and was chosen Captain. This company was accepted by Gov. Yates, under the State's quota of 75,000 men in 1861, and was the nucleus of the 1st Reg., Ill. Vol. Inf., of which he was chosen Colonel, and which was called No. 7, in honor of the six regiments furnished by Illinois for the Mexican war. Col. Cook's commission was dated April 24, 1861, and the regiment was mustered in at Camp Yates, April 25, 1861, by Capt. John Pope of the regular army, and was, consequently, the first regiment to enter the field from Illinois for suppressing the rebellion. They were ordered to several different points, and at Fort "Joe Holt," Ky., Col. John Cook was assigned command of a Brigade. Feb. 3, 1862, he was assigned to the command of Gen. Charles F. Smith, in the movement up the Cumberland and Tennessee rivers. After the capture of Fort Donelson Col. Cook was commissioned Brigadier General, for gallant conduct. During the advance on Corinth he was ordered to report to the Secretary of War, and was assigned a command consisting of his brigade, with two brigades from Gen. Shields division, eleven batteries of Artillery, and two regiments of cavalry. After McClellan's retreat from Harrison's Landing and Pope's retreat from the valley, Gen. Cook was relieved, at his own request, and the following fall was ordered to report to Major Gen. John Pope, commanding the military department of the northwest, under whom he remained until Oct. 9, 1864, when he was assigned command of the military district of Illinois, with headquarters at Springfield. He was there mustered out, having been previously commissioned by President Johnson, Major General by brevet. He was elected in the fall of 1868, Representative in the Illinois State Legislature, from Sangamon county. He was instrumental in securing the second appropriation for the erection of the New State House. Gen. Cook and family reside in Springfield, Illinois.

CAROLINE E., born Feb. 8, 1831, was married in Springfield, Dec. 19, 1855, to William J. Black, who was born in Vandalia, Ill., Nov. 11, 1828. He died, Nov. 24, 1861, leaving a widow, who resides with her mother in Springfield.

HANNAH M., born July 6, 1838, in

Springfield, was married there, June 18, 1862, to Legh R. Kimball, who was born Aug. 7, 1826, in New Hampshire. They had one child JULIA L., who died in infancy. Mr. Kimball was paymaster on the Chicago & Alton railroad, and afterwards General Agent on the T. W. & W. railroad. He died May 30, 1865, in Springfield, Ill., and his widow resides there with her mother also.

ELIZABETH T., born July 29, 1841, in Springfield, was married June 8, 1864, to Gideon R. Brainerd. They have four living children, LEGH KIMBALL, BENJAMIN H., JAMES L. L. and SUSAN L. Mr. Brainard was book-keeper in the Marine and Fire Insurance Company's Bank. He is now engaged in farming, two miles west of Springfield, Illinois.

James L. Lamb was an elder in the First Presbyterian church of Springfield, and a director of the Theological Seminary of the Northwest, at Chicago. He was an active, earnest, christian gentleman, always interested in education, and a friend to those in need, as the writer of this can testify from personal knowledge. He was in the pork packing business, in Springfield, from 1842 to the time of his death, which occurred Dec. 3, 1873. His widow and children reside in Springfield, Illinois.

LAMB, HANNAH G., a native of Pennsylvania, and sister to George and James L. Lamb, was married to Col. Thomas Mather. *See his name.*

LAMUN, JAMES, was born Dec. 12, 1802, in Ross county, Ohio, and was married May 25, 1822, in that county, to Ann McCafferty, had three living children, and Mrs. Lamun died there, May 31, 1830. Mr. Lamun came to Springfield alone in 1839, and four or five years later returned to Ohio and brought out his three children, namely—

JOHN, born July 2, 1823, in Ross county, Ohio, and after spending several years in Sangamon county, returned to Ohio, and was there married; has six children, and lives in the northwest corner of Cooper township, two and a half miles southeast of Mechanicsburg.

ELEANOR, born March 3, 1825, in Ohio, married in Sangamon county to Flemuel Prickett, and lives near Mt. Auburn, Christian county, Illinois.

ANDREW, born March 25, 1829, in Ohio, married in Sangamon county to Hettie Robbins. They moved to the vicinity of Shady Grove Postoffice, Dallas county, Mo., where he died in 1870, leaving a widow and six children.

James Lamun has remained a widower forty-five years, and resides in the northeast corner of Cooper township, two and a half miles southeast of Mechanicsburg, Illinois.—1874.

LACY, CLAWSON, was born April 1, 1800, in Morris county, New Jersey. Phebe Force was born March 23, 1799. They were there married, Dec. 24, 1820, and had five children in that county. The family moved to Sangamon county, Ill., arriving June 5, 1830, in what is now Salisbury township, where they had five children. Four of their children died young. Of the other six—

HARRIET, born May 27, 1822, in New Jersey, married Jacob Carman in Sangamon county, and she died August, 1859, in Christian county. Mr. Carman and his three daughters, all married, live in Missouri.

SARAH E., born Feb. 14, 1828, in New Jersey, married in Sangamon county, March 19, 1848, to John Hale, who was born April 1, 1818, in Muskingum county, Ohio. They had three living children, OSCAR A., ELLIS A. and ELMER E., live with their parents in Salisbury township. John Hale enlisted August 12, 1862, in Co. H, 114th Ill. Inf., for three years, served full term, and was honorably discharged August 8, 1865.

MAHLON S., born Feb. 20, 1830, in New Jersey, died in Sangamon county, Jan. 25, 1855.

JACOB C., born Nov. 3, 1835, in Sangamon county, married Mrs. Susan Stone, whose maiden name was Gard. They have four living children, LOTTIE, HARRIET C., MARY J. and MAGGIE D., and live in Salisbury township. Jacob C. Lacy enlisted August 12, 1862, in Co. H, 114th Ill. Inf., for three years, was captured at the battle of Guntown, Miss., June 10, 1864, was more than nine months in Andersonville prison. His hearing and health is impaired from privation and suffering.

JOHN, born March 31, 1840, in Sangamon county. He enlisted August 12,

1862, for three years, in Co. H, 114th Ill. Inf., was captured at the battle of Guntown, June 10, 1864, taken to Andersonville, remained seven months and eighteen days, and was exchanged; served full term, and was honorably discharged. He weighed one hundred and sixty-five pounds when he went into Andersonville, and ninety pounds when he came out. He was married to Elizabeth Cox. They had one child, JAMES H., who died, aged three years. John Lacy and wife live with his parents, near Salisbury.—1874.

PHŒBE, born June 20, 1843, in Sangamon county, married Alvetus Jackson, who was born at Jay, Oxford county, Maine, about 1830. They have four children, BENJAMIN F., ORPHA, ANNIE and ADA, and reside in Salisbury township.

Clawson Lacy lives, now—1871—in Salisbury township, near where they settled in 1830.

LAKE, BAYLISS G., was born Nov. 1, 1795, in Fauquier county, Va. He was married in Frederick county Oct. 5, 1820, to Eliza Glascock, who was born in Loudon county Oct. 31, 1800. They at once moved to Clark county, Ohio, where they had three children. B. G. Lake and John McBeth started April 3, 1827, on foot, to see Illinois. They arrived at Springfield April 14th. Mr. Lake had some friends in the county. After spending about one month with them, he made an engagement to help herd some cattle and drive them east, arriving at his home in June with more money than when he started. He moved his family in a wagon drawn by four horses, arriving in the fall of 1827, in what is now Fancy Creek township, where they had six children. Of their nine children—

MARY, born May 16, 1823, in Ohio, married in Sangamon county to Stephen Wilcockson. See his name.

THOMAS W., born July 4, 1825, in Clark county, Ohio, married in Sangamon county June 27, 1847, to Julia A. England. They had ten children. Four died in infancy, and DANIEL was drowned when ten years old. Of the other five, MARY F. married Eugene Hockaday; has two children, NOURMA and WILLIAM E., and live near Champaign city, Ill. WILLIAM F. married Annie Driskill; has one child, OLLIE MAY, and live near Lincoln, Ill. LAURA E., MARGARET E. and JOSEPH A. live with their parents in Williamsville, Sangamon county, Illinois.

PHŒBE, born June 23, 1827, in Ohio, married in Sangamon county to William Mount, who was born April 20, 1826, in Monmouth county, New Jersey. They had three children. JOHN W. and TOM E. live with their parents. AUSTRALIA died, aged eight years. Mr. and Mrs. Mount reside in Menard county, six miles northwest of Williamsville, Illinois.

HARRID, born April 11, 1830, in Sangamon county, was killed in 1843 by a horse running away with himself and sister, Mary.

EDNA, born June 7, 1831, in Sangamon county, married John H. Council. See his name.

HENRY, born April 24, 1834, in Sangamon county, lives near Lawndale, Logan county—1874.

JOHN S., born Jan. 9, 1840, in Sangamon county, married Feb. 26, 1867, to Charlotte Brittin. They have one child, DORA E., and live in Fancy Creek township.

MARGARET, born Dec. 15, 1843, in Sangamon county, married Andrew J. Barber, who was born Oct. 5, 1836, in Fauquier county, Va. They have two children, JOHN and BAYLISS L., and live in Fancy Creek township.

HARRIET C., born Oct. 22, 1845, in Sangamon county, married Evans E. Brittin. See his name.

Mrs. Eliza Lake died Aug. 28, 1864, and Bayliss Lake was married Sept. 26, 1865, to Sallie McKendree. She was born Dec. 6, 1804, in Jefferson county, Va. They reside four and a half miles northwest of Sherman, Sangamon county, Illinois.

LAKE, THOMAS, was born Dec. 30, 1800, in Fauquier county, Va. Harriet Dillon was born Nov. 27, 1808, in the same county. They were there married, Jan. 4, 1826, and had two children there. The family moved to Sangamon county, Ill., arriving in what is now Fancy creek township, where seven children were born. Of the nine children—

ANN E., born July 17, 1830, in Virginia, died unmarried in Sangamon county, aged thirty-two years.

BAYLISS E., born August 10, 1832, in Fauquier county, Va., raised in Sangamon county, married Sarah Rogers. They have one child, JAMES, and live near Winterset, Iowa. Bayliss E. Lake enlisted in July, 1861, in Co. D, 1st Iowa Cav., for three years, re-enlisted as a veteran, served to the end of the rebellion, and was honorably discharged.

SUSANNA, born Nov. 20, 1834, in Sangamon county, married John L. Harris. They have two children, THOMAS M. and HATTIE, and live near Bedford, Taylor county, Iowa.

JAMES, born June 1, 1837, in Sangamon county. He enlisted in Sept., 1862, for three years, in Co. G, 114th Ill. Inf., and was appointed Sergeant. He was wounded at the battle of Guntown, Miss., June 11, 1864, captured, and died in rebel prison at Mobile, Alabama.

JOHN F., born June 6, 1839, in Sangamon county. He enlisted August 9, 1861, for three years, in Co. A, 3d Ill. Cav., and was discharged on account of physical disability, Dec. 25, 1861. He was married Nov. 29, 1865, to Matilda Lemon, who was born June 11, 1847, in Ireland. They have two children, CHARLES W. and CORA A., and live in Fancy Creek township.

ELIZABETH A., born May 13, 1842, in Sangamon county, married Wm. F. Constant. *See his name.* They have one child, MARY E.

AGNES C., born June 5, 1844, in Sangamon county, married Charles Unsby. She died March 16, 1871, in Williams township.

WILLIAM B., born August 23, 1847, in Sangamon county, resides with his mother.

MARY M., born June 28, 1850, in Sangamon county, married John W. Jones. They have one child, DORA A., and reside in Logan county.

Thomas Lake died April 10, 1853, and his widow lives two and a half miles west of Williamsville, Illinois.

LANGSTON, JECHONIAH,

was born in the year 1769, in South Carolina. His father was a Whig, and Jechoniah was often sent by his father to convey information to Whigs of the whereabouts and doings of the Tories. On one occasion the Tories were about to kill his father, and he informed the Whig soldiers in time to save his life. He was then about ten years old, and soon after, some of the Tory soldiers caught him, and taking a leather strap used for fastening their extra clothing behind them on their saddles, they hung him to a beam outside his father's barn, and watched him until he ceased to manifest any signs of life; and then took him down to save the strap, and left him on the ground dead, as they supposed; but after a long time he came to life. He was married in South Carolina, and after the birth of one child, his wife died. He left the child there, and went to Wayne county, Ky., where he was married to Nancy Dodson. They had three children in Kentucky, and moved to Champaign county, Ohio, where two children were born; and then moved to Sangamon county, Ill., arriving Feb., 1820, in what is now Fancy Creek township, where they had four children. Of their children—

JOSEPH D., born Dec. 25, 1805, in Wayne county, Ky., married July 23, 1829, to Elizabeth Cantrall. She was born Aug. 29, 1808, in Ohio. They had five living children in Sangamon county. WILLIAM C., born April 25, 1830, married Oct. 28, 1851, to Elizabeth J. Fagan, who died Dec. 26, 1853, and he married June 17, 1855, to Eliza J. King. They live in Fancy Creek township, seven miles north of Springfield. EMILY, born in 1832, married Asaph Bates. They had five children, THERESA E., JOHN T., ELIZABETH A., EMILY S., and JOSEPH W., and Mrs. Bates died May 8, 1872. THERESA and JOHN, twins, born May 11, 1834. She died June 22, 1856. JOHN married April 11, 1862, to Martha Price. They had one child, EVA JANE, and he enlisted Aug., 1862, in Co. C, 114th Ill. Inf., for three years. He was killed at the battle of Nashville, Tenn., Dec. 15, 1864. JAMES B. born Nov. 29, 1836, married Eliza Taylor; have five children, SARAH A., MARY A., JOHN O., IDA S., and BEULAH, and live near his father, in Menard county. Joseph D. Langston and wife reside in Menard county, one mile north of Sangamon county line, and one mile west of Peoria road, and fifteen miles north of Springfield.

Joseph D. Langston remembers that during the fourteen months from the time his father moved into his new home until Sangamon county was organized, they were under the jurisdiction of Madison county, and the authorities at Edwardsville claimed that they were entitled to some revenue from the isolated settlers. They were so scattered that it was not thought advisable to send out an assessor, and after him a collector, but the sheriff, Bowling Whitesides, would send out a deputy, with instructions to assess and collect as he went. Mr. Langston remembers that late in 1820 or early in 1821, the deputy came, riding one horse and leading another, with a pack saddle on it. He would engage in a promiscuous conversation, and without making his business known, would fix some value on their property. He would direct the conversation in such a manner as to ascertain how many coon skins they had on hand. He would then make his business known, and proceed to make his assessment and collection. Mr. Langston said it was a remarkable fact that the tax in almost every case amounted to *exactly the number of coon skins they had on hand.* When the officer had accumulated all his horse could carry, he would go to Edwardsville, make a deposit, and return for another load. And that was the way the first revenue was collected in Sangamon county.

JAMES W., born June 15, 1808, in Wayne county, Ky., married in Sangamon county, Nov. 11, 1838, to Mrs. Harriet L. Skinner, whose maiden name was Constant. They had five children in Sangamon county. WILLIAM H., born July 6, 1841, enlisted June 10, 1862, in Co. H, 70th Ill. Inf., for three months, served four months and thirteen days as Sergeant, and was honorably discharged Oct. 23, 1862. He again enlisted, Jan. 30, 1864, in the naval service for one year, at Mound City, Ill., served until May 4, 1865, when he was honorably discharged at Philadelphia. He was married Nov. 3, 1870, at Jacksonville, Ill., to Belle B. Rowe, who was born Sept. 12, 1848, at Hazleton, Luzerne county, Pa. They have one child, IRENE, and reside at Louisana, Pike county, Mo. MARY G., born July 19, 1843, married April 10, 1866, to George W. Thompson, who was born March, 1837, in Washington county, New York. He was Captain of a company in the 16th Ill. Inf., and served from 1862 to the end of the rebellion. They have four children, HARRIET M., LAURA L., LILIAN GRANT and GERTRUDE, and reside near Warrensburg, Macon county, Illinois. ELIZA J., born April 23, 1846, is unmarried, and lives with her mother. MARTHA E., born Oct. 3, 1849, and died in her eleventh year. LAURA died in her second year. James W. Langston died March 16, 1855, and his widow, Mrs. Harriet Langston, resides in Mechanicsburg, Illinois.

JECHONIAH, Jun., born in Wayne county, Ky., married in Sangamon county to Mary Martin. They had eight children. Mr. Langston died, and his family live near Macomb, McDonough county, Illinois.

MARTHA, born April 20, 1816, in Champaign county, Ohio, married in Sangamon county, Dec. 1, 1844, to John R. McKee, who was born Nov. 10, 1820, near Cincinnati, Ohio. They had one child, EMMA, who died in her third year. Mr. McKee enlisted, Aug. 1, 1861, in Co. F, 33d Ill. Inf., for three years. He re-enlisted Dec. 31, 1863, at Indianola, Texas, and served until Oct., 1865, when about one month before his regiment he was mustered out. Mr. and Mrs. McKee live at Williamsville, Illinois.

MARY G., born in Ohio, married in Sangamon county, Aug. 13, 1840, to Alexander M. Doake, who was born in Kentucky. They both died, leaving one child, MARGARET J., who married to Lewis Ludy. They have five children, and live at Emporia, Kansas.

MARGARET, born in Sangamon county, married Isaac Booth. They both died, leaving one child, ALICE, who married George Simpson. They live in Missouri.

NANCY H., born in Sangamon county, married Joseph Shepherd. They had one child, CHARLES, who died, aged seven years. Mr. S. died, and she married Samuel Yocom. *See his name.*

ELIZABETH, born in Sangamon county, married John Ludy, moved to Emporia, Lyons county, Kansas. Mrs. Ludy died, leaving five children, three of whom died. The family live at Emporia, Kansas.

JANE, born in Sangamon county, married Lewis Ludy, and died in Sangamon county, leaving two children.

Jechoniah Langston died, Feb., 1852, in Sangamon county. His widow moved to Kansas, and died, Aug. 19, 1866, near Emporia, Lyons county.

LANHAM, MRS. ANN E., whose maiden name was Havner, was born May 29, 1800, in Loudon county, Va. She was married in Harrison county, Ohio, to Walter Lanham, and moved to Perry county, Ohio, where they had three children, and Mr. Lanham died there. Mrs. Lanham, with her children, came to Sangamon county, Ill., arriving in the fall of 1840, at Mechanicsburg. Of her three children—

SOLOMON, born May 4, 1821, in Perry county, Ohio, married in Sangamon county, Nov. 25, 1846, to Mary E. Sparks. They had seven living children, ANNIE, WILLIAM T., MINNIE M., LEWIS A., LUELLA A., CHARLES W. and HARVEY O., and live with their parents, two and one-half miles southwest of Dawson, Illinois.

WESLEY, born May 26, 1823, in Ohio, married, Aug. 4, 1844, in Sangamon county, to Nancy A. Steele. They had four children—FRANCIS M., born Dec. 8, 1847, married, May 26, 1871, to Emma Skinner, had one child, and mother and child died. He lives near Harristown, Ill. EDWARD W., born July 1, 1850, married, March 26, 1874, to Frances M. Leeds, and live near Harristown, Illinois. CHARLES O., born April 27, 1854, lives near Harristown. ANNA L., born July 2, 1856, lives with her mother. Wesley Lanham died Aug. 26, 1861. His widow married William Graham, and reside one mile northeast of Illiopolis.

NANCY, born in 1825, in Ohio, married in Sangamon county, Aug., 1844, to Asa Maxfield. They have two living children, MINERVA A. and EDGAR, and live in Carrollton, Missouri.

Mrs. Ann E. Lanham died Feb. 27, 1874, in Sangamon county.

LANHAM, ELIJAH T., was born Jan. 28, 1801, in Frederick county, Md. His grandfather on his mother's side was Benjamin Penn, who was a relative of William Penn, the founder of the colony of Pennsylvania. E. T. Lanham was married in 1823, in Clermont county, Ohio, to Eleanor Constant. See her name. They had two children in Ohio, and moved to Sangamon county, Ill., with her parents in 1826. They had seven children in Sangamon county. Of their nine children—

NANCY ELLEN, born May 15, 1824, in Ohio, married in Sangamon county, to A. W. May. They have six children, and live near Cornland, Logan county.

RACHEL A., born March 8, 1826, in Clermont county, Ohio, married in Sangamon county to John W. Mathews. See his name.

BENJAMIN F., born July 8, 1827, in Sangamon county, married Miranda Stockton. They have five living children, and reside at Decatur, Ill.

HARRIET, born July 25, 1830, in Sangamon county, married Ebenezer Coe. See his name.

JOHN H., born July 18, 1833, in Sangamon county, married April 1, 1856, to Elizabeth M. Matthews. They have three living children, ELEANOR J., JOHN W. and ELIJAH, live with their parents near Barclay, Illinois.

GEORGE W., born Sept. 4, 1835, in Sangamon county, married in 1862, to Pauline Blankenbaker, and enlisted soon after, at Springfield, in Co. C, 124th Ill. Inf., for three years. He was killed in battle at Vicksburg, Miss., June 27, 1863.

WILLIAM N., born Oct. 21, 1837, in Sangamon county. He enlisted in 1861, in Co. H, 30th Ill. Inf., for three years, served full term, and was honorably discharged. He was married August 1, 1865, to Rebecca Hartsman, who was born Sept. 27, 1845, in Cumberland county, Pa. She died Feb. 11, 1874, in Decatur, Ill., and he resides there.

MARY J., born Nov. 20, 1839, in Sangamon county, married James Cantrall, have one child, and live in Decatur, Illinois.

CAROLINE H., born May 24, 1842, in Sangamon county, married Jesse Henard, have two children, and live near Forsyth, Macon county, Illinois.

Elijah T. Lanham died Sept. 16, 1847, in Sangamon county, and Mrs. Eleanor Lanham died Nov. 3, 1869, at Decatur, Illinois.

—56

LANPHIER, CHARLES H., was born April 14, 1820, in Alexandria, Va. He went to Vandalia, Ill., in May, 1836, and from there to Springfield, arriving Aug. 6, 1839. He was married, Feb. 25, 1846, in Gallatin county, near Equality, Illinois, to Margaret T. Crenshaw, who was born there, Dec. 4, 1828. Her father, John Crenshaw, settled there in 1812, being one of the earliest pioneers in that part of the State. Mr. and Mrs. Lanphier had seven children in Springfield, two of whom died young. Of the other five—

FRANCINE E., born Dec. 24, 1846, in Springfield, married James W. Patton. See his name.

ROBERT G., born Oct. 21, 1848, in Springfield, is farming in Gallatin county, Illinois.

JOHN C., born Oct. 19, 1850, in Springfield, is a practicing lawyer with his brother-in-law, J. W. Patton, in Springfield, Illinois.

CHARLES H., Jun., born Sept. 26, 1854, in Springfield, is in the drug business in his native city.

MARGARET C., resides with her parents.

Charles H. Lanphier, Sen., came to Springfield as an apprentice in the Register office. On the death of one of the proprietors (Mr. Walters), in 1846, he, in connection with George Walker, purchased the office. From that time he was part or entire owner, and published the *Illinois State Register* until 1863, when he sold out to a company, who afterwards published the paper about one year, and sold it to E. L. Merritt & Bro., the present proprietors. During the time Mr. Lanphier was publishing the *Register*, he was once elected State Printer, being the last one elected under the constitution of 1818. He was also elected Printer to the Constitutional Conventions of 1847 and 1861. Mr. Lanphier was elected, in 1864, clerk of the circuit court of Sangamon county, for one term of four years, and in 1868, re-elected for another term of four years. He has also served several terms as alderman in the city council. He now—1876—resides in Springfield, Illinois.

LANTERMAN, PETER, was born Jan. 8, 1749, in Germany, but when he came to America is not known by his descendants. He was married about 1779 to Alletta Applegate. They had nine children in Maryland, and came to Sangamon county in 1819. I find in the family record, in the hands of Mrs. Martha H. Britt in Springfield, that Peter Lanterman died June 14, 1821. The probate court of Sangamon county admitted his will to record Aug. 26, 1821, the first ever recorded in the county. *See page 41.* His widow, Alletta Lanterman, died Dec. 30, 1839. From the record in the hands of Mrs. Britt, I copy the date of the birth of each of their nine children, as follows—

LANTERMAN, SOPHIA, was born July 7, 1780, and married John Lindsay. *See his name.* They are both dead, but left two sons, *JOHN* and *ABRAHAM*. *See the Lindsay family.*

LANTERMAN, RICHARD, born Sept. 13, 1782, never came to Sangamon county.

LANTERMAN, JOHN, was born Oct. 18, 1784; his sons think in Maryland. He was married Nov. 28, 1811, in Fleming county, Ky., to Elizabeth McKinnie, who was born June 30, 1793. They had five children in Fleming county, and moved to Sangamon county, arriving in the fall of 1819, two and a half miles northwest of where Springfield now stands, where they had eight children. Of their thirteen children—

ABRAHAM, born Dec. 22, 1812, in Fleming county, Ky., was married in Sangamon county to Catharine Cabanis. They had several children, and moved to Kansas, in the vicinity of Medoc, Missouri. Their son, JOHN L., enlisted in a Wisconsin regiment, and died in the army, during the war for the suppression of the rebellion.

NANCY, born March 30, 1815, in Fleming county, Ky., was left there with her grandmother until 1822. She was married in Sangamon county Oct., 18, 1832, to Joseph W. Duncan. *See his name.* J. W. Duncan died, and she married Harrison Bishop. He died; she is now living with her son, David Duncan, at Williamsville, Illinois.

ANDREW J., born May 6, 1816, in Fleming county, Ky., was brought up in Sangamon county, and married in Marshal county, Ill., to Elizabeth Bell. They had four children; two died young. NANCY E., and JOHN R., live with their father. Mrs. Elizabeth Lanterman died in 1855, and A. J. Lanterman married Martha M. Berry. They have three children, JANE, McCLELLAN and LYCURGUS, and live near Elkhart, Logan county, Illinois.

PETER, born Sept. 4, 1817, in Fleming county, Ky., was married in Sangamon county, Ill., to Dolly A. Lightfoot. They had ten children, five of whom died young. Of the others, SUSAN J., married Jacob Yocum. *See his name.* JOHN H. married Isabel Dunham. They have five children, FRANCIS R., CHARLES P., EDWARD S., W. GROSS, and EARNEST H., who reside with their parents, near Elkhart, Logan county, Ill. JOSEPH M. married Lizzie Constant, and lives at Colorado Springs, Colorado. SCOTT and JAMES live with their parents, four and a half miles southeast of Elkhart, Logan county, Illinois.

ALLETTA J., born June 13, 1819, in Kentucky, and brought up in Sangamon county, was married in JoDaviess county, to Sutton Gott. They have five children, three of whom are married. Sutton Gott died Sept. 17, 1873. His widow and children reside near Elizabeth, JoDaviess county, Illinois.

MARY A., born Feb. 17, 1821, in Sangamon county, married George Cabanis. They had two children. JASPER N. was captured in a Wisconsin regiment, and died in the army, leaving a widow and one child. JAMES H. resides with his parents, near Big Patch, Grant county, Wisconsin.

ELEANOR A., born Nov. 14, 1822, in Sangamon county, married Milton Carpenter. They had four children, and Mr. Carpenter died. His widow married Russell Godby. They have two children, and reside near Petersburg, Menard county, Illinois.

SOPHIA L., born Oct. 25, 1824, in Sangamon county, married Calvin Cloyd. *See his name.*

JAMES, born 1826, in Sangamon county, married twice. Has children, and resides in Georgetown, Grant county, Wisconsin.

LEWIS McK., born Jan. 31, 1827, died Sept. 4, 1835.

JOHN L., born June 30, 1829, in Sangamon county, married Mary Withrow. She had one child, and mother and child died. J. L. Lanterman married Ann Lindsay. He enlisted in the 73d Reg., Ill. Inf., and died at Murfreesboro, Tenn., leaving his widow and children in Logan county, Illinois.

SARAH E., born Dec. 30, 1830, in Sangamon county, married John Askins. They had one child, and Mrs. A. died.

MELINDA, born May 13, 1833, in Sangamon county, married William Mergethaler. They had one child, and Mrs. M. died.

CHARLOTTE T., born May 17, 1836, in Sangamon county, married Wallace Reed. They had four children, and she died. Her husband and children reside near Petersburg, Illinois.

John Lanterman died March 14, 1842, and his widow died May 10 or 11, 1857—he in Sangamon county and she in Logan county, Illinois.

LANTERMAN, DANIEL A., born Dec. 24, 1786, in Maryland, was twice married, and lived in Madison county, Ill. He never resided in Sangamon county.

LANTERMAN, JAMES, born April 15, 1789, in Maryland. He brought up a family in Lawrence county, Ill., but never lived in Sangamon county.

LANTERMAN, ABRAHAM, was born Jan. 20, 1792, in Maryland, came with his parents to Sangamon county, about 1819, and was married Jan. 12, 1826, in Menard county, to Martha White, who was born Sept. 30, 1795, in Green county, Ky. They had six children, namely—

ELIZABETH J., born Aug. 10, 1827, in Sangamon county, was married, June 24, 1847, to Hiram Westlake. They have six children—CLARA B., CHARLES, SAMUEL, MARTHA, WILLIAM and FRANK, and reside in Salinas, Monterey county, California.

ALLETTA M., born May 23, 1829, died about 1849.

SOPHIA, born May 3, 1831, in Sangamon county, was married, Feb. 2, 1854, to David N. McCandless, who was born Feb. 9, 1828, in Butler county, Penn. They have six children, EDMONDSON S. resides with his parents. JULIA E. was married, Feb. 24, 1876, to Dudley Jones. MARTHA E., HELEN B., MARY F. and CHARLES N. live with their parents, six miles southeast of Springfield, Illinois.

NANCY G., born Jan. 26, 1834, was married in Springfield, June 24, 1853, to James A. McCandless, cousin of David N. They have six children—EDITH married Albion Baker. GEORGE, GRACE, ALBERT and CARL, all live in Salinas, Montery county, California.

MARTHA H., born April 27, 1837, in Sangamon county, was married, July 1, 1859, in Springfield, to Henry Britt, who was born April 2, 1826, in Sussex, England. They have four children—CHARLES A., MOLLIE E. HANNAH M. and CLARA E., and reside in the northwest part of Springfield, on part of the land entered by Mrs. Britt's father.

ISABEL W., born Dec. 23, 1841, in Sangamon county, was married, Nov. 30, 1865, to Wm. Albert Crowder. See his name.

Mrs. Martha Lanterman died, June 14, 1861, and Abraham Lanterman died May 28, 1863, both near Springfield, Illinois.

LANTERMAN, HETTY, born Dec. 8, 1793, in Maryland, never lived in Sangamon county, Illinois.

LANTERMAN, PETER, Jun., was born July 26, 1795, in Maryland, came to Springfield with his parents, in 1819, married Eliza Purviance, and moved to Dewitt county, Illinois.

LANTERMAN, ALLETTA, born March 19, 1799, in Maryland, was married in Sangamon county to Thomas Earnest. See his name.

LARD, JOHN, was born Feb. 12, 1792, near Charleston, S. C., was taken by his parents to Kentucky, where his father died. At fifteen years of age he went to St. Louis to visit an uncle, and was married there in 1812, to Lydia Todd. She died in Feb., 1824, leaving one child. John Lard went to Wayne county, Ill., and was there married to Elizabeth Kelly, and returned to St. Louis about 1830, and came to Sangamon county in March, 1835, and settled in what is now Ball township. They had six children. Of his seven children—

JOSIAH, born May 12, 1819, in St. Louis, Mo., married Sept. 22, 1842, in Sangamon county, to Jemima J. Crowder. She had six children, and died April 3, 1855. Mr. Lard was married Nov. 25, 1857, to Amelia Funderburk. They had four living children. Of all his children, MARTHA A., married John Marshall, and lives in Missouri. JOAB J. married Mary J. Stroud, has three children, ELECTA A., JAMES J. and PHILEMAN S., and live in Ball township. LYDIA E married J. J. Jones, and lives in Montgomery county, Kansas. SARAH T., married Alfred Curtis, have one child, LAURA, and live in Ball township. ALCY or ALICE, GEORGE R., JACOB F., JOHN H., EMMA and MINNIE live with their parents. Josiah Lard lives on the farm where his father settled in 1835, in Ball township, twelve miles south of Springfield.

CYNTHIA A., married Robert Maher, have one child, LOUISA P., and reside in Ball township, six miles south of Springfield.

THOMAS K. died in 1851, aged seventeen years.

AMELIA married William J. Atterbery, and lives in Christian county, Missouri.

ROBERT J., married Sarah Rupert, have two children, MARY E. and LUELLA MAY, and live in Ball township.

MAHALA married Ninian M. Taylor. See his name.

HEZEKIAH is unmarried, and lives with his sister, Mrs. Maher.

Mrs. Elizabeth Lard died Feb. 9, 1843, and John Lard died Nov. 16, 1845, both in Sangamon county.

LASWELL, ANDREW, was born in Feb., 1781, in Loudon county, Va. When thirteen years old, he went on a pack-horse, in company with his brothers and sisters, to Shelby county, Ky. When a young man he went to Greene county, and was there married to Nancy Wright, who was born in 1784, in Culpepper county, Va., and taken by her parents to Green county, Ky. They had nine children in Kentucky, and moved to Sangamon county, Ill., arriving in Nov., 1824, and settled one mile west of Springfield. Of their children—

POLLY, born in 1805, in Kentucky, married to John Crowder. See his name.

THOMAS, born Nov. 13, 1806, in Green county, Ky., married Feb. 4, 1830, in Sangamon county, to Sally Henry, who was born June 4, 1811, in Gallia county, Ohio. They had ten living children. MARY married James Tomlinson, has six children, and lives in Gardner township. ANDREW J. married Eveline Jones in Missouri. She died, leaving three children, and he married Drucilla Rick, has one child, and lives in Gardner township. NANCY married Jules Beauloss, and died, leaving three children. AMANDA married John Turner, has five children, and lives in Labette county, near Fort Scott, Kansas. EMILY married Thomas Vance; has four children, and live in Labette county, Kansas. ELIZABETH married Jacob Hurst, and lives in Labette county, Kansas. LUCINDA married Newton Simpson, who died, leaving one child. Mr. Simpson served three years in the 10th Ill. Cav. His widow married John Ryan, who was a veteran soldier, and was "with Sherman in his march to the sea." Mr. and Mrs. Ryan have two children, and live in Springfield. JOHN, HENRY and LAURA E. live with their parents, five miles northwest of Springfield.

MOSES, born May, 1809, in Kentucky, married in Sangamon county to Mary Enyart. His wife and children are all dead. He lives in Springfield.

PETER, born in 1811 in Kentucky, has been twice married, and lives in Oregon.

SALLY died, aged nineteen years.

ELLEN married Martin McCoy, who died in 1870, leaving a widow and child, near Auburn, Illinois.

JOHN, born in 1815 in Green county, Ky., married in Sangamon county to Virginia Barrett. He died in Dec., 1871, leaving three children. His family lives in Springfield.

ELIZABETH married William Robbins. *See his name.* They have four children, and live near Mechanicsburg.

Andrew Laswell died April 11, 1853, and his widow died April, 1855, both near Springfield.

LATHAM, JAMES, was born Oct. 25, 1768, in Loudon county, Virginia, of English parents. He emigrated when a young man, to Kentucky, and was there married, June 21, 1792, to Mary Briggs, who was born Feb. 3, 1772, in Virginia, of Scotch parents. They had nine children in Kentucky, and moved to Elkhart Grove, in what is now Logan county, but was formerly a part of Sangamon county, Ill., arriving in 1819. Mr. Latham and his son Richard built a horse mill, at Elkhart, in 1823. It was the first mill north of the Sangamon river. When he settled at Elkhart, their nearest mill was at Edwardsville, more than one hundred miles south. When Sangamon county was organized, James Latham was appointed Judge of the Probate Court, May 27, 1821. He was also Justice of the Peace. Of his children—

ELIZABETH, born Nov. 25, 1793, in Kentucky, was married there, May 9, 1810, to James W. Chapman. They moved to Illinois with her parents, and settled north of the Sangamon river, near the mouth of Fancy creek, where Mr. Chapman established a ferry, in 1818, on the Sangamon river, near Bogue's mill. He remained there two or three years, and moved farther north. Two only of their children are living. ELIZA married Hiram Lloyd, and lives near Broadwell, Logan county, Ill. ADALINE married Thomas Gale, and lives in Memphis Tenn. The parents both died at Elkhart. Mr. Chapman, in 1871, being the last of the two.

LUCY, born Aug. 18, 1797, in Kentucky, came with her parents to Sangamon county, and married Grant Blackwell. They returned to Kentucky in 1827, and died there, leaving one child, THOMAS, who lives near Morganfield, Union county, Kentucky.

RICHARD, born Dec. 23, 1798, in Bowling Green, Warren county, Ky. came with his parents in 1819 to Sangamon county, He was married, Sept. 16, 1824, at Elkhart, Ill., to Emily Hubbard, a native of Kentucky. They had one child, and mother and child died, in 1825, at Elkhart. Richard Latham was married, Nov. 27, 1825, to Mrs. Margaret Broadwell, whose maiden name was Stephenson. She was a sister of James C., John and Robert Stephenson, *See their names.* Mr. and Mrs. Latham had thirteen children, seven of whom died young. Of the other six—MARY A., born Feb. 25, 1829, was married, Nov. 25, 1848, to Dr. Timothy Leeds. *See his name.* MARTHA E. married James S. Major.

She died Sept. 20, 1852. HENRY C., born April 11, 1837, at Elkhart, is dealing in conveyancing and furnishing abstract titles to real estate. He resides in Springfield. LUCY lives with her mother. KITTIE S., born Jan. 24, 1841, at Elkhart, was married in Springfield, Jan. 30, 1868, to Elder J. H. McCullough, a minister of the Christian church, and resides in Denver, Colorado. NANNIE, born Dec. 6, 1843, at Elkhart, was married Sept. 16, 1873, in Springfield, to George H. Souther. They have one child, LATHAM, and reside in Springfield. Richard Latham died, June 5, 1868, and his widow lives with her son Henry C. in Springfield, Illinois.

MARY L., born in Kentucky, married John Constant. *See his name.*

PHILIP C., born Jan. 25, 1804, in Bowling Green, Ky., came to Elkhart Grove with his father, in 1819. In Feb., 1827, he entered the county clerk's office, in Springfield, under C. R. Matheny, county clerk. He remained there eight years, and was married in Springfield, May 15, 1831, to Catharine R. Taber, who was born Feb. 25, 1812, in Champaign county, Ohio. They had five living children in Springfield. MARY E., born in 1836, married Dr. Alexander Halbert. *See his name.* JULIA M., born Jan. 11, 1838, was married in Springfield to B. D. Magruder, a native of Baton Rouge, Louisiana. They have two children, ELLA and HARRY L., and live in Chicago. WM. HENRY, born Nov. 27, 1839, enlisted in 1862 for three years, in Co. B, 114th Ill. Inf., was elected 1st Lieutenant at the organization, and at once promoted to Adjutant. He died Dec., 1863, in Springfield, of disease contracted in the army. GEORGE C., born May 16, 1842, was married, Oct. 2, 1867, to Olive Priest. They have three children, OLIVE, MARY M. and JOHN P., and live in Springfield. G. C. Latham is connected in business with his father-in-law, John W. Priest. PHILIP C., Jun., born July 18, 1844, was married to Lucy George, a native of Canada. He died suddenly, Feb. 16, 1871, leaving one child, HENRY I. Mrs. Lucy Latham married, and resides in Nebraska. Mr. Philip C. Latham, Sen., was killed by lightning, near Shawneetown, Ill., May 25, 1844.

His widow resides in Springfield, in a house built by her husband in 1838.

NANCY resides with Mrs. Richard Latham.

MARIA, born Nov. 14, 1809, in Bowling Green, Ky., was married to Archibald Constant. *See his name.*

JOHN, born Sept. 9, 1812, in Bowling Green, Ky., was married in Sangamon county to Lucy Bennett, a native of Kentucky. They had two children—MARY E. married William Dustin, a banker, and resides in Lincoln, Ill. MARGARET E. married Morgan H. Bailhache, and resides in Martinez, California.

ROBERT B., born June 21, 1818, in Union county, Ky., was married in Sangamon county, Nov. 5, 1846, to Georgiana Gillette, a native of New Haven, Conn. She died in 1853. R. B. Latham w. married July 24, 1857, in Logan county, to Savilla Wyatt, a native of Morgan county, Ill. They have five children, MARY, RICHARD, ROBERTIE, WILLIAM W. and GEORGIANA, and reside in Lincoln, Ill. Robert B. Latham was elected Sheriff of Logan county in 1850, and served two years. He was elected Representative in Illinois Legislature for 1861-62. He raised a regiment and became Colonel of the 106th Ill. Vol. Inf., and served twenty months in the war to suppress the rebellion, and then resigned on account of impaired health. He is now a dealer in real estate in Lincoln, Logan county, Illinois.

After James Latham had served a year or two as Judge of the Probate Court of Sangamon county, he was appointed, on the part of the U. S. Government, to superintend the Indians around Fort Clark. Soon after, he moved his family there, making that place his headquarters. The town of Peoria was laid out, on land including the fort. Judge Latham died there, Dec. 4, 1826. His widow returned with her family to Elkhart, where she died.

LAUGHLIN, JOHN, was born in 1757, place not known, and was married in South Carolina to Elizabeth Orr, who was born in 1779. They went to Caldwell county, Ky., and had eight children there, and moved to Sangamon county, Ill., arriving in 1828, in what is now Ball township. Of their children—

MARGARET, born in Kentucky, married in Sangamon county to William S. Viney. *See his name.*

WILLIAM L. married Isabel Holland, and both died without children in Sangamon county.

JANE married Matthew Crowder. *See his name.*

LEWIS A. married; has five children, and lives near New London, Iowa.

THOMAS married Nancy Lowrey. They had two children. He was a practicing physician, and died in Clinton, Ill., leaving his family there.

JOHN married Catharine Lowrey. He died, leaving a widow in Ball township.

JAMES died, aged eleven years.

ISABEL, born in Caldwell county, Ky., married Washington Crowder. *See his name.*

John Laughlin died Nov., 1829, and his widow died in Feb., 1833, both in Sangamon county.

LAVELY, WILLIAM, born Aug., 1811, in Baltimore, Maryland. His father and uncle were captains of war vessels during the war of 1812-15 with England. When a young man, William Lavely came west, by the way of Cincinnati, arriving in Springfield during the summer of 1830, where he joined his sister, Mrs. Dr. Merriman. He was married April 2, 1839, in Menard county, Ill., to Lavinia Constant. They had three children, namely—

SUSAN died in infancy.

WILLIAM T., born July 19, 1843, in Springfield, married in his native city Feb. 5, 1868, to Lora Dunton, who was born June 1, 1850, in Racine, Wisconsin. They have one child, RUFUS W., and reside in Springfield, Illinois.

ELLEN MAY, born July 14, 1848, in Springfield, was married in her native city Feb. 28, 1871, to Park E. Temple, who was born April 29, 1845, in Bloomington, Ill. He graduated in the law department of Michigan University, Ann Arbor, in 1870. They have two children, MAI and DAISY. Mr. Temple, after his marriage, served one year as City Attorney of Springfield. He is now a newspaper correspondent, and practices law in Bloomington, Ill., where he and his family reside.

William Lavely has filled a number of civil offices, such as Justice of the Peace ten or twelve years, Mayor of the city of Springfield for the year 1852, chairman of the Board of Supervisors of Sangamon county three years, etc. He was Grand Master of the Masonic Grand Lodge of Illinois for the years 1847 and '8. During the greater part of his life, he has been engaged in mercantile pursuits, and now —1876—resides in Springgeld.

LAW, BENJAMIN C., was born March 31, 1805, in Huntington county, Penn. His parents moved to Ohio, thence to Bath county, Ky., where he was married Sept., 1824, to Janetta McClees. They had one child in Kentucky, and moved to Dickson county, Tenn., where three children were born; and from there to Sangamon county Ill., arriving April, 1836, five miles east of Springfield, where six children were born. Of their ten children—

ANNA, born March 5, 1827, in Kentucky, married in Sangamon county to J. Perry, and both died of cholera in 1851, leaving two children.

THOMAS, born Sept. 21, 1831, in Tennessee, married in Sangamon county to Louisa Gibson; have five children, and live in Mechanicsburg township.

REBECCA, born June 3, 1833, in Tennessee, married Henry Harwood, an engineer of the T., W. & W. They have six children, and live in Springfield.

MARY, born March 31, 1835, in Tennessee, married David McCarthy; have five children, and live in Mechanicsburg.

JANE, born Dec. 5, 1837, in Sangamon county, and lives with her parents.

MATTHEW and *MARK*, twins, born Sept. 30, 1839, in Sangamon county, both live with their parents, five miles east of Springfield.

MARK enlisted July, 1862, for three years, in Co. I, 114th Ill. Inf. Served to the end of the rebellion, and was honorably discharged with the regiment in July, 1865.

NARCISSA, born June 9, 1842, in Sangamon county, married May 19, 1872, to Silas Thomas, a native of Clermont county, Ohio. She died Dec. 31, 1873. Silas Thomas enlisted in July, 1861, in Co. G, 7th Ill. Inf.; re-enlisted as a veteran, served until July, 1865, when he was honorably discharged. Himself and four brothers served through the whole war, and came out without a wound.

GRIZELLA, born Feb. 17, 1844, died, aged seven years.

LYDIA C., born Feb. 17, 1846, lives with her parents.

Benj. C. Law and wife—1874—live on the farm where they settled in 1836, five miles east of Springfield.

Mark Law, the father of Benjamin C., was born March 6, 1762, in county Tyrone, Ireland, came with his son to Sangamon county, and died Feb. 23, 1840.

LAWLEY, STEPHEN, born July 22, 1777, in North Carolina, was married there to Mrs. Abigail Wilson, and moved to Smith county, Tenn., where they had four children, and moved to Springfield, Ill., arriving in the spring of 1828. He remained one year near Springfield, and in the spring of 1829 moved to what is now Ball township, ten miles south of Springfield. Of their four children—

MARY, born in Tennessee, was married there to William Wright. They came to Sangamon county in 1827, one year before her father, lived two years near Springfield, and in the spring of 1829 moved to what is now Ball township. The next year the family returned to Tennessee. The parents died there, leaving five children.

ELIZABETH, born in Tennessee, was married there to Paschal Wright. They came to Sangamon county in 1828, with her father. About 1835, the family returned to Tennessee. They had seven children; all lived to be men and women.

PRUDENCE, born in Smith county, Tennessee, was married there to Leonard Fry. They moved to Sangamon county, in 1827, first living in what is now Cotton Hill township, and afterwards moved to Ball township, where they raised a family of eight children. In the fall of 1870, they moved to Bates county, Mo., except one daughter, Mary, who married Barnes Peak, have three children, and live near Edinburg, Christian county, Illinois.

WILLIAM B., born June 24, 1811, in Smith county, Tennessee, came to Springfield with his father, in 1828, and in 1829 went to what is now Ball township. He was married, Dec. 25, 1831, to Amy Meredith. They had two children. DAVIS W., born Nov. 15, 1832, in Sangamon county, was married there to Cassandra Peddecord. They had two children, MARY E. and DAVIS F. D. W. Lawley enlisted Aug. 15, 1862, in Co. E, 114th Ill. Inf., for three years; served full term, and was honorably discharged Aug. 3, 1865. For a second wife, he married Mary Ann Ray. They had four children, IDA F., JAMES W., LUELLA MAY and EVA I. D. W. Lawley lives in Cotton Hill township. STEPHEN T., born Nov. 23, 1836, married in 1859 Mary A. Gaines, a native of Indiana. They have six children, SARAH E., AMY J., MARY M., MARGARET L., ALBERT W., CHARLES A., and LAURA H., and live in Cotton Hill township. Mrs. Amy Lawley died Sept. 12, 1838, and William B. Lawley was married Nov. 28, 1839, to Sarah M. Duncan. They have eight living children. RUTH J., born Sept. 13, 1840, in Sangamon county, married in 1850 to Lawrence Saltenger. They have six children, WILLIAM S., ELMER E., JAMES E., FRANCIS E., MINNIE C., and MARY V., and live near Palmer, Christian county, Ill. ELIJAH D., born Sept. 9, 1842, in Sangamon county, enlisted in Aug., 1862, in Co. E, 114th Ill. Inf., for three years. He was wounded and taken prisoner at the battle of Guntown, Mississippi, June 10, 1864. He was a prisoner to the close of the rebellion, and was disabled for life. He was married in 1868 to Sarah J. Boyd. They have two children, LEWIS E. and FREDDIE, and live at Macon, Macon county, Ill. JAMES P., born Dec. 10, 1844, in Sangamon county, was too young to enlist with his brothers, but ran off, and enlisted July, 1863, in Co. E, 114th Ill. Inf., at Black River. Miss. Served to the end of the rebellion, and was honorably discharged. He was married in 1869 to Nancy J. Jones. They have one child, ROBERT W., and live in Palmer, Christian county, Illinois. AMANDA E., born June 9, 1849, in Sangamon county, married in 1868 to John B. Matthew. See his name. They have two children, CHARLES E. and GEORGE R., and live at Mt. Auburn, Ill. SARAH M., LEONARD W., FRANCIS J., JEROME F. and PRUDENCE A. live with their parents. William B. Lawley and wife live ten miles south of Springfield, in Ball township, Sangamon county, Illinois.

Mrs. Abigail Lawley died Jan. 6, 1853, and Stephen Lawley died Dec. 28, 1861, both on the farm where they settled in 1829, in Ball township, Sangamon county, Illinois.

LAWSON, WILLIAM P., was born Nov. 19, 1794, at what was then called Grassy Lick, Kentucky. Priscilla Duncan was born Dec. 12, 1797, in Bath county, Kentucky. They were married Feb. 3, 1820, and had two children, and Mrs. Lawson died in Fleming county, Ky, Aug. 20, 1824. Mr. Lawson was married Oct. 19, 1826, in Fleming county, to Frances Dunn. They had one child, and moved to Sangamon county, Ill., arriving Nov. 18, 1828, at Buffalo Hart grove, where they had eight living children. Of all his children—

MARGARET, born Jan. 8, 1821, in Fleming county, Ky., married in Sangamon county Aug., 1852, to John Fletcher. They have three children, and live one and one-quarter miles southeast of Buffalo Hart station, Sangamon county.

SARAH J., born Dec. 25, 1823, in Fleming county, Ky., married in Sangamon county to Robert Cass, Jun. *See his name.*

JACOB, born Oct. 4, 1827, in Fleming county, Ky., raised in Sangamon county, married to Martha Davis. They have nine children, and live near Catlin, Vermilion county, Illinois.

NANCY A., born Aug. 7, 1830, in Sangamon county, married James Timmons; have six children, and live four miles northwest of Illiopolis.

MARTHA A., born July 10, 1833, in Sangamon county, married Henry Bell. They had six children, and Mr. Bell died June, 1868, in Petersburg, Ill. His widow and children reside there.

CLARINDA, born Aug. 3, 1836, was drowned by crawling in an open well the very day she was one year old.

LUCINDA, born Aug. 29, 1839, in Sangamon county, married Marcus Costilla, a native of Ireland, have four children, and live in Buffalo Hart township.

CHRISTIANA, born May 9, 1842, in Sangamon county, married Lewis Cass. *See his name.*

ELIZA J., born July 14, 1845, in Sangamon county, married Lafayette Ball; have four children, and live at Fairmount, Vermilion county, Illinois.

—57—

JULIA C., born Feb. 6, 1848, in Sangamon county, married Hiram Amos, and lives at Jacksonville, Illinois.

ISABEL, born Feb. 13, 1851, in Sangamon county, married John Shaver.

Mrs. Frances Lawson died Oct. 10, 1867, in Sangamon county, and Wm. P. Lawson lives with his daughter, Mrs. Robert Cass, Jun.—1874.

LEEDS, PETER T., was born March 29, 1801, near Leeds' Cove or Leeds Landing, in Gloucester county, N. J. His ancestors emigrated from Leeds, England, about the year 1700. His parents, James and Rhoda Leeds, were members of the Society of Friends. They had five sons and three daughters in New Jersey, and with their family left there, May 15, 1806, and settled near Moscow, Clermont county, Ohio. The girls married farmers, and three of the sons became farmers also; the whole six settling in Clermont county. One son, Josiah, learned the hatter's trade, and Peter T., the subject of this sketch, selected a profession, and commenced the study of medicine at the age of twenty. Not having the means to attend medical school, he taught during the day and read medicine at night until he was theoretically qualified for practice. While teaching, he had one pupil who attended his school two summers, and who has since been known as Gen. Ulysses S. Grant, the leader of the U. S. armies in crushing the great rebellion, also twice President of the United States. Dr. P. T. Leeds remembers having seen the first steamboat that ascended the Ohio river as far as Moscow. He was married, in 1821, to Jane Harden. They had six children in Ohio, one of whom died young. Dr. Leeds moved with his family to Illinois, arriving at Mechanicsburg, Sangamon county, April 1, 1836. Of his children—

DAVID, born Oct., 1822, in Clermont county, Ohio, studied medicine with his father, and located in Mt. Pleasant, Iowa. He was married there to Martha Shaw. They had three children, JOHN, MATTIE and ARTEMAS. Dr. David Leeds died in Mt. Pleasant, September, 1853.

TIMOTHY, born Jan., 1825, in Ohio, studied medicine with his father, and graduated at St. Louis Medical College. He married Mary A. Latham. Dr. Timothy Leeds practiced medicine in Mt. Pulaski, until 1856, when he moved to Lincoln, Ill. He died there May 1, 1857, and was buried at Mt. Pulaski with Masonic honors. His widow died in Springfield, Dec. 11, 1857, leaving her two children, MAGGIE and TIMOTHY, with their grandmother, Mrs. Margaret Latham, in Springfield.

LYDIA, the only daughter, born March, 1827, in Clermont county, Ohio, and brought up in Sangamon county, married to her cousin, John M. Leeds, at Mt. Pleasant, Iowa, and moved to Clinton, Illinois. They had five children—DARTHULA J., born Jan. 5, 1847, in Glasgow, Jefferson county, Iowa, married April 21, 1871, in Clinton, Ill., to A. H. C. Barber, formerly of Portsmouth, Ohio. They have three children, VIOLET, JOHN and FANNIE, and reside in Clinton, Ill. ALICE A., was born in Mechanicsburg, and died, aged two years. MARY E., born Dec. 24, 1850, in Marion, Dewitt county, Ill., was married, March 1, 1871, to J. H. Morse, formerly of Milford Centre, Union county, Ohio. They have one child, GEORGE B., and live in Clinton, Ill. SARAH ARGILLIA, born Jan. 9, 1855, and LYDIA LENORAH, born Sept. 3, 1857, in Clinton. The two latter live with their mother. John M. Leeds went to California, in 1862, and on returning he was killed by Indians, in the Sierra Nevada mountains. His widow and two unmarried daughters reside in Clinton, Dewitt county, Illinois.

DANIEL K., born Nov., 1829, in Ohio, enlisted in the regular army during the Mexican war, was wounded in the battle of the City of Mexico, and died in that city, in 1847, of inflammation of the lungs.

LUCIAN LAVASSA, was born April, 1831, in Clermont county, Ohio, commenced the study of medicine with his father, at seventeen years of age, and graduated at Rush Medical College, Chicago, Ill., in 1852. He practiced medicine with his father three years, and during that time he married Susan Shoup, of Logan county. She died, in 1854, leaving one child, SARAH ALICE. He then located in Lincoln, Ill., and in 1855 married Sarah J. Shoup; she only lived ten weeks, and in the autumn of 1856 he married Hannah Wilson, of Logan county. They have three children, viz: ANNIE M., MYRTIE J. and HANNAH E. The eldest child, Sarah Alice, married E. Spellman, and lives in Lincoln. Dr. L. L. Leeds has owned one horse thirteen years, and kept a record of his travels, which has been 82,000 miles, to January, 1876. His name is Gray Bill, and he is yet able, ready and willing to travel, and he will probably yet make his 100,000 miles. Dr. L. L. Leeds continues in the practice of his profession, at Lincoln, Logan county, Illinois.

Dr. Peter T. Leeds moved from Mechanicsburg to Buffalo, Sangamon county, Illinois, August 19, 1859; remained in active practice until 1865, but has now partially withdrawn, and only attends to office business. He has been a successful practitioner, and is strictly a self-made man.

LEMON, JOHN I., born March 6, 1803, in Scott county, Kentucky, came to Sangamon county, arriving at Berlin in 1834 or '5. He was married near Washington, Tazewell county, to Ann Maria White. They made their home in Sangamon county until they had five living children. The family moved to Farmer City, and from there to El Paso, where three children were born. Their eldest children, *JAMES D., WILLIAM U.* and *JOHN I., Jun.*, were all born in Sangamon county, and were Union soldiers in Co. A, 107th Ill. Inf.

JAMES D. was Lieutenant, and was killed in battle on the Potomac.

WILLIAM U. and

JOHN I. died of disease in the army, the former near Paducah, and the latter in Tennessee.

John I. Lemon resides at El Paso, Illinois.

LEMON, MARY ANN, sister to John I., was born Nov. 3, 1805, in Scott county, Ky., came to Sangamon county in 1835 or '6, married to William Hickman. *See his name.* They had one son, Euclid.

LEMON, ELIZA, sister to John I., born March 29, 1808, in Scott county, Ky., came to Sangamon county in 1835 or '6, married William Underwood. *See his name.* He died, and she married John Churchill. *See his name.*

LEMMON, ULICK, was born July 30, 1791, in Baltimore, Md. He visited the western States, and entered land in Sangamon county. He was married in Sangamon county, in 1826 or '7, to Mrs. Susan Bachus, whose maiden name was Pearce. She was born Sept. 19, 1799, near Nashville, Tenn. She had one child by her first marriage—

NANCY BACHUS, born Oct. 28, 1823, and married Willard Mitchell. They had two living children. Mr. Mitchell was at one time employed on the Panama railroad, contracted disease, went to California, and died there in 1850. His widow married Benjamin Force, had three children, and lives in Athens, Menard county, Illinois.

Mr. and Mrs. Lemmon had six children in Sangamon county, namely—

WILLIAM E., born Nov. 17, 1828, married Elizabeth Martin, have seven children, and live in Logan county, Illinois.

MARGARET A., born March 5, 1830, in Sangamon county, married Alfred N. Hinsley. *See his name.*

ELVIRA, born June 22, 1835, married May 1, 1853, to Alexander Hale. They have ten children, and live in Athens, Menard county, Illinois.

JAMES and *JOHN*, twins, born May 19, 1838. They are both preachers in the Christian church, and reside at Athens, Menard county, Illinois.

CYNTHIA S., born Sept. 25, 1840, married Madison Batterton. *See his name.*

Ulick Lemmon died Jan. 6, 1852, and his widow died Jan. 18, 1866, both in Sangamon county.

LEVEL, JAMES M., was born Dec., 1817, in Pickaway county, Ohio. His parents died when he was a child, and he was brought to Sangamon county by Abel Powell. They arrived June 27, 1828. James M. Level was married Dec. 2, 1855, to Margaret Sawyers, who was born Nov. 3, 1830, in Fayette county, They had six children, two of whom died—

CLARISSA E. in her eighth year; and *WILLIAM T.* in infancy. The other four—

JOHN S., born April 5, 1858,

JAMES H., born Sept. 23, 1859,

MARY E., born July 15, 1861, and

CLARA M., born May 28, 1866, live with their parents. James M. Level resides on the farm settled by Levi Cantrall in 1820. It is adjoining Cantrall on the southwest.

James M. Level remembers that about 1838 he helped to cut wheat with the old-fashioned sickle or reap-hook, tramped it out with horses, fanned the chaff out by two men taking a linen sheet and using it for a fan, while a third one stood on some elevated place, and poured the wheat and chaff down before the fan. This fanning operation cannot be described to a person who never saw it; and, therefore ought to be enacted at some Old Settlers' meeting. He then drove a four-horse team and hauled fifty bushels of the wheat to St. Louis, one hundred miles, and sold it for twenty-five cents per bushel. It required from ten to twelve days to make the trip.

LEVI, JOHN M., born about 1800, came to what is now Ball township, with his parents, among the early settlers, and was married to Eliza J. Hurley. They had five children—

MARY married John Hartsock, and lives in Christian county.

GRACIE J. married James Smith, had one child, FRANCIS A., and Mr. Smith died August 23, 1869, and his widow married Oct. 15, 1872, to John H. Hermon. *See his name.*

SARAH married Daniel H. Funderburk, has four children, and lives in Christian county.

LOUISA married Rev. Franklin Doughty, of the M. E. Church, have five children, and live at Fairfield, Iowa.

ELIZABETH married Joseph C. Dodds. They have two children, JOHN and IVY PEARL, and live in Ball township, Sangamon county.

Mrs. Eliza J. Levi died, and Mr. Levi married Fannie Clemons, and he died Dec. 23, 1872. His widow lives in Rochester, Illinois.

LEWIS, JOHN R., was born in 1806 in Farmington, Connecticut. He studied medicine at New Haven, came West in 1831 or '2, and established himself in practice at Carlinville, Ill. He returned to his native place, and was there married Nov. 16, 1835, to Mrs. Ruth Stanley, whose maiden name was Crampton. He brought his wife to Carlinville, ceased practicing medicine, and engaged in farming. Mrs. Ruth Lewis died Aug. 28, 1839, at Carlinville, leaving one child.

Dr. Lewis soon after moved to Chatham, in Sangamon county, and engaged in practice there. His son—

CHARLES H., born April 4, 1837, near Carlinville, brought up in Chatham, graduated in 1862 from the academical department of Yale college, and from the medical department of the same college in 1867. He spent the intermediate time in the army, and afterwards practiced a short time in Chatham. Dr. Charles H. Lewis was married April 11, 1869, in Oswego, Kansas, to Imogene Lewis. They have two children, EDWARD H. and FLORENCE M., and reside near Cedar Vale, Chautauqua county, Kansas. Dr. Lewis is engaged in farming and the drug business.

Dr. John R. Lewis, soon after removing to Chatham, became acquainted with Miss Sarah M. Thompson, a native of Monson, Massachusetts, whose home in the West was with her brother-in-law, Rev. James A. Clark, in Fort Madison, Iowa, where Dr. Lewis and Miss Thompson were married Aug. 25, 1844, and at once came to Chatham. They had five children. Of the three living—

MARIA L. was married Jan. 1, 1874, to Dr. Charles B. Johnston, a practicing physician at Tolono, Champaign county, Ill., where they reside.

JOHN T. and EDWARD V., both born in Chatham, and live there with their mother.

Dr. J. R. Lewis assisted in organizing the First Presbyterian church in Carlinville, and was one of the ruling Elders as long as he lived there. He was elected to the same office in the church at Chatham, and continued to discharge its duties to the end of his life. He died Aug. 5, 1858, in Chatham, where his widow and two sons now reside—1876.

LEWIS, EDDIN, was born Dec. 23, 1803, in Caldwell county, Ky. He was there married, about 1825, to Winnifred Easley, who was born in the same county, March 10, 1806. They had two children in Kentucky, and moved to Sangamon county, Ill., in the fall of 1830, in what is now Ball township, where they had six children—

WILLIAM R., born Oct. 11, 1826, in Kentucky, died in Sangamon county, aged twenty years.

JAMES M., born May 27, 1828, in Caldwell county, Ky., married March 6, 1851, in Sangamon county, to Perrilla M. Lockridge. She died May 1, 1857, leaving one child, CYRUS E. James M. Lewis married August 30, 1860, to Mrs. Emily Ricks, whose maiden name was Simpson. She died April 20, 1864, leaving one child, LAURA BELLE, who resides with her uncle, Andrew Simpson, in Taylorville. James M. Lewis married Mary A. Clayton. She died June 20, 1868, leaving two children, JULIA M. and MANFORD S. J. M. Lewis was married August 30, 1869, to Jane Burris. They have one child, MINNIE ALICE, and reside five miles southeast of Auburn. James M. Lewis remembers one event connected with the deep snow, beginning in December, 1830. His father had just finished his first cabin, and moved into it, as the snow began falling. In building it he dug the earth out in front of the hearth and used it in forming the side walls to his fireplace. That hole under the floor was for keeping vegetables, but he had none. When the snow became quite deep, he found that he would certainly loose a fine litter of pigs unless he could find protection for them. He could think of no other place than his rude cellar. He raised a puncheon, dragged the sow in, and pitched her, with the pigs, down that cavity. The record shows that James M. was but two and a half years old, but the squealing of the hog almost frightened him into fits, making an impression on his mind that remains indelible. If all history was written it would be found that many of the best families and fortunes were built on as rude foundations as this incident implies.

JOHN W., born May 27, 1831, in Sangamon county, spent six years in California, returned home, started for Pikes Peak, and died at St. Joseph, Mo., in 1860 or '61.

MARGARET E., born in Sangamon county, married George F. Kessler, who was accidentally shot dead, while on a hunting excursion, in 1858. She married Sylvanus Wineman, who died July 29, 1875. She resides near Auburn.

SARAH J., born in Sangamon county, married George W. Armstrong. They have two children, LAURENTI-

US B. and ALONZO W., and reside in Auburn.

MARTHA A., born in 1838, in Sangamon county, married Abraham Gish, has two children, namely: CHARLES and ARRAH, and reside in Virden.

SAMUEL, born Sept. 17, 1840, in Sangamon county. He was married Feb. 7, 1861, in Auburn, to Emma Wheeler. Mr. Lewis enlisted August 9, 1862, for three years, in Co. B, 114th Ill. Inf., and was commissioned 1st Lieutenant of his company in April, 1865. He was wounded and captured at the battle of Guntown, Miss., June 10, 1864, was taken to Andersonville prison, and enjoyed its hospitalities for ten months; sent to Vicksburg for exchange, where he first heard of the assassination of President Lincoln. He had a silver ring, with a quarter dollar gold piece set in it. By giving that to the rebel guard he was permitted to escape before the time for exchange. He was honorably discharged at Camp Butler, August 12, 1865. Mr. and Mrs. Lewis have five children, EDITH M., MARY B., FREDERICK L., MAGGIE J. and JAMES H., and reside in Auburn. Mr. Lewis is a merchant there, and President of the Auburn Bank.

MARY M., born in Sangamon county, was married there to Thomas Black. See his name.

Mrs. Winnifred Lewis died Nov. 15, 1843, and Eddin Lewis was married May 28, 1844, to Permelia A. Fletcher. They had two children—

EDWARD H. was married Nov. 4, 1869, to Margaret Whetstone. She died Feb. 8, 1872, leaving one child, CHARLES D. E. H. Lewis lives in Auburn.

PERMELIA F., married Jan. 7, 1864, to James A. Ogg, who was born Oct. 9, 1842, in Madison county, Ky. He enlisted for three years, March 29, 1862, in Co. F, 12th Ill. Cav., served until Apr. 2, 1865, when he was honorably discharged. Mr. and Mrs. Ogg have three children, JAMES F., WILLIAM A. and MARY E., and live in Auburn, Illinois.

Eddin Lewis died Jan. 29, 1850, and his widow married Larkin H. Lewis, and resides in Auburn.

Eddin Lewis was an energetic farmer and business man. He was one of the earliest men engaged in buying and droving fat hogs and cattle, and packing pork in Sangamon county.

LEWIS, LARKIN, brother to Eddin Lewis, was born in Caldwell county, Ky., married there to Elizabeth Welch. They had three children in Kentucky, and she died there, May 17, 1835. He moved with his children to Sangamon county, in 1838 or '9, and was married, Feb. 28, 1856, to Mrs. Permelia A. Lewis, whose maiden name was Fletcher. They had two children. Of his children—

WILLIAM J., married Sarah Clayton, have two children, ALFRED and SARAH, and live in Ball township.

SAMUEL married Mary Henderson, have three children, and live in Kansas.

DAVID married Margaret Henderson, have three children, MARY, NETTIE and LOTTIE, and live in Pawnee township.

By the second wife—
GEORGE W., and
JAMES L., live with their parents, in Auburn, Illinois.

LEWIS, WILLIAM, born in Kentucky, married in Sangamon county to Jemima Easley, and lives at St. Joseph, Missouri.

LEWIS, NANCY, born in Kentucky, married in Sangamon county to James O. Wilson, and lives in Bates county, Missouri.

LEWIS, MORGAN, born in Kentucky, married in Sangamon county to Sarah Walters, and both died, without children.

LEWIS, JOHN, born in Kentucky, married Nancy Campbell, and have four children—

WILLIAM H. married Lorilla Wilson, and lives in Ball township.
ELIZABETH,
JOHN F., and
AMANDA, live with their parents, in Ball township.

Mrs. Elizabeth Lewis, the mother of Eddin, Larkin, William, Nancy, Mary Morgan and John, died in 1857, in Ball township, in the seventy-fifth year of her age.

LEWIS, OBED, was born April 25, 1812, in Chester county, Penn. He came to Springfield, Ill., in 1838, was married, Sept. 23, 1851, to Cordelia M. Iles. They have three children—

**WILLIAM T.,
KATE**, and
MARY, and reside in Springfield.

From 1839 to 1868 Mr. Lewis was engaged in manufacturing carriages and wagons. He served the city as alderman, from 1862 to 1864, and from 1868 to 1873. He was elected mayor, in April, 1874, serving a term of one year. Obed Lewis and family reside in Springfield.

LEWIS, SAMUEL, born Feb. 16, 1767, in Pennsylvania, about sixteen miles above Philadelphia, on the Delaware river. He crossed the Allegheny mountains on horseback five times, and was married on the Kanawha river, West Virginia, about 1799, to Sally Floro, who was born there in 1785. They moved in 1814, to St. Francis county, Mo., and from there to Sangamon county, Ill., arriving May, 1830, in what is now Cotton Hill township. They had children in West Virginia, in Missouri, and in Sangamon county, making a total of fifteen. In June, 1844, Mr. Lewis moved his family to Delaware county, Iowa. Mrs. Sally Lewis died there in 1847, aged sixty-two years. Her mother lived to be one hundred and six years of age, and was living at Strawberry, Texas, at the time of her daughter's death. Samuel Lewis died in Iowa, Aug. 9, 1867, being in his one hundred and first year. His mother lived to be one hundred and fourteen years old. Of their fifteen children, six only are living—four of them in Iowa. One only resides in Illinois, the seventh child.

ALFRED, born March 26, 1823, in St. Francis county, Missouri, raised in Sangamon county, married March 14, 1850, in Loami, to Eliza J. Abell, a granddaughter of Adam Barger. Mr. and Mrs. Lewis had nine children in Sangamon county, four of whom died young. SARAH S., MARIA A., JOHN S., LOUISA F. and CORNELIA E. J. live with their parents. Alfred Lewis made his home in Sangamon county, near Breckinridge mill, until the fall of 1872, when he moved to Taylorville for the purpose of educating his children, and now resides there. He carries the first month's wages he ever earned in his pocket to the present time. It is in the shape of a watch.

LEWIS, MARIA, sister to Alfred, born April 6, 1815, married in Missouri to William Cooper. He died Sept., 1836, in Sangamon county, leaving four children, two of whom are living in Benton county, Mo. His widow married Hamilton McCoy. *See his name.*

LEWIS, LEVI D., born Aug. 26, 1801, near Morristown, N. J. Eliza Sutton was born Feb. 4, 1804, at the same place. They were there married Aug. 13, 1823, and had six children, one of whom died, aged five years. The family moved to Springfield, Ill., in Nov., 1835, where they had one child. Of their six children—

WILLIAM C. B., born Sept. 11, 1824, in New Jersey, went as musician in an Illinois regiment, to the Mexican war, returned, and died Oct. 6, 1847, in Springfield.

SARAH, born July 30, 1826, near Morristown, N. J., married in Springfield to Reuben Coon, who was born July 22, 1821, in New Jersey. They had eight children in Springfield, one of whom died young. LEVI L., born June 11, 1849, married in Springfield, Jan. 8, 1872, to Mary J. Tully, who was born Jan. 8, 1855, at Little Rock, Arkansas. Mr. L. L. Coon is engaged in the manufacture of boots and shoes, in Springfield. ANN ELIZA, born July 27, 1851, married in Springfield, Feb. 25, 1873, to William H. Billington, who was born March 31, 1849, in Shrewsbury, England. They have one child, LINA MAY, and reside in Springfield. Mr. Billington is conductor on the T. W. & W. railroad. FRANKLIN P., born May 12, 1853, is farming. CHARLEY, LINA, SUSAN and GEORGE reside with their mother. Mr. Reuben Coon was for several years engaged in the leather trade, and the manufacture of boots and shoes. He died, Nov. 7, 1871, and his widow and children reside in Springfield, Illinois.

MARY E., born Sept. 19, 1834, in N. J., married in Springfield, in 1853, to Thomas H. Palladay. She died May 18, 1855.

JAMES S., born Feb. 10, 1837, in Springfield, was married March 27, 1862, to Mary A. Smith, in Monmouth, Warren county, Ill., and reside there.

JOHN BERGEN, born Nov. 15, 1843, in Springfield, married in Nov.,

1871, near Monmouth, Ill., to Eliza Smith, and resides at Lenox, Iowa.

Levi D. Lewis was connected with his brothers, Joseph and Thomas, in the boot and shoe business for several years. In 1849 he went to California, and died there Feb. 24, 1850. Mrs. Eliza Lewis resides with her daughter, Mrs. Coon, in Springfield.

LEWIS, THOMAS, born July 9, 1808, near Baskingridge, Somerset county, New Jersey, was married at New Brunswick, N. J., April 4, 1832, to Margaret A. VanNorstrand, who was born in Somerset county, N. J., Oct. 4, 1810. In July, 1836, Mr. Lewis took a trip West, with the view of selecting a future home. After passing through Indiana, Illinois and Missouri, he selected Springfield, Ill., and returned to New Jersey for his family, consisting of his wife and two children. They started West June 9, 1837, in company with Mr. Lewis' two brothers, John and Eliphalet C., with their families; his sister, Susan A., and his brother-in-law, C. VanNostrand, in all twenty-seven persons. They arrived in Springfield Aug. 1, 1837. Mr. and Mrs. Lewis had five children; one died in infancy. Of the others—

ADALINE, born Sept. 12, 1833, in New Brunswick, New Jersey, married in Springfield March, 1858, to Stephen D. Ayres, who was born May 20, 1829, in Trumansburg, N. J. They have six children living. WILLIAM J., NETTIE, LEWIS C., STELLA, ALBERT T. and OLIVE. S. D. Ayres and family reside in Cairo, Illinois.

WILLIAM T., born Sept. 25, 1836, in New Brunswick, New Jersey, was married April 20, 1862, in Macon county, Ill., to Sarah C. Sprouse, who was born April 20, 1843. They have six children living—CHARLES A., SARAH M., EDWARD P., OWEN, STELLA A. and ANNIE. W. T. Lewis and family reside in Chilicothe, Missouri.

CHARLES H., born Aug. 12, 1839, in Springfield, Ill., died Feb. 6, 1855.

ALBERT, born Aug. 1, 1849, in Springfield, is unmarried, and resides in Cairo, Illinois.

Thomas Lewis had nine brothers and one sister. His brothers all died, each leaving a widow. For several years Mr. Lewis had nine widowed sisters-in-law, and eight are still living. His brothers, Eliphalet C. and John, settled in Warren county, Ill., and died there. Thomas Lewis has been an active, energetic business man all his life. He lived in Springfield until 1875, when he moved to Cairo, Ill., where he now resides—1876.

LEWIS, SUSAN, born April 19, 1814, in New Jersey, the only sister of Thomas Lewis, was married in Springfield, Ill., to Henry VanHoff. *See his name.* Mr. VanHhff died, and his widow married Rev. J. G. Bergen. *See his name.*

LIGHTFOOT, HENRY F., was born Feb. 22, 1787, near Madison Court House, Virginia, and was there married Feb. 21, 1811, to Mary T. Jones, who was born Jan. 6, 1792, at the same place. They moved to Adair county, Ky., where they had three children, and from there to Warren county, near Bowling Green, where three children were born; thence to Sangamon county, Ill., arriving Oct. 23, 1830, near Springfield. Two children were born in Sangamon county. Of their children—

JOHN A., born Sept. 3, 1814, in Adair county, Ky., was married Sept. 24, 1838, to Susan J. Jones. She died Sept. 5, 1844, in Chester, Ill., leaving one child, HENRY F., who was born Sept. 1, 1840, at Georgetown, Randolph county, Ill. He was married in the fall of 1864, at Rock Island, Ill., to Fannie F. Kelly. H. F. Lightfoot died in St. Louis, leaving two children, HENRY W., and ———, who live with their mother in St. Louis, Mo. John A. Lightfoot married Cornelia Sigler. She died, leaving three children, CHARLES W., MARY A. and SUSAN M., with their relatives in Jacksonville, Ill. J. A. Lightfoot is employed in the U. S. Custom House at New Orleans.

GOODRICH, born April 19, 1817, in Adair county, Ky., married in Sangamon county Dec. 1, 1842, to Nancy Callerman. They had eight living children. MARY E., born Sept. 18, 1847, married Sept. 2, 1868, to John F. Fagan. *See his name.* ELIZABETH J., born June 22, 1849, married Sept. 6, 1870, to Richard T. Lewis, who was born April 18, 1838, in Delaware county, Ohio, came to Sangamon county in 1844. He enlisted at Springfield, Sept. 28, 1861, in Co. G, 10th

Ill. Cav., for three years. Re-enlisted as a veteran Dec. 12, 1863; served until the end of the rebellion, and was honorably discharged Nov., 1865, at San Antonia, Texas, and mustered out at Springfield Jan. 6, 1866. He resides at Elkhart, Logan county, Illinois. JAMES R., born April 17, 1852, married Dec. 24, 1873, to Julia A. Plunkett, and live near Marysville, Nodaway county, Mo. SUSAN M. married Jan. 8, 1874, to John L. Callerman, Jun. *See his name.* JOHN L., JUDITH L., ALICE B. and JULIA ANN live with their parents, three miles north of Springfield, Illinois.

DOLLY A., born Feb. 9, 1820, in Adair county, Ky., married Dec. 6, 1839, to Peter Lanterman. *See his name.*

MARGARET S., born Nov. 16, 1822, in Kentucky, married in Sangamon county to Philip F. Lightfoot. They had two children. REUBEN enlisted in 1862, for three years, in Co. A, 38th Ill. Inf. He was wounded at the battle of Stone's river, and died Jan. 4, 1863. GABRIEL lives near Springfield, Ill. Mrs. Margaret S. Lightfoot died Dec. 15, 1847, while on a visit in Alabama.

ROBERT S., born March 13, 1825, in Kentucky, came to Sangamon county with his parents, went to California soon after the discovery of gold, and died there.

ELIZABETH M. married in Sangamon county to Henry Shuck, and died, leaving one child, ANNIE, who lives with her father in Springfield.

PHILIP H., born August 24, 1829, in Kentucky, died in Sangamon county in his seventh year.

GABRIEL M., born August 8, 1832, died March 12, 1846.

Henry F. Lightfoot died Feb. 10, 1846, while on a visit to Kentucky near Danville. His widow died Oct., 1858, in Sangamon county.

LILLARD, THOMAS, born in North Carolina, married there to Temperance Duncan. They moved to Tennesee with her father, and from there to Sangamon county, Ill., arriving in 1830 in what is now Woodside township. Mrs. Lillard died, and he married again, and moved to Missouri, taking all except two of his children—

MARTHA A. married William Jones, Jun. *See his name.*

The other is the wife of Burril McKinney, and lives in Wisconsin.

LINCOLN, ABRAHAM, was born Feb. 12, 1809, in that part of Hardin, which is now Larue county, Ky. He was taken by his parents, in his eighth year, to Spencer county, Indiana. His mother died there, and his father returned to Kentucky, and married again. In 1830 the family moved to Macon county, Ill., and spent the winter of the "deep snow" there. In the spring of 1831, Abraham Lincoln passed through Springfield and went to New Salem, near where Petersburg, Menard county, now stands. He labored at boat building, rail making and like employments, also clerking in a store, until the Black Hawk war came on, when he was elected captain of a volunteer company. After the war he was elected to the Legislature four times. He studied surveying and practiced that, usually in summer, after having spent the winter in the legislature. During all the intervals between other employments for gaining a livelihood, he studied law, and when qualified to practice he sold his surveying implements, and in 1837 moved to Springfield He was married in Springfield, Nov. 4, 1842, to Mary Todd. They had four children—

EDDIE, WILLIE and *THOMAS* (Tad) are all dead.

ROBERT T., born in Springfield, graduated at Harvard College, married in Washington, D. C., to the daughter of Senator Harlan, of Iowa, is now a practicing lawyer in Chicago.

Abraham Lincoln was elected, in 1846, Representative in Congress, serving one term of two years. From the close of that term until 1854, he "practiced law more assiduously than ever before." During that time he took but little interest in politics, but the repeal of the Missouri compromise aroused him to the encroachments of slavery, and he united with kindred spirits in organizing the Republican party, at Bloomington, Ill., in 1856. In 1858 he was a candidate for United States Senator to succeed Stephen A. Douglas, whose term was drawing to a close. Contrary to the usual custom with candidates for that office, instead of aiming to influence the members of the legislature, by whose votes the choice is made, the contest was brought directly before the people, in order to influence their action in choosing members of the legislature, who were to choose a United States Senator. That led to seven joint debates between Mr. Lincoln and Mr. Douglas, in different parts of the State of Illinois. Mr. Douglas was elected as his own successor, but Mr. Lincoln's speeches in that campaign gave him a national reputation, and proved that his understanding of the slavery question was more clear and comprehensive than that of any other man in the nation. That led to his being chosen by the Republican National Convention, assembled in Chicago, in June, 1860, as the candidate of that party for the office of President of the United States. He was elected in November of that year. When he took his seat at Washington, D. C., March 4, 1861, he found fifteen States in armed rebellion against his authority, the treasury of the nation empty, its arsenals plundered, and its ships of war scattered to the most remote parts of the globe. War—cruel, bloody and relentless, followed. He was re-elected President in November, 1864, and when he took the oath of office for the second time, March 4, 1865, the armed hosts of the rebellion had almost melted away, and in his heart he was beginning to sing the glad anthem of "Peace on earth and good will to men," when he was shot by the hand of an assassin on the evening of April 14, and breathed his last on the morning of April 15, 1865, at the capital of the nation.

His remains, accompanied by a large delegation of the most distinguished men of the nation, civilians, statesmen and soldiers, occupying a railroad train of nine cars, were conveyed to his former home. For twelve days and nights the train moved on, and was hailed everywhere more like a triumphal procession than a funeral cortege. May 4, 1865, his body was deposited in the receiving tomb at Oak Ridge Cemetery, Springfield, Illinois.

A grateful people have erected to his memory a monument, and upon it placed his statue, in bronze, of heroic size. It was unveiled Oct. 15, 1874, in the presence of the Society of the Army of the Tennessee, at their eighth annual re-union, with a host of citizens, making an assemblage of about twenty-five thousand persons. When the four groups of statuary, representing the Infantry, Cavalry, Artillery and Navy, are put in position on the monument, the total cost will be about two hundred and twelve thousand dollars.

Mrs. Lincoln resides with her sister, Mrs. Edwards, in Springfield, Illinois.—July, 1876.

The following are the only words Mr. Lincoln ever wrote concerning himself or his ancestors. They were not intended for publication, but were written as an act of personal regard for an old friend, and placed in the hands of Hon. Jesse W. Fell, of Bloomington, Ill., in December, 1859. It is very properly termed by Mr. Fell, the

AUTOBIOGRAPHY OF ABRAHAM LINCOLN.

"I was born Feb. 12, 1809, in Hardin county, Kentucky. My parents were both born in Virginia, of undistinguished families—second families—perhaps I should say. My mother, who died in my tenth year, was of a family of the name of Hanks, some of whom now reside in Adams, and others in Macon counties, Illinois. My paternal grandfather, Abraham Lincoln, emigrated from Rockingham county, Va., to Kentucky about 1781 or '2, where, a year or two later, he was killed by Indians, not in battle, but by stealth, when he was laboring to open a farm in the forest. His ancestors, who were Quakers, went to Virginia from Berks county, Pennsylvania. An effort to identify them with the New England family of the same name ended in nothing more definite than a similarity of christian names in both families, such as Enoch, Levi, Mordecai, Solomon, Abraham, and the like.

"My father, at the death of his father, was but six years of age, and he grew up literally without education. He removed from Kentucky to what is now Spencer county, Indiana, in my eighth year. We reached our new home about the time the State came into the Union. It was a wild region, with many bears and other wild animals still in the woods. There I grew up. There were some schools, so-called, but no qualification was ever required of a teacher, beyond "readin', writin' and cipherin'" to the rule of three. If a straggler, supposed to understand Latin happened to sojourn in the neighborhood, he was looked upon as a wizard. There was absolutely nothing to excite ambition for education. Of course, when I came of age, I did not know much; still, somehow I could read, write, and cipher to the rule of three, but that was all. I have not been to school since. The little advance I now have upon this store of education, I have picked up from time to time, under the pressure of necessity.

"I was raised to farm work, which I continued till I was twenty-two. At twenty-one I came to Illinois, and passed the first year in Macon county. Then I got to New Salem, at that time in Sangamon, now in Menard county, where I remained a year, as a sort of clerk in a store. Then came the Black Hawk war, and I was elected a captain of volunteers, a success which gave me more pleasure than any I have had since. I went the campaign, was elated; ran for the legislature the same year—1832—and was beaten, the only time I ever have been beaten by the people. The next, and three succeeding biennial elections, I was elected to the legislature. I was not a candidate afterwards. During this legislative period I had studied law, and removed to Springfield to practice it. In 1846, I was once elected to the lower house of congress; was not a candidate for re-election. From 1849 to 1854, both inclusive, practiced law more assiduously than ever before. Always a Whig in politics, and generally on the Whig electoral tickets, making active canvasses; I was losing interest in politics, when the repeal of the Missouri Compromise aroused me again. What I have done since then is pretty well known.

"If any personal description of me is thought desirable, it may be said, I am in height, six feet four inches, nearly, lean in flesh, weighing on an average one hundred and eighty pounds, dark complexion, with coarse black hair and gray eyes; no other marks or brands recollected.

"Yours, very truly,
"A. LINCOLN."

Hon. J. W. Fell.

During the war to suppress the rebellion, as is well known, Mr. Lincoln was frequently waited upon by delegations from religious bodies. Among others, a large number of women belonging to the Society of Friends gave him a call. One of their number, the widow of Joseph John Gurney, a distinguished Quaker preacher of England, wrote him a letter. The following is Mr. Lincoln's reply. It will be highly prized, because it contains such emphatic and unequivocal expressions of his belief in the overruling providence of God.

"EXECUTIVE MANSION,
"WASHINGTON, Sept. 4, 1864.

"*Eliza P. Gurney:*

"MY ESTEEMED FRIEND—I have not forgotten—probably never shall forget—the very impressive occasion when yourself and friends visited me, on a Sabbath forenoon, two years ago; nor has your kind letter, written nearly a year later, ever been forgotten. In all, it has been your purpose to strengthen my reliance on God. I am much indebted to the good Christian people of this country for their constant prayers and consolations; and to no one of them, more than yourself. The purposes of the Almighty are perfect, and must prevail; though we erring mortals may fail to accurately perceive them in advance. We hoped for a happy termination of this terrible war long before this; but God knows best, and has ruled otherwise. We shall yet acknowledge His wisdom and our own error therein. Meanwhile, we must work earnestly in the best light He gives us, trusting that so working still conduces to the great ends He ordains. Surely, He intends some great good to follow this mighty convulsion, which no mortal could make, and no mortal could stay.

"Your people, the Friends, have had, and are having, a very great trial. On principle and faith, opposed to both war and oppression, they can only practically oppose oppression by war. In this hard dilemma, some have chosen one horn and some the other. For those appealing to me on conscientious grounds, I have done, and shall do, the best I could and can, in my own conscience, under my oath to the law. That you believe this, I doubt not; and believing it, I shall still receive, for our country and myself, your earnest prayers to our Father in Heaven.

"Your sincere friend,
"A. LINCOLN."

LINDLEY, SIMON, was born Jan. 20, 1769, in Orange county, N. C. Anna Standley was born Feb. 3, 1766, in Kent county, Del. Her parents moved to Pendleton District, S. C. Simon Lindley and Anna Standley were there married, July 14, 1789. Their home was in Orange county, N. C., until four children were born, and they moved to Christian county, Ky., where they had three children. In the fall of 1807 they moved to Madison county, Ill., and the next spring to what is now Bond county. All was quiet there for about three years, but in the latter part of 1811 the Indians became hostile, and began to murder the settlers and steal property. Mr. Lindley was warned by a very old, whitehaired Indian, of the threatened danger. Then the settlers united in building a fort or stockade, about two and a half miles from where Greenville now stands. They lived in that fortification during the whole time the war with Great Britain was raging. They could not have held their ground and provided for their families, but the soldiers who were stationed there guarded the men while they worked in the fields. They lived that way four years, many of their members being murdered. The Indians continued to swarm about them in greater numbers, and they abandoned the fort, and all went back to the vicinity of Edwardsville, in September, 1814, and the next spring, 1815, a treaty was made, in consequence of which, hostilities ceased. Mr. Lindley remained near Edwardsville four or five years, and moved to what became Sangamon county, arriving April 14, 1820, in what is now Chatham township. The farm is now owned by the heirs of Benjamin F. Darnielle. Of his seven children—

JOHN, born Jan. 23, 1791, in North Carolina, married twice, and died in Madison county, Illinois.

JOSEPH, born Jan. 7, 1793, in North Carolina, married in Bond county to Nancy Hicks, moved to Sangamon county, then to Tennessee, and from there to Freestone county, Texas.

MARY, born May 11, 1795, married George Bridges, raised a family, and died in St. Clair county.

SARAH, born Dec. 4, 1797, married Allen Bridges. They raised a family and live in Polk county, Mo.

SIMON, Jun., born August 16, 1799, in Christian county, Ky., came to Sangamon county with his parents, went to South America when a young man, married there, and has not been heard of for several years.

ELIZABETH, born Sept. 3, 1803, in Christian county, Ky., married July 30, 1826, in Sangamon county, to Samuel Harbour. *See his name.*

ANNA, born May 9, 1806, married April 13, 1826, to Thomas Greenwood. *See his name.*

Simon Lindley died August 30, 1827, and his widow died Jan. 23, 1849, both near where they settled in 1820.

Simon Lindley was a minister of the Regular, or Predestinarian Baptist church. In July, 1821, himself and wife, John Bridges and wife, united with others for the purpose of keeping up worship, and on the second Saturday in June, 1826, the Liberty Baptist church, on Lick creek, was organized by Elders William Crow, Thomas Ray and Micajah Rowland, and brethren Austin Sims and Peter Robeson. There were thirteen members:—

Males.	Females.
John Morris,	Ruth Greenwood,
John Hilyard,	Elizabeth Hilyard,
Wm. D. Morris,	Clarissa Huffmaster,
Levi Harbour,	Polly Harbour,
Simon Lindley,	Polly Hilyard,
Joseph Hilyard,	Clarinda Morris.
Morris Hilyard.	

The church worships now in a school house in Curran township, and is under the pastoral care of Elder C. C. Purvines.

Mr. Lindley was a very eccentric man, and many anecdotes are related of him, both in connection with his preaching and in private life. Mr. Lindley was also a man of liberal education. He was educated at some college in Philadelphia, but whether he was a graduate or not, I cannot say. After the town of Springfield was laid out, there was a discrepancy between the surveyors of that and the former town of Calhoun, and Mr. Lindley was called on to re-survey it and harmonize the differences, which he did, to the satisfaction of all parties.

LINDSAY, JOHN, was born in Virginia, and married Sophia Lanterman. *See his name in Omissions.*

LINDSAY, ISAAC, born May 16, 1819, in Franklin county, Penn., was married in Jacksonville, Ill., in 1841, to Mary Dyer. Their four children all died young, and Mrs. Mary Lindsay died in the spring of 1850. Mr. Lindsay was married in Jan., 1851, in Springfield, to Mercy Elder, a native of Kentucky. *See Elder family.* They had three children, and all died young. Mrs. Mercy Lindsay died Jan. 27, 1858. Mr. L. was married in Springfield, Ill., to Mrs. Sarah Rogers, whose maiden name was Elder, a sister of his second wife. They have five living children, MARTHA A., FRANK R., WILLIAM E., ADA and IDA, twins, who all live with their parents.

Isaac Lindsay was a bricklayer by trade, and was for about seven years, from 1858, clerk in the recorder's branch of the circuit court of Sangamon county. He was assessor and collector for the city two years—1856 and 1857. He and his family reside in Springfield, Illinois.

LINDSAY, MORRIS, born June 30, 1818, in Franklin county, Penn. He came to Springfield with his brother, Isaac, in 1836, and was married April 2, 1844, at Salisbury, to Sarah Miller, a daughter of Solomon Miller. They had four children, two of whom died young. Of the other two—

SOLOMON L., born March 12, 1846, in Sangamon county, was married Jan. 8, 1872, in Arkansas, to Dora Moore, a native of Tennessee. They have two children, MORRIS W. and ALBERT CHARLES, and reside in Springfield, Illinois.

ALLIE, born Aug. 26, 1850, in Sangamon county, and resides with her mother.

Morris Lindsay was appointed postmaster, at Springfield, in 1858, and served until 1861. He also served several terms as a member of the city council of Springfield. In 1863 or '4 he moved to Carbondale, Ill., where he died March 25, 1869. His remains were brought to Springfield, and interred in Oak Ridge Cemetery. His widow and daughter reside in Carbondale, Jackson county, Illinois.

LITTLE, SAMUEL, born in 1776, in Virginia. He was married in the year 1797, in Fleming county, Ky., to Mary Newcomb. They had nine children in Kentucky, and moved to St. Clair county, Illinois, where two of their children died. Mr. Little moved with his family to what became Sangamon county, arriving in 1819 or 1820, and settled two and one-half miles southwest of the present State House. Six of their children married and raised families, and all except one has died, and their children have moved away from the county. The only remaining one—

SAMUEL N., born March 1, 1814, in Fleming county, Ky., married in Sangamon county, Jan. 29, 1843, to Eliza M. Morgan. They have seven children—WILLIAM H., born March 16, 1845, near Springfield, married, Oct. 31, 1872, to Delia Pirkins. Wm. H. Little was killed Aug. 16, 1873, by an accident on the Chicago & Alton railroad, at Sag Bridge, near Chicago, and interred in Oak Ridge Cemetery. His widow resides with her father, R. Pirkins. *See his name.* GERSHOM J., born Feb. 19, 1847, near Springfield, married, Jan. 2, 1867, to Nellie Crafton. She died Jan. 14, 1868. G. J. Little was married, Oct. 27, 1874, to Maggie E. Conner, who was born June 22, 1851, in Springfield. G. J. Little is of the firm of S. N. Little & Sons, and resides in Springfield. SANFORD H., born June 21, 1849, lives in Springfield, and is of the firm of S. N. Little & Sons. HARRIET C., born Dec. 12, 1853, near Springfield, married Feb. 14, 1867, to John W. Crafton. They had one child, WILLIAM H., who died in his third year. Mr. and Mrs. Crafton reside in Springfield. MARY E., born May 10, 1851, died Oct. 30, 1855. MINERVA C., died Aug. 1, 1857. FANNIE Z., born Jan. 8, 1869, resides with her parents. Samuel N. Little owns and resides on the farm where his father settled in 1819, and received the title from the United States government soon after it came into market, in 1823. He is also engaged in the livery business, in Springfield, with his sons, Gershom J. and Sanford H., under the firm name of S. N. Little & Sons.

Of his parents—Mrs. Mary Little died in July, 1823, and Samuel Little died Jan. 1, 1847, both near Springfield.

LITTLE, THOMAS S., born March 16, 1820, in Northampton, Mass., came to Springfield, Ill., Aug., 1838, where he was married, May 30, 1844, to Ann M. Watson. They had five children, two of whom died in infancy. Of the other three children—

MARIA W., born Jan. 27, 1846, in Springfield, was married, Aug. 7, 1865, to Samuel A. Slemmons, who was born Jan. 28, 1842, at Cadiz, Harrison county, Ohio, and came to Springfield in 1859. Mr. and Mrs. Slemmons have three children, GEORGE B., ELLA L. and ALICE H. Mr. Slemmons was a member of an independent military company, of which John Cook was captain, and it was part of a regiment of which E. E. Ellsworth was Colonel. In connection with that company, Mr. Slemmons volunteered on the first call for 75,000 men, in April, 1861, but being under age he was prevented by his father from going. He returned to Ohio, in 1862, and became Lieutenant of Co. E, 88th Ohio Inf., a three months regiment, in which he served four and one-half months. During that time he was appointed Major of a three years regiment, but could not serve on account of a crippled arm. He came back to Springfield, and engaged in business. Mr. Slemmons was one of the original projectors of the Springfield Spice and Hominy Mills, and aided in building and running the same, as a member of the firm of Conkling, Slemmons & Co. He went out of the firm in April, 1876, and is now—July 1876—residing in Springfield.

ELLEN C., born Dec. 14, 1847, in Springfield, was married, Oct. 20, 1870, to William O. Converse, who was born June 30, 1840, in Painesville, Lake county, Ohio, and was brought with the family of his father, Henry Converse, to Springfield, in 1846. Mr. and Mrs. Converse have two daughters, NIANA and ———, and reside in Springfield. Mr. Converse is a farmer, and trader in stock, land, etc. He united with A. M. Garland, who first suggested it, in obtaining a pledge from the board of supervisors of Sangamon county, that they would lease the old poor house grounds to an Agricultural Society. Mr. Garland and Mr. Converse induced others to unite with them in organizing the present Sangamon county Agricultural Society, and securing the lease for the grounds for twenty-five years—from 1872. Wm. O. Converse served the society four years as secretary, and is now—1876—its treasurer, elected for two years.

EMMA B., born March 2, 1850, in Springfield, was married, Dec. 9, 1869, to Charles E. Blake. They have one child, PAUL, and reside at Anoka, Minn. He is cashier and manager of the Anoka Bank.

Thomas S. Little was in business as a merchant tailor and clothier, from 1844 to the spring of 1876, when he retired in consequence of impaired health, and resides in Springfield.

LOCK, JOHN, was born Jan. 10, 1799, in the town of Farrisburg, Addison county, Vermont. Maria Jaquays was born Aug. 31, 1802, in the same county. They were there married Jan. 5, 1820, had three living children in Vermont, and moved to Essex county, N. Y., where two children were born. The family moved to Sangamon county, Ill., arriving May 2, 1832, at Rochester, where they had six children. Two died young. Of their nine children—

HANNAH, born Jan. 13, 1821, in Vermont, was twice married in Sangamon county, and died there Nov. 27, 1844.

JONATHAN, born Feb. 3, 1823, in Vermont, died in Sangamon county July 8, 1838.

MERCY, born June 4, 1825, died in her eleventh year.

RACHEL S., born May 30, 1829, in New York, married in Sangamon county Aug. 17, 1852, to Isaac May. They have a family, and live near Greenville, Dade county, Missouri.

ADELINE E., born Aug. 3, 1831, in Essex county, N. Y., married in Sangamon county Nov. 19, 1853, to Samuel Grubb. See his name.

SYLVESTER, born June 14, 1834, in Sangamon county, died in his fourteenth year.

WILLIAM H., born Aug. 16, 1840, in Sangamon county, married Nov. 28, 1861, to Amanda M. Delay. They had two children, LOLA and WILLIAM H., Jun., and Mr. Lock died Jan. 25, 1871. His family live in Rochester.

VILROY, born Nov. 21, 1843, died in in his fourth year.

JOHN, *Jun.*, born Feb. 26, 1848, in Rochester, lives with his parents.

John Lock and his wife have been living together nearly fifty-six years, and reside in Rochester. May 3, 1832, the day after his arrival, and before he had unloaded his wagon, he was notified to appear at Springfield on the morning of the 4th, to stand draft to fight the Indian under Black Hawk. He was there in time, but more men had volunteered than had been called for, and his services were not wanted. There was no corn in Sangamon county at the time, and Mr. Lock went thirty miles below St. Louis, paid five dollars for ten bushels, and hauled it home for seed, and bread for his family. He has known corn to sell for four dollars per bushel, and has seen equally as good corn sell at eight cents per bushel, a difference of fifty fold. Mr. Lock donated timber and labor to aid in building the first steam mill in Rochester. After it was built, the proprietors refused to grind for toll, and demanded twenty-five cents per bushel for grinding. Mr. Lock offered two bushels for grinding one, but the miller refused. The price of corn was ten cents. He was forced to the necessity of hunting a purchaser for two and one-half bushels, take the twenty-five cents and pay it for grinding one bushel. The usual toll is one-eighth of the grain.

LOCKRIDGE, JOHN, was born about 1758, in Augusta county, Va. He enlisted about 1775, in the revolutionary army, and was in the battles of Guilford Court House, the Cowpens, and many others. For his services he drew a pension to the end of his life. Mr. Lockridge married in his native county, and moved to Montgomery county, Ky., raised a large family, and came to Sangamon county, Ill., with his son, William A., arriving in 1835. He died in 1848. He had four sons and four daughters, who came to Sangamon county, namely—

JOSEPH H., born Dec. 10, 1791, in Montgomery county, Ky., was married there to Martha Cassity. They moved to Sangamon county in 1835, in what is now Ball township, where he died. His widow married James Phelps, and lives in Auburn.

ELIJAH, born Dec. 19, 1806, in Montgomery county, Ky., married in Kentucky, to Lavina Cassity, and moved to Sangamon county, Ill., arriving in 1835, in what is now Ball township. They had eight children, namely: ELIZABETH A. married Charles Bridges, moved to Missouri, and Mr. Bridges died there. JOSEPH W. married Oct. 1, 1848, to Eleanor Haley. They had two living children, EDWARD and JULIETTE, who live with their mother. Joseph W. Lockridge died Dec. 27, 1865, in Sangamon county. His widow married July 19, 1867, to George Young, who was born November, 1832, in Pittsylvania county, Va. They had three children, WILLIAM E., LUELLA and THOMAS M., and live half a mile north of Pawnee. JOHN married Elizabeth A. Hart. They have two children, ROSE and ROBERT, and live in Henry county, Mo. He served three years in an Illinois regiment, nine months of the time in Libby prison, and came as near starving to death as it was possible to do, and live. FRANCIS M., served three years in an Illinois regiment, and was honorably discharged. He lives in Henry county, Mo. ROBERT enlisted in an Illinois regiment, and died in the army. MARTHA J. married Henry Kitch. They moved to Missouri, where he died, and she married again. MARY married James Molliborn. They have three children, AMBROSE, CORDELIA and LILLIE BELLE, and live three miles northwest of Pawnee. AMANDA L. married John Forahner, and lives in Missouri. Elijah Lockridge died in Ball township, about 1856. His widow lives with her children, in Missouri.

LOCKRIDGE, WILLIAM A., was born Jan. 17, 1810, in Montgomery county, Ky. He was married there to Sally Moore, June 3, 1830. They had two children in Kentucky, and moved in company with his father, John Lockridge, to Sangamon county, Ill., arriving Oct. 22, 1835, in what is now Ball township, where five children were born. Of their seven children—

BURRILLA N., born June 11, 1832, in Kentucky, married in Sangamon county, to James M. Lewis. *See his name.*

JULIA A., born in Kentucky, married to Napoleon Lloyd. They have three children, WILLIAM, ROBERT and HATTIE, and reside at Mt. Sterling, Kentucky.

MARY E., born March 14, 1836, in Sangamon county, married William Gardner. They reside in Chatham, Illinois.

MARGARET, born in Sangamon county, is an invalid, and resides with her sister, Mrs. Ingels.

SARAH B., born Jan. 1, 1841, in Sangamon county, married Nathaniel Ingels, who was born Jan. 1, 1837, near Paris, Ky. They have five living children, SARAH P., HENRY G., FREDERICK L., JOHN A. and JESSIE N., WILLIAM B. died, aged two years. They live in Ball township, two and a half miles southeast of Chatham, Illinois.

WILLIAM R., born in Sangamon county, married April 22, 1869, to Mary Nuckolls. They had one child, CHARLES W., and reside adjoining Pawnee on the north. William R. Lockridge is a farmer, stock-raiser and merchant.

JOHN R., born in Sangamon county, married to Sarah J. Headley. They have one child, JAMES W., and live in Ball township, near Sugar creek Cumberland Presbyterian church, on the farm settled by Joseph Dodds in 1818.

Mrs. Sally Lockridge died Nov. 23, 1857, in Sangamon county, and Wm. A. Lockridge was married June 10, 1858, to Amanda E. Goodbar, who was born in Kentucky, June 2, 1826. They have three children, *EMMA*, *RACHEL L.* and *MARY M.*

Wm. A. Lockridge resides in Ball township, two and a quarter miles south of Chatham, Ill. When Mr. Lockridge came to Sangamon county the timber land was all taken, and it was almost impossible to buy it at any price. Prairie land could be obtained for two or three dollars per acre, and at the same time he has known timber land to sell as high as eighty dollars per acre. Timber land equally good can now be bought for forty dollars per acre, while the prairie land that was then so cheap sells from forty to sixty dollars per acre. Railroads, coal and the hedge plant have wrought the change. Mr. Lockridge says he raised wheat, tramped it out with horses, hauled it ninety miles to St. Louis, and sold it for thirty-seven and a half cents per bushel. It required ten days to make the trip, and a full four-horse load would bring about seventeen dollars and fifty cents. The best he could do in selling net pork in Springfield was one dollar and a quarter per hundred pounds, and half of that in trade at very high prices. Mr. Lockridge is now one of the most extensive farmers in the county.

LOCKRIDGE, JOHN, was born July 17, 1799, either in Montgomery or Fayette county, Kentucky. He was married in Kentucky Sept. 3, 1811, to Margy Killough, and moved in 1826 to Owen county, Indiana, and from there to Sangamon county, Illinois, arriving Oct. 20, 1838. Of their eight children—

NANCY, born in Kentucky, married in Indiana to John M. Hart, and died, leaving a family in Putnam county, Indiana.

JOHN MILTON, born Jan. 15, 1814, in Montgomery county, Kentucky, came to Sangamon county, near Auburn, in 1837, one year before his father came. He was married July 2, 1840, to Jane Nuckolls. They had five living children in Sangamon county. ROBERT H., the fourth one, born Jan. 17, 1850, married May 3, 1871, to Ella Hough, who was born July 22, 1853, in Lewis county, New York. They live two and a half miles southeast of Chatham. The other four, JOHN W., JAMES M., ANDREW H. and CHARLES E., live with their parents. J. Milton Lockridge and family reside one mile west of Auburn, Illinois. Mr. Lockridge has served several years as a member of the Board of Supervisors of Sangamon county.

JAMES W., born in Kentucky, married Margaret A. Bridges. She died, and he married Jane Foster. They reside at Elkhart, Logan county, Illinois. He has children by both marriages.

MARGARET married Alexander Smith, and died, leaving seven children in Chatham.

MATTHEW K. married Pauline Landers. She died, and he lives in California.

JOSEPH H. married Mrs. Elizabeth Frazier, whose maiden name was Wallace, and live in Auburn, Illinois.

ELIZABETH married Madison Curvey, and died without children.

LOUISA married Franklin Steele, and lives in Owen county, Indiana.

John Lockridge died in Oregon Sept. 20, 1852, having left his family in Sangamon county, expecting to return. His widow, Mrs. Margy Lockridge, died in Montgomery county, Illinois, November 2, 1864.

LOCKRIDGE, ELIZABETH, born in Kentucky, married Alexander Cassity. *See his name.*

LOCKRIDGE, ISABEL K., born July 4, 1815, in Kentucky, married William Bridges. *See his name.*

LOCKRIDGE, MARGARET, married James Bridges. *See his name.*

LOCKRIDGE, REBECCA, born in Kentucky, married George Bridges. *See his name.*

LONG NINE.—In the State Legislature of Illinois that assembled at Vandalia, in December, 1836, and continued until March, 1837, the delegation from Sangamon county was composed of two Senators and seven members of the House of Representatives. They were the most remarkable body of men from any one county, for the reason that they were much taller than the average of human stature. Some of them were a little less and some a little more than six feet, but their combined height was exactly fifty-four feet. They were then, and are yet, spoken of as the "Long Nine."

The names of those in the Senate were Archer G. Herndon and Job Fletcher; in the House of Representatives, Abraham Lincoln, Ninian W. Edwards, John Dawson, Andrew McCormack, Dan Stone, William F. Elkin and Robert L. Wilson. One or two were as tall, but none taller, than Abraham Lincoln, who it will be seen, by reference to his Autobiography, could add four inches to be divided among those who fell below the average. A sketch of each of them will be found in their appropriate places, in the alphabetical arrangement.

The settlement of the State began in the southern part, and Kaskaskia was made the capital of the territory because it was more easy of access to a majority of the inhabitants than any other point. Settlements moved northward, and Vandalia was created for the purpose of making it the capital. A feeling prevailed at the time that it would again be necessary to move further north. For that reason a clause was inserted in the law establishing the capital at Vandalia, that it should not be moved from there for twenty years.

Before the expiration of that time, it was everywhere conceded that the capital must again be moved north. Springfield was early a candidate, and the members of the legislature from Sangamon county were chosen with direct reference to that subject. The people of Illinois were at that time nearly insane on the subject of internal improvements. The previous session of the legislature commenced chartering railroad companies, but the session of 1836-'7 was devoted largely to business of that kind. The capital stock authorized to joint stock companies, chiefly railroads, down to the end of the session of 1836-'7, was twelve millions of dollars. The internal improvement act of Feb. 27, 1837, appropriated ten million, two hundred thousand dollars, directly from the State treasury; more than nine millions of that sum was for railroads. At the same session private laws were enacted, chartering joint stock companies with authorized capital stock, to the amount of nearly eight millions, making an aggregate of nearly thirty millions of dollars involved in efforts to legislate railroads into existence, before the business of the country would justify it.

In order to accomplish this legislation, a great amount of what is understood among politicians as "log rolling," was done. That is, you help me to get my pet scheme through, and I will help you. The "Long Nine" did not ask much for their section in the way of internal improvements, but they never lost an opportunity to make a vote for the removal of the capital to Springfield. It is only surprising that, with such opportunities, they did not accomplish more. It will be seen, by reference to the forty-third page, that there were seven candidates for the location, and that on the first ballot Springfield received thirty-five of the one hundred and twenty-one votes cast, and continued to gain until the fourth ballot, when she received seventy-three of the one hundred and eight votes cast. It was thus decided that Springfield was to be the future capital of the State, and as surely determined that the men who secured that result should ever after be known as the "Long Nine."

LONG, THOMAS, was born May 6, 1775, in Nelson county, Ky.; went to Caldwell county, married there Feb. 4, 1819, to Annis Hurlbut, who was born in Vermont Feb. 14, 1801. They had three living children in Kentucky, and moved to Sangamon county, Ill., arriving April 19, 1824, seven miles south of Springfield, where three children were born, and they moved to Rochester, in the same county, where they had two children. Of their nine children—

MATTHEW E., born June 12, 1820, in Kentucky, married in Sangamon county Feb. 4, 1844, to Eliza Thompson, daughter of General Lewis Thompson. Mr. Long moved to Taylorville in the spring of 1850. Mrs. Eliza Long died Nov., 1857, in Taylorville, and he was married July 4, 1861, to Mary Sattley. Mr. Long was elected Justice of the Peace in 1869, and is now serving his second term. Matthew E. Long and wife reside in Taylorville, Illinois.

JOHN H., born Aug. 26, 1822, in Kentucky, died March 1, 1841, in Sangamon county.

JAMES G., born Dec. 8, 1824, married Feb. 3, 1857, in Washington, D. C., to Virginia Stone. They had one child, VIRGINIA. Mr. Long was Sheriff of Menard county two terms, after which he obtained a clerkship in the pension office, and served sixteen years. He was then elected and served one term in the legislature of the District of Columbia. Mrs. Virginia Long died Sept. 15, 1860, in Washington, D. C. Mr. Long and daughter reside there.

THOMAS W., born March 8, 1830, in Sangamon county, married Oct. 19, 1854, to Mary Trotter, who was born Aug. 6, 1835. *See Trotter family.* They had one child, JAMES E., and Mrs. Long died March 21, 1856. T. W. Long was married May 15, 1864, to Harriet Logan, a native of Ohio. They had one child, FLORA B., and Mrs. Long died Jan. 6, 1871. Mr. Long was Deputy Sheriff of Christian county in 1863 and '64, and is now keeping the Long House in Taylorville, Illinois.

GEORGE W., born March 3, 1833, in Sangamon county, married in Taylorville, June 22, 1852, to Sarah J. Stockdale, a native of Kentucky. They had one child, WILLIAM F., and Mrs. Sarah Long died April 2, 1861. Mr. Long was married in 1871, to Millie Tickle, a native of New York State. They have one child, FLORENCE E., and reside in Taylorville, Illinois.

ELIZABETH A., born Aug. 27, 1835, in Sangamon county, married in Taylorville, Oct. 2, 1861, to Charles A. Manners, who was born Aug. 2, 1827, in Somerset county, New Jersey. His mother was a Stout, a descendant of "Penelope." *See Stout family.* Her own name was Penelope, also. Mr. Manners came to Christian county, and settled in Taylorville, July, 1851. He was county surveyor from 1852 to '54, and then was appointed Government surveyor in Kansas and Nebraska, and was there from 1855 to '60. He was then elected sheriff, in 1862, in Christian county for one term, since which time he has been engaged in the construction of railroads and farming. They have two children, FRANCES C. and TOM, who reside with their parents, in Taylorville, Illinois.

BENJAMIN F. and *FRANCIS M.*, twins, born Oct. 21, 1837, in Rochester, Sangamon county.

BENJAMIN F. married in Taylorville, April 17, 1862, to Eliza Rice, of Kentucky. They have one child, VIRGINIA, and reside in Taylorville.

FRANCIS M. was Captain of Co. G, 41st Ill. Inf., was promoted to Major, at Memphis, in 1862. Was wounded at Jackson, Miss., July 12, 1863, from which he died the sixteenth of the same month.

Thomas Long was Major in the Black Hawk war—first campaign. He left Springfield as Captain, and was elected Major, at Beardstown, and commanded what was known as Long's Odd Batalion. He died July 13, 1875, in Taylorville. His widow still resides there—1876.

LOGAN, JAMES M., born Sept. 22, 1815, in Bourbon county, Ky. He came to Springfield in May, 1840, and was married April, 27, 1843, near Rochester, to Elizabeth W. Bowling. She was born Sept. 22, 1818. They had five children, two of whom died young.

NANCY M., born March 31, 1845, in Springfield, married Jan. 2, 1868, to Samuel F. Ridgeway. *See his name.*

JAMES C. and *COLUMBIA J.*, twins, were born June 2, 1848, in Springfield.

—59

JAMES C. was married Dec. 3, 1873, in Marysville, California, to Libbie Wilbur. They have one child, JAMES W., and reside in Oroville, Butte county, California.

COLUMBIA J. was married in Springfield Dec. 7, 1871, to Isaac C. Preston, of Maryland. They live in Essex, Page county, Iowa.

James M. Logan resides in Springfield.

LOGAN, STEPHEN T., was born Feb. 24, 1800, in Franklin county, Ky. His parents moved to Lincoln county in 1802. Stephen T. attended school at Frankfort, and became a clerk in the office of the Secretary of State, under Martin D. Hardin, the father of Col. John J. Hardin, who fell at the battle of Buena Vista, Mexico, in 1846. Although Stephen T. Logan was but thirteen years old at the time, it so happened that in the discharge of his duties he issued all the commissions to the officers under Governor and Gen. Shelby in his campaign to the northern frontier in the war of 1812. The office of the Secretary of State was kept in the third story of the capitol, which was burned soon after, and S. T. Logan came very near being burned with it. In 1817 he went to Glasgow, Ky., studied law and practiced there. He was married in Glasgow, in June, 1823, to America T. Bush, who was born there in 1806. They had four children in Glasgow, two of whom died young. Mr. Logan moved his family to Springfield, Ill., arriving May 16, 1832. They had four children in Springfield. Their children were two sons and four daughters. Both sons and two daughters are dead.

Mrs. America T. Logan died Feb. 24, 1868, and Stephen T. Logan resides in Springfield. He has lived in the same house forty years.

Stephen T. Logan was elected Judge of a circuit that included about one-fourth of the State. After serving a short time, he resigned in 1837. He was again elected, in 1839, without his consent, but resigned in a few weeks, both times because he could not live on the salary, and could do better by private practice. Judge Logan served four terms in the State Legislature, and was a member of the State Constitutional Convention of 1847. early in life he established a reputation as one of the most able lawyers in the country, and long enjoyed a lucrative practice. He retired several years ago, and is now in his seventy-seventh year. He was at one time a partner with Abraham Lincoln. Success never affected him injuriously. His whole life has been plain and unostentatious.

LOGSDON, JOSEPH, was born about 1780, in Madison county, Ky. He was there married to a Miss Simmons. They had several children born in Kentucky, and moved to Sangamon county, Ill., arriving in 1824, in what is now Ball township, near where St. Bernard church now stands. In 1832 or '33, he moved his family to Missouri, and from there to Texas. He died in 1848 on his road from Texas to California. He is particularly remembered in the vicinity of St. Bernard church from the fact that the first religious services ever conducted by a Catholic priest in Sangamon county was held at his house, in 1829.

LOOSE, JACOB G., born about 1812, in Washington county, Penn., and came to Springfield, Ill., in 1836 or '7. He was married in Springfield, Dec. 18, 1845, to Elizabeth Iles. They had ten children in and near Springfield, three of whom died young. Of the other seven children—

SALLIE C., born Dec. 25, 1848, in Springfield, was married, Jan. 9, 1865, to Junius D. Crabb, a native of Harrison county, Ohio. They have five children, and reside adjoining Springfield on the south.

JESSIE V., born Nov. 2, 1850, in Springfield, was married there, Feb. 7, 1872, to Dr. Jacob S. Price, who was born in Kentucky. They have two children, and reside in Springfield, Illinois.

JOSEPH I., FRANK E., GEO. PASFIELD, ROBERT D. and ELIZABETH, the five latter live with their mother.

Jacob G. Loose died Nov. 4, 1874, and his widow and children reside two miles southwest of the State House, Springfield, Illinois.

When Mr. Loose came to Springfield, he first engaged as clerk in a dry goods store, and later engaged in business on his own account, at one time in partnership with Col. John Williams, again with E. B. Hawley. He afterwards purchased land and engaged in farming and stock raising, which he continued until he became the owner of seventeen hundred acres of land adjoining Springfield, south and southwest. Becoming satisfied that his land contained coal, he made arrangements with Mr. P. L. Howlett, who was then boring for coal at Riverton, to use his machinery, but afterwards decided not to wait, and sent to the oil regions of Pennsylvania, obtained a complete outfit, and commenced boring in June, 1866. He bored down to coal, satisfied himself that it would pay to mine it, and commenced sinking a shaft in September. He commenced taking coal from the shaft in April, 1867, being the first shaft within fifteen miles of Springfield to supply the market with coal. The mine is 237 feet deep, reaching a bed of coal five feet ten inches in thickness. The entire cost when first fitted up, including steam engine, hoisting machinery, etc., was eighty thousand dollars. The mine is at the junction of the C. & A., and the T. W. & W. railroads, two miles south of the State house, and is yet owned by his heirs. This was only the beginning of the development of the underground treasures of Sangamon county. There are now—1876—seven shafts in the county.

LYMAN, JOHN, was born Apr. 2, 1780, at Lebanon, New Hampshire. The Lyman family in America trace their origin to Richard Lyman, of High Ongar, near London, England, who emigrated to America in 1631, and settled at Northampton, Mass. He had three sons, one of whom, Richard, removed to Lebanon, N. H. He had five sons, Ebenezer, Thomas, David, John and Richard. John was married in 1731 to Hannah Burchard. They had one child, Mary, and Mrs. Lyman died. He married in 1747 to Mary Strong. They had one daughter and six sons. Four of their sons, John, Abel, Elijah and Josiah, moved to Brookfield, Vermont. Abel had six sons, five of whom—John, Azel, Alvan, Ezra and Cornelius—emigrated to Sangamon county, Illinois. It was the latter John whose name heads this sketch. He was married Nov. 13, 1864, at Lebanon, New Hampshire, to Martha Storrs, a native of that town. They made their home at Randolph, Vermont, until they had two living children. He was, meantime, privately studying medicine, and took his family to his father's house at Brookfield, while he attended medical lectures at Dartmouth college. Having completed his studies about 1808, he commenced practice at New Haven township, Vt. During the war of 1812, he was part of the time surgeon in the United States army, and was stationed at Swanton, Vt. In 1817, he removed to Williston, Vt., and in 1824 to Potsdam, N. Y. In 1832 he and his brother, Azel, traveled over the Western country; and in the fall of 1833, in company with fifty-two persons, including his four brothers, he removed to Sangamon county, and settled on Prairie creek, in what is now Gardner township, nine miles northwest of Springfield. They were eight weeks on the road, and observed the fourth commandment by resting every Sabbath and assembling for divine worship, which was conducted by Rev. Billious Pond, who fell in with the company at Oswego, N. Y. Dr. John Lyman and wife had eight children, three of whom died young. Of the other five—

HENRY P., born Aug. 10, 1805, at Randolph, Orange county, Vt., married Aug. 7, 1833, at Madrid, St. Lawrence county, N. Y., to Mercy Sanders, who was born Dec. 4, 1805, at Bethel, Windsor county, Vt. They started soon after marriage to Sangamon county, arriving in the fall of 1833. They had four children in Sangamon county, namely: CALISTA M., born July 14, 1834, married March 5, 1864, to R. C. Curtis, and resides in Waverly, Illinois. JOHN STORRS, born July 31, 1841, enlisted Aug. 9, 1862, for three years, in Co. G, 101st Ill. Inf.; served to the end of the rebellion, and was honorably discharged June 22, 1865, at Springfield. He was married Sept. 13, 1870, to Mary Carrie Happer, who was born July 26, 1849, in Sangamon county. They have two children, EDWARD H. and NELLIE C., and reside one and three-quarters miles northwest of Farmingdale—1876. SARAH A., born Jan. 16, 1844, married Aug. 15, 1865, to Rev. James D. Kerr. They have three children, HARRY P., JAMES M. and RALPH C., and reside at Nebraska City, Neb. He is pastor of the First Presbyterian church there—1876. GEORGE H., born Oct. 4, 1850, married Jan. 16, 1873, to Emelie Stewart, and resides at Carmi, Ill.

—July, 1876. Henry P. Lyman and his wife reside at Farmingdale, Sangamon county, Illinois—1876.

HANNAH, born Sept. 16, 1807, at Randolph, Vt., married Stephen Child. See his name.

BENJAMIN RUSH, born March 10, 1815, at New Haven, Vt., married in Sangamon county Dec., 1837, to Eliza Estabrook. They had three children, and Mr. Lyman died Feb. 16, 1847, in Sangamon county. His widow married Seth Child, and moved to Manhattan, Kansas, taking two of her children. Her son, LEWIS J. LYMAN, went there later, and is now—1876—a practicing physician at St. George, Pottawattomie county, Kansas.

MARTHA, born March, 1817, married Lewis Judd, and died Dec., 1835, in Madison county, Illinois.

LAURA, born Jan. 14, 1819, married Augustin Curtis, and died Aug., 1847, at Waverly, Ill., leaving one daughter, LAURA, who married Wm. Brown, and died Jan., 1870. Mr. Brown lives in Waverly, Illinois.

Mrs. Martha Lyman died March 8, 1862, and Dr. John Lyman died Aug. 4, 1865, after one hour's illness. Both died near Farmingdale, Sangamon county.

LYMAN, AZEL, was born Aug. 1, 1784, at Lebanon, Conn., and was taken by his parents two years later, to Brookfield, Vt. He was married in 1808, in Randolph, Vt., to Roxana Fisk, who was born there, Dec. 12, 1788. They moved to Potsdam, N. Y., in 1810, had three living children, and Mrs. Lyman died there, June 7, 1829. He was married in 1830 at Potsdam, to Mary P. Bates, who was born there, Feb. 2, 1809. They moved to Sangamon county with his four brothers, arriving in 1833, at what is now Farmingdale They had eight children, six of whom were born in Sangamon county. Four only of their children are living. Of his children—

AZEL S., born in New York, married in Cincinnati, Ohio, raised a family, and resides in New York City. He invented a way of making paper from wood, a refrigerating vessel and a historical chart, all of which are valuable.

ROXANA, married, and died in Chicago about the time of the great fire.

MARY is unmarried, and resides with her brother, Azel S., in New York City. She was educated in Jacksonville by Rev. Theron Baldwin.

By the second wife—

ELLEN, born April 2, 1831, in Potsdam, N. Y., married in Sangamon county, May 1, 1852, to S. Simonson, who was born March 22, 1824, in Norway. They have one child, and reside at Green Valley, Tazewell county, Illinois.

THERON B. married Miss Mundy, has three children, and lives in Tallula, Menard county.

ALMYRA, married, has two children, and resides with her mother.

OTTO married and resides near Green Valley Postoffice, Tazewell county.

Azel Lyman died Jan. 3, 1873, near Delavan, Ill., and his widow resides there. The family moved from Sangamon to Tazewell county in 1852. Azel Lyman was an active Sunday school worker. He established Sunday schools in thirty-five counties of Illinois.

LYMAN, ALVAN, born Mch. 5, 1786, at Brookfield, Vt. He was married, February, 1813, at Royalton, Vt., to Lucy Perrin, who was born there Dec. 22, 1790. They became acquainted in St. Lawrence county, N. Y., and returned to Vermont to be married. They had two children born and died in St. Lawrence county, N. Y., and moved with a colony of fifty persons to Sangamon county, arriving in the fall of 1833 near Farmingdale. Mr. Lyman helped to haul the silver coin from Alton to Springfield, to establish the State Bank of Illinois. He arrived with one of four loads of coin, July 4, 1835. Alvan Lyman lived thirty-three years in Sangamon county, and died September, 1866, near Farmingdale. His widow resides with her niece, Mrs. T. H. Ferry, four miles southwest of Pleasant Plains.—1874.

LYMAN, EZRA, born Feb. 23, 1789, at Brookfield, Vt. He went to Potsdam, N. Y., in May, 1809, and in 1811 went back to Brookfield, Vt., and was married to Mercy Cushman. They made their home in Potsdam, until four children were born, one of whom, BETSY, died at three years of age, and the family moved to Sangamon county, Ill., in 1833, with a colony, and settled in what is now Gardner township. Of their children—

EZRA C., born May 19, 1814, in Potsdam, N. Y., married in Sangamon county, March 28, 1840, to Caroline Van Patten. They had eight children in Sangamon county. ALVAN, born June 23, 1842, died, aged seven years. HANNAH H., born Oct. 14, 1844, married, Nov. 15, 1863, to Thomas H. Earnest. See his name. MARY E., born Feb. 23, 1846, married, Dec. 12, 1867, to Robert Morris, a native of New Jersey. They have two children, ETTIE C. and WILLIAM E., and reside near Maroa, Macon county. CORNELIUS, born Oct. 14, 1849. CUSHMAN, born Oct. 21, 1851. ALVAN, born Jan. 31, 1853. JOHN D., born Oct. 7, 1856. LAURA A., born Oct. 16, 1858; the five latter reside with their parents, near Maroa, Macon county, Ill., where they moved from Sangamon county in 1874.

MERCY S., born May 19, 1820, in New York, married in Sangamon county to Jeremiah D. Low. (He was one of the fifty-two colonists, and was a teacher.) They had three children—CORNELIA A. died in St. Louis, aged eleven years. LAURA T., born July 16, 1848, and CHARLES H., born Oct. 11, 1851, reside with their parents, in Chicago.

ZERVIAH H., born about 1831, is unmarried, and resides with her brother, Ezra C.

Ezra Lyman died, Oct. 1, 1851, and Mrs. Mercy Lyman died in 1864, both in Sangamon county.

LYMAN, CORNELIUS, was born August 10, 1792, in Brookfield, Vt. He was there married, about 1814, to Betsy Cushman, and moved to Potsdam, N. Y., where they had two children. The family moved to Clinton county, and from there to Sangamon county, Ill., in 1833, as part of the colony of fifty-two persons. After residing in Sangamon county many years, they moved to Minnesota with the first emigration, and settled at St. Croix Lake. Of their two sons—

CORNELIUS S., born in 1816, in New York, married at Chatham, Sangamon county, to Emily Kincaid. They have a large family, and reside near Stillwater, Minn.

DAVID P., born in New York, married in Sangamon county to Ann J. Hannah. They have a family, and reside near Stillwater, or Marine Mills, Minn.

Cornelius Lyman died Jan. 31, 1864, and his widow died, both near Stillwater, Minn.

LYON, HENSON, was born July 28, 1790, in Loudon county, Va., was taken by his parents about 1800 to Clark county, Ky. Nancy McCann was born Jan. 8, 1795, in Clark county, and they were there married Aug. 10, 1814. They moved to Shelbyville, where they had nine children, and the family moved to Sangamon county, Ill., arriving Oct., 1834, in what was then called Portland, south of the Sangamon river, and seven miles northeast of Springfield, where one child was born. In March, 1835, they moved to a farm, two and one-half miles east of Springfield. Of their ten children—

HARRISON D., born May 7, 1815, in Shelbyville, Ky., married in Sangamon county April 6, 1843, to Mary E. Hickman. They had four living children. MARY E. lives with her parents. WILLIAM H. married March 12, 1874, to Sarah A. Day, a native of New York, and resides three miles northeast of Springfield. EUCLID F. and JAMES F. reside with their parents, three and one-half miles northeast of Springfield.

LUCINDA M., born Feb. 20, 1818, in Shelbyville, Ky., married there to Clifton L. Burge, and came to Sangamon county in 1836. She died July 27, 1860, leaving three children in Sangamon county. GEORGE W. married in Springfield to Martha Clarke, and lives in Ottawa, Kansas. SOPHRONIA E. married in Kansas to Willis P. Broadwell, and lives in Rockport, Boone county, Mo. CLIFTON L., Jun., lives in Ottawa, Kansas.

JAMES O., born Oct. 15, 1821, in Kentucky, died, unmarried, in Springfield, Feb. 5, 1860.

HESTER A. R., born Nov. 13, 1823, in Kentucky, married in Sangamon county to James S. Dawson. They have seven children, and live near Paris, Mo.

ELIZABETH M., born June 21, 1825, in Kentucky, married in Sangamon county to Morgan Mace, and live near Ironton, Mo.

HARVEY M., born Feb. 25, 1827, in Ky., died Oct. 22, 1859, unmarried, in Springfield.
BENJAMIN N., born Oct. 26, 1829, in Kentucky, died, unmarried, in Springfield, Sept. 5, 1857.
EUCLID F., born Sept. 27, 1830, in Kentucky, died, unmarried, near Springfield, Feb. 22, 1848.
THOMAS L., born Sept. 28, 1832, in Kentucky, died, unmarried, at the house of his brother, Harrison D., Aug. 16, 1866.
CLIFTON B., born Jan. 15, 1835, in Sangamon county, died, unmarried, near Springfield, Feb. 21, 1857.

Mrs. Nancy Lyon died Dec. 5, 1845, and Henson Lyon died Sept. 29, 1867, both near Springfield.

LYON, TALBOTT, was born in 1805, in Shelby county, Ky. He came to the house of his uncle, Henson Lyon, in Sangamon county, in 1834. He married Elizabeth Fullinwider; had six children, and she died; and he married Eliza Correll, had four children, and he died Sept., 1845. His children are all dead, and his widow married, and lives in Atchison, Kansas.

LYON, ELIZABETH, sister to Talbott, born Dec. 21, 1823, in Shelby county, Ky., came to Sangamon county in 1840, married George T. Hickman. *See his name.*

LYNN, JAMES, was born Feb. 24, 1788, in Rowan county, N. C. In 1809 he went to Muhlenberg county, Ky., and when the war between the United States and England commenced, in 1812, he enlisted in a regiment at Russelville, Ky., and served eighteen months. He was severely wounded by a gunshot in Canada. After leaving the army he returned to Muhlenberg county, Ky. Sarah DePoyster was born April 29, 1795, in Iredell county, N. C. When she was a child her parents moved to Butler county, Ky. James Lynn and Sarah DePoyster were married Nov. 27, 1814, in Butler county, and at once visited his parents in North Carolina, remaining one year, and in the fall of 1815 moved to Barren county, Ky., where they had four children, and moved to Sangamon county, Illinois, arriving in the fall of 1825, at the north end of Buffalo Hart Grove. Mrs. Lynn says that the country looked so new and wild, it required three days to look around and consult before they could decide to unload their wagons. Her husband would willingly have gone back, but she would not consent to it. Indians were very numerous, but never did them any harm. They had four children in Sangamon county. Of their eight children—

MARY ANN, born Nov. 7, 1816, in Kentucky, married in Sangamon county, Feb. 28, 1840, to Garrett Laughlin. They had eight children. JAMES H., born Dec. 6, 1842, and JOHN W., born Nov. 1, 1845, are unmarried, and reside with their parents. SARAH J., born April 9, 1848, married April 9, 1870, to Alexander McMurray, who was born in 1843, in county Donegal, Ireland. She died Sept. 29, 1873. ISABEL, born March 14, 1850, married Jan. 13, 1869, to Samuel Remines, have two children, MINNIE and MARY. WILSON D., GEORGE P., GARRET F. and EMMA C.—the four latter live with their parents, half a mile southwest of Cornland, in Sangamon county.

R. PERRY, born July 20, 1819, in Barren county, Ky., raised in Sangamon county, married May, 1865, at Sedalia, Mo., to Emily Dickson, a native of Arkansas. They had three children; two died in infancy. CATHARINE lives with her parents at the homestead settled by his father in 1825, near Buffalo Hart Station, Sangamon county, Illinois.

CALYOU JANE, born Feb. 2, 1822, in Kentucky, married March, 1868, in Sangamon county, to William Beck. They live in Vernon county, Mo., near Appleton, Kansas.

JOHN W., born May 24, 1824, in Barren county, Ky., raised in Sangamon county, married Aug. 5, 1858, to Sarah Matthews, at Decatur, although they both lived at the time in Sangamon county. She was born Sept. 14, 1835, in Clermont county, Ohio. They had eight children; two died in infancy. LUE BELLE died March 23, 1871, in her twelfth year. The other five, ALICE A., SARAH F., CLARA D., MARY E. and ADA MARIA live with their parents, two and a half miles east of Buffalo Hart Station, Sangamon county, Illinois.

MARTHA, born Dec. 29, 1826, in Sangamon county, died Sept. 25, 1830.

SUSAN, born Feb. 2, 1829, in Sangamon county, married Feb., 1851, to Lewis Dyer. They have five children, and live in Vernon county, Mo., near Appleton, Kansas.

SARAH F., born May 4, 1834, in Sangamon county, married Sept., 1857, to Monroe Lynn, have one child, LAURA, and live at Niantic, Illinois.

MARIA K., born Sept. 22, 1836, married Feb., 1867, to John G. Lynn, and died June 11, 1870, in Missouri.

James Lynn died March 11, 1860. He carried the musket ball received in 1814, in Canada, in his flesh to the grave. His widow resides—1874—with her son, R. Perry Lynn, on the farm where herself and husband settled in 1825. It is half a mile northeast of Buffalo Hart Station.

M

MALLORY, VALENTINE R., was born Dec. 16, 1798, near Paris, Bourbon county, Ky. He was a soldier in the war of 1812, and was at the battle of the river Thames. Nancy Dawson was born Sept. 20, 1802, in Fairfax county, Va., and in 1804 was taken by her parents to Bracken county, Ky. V. R. Mallory and Nancy Dawson were there married, June 28, 1821. They had three children, and in March, 1827, united with the Baptist church. They moved, in company with her brother, John Dawson (*see his name*) to Sangamon county, Illinois, arriving Oct. 22, 1827, in what is now Clear Lake township, where they had six children. Of all their children—

WILLIAM A., was born Oct. 25, 1822, in Bracken county, Ky. At nineteen years of age he commenced teaching school, and reading medicine, first under Dr. John Todd, of Springfield, then at Laporte, Ind. His first practice was at Beloit, Wisconsin, one year. He spent some time at Louisville Medical College, in 1846, and Cincinnati Eclectic Medical College, in 1847, and located at Fort Madison, Iowa, in 1848. He was married at Denmark, five miles from Fort Madison, Lee county, Iowa, June 6, 1848, to Susan A. Johnson, who was born Feb. 21, 1824, at Bedford, Penn., of Scotch parents. Dr. Mallory and his wife had one child in Iowa, and returned to Illinois. He commenced practice, in Springfield, Dec. 21, 1849. In Aug., 1852, he commenced publishing the *Christian Sentinel*. It was sold to Eureka College, in February, 1856. March 20, 1856, he went into the employ of the Illinois State Christian Association, preaching and teaching at Pittsfield and Rushville, and then to the churches in Sangamon and Menard counties, until the beginning of the rebellion, when he resumed the practice of medicine in Clear Lake township. In June, 1862, he was commissioned, by Governor Yates, as a recruiting officer, which culminated in the organization of the 114th Ill. Inf. Dr. Mallory became Captain of Co. C, at the organization of the regiment. He served until Sept. 11, 1863, when he resigned on account of ill health. On recovering, he resumed practice, preaching and Sunday school work, at Howlett, now Riverton. Dr. Mallory and his wife had two children in Sangamon county. Of their three children—ROLLIN V., born March 26, 1849, at West Point, Lee county, Iowa, married in Sangamon county, Sept., 1872, to Miranda Cantrall. They have one child, WILLIAM C., and live at Cantrall, Sangamon county. ALEXANDER J., born Apr. 28, 1857, and INA SUE, born March 16, 1863, reside with their parents, near Riverton, and within half a mile of where his parents settled, in 1827.

JOHN T., born April 27, 1825, in Bracken county, Ky., married in Sangamon county, April, 1847, to Elizabeth Myers. They had two children—CLARENCE A. married Mary Strode, and reside in Fancy Creek township. HERP L. is unmarried, and resides in Abilene, Kansas—1874. Mrs. Elizabeth Mallory died in Macon county. J. T. Mallory married Mrs. Ellen Simpson, whose maiden name was Holden. They have seven children, and live near Ottawa, Franklin county, Kansas.

ELIZABETH, born May 28, 1827, in Bracken county, Ky., married in Sangamon county, Jan. 8, 1857, to John C. Anderson, who was born Dec. 2, 1833, near Bloomington, Ind. They had three children, ELIJAH H., CLARA M. and JOHN C. Mr. Anderson died Dec. 6, 1860, near Williamsville. His widow and children reside with her mother, near Riverton.

REUBEN, born Sept. 7, 1829, in Sangamon county, married, April, 1854, to Mary J. Nesbitt. They have seven children, and reside near Buffalo, Wilson county, Kansas.

EGBERT O., born Dec. 21, 1831, in Sangamon county, married, August, 1858, to Nancy A. Cantrall. They have five children. E. O. Mallory enlisted July, 1862, in Co. I, 114th Ill. Inf., for three years. He was elected Lieutenant at the organization of the company, promoted to Captain, in 1863; served as such to the end of the rebellion, and was honorably mustered out, at Springfield, in 1865. He moved to Knox county, Mo., and was elected Judge of the County Court of that county, and now resides near Greensburg, Missouri.

ELIZA F., born Sept. 15, 1834, in Sangamon county, married G. W. Brittin. See his name. He died, and she married Thomas Glascock. See his name.

NANCY D., born Sept. 17, 1836, in Sangamon county, married Henry Britin. See his name.

JAMES D., born May 9, 1839, in Sangamon county, married April 25, 1861, to Frances P. Cantrall. They have two children, HENRY E. and EDWIN O. James D. Mallory enlisted July 25, 1862, for three years, in Co. I, 114th Ill. Inf., and was elected orderly Sergeant at the organization of the company. He was taken prisoner at the battle of Guntown, June 10, 1864, was in hospital one month at Mobile, and in Andersonville prison from August 1 to Sept. 13; while there he saw the inhuman rebel, Gen Winder, fall dead, from either heart disease or apoplexy. Mr. Mallory was sent to Charleston and kept three weeks under the fire of the Union artillery while the bombardment was progressing. He saw a Union soldier who tried to escape, hung by the thumbs with a small cord and drawn up until his feet barely touched the ground. He was whirled around until circulation ceased, and he was dead in fifteen minutes. He was sent from Charleston to Florence in Oct., 1864, remaining five months. Rations was half a pint of corn meal, corn and cob ground together, and half a pint of peas. Had one small ration of meat soon after entering, and no more until March, 1865, when six cows heads were sent in with the tongues and brains taken out. He was hospital steward at the time, and issued them himself. At Florence a soldier had no blanket, and when he asked for one he was tied up and whipped one hundred lashes by a New York tough named Stanton, under direction of the prison authorities. The soldier lived through it. Stanton received some favor for it, but was watched and killed at Annapolis, Md. When Sherman's army approached the prison in March, 1865, Mr. Mallory was among those who were too much emaciated to march, and was released, paroled, and fell into the hands of the Union soldiers. J. D. Mallory resides in Clear Lake township, near Riverton, Sangamon county, Illinois.

MARK C., born Jan. 16, 1844, in Sangamon county, married Nov. 28, 1869, in Menard county, to Emily Jordan. They live near Olathe, Johnson county, Kansas.

Valentine R. Mallory died Nov. 21, 1864, and his widow resides on the farm where they settled in 1827. It is three miles southeast of Riverton, formerly Howlett, and previous to that Jamestown, Sangamon county, Illinois.

MALONE.—Three brothers of that name were among the early settlers of Sangamon county, namely:

JOHN W. was born about 1816 near Richmond, Va.; was taken by his parents to McMinn county, Tenn., in 1824; went to Brown county, Ill., about 1832; was married there to Caroline Phillips, and moved to Springfield in 1834. They had five children in Springfield, and moved to St. Louis, where Mr. Malone died. His widow resides near Mt. Sterling, Brown county. Her son, Joseph Malone, is a dentist, and practiced in Springfield. He is now practicing at Mt. Sterling, Brown county, Illinois.

JESSE J., born Jan. 21, 1818, near Richmond, Va., moved to McMinn county, Tenn., in 1824; came to Sangamon county about 1836; went to Crawford county, Mo., two years later; there married May 3, 1842, to Harriet Patton; returned to Sangamon county in 1846; practiced medicine in Chatham; moved to Waverly, Ill., and died there of cholera, July 15, 1851. His widow returned to her friends in Missouri. Their daughter, MARY F., married George W. Trumbo. See his name. LAURA married Hugh

M. Frazier, and lives near Monticello, Mo. CHARLES F. is unmarried. Mrs. Harriet Malone married in Missouri, April 12, 1855, to Benjamin Ruggles. Had two children, JOHN C. and WILLIAM N., and Mr. Ruggles died in 1868. Mrs. Ruggles resides with her daughter, Mrs. Trumbo, eight miles south of Springfield, Illinois—1874.

ALFRED C., born March 23, 1822, near Richmond, Va., was taken by his parents to McMinn county, Tenn., and came to Springfield Sept. 2, 1840. He was married Sept. 18, 1845, to Amanda M. Bridges. They had ten living children in Sangamon county, namely: WILLIAM B., EMMA J., LOUISA D., MARTHA E., MIRANDA E., AMANDA R., MARIA E., CHARLES E., MARY J. C. and ALBERT H. reside with their parents, in the northeast corner of Chatham township, one and a half miles north of Chatham, Sangamon county, Illinois.

MALTBY, JOSIAH, was born in 1779, in Connecticut. Mary McArthur was born in 1783 in New Hampshire. They were married in Orange county, Vt., moved to Oneida and Tioga counties, N. Y., and came to Sangamon county, Ill., in 1822, on Spring creek. Their daughter—

SARAH, married Sylvanus Massie. See his name.

Mrs. Mary Maltby died in 1827, and Josiah Maltby died Jan., 1841; she in Sangamon, and he in Brown county, Illinois.

MANN, CHRISTOPHER C., born Jan. 2, 1819, in Bracken county, Ky., came to Sangamon county later than his brother, Uriah. He was married in Sangamon county Nov. 10, 1843, to Ann R. King. They had six children, namely—

HENRY F., born Nov. 10, 1844. He went from Springfield and enlisted in Chicago June 17, 1861, in Co. E, 24th Ill. Inf., for three years. He was captured by John Morgan at Pulaski, Tenn., in 1862, and escaped in about twenty-four hours. He was slightly wounded at Rocky Face Ridge, Ga., in May, 1862; served until Aug. 6, 1864, when he was honorably discharged at Chicago. He was married Jan. 30, 1868, in Sangamon county, to Jeanetta Snodgrass, who was born Dec. 22, 1848. They have three children,

LUAMMA, MARETHA J. and CHARLES E., and reside seven miles east of Springfield, in Clear Lake township.

WILLIAM, born July 9, 1847, enlisted Aug., 1862, in Co. I, 114th Ill. Inf., for three years; served until the suppression of the rebellion, and was honorably discharged at Springfield. He lives at Carthage, Missouri.

MARY, born Nov. 25, 1849, married Oct. 1, 1869, to John Huffman in Sangamon county. They have two children, and live at Carthage, Missouri.

ALICE J., born April 28, 1852, married April 2, 1869, to John B. Allen; have three children, and live at Carthage, Missouri.

MARETHA, born Oct. 17, 1853, married May 11, 1872, to James Farley, who was born May 14, 1845, in county Dublin, Ireland, and raised in Louisville, Ky. They have one child, GLENARA, and reside at Riverton, Sangamon county, Illinois—1874.

EMILY E., born Sept. 6, 1857, married Dec. 24, 1873, to Franklin Steele, and reside at Riverton, Illinois.

Christopher C. Mann died Jan. 31, 1859, and his widow resides at Riverton, Sangamon county, Illinois.

MANN, URIAH, was born Sept. 17, 1810, in Bracken county, Ky. He came to Sangamon county with his sister, Anna, and her husband, Thomas A. King, arriving the first Sunday in Oct., 1831. He was a soldier in the Black Hawk war, in 1832, in the same regiment with Capt. Abraham Lincoln, with whom he had many a wrestling match. Uriah Mann was married Jan. 6, 1832, in Sangamon county, to Elizabeth King. They had seven children in Sangamon county, two of whom died young.

PETER, born July 23, 1833, married Sept. 17, 1854, to Carrie J. Knox. They had five living children. URIAH died Feb., 1870, in his ninth year. CLARENCE A., LUELLA B., ALLEN and OLIVER live with their parents, adjoining Camp Butler National Cemetery on the east.

SARAH A., born Jan. 27, 1836, married George W. Black. See his name.

THOMAS H., born April 6, 1843, in Sangamon county, enlisted Aug., 1862, for three years, in Co. I, 114th Ill. Inf. He was taken prisoner at the battle of Guntown, Miss., June 10, 1864; was ten months in Andersonville prison pen, exchanged about the close of the rebellion, and honorably discharged June 14, 1865, at Springfield, and died at home Feb. 16, 1867, of disease contracted in the rebel prison.

CHARLES V., born Dec. 26, 1846, lives with his father.

MARY F., born March 2, 1853, lives with her father.

Mrs. Elizabeth Mann died Sept. 9, 1861, and Uriah Mann was married Aug. 25, 1862, to Ellen Brimbarger, who was born Sept. 8, 1839, in Gallatin county, Ky. They had eight children. URIAH GRANT and ELIZABETH S., died in their seventh and third years, respectively. FANNIE B., BETTIE, ETHEL M., SONORA, PERCES ANN and RICHARD OGLESBY live with their parents, on the farm where Mr. Mann settled in 1835. It is five miles east of Springfield, adjoining Camp Butler.

Uriah Mann hauled all the rails and timber, for improving his farm, on a wagon constructed by himself, without any iron, the wheels being hewn each from a single piece of timber, from the largest tree he could find. His house was built by himself, of round logs. His tables, cupboard and other furniture were made from wild cherry lumber. In the absence of saw-mills, he split the timber into broad slabs, fastened them into a snatch block, hewed them to a uniform thickness, and after waiting a sufficient time for them to season, worked them into his household furniture. The first meal he ate in his own house, the meat was hog's jowl, and the bread made from frostbitten corn. He hauled the first wheat he raised for sale to St. Louis, and sold it for thirty-five cents in trade. He is now among the most successful farmers of the county.

MANN, MELINDA, born Aug., 1807, in Bracken county, Ky., married there to Thomas Threlkeld, had five children, and Mr. T. died. She married Wm. Summers, had two children, and he died. Mrs. Melinda Summers and her seven children all came to Sangamon county, arriving Oct. 20, 1847. Her daughter, Rebecca, married Stephen L Cooper. See his name.

MANN, ANN, born Jan. 1, 1813 in Bracken county, Ky., married Thomas A. King. See his name.

MANN, PETER, the father of Melinda, Uriah, Ann and Christopher was a soldier from Bracken county, Ky. in the war of 1812, and came near dying of disease in Canada. He returned to Kentucky and died there.

MARSH, WILLIAM H., was born Dec. 15 1804, in Lancaster county, Penn. He was married May 14, 1829 in the city of Lancaster, to Lydia Brady who was born April 7, 1810, in Chester county, Penn. They had two children and Mrs. Marsh died, July 24, 1833 Wm. H. Marsh was married, April 9 1835, to Mary Lytle, in Lancaster. She was born in that county March 17, 1808 The family moved to Sangamon county Ill., arriving May 16, 1837, at Springfield where four children were born. Of his six children—

LUCY A., born Sept. 2, 1830, in Lancaster county, Penn., married in Sangamon county, Aug. 26, 1857, to Mitchell Graham. See his name.

DEWITT C., born Oct. 21, 1832, in Lancaster county, Penn., married in Sangamon county, Aug. 29, 1855, to Harriet M. Bryant, and have four children, EVANGELINE M., MARY A., VIVI I. and JULIA A. Mrs. Marsh died, Dec. 29, 1869, and he married Rebecca Snyder, who was born July 24, 1836, in Bedford county, Penn. They have two children, CHARLES W. and WILLIAM D., and live one and one-half miles north of Springfield.

By the second marriage.

LYDIA C., born May 15, 1838, in Springfield, died March 10, 1854.

MARTHA A., born Aug. 13, 1840, in Springfield, married, Oct. 10, 1866, to Charles Reed. They have one child, MARY, and live at 1061, North 5th street, Springfield.

ISABEL, born April 17, 1842, in Springfield, lives with her father.

DELIA, born Sept. 7, 1845, in Springfield, married, Dec. 18, 1872, to Albert Jennings, and died, in Springfield, Aug. 9, 1873.

Mrs. Mary Marsh died, March 25, 1872, and Wm. H. Marsh resides two miles north of Springfield.

When Wm. H. Marsh came to Springfield, he was employed by the State House Commissioners as foreman in erecting that edifice, under direction of the architect. He was thus engaged, part of 1837, all of '38, and part of 1839. He was next employed as foreman on the abutments of the bridge at the Sangamon river, for the Northern Cross railroad, now the T. W. & W., road, at Riverton. When gold was discovered on the Pacific coast, he attempted to go to California, but became disabled at the Rocky mountains, and returned. He was keeper of the Sangamon county poor house for ten years, ending in the fall of 1859.

MARTIN, ABRAHAM, was born about 1787, in Kentucky, of parents from North Carolina. He was married in Kentucky, about 1807, to Melinda Lewis. They had three children in Kentucky, and moved to the vicinity of Bedford, Lawrence county, Ind., where nine children were born, and the family moved to Sangamon county, Ill., arriving in the fall of 1830, in what is now Cooper township, where one child was born. Of their children—

LEWIS, born in Kentucky, married in Indiana, moved with his father to Sangamon county, and after two years returned to Indiana, where his wife died; and he was married there to Mrs. Martha Stotts. In 1848, he came back to Sangamon county. He has five living children, nearly all married, and lives near Sharpsburg, Christian county. He had one son who served in the Union army through the rebellion.

MARGARET, born in Kentucky, married in Sangamon county to Henry Judy. They had five children, two of whom died young, and Mr. Judy died. The widow and two of her children live in Atchinson county, Kansas. She had two sons in the Union army, one of whom was killed while bearing a flag in battle; the other was since killed by an accident on a railroad.

JOHN, born in Kentucky, married Rachel Harvey. He died, and his widow and five children live in Christian county, Illinois.

SUSAN, born in Indiana, married in Missouri to David Driscoll. He died, Sept., 1845, leaving two children. Her son, LEWIS S. DRISCOLL, was a member of Co. D, 33d Ill. Inf., and died, at Ironton, Mo. His remains were buried in Cooper township. The widow has been twice married since; the last time to Hugh Turner. *See his name.*

SAMUEL, born in Indiana, raised and married in Sangamon county to Mary Bragg. They moved to Buchanan county, Mo., and from there went to the mouth of the Platt river, Neb., and in company with another man, laid out the town of Plattsmouth, where he died, in 1853, leaving a widow and three children by the first, and one by the second wife. He had two sons in the Union army.

JEFFERSON, born in Indiana, moved to Sangamon county, married in Mills county, Iowa, to Fidelia Clark, and died there, without children, June, 1864.

RACHEL, born in Indiana, raised in Sangamon county, married in Buchanan county, Mo., to James W. Berry. He died, leaving four children, and she married George L. Atwood, had one child, and died in Sangamon county. Two of her sons were in the Union army during the rebellion. One has since died, and the other is in the regular army.

MOSES, born in Indiana, raised in Sangamon county, married Mary J. Crull. They have eight children, and live in Bates county, Mo.

MESSENGER, born Feb. 22, 1833, in Sangamon county, married, Dec. 23, 1858, to Eliza Craig, who was born May 12, 1837, in Scotland. They have four living children, MARY M., SARAH J., AMANDA and SUSAN BELL, and reside on the farm where his parents settled in 1830, in Cooper township, near Breckenridge.

Abraham Martin moved, in 1839, to Buchanan county, Mo., and returned in 1845. Mrs. Melinda Martin died, Feb. 19, 1860, and Abraham Martin died, Oct. 24, 1864, both in Cooper township, Sangamon county, Illinois.

MARTIN, GEORGE, was born in 1805, in Hampshire county, Va., and was there married to Leah Fahs. They had two children, and moved to Licking county, Ohio, where one child was born; and then moved to Sangamon county, arriving in the spring of 1834, in German Prairie, and in 1836 moved to what is now Cotton Hill township, where three children were born. Of their six children—

MARGARET A., born in Virginia, died Feb. 19, 1849, in Sangamon county.

JOHN W., born Feb. 22, 1830, in Virginia, married in Sangamon county to Mary Wood. He died July 2, 1862.

JAMES M., born June 15, 1832, in Licking county, Ohio, married in Sangamon county Feb. 1, 1855, to Mary Williams. They had six children, four of whom died under six years. MARY F. and JAMES H. reside with their parents, in Cotton Hill township, near old Ricnzi, Sangamon county.

MARY C., born in Sangamon county, married David H. Stewart, and died.

MELINDA J., born in Sangamon county, died, aged ten or twelve years.

RACHEL L. died, aged three years.

George Martin died Oct. 25, 1841, and Mrs. Leah Martin died Aug. 8, 1860; both in Cotton Hill township.

MARTIN, WILLIAM, a brother to George Martin and Mrs. Milslagle, was born in Hampshire county, Va.; came to Sangamon county in 1834 or '35. He married Nancy Torrence. They had four children.

MARY J. married Edward George, and died.

SARAH E. married D. F. Chapman.

JOHN W. died young.

RACHEL married Melvin Bell. See his name.

Wm. Martin died, and his widow married John Adams.

MASON, JOHN A., born June 14, 1814, in Swanton, Franklin county, Vt. When quite young he went to Buffalo, N. Y., and there joined his brother, and came from there to Springfield, Ill., arriving May 20, 1837. He learned the business of a chair maker in Springfield, and from that worked into the manufacture of cabinet furniture. He retired from business in 1869, with ample means and impaired health. He is not yet married, and resides at Buffalo, Sangamon county, Illinois, but spends much of his time among his old friends in Springfield.

MASON, NOAH, was born Jan. 15, 1782, at Mendon, Worcester county, Mass. He was bound to a hard master, ran away, and followed the life of a sailor for about five years. Lucinda Stetson was born June 14, 1782, in Hanover, Plymouth county, Mass. They were married July 15, 1804. Soon after marriage Mr. Mason left on a voyage to China and the East Indies, and was absent twenty-one months. On his return they moved to the vicinity of Belfast, Hancock county, Maine, where they had three children. In 1812 he moved to Madison county, N. Y., thence to Genesee county, in the same State, in 1814, where two children were born. In the spring of 1819 he moved to Olean Point, on the Allegheny river, and in the autumn of 1821 united with two other families in building a boat, in which the three families descended the Allegheny and Ohio rivers, landing in Pope county, Illinois, where another son was born, and they called his name Seth. After remaining two and a half years, the family left for what is now Tazewell county, but on reaching Sugar creek, in what is now Auburn township, April 10, 1824, decided to settle there. Of the six children—

NOAH, Jun., born Feb. 25, 1807, fifteen miles from Belfast, Maine, married in Sangamon county, Feb. 19, 1835, to Martha Nuckolls. They had six children, and Mrs. Martha Mason died, Mar. 24, 1852. Noah Mason, Jun., was married Aug. 9, 1853, to Elizabeth Talbott. They had one child. Of all his children, GEORGE T., born Feb. 11, 1836, married June 9, 1861, to Anna Brooks. They have three children, and reside in Auburn township. JANE, born July 22, 1837, married William R. Hill, Oct. 8, 1858. They have four children, and reside in Auburn township. JOHN L., born March 15, 1839, has represented Chatham township for several years in the County Board of Supervisors. He was married May 4, 1876, in Springfield, Ill., to Mildred Harker, and resides one mile northwest of Auburn, Sangamon county, Illinois. MARY ANN, born Jan. 1, 1842, was married Jan. 1, 1861, to James M. Stout. See his name. AMANDA died, aged seven years. ELMINA E., born Oct. 4, 1847, was married April 25, 1866, to Ira Ryan. They have three children, and reside in Girard. MARTHA C., born April 11, 1849, was married May

30, 1872, to James P. Brasfield, have one child, NOAH W., and reside at Loami. NOAH D., the only child by the second wife, born Oct. 3, 1854, resides with his parents. Noah Mason, Jun, has met with some narrow escapes from death. He still exhibits a spot on his head, whiter than the rest, as the mark of a severe fall in childhood. Once, in New York, he accompanied his father to the woods, where he was clearing timber from the land, when the weather was extremely cold. Noah became sleepy and sat down under a tree. When his father's attention was called to him he could not be wakened. He was carried to the house, and with the utmost exertion of all the members of the family, he was aroused and his life saved. His first business transaction was in Pope county, Ill. He was paddling about in the Ohio river in a boat of his own building, when a stranger hailed him with "What will you take for your boat?" He replied, one dollar. The man handed him a two dollar bill, and Noah, with much running to and fro, returned the change, only to find, after his boat was gone, that the two dollar bill was a counterfeit. From childhood Mr. Mason has been remarkable for presence of mind. While the Mason family were at Olean Point, N. Y., on the Alleghany river, Noah was one day engaged in his favorite amusement of paddling about on a slab in the river, and had gone with the current some distance down the stream, when suddenly he heard a noise, and looking up he saw a tree falling towards him. He was a good swimmer, and quick as thought he jumped off his slab, diving to the bottom. He heard the tree splash in the water above him, and he came to the surface among its branches, unhurt. Again, his father, with another man, were felling trees, and the limb of one tree had lodged against a knot on another, balancing in mid-air. Noah was trimming the branches from those that had fallen, and unconsciously came under this loose limb, and it fell. He heard it coming, and threw himself down beside a large log, which the limb fell across, immediately over his head, and he escaped with only a fright. Again, he was hauling stakes for a fence, when he came to the deep ford on Sugar creek, Sangamon county. On driving in, the load slipped forward on the horses, and Noah landed on the wagon tongue. The The horses began kicking and running, and he thought his time had come; but he made one desperate jump, clearing the horses' heels and front wagon wheel, and landed head-first in the water. Fortunately he took the lines with him, which enabled him to stop the horses. When the Masons arrived in Sangamon county, horse-mills were the only kind in use; but soon other kinds were built. Nearly all the bread used was made from Indian corn. Mr. Mason, Sen., raised cotton for many years after coming to Sangamon county, and there were two cotton-gins built near him. The nearest carding machine was at Sangamo, and owned by a Mr. Broadwell. After the wool and cotton were carded, the different families manufactured their own cloth, and this constituted the wearing apparel of both males and females. Peaches were almost a sure crop, and Mr. Thomas Black had a copper still attached to his horse-mill; and Noah M., Jun., assisted him in making pure whisky from corn, and pure brandy from peaches. He also cut hickory wood for Mr. Black at thirty-seven and one-half cents per cord, and made rails the summer he was twenty-one years old, for thirty-seven and one-half cents per hundred, and cut corn in the fall, sixteen hills square, for five cents per shock or fifty cents per day. In this way he clothed himself, and had sixteen and one-half dollars—all in silver half dollars —when he started, with a number of others, March 19, 1829, for the Galena lead mines; was there six summers and two winters including the winter of the deep snow. Mr. Mason served in four different companies during the Black Hawk war. In 1834 he had five eighty-acre tracts of land, bought with money earned by himself in the lead mines. The prairie-flies were a great annoyance in summer, and in order to avoid them plowing among the corn was frequently done at night. Whisky was thought to be indispensable in early times in the harvest field, but Mr. Mason proved to the contrary. He threshed his wheat with horses, and cleaned it with a fanning mill. With the help of a boy, one season he prepared one load of wheat per week for four weeks, and sold it in Alton for forty cents per bushel. He has hauled wheat to St. Louis, selling it for thirty-eight cents per bushel. The merchants had their goods hauled on wagons from St. Louis and Chicago. Mr. Mason and nine others brought goods from the latter city for Mr. Bela Webster, of Springfield, at one dollar per hundred pounds, and were three weeks going and coming. Mr. Mason is one of the successful farmers of Sangamon county. He has retired from active business, and now—1876—resides in Springfield, Illinois.

LUCINDA, born July 24, 1809, in Maine, married in Sangamon county to B. F. Hutton. They reside in Chatham township, Sangamon county, Illinois.

THOMAS, born Aug. 2, 1812, in Maine, married in Sangamon county to Elizabeth Husband. They had four children, namely—NOAH died, aged sixteen years. EMILY married Jacob Brunk. *See his name.* ELIZABETH married William Epling, who was born in 1840, in Giles county, Va. They have two children, THEODORE ULYSSES and CHARLES W. Mr. Epling has recently brought from Virginia his two sisters, Adaline and Hesiltine, and his brother, John H. He resides three and one-half miles south of Chatham. WILLIAM T. married Nancy Dodds. They have one child, and live two miles northwest of Auburn, Illinois. Mrs. Elizabeth Mason died in 1851, and Thomas Mason died, Sept. 5, 1871, both in Sangamon county.

ELIZABETH, born Feb. 4, 1816, in New York, married in Sangamon county to Ezra Barnes. *See his name.*

CAROLINE, born Feb. 13, 1819, married in Sangamon county to Madison Curvey. They had four children, and Mrs. Curvey died in the spring of 1854. Her son, ORRIN, married Ann Roberts, and lives in Chatham township.

SETH, born Jan. 3, 1823, in Pope county, Ill., married, Aug. 21, 1851, to Eleanor Kent, who was born May 28, 1831, in Harrison county, Ohio. They have no family. Seth Mason resides on the farm where his father settled in 1824, in Auburn township. He has in his possession a trunk made of camphor wood which his father brought from China, with a set of table ware made to order there, with the initials of himself and wife (N. L. M.) on each piece. The chest was filled with silks and other rich goods.

Noah Mason, Sen., died, Nov. 18, 1831, and his widow died, October, 1862, both in Sangamon county, Illinois.

MASSIE, THOMAS, was born Dec. 26, 1759, in Albemarle county, Va. He was a Revolutionary soldier, for which he drew a pension near the close of his life. He went to Kentucky after the Revolution, and there became personally acquainted with Simon Kenton, one of the associates of Daniel Boone in the early settlement of Kentucky. Thomas Massie was married to Fanny Hudson, either in Kentucky or Virginia. They had four children, none of whom ever came to Sangamon county. Mrs. Fanny Massie died in Kentucky, and Thomas Massie married Rebecca Collyer, a native of Virginia, also. They had eight children, all born in Montgomery county, Ky., and the family moved to Sangamon county, Ill., arriving in 1828, in what is now Curran township. Of their eight children—

ABSALOM, born in Kentucky, married in Tennessee, and died there.

JOHN C., born Aug. 11, 1795, in Kentucky, married Aug. 13, 1815, in Tennessee, to Elizabeth Freeman. He moved to Sangamon county soon after his father, in 1828, and after a stay of five or six years, moved to Pike county, Ill., where Mrs. Massie died. Mr. Massie married again, and died there. His son, MELVIN MASSIE, was a Representative from Pike county, to the Legislature of 1873.

HUDSON, remained in Kentucky.

SYLVANUS, born Sept. 12, 1799, in Kentucky, married in Sangamon county, Aug. 11, 1829, to Sarah Maltby, and had seven children. He died, June 28, 1856, and his widow lives in Gardner township, Sangamon county.

FRANCES J., born June 25, 1802, married Wm. Ralston, Jun. *See his name.*

THOMAS, Jun., born in Kentucky, was educated as a physician, and died, unmarried, in Tennessee.

JESSE E., born in Kentucky, in 1810, is unmarried, and lives in Gardner township.

MARTHA, born Feb. 1, 1813, in Kentucky, married, July 14, 1829, to Thomas Morgan. *See his name.*

Thomas Massie, Sen., died, Aug. 19, 1835, and Mrs. Rebecca Massie died Sept. 7, 1835, both in Sangamon county.

SANGAMON COUNTY.

MATHENY, CHARLES R., born March 6, 1786, in Loudon county, Va. When a young man he visited his brother at Crab Orchard, Ky., and was there licensed to preach, by the proper authority, in the M. E. church. He went, in 1805, as missionary, under the auspices of that church, to that part of the North-Western territory which afterwards became St. Clair county, Ill. In addition to preaching he studied and practiced law. He was married in 1806, in St. Clair county, Ill. to Jemima Ogle, who was born in that county, Oct. 26, 1787. Her father, Captain Joseph Ogle, emigrated from Pennsylvania very early, and was a prominent actor in the Indian wars and other events connected with the early history of the country. Ogle county, in the northern part of Illinois, was named in honor of his memory. C. R. Matheny was elected in 1817, representative in the Territorial Legislature, which met at Kaskaskia, Ill., and was clerk of the House during the winters of 1820 and '21. C. R. Matheny and wife had seven children in St. Clair county, Ill., and when the law was enacted for the organization of Sangamon county, he was induced by the tender of the office of county clerk, county auditor, circuit clerk, and some other prospective advantages, to come to Springfield, arriving in the spring of 1821, where four children were born. Of their eleven children—

MARY, born April 13, 1837, in St. Clair county, was married in Springfield to Robert Thompson. *See his name.*

MATILDA, born August 29, 1809, in St. Clair county, was married in Springfield, Illinois, to Gershom Keyes. *See his name.*

LUCY, born Mar. 13, 1811, in St. Clair county, was married in Springfield to P. Asbury Sanders, who was born in Loudon county, Va., and came to Sangamon county in 1828. Mrs. Lucy Sanders died, Feb. 8, 1836, leaving one son, CHARLES M., who went to California in 1857, and was last heard from by his friends in Springfield in the Union army. P. A. Sanders married Margaret Ogden. They have two sons in Springfield.

LORENZO DOW, born March 25, 1813, in St. Clair county, Ill., studied medicine in Springfield, Ill., under Dr. J. M. Early, and served in the Black Hawk war. He graduated in the spring of 1836, in the medical department of Transylvania University, Lexington, Kentucky, the first native of Illinois to obtain that distinction, and the second citizen of Sangamon county to graduate in any medical college, Dr. Geo. M. Harrison being the first. *See his name.* Dr. L. D. Matheny had just engaged in the practice of medicine under flattering circumstances, when he died, Feb. 7, 1837, in Springfield, Illinois.

NOAH W., born July 31, 1815, in St. Clair county, Illinois. He assisted his father in the county clerk's office as soon as he could write. At his father's death Noah was appointed clerk *pro tem.*, by the county court, and in Nov., 1839, he was elected to fill the unexpired term of his father. He was afterwards elected for eight successive terms, of four years each. He was married in Springfield, August 22, 1843, to Elizabeth J. Stamper, daughter of the Rev. Dr. Jonathan Stamper, of the M. E. church. She was born April 18, 1825, in Bourbon county, Ky. Noah W. Matheny and wife have four children, all born in Springfield. WILLIAM S., SAMUEL O., EDWARD C. and FANNIE, who reside with their parents. Mr. Matheny served as county clerk until 1873. He served ten or twelve years as deputy for his father, and thirty-four years by election. He is now—1876—President of the First National Bank, Springfield, Ill., and resides in the city.

JAMES H., born Oct. 30, 1818, in St. Clair county, was brought up in Springfield. At fifteen years of age he we employed as clerk in the Postoffice and Recorder's office, transacting the business of both offices. The two now have grown to require the services of at least twenty men. J. H. Matheny was appointed deputy clerk of the State Supreme Court for 1839 and '40. In 1841 he became deputy in the circuit clerk's office. He was married in Springfield, Feb. 11, 1845, to Maria L. Lee, who was born in 1827, in Carrolton, Ill. They have seven children, all born in Springfield. LEE is now clerk in the Postoffice, Springfield, Ill. EDWARD DOW, born Dec. 4, 1847, studied law with his father, and is a member of the law firm of Matheny, McGuire & Matheny, Springfield, Illinois. LUCY, NORA, JAMES H., Jun.,

RALPH C. and ROBERT W; the five latter live with their parents. J. H. Matheny was a member of the constitutional convention of 1848. He was elected circuit clerk in 1852 for four years, after which he was commissioned Lieutenant Colonel of the 130th Ill. Inf. After the capture of Vicksburg he was on detached duty, holding military courts until 1864, when his regiment was consolidated with another, and he resigned. In Nov., 1873, he was elected Judge of Sangamon county for four years, and resides in Springfield, Ill.

In 1840 ten young men, who had been brought up in the vicinity of Springfield, and had not seen much of the world, or heard a great man speak, learned that Henry Clay was to make a speech at Nashville, Tenn., at a certain time. They fitted up an old prairie stage, put on a cover, provided themselves with tents and provisions, and in August, 1840, Benjamin A. Watson, Henry Oswald, Daniel Woodworth, Edna Moore, Stanislaus P. Lalumere, John H. Craighead, Oliver P. Bowen, Benoni Bennett, Moreau Phillips and James H. Matheny started in their wagon, drawn by four horses, and driven by Phillips. They camped out at night, did their own cooking, and sung the stirring campaign songs of that year in passing through every town and village. In some places they were applauded, at others jeered, and occasionally they were pelted with stale eggs, but they sang through it all, were on time to hear Clay's speech, and were invited on the platform. They sung some of their spirited songs, creating quite a furore, saw a crowd of forty thousand men, ten times as many as they had ever seen before, and returned home as they went, having been out five weeks, and traveled about one thousand miles. They felt well paid for their time, labor and expense. James H. Matheny delivered the oration at the first meeting of early settlers in Sangamon county, Ill. He is the senior member of the firm of Matheny, McGuire & Matheny, of Springfield, Ill., and is now (1876) Judge of the Sangamon county court.

CHARLES W., born Sept. 27, 1820, in St. Clair county, was married in Springfield, Feb. 13, 1845, to Margaret Condell, a native of Pennsylvania. They had three children—HELEN, born Jan., 1846, died Jan., 1864. CHARLES O. and GEORGE H. reside with their parents. Charles W. Matheny was for many years engaged in merchandizing in Springfield, and now—1876—resides in the city.

A. ELIZABETH, born Nov. 28, 1823, in Sangamon county, resides with her sister, Mrs. Whitehurst.

ELIJAH COOK, born June 13, 1826, in Springfield, crossed the Plains in 1849, and remained on the Pacific coast until 1854, when he returned, and was married Feb. 3, 1857, in Springfield, to Alletta L. Vannordstran. They had two children, JOHN R. and LOUISA I. Mrs. Matheny died in June, 1864, and he was married, in 1865, to Mrs. Naomi L. Rittenhouse, a native of Pennsylvania, whose maiden name was Schroyer. She has two children by a former marriage, CHARLES E. and LOUIS PERCY Rittenhouse. Mr. and Mrs. Matheny have three children, MIMA, PHILLIPS G., and ADA L., who reside with their parents. E. C. Matheny was deputy United States Marshal about nine years, for the southern district of Illinois, and during that time sold over $2,000,000 worth of confiscated property, at Cairo. He resides in Springfield, Illinois.

MARIA C., born Aug. 10, 1829, in Springfield, was married, June 12, 1849, to Stephen S. Whitehurst. They had seven children—MIMI, born April 13, 1854, in Springfield, Ill., was married there, Jan. 13, 1876, to George H. Helmle, who was born Feb. 5, 1853, in Springfield. G. H. Helmle was elected town clerk, in the spring of 1874, and again in 1875, and was elected assessor in 1876. He is an architect, and resides in Springfield. MARY, MEREDITH HELM, LIZZIE M., CARRIE M., SUSIE M. and REGINALD GWYNN, live with their mother. Stephen S. Whitehurst died, May 19, 1875, and Mrs. Whitehurst and family reside in Springfield, Illinois.

EMILY R., born March 16, 1832, in Springfield, was married there, Sept. 25, 1860, to Benjamin C. McQuesten. They have one child, BENJAMIN, and moved in 1869 to Ottawa, Kansas, where Mr. McQuesten is engaged in banking, and where he and his family reside.

Charles R. Matheny held the office of county clerk until his death, which occurred Oct. 10, 1839. Mrs. Jemima Matheny died Feb. 23, 1858, both in Springfield, Illinois.

MATTHEWS, JOSEPH, was born in Buckingham county, Va., and when a young man went to Fayette county, Ky., where he was married to Tabitha Rutherford, a native of that county. After spending a few years each in Wayne and Cumberland counties, Ky., they moved to Sangamon county, Ill., arriving Oct. 20, 1830, in what is now Cooper township. They had eleven children, some of whom died, and some married and remained in Kentucky and Tennessee.

SALLY married in Kentucky to Charles Thomas. She died in Mechanicsburg in 1865, leaving one son, ROWLAND D. Thomas, who is married, and lives in Cooper township.

ELIZABETH, born in Kentucky, married there to Dr. Joel Hughes, came to Springfield in 1834, and in 1837 went to Ashley, Mo., where Dr. Hughes died. His widow married in Springfield to William Brown, and died Oct. 19, 1859, in Cotton Hill township.

WILLIAM S., born in Kentucky, married in 1833, in Sangamon county, to Mrs. Lucinda Ashley, whose maiden name was Cooper. He died in 1834, leaving one child, WILLIAM S., Jun. He served three years in the 130th Ill. Inf., part of the time in Andersonville prison. W. S. Matthews, Jun., lives near Edinburg, Illinois.

LOT P., born Oct. 11, 1811, in Cumberland county, Ky., married in Sangamon county June 28, 1838, to Eliza Forrest, who was born in 1815. They had four children in Sangamon county. SARAH J., born April 30, 1839, married Joseph Breckinridge. *See his name.* He died, and she married Thomas Pike. LAVINA A. died, aged twenty-two years. JOHN HENRY, born June 8, 1848, is a minister in the Christian church at Toledo, Ohio—1874. JAMES J., born March 4, 1854, lives at Illiopolis. Mrs. Eliza Matthews died July 13, 1866. Lot P. Matthews lived in Cooper township until the death of his wife. Since that time he has been traveling as a colporteur in the Christian church.

JOSEPH H., born Nov. 2, 1813, in Cumberland county, Ky., married in Sangamon county, Oct. 20, 1843, to Sarah A. Hayley. They had eight children in Sangamon county. FRANCES A., born July 11, 1844, married Dec. 4, 1859, to Charles H. Bridges. *See his name.* JAMES F., born Jan. 1, 1846, died in his nineteenth year. THOMAS P., born Nov. 18, 1848, married Silence A. Pearce, and live in Niantic, Macon county, Ill. MARY E. died in her third year. AMELIA and CORLELIA, born July 2, 1854; WILLIAM A., born June 10, 1857, and ALICE, born Dec. 26, 1859. The four latter live with their mother. Joseph H. Matthews died Oct. 16, 1861, in Pawnee, and his widow and children reside in Illiopolis, Sangamon county, Illinois.

JAMES J., born in Kentucky, married in Sangamon county to Ann Dozier, and both died.

Mrs. Tabitha Matthews died August, 1835, and Joseph Matthews died Dec. 15, 1844, both in Cooper township, Sangamon county, Illinois.

MATTHEWS, SCHUYLER B., was born Aug. 11, 1821, in Greene county, Kentucky, and came to Sangamon county, arriving Oct. 18, 1834, in what is now Island Grove township, two miles east of Berlin. S. B. Matthews and Elizabeth Batty were married in Sangamon county June 1, 1854. She was born Oct. 16, 1825, in Lancashire, England. They have three children, JOHN W., WILBER B. and SCHUYLER A.; all reside with their parents, three miles south of New Berlin, Ill.

MATHEW, SIMON, was born Feb. 12, 1787, in Virginia, and was married in Franklin county, Ohio, April 7, 1812, to Anna Deardorff. They had two children in Ohio, and in 1816 or '17 moved to Washington county, Indiana, where they had six children, and moved to Sangamon county, Ill., arriving Nov., 1833, in what is now Ball township, where they had one child. Of their children—

JAMES D., born about 1813, in Ohio, married in Sangamon county to Dorcas Hamilton. They have ten children, and reside near Chandlerville, Cass county, Illinois.

JOHN M., born in 1815, in Franklin county, Ohio, married in Sangamon county to Mrs. Sarah Crowder, whose maiden name was Woozley. They had five children in Sangamon county. JAMES H., born Oct. 13, 1838, married March 28, 1860, to Sally A. Handlin. They have two children, EVERETT S. and JENNIE M., and live in Springfield. SIMON T., married Mary A. Clayton. They have three children, ETTA E., LUTHER F. and CHARLES CARROLL, and reside in Ball township, Sangamon county, Ill. SUSAN ANN, born August 29, 1844, married Marcus D. Clayton. *See his name.* WILLIAM O. married Mary E. Lamb, have two children, IDA MAY and FANNIE A., and live four miles north of Pawnee, Illinois. LEONARD S., married Sept. 24, 1874, to Alice Galloway. Mrs. Sarah Matthew died, and John M. Matthew married Mary A. Scott. They have five children, FANNIE, JOHN M., Jun., LAURA, LUCY and JOSEPHINE, and reside in Ball township, three and a half miles southeast of Chatham, Illinois.

SILAS D., born in 1818, in Washington county, Indiana, married in Sangamon county to Ellen Deardorff, who died, and he married Mrs. Elizabeth Wood. They had five children. Their son, JOHN F., served two enlistments in the army, and died at home of disease contracted in the service. Silas D. Matthew and family reside near Edinburg, Christian county, Illinois.

CATHARINE A., born in 1820, in Washington county, Indiana, married in Sangamon county to John Deardorff, who died, leaving two children, and she married Daniel Fetters. They have one child, and reside near Macon, Macon county, Illinois.

OSCAR F., born in 1822, in Washington county, Indiana, married in Sangamon county to Margaret Britton. They had nine children. ANNA E. died at seventeen years of age. WINFIELD SCOTT, born May 6, 1848, is now—1875—a student in the Senior class of the Northwestern University, Chicago, with the intention of entering the ministry in connection with the M. E. church. JOHN B. married in 1868 to Amanda E. Lawley. They have two children, CHARLES K. and GEORGE R., and live at Mt. Auburn, Christian county, Illinois. REBECCA J. married Daniel Poffenberger. *See his name.* THOMAS L.

lives with his parents. LOUISA L. died, aged seventeen years. OSCAR M. died young. LAFAYETTE LINCOLN, and MATILDA M. live with their parents. Oscar F. Matthew and wife reside near Cotton Hill Postoffice, Sangamon county, Illinois.

FRANCIS M., born in 1825, in Washington county, Indiana, married in Sangamon county to Nancy VanOsdol. They have five children, and reside at Los Nietos, Los Angeles county, California.

SARAH E., born in 1827, in Indiana, married in Sangamon county to John Smith, who died, and she married Isaac Grimes, and lives near Chatham, Illinois.

DAVID L., born in 1829, in Washington county, Indiana, married in Sangamon county to Caroline Matthew, who died, and he married Hannah Conyer, and resides near Chandlerville, Cass county, Illinois.

WILLIAM P., born July 25, 1834, in Sangamon county, married July 14, 1853, to Mary Safley. They have four living children, MARTHA V., STEPHEN L., U. S. GRANT and IDA A., and reside in Cotton Hill township, Sangamon county, Illinois.

Mrs. Anna Matthew died Oct. 24, 1834, and Simon Matthew was married in 1835 to Mrs. Elizabeth Deardorff. They had three children in Sangamon county—

THOMAS G. married Ann Ferrigo, and lives near Mapleton, Bourbon county, Kansas.

MATILDA J. married Brigham Pease, have four children, and live in Ball township.

ELIZA died, aged seventeen years.

Simon Matthew died June 18, 1848, and Mrs. Elizabeth Matthew died Oct., 1849, both in Sangamon county, Illinois.

MATTHEW, WILLIAM, was born June 9, 1802, in Bracken county, Ky. He was married Jan. 4, 1824, to Sarah McDaniel, who was born August, 1808. They had six children in Kentucky, and moved to Marion county, Ind., in 1834, and to Sangamon county, Ill., arriving October, 1836, in what is now Mechanicsburg township, where two children were born. Of their eight children—

JOHN W., born Oct. 4, 1824, in Bracken county, Ky., married in Sangamon county, August, 1848, to Rachel

Lanham. They have eight children—MARTHA E. married Blackstone McDaniel. *See his name.* WILLIAM H. married Edna Vaughn, have one child, ESTELLA, and lives with his father. ELIJAH T., SARAH F., IRENE, HARRIET E. and MARY F., live with their parents. JOSEPH died, aged three years. John W. Matthew has no education from books, but has been a good business man in farming and stock dealing. In 1872 he took an over dose of quinine which totally destroyed his hearing. Not being able to read or write, and knowing nothing of sign language, he is utterly unable to receive or communicate a thought. He lives near Dawson, Illinois—1874.

ROBERT W., born Jan. 27, 1826, and died Sept., 1853.

NATHANIEL F., born Nov. 4, 1827, in Bracken county, Ky., married Nov. 26, 1856, in Sangamon county, to Mary McDaniel. They had seven children; the first and third, ALBERT and DOUGLAS, died young. OLIVER F., BELLE M., ROBERT S., GEORGE M. and WILLIAM J., live with their parents, four and one-half miles southeast of Buffalo Hart station, Sangamon county, Illinois.

LUANNE, born Dec. 10, 1829, in Kentucky, married in Sangamon county, Jan., 1855, to A. J. Newhouse, have five children, and live in Marion county, Indiana.

JAMES H., born March 20, 1832, in Bracken county, Ky., brought to Sangamon county, in 1835, married Nov. 14, 1854, in Hillsboro, to Sarah C. House, who was born Sept. 2, 1835, in Cabarras county, N. C. They have four children, JOHN L., ALICE M., MARY A. and ILLNOY C., and live one-half mile northwest of Barclay, Illinois—1874.

ELIZABETH M., born in Kentucky, Aug. 15, 1834, married John H. Lanham. *See his name.*

MARY E., born Sept. 15, 1837, in Sangamon county, married, Feb., 1857, to William D. Turner. They have five children, and live in Wayne county, Illinois.

MARTHA J., born Feb. 1, 1840, in Sangamon county, married, Sept., 1857, to John Turner, had one child, and Mr. Turner died. She married John Goodman, has two children, and lives in Wayne county, Illinois.

William Matthew died, April 12, 1841, and his widow died Sept. 26, 1851, she, in Sangamon, and he, in Logan county, Illinois.

MAXWELL, ARCHIBALD, was born July 11, 1808, in Donne, Perthshire, Scotland. He crossed the Atlantic ocean in 1830, first landing at Quebec, Canada, went to Halifax, Nova Scotia, thence to New York city, landing Nov., 1831. He left there in June, 1832, while the cholera was raging. After a short stay in Trenton, N. J., he went to Philadelphia, and spent a whole day trying to find a lodging place. He had plenty of money, and could obtain all the food he wanted, but fear of cholera prevented his finding a resting place; and he was compelled to leave the city for one night, but returned the next day and obtained employment at his trade, stone cutting. In the summer of 1833 he went to Raleigh, N. C., and was employed on the State House, being erected there. From Raleigh he came to Springfield, Illinois, arriving in April, 1838, and soon after went to work on the State Capitol, then in course of construction. It is now the Court House of Sangamon county. Margaret Wilson was born Oct. 10, 1818, in Dumfriesshire, Scotland, and came to America, with her brother William C. Wilson, landing in New York, in 1836, and came to Springfield, Ill., in November, 1837. Archibald Maxwell and Margaret Wilson were married, Nov. 26, 1840, in Springfield. They had nine children in Sangamon county, two of whom died young. Of the other seven children—

JOHN, born Sept. 11, 1842, in Sangamon county, resides with his parents.

ARCHIBALD and *MARGARET C.*, twins, born July 16, 1844, in Sangamon county.

ARCHIBALD is a teacher, and resides with his parents.

MARGARET C., was married July 31, 1866, to Calvin L. Finley, who was born July 3, 1841, in Ohio. They have five children, MARGARET E., ETTA R., ARCHIE C., ROBERT J. and MOLLIE G., and live one mile north of Illiopolis.

ROBERT W., born Dec. 13, 1845, in Sangamon county, graduated March 25, 1874, in the law department of Michigan University, at Ann Arbor. He is now practicing law at Decatur, Illinois.

WILLIAM C., was born Oct. 21, 1850, in Sangamon county. He graduated, Feb. 26, 1874, at Bellevue Hospital Medical College, New York city, and commenced practice in Chesnut, Logan county, Illinois. Dr. Maxwell is now practicing in Springfield—1876.

ELIZABETH M., born June 18, 1852, died in her fifth year.

JAMES T., born July 15, 1859, resides with his parents.

Archibald Maxwell and wife reside two miles west of Illiopolis. Their marriage and the marriage of their eldest daughter were both solemnized by Rev. John G. Bergen, D. D.

MAXWELL, ELIAS, was born in Green county, Ohio. He was there married to Mrs. Nancy Morgan, a native of the same county. They moved to Sangamon county, Illinois, about 1825, and had six children in Island Grove—

SARAH A., born in Sangamon county, married, had one child, and mother and child both died.

JULIA A., born in Sangamon county, married Thomas D. Smith. He died Feb. 10, 1873, leaving a widow and seven children at Humboldt, Kansas.

WILLIAM, born May 4, 1830, in Sangamon county, married Oct. 27, 1852, to Hannah H. Batty, a native of England. They had eight children; three died young, and WILLIAM H. died, aged twelve years. RICHARD E., JOHN E. and EMMA E. reside with their parents in New Berlin, Illinois.

ANTHONY P., born in Sangamon county, went to the Pacific coast in 1859, married in Oregon to a Miss Powell, has a family, and lives near Salem, Oregon.

GEORGE M., born May 1, 1837, in Sangamon county, married March 27, 1860, to Adaline Meacham. They have two children, LUELLA and GEORGE H., and reside one mile north of New Berlin, Illinois.

EDSON died, aged twelve years.

Mrs. Nancy Maxwell died Nov., 1837, and Elias Maxwell married Minerva Grant. They had one child—

LUDLOW W., born in Sangamon county, married Ada Record. They have one living child, and live at Shapier, Wisconsin.

Mrs. Minerva Maxwell died, and Elias Maxwell married Mary Ellis. They had one child—

ABNER, born in Sangamon county, enlisted April, 1861, for three years, in Co. D, 26th Ill. Inf., re-enlisted as a veteran, was taken sick in the army, came home, and died in 1864.

Elias Maxwell died April, 1848, in Sangamon county. His widow married Andrew Scott. *See his name.*

MAXCY, JOEL, was born about 1759, in Rockingham county Va. He was a soldier in a Virginia regiment in time of the Revolution, and was in the battle of Guilford Court House. He remembered having seen Generals Marion, Morgan, DeKalb and Gates. He was married after the war in Prince Edward county, to Mrs. Susan Hill, whose maiden name was Davis. She had five children by her first marriage. Mr. and Mrs. Maxcy had three children in Virginia; and in 1798 moved to Warren county, near Bowling Green, Ky., where one child was born. Mrs. Susan Maxcy died there Aug. 27, 1812. Of her four children, one only ever came to Sangamon county.

JAMES, born Nov. 17, 1791, in Prince Edward county, Va., and was taken by his parents in 1798 to Warren county, Ky. He enlisted at Bowling Green, in 1812, in the United States army. His regiment started the day of his mother's death, Aug. 27, 1812,—and returned in four months. He enlisted again Aug. 25, 1813. His regiment marched the next day. At Newport, Ky., he was elected Second Lieutenant. The march continued north, and he was in the battle of the river Thames, Oct. 5, 1813, and was honorably discharged in November following. He returned home, and was married Dec. 29, 1813, near Bowling Green, to Maria C. Cook. She was born Feb. 20, 1794, near Danville, Ky. They had four children in Kentucky, and moved to Springfield, Ill., arriving May 3, 1834. Of their children—
JOHN C., born Nov. 22, 1814, in Bowling Green, Ky., married Sept. 22, 1835, in Springfield to Farnetta C. Lloyd.

They had six children. Of their five living children, MARGARET D. married Charles S. Zane. *See his name.* JAMES R. was married in Chicago to Harriet Dickson. MARY AGNES was married in Springfield, Ill., to R. D. Lawrence. They have one living child, *Susie C.*, and live in Springfield. MARIA C. married George A. Davis. They have one child, *Georgia.* ZACHARY T., born in 1851, in Springfield. John C. Maxcy has filled several local offices; among others, he has been a member of the Board of Supervisors of Sangamon county, and resides in Springfield, Ill. JAMES M., born Sept. 16, 1816, in Kentucky, lived in Springfield from 1834 to 1849, when he went to California. He was Quartermaster in the United States army during the rebellion, and died there in 1866. MARGARET E., died in her fifth year. MARY J., born July 27, 1822, in Kentucky, married in Springfield to Wm. H. Herndon. *See his name.* Mrs. Maria C. Maxcy died in 1876, and James Maxcy lives in Springfield. He was the first City Marshal of Springfield, and for twenty-six years in succession filled some one of the city offices. He is now in his eighty-fifth year.

Joel Maxcy was married in Butler county, Ky., to Mrs. Betsey A. Howard, whose maiden name was Brown. She was born Feb. 14, 1795, in Prince Edward county, Va. She had two children, Mordecai and America Howard, both of whom married and died in Shelby county, Ill. Mr. and Mrs. Maxcy had two children born in Butler county, Ky., and moved to Logan county—same State,—where three children were born; and the family moved to Sangamon county, Ill., arriving Nov., 1827, at Springfield, and soon after moved to Island Grove township, north of Little Spring creek. Of their five children—

NELSON, born Dec. 26, 1814, in Butler county, Ky., married in Sangamon county April 27, 1829, to Mary Campbell. They had one child, ERASTUS, who now resides near Washington, Texas. Nelson Maxcy married, as his second wife, Melinda Maxcy, in Arkansas. They had two children, CYRILDA and IRENE, and Mr. Maxcy died Nov., 1869, near Washington, Texas, leaving his family there.

BURRELL J., born Sept. 29, 1818, in Kentucky, died in Sangamon county, in his twenty-first year.

HARRISON B., born Sept. 26, 1820, in Kentucky, died in Sangamon county, Dec. 7, 1845.

NAPOLEON B. died in Kentucky, aged four years.

SAMUEL O., born Aug. 19, 1825, in Logan county, Ky., married in Sangamon county Nov. 16, 1848, to Nancy Archer. They had two children in Sangamon county. JAMES H., born Sept. 18, 1849, married Feb. 19, 1873, to Alice S. Jameison, who was born April 7, 1846, in Licking county, Ohio. They reside four miles east of Berlin. WILLIAM J., born Oct. 13, 1856, lives with his parents. Samuel O. Maxcy and wife reside on the farm where his father settled in 1827. It is four miles east of Berlin.

Joel Maxcy died Dec. 27, 1827, in Sangamon county. His widow lived with her son, Samuel O., but went to visit her children by the first marriage, and died in Shelby county Feb. 11, 1856.

MAY, WILLIAM L., was an early settler of Springfield, and was a member of Congress from this district, as early as 1836. I am unable to obtain the information for a complete sketch.

McATEE, ANDREW, was born in Kentucky, came to Sangamon county with his brother, Smith, married Mary A. Rape, had two children, and the family moved to Polk county, Missouri.

McATEE SMITH, was born in 1801 or '2, in Kentucky, came to Sangamon county, about 1825, and entered what is now part of Daniel G. Jones' farm, in Cotton Hill township. He went to Galena and worked in the lead mines until he earned money to make improvements on his land. He was married, in 1829, to Elizabeth Rape, in Sangamon county. She had one child—

HENRY R., born in 1830, and died, unmarried, Nov. 14, 1856.

Mrs. Elizabeth McAtee died, and he married her sister, Tennessee Rape, in 1831. They had seven living children in Sangamon county.

ELIZABETH, born March 5, 1832, married John W. Greenawalt. *See his name.*

JOHN W., born Jan., 1852, died in his nineteenth year.

SUSANNAH, born April 2, 1836, died in her fourteenth year.
BENJAMIN F., born March 3, 1838, married Feb. 26, 1863, to Almyra Marshall. They have three children, NORMAN A., LAURA BELL and EUGENE CARROLL, and live three miles north of Pawnee, in Ball township—1874.
THOMAS J., born November 22, 1839, died, unmarried, Sept. 3, 1865.
SARAH, born Dec. 14, 1841, died at twelve years of age.
MARTHA, born Oct. 31, 1844, died, unmarried, Aug. 19, 1865.

Mrs. Tennessee McAtee died March 9, 1847. Smith McAtee was married, Nov., 1847, to Mrs. Margaret Wall, whose maiden name was Jones. They had two children—
JANE, born Dec. 17, 1849, is unmarried, and lives with her mother.
MARY, born July 6, 1850, in Sangamon county, married, Jan. 23, 1869, to Henry B. Rose, who was born March 12, 1844, in Floyd county, Ky. He was a soldier in Co. C, and transferred to Co. G, 14th Ky. Cav.; enlisted for one year, served fourteen months, and was honorably discharged. Mr. and Mrs. Rose have two children, EDGAR J. and HENRY E., and reside near Independence, Montgomery county, Kan.—1874.

Smith McAtee died May 19, 1851. His widow married Felix Stovall. He died, and she lives in Cotton Hill township, Sangamon county.

Hezekiah McAtee, the father of Smith and Andrew, came with them to Sangamon county, and after tarrying a few days moved on with the other members of his family, to Pike county, Illinois.

McBRIDE, JAMES, was born April 11, 1782, in Bedford county, Va. He was there married to Elizabeth Boyd, who was born April, 1783, in the same county. They had two children in Virginia, and moved to Madison county, Ky., in 1807, where eight children were born. James McBride went to South Carolina on business, and died there, Nov., 1826. His family moved to Montgomery county, Ky., where two of the children died, and one married and settled there. Mrs. McBride and seven of her children moved to Sangamon county, Illinois, arriving in Nov., 1837, in what is now Cooper township, north of Sangamon river. Of her children—

JOHN, born Oct 23, 1803, in Virginia, married in Montgomery county, Ky., to Nancy Pebworth. She died March, 1865, in Missouri. Their only child, JAMES, is married and lives in Indiana. John McBride lives in Illiopolis township with the Gragg family.
AMELIA, born March 20, 1806, in Virginia, died in Kentucky, May, 1834.
NANCY, born Dec. 11, 1808, in Kentucky, died in Sangamon county, Sept., 1838.
JAMES, born March 26, 1811, in Madison county, Ky., is unmarried, and lives in Mechanicsburg.
SOPHIA, born March 11, 1813, in Madison county, Ky., married in Sangamon county, to William Gragg. *See his name.*
THOMAS, born March 11, 1816, in Kentucky, died there, March, 1834.
CORRENA, born July 27, 1818, in Kentucky, died in Sangamon county, Sept., 1838.
WILLIAM, born Sept. 22, 1820, in Kentucky, is unmarried, and resides in Illiopolis township.
ELIZABETH, born June 17, 1824, in Madison county, Ky., is unmarried, and resides with her brother-in-law, William Gragg.
JEFFERSON, born June 8, 1826, in Madison county, Ky., married in Sangamon county, Jan. 5, 1847, to Ann M. Hesser. They had ten children; the eldest died in infancy. ALBERT O., born March 12, 1851, resides at Buffalo. MARIA L., born April 20, 1853, married August 27, 1872, to Jasper Daley, have one child, and reside at Moravia, Iowa. GEORGE W., born March 20, 1855, resides with his parents. ELIZABETH E., born April 20, 1857, married Jan. 15, 1873, to Caleb Duvall, and resides near Asherville, Kansas. FRANCES C., SAMUEL J., NOAH E., JESSE T. and FLORA ANNIE MAY; the five latter reside with their parents at Moravia, Appanoose county, Iowa.

Mrs. Elizabeth McBride died March 27, 1856, in Sangamon county.

McCORMACK, ANDREW, was born April 27, 1801, in Nashville, Tenn. His father was born near Dublin, Ireland, and his mother (whose maiden name was McFarren) came from the north of Ireland. They were Protesants, and left their native country during the rebellion of 1798, and were married in America, probably in Tennessee. They moved with their family from Nashville, Tenn., to Fleming county, Ky., and Mr. McCormack died there about 1815, leaving the family, consisting of the mother, four brothers and three sisters, to the care of Andrew, whose name heads this sketch. He managed to keep them together until they were able to take care of themselves. Being studiously inclined, he worked in the day and studied at night. He brought his mother and all the children to Sangamon county about 1829, settling on Fancy creek. Shortly after he went to work in the Galena lead mines, and during some Indian troubles there, he was Captain of a company of volunteers. On his return he moved to Springfield, and was married July 27, 1834, on Sugar creek, to Ann S. Short—daughter of James Short,—who was born Jan. 3, 1810, in Green county, Ky. They had ten children, three of whom died in infancy. The eldest died, aged eighteen years. Of the other children—

MARGARET J., born Jan. 10, 1838, in Springfield, was married Aug. 23, 1866, to David Caldwell, who was born Oct. 16, 1839, in Dearborn county, Ind. He enlisted Aug., 1861, in Co. B, 26th Ind. Inf., and served three years. They have two children living, JOHN A. and GEORGE D., who reside with their parents, in Springfield, Illinois.

LUCRETIA B., born Jan. 6, 1841, was married June 21, 1867, in Springfield, to William C. Poffenbarger, who was born in Sangamon county. They have four children, ELIZABETH A., MARY A., IRA D. and HENRIETTA A., who reside with their parents, on a farm near Taylorville, Illinois.

MARY E. resides with her mother.

JOHN A., born July 8, 1845, was married Aug. 10, 1870, in Springfield, to Matilda Morganroth, a native of McLean county, Ill. J. A. McCormack is a carpenter, and is now employed at the T., W. & W. R. R. shops. He resides in Springfield, Illinois.

ALEXANDER R., born Sept. 25, 1847, was married Oct. 12, 1875, in Springfield, to Mrs. Fannie Rivers, whose maiden name was Creamer. They reside in Springfield.

ANN C., born Jan. 14, 1850, was married May 3, 1874, in Springfield, to Henry Schneider, a native of Switzerland. She resides with her mother.

Andrew McCormack was a stonecutter and brickmason. He represented Sangamon county three times in the State Legislature, and was one of the "Long Nine." He was Mayor of the city for 1843 and '44, and was a man of great physical strength, standing six feet two and a half inches in height, and weighing two hundred and eighty pounds. Andrew McCormack's mother died at his house in Springfield, Jan. 21, 1842, and he died January 24, 1857. His widow still resides in Springfield, Ill.—1876.

McCORMACK, JOHN, brother of Andrew, married Miss Sherrill, on Sugar creek, Sangamon county, Illinois, in 1833. He resides at New Buda, Iowa.

McCORMACK, WILLIAM, brother of Andrew and John, married Miss White, on Fancy creek, Sangamon county, Illinois, moved to Missouri, and died there.

McCORMACK, ALEXANDER, brother of Andrew, John and William, married in 1834, in Springfield, Ill., to Miss Gillock. They reside in Princeton, Missouri.

McCORMACK, JAMES, brother of Andrew, John, William and Alexander, went to Lexington, Ky., when a young man, and resides there. The sisters of Andrew McCormack are dead.

McCOY, DAVID, was born in 1790, in the State of Georgia. His parents moved to Tennessee, and both died there when he was quite young. He went with a married sister to Ohio, and from there to Montgomery county, Ill. Mary Kilpatrick was born March 29, 1800, in Fayette county, Ky. In 1817 her parents moved to Montgomery county, Ill. David McCoy and Mary Kilpatrick were there married in the fall of 1818, and moved to the south side of Richland creek, in what became Gardner township, Sangamon county, arriving in the spring of 1819. They came in company with her brother, Wm. Kilpatrick, and his wife, both couple having just been married. They lived there one year before they had any knowledge of another family coming into that region of country. His improvements were on a piece of school land, which was not for sale when the other land came into market. In the fall of 1823 Mr. McCoy moved five miles south, to the north side of Spring creek, in what is now Cartwright township. They had three children on Richland creek and eight on Spring creek; two of the latter died in infancy. Of their nine children—

OWEN F., born Feb., 1820, went to California in 1849, and died there in 1856.

HUGH, born March, 1821, died unmarried, March, 1848, in Sangamon county.

POLLY A., born April 8, 1823, on Richland creek, married in Sangamon county, Oct. 29, 1844, to Elihu Scott, who was born August 18, 1821, in Tennessee. They had six children; one died in infancy. MARY E., born July 30, 1845, married April 16, 1868, to C. Howard Sowle, who was born Jan. 8, 1839, near Rochester, N. Y. They have two children, JOSEPHINE and CHARLEY, and reside one mile northeast of Richland station, Sangamon county, Ill. MARTHA J. lives with her mother. JOHN B. resides at Kansas City, Mo, OWEN M. and ELIHU, Jun., live with their mother. Elihu Scott died May 21, 1869, in Sangamon county, and his widow resides one mile northeast of Richland Station, Sangamon county, Illinois.—1876.

NANCY, born Feb. 1, 1825, on Spring creek, married Feb. 9, 1843, to Robert Bone. They have a family of children, and live in Menard county, five miles north of Richland station.

THOMAS K., born in 1827, in Sangamon county, married in 1848, to Margaret A. Kendall, have five living children, and live in Umatilla county, Oregon, near Walla Walla, Washington Territory.

WILLIAM K., born April, 1829, in Sangamon county, is unmarried, and resides at Bancroft, Daviess county, Mo.

JAMES P., born July 3, 1832, in Sangamon county, married Jane L. Seeley, had eight children, five of whom are living with their parents in Topeka, Kansas.—1874.

RACHEL, born in Sangamon county, married Rev. John C. VanPatten. See his name.

JOSEPH G., born Dec., 1838, in Sangamon county, married Sarah Epler, had five children; two died in infancy. The three living reside with their parents in Kansas City, Mo.—1874.

Mrs. Mary McCoy died Jan 20, 1848, and David McCoy died Jan 22, 1868, both in Sangamon county.

David McCoy had some experience in breaking prairie before he came to Sangamon county. He was one of the few early settlers who never cleared the timber from his land, but made his farm in the prairie. He brought a plow with him suitable for breaking prairie. He hung it under the axle of his wagon, and thought he could drive the oxen and hold the plow himself, but found that he could not. His wife volunteered to drive while he held the plow, but then another difficulty arose. The baby could not be left alone long at a time. In that dilemma Mr. McCoy made a box similar to a cradle, made it fast on the beam of the plow, put the babe into it, and in that way broke his land. He built a saw mill on Spring creek, about 1825 or '26, and added grinding machinery soon after. When that mill was put in operation, there was great joy in the settlement, as it was the only place where grinding could be obtained. He adopted as a rule that a grist belonging to a widow should never be tolled. He would loan money without interest for the purpose of entering land. Mr. McCoy went annually to St. Louis, with strained honey and deer-skins, and exchanged them for groceries and other necessaries for the family. His daughter, Mrs. Scott, remembers when the first shoes were made for the children. The eldest one was seven years old.

McCOY, JAMES, was born July 25, 1791, in Nicholas county, Ky. He was a soldier in the war of 1812, from Kentucky, in the Dragoons under Col. Dick Johnson, and was in the battle where Tecumseh was killed. He returned to Kentucky, and was married in Nicholas county, Sept. 15, 1814, to Jane Murphy, who was born in that county, March 29, 1494. They had two children in Kentucky, and moved to Sangamon county, Ill., arriving in the fall of 1818, on Horse creek, in what is now Cotton Hill township. Mr. McCoy and Levi W. Goodan owned a wagon together, and each had a horse, a wife and two children, and both families moved from Kentucky in that wagon together. Their wives were two of the six women who came to Sangamon county that year. The wives of the two Drennans, Joseph Dodds and Mr. Vancil being the other four. Mr. and Mrs. McCoy had twins there, one of whom died in infancy. In the spring of 1819 they moved to what is now Rochester township, where seven children were born. Of their ten children—

CAROLINE M., born July 16, 1815, in Nicholas county, Ky., was married in Sangamon county, Ill., August 17, 1834, to Lewis A. Grimsley. They had two children—ELIZA J., born May 19, 1838, was married, June 23, 1857, to Henry Jacoby. They had one child, AMELIA, and Mr. Jacoby died Oct. 3, 1859. His widow and daughter reside in Springfield. WILLIAM P., born May 9, 1840, in Rochester, is now chief clerk in the county clerk's office, Springfield, Ill.—May, 1876. Lewis A. Grimsley died Sept. 23, 1842, in Logan county. Mrs. Caroline M. Grimsley died March 28, 1843, at her father's house, near Rochester.

SYLVESTER G., born April 28, 1817, in Nicholas county, Ky., was married in Sangamon county, Nov., 1841, to Mary Robinson. They had two children—JAMES B., born Oct. 5, 1842, in Rochester, Ill., served in the war to suppress the rebellion, and was honorably discharged. He was married, Jan. 8, 1857 to Nellie Gillett. They had four children, CHARLES A., TAYLOR L., SYLVESTER A. and MARY ARMINTA, who reside with their parents, near Abington, Jefferson county, Iowa. CAROLINE, born Oct. 2, 1844, married Hall McReynolds, Jan., 1870. They have three children, LEE, HILDA and IRA, who reside with their parents, near Maryville, Wapella county, Iowa. Sylvester G. McCoy died March 5, 1844, in Sangamon county, Ill. His widow and children moved to Iowa, in December of that year. She was married, in 1859, to P. A. McReynolds, and resides at Abington, Jefferson county, Iowa.

—62

JOSEPH E., born March 12, 1819, in what is now Cotton Hill township, and is believed to have been the FIRST WHITE CHILD BORN WITHIN THE PRESENT LIMITS OF SANGAMON COUNTY. He had a twin, who died in infancy. Joseph E. McCoy was married, July 14, 1841, in Sangamon county, to Eveline Jones. They had two children—ELIZA A., born in Sangamon county, is unmarried, and resides in Jewell county, Kansas. JANE E., born in Sangamon county, was married there to James B. Ward. They have two children, ALBERT and OTTO, and reside in Jewell county, Kansas. Mrs. Eveline McCoy died, Jan. 6, 1849, in Decatur, Ill., and J. E. McCoy was married, April 22, 1863, in the same place, to Mary F. Hudnut, a native of Washington, Ky. They have two children, JOSEPH E., Jun., and JOHN E. J. E. McCoy and family moved, in 1872, to Jewell county, Kansas, near Cawker city, Mitchell county, where they now reside—1876. When Joseph E. McCoy and his twin sister were born, there were twins in another family, and triplets in still another, making seven children in the three first births in Sangamon county.

ISAIAH T., born May 16, 1821, near Rochester, married Lucilla Robinson. They had four children. The eldest son, LEWIS GRANVILLE, enlisted in the second Iowa Infantry, and was Orderly Sergeant on Gen. Grant's staff. He was married in Logan county, Ill., and resides at Cincinnati, Arkansas—1874. Mrs. Lucilla McCoy died, April, 1855, in Rochester. Isaiah T. McCoy married Helen Thompson, and she died in less than a year. He then married Isabel Kinney. They have five children, and reside near Lincoln, Logan county, Illinois.

MILTON D., born Oct 16, 1823, near Rochester, was married in Sangamon county, Ill., March 29, 1848, to Malcina A. Cooper. They had seven children, all born near Rochester. The fourth one, VALMORE B., died Sept. 25, 1857, in his third year. Of the other six—SYLVESTER J., born May 3, 1849, was married, Jan. 8, 1874, to Pauline Abel, and resides in Macon county, near Warrensburg. JACOB C., born Oct. 19, 1850, resides near Cawker city, Mitchell county, Kansas. LOUVILTA JANE, JESSE K., MARY M. and LILLIE

C. reside with their parents, at the family homestead settled by Mr. McCoy's parents, in 1819, adjoining Rochester on the east.

MARY J., born Aug. 22, 1825, was married near Rochester, November, 1847, to Alexander T. Giger. See his name.

ANDERSON A., born Oct. 22, 1827, was killed by a fall from a horse, August 1, 1846, near Rochester.

JAMES M., born March 6, 1830, was married, in 1850, to Louisa, sister of O. N. Stafford. They had three children. MALCINA married John McBride, and resides near Kansas City, Missouri. CHARLES C. resides near Mt. Pulaski, and JAMES M., Jun., lives near Rochester. James M. McCoy died in September, 1855. His widow married James Huston, and reside near Carrolton, Missouri.

JOHN W., born Feb. 19, 1832, enlisted, in 1861, in the 7th Ill. Cav., for three years; served more than his full time, and was honorably discharged in 1864. He married Deborah McBride, and mother and child died. He was married, in 1869, to Minerva Kearns; each marriage occured near Broadwell, Logan county. They have two children, and reside near Cawker City, Kansas.

JULIA A., born March 31, 1834, died Feb. 25, 1852.

James McCoy died March 25, 1844, and Mrs. Jane McCoy died Jan. 22, 1852, both on the farm where they settled in 1819, adjoining Rochester on the east.

James McCoy bought the first full sack of salt ever sold in Springfield. He paid for it in coon skins. Salt was brought in sacks of about four bushels. His brother, Joseph E., says that he assisted in catching the coons, and it took all winter to procure a sufficient number to buy that sack of salt. This occurred in 1821 or 1822.

McCOY, JOSEPH E., born Oct. 5, 1797, in Nicholas county, Ky.; came to Sangamon county, arriving at the house of his brother James in 1821. He was a soldier from Sangamon county in the Black Hawk war of 1831-2. He never married, and resides with his nephew, Isaiah T. McCoy, near Lincoln, Logan county, Illinois.

McCOY, HAMILTON, was born March 22, 1815, in Mason county, West Virginia; came to Sangamon county (Cotton Hill township) in 1836; was married Jan. 3, 1838, to Mrs. Maria Cooper, whose maiden name was Lewis. They had ten children,—two died young. Of the other eight children—

JOHN married Elizabeth Abell, and died, leaving two children, WILLARD and JOHN.

SAMUEL, born in Sangamon county, enlisted in Feb., 1862, in the 33d Ill. Inf., and was discharged on account of physical disability, Sept. 1862. Enlisted in 1863 in the 16th Ill. Cav.; was captured in Virginia, taken to Libby prison, exchanged, and died in Baltimore, Md., from the effects of his prison treatment.

POLLY died in Sangamon county April 3, 1864, aged twenty-two years.

WILLIAM died, aged twenty-two years, in Sangamon county.

JAMES A. died, aged twenty-two years.

ALFRED, born in Sangamon county, served a term in the 10th Ill. Cav., and was in Washington at the time of President Lincoln's assassination. He married Jane Rhodes, and lives at Columbus, Ohio—1874.

DAVID, born in Sangamon county, and went to California in 1873.

THOMAS PRESTON, born in Sangamon county, married Margaret Berry, and reside one and one-half miles southwest of Breckenridge.

Mrs. Maria McCoy died Sept. 14, 1872, in Sangamon county, and Hamilton McCoy resides near the old Breckenridge mill, in Cotton Hill township, Sangamon county, Illinois.

McCONNELL, JAMES, was born in 1789, near Belfast, Ireland. Sarah Smith was born at the same place, in 1787. They were married in 1811, and soon after embarked for America, landing in New York City. In a short time he went to Belleville, New Jersey, where he labored in a powder mill three years, without losing a day. The war with England, from 1812 to 1815, was then in full force, and caused a great demand for powder. Mr. McConnell having learned all the processes of manufacturing the same, and was an especial adept in the most difficult part—that of refining saltpetre. He went to Madison county, New York, and established works on his own account, and continued to manufacture powder there, seven or eight years, when he turned his attention to farming and raising fine stock in the same county. After making several trips to Kentucky, selling stock, he was advised to take some to Illinois. Acting upon this advice, he embarked at Pittsburg with a lot of jacks and jennets, landed them at Shawneetown, and drove them from there to Springfield, arriving in the fall of 1840. He had no thought of making his home here, but was so well pleased with the country that he bought the land about three miles south of Springfield, making part of the farms on which two of his sons now reside. He went back to New York, settled up his business, and came with his family the next year. His removal was the cause of several other families coming, also. Mr. McConnell brought a flock of about two hundred fine merino sheep, and at the same time some thorough-bred Berkshire hogs. His son, Edward F., brought a flock of merino sheep, also. This was about the first effort to introduce fine blooded sheep and hogs into Sangamon county.

Mr. and Mrs. McConnell had one child in New Jersey and seven in New York, namely—

MARY, born in 1812, in New Jersey, married in New York to John Buck, and died there. Mr. Buck married again and resides in Auburn, Illinois.

SARAH, born in 1814, in Madison county, N. Y., was married there to Franklin B. Hoppin. *See his name.*

EDWARD F., born April 30, 1816, in Madison county, N. Y., married there to Ann M. Hoppin. They had one son. JAMES S., born Feb. 9, 1843, at the home of his grandfather, near Springfield, Ill., married June 21, 1866, in Galesburg, Ill., to Laura Lavinia Pike, who was born Feb. 18, 1845, at Middleburg, Elkhart county, Indiana. They had two children, EDWARD PIKE and MARY LAVINIA; the latter died Dec., 1875, in her sixth year. James S McConnell, son and wife reside near Chatham, Ill. Mrs. Ann M. McConnell died June 14, 1853, near Chatham, aged thirty-two years. Edward F. McConnell was married March 13, 1855, at Eaton, N. Y., to Mary P. Hoppin. They have no living children, and reside two miles southwest of Chatham, Sangamon county, Ill. E. F. McConnell has, from the time he came to the county, been engaged in farming, making wool growing a specialty. Previous to 1866 the McConnell and Hoppin flocks of sheep had been developed and brought up to a standard of excellence not equaled in any of the older eastern States for weight of carcass, length of staple, density of fibre, and average weight of fleece per head. These essential merits were brought forth by the highly nutritious grasses and fattening properties of the corn raised in Sangamon county. Mr. McConnell was Major in the New York State Militia previous to his removal west. When he came it was by private conveyance, that being before the days of railroads. He has since returned in as many hours as it required days to travel over the route the first time.

ANDREW B., born Jan., 1819, in Madison county, N. Y., was married there to Augusta Rogers. They have eight children born in Sangamon county, namely: MERCY ADELIA married DeWitt Smith. *See his name.* FRANK R., married Belle Merriman, has two children, and lives near Victoria, Victoria county, Texas. EDWARD O. married Luella Patteson, has one child, and lives at Bates, Sangamon county, Ill. SARAH A. married S. Willis Merriman, has one child, and lives near Victoria, Texas. JOHN D., WILL A., AUGUSTA and ANDREW; the four latter reside with their parents. A. B. McConnell was elected President of the Illinois State Agricultural Society four years in succession, 1865-'66-'67 and '68. In 1870 he was elected Sheriff of Sangamon county for two years. He resides now—1876—three miles south of Springfield, on part of the land purchased by his father in 1840.

ELIZA, born in Madison county, New York, married there to Charles T. Hoppin. *See his name.*

JOHN, born Dec. 5, 1824, in Madison county, N. Y., married in 1848, at Chatham, Illinois, to Elizabeth Parsons, who was born March 10, 1831, in Connecticut. They have two sons born in Sangamon county, SAMUEL P., born July 5, 1849, married Feb., 1876, in Chicago, to Sarah Rogers, daughter of Judge J. G. Rogers. S. P. McConnell is a practicing lawyer in Chicago, and resides there. JAMES H. is engaged in business in Springfield. At the beginning of the rebellion John McConnell raised a company, which was assigned as Co. A, 3d Ill. Cav. He was promoted, Sept. 11, 1861, to Major of the regiment, with which he served until until March 18, 1863, when he resigned. While connected with the Third Cavalry, Major McConnell commanded the only cavalry engaged in the battle of Pea Ridge, Mar. 6, 7 and 8, 1862. Col. G. M. Dodge, of the Fourth Iowa Infantry, commanding the brigade, in his report says: "Where so many fought gallantly, it would be hard to distinguish; but I noticed the daring bravery of Major McConnell, of the Third Illinois Cavalry, who supported me on my right." Gen. E. A. Carr, who commanded the Fourth Division, in a letter dated April 14, 1862, after apologizing for the delay on account of a wound in his right hand, says: "Otherwise, I should have taken the liberty of writing to you long before this, to congratulate you on having such a noble man for a husband. His conduct on the day of battle, and all other days, was admired by every one. With about two hundred and seventy-five men he kept back a line of the enemy four or five deep and three-quarters of a mile long, comprising several thousand, and prevented them from getting around so as to fall on our flank and rear. Tell his father that he has great reason to be proud of such a son." Major McConnell was appointed, June 15, 1863, Colonel of the 5th Ill. Cav. He was physically unable for duty until May 27, 1864, when he was mustered in and took command, the regiment then being in Mississippi. Col. McConnell was appointed, March 13, 1865, to Brev. Brig.-General. His commission was issued April 14, 1865, having been signed on the morning of that day by President Lincoln, being one among the last acts of his official life, as he was assassinated on the evening of that day. Gen. McConnell's regiment was assigned to the First Brigade, Second Division, Major-Gen. Custer commanding. They moved by way of Red river to Hempstead, Texas, where they remained from August to October 6, and then moved to Springfield, Ill., where Gen. McConnell was mustered out with the Fifth Cavalry, Oct. 27, 1865. Gen. John McConnell is a farmer, and resides on part of the land bought by his father in 1840, three miles south of Springfield.

JANE, born April 15, 1829, in Madison county, N. Y., married in Sangamon county, in 1842, to Franklin Fassett, a native of Ohio. They have two daughters, SARAH E. and JENNIE, and reside on south Sixth street, Springfield, Ill. Mr. Fassett is a farmer, and is engaged in business in Springfield.

Mrs. Sarah McConnell died Jan. 17, 1855, and James McConnell died Jan. 7, 1867, both in Woodside township, three miles south of Springfield, Ill.

In consequence of his efforts to introduce improved stock, and his advanced ideas generally on the subject of cultivating the soil, James McConnell was by common consent assigned an honorable position among the farmers of Illinois. He was one of the earliest farmers who were in favor of forming a State Agricultural Society, and was president of the convention assembled in 1852, in Springfield, that organized the Illinois State Agricultural Society, now called the Illinois State Board of Agriculture.

McCLEES, THOMAS, was born about 1775, in Pennsylvania, and went to Fleming county, Ky., and from there to Ohio, where he was married Sept. 9, 1804, to Mary Jameison, who was born in Fleming county, Ky. They had two children in Ohio, and returned to Kentucky, where six children were born. The family moved to Sangamon county, Ill., arriving in the fall of 1830, and settled five miles southeast of Springfield. Of their eight children—

JANETTA, born Nov. 18, 1805, in Ohio, married Benj. C. Law. *See his name.*

JOHN, born Jan. 25, 1807, in Ohio, never came to Illinois. History not known.

WILLIAM, born in Fleming county, Ky., came with the family to Sangamon county, and died at Mineral Point, Wis., in 1851.

DANIEL, born about 1812 or '13, in Fleming county, Ky., married in Sangamon county to Margaret Clark. They had three children, and he went to California in the early gold-digging times, and his family went to him. His daughter MARY J., married John Spence. He served three years in a Wisconsin regiment; was starved in Andersonville prison, and died after coming home. His widow lives in Springfield. CHRISTIANA married Thomas Petty, and lives near Sangamon station. Daniel McClees lives in Washington Territory, near Puget Sound.

LOUISA, born about 1815, in Fleming county, Ky., married in Sangamon county to John Lewis, who died, and she married Peter Carril, and had one child, JAMES T., who is married, and resides near Quincy, Mo. Peter Carril died, and his widow lives with her sister, Mrs. Law.

GRACE, born Feb. 22, 1817, in Fleming county, Ky., married Levi W. Jones. See his name.

THOMAS, born Nov. 18, 1818, in Kentucky, died in Sangamon county, in his twenty-fourth year.

JAMES, born Oct. 17, 1820, in Kentucky, went from Sangamon county to California soon after the discovery of gold, and has not been heard of since about 1850.

Mrs. Mary McClees died in Sept., 1831, and Thomas McClees died in 1852, both in Sangamon county, Illinois.

McCLELLAND, ROBERT, was born about 1789, in Ohio. His mother died when he was quite young, and his father died a few years later. He went to White county, Ill., when he was a young man. Charlotte Council was born about 1797, near Tarboro, N. C., and was taken by her parents to White county, Ill. Robert McClelland and Charlotte Council were there married, had two children in that county, and moved to what became Fancy Creek township, Sangamon county, Sangamon county, arriving in Aug., 1819, where ten children were born. Of their children—

ELIZABETH, born in White county, Ill., married in Sangamon county to Conrad Crawley. They had four children, and moved to St. Joseph, Mo., and from there to Liberty, Mo., where Mrs. Crawley died. Mr. Crawley returned to Sangamon county with their children. Their son, JAMES M. Crawley, married Miss Shoup, and resides half a mile east of Crow's Mill. See Shoup family. Thomas died early in 1872, at the house of his brother, James M.

JAMES, born in 1818, in White county, Ill., married in Sangamon county to Mary Brown. She was born Dec. 25, 1818. They had nine living children in Sangamon county. ROBERT married Ann Groves. They have one child, MINNIE, and reside two and a half miles northeast of Williamsville. THOMAS L. enlisted Aug. 12, 1862, for three years, in Co. C, 114th Ill. Inf. He was taken prisoner at the battle of Guntown, Miss. June 11, 1864. Spent four months in Andersonville prison, and was reduced from 160 to 100 pounds by starvation. He was taken to Millen, Ga., and remained two months. He was paroled and exchanged Dec., 1864; served his full term, and was honorably discharged Aug. 12, 1865. He was married to Nancy J. Jones. They had three children, CHARLES H., NOAH F. and IRWIN S., and reside two miles north of Williamsville. MARTHA J. died, aged eleven years. JOHN W., married Susan Groves. They have one child, MABEL, and reside three-quarters of a mile southeast of Williamsville. CHARLES lives with his mother. NANCY A. married Walter S. Redford, and lives in Illiopolis. GEORGE, MARY and JAMES live with their mother. James McClelland died Sept. 25, 1865, and his widow resides one and a half miles northeast of Williamsville.

WILLIAM born Jan. 19, 1820, in Sangamon county, married Aug. 29, 1844, to Margaret Sales. She was born Aug. 10, 1829, in Sangamon county. They have nine children. MARY E. married Homer N. Bryant. He served three years in the 114th Ill. Inf., and was honorably discharged. They reside at Lone Tree, Neb. LUCINDA J. married David F. Hurst. He was a soldier in a Pennsylvania regiment. They live near Elkhart, Ill. GEORGE married Mary E. Shively, and live near Lone Tree, Neb. THOMAS lives with his mother. MELISSA married March 12, 1872, to Asa Canterberry, and live near Athens, Ill. EMMA, EDGAR, WILLIAM, and FLORENCE live with their mother.

William McClelland died April 17, 1876, and his widow resides three and one-half miles northwest of Sherman, Illinois.

NANCY, born Aug. 17, 1821, in Sangamon county, married in 1846, to Charles

McCrea, who was born in 1818, in Penn. They moved to Beardstown, and resided there until two children were born. JAMES E., born Jan. 4, 1847, unmarried, and resides at Long Valley, California. MARY F., born Dec. 3, 1849, married William F. King. *See his name.* Charles McCrea went to California in 1849, was about starting for home when last heard from in 1855, and it is believed by his friends that he was murdered for his money. Mrs. McCrea was married in 1856 to John W. Beck. They had three children, HARRY, ANNA and EMMA. Mr. Beck died in 1868, and his family reside in Petersburg.

JANE, born in Sangamon county, married Stephen Brittin. They had six children. CHARLOTTE married John Lake. EVANS married Catharine Lake, and reside in Iowa. Mr. and Mrs. Brittin both died in Fancy Creek township.

JOHN, born Sept. 1, 1824, in Sangamon county, married Oct. 12, 1848, to Elizabeth Mitts. They have seven children. JANE married S. Sanford Turley. They have four children, NORA L., LUELLA, JOHN E. and OLLIE M., and reside one and a half miles south of Williamsville. Mr. Turley enlisted in Co. B, 11th Mo. Inf., in July, 1861; served full term, and was honorably discharged Aug. 4, 1864. ROBERT E. is a practicing physician. MARTHA E., CHARLOTTE F., ANNIE and ALICE, twins, and MARY L., are unmarried, and reside with their parents, at Williamsville—1874.

ROBERT, born April 17, 1827, married Nov. 23, 1854, to Martha Mitts. They have five children, MARIETTA, GEORGE A., WILLIAM H., KATE and LEWIS, and reside two and a half miles northwest of Williamsville.

LUCINDA died in 1850, at twenty-two years of age.

MARY, born in Sangamon county, married Mr. Harper, who died, and she married James Washington. She resides in St. Joseph, Missouri.

GEORGE W., born Feb. 27, 1832, in Sangamon county, married Dec. 21, 1858, to Mary C. Brown, who was born July 10, 1837. They have four children, FREDERICK, FRANK, PAUL and ARTHUR, and reside three miles northwest of Sherman.

THOMAS, born March 26, 1835, in Sangamon county, married Oct. 2, 1860, to Sarah J. Brown, who was born Nov. 3, 1839, in Sangamon county. They had three children. MINNIE K. died in her fourth year. CHARLIE B. and EDWIN live with their mother. Thos. McClelland died April 24, 1876, on his farm, six miles southeast of Springfield, Ill., where his family reside.

JULIA A. is unmarried, and lives at Petersburg, Illinois.

Robert McClelland died Oct., 1860, and Mrs. Charlotte McClelland died May, 1868, both in Sangamon county, Illinois.

McCOLLY, JOHN, a native of New York, was married in St. Lawrence county to Sarah Bryant, a sister to Mrs. Isaac Bates, and cousin to William Cullen Bryant. They came to Sangamon county in 1837, with the family of Isaac Bates, settled in Fancy creek township, raised a family, and in 1856 moved to Lynn county, Iowa.

McCOMAS, ELISHA, was born March 25, 1803, in Cabell county, West Virginia. He was there married, March 30, 1825, to Sophia Shelton, who was born there, Oct. 9, 1809. They moved to Sangamon county, Ill., arriving April 30, 1825, in what is now Curran township. They had nine living children in Sangamon county, namely—

DIKE, born April 18, 1827, married May, 1848, in Sangamon county, to Nancy Murphy. They moved to Wayne county, Iowa, in April, 1853. He was killed March 6, 1856, by the fall of a tree, leaving a widow and three children, two of whom have since died. The living child, GEORGE, married Lorena McMurray, and lives in Wayne county, Iowa. His mother is married, and lives in the same county.

JINCY, born May 15, 1829, married Henry Davis. She died, Nov., 1864, leaving her husband and five children in Wayne county, Iowa.

CYNTHIA, born April 8, 1831, married Sept. 7, 1854, to James M. Gibson. *See his name.*

MARY E., born Sept. 1, 1835, married Dec., 1853, to Andrew J. Davis. They have five children, and live in Wayne county, Iowa.

SARAH J., born March 14, 1838, married Sept. 7, 1865, to William H.

Featherston. She had three children, and died in Missouri. Mr. F. and two children live in Curran township, Sangamon county. The other child lives with her aunt, Mary E. Davis, in Wayne county, Iowa.

ELISHA T., born Sept. 14, 1840, enlisted August 5, 1862, in Co. I, 73d Ill. Inf., for three years. He was wounded at the battle of Stone's river, Dec. 31, 1862, and died in hospital, Jan. 6, 1863, near Murfreesboro, Tenn.

SOPHIA A., born Dec. 24, 1842, married March 7, 1864, to Thomas B. Gibson. *See his name.*

FRANCES I., born April 19, 1845, married Nov. 13, 1867, to Ebenezer H. VanDoren. *See his name.*

JESSIE M. is unmarried, and lives with her mother.

Elisha McComas died Nov. 30, 1863, and his widow resides two and a half miles south of Curran, Sangamon county, Illinois.—1876.

McCOMAS, DAVID, a brother to Elisha, born about 1813, in Cabell county, West Virginia, came to Sangamon county in 1827, was married in the spring of 1831, to Nancy Shelton. They had seven children. The father died in LaSalle county, and the mother in Iowa. Their daughter—

LOUISA married James M. Shelton. *See his name.*

McCUNE, GAVIN, was born July 7, 1788, in Pennsylvania, and was taken by his parents in 1796 to Nicholas county, Ky. He was there married to Hannah Ardry, a native of that county. They had six children in Kentucky, and moved to Sangamon county, Ill., arriving in the fall of 1832 in what is now Cooper township. Of their six children—

MARY, born Dec. 27, 1811, in Ky., married James Bashaw. *See his name.*

ISABEL, born Oct., 1813, in Ky., married William S. Bashaw. *See his name.*

JANE, born about 1815 in Kentucky, lives with Solomon Reed, near Rochester, Illinois.

JAMES M., born Feb. 27, 1817, in Nicholas county, Ky., married in Sangamon county Feb. 24, 1842, to Nancy Whitford. She was born June 15, 1823, in Wayne county, Illinois. They had eight children in Sangamon county.

WILLIAM, born Dec. 29, 1842, enlisted Aug., 1862, for three years, in Co. I, 114th Ill. Inf. He was captured June 10, 1864, at the battle of Guntown, Miss.; spent nine months in a rebel prison in Alabama, exchanged at Vicksburg, and honorably discharged at the end of the rebellion. He was married Jan., 1870, to Mary E. Frankeberger; have one child, and live near Nashville, Barton county, Mo. HENRY C., born Feb. 3, 1844, married June 7, 1865, to Margaret Thompson, who was born April 26, 1841, in Fairfax county, Va. They have two children, ALMA and IONA, and live five miles east of Rochester. ELMIRA J., born June 3, 1847, married Sept. 1, 1864, to Charles Flagg; have two children, and live near Nashville, Mo. CHARLES A. lives at Decatur, Ill. MARY A., AMANDA A. and ROBERT W. live with their parents. JOHN W. died Sept. 23, 1875. James M. McCune and family live three miles east of Rochester, Sangamon county, Illinois.

JOHN M., born May 20, 1820, in Nicholas county, Ky., married in Sangamon county, Jan. 25, 1844, to Jane Baker. They have five children. CAROLINE. born Nov. 19, 1844, married Aug. 28, 1866, to Robert Martin, who was born July 3, 1840, in county Down, parish of Killylaigh, Ireland; came to America and to Sangamon county in 1856; enlisted July 25, 1862, in Springfield, in Co. I, 114th. Ill. Inf.; served three years, and was honorably discharged July, 1865. Mr. and Mrs. Martin have three children, JOHN W., CHARLES E. and JAMES A., and reside eight miles due east of Springfield. MARY E., born Aug. 3, 1848, married April 7, 1867, to William J. Nutt, who was born July 10, 1841, in Orange county, N. Y.; came to Sangamon county in 1857; enlisted July 25, 1862, for three years, in Co. I, 114th Ill. Inf.; served to the end of the rebellion, and was honorably discharged Aug. 3, 1865, with the regiment. Mr. and Mrs. Nutt have three children, CHARLES E., OTHO L. and ROBERT E., and reside eight miles east of Springfield. ELIZA A., born March 3, 1851, married Sept. 11, 1873, to David H. Gobin, who was born Oct. 8, 1844, in Shelby county, Ill.; came to Sangamon county in 1856; enlisted Oct. 8, 1862, as musician in Co. I, 114th Ill. Inf.; served three years, and was honorably discharged Oct. 8, 1865. Mr. Gobin is a preacher in the United Brethren church, and resides at Taylorville, Illinois. LUELLA A., born June 16, 1858, and IDA B., born Jan. 9, 1865; reside with their parents, three miles east of Rochester, Sangamon county, Illinois.

ROBERT, born in Kentucky in 1822, died in Sangamon county Sept. 1843.

Mrs. Hannah McCune died April 22, 1848, and Gavin McCune was married to Ruth Hamm. He died Aug. 29, 1853, in Sangamon county, Illinois.

McDANIEL, HENRY, was born May 20, 1781, near Harrisburg, Pa., and about 1786 he was taken by his parents to Clark county, Ky. In 1809 he entered the ministry in connection with the M. E. church. From that time until 1822 he gave his entire time to preaching, so far as his health would permit. He was stationed at Georgetown, Lexington, Louisville and Danville, respectively. His wife died in Kentucky without children, and he came to Sangamon county in 1834, returned to Kentucky, and brought out some of his brothers in 1836. He was married in 1838, in Sangamon county, to Amanda Carrico. They had five children—

CATHARINE, born Feb. 22, 1839, married Thomas Hunter. They had two children. FRANCES E. lives with her mother, and CLARETTA lives with her grandmother McDaniel. Thomas Hunter died in 1866, and his widow married Austin Phelps, and lives in Springfield.

ANGELINE, born July 9, 1841, in Sangamon county, married John T. McElfresh, have three children, and reside in Decatur, Ill.

CHARLES B., born Feb. 7, 1845, in Sangamon county, enlisted in 1862, for three years, in Co. A, 73d Ill. Inf., was wounded at the battle of Stone's river, Dec. 31, 1862, recovered, and was transferred to Bat. G, First Mo. Art., was with Sherman in his march to the sea, and was with the force that liberated the last of the Union men from Andersonville prison. He was honorably discharged, in 1865, was married, Jan. 22, 1866, in Springfield, to Martha E. Matthews, have three children, JOHN L., JENNIE F. and HENRY H., and live in Mechanicsburg, Illinois.

JOHN N., born March 19, 1848, and
REUBEN T., born Aug. 24, 1852, resides with their mother.

Rev. Henry McDaniel died, Aug. 10, 1863, in Mechanicsburg, and his widow resides two and one-half miles southwest of Dawson.

The mother of Henry, James, William, Jonathan and Robert McDaniel, came with her two youngest sons to Sangamon county, and died, aged near one hundred years.

McDANIEL, WILLIAM, was born Oct. 20, 1786, in Clarke county, Ky. He was married there to Margaret McDonald. They had twelve living children in Clark and Harrison counties. The family moved to Sangamon county, Ill., arriving in Nov., 1833, and settled near Mechanicsburg. Of their children—

LUANNA, born March 22, 1809, in Clark county, Ky., married there May 15, 1828, to Thomas Sparks, and came with her parents to Sangamon county, in 1833. They had seven children—MARY E., born March 8, 1829, in Kentucky, married in Sangamon county to Solomon Lanham. See his name. MARGARET A. married James Lawyer, and lives in Salisbury. CYNTHIA A. married George Bowers. EMILY W. married H. H. Clemons, and lives near Dover, Shawnee county, Kansas. JOHN W., born June 11, 1838, served three years as a Union soldier, from Illinois, about one year in rebel prisons. He was married to Mrs. Sarah Myers, whose maiden name was Curry. They have two children, MARY C. and SARAH M., and live near Dawson, Ill. MARTHA died, in 1865, aged twenty-two years. HARRIET B. married D. W. Walters, had one child, MATTIE E., and Mrs. Walters died, Feb. 2, 1872. Thomas Sparks died, Feb. 14, 1851, in Sangamon county, and Mrs. Luanna Sparks died, June 22, 1873, in Missouri, caused by an accident while riding in a spring wagon.

SALLY, born Aug. 28, 1811, in Clark county, Ky., married there to Thomas Correll. See his name.

ELIZABETH, born in 1811, in Kentucky, married there to Frederick Sutcliffe, and came with her parents to Sangamon county, had three children, and Mr. S. died. The was twice married after, and died, leaving two children, in Iowa.

MARY A., born Aug. 4, 1813, in Clark county, Ky., married James Herrin. See his name.

DAVID S., born in Kentucky, married in Sangamon county to Matilda A. Shinkle. He died, and his widow married Aaron Morgan. See his name.

CLARK, born in Kentucky, died in Sangamon county, in his twentieth year.

ROBERT P., born Sept. 4, 1819, in Harrison county, Kentucky, married in Sangamon county, Jan. 18, 1844, to Elizabeth R. Correll. He died, Aug. 5, 1851, leaving two children—RUFUS died, aged eighteen years, and ROBERT W., aged two years. His widow married James H. McDaniel. See his name.

MARTHA, born in Kentucky, married in Sangamon county to Aaron McIntire. They both died in Fulton county, Mo., leaving several children.

MARGARET, born in Kentucky, married in Sangamon county to Jacob Maxwell, and died, without children.

WILLIAM, born in Kentucky, died in Sangamon county, aged nineteen years.

JAMES H., born May 12, 1827, in Harrison county, Ky., married in Sangamon county, Nov. 3, 1853, to Mrs. Elizabeth R. McDaniel, whose maiden name was Correll. They had three children—IRVIN died, aged four years. JENNIE and LIZZIE live with their parents, two miles south of Dawson, Sangamon county, Illinois.

JOSEPH, born in Kentucky, raised in Sangamon county, is unmarried, and lives at Farmington, Iowa.

William McDaniel died, January, 1852, and his widow died, Dec. 31, 1856, both in Sangamon county.

McDANIEL, JONATHAN, was born April 8, 1796, in Clark county, Ky. He was married March 23, 1820, in Harrison county, Ky., to Elizabeth Correll. They had five living children in the latter county, and the family moved to Sangamon county, Ill., arriving in the fall of 1835, in what is now Mechanicsburg township, where they had two children. Of their children—

LUANN, born Jan. 6, 1823, in Kentucky, married Jonathan Huckleberry. See his name. She died Jan. 2, 1855.

MARTHA, born August 1, 1825, in Kentucky, married in Sangamon county to John Langley. She died in 1850, and Mr. L. married Mrs. Elizabeth Smith, whose maiden name was Huckleberry.

ROBERT, born Oct. 30, 1827, in Kentucky, died in Sangamon county, Feb. 22, 1855.

ELIZABETH, born Sept. 23, 1834, in Harrison county, Ky., married in Sangamon county, April 9, 1861, to Jacob Myers, who was born Oct. 22, 1831, in Berks county, Pa. He has three children by a former marriage, WILLIAM, ELI and MARIA, and by the present wife, EDWIN, OLIVER and LENA. Mr. and Mrs. Myers reside three miles north of Illiopolis, Sangamon county, Illinois.

JAMES, born Sept. 22, 1837, in Sangamon county, died in his sixth year.

MARIA, born Nov. 26, 1838, in Sangamon county, married John W. North. See his name.

Jonathan McDaniel died Jan. 1868, in Sangamon county, and Mrs. Elizabeth McDaniel resides with her daughters, Mrs. Myers and Mrs. North.—1876.

McDANIEL, JAMES, an elder brother to Robert, was born Sept. 2, 1781, in Pennsylvania. His father, Robert McDaniel, was a Revolutionary soldier, served three years and six months, and was present when Cornwallis surrendered at Yorktown, Va. When James was a child the family moved to Stroude's station, Clark county, Ky. He was there married to Mary Matthews. They had one child there, and moved to Bracken county, where they had three living children, and the family moved to Sangamon county, Ill., arriving, in 1838, at Buffalo Hart Grove. Of their four children—

JEPTHA, born in 1806, in Clark county, Ky., married in Bracken county, and came to Sangamon county with his father in 1838. They had one child in Kentucky and seven in Sangamon county. ELIZABETH married Levi McDaniel. See his name. MARY married William Matthews, have five children and live in Buffalo Hart township. MARTHA married Oliver McDaniel. See his name. JOHN T., unmarried, is a teacher. Mrs. Sarah McDaniel died in 1852, and Jeptha

MARY, born Dec. 16, 1820, in Kentucky, died in Sangamon county, in her twenty-seventh year.

McDaniel died in 1856, both in Sangamon county.

LUANN, born March, 1810, married Glover Matthews, and had eleven children. He died August, 1855, and his widow resides in Buffalo Hart township.

MARY, married Thomas Elliott, and both died.

WILLIAM married Nancy A. Smith, had two children, and he died. She married again, and is now a widow near Riverton.

Mrs. Mary McDaniel died in 1845, and James McDaniel died in 1861, both in Sangamon county.

McDANIEL, ROBERT, was born Feb. 14, 1799, in Clark county, Ky. He was married in Bracken county, March 25, 1825, to Jemima Correll. She was born July 10, 1799, in Montgomery county, Ky. They had five children in Bracken county, and moved to Sangamon county, Ill., arriving in the fall of 1835, in Mechanicsburg township, and the next year to Buffalo Hart grove, where one child was born. Of their six children—

GEORGE, born June 9, 1826, in Bracken county, Ky., married Oct. 31, 1854, in Sangamon county, to Louisa J. Constant. They had two children, EDWIN A. and ELMER W., and live three miles southeast of Buffalo Hart Station, Sangamon county, Illinois.

LEVI, born Dec. 3, 1827, in Kentucky, married Feb. 16, 1871, to Elizabeth McDaniel, and lives with his parents.

JOSEPH, born Dec. 12, 1830, in Kentucky, married Feb. 16, 1864, in Sangamon county, to Mary E. Furrow. She was born August 7, 1836, near Piqua, O. They live in Buffalo Hart township, Sangamon county, Illinois.

MARY H., born Jan. 24, 1833, married Nov. 26, 1856, to Nathaniel F. Matthews. *See his name.*

HARRISON, born June 2, 1835, in Bracken county, Ky., married in Sangamon county, Feb. 6, 1868, to Clarrissa M. Priest, who was born Oct. 20, 1846, in St. Lawrence county, N. Y. They had three children, two of whom died in infancy. ROBERT F. resides with his parents, one mile east of Buffalo Hart Station, Sangamon county, Illinois.

OLIVER, born Dec. 27, 1837, in Sangamon county, married July 16, 1867, to Martha McDaniel. They have three living children, BERTHA MAY, GRACE LOU and JOSEPH A., and live in Buffalo Hart township, Sangamon county.

Robert McDaniel and his wife now—1876—reside three miles east of Buffalo Hart Station, on the farm where they settled in 1836.

McDANNOLD, MRS. ELIZABETH C., whose maiden name was Iles, a sister of Elijah and Washington Iles, was born Dec. 16, 1802, in Bath county, Ky., and married there Oct. 8, 1822, to John E. McDannold, who was born Nov. 7, 1795, in Kentucky. Mr. McDannold died Nov. 6, 1833, in Kentucky, leaving five children. Mrs. McDannold came with her family to Springfield, Ill., in Oct., 1836. Her daughter—

PARTHENIA, born July 6, 1823, in Mount Sterling, Montgomery county, Ky., was married April 9, 1845, to Gen. James W. Singleton. They have two children, LOUISA E. and JAMES J., and live at Quincy, Illinois.

Mrs. E. C. McDannold married —— Strawbridge. *See his name.*

McELVAIN, SAMUEL, was born Feb. 22, 1791, in Augusta county, Va. Arriving at manhood, he went to Adair county, Ky. He enlisted in the army against Great Britain, and was in the battle of New Orleans, Jan. 8, 1815. Returning to Adair county, after the war, he was married Jan. 4, 1816, to Penelope Abell. They had five children, and the family moved to Sangamon county, Ill., arriving Sept., 1828, in what is now Auburn township. Of their children—

HARRIET N., born Oct. 23, 1816, in Kentucky, married May 4, 1844, in Sangamon county, to Harvey Walker, of Cass county, and died while on a visit to the old homestead, in Sangamon county, June 17, 1849, leaving three children, viz: SUSANNAH married a Mr. Wood, of Iowa. They have six children, and live at Indianola, Warren county, Iowa. WILLIAM studied law, and died in 1868. HARRIET N. finished a collegiate course, and died Sept., 1874.

MARGARET J., born Sept. 1, 1819, in Kentucky, married Feb. 1, 1844, in

Sangamon county, to Mathew Patton. *See his name.*

WILLIAM A., born Dec. 1, 1822, in Kentucky, married Nov. 1, 1853, in Sangamon county, to Angeline A. Sowell. They have six children, namely: HOWARD A., SAMUEL S., JAMES W., NELLIE J., MARGARET A. and LIZZIE G. W. A. McElvain resides one and a half miles southwest of Auburn, Sangamon county, Ill., near where his father settled in 1828.

JAMES E., born Nov. 16, 1825, in Kentucky, married in Sangamon county to Nancy Sowell, and moved to Missouri in Oct., 1857, and from there to Butler county, Neb., in March, 1871. They have eight children,—seven sons and one daughter. WILLIAM married Miss Richardson, of Missouri, in 1871, and resides near Hiawatha, Butler county, Neb. The other seven live with their parents, near Hiawatha, Butler county, Nebraska.

THERESA M. H., born Nov. 7, 1827, in Kentucky, married in Sangamon county Oct. 18, 1849, to B. M. White. They had eight children,—five sons and three daughters, and live at Fountain, Miami county, Kansas.

Samuel McElvain died April 1, 1848, and his widow died Sept. 28, 1855, both in Sangamon county. Mr. McElvain and his wife united with the First Presbyterian church, Springfield, in 1829. It was then in charge of Rev. John G. Bergen. Dr. Bergen organized a Presbyterian church at the residence of Mr. McElvain, in 1830. It was composed of twelve members. Mr. McElvain was elected one of the Ruling Elders, and continued to discharge the duties of his office to the end of his life.

McGINNIS, DAVID, was born in 1798, in Mercer county, Ky. He was married Dec. 24, 1820, in Boone county, to Eliza Gibson, a native of that county. They had three children in Boone county, and Mr. McGinnis visited Sangamon county, in the fall of 1826, selected a location for a home, returned to Kentucky, and brought his family, accompanied by his brother, G. Dawson, arriving Nov. 18, 1827, in what is now Island Grove township, where six children were born. Of all his children—

MARY J., born Oct. 9, 1821, in Kentucky, married in Sangamon county to Bernard A. Vanderen. *See his name.* She died, Aug. 5, 1842. Her only living child, JOHN D., is married, and reside in Labette county, Kansas.

WILLIAM, born July 7, 1823, in Boone county, Ky., married in Sangamon county, June 19, 1845, to Lorinda Darneille. They had three living children—ZACHARAY T. married, Nov., 1871, to Fannie Wright, daughter of Dr. N. Wright, have two children, JENNIE B. and a babe, and live in Chatham, Ill. EMMA was married, Dec. 24, 1874, to Jacob Staley. CHARLES lives with his parents, five miles southwest of Chatham, Sangamon county, Illinois.

MARTHA A., born Sept. 1, 1827, in Kentucky, married in Sangamon county to Thomas J. Darneille. *See his name.* She died, Dec. 2, 1853.

ELIZABETH, born Oct. 25, 1829, in Sangamon county, married James A. Hall. *See his name.*

JOHN J., born Feb. 8, 1832, in Sangamon county, married, July 16, 1855, to Elizabeth Green, who was born Feb. 5, 1838, in Owen county, Ky. They had two living children, DAVID R. and WILLIAM, who reside with their mother. John J. McGinnis died Feb. 15, 1866. His widow and child reside where his father settled in 1827, in a brick house he built in 1836. It is four miles southwest of Curran, Sangamon county.

AMERICA died, at ten years of age.

MARGARET married R. R. Roberts, had one child, and mother and child died, at the family homestead.

DAVID S., born Dec. 15, 1838, died in 1860.

ELIZABETH J., born March 29, 1840, married April 2, 1867, to John J. Green, who was born Oct., 1842, in Owen county, Ky. They had two children, DAVID M. and JOHN M., and she died, Feb. 3, 1873. Mr. Green and the children live at the David McGinnis homestead.

Mrs. Elizabeth McGinnis died, Nov., 1844, and David McGinnis was married, in 1851, in Warsaw, Ky., to Mrs. Sally M. King, whose maiden name was Spencer. David McGinnis died, July 2, 1867, from the effects of being thrown from a buggy by a runaway horse. His widow resides at her old homestead, three miles southwest of Curran.

David McGinnis stall fed about sixty head of cattle, in 1838, which was the first thing of the kind done in the county, so far as my informant knows. He drove them to St. Louis, and sold them for $18 per head. They averaged 1600 pounds each, so that they brought a little more than one dollar per hundred pounds. The money was brought home in silver, kept for months in an old business secretary, without locks on that or the house. The doors of the desk were often open so the money could be seen, and several hired men were about, and there never was a dollar stolen. The brick house built by David McGinnis, in 1836, in what is now Island Grove township, is in a good state of preservation. It was about the first, if not the first, brick house built in Sangamon county outside of Springfield.

William McGinnis remembers that his father, two hired men and himself, each put a sack of corn on a horse and rode to a water mill on Spring creek, eight miles distant. This required the labor of four men and four horses a whole day to get about ten bushels of grain ground. That was the prevailing custom. It was thought to be an almost unpardonable innovation when a Yankee came in and would put more grain in his wagon, and with two horses and one man accomplish more easily what had required four men and four horses.

David and William McGinnis were the inventors of a device for guiding prairie plows by wheels and a lever. They put it in operation in the summer of 1829. It was adopted throughout the prairie country, and might have made them a large amount of money, but it was never patented.

McGINNIS, GREENBERRY DAWSON, brother to David and William. He was born Feb. 16, 1800, in Mercer county, Ky. Sally Barkley was born August 7, 1806, in Bracken county, Ky. Her parents moved to Boone county. G. Dawson McGinnis and Sally Barkley were married in Boone county, Ky., Sept. 13, 1827. A few weeks later they moved to Sangamon county, Ill., arriving Nov. 18, 1827, in what is now Island Grove township, and soon after into Curran township. He prepared his logs and hauled them together to build a house. By that time all his money was gone except one quarter of a dollar. They did not like to part with their last cent, not knowing where the next was to come from, but it was the universal custom to have whisky at their house raisings. The raising was delayed, hoping to find some way to obtain the whisky and save the money. The thought was entertained for a time of inviting their neighbors to assist without the accustomed stimulant. It was doubtful if they would come, but the husband and wife held a consultation, and decided that even though they responded to the call and helped them, he would always be regarded as the stingiest man in the whole county, and that it would be better to part with his money than to have such a name. The whisky was purchased and the house raised. That house was less than one-fourth of a mile north of the Lick creek timber. His neighbors wondered at his going so far from timber, and assured him that he could never raise any except muley cattle, because the weather would be so cold out on the prairie that it would freeze the horns off. They had nine living children at that place, namely—

DAVID ERVIN, born August 24, 1828, married August 1, 1850, to Matilda Miller. They had four children, PERMELIA A., the third child, died in her eighth year. The other three, WILLIAM J., GREENBERRY D. and ROBERT E. live with their father Mrs. Matilda McGinnis died May 3 1858, and he was married Jan. 20, 1859 to Mrs. Ruth A. Forrest, whose maiden name was Greenwood. They have six children, SCOTT, THOMAS H., JEROME, CAROLINE, CLIFTON and a boy babe. David E. McGinnis resides in Loami township, three miles southeast of Bates, Sangamon county, Illinois.

W. WASHINGTON, born March 15, 1830, married April 2, 1857, to Charlotte Jacobs. They have five living children, TABITHA, TEDORSIS, ULYSSES GRANT, LUTHER and a babe W. W. McGinnis lives at the family homestead, where he was born.—1874.

ELIZABETH, born Sept. 2, 183 died in her eleventh year.

PEYTON M., born August 9, 1833, married Oct. 22, 1857, to Caroline Neal. She was born April 18, 1840. They reside in the southwest corner of Curran township, Sangamon county, Illinois.

MARTHA A., born March 24, 1835, married April 2, 1857, to James Brawner. See his name.

GREENBERRY D., Jun., born May 4, 1837, married Catharine Jacobs. They have seven children and live in Bates county, Mo.

SARAH, born August 5, 1839, married John E. Gibson. See his name.

ROBERT SMITH, born July 23, 1841, enlisted August 13, 1862, at Springfield, for three years, in Co. B, 130th Ill. Inf., served full term, and was honorably discharged at Springfield, August 30, 1865. He was married Nov. 1, 1866, to Mary E. Bacon, a native of Ohio, and resides one and a half miles south of Bates, Sangamon county, Illinois.

MARY E., born August 12, 1849, lives at the family homestead.

Greenberry Dawson McGinnis died Jun. 29, 1869, of heart disease, and his widow resides with her son W. Washington McGinnis, at the homestead settled by herself and husband in 1827. It is four miles southwest of Curran, Sangamon county, Illinois.—1874.

McGINNIS, WILLIAM S., was born March 30, 1810, in Mercer county, Ky.; came to Sangamon county, Ill., in 1827, with his brothers, David and G. Dawson. He was married the latter part of 1833 to Mary M. Kelly. They had one child.

JOHN G., born Dec. 4, 1834, in Sangamon county; raised in Jasper county, Mo., and married there July 10, 1860, to Sarah F. Vestal, who was born Feb. 24, 1843, in Hardin county, Tenn. They had two children. LAURA E. died in infancy. DELILAH MAY lives with her parents in Chatham township, two miles east of Loami.

Mrs. Mary M. McGinnis died August, 1835, and W. S. McGinnis married Alta M. Kelly, a cousin to his first wife. They had one child in Sangamon county, and the family moved, in 1837, to what was Barry, but is now Jasper county, Mo., where five children were born. William S. McGinnis died Oct. 20, 1845, and his widow and four children reside in Jasper county, Missouri.

McGINNIS, SMITH, born and married in Mercer county, Ky., came to Sangamon county, stopping a short time with his brothers, David, G. Dawson and William S., and moved to Adams county, Ill.; thence to Andrew county, Mo. His daughter is the wife of Dr. E. Artzman, of Springfield.

McGRAW, ABSALOM D., brother to Charles G., was born May 30, 1812, in Harrison county, Ky. At twenty-four years of age, he left his native county, and came to Springfield, Ill., arriving Nov. 28, 1836, just in time to encounter the "sudden change" of Dec. 20, 1836. He was married April 30, 1839, in Springfield, to Rebecca Hunter, who was born July 17, 1815, in Hardin county, Ky. They had seven living children—

ORVILLE H., born Oct. 15, 1841, in Springfield, married March 4, 1868, to Annie Gourley. They had one child, MINNIE F., and Mrs. McGraw died Jan. 5, 1872. He was married July 3, 1873, to Abbie V. Mason, and lives in Decatur. He is so severely crippled as to lose the use of one arm, and nearly lose the use of one leg.

DALLAS J., born April 12, 1845, in Springfield. He was injured by a railroad accident March 31, 1871, and died April 9, 1871, at Brownsburg, fourteen miles west of Indianapolis, Indiana.

HELEN J., born Sept. 27, 1847, in Springfield, married Oct. 14, 1868, to William Trimble. See his name.

AMBRO D., born Jan. 6, 1850; *MARY E.*, born April 12, 1852; *MARIA*, born Jan. 19, 1855, and *LINNÆUS*, born Aug. 15, 1857;—the four latter live with their parents.

A. D. McGraw engaged in farming, March, 1848, and now resides five miles due south of Springfield.

McGRAW, CHARLES G., was born Feb. 13, 1801, in Mason county, Ky., near Washington. His parents moved to Harrison county in 1810 or '11. He spent a few years, when a young man, in Nashville, Tenn., and St. Louis, Mo.; came to Springfield in March, 1836, and engaged in the mercantile trade, as a member of the firm of Hill & McGraw. C. G. McGraw was married April, 1839, to Vienna Adams, daughter of James

Adams. See his name. They had one child—

JAMES A., born March 8, 1840, in Springfield, Ill., is unmarried, and is a merchant in his native city.

Mrs. Vienna McGraw died Feb. 12, 1844. C. G. McGraw was married Dec. 15, 1848, to Almira Walker. They had two children—

ALIDA, born Feb. 26, 1850, in Springfield, was married in Logan county, Ill., Sept. 8, 1869, to Alexander Downey. They had one child, RUSH V., who lives with his mother. Mr. Downey died in Pontiac, March 22, 1872, and his widow was married Jan. 6, 1875, to R. Fenwick, in Bloomington, Ill., where they now reside—1876.

FANNIE M., born May 5, 1852, in Springfield, is unmarried, and lives in Bloomington, Illinois.

Charles G. McGraw died Aug. 1, 1858, near McLean, and his widow died July 22, 1872, in Bloomington, Illinois.

McHENRY, JOSEPH, moved from Kentucky, and settled on Richland creek, among the earliest settlers. He brought seven children, and left one married in Kentucky. His son—

HENRY, lives in Petersburg.

MARTIN, lives in Menard county.

ELIZABETH married Matthias Yoakum, and lives in Menard county.

FRANCES married Uriel Greene, had six children, and Mr. Greene died in 1835; and the widow married Alex. McMurphy, had two children, and he died; and she married Jesse Whitlow, and she died March 2, 1870. Her daughter, Catharine Greene, married Ebenezer Preston, Jun. See his name.

McKEE, JOHN, was born Jan., 1802, in Harrison county, Ky., came to Sangamon county with his sister and brother-in-law, Ivins Foster. He was married in Sangamon county to Mary Browning, who was born in Boone county, Ky. They had four children, namely—

WILLIAM D., born Sept. 14, 1836, in Sangamon county, married April 23, 1863, to Sophronia Sweet. They have two living children, ELIZABETH D., and MORRIS E., and live near Sweet Home, Nodaway county, Mo.—1874.

REBECCA, born March 25, 1838, in Sangamon county, married August 5, 1862, to J. W. Woods, who was born August 5, 1839, in Belmont county, Ohio. They have one child, WILLIAM W., and reside at Loami, Sangamon county, Illinois.—1874.

JAMES, born in Sangamon county, married to Nancy J. Barbre, have two children, and live near Sweet Home, Nodaway county, Mo.—1874.

JOHN, born Sept. 30, 1844, in Sangamon county, married Sept. 29, 1863, to Caroline Williams, have one child, MARTHA, and live in Loami, Illinois.

Mrs. Mary McKee died in 1846. Mr. M. is married again, and lives one and a half miles east of Loami, Illinois.—1874.

McKEE, JAMES, brother to Mrs. Ivins Foster, came to Sangamon county in 1829, and settled on Lick creek, and now lives in Cooper township, Sangamon county, Illinois.

McKINNIE, LEWIS, was born Oct. 11, 1767, in Virginia; it is believed that it was in Culpepper county. His father was born on board a ship in the Atlantic ocean, while his parents were on the way from Scotland to America. Nancy Saunders was born Oct. 12, 1771, in Loudon county, Va. Lewis McKinnie and Nancy Saunders were married in Fayette county, Ky. They had nine living children there. Some of their children married in Kentucky and preceded him to Sangamon county. He came to visit two of them in 1820, and moved his own family, arriving Nov. 15, 1826, near Springfield. He commenced at once to build a house, and moved into it Feb., 1827. It was four miles northwest of Springfield. Of their nine children—

ELIZABETH, born June 30, 1793, in Fayette county, Ky., married there to John Lanterman. See his name. They came to Sangamon county in 1819.

ANDREW, born Feb. 2, 1795, in Fayette county, Ky., married there to Martha Tomlinson, and came to Sangamon county with Captain Jonathan Saunders in 1824, settling four miles northwest of Springfield. They had one child in Kentucky, and eight in Sangamon county. Two died young. ELIZABETH A., born in Kentucky, married in Sangamon county to William B. Jones. See his name. REBECCA married John Morgan, and died. ANDREW is unmarried, and lives near Leroy, McLean county, Ill. THOMAS married Nancy Little, and died in 1873, leaving a widow and two children, near Leroy. CHARLES A. married Elizabeth Land, has three children, and lives near Farmer City. MARTHA died, aged eighteen years. SARAH M. married William Morgan, has six children, and lives near Farmer City, Illinois. Andrew McKinnie died June, 1855, and his widow resides near Farmer City, DeWitt county, Illinois.

GUNNELL S., born March 26, 1897, in Fayette county, Ky., married in Sangamon county, April 25, 1824, to Elizabeth Little. They had five children. MARY, born Feb. 21, 1826, married Dec. 5, 1848, to William J. Sinnard. They had seven children, WILLIAM T., GUNNELL M., E. E., ALLISON D., SARAH E., MARY F. and LEWIS H., and live near Blue Mound, Christian county, Illinois. NANCY, born April 1, 1828, married Dec. 10, 1848, to C. C. Hollier. They had twelve children, six of whom died under three years. The six living are: LEWIS S.; MARY E. married Jacob Bliler, have one child, *Clarence S.;*— EDMUND A., ALICE B., IDA J. and LUCY. C. C. Hollier and family reside near Blue Mound, Illinois. LEWIS H., born Sept. 10, 1832, married Feb. 18, 1862, to Margaret J. Fletcher. They had three children, CHARLES A. E. lives with his parents; MARY E. and ALICE T. died young. L. H. McKinnie resides near Blue Mound, Ill. SAMUEL H., born Dec. 5, 1834, died March, 1860. ALLISON S., born July 26, 1837, was married Sept. 15, 1863, to Clarissa Reed. They have one living child, BENJAMIN F., and live two miles north of Springfield. Mrs. Elizabeth McKinnie died Aug. 15, 1869, and Gunnell McKinnie died Oct. 14, 1875, near Blue Mound, Christian county, Ill.

ELEANOR, born Feb. 22, 1799, in Fayette county, Ky., married Uriah Callerman. *See his name.*

SARAH, born Jan. 16, 1801, in Fleming county, Ky., married there to Jonathan R. Saunders. *See his name.*

NANCY, born June 15, 1803, in Fleming county, Ky., married in Sangamon county to Hiram Duncan. They moved to southwest Missouri, where three children were born, then moved to the vicinity of Stockton, California, and reside there.—1876.

MARY, born Feb. 8, 1806, in Fleming county, Ky., married in Sangamon county to John Humphrey. *See his name.* He died, and she married John Branson. *See his name.*

THOMAS L., born Feb. 4, 1808, in Fleming county, Ky., married in Sangamon county, August 27, 1840, to Sarah A. M. Jones. They had five children in Sangamon county. MARY E., born Nov. 27, 1841, married Waldermer F. Helvety, and lives near Forsythe, Macon county, Ill. WILLIAM L., born Feb. 1, 1844, was married Jan. 8, 1874, to Eleanor Hood, and has one child, MAUD E. HENRY H., born March 7, 1846, died March 7, 1860. COLUMBIA A., born April 29, 1850, married Henry B. Drake. They have one child, MABEL L., and reside near Elkhart, Ill. JULIA F., born April 2, 1856, resides with her parents. Thomas L. McKinnie, and his wife reside on the farm where his parents settled in Feb., 1827, four miles northwest of Springfield.

WILLIAM P., born May 20, 1810, in Fleming county, Ky., married May 12, 1839, to Sarah J. Threlkeld, who was born Oct. 16, 1817, in Shelby county, Ky. Her home was in Sangamon county from about 1832, but the marriage took place while she was on a visit near Burlington, Iowa. They had ten children, all born in Sangamon county, Ill. MARY A., born May 11, 1840, married Nov. 9, 1865, to William A. Montgomery. They had two children. The second, CHARLES E., died young. EDWARD P. lives with his parents, near Assumption, Christian county, Ill. THOMAS L. S., born June 13, 1841, married Jan. 1, 1868, to Harriet Clark, in Springfield. They had two children. GEORGE T. died young. EDWIN E. lives with his parents near Buffalo Hart Station, Sangamon county, Illinois. LUCY J., born Nov. 5, 1842, married Nov. 9, 1865, to Charles H. Judd. They had one child, FRANCIS E., and Mr. Judd died August 30, 1870. His widow and son reside with her parents. SARAH E., born Sept. 4, 1844, married Dec. 25, 1862, to Joseph E. Corbin, and have three children, OLIVER E., WILLIAM and JENNIE B., and live near Rockville, St. Clair county, Missouri.

WILLIAM A., born March 11, 1846, was married Sept. 16, 1874, to Emma Marshall, and lives near his father. VIRGIL U., born May 4, 1848, was married Sept. 10, 1872, to Elizabeth Hood. They have two children, and reside near Forsythe, Macon county, Ill. NANCY E., born June 7, 1850, married John W. Taylor. *See his name.* FRANCES M., born March 4, 1852, was married Sept. 11, 1872, to Victor F. Hilvety. They have two children, EARNEST and a babe, and live near Forsythe, Macon county, Ill. HARRIET M., born Nov. 25, 1855, was married Feb. 12, 1874, to Isaac Hazlett, and live near Farmer City. CHARLES E., born Oct. 13, 1859, lives with his parents. Wm. P. McKinnie and wife reside four miles northwest of Springfield, on the farm where they settled in 1840, and adjoining where his father settled in 1827.

Lewis McKinnie died Oct. 7, 1841, and Mrs. Nancy McKinnie died Oct. 8, 1843, both near Springfield, Illinois.

McLOUD, JOHN K., was born in 1809 or '10, in Washington county, Tenn. He came to Sangamon county in 1837 or '8, and was married to Mrs. Margaret McNabb, whose maiden name was Dunlap. They had six children, namely—

LOUISA married Collin H. Cowardin, have six children, and live in Sullivan county, Mo.

LUZETTA, married Oct. 13, 1863, to Cyrus Lilly, a native of Augusta county, Va. They have four children, LAURA B., NORA E., MARY M. and GRACE M., and reside three miles west of Sherman, Illinois.

DRUCILLA married Augustus Young. They have five children, and live in Logan county, Illinois.

WILLIAM P., born April 9, 1844, in Sangamon county, married March 9, 1871, to Mayne E. Myers, who was born in Licking county, Ohio, Dec. 13, 1849. They have one child, CLARENCE P., and reside at the family homestead, two and a half miles west of Sherman, Illinois.—1874.

MARY E., married Bernard Henley, have two children, and live in Sullivan county, Mo.

MARGARET E., married Adolphus Allen, and lives in Sullivan county, Mo.

Mrs. Margaret McLoud died April 7, 1860. John K. McLoud resides in Fancy Creek township, two and a half miles west of Sherman, Sangamon county, Illinois.—1874.

McMURPHY, DAVID, was born Aug. 20, 1794, in Windsor county, Vermont, married in St. Lawrence county, New York, to Elizabeth White, who was born in Harrisburg, Pennsylvania. They had three living children in New York. Mr. David McMurphy visited Sangamon county in 1837, and moved his family, in 1839, to what is now Salisbury township. Of his children—

GEORGE, born Jan. 6, 1823, in St. Lawrence county, N. Y., married at Salisbury, Sangamon county, March 29, 1845, to Mary A. Miller, who was born Dec. 18, 1827. They had eight children in Sangamon county, two of whom died young. ALBERT, born March 29, 1846, at Salisbury, married near Carbondale, Ill., to Julia A. Prickett. They have one child, DAISEY IRENE, and reside in Springfield. Mr. Albert McMurphy is engaged in the grocery trade. GEORGE W., born July 31, 1850; WILLIAM H., born Oct. 17, 1853; ISAAC H., born January 20, 1855; SARAH A., born July 11, 1860; the four latter at Salisbury. MARY O., born March 3, 1864, in Springfield. The five latter reside with their parents. Mr. George McMurphy moved from Salisbury to Springfield, in 1863, and is in the grocery business, corner of Madison and sixth streets.

WILLIAM H., born Nov. 20, 1826, in St. Lawrence county, N. Y., partly raised near Salisbury, Sangamon county, and married, in 1854, in Mason county, to Lucinda M. Holland. They have three children, JOHN, NELSON and JENNIE, and reside near Burton View, Logan county, Illinois.

LESTER, born Jan. 28, 1833, in St. Lawrence county, N. Y., married near Salisbury, Sangamon county, March 13, 1853, to Eliza J. Parvin, who was born March 30, 1830, on the farm where she was married. They had four children, two of whom died young. DAVID V., born May 5, 1856, and CHARLES, born June 22, 1862, reside with their father. Mrs. Eliza J. McMurphy died in Springfield, March 3, 1865, and Lester

McMurphy was married March 26, 1867, in Jacksonville, Ill., to Mary E. Gass, a native of that city. They have two children, FRANK P. and HERBERT L., who reside with their parents, in Springfield. Lester McMurphy was acting post master at Salisbury for five years, and came to Springfield in 1860, and from that time to the present has been employed in the Post Office. He is now chief clerk—1876.

David McMurphy was a practical millwright for many years before coming to Illinois, and he built many mills in Sangamon and adjoining counties.

Mrs. Elizabeth McMurphy died Oct. 18, 1868, in Springfield, and David McMurphy died Oct. 29, 1875, in Logan county, Illinois.

McMURRY, MRS. ELIZABETH, whose maiden name was Logue, was born Dec 6, 1775, in Virginia. She was married in Botetourt county, Virginia, to Robert McMurry, who was born about 1773 in that county. They had four children there, and in the autumn of 1801 moved to Washington county, Ky., where three children were born. In the autumn of 1810 they moved to St. Clair county, Ill., where they spent one winter in camp. In the spring of 1811 they moved to a place called Turkey Hill, near the present city of Belleville. Robert McMurry died there, in Feb., 1812. The Indians were manifesting signs of hostility as the allies of Great Britain, in the war of 1812, and Mrs. McMurry very wisely decided to return to Kentucky with her seven children. After the war she moved to St. Clair county again, and from there to Sangamon county, Ill., arriving in the fall of 1821, settling north of Spring creek, and eight miles west of Springfield. Mrs. Elizabeth McMurry died in 1857, in Curran township. Of her seven children:—

WILLIAM, born Dec. 29, 1793, in Botetourt county, Virginia, remained with his mother until her return to Kentucky, after the death of his father. He was married Oct., 1817, in Washington county, Ky., to Elizabeth Clampit, who was born March 22, 1801, in Kentucky. They came to St. Clair county, Ill., in 1818, where one child was born, and moved, in the fall of 1820, to what became Sangamon county, settling north of Spring

—64

creek, and eight miles west of Springfield, where they had nine living children. In 1849 Mr. McMurry moved to DeWitt county, Ill. Of his children: JAMES L., born Jan. 31, 1819, in St. Clair county, married three times, without children by either marriage. He was married the fourth time in Iowa. They have two children, WILLIAM and JOSEPH, and live in Urbana, Ill. ELIZABETH, born Feb. 17, 1821, was married to Caswell Hall. They had four children. EDITH M. died in 1863. EMMA married Mr. Stout, May 19, 1868, and lives at Leroy, Ill. PETER C. is married, and lives at Leroy, Ill. WILLIAM lives at Leroy. Mrs. Elizabeth Hall died Oct. 16, 1853, near Clinton, Ill. Caswell Hall was married in 1855 to Miss Edwards, and lives at Leroy, McLean county, Ill. NANCY, born March 5, 1823, died June 16, 1851. WILLIAM C., born Oct. 2, 1826, in Sangamon county, was married there, April 24, 1850, to Elizabeth J. Cummings. They had four children. ANN E. married Joseph Jackson, Feb. 26, 1875. IDA G., MARTHA A. and JAMES M. live with their father. Mrs. McMurry died Oct. 7, 1860, and W. C. McMurry enlisted Sept. 4, 1861, in Co. I, 39th Ill. Inf., for three years. He was taken prisoner, May 16, 1864, at Drury's Bluff, Virginia, and imprisoned one week at Libby, three and a half months at Andersonville, two weeks at Charleston, five months at Florence, South Carolina, was exchanged, and entered the Union lines, Feb. 26, 1865, and was honorably discharged, March 14, same year, being six months and ten days over his full time. He was married Apr. 20, 1865, to Mrs. Lucinda B. Cummings, whose maiden name was McCord. They have one child, LOT, and reside in Farmer City, Ill. LEWIS R., born May 25, 1829, died Sept. 18, 1851. MOSES C., born April 15, 1831, in Sangamon county, enlisted June, 1864, for one hundred days, in Co. A, 135th Ill. Inf., served full time, and was honorably discharged, Oct., 1864. He was married Nov. 17, 1868, to Almeda Warner, who was born April 30, 1844, in Ohio. They have two children, JAMES O. and OTTO F. M. C. McMurry and family live near Saybrook, Champaign county, Ill. SAMUEL B., born Sept. 6, 1833, in Sangamon county, enlisted in 1861, in Co. E, 20th Ill. Inf., for three years, and died at Mound City, Ill., March 21, 1862, was taken home, and buried at Clinton. JOSEPH D., born April 7, 1838, lives at Farmer City. ANN J. P., born Feb. 29, 1840, in Sangamon county, was married at Clinton, March 5, 1867, to T. H. Benton McElhaney, who was born Feb. 4, 1842, in DeWitt county, Ill. He enlisted August 11, 1862, in Co. D, 107th Ill. Inf., for three years, served until the close of the rebellion, and was honorably discharged, July 11, 1865. Mr. and Mrs. McElhaney have three children, WILLIAM A., LOU C. A. and BENTON M., and live at Clinton, Ill. PETER A., born July 14, 1843, in Sangamon county, enlisted June, 1864, for one hundred days, in Co. A, 135th Ill. Inf. served full time, and was honorably discharged, Oct. 1865. He was married in June, 1874, to Olie McMahon, and resides at Clinton, Ill. Mrs. Elizabeth McMurry died Sept. 17, 1850, and William McMurry was married August 14, 1853, in Sangamon county, to Mrs. Agnes Bryant, whose maiden name was Sims. William McMurry died Feb. 13, 1876, at Clinton, Ill., and his widow resides there.

SAMUEL, born Oct. 21, 1795, in Botetourt county, Va., was married Nov. 20, 1821, in St. Clair county, to Mary Rittenhouse. She was born Oct. 1, 1800, in Madison county, Va. They moved to Sangamon county in 1823, settling south of Spring creek and eight miles west of Springfield. They had nine children in Sangamon county. JOHN D., born Aug. 6, 1824, was married Jan. 9, 1846, to Catharine Bormann, who was born Feb. 14, 1825, in the Kingdom of Bavaria. They had four living children. SAMUEL B., born March 1, 1848, was married Sept. 2, 1874, to Matilda Roots, of Mannsville, Taylor county, Ky. They live two miles west of Curran, Ill. LAURETTA A., born December 25, 1850, was married February 22, 1872, to George F. Allen. They had one child, Arthur F. Mrs. L. A. Allen died, November 12, 1874. BARTHENA D. and CHARLES W., live with their father. Mrs. Catharine B. McMurry died May 31, 1872, and John D. McMurry was married Jan. 7, 1875, in Springfield, Ill., to Mrs. Rebecca McKechnie, who was born in 1826 in Yorkshire, England, and whose maiden name was Snape. They reside three miles northwest of Curran, Sangamon county, Ill. PETER C., born Jan. 29, 1826, married Almeda Davis. They had two children. He died Oct. 22, 1853. Of their children, CHARLES S. and JOHN L. live with their mother, who married W. W. Kelly. See his name. ROBERT T., born Jan. 6, 1828, married Margaret Davis. They have four children. MARY E. was married March 16, 1875, to Boswell Thatcher, of Wayne county, Iowa. SAMUEL O., DAVID L. and JAMES live with their parents, near Bethlehem, Iowa. WILLIAM L., born Jan. 26, 1830, married Barbara A. Bormann. They have seven children. VERLINDA C. married George McComas in 1872, and lives near Bethlehem, Iowa. GEORGE F., LENORE, MELISSA M., MOSES S., ELMORE and JOHN L. live with their father. Mrs. McMurry died June 11, 1875, and the family live near Bethlehem, Iowa. ARTHUR B., born Jan. 30, 1832, died, aged ten years. GEORGE L., born Feb. 19, 1834, married Julia F. Head. They have two living children. Mrs. Julia McMurry died Sept. 16, 1875. Mr. McMurry and the children live near Bethlehem, Iowa. JAMES O., born March 19, 1837, married Elizabeth Pearce. They had four children, ROBERT, DEBORAH C., BARTHENA and JAMES. Mrs. Elizabeth McMurry died April, 1873. He married Matilda Chrisman. They have one child, EARNEST, and live near Bethlehem, Iowa. ELIZABETH E., born Jan. 20, 1839, married Debold Paulen. See his name. MARY J., born Sept. 23, 1842, married George Mentzer. They have three children, JOHN D., LAURA and ——, and reside near Cerro Gordo, Ill. Mrs. Mary McMurry died April 5, 1863, and Samuel McMurry died April 19, 1863.

JAMES, born April 5, 1798, in Botetourt county, Virginia, was married in Sangamon county, Ill., to Lavina Earnest. They had six children in Sangamon county, and moved to Keokuk, Iowa; from there to Independence, Mo., thence to California, about 1855. Of their children, SARAH married Rev. Mr. James. She died in 1854, leaving one child. MARTHA J. married Inglefield Gregory. ROBERT S. married in 1849, and his wife died Nov. 16, 1863, leaving six children, LUELLA, ALTA, SARAH, MARY L., WILLIAM H. and OLIVE M. THOS.

FRANK, JAMES and ELIZA,—the three latter are married. James McMurry died near lone City, California, and his family reside there.

LEWIS, born April 15, 1801, in Virginia, came to Sangamon county, Ill., with his mother in 1823. He married Leanna DeMula, a French lady of St. Louis, and died there, without children, in 1853.

ESTHER, born Oct. 28, 1803, in Kentucky, was married in Sangamon county to John Turner. See his name.

ARTHUR B., born Nov. 7, 1807, in Washington county, Ky., was married in Sangamon county, Ill., to Sarah Enyart. They had six children. ROBERT died in his twenty-first year. MARTHA J. married Robert Elder, and live in Butler county, Neb. ELIZABETH A. married Wesley Huggins, and died June 12, 1862. MARY F. married John F. Crowder. See his name. She died in June, 1873. LEWIS S. married Melissa Griffin. They have three children, and reside in Butler county, Neb. SARAH M. was married in 1866 to Dr. Charles Kerr. They had four children, CHARLES, MABEL, MAUD and NETTIE; the latter died in infancy. Mrs. S. Melissa Kerr died March 22, 1876, in Pawnee, and was buried in Oak Ridge Cemetery. See Dr. Kerr's name, with Elisha Sanders. Arthur B. McMurry died Feb. 28, 1855, and his widow was married June 7, 1875, to William Parkes. See his name.

LOGAN, born March 22, 1810, in Washington county, Ky., was married in Sangamon county Dec. 22, 1831, to Melissa Robison, who was born Nov. 11, 1813. They had ten children in Sangamon county. EDWARD S., born Nov. 13, 1832, was married Jan. 10, 1858, to Susan Reid; have four children, J. J., ANNA, MARTHA E. and G. E. LEWIS, and live at Leghorn, Kansas. E. S. McMurry is Postmaster there. JOHN L., born Mar. 31, 1835, died in his third year. MARY E., and MARTHA J., twins, born July 10, 1838. Mary E. was married July 26, 1868, to Hiram F. Robbins, born in Warren county, Penn. They have three children, SANDFORD L., FANNIE A. and ANNIE M., and reside near Maple Grove, Pottawatomie county, Kansas. Martha J. was married July 1, 1868, to James Siddens, who was born in Putnam county, Indiana, February 9, 1836. They have three children, IDA B., SADIE M. and MARY F., and reside near Westmoreland, Pottawatomie county, Kansas. ANGELINE, born May 23, 1841, died in her second year. ELIHU J. L., born Aug. 9, 1844, enlisted in Capt. Pratt's Co., 130th Ill. Inf., Aug. 11, 1862, for three years. The company disbanded, and he joined Co. B, 10th Ill. Cav., in October of the same year. Served three years and three months, and was honorably discharged. GEORGE F., born Aug. 21, 1847, resides near Westmoreland, Pottawattomie county, Kansas. SARAH A., born June 20, 1850, EMILY F., born March 5, 1854, and ROSELLA, born March 21, 1858, all reside with their parents, half a mile south of Farmingdale, Sangamon county, Illinois.

McNABB, WILLIAM, was born about 1760, in Ireland, and emigrated to America before the Revolution. The family settled in that part of Amherst which is now Nelson county, Virginia. He was there married to Mary Crawford, a cousin of Wm. H. Crawford, of Georgia, who was one of the four candidates for President, in 1824. Mr. and Mrs. McNabb moved from Virginia to Green county, Ky., where they had six children, and moved to Illinois, in 1819, first stopping in Logan county, and in 1820 moved to a point about three miles west of Springfield, and settled the farm now owned by Washington Rickard. Of their six children—

SAMUEL, born in Kentucky, married there, came to Sangamon county about 1826, and in the spring of 1831 moved to the vicinity of Petersburg, Ill., and died there in 1872.

HESTER, born Dec. 10, 1789 in Green county, Ky., married there to Robert White, July 17, 1806, and came to St. Clair county, Ill., in 1814, and in 1818 came to what was afterwards Sangamon, and still later Menard county, and settled near what is now Athens. Mr. White was born Oct. 18, 1779. They had five children, namely: MARY P., born in Green county Ky., married Mr. Miner, who lived but a few months, and she married William McDougal in 1827. They had thirteen children, all except one lived to maturity: ten of whom are yet living, and have families. Mr. and Mrs. McDougal reside near Athens, Illinois. ELIZA, born in 1810, in Green county, Kentucky, married near Athens, Illinois, March 15, 1834, to Jacob C. West, a native of Tennessee. They had eight children, five of whom died young. Of the other three—WILLIAM F., born June 19, 1835, married Miranda England, and had three children, all of whom died young. Wm. F. West was a graduate of the Missouri Medical College. He was appointed, Sept., 1861, Assistant Surgeon, and soon after promoted Surgeon of the 28th Ill. Inf. He served until June, 1863, when he resigned on account of impaired health, and died March 27, 1864, near Athens. JOHN M., born Dec. 22, 1836, became first Assistant Contract Surgeon to the 28th Ill. Inf., in April, 1862, and in December of the same year resigned, in consequence of impaired health. He completed his medical course, and graduated in February, 1864, at Rush Medical College, Chicago. He was married, Feb., 1863, to Harriet L. Bishop, at Williamsville, Ill. She died, June 7, 1875, leaving one child, J. Hal. Dr. West was married, Feb. 1, 1876, in Pittsburg, Penn., to Susie Lockwood, a native of Norwalk, Conn. Dr. J. M. West is a practicing physician, in Springfield, Ill. JACOB R., born in 1848, lives with his parents. Jacob C. West and wife reside near Athens, Ill. JOHN R., born in Green county, Ky., died near Athens, aged twenty-two years. WILLIAM H., born in Kentucky, married near Petersburg to Elizabeth Bone. They had seven children, four of whom are yet living. Mrs. White died, and Wm. H. White married Mrs. Elizabeth Sewell. They had three children, and he died Nov., 1864, near Athens, Ill. ROBERT F., born near Athens, Ill., married in Morgan county to Rachel Roach, daughter of Rev. N. Roach. They had seven children, four of whom died early in life. MARY E. and JOHN R. live with their parents. ESTHER married William Moore, and lives in DeWitt county. Rober F. White and wife reside near Athens, Ill. Robert White died Nov. 27, 1847, and Mrs. Hester White died April 2, 1867, both near Athens, Menard county, Illinois.

CATHARINE, born, and married in Kentucky to Mr. Blakeman, spent a short time in Illinois, and returned to Kentucky.

ISABELLA, born, and married in Kentucky to Benjamin Wilcox, raised a large family near Petersburg, Illinois.

MARTHA, born in Kentucky, married John Jeneson, near Springfield, raised a family of six children, and both died, near Petersburg, Illinois.

JAMES CRAWFORD McNABB, born Dec. 27, 1800, in Green county, Ky., married in Sangamon county, Nov. 8, 1825, to Ann R. Watson. They had four children in Sangamon county—EVELINE, born Sept. 15, 1826, married, Oct. 24, 1843, to John G. Elkin. See his name. ADELAIDE C., born March 1, 1829, married, in 1847, to Henry Beers. See his name. Mr. Beers died, August, 1851, and she married, Oct. 28, 1858 to Adolphus Rogers. They have two children, HENRY C. and ADELAIDE, and reside in Cincinnati, Ohio. JAMES H., born Sept. 17, 1831, in Sangmon county, went to California in 1849, and was married there, in 1859, to Mary Scudder, a native of New Jersey. They have three living children, ADELAIDE, JAMES and MARY E. James H. McNabb was twelve years editor of the *Petalonma Argus*, was State Senator, from 1862 to 1868. He is now—1876—and has been for the last five years, deputy collector in the United States Custom House, at San Francisco, California, and resides there. LUCILLA H. died, aged nine years. James C. McNabb died, January, 1835, in Sangamon county, and his widow resides in Mechanicsburg, Illinois.

William McNabb died, early in 1831, near Springfield, and his widow died about 1836, in Petersburg, Menard county, Illinois.

McNEILL.—The origin of this family in America was with two brothers, John and Archibald McNeill, who emigrated from Scotland in 1770. Archibald was a physician, and settled in Georgia. John was a General in the British army. He took leave of absence, and settled in Kent county, Maryland. When the war began, which ended in the American Revolution, General McNeill was ordered home to duty, but refused to go, his sympathies being with the colonists. He aided them all he could without entering the army. At one time some

American officers were at his house in consultation. Gen. McNeill discovered a man at the window eavesdropping. He walked back and forth by the window, and at a favorable moment plunged a cane through the glass into the face of the eavesdropper, who escaped with the loss of an eye. Gen. John McNeill had two sons, Archibald and John, the latter of whom had two sons, who were among the early settlers of Sangamon county, and are the subjects of the following sketches:—

McNEILL, FRANCIS A., born Jan. 1, 1809, in Allegheny county, Md. He was baptized in infancy by Rev. Francis Asbury, the first Bishop of the M. E. church in America. He was converted in early life, and at twenty years of age was in the ministry and stationed at Frederick City, Md. His health failing, he commenced the study of medicine, and in 1834 graduated at the University of Maryland, in Baltimore, and located at Shepherdstown, Va. He was married Feb. 1, 1830, in Frederick City, Md., to Mary E. Cronise, who was born there, March 4, 1812. Dr. McNeill and wife moved from Shepherdstown, Va., to Springfield, Ill., in the spring of 1835. He practiced medicine in Springfield twelve years, and at the same time retained his ministerial connection. He was ordained deacon in 1833, at Baltimore, by Bishop Hedding, and ordained Elder in 1837, at Jacksonville, Ill., by Bishop Soule. In 1847 Dr. McNeill moved to Peoria, and became pastor of the Methodist church at that place. From there he was appointed to Racine, Wisconsin, and from there to Mt. Morris, Ogle county, Ill., October, 1852. His labors in the ministry had again impaired his health, and at Mt. Morris he resumed the practice of Medicine. Dr. McNeill had ten children, five of whom died young, and

MARY F. died, aged eleven years.

Of the other four—

ANN NORVELLA, born June 26, 1835, in Shepherdstown, Va., partially brought up in Springfield, was married at Mt. Morris, Ill., Feb. 1, 1854, to Henry I. Little, who was born Nov. 25, 1826, in Washington county, Md. They have nine children, WILLIAM F., CHARLEY F., ELDRIDGE H., MARY E., ARTHUR B., ELLEN L., WILLIAM McN., NORVELLA L. and KITTIE L. Mr. Little is a dry goods merchant, and resides at Mt. Morris, Ogle county, Illinois.

JAMES F., born Oct. 15, 1841, in Springfield, Ill., enlisted August 12, 1862, for three years, in Co. G, 114th Ill. Inf. He was promoted to Sergeant-Major, served to the close of the rebellion, was honorably discharged, August 15, 1865, and was afterwards clerk in the Adjutant-General's office until that office was abolished. He was married Nov. 18, 1872, to Julia E. Hibbs, a native of New York City. They have two children, WALTER F. and MABEL. James F. McNeal is corresponding clerk in the first National Bank, of Springfield, Ill., and resides in the city.—1876.

WILBUR A., born June 12, 1843, in Springfield, Ill., resides at Machachinock, Mahaska county, Iowa.

HOBART W., born June 18, 1847, in Peoria, Ill., was married May 15, 1869, at Eldora, Iowa, to Lizzie Phillips. They have one living child, ANNA M., and reside at Oscaloosa, Iowa.

While Dr. F. A. McNeill was living in Peoria, his wife, Mrs. Mary E. McNeill visited friends in Springfield, and died there Nov. 24, 1849. Dr. McNeill was married Feb. 2, 1857, at Mt. Morris, Ill., to Barbara E. Wagner, who was born Oct. 6, 1834, in Washington county, Maryland. They had four children, two of whom only are living, namely—

KITTIE M. and

FRANK S., who reside with their mother.

Rev. Francis A. McNeill, M. D., died Feb. 3, 1872, at Mt. Morris, Ogle county, Ill., and his widow resides there. Dr. McNeill was a man of much more than ordinary ability, and of untiring industry. In addition to the labors of two professions, he found time to devote to political matters. Having from childhood witnessed the pernicious influence of slavery, he very early in life became an opponent of its extension. It was partly to avoid its influence that he moved West. While practicing medicine in Springfield, he took an active part in the politics of the day. As a public speaker, he advocated the election of Harrison for President in 1840, and in 1844 was a delegate to the convention that nominated Clay for President. He was one of the delegates from Ogle county to the convention that assembled in Bloomington in 1856, which gave birth to the Republican party. Being a warm friend of Mr. Lincoln, while living in Springfield, when the latter became a candidate for President, he had not a more ardent supporter than Dr. McNeill.

Before the convention assembled that nominated Mr. Lincoln, Dr. McNeill was editing a paper at Mount Morris, and was among the first to hoist the name of Abraham Lincoln for President. In 1860 he was elected Representative from Ogle county, for two years, in the State Legislature; and was, consequently, in that body when the rebellion broke out. He was appointed Oct. 12, 1861, by Governor Yates, army surgeon, and was with the 34th Ill. Inf. about six months, when he resigned on account of impaired health. He was commissioned July 18, 1862, hospital chaplain, and assigned to the post at Paducah, Ky., where he remained until 1864, when he was transferred to Louisville, as chaplain of the post there. He resigned August, 1865, returned home, and resumed the practice of medicine, which he continued until stricken down with paralysis, which, after a year's suffering, terminated in death—as previously stated—thus closing a well-spent life.

McNEILL, WILLIAM, born Aug. 15, 1811, in Cumberland, Allegheny county, Maryland. Rev. F. A. McNeill, M. D., was his brother. William McNeill studied medicine in his native town, and graduated at Jefferson Medical College, Philadelphia, in Feb., 1835. He was married Aug. 1, 1837, in Cumberland, to Civilia McNamee, who was born July 6, 1817, in Hagerstown, Maryland. They had one child in Cumberland, and in the spring of 1839 moved to Petersburg, Illinois. In the autumn of that year he moved to Mechanicsburg, Sangamon county. They had eight living children in Illinois. Of their nine children—

THOMAS H., born May 17, 1838, in Maryland, is unmarried, and is farming near Cornland, Logan county, Illinois.

RICHARD J., born Dec. 23, 1840, in Mechanicsburg, Ill., graduated Feb., 1863, at the Eclectic Medical College, of Cincinnati, Ohio. Dr. R. J. McNeill was married Dec. 18, 1873, near Rochester, Ill., to Eliza Taft. They have one child, WILLIAM T., and live in Rochester.

LAURA, born December 12, 1842, at Bolivia, Christian county, Ill., was married in Mechanicsburg to George W. Hall. *See his name.* He died, and she lives at Illiopolis.

ROBERT B., born April 28, 1846, in Mechanicsburg, is a druggist, in Pana, Illinois.

FRANCIS A., born Oct. 23, 1849, near Rochester, graduated at the Eclectic Medical College, Cincinnati, Feb., 1874, and is practicing medicine at Pana, Illinois.

MARY F., born Oct. 19, 1853, and

CHARLES, born Jan. 3, 1855, both near Rochester.

NELLIE, born July 17, 1858, and

LUTIE, born Jan. 27, 1864, both in Mechanicsburg. The four latter reside with their parents in Taylorville, Ill. Dr. William McNeill is practicing his profession there.—Aug., 1876.

MATHER.—The origin of the Mather family in America was with REV. (1) RICHARD MATHER, who was born in 1596, at Lowton, Lancashire, England. He came to America, landing in Boston, Aug. 17, 1635, and the next year became pastor of a church, at Dorchester, Mass., where he remained until his death, April 22, 1669. His son, (2) INCREASE MATHER, born June 21, 1639, at Dorcester, Mass., became pastor of North street church, Boston, in 1664, and continued in charge of that church until the day of his death, Aug. 23, 1723. He was President of Harvard College, from 1685 to 1701, and received the degree of Doctor of Divinity from its board of trustees in 1692, the first title of the kind ever conferred in America. His son, (3) COTTON MATHER, born Feb. 12, 1663, in Boston, became the colleague of his father in the pastorate in 1684. He was elected in 1713 a member of the Royal Society of London, being the first American ever thus honored. Rev. Cotton Mather died Feb. 13, 1728, and in 1729 his life was written by his son, (4) SAMUEL MATHER. His son, Dr. (5) THOMAS MATHER, had a son, (6) WILLIAM MATHER, who was a soldier from Connecticut in the Revolution. His son—

MATHER, (7) THOMAS, was born April 24, 1795, in Simsbury, Hartford county, Conn. Inheriting much of the intellectual ability and integrity of character of his ancestors, and impelled by the New England spirit of enterprise, on arriving at the age of manhood, he left his native State and engaged in business in New York city, where he remained but a short time. In the spring of 1818, he went to Kaskaskia, the capital of the Territory of Illinois. There he subsequently became associated in business with Edmund Roberts, James L. Lamb and Stacy B. Opdycke. Some years later they laid out the town of Chester, Randolph county, Ill., and engaged in business there also. Thomas Mather was married Dec. 5, 1825, in Kaskaskia, to Hannah G. Lamb, who was born March 23, 1798, in Connellsville, Fayette county, Penn. She was a sister to George and James L. Lamb. In addition to his mercantile pursuits, Mr. Mather found time to look after the interests of the government. He served a number of times in both branches of the Legislature, was a member of the lower house during the session of 1822-3, when the resolution was adopted to submit to the people a proposition for a convention, to be called for the purpose of amending the constitution, with the view of admitting slavery into the State. He opposed the resolution submitting it, and when it was before the people he bore a conspicuous part in the public discussion against adopting the measure. It was through the persistent opposition of Mr. Mather and kindred spirits, that Illinois was saved by the small majority of 1,800 votes from becoming a slave State. In 1825 he was appointed by President John Quincy Adams, one of the commissioners to locate a military road from Independence, Mo., to Santa Fe, New Mexico, and to negotiate treaties with the Indian tribes along the line. He acquired the title of Colonel during the administration of Governor Coles—1822-26—by being assigned an honorary position on his staff, and wore the title ever after. He once declined an appointment to fill a vacancy in the United States Senate. When Col. Mather moved to Springfield in 1835, the mercantile firm with which he was associated was reorganized, and opened under the firm name of Mather, Lamb & Co., and thus it continued for many years. The State Bank of Illinois was chartered by the Legislature, at Vandalia, during the session of 1834-5. The bank was organized at Springfield May 11, 1835, with Thomas Mather President, and N. H. Ridgely Cashier. They continued in office the whole time the bank was in existence— about seven years. The Northern Cross Railroad, from Meredosia, through Jacksonville, to Springfield, having run down so as to be practically useless, it was purchased of the State by Thomas Mather, N. H. Ridgely, James Duncan and others. They put it in good running order, and extended it to the Indiana State line. It is now part of the Toledo, Wabash & Western Railroad. He was afterwards connected with the organization of the Illinois Central and Galena Union Railroad Companies, and induced eastern capitalists to furnish the means for building the former. Col. Mather was a true friend of education, which he manifested by serving a number of years as a member of the Board of Trustees of the Illinois College, at Jacksonville, and contributing liberally toward the endowment of that and other institutions of learning. His parents were Congregationalists, and he never forgot his New England training; but on coming to Illinois, he identified himself with the Presbyterian church, differing from that of his father's not in doctrine, but in government only. His religious principles were not the result of education alone, but originated in a profound conviction of the divine claims of christianity. His benefactions to the church were large and judiciously bestowed. He retired from active business in consequence of impaired health; but continued to reside in Springfield, and died March 28, 1853, in the city of Philadelphia. His remains lie buried in the place of his nativity, surrounded by generations of his ancestors. His widow lived in Springfield until 1866, when she moved to Chicago, where she now—1876 —resides, in the seventy-eigth year of her age, and in the full possession of her mental and physical powers, venerated and loved not only by those to whom she has so long been a mother, but by their children also. Their house was truly the home of the orphan. More than one bereaved of natural protectors was fondly and lovingly cherished beneath their roof. There are those yet living in whose memories Col. Mather is enshrined as a true friend and a second father. Not having any children of his own, he adopted the following:

R. PENNELL LAMB, son of Dr. Thos. G. Lamb, of Fayette county, Penn., was born in 1822. He studied medicine, and graduated at the University of Pennsylvania, in 1849. In 1852 he was married to Mary Johnson, of Springfield, and removed the same year to Butler county, Ohio, where he died in 1866, leaving no children.

SUSAN R. LAMB, born in Kaskaskia, Ill., was married in 1855 to Dr. C. Perry Slater, of Springfield, who died in 1858. *See his name*. She was married in 1870 to James H. Roberts. *See his name*.

THOMAS C. MATHER was born in Illinois in 1839. He studied law and graduated from Ann Arbor University, Michigan. In 1871 he was married to Mary Horine, of Missouri. They have three children, THOMAS, Jun., LINA and MAY. Mr. Mather is practicing his profession and resides in Springfield.

Gen. THOMAS S. MATHER, of Springfield, was not adopted, but is a son of William Mather, a younger brother of Col. Thomas Mather.

MEADER, TIMOTHY E., was born Nov. 25, 1800, in Rochester, N. H. When a young man he spent several years in Maine, part of the time in teaching, and part of the time in the tanning and currying business. In 1834 he set out for a visit to the west. He traveled by stage and canal to Buffalo, and from there to Chicago by sailing vessel, and was seven weeks traveling from Maine to Chicago. He went down DesPlaines river in a canoe, and found a tribe of Indians camped at the mouth of the river. He went from Hennepin to Beardstown by steamboat, and walked from the latter place to Springfield, arriving in June. He next went to St. Louis, thence to New Orleans, and embarked on a sailing vessel for Boston, arriving in that city in Jan., 1835. He returned to Springfield in 1836, and remained until 1839, during which time he bought and improved a piece of land in what is now Pawnee township. In the fall of 1839 he returned east, and was married Nov. 9, 1839, at Dover, N. H., to Miriam H. Trickey. She was born Feb. 8, 1802, at Brookfield, N. H. They went the same fall they were married to Plattsville, Wis., and in the winter of 1840-'41 started for Sangamon county in a sleigh, and came the whole distance that way, although they had to wait several times for snow, but they arrived safely at their home in Pawnee township. They have only one child—

VIENNA, born April 21, 1843, in Sangamon county, married George P. Weber. *See his name*.

Timothy Meader and wife are both living on Brush creek, between Pawnee and Auburn, Sangamon county, Illinois. —1876.

MEADER, WILLIAM W., born April 22, 1820, in New Hampshire, came to Springfield in 1839, resided two years at Springfield and Pawnee, returned east, and was married at Dover, N. H., in 1845, to Lavina Trickey. He brought his family to Sangamon county in 1866, engaged in farming and selling dry goods, moved to Christian county in 1868, and Mrs. M. died, Nov., 1872, at Clarksdale. Their only child—

EDWARD E., is now of the firm of Brock & Meader, Clarksdale, Christian county, Illinois. Wm. W. Meader lives in Clarksdale also.

Mrs. Vienna Bodge, widow of James Bodge, late a merchant of Pawnee, is a sister to Timothy E. and Wm. W. Meader.

L. M. Babb, who lives three miles northeast of Pawnee, is a nephew of the Meaders.

MEACHAM, ADIN E., was born March 10, 1789, at Benson, Rutland county, Vermont. His father started with his family to move west, July 30, 1812, and halted at Chillicothe, Ohio, Sept. 24. They resumed their journey May 20, 1813, passing through Cincinnati, Ohio, Lexington, Ky., thence to Shawneetown, Ill., from there to Kaskaskia, thence up the Mississippi river to the American bottom, about ten miles above St. Louis, arriving July 26, 1813, and on the 12th day of September, the father died. The family remained there until the close of the war with Great Britain. Adin E., with his mother, moved to the vicinity of the present town of Loami, Sangamon county, Ill., in 1819. He was married there to Isabel Colburn, and had six children—

FIDELIA, born Aug. 1, 1820, married James D. Weir. They had seven living children—OLIVER B. was married in Missouri to Martha Blackwell. They had two children, JOHN and LAURA. At the breaking out of the rebellion, he left Missouri, brought his family to Sangamon county, and enlisted in the 73d Ill. Inf., for three years. He was wounded at the battle of Chattanooga, Sept. 19, 1863, and died seven days later. His children reside with their mother, who is married to Charles Preddy. They have four children, and live in Green county, Missouri. MARY J. married John Hunter. They have five children, and live at Plattville, Taylor county, Iowa. MARTHA E. married John Frank. They have two children, and live in Carthage, Missouri. HENRY is unmarried, and lives at Carthage. ISABEL married Mr. McMaster. They have two children, and live in Springfield, Missouri. MARION and AGNES live with their parents at Carthage, Missouri.

EUNICE M., born Oct. 13, 1822, married Isaac R. Mengel. See his name.

JANE L., born Oct. 12, 1824, married Levi B. Mengel. See his name.

Mrs. Jane L. Mengel has a commission held by her father, Adin E. Meacham, as Lieutenant in the 7th Reg. Ill. Militia, dated at Kaskaskia, Aug. 17, 1817, and signed by Ninian Edwards, Governor. On the back of the same is the endorsement that Adin E. Meacham has taken the oath of fidelity and of office, as prescribed by "An act to suppress dueling," dated Sept. 1, 1817, attested by John H. Randle, District Clerk. A. E. Meacham served sixty days in a company of Indian Rangers, and received for that service $40 37½.

JULIA A., born Dec. 16, 1827, married May 23, 1844, to Charles H. Dawson, who was born Feb. 26, 1820, in Vermont. They had eight children, two of whom died in infancy. RICHARD H., born March 14, 1845, married Lizzie C. Ruckle. They have two children, KATIE and ALICE, and live in Springfield, Illinois. GEORGE E., born June 23, 1847, graduated at Ann Arbor, Michigan University, was Professor of Languages, in the High School, at Buffalo, N. Y., for some time, and is now—1875—leaving for a two years' tour of Europe, studying and perfecting himself in the law. LYDIA L., was born May 12, 1847, and married Joseph E. Coleman. See his name. OLIVE A., born Sept. 2, 1853, married, Oct. 7, 1873, to Robert E. Short. See his name. They have one child, OLIVE IRENE, and live near Loami. ANDREW L. and WALTER L. live with their mother. Charles H. Dawson died July 22, 1820, and his widow lives near Loami, Sangamon county, Illinois.

ADIN E. A., born July 16, 1831,, in Sangamon county, was married Jan. 1, 1852, in Stoughton, Wisconsin, to Martha Renshaw, who was born April 22, 1836, in St. Lawrence county, N. Y. They have six living children, CHARLES W., AUSTIN S., ADA BELLE, MAGGIE E., MARIETTA and ORRIN R., and live at Loami, Sangamon county, Ill. Adin E. A. Meacham has in his possession a powder horn that has been in the family three generations before it came into his hands. It bears the following inscription, elaborately carved: "John Herolt's Horn, 1756." The only other letters on it are "A Muscovy Cat," over a figure supposed to represent an animal known by that appellation. It also contains figures of other animals, ships, and various hieroglyphics, and must have occupied many leisure hours of some soldier engaged in the French and English wars on this continent before our nation was born. A. E. A. Meacham has also a gourd raised by his father in 1826, near where he now resides; it holds an even half bushel. How a Yankee came to grow a gourd, such as our early education led us to believe could only be done by some person with southern blood in their veins, is a mystery.

HARRIET I., born Oct. 3, 1834, was married Oct. 7, 1857, to Andrew J. Parker. They have two children, DORA I. and IRA M., and live in Loami.

Mrs. Isabel Meacham died Nov. 25, 1861, and her husband, A. E. Meacham, died March 9, 1866, both near Loami, Sangamon county, Illinois.

MEACHAM, EDOM, was born in Kentucky, and married there to Nancy Cavenah. They had three children, and

—65

moved to Sangamon county, Ill., arriving Dec., 1830, just in time for the "deep snow," on Lick Creek, in what is now Loami township, where they had three children. Of their six children—

MARTHA E., born Jan. 27, 1827, in Kentucky, married in Sangamon county Jan. 23, 1846, to Jonathan Morris. *See his name.*

WILLIS, born in Kentucky, and married in Sangamon county to Rachel C. S. Hudson. They have two children, ADALINE and MARGARET, and reside in Waverly, Ill.

M. MARGARET, born in Kentucky, married in Sangamon county to Peter L. Jarrett. *See his name.*

FRANKLIN, born in Sangamon county, married Mary Hutchinson, has one child, and lives in Waverly, Illinois.

LUCINDA, born July 29, 1838, in Sangamon county, married Aug. 12, 1853, to Wellington B. Huffaker, who was born Oct. 22, 1829, in Morgan county, and came to Sangamon county in 1851. They had seven children. JESSIE B., the second child, died when she was seven years old. WELLINGTON L., the fourth child, died in his third year. GEORGE G. was married June 2, 1875, in New Berlin, to Clara J. Manson, and lives near New Berlin, Ill. LIZZIE M., JENNIE, FRANCIS M. and LOULU A. live with their mother. Wellington B. Huffaker died March 3, 1873. His widow and children reside four miles south of New Berlin, Sangamon county, Ill. Mr. Huffaker was a successful farmer and stock raiser, and had just completed the finest private residence in Sangamon county, outside of Springfield.

ADALINE, born Oct. 4, 1844, in Sangamon county, married March 27, 1860, to George Madison Maxwell. *See his name.*

Mrs. Nancy Meacham died Sept. 11, 1853, and Edom Meacham was married in 1855 to Margaret McCormick. They have nine children, and reside in Waverly, Morgan county, Illinois.

Willis L. Meacham, the father of Edom, was a native of North Carolina. He moved from Kentucky to Sangamon county with his son, Edom, both families arriving just as the deep snow commenced falling in Dec., 1830. He brought several other children with him. His daughter Annis, married Dr. West, who died, leaving three children; and she married William Sims, and lives in Jacksonville, Ill. His son, Tandy, married Julia Littrall, and lives in Waverly, Ill. Willis L. Meacham and wife both died in Sangamon county.

MEACHAM, JOSEPH K., was born in Kentucky, came to Sangamon county among the earliest settlers, and married Ann Hodgerson. They had four children in Sangamon county, namely—

WILLIAM C., born Jan. 8, 1833, married Narcissa Parsley. They have five children, and reside near Maroa, Macon county, Illinois.

JOHN H., born Feb. 12, 1834, married Jan. 4, 1861, to Leah Jarrett. They had six children; two died in infancy. JOSEPH K. died in his eighth year. JAMES W., LUANNA J. and ADA E. live with their parents, three miles south of New Berlin, Illinois.

WILLIS died at ten years of age.

REBECCA E., born April 8, 1838, married Rowan Morris, Jun., and live in Ray county, Missouri.

Joseph K. Meacham died July 28, 1838, and his widow died April 12, 1867, both in Sangamon county, Illinois.

MEACHAM, JOSEPH, was born in 1794 in Christian county, Ky. Thankful Finley was born in 1795 in the same county. They were married, and had seven children there. The family moved to Sangamon county, arriving Oct., 1840, at Springfield, and the next spring moved to what is now Loami township. Of their children—

ELCEY F., born Oct. 2, 1820, in Christian county, Ky., married in Sangamon county Nov. 7, 1844, to Jackson Archer. *See his name.* He died, and she married William Duff. *See his name.*

JOHN W., born Aug. 1822, in Christian county, Ky., came to Sangamon county in 1838, preceding his parents. He was married in Springfield to Ann Young. They had seven children; one only is living, ROBERT P. He married Sarah Jumper in Jacksonville. The family reside in Waverly, Illinois.

MARY H., born in Kentucky, married in Sangamon county to A. S. Har-

SANGAMON COUNTY.

mon. She died, and Mr. Harmon married again. He lives in Waverly.

ELIZABETH E. was twice married. She and both husbands died in Waverly.

MINERVA L., born in Christian county, Ky., married in Sangamon county to Young Hudson. See his name.

ABNER W., died in Kentucky, and AMERICA J., died in Sangamon county, each at ten years of age.

Mrs. Thankful Meacham died Oct. 7, 1844, and Joseph Meacham died Oct. 19, 1845, both near Loami, Sangamon county, Illinois.

MEGREDY, ENOCH, born in 1794, in Cecil county, Maryland, was married there, Aug. 20, 1816, to Mary S. Jones, who was born in Cecil county, April 7, 1798. Mr. Megredy was engaged in merchandizing, and they had four children there. About 1823 they moved into the adjoining county, in Pennsylvania, where Mr. Megredy continued in the mercantile business. Four children were born in Pennsylvania, and about 1831 they returned to Maryland, where they had three cnildren. Mr. M. moved his family to Springfield, Ill., arriving June 16, 1837, and in December following moved to what is now Ball township, six miles south of Springfield, where two children were born. Of all their children; the eldest—

ELIZABETH died Dec. 14, 1821, in Maryland, aged four years.

JAMES J., born Feb. 1, 1819, in Cecil county, Md., was married in Sangamon county, Ill., Dec. 30, 1841, to Ann R. Hall. They had ten children, three died under four years, and JOHN B. in his fourth year. Of the other six—CHARLES L. married Virginia Weber, and lives at Belleville, Kansas. ANNA, WILLIAM P., SAMUEL E., MILLARD F. and FANNIE, live with their parents, three and three-fourths miles northwest of Pawnee. James J. Megredy represented Sangamon county in the State Legislature, for the session of 1857 and '8.

MARY A., born Nov. 3, 1820, in Cecil county, Maryland, was married Nov. 25, 1847, in Sangamon county, Ill., to Dr George M. Harrison. See his name.

DANIEL, born Aug. 30, 1822, in Maryland, was married in Sangamon county, Feb. 22, 1849, to Sarah N. Harrison, who died, and he married Catharine Kennedy. Daniel Megredy died in Ball township, leaving three children, WILLIAM ARTHUR, MARY and SARAH.

ELIZABETH, born Sept. 11, 1824, in Lancaster county, Penn., is unmarried, and lives at the family homestead, in Sangamon county.

ENOCH, born June 16, 1826, at Conestoga, Lancaster county, Penn., raised in Sangamon county, married, Oct. 16, 1850, to Lucinda P. Harrison, who was born Sept. 10, 1828, in that part of Sangamon which is now Menard county. They had four children—MARY A., the second child, died in her fifth year. ENOCH E., ADA and LESLIE E. live with their parents, in Menard county, three and one-half miles northwest of Salisbury.

JOHN, born July 11, 1828, in Conestoga Center, Pennsylvania, married Priscilla L. Miller. They had four children, and Mr. Megredy died, near Springfield. His widow and children live in Kansas City, Missouri.

SARAH died, aged twenty years.

ABIGAIL, born July 18, 1832, in Cecil county, Maryland, was married in Sangamon county, April 14, 1858, to Morgan B. Pettus. They have three children, and live in Lincoln, Illinois.

WILLIAM R., born Dec. 31, 1833, in Wakefield, Cecil county, Maryland, was married in Iroquois county, Ill., Oct. 8, 1872, to Joanna Harlan, who was born Oct. 21, 1850, in Morgan county, Ill. They have one child, WILLIAM, and live in Chatham, Sangamon county, Illinois.

ADALINE B., born Nov. 21, 1835, in Cecil county, Maryland, was married Nov. 21, 1855, in Sangamon county, Illinois to Robert S. Graham. See his name.

ARCHIBALD JOB, born January 30, 1838, in Sangamon county, lives at the homestead.

MARGARET R., born April 20, 1840, in Sangamon county, is unmarried, and lives at the homestead.

Enoch Megredy, Sen., died December 28, 1851, and his widow died Aug. 11,

1866, both on the farm where they settled in 1837, six miles south of Springfield.

Archibald Job, a cousin of Mr. Megredy, had a contract for furnishing stone to build the State House, in Springfield, which was commenced the year Mr. Megredy came to the county. The stone was obtained in Ball township, near Crow's mill, and Mr. Megredy was employed to superintend the quarries. He was experienced in the business before he came west. Mr. Megredy was a local Methodist preacher, and a consistant temperance man. He lectured on temperance on all suitable occasions.

MENGEL, ISAAC R., was born about 1820, in Lancaster county, Penn. He left home with his brother, Levi B., April 17, 1838, and arrived at Springfield, Ill., early in May, and a few days later went to Lebanon, now Loami, in the employ of J. P. Langford, who had a contract for furnishing timber for the State House, then being built in Springfield. He was married near Loami to Eunice M. Meacham. They had twelve children, among them two pairs of twins, and once three at a birth, two boys and a girl; the latter and one of the boys died young. The other boy—

ELLIS, lives with his parents in Nebraska.

LEVI enlisted in Co. K, 124th Ill. Inf., and died in the army.

ETHAN M., enlisted in Co. K, 124th Ill. Inf. He lost an eye by an accidental shot from a weapon in the hands of his Captain, near the close of his term of service. He married Amanda M. Weber, in Sangamon county, and lives in Nebraska.

ARMINDA J., married a Mr. Griffin, in 1865. They have three children, and live near Lincoln, Neb.

HATTIE lives with her parents in Wahoo, Neb.

Isaac R. Mengel resides at Wahoo, Saunders county, Nebraska. He is Probate Judge of that county—1875.

MENGEL, LEVI B., born in 1822 in Lancaster county, Penn., and came with his brother, Isaac R., to Springfield, thence to Loami, in 1838. He was married Nov. 13, 1842, to Jane L. Meacham. They had ten living children in Sangamon county.

ELIZABETH, born June 12, 1843, married June, 1869, to James Coleman. They have twins, NINA MAY and LINA JANE, and live in Christian county, Illinois.

TIRZAH married David P. Colburn. See his name.

ANTHONY W. died Aug. 27, 1874, in his seventeenth year.

EUNICE married Oct. 29, 1874, to Ezra D. Fuller. They have one child, LULU, and live near Loami, Illinois.

FRANCIS, ALICE C., JOSEPH W., KATE M., ANNA L. and *HARRY S.* live with their mother.

Levi B. Mengel died Sept. 10, 1874, near Loami, Sangamon county, Ill., and his widow and children reside there.

MEREDITH, ABSALOM, born about 1785, in Virginia, was married there about 1807, to Mary Royal, a native of the same State. They moved to Butler county, Ohio, where they had four children, and then moved to Miami county, where two children were born. The family moved to Sangamon county, Ill., arriving Oct. 27, 1829, in what is now Ball township. The company in which they came numbered sixty-three persons. Of their six children—

THOMAS, born in Butler county, Ohio, was married in Sangamon county to Priscilla Fields, who died, and he married Jane Basil. They had two children. DAVIS was a soldier in an Ill. Reg., and was killed at the battle of Resaca, Georgia, May 15, 1864. NANCY E. married a Mr. Buck. He was a Union soldier, and died in the army. His widow resides with her mother. Thomas Meredith was drowned in Sacramento river, Cal. His widow and widowed daughter reside near Elizabeth, JoDaviess county, Illinois.

AMY, born in Butler county, Ohio, was married in Sangamon county to William B. Lawley. See his name.

DAVIS, born June 14, 1812, in Butler county, Ohio, was married June 29, 1836, in Sangamon county, to Mary Newcomer. They had eight children; one died in infancy. Of the other seven—
SUSANNAH, born May 4, 1837, married Drury Jones. See his name.
CHARLES N., born July 23, 1839, enlisted in Co. E, 114th Ill. Inf., August 11, 1862. He was taken sick at Camp Butler,

and was out of the service six months. He was married March 8, 1863, to Laura Wagoner, who was born Sept. 3, 1841, in Menard county, Ill. He rejoined his regiment, March 20, of same year, and after the siege of Vicksburg, was sent to Memphis, where he was detailed as Orderly at headquarters of the Sixteenth Army Corps. Charles N. Meredith was honorably discharged, Oct., 1864, at Memphis, Tenn. Mr. and Mrs. Meredith have two living children, MARY F. and IDA J., who live with their parents. C. N. Meredith is engaged in the clothing business at Taylorville, Ill., and resides there. MARY J., born Dec. 3, 1842, was married Jan. 1, 1863, to John R. Kincaid, who was born Nov. 14, 1833, in Virginia, and brought up in Gallia county, Ohio. Mr. and Mrs. Kincaid have four living children, LUTHER E., JAMES W., CATALINA MAY and FRED CARROLL, and live five miles north of Pawnee, Sangamon county, Ill. SARAH A., born Nov. 2, 1844, was married Oct. 19, 1865, to Lewis R. Hedrick. They have three living children, namely, MARY S., FRANCIS R. and ALICE J., and live in Taylorville, Christian county, Ill. CHRISTOPHER C., born June 3, 1848, resides with his parents. LUTHER OSBORN, born July 7, 1851, was married Sept. 4, 1873, to Eliza A. Poffenberger. They have one child, CHARLES NOAH, and live in Cotton Hill township, Sangamon county, Illinois. FANNIE L., born Jan. 27, 1857, lives with her parents. Davis Meredith lives in Ball township, ten miles southeast of Springfield, Ill. He remembers that, after the deep snow, when it had entirely disappeared except on the roads, where the snow had been packed down, they looked like ribbons stretched over the prairie, and the sight was beautiful. These strips were from one to three feet wide, and it was weeks after the other snow was gone before they disappeared.

WILLIAM, born in Butler county, Ohio, brought up in Sangamon county, is a minister in the United Brethren church, and lives at Fort Scott, Kansas.

SARAH A., born in Miami county, Ohio, was married in Sangamon county, Ill., to James Dillon. They have two children, OLIVER and DAVIS, who live with their father. Mrs. S. A. Dillon died at Hittle's Grove, McLean county, Illinois.

JOSEPH, born in Miami county, Ohio, was married in Sangamon county, Ill., to Susan Dillon, who died, leaving five children, SARAH A., LESLIE C., THOMAS J., CHARLOTTE J. and MARY C. live with their father. He married Mary Adams. They have one child, MELISSA. Joseph Meredith and family live near Taylorville, Ill.

Absolom Meredith died in Rochester township, Sangamon county, Ill., in 1842, and his widow died in 1844, in Ball township, Sangamon county, Illinois.

MERRIMAN, ELIAS H., was born Jan. 20, 1802, in Baltimore, Maryland. He graduated at William and Mary College about 1820, and at the Baltimore Medical University soon after. He was married in Baltimore Aug. 16, 1822, to Susan H. Lavely, a sister to William Lavely. *See his name.* She was born Dec. 9, 1804, in that city. They had one child there, also. After practicing for a time in the vicinity of Baltimore, Dr. Merriman moved to St. Louis, Mo., and from there to Springfield, Ill., arriving in March, 1830. They had one child in St. Louis, and two in Springfield. Of their children—

JAMES H., born Jan. 27, 1827, in Baltimore, Md., was raised in Springfield, Ill. He enlisted in Co: A, 4th Ill. Inf., in 1846, and was appointed by Col. E. D. Baker Sergeant-Major of the regiment, and served as such during the war with Mexico. He was appointed under President Taylor to a clerkship in the United States General Land Office, and was later appointed Lieutenant in the United States Revenue Service, in which he served about twenty-four years, the last twelve as Captain. He is now Inspector of the Life Saving Service, having charge of all the stations on the Atlantic coast, with headquarters in New York city—1876.

WILLIAM J. N., born Feb. 10, 1830, in St. Louis, Mo., and raised in Springfield. In 1852, he went to California, and in 1855 went from there with Gen. Walker on his expedition to Central America, after which he returned to the United States. He now resides in Springfield, Ill.

ELLEN M., born May 1 1832, in Springfield, married in 1854 to Thomas H. Murphy, a native of Quebec, Canada. They moved in 1859 to New Orleans, and returned to Springfield in 1873. She resides with her mother, in Springfield.

Dr. E. H. Merriman was engaged in one of the campaigns of the Black Hawk war, and was bearer of dispatches from General Henry to General Atkinson. *See page 85.* He was in successful practice in Springfield for twenty years. In 1851 he went to San Francisco; spent four years there, and in 1855 went to Costa Rica, in search of coal. He had commenced mining, but the yellow fever breaking out among the men, he treated them successfully, but afterwards fell a victim to the disease himself, and died there on the Island of Cano, May 8, 1855. His widow resides in Springfield, Illinois.

MERRIMAN, REUBEN, was born Sept. 6, 1790, in Connecticut. When a young man, he went to Kentucky, and after a stay of one year, returned to Connecticut, and was married, May 4, 1812, about twenty miles from Bridgeport, to Betsy Bennett. They went at once to Scott county, Ky., settled on Big Eagle creek, and engaged in milling and coopering with his younger brother, Lyman, and their father, who all moved at the same time. They had five living children. The father died there, and the two brothers, with their families and their sister, and widowed mother, moved to Sangamon county, Ill., arriving in the fall of 1829, in what is now Williams township, where twins were born. Of all their children—

LUCINDA, born Feb. 21, 1813, in Scott county, Ky., married in Sangamon county to Isaac Constant. *See his name.* They had four children, and moved to Jackson county, Oregon, Rogue River Valley, in 1852.

LAVINA J., born April 2, 1817, in Kentucky, married to William T. Jones. *See his name.*

GEORGE B., born Sept. 8, 1818, in Scott county, Ky., came to Sangamon county, in 1829, married, Jan. 1, 1844, to Maria L. Dawson. They had six living children in Sangamon county—JOHN W. married Maria J. Brittin, have two children, DORA B. and HARRY W., and reside in Marion county, Iowa. REUBEN A. resides in Williams township. BELBERT, LUCY T., BERTHA E. and GEORGE A. reside with their parents, four miles southeast of Williamsville, Sangamon county, Illinois.

JOHN S., born Nov. 29, 1821, in Scott county, Ky., married in Sangamon county, Nov. 7, 1848, to Mary J. Dawson. They had ten children; one died in infancy, and NOAH W., the youngest child, died March 4, 1873, aged six years. MARY FLORENCE died, Aug. 12, 1874, and ANN ELIZA died, June 13, 1876, at their father's house, near Williamsville, Illinois. Of the other six— MARTHA V., CHARLES B., LELIA L., CLAY S., CORA E. and ABRAHAM L. live with their parents, three miles west of Williamsville, Sangamon county, Illinois.

WILLIAM H., born March 4, 1825, in Kentucky, was married in Sangamon county to Mary A. Lewis. They had two children, and in 1852 started overland for Oregon. Mrs. Merriman and one of the children died on the way. Mr. Merriman and the other children went on to their destination. Wm. Merriman was there married to Mrs. Artamesia Chapman, whose maiden name was Riddle. They have several children, and reside near Jacksonville, Jackson county, Oregon.

ROBERT F., and *FRANCIS A.*, twins, born Sept. 5, 1830, in Sangamon county, Illinois.

ROBERT F., married Sept. 17, 1862, in Sangamon county, to Elizabeth Thompson, who was born Jan. 28, 1840, in Wayne county, Ohio. They have one child, WILLIE, and reside five miles southeast of Williamsville.

FRANCIS A. married, Oct. 7, 1858, to Emma Bishop, who was born Dec. 12, 1838, in Clark county, Ohio. They had five children, EDDY F., MARY L. MYRTILLA, and BYRON and ROSE twins; the two latter died in infancy. Mrs. Emma Merriman died May 9 1866. F. A. Merriman was married Nov. 25, 1868, to Chloe Sparklin, a native of Elkhart county, Indiana. They reside five miles southeast of Williamsville, and two and one-half miles north of Barclay, Illinois.

Mrs. Betsy Merriman died Feb. 27, 1842, and Reuben Merriman died Feb. 28, 1842, both in Sangamon county.

MERRIMAN, LYMAN, was born in 1792, in Connecticut. He went with his brother Reuben to Scott county, Ky., in 1812, and was there married to Sarah R. Howard, who was born there in 1794. They had four living children, and moved to Sangamon county, Ill., arriving in the fall of 1829, in what is now Williams township, where one child was born. Of their five children—

MADISON M., born March 11, 1817, in Scott county, Ky., married Elizabeth Fletcher. They have seven living children. Their daughter, ELIZABETH A., married Irvin J. Houtz, and reside in Williams township, two and a quarter miles north of Sherman. The other six reside with their parents, in Logan county, Illinois.

SARAH J., born Aug. 22, 1819, in Scott county, Ky., married William Yocom. *See his name.*

ELVIRA married Francis M. Young, had one child, and died in 1851.

CORDELIA L., born in Kentucky, married in Sangamon county March 10, 1862, to B. F. Fletcher. *See his name.*

MARY A., born in Sangamon county, married Hiram J. Young. She died Aug., 1867, leaving four children, LAURA A. and MARY A. reside with their aunt, Mrs. Wm. Yocom. The two sons live with their father, in Montgomery county, Illinois.

Lyman Merriman died in March, 1865, and his widow died Sept. 20, 1869.

LAURA, the sister of Reuben and Lyman Merriman, who came with them from Kentucky, married in Sangamon county in 1829 to Francis Arenz, went to Beardstown, and died within a year after she was married. The mother of the Merriman brothers and sister died in Beardstown, also.

MESLER, CORNELIUS, was born Oct. 7, 1798, in Morris county, New Jersey. Phœbe Shepard was born July 15, 1804, at Green village, Morris county, New Jersey. They were married Dec. 25, 1822, in Newark, New Jersey. They came to Springfield, Ill., in June, 1830, and settled one and one-half miles east of the city. In 1834 they moved to what is now Cooper township,

south of Sangamon river. Cornelius Mesler died July 7, 1854, and his widow resides on the farm where they settled in 1834. It is in Cooper township, three miles northeast of Clarksville, Sangamon county, Illinois.

MERRIWEATHER, JOHN H., was born July 2, 1808, in Baltimore county, Md. He migrated to the vicinity of Springfield, Clark county, Ohio, and was there married in 1834 to Elizabeth Hummell. They had two children there, and came to Springfield, Ill., arriving in May, 1839, where six children were born, one of whom died. Of their seven children—

ELIZABETH H., born in 1836 near Springfield, Ohio, was married May 2, 1864, in Springfield, Ill., to Edward L. M. Johnson, a native of Virginia. He was a contractor, and superintended the carpenter work on the Springfield and Illinois Southeastern—now O. and M.—railroad. He died November, 1874. His widow resides in Pana, Illinois.

WILLIAM H., born April 28, 1838, in Clark county, Ohio, was married Sept. 20, 1860, in Springfield, Ill., to Sarah J. Bateman, who was born there Sept. 13, 1842. He served seventeen months in Co. B, 114th Ill. Inf. Mr. and Mrs. Merriweather have five children, and live near Gerard, Crawford county, Kansas.

ELIZA W., born May 5, 1840, was married in Springfield, Ill., April 19, 1860, to John T. Rhodes, who was born Jan. 14, 1831, in Frederick county, Md. They have two children, WILLIAM R. and ELLA M. J. T. Rhodes is a contractor and builder. He was a member of the Board of Supervisors of Sangamon county for three years, and was elected in the spring of 1874 a member of the City Council for three years, and resides in Springfield, Illinois.

JAMES, born Sept. 30, 1844, in Springfield, was married Oct. 20, 1870, in Sangamon county, to Minerva Enyart. They have one child, ANN E., and live near Pawnee, Illinois.

JOHN H., Jun., born Sept. 7, 1846, in Springfield, and resides in Pawnee, Sangamon county, Illinois.

ELLA L., born April 18, 1851, in Springfield, was married there Nov. 4, 1874, to Charles W. Post, who was born Oct. 26, 1854, in Springfield, Ill. C. W.

Post is with his father, C. R. Post, in the agricultural implement business, in Springfield, Illinois.

GEORGE W., born April 29, 1855, in Springfield, lives with his sister, Mrs. Johnson, in Pana, Illinois.

John H. Merriweather, Sen., was a merchant in Springfield for many years, but the latter part of his life was spent on his farm, near Pawnee, Ill., where he died Oct. 15, 1863. His widow died Aug. 18, 1868.

MESSICK, JOSEPH W., was born in Christian county, Ky., and came to Sangamon county in 1829, with his sisters, Matilda and Melinda. He returned to Kentucky in 1840, married there, and brought his wife and youngest sister, Julia A., to Sangamon county. He makes his home in Macoupin county, near Nilwood. His sister—

ELIZABETH, came before, and married Silas Harlan. See his name. He died, and she married George Roberts, and resides in Chatham township.

MATILDA is unmarried, and resides with her niece, Mrs. J. F. Irwin.

MELINDA married M. F. Cannon, and both died in 1850 in Chatham township.

JULIA A., married William D. Crow. See his name.

MILLER, CHRISTIAN, was born Jan. 12, 1771, in Loudon county, Va. Sarah Neer was born June 28, 1786, in the same county, and they were there married in 1807. They had eight children in that county. The whole family left Loudon county Sept. 4, 1833, traveling in wagons; they reached Champaign county, Ohio, and stopped with a brother. Mr. Miller and his eldest son, David, set out on horseback for Illinois, via Indianapolis, Crawfordsville, Vermilion Salt Works, thence through Illinois to Pekin, Lewiston and Canton, and returning, crossed the Illinois river at Fort Ross—now Havana—thence to Springfield, Paris, Terre Haute, Ind., and back to Ohio. He purchased a farm in Miami county, Ohio, and commenced moving to it on the morning after the great meteoric shower, Nov. 13, 1833. One year later he sold out in Ohio, and started, Nov. 17, 1834, with his family; passing through Springfield they reached Alton in December. From there they moved back to Sangamon county, arriving in Springfield, Jan. 20, 1835. Mr. Miller entered two thousand one hundred acres of land in the vicinity of the mouth of Buckhart creek, in what is now Cooper and Rochester townships. On the 19th of March, 1835, the family moved to what is now Cooper township. All the Miller family except David and John C., moved, in Nov., 1838, to Coles county, six miles from Jefferson City, Mo., and all returned to Sangamon county in Dec., 1841. Of the eight children of Christian Miller—

DAVID, born April 18, 1809, in Loudon county, Va., came to Sangamon county in 1835, married April 26, 1838, to Eliza D. Jackson, who was born July 10, 1808, in Shelby county, Ky. She died without children, in Sangamon county, Oct. 10, 1871. David Miller was married Feb. 1, 1872, in Sangamon county, to Fannie Jackson, who was born Oct. 28, 1841, in Nelson county, Ky., and raised in Missouri. They had two children. FANNIE E. died in infancy. David Miller died Jan. 23, 1875. His son, DAVID EDWIN, born August 31, 1875, seven months and eight days after the death of his father. The widow and infant son of David Miller reside at Sangamon Station, five miles east of Springfield, Ill.

ANN, born Nov. 11, 1810, in Virginia, resides with her brother, Jacob C. She never married, has been an invalid for fifteen years, and has been blind since Nov. 30, 1868.

JOHN C., born Oct. 19, 1812, in Loudon county, Va., came to Sangamon county in 1835, married at Rochester, Feb. 5, 1837, to Melvina Sattley. They had six children in Sangamon county, namely: GEORGE H., born March 19, 1838, married March 13, 1863, to Louisana Archer. They had one child, JOHN E., and Mrs. Miller died Jan. 1, 1874. Mr. Miller and his son reside at the family homestead, three miles east of Rochester. HARRIET V., born Oct. 13, 1840, married Feb. 9, 1862, to Daniel Waters, who was born Sept. 14, 1830, in Loudon county, Va., and came to Sangamon county in 1852. They had five children, two of whom died, GEORGE E. in his third year, and LULA in infancy. The other three, ANNIE A., CHARLES M. and LILLA M., a twin to Lula, reside with their parents, five miles east of Rochester. EDMOND, born Feb. 1, 1843, married Oct. 13, 1870, to Louisana Whitesides. She died Nov. 23, 1871, and he resides three miles east of Rochester, where his parents settled in 1837, and where he was born. SARAH ANN, born Sept. 20, 1845, married August, 1866, to George Lucas, have two children, JOHN H. and MARY E., and live five miles west of Mechanicsburg. ELIZA E., born Feb. 23, 1848, married Dec. 27, 1870, to John Archer, have one child, LOUETTA, and live three miles north of Edinburg, Ill. MARY ALICE, born March 2, 1851, lives with her mother. John C. Miller died Jan. 13, 1853, and his widow resides three miles east of Rochester, Ill., where she and her husband settled in 1837.

SAMUEL, born Aug. 27, 1815, in Loudon county, Va., married in Sangamon county, June 30, 1841, to Eliza Jones. They had four children. ANDREW died August 20, 1845, in his fourth year. EVELINE, born May 28, 1846, married Sept. 26, 1866, to George H. Waters. Mrs. Waters died, Dec. 18, 1870, leaving a son, ORVAL E., who lives with his father, near Sangamon Station. SARAH ELEANOR, born Nov. 6, 1850, married Jan. 10, 1871, to William H. Crowl. *See his name.* They have two children, LAURETTA and SAMUEL, and reside near Taylorville, Ill. MARY, born Sept. 19, 1855, lives with her parents, one and a quarter miles west of Rochester, Illinois.

NATHAN, born March 24, 1822, in Virginia, died in Sangamon county, June 9, 1848.

JACOB C., born April 9, 1824, in Loudon county, Va., married in Sangamon county, June 10, 1869, to Charlotte Prather. She was born Jan. 4, 1843, in Washington county, Md. They have two children, SAMUEL J. and DON WILLIAM, and live in Sand Prairie, five miles east of Rochester, Illinois.

JOSEPH, born August 18, 1826, in London county, Va., married in Sangamon county, Oct. 4, 1849, to Louisiana Branch. They have ten children, SAMUEL J., DAVID F., WILLIAM E., GEORGE W., ALBERT J., IDA E., DELLA ANN, REBECCA, JOSEPH, Jun., and MIRTIE, and reside in Cooper township, four miles east of Rochester, Sangamon county, Illinois.

—66

ELIZABETH, born Nov. 3, 1829, in Virginia, married in Sangamon county to Samuel Neer. She died April 2, 1854, leaving one son, NATHAN JESSE NEER, born March 7, 1854, in Sangamon county, raised and educated by his aunt, Ann Miller. He is telegraph operator and station agent at Rochester, Illinois.

Christian Miller died Sept. 14, 1842, and Mrs. Sarah Miller died August 20, 1864, both in Sangamon county.

MILLER, ADAM, Sen., younger brother to Christian, Sen., was born, raised a family, and died in Loudon county, Virginia, Aug. 6, 1828. His three sons and five daughters all came to Sangamon county, as follows—

ELIZABETH married John Jacobs in Virginia. She is a widow in Cooper township, where she came in 1839.

CATHARINE married in Virginia to Israel Dulaney. She died in 1844 in Rochester township, Sangamon county.

CHRISTIAN, Jun., born Dec. 25, 1805, in Loudon county, Va., came to Sangamon county in 1835. He never married, and died at the house of his brother, John A., Sept. 23, 1874.

BARBARA, born Feb. 20, 1808, in Loudon county, Va., came to Sangamon county in 1835, and married Samuel A. Jones, and both died near Rochester, Illinois.

JOHN A., born Nov. 11, 1810, in Loudon county, Va., came to Sangamon county in 1835 with his uncle, Christian Miller, Sen. He was married July 14, 1842, in Sangamon county, to Mary Ann Norwood. She was born June 7, 1811, in Loudon county, Va., and came in 1838 to Sangamon county with her brother, William, who writes his name Norred. John A. Miller and wife had four children in Sangamon county, MARY V., born April 9, 1846, married Aug. 10, 1864, to Andrew B. Surber who was born June 8, 1836, in Pulaski county, Ky. They have three children, WILLIAM F., MARY E. and JOHN, and live three miles east of Rochester, Illinois. JOHN F., born Oct. 5, 1848, married Dec. 22, 1873, in Galesburg, Ill., to Laura J. Highmore, daughter of John S. Highmore. They live in Edinburg, Ill. CHRISTIAN E., born March 12, 1850, and SUSAN E., born April 18, 1852, reside with their parents, two and a half miles east of Rochester, Sangamon county, Illinois—1874.

MARY, born in 1812 in Loudon county, Va., married George M. Greene. See his name.

SARAH, born in Loudon county, Va., married there to Abraham E. Nickolls. They came to Sangamon county in 1842, and she died in 1844, leaving two children. Her son, GEORGE Nicholls, lives near Rochester, Illinois.

ADAM, born July 13, 1819, in Loudon county, Va., came to Sangamon county in the fall of 1835. He was married in Rochester Dec. 31, 1856, to Cynthia Elgin. She was born Nov. 19, 1839, in Greene county, Ind. They had six children, five of whom, GILES E., FRANCISCO, DON L., WILLIE, EDNA and a babe, all died under ten years. JESSE E., born March 15, 1864, lives with his parents, in Pana, Christian county, Illinois.

MILLER, GEORGE, a brother to Christian and Adam, Sen., was captain of a company in the war of 1812. He had a son—

JOHN G., born Aug. 27, 1810, in Loudon county, Va., and married there, Nov. 1833, to Amanda A. Russell. They had five children, and came to Sangamon county in 1854. Their daughter, MINERVA, married Benj. H. North. See his name. John G. Miller moved, in 1873, to the vicinity of New Scandinavia, Kansas. His brother—

JACOB, lives south of Springfield.

MILLER, VALENTINE, brother to Christian, Sen., never came to Sangamon county, but has a son—

NATHAN, who resides near Dawson. He was not in time to be included as an early settler.

MILLER, JACOB, was born in 1789, in Kentucky. He was a soldier in the war of 1812, mustered in at Winchester, Ky., and was in the battle of Tippecanoe. Lucina Poats was born Dec. 18, 1793, in Stafford county, Va., and was taken to Clark county, Ky., when she was quite young. Jacob Miller and Lucina Poats were there married in 1812. They had five children in Kentucky, and moved to Sangamon county, Ill., arriving Dec., 1824, in what is now the northwest corner of Chatham township, where they had five children. Of their children—

ELIZA, born June 1, 1815, in Kentucky, married in Sangamon county, Oct. 20, 1832, to John Greenwood. See his name.

EUNICE, born May 29, 1819, in Kentucky, married in Sangamon county, Feb. 22, 1839, to John D. Foster. See his name.

JOHN H., born Dec. 6, 1821, in Clark county, Ky., married in Sangamon county, Feb. 14, 1849, to Elizabeth Greening. They have three children—CAROLINE married William H. Shumate, have one child, ROBERT R., and live in Marshall county, Kansas. ELIZA married George W. Stubbs. See his name. JOHN T. J. lives with his parents, in Chatham, Illinois.

EMILY T., born Jan. 13, 1824, in Kentucky, married in Sangamon county, March 7, 1843, to John Greenwood. See his name. She died, April 21, 1866.

SALLY, born March 20, 1826, in Sangamon county, lives with her mother.

MATILDA, born Sept. 25, 1828, in Sangamon county, married Aug. 1, 1850, to David Erving McGinnis. See his name.

JAMES F., born Aug. 7, 1831, in Sangamon county, married July 6, 1854, to Melinda E. Shutt. They have four children living, THOMAS J., WILLIAM A., CHARLES H. and OLLIE MAY, and live in Loami township, Sangamon county, Illinois.

EDMUND T., born Feb. 15, 1834, in Sangamon county, married Oct. 20, 1859, to Elizabeth Trimble. She had one child, and mother and child died. Mr. Miller was married Jan. 27, 1870, to Elizabeth A. Stubbs. They have one child, MINNIE F., and live on the farm where his parents settled in 1824. It is five miles west of Chatham, Illinois.

FRANCIS M., born Feb. 11, 1836, in Sangamon county, married Oct. 1, 1858, to Eliza J. Trimble. They have seven daughters, FLORA A., SARAH E., MARY F., LILLIE, LUELLA, LYDIA B., and a babe, and live in Chatham township, Sangamon county, Illinois.

WILLIAM G., born in Sangamon county, married Jan. 14, 1858, to Nancy Baker. She died, leaving two children,

HENRY E. and MARY A. William G. Miller married Sarah Hall. They had two children, WILLIAM M. and MINNIE M., both of whom died young. W. G. Miller enlisted, Aug. 9, 1862, in Co. I, 73d Ill. Inf., for three years. He was wounded at Mission Ridge, Nov. 24, 1863, served to the end of the rebellion, and was honorably discharged, June 24, 1865, and resides three miles south of Loami, Sangamon county, Illinois.

Jacob Miller died, July 27, 1862, and his widow, Mrs. Lucina Miller, resides at the homestead where they settled in 1824, in Sangamon county, Illinois.

MILLER, SOLOMON, was born about 1796, in Adair county, Ky. He was married there to Nancy A. Antle. They had four children in Kentucky, and moved to St. Clair county, Ill., and from there to Sangamon county, arriving in the spring of 1820, at what is now Salisbury, where five children were born. Of their children—

BARBARA, born March 15, 1812, in Cumberland county, Ky., married Reuben Buchanan. See his name.

EVE, born Dec. 11, 1813, in Kentucky, married in Sangamon county to Wm. T. H. Duncan. See his name.

MELINDA, born in Kentucky, married in Sangamon county to William C. Hoag. See his name.

SARAH, born in Kentucky, married in Sangamon county to Morris Lindsay. See his name.

JASON, born Nov. 6, 1819, in Kentucky, married in Sangamon county, Feb. 10, 1853, to Sarah E. Willis. They have five children, FRANCIS M., MARY E., HARRIET A., THOMAS W. and SARAH IDA, and reside at Salisbury, Illinois.

JOHN A., born April 8, 1822, in Sangamon county, married in 1847 to Hannah J. Jackson, a native of Massachusetts. They had three children in Sangamon county. ALLEN A., born May 8, 1850, married Nov. 9, 1871, to Margaret A. Crawford, who was born May 3, 1850, in Laurel county, Ky. They have one child, EDWARD, and reside two miles northwest of Bradford station. MORRIS R. and HARVEY reside with their parents, two miles north of Salisbury, Illinois.

DOCIA, born in Sangamon county, married Rev. Tilford Clarke, have nine children, and live in Gardner township, Sangamon county, Illinois.

ALLEN, born in Sangamon county, married Clarissa Keys. They have seven children, and live in Springfield.

NANCY A., born in Sangamon county, married George McMurphy. See his name.

GEORGE W., born May 18, 1833, in Sangamon county, married June 8, 1854, to Abigail Baker. They had three children, JOHN B., JENNETTE and MAY. Mrs. Abigail Miller died May 11, 1867, and George W. Miller lives in Salisbury, Illinois.

Mrs. Nancy A. Miller died April, 1854, and Solomon Miller married Lucinda Gard. He died in 1858, near where he settled in 1820, at Salisbury, Illinois.

MILLER, MICHAEL, was born March 16, 1800, in Rowan county, North Carolina. Eleanor Turner was born about 1801 in the same county. They were married, and had two children there. In 1823 the family moved to Monroe county, Ky., where two children were born; and in 1827 moved to Morgan, and in 1837 to Sangamon county, in what is now Curran township, where they had six living children. Of their children—

RICHMOND married Charity Hart, and lives in Iowa.

ELIZABETH married Pleasant Prather, moved to Adams county, Iowa. He was a Union soldier, re-enlisted as a veteran, and while at home on a furlough, was killed on his own farm by a rebel bushwhacker, in 1864. The murderer was his nearest neighbor, and was caught by other neighbors and hung near where the murder was committed. He had two sons, Union soldiers, one of whom was killed in battle after his father's death. The widow and children reside on the same farm, in Adams county, Iowa.

BURRELL died, at sixteen years.

JOHN A., born April 4, 1821, in Rowan county, North Carolina, came with his father to Morgan county, Ill., in 1827, and to Sangamon county in 1837. He was married Nov. 24, 1842, to Louisiana Clements. They had nine children, three of whom died young. FRANCIS M., born Oct. 11, 1844, was teaching school near Mechanicsburg, abandoned it, and enlisted in June, 1862, in Co. H, 69th Ill. Inf., for one hundred days, and died at home on sick furlough July 17, 1862. JOHN A., Jun., born Aug. 26, 1852, in Sangamon county, married June 25, 1874, in Adams county, Iowa, to Margaret E. Prather, who was born in that county Feb. 26, 1852. They live near Chatham, Ill. THOMAS P., born Jan. 26, 1855, married Aug. 30, 1874, to Martha V. Graham, at Franklin, Morgan county, Ill., where she was born Sept. 8, 1859. They live near Chatham, Ill. CHARLES O., OSCAR C. and ANN E. live with their father. Mrs. Louisiana Miller died Aug. 5, 1874, and John A. Miller resides near Chatham, Ill. —1874.

CHARLOTTE married Joseph Little. She lives with some of her children, in Mechanicsburg.

HENRY A. married Jane Mason. She died, and he married Elizabeth Martin, and lives in Mechanicsburg, Illinois.

SARAH married William Robbins. See his name.

MELVINA married Joseph White, and she died.

CORNELIA J. married Lewis Hauser, and lives in Adams county, Iowa.

GEORGE W. lives in Iowa.

Michael Miller died Jan. 5, 1863, and his widow lives in Adams county, Iowa.

MILLS, JAMES, was born Oct. 20, 1794, in Augusta county, Va. When he was nineteen years old he, with two brothers, went to Pickaway county, Ohio. Elizabeth Mitts was born Oct. 17, 1793, in Virginia, went to Kentucky with her parents, and from there to Pickaway county, Ohio. James Mills and Elizabeth Mitts were there married and had seven children, and moved to Tippecanoe county, Ind., in 1834, where one child was born, and from there to Sangamon county, Ill., arriving in the fall of 1840, in what is now Fancy creek township. Of their children—

JOHN, born April 24, 1823, in Ohio, married there to Jane Wiley, had five or six children, and the parents died in Pickaway county.

ELIZABETH, born Oct. 12, 1824, in Ohio, married in Sangamon county to John W. Morrison, who was born March 17, 1823, in Edinburg, Scotland. They had four children, ORVILLA W., ESTELLA died young; JOHN W. and JAMES W. The three living reside with their mother. Mr. Morrison started July 9, 1862, for Idaho, and his fate is not certainly known, but it is believed he died there. His family reside in Williamsville, Illinois.

ADAM, born June 30, 1826, in Ohio, married in Sangamon county, March 23, 1853, to Louisa A. Kerns, who was born August 8, 1830, in Ross county, Ohio. They have five living children, JOHN, HATTIE, EDWARD, ADAM and ELLEN, and live two and a half miles north of Cantrall.—1874.

WILLIAM, born August 1, 1828, in Ohio, died in 1850.

MARCUS AURELIUS, born Sept. 19, 1830, in Ohio, enlisted at Springfield, in 1861, in Co. G, 10th Ill. Cav., for three years, re-enlisted as a veteran, served until July 5, 1865, when he was honorably discharged. He is unmarried, and resides with his sister, Mrs. Morrison, at Williamsville, Illinois.

SARAH, born Nov. 23, 1832, in Ohio, married in Sangamon county to William Newell. They had three children, and he and two of the children died. She married Clay Gaines. They have one child, and live near Odell, Ill.

DEBORAH, born Sept. 30, 1834, in Ohio, married in Sangamon county to David C. Duncan. See his name.

DORCAS A., born Sept. 3, 1837, in Indiana, married John J. Alexander. See his name.

James Mills died Jan. 17, 1867, and his widow died June 27, 1870, both in Williamsville, Sangamon county, Ill.

MILLINGTON, PETER, born July 6, 1737, in Vermont, was married in Boston, Mass., in 1759, to Henrietta Boulden, of that place. She died within two years, and Mr. Millington was married in 1769 to Mehetible Glass, a native of Massachusetts. Mr. Millington was Captain in the Revolutionary army, and accompanied Ethan Allen and Benedict Arnold on their expedition into Canada. He was taken prisoner at Quebec, and remained in captivity until the close of the war. Two years later he moved to Millington Spring, New York, where a son —

MARCUS, was born, March 14, 1801, he being the youngest of five children and the only one who came West. He accompanied his father to Ohio, and was married June 3, 1827, at Worthington, to Jane Justice, a native of that State. They had two children there, and came with his father to Sangamon county, Ill., arriving Oct., 1839, and stopping for a short time at Mazeppa, in Cotton Hill township, where one child was born. He soon after moved into Springfield. Of the three children, AUGUSTUS O., born June 7, 1828, in Worthington, Ohio, enlisted in 1846 as a private in Co. A, 4th Ill. Inf., and was promoted by General Scott, at the battle of Cerro Gordo, to Second Sergeant, for meritorious conduct on the battle field. He served in that capacity until the close of the war. He was married in Springfield, Ill., to Almira Marshall, who was born in 1830, in Ohio. They had five children, four of whom died young. Mrs. Almira Millington died Nov. 5, 1856. Augustus O. Millington was married May 10, 1857, to Mrs. Harriet E. Doud, whose maiden name was Halliday, a native of Ohio. He raised a company Aug. 10, 1861, for the Union army, in one day, which was mustered in as Co. I, 29th Ill. Inf., of which he was commissioned Captain. After the battle of Shiloh, he was promoted by Governor Yates, for meritorious conduct, to the rank of Major. He received his commission as Colonel, Aug. 19, 1863, and was in command of a provisional brigade about eighteen months. When Gen. Sherman started on his "march to the sea," he left thirty-five detachments of invalid troops with Colonel Millington at Bridgeport, Ala. He remained there eight months, when he was ordered to Chattanooga, where he was mustered out May 22, 1866. According to the statement of Gen. McClernand, Col. Millington was distinguished for good conduct in battle, and especially as a drill officer, his regiment being the best drilled in the brigade. Since the war Col. Millington has been engaged as a contractor and builder, part of the time in Chicago. He resides in Springfield. His only living child, OZRO L., born March 14, 1852, is a conductor on passenger train to and from Little Rock Arkansas. CAROLINE, born May 28, 1830, in Ohio, married John Beard, a native of Ohio. They have two children, and reside in St. Louis, Missouri. ELIZA is married, and resides in Manchester, Mo. Marcus Millington died Aug., 1863. His widow died in 1865, both in Springfield, Illinois.

Peter Millington died in 1839; his widow died the same year, both in Sangamon county.

MILSLAGLE, ANDREW., was born March 25, 1801, in Hampshire county, Va. He was there married, July 4, 1832, to Mary Martin, a native of the same county. They had one child, and came to Sangamon county, Illinois, arriving early in 1834, near Springfield, where they had one living child. Of their two children—

ELIZABETH A., born May 8, 1833, in Virginia, married in Sangamon county to Thomas Moppin. She died, July 7, 1867, leaving two children, who reside with their father in Kansas.

JACOB M., born Oct. 22, 1838, in Sangamon county. He enlisted, Aug. 11, 1862, in Co. E, 114th Ill. Inf., served until June 5, 1865, when he was honorably discharged. He was married October 5, 1865, in Christian county, to Elizabeth A. Peek. They have two children, MINNIE MAY and GRACIE, and live in Cotton Hill township, near old Rienzi, Sangamon county, Illinois.

Mrs. Mary Milslagle died Oct. 29, 1838. Andrew Milslagle married Mrs. Jane Beatty, whose maiden name was Waddell. They had two living children.

WILLIAM, born Sept. 18, 1839, in Sangamon county, enlisted, Aug. 11, 1862, in Co. E, 114th Ill. Inf., for three years. He was discharged on account of physical disability, in April, and died at home, July 9, 1863.

MARY, born Dec. 7, 1842, in Sangamon county, married Nelson Price. They have three children, NELLIE, AMY W. and ALICE, and live in Cotton Hill township, near old Rienzi, Sangamon county.

Mrs. Jane Milslagle died, Oct. 23, 1846, and Andrew Milslagle resides in Cotton Hill township, where he settled in 1836. It is near old Rienzi, Sangamon county, Illinois.

MISCHLER, PHILIP, was born Feb. 16, 1820, in Heppenheim, Hesse Darmstadt, Germany. His father's family came to America, landing in New York city, Sept. 17, 1839, and moved at once to Randolph, Portage county, Ohio. Philip started with Adam Kessler, in the spring of 1840, to Wellsville, thence by the Ohio river, to Cincinnati, and from there to Louisville, Ky., where his money was stolen. They managed to reach St. Louis, where they spent the summer at work. They went up the Mississippi and Illinois rivers to Beardstown, and walked from there to Springfield, without anything to eat on the road, arriving Sept. 7, 1840. His father, Martin Mischler, with his wife and three daughters, came the next spring. The daughters—Mary married George Spath. *See his name.* Margaret married Andrew Lump. Catharine married Henry Ramstetter.

Philip Mischler married in Springfield, Aug. 20, 1847, to Elizabeth Hoechster, who was born Feb. 14, 1822, at Hemsbach, Baden, Germany, and came, in 1845, to Springfield. They had two children in Springfield.

PHILIP, Jun., born Jan. 9, 1848, is a clerk in Bressmer's store.

HENRY, born June 11, 1860, lives with his parents.

Philip Mischler and his wife live at the corner of Eighth and Edwards streets, Springfield, Illinois.

He learned the business of coopering, in Springfield, and carried it on quite extensively from 1844 to 1868.

MITCHELL, EDWARD, was born Dec. 13, 1794, in Botetourt county, Virginia, and came west when he was quite young. Early in 1824 he came to Springfield, Illinois, where he was married on the 6th of June, the same year, to Mary Bartlett, a native of Connecticut. They had three children, and Mrs. Mary Mitchell died in Springfield in 1830. Edward Mitchell was married Nov. 10, 1831, in St. Louis, Mo., to Eleanor Essex, a native of England. They had one child. While living in Springfield Mr. Mitchell took part in the Winnebago Indian war of 1827. In 1825 or '6 he was appointed by President John Quincy Adams, Postmaster of Springfield, and was retained in office by President Jackson, although he was outspoken in his opposition to Jackson politically, being a Whig. From April 5, 1827, to August 9, 1835, Mr. Mitchell was Recorder of Sangamon county. He died in Springfield, Sept. 12, 1836. Soon after his death, Mrs. Mitchell, with all his children, moved to St. Louis, Mo. Of his children—

MARY ANN, born April 28, 1825, in St. Clair county, Ill., brought up in Springfield and St. Louis, was married in the latter city, Nov. 28, 1853, to William M. McPherson. They had six children, WILLIAM M., Jun., LAURA, EDWARD, MARY, PAGE and SOPHIA. The two eldest are married. Mr. McPherson was a lawyer and a prominent business man for many years. He died in St. Louis since the close of the rebellion. His widow and children reside in that city.

LAURA R., born July 4, 1828, in Springfield, Ill., was married March 28, 1848, in St. Louis, to J. H. Page Blackwood. They had three children, MARY, SALLIE GLASGOW and LAURA. J. H. P. Blackwood died August 15, 1858, and his widow and children reside at St. Louis, Mo.

EDWARD J., born August 3, 1830, in Springfield, Ill., married March 5, 1856, in St. Louis, to Theresa Cromwell. They had one child, MARY, and Edward J. Mitchell, died Jan. 29, 1871. His widow and daughter reside in St. Louis, Mo.

Mrs. Eleanor Mitchell, after the death of her husband in Springfield, lived in St. Louis ten or twelve years, and then moved to Louisiana, Mo., with her daughter—

VIRGINIA, born Oct. 23, 1835, in Springfield, Ill., married Dec. 4, 1851, in Louisana, Mo., to Dr. J. D. Harper, who was born Aug. 7, 1824, in Fayette county, Ohio. He had previously been married at Mt. Pleasant, Iowa, to a Miss Saunders, who died in 1850. Soon after their marriage Dr. Harper and wife, with her mother, moved to Springfield. Dr. and Mrs. Harper have three living children, JOHN E., ANNIE E. and HARVEY M., and reside in Springfield.

Mrs. Eleanor Mitchell died July 21, 1861, in Springfield, Illinois.

MITTS, CYRUS, born May 19, 1798, near Chillicothe, Ohio. Martha Burbridge was born Aug. 16, 1798, in Bath county, Kentucky. They were there married Sept. 22, 1818, and had two children, when they moved to Pickaway county, Ohio, where three children were born; and then moved to Sangamon county, Illinois, arriving in June, 1828, in what is now Fancy Creek township, where they had six children. Of their eleven children—

JAMES M., born July 23, 1819, in Bath county, Ky., married in Sangamon county to Eveline B. England. They had six children in Sangamon county.

THOMAS J. married Minerva Stratton. They have two children, and live in her native city, Chillicothe, Ohio. MAGGIE E. married James Symms, have three children, and live in Clarke county, Iowa. DAVID H. married Mary Josephine Nelson, and lives with his mother. LEWIS P., JAMES E. and BELLE M. live with their mother. James M. Mitts died Feb. 10, 1858, and his widow resides four and a half miles northwest of Williamsville, Illinois.

JESSE B., born Dec. 17, 1820, in Bath county, Ky., raised in Sangamon county, married in Iowa to Julia Russell. They had four children. Mr. Mitts was a member of 37th Iowa Inf., (Grey Beards), and died Dec., 1864, in the army. His widow and children live in Keokuk county, Iowa.

JANE, born Oct. 20, 1822, in Ohio, married in Sangamon county to George W. Council. See his name.

ROLAND, born in Ohio, died Dec. 6, 1862, aged thirty-eight years.

ELIZABETH A., born March 19, 1828, in Ohio, married in Sangamon county to John McClelland. See his name.

CARLISLE, born March 12, 1830, in Sangamon county, married June 4, 1863, to Margaret Hall, who was born Nov. 23, 1838, in Menard county, Ill. They reside in Fancy Creek township, four miles northwest of Williamsville, Illinois.

CYRUS, Jun., born Jan. 28, 1832, in Sangamon county, married Sarah Layton. They have nine children, and live in Keokuk county, Iowa.

ROBERT, born July 24, 1835, in Sangamon county, is unmarried, and lives in Clarke county, Iowa.

MARTHA, born March 31, 1837, in Sangamon county, married Robert McClelland. See his name.

MARY A., born June 25, 1839, in Sangamon county, married Jefferson Perce. They had two children, and Mr. Perce died in Sangamon county. His widow and children live in Clarke county, Iowa.

JOHN, born Sept. 10, 1841, in Sangamon county, was a soldier three years in Co. C, 114th Ill. Inf., married Susie D. Hay, has three children, and lives in Clarke county, Iowa.

Cyrus Mitts died Aug., 1852, and his widow died Dec. 19, 1862, both in Sangamon county, Illinois.

The Union General, Burbridge, of Kentucky, was a nephew of Mrs. Mitts. Her father was a Revolutionary soldier from Virginia, and four of her brothers were soldiers in the war of 1812 from Kentucky.

MOFFITT, GEORGE, was born about 1780, in Augusta county, Va., was married to Rebecca Gilkison, had two children there, and then moved to Fayette county, Ky., where six children were born. The family moved to Christian county, Ky., and from there to Sangamon county, Ill., arriving in what is now Ball township in 1829. Of their children—

JOHN, born in Virginia, died in Sangamon county, unmarried, aged about forty-five years.

MYRA, born in Virginia, married in Sangamon county to Moses Archer. See his name.

SALLY, born in Kentucky, married in Sangamon county to David Black. They had six children, and Mr. Black died in 1857. His widow lives with her son GEORGE, who married in St. Clair county to Lavina Broom. They have six children, and live near Blue Mound, Macon county, Illinois.

EVELINE, born in Kentucky, married in Sangamon county to Thomas Drennan. See his name.

MARGARET, born May 18, 1808, in Fayette county, Ky., married in Sangamon county to Thompson Pyle. See his name.

GEORGE, born in Kentucky, married in Sangamon county to Mahala Peters, moved to Jefferson county, Iowa, and died, leaving a widow and three children there.

MARTHA, born in Kentucky, married in Sangamon county, to Calvin Stevenson, had one son, and Mr. S. died. His widow married James Mitts. They had seven children, and she died near Mt. Pleasant, Iowa.

REBECCA, born in 1814, in Kentucky, married in 1826, in Sangamon county to Smith Ball. See his name.

Mrs. Rebecca Moffitt died in 1829, in Sangamon county, and Mr. Moffit married Mrs. Betsy Dawdy. They had two children—

JAMES and EMILY, and George Moffitt died in 1860, in Jefferson county, Iowa. His widow lives with her son James, in Mt. Pleasant, Iowa.—1874.

MOFFITT, THOMAS, was born April 13, 1797, in that part of Montgomery, which is now Bath county, Ky., and came to Springfield, Ill., Nov. 14, 1826. He was married Jan. 22, 1829, in Morgan county, Ill., to Eliza A. Gatton, who was born July 26, 1810, in Kentucky, also. They had eight children in Springfield, four of whom died young. Of the other four—

JAMES W., born June 4, 1830, was admitted to the bar, and practiced law with his father for a short time, and died Sept. 18, 1864.

JANE ELIZA, born Dec. 4, 1834, and died March 14, 1858.

SARAH R., born Jan, 7, 1837, died Feb. 16, 1864.

THOMAS G., born Nov. 3, 1839, in Springfield, and was clerk in the office of the Auditor of State four and a half years. He enlisted in 1861, in Co. A, 7th Ill. Inf., was commissioned Lieutenant, promoted to Adjutant of the regiment, and died March 29, 1862, in Springfield.

Mrs. Eliza A. Moffitt died, Nov. 11, 1867, and Mr. Moffitt resides in Springfield. He is in his eightieth year, and bereft of all his children, and finally of his wife.

Thomas Moffitt taught school when he came to Springfield, devoting all the time at his command to the study of law, and was licensed to practice in 1828 or '9. He was Orderly Sergeant in a company from Sangamon county in the Winnebago war of 1827, and in 1832 was captain of a company in the Black Hawk war. He served two years as county commissioner, and from 1843 served as Judge of the Probate Court. Under the constitution of 1848, he was elected County Judge for four years. He has for many years been a Ruling Elder in the Second Presbyterian church of Springfield, Illinois.

MOORE, CHARLES, came from one of the Southern States, built a cotton gin at the east side of Buffalo Hart Grove, in 1823 or '4, ran it for several years, and then moved farther north. He had been a Revolutionary soldier, and while going to draw a pension, the stage upset, and caused his death.

MOORE, ENOCH, was born March 26, 1802, near Waterloo, in what is now Monroe county, but then St. Clair county, Ill. His parents settled there about 1781. His father, John Moore, was a brother of General James B. Moore—they were natives of Virginia—and his mother a sister of General J. B. Whitesides;—she was a native of South Carolina; each of whom were influential men in the early history of Illinois. Enoch Moore was married near Waterloo, Illinois, Sept. 10, 1833, to Charlotte Sherman, who was born August 10, 1804, in one of the eastern States, and came to Illinois when quite young. They had three children, two of whom died in infancy. Of the third—

HESTER A., born Nov. 1, 1834, was married in Springfield, Nov. 20, 1854, to J. N. Underwood, a native of Illinois. Mrs. Underwood died Nov. 4, 1855, at Bloomington, Ill. Mr. Underwood was editorially connected with one of the Bloomington papers. He has since married, but his residence is not known.

Mrs. Charlotte Moore died April 2 1839, at Vandalia, Ill. Enoch Moore was married near Richmond, Ky., March 31, 1845, to Matilda Wakefield, who was a native of Massachusetts.

Enoch Moore lived in Alton a short time after his first marriage, then moved to Vandalia, where he was employed as clerk in the office of the State Treasurer When the records were removed to Springfield, in 1839, he came with them and was engaged principally in the Fund Commissioner's office, through all the changes of administration. His strict integrity, unfeigned conscientiousness, humility and consistent christian deportment, was so apparent that no political partisan ever felt justified in displacing him, and he continued to the end of his life in connection with some one of the State offices. His careful and methodical business habits led to the detection of the spurious indebtedness issued in the name of the Fund Commissioners, to the amount of hundreds and thousands of dollars, many years after it took place. He also discovered the fraudulent re-issue of canal bonds by Governor Matteson.

Mrs. Matilda Moore died March 23, 1863, in Springfield. Enoch Moore died March 28, 1876, in Chicago, while undergoing an operation for cataract of the eye. His remains were brought to Springfield, and buried in Oak Ridge Cemetery. The only surviving member of the family is their daughter—

CHARLOTTE M., who was born in Springfield, and now—1876—resides in her native city. She has been an energetic and efficient laborer in city missionary work, temperance and prison reform.

Enoch Moore will be remembered by all who visited the State House during the thirty-six years he spent there, by his stature. He was but four feet two inches high, yet his body was so fully developed that in a sitting posture he looked quite as large as the average of mankind. His weight was about one hundred and seventy pounds when in ordinary health. The deficiency was in the length of his lower limbs. He leaves a sister, Mrs. Hester A. Allyn, residing at the corner of Third and Monroe streets, Springfield. Her husband, Rev. Norman Allyn, was a traveling preacher in the Southern Illinois Conference M. E. church, at the time of his death, at Bunker Hill, Ill., in March, 1864.

MOORE, JOHN, was born Apr. 20, 1796, in Shoreham, Vermont. He came to Springfield, Ill., and was married Aug. 9, 1823, to Mrs. Elizabeth Hawley, whose maiden name was McMurdy. They had four children in Springfield, and moved to Schuyler county about 1835, where one child was born. Of their children—

JOHN L., born July 5, 1824, is understood to have been the first male child born in Springfield. He was married in Schuyler county Jan. 3, 1855, to Jemima J. Doyle. He died in the latter county March 14, 1864, leaving a widow and five children, who now live in Rushville, Illinois.

SARAH E., born March 17, 1826, in Springfield, was married in Schuyler county, Ill., to Rev. George F. Davis, of the Presbyterian church. They reside at Casey, Clarke county, Illinois.

MARY E., born Oct. 22, 1830, in Springfield, has been a teacher for many years, and resides with her relatives, partly, in Springfield, Illinois.

HENRY P., born Jan. 7, 1833, in Springfield, was brought up in Schuyler county, and married in Logan county, Ill., to Jennie Bock. They have two children, and live near Elkhart, Illinois.

CARRIE P., born Nov. 25, 1835, in Schuyler county. She and her sister, Mary E., were educated at Normal for the profession of teaching. She resides in Springfield.

Mrs. Elizabeth Moore died Jan. 24, 1858, and John Moore died June 14, 1873, both in Schuyler county, Illinois.

MOORE, BUSHNELL B., was born Jan. 6, 1801, in Shoreham, Vt. Melissa Northrope was born Jan. 30, 1803, in the same town. They were there married Jan. 7, 1824. Mr. Moore had previously established himself in business at Hopkinton, St. Lawrence county, N. Y. They had two living children there, and the family moved to Sangamon county, Ill., arriving July, 1836, in what is now Gardner township. Of their children—

MARCIA A., born Oct. 7, 1826, is unmarried, and resides with her mother, at Farmingdale, Illinois.

MARIA L., born June 29, 1828, at Hopkinton, New York, married in Sangamon county May 15, 1849, to Eben Dutch. He was born Oct. 18, 1819, in Augusta, Maine. They had four children in Sangamon county. FLORENCE MAY is a teacher in the public schools, and resides at Farmingdale. FREDERICK and WINTHROP live with their uncle, Henry S. Dutch, in Oxford, Johnson county, Iowa. RALPH E. lives at Farmingdale, Ill. Eben Dutch died Aug. 29, 1864, in Sangamon county, and his widow died in 1876, near Farmingdale, Sangamon county, Illinois.

Bushnell B. Moore died June 18, 1838, in Sangamon county, and his widow married Rev. Billious Pond. *See his name.*

—67

MOORE, JOHN B., was born July 11, 1803, in Warren county, N. J. Rachel L. McCarty was born Feb. 7, 1812, in Morris county, N. J. They were married in the latter county, Dec. 8, 1831, and had four children there. They moved to Sangamon county, Ill., arriving July 28, 1838, in what is now Gardner township, where one child was born. Of the five children—

ELIJAH V., born Sept. 19, 1832, in New Jersey, married in Sangamon county to Margaret Jones. They had two children, JOHN B. and ANN E. Elijah V. Moore enlisted August 5. 1861, in Co. C, 2d Ill. Art., was appointed Sergeant Major, and promoted to 1st Lieutenant, April 20, 1862. He was killed at the second battle of Fort Donelson, Feb. 5, 1863. His widow and children live one mile east of Bradfordton, Sangamon county, Illinois.

MOSES H., born Feb. 28, 1834, in New Jersey, married in Sangamon county, Feb. 24, 1870, to Lenora Crowder, who was born March 14, 1852, in Missouri. They have one child, ANN E. and live one mile east of Bradfordton Sangamon county, Illinois.

DELIA V., born Feb. 5, 1836, in New Jersey, married Dec. 1, 1870, to Isaac Gregory. *See his name.* They have one child, FANNIE, and live near Blue Mound, Macon county, Illinois.

JOHN B., Jun., born Dec. 14, 1837, in New Jersey, and raised in Sangamon county. He engaged in freighting over the plains from Nebraska City to Denver, and died March 21, 1864, on Platte river, one hundred and eighty miles east of Denver, and twenty miles from Julesburg.

JULIA A., born Dec. 23, 1839, in Sangamon county, married Nov. 11, 1858, to William H. Miller, General Superintendent of C. and A. telegraph line. She had one child, MARY R., and Mrs. Miller died Nov. 16, 1871, at Bellefountaine, Ohio.

John B. Moore, Sen., died Aug. 18, 1839, in Sangamon county, and his widow married Oct. 25, 1842, to Josiah Broadwell, Sen. *See his name.*

MOORE, JOSEPH, was born Aug. 12, 1780, in Shenandoah county, Virginia. He was there married, Sept. 15, 1803, to Julia Ann Duck. They had six children in Virginia, and then moved, in 1815, to Bath county, Ky., where two children were born. After a residence of twenty-one years in Kentucky, Mr. Moore moved his family to Sangamon county, Ill., arriving in what is now Auburn township, in the fall of 1836, and four years later moved to Ball township. Of their children—

REUBEN, born in Virginia, married Charlotte Coaley, moved to Texas, about 1847, and died there, in 1862, leaving a wife and five children.

MARY, born in Virginia, married to Daniel Hannah, who died, leaving a widow and one child in Mt. Sterling, Kentucky.

SARAH, born April 27, 1807, in Shenandoah county, Virginia, married in Kentucky to Wm. A. Lockridge. *See his name.*

JOHN H., born in Virginia, married in Kentucky to Louisa Boyd, and remained there.

ABRAHAM, born in Virginia, died in Mississippi, aged twenty-six years.

ELIZABETH, born in Shenandoah county, Va., married Wm. M. Patton. *See his name.*

MORRISON M., born in Bath county, Ky., married in Sangamon county to Elizabeth Crow. They have eight children—JOSEPH M. lives in Minnesota. JOHN H. and CHARLES live with their parents. MARGARET A. married William D. Nuckolls. *See his name.* GEORGE L., WILLIAM D., ASA B. and SARAH E., live with their parents, on the farm where his father settled in 1840. It is two miles south of Chatham, Sangamon county, Illinois.

JAMES W., born in Virginia, married Mary A. Walker, who died, and he married Virginia Lane, and is a practicing attorney in Washington City, D. C.

RILEY, died, at ten years of age.

Mrs. Julia A. Moore died, July 23, 1853, and Joseph Moore died Sept. 7, 1856, both in Sangamon county.

MORGAN, CHARLES, was born Sept. 5, 1781, in Hampshire county, Va. His parents moved to Fleming county, Ky., in 1793. Charles Morgan and Elizabeth Constant were there married in 1807, and had four children in Kentucky. The family moved in March, 1814, to Clermont county, Ohio, where they had four living children, and then moved to Sangamon county, Ill., arriving in Oct., 1826, in what is now Mechanicsburg township, where two children were born. Of their ten children—

JACOB, born May 20, 1808, in Fleming county, Ky., married in Sangamon county May 17, 1832, to Susan Correll. They had three living children. JOSEPHUS, born March 30, 1833, is unmarried, and resides five and a half miles northwest of Illiopolis, Ill. MINERVA, born Nov. 8, 1834, died April 3, 1854. CAROLINE, born July 21, 1837, married George W. Hesser. See his name. Mrs. Susan Morgan died Oct. 15, 1848, and Jacob Morgan was married Nov. 22, 1855, to Mrs. Mary A. Wilson, whose maiden name was Stickel. She was born April 16, 1825, in York county, Penn. They have four children, LUELLA, SELINA B., ANNA M. and CHARLES W. Mrs. Morgan has one son by her first marriage, ANDREW S. WILSON, born Mar. 23, 1847, in Macon county, Ill., married in Bloomington, Ill., to Mary Hamilton; had one child, and resides in Washington, Kansas. He has represented Washington county in the Kansas Legislature two terms, and is now —1874—Judge of the Twelfth judicial district in that State. Jacob Morgan resides two and a half miles west of Mechanicsburg, Illinois.

WILLIAM, born in 1810 in Fleming county, Ky., died in Sangamon county in 1828.

JOHN C., born May 19, 1812, in Fleming county, Ky., married in Sangamon county Jan. 28, 1836, to Elizabeth Bridges. They had eight children in Sangamon county. MARTHA E., born June 23, 1837, died Oct. 6, 1857. LAVINA J., born Feb. 19, 1839, married Oct., 1857, to Zenas Crawford. They have five children, MARTHA E., CHARLES H., ANNIE F., WM. GRANT and JOHN T., and live near Princeton, Franklin county, Kansas. CHARLES W., born Nov. 11, 1841, enlisted July, 1861, for three years, in Co. I, 41st Ill. Inf. He was killed at Fort Donelson Feb. 15, 1862. His remains were brought home and interred near Mechanicsburg. SARAH A., born Feb. 21, 1844, married July 22, 1865, to Victor Bechtel. He served three years, from July, 1861, in Co. I, 41st Ill. Inf.

They have five children, IDA MAY, LILLIE A., HARVEY T., ALVA E. and ALTA I., and live near Ottawa, Kansas. NORMAN C., born Sept. 23, 1846, married Aug. 31, 1871, to Emily Peak, have one child, JOHN T., and live near Richmond, Kansas. AARON T., born July 22, 1849, died Jan. 12, 1865. FIDELIA ADALINE, born July 5, 1852, and RUTH EMELINE, born July 10, 1854, reside with their parents, three miles southwest of Illiopolis, Illinois—1874.

DANIEL, born Feb. 28, 1813, in Fleming county, Ky., married in Sangamon county Jan. 9, 1834, to Melinda Morgan. They had seven children; one died in infancy. ELIZA J., born Dec. 31, 1834, married Aug. 26, 1858, to Jeremiah Kelly, have two children, and live in Madison, Greenwood county, Kansas. MARY, born Nov. 22, 1836, married Dec. 6, 1860, to James Lockhart, and died July 14, 1861. FRANKLIN B., born March 14, 1839, married Oct. 13, 1870, to Margaret A. Ficklin, had one child, FRANKLIN, and live two and a half miles west of Mechanicsburg. WILLIAM W., born Nov. 24, 1841, married Jan. 12, 1868, to Emily A. Patterson, have one living child, EDGAR, and live three and a half miles west of Mechanicsburg. ERSKINE, born June 3, 1849, and EMMA A., born May 12, 1854, reside with their parents, two and a half miles each from Mechanicsburg, Dawson and Buffalo—1874.

AARON, born March 3, 1816, in Clermont county, Ohio, married in Sangamon county Jan. 12, 1837, to Matilda A. McDaniel, whose maiden name was Shinkle. They had eleven children, four of whom died under seven years. Of the other seven—MARIA L., born April 26, 1840, married George H. Grabendich, had one child, WILLIAM F., and Mr. G. enlisted in 1862, for three years, in Co. C, married Robert Alls, and died, leaving 124th Illinois Infantry. He was wounded at Vicksburg, June 26, and died June 27, 1863. Mrs. Grabendich one child, CHARLES A. MINERVA E., born Nov. 30, 1844, married James Moore, have two children, and live two and a half miles west of Mechanicsburg. CHARLES W., born June 30, 1849, married Matilda Moon, have one child, and lives three miles northwest of Mechaniesburg. MARY F., JAMES A., JANETTA and MARTHA J. reside with their parents, two and one half miles southeast of Dawson.

WASHINGTON, born Feb., 1818, in Ohio, died in Sangamon county Sept. 26, 1838.

LAVINA, born in Ohio, married in Sangamon county to G. W. Carrico, and live in Missouri.

CHARLES W., born May 23, 1829, in Sangamon county, married Oct. 15, 1850, to Elizabeth E. Derry, who was born Oct. 26, 1830, in Loudon county, Va. They had eleven children, five of whom, GEORGE E., JOHN R., WILLIAM A., CORDELIA S. and EMMA F., died under six years of age. MINERVA J., born Dec. 28, 1851, married March 9, 1871, to Benjamin Cox, have two children, EVELINE and ALVA, and live three miles north of Illiopolis. JAMES R., ELIJAH A., LAURA A., LUELLA L. and CHARLES A. reside with their parents, in Macon county, three and a half miles northeast of Illiopolis, Illinois.

JAMES A., born March 13, 1834, in Sangamon county, married Nov. 14, 1856, to Sarah A. Lee, who was born March 15, 1841, in Gallatin county, Ohio. They had seven children. The first, second and fifth, HENRIETTA, IDA E. and HENRY L., died under four years. CHARLES F., VIOLA E., EDWIN O. and MELVIN A. reside with their parents, in Macon county, four miles northeast of Illiopolis, Illinois.

Charles Morgan died Jan. 25, 1866, and Mrs. Elizabeth Morgan died Oct. 9, 1868, both in Sangamon county, near where they settled in 1826.

MORGAN, DANIEL, brother to Charles, was born March 10, 1785, near Warm Springs, Hampshire county, Va., and was taken by his parents, in 1793, to Fleming county, Ky. Mary S. Woods was born June 17, 1786, in Burke county, N. C., and was taken by her parents to Wilkes county, in the same State. In the fall of 1794 they moved to Clark county, Ky., and in 1799 to Chillicothe, Ohio, and in 1801 to Fleming county, Ky. Her father, Andrew Woods, was born in Pennsylvania, taken by his parents to South Carolina, and was Captain of a company from that State, and served nine months in the war for Independence. He died March 26, 1803, in Fleming county, Ky. Daniel Morgan and Mary S. Woods were married Oct. 24, 1810, in Kentucky, and had three children there. They moved to Monroe county, Indiana, in 1822, where one child was born, and then moved to Sangamon county, Illinois, arriving Nov. 21, 1828, in what is now Mechanicsburg township. Of their five children—

MELINDA, born May 18, 1811, in Fleming county, Ky., married in Sangamon county, Ill., to Daniel Morgan. See his name.

MARY, born Nov. 5, 1815, in Fleming county, Ky., died Aug. 24, 1835, in Sangamon county, Illinois.

ELIZA M., born August 24, 1822, in Fleming county, Ky., married Jan. 29, 1843, in Sangamon county, to Samuel N. Little. See his name.

MAHALA C., born July 19, 1824, in Fleming county, Ky., married in Sangamon county, June 29, 1854, to Rev. James B. Houts, who was born May 31, 1817, in Salem, Livingston county, Ky. They had two children, MARY F. and MINERVA L. Rev. J. B. Houts died Nov. 10, 1872, at Myersville, Vermilion county, Ill. At the time of his death he was filling his 33d appointment as circuit preacher in the M. E. church. His widow and daughters reside in Springfield, Illinois.

WILLIAM H., born June 26, 1826, in Monroe county, Indiana, is unmarried, and resides one mile west of Mechanicsburg, adjoining the farm on which his parents settled in 1828. He remembers going with his father to a water mill on the Sangamon river, and that the mill was roofed by first covering it with logs and slabs, and earth was thrown on that. Weeds were growing on top of the mill, which he thought was very strange.

Daniel Morgan was a soldier from Fleming county, Ky., in the war with England, from Aug., 1812, to March, 1813. He died in Sangamon county, Sept. 6, 1866, and his widow resides with her son, William H. She draws a pension for the services of her husband in the war of 1812.

MORGAN, THOMAS, was born about 1783, in Kentucky. He was married near Cincinnati, Ohio, to Mrs.

Elizabeth Butler, whose maiden name was Bell. She was born in 1773, in Maryland. They had seven children in Hamilton county, Ohio, and moved to Sangamon county, Ill., about 1822, and settled south of Spring creek, in what is now Gardner township. Of their children—

EVAN, born in Ohio, married in Sangamon county to Elizabeth Ditson, had five children, and he died August 15, 1834. His widow married M. S. Skidmore, and lives near Hamburg, Fremont county, Iowa.

ELIZABETH, married in Ohio to John Bartlow, came with her parents to Sangamon county, and moved to Schuyler county, Ill., about 1830, where they both died, leaving seven children.

MARTHA, married in Ohio to John Moffatt, came to Sangamon county, and died, leaving two children, who are married, and reside near Decatur, Illinois.

JOHN, born Jan. 19, 1806, near Cincinnati, Ohio, came to Sangamon county, in 1822, and married, Feb. 24, 1825, to Camely Duff. They had twelve children, in Sangamon county. WILLIAM H., born Jan. 9, 1826, married Emily Robinson, had one child, Edward W., born Sept. 17, 1851, resides in Gardner township. Mrs. Emily Morgan died, March 28, 1852, and Mr. M. married Mrs. Elmira King, whose maiden name was Bradley. They started to Kansas, and he died Nov. 10, 1867, at Rockport, Missouri. His widow lives in Wilson county, Kansas. FINIS E., born Oct. 21, 1827, married Elizabeth Day. They have five living children, and live at Clinton, Illinois. JOSIAH B., born Nov. 26, 1829, married Mary A. Reed, have four children, and live near Neodesha, Wilson county, Kansas. MARY A., born Oct. 17, 1831, married Edward C. Sackett, and died at her mother's. Mr. S. was a Union soldier, and lives near Carrollton, Ill. AMANDA J., born Sept. 30, 1833, married Alfred Moulton, and died, in 1864, leaving two children. ELIZA A., born May 31, 1835, married, Oct. 28, 1850, to John Hardin, and has five children, JULIET, CAMELY F., MARGARET E., IDA and EDWARD L. Mr. Hardin has not been heard of for eight or nine years—supposed to be dead. JOHN F., born May 13, 1837, lives with his mother. CAMELY F. died in her eighteen year. GREEN B. died in his seventeenth year. URIAH, LYMAN T. and RUFUS M. live with their mother. John Morgan died Dec. 25, 1856, and his widow resides—1874—one and one-half miles south of Farmingdale, Sangamon county, Illinois.

RUTH, born near Cincinnati, Ohio, married in Sangamon county to DeLos Brown. They had three children, and he died, near Sidney, Fremont county, Iowa. His widow and child live there.

THOMAS, Jun., married Martha Massey, and both died in Hancock county.

MARGARET, married Richard Quinton, and moved to California.

Thomas Morgan, Sen., moved to Schuyler county, and he and his wife died there in 1858.

MORRIS, ACHILLES, a cousin to Bishop Morris, of the M. E. church, was born in Kanawha county, West Virginia, married there, and came with his family to Sangamon county, Illinois, arriving in the fall of 1826, in what is now Loami township. He was a soldier in the Black Hawk war, and was afterwards elected as one of the representatives of Sangamon county in the State legislature. He raised a company in the vicinity of Loami, of which he became Captian, in the 4th Ill. Inf., under Col. E. D. Baker, and died of disease at Camargo, Mexico, in 1847. He left a widow and eleven children in Sangamon county. His eldest son—

JONATHAN, was born July 21, 1825, in Kanawha county, Va., married in Sangamon county, Jan. 23, 1846, to Martha E. Meacham. He enlisted in the company of which his father was Captain, int he 4th Ill. Inf. He was promoted to Major of the regiment in Mexico, and was one of the party that captured Santa Anna's cork leg. Served to the close of the Mexican war. Mr. and Mrs. Morris had nine children; four died under three years. Of the other five: NANCY married John Goldsmith, who is editor of the *Waverly Times*, and resides there.—1874. EDOM D., DOUGLAS, RICHARD N. and WILLIS GRANT live with their mother in Waverly. Jonathan Morris raised a company in Waverly, in 1861, and was commissioned Captain of Co. —, 14th Ill. Inf. He was promoted to Major of the regiment. After eighteen months service a horse fell with him and crushed an ancle, in consequence of which he resigned Sept., 1862, and died suddenly at Waverly, Nov. 12, 1871.

I have no history of the other members of the family of Achilles Morris.

MORRIS, WILLIAM D., brother to Bishop Thomas A. Morris, was born in Cabell county, West Va. He was married there, and brought his family to Sangamon county in the fall of 1825, and settled on Lick creek, in what is now Loami township. His daughter Melissa married William Heredith. *See his name.*

MORRIS, JOHN, was born and married in Cabell county, West Va., and moved, in company with his brother, William D., to Sangamon county in the fall of 1825, settled on Lick creek, and raised a family there. He was a preacher in the anti-mission or predestinarian Baptist church. His brother, Wm. D., was a member of the same church. They were brothers to Bishop Morris, of the M. E. church. John Morris is dead, and has no representative in the county.

MORSE, JAMES M., was born Feb. 4, 1807, in Newburyport, Mass. He was married April 7, 1831, in West Newbury, to Sarah C. Sawyer, who was born there, Nov. 25, 1807. He moved, in 1831, to Vandalia, Ill., where they had three children. Mr. Morse was employed in the office of the Secretary of State, and when the State government was removed to Springfield, in July, 1839, he came with it. They had three children in Springfield; one died in infancy. Of their five children—

LYMAN C. B., born Feb. 15, 1834, in Vandalia, died Feb. 27, 1855, in Springfield.

SARAH E., born Feb. 13, 1836, in Vandalia, Ill., married June 4, 1857, in Springfield, to Joseph E. Woods. They had two children—ANNIE died in infancy. SARAH C. lives with her father. Mrs. Woods died July 9, 1860. Mr. Woods married again, and is living in Springfield, Illinois.

HARRIET M., born March 9, 1839, in Vandalia, married, Sept. 24, 1857, to William T. Church. They had three children, ALLIE and ANNIE died young. JULIA G. lives with her grandfather Morse. Mrs. Church died, Dec. 9, 1873, at Elkhart, Ill., and was buried at Oak Ridge.

ELLEN F., born Aug. 2, 1841, in Springfield, married Feb. 20, 1862, to Daniel Winters, who was born in Chambersburg, Penn., Jan. 30, 1832, and came to Springfield in 1851. They had four children—CHARLES E. and JAMES B. live with their parents. MARY C. and LILIAN M. died young. NELLIE is the babe. Mr. Winters is in business, and lives in Springfield.

CHARLES E., born Nov. 1, 1844, in Springfield, married, March 19, 1868, in Logan county, to Ellen E. Long. They have five children, JAMES H., ANNA B., CHARLES E., JOHN B. and a boy babe. Mr. Morse is engaged in farming, near Elkhart, Logan county, Illinois.

JULIETT E., born July 17, 1848, in Springfield, died in infancy.

Mrs. Sarah C. Morse died July 28, 1848, in Springfield, and James M. Morse was married in Springfield, Oct. 30, 1850, to Emma M. Holton, who was born in 1814, at Danbury, Conn. They had four children—

JAMES Wm. died, aged two years.

JAMES Wm., born Sept. 3, 1853, in Springfield, married Sept. 17, 1872, to Alice B. Schmutz, a native of Bloomington, Ill. They have two children, FLORENCE B. and ETHEL G., and reside in Springfield, Illinois.

EMMA G., born Jan. 16, 1856, in Springfield, resides with her parents.

ANNA C., born Sept. 9, 1859, in Springfield, died March 23, 1866.

James M. Morse was in the office of the Secretary of State when the office was held by A. P. Fields, Stephen A. Douglas, Lyman Trumbull and Thompson Campbell. From 1846 to 1852 Mr. Morse was Assessor and Treasurer of Sangamon county, and for fifteen years was Public Administrator of the county. He is now retired from business, and resides in Springfield, Illinois.

When the seat of government was moved from Vandalia to Springfield, James M. Morse came with A. P. Fields, Secretary of State, in whose department he was employed. They were accompanied by Levi Davis, Auditor of Public Accounts, with his clerk, Wm. S. Prentiss, now Presiding Elder in the M. E. church; John D. Whitesides, State Treasurer, and Enoch Moore, his clerk; William Walters, Public Printer, and Charles H. Lanphier, his assistant. From 1842 to 1844 Mr. Morse was engaged in rewriting the Territorial records; and during that time roomed with Enoch Moore at the State house. A friendship was thus cemented that could only end with their lives.

MOSTELLER, CHRISTOPHER, was born in Buncombe county, North Carolina, went to Butler county, Ohio, when a young man; and was there married to Phœbe Sackett. They had two children in that county, and moved to Union county, Ind., where they had two children; returned to Butler county, Ohio, and from there came to Sangamon county, Ill., arriving in the spring of 1830, in what is now Salisbury township. Of their children—

THOMAS, born Oct. 8, 1807, in Butler county, Ohio, was married in Franklin county, Ind., July 21, 1827, to Charlotte Morris. They moved with his parents to Ohio, where they had two children, and came in the spring of 1830 to Sangamon county, where six children were born. Of their eight children— PHŒBE A. died, aged fifteen years. ALICE J., born Nov. 29, 1829, in Butler county, Ohio, was married Dec. 4, 1845, to Job Davenport. See his name. DORCAS, born Feb. 14, 1832, in Sangamon county, married Dr. Francis T. Antle. They had four children: HARRIET died in 1874; THOMAS P., IONA O. and MARY ELLA live with their parents, in Petersburg, Ill. JAMES, born Dec. 5, 1833, in Sangamon county, enlisted in 1862, in Co. F, 114th Ill. Inf., for three years, and died of disease, near Vicksburg, Miss., Sept. 18, 1863. His remains were buried at the Baptist cemetery in Cartwright township. EDWARD C., born June 22, 1841, in Sangamon county, enlisted in 1861 in Co. A, 10th Ill. Cav., for three years, and was discharged on account of physical disability. He was married in Kansas to Love B. Holladay. She died, and E. C. Mosteller was married again in Iowa, and has one child. He studied medicine, and attended one course of lectures at Rush Medical College, Chicago, Ill., graduated at the Eclectic Medical Institute, Cincinnati, Ohio, and is practicing his profession at Adelphia, Polk county, Iowa. MARTIN S., born April 21, 1843, in Sangamon county, was married Oct. 4, 1864, to Sarah M. Antle, in Petersburg. They had four children: FRANKIE H. died April 7, 1869, in Macon county, Ill.; FREDDIE F., ALBERT A. and MAUD M. live with their parents. M. S. Mosteller is a graduate of the Eclectic Medical Institute at Cincinnati, Ohio, and is a practicing physician at Pleasant Plains, Ill. JOHN H. A., born April 21, 1847, in Sangamon county, enlisted in 1862, for three years, in Co. F, 114th Ill. Inf., and was discharged on account of physical disability in Aug., 1863. He re-enlisted in 1864 in Co. D, 33d Ill. Inf.; served to the close of the rebellion, and was honorably discharged in 1865. He lives at Tallula, Menard county, Ill. ELIZA W., born June 19, 1852, was married in Petersburg to Thomas Davis. He is a telegraph operator, and lives at Vandalia, Audrain county, Mo. Mrs. Charlotte Mosteller died March 2, 1865, and Thomas Mosteller lives now—1876— at Pleasant Plains. He remembers being present on Richland creek when Abraham Lincoln was waiting to make a speech. Josiah Grady said: "Lincoln, they have the story in circulation that you are a Deist." Mr. Lincoln immediately answered: "That is not so: my father was an old Baptist, and taught me to believe in the Christian religion, and I do believe in it as much as anybody; but I confess I have no religion."

DORCAS, born June 15, 1810, in Butler county, Ohio, was married Sept. 18, 1835, in Illinois, to Benjamin McElwain. They are without family, and live in Petersburg, Menard county, Illinois.

SAMUEL died in 1844.

AARON P., born May, 1820, in Union county, Indiana, was married in 1845 in Sangamon county, Ill., to Emily Campbell. They had six children. JANE, born in 1846, was married to Thomas Gorrell. They are without family, and live in Crawford county, Kansas. GEORGE W., born in 1848, married Mary Lindsay. They have two living children, and live in Crawford county, Kansas. LOUIS, born in 1850, is unmarried, and lives in Kansas. ANN, born in 1853, died, aged ten years. JOHN C., born in 1856, is unmarried, and lives in Kansas. LAURA, born in 1861, died, aged two years. A. P. Mosteller moved to Kansas in 1861, where Mrs. Emily Mosteller died Dec. 8, 1872. A. P. Mosteller was married Feb. 8, 1874, to Mrs. Mary Hooper, and lives at Osage mission, Neosho county, Kansas.

GEORGE S., born Nov. 9, 1822, in Franklin county, Ind., was married in Mason county, Ill., Nov., 1856, to Martha Simmons, who died without family in March, 1858. G. S. Mosteller was married Nov., 1860, to Roxana Reese. They have three living children, FRANK, MARY and IDA, and live at Forest City, Mason county, Illinois.

REBECCA, born Oct. 16, 1827, in Butler county, Ohio, was married Aug. 2, 1849, in Illinois, to Thomas A. Gibson. They had two children. GEORGE L., born Oct., 1850, lives with his parents. JOHN died in his ninth year. T. A. Gibson and family live in Forest City, Illinois.

Christopher Mosteller died in 1844, and his widow married Rev. John Antle. She died August, 1863; both in Salisbury, Sangamon county, Illinois.

MOTT, JAMES, was born Nov. 27, 1803, in Kent county, England, and came to America in 1821, landing in New York. He went to Sacketts Harbor, learned cabinet making, and was married there, Jan. 9, 1830, to Amanda M. Brown, who was born March 18, 1813, at Woodstock, Vermont. They had three children; two died there, and they moved, in 1834, to Cleveland, Ohio. They went from there to St. Louis by water, thence to Jacksonville, Ill., in a wagon, and after visiting some relatives in Cass county, came to Springfield, arriving Jan. 1, 1836, where one child was born, and in 1838 moved to Menard county, near Petersburg, thence to Athens, Feb. 20, 1843, where twelve children were born, nine of whom died under five years of age. Of the other five—

JAMES W., born July 19, 1833, at Sacketts Harbor, N. Y., partly brought up in Springfield, was married near Athens, April 18, 1856, to Millie J. Hurt, who died June 24, 1857. J. W. Mott was married May 15, 1859, to Mrs. Mary A. Holland, whose maiden name was England. They had eight children, ALLEN, EDGAR, AGNES, MARGARET, JAMES, CHARLES, MILAM and EUGENE. Mrs. Mott died Nov. 19, 1872, and J. W. Mott resides in Athens, Sangamon county, Ill.—1874.

GEORGE E., born July 25, 1836, in Springfield, was married there April 19, 1865, to Eliza P. Smith, a native of the same place. They have three children, WILLIAM R., HARRY W. and LAURA E., and live at 635, north 5th street, Springfield.

HARRIET EMMA, born July 12, 1843, in Athens, married David A. England. See his name.

MARY A., born in Athens, married James M. England. See his name.

HENRY W., born August, 1847, in Athens, is now—July, 1876—clerk of the Matteson House, Chicago, Illinois.

James Mott died Sept. 24, 1873. His widow lives at Athens, Menard county, Illinois. Mr. Mott was associate Judge of Menard county one term of four years.

MOURER, WILLIAM, was born about 1807, in Berkley county, Va. His parents emigrated to Muskingum county, Ohio, where his father died. In 1823 or '4 he went to Washington county, Maryland, where he was married Dec. 12, 1833, to Jane I. Ensminger, who was born May 8, 1815, in that county. They had one child in Maryland, and moved to Springfield, Ill., arriving in the fall of 1836, where they had four children. Of their five children—

GEORGE W., born Oct. 29, 1834, in Washington county, Maryland, and brought up in Sangamon county, Illinois. He enlisted in Springfield, Aug. 27, 1862, for three years, in Co. E, 114th Ill. Inf. At the organization of the regiment, he was promoted to Quarter-Master, and was with the regiment until after the battle of Nashville, in Dec., 1864, when he was honorably mustered out on account of physical disability. He is now a farmer, and resides with his mother, five and one-half miles southeast of Springfield, Ill.

ALICE J. and MARGARET E., twins.

ALICE J. married, Nov. 18, 1857, to Samuel N. Shoup. See his name.

MARGARET E., MARYLAND and VIRGINIA reside with their mother.

EUGENIE G. married John N. Gatton. See his name.

Mr. William Mourer formed a partnership with Benjamin Ferguson, as carpenters and builders, soon after coming to Springfield. Their first work was the building of the American Hotel, at the southeast corner of Adams and Sixth streets; when finished, the finest hotel in the State of Illinois. They were contractors for part of the work on the State House, then in course of construction, now the Sangamon county Court House. After the death of Mr. Ferguson, Mr. Mourer continued in the business for about seventeen years. In 1850 he took the contract, and built the north and south porticos to the State House. He bought a farm, and moved in the spring of 1853 to Woodside township. While discharging the duties of grand juror, he was taken violently ill, of pneumonia, and died in Springfield, June 10, 1867. His widow resides five and one-half miles south of Springfield, on the farm where they settled in 1853.

MOWRY, JOHN H., born Feb. 26, 1829, in Charleston, S. C. Accompanied his father to Chicago in 1836, came to Springfield, Ill., in 1839, and learned the carpenter's trade. In 1856 he was elected Sheriff of Mason county, but resigned, after serving fifteen months, to avoid hanging a man convicted of murder. He was married, Jan. 2, 1858, in Dixon, Lee county, Ill., to Martha Grimm, who was born March 6, 1832, at Harpers Ferry, Va. They have six children living, *ANN E., IDA E., ELEANORA, MARY, HARRIET,* and *GRACE.* During the rebellion J. H. Mowry was employed in the mechanical department of the government at Camps Yates and Butler, near Springfield, and being ordered to Camp Douglas, at Chicago, moved his family to that city. He was also engaged at Camp Fry, and at the arsenal at Rock Island, and on the public works at Wilmington, Delaware, in 1863 and '64. In 1866 he made a two-years tour through England and the continents of Europe, Asia and Africa. He lost all his property in the great Chicago fire, Oct. 9, 1871. In July, 1874, he took charge as first foreman of the addition to the State prison of Michigan, then in course of construction. He remained
—68

there until 1875, when he returned to Springfield, where he is now engaged in the business of a contractor and builder.

MULKEY, JESSE H., was born in Dec., 1818, in Kentucky or Tennessee, married Nancy Simpson, a sister to Wm. Simpson, and came to Richland creek, Sangamon county, in 1829, and one year later moved to DeWitt county. He died Oct., 1858, and she died April 5, 1872—both in DeWitt county, leaving a large family. Their son—

SAMUEL W., born March 1, 1828 in Tennessee, married July 2, 1865, to Almarinda Harrold, and was married the second time, Dec. 1, 1869, to Mrs. Elizabeth B. Combs, whose maiden name was Foster, a half-sister to Mrs. Hannah F. Stubbs. S. W. Mulkey enlisted July, 1861, in Co. F, 41st Ill. Inf., for three years, served full term, and was honorably discharged, August 1, 1864, at Springfield. He lives four miles east of Berlin, Sangamon county, Illinois.

MYERS, HENRY C., was born Dec. 6, 1817, in Chambersburg, Pa., and came to Springfield, Ill., in 1838. In 1841 he went to Boone county, Mo., and was there married in 1843 to Eleanor D. Robards, a native of Lexington, Ky. Mr. Myers moved back to Springfield, Ill., where they had three children, one of whom died young—

FRANKLIN, born August 5, 1847, in Howard county, Missouri, was trained to the mercantile business by his father, and became his successor. He is now engaged in miscellaneous merchandising in Springfield, Illinois.

ELLA D., born in Springfield, resides with her mother.

Henry C. Myers was first in the grocery trade, changed to confectionery, and from 1861 to 1865 was sutler at Camp Butler. After the close of the rebellion he engaged in general merchandising, and died Jan. 24, 1871. Mrs. Eleanor D. Myers and her two children reside in Springfield, Illinois.

N

NAVE, HENRY, was born Sept. 22, 1812, in Carter county, Tenn. Margaret C. Bowers was born Sept. 12, 1812, in the same county. They were there married, April 9, 1831, had one child, and then moved to Washington county, Ind., where one child was born. Both children died there, MARTHA in her fourth year, and ELIZABETH in infancy. Mr. Nave and his wife moved to Sangamon county, Ill., arriving Sept. 22, 1839, in what is now Fancy Creek township. They reside one and three-quarter miles north of Cantrall, Sangamon county, Illinois.—1874.

NEAL, DANIEL, was born about 1770, in Bedford county, Va. He was married there to Polly Booth, a native of the same county. They had ten children in Virginia, and moved to Franklin county, Tenn., in the fall of 1808, where one child was born. The family then moved to Bourbon county, Ky., where they had five children, and they moved to Sangamon county, Illinois, arriving Nov. 10, 1828, in what is now Chatham township. Of their sixteen children—

ACHILLES, born about 1793, in Virginia, died in 1809 in Tennessee.

FANNY, born in Virginia, married in Kentucky to Barton Darneille, and moved to Sangamon county before her parents. He died in Macon county. His widow died, in 1852, in Chatham township, Sangamon county.

WINSTON, born in Virginia, married in Kentucky to Melinda Miller, came to Sangamon county in 1829, moved back about 1839, and died, leaving a large family.

MARY, born in Bedford county, Va., March 18, 1799, married to Andrew Starr. See his name.

NANCY, born in Virginia, married in Kentucky to Joseph Jackson, and came to Sangamon county with her father, Mr. Jackson died at Galena, and she married John Hodge, who died, and she married Andrew Steele, who was born Feb. 6, 1795, in Davidson county, Tenn. She never had children. They live in Loami township.

WILLIAM, born in Virginia, married Rachel Daisey, in Nicholas county, Ky., and lives with his third wife.

JUDITH, born in Virginia, about 1804, married in Sangamon county to Stephen Shelton. See his name.

PRUDENCE, born April 9, 1806, in Bedford county, Va., married in Sangamon county to Wm. Shelton. See his name.

CATHARINE lives with her sister, Mrs. Steele.

STEPHEN B., born Dec. 25, 1808, in Virginia, married in Sangamon county to Julia A. Wyckoff. They had four children—FIELDING M., born Oct. 29, 1832, married Leah M. Greenwood. They had seven children, JULIA A. died at two years. WILLIAM A., JOHN S., ELIZA A., RUTH J., HENRY R. and CORA L. live with their parents, four and one-half miles west of Chatham, Illinois. SAMUEL M. enlisted in 1862, in Co. B, 11th Mo. Inf., for three years. Served to the end of the rebellion, and was honorably discharged. He was married, in 1869, in Sangamon county, to Clarissa Underwood, have three children, and live in Green county, Mo. MAHALA A. married John W. Greening. See his name. WILLIAM A. enlisted in 1861, in Co. I, 14th Ill. Inf., for three years, re-enlisted as a veteran, Jan., 1864; served to the end of the rebellion, was honorably discharged, and lives near Chatham, Illinois. Mrs. Julia A. Neal died, and S. B. Neal married Elizabeth Proctor. They had six children, four of whom, STEPHEN B., JUN., SIMON N., GEORGE W. and MARY JANE, died under fifteen years. HENRY C. enlisted, Aug. 9, 1861, in Co. B, 30th Ill. Inf., for three years. He was captured at the battle of Atlanta, Georgia, July 22, 1864, and died in Andersonville prison pen about one month later. Mrs. Elizabeth Neal died, and S. B. Neal was married, April 28, 1862, to Mrs. Lucinda Whited, whose maiden name was Bridges. They had one child, EMMA. Stephen B. Neal died, and his widow lives in Loami township, Sangamon county, Illinois.

JOHN A., born July 31, 1809, in Franklin county, Tenn. married in Sangamon county, Aug., 1837, to Eliza A. Greening. They had two children. MARY E. married James Jacobs. See his name. CAROLINE married Peyton M. McGinnis. See his name. Mrs. Eliza A. Neal died in 1846, and John A. Neal was married, Jan. 13, 1859, to Mrs. America Darneille, who had previously been Mrs. Gibson, and whose maiden name was Forrest. Mr. Neal was a member of the Sangamon county Board of Supervisors, from 1862 to 1865, and is now a justice of the peace for Chatham township, and resides in Chatham—1874. John A. Neal is authority for the statement that about three and one-half miles north of the present town of Rochester, five hogs were confined in a snow drift, about the fifth of Jan., 1831, and escaped from it the latter part of February, when the snow was going off. They had been nearly two months where it was impossible for them to obtain food. They were skeletons, but afterwards became good hogs.

GEORGE W., born in 1811, in Bourbon county, Ky., came to Sangamon county in 1828. He went to LaFayette county, Mo., was engaged to be married, bought a farm of a man named James Bowman, made one payment on it, and had some money left. He was murdered for the money by Bowman, May 6, 1846. The murderer escaped, was captured two years later, and when within six miles of the county seat, one of the guards carelessly left a pistol in a pocket of his overcoat, which he hung up while partaking of his breakfast. The prisoner watched his opportunity, took the pistol and shot himself dead.

LUCY, born in Kentucky, married Daniel Richardson, had five children, and lives in Monroe county, Iowa.

BERTHENA, born in Kentucky, has been twice married, and lives in Nebraska.

ELIJAH B., born in Kentucky, married in Sangamon county to Mary Heredith. They had seven children, four of whom died. GEORGE W. married Carrie Greening, and lives in Chatham township. JOHN and ELIJAH also live in Chatham township. The parents both died in 1853.

BARBARA A., born Jan. 31, 1819, in Kentucky, married in Sangamon county to Sidney S. Campbell. *See his name.*

Daniel Neal died, Aug. 26, 1838, and his widow, Mrs. Polly Neal, died in 1854, both in Sangamon county, Illinois.

NEAL, JAMES W., was born Sept. 26, 1806, in Bourbon county, Ky., and was married in Nicholas county, Jan. 4, 1827, to Mary Cassity. They had two children in Bourbon county, and moved, in company with her father, to Sangamon county, Ill., arriving in the fall of 1830, in what is now Rochester township, where three children were born. Of their five children—

ALMIRA J., born Nov. 3, 1827, in Kentucky, married Feb. 13, 1851, in Sangamon county, to Isaac Keys. *See his name.*

ELIZA E., born Sept. 10, 1829, in Kentucky, married in Sangamon county to H. Cicero St. Clair. *See his name.*

NANCY E., born March 14, 1833, in Sangamon county, married Feb. 10, 1853, to Oscar L. St. Clair. *See his name.*

WILLIAM H., born April 12, 1835, in Sangamon county, lives at the family homestead, one mile west of Rochester, Illinois.

JAMES H., born Sept. 5, 1838, in Sangamon county, married in Taylorville, Nov. 13, 1866, to Lizzie H. Moore. They had two children, NELLIE and MARY R. The latter died May 8, 1875, aged two years. James W. Neal resides at Lamar, Barton county, Mo. He was elected Treasurer of that county in the fall of 1872, for two years, and is a banker in Lamar.

James W. Neal died June 20, 1870, and his widow resides on the farm where the family settled in 1825, one mile west of Rochester, Sangamon county, Illinois—1876.

NEAL, NATHANIEL B., was born in Bourbon county, Ky., and came to Sangamon county in 1835 or '6. He was married in 1839 to Sarah A. King. They had one child—

HENRY H., born Sept. 25, 1840, five miles northeast of Springfield. He enlisted April 16, 1861, on the first call for 75,000 men, for three months, in Co. F, 9th Ill. Inf.; re-enlisted July 28, 1861, same company and regiment, for three years; served full term, and was honorably discharged, Aug. 25, 1864, at Camp Butler. He was married Oct. 4, 1864, in Springfield, to Lorena Hill, a granddaughter of Philip Smith. They have four children, IDA B., ALVA, EVA, and a boy babe, and live four miles northwest of Chatham, on the old Starr farm. —1874.

Nathaniel B. Neal died, and his widow married Hudson Lanham. *See King family name.*

NEALE, TOM M., was born in 1796 in Fauquier county, Va. His parents moved when he was a boy to Bowling

Green, Ky. He enlisted there and served the latter part of the war with Great Britain which began in 1812. He studied law in Bowling Green, and early declared himself opposed to slavery. He was married there in 1821 to Harriet Blakemore. They had two children in Kentucky, and moved to Sangamon county, Ill., arriving at Springfield Nov. 26, 1824, where eight children were born. Of their children—

SINAI A., born Nov. 26, 1822, in Kentucky, married in Sangamon county to Thomas Beerup. See his name.

MARY E., born March, 1824, in Kentucky, is unmarried, and resides in Carlinville, Illinois.

RICHARD D., born Feb. 22, 1826, in Springfield, married Mrs. Lucy Williams, whose maiden name was Patten. He died, leaving a widow and one child, JULIA C., who reside near Shelbyville, Illinois.

THOMAS O., born June 4, 1828, in Springfield, died in California, aged twenty-four years.

HARRIET B., born Nov. 29, 1830, in Springfield, married Hickison Grubbs. They have five children, FLORA K., NEVILLE C., FRANK P., EDWARD and HARRY, and reside in Springfield, Missouri.

SARAH M. and MARTHA K., twins, born Sept. 15, 1834, in Springfield, Illinois.

SARAH M. married John Dugger. They have four children, JEFFERSON L., RICHARD N., PATTIE M. and WILLIAM, and reside in Carlinville, Illinois.

MARTHA K. married Milton McClure. They have two children, JAMES A. and HATTIE B., and reside in Carlinville, Illinois.

CATHARINE, born Jan. 15, 1836, in Springfield, Ill., married George Gilbert. They are without family, and reside at Springfield, Missouri.

MIRIAM C., born May 28, 1838, in Springfield, Ill., married Joseph Edwards. They are without family, and reside in Columbus, Kentucky.

MARGARET, born April 15, 1840, in Springfield, married John Krugg. They have one child, BERTIE, and reside in Wichita, Kansas.

Gen. Tom M. Neale died Aug. 7, 1840, and his widow died Aug. 27, 1859 both in Springfield, Ill. Gen. Neale was a lawyer by profession. He was the highest military officer from Sangamon county in the campaign against the Winnebago Indians in 1827, being the Colonel commanding the four infantry companies. He acted as Justice of the Peace for several years, and united many couples in marriage about the time of the "deep snow." Sometimes the only fee tendered him was a saddle of venison. Col. Neale surveyed and laid out into lots the land that was donated to secure the county seat at Springfield. See page 36. He was three times elected County Surveyor, and held that office at the time of his death. Gen. Neale appointed Abraham Lincoln his deputy when he was first elected County Surveyor.

NELSON, WILLIAM, came from St. Clair county with Henry Funderburk, and settled on Horse creek in the spring of 1817, raised a family of seven children, and moved to Texas. His daughter, Nancy, married James Funderburk. See his name. They live near Taylorville, Illinois.

NESBITT, SAMUEL G., was born August 18, 1808, in what is now Juniata county, Penn. Mary B. Turner was born Sept. 28, 1814, in the same county, and her parents moved into the adjoining county of Mifflin. Samuel G. Nesbitt and Mary B. Turner were there married, June 6, 1833. They had two children in Juniata county, and moved to Sangamon county, Ill., arriving June 26, 1837, at Springfield, and in a few weeks moved to Mechanicsburg, where one child was born. The family then moved to Decatur, where they had four children, and then moved back to Sangamon county, Clear Lake township, where four children were born. Of all their children—

MARY J., born April 11, 1834, in Pennsylvania, was married in Sangamon county, April, 1854, to Reuben Mallory. See his name.

MARTHA T., born Dec. 9, 1835, in Pennsylvania, was married March 20, 1861, in Sangamon county, to Isaac O. Eyman, who was born May 20, 1837, in St. Clair county, Ill. They have five living children, namely: LAURA E., CLARA E., LEWIS E., IDA A. and

CHARLEY M., and live at Harristown, Macon county, Illinois.

WILLIAM CAMERON, born May 8, 1838, at Mechanicsburg, Sangamon county, enlisted in Co. E, 145th Ill. Inf., and was mustered in, June 9, 1864, as 1st Lieutenant, for one hundred days; served full term, and was honorably discharged, Sept. 23, 1864. He was married Feb. 23, 1865, to Sarah C. Bailey, who was born Oct. 14, 1845, in Hawkins county, Tenn. They have three children, CHARLES E., SAMUEL G. and MARY J., and live four miles north of Rochester, Sangamon county, Illinois.

MARGARET R., born Feb. 28, 1840, in Decatur, was married in Sangamon county, Jan. 3, 1867, to James W. Richardson, who was born April 22, 1841, in New Haven, Conn. They have four children, JENNIE B., MARY B., THOMAS and SAMUEL, and live in Clear Lake township, west of Sangamon river and north of Sugar creek. Mr. Richardson enlisted July 18, 1862, in Co. I, 114th Ill. Inf., for three years, and served one year in the ranks. He was transferred, March 28, 1864, to the signal corps, and served as such to the end of the rebellion. He was honorably discharged at New Orleans, July 4, 1865.

SARAH G., born May 1, 1842, in Decatur, was married Dec. 24, 1868, to Jacob F. Cromley. She died March 5, 1870, in Sangamon county.

HELEN M., born May 8, 1844, in Decatur, raised in Sangamon county, was married in Decatur, Oct. 31, 1865, to John S. Windsor. They have three children, LILLIE B., MARY L. and HELEN M., and live at Mulberry, Clermont county, Ohio. J. S. Windsor was born Sept. 10, 1836, near Cincinnati, Ohio. He enlisted in Co. K, 116th Ill. Inf., and was mustered in, Dec. 30, 1862, as 1st Lieutenant, promoted to Captain of Co. E, Jan. 31, 1863; promoted to Major, Sept. 26, 1864, and Lieutenant-Colonel, May 27, 1865. He was mustered out with the regiment, June 7, 1865.

ALICE E., born in Decatur, and lives with her parents.

EMMA K., born Feb. 25, 1849, in Sangamon county, died Sept. 29, 1856.

EVELINE H., born July 30, 1851, in Sangamon county, was married Feb. 20, 1872, to Frank K. Springer. See his name.

SAMUEL T., born July 12, 1854, and

LAURA B., born Jan. 31, 1859, live with their parents.

Samuel G. Nesbitt learned the art of printing under Simon Cameron, in Pennsylvania. He was for many years connected with the *Illinois State Journal* office, but is now giving his attention entirely to farming. While living at Decatur he was elected to represent Macon county in the legislature of 1842. He acted with the Democratic party until 1861, when the rebellion broke out. From that time he acted with the Republican party. He served five years, from 1865 to 1870, as the representative of Clear Lake township in the Sangamon county Board of Supervisors, and now resides two and a half miles southeast of Riverton, Illinois.

NEWCOMER, CHRISTOPHER, was born in Huntington county, Penn., Oct. 9, 1791. Susan Sells was born March 17, 1794, in the same county. They were married July 1, 1813, in Franklin county, Ohio, and had five children there. The family moved to Sangamon county, Ill., arriving Dec. 9, 1824, in what is now Woodside township, where they had five living children. Of their children—

MARY, born June 7, 1814, in Ohio, married Davis Meredith. See his name.

CHARLES S., born in 1816, in Ohio, raised in Sangamon county, and died June 14, 1839, at the Galena lead mines, where he was engaged in smelting lead.

SAMUEL, ELIZA and SUSANNAH all died young in Ohio.

ARMENIA, born in 1825 in Sangamon county, died Sept. 4, 1845.

JANE M., born in 1826, in Sangamon county, died September 10, 1845.

The two latter were engaged to be married, which was to have taken place just about the time of their deaths, if they had lived.

AMANDA E. died April 23, 1839, in her tenth year.

DOW, born May 26, 1832, in Sangamon county, married Nancy M. Fry, who died Feb. 23, 1852, and he married July 4, 1854, to Catharine M. Brunk. They have two living children, CHARLES W. and MARY JOSEPHINE, and live on the farm settled by Mr. Newcomer's father in 1824, in the southeast corner of Woodside township, seven miles southeast of Springfield, Illinois.

Christopher Newcomer died Feb. 12, 1852, and his widow died Jan. 12, 1872, both on the farm where they settled in 1824.

NEWMAN, HENRY, was born Aug. 18, 1787, in Baltimore, Md. In 1795 he was taken by his parents to Knox county, Tenn. During the war of 1812-13-14 with England, he served in three different companies; once for himself and twice in the place of relatives, who had been drafted. He was under Gen. Jackson at the battle of New Orleans. Henry Newman was married in Knox county, Tenn., Dec. 15, 1815, to Priscilla Plumlee, who was born May 13, 1791, in Burke county, North Carolina. They had seven children in Tennessee, and moved to Springfield, Ill., arriving in Dec., 1828, where they had two living children. Of their nine children—

ELIZABETH E., born Jan. 9, 1817, in Knox county, Tenn., married July 13, 1858, in Springfield, to John Haines. They have one child, CHARLES HENRY, and reside in Cotton Hill township, near New City, Sangamon county, Illinois.

MINERVA W., born April 29, 1820, in Knox county, Tenn., married April 26, 1839, in Springfield, Illinois, to Henry Teed, who was born in 1818 in Springfield, Mass. They had four children, one of whom was drowned at about fifteen years of age. The other three, ALBERT, MINERVA A. and CHARLES, live with their mother in San Francisco, Cal., whither the family went in 1852.

MARY ALMIRA, born Feb. 3, 1822, in Knoville, Tenn., married Dec., 1842, in Springfield, Ill., to Josiah Moore, a native of Hagarstown, Md. Mr. Moore died in 1857, and she died July, 1858. Their only living child, ANDREW J. Moore, lives in San Antonio, Texas.

JACOB S., born Jan. 6, 1825, in Knoxville, Tenn., raised in Sangamon county, and was assassinated by an unknown hand April 23, 1873, at Springfield, Missouri.

JOHN W., born Jan. 11, 1826, in Knoxville, Tenn., raised in Springfield, married in St. Louis, Mo., May 13, 1852, to Caroline M. Field, who was born April 13, 1834, in Auburn, New York. They have three living children, HERBERT S., JOHN B. and ANNA G., and reside in Springfield. Mr. Newman is a member of the firm of Thompson & Newman, planing mill and door, sash and blind factory, Springfield, Illinois.

JOSEPH PLUMLEE, born Nov. 18, 1827, in Springfield, enlisted in the 4th Ill. Inf., under Col. E. D. Baker, and was killed at the battle of Cerro Gordo, Mexico, in 1847.

JAMES F., born July 29, 1829, in Springfield, and died Sept. 20, 1861, in his native city.

MARY A., born April 15, 1831, in Springfield, married Nov., 1852, to William Fooshe. They had one living child, JOSEPH P., a machinist, and reside with his mother in Springfield.

WILLIAM H., born Jan. 1, 1835, in Springfield, and died March 8, 1873.

Henry Newman died March 20, 1861, and his widow died Aug. 10, 1873, both in Springfield, Illinois.

NEWSOM, DAVID, was born Dec. 28, 1805, in Greenbrier county, Va. He was the youngest of twelve children, of William and Margaret Newsom, whose maiden name was Spicer. The father was of English and the mother of German parentage, but both born in Virginia. William Newsom died when his son David was seven years old. In his fourteenth year David was thrown upon his own resources, with four dollars in money, some clothes and a limited amount of education. He learned the tanner's trade in Gallipolis, Ohio, but never liked the business. He taught school two years in Meigs county, Ohio, and applied the proceeds in improving his own mind. He returned to Virginia, and was married July 12, 1827, in Monroe county, to Polly Houston. They had one child in Virginia, and in company with his father-in-law moved to Sangamon county, Illinois, arriving Nov. 14, 1828. Mr. Newsom at one time owned and lived on what is now part of Oak Ridge Cemetery, but sold it at a large profit. He then entered land and made a farm near Springfield. Mr. and Mrs. Newsom had nine children in

Sangamon county, Ill., and in April, 1851, started overland for Oregon. One son was born on the road, and after a journey of six months arrived, Oct., 1851, at the Old Methodist Mission, founded in 1834, about ten miles northwest of the present city of Salem, Oregon. There he received a donation of 325 acres of land, upon which they made a farm, and where one child was born. Three of their children died young. Of the others—

JOHN W., born April 30, 1828, in Monroe county, Va., brought up in Sangamon county, Ill., was married Dec. 21, 1865, in Oregon, to Olive Greenwood. They have two living children, MINNIE M. and ROY, and live near Salem, Oregon.

ROBERT L., born Jan. 22, 1832, in Sangamon county, Illinois, was married in 1856, in Hardinsburg, Ky., to Annie Lightfoot. They have five living children, WILLIAM WAVERLY, ALFRED LANDER, PERCY LEE, LUELLA and IRENE. R. L. Newsom is a druggist, and lives in Cloverport, Kentucky.

SAMUEL J., born March 13, 1834, in Sangamon county, is a stock raiser. He is unmarried, and lives near Prineville, Wasco county, Oregon.

VIRGIL H., born Aug. 29, 1836, in Sangamon county, Illinois, is a stock raiser. He is unmarried, and lives near Salem, Oregon.

MARGARET J., born in Sangamon county, Ill., was married in Oregon, May 7, 1854. to Elisha Veazey, and died March 24, 1861, leaving four children, all died young but JAMES M., who lives with his father, near Gervais, Marion county, Oregon.

MARY E., born April 2, 1841, in Sangamon county, Ill., was married Dec. 23, 1857, in Oregon, to John W. Greenwood. They have four children, ALICE A., FANNIE, JOHN L. and WINNIE, and live near Salem, Marion county, Oregon.

ANN M., born Sept. 25, 1844, in Sangamon county, was married, Dec. 31, 1863, to J. P. Munkers, near Salem, Oregon. They have three living children, FRANK, LENA and IVY, and live near Heppner, Umatilla county, Oregon.

GEORGE H., born July 9, 1851, at Independence Rock, on the Sweetwater river, on the wagon road to Oregon. He was married Sept. 5, 1875, in Oregon, to Lauretta Williams. They are without family, and live at the homestead, ten miles northeast of Salem, Oregon.

HARVEY M., born April 18, 1854, in Marion county, Oregon, died there May 24, 1875.

David Newsom and wife are living in Marion county, Oregon, on the farm where they settled, Oct. 29, 1851. Mr. Newsom was always fond of literature, and is extensively known in western Oregon as an able writer on general topics. He was appointed by President Lincoln, Statistician for the Williamette valley, and served with honor until 1870, when he resigned in consequence of advancing years. He is engaged in farming and fruit growing. His address is Salem, Marion county, Ohio.

NIPPER, WILLIAMSON, was born Sept. 19, 1796, in Virginia. His father moved to Alabama when he was twelve or fifteen years of age, and from there to the vicinity of Nashville, Tenn. He was there married to Nancy Moore. She had twins, and the mother and children died. He was then married to Hepsey Gibson, who was born Feb. 14, 1803, in Franklin county, Tenn. They had three children, and moved to Sangamon county, Ill., arriving in the fall of 1829, about one mile east of the present town of Loami, where six children were born. Of all the children—

ELIZA C., born Oct. 26, 1823, in Tennessee, married in Sangamon county, March 19, 1844, to George W. Legrand. He was born March 12, 1823, in Breckenridge county, Ky., and came to Sangamon county in 1843. They had eleven children, six of whom died young. Of the other five: SARAH married Oct. 19, 1867, to R. Wickliffe Price, who was born Feb. 11, 1825, at Georgetown, Ky., have three children, ROBERT W., PHILEMON BIRD and CHARLES W., and live near Loami. Mr. Price is a lawyer. WILLIAMSON A., ROBERT M., ELSIE M. and LUCY A. live with their parents, five miles west of Loami, Sangamon county, Illinois.

NANCY F., born March 16, 1825, in Tennessee, married Miles Meacham, in Sangamon county, had four children, and died in Warren county, Illinois.

HARRIET M., born Jan. 17, 1829, in Tennessee, married in Sangamon county, to William E. Hudson. See his name.

ELMIRA J., born May 31, 1831, in Sangamon county, married John Evans, and both are dead.

AMERICA A., born August 2, 1833, in Sangamon county, married Abner Clark, have seven children, and live in Worth county, Mo.

WILLIAMSON M., born Sept. 22, 1835, in Sangamon county, married Mary Staley. They had one child, NANCY M. F., and Mrs. Mary Nipper died. W. M. Nipper married Louisa Cline, who was born Oct. 22, 1840, in Scott county, Ill. They have three children, ELMIRA S., PHILIP and JOSEPH W., and live four miles west of Loami, Sangamon county, Illinois.

HEPSEY A., born Dec. 13, 1837, married Abner W. Knight. See his name.

THOMAS H., born Oct. 1, 1840, died aged twenty-three years.

MARY M., born March 26, 1843, in Sangamon county, married Oct. 19, 1863, to Wilson Cline, who was born March 3, 1836, in Scott county. They have three children, BENJAMIN F., JOHN H. and HARRIET M., and live near Loami, Illinois.

Williamson Nipper died August 24, 1843, and his widow married Daniel Staley, (see his name) and she died Mar. 8, 1873, both near Loami, Sangamon county, Illinois.

NORRED, RICHARD C., was born about 1795 in Loudon county, Va., married in Frederick county, Md., to Elizabeth Jenkins; moved to Ohio, and from there to Sangamon county, Ill., arriving in 1836. They had children in Maryland, Ohio and Sangamon county. The parents and most of the children died in Sangamon county. One son, only, lives in the county.

PARIS is married and lives three miles south of Illiopolis, Illinois.

JAMES T., last heard from at Marysville, Yuba county, Cal., in 1869.

NORRED, MARY A., sister to William and Richard C. Norred, was born in Loudon county, Va., came to Sangamon county, Ill., and married John A. Miller. See his name.

NORRED, WILLIAM, was born March 9, 1809, in Loudon county, Va. He was married in 1834 in that county to Elizabeth E. Dowdall, who was born there March 9, 1814. They lived in Frederick county, Md., until they had two children, and moved to Sangamon county, Ill., arriving Nov. 6, 1838, and settled three miles northeast of Rochester, at the mills of Darling & Baker, where a child was born. Of their three children—

CHARLES W., born April 11, 1836, in Maryland, died in Sangamon county in his third year.

SAMUEL T. born July 6, 1838, in Maryland, died in Sangamon county in his fourteenth year.

CHARLES H., born Jan. 19, 1842, in Sangamon county. He was a medical student, but laid aside his books in Aug., 1862, and enlisted in Co. —, 114th Ill. Inf. He was placed in charge of a medical dispensary for the regiment, and later, of a hospital, served until the close of the war, when he was honorably discharged, attended McDowell College at St. Louis, and graduated there. He was married in Logan county to Elizabeth Dalbey. They have two children, CHARLES ELMER and WILLIAM ASBURY. Dr. Norred commenced practice at Dawson, but removed to Middletown, Logan county, where he now resides.

Mrs. Elizabeth E. Norred died Sept. 1, 1843, in Sangamon county, and William Norred was married in 1845, in Loudon county, Va., to Mary Ann Doneil, who was born in that county, April 22, 1820. She died Oct. 21, 1851, leaving one child—

JOHN W., born June 17, 1847, in Sangamon county. He married Mary Richardson, and lives in Middletown, Logan county, Illinois.

William Norred was married Dec. 18, 1853, in Sangamon county, to Mrs. Martha Dowdall, whose maiden name was Enlow, a native of Washington county, Pa. She has one child by her first marriage, Silas R. Dowdall. Mr. and Mrs. Norred have four children—

FENTON M., LAURETTA, MARY E. and *ELIZABETH C.*, and reside half a mile northwest of Dawson, Sangamon county, Illinois.

NORRIS, AQUILLA, was born Jan. 1, 1776, near Baltimore, Md. He was there married to Eleanor Norris. They had eight children in Maryland, three of whom died young, and Edward, the eldest, died there Aug. 30, 1830, aged nineteen years. The parents, with four children, came to Sangamon county, arriving in Round Prairie, six miles east of Springfield, in April, 1835. Of their four children—

JAMES L., born July 18, 1813, in Maryland, married in Sangamon county, Oct. 17, 1841, to Sarah E. Cole. They had one living child, PRISCILLA, who married Jesse Estes, has five children, and lives in Winchester, Scott county, Illinois. James L. Norris and wife live near Cotton Hill Postoffice, Sangamon county, Illinois.

JOHN, born Oct. 17, 1814, in Maryland, married in Sangamon county, Oct. 17, 1841, to Mary W. Cole. The two brothers and sisters were married by the same ceremony. John Norris was a soldier in the Springfield Cadets, was on duty at Nauvoo, in the Mormon war, and was shot dead accidentally, Sept. 28, 1844. His widow married John Fagan. *See his name.*

PRISCILLA, born Aug. 19, 1820, in Baltimore, Md., was married in Sangamon county to Gershom Keyes. *See his name.*

MARY A., born Feb. 3, 1822, in Maryland, married to Bedford W. Higgins. *See his name.*

Mrs. Eleanor Norris died Oct. 28, 1852, and Aquilla Norris died March 4, 1856, both in Sangamon county, Illinois.

NORRIS, ELIZABETH, was born March 22, 1776, near Baltimore, Maryland. She was sister to Mrs. Eleanor Norris. She died Dec. 20, 1872, in Springfield, at the house of A. R. Robinson. She was nearly ninety-six years of age, and never married.

NORTH, JOHN, born Nov. 22, 1806, near the village of Bent creek, on James river, Buckingham county, Va. His grandfather, Richard North, was born in England, and trained to the business of a cutler. He came to America, and worked at his business at Bent creek. His wife's maiden name was Thornton, but whether they were married in England or America is unknown to their descendants. Their third son, Peter, born in Virginia, was married there to Elizabeth Franklin, a daughter of Robert Franklin, of Campbell county, Va. Peter North was a soldier from Virginia in the war with England in 1812. In 1819 or '20 he moved to Jefferson county, near Dandridge, Tenn., taking with him six children. The second son, John, whose name heads this sketch, was there married, Sept. 22, 1828, to Anna Giger, who was born Nov. 4, 1807, in that county. They came to Sangamon county, Ill., arriving April 12, 1829, in what is now Cooper township, north of Sangamon river, where they had four living children. Of their children—

BENJ. HOUSTON, born Nov. 19, 1832, in Sangamon county, married Nov. 15, 1855, to Minerva A. F. Miller, who was born May 18, 1836, in Loudon county, Va. They have three children, JOHN H., MARY A. and ALMEDA S., and live in Cooper township, Sangamon county, Illinois.

HARVEY N., born Jan. 26, 1835, married Nov. 13, 1856, to Sarah E. Prather. They have four children, TONY, EMERY, CLYDE and PETER, and live in Christian county, four miles northeast of Breckenridge, Sangamon county, Illinois.

JOHN W., born Nov. 9, 1837, in Sangamon county. He enlisted August 7, 1862, in Co. A, 73d Ill. Inf., for three years, was captured Sept. 20, 1863, at the battle of Chickamauga, taken to Richmond, Va., was one month in Libby prison, thence to Danville, Va., thence to Andersonville, Ga., arriving at that prison pen March 20, 1864, where he remained to Dec., 1864. He was then taken to Charleston, S. C., where he spent six weeks in prison, thence to Florence, S. C., where he was released on parole, and started from Wilmington, N. C., March 4, 1865, for home, via Annapolis, Md., and reached home March 17, 1865, and was honorably discharged. John L. Hesser, relating his prison experience, speaks of John W. North as "a man of peculiar form or stature, six feet four inches in height, two hundred and ten pounds in weight, and a heart in proportion. In Andersonville he generally went by the name of The Infant. He was very kind and obliging to all the sick and weakly

—69

souls; never allowed any imposition on those poor, feeble forms who were not able to defend themselves. We lived as two brothers, commingled our sorrows together for eighteen dreary months, never were separated but one night during our imprisonment. * * * Lived through all the trying and heart-rending scenes of the many kinds of disease and death, where so many more died than lived, astonished that even one could live." John W. North was married March 8, 1866, to Maria McDaniel. They had three children, LOU IDA, ANN ELIZABETH and GERTIE LEE, and live two and a half miles south of Mechanicsburg, Illinois.

ANDREW J., born March 18, 1841, died April 26, 1857.

Mrs. Anna North died Feb. 24, 1844, and John North was married Sept. 19, 1844, to Susannah Eckel. They had six children; all died under five years. Mrs. Susannah North died July 1, 1855, and John North was married Feb. 19, 1856, to Mrs. Amelia Woodruff, who had previously been Mrs. West, and whose maiden name was Taylor. They had four children, PETER F. died in his second year. ROBERT F., born Mar. 31, 1859, EDWARD E., born Jan. 14, 1861, and PERMELIA A., born Jan. 24, 1864. John North resides on the farm where he settled in 1829, three miles south of Mechanicsburg, Sangamon county, Illinois.

NORTH, ROBERT, was born in Oct., 1814, in Buckingham county, Va., and taken by his parents to Jefferson county, Tenn., when he was a boy. He came to Sangamon county with his brother, John North, who had been back to Tennessee. They arrived in Sept., 1832, in what is now Cooper township. Robert North was married in Sangamon county March 29, 1838, to America Schmick. She was born Feb. 10, 1816, in Lincoln county, Ky., and came to Sangamon county in company with her mother, brother-in-law—John Clemons, one brother, two sisters and two nephews, arriving in the fall of 1829, and settled three miles south of Springfield. Robert North and wife had six living children in Sangamon county. Of their children—

JOHN W., born May 4, 1840, married Feb. 23, 1865, to Mary E. Troxell. They have two children, WILLIAM R. and SUSAN E., and reside two miles southwest of Clarksville, or Berry station, Sangamon county, Illinois.

MARY A., born Dec. 31, 1842, married Sept. 10, 1863, to William F. Herrin. See his name. They had five children, BELLE N., JAMES E., CHARLES F., BURT A., and CARRIE F. BURT A. died May 7, 1876.

SARAH J., born Nov. 17, 1844, married May 22, 1862, to David C. Herrin. See his name. They had five children, ROBERT E., JAMES W., GEORGE E., DAVID A. and JESSIE LEE; the youngest died Jan. 23, 1875.

CHRISTIANA, born July 17, 1849, lives with her parents.

ALBERT, born April 7, 1851, married Dec. 31, 1873, to Mary A. Lord, who was born Jan. 10, 1852, in Sangamon county. They live three-fourths of a mile east of Clarksville, Sangamon county, Illinois.

LAURA F., born Nov. 7, 1859, lives with her parents.

Robert North and wife reside two miles northeast of Berry station or Clarksville, Sangamon county, Illinois. He is one of the most extensive farmers in Sangamon county.

NOTTINGHAM, JONATHAN, was born Sept. 25, 1808, in Cape May county, New Jersey. Clark Nottingham emigrated from England, and settled in Delaware, about 1760. He moved to New Jersey soon after the Revolution, and raised a family. His son Jonathan was Colonel of a New Jersey regiment in the war of 1812. He was there married, and was the father of the subject of this sketch. Jonathan Nottingham number two was married, Jan. 30, 1831, to Hannah Smith, who was born July 10, 1807, in the same county. They had four children in New Jersey, and moved to Sangamon county, Illinois, arriving in Oct., 1837, and stopped south of Richland creek, where they lived two years, and in the spring of 1840 moved to a farm he had purchased, two and one-half miles northwest of Pleasant Plains. Seven children were born in Sangamon county. Of their children—

REUBEN L., born Dec. 14, 1832, in New Jersey, married Lutheria Hubbard. He enlisted, Aug. 8, 1863, for three years, in Co. —, 101st Ill. Inf., and died of disease, at Cairo, Ill., Dec., 1863.

JOHN, born in New Jersey, married Mary A. Corson, have three children, and live in Menard county.

ABIJAH S., born in New Jersey, married Mary Eaton, and lives near Pleasant Plains.

FRANCIS A., born June 22, 1837, in New Jersey, raised in Sangamon county, went to Pike's Peak, in 1858, and now lives in Mendocino county, California.

RACHEL, born in Sangamon county, married Reuben Corson, have four children, and live in Menard county, Illinois.

ALMARIN, born March 31, 1840, in Sangamon county. Served three years in the 1st Oregon Cavalry, and was honorably discharged. He is a stock dealer at Oskaloosa, Kansas.

CLARKE, born Feb. 26, 1842, in Sangamon county, married in Dayton, Ohio, in May, 1873, to Annie Christian, and lives two and one-half miles northwest of Pleasant Plains, Illinois.

JANE, born Oct. 29, 1843, in Sangamon county, married Henry K. Hoff, has three children, and lives in Golden City, Colorado.

JAMES S., born Jan. 17, 1845. Served three months in Co. I, 71st Ill. Inf., and is now—1873—an attorney at Silver City, New Mexico.

ELIZABETH, born Jan. 22, 1847, married Alexander Higgins. See his name.

CHARLES W., born June 29, 1848, in Sangamon county, married March 26, 1873, to Georgia Pellet, and lives near Pleasant Plains, Illinois.

Mrs. Hannah Nottingham died July 9, 1850, and Jonathan Nottingham was married, Aug., 1852, in Cape May county, N. J., to Mrs. Mary A. Townsend, whose maiden name was Sutton. Jonathan Nottingham resides on the farm where he settled in 1840, two miles northwest of Pleasant Plains, Sangamon county, Illinois.

NUCKOLLS, JAMES, was born Jan. 5, 1777, in Botetourt county, Va., and the family moving to Grayson county, same State, he was there married Jan. 5, 1804, to Janey Swift, who was born March 2, 1781, in that county. They had six children in Virginia, and in 1818 moved to Madison county, Illinois, where they had one child, and moved to what became Sangamon county, arriving in 1820, in what is now Auburn township, where they had one child. Of their children—

CHARLES D., born March 2, 1805, in Grayson county, Va., was married March 10, 1832, in Sangamon county, to Mary Wilson, who was born Jan. 3, 1812, in Buncombe county, N. C. They had eight children in Sangamon county. MARGARET J., born March 19, 1833, married Richard Ricks, and both died, leaving one child, MANFORD J. THOMAS J., born Dec. 6, 1834, was married Jan. 19, 1871, to Martha A. Brunk. They have three children, LILLY JANE, LUCY M. and GEORGE T; the latter died Feb. 10, 1876. T. J. Nuckolls lives in Auburn township, near where his grandfather settled in 1820. JAMES M., born Dec. 28, 1836, married Nancy Drennan, and died August 24, 1866, leaving one child, LAURA MAY, who lives with her mother. Mrs. Nancy Nuckolls married James M. Bennington. See his name. JOHN W., born March 30, 1838, married Louisa Pyle. They have three children, MARY M., CHARLES F. and MILLY ANN, and live four miles west of Pawnee, Ill. GEORGE W., born April 23, 1843, lives with his mother. MARY E., born Sept. 28, 1845, married William R. Lockridge. See his name. CHARLES Wm., born May 27, 1848, married Margaret J. Moore. They have one child, MINNIE, and live six miles east of Auburn, Illinois. Charles D. Nuckolls was a farmer and builder in early life. In the early settlement of Springfield he was engaged in the leather business. He purchased a lot at the southeast corner of Sixth and Washington streets for twelve dollars, and several years later sold it to Sangamon county for twelve hundred dollars. A court house was built on it, which was occupied as such from 1845 to 1876. Late in life Mr. C. D. Nuckolls studied medicine, and graduated in 1856, at McDowell College, St. Louis, Mo. He practiced several years, and died Nov. 19, 1865. His widow lives four miles east of Auburn.

THOMAS J., born Oct. 12, 1806, in Virginia, died in Madison county, Ill., aged fourteen years.

MARY, born Jan. 6, 1809, in Grayson county, Va., was married in Sangamon county, Ill., to Alfred Curry, who died, and she married Jesse Elgin. They live in Pana, Illinois.

MARGARET, born April 2, 1811, in Virginia, was married in Sangamon county, to James Wilson, and died. See his name.

MARTHA, born Feb. 20, 1813, in Grayson county, Va., was married in Sangamon county to Noah Mason. See his name.

JAMES M., born March 11, 1815, died in his sixth year.

JOHN, born March 24, 1817, in Grayson county, Va., was married in Sangamon county, Ill., to Elizabeth Ricks. They had one child, MYRA J., who died, aged seventeen years. Mrs. Elizabeth Nuckolls died, and John Nuckolls married Adaline Rice, and lives at the family homestead settled by his father in 1820, four miles east of Auburn.

JANE, born Oct. 11, 1819, in Madison county, Ill., was married in Sangamon county to John Milton Lockridge. See his name.

ANN, born August 23, 1822, in Sangamon county, was married there, in 1843, to William Graham. He was drowned in July, 1844, while attempting to cross a stream of water in Christian county. His widow was married July 30, 1849, to Thomas P. Bond, who was born July 11, 1812, in Burton county, N. C., raised in Kentucky, came to Montgomery county, Illinois, in 1835. In 1839, he, in company with G. R. Jernigan and Wm. S. Ricks, circulated a petition, obtained the requisite number of signatures, and Mr. Bond took it to Vandalia, presented it to the legislature, and secured the passage of the law creating Dane county, which was afterwards changed to Christian county. In 1848 he was elected to fill an unexpired term as county clerk, and then to a full term; was elected in 1868 to an unexpired term as county treasurer, and then to a full term. Thomas P. Bond acquired the title of Col nel by being elected to that position in the State Militia in 1840. Mr. Bond has two daughters by a former marriage, both married. One resides in Nebraska, the other at Fairplay, Park county, Col.

Thomas P. Bond and wife reside in Taylorville, Christian county, Illinois.

Mrs. Janey Nuckolls died June 15, 1836, and James Nuckolls died Sept. 15, 1859, both on the farm where they settled in 1820. It is five miles east of Auburn.

NUCKOLLS, JOHN, born March, 1781, in Hanover county, Va., was married March 10, 1809, in Grayson county, Va., to Ann Collins, who was born Dec. 11, 1786, in North Carolina. They had ten children, three of whom died young. They moved with five children to Sangamon county, Ill., arriving in 1826, in what is now Auburn township, where his brother James had settled six years before. They had two children in Sangamon county. Of their seven children—

CLARK, born Feb. 22, 1811, in Grayson county, Va., was married in Sangamon county April 30, 1835, to Orlena Shellhouse. Clark Nuckolls died Oct. 5, 1854, in Christian county.

MATILDA, born Nov. 16, 1813, in Grayson county, Va., was married Dec. 18, 1834, in Sangamon county, to Irvin S. Pulliam. See his name.

MARTHA, born July 3, 1819, in Grayson county, Va., was married March, 1844, in Sangamon county, to Willis Shellhouse. See his name.

CHARLES, born Dec. 11, 1822, in Grayson county, Va., was married in Sangamon county Aug. 29, 1849, to Cassandra Clayton, who was born Feb. 8, 1832. They had three children, AMANDA E., "M." and EMILY J. Mrs. Cassaranda Nuckolls was killed by lightning May 25, 1858. Charles Nuckolls was married Oct. 19, 1858, to Susan Baker, who was born Jan., 1832, in Bertie county, North Carolina, and moved to Sangamon county, Ill., in 1850. They have seven children, CHARLES S., JOHN H., SARAH N., JAMES A., LYDIA M., ROBERT J. and WILLIAM W. Charles Nuckolls and family reside near Auburn, Illinois.

JAMES D., born Dec. 22, 1824, in Grayson county, Va., was married in Sangamon county March 22, 1849, to Lydia Easley. They had six children, JOHN W., JAMES M., THOMAS J., EMMA A., WARHAM E. and CHARLES D. Mrs. Lydia Nuckolls died in Missouri, and J. D. Nuckolls was married June 16, 1870, to Louisa J. Voshell. They have one child, LYDIA A., and reside near Auburn, Illinois.

JANE, born Jan. 2, 1828, in Sangamon county, was married there March 26, 1846, to James Blount, who was born Aug. 8, 1822, in Tennessee. They had three children: JOHN, born Dec. 25, 1849, in Sangamon county, and JAMES H., born Jan. 22, 1851, in Sangamon county, both live in Edinburg; IDA M., born March 28, 1857, was married April 7, 1874, to Thomas Bell, who was born April 5, 1841, in Champaign county, Ohio. They live in Edinburg, Ill. Mr. and Mrs. Blount reside in Edinburg, Christian county, Illinois.

AMANDA, born Oct. 16, 1831, in Sangamon county, married Samuel Davidson. See his name.

John Nuckolls died Aug. 2, 1844, in Sangamon county, and his widow, Mrs. Ann Nuckolls, resides with her children in Ball and Pawnee township. She is in her nintieth year, and enjoys excellent health—March, 1876.

O

OGDEN.—Two brothers, John and Joseph Ogden, were born and married in Maryland. John moved to Logan county, Ky., and raised a family there. Several years later, Joseph died in Maryland. John moved the family of his brother Joseph to Grayson county, Ky. John's daughter—

SARAH, married Nathaniel Rames. See his name.

Joseph's son—

OGDEN, ZACHARIAH, was born Nov. 11, 1794, near Frederick City, St. Mary's county, Maryland. His father died there when he was quite young, and his mother moved to Washington county, Kentucky. Zachariah was married, in 1815, in Grayson county, to Elizabeth Peerce. They had six children in Kentucky, and the family moved to Sangamon county, Ill., arriving Oct 13, 1827, in what is now Ball township, where they had five children. Of their children—

MELINDA, born in Kentucky, married in Sangamon county to Stephen Gatton. They had two children, and the whole family died.

WINNIE, born in Kentucky, married in Sangamon county to James Clark. They have eleven children, and live in Decatur county, Iowa.

JAMES, born in Kentucky, married in Sangamon county to Jane Ogden. They had six children in Sangamon county, four of whom died, namely: ELIZABETH, at seventeen; MARY A., at two; SARAH M., in infancy, and ZACHARIAH P., in his thirteenth year. JAMES WM. and JOSEPH RAMES live with their father. Mrs. Jane Ogden died May 28, 1869, and James Ogden lives one and one-quarter miles southwest of Pawnee, Illinois.

WILLIAM L., born in Kentucky, married in Sangamon county to Eliza J. Davis, who died, Jan., 1842, leaving one child. He married Lucy Durbin. They had six children. Mr. Ogden died, May 1, 1858, and Mrs. Ogden died, June 9, 1869, and all the children are dead except three. MIRANDA I. lives with her uncle, J. B. Ogden. ELIZABETH A. lives with J. T. Burtle, Sen., and MARGARET M. with her uncle, James Ogden.

JOSEPH B., born in Kentucky, married in Sangamon county to Mary E. Brawner. They had five living children. MARY M. married James Shively, has one child, DORA, and lives in Pawnee township. BETTANEY E., JAMES W., ANN E. and SARAH M. live with their parents, one mile southwest of Pawnee, Illinois.

JOHN C., born in Kentucky, married in Sangamon county to Minerva J. Clayton. He died, July, 1850, leaving a widow and one child, JAMES HARDIN. The widow married, and lives in Missouri.

SARAH, born in Sangamon county, in 1828, died Aug., 1835.

FRANCIS M., born in 1830, in Sangamon county, married Elizabeth Durbin. They had two children, ZACHARIAH and JAMES M. Mrs. Ogden died, and he married Maria Riney, has four children, SUSAN E., EDNA F., GERTRUDE I. and FANNIE B., and live four miles southeast of Pawnee, Illinois.

ELIZABETH E., born in Sangamon county, married James Durbin, who died, leaving a widow and one child, MARGARET J., who married James

Riney, and lives four miles south of Pawnee, Illinois.

MARY J. died, aged sixteen, and *SARAH M.* died, aged five years.

Mrs. Elizabeth Ogden died, October 4, 1858, and Zachariah Ogden died Aug. 4, 1869, and were both buried at St. Bernard Catholic church, Sangamon county, Illinois.

O'NEAL, SAMUEL, was born Oct. 11, 1811, in Kentucky, and came to Sangamon county, Ill., when he was a young man. He married three times, and his wives all died. His son—

JAMES HENRY, disappeared very mysteriously. He left a wife, but no children. After the death of his father, advertisements were kept in the papers for two years, in order to ascertain where he was, that he might obtain his proportion of his father's estate. At the end of that time, his debts were paid from it, and the remainder divided among the other heirs. Samuel O'Neal's daughter—

SARAH, married Jan. 6, 1862, to Charles H. Willison. She died May 8, 1864, leaving one child, MARY E., who lives with her father. He married Sarah J. Henkle. *See Jacob Henkle.*

Samuel O'Neal was married June 5, 1847, to Lucy Scott. They had six children, four of whom died under eleven years. Of the other two—

MINERVA E., born Aug. 25, 1854, and

WILLIAM F., born June 15, 1862, live with their mother.

Samuel O'Neal died in 1863, and his widow and children reside in Ball township, four miles southeast of Chatham, Illinois.

ORGAN, MICAJAH, was born Sept. 11, 1793, near Nicholasville, Jessamine county, Kentucky. He was married Dec. 18, 1817, to Susannah Donner, a sister of George and Jacob Donner. They had five children in Kentucky, one of whom, *WILLIAM R.*, died at eight years of age. The family moved to Sangamon county, Ill., arriving in the autumn of 1828, on German Prairie, five miles northeast of Springfield, and in 1829 moved to what is now Auburn township, where they had six living children. Of their children—

GEORGE L., born Dec. 29, 1820, in Kentucky, married in Sangamon county to Mary Foster. They had five children, MINERVA J., SARAH F., WILLIAM, IDA and LESLIE. Mrs. Mary Organ died, and he married Mrs. Wyatt, whose maiden name was Jacobs. They have one child, EFFIE M., and live in Virden, Illinois.

ATHA, born April 7, 1823, in Kentucky, married in Sangamon county to Elijah A. West. *See his name.*

HEZEKIAH B., born April 1, 1825, in Kentucky, married in Sangamon county to Catharine A. Gates. They have three children, DAVID, ANDREW and GEORGE A., and live five miles southwest of Auburn, Illinois.

SUSAN, born Jan. 25, 1827, in Kentucky, married to David H. Patton. *See his name.*

DANIEL F., born April 16, 1829, in Sangamon county, Illinois, married Elizabeth Kossner, have five children CHARLES, WILLIAM, MICAJAH ATHA M. and FRANK, and live near Longton, Elk county, Kansas.

JORDAN S., born August 16, 1832 in Sangamon county, married Margaret ret C. Wineman, daughter of Philip Wineman. They have two children IVY JANE and LELIA GRACE. Jordan S. Organ has for several years represented Auburn township in the Board of Supervisors of Sangamon county. He resides two miles south of Auburn, Sangamon county, Illinois.

THOMAS H., born Dec. 11, 1834, in Sangamon county, married Hannah J Brown. They have six children, WALTER, CHARLES S., SUE A., JENNIE M., MILLIE and DAISEY, and reside in Pontiac, Livingston county, Illinois.

ELIZABETH T., born Oct. 15 1837, in Sangamon county, died unmarried.

SARILDA and *SARENA*, twins, born Dec. 29, 1839, in Sangamon county

SARILDA married Edgar Cincebox have two children, EDGAR S. and HETTIE D., and reside in Virden, Illinois.

SARENA married George C. Houchens, have one child, SARENA L., and reside in Springfield, Illinois.

Mrs. Susannah Organ died March 3, 1866, and Micajah Organ died March 27, 1867, both in Sangamon county, Illinois.

OPDYCKE, STACY B., born Jan. 1, 1795, at New Castle, New Jersey, learned the trade of a carpenter there, and went to Kaskaskia, Ill., in 1816, walking nearly the whole distance. He was married in Kaskaskia, April 25, 1833, to Hannah G. Griffith, who was born Feb. 11, 1804, in Pennsylvania. She was a daughter of Dr. Thomas Griffith, of Tazewell county, Ill., and sister of Mrs. Charlotte Pricket, of Springfield, Ill. Mr. and Mrs. Opdycke moved from Kaskaskia, Randolph county, to Chester, in the same county, where they had one child, and from there to Springfield, Ill., in 1835, where three children were born, two of whom died young. Of their two children—

CHARLOTTE, born March 19, 1835, was married in Springfield, Ill., to John D. Keedy. See his name.

THOMAS G., born April 9, 1847, died in Nov., 1864, in Springfield.

Stacy B. Opdycke was engaged in porkpacking with James L. Lamb for several years, and was afterwards merchandizing with Tinsley & Fonday.

Mrs. Hannah G. Opdycke died Oct. 9, 1847, and Stacy B. Opdycke died June 18, 1858, both in Springfield, Illinois.

OVERSTREET, JOHN, was born in 1784 or '5, in Bedford county, Va. His father, John Overstreet, was born in 1758, in the same county, and was a soldier in the Revolutionary army during the whole seven years war for Independence. In 1783 he was married to Nancy Dabney. They had four children in Bedford county, and moved to Cabell county, West Virginia, and died there. His son, whose name heads this sketch, was married in Cabell county to Susan Roberts. He became a soldier in the war with England, in 1812. While in the army, he heard that his wife had been killed by Indians, and soon after was himself captured by Indians. Not long after his capture the Indians were preparing to burn him alive, and while doing so one of their number offered him such a gross insult that he knocked the savage down and he fell in the fire prepared to burn his victim. This act of brave daring in the face of death, inspired the other Indians with respect, and a feeling that he was too noble to be thus treated, and they saved his life. He was next sold and taken to Canada, where he fell into the hands of white men, with whom he was retained for a few years in rather easy restraint, and by the time he had gained his liberty, he had formed attachments, and married there. One child was born, and the wife and child died. Finding himself once more alone in the world, a yearning desire for the scenes of his younger days sprang up, and he returned to Cabell county, Virginia. He paid his first visit to the old cabin where he had spent the years of his early married life. Seeing the smoke curling up from the chimney, he sauntered, half dreamily, to the door, and without having framed any excuse for his visit he knocked at the door, and after a short pause it turned on its rude wooden hinges, and the wife of his youth stood before him! Having long before given him up for dead, his sudden appearance in bodily form was more than she could bear, and she sunk in a swoon. Mr. Overstreet soon discovered that she had another husband, and when she revived, the three held a council. The two husbands agreed to leave it for her to say which should be her husband, each giving his word that if he was rejected, he would go away and offer no annoyance to the favored one. She decided to retain her first love. The rejected husband, true to his word, bade them adieu, disappeared, and they never heard of him again. Mr. and Mrs. Overstreet came to Sangamon county, in 1819, and settled not far from where Athens now stands. A few years later, being a millwright, he built a horse mill at Athens, manufactured flour, loaded a small flat boat, in the Sangamon river, and with two brothers, Jesse G. and David Hurt, floated down the Sangamon into the Illinois, thence to the Mississippi river, and down that stream to New Orleans. The trip was a successful one, but Mr. Overstreet died in New Orleans, in 1835. The two brothers started home, and David died at the mouth of the Ohio river. Jesse G. Hurt, the only survivor, is yet living, and resides in Menard county. He married a niece of Mr. Overstreet. See name of Dabnay Overstreet. Mr. Overstreet was for several years a local preacher in the M. E. church. His widow died in Athens in 1869, in her seventy-fourth year.

OVERSTREET, DABNEY, brother to John, was born about 1786 in

Bedford county, Va., and married in Greenbrier county to Jennie Rogers. They had seven children in Virginia, and moved to Sangamon county, Ill., arriving in 1830, where seven children were born. Of their children, I can give the sketches of two, only—

NELLIE, born in Virginia, married in Illinois to Jesse G. Hurt. They had eleven children, and she died. Mr. Hurt and the children live near Athens, Menard county, Illinois.

JOHN, born Oct. 10, 1819, in Cabell county, West Virginia, married May 11, 1839, in Sangamon county, to Rachel Cantrall. They had four living children. LOUISA J., born May 11, 1841, in Sangamon county, married Henry F. Shepherd. See his name. JAMES W., born Feb. 5, 1844, married Mrs. Martha E. Dunlap. She had one child by her first marriage, JANE DUNLAP. They had three children, JENNIE, MARY and NELLIE —and live near Cantrall. ELIZABETH A., born June 13, 1848, married Dec. 5, 1866, to Sebastian B. Shepherd. See his name. JOHN T., born Nov. 15, 1851, married Dec. 24, 1872, to Maggie Brenan, and live in Ford county, Illinois. John Overstreet and wife reside two miles north of Cantrall, Sangamon county, Illinois.—1874.

OWEN, THOMAS J. V., was born July 23, 1824, in Kaskaskia, Illinois. His grandfather, Major Ezra Owen, was born March 17, 1770, in Halifax county, Virginia, we t to Kentucky when a young man, and fought the Indians with Daniel Boon . In 1809, the year the Territorial government was organized, he moved with his family from Kentucky to Kaskaskia, Illinois. His eldest son, Thomas J. V. Owen, born in Kentucky, was married in Kaskaskia, July 15, 1823, to Emeline Hotchkiss. Their eldest son is the one whose name heads this sketch. His brother William, enlisted in Springfield, in 1862, in Co. M, 2d Ill. Art., was wounded at Rogerville, Tenn., captured and taken to Libby prison, where he starved to death. His brother, George S., was assassinated in Randolph county in 1864, during the rebellion. His brother, Elias K., entered the U. S. Navy in 1848, was taken from Springfield by Abraham Lincoln, at that time member of congress from this district. He is yet in the navy.

He married, in Kaskaskia, to Sarah Jane Riley, and resides in Baltimore, Maryland. —1875. Thomas J. V. Owen, Sen., was a member of the legislature in 1831, and during that year was appointed Indian agent in Chicago, where he died Oct. 15, 1835. Thomas J. V. Owen, the subject of our sketch, was educated at St. Mary's college, Perryville, Mo., and came to Springfield, June 4, 1840, where he commenced the study of medicine. He went with Gen. Ford's army to Nauvoo, at the time the Mormon prophet, Smith, was killed, in 1844. In 1846 he went to Bloomington, Illinois, and aided in organizing Co. B, 4th Illinois Infantry, was enrolled hospital Steward, and afterwards appointed assistant Surgeon to the regiment. He served the full term of the regiment in Mexico, returned to Springfield, and engaged in the drug business. He was married Aug 15, 1848, in Jacksonville, Illinois, to Mary Eliza Hurst, eldest daughter of William S. Hurst, of that city. They had two children—

MARY EVELINE, born Sept. 23, 1849, and died May 12, 1855.

WILLIAM H., born Feb. 6, 1852, in Springfield, was married Dec. 17, 1874, in Taylorville, Ill., to Jeanette Denton, who was born there, Nov. 10, 1852. They have one child, WILLIAM H., and reside in Taylorville, Illinois.

Thomas J. V. Owen died March 19, 1876, at Decatur, Ill. His remains were brought to Springfield, and buried in Oak Ridge Cemetery. Soon after his death his widow moved to Springfield, Illinois, where she now resides. Mrs. Emeline Owen, the mother of T. J. V. Owen, Jun., lives with his widow, in Springfield.

ORENDORFF.—For family sketch, see Ommissions or Appendix.

P

PARKS, BEAUMONT, was born Jan., 1775, in Norwich, Conn. He was an orphan at twelve years of age, and resolved to educate himself. In order to obtain the means to do so, he began trading with the French Canadians and Indians. He worked his way out, in company with his brother-in-law, Rev.

Mr. Bacon, father of Rev. Leonard Bacon, D. D., of New Haven, Conn., through the rivers and lakes, from Vermont to the region of Georgian Bay and Lake Huron. As winter approached, he commenced building a house with the intention of remaining in it until spring. He was discovered by Col. Dunham, commander of the U. S. Fort, at Michilimacinac. Col. Dunham was astonished at seeing a boy of fourteen or fifteen years preparing to winter alone in that inhospitable region, and enquired what he was aiming to do. On being told by young Parks that he was trying to raise money to defray the expense of an education, Col. Dunham offered him a home in his own family, with the promise of assisting him in his purpose. He accepted the kind proposition, went to the Fort and remained there between three and four years. During that time his savings amounted to about $80. Expressing his determination to set out for College, Col. Dunham sent some friendly Indians to accompany him a portion of the distance. He traveled in a birch canoe through the upper lakes and portions of Canada, and thence east. When he had gone about two-thirds of the distance, he was taken sick with small pox, and was compelled to travel alone until he could find shelter, although he was then in a part of the country more or less settled by white men. At Montreal, a French Canadian took him in and nursed him for nearly a month, until he was able to pursue his journey. His savings were now reduced to about thirty dollars, but his hospitable friend would not receive anything for his trouble. His exhausted condition required the expenditure of more money, and when he arrived at his destination his money had all vanished. Notwithstanding so much time was lost, after a journey of one thousand six hundred miles, he found himself at Dartmouth College, a stranger, and destitute. Yet he boldly knocked at the doors of that institution of learning for admittance. That was about the year 1798. By diligent study while in the family of Col. Dunham, he was enabled to teach the lower branches. He then made arrangements to continue teaching in summer and attend college in the winter, and prosecuted his studies while teaching, so as not to fall behind in his class. He was thus enabled to defray his expenses, with some aid furnished by Col. Dunham., and in that way went through college on equal terms with Daniel Webster, Levi Woodbury—the latter of whom was his class-mate—and other world-wide celebrities. After passing through college he entered the law office of Judge Slade, of Middlebury, Vt., and in due time was admitted to the bar. He was married in 1811, at Windsor, Vt., to Nancy Conant. He soon acquired a large and lucrative practice, which he held for about ten years, when—however others might think—he became convinced that it was impossible to be a successful lawyer and a thoroughly honest man. That, with other causes, induced him to abandon his practice and move west. He left Vermont, and in August, 1821, landed at Madison, Ind., where he opened an academy for the education of young men, which was one of the earliest institutions of the kind established west of the Allegheny mountains, and probably the first school in the State of Indiana where the Greek and Latin languages were taught. It was attended by many who have become distinguished at the bar, on the bench, and in the councils of the nation, such as the Hendricks, Sullivans, Brights, Sheets, Cravens, and many others. After ten years success in Madison, he was appointed Professor of languages in the Indiana State University, at Bloomington, and was in that position about seven years. He came to Springfield, Ill., in the autumn of 1840, and at once opened a private school or academy, which was generally supported by all the leading citizens, and many of the students have become distinguished in the learned professions, in politics and business. When the city schools of Springfield were organized on the present plan, he was the first Superintendent, and continued teaching in Springfield for nearly twenty years, when old age caused him to relinquish his chosen field. Mr. and Mrs. Parks had four children in Vermont, one of whom died there, and five in Indiana, one of whom died there. Of the other seven children—

SUSAN, born Dec., 1812, in Vermont, was married Dec. 29, 1832, in Indiana, to John Bennett. They moved to Liberty, Mo., and she died there in March, 1852. Of their children, WARWICK S. went

—70

to California about the close of the rebellion, and has not been heard from since. RICHARD married, and died from a wound received in the Kansas troubles. FRORENCE J. was married in 1856 to George Challis. They have several children, and reside in Atchison, Kansas. BEAUMONT J. married in Atchison, Kansas. Himself, his wife and his father moved to Colorado, and reside on a dairy farm. FRANK W. was married near Auburn, Illinois, to Sarah J. Davidson. They have one child, EDITH, and reside near Mt. Liberty, Reno county, Kansas. LILLIE is the youngest of the family.

NANCY C., born Feb. 5, 1818, in Vermont, was married in Springfield, Jan. 28, 1852, to Rev. Joseph E. McMurray, of the Presbyterian church. They had four children, ALICE R., EDWARD P., THOMAS B. and WALTER S. The latter died young. Rev. Mr. McMurray died Jan. 27, 1868, at Cerro Gordo, Piatt county, Ill. His widow and children reside in Auburn, Illinois.

SAMUEL C., born March 25, 1820, in Windsor, Vermont, came to Springfield, Ill., in 1840, six months before his parents. He was married Nov. 13, 1853, in Logan county, Ill., to Elizabeth A. Turley. They have four children, LULA H., HENRY C., SAMUEL C., Jun., and MARY L. and reside in Lincoln, Ill. Samuel C. Parks was appointed, March, 1863, by President Lincoln, Associate Judge of the U. S. Court for the Territory of Idaho. He discharged the duties of the office until May, 1865, when he resigned and returned to Lincoln. He was elected one of the delegates representing the district composed of Logan and Sangamon counties, in the Illinois Constitutional Convention of 1870. Judge Parks is now a practicing lawyer at Lincoln, Illinois.

THOMAS S., born May 22, 1822, at Madison, Ind., married in Sangamon county, Oct. 23, 1851, to Nancy C. Poley. They have four children. LETITIA is now (1876) in the second year of her course at Illinois Female College, at Jacksonville. SAMUEL is a clerk in his uncle Isaac Poley's bank, at Auburn. MINNIE and MARY; all four live with their parents. Thomas S. Parks taught school in Sangamon county eleven years. He is a farmer, stock dealer and Police Magistrate. He and his family reside in Auburn, Sangamon county, Illinois.

ELIZA A., born Dec. 15, 1825, at Madison, Indiana, was married in Springfield to Stephen Conkling. She died at Leroy, McLean county, Ill., in 1859.

WILLIAM J., born Dec., 1832, in Indiana, died in Springfield in his tenth year.

LETITIA, born Dec. 25, 1835, in Bloomington, Ind., married in Springfield, Ill., in 1857, to Dr. Albert H. Lanphear, a native of New York. They have two children, ALBERT MOTT and SAMUEL P., and reside in Atchison, Kansas. Dr. Lanphear is practicing his profession there.

After Professor Beaumont Parks retired from teaching he resided a few years in Springfield, and then determined to spend the remainder of his days in the families of his children. Mrs. Parks died at Cerro Gordo, Ill, Sept. 11, 1865. Prof. Parks continued active and energetic to the last day of his life, and died April 8, 1870, without an hour of sickness, at the residence of his son, Judge S. C. Parks, in Lincoln, Ill., and was buried at that place.

PARK, JOHN, born about 1762, in county Antrim, Ireland. Sarah Mayben was born in Ireland also. They were both brought to America when quite young, without any knowledge of each other. They were married in South Carolina, and had nine children there, one of whom died young. The family moved to that part of Logan county which afterwards became Todd county, Ky., and from there to Sangamon county, Illinois, arriving Nov. 28, 1828, at Island Grove. Four of their children were married in Kentucky, but all came with them to Sangamon county. Of their children—

THOMAS, born in South Carolina, was married, Jan. 19, 1813, in Kentucky, to Jane Mayben. They had seven children there, and moved, in 1828, to Sangamon county, Ill., where one child was born. They moved to Morgan county, Ill., in 1831. Of all their children—One died young. JOHN J., born Nov. 18, 1814, was married April 4, 1839, in Morgan county, Ill., to Jane E. Caldwell, who was born in Nicholas county, Ky. They had seven children in Morgan county, and moved to Sangamon county, Ill., March 22, 1855, where three children were born. Of their children—NANCY J., born Jan. 23, 1840, was married, July 11, 1861, in Sangamon county, to Charles H. Knapp. They have two children, *Fannie L.* and *Carrie*. C. H. Knapp died in Macon county, in 1867, and his widow was married, Dec. 14, 1869, to John Carder, of Ohio. They have one child, *Josie E.* SARAH A., born Aug. 29, 1844, was married, July 1, 1875, to L. R. Tracy. DAVID T., JOHN H., MARY C., JAMES M., ELIZA M., SAMUEL C. and WILLIAM M. John J. Park moved to Macon county, near Decatur, April 6, 1864, and his unmarried children reside there with him. HENRY M., born Nov. 29, 1816, in Kentucky, married Nancy Miller, of same State. JAMES A., born Oct. 8, 1818, in Kentucky, is unmarried. ELIJAH M., born Dec. 10, 1820, in Kentucky, married Nancy A. Armstrong, of same State. WILLIAM R., born Aug. 23, 1824, in Kentucky, was married, Nov. 22, 1850, to Nancy E. Graham, who was born June 9, 1828. They have four children, JOHN T., ELMIRA A., WILLIAM R. and JAMES H., and reside near Harristown, Macon county, Illinois. ROBERT V., born Sept. 20, 1828, in Kentucky, was married to Angeline Scott. SARAH J., born Oct. 8, 1830, in Sangamon county, married William M. Gaddis, of New York. Thomas Park died, March 30, 1852, and Jane Park died Dec. 6, 1873, both in Morgan county, Illinois.

MARY, born in South Carolina, married in Kentucky, April 4, 1816. They had one child, and both died in Sangamon county. Their daughter, SARAH, married A. P. Wyckoff. *See his name.*

HUGH, born in South Carolina, married in Kentucky, March 25, 1816, to Jane Gibson, moved to Sangamon county, in 1828, and from Sangamon to Macon county, where Hugh Park died, Sept. 28, 1845, leaving four children.

GRIZETTE, born Aug. 26, 1797, in South Carolina, married Joseph McNew, and for a second husband, married in Sangamon county, to John Hudson. *See his name.*

JAMES, born Dec. 25, 1799, in South Carolina, married April 25, 1820, in Kentucky, to Mary Modrell, who was born June 19, 1800. They had six children in Kentucky, and emigrated with his parents to Sangamon county, in 1828, where eight children were born. Of their fourteen children—SARAH J., born July 21, 1821, married in Sangamon county to Demarcus Gibson. They had eight children, four of whom died young. The other four reside with their parents, in Knoxville, Illinois. JOHN G., born July 7, 1822, in Kentucky, married in Sangamon county, March 1, 1855, to Elizabeth Rigg. They had five children, JAMES E., CHARLES F. and SAMUEL H. died young. HENRY A. and JOHN W. reside with their parents, four miles west of Loami, Sangamon county, Illinois. HARRIET A., born Sept. 12, 1823, in Kentucky, married in Sangamon county to Allen Short. They have nine children, and live in Marion county, Iowa. ROBERT M., born Dec. 13, 1824, in Kentucky, married Mary Reynolds. They had seven children, and Mrs. Park and six of the children died. He married Elizabeth Bower. They have six children, and live in Macon county, Illinois. MARY L., born Dec. 25, 1825, in Kentucky, married Francis George. They have three children, MARY A., HEPSIRA E. and RACHEL A., and live near Edinburg, Illinois. ELIZABETH H., born Feb. 10, 1827, in Kentucky, married in Sangamon county, Aug. 8, 1844, to John A. Burton. *See his name.* Mr. Burton died, and his widow married March 8, 1860, to Wm. S. Morris, who was born June 17, 1829, in Meade county, Ky. They have two children, EMMA L. and DORA L., and live two and one-half miles northwest of Loami, Illinois. JULIA A., born April 17, 1829, in Sangamon county, married James R. Rigg. *See his name.* THOMAS N., born Feb. 16, 1831, married Mary Fowler. They had two children, and mother and children died. Mr. Park married Sarah E. Hudson. They had two children; one died in infancy. LURENA MAY lives with her father. Mrs. Sarah E. Park died, and Mr. Park married Elizabeth Franklin. They have one child, and reside three miles west of Loami, Ill. RACHEL G., born March 9, 1833, married Benjamin W. Burton. *See his name.* HUGH A., born February 2, 1835, married Elizabeth Turpin. They have four children, WILLIS C., EDWARD M., CHARLES L. and LINDA F., and reside two miles southwest of Loami, Illinois.

NANCY H., born Jan. 18, 1837, married George W. Hudson. He died, and she married James L. Short. They have one child, HUGH F., and reside in Loami township. JAMES W., born Jan. 24, 1839, married Martha Hodgerson, and he died in two weeks after marriage. MARTHA E., born July 1, 1841, married Young Hodgerson. She died, without children. WILLIAM L., born Oct. 13, 1843, married, Sept. 6, 1866, to Mary Rigg. They have two children, JAMES R. and MARY J., and reside on the farm where his parents settled in 1835, and where he was born, three miles west of Loami, Illinois. James Park died, Oct. 25, 1865, and his widow died, Feb. 7, 1869, both in Loami township, Sangamon county, Illinois.

JANE, born in South Carolina, married in Sangamon county to William Earnest, moved to Louisa county, Iowa. He died there, leaving a widow and four children.

JOHN S., born in South Carolina, married in Sangamon county to Mary A. Morrison, moved to Morgan county, brought up seven children, and Mr. Park died, in May, 1847. Of his children— ELVIRA married J. A. Haney, and lives in New Berlin, Illinois.

SARAH, born in South Carolina, married in Sangamon county to Zaza Bowen. *See his name.*

Mrs. Sarah Park died, Sept. 9, 1853, and John Park died, Sept. 23, 1853, both at the house of their son James, in Sangamon county, Illinois.

PARKES, WILLIAM, was born Jan. 29, 1807, at Jonesboro, Washington county, Tenn. He was married April 14, 1830, in Jefferson county, to Polly North, a sister to John and Robert North. She was born about 1810 or '11 in Buckingham county, Va. They had two children in Tennessee, and moved to Posey county, Ind., where one child was born; and moved to Sangamon county, Ill., arriving in the spring of 1836, in what is now Cooper township. Two years later he went to Mechanicsburg, and in Feb., 1848, moved to Cooper township, south of Sangamon river. They had nine children in Sangamon county; and five of their children died under six years. Of the other seven, all born in Sangamon county—

CAROLINE, born Jan. 12, 1839, in Sangamon county, married Sept. 24, 1857, to Charles Boehme; have five children, and live near Linwood, Butler county, Nebraska.

EVELINE, born Jan. 1, 1841, married Jan. 8, 1863, to J. South; have two children, MATTIE B. and MARY E. She and the children live with her father.

HENRY, born Jan. 15, 1843, in Mechanicsburg, Ill., enlisted Aug., 1862, for three years, in Co. C, 114th Ill. Inf.; served until June 29, 1863, when he died at Chickasaw Landing, Tennessee.

MINERVA, born April 6, 1845, married Aug. 14, 1867, to Charles Roberts; have one child, and live near Princeton, Franklin county, Kansas.

ELIZABETH, born Jan. 3, 1847, married Jan. 14, 1869, to Edgar Eckel. *See his name.*

JAMES, born April 2, 1851, and *HIRAM*, born April 8, 1864, live with their father.

Mrs. Polly Parkes died Sept. 12, 1873, and William Parkes was married June 7, 1875, to Mrs. Sarah McMurry, whose maiden name was Enyart. They reside near Berry Postoffice, or Clarksville, Sangamon county, Illinois.

PARKINSON, JAMES, was born Dec. 22, 1805, in Belmont county, Ohio, twelve miles below Wheeling, West Virginia. His parents were from Washington county, Penn.; and when James was an infant they moved back, across the Virginia Pan Handle, to their home in Pennsylvania, and a few years later, moved to what is now Marshall county, West Virginia, in the Pan Handle. James Parkinson came to Sangamon county, Ill., arriving at Springfield in Nov., 1830, just in time for the "deep snow." He returned to Virginia in the spring, and came again to Sangamon county in the fall of 1831. He made his home at the house of David McCoy, on Spring creek, until Nov. 7, 1833, when he was married to Mahala Earnest. They had five living children in Sangamon county, namely—

MARY J., born Nov. 1, 1834, married William Baldwin. *See his name.*

GRIZZELLA A., born March 22, 1836, married William T. Bradford. *See his name.*

CLARINDA A., born Jan. 22, 1838, married June 23, 1859, to Thomas B. Petefish, who was born Aug. 7, 1833, in Shenandoah Valley, Virginia. They have five children, MARION P., LOTTIE LOU, ELIZABETH M., MELINDA E. and PEARLIE M., and reside near Belvoir, Douglas county, Kansas.

JOHN J., born Jan. 23, 1840, enlisted in the fall of 1861, for three years, in Co. B, 10th Ill. Cav.; served full term, and was honorably discharged in 1864. He was married Nov. 9, 1865, to Augusta Patteson, daughter of Dr. Alex. A. Patteson. They had three children—JOHN L. died, aged four years; and ALEXANDER died in his second year. EARNEST resides with his parents in Gardner township, south of Spring creek, Sangamon county, Illinois.

WILLIAM H., born Oct. 31, 1842, married Feb. 12, 1868, to Sarah J. Bradford. They have two children, JAMES B. and WILLIAM W., and reside south of Spring creek, nine miles west of Springfield, Illinois.

James Parkinson and wife reside in Curran township, eight miles west of Springfield, Ill.—south of Spring creek, and within one mile of where they were married. This sketch was written at their residence on the evening of Nov. 7, 1873, the fortieth anniversary of their marriage. They had at their table that day all their five children, fourteen of their seventeen living grandchildren—three being in Kansas,—and all their sons and daughters-in-law except Mr. Petefish, of Kansas.

The courtships of George Bryan—see *his name*—and that of James Parkinson and Mahala Earnest are, so far as I am informed, the two shortest on record. For two years previous to their marriage, Mr. Parkinson "waited on" Miss Earnest. Adopting a custom then quite prevalent, he would start on horseback, call for her, and propose that they go to church, to a wedding, to a social gathering or a dancing party. If she assented, he would take her behind himself on the horse, and set out. If she declined, he would usually spend the day or evening, as the case might be, with her. This was the practice with them for about two years, and I have it from their own lips that the subject of their marriage was never mentioned between them. Finally Mr. P. made up his mind to change the programme. He first, without consulting the lady or any friend of hers, went to Springfield and obtained a license for the marriage of James Parkinson and Mahala Earnest. He called at her father's house on the morning of Nov. 7, 1833, and told her that he would be there that evening, and wished her to be at home. That was the first time he ever notified her beforehand to expect him. He then departed hurriedly, without giving the slightest intimation of the object of his proposed visit. The next movement was to call on a Justice of the Peace by the name of Robison, and request that officer to meet him the same evening at the house of David McCoy, where Mr. P. boarded. The Esquire wanted to know if it was necessary for him to take any papers or legal forms. Mr. P. replied, as he departed hurriedly, that *he* had all the papers necessary. The Justice met him at the appointed time and place, when he was informed that he was expected to solemnize a marriage. 'Squire Robison, Mr. McCoy and Mr. Parkinson set out on horseback, crossing Spring creek from north to south, and arrived about sundown at the residence of Miss Earnest's father, to find the young lady out on the open prairie milking the cows. Mr. P. had not intimated to the other gentlemen that he had *his courting yet to do*. They separated to find hitching places for their horses; and as they did so, Mr. P. went to Miss Earnest and told her that he had come to marry her, and asked if she would have him. She stood, milk pail in hand, and, after a few moment's meditation, said, "Go in the house, and I will be there directly." These were the only words that ever passed between them by way of courtship. She then resumed her milking, and finished it as though nothing unusual had occurred. The father of Miss Earnest was attending to some outdoor work, and Mr. P. approached and told the old gentleman that he had come to marry his daughter, and asked his consent to the union. Mr. Earnest replied that he had no objection to the marriage, but regretted that he had not been notified in time to make suitable preparations for so important an event. Mr. Parkinson said, "I have made all the preparations necessary, as I have the license in my pocket, and the 'Squire is here, ready to perform his part." They were married that very evening, and the notes from which this sketch was written were taken in their presence, on the evening of the fortieth anniversary of their wedding.

His reasons for taking such a course were secreted in his own breast for forty years, and were revealed, for the first time, to the writer on the evening of the anniversary above named. I can assure the reader that there was nothing in it calculated to cast the slightest shadow of reproach on the character of either of the parties. It was a method of his own for solving a problem, entirely right in itself, but not such a mode as I should have adopted, for the reason that the courting was too soon over. I would much prefer to prolong so pleasant a pastime. I may divulge his secret if he fails to invite me to his golden wedding Nov. 7, 1883; but if he invites me to help celebrate that day, and treats me as well as he did on the fortieth anniversary, he may retain it forty years longer, if he wishes to.

Mr. Parkinson served as Justice of the Peace twelve years, by successive re-election from 1848. When the township organization was adopted, he was elected the first representative of Curran township in the county Board of Supervisors, and was twice re-elected. Edward Robison was the 'Squire who solemnized the marriage. *See his name.*

PAINE, ENOCH, was born March 14, 1821, in Kaskaskia, Ill. The family moved from there to Macoupin Point, and to Springfield in 1835. His mother was a daughter of John Grosvenor, a prominent early settler of Kaskaskia. Enoch Paine learned the bookbinding business with Birchall & Johnson. He there helped to bind the work of the last session of the legislature at Vandalia. He continued in the employ of that house until 1859, which in that time changed to Johnson & Bradford. In 1860 Mr. Paine established a bindery for himself, and did the State binding for about ten years, working, at some times, forty hands. Enoch Paine was married in Springfield, March 14, 1843, to Emily Sholtz, who was born March 14, 1820, in Edwardsville, Ill. They had seven living children, namely—

MARY A., born Oct. 19, 1845, resides with her parents.

LUCY A., born Jan. 4, 1847, married Oct. 17, 1871, in Springfield, to A. Judson Gunnell. They have one child, PEARL J., and reside at Moberly, Mo. He is locomotive engineer on the Northern Missouri Railroad.

ALICE F., born July 28, 1849, married Oct. 5, 1872, in Springfield, to William Mosely. They have two children, GUY DeFOREST and VIDA P., and reside at Stonington, Ill. He is a merchant there.

RUFUS E., born Jan. 11, 1852, married in Springfield, May, 1873, to Emma Pride. They have one child, GRACE, and reside five miles northeast of Springfield, on the farm.

LILLIE E., born Nov. 25, 1854, married June 16, 1873, in Springfield, to John L. Phillips, who was born Aug. 1, 1851, in Belleville, Ill. Mr. Phillips is foreman in the *Journal* job printing department, and resides in Springfield, Illinois.

JULIA E., born Jan. 23, 1857, graduated at the Springfield High School in 1874, and resides with her parents.

CLARA resides with her parents.

Enoch Paine and wife reside in Springfield, Illinois.

During the rebellion Mr. Paine had charge of the manufacture of cartridges, working from two hundred and fifty to three hundred operatives. Cartridges made there cost only one-seventh of what they did at other places.

PARRISH, SAMUEL, was born June 22, 1809, in Franklin county, Ohio. He married Sarah Manning. They had three living children in Ohio. The family moved to Sangamon county, Ill., arriving in the fall of 1839, in what is now Gardner township, where six children were born. Of their children—

SYNDISA, born Dec. 23, 1831, in Franklin county, Ohio, was married Feb. 26, 1852, in Sangamon county, to William Wilson. They had three children, MARGARET A., MOLLIE, died in her tenth year, and CHARLES. Mr. Wilson died Dec. 18, 1864. His widow married May 31, 1866, to James L. Carman. They have one child, CORA, and reside at Kenny, DeWitt county, Ill.—

Dec., 1875. James L. Carman went from Salisbury, and enlisted in 1861, in Co. E, 14th Ill. Inf., for three years; re-enlisted as a veteran, Jan. 4, 1864, served to the end of the rebellion, and was honorably discharged, May 21, 1865.

CORNELIUS, born Jan., 1836, in Ohio, died in Sangamon county, aged twenty-two years.

REBECCA, born Feb., 1838, in Ohio, was married in Texas to John Byford, and resides at Springfield, Arkansas.

JAMES, born Dec., 1841, in Sangamon county, enlisted in Co. —, 114th Ill. Inf., in 1862, for three years. He was taken prisoner at the battle of Guntown, Miss., June, 1864, taken to Andersonville prison-pen, where he remained nine or ten months, was released, and died May 15, 1865, at Jacksonville, Florida.

SAMUEL, born May, 1843, in Sangamon county, enlisted in an Ill. Art. Co. for three years, re-enlisted as a veteran, and served to the end of the war. He was married in Tennessee to Jane Richardson. They have three children, JOSEPH, CHARLES and FLORENCE. Samuel Parrish is Superintendent at the National Cemetery, at Fort Donnelson, Tenn.—1874.

AMANDA, born Feb., 1845, in Sangamon county, married S. Neff. They had seven children, FRANKLIN E., JOHN S., FRANCES M., LUELLA, ROSCOE C., ANNA M. and another. They reside near Chinkapin Hill, Sangamon county, Illinois.

JOSEPH, born June, 1848, in Sangamon county, married Eliza Richardson. They have one child, and reside at Dover, Tenn.

CHARLES, born July, 1853, in Sangamon county, is unmarried, and lives in Arkansas.

Mrs. Sarah Parish died Dec., 1861, and Samuel Parish married Mrs. Mahala Legget. He died May 28, 1873, in Springfield. Mr. P. is believed to have chopped more timber than any other man in Sangamon county.

PASFIELD, GEORGE, was born October, 1792, in London, England. His parents came to America when he was a child and settled in Philadelphia, where they both soon died of yellow fever, leaving their son George without a relative in America. By his own exertions, he obtained a good practical education, and learned a trade which he did not long pursue, and afterwards went to Matanzas, Cuba, as agent for a shipping house. He remained there some time, but the climate not agreeing with him, returned to Philadelphia, where he invested in real estate, and bought an interest in a nail mill. The results were unfortunate. He came to Cincinnati, about 1817, and engaged in shipping pork and flour from that point and Louisville, on flat boats, for New Orleans. Later he established himself in the grocery business, at Paris, Bourbon county, Ky., and continued packing pork and shipping. He was married in Paris, Jan. 5, 1821, to Mary Forden, sister of John Forden. *See his name.* She was born Oct. 22, 1805, in Hagerstown, Md. Mr. and Mrs. Pasfield moved to Springfield, Ill., in the spring of 1821, where one child—

GEORGE, was born Nov. 30, 1831. He studied medicine, and graduated at St. Louis Medical College, in the class of 1855-'6. Dr. George Pasfield was married Sept. 19, 1866, at Mechaniesburg, Ill., to Hathaway Pickrell. They have two children, EMMA and GEORGE L., and live in Springfield, Ill. Dr. Pasfield is not practicing his profession.

George Pasfield was an enterprising and successful merchant, and was a member of the town board of Springfield before the city organization. He was one of the signers of the fifty thousand dollar note to secure the location of the capital at Springfield, and was one of the first to commence business on the State House square, doing much in the way of building to improve the city. He died, Nov. 9, 1869, and his widow lives with her son, Dr. George Pasfield, in Springfield, Illinois.

PATTON, JAMES, born Mch. 17, 1791, in the city of Baltimore, Md. When a child, his parents moved to Stanton, Va., and from there to Clark county, Ky., in 1798. There James was apprenticed to the tanning business, and in 1808 the family moved to Christian county, where he joined them in 1810, having finished his apprenticeship. James Patton and Polly Husband were there married, April, 1815. They had three children in Kentucky, and moved to what became

Sangamon county, Ill., arriving October, 1820, in what is now Auburn township, where two children were born. Of their five children—

WILLIAM M., born March 10, 1816, in Christian county, Ky., married in Sangamon county to Elizabeth A. Moore. They had three children. JAMES W., born Feb. 15, 1840, in Sangamon county, was married there, Dec. 8, 1869, to Francine E. Lanphier. They had three children—LANPHIER M. died Sept. 9, 1874. WILLIAM L. and JAMES M. live with their parents. James W. Patton studied law with Hay & Cullom, and was admitted to practice in 1861. He was elected in 1864 to represent Sangamon and Logan counties in the Illinois State Legislature. He has associated with him his brother-in-law, John C. Lanphier, in the practice of law, in Springfield, Ill., and resides there. MATHEW, Jun., born Aug. 22, 1841, in Sangamon county, was married June 7, 1876, near Virden, to Barbara A. Rauch. See Rauch family. Mr. and Mrs. Mathew Patton live in Chicago, Illinois. JULIA A., born April 25, 1843, in Sangamon county, was married there, January 5, 1870, to Basil Hill, who was born October 21, 1838, in Vanburensburg, Fayette county, Illinois. Mr. and Mrs. Hill moved to Missouri, Feb., 1870, and have one child, MATHEW M., born Dec. 28, 1870, and resides in Newtonia, Newton county, Mo. William M. Patton died, Jan. 7, 1848. His widow resides in Auburn township, Sangamon county, Illinois.

REBECCA ANN, born Oct. 5, 1817, in Kentucky, married Elihu Stout. See his name. She died Sept. 21, 1852.

MATHEW, born March 14, 1819, in Kentucky, married Feb. 1, 1844, in Sangamon county, to Margaret J. McElvain. They had six children, namely: WILLIAM D., born Jan. 23, 1845, in Sangamon county, married Adaline M. Black. They had one child, MINNIE F. Mrs. Patton died Jan. 26, 1875, and W. D. Patton was married Feb. 16, 1876, to Caddie A. Jones. He is a druggist, and resides in Auburn, Illinois. MARY E. died, aged three years. ELIZABETH, born in Sangamon county, married James Fletcher. They are without children, and reside three miles southwest of Auburn, Ill. JAMES SAMUEL, CHARLES M., ROBERT H. and MARGARET S. reside with their father. Mrs. Margaret J. Patton died May 2, 1865, and Matthew Patton was married Jan. 23, 1867, to Sarah J. Mackey. They reside in Auburn, Sangamon county, Illinois.

ELIZABETH, born April 15, 1821, in Sangamon county, married March 5, 1845, to William Orr, and died July 29, 1847.

DAVID H., born April 19, 1824, in Sangamon county, was married March 4, 1846, to Susan Organ. They have six children—SUSAN A. married William Moomaw. They have one child, ADA, and live in Auburn township. WILLIAM, born April 21, 1850, in Sangamon county, was married Feb. 4, 1873, to Sarah Jane Savage. They have one child, WILLIE, and live in Auburn, Ill. MATTHEW DANIEL, BENJAMIN F., BETTIE O. and MARGARET F. live with their parents. David H. Patton resides on the farm where his father settled in 1820, three miles southeast of Auburn, Illinois.

Mrs. Polly Patton died Feb. 15, 1844, and James Patton was married in 1846 to Mrs. Lettie Nifong, who died Feb. 6, 1856, and he was married Aug. 1, 1865, to Mrs. Elizabeth Gregory. She died June 23, 1875, and James Patton resides where he settled in 1820, four miles southeast of Auburn. He has always been known as Col. Patton, a title he acquired in connection with early military training in the county. He established a tannery soon after he settled in the county, and supplied the early settlers with leather for many miles around. The nearest mill to him at the time he settled there was at Edwardsville, sixty miles south. He was in better circumstances than most of the early settlers, and when he saw a family laboring under disadvantages, he interested himself in their welfare, and assisted them in many ways. Noah Mason, of Springfield, speaking of their early experience in the new country, says, "My father found a true friend in the now venerable Col. James Patton, which lasted to the end of his life, and is gratefully remembered by his descendants."

PATRICK, JOHN H., was born Nov. 1, 1789, in Clarke county, Ky., married Jane Foster. They had three children, and Mr. Patrick died while on busi ness in the State of Mississippi. His widow married John Armstrong, and they moved, with her three children, in company with her brother, George Foster, to Sangamon county, Ill., arriving in the fall of 1827, in what is now Loami township. Of the three Patrick children—

SOPHIA, born in Kentucky, in 1813, married in 1828, in Sangamon county, to William Easley.

MARGARET F., born Jan. 5, 1815, in Kentucky, married Albartes Barger. See his name.

LAVICA, born in 1817, in Kentucky, married there to Joseph Burch, and lives in Lafayette county, Mo.

Mrs. Jane Armstrong died Aug. 27, 1870, in Macon county, Mo. Both her husbands were soldiers in 1812. She drew a pension to the end of her life as the widow of John Armstrong.

PAULEN, DEBOLD, was born March 25, 1800, in the village of Eingenheim, twelve miles nearly north of Strasburg, France, now Germany. He was there married to Margaret Walter, who was born Nov. 11, 1806, in the same province. They had one child in France, and emigrated to America, landing at New Orleans, Feb. 18, 1837. In the fall of that year the yellow fever raged as an epidemic in New Orleans. Of the one hundred and sixty-three passengers who came over in the ship with Mr. Paulen, all except thirty died. Mr. Paulen, his wife and child all had the disease, but escaped death. Their money was gone, but they came up the Mississippi and Illinois rivers to Beardstown, Illinois, and from there by wagon to Sangamon county, arriving April 20, 1838, in what is now the southeast corner of Island Grove township. They had two children in Sangamon county. Of their three children—

DEBOLD, Jun., born Sept. 11, 1828, in Alsace, France, now Germany, came to Sangamon county in 1838 with his parents, married Jan. 26, 1854, to Alpha C. Rigg, who died without children, Jan. 18, 1856. Mr. Paulen was married Mar. 10, 1857, to Elizabeth McMurry. They have four children, namely: GEORGE R., MARGARET A., JACOB W. and JOHN LEW, and reside two and three-quarter

—71

miles northwest of Curran, Sangamon county, Illinois.

JACOB W., born Sept. 8, 1839, in what is now Curran township, Sangamon county, enlisted in 1862, in Co. B, 130th Reg. Ill. Inf., was elected 2d Lieut. upon the organization of the company, served in the Vicksburg campaign in the 4th division of 15th Army Corps, was promoted to 1st Lieut. at DeCrow's Point, Texas, Feb. 21, 1864. He was taken prisoner in Gen. Bank's expedition, at the battle of Mansfield, La., April 8, 1864; was fourteen months a prisoner at Tyler, Texas, and released soon after the close of the rebellion. He was commissioned Capt. of Co. E, 130th Ill. Inf., after the war, for meritorious conduct, and was honorably discharged the latter part of June, 1865. He was married June 18, 1866, to Lucy B. Johnson, who was born near Frankfort, Ky., March 5, 1848. They had three children, namely: BENJ. R. S., born in DeWitt county, Ill., July 14, 1869; LAURA E., born June 25, 1871; MINNIE M., born June 28, 1873. The two latter near Fredonia, Wilson county, Kan., where Mr. Paulen and family reside.

MARY F., born March 26, 1844, in Sangamon county, married in the same county to Ebenezer F. Hatfield, who was born Dec. 8, 1841, in Warren county, O., enlisted Sept. 10, 1861, in Co. A, 4th Ohio Cav., for three years. He was wounded at the battle of Chickamauga, Sept. 20, 1863, captured, and released ten days later; served his full time, and was honorably discharged. He now draws a pension. Mr. and Mrs. Hatfield have three children, EDWARD E., CHARLES C. and SILAS G., and reside two miles west of Curran, Illinois.

Mrs. Margaret Paulen died April 7, 1863, in Sangamon county, and her husband resides with their son, Debold, Jun.

Debold Paulen was not out of Sangamon county from the time he came, in 1838, for thirty-two years. In 1870 he went to visit a brother and sister in Canada, whom he had not seen for forty years. He is now—1876—in his seventy-seventh year, teeth all sound, good health, and says he does not know of an ancestor dying under eighty years.

PEACOCK, CALEB, was born Nov. 3, 1813, in Hardy county, Virginia.

He came to Springfield, Ill., in the fall of 1836, and was married, Feb. 27, 1840, to Susannah Stacy. She died July 8, 1842. Mr. Peacock was married, Dec. 3, 1844, to Phebe Dill. They moved to Plymouth, Hancock county, in 1855, and returned in 1863. They have four living children, namely—

BENJAMIN F. married Rebecca J. Eades, and live in Auburn, Illinois.

MILLARD F., ALVA B. and *SAMUEL E.* live with their parents.

Caleb Peacock and family reside in Auburn, Sangamon county, Illinois.

PEASE, ABRAM, born July 22, 1791, in Martha's Vineyard, Dukes county, Mass. The ancestors of this family were from Wales, and came to America more than two hundred years ago, settling in Massachusetts. Abram Pease, whose name heads this sketch, went to the State of New York, when a young man, and was married there, Aug. 18, 1811, to Orpha Southwick. He was a soldier in the war of 1812, from Cayuga county, N. Y. Abram Pease and wife came to Sangamon county with the family of Jesse Southwick, arriving in 1818 in what is now Ball township. They had four children—

DEXTER, born July 14, 1817, in New York, *THEODORE, BRIGHAM* and *NANCY*; the latter died August 11, 1820.

Mrs. Orpha Pease died Feb. 22, 1820, in Sangamon county, and Abram Pease was married, June 21, 1827, in Sangamon county, to Dorotha Lathrop, who was born April 12, 1805, in New York. They had one living child—

SHAW, born April 23, 1828, in Sangamon county, was married July 6, 1851, in same county, to Amanda H. Pettus, who was born June 24, 1832, in Nicholas county, Ky., and came to Sangamon county with her father, Thomas P. Pettus, and her grandfather, George Bryan, of Bryan's station, Ky. Shaw Pease and wife have eight living children. LESLIE T., born Aug. 5, 1852, in Sangamon county, studied medicine, and was married, May 9, 1875, to Mary L. Halsted, who was born Feb. 7, 1854, in Castile, Wyoming county, N. Y. Dr. Leslie T. Pease is practicing medicine at Blue Mound, Macon county Ill., and resides there. Of the other seven children—A.

JUDSON, FRANCIS W., IDA, LUELLA and LINCOLN, were born in Sangamon county, and GEORGE and CHARLES P. were born in Macon county, Ill. Hon. Shaw Pease was a farmer in Woodside township, Sangamon county, until 1867, when he removed to the vicinity of Niantic, Macon county, where he now resides. He served one term as member of the Board of Supervisors of Macon county. In Nov., 1874, he was elected to the twenty-ninth district in the State Legislature for two years. Mr. Pease nor either of his sons chew tobacco, drink whisky or use profane language.

Mrs. Dorotha Pease died, Aug. 13, 1832, and Abram Pease died September 1, 1843, both in Sangamon county, Illinois.

PENNY, HIRAM, was born Oct. 5, 1790, in North Carolina, and was taken, when quite young, by his parents to Pope county, Illinois. He was married in Kentucky, opposite where they lived in Illinois, to Catharine McHenry. They had five children in Pope county, and moved to Sangamon county, arriving in the fall of 1822, in what is now Cartwright township, where they had four children. Of their children—

ALEXANDER, born March 1, 1815, in Pope county, Illinois, married in Sangamon county to Mary Archer. They had one child, WILLIAM H., who enlisted Sept. 18, 1862, for three years, in Co. F, 114th Ill. Inf., was captured at Guntown, Miss., June 10, 1864, and was starved to death in Andersonville prison. Alexander Penny married for a second wife, Elizabeth Hennings, and died, in Wilson county, Kansas, in 1870, leaving a widow and one child.

HENRY J., born May 22, 1817, married Louisa Hannahs, have two children, and live in Carroll county, Missouri.

ELIZABETH J., born March, 1819, died at eighteen years of age.

WILLIAM G., born Jan. 5, 1821, married Eleanor Duff, had six children, and he enlisted in an Illinois regiment, and died at Little Rock, Arkansas. His widow died, and his sons live in Webster county, Nebraska.

JEMIMA, born Sept. 11, 1822, married James Ross. They had two children, and Mrs. Ross died. Mr. Ross was a soldier, and died in the Union army. Their son lives in Logan county, and their daughter in Iowa.

SOLOMON A., born Sept. 15, 1824, in Sangamon county, married Polly Duncan, had one child, and Mrs. Penny died. He moved to Kansas, married again, and died there.

CAROLINE, born Nov. 21, 1828, married Samuel Campbell. They have two children and live in Kansas.

HIRAM D., born Oct. 16, 1830, married Jane Irwin, who died, and he married Laura Graves, and lives in Wilson county, Kansas.

Hiram Penny died Dec. 10, 1852, in Sangamon county. His widow died April 30, 1873, in Wilson county, Kansas.

William Penny, the father of Hiram, was born in 1751, and was captain of a company from North Carolina in the Revolutionary army. He moved to Pope county, Ill., and from there to Sangamon county, and died, March 15, 1821, on Richland creek, in what is now Cartwright township. He had two brothers, Solomon and Robert. Solomon married Jane Renshaw, raised a family, and died after leaving the county. Robert raised a family and died. His widow, more than ninety years old, lives with her daughter, Mrs. Abraham Freeman, in Springfield.

PELHAM, JOHN, was born July 14, 1804, in Hamilton county, near Cincinnati, Ohio. Anna M. Judd was born Oct. 20, 1806, in Chenango county, near Oxford, N. Y. In 1818 her parents moved to Westport, Oldham county, Ky., and in 1821 moved to the vicinity of Shawneetown, Ill. In 1823 they moved up the Ohio river to Evansville, Ind. John Pelham and Anna M. Judd were there married, Jan. 23, 1827. They soon after went to St. Clair county, Ill., thence to Quincy, and from there to Sangamon county, arriving Sept. 11, 1827, at Sangamo town. They had seven living children, namely—

JAMES M., born May 5, 1829, married Mrs. Demaris Stone, whose maiden name was Gard. They had three children, ALAMANDA, FRANKLIN and JAMES M. In 1859 James M. Pelham went to Pikes Peak, and from there to California. In 1862 he united with a body of men, styling themselves the "One Hundred Californians." They went in a body from San Francisco to Boston, Mass., and became a Co. of the 2d Mass. Cav. He served full three years, and was honorably discharged, June, 1865. He received a gun shot wound in the Shenandoah Valley. That and exposure so impaired his health that he died, Jan. 14, 1866, near Salisbury, within three miles of where he was born. His widow and children live in Gardner township, Sangamon county, Illinois.

WILLIAM B., born April 18, 1834. He enlisted April, 1861, on the first call for 75,000 men, in the 7th Ill. Inf.; served three months, and was honorably discharged August. 16, 1861. He enlisted in Co. D, 33d Ill. Inf., for three years, was wounded at the battle of Black river bridge, May 17, 1863. Dec. 31, 1863, he re-enlisted as a veteran, was transferred to the Invalid Corps, and was discharged on account of physical disability, in Nov., 1864. He was married June 1, 1865, to Elizabeth White. They have four children, and live in Tazewell county, Illinois.

DANIEL C., born Jan. 11, 1837, enlisted Aug. 16, 1861, in Co. D, 33d Ill. Inf., for three years, was re-enlisted as a veteran, Dec. 31, 1863, at Indianola, Texas, served until the end of the rebellion, and was honorably discharged. He was married Dec. 27, 1866, to Mildred P. Batterton. They have four children, ARTHUR, ADA L., ALBERT and HARRY; the latter died Aug. 10, 1873. D. C. Pelham resides at Salisbury, Sangamon county, Illinois.

MARY E., is unmarried, and lives with her mother.

ELIZA A., born Feb, 6, 1843, married Oct. 4, 1866, to Josiah Mitchell. He enlisted for three years, in 1861, in Co. E, 14th Ill. Inf., was wounded at the battle of Pittsburg Landing, April 6, 1862, and was honorably discharged. He re-enlisted as a veteran Dec., 1863, and was honorably discharged Nov., 1865. Mr. and Mrs. Mitchell have two children, ARTHUR C. and CHARLES O., and live at Tallula, Illinois.

JOHN H., born August 22, 1846, enlisted Feb., 1864, in Co. A., 10th Ill. Cav., served until Nov., 1865, when he was honorably discharged, at San Antonio, Texas, and resides with his mother at Salisbury, Illinois.

ROBERT E., born Oct. 22, 1848, enlisted August 19, 1871, in Co. G, 6th U. S. Inf. for five years, now—May, 1873—at Buford, Dacotah Territory.

John Pelham died in St. Clair county, July 21, 1850. His widow married Oct. 3, 1867, to Wm. B. Gaines. He died Oct. 21, 1871. She resides at Salisbury, Sangamon county, Ill., and is known as Mrs. Pelham.—1874.

PETER, ZACHARIAH, was born in Amherst county, Virginia. His parents moved, when he was two years old, to Washington county, Ky. He was married near Danville, Ky., to Nancy Spaulding. They had five children in Kentucky, and moved to what afterwards became Sangamon county, Ill., arriving Sept., 1818; and finding an empty cabin in what is now Ball township, Mr. Peter moved his family into it. That was the cabin built by Robert Pulliam, in the fall of 1817, the first ever erected in Sangamon county. Mr. Peter lived there until the spring of 1819, when Mr. Pulliam came with his own family. Mr. Peter then vacated it and built a cabin about three miles further north, on what is now —1876—known as the Megredy homestead. They had one child in Sangamon county. Of their six children—

MARY T., born Sept. 13, 1806, in Danville, Ky., married in Sangamon county, Sept. 10, 1826, to Robert Withrow. See his name.

SAMUEL, born in 1808 in Kentucky, married in Sangamon county to Margaret Pulliam. They had five children, and she died, in Iowa, leaving her children there.

JOHN N., born in 1810 in Kentucky, married in Sangamon county to Emily Waldrup. They had seven children. The living members of the family reside near Butler, Montgomery county, Illinois.

MAHALA D., born in 1813 in Kentucky, married in Sangamon county to George Moffatt. They had five children, and Mr. Moffatt died. She, with some of her children, live in Glasgow, Iowa.

THERZA or (*THERESA*), born in 1815 in Kentucky, married in Sangamon county to Brinsley Ball. They had eight children, and Mr. Ball went to California and died there. Mrs. Ball and some of their children live near Galena, JoDaviess county, Illinois.

JAMES M., born in 1819 in Sangamon county, and married Milly A. Peter. They have four children, and live near Mattoon, Moultrie county, Illinois.

Mrs. Nancy Peter died, and Zachariah Peter married Mrs. Margaret Kelly, widow of John Kelly. See his name. They had one child—

PETER CARTWRIGHT, born in Sangamon county. He was a soldier from Sangamon county in the war with Mexico, in 1846 and '7. He went to Washington Territory, where he was married; went from there to California, and was killed by Indians, leaving a widow and one child in California.

Mrs. Margaret Peter died, and Zachariah Peter married Mrs. Elizabeth Thomas, whose maiden name was Keyes. She died, and he married Eliza Gordan.

Zachariah Peter died Aug. 5, 1864, in Springfield, and was buried in Hutchinson cemetery. His widow went to California.

Mr. Peter was one of the three commissioners appointed to organize Sangamon county, and locate the tempory county seat. It was he and William Drennan who wrote their initials on the stake driven in the ground, and marked it Z., P. & D. That was the way the county seat was located, April 10, 1821, and called Springfield. See page 32.

PETTUS, THOMAS P., was born March 31, 1790, in Nicholas county, Ky. He was married there, in 1830, to Mrs. Matilda W. Todd, whose maiden name was Bryan, a daughter of George Bryan. See his name. Mr. and Mrs. Pettus had two children, came to Sangamon county, in 1834, and settled in what is now Woodside township. Of their children—

AMANDA H., born June 24, 1832, in Nicholas county, Ky., married in Sangamon county to Shaw Pease. See his name.

MORGAN B., born Oct. 2, 1834, in Frankfort, Ky., married in Sangamon county, April 14, 1858, to Abigail Megredy. They have three living children, namely—FRANCES O., M. MALINDA and CHARLES ARCHIBALD. LAURA, the third child, died May 11, 1871, aged four years. Mr. Pettus, in

1866, moved from Sangamon county to Lincoln, Logan county, Illinois, where he now resides, and is engaged as contractor and builder.

Thomas P. Pettus died April 2, 1852, near Woodside, Sangamon county, and Mrs. Melinda W. Pettus died, Nov. 22, 1872, at the residence of her son, Morgan B. Pettus, in Lincoln, Logan county, Illinois.

PHELPS, ADNA, Sen., was born April 30, 1792, at Hebron, Grafton county, N. H. He was there married to Mary Colburn. They had eight children, all born in New Hampshire, three of whom died in infancy. Some of their children came to Sangamon county before 1840. The parents did not come until July 23, 1844, when they arrived at Loami. Of their five children—

JONATHAN, born June, 1814, married in Massachusetts to Mrs. Nancy Pease, whose maiden name was Turrell. He was a Universalist preacher. He died Oct. 8, 1862, at Loami. His widow resides with her daughter by her first husband, Mrs. D. S. Lombard, in Springfield.

DAVID, born Dec., 1815, at Hebron, N. H., came to Loami in 1836 or '7, married Dec. 16, 1838, to Mehetabel Colburn, who died March 7, 1842, and Mr. Phelps was married Jan. 28, 1843, to Fanny Colburn. They had two children; one died in infancy. He went to California in 1849. Their daughter, ELMINA, married A. J. McDonald, and lives at Grass Valley, Nevada county, California. David Phelps was crushed while going through a mine, of which he was part owner, July 6, and died July 8, 1866. His widow married George Hutchinson, and lives in California.

LAURA, married in Massachusetts to James Herrin, had one child, and died in New Hampshire.

ADNA, Jun., born Dec. 28, 1832. at Hebron, N. H., married Nov. 16, 1856, at Loami, to Martha Meigs, who was born Nov. 14, 1840, at an Indian trading post in Iowa. They had eight children, CLARENCE E. and SHERMAN, third and seventh, died in infancy. The other six, LILLIAN A., DAVID B., MATILDA M., LAURA E., VIOLA and DAISY M. live with their parents, three miles west of Springfield, Ill. Adna Phelps enlisted Aug. 5, 1862, for three years, in Co. I, 73d Ill. Inf., was appointed Orderly Sergt., promoted, May 15, 1863, to 2d Lieut., promoted Nov. 22, 1863, to 1st Lieut., served until June 12, 1865, when he was honorably discharged.

MANDANA, born August 12, 1835, at East Lebanon, N. H., married at Loami to Isaac Colburn. See his name.

Adna Phelps, Sen., died March 5, 1852, and his widow died Feb. 13, 1859—he in Springfield and she in Loami.

PHILLIPS, MRS. CHARLOTTE, whose maiden name was Smith, a sister to Jonas Smith and Mrs. Ebenezer Colburn. She was born Dec. 18, 1799, in Suffolk county, L. I., New York, married in 1816, at Marietta, Ohio, to Burfit Goldsmith, a native of Maryland. They had four children, and Mr. G. died in 1837 at Cincinnati. The widow was married in 1838 to Joel D. Phillips. They had one child, and father and child died in 1854, in Tipton county, Ind. All her children are dead except her son, W. H. O. Goldsmith. He was a member of the 1st U. S. Dragoons for five years, and served through the war to suppress the rebellion. He is married, and lives in Rush county, Ind. Mrs. Phillips resides with her brother, Jonas Smith, at Loami, Illinois.

PHILLIPS, FRANCIS, was born in 1785, in Maryland. He went to Green county, Ky., and was there married, in 1810, to Mary Duggin, a native of Virginia. They had five children in Kentucky, one of whom died young. The family moved to Sangamon county, arriving in 1829, near Springfield. Of their children—

MOREAU, born May 26, 1811, in Green county, Ky., came with his parents to Sangamon county in 1829, and was in the Black Hawk war in a Sangamon county company in 1831. He returned to Kentucky, and was married in Green county, in 1836, to Melissa Lee, a native of that county, also. They had nine children in Sangamon county, two of whom died young. F. MORTIMER, born Nov. 7, 1837, married in 1861 to Mattie A. Troxell, a native of Maryland. They have two children, ALICE BELL and WILLIE, and reside in Springfield. THOMAS J., born Dec. 3, 1839, died April, 1871. MOREAU J., born Feb. 16, 1843, and WILLIAM O., born in 1846, reside in Springfield with their parents. CHARLES J., born in 1848, married, Oct. 1873, to Etta Snow, a native of Maine. They have two children, BERTHA and ETTA, and reside in Springfield. MARY, born Sept., 1853, died March, 1873. URIAH EDWIN, born June, 1851, and ROBERT EMMET, born Feb. 8, 1858, reside with their parents, in Springfield. Moreau Phillips was one of the ten young men who went to Nashville, Tenn., to hear Henry Clay make a political speach in 1840. *See sketch with name of J. H. Matheney.*

JEFFERSON, born in 1813, in Green county, Ky., married in Springfield, in 1836, to Elizabeth Dillman, a native of Ohio. They had four children, two of whom died young. WILLIAM A. and FRANCIS reside at Winona, Illinois. Jefferson Phillips died about 1845.

MARY, born in 1815, in Green county, Ky., married in Springfield, in 1836, to Stephen G. Ubanks. They had two children—SUSANNAH, born in Petersburg, married there to Theodore S. Rogers. They reside near Zanesville, Montgomery county, Ill. MARGARET G., born Oct. 2, 1839, married, Jan. 30, 1860, to Wm. H. Wickersham. They have five children, LILLIE B., NETTIE, MAUDE, OLIVER and CHARLES S. Mr. Wickersham was born March 7, 1836, in Versailles, Ky., learned the business of printing in the *State Journal* office, went to California, in 1853, returned to Springfield in 1859, enlisted, Aug., 1862, for three years, in Co. C, 124th Ill. Inf., served until the end of the rebellion, and was honorably discharged. He is now engaged in the *Journal office*. Mrs. Ubanks died in 1845.

WILLIAM, born in 1826, in Green county, Ky., raised in Sangamon county, married about 1846, in Petersburg, Ill., to Margaret White. They had two children, FRANK and JEFFERSON, both living in Petersburg. William Phillips died in 1852, in Petersburg.

Mrs. Mary or Margaret? Phillips died in 1834, in Springfield. Francis Phillips went back to Kentucky, married a Mrs. Lambkin, came to Springfield on business, and was returning to Kentucky when he died on the road.

Francis Phillips was something of a genius. Farming and chair making was his main business, but he would do any kind of a job of painting, plain or ornamental. A hotel sign painted by him for Archer G. Herndon, is remembered by some of the old men, who in their boyhood days regarded it with an awe inspiring reverence that seems not to have left them to the present time. The name of the hotel was the "Indian Queen," and the sign was the painter's idea of that imaginary personage.

PICKRELL, ABEL, was born March 14, 1782, in Loudon county, Va. His father died when he was quite young, and he was taken by his mother to Fleming county, Ky., about 1793. He went to Montgomery county, in the same State, when a young man, and was there married, in 1804, to Sarah Taylor, who was born Oct. 31, 1784, at a place called Red Stone Fort, Penn. Mr. Pickrell was a soldier in the war of 1812, and went from Montgomery county, Ky. They had six children in that county, and in the fall of 1818, moved to Shelby county, in the same State, and from there moved to Sangamon county, Ill., arriving in the fall of 1831, in what is now Williams township. Of their children—

JESSE A., born June 13, 1805, in Montgomery county, Ky., came to Sangamon county, Illinois, arriving in the spring of 1828, being the first of the family to come to the county, stopping in what is now Mechanicsburg township. He was married Dec. 18, 1828, in Sangamon county, to Elizabeth Churchill. They had ten living children in Sangamon county. WILLIAM O., born Feb. 27, 1830, in Sangamon county, married near Keokuk, Iowa, to Hannah Reed. They have seven children, IDA M., FANNIE H., JESSE, ELIZABETH, OLLIE and WALTER C., and reside near Ottawa, Kansas. ABEL GEORGE, born Feb. 19, 1832, in Sangamon county, enlisted July 20, 1861, in Co. C, 11th Mo. Inf., for three years, was commissioned Quartermaster of the regular army, July 24, 1862, and mustered out August 15, 1864. He was married Dec. 27, 1864, in Jacksonville, Ill., to Emma H. Winn. *See Branson family.* They have three children, CORILLA, ALICE and GERTRUDE, and reside one and a half miles south of James-ville, or Wheatfield Postoffice, Sangamon county, Ill. MILLER H., born March 31, 1835, married in Sangamon county to Sophronia Fry. ANN M., born Sept. 14, 1840, married Sept. 25, 1866, to Henry H. Lee, who was born August 10, 1834, in Gallia county, Ohio, and died Aug. 10, 1867, in Sangamon county. She lives with her parents. MARY V., born Dec. 11, 1842, married Sept. 6, 1865, to Samuel T. Rogers. They have one child, ROBERT, and live at El Paso, Ill. AMANDA P., born August 31, 1844, married Walter F. Swift, Oct. 13, 1870. She died June 19, 1872, in Ottawa, Kansas. Mr. Swift married March 6, 1874, to Bertha Burkhardt. See her name. JOHN C., born Oct. 27, 1846, enlisted July 26, 1864, for three years, in Co. B, 25th U. S. Inf.; served full time, a portion of it as Orderly on Gen. George H. Thomas' staff. He was honorably discharged July 26, 1867, and died at home, March 25, 1873. BENJAMIN F., born Dec. 10, 1848. M. GERTRUDE, born Dec. 29, 1850, and SALLIE E., born March 6, 1855. The two latter live with their parents. Jesse A. Pickrell and family reside near Lanesville, or Wheatfield Postoffice, Sangamon county, Ill. He was among the earliest to introduce improved breeds of cattle, hogs and other stock into Sangamon county, and is one of the most extensive farmers and stock raisers in the county.

WILLIAM S., born March 28, 1807, in Montgomery county, Ky., came to Sangamon county in the fall of 1828, in company with his brother Jesse A., who had returned to Kentucky on a visit. W. S. Pickrell volunteered and served three terms in the Black Hawk war; one term in 1831 and two in 1832. He was Lieutenant, afterwards Major, and Lieutenant-Colonel of militia. He was married near Springfield, June 4, 1833, to Amanda P. Watson. *See Watson family.* They had ten living children. JAMES H., born March 20, 1834, in Sangamon county, was married Sept. 20, 1860, near Paris, Ky., to Margaret T. Bedford, who was born there, March 4, 1840. They had seven children; one died in infancy. AMANDA W., ANNA L., ELLEN H., HARVEY E., WILLIAM B. and JESSE G; the latter died August 5, 1876. The other five live their parents at Harristown, Macon county, Ill. ANNELIZA, born August 20, 1839, was married Dec. 15, 1858, to Harvey N. Edwards, who was born Nov. 9, 1824, in Madison county, N. Y. They reside in Springfield, Ill. HATHAWAY, born Nov. 13, 1841, married Dr. George Pasfield. *See his name.* H. CLAY, born Jan. 27, 1844. LAURA, born Oct. 3, 1846. EMMA, born Jan. 11, 1849. WILLIAM, born Feb. 9, 1851. WATSON, born Oct. 4, 1853. ARTHUR, born Dec. 29, 1856. SCOTT, born Sept. 19, 1860. The last seven children reside at the homestead adjoining Mechanicsburg. William S. Pickrell died Feb. 4, 1870, and Mrs. Amanda P. Pickrell died Mar. 1, 1876, both on the farm where he settled in 1829. Wm. S. Pickrell entered the land on which Mechanicsburg now stands, laid out the original town, and made two additions afterwards. The first sale of lots took place Nov. 16, 1832. He was one of the most successful farmers and stock raisers of Sangamon county. His sons are all well trained to the same business.

OLIVER B., born Jan. 31, 1809, in Kentucky, died there Dec. 8, 1829.

BENJAMIN F., born March 10, 1811, in Montgomery county, Ky., came with his father to Sangamon county, and was married Oct. 5, 1834, to Mary A. ELKIN. They had three children. WILLIAM T., born March 6, 1836, was married in Ottawa, Kansas, to Virginia Whetstone. They have one child OTTOE K., and reside in Ottawa, Kansas. FRANCIS M., born Oct. 11, 1837, married near Williamsville, Ill., to Mary C. Poorman. They have two children, JOHN and PERCY. ELIZA F., born Jan. 30, 1839, was married May, 1874, in Decatur, Ill., to John L. Routt, the present Governor of Colorado.—January, 1876. They reside in Denver, Colorado. B. F. Pickrell died August 28, 1838, in Sangamon county. His widow married Abner Riddle. *See his name.*

EVELINE, born April 1, 1813, in Montgomery county, Ky., married B. Logan Hall. *See his name.*

MARY A., born Oct. 11, 1815, in Montgomery county, Ky., married John Bice. *See his name.*

Mrs. Sarah Pickrell died April 9, 1861, and Abel Pickrell died Jan. 3, 1862, both in Sangamon county, near Mechanicsburg, Illinois.

PIERSON, MOSES, born June 7, 1802, in Warren county, near Lebanon, Ohio. Clarissa Morris was born June 18, 1808, in the same county. They were married, Nov. 3, 1824, and had two living children there. They moved to Sangamon county, Ill., arriving in the fall of 1833, at Springfield, and a year or two later settled two and one-half miles northeast of Springfield. They came to the west hoping that Mrs. Pearson's health would be improved, but finding that it was not. They were returning to Ohio, and stopped at Paris, Ill., to visit some friends, when Mrs. Pierson suddenly died there, June 9, 1836. Mr. Pierson took his two children to their relatives in Ohio, and returned to Sangamon county, where he was married, Oct. 18, 1837, to Harriet Kilbourn, who was born Oct. 18, 1818, near Chillicothe, Ohio. They had nine children in Sangamon county. Of all his children—

DAVID M., born Nov. 12, 1827, near Lebanon, Ohio, was married Dec. 27, 1865, in Sangamon county, to Celestia E. Wilson, who was born Sept. 5, 1839, in St. Lawrence county, N. Y. They had two children. LAWRENCE L., the youngest, died in his second year. GILMAN M., born Oct. 9. 1866, resides with his parents, at his grandfather Wilson's, two miles northeast of Springfield.

SARAH LAVINIA, born April 4, 1831, near Lebanon, Ohio, was married in Sangamon county, June 27, 1867, to Richard H. Beach. *See his name.*

Children of Moses Pierson by the second marriage—

CLARISSA, born Aug. 27, 1838, in Sangamon county, married Lucius C. Francis. *See his name.*

JOHN G., born Sept. 3, 1840, in Sangamon county, is unmarried, and resides at the family homestead, two and one-half miles northeast of Springfield.

JANE MARY, born Sept. 30, 1842, resides at the family homestead.

THEODORE F., born June 7, 1844, enlisted Aug. 5, 1862, for three years, in Co. G, 114th Ill. Inf. He was taken prisoner June, 1864, at the battle of Guntown, Miss., spent four months in Andersonville prison, and taken from there to Savannah Ga., and paroled. On being exchanged he returned to duty, at Benton Barracks, St. Louis, where he was honorably discharged, July 27, 1865. He was married at Jacksonville, Ill., Sept. 15, 1874, to Josephine E. Morrison, who was born Nov., 1847, near Naples, Scott county, Ill. They reside four miles north of Illiopolis, Sangamon county, Illinois.

FRANK, born Sept. 25, 1846, resides four miles north of Illiopolis, Illinois.

JOSEPH, born March 22, 1848; *EDWARD*, born May 13, 1849; *JESSIE A.*, born Jan. 6, 1854, and *HARRIET*, born Feb. 27, 1857, reside at the family homestead, near Springfield, Illinois.

Mrs. Harriet Pierson died Feb. 18, 1858, and Moses Pierson died Dec. 20, 1860, both on the farm where he settled in 1834 or '5, two and a half miles northeast of Springfield, Illinois.

PIKE, JOHN, was born in Virginia, and when a young man went to Bourbon county, Ky., where he was married to Mary Moon. They had three children in Bourbon county. In the spring of 1828 Mr. Pike started, with his household goods loaded on a wagon made entirely of wood, each wheel being hewn from a solid piece of timber. It was drawn by a yoke of oxen, with one horse in the lead. The wagon was many times taken to pieces and formed into a raft to float the wife, children, and household goods across the unbridged streams. They traveled in that way until they reached Jacksonville, Ill. He was not satisfied with the country, and started back to Kentucky. On reaching White river, Ind., they halted, and again started for Illinois. Late in the fall of 1829 they stopped near the South Fork timber, about three miles south of the present town of Rochester. The weather being too cold to travel, and it was too late in the season to build, the family spent that winter in the tent they had used all summer. In the spring of 1830 Mr. Pike had twenty acres under cultivation. He also built a log cabin in the edge of the prairie, and lined it with clap boards. The next winter being the time of the "deep snow," when it fell the wind drifted it around the house until it was almost covered, thus making it very warm. Mr. Pike made rails at twenty-five cents per hundred, until he earned one hundred dollars, with which he entered his first eighty acres of land. That required the making of forty thousand rails. Mr. and Mrs. Pike had three children in Sangamon county. Of their six children—

MILTON, born in Bourbon county, Ky., married in Sangamon county, June 12, 1845, to Martha J. Porterfield. They had three children, and Mrs. Pike died March 25, 1855. He was married July 29, 1857, to Elizabeth M. Brownell. They have eight children, and reside in Auburn, Sangamon county, Illinois.

GEORGE H., born in Kentucky, lived with the family in Sangamon county until he was twenty-one years old. He was married in Bureau county, but if living, his residence is not known.

THOMAS, born in Kentucky, married in Sangamon county to Elizabeth Baker, and had two children. He married Mrs. Sarah J. Breckenridge, whose maiden name was Mathews, and lives near Edinburg, Illinois.

ELMIRA J., born in Sangamon county, married Isaac Baker, who died, leaving one child, and she married Samuel Woodrow, has two children, and lives at the place where her parents settled in 1829, three miles south of Rochester, Illinois.

LUCINDA, born Nov. 29, 1833, in Sangamon county, married John F. Jones. They had one child, CHARLES T., who married Missouri Reavis, and lives at Campbellsburg, Ill. J. F. Jones died, and his widow married Edward George. See his name.

WILLIAM, born in Sangamon county, married Alvira White, and lives in Kansas.

John Pike died in 1833 or '4, in Sangamon county. His widow married in 1836 to James Martin. They had one child—

NANCY, who married Jefferson Smith, and lives two and a half miles south of Dawson, Sangamon county, Illinois.

Mrs. Mary Martin died in 1858.

PIPPIN, JOSEPH, was born April 2, 1782, in Cecil county, Md., and taken by his parents to Russell county, Va. He was there married, Dec. 12, 1812, to Sarah Haines, sister to Christopher Haines. See his name. She was born in Russell county, June 5, 1785. In August, 1813, they moved to Allen county, Ky., where they had ten children, and moved to Sangamon county, Ill., arriving Nov. 10, 1830, in what is now Cotton Hill township, where one child was born. Of their children—

MARGARET, married to John Ashford, and died, leaving a family in Kentucky.

TELITHA, born Sept. 29, 1815, in Kentucky, married in Sangamon county to James A. Snodgrass. See his name.

MARY, born in Kentucky, and died in Sangamon county, aged twenty years.

CHRISTOPHER, born Oct. 12, 1819, in Kentucky, died in Sangamon county, Feb. 14, 1848.

MARTHA A., born April 11, 1821, and

JOHN L., born March 10, 1823, in Kentucky, both live with their mother.

WILLIAM died under five years.

JESSE, born Feb. 11, 1827, in Allen county, Ky., married in Sangamon county, June 25, 1862, to Isabel Craig. She was born August 28, 1840, in Glasgow, Scotland. They had five children; two died under six years. MARY E., JOHN A. and Burgess R. live with their parents, near New City, Sangamon county, Illinois.

CATHARINE, born Feb. 14, 1829, married Jackson Ryan. She died Jan. 7, 1849.

NANCY A., born Feb. 11, 1830, in Kentucky, married in Sangamon county to John Benjamin.

MELINDA J., born March 5, 1833, in Sangamon county, married John Allen, and she died Sept. 2, 1865.

Joseph Pippin died August 10, 1873, in his ninety-second year. His widow lives in Cotton Hill township, near where they settled in 1830. Their married life extended over more than sixty years.

PIRKINS, EDWARD, was born March 15, 1791, on the river Yadkin, Wilkes county, North Carolina. His parents moved, when he was quite young, to Adair county, Ky. He was married Aug. 20, 1812, in Campbell county, Tenn., to Anna Pierce, who was born March 28, 1796, in Blount county, Tenn. They made their home in Campbell county, Tenn., until they had four children, and they moved in company with the family of his father-in-law, Robert Pierce, to Madison county, Ill., arriving in the fall of 1819. The next spring the two families moved to Sangamon county, arriving in April, 1820, on Richland creek, in what is now Cartwright township, where seven children were born. Of their eleven children—

POLLY, born June 25, 1813, in Campbell county, Tenn., married Tavener B. Anderson. See his name.

LEAH, born March 29, 1815, in Campbell county, Tenn., married in Sangamon county, Dec. 16, 1841, to James W. Beekman, who was born Dec. 9, 1816, in Somerset county, N. J. They had five children, all born in Sangamon county. MARY E., born Dec. 7, 1842, died Feb. 4, 1847. CORNELIUS T., born Oct. 16, 1846, died Nov. 11, 1867. JANE E. and SARAH L., twins, born Mar. 26, 1850. JANE E. married, Sept. 18, 1872, to Thomas C. Richardson, had one child, MARY L., who died in infancy. They reside with Mrs. Richardson's father. SARAH L. married, Oct. 12, 1871, to Winfield S. Caldwell, and reside in Menard county, five miles north of Pleasant Plains. WILLIAM E., married Jan. 1, 1874, to Julia S. Harrison. She died, leaving one child, EDWARD J. Mr. Beekman resides with his father. Mrs. Leah Beekman died, Feb. 21, 1873. James W. Beekman resides three and one-half miles northeast of Pleasant Plains, Sangamon county, Illinois.

ELIZA, born Dec. 25, 1816, in Campbell county, Tenn., married in Sangamon county to Edmund Crafton. They had nine children, and Mrs. Crafton died, in 1869, in Springfield.

ROBERT L., born April 29, 1819, in Campbell county, Tenn., married March 11, 1841, in Menard county, to Harriet E. Bone, who was born Sept. 19, 1819, near Petersburg. They had five children, two of whom died in infancy. Of the other three—CHARLES R. lives in Curran township, near his father. FRANCES JENNIE, born March 7, 1844, married, Feb. 8, 1866, to John F. Purvines. See his name. THOMAS M. lives in Curran township, near his father. Mrs. Harriet E. Pirkins died Sept. 22, 1851, and R. L. Pirkins was married, Nov. 3, 1853, to Emma M. Dorand, who was born July 15, 1825, in St. Lawrence county, N. Y. They had one child, HARRIET E., who died, Nov. 16, 1860, in her seventh year. R. L. Pirkins and wife reside in Curran township, seven miles southwest of Springfield, Sangamon county, Illinois.

EDWARD RILEY, born Sept. 25, 1821, in Sangamon county, married June 16, 1846, to Rachel R. Butler. They had six children in Sangamon county. WILLIAM EDWARD, born March 21, 1849, married, Dec. 16, 1869, to Rose H. Cooper, who was born April 19, 1849. They have two children, ROSE BELLE and NELLIE, and reside five miles southeast of Pleasant Plains, Sangamon county, Illinois. CORDELIA E., born May 23, 1851, married, Oct. 31, 1871, to Wm. H. Little. See his name. He died at Chicago, Aug. 17, 1873, from an accident on the Chicago & Alton railroad, the night before. EMMA L., FANNIE M. and SALLIE B. reside with their parents. JULIA died in her fourth year. E. R. Pirkins lived in Cartwright township, three and one-half miles southwest of Richland station, until he was elected treasurer of Sangamon county, Oct., 1873, for two years, and now—1876—resides in Springfield, Illinois.

JOSEPH B., born May 15, 1824, in Sangamon county, married Aug. 29, 1849, to Melinda A. Iles. They had four children, one died in infancy. The other three—ANNIE C. P. married, October 20, 1869, to William E. Morrison. They had one child, JAMES DON, and Mrs. Morrison died, in 1874, at Morrisonville, Christian county, Illinois. JULIA R. and LOUISA M. reside with their father. Mrs. M. A. Pirkins died, Jan. 12, 1857, and J. B. Pirkins was married June 8, 1864, at Nicholasville, Ky., to Ann Mary Price, who was born Jan. 17, 1842, in Woodford county, Ky. They had three children, one of whom died in infancy. JOSEPH B., Jun., and ROBERT L. live with their parents. J. B. Pirkins resides near Woodside, Sangamon county, Illinois. He was a member of Co. A, 4th Ill. Inf., and served one year in the war with Mexico, under Col. E. D. Baker. He was elected, in Nov., 1858, sheriff of Sangamon county, for two years, and was President of the Sangamon county Agricultural Society, in 1872. He was the first President of the Society as now organized.

WILLIAM E., born Feb. 18, 1827, in Sangamon county, married, April 5, 1860, to Mary Sayre. They had three children, viz: CLARENCE F., the second one, died in his second year. ANNIE L. and JENNIE E. reside with their parents, four miles northeast of Richland station, Sangamon county, Illinois.

RACHEL L., born Jan. 7, 1830, in Sangamon county, died March 9, 1853.

FRANCIS M., born Nov. 19, 1832, in Sangamon county, went, in the summer of 1862, to California and Oregon, and from there to Idaho. He left Fort Berthold, on the Missouri river, for home, with about twenty others in a boat, and all of them were massacred by Sioux Indians, below that Fort, August 3, 1863.

JAMES M., born Sept. 5, 1835, in Sangamon county, died unmarried, Sept. 27, 1869, at the family homestead.

REBECCA E., born Jan. 24, 1840, in Sangamon county, married Dec. 15, 1857, to William H. Wilton, who was born March 31, 1827, at Carlisle, Clinton county, Illinois. They had nine children. ANNA and EMMA, twins, FRANK, NED and HARRY, twins, WILLIE, LIZZIE and ELLA. They reside two and one-half miles north of Richland station, Sangamon county, Illinois, on the farm where her father settled in 1820.

Mrs. Anna Pirkins died Nov. 1, 1854, and Mr. Edward Pirkins, now in his 84th year, resides with his children, principally at the farm where he settled in 1820.

ROBERT PIERCE, the father-in-law of Edward Pirkins, was an early settler of Sangamon county.

Edward Pirkins remembers that when himself and his father-in-law, Mr. Pierce, were looking at the country they were at Island Grove, and Mr. Pierce thought it ought to be called lost grove because there was not more than enough timber for one family, and as one family could not live alone, it would be lost. They went to Richland creek because there was more timber there. Claims were laid to it all before it came into market, and when it was ready for entry the timber land was all taken very soon. It had been a source of great anxiety because there were no pre-emption laws to protect the settlers, and they felt very much relieved when they had generally secured their homes. This happiness did not last long, for they soon began to worry about how long the timber would last. Mr. Pirkins remembers meeting four or five of his neighbors when the timber question came up. He gave it as his opinion, that he would cut the last stick of his timber in twenty years, and he would have to leave the country. One man who had read something about "Peat" or turf, tried to console those present with the thought that before the timber was exhausted a plan would be invented to break the prairie, and they could dry the sod, call it peat and burn it. There is more wood on his land now than when he entered it.

Edward Pirkins took the premium of a gold headed cane, at the Sangamon county Fair, Sept., 1875, for the best equestrianism by aged gentlemen. There were eleven entries, all over sixty years of age. Rev. A. Gross, on behalf of the society, said: "Mr. Pirkins, the committee chosen by the Sangamon county Fair, consider you the most graceful rider, and on behalf of the Society, I present you with this beautiful cane, to which we feel you are justly entitled."

PLAIN, DAVID S., born Feb. 27, 1824, near Greenville, Mechlenburg county, Ky. His mother died when he was two weeks old, and in 1835 he was brought to what is now Auburn township, by Samuel Short, who brought him up. David S. Plain was married Sept. 4, 1845, to Eliza Roach, who was born April 14, 1823, in Christian county, Ky. They have ten children—

EMILY J., born Feb. 9, 1847, was married Feb. 26, 1873, to W. A. Lowdermilk, of Auburn township. They have one child, CHARLES O., and reside in Cass county, Missouri.

MIRANDA, born June 12, 1848, in Sangamon county, Ill., was married May 11, 1870, to Thomas R. Stroud. They moved to the vicinity of south Carrolton, Ky., but returned August 16, 1875. They have two children, ELIZA M. and EDGAR L., and reside in Auburn township, Sangamon county, Illinois.

JESSE S., born Feb. 20, 1850, in Sangamon county, was married Sept. 16, 1873, to Fannie Briant, who was born in

McLean county, Ky. They live in Mechlenburg county, Ky.

SAMUEL S., born Dec. 17, 1851, was married Sept. 3, 1872, to Mattie Jeringan. They live in Radford, Christian county, Illinois.

AMERICA R., born Feb. 24, 1854, was married Dec. 24, 1873, to W. C. McGlothlin, who was born in Green county, Ill. They reside in Auburn township, Sangamon county, Illinois.

DAVID E., born Nov. 20, 1855, lives with his parents.

CHARLES, born Oct. 1, 1857, died Oct. 7, 1875.

ELIZA J., born Nov. 5, 1859,

MARY C., born Dec. 26, 1861, and

MARGARET M., born May 4, 1864, all in Sangamon county, and the unmarried children reside with their parents, five miles southeast of Auburn, Sangamon county, Illinois.

PLANCK, JACOB C., born Jan. 27, 1804, in Maryland, went, when a boy, to Kentucky, and was married in Flemingsburg, Fleming county, Ky., about 1826, to Mary M. Rogers, who was born there, April 4, 1806. They moved to Springfield, Ill., in the autumn of 1826, where they had nine children, one of whom died in infancy, and one aged seven years, Of the other seven—

EMILY R., born Jan., 1828, in Springfield, Ill., was married there, Feb., 1845, to Benjamin A. Watson. See his name.

EMELINE, born Dec. 4, 1829, in Springfield, was married Dec., 1848, to Walter Davis, a native of Richmond, Virginia. They had four children, three of whom died young. Mr. Davis died Jan. 6, 1861, and Mrs. Davis died Oct. 4, 1863, both in Springfield, Illinois, leaving one child, CLARA, born May 21, 1854. She was married March 25, 1875, to James Hoyt, a native of Williamsburg, New York. They live in Springfield, Illinois.

JULIA J., born July 24, 1832, in Springfield, was married there, Oct. 6, 1852, to Joseph B. Fosselman, who was born March 4, 1830, in Perry county, Penn. They have two living children, ANNA M. was married Feb. 23, 1876, to Emery Wolgamot. See his name. EDWARD lives with his parents. J. B. Fosselman came to Springfield in 1850, and being an experienced druggist, he engaged in that business, and prosecuted it for ten years, when he changed to the wholesale grocery trade, which he continued thirteen years. He is now in the drug business in Springfield, Ill.

WILLIAM H., born Oct. 16, 1835, in Springfield, was married there in 1863, to Mrs. Elizabeth Robinson, whose maiden name was Abrams. They have one child, KATIE, and live in St. Louis, Missouri.

AMELIA R., born May 25, 1839, in Springfield, was married Dec. 24, 1860, to Alexander R. Dodds. See his name. They had one child, EVA MAY, and Mr. Dodds died Jan., 1864. Mrs. Amelia R. Dodds and her daughter live in Springfield, Illinois.

CHARLES, born Dec. 10, 1842, in Springfield, was married Dec. 1, 1868, to Mrs. Hattie Bailey, whose maiden name was Stevens, a native of Rochester, New York. They live in Holland, Ottawa county, Michigan.

MARY E., born Sept. 13, 1849, in Springfield, was married there, Feb. 18, 1865, to James Smith, who was born May 20, 1841, in Vermont. They had one child, LILLIE MAY, and Mr. Smith died Nov., 1874, in Sandusky, O. Mrs. Smith and her daughter live in Holland, Ottawa county, Michigan.

Mrs. Mary Planck died Jan. 14, 1867, and Jacob C. Planck died August 3, 1867, both in Springfield, Illinois.

PLUNKETT, JOHN H., was born Oct. 3, 1782, in Cabarras county, N. C. Elizabeth Purviance was born March 17, 1785, in the same county. They were married Feb. 19, 1804, and had seven children there. The family then moved to Sangamon county, Ill., arriving in May, 1823, at the north side of Richland creek, in what is now Cartwright township, where, two children were born. Of their nine children—

NANCY, born June 15, 1806, in North Carolina, married Maxwell Campbell. See his name.

ROBERT S., born June 15, 1808, in North Carolina, married in Sangamon county, Nov. 5, 1829, to Ruth Combs, who was born in Green county, Ky. They had six living children. MARTHA A., born July 4, 1832, married Wm. Bumgardner, and both died in Effingham county, leaving five children. ASA W., born April 3, 1834, married Jan. 12, 1853, to Nancy J. Willis, who was born July 21, 1831, in Kentucky. They had seven children; two died in infancy, and MARY ETHEL died in her ninth year. ROBERT S., EMMA I., JOHN W. and LILLIE MAY live with their parents, near Pleasant Plains, Ill. JASON D., born Jan. 1, 1836, was married Mar. 5, 1857, to Catharine Dunkel. They have four living children, HARLEM O., WILLIAM H., HATTIE C. and RUTH C., and live four miles east of Pleasant Plains, Sangamon county, Ill. RICHARD M., born Dec. 13, 1838, died April 28, 1852. JOHN N., born Sept. 30, 1840, enlisted on the first call for seventy-five thousand men, April, 1861, for three months, in Co. E, 7th Ill. Inf., and served full term. He enlisted August 11, 1862, in Co. F, 114th Ill. Inf., for three years, served until Oct. 18, 1864, when he was discharged on account of physical disability, by the special order of Abraham Lincoln, on the personal application of his father, who was a soldier in Capt. Lincoln's company, in the Black Hawk war. John N. Plunkett was married August 24, 1865, to Mary C. Sutton, who was born Oct. 22, 1843. They have four children, ITHA E., MINNIE E., MELINDA J. and JOHN C., and live one mile west of Salisbury, Sangamon county, Ill. REBECCA J., born Oct. 15, 1841, married March 13, 1862, to Amos D. Irwin. *See his name.* Mrs. Ruth Plunkett died Feb. 23, 1844, and Robert S. Plunkett married Anna Alexander, who died without children, and Mr. Plunkett was married Nov. 11, 1850, to Mrs. Marilda Gateley, whose maiden name was Hind. They have two children, LAURA N. and RUTH D., and reside three and a half miles east of Pleasant Plains, Sangamon county, Illinois.

ELLEN married Zachariah Wilbourn. They had six children, and moved to the vicinity of Mt. Pleasant, Iowa, where Mrs. Wilbourn died. Her children are all married, and live in Iowa. Mr. Wilbourn resides near Mt. Pleasant, Henry county, Iowa.

ELIZABETH MATILDA, born in Cabarras county, North Carolina, married in Sangamon county to William C. Irwin. *See his name.*

JOHN B., born in 1818, in North Carolina, married in Sangamon county, Ill., to Mary Conner. They have six children. Their son, WILLIAM, is married and lives two and a half miles south of Pleasant Plains, Ill. John B. Plunkett and family moved to the vicinity of Edina, Sullivan county, Missouri, where they now reside.

JOSEPH M., born Sept. 6, 1820, in North Carolina, married in Sangamon county to Lucy Cone. He died May, 1873, in Petersburg, Ill., leaving a widow and three children.

JAMES L., born Sept. 16, 1822, in North Carolina, married June 15, 1848, in Sangamon county, to Martha A. King. They had five children. MARTHA A., the third child, died in infancy. LUCETTA married William R. Strode. *See his name.* They live near Bluff City, Nodaway county, Mo. JULIA A., born March 5, 1852, married James R, Lightfoot. *See his name.* They moved to the vicinity of Marysville, Nodaway county, Mo., and returned to Sangamon county in 1876. LUCY E. and CHARLES live with their parents, near Chinkapin Hill, four miles northwest of Springfield, Ill. James L. Plunkett accompanied his father to North Carolina in 1839 or 40, when they brought with them his grandfather, James Plunkett.

BENJAMIN H., born June 15, 1825, in Sangamon county, married Eliza Cone, had eight children, and he died, in Petersburg, in 1868. His widow married Thomas Hobbs. He died, and she lives near Petersburg, Illinois.

SILAS PINKNEY, born June 15, 1828, in Sangamon county, married, Feb. 26, 1851, in Menard county, to Salina Keltner, who was born May 14, 1833, in Cass county, Ill. They have four living children, CORNELIUS A., JAMES H., EMMA E. and NANCY E., and live three miles east of Pleasant Plains, Ill. It is on the farm where he was born.

John H. Plunkett died Feb. 13, 1849, and his widow died May 8, 1858, and both are buried in Cartwright township. He was the eldest son of James Plunkett, who was born Feb. 4, 1767, and his wife, Agnes Huston, born Sept. 19, 1765. She died in North Carolina, Feb. 26, 1838, and her husband came to Sangamon county, in company with their son, John H., whose name heads this sketch, on his return from a visit to North Carolina. James Plunkett died in Sangamon county, in 1841, aged seventy-three years.

POFFENBERGER, CHRISTIAN, was born in Washington county, Md., and was there married to Mary Brantner. They had seven children in Maryland, and moved, in 1826, to Franklin county, near Columbus, O., where four children were born. The family moved to Sangamon county, Ill., arriving Oct., 1839, in Round Prairie, five miles east of Springfield. Of their children—

LAVINA, born in Maryland, died in Ohio, aged fourteen years.

BARBARA, and a twin that died in infancy, were born in Maryland. She married in Sangamon county to Daniel Price. They have two children, and live in Abingdon, Iowa.

GEORGE W., born Oct. 16, 1817, in Washington county, Md., married in Sangamon county, Feb. 9, 1841, to Rachel Jones. They have six children born in Sangamon county. JOHN A., born March 4, 1843, married Feb. 4, 1869, to Mary E. Keys. She died March 7, 1871, and he lives with his parents. DANIEL, born July 19, 1846, married Jan. 4, 1870, to Rebecca J. Matthews. They have two children, and live in Cotton Hill township. MARY E., born July 30, 1848, lives with her parents. GEORGE W., Jun., born Feb. 15, 1852, married in 1874 to Belle Fairchild, daughter of Charles Fairchild. *See his name.* They have one child, and live at the old George Brunk homestead, in the northwest corner of Cotton Hill township. ELIZA A., born April 1, 1854, married Sept. 4, 1873, to Luther Osborn Meredith. *See his name.* EDWIN, born May 22, 1857, lives with his parents. George W. Poffenberger and wife reside two and a half miles west of Rochester, Sangamon county, Illinois.

SAMUEL, born in 1819, in Maryland, married in Sangamon county to Louisa Dockum, moved to Iowa in 1846, had one child, and Mrs. P. died. He married Hannah Smith, had two children, and she died. Mr. Poffenberger is married again, and resides near Winterset, Iowa.

SARAH A., born August 20, 1821, in Maryland, married in Sangamon county, Dec. 24, 1840, to Adam Unclebee. They had two children. CHARLES served three years in the 3d Ill. Cav.; married Agnes C. Lake, and she died March 16, 1871. *See Lake family.* Charles Unclebee is married again, and lives in Cotton Hill township. Adam Unclebee died March 20, 1842, and his widow married John S. Hillman. *See his name.*

EMANUEL, born and died in Maryland, aged eleven years.

MARY A., born in Maryland, married in Sangamon county to Joseph Price, have a large family, and live in Missouri.

JOHN, born in Ohio, raised in Sangamon county, has a family, and lives in Keokuk county, Iowa.

JANE, born in Ohio, brought up in Sangamon county, was married in Jefferson county, Iowa, to John Carson, and lives near Winterset, Iowa.

WILLIAM C., born March 22, 1834, in Columbus, Ohio, was married Oct. 29, 1858, in Sangamon county, Ill., to Lucinda Salley. They have five children, GEORGE W., MARY ANN, JOHN McC., MAY and WILLIAM D., who live with their parents in Springfield, Illinois.

ANDREW, born in Ohio, died, aged ten years, in Iowa.

Christian Poffenberger moved his family to Jefferson county, near Fairfield, Iowa, in 1846. His wife died February, 1853, and he died October, 1857, aged seventy-one years. They both died in Iowa.

POFFENBERGER, WILLIAM, a brother to Christian, was born in Washington county, Md., married there to Elizabeth Harris, moved to Ohio, and to Sangamon county, with his brother in 1839. Their daughter—

MATILDA, was married in Sangamon county, to Archibald Turner. *See his name.* They live in Springfield.

ANDREW J., born in Sangamon county, enlisted in 1864, in Co. A, 145th Ill. Inf., for one hundred days, served one hundred and sixty days, and was honorably discharged. He was married Oct. 21, 1868, to Phebe Robb. They have two children, WILLIAM and PARSETTA, and live one mile west of

Breckenridge, Sangamon county, Illinois.—1874.

POLEY, JOSEPH, was born Feb. 1, 1802, in Logan county, Ky. His father, Charles Poley, or Pouley, was a native of Paris, France, and was educated there with the view of his becoming a preacher in the Lutheran church. When he came to America he abandoned the ministry, married, moved to Logan county, Ky., and brought up a family there. He then moved to Muhlenburgh county, in the same State, where his daughter, Pauline, married John Jacob Rauch. *See his name.* Joseph Poley, whose name heads this sketch, was married there, Nov. 20, 1825, to Hannah Gossett, and moved to Sangamon county, Ill., arriving in the fall of 1829 in what is now Auburn township. They had four children—

ELISHA, born Sept. 20, 1826, in Muhlenburgh county, Ky., and married in Sangamon county to Sally Shaver, who died, and he married Mary E. Thrasher. They moved overland, in company with his brother-in-law, Abram Gamble, arriving with their families in Solano county, California, in Sept., 1860. In November, Mr. Poley and Mr. Gamble rode five miles on horseback, without saddles, to vote for Abraham Lincoln. A few years later, Mr. Poley moved back to Auburn, Sangamon county. They have three children—JOSEPH G. and ELBERT, born in California, and HARRY, born in Sangamon county. Elisha Poley is a member of the firm of Poley & Butler, commission merchants, Chicago, Illinois, and now—August, 1876—expects to move his family there, from Auburn, soon.

NANCY C., born March 24, 1828, in Muhlenburgh county, Ky., was married at the homestead in Sangamon county, Oct. 23, 1851, to Thomas S. Parks. *See his name.*

LIZZIE and *WILLIE* both died young.

Mrs. Hannah Poley died in 1832, in Sangamon county, and Joseph Poley was married, Nov. 6, 1834, in the same county, to Frances Gates. *See Gates family.* They had ten children in Sangamon county.

ALONZO G., the youngest, died in infancy.

Of the other nine—

BENJAMIN F., born Aug. 8, 1835, in Sangamon county, married, Dec. 30, 1863, to Nancy E. Groves, who was born April 1, 1843, in Macoupin county, Ill. They have three living children, FLORA, ANSON and ORVILLE, and reside four and one-half miles southeast of Auburn, Sangamon county, Illinois.

PETER J., born in 1836, and died Nov. 15, 1859.

MARY C., born May 5, 1838 in Sangamon county, was married, June 4, 1857, to Abram Gamble, who was born Dec. 25, 1825, in Carroll county, Ohio. They have three living children, CHARLES E., FANNIE L. and GEORGE A. In 1859 Mr. and Mrs. Gamble moved to Kansas, and in the spring of 1860 they were joined by Elisha Poley with his family and Benjamin F. Poley, and moved overland to California. Mr. and Mrs. Gamble returned to Auburn in 1866. Not enjoying good health here, they started, in the spring of 1867, and crossed the plains to California. They now—1876—reside in Napa City, Napa county, California.

CAROLINE, born Dec. 16, 1839, in Sangamon county, married, March 9, 1864, to B. O. Foster. They have three children, FLORENCE P., CARRIE A. and FRANK L. Mr. and Mrs. Foster lived several years in California, but now—1876—they reside in Auburn, Sangamon county, Illinois.

ISAAC J., born April 14, 1842, in Sangamon county, was married Oct. 31, 1865, in Adams county, Illinois, to Mary C. Wolf, a native of that county. They had four children—LORENA died in infancy. LENA A., GENEVRA and LEWIS ELMORE live with their parents. Isaac J. Poley is a banker in Auburn, Sangamon county, Illinois, and resides there.

MATILDA F., born Jan. 10, 1844, in Sangamon county, was married, Nov. 20, 1862, to G. W. Barnett. They have three living children, ADAH F., FREDDIE C. and ARTHUR, and reside near Carlinville, Illinois.

JOSEPH, Jun., born May 13, 1846, in Sangamon county, was married April 15, 1873, at Liberty, Adams county, Illinois, to Josephine Collins, who was born June 28, 1852, in that county. They have one child, WILMER M., and reside on his farm, near Auburn, Illinois.

LOUISA E., born July 4, 1848, in Sangamon county, married, April 1, 1868, to J. K. Reeder, and reside near Auburn, Illinois.

CHARLES M., born Nov. 30, 1850, in Sangamon county, is not yet married—August, 1876—and resides with his mother.

Joseph Poley died Aug. 17, 1866, and his widow, Mrs. Frances Poley, resides at the family homestead, two and a half miles southeast of Auburn, Sangamon county, Illinois. Joseph Poley acted as justice of the peace for many years; he was a man whose counsels were often sought by his neighbors. His advice, when followed, always led to the settlement of difficulties without litigation, and in a peaceful and friendly manner. His five sons and five sons-in-law are all, with perhaps one exception, free from the use of tobacco, and all avoid intoxicating drinks. Neither of them was ever charged with an act in violation of law; and it is averred by one of the sons-in-law, that, as a logical sequence, they all invariably vote the Republican ticket.

Mr. Poley brought some money with him to the county, but his greatest success was after coming here. He left his heirs the title to three thousand acres of land, two thousand five hundred of it was in one body.

POLLOCK, THOMAS, born April 15, 1812, near Brownsville, Penn. He came to Sangamon county about 1837, and was one of the engineering corps that surveyed and located the Northern Cross railroad, now the Toledo, Wabash and Western railroad. He was married Dec. 5, 1839, to Elizabeth A. Foutch. They had ten children in Sangamon county, three of whom died under seven years—

THOMAS, Jun., born Sept. 22, 1840, in Sangamon county, enlisted Aug. 12, 1862, for three years, in Co. A, 106th Ill. Inf. He was appointed Corporal, promoted to Orderly Sergeant, 2d Lieutenant, and was commissioned 1st Lieutenant on his birth day, in 1864. He served to the end of the rebellion, and was honorably discharged, August, 1865. He resides with his mother, (1876), near Berlin, Illinois.

SARAH J., born Sept. 17, 1847, in Sangamon county, married Oct. 1, 1865, to James H. Malyon, who was born in 1840 in London, England. He was a bugler in the British army, at the siege of Sevastopol, Russia, in 1854, came to America soon after, and to Sangamon county in the fall of 1857. He enlisted August 12, 1861, at Springfield, in Co. D, 26th Ill. Inf., for three years. Re-enlisted as a veteran, Jan., 1864, served to the end of the rebellion, and was honorably discharged at Springfield, July, 1865. They have four children, LIZLIE J., KITTIE F., HARRY D. and an infant, and live in St. Louis, Missouri. —1873.

HUGH, JOHN W. and HENRY V. live with their mother.

Thomas Pollock died Oct. 15, 1867, in Sangamon county, and his widow resides three miles west of Berlin, Sangamon county, Illinois.

POND, BILLIOUS, was born June 26, 1781, in Northbury, now Plymouth, Litchfield county, Conn. Rhoda Orton was born in the same county, April 17, 1786. They were married Oct. 11, 1801, in Niagara county, N. Y., and had nine children there. A colony left Potsdam, St. Lawrence county, N. Y., and by previous arrangement, through the agency of Mr. Timothy Turner, Mr. Pond joined the colony at Oswego, and acted as its pastor or minister. They arrived Nov. 26, 1832, at old Sangamo town, in Sangamon county, Illinois, and the next spring all moved to the vicinity of the present Farmingdale station. Mr. Pond preached during the winter of 1833 and '4, near Carrolton, Greene county, and in the spring of 1834 returned to his family at Camden, N. Y. He moved his family, bringing all his living children, and arrived July 27, 1837, at what is now Farmingdale, Sangamon county. Of their children—

AMANDA, born, married and died in New York.

MARVIN B., born Nov. 3, 1807, in New York, married there twice, came to Sangamon county in 1837, and in 1839 moved to Menard, and from there to Mason county, where he died in July, 1871, leaving a family. His widow's maiden name was Jane Beerup. She lives in Havana, Ill.

RHODA, born August 17, 1810, and married April 12, 1829, in Camden, N. Y., to Truman M. Catlin, and reside one mile north of Farmingdale.

ADALINE, born August, 1813, in New York, died in Sangamon county in 1838.

SAMUEL S., born August 9, 1816, in New York, married Emily Dufer, and she died, leaving three children. He married Mrs. Hester Durrell, whose maiden name was Moore. They have three living children, and reside near Greenview, Menard county.

FRANCIS N., born March 17, 1819, in New York, came to Sangamon county with his parents, married in Galesburg, Ill. They have no living children, and reside near Greenview, Menard county.

DAVID B., born July 5, 1822, in New York, married in Sangamon county, March 25, 1845, to Susan Moore. They had five children.—FRANCIS A. fell from a fence and broke his neck, in his third year. Two died in infancy. TRYPHENA S. lives with her father. JOHN E., born August 4, 1851, in Sangamon county, married Nov. 5, 1874, to Alice Buchanan. They have one child, NELLIE E., and live at Greenview, Menard county, Illinois. Mrs. Susan Pond died March 10, 1855, and David B. Pond was married to Mary E. Watson, who was born Jan. 1, 1833, in Erie county, N. Y. They reside adjoining Farmingdale, Sangamon county, Illinois, on the east.

ANN P., born May 24, 1825, in N. Y., married in Sangamon county to John Burris, have two children, and live near Fredonia, Kansas.

HANNAH S., born April 23, 1829, in New York, married Melvin Cushion, and died, without children.

Mrs. Rhoda Pond died Oct. 8, 1838, and Rev. Billious Pond was married, Oct., 1839, to Mrs. Melissa Moore, whose maiden name was Northrope. They had one living child—

HENRY S., born Aug. 16, 1841, in Sangamon county, went to Montana Territory, in 1862, and was married there to Delia Kirkpatrick. They have two children, MARY and MAURICE E., and reside in Bannock City, Motana.

—73

Rev. Billious Pond died Dec. 8, 1874, and his widow resides at Farmingdale, Sangamon county, Illinois.

POOR, EVAN, was married in Tennessee to Mahala Enochs, a native of that State. They had one child in Tennessee, and moved to Sangamon county, Ill., arriving in the fall of 1829 at Springfield. One child was born in Sangamon county, and Mrs. Mahala Poor died. Evan Poor was married to Mary Moris. They had one child. Of his three children—

WILLIAM, born Nov. 28, 1827, in Tennessee, married in Sangamon county, July 13, 1848, to Elizabeth C. Smith. They had six children—JAMES MADISON, born April 21, 1849, was killed Nov. 16, 1862, by a horse that he was riding, falling on and crushing him. MARY C., born Sept. 18, 1852, married April 20, 1871, to William Cortwright, have one child, WILLIAM S., and live near Curran, Illinois. MARTHA J. lives with her parents. MELISSA A. died, March 25, 1871, in her tenth year. JOHN CARROLL and THOMAS M. reside with their parents, one mile north of Curran, Sangamon county, Illinois.

JAMES A., born Feb. 8, 1830, in Sangamon county, married, March 12, 1857, to Sarah A. Smith. They had three children, ELLIS A., WILLIAM R. and EMMA M. James A. Poor died Nov. 12, 1867. His widow married, Dec. 24, 1868, to James McCausland, and live one mile north of Curran, Sangamon county, Illinois.

MARGARET C., born in Springfield, died at sixteen years of age, in Iowa.

Evan Poor died in Springfield, in 1834. Mrs. Mary Poor, after living a widow twenty-seven years, married Rev. Mr. Lynn, a Presbyterian minister, and resides near Glasgow, Jefferson county, Iowa—1874.

PORTER, JOSIAH, was born April 10, 1802, in Chester District, South Carolina. Mr. Porter attended Bourbon Academy and Centre College, Ky., and completed his literary course by graduating at the Indiana State University, at Bloomington, in Sept., 1832. He received his theological education at Lane Seminary, Cincinnati, and was licensed to preach, by Shiloh Presbytery, at Murfreesboro, Tenn., Oct. 3, 1835. After a few months' missionary labor, in Tennessee, he came to Chatham, Sangamon county, Ill., arriving Oct. 1, 1836. After spending one year with the Chatham and Sugar Creek churches, he went within the bounds of Crawfordsville Presbytery, and was ordained by that Presbytery, at Waveland, in April, 1838. In Nov., 1838, he took charge of the church at Wayneville, Dewitt county, Ill., and solemnized the first marriage in that county. In the spring of 1845 he returned to Sangamon county, and acted as colporteur, until Jan. 1, 1846, when he entered upon the missionary work of supplying the vacant churches of Illinois Presbytery, which was then New School. In the fall of 1846 he became stated supply to Winchester Presbyterian church. In the spring of 1849 he took charge of the Presbyterian church at Chatham, and this has been his home to the present time. In 1851 he took charge of the Spring creek Presbyterian church, for two years, and served the church at Virden one year. He is now without charge—1874.

Rev. Josiah Porter was married at Chatham, July 18, 1837, to Martha W. Thornton. They have two children—

MARY L. and

MARTHA A. They both reside with their parents, on a farm adjoining Chatham, Sangamon county, Ill., on the west. For Mr. Porter's recollection of events connected with the "sudden change," *see page 66.*

POTTLE, JEREMIAH, was born about 1800, near Camden, Knox county, or Waldo, Waldo county, Maine. When he was twelve years old his parents moved to Bracken county, Ky. Martha McDaniel was born Oct. 13, 1794, near Stroude station, Clark county, Ky. They were married April 2, 1828, in Bracken county, Ky., and had four children there. They then moved to Indianapolis, Ind., where one child was born, and from there to Sangamon county, Ill., arriving in the fall of 1836, at Buffalo Hart Grove, where one child was born. Of their six children—

JONATHAN, born Feb. 6, 1829, in Kentucky, died August 29, 1866, in Sangamon county.

ELIZABETH, born May 13, 1830, is unmarried, and lives with her mother.

JAMES H., born Nov. 13, 1831, is unmarried, and resides with his mother.

DANIEL, born April 12, 1834, in Bracken county, Ky., was married in Sangamon county, Ill., Feb. 23, 1859, to Mary E. Jones. They had four children, JEREMIAH and HOMER died young. LAURA and STROTHER live with their father, Mrs. Mary E. Pottle died Jan. 24, 1868, and Daniel Pottle was married Nov., 1874, to Sarah E. Ford, and reside three miles east of Buffalo Hart Station. Daniel Pottle served in Co. I, 9th Ill. Cav., from Feb., 1865 to Nov. 18, 1865, when he was honorably discharged.

JOSEPH, born July 3, 1836, in Indianapolis, Ind., died Nov. 18, 1868, in Sangamon county, Illinois.

ABNER, born Oct. 15, 1842, in Sangamon county, is a school teacher, and lives with his mother.

Jeremiah Pottle died August 9, 1861, and his widow lives three miles east of Buffalo Hart Station, Sangamon county, Illinois—1784.

POWER, GEORGE, was born Feb. 18, 1798, in Fayette county, Ky. His father was born in Virginia, and had spent some time in North Carolina before he went to Kentucky. When George was about ten years old, his parents moved to Bath county. He was there married, Feb. 10, 1820, to Nancy Wilcockson. They had one child in Bath county, and moved to Sangamon county, Ill., arriving in the fall of 1821, in what is now Fancy Creek township, where one child was born. Of their two children—

WILLIAM D., born May 2, 1821, in Bath county, Ky., brought by his parents to Sangamon county the same year, and was married, Jan. 6, 1843, to Nancy J. Barnett. They had five children, namely: ARMINTA L., born Oct. 8, 1843, married, March 3, 1869, to Joel Dalbey, who was born August 28, 1829, in Pickaway county, Ohio. They had one child, JENNIE EMELINE. She died in the spring of 1875, and Mr. and Mrs. Dalbey live in Springfield, Illinois. JAMES L., born May 4, 1847, died in infancy. GEORGE D., born May 14, 1851, married, Oct. 25, 1871, to Eliza J. Dunlap. They have one child, WILLIAM D., Jun., and live near Cantrall, Illinois. MARY E. and WILLIAM E. live with their mother. William D. Power was elected County Judge in 1857, re-elected in 1861, served until March 2, 1863, when he died in office. His widow and children reside in Springfield, Illinois.

JAMES E., born Dec. 1, 1824, in Sangamon county, is unmarried, and resides with his parents, near Cantrall, Illinois.

George Power and his wife now—1876 —reside near Cantrall, Sangamon county, Illinois, where he settled in 1821. He has held civil and military offices, among which are the following: Commission from Governor Ninian Edwards, dated Sept. 15, 1827, as Major of the 25th Reg. Illinois Inf., under the old military laws. He was commissioned, June 4, 1831, by Gov. Reynolds, as 2nd Lieut. of a company of mounted volunteers, in the Black Hawk war. He has an old commission as justice of the peace, from Gov. Edwards, dated July 25, 1828. For the same office from Gov. Reynolds, Sept. 3, 1831. From Gov. Joseph Duncan, Aug. 27, 1835. From Gov. Thomas Carlin, Aug. 27, 1839. From Gov. Thos. Ford, Aug. 14, 1843; the whole covering a period of nineteen years, as justice of the peace. He built the first frame house in Sangamon county north of the Sangamon river. He commenced business in Sangamon county with a total cash capital of five dollars. He has now a stock farm in one body of two thousand acres. His family vault cost five thousand dollars, is situated on the farm where he resides. It was built soon after the death of his son, Judge William D. Power. His remains were the first placed in it.

POWELL, ABEL, was born June 28, 1785, in Virginia. He was married in Bath county, Ky., Sept. 13, 1806, to Dorothy Mitts. They emigrated to Pickaway county, Ohio, where two children were born, and moved to Sangamon county, Ill., arriving June 27, 1828, in what is now Fancy Creek township. Of his two children—

HIRAM, born June 22, 1807, married Lucy L. Willcoxon.

MAHALA, born April 5, 1809, married A. J. Hornback.

JAMES M. LEVEL, came with Mr. Powell to Sangamon county. See his name.

Abel Powell died March 8, 1836. His widow died Feb. 7, 1858, both on the farm where they settled in 1828, near Cantrall, Illinois.

PRENTICE.—The Prentice family in Illinois descended from Thomas Prentice and Grace, his wife, who came from England in 1648. There is a tradition in the family that he served in the army of the Commonwealth, and was one of Oliver Cromwell's Life Guard. However that may be, soon after he came to this country, "in 1656, he was chosen Lieutenant of a troop of horse, and chosen Captain in 1662." The brilliant exploits of the "old trooper" are fully recorded in Hubbard's history of the early Indian wars. He settled in Newton, Massachusetts, and died there in 1709. The stone is still there which marks his grave, and bears the following inscription: "Here lies ye body of Capt. Thomas Prentice, dec'd July ye 7th, 1709, in ye 89th year of his age." His death was caused by a fall from his horse, while returning from church on Sunday. Capt. Thomas Prentice and his wife, Grace, had eight children, one of whom was Thomas Prentice, Jun., who was born in Newton, Mass., Nov. 11, 1649, and who married Sarah Stanton, Jan. 1, 1675. They had four children, one of whom was Samuel, who was born in 1680. He married Esther Hammond, and in 1709 moved to Stonington, Conn. They had nine children, one of whom was Samuel Prentice, Jun., who was born Nov. 25, 1702. He married Abigail ———. They had thirteen children, one of whom was Amos, who was born April 24, 1748, and who married Anna Owen. He was a physician, and was for some time Surgeon in the Revolutionary army. He resided in New London, Conn., at the time that town was burned by the traitor, Arnold, and lost his residence, drug store, and very near all he had, by that act of vandalism. After the close of the war he removed to Milltown, on the Susquehanna river, near the spot where the little city of Waverly, N. Y., now stands, and died there, July 19, 1805. Dr. Amos Prentice and his wife, Anna, had five children, one of whom was John Owen Prentice, who was born in Groton, Conn. Dec. 25, 1776. He married Rachel Swain in 1799, emigrated to St. Clair county, Ill., in 1816, and died at his residence, at Cold Spring, Shelby county, Jan. 1, 1838, leaving seven children. The following are their names, with the dates of birth: Charles, born in 1800; Owen, in 1802; Amos, in 1804; Harriet, in 1809; Julia, in 1814; William Swain, in 1819; and James B., in 1821. We will continue the history of but one member of this family:—

PRENTICE, WILLIAM SWAIN, was born May 21, 1819, in St. Clair county, Illinois, moved with his father to Hillsboro, in 1827, and in 1829 to Shelby county, both in the same State. In 1836 he was employed by his brother, Col. Charles Prentice, who was Register of the Land Office at Vandalia. After the death of his brother Charles, in 1837, he was employed as chief clerk in the office of the Auditor of Public Accounts, and removed with the seat of government of the State of Ill., from Vandalia to Springfield, in 1839. Wm. S. Prentice was married in 1842, in Springfield, to Martha A. Wash, sister to Milton H. Wash. *See his name.* She was born Jan. 8, 1823, near Russelville, Logan county, Ky. Mr. and Mrs. Prentice had six children, namely—

OWEN D., born Sept. 21, 1844, at Cold Spring, Shelby county, Ill., and raised principally in Springfield.

ELLEN, born March 25, 1848, in Shelbyville, Ill., was married May 6, 1868, in Springfield, to Albert E. Peppers. They have two children, LULA and ALBERT PRENTICE, and reside in Detroit, Michigan.

HIRAM B., born May 21, 1853, in Paris, Ill., is now—1876—clerk in the United States Pension Office, in Springfield, Illinois.

LAURA, born May 19, 1858, in Springfield, resides with her parents.

WILLIAM C., born June 18, 1863, died Jan. 3, 1869.

LIZZIE M., born Sept. 5, 1866, in Springfield, lives with her parents.

In 1849 Wm. S. Prentice entered the ministry, in connection with the Methodist Episcopal church. He spent two years preaching at Paris, two years at Danville, two years at Carlinville, one year at Quincy, and one year at Jacksonville, all in Illinois. In the autumn of 1857 he was appointed Presiding Elder of Springfield District, where he served one term of four years. He was then four years Presiding Elder of Jacksonville District, three years pastor of the Second M. E. church of Springfield, and again four years as Presiding Elder of Springfield District. He is now—1876—near the close of a four years term as Presiding Elder of the Decatur District. Rev. Mr. Prentice was a delegate from Central Illinois Conference to the General Conference of the M. E. church, which convened in Buffalo, N. Y., in 1860. He was again a delegate to the General Conference that assembled in Brooklyn, N. Y., in May, 1872; also to the General Conference at Baltimore, Md., in May, 1876. He received the honorary degree of D. D. from the Illinois Wesleyan University, in Bloomington, June, 1876.

From the time Rev. Wm. S. Prentice became Presiding Elder in 1857, his home has been, and is now, in the city of Springfield, Illinois.—August, 1876.

PRESTON, EBENEZER, was born in 1786, in Cape May county, N. J. Mahala Tomlin was born April 7, 1789, in the same county. They were there married, about 1809, and had nine living children in New Jersey. The family moved to Sangamon county, Ill., arriving Oct. 16, 1839, on Richland creek. Of their nine children—

RICHARD was a navigator, never married, and little is known of him since the family came west.

DAVID married Amelia Corson in New Jersey, came to Sangamon county, raised a family, and moved to Carroll county, Missouri.

EBENEZER, Jun., born May 14, 1821, in New Jersey, married February 15, 1849, in Sangamon county, to Catharine Greene, who was born September 22, 1827, in Greene county, Ill. They have two living children—ALMEDA married Robert Corson, have two children, MINNIE B. and CYNTHIA C., and live in Cartwright township. JULIA A. lives with her parents, three miles northwest of Pleasant Plains, Sangamon county, Illinois.—1874.

ELIZABETH married David Wright. He died, Oct., 1870, leaving a widow and four children, five miles north of Illiopolis, Sangamon county, Illinois.

WILLIAM, born July 26, 1827, married in Sangamon county to Margaret Hatch, have seven children, and live in Mason county, Illinois.

SARAH married Haythorn Tomlin, have five children, and live in Mason county, Illinois.

ROBERT married Mary Henderson, have three children, and live in Mason county, Illinois.

LYDIA married Jeremiah Corson, have two children, and lives in Mason county, Illinois.

OTHNEIL died, in 1855, in Mason county, aged eighteen years.

Ebenezer Preston died May 10, 1849, and his widow died Feb. 17, 1872, he in Sangamon, and she in Mason county, Illinois.

PRICKETT, DAVID, was born Sept. 21, 1800, in Franklin county, Georgia, and came to Edwardsville, Madison county, Ill., in 1816. He graduated in the law department of Transylvania University, at Lexington, Ky., in his twenty-first year, and was admitted to practice at Edwardsville, Nov. 15, 1821. He was Judge of the probate court of Madison county, and in 1826 was elected to the General Assembly of Illinois, at Vandalia. In 1831 he was aid-de-camp to Gen. John D. Whitesides, in the Black Hawk war. David Prickett was married Jan. 24, 1834, at Tremont, Tazewell county, Ill., to Charlotte G. Griffith, who was born May 9, 1806, in Chester county, Penn. She was a sister to Mrs. Hannah G. Opkycke, and daughter of Dr. Thomas Griffith, of Tremont, who was formerly of Pennsylvania. Mr. and Mrs. Prickett moved to Springfield, Ill., in 1835. They had five children, all born in Springfield. Susan, the youngest, died in infancy. Of the other four—

CHRISTINA G., resides in Springfield, with her mother.

THOMAS G., born in Springfield, was elected city attorney three times, was elected alderman from the third ward, is now—1876—a member of the city council, is a practicing lawyer, and resides with his mother in Springfield, Illinois.

GIBSON R. and *HANNAH O.* live with their mother.

David Prickett died March, 1847, and Mrs. Charlotte G. Prickett resides in Springfield, Illinois.

Hon. David Prickett was the first reporter to the Supreme Court of Illinois, having been appointed to that office as soon as it was created. He was elected, by the General Assembly, State's Attorney for the judicial circuit of Illinois in 1837. In 1840 he was Treasurer of the Board of Commissioners of the Illinois and Michigan Canal. In 1842 he was appointed a director of the State Bank of Illinois, on behalf of the State. He was assistant clerk of the House of Representatives of Illinois at the time of his death. He was a man whose integrity was above suspicion, very genial, rich in anecdote, addicted to witticisms, frequently pointing them against himself. Every public man of Illinois knew him to speak kindly of him.

PRIEST, JOHN W., was born Oct. 18, 1809, in Pomfret, Windsor county, Vermont. He was taken, in 1816, by his parents, to Parishville, St. Lawrence county, N. Y., where he was married, Aug. 27, 1835, to Alice Wakefield. They moved at once to Montgomery, Alabama, and in the fall of 1836 to Columbus, Miss., where he engaged in the manufacture and sale of tin ware. Mrs. Priest died there, May 14, 1840, leaving one child:

FRANKLIN G., who died in his fourth year.

Mr. Priest came to Springfield, Illinois, in June, 1840, and was married, March 30, 1845, to Lucinda M., daughter of Caleb Stafford, of Rochester, Ill. They had four children, two of whom died young—

OLIVE L., born in Springfield, married, in 1867, to George C. Latham. See his name.

MARY E., resides with her father.

Mrs. Lucinda M. Priest died Sept. 10, 1851, and John W. Priest was married, Sept., 1853, to Catharine Wright, a native of St. Lawrence county, N. Y. She died July 9, 1875.

Hon. John W. Priest was elected eight successive years, alderman of the city, was several years President of the city School Board, and is now President of the Board of Water Works Commissioners. He was elected Mayor of Springfield for three successive years, 1856, '57 and '58, and again in 1870. He is now keeping a stove and tin ware store, in Springfield, Illinois.

PRIMM, JOHN, was born July 25, 1780, in Stafford county, Va. When a young man he went to what became St. Clair county, Ill., and was there married, Oct. 10, 1809, to Ruth Cox, who was born March 9, 1783, in Delaware, and came to Monroe county, Ill., with her parents in 1808. They had five children in Monroe county, and moved to Sangamon county, arriving May 1, 1820, in what is now Fancy Creek township, where two children were born. Of their seven children—

ELIZABETH, born Oct. 14, 1810, married in 1828, in Sangamon county, to Christopher Hussey. See his name. He died, and she married Wm. B. Preston. They had six children. Mr. Preston died, and the widow married Lyman Olds. She died in Middletown, Logan county, in 1869 or '70.

MARY, born Sept., 1812, married in Sangamon county, Nov. 30, 1829, to Isaac Preston. They had six children, and Mr. Preston died, and she married Felix Green. He died, and she married David Lee, had one child, and Mr. Lee died. She lives in Logan county, Illinois.

ELISHA, been Oct. 24, 1814, in Monroe county, Ill., married in Sangamon county, Sept. 19, 1837, to Lucinda C. Glascock. She was born August 12, 1819, in Fauquier county, Va. They have one child, SUSAN, who married Wm. L. Rankin, being his second wife. They have five children, ANNIE M., GEORGE M., WILLIAM, LEWIS T. and LUCINDA, and live in Menard county, near Athens, Ill. Elisha Primm and his wife reside in Menard county, three miles southwest of Cantrall, Sangamon county, Illinois.

ENOCH, born August 2, 1816, in that part of Monroe which is now part of St. Clair county, came to Sangamon county with his parents. He was married May 23, 1839, to Lucinda ———. They had fourteen children; two died under five years. MARY H. lives with her parents. BENJAMIN F. married Martha Crowder. They have two children, and live near Longton, Elk county, Kansas. EMILY J. married William T. Hutchinson. They have three children, and live in Petersburg, Ill. MARGARET E. married D. A. Rankin, has three children, and lives at Tallula, Illinois. FRANCES E. married H. H. Irwin, had one child, and Mrs. Frances E. Irwin died Nov. 12, 1873. Mr. Irwin lives in Menard county, Ill. AMANDA lives with her parents. ROBERT L. died Dec. 4, 1873. JOHN Q., ELVIRA E., THEOPHILUS B. and WILLIE reside with their father. Mrs. Lucinda R. Primm died March 4, 1874, and Enoch Primm resides in Menard county, northeast of Pleasant Plains, Illinois.

SUSAN, born Sept., 1818, married Feb. 24, 1848, to James Henton; have seven or eight children, and live in Kansas.

JOHN H., born June 15, 1820, married Jan., 1848, to Mary A. King, have three children, and reside in Menard county, four miles southwest of Cantrall, Illinois.

ELIJAH S., born Oct. 27, 1822, in Sangamon county, married August 20, 1844, in McLean county, to Mary E. Glascock. They had two children, JOSEPH H. died Jan. 30, 1863, in his eighteenth year. ELIJAH S., Jun., born June 20, 1847, married April 5, 1866, to Alice M. Myers, who was born Oct. 8, 1846, in Licking county, Ohio. They have three children, JOSEPH T., JAMES E., and FREDERICK, and live in Menard county, within two hundred yards of the Sangamon line, and two and a half miles southwest of Cantrall, Ill. Elijah S. Primm died Feb. 25, 1847, three months before the birth of his son, of the same name. His widow married Oct. 3, 1850, to James Driskell. They had three children. MARGARET A. married William F. Lake. See his name. They have one child, OLIVE MAY, and reside in Logan county. JAMES E. lives with his uncle, Thomas Glascock, and MARY L., with her aunt, Lucinda C. Primm. Mrs. Mary E. Driskell died April 20, 1858, and James Driskell died Nov., 1862.

John Primm died August 9, 1848, where he settled in 1820, and his widow died Feb. 3, 1856, at the house of her son, Elisha.

When Elisha Primm was married, his wife remembers that they bought a feather bed for seventy-five cents per pound, and paid for it by selling corn at ten cents per bushel. They sold bacon for three cents per pound, and at the same time bought calico for forty cents per yard. More recently they sold bacon for forty cents per pound. Mr. Primm has sold pork, neatly dressed, in Springfield, for one dollar and fifty cents per one hundred pounds, and has sold the same quality at fourteen dollars per hundred. For his account of cotton raising in Sangamon county. See page 73.

PRIMM, THOMAS, was born May 11, 1782, in Stafford county, Va., moved with his father's family, in 1801, to St. Clair county. Elizabeth Stallions was born Aug. 19, 1792, in Wheeling, Va. Her parents moved to St. Clair county, Ill., arriving May 13, 1796, at Whiteside station. Thos. Primm and Elizabeth Stallions were there married, Mar. 12, 1807. She was less than fifteen years old. They had six living children in that county. The family moved to Sangamon county, arriving Oct. 8, 1820, where three children were born. Of their nine children—

WILLIAM, born Jan. 11, 1808, in St. Clair county, married in Sangamon county to Maria Canterbury. They had seven children—ASA C. married Fidelia Hall, who died, in 1859, leaving two children, and he married Mrs. Mary A. Ryker, whose maiden name was Moore. They have four children, and live in Bourbon county, Kansas. MARGARET J. married, in 1866, to Wm. Warfield. They have two children, and live in McLean county, Illinois. WILLIAM H. enlisted in Aug., 1862, in Co. C, 114th Ill. Inf., served full term, and was honorably discharged. He was married to Catharine Perrine, have two children, and live in Lucas county, Iowa. THOMAS N. enlisted Aug. 3, 1861, in Co. F, 28th Ill. Inf., for three years, served more than full term, and was honorably discharged. He was married to Adelia Perrine, had two children, one died, aged six years. They live in Lucas county, Iowa. ISAAC H. married Ann M. Roberts. They have two children, MAGGIE M. and ELVIRA M., and live one mile east of Athens, and three miles north of Cantrall, Illinois. Mrs. Maria Primm died April 30, 1872, and William Primm lives three-quarters of a miles southeast of Athens, Illinois.

JAMES, born Sept. 4, 1809, in St. Clair county, married Maria Russell, who was born at Harper's Ferry, Va. They had nine children, five of whom only are living. THOMAS F. and JOHN J. were Union soldiers in an Illinois regiment, and live with their mother. EDWARD T., WILLIAM R. and RUTH E. live with their mother. James Primm died, Jan. 4, 1872, and his widow and children live two and one-half miles south of Lincoln, Logan county, Illinois.

ABRAHAM S., born Dec. 25, 1812, in St. Clair county, raised in Sangamon county, married, June 18, 1839, to Lucinda Hall, who was born April 28, 1820, in Ohio, opposite Guyandotte, Va. They had eleven children, six of whom died under five years. Of the other five—MARY married Henry Cline. See his name. MELISSA married Michael T. Hargrave, who was born March 17, 1842, in Guilford county, N. C. They have one child, LILLIE M., and live near Athens, Illinois. MINNIE E. married Andrew P. West, and live in Atlanta, Illinois. ROSE A. and LILLIE M. live with their parents, adjoining Athens, Illinois, on the northeast.—1874.

JOHN L., born Oct. 31, 1814, in St. Clair county, married Hannah M. Rankin. She died, August, 1846, leaving three children. He was married, Aug., 1847, to Mrs. Sinai Davis, whose maiden name was Allen. They have four children, and live two and one-half miles southeast of Lincoln, Illinois.

DANIEL C., born Jan. 3, 1817, in St. Clair county, married Elizabeth Tice. He died, Oct., 1864, leaving a widow and six children in Menard county, Illinois.

MARY A., born April 19, 1819, married Augustus Rankin, and died, Nov. 21, 1852, leaving one child in Logan county, Illinois.

THOMAS J., born Jan. 25, 1822. He has practiced medicine more than a quarter of a century, is unmarried, and lives in Athens, Illinois.—1874.

ELIZABETH, born Jan. 12, 1824, married George W. Cline. See his name. He died, and she married Jacob Barnsback, who died, in 1861, leaving a widow and four living children in Madison county, Illinois.

NINIAN E., born April 6, 1830, married Elizabeth Wood. He died, in 1857. His widow lives in Athens, Illinois.

Thomas Primm died May 14, 1856, and his widow, familiarly known as Aunt Betty Primm, lived with her son, Abraham S. Primm, near Athens, Illinois, until her death in 1871. She was eighty-three years old. Her recollection of early events was remarkably vivid. She remembered passing over the ground where Springfield stands when the grass was higher than her head as she sat on horseback. She carried a child on one arm and used the other to keep the grass out of her face, and lived to see that spot of land occupied by a city of more than twenty thousand inhabitants.

PROCTOR, SIMON L., born Jan. 12, 1793, in Shelby county, Ky. He was a soldier in the war of 1812, and was in the battle of Tippecanoe; was married in Nelson county, Ky., May 16, 1813, to Jane Seifers, who was born April 5, 1795, in that county. They had one child, and moved to Green county, Ind., where two children were born, and moved to Hardin county, where they had eight children, and from there to Sangamon county, Ill., arriving May 18, 1837, at Springfield. Three years later they moved to Lick creek, and in 1845 to what is now Cotton Hill township. Of their eleven children—

SARAH, born February 5, 1815, in Nelson county, Ky., married in Sangamon county, in 1846, to William Hays, who died, and she married Wm. George, who died, July, 1872, aged ninety-three years. She lives in Rochester, Illinois.

RICHARDSON H., born Oct. 28, 1816, in Indiana, married in Sangamon county to Elizabeth Young, had two children, and she died March, 1851, and he married Sibbie A. Young, had two children, and R. H. Proctor died, in 1858, at Springfield, Illinois.

MARGARET, born Oct. 7, 1818, in Green county, Ind., married in Sangamon county to John Williams, have a family, and live near Milton station, Mills county, Iowa.

ELIZABETH, born May 12, 1821, in Hardin county, Kentucky, married in Sangamon county to Stephen B. Neal. See his name.

JANE, born June 15, 1823, in Kentucky, died in Sangamon county, Oct. 10, 1850.

BARBARA, born May 12, 1825, in Hardin county, Ky., married in Sangamon county to Elisha T. Sanders. See his name.

SAMUEL C., born June 14, 1827, in Kentucky, married in Sangamon county to Dorcas A. Crowder, a daughter of Chandler Crowder. They had eight children, two only are living, MARY E. and JOHN. Mrs. Proctor died Jan. 9, 1869, and he died June 28, 1871. Samuel C. Proctor was ordained, May 16, 1868, as a minister of the gospel, at the Horse Creek Baptist church.

LOUISA, born July 4, 1828, in Kentucky, married in Sangamon county, Nov. 17, 1851, to Marion F. Greenawalt. They have seven children, and live near Rochester, Illinois.

LUCINDA, born Sept. 28, 1831, in Kentucky, married in Sangamon county to George W. Sanders. See his name.

BRYANT R. W., born May 11, 1834, in Kentucky, was drowned while bathing, in Sangamon county, June 28, 1851.

BENJAMIN K., born May 28, 1836, in Kentucky, raised in Sangamon county, enlisted July, 1862, in Co. K, 114th Ill. Inf., for three years, and died, Jan., 1864, at Pawnee, Ill., while at home on sick furlough.

Simon L. Proctor died Sept. 18, 1845, and his widow died June 14, 1853, both in Sangamon county.

PULLIAM, ROBERT, was born April 12, 1776, in Henry county, Va. His father, John Pulliam, emigrated to Kentucky when Robert was a boy, and the family moved from there to Illinois, arriving in 1796, in what was then called the New Design settlement, now a part of Monroe county. The next year they moved into a settlement in the district of St. Louis, in what was then locally known as "New Spain." They moved to Cape Girardeau, Missouri, and a few years later to Randolph county, Ill., near where the town of Red Bud now stands. In 1802 Robert Pulliam improved a farm a few miles east of Belleville, St. Clair county, and about 1803 he settled in the American Bottom, near the Bluff, six or seven miles below the present city of Alton. Mary Stout was born April 9, 1776, but the locality is not known. Robert Pulliam and Mary Stout were married Sept. 13, 1804. In 1815 they moved to St. Clair county, and in the fall of 1817, leaving his family in St. Clair county, he, with two or three hired men, and a woman by the name of Strickland—sister of one of the hired men—to cook for them, he came to Sugar creek and *built a cabin* in the timber, on the east side of the creek. The land is now owned by James Scott, and is situated nearly three-quarters of a mile west of a point ten and a half miles due south of Springfield, on a line with Sixth street. When the government survey was made it was found to be on the southwest quarter of section twenty-one, township fourteen north, range five west, and is now in Ball township. That is believed to have been, without doubt, the first habitation of any kind built by white men in what is now Sangamon county. Mr. Pulliam brought with him a herd of cattle and some horses. The growth of grass, which had been luxuriant for ages, afforded ample grazing when there was not any snow. When that covered the ground Mr. P. had the men cut down elm trees, and the stock would live on the buds until the snow passed away. The cabin was built in a forest, composed principally of sugar trees. As the spring approached, Mr. Pulliam put his men to work and made sugar. As the season advanced, and caused the grass to grow, he collected his horses and cattle and returned to his family in St. Clair county in the spring of 1818. He remained there until the spring of 1819, when he came, with all his family, back to Sugar creek, to find his cabin occupied by Zachariah Peter. *See his name.* Robert Pulliam had six children in Madison and St. Clair counties, namely—

NANCY, born July 26, 1805, in Madison county, married in Sangamon county to John Brownell. *See his name.*

MARTIN G., born Sept. 17, 1807, in Madison county, married in Sangamon county, Nov. 25, 1827, to Lucy Knotts. They had twelve children in Sangamon county, two of whom died young. THOMAS J. married Elizabeth McLaughlin, and resides in Girard, Macoupin county, Ill. ROBERT L. married Rebecca Wilson, and lives in Iowa. SARAH married Basil Brawner. *See his name.* They live in Iowa. GEORGE S. married Ellen Knotts, has a family of children, and lives in Ball township, within three-quarters of a mile of where his grandfather built the first house in the county. His postoffice is Chatham, Ill. MARTIN H. died unmarried, in Iowa, aged twenty-four years. JOSEPH O. married Sarah A. Stewart, and lives in Iowa. DOROTHY is unmarried, and lives near Chatham, Ill. MARY E. married Harvey Hegler, and lives near Virden, Ill. CHARLES M. is unmarried, and lives near Chatham, Ill. Martin G. Pulliam died in June, 1872, and his widow, Mrs. Lucy Pulliam, resides with her son, George S., in Ball township, near Chatham, Sangamon county, Illinois.—1874.

IRWIN S., born Sept. 12, 1811, in Madison county, Illinois, married in Sangamon county, Dec. 18, 1834, to Matilda Nuckolls, who was born in Grayson county, Va., Nov. 16, 1813. They had nine children in Sangamon county, namely: JOHN R., born Jan. 2, 1836. He enlisted, May, 1864, for one hundred days, served full time and one month over, and was honorably discharged. He is unmarried, and lives in Ball township, four miles southeast of Chatham, Sangamon county, Ill. MARY A., born August 19, 1837, married Benjamin H. Taylor, who was born Oct. 2, 1835, in Morgan county, Ill. They have two children, EDWARD C. and WILLIAM SHERMAN, and live in Pawnee township, six miles east of Auburn, Ill. Benjamin H. Taylor enlisted August 2, 1861, in Co. B, 30th Ill. Inf., served two years, was wounded, suffered amputation of a leg twice, and was honorably discharged August 7, 1863. JAMES H., born Nov. 6, 1839, enlisted Aug., 1862, in Co. B, 114th Ill. Inf., for three years, and was captured at the battle of Guntown, June, 1864. On the 18th of that month he was imprisoned at Andersonville, and was released April 28, 1865, by the collapse of the rebellion. After returning home he was honorably discharged. His weight, in health, was from one hundred and sixty-five to one hundred and seventy-five pounds. When he reached home, one month after his discharge, he weighed one hundred and twenty pounds. He was not sick a day, but the loss of flesh and muscle was wholly caused by starvation. James H. Pulliam unites with R. F. Fletcher in confirming the statement made by Stephen Bell about the breaking out of a spring in Andersonville prison. *See name of Bell.* Mr. Pulliam was married Nov. 26, 1868, to Addie Fairbanks. They had one child, ORA V., and Mrs. Addie Pulliam died

March 25, 1870. James H. Pulliam was married March 4, 1873, to Lydia Shellhouse, and lives now—1876—in Ball township, at his grandfather's old homestead, not where he built the first cabin, but the second. MARGARET J. died young. CHARLES IRWIN, born August 22, 1844, was married Nov. 19, 1872, to Emily J. Drennan, and lives in Pawnee township, five miles east of Auburn. GEORGE W., born March 31, 1847, was killed by a kick from a horse, aged five years. THOMAS J., born Oct. 27, 1849, lives at the family homestead. WILLIAM S., born April 3, 1852, lost his right hand by being crushed in a corn mill when a boy. He lives at the homestead with his brother, Charles I. FRANCIS M., born Sept. 16, 1858, lives at the homestead. Irwin S. Pulliam died May 8, 1869, and his widow resides with her son, Charles I., at the family homestead in Pawnee township, five miles east of Auburn, Sangamon county, Illinois.

MARY, born Oct. 7, 1814, in Madison county, married in Sangamon county, April 19, 1835, to Ludwell P. Fariss. They had four children, and both died at Mt. Pleasant, Iowa. One of the daughters is now the wife of Dr. McBride, of Decatur, Illinois.

MARGARET, born Oct. 13, 1816, in St. Clair county, married in Sangamon county to Samuel Peter, a son of Zachariah. She died at Winterset, Iowa, leaving four children, namely: ELIZABETH, NANCY J., WILLIAM and JOHN.

GEORGE W., born Sept. 12, 1822, in Sangamon county, died June 18, 1872, after having been thirty years an invalid, though the immediate cause of his death was being thrown from a wagon by a runaway team. He lived with his brother, Irwin S., until the death of the latter, and remained with the family until his own death.

Robert Pulliam died July 31, 1838, seven miles south of Carlinville, in Macoupin county. His widow died July 1, 1847, in Sangamon county, Illinois.

A paper was prepared by Gov. John Reynolds, to be read at the first old settlers' meeting in Sangamon county, in 1859. In that paper Gov. Reynolds related some incidents in the life of Robert Pulliam. It was not read, as intended, but came into my hands. It is known to all the old settlers that Mr. Pulliam wore an artificial leg. Gov. Reynolds says that one of Mr. Pulliam's legs became diseased, and in the summer of 1808 it was found to be absolutely necessary to amputate it in order to save his life. Dr. Tuthill, of Cahokia, performed the operation. The Governor says: "I resided with my father in the neighborhood of Mr. Pulliam, and knew the circumstances of the amputation. The patient possessed such courage that he held his body as firm as a rock, without assistance, during the operation. I presume this was the first amputation of a limb that occurred in Illinois, and at that time was considered a surgical operation almost superhuman." Gov. Reynolds describes Mr. Pulliam as a man of fine proportions and perfect physical development. He says the circumstances of his life prevented his obtaining an education from books, to any considerable extent, but his natural good sense and opportunities for studying men, enabled him to hold a place in the front rank of business men of that time. He was fond of the rude sports of the times; such as horse racing, hunting, and games of various kinds, but later in life he felt that the example was injurious, and changed his course. He first united with the Baptist church, and then, for greater convenience, connected himself with the Methodist church, and his wife did the same. They continued in its communion to the end of their lives. Mr. Pulliam understood the advantages of improved machinery, and endeavored to introduce it into the settlement whenever it was practicable. He was one of the earliest to build a mill in the county. It was run by tread wheel, and the motive power was either horses or oxen. All the early settlers raised cotton quite extensively, and he was one of the first, if not *the* first, to introduce a cotton gin into the settlement.

PURVIANCE, JOHN, was born June 19, 1760. The place of his birth is not known, but he went from Pennsylvania to the vicinity of Concord, Cabarras county, North Carolina. He was a soldier in the colonial army that achieved American Independence, but whether he went from Pennsylvania or North Carolina is not known. John Pur-

viance and Nancy Ferguson were married and had three sons and three daughters in North Carolina, namely—
DAVID SIMPSON, ALEXANDER C., JOHN G., ELIZABETH, MATILDA and MARGARET.

Mrs. Nancy Purviance died, and he married Elizabeth Lisenby. They had two sons and two daughter—
JAMES, SAMUEL, NANCY and ELIZA.

All except one of his children—who married and died in North Carolina—came to Sangamon county, and their histories are given each as the head of a family of early settlers. He came to Sangamon county after nearly all his children were settled here, and died Sept. 27, 1833. His remains were buried at Richland Baptist church, in Cartwright township. From the earliest records in some branches of the family in this county, I found the name spelled as it is at the head of this sketch, but they have very generally permitted it to be changed to Purvines, probably because without precision in speaking the original name, the sound would be that produced by the modern spelling which is now adopted by all the descendants in Illinois, as follows:

PURVINES, DAVID SIMPSON, was born May 18, 1787, in Cabarras county, N. C. Elizabeth Weddington was born Dec. 25, 1790. They were married, and had three children in North Carolina, and the family moved to Richland creek, in what became Sangamon county, and Cartwright township, arriving in the fall of 1820, where they had five children. Of their seven children—

JOHN L., born Feb. 6, 1814, in North Carolina, married in Sangamon county to Elizabeth Earnest. They had two children—HENRY married Jane Thompson, and lives near Clinton, DeWitt county, Illinois. JOHN died, at twenty years of age. John L. Purvines died, Jan. 6, 1842, in Sangamon county. His widow has been twice married, since, is now a widow—1873—and lives near Clinton, Illinois.

MATILDA, born May 3, 1816, in Cabarras county, N. C., brought up in Sangamon county, married Madison A. Cartwright. See his name.

WILLIAM H., born Dec. 13, 1819, in North Carolina, married Feb. 25, 1847, in Sangamon county, to Frances A. Harrison. They had four children—ALFRED B., born May 11, 1848, married, Sept. 13, 1870, to Nannie C. Martin, who was born Nov. 27, 1850, in Robertson county, Tenn. They have one child, LEVI PERRY, and live two and one-half miles northeast of Pleasant Plains—1873. PEYTON A. lives with his mother. SARAH E. married Henry Welland, has one child, HARRY A., and lives one mile west of Pleasant Plains, Illinois. WILLIAM H., Jun., lives with his mother. William H. Purvines died, Sept. 25, 1855, and his widow married Wm. H. Harrison. They had one child, FIELDING T., who lives with his mother, one and one-half miles west of Pleasant Plains, Illinois.

SAMUEL F., born March 24, 1822, in Sangamon county, married April 16, 1845, to Elizabeth Bryant, and had two sons. CHARLES married Miss McAtee, and lives at Greenview, Menard county, Illinois. JOHN lives with his mother. Samuel F. Purvines died July 22, 1849. His widow has been twice married, and lives in Iowa or Kansas.—1873.

NATHAN S., born March 3, 1829, in Sangamon county, married, Dec. 6, 1849, to Wealthy M. J. Harrison. They had seven children, one died in infancy. EMILY F., born Oct. 13, 1850, married Feb. 25, 1868, to Wm. Fletcher Correll. See his name. JOHN Q., NORMAN M., ELIZABETH P., PEYTON L. and NATHAN L., reside with their parents, near Pleasant Plains, Sangamon county, Illinois.

DAVID P., born Jan. 17, 1832, in Sangamon county, married, May 20, 1852, to Amanda Crafton. She died, Aug. 29, 1865, and he lives in Springfield, Illinois—1873.

David Simpson Purvines died March 14, 1852, and his widow died Jan. 6, 1872, both in Cartwright township, Sangamon county, Illinois.

PURVINES, ALEXANDER C., born March 16, 1794, in Cabarras county, N. C., married Margaret Weddington, and had one child there. They moved to what became Sangamon county, Ill., arriving in 1819, and settled on Richland creek, where they had three children—

ALFRED B., born Oct. 25, 1818, in North Carolina, died in Sangamon county March 11, 1839.

JOHN W., born Oct. 25, 1821, in Sangamon county, died, aged twenty-three years.

ELIZABETH J., born June 23, 1824, in Sangamon county, married John C. Bone. She had one child, ALMEDA J., who married Robert P. Harrison. See his name. Mrs. E. J. Bone died in 1852.

ORAMEL G. L., born Nov. 10, 1826, in Sangamon county, married, February 4, 1862, to Louisa Potter. They have two children, MARY E. and ELIJAH A., and live in Menard county, three miles northeast of Pleasant Plains, Illinois.

Mrs. Margaret Purvines died January, 1831, and Alex. C. Purvines married, Oct., 1831, to Mrs. Jane Hamilton, whose maiden name was Coleman. They had eight children—

MARGARET A., born Sept. 5, 1832, married Abraham J. Duff, have six children, and live in Logan county, Illinois.

WILLIAM G., born Sept. 3, 1834, married Emily F. Eaton. They have four children, VIOLA, LOREN, ALICE and CARROLL, and reside one and three-quarter miles northeast of Pleasant Plains, Illinois.

NANCY S., born Aug. 9, 1836, died, aged sixteen years.

SARAH A., born July 17, 1838, married Samuel H. Armstrong, and lives in Menard county, Illinois.

ALEXANDER J., born August 3, 1840, married Susan Jones. They have seven children, and live in Iroquois county, Illinois.

ITHA L., born Sept. 12, 1843, married E. L. Bone, have five children, and live in Menard county, Illinois.

JAMES O. and

EDGAR C. live with their mother.

Alexander C. Purvines died July 16, 1861, from injuries received by being thrown from a wagon, by a runaway team. His widow, Mrs. Jane Purvines, resides one and one-half miles northeast of Pleasant Plains, Sangamon county, Illinois.—1873.

PURVINES, JOHN G., born July 8, 1796, in Cabarras county, N. C., came to Sangamon county, when a young man, with his brother Simpson, or Alex. C., and was married, Jan. 1, 1823, to Elizabeth Coleman. They had ten children in Sangamon county, namely—

EVAN E., born Sept. 30, 1823, died at seventeen years of age, caused by a runaway ox team.

NANCY M., born Oct. 20, 1824, married Hiram Stevens, has two living children, LOUISA F. and WILLIAM H. and live at Pleasant Plains, Illinois.

JOHN R., born Jan. 10, 1827, married Mary Coleman, had four children, and Mrs. Purvines died. His children, JOHN G., DAVID S., NOAH G. and MARSIA J. live in Sangamon county. J. R. Purvines lives in Crawford county, Missouri.

WILLIAM H., born Feb. 19, 1829. He was killed, in his twenty-fifth year, by the accidental discharge of a gun.

FRANCIS M., born June 28, 1831, married Lucretia J. Trask, had three children, and she died, and he married Mrs. Lucinda Coleman, whose maiden name was Walton. They had seven children, and live in Missouri.

CORNELIUS C., born Oct. 26, 1833, married, Nov. 22, 1855, to Martha E. Irwin, born Feb. 27, 1837. They had seven children, AZRO A., CHARLES R., CHURCHILL G., LOLA J., LEWIS C., MARY E. and WILLIAM H., and live near Loami, Illinois. Elder C. C. Purvines is pastor of Liberty Baptist church.—1874.

JAMES A., born July 23, 1835, married Margaret S. Purvines. He died, leaving two children. His widow married David Crezy, and lives in Nebraska City, Nebraska.

ALEXANDER F., born June 11, 1839, in Sangamon county, married, May 7, 1868, to Margaret S. Duncan, and have one child, GILBERT C. Dr. A. F. Purvines is a practicing physician, at Salisbury, Sangamon county, Illinois.

JOSHUA C., born June 9, 1842.

MARCIA A., born Jan. 11, 1846, married, Sept. 18, 1864, to John W. Foley. See his name.

John G. Purvines died Jan. 1, 1863, in Sangamon county, on the fortieth anniversary of his marriage, and his widow lives with her son-in-law Foley, at Pleasant Plains, Illinois.—1874.

PURVINES, ELIZABETH, born in Cabarras county, North Carolina, married John H. Plunkett. See his name.

PURVINES, MATILDA, born in North Carolina, married Samuel Irwin. See his name. She died in North Carolina.

PURVINES, MARGARET, born in North Carolina, married William Irwin. See his name.

PURVINES, JAMES, born about 1798, in Cabarras county, N. C., came to Sangamon county when a young man, married in Morgan county to Mary Cox, had eight children, moved to Bonaparte, Iowa, and died there.

PURVINES, SAMUEL, was born Aug. 1, 1801, in Cabarras county, N. C., came to Sangamon county, when a young man, and was married to Mary Irwin, daughter of Samuel L. Irwin. See his name. They had eight children in Sangamon county—

TABITHA JANE, born Dec. 18, 1827, married Robert F. Hamilton. See his name.

LYDIA A., born Jan. 16, 1831, married, March, 1854, to John C. Bone. They had one child, MARY E., who married in Springfield, July, 1875, to Thomas Long, a native of Morgan county. They live in Chicago. Mrs. Lydia A. Bone died Aug., 1862.

ACHILLES NEWTON, born Dec. 1, 1832, in Sangamon county, enlisted Aug. 8, 1862, for three years, in Co. F, 114th Ill. Inf., was appointed Orderly Sergt., Oct. 1, 1863, was wounded in the left ankle, at the battle of Guntown, Miss., June 10, 1864, but escaped capture, served to the end of the rebellion, and was honorably discharged, Aug. 3, 1865. He is unmarried—1873—and lives near Pleasant Plains, Illinois.

ELIZABETH M., born July 23, 1834, married, Feb. 18, 1861, to Thomas E. White, who was born June 13, 1832, in Bond county, Illinois. They have two children, LOLA A. and ROBERT E., and reside near Pleasant Plains, Sangamon county, Illinois.

NANCY F., born Dec. 6, 1836, in Sangamon county, married, Feb. 4, 1864, to John C. Bone. They had four children—JOHN C., Jun., died young. CHARLES R., CARRIE A. and OR-

LENA S. live with their parents. John C. Bone was born Sept. 7, 1817, in Rutherford county, Tenn., brought by his father to Sangamon county, who after a short stay moved to Rock creek, Menard county. J. C. Bone has been married four times: first to Catherine S. Foster, who died March 25, 1841. See Constantine Foster. Second, Elizabeth J. Purvines, who died August, 1852. See Alexander C. Purvines. Third, Lydia Ann Purvines, who died August, 1862. See Samuel Purvines. Fourth, Nancy F. Purvines, his present wife. John C. Bone has been a stock raiser and dealer all his life, in Sangamon and Menard counties. He moved to Chicago, in October, 1872, and is now—1876—in the live stock commission business, at the Union Stock Yards.

JOHN F., born April 6, 1839, in Sangamon county, married Francis J. Pirkins. They have two children, HATTIE B. and JESSIE E., and live in Cartwright township, near Richland station, Sangamon county, Illinois.—1873.

RACHEL M., born Aug. 25, 1840, married James S. Zane. See his name.

SAMUEL S., born Feb. 26, 1844, is unmarried—1873—and lives near Pleasant Plains, Illinois.

Samuel Purvines died Sept. 26, 1852, and in less than one month—Oct. 20, 1852—his widow died; both near Pleasant Plains, Sangamon county, Illinois.

PURVINES, NANCY, born in North Carolina, married in Sangamon county to Peter Shepherd, and lives near Quincy, Adams county, Illinois.

PURVINES, ELIZA, born in North Carolina, married in Sangamon county to Peter Lanterman. See his name.

PURVINES, JAMES S., was born Dec. 18, 1805, in Cabarras county, North Carolina. He was a cousin to David S., Alexander C., John G., etc., and came with some of his relatives to Sangamon county in 1820 or '21. After remaining six years he returned to North Carolina, visited some of his brothers and sisters in Georgia, and at the end of one year came back to Sangamon county. James S. Purvines was married in the fall of 1829 to Mary Ann Hughes, of Morgan county, Ill. They had eight children, namely—

GEORGE C., died, aged twenty years.

JOHN G. was drowned at nine years of age.

WILLIAM B. married Mrs. Mary Benner, whose maiden name was Foreman. They have one child, and live in Menard county, three miles northwest of Salisbury, Illinois.

FRANCIS M. married Permelia Wetherby, have one child, CARRIE, and live in Menard county, three and a half miles northwest of Salisbury, Sangamon county, Illinois.

MARGARET S. married James A. Purvines. See his name. He died, and she married David Crezy, has two children, and lives in Nebraska City, Neb.

ELVIRA married Alexander Carper, and lives near Nebraska City, Neb.

MARTHA J. married Isaac N. Ball, has three children, BENJAMIN, MAMIE and JAMES, and live in Menard county, three and a half miles northwest of Salisbury, Illinois.

ELIZABETH R. married George Anderson, and died.

Mrs. Mary A. Purvines died in 1849, and James S. Purvines married Martha Donovan, who died, in 1872, and he was married to Mrs. Harriet M. Harris, whose maiden name was Barzel, a native of Upper Canada. They reside in Menard county, three and a half miles northwest of Salisbury, Sangamon county, Illinois. —1873.

PURSELL, WILLIAM, was born Jan. 23, 1820, at White Park, near Belfast, Ireland. His parents emigrated to Bytown, now Ottawa City, Canada, in 1824. His mother died there, and he was taken to raise by Heraldus Eastabrook, of Vermont. He was brought by Mr. Eastabrook to Sangamon county, Ill., arriving at Old Sangamo, Oct. 25, 1833. William Pursell was married, Jan. 1, 1846, to Elizabeth Van Patten. They had thirteen children—

ROBERT H. died March 1, 1860, in his fourteenth year.

MARY A. died Jan 16, 1860, in her twelfth year.

ALBERT H. died Nov. 1, 1871, in his twenty-second year.

JENNIE ADA died Dec. 28, 1859, in her second year.

JOHN C. died Dec. 4, 1871, aged ten years.

The other eight children—
CARRIE L., LAURA E., ALICE B., CHARLES W., HATTIE L., ROBERT R., FANNIE E. and JESSIE T. live with their parents, three and three-quarters miles southwest of Farmingdale, Sangamon county, Illinois.

Mr. Pursell was present at the organization of the Sunday school in connection with Farmington Presbyterian church, in Dec., 1833. For forty years—until 1873—his connection with the school, as pupil, librarian, teacher and superintendent, continued unbroken. He is one of the substantial farmers of Sangamon county.

PYLE, NICHOLAS. The family came from England, and he was married in South Carolina, during the American Revolution, to Ann Black, a sister of Thomas Black. See his name. Some of their children were born in South Carolina, and the family moved on pack horses to Christian county, Ky., where more children were born, making a total of fourteen sons and five daughters, some of whom married in Kentucky. The parents and part of the children moved to St. Clair county, Ill., where some of the children married. The aged couple, with their two youngest sons, came to Sangamon county in 1825, and settled about three miles east of Auburn. Of the two sons—

THOMPSON, born about 1804, in Christian county, Ky., married in Sangamon county, in 1828, to Margaret Moffitt. They had nine living children. MATILDA, born Jan. 26, 1829, died Jan. 4, 1845. WM. ALFRED, born Nov. 13, 1830, is unmarried, and lives with his mother. SARAH ANN, born April 10, 1832, married Solomon Taylor, has five children, and resides in Macoupin county, near Zanesville, Montgomery county, Ill. ELIZABETH I., born Jan. 26, 1834, married Samuel H. Meteer, have three children, and live near May Postoffice, Martin county, Minn. GEORGE M. born April 22, 1837, married Susan Bridges, have three children, and live near Elgin, Howard county, Kansas. LAWSON, born July 7, 1842, married August 17, 1869, to Mary E. Shepherd, have one child, MILDRED, and live six miles south of Springfield, Ill. REBECCA, born July 6, 1844, married George Bridges. *See his name.* ELLEN S., born Sept. 7, 1846, married Sept. 4, 1867, to George D. Crane, and live near Woodside, Illinois. EVELINE, born April 20, 1849, lives with her mother. Thompson Pyle died Dec. 19, 1870, and his widow resides near where they settled in 1828, six miles south of Springfield, Sangamon county, Illinois.

ALFRED, born Oct. 12, 1806, in Christian county, Ky., and was the youngest of nineteen children. He was brought by his parents to Sangamon county in 1825, married in St. Clair county to Melinda Padfield. They had eight children, three died young. DAVID, born March 8, 1838, married Harriet A. Scott, have three children, IDA C., ROBERT E. and DAVID H., and live eight miles south of Springfield, Ill. ARMINDA, born Oct. 13, 1839, married Thomas R. Shepherd. *See his name.* WILLIAM married Jennie Jackson, and both died. ANN married John H. Shepherd. *See his name.* LOUISA R. married John W. Nuckolls. *See his name.* Mrs. Melinda Pyle died Sept. 19 1849, and Alfred Pyle died March 3, 1852, both in St. Clair county, although they had spent the greater part of their lives in Sangamon county.

Nicholas Pyle died in 1829, in Sangamon county, and his widow died at the house of their son, Alfred, in St. Clair county, Illinois.

R

RALSTON, WILLIAM, born in 1759, in Virginia, was a Revolutionary soldier, enlisting near the close of the war. He was then quite young for a soldier, but was at the siege and capture of Yorktown, and was present when Lord Cornwallis surrendered to Gen. Washington. He was married in Virginia to Nancy McClure, and soon after moved to the vicinity of Crab Orchard, Kentucky, and later to the vicinity of Mt. Sterling, Montgomery county, in the same State. They had twelve children in Kentucky, and moved to Sangamon county, Illinois, arriving in 1828, on Spring creek, accompanied by five of his children, and the sixth came a year or two later. The others remained in Kentucky. Of the six who came to Sangamon county—

WILLIAM, Jun., born May 20, 1796, in Montgomery county, Ky., was married there to Frances J. Massie, Sept. 13, 1825. They had one child that died in Kentucky, and the family moved to Sangamon county, Illinois, in 1828, settling on Spring creek in 1829, where seven children were born. MARY E. married Thomas Hessey, and died, leaving six children, who live with their father in Gardner township, Sangamon county, Illinois. EMILY M., born Dec. 30, 1831, was married, Nov. 24, 1850, to Jacob J. Brown. *See his name.* WILLIAM T. died May 26, 1858, in his twenty-fifth year. JOHN H. died June 9, 1861, in his twenty-sixth year. NANCY A., born Dec. 23, 1837, was married, Oct. 12, 1858, to Daniel Taylor. *See his name.* JAMES H., born Aug. 27, 1840, lives with his mother one and three-quarter miles south of Farmingdale, Sangamon county, Illinois. CHARLES F., born April 10, 1844, was married Dec. 3, 1867, in Sangamon county, to Clara A. Conklin, and live at Colorado Springs, Colorado. William Ralston, Jun., died Oct. 17, 1851, in Sangamon county, Ill., and his widow resides now—1873—on the farm where they settled in 1829, one and three-quarter miles south of Farmingdale, Sangamon county, Illinois. She has been a member of the Baptist church nearly half a century.

JOSIAH, born in Kentucky, was married in Sangamon county to Roxana Smith. They have eight children, and live in Hancock county, Illinois.

NATHANIEL, born in Kentucky, was married in Sangamon county to Clemantine Kelly. They moved to Missouri, but returned during the rebellion to Sangamon county, where he died. His widow and eight children live near Carthage, Jasper county, Missouri.

ELLEN, born in Kentucky, was married in Sangamon county, Illinois, to James Douglas. *See his name.*

SAMUEL, born in Kentucky, was married there to Nancy Ellis. They had two children in Kentucky, and came to Sangamon county in 1835. One child was born in Sangamon county, and one in Petersburg, Menard county, Illinois. Samuel Ralston and family reside in Washington, D. C.

JOSEPH, born Sept. 10, 1813, in Kentucky, was married in Sangamon county, Ill., Nov. 13, 1833, to Mrs. Susan Earnest, whose maiden name was Kendall. They had two living children—MARGARET J. married David Vulgamott, and have six children. They live in Fairfield, Jefferson county, Iowa. JOSEPH H., born Dec. 21, 1838, in Sangamon county, studied medicine in Springfield, Illinois, was married, Sept., 1865, at Placerville, Idaho Territory, to Lida Keck. They have two children, HENRY H. and EMIL. Dr. Ralston and family reside at Bentonsport, Van Buren county, Iowa. Joseph Ralston died July 31, 1839, in Sangamon county, and his widow married James E. Reed. *See his name.*

William Ralston, Sen., died July, 1835, and his widow died eight or nine years later, both in Sangamon county, Illinois.

RAMES, NATHANIEL, was born April 19, 1806, in Tennessee. Sarah Ogden was born Oct. 18, 1806, in Logan county, Kentucky. They were married March 8, 1829, in St. Louis, Mo., had one child there, and moved to Springfield, Ill., arriving April 16, 1830, where they had two children. Of their three children—

MARTHA T., born Dec. 17, 1829, in St. Louis, died in Springfield in her seventh year.

JOHN O., born August 20, 1831, in Springfield, married Oct. 7, 1852, to Mary J. Connelly, who died in 1854. Mr. Rames was married April 14, 1859, in St. Louis county, Mo., to Mary E. Redman, who was born there, June 14, 1839. They had six children in Springfield; two died young. MATTIE M., CORA B., MARY J. and JOHN O., Jun., live with their parents. J. O. Rames was a member of the city council three years, and has been a member of the School Board since 1870, with the exception of two years. He has been engaged in harness making for seventeen years, and resides in Springfield, Illinois.

WILLIAM N., born May 22, 1834, in Springfield, died March, 1853.

Nathaniel Rames died Feb. 29, 1836, in Springfield, and his widow lives with her son, John O., in Springfield.—1876.

RANDALL, THOMAS E., was born in 1785, in Virginia, was taken to Crab Orchard, Ky., when a child. He was married and had three children in Fleming county, Ky., and moved from there to Sangamon county, Ill., in 1827. His son—

MARSHAL S., born Jan. 26, 1813, in Fleming county, Ky., married in Sangamon county, in 1837, to Deborah Cantrall. They had twelve children. Their daughter, MARY J., married William G. Cantrall. *See his name.* Marshal S. Randall and family reside near Blue Mound Station, Christian county, Illinois.

RANSOM, JOHN G., was born April 27, 1808, at Chazy, Clinton county, N. Y., and was there married, Sept 30, 1830, to Lucy M. Gregory. They moved to Springfield, Ill., arriving June 6, 1835. Mr. Ransom commenced work as a journeyman wagon and carriage maker, and in a short time established the business on his own account. He made, as he believes, the first buggy ever put up in Springfield. In 1838 Mr. Ransom moved to Chatham, which had just been laid out, and he was among the first to erect permanent buildings in the town. He engaged in carriage and wagon making there. In 1840 he moved to Whitehall, Ill., and back to Chatham in 1842. In 1845 he moved to Galena, Ill., where Mrs. Lucy M. Ransom died, Mar. 18, 1846, leaving three living children, with whom Mr. Ransom returned to Chatham. Of those children—

EDWARD H., born in Sangamon county, married Gazena A. Brurink. He was a soldier in Co. B, 114th Ill. Inf., and spent several months in prison at Andersonville, Georgia. The privation and disease contracted there caused his death in Feb., 1869. He left a widow and four children in Virden, Illinois.

AMELIA M. married William Montgomery. They have seven children, and live at Stonington, Christian county, Illinois.—1874.

MARTHA married in Plattsburg, New York, to William L. Wood. They have one child, and live at Stonington, Christian county, Illinois.

John G. Ransom was married July 1, 1817, in Chatham, to Mrs. Elizabeth Bradley, whose maiden name was Hand. They had seven children, two of whom died young. Of the other five—

AUGUSTA E., born in Chatham, married Henry D. Cogswell, has one child, and lives in Bloomington, Illinois. —1873.

EMMA, CHARLES, JOHN E. and MARIA T. live with their parents.

John G. Ransom and family reside in Chatham, Sangamon county, Illinois.

RANSOM, LORING, was born April 13, 1806, in Chazy, Clinton county, N. Y., and came with a colony of fifty-three persons to Sangamon county, arriving at what is now Farmingdale, in Sept., 1833. He was married Oct. 29, 1839, at a place called Millville, north of Lick creek, and three miles west of Loami, to Mary Wariner, who was born April 20, 1817, in Barren county, Ky., and came to Sangamon county in the spring of 1834, with her father. Mr. and Mrs. Ransom had three living children—

ISABELLA W., born Sept. 13, 1840, in Chatham, married in Springfield, Feb. 24, 1861, to George W. Johnson, who was born Aug. 7, 1835, in Henniker, Merrimack county, N. H. He is an engineer on the G. C. & S. railroad, and resides in Springfield.

WILLIAM A., born Jan. 7, 1843, in Chatham, was married Nov. 23, 1872, in Hannibal, Mo., to Kittie Shelton Kiger, who was born July 29, 1843, in Nelson county, Va. They live in Springfield, Illinois.

ISAAC N., born May 12, 1846, in Springfield, married, Nov. 10, 1870, to Annie E. Crary, and live in Springfield, Illinois.

Loring Ransom was farming a few years and then went to Chatham, from there to Berlin, and from there to Springfield, where he died, Sept. 13, 1867. Mrs. Mary Ransom resides with her children, in Springfield, Illinois.

RANSOM, LUTHER N., was born about 1800, at Chazy, Clinton county, N. Y. He was there married to Zerviah Ransom. They had two children in New York, and moved to Sangamon county, Ill., with a colony, arriving in Sept., 1833, at Farmington, in what is now Gardner township. In 1835 Mr. R. sold out at that place, and entered two thousand one hundred acres of land eight or ten miles south of Springfield, and laid out the town of Chatham. In 1840 he moved to Springfield, where Mrs. R. died. Previous to this time Mr. R. had been a member of and an officer in the Presbyterian church, and was the principal means of establishing the church in Chatham. After the death of his wife he adopted communist principles as expounded by Fourier, went to Economy, Ohio, and united with the Fourierite community there, believing it would be a good place to bring up his children. He was married while there to a widow lady, by whom he had one child. At a time of excessive high water in the Ohio river, late in 1847, a very large brick building, owned and occupied by the Fourierites, was surrounded by water, weakening the foundations, and it fell, burying in its ruins a large number of persons. The two eldest children and the wife of Mr. Ransom were among the lost. She had just handed her babe out of a window, by which it was saved. Mr. Ransom was not at the place when the calamity came, but he soon after took his babe, left the Fourierites, and joined the Shakers at Lebanon, Ohio. This was in 1848. He remained with the Shakers until August, 1859, when he took his son, ALBERT, and went to Lawrence, Kansas, where he resided until July, 1872, when he died, a spiritualist, and an open disbeliever of the Bible. He was an original abolitionist, an uncompromising temperance man, scrupulously honest in his dealings, and it was believed by those who knew him well, that he was honest and conscientious in all he did. His erratic course was regarded more as the manifestations of an unsettled mind than of a depraved disposition.

RAPE, JOHN, was born about 1794, in South Carolina, and taken to Tennessee by his parents, at eight years old. He was a soldier from Tennessee, in the war of 1812, and arrived at New Orleans the day after the battle of Jan. 8, 1815. His father, Gustavus Rape, was a soldier from North Carolina during the war of the American Revolution. John Rape was married Aug. 18, 1818, in Tennessee, had two children there, and moved to Sangamon county, Ill., arriving

—75

in what is now Cotton Hill township, in Feb., 1826, where they had five children. Of their children—

CATHARINE, born Dec. 31, 1821, in Tennessee, married in Sangamon county to Benjamin R. Ridgeway. See his name.

AMELIA, born May 29, 1823, in Tennessee, married in Sangamon county, Dec. 25, 1840, to Wesley Beam. See his name. He died, leaving five children, and she married, July 17, 1855, to James Howlett. They have six children, WILLIAM M., DANIEL N., AMELIA L. and MARTHA E., twins, JAMES F. and GEORGE B. McL. Mr. Howlett had three children by a former marriage. They reside in Cotton Hill township.

DANIEL, born March 30, 1826, in Sangamon county, married, July 7, 1853, to Myrah Snodgrass. They had three children, CHARLES F., MOSES F. and FLETCHER E. Mrs. Rape died March 10, 1869, and he married, Sept. 2, 1869, to Mrs. Rebecca J. Hardin, whose maiden name was Snodgrass. They have one child, EDWIN, and live near New City, Sangamon county, Illinois.

JACOB, born Nov. 5, 1827, in Sangamon county, married, Dec. 26, 1850, to Rachel Beam. They have five children, THOMAS J., MELINDA J., CHARLES W., JOHN W. and LEWIS M., and live in Cotton Hill township, two and one-half miles south of New City, Sangamon county, Illinois. Jacob Rape says that it was so difficult to obtain farming implements, that himself and a brother covered corn many days with *wooden hoes*, made for the purpose by their father.

ALFRED N., was born May 5, 1830, in Sangamon county. He enlisted, Aug. 12, 1862, in Co. K, 124th Ill. Inf., for three years, served full term, was in fifteen battles, and was honorably discharged, Aug. 15, 1865. He was married, Oct. 17, 1871, to Mary A. Constant. They had one child, WM. EDWARD, who died in infancy. They live three miles southwest of New City, in Cotton Hill township, Sangamon county, Illinois.

FRANCIS M., born Nov. 20, 1831, in Sangamon county, married Melvina Snodgrass, had two children, MARY D. and NANCY I., and Mrs. Rape died, and he married, Oct. 8, 1869, to Mary J. Hayden, a grand-daughter of Pentod Vancil. They have two children, ROSA E. and FLORA E., and live in Cotton Hill township, near New City, Sangamon county, Illinois.

AMANDA, born Oct. 25, 1835, in Sangamon county, married, Aug. 5, 1852, to Preston Haines. They had three children—NANCY J., born April 9, 1855, married, June 9, 1873, to Benj. K. Haines. See his name. AMELIA C. and JOHN W. live with their mother. Preston Haines enlisted in 1861, for three years, in Co. B, 11th Mo. Inf. He died Feb. 14, 1863, in Military Hospital, at Keokuk, Iowa. His widow married, June 14, 1871, to W. T. Williams, have one child, MARTIN L., and live in Cotton Hill township, Sangamon county, Illinois.

Mrs. Polly Rape died, July 19, 1838, and John Rape was married, Feb. 3, 1839, to Elizabeth Snodgrass. They had seven children in Sangamon county—

JOSEPH, born Jan. 25, 1840, married, March 7, 1872, to Frances M. Reavis, who was born Feb. 23, 1856, in Fayette county, Ill. They have one child, NOAH F., and live near New City, Sangamon county, Illinois.

JOHN, born Dec. 16, 1843, lives near New City, Illinois.

JAMES T., born Sept. 27, 1845, married Mary West, have two living children, and lives near Cotton Hill P. O., Sangamon county, Illinois.

MARY E., born Oct. 18, 1848, married, Sept. 13, 1863, to Thomas McLoon, a native of Ireland. They have three children, MARY B., LAURA A. and JOHN E., and live near New City, Illinois.

SAMUEL D., born Jan. 20, 1853, lives with his mother.

NANCY E., born April 27, 1856, married, Feb. 19, 1874, to B. F. Young, and lives in Cotton Hill township.

EMILY J., born Aug. 12, 1859, lives with her mother.

John Rape died Jan. 29, 1872, and his widow lives on the farm where he settled i 1826. It is in Cotton Hill township, near New City, Sangamon county, Illinois.

RAPE, HENRY, born in 1784, in South Carolina, came with his brother

Peter to Sangamon county, Ill., about 1825, preceding their brother John one year. Henry Rape was married June, 1836, in Sangamon county, to Polly Snodgrass. They had six children in Sangamon county—

JAMES H., born July 23, 1837, in Sangamon county, enlisted in 1861, for three years, in Co. I, 7th Ill. Inf., served full time, and was honorably discharged, July 24, 1864, at Chattanooga, Tenn. J. H. Rape was married Dec. 7, 1875, at the Revere House, Springfield, Ill., to Mrs. Maria L. Campbell, whose maiden name was Brownell. *See Brownell family.* Mr. and Mrs. Rape live in Christian county, near Taylorville, Illinois.

GUSTAVUS F., born April 28, 1840, was married July 28, 1870, to Sarah Raney. They had two children, ORA VERNON and RALEIGH, and moved to the vicinity of Virginia, Bates county, Missouri. Their children both died there.

THOMAS J., born Dec. 20, 1842, was married July 29, 1869, to Clara A. Pettibone. They have one child, EARNEST R., and live in Cotton Hill township, Sangamon county, Illinois.

WILLIAM L., born Nov. 23, 1845, was married April 29, 1874, to Jennie Beaty. They have one child, ROLLA E., and live near Taylorville, Christian county, Illinois.

ELIZABETH J., born April 23, 1844, was married Dec. 29, 1874, to Richard Hillman. *See his name.*

Henry Rape died Nov. 11, 1851, and his widow married George Hamilton. They had one child—

ROBERT RAPE, born May 5, 1855, lives with his mother, three-fourths of a mile west of New City, in Cotton Hill township, Sangamon county, Illinois.

Mrs. Polly Rape had never formed a letter with a pen until her sixtieth year. Her son, James H., was in the army, and she found it difficult to induce others to write to him as often as she desired, so she resolved to learn, and commenced by copying letters and other documents, and was soon able to communicate with him. She continued this correspondence, to the great satisfaction of both, until his three years of service terminated.

RAPE, JACOB, was born Mar. 1, 1778, married Patsy Thornton, raised a family, and died April 28, 1865, in Sangamon county. His widow lives in Christian county. Their granddaughter married George Morgan, and lives in Taylorville, Illinois.

RAPE, POLLY, born in 1786, in South Carolina or Tennessee. She was a sister to John, Peter, Henry and Jacob. She was married in Sangamon county to Henry Funderburk. *See his name.*

RAPE, PETER, was born Mar. 15, 1790, married and raised a family. His wife, Sarah Rape, died July 23, 1841, in her forty-sixth year. He died March 29, 1847.

RAUCH, JOHN JACOB, was born July 25, 1796, in Stutgardt, Wirtemburg, Germany. He came to America in 1818, and was eleven weeks on the passage from Amsterdam, arriving at Philadelphia in September. He entered into an agreement, before starting, with a man who came on the same vessel, by which that gentleman was to pay his passage across the ocean in exchange for labor Mr. Rauch was to perform. He had fulfilled part of the agreement before starting, and acted as servant to the gentleman and his wife on board the vessel. On arriving in Philadelphia he found that the money had not been paid. The only excuse the man made was that his wife objected to it. In the early history of the American colonies some of them enacted laws under which emigrants might be sold at auction to pay for their passage across the ocean. The custom still prevailed at the time Mr. Rauch arrived in the country, but I have thus far failed to learn that there was any law for it at that time. Seventy dollars was the amount demanded by the owners of the vessel, and he was put up at auction to raise the money. The lowest, and perhaps the only bid was to pay the money on consideration of his serving three years in return, at hard labor, as the following paper will show:

PHILADELPHIA.

This Indenture Witnesseth: That Johan Jacob Rauch, of his own free will, to go to Alabama Territory, hath bound himself servant to Francis C. Clapper, of Philadelphia, merchant, for the consideration of seventy dollars, paid to Lewis, Haven & Co., for his passage from Amsterdam; as also, for other good causes, he, the said Johan Jacob Rauch, hath bound and put himself, and by these presents doth bind and put himself, servant to the said Francis C. Clapper, to serve him, his executors, administrators and assigns, from the day of the date hereof, for and during the full term of three years, from thence next ensuing. During all which term the said servant, his said master, his executors, administrators and assigns, faithfully shall serve, and that honestly and obediently in all things, as a good and faithful servant ought to do. And the said Francis C. Clapper, his executors, administrators and assigns, during the said term, shall find and provide for the said servant sufficient meat, drink, apparel, washing and lodging, and to give him, at the end of the term, two complete suits of clothes, one thereof to be new. And for the true performance hereof both the said parties bind themselves firmly unto each other by these presents. In witness whereof they have interchangably set their hands and seals. Dated the second day of October, A. D. one thousand eight hundred and eighteen.

F. C. CLAPPER.

Bound before Conrad Wile, Register.

Mr. Rauch was at once sent to Alabama, and labored faithfully for two and a half years, the principal part of the time at boat building, and must have earned many times the value of the money paid out for him. His food and clothing during the whole of that time was of the very worst description, in addition to which he was treated to all manner of indignities on account of his lack of knowledge of our language, and for any other cause which the caprice or malignity of those with whom he was associated might suggest. Six months before the expiration of his time his hardships became intolerable. He left Alabama and made his way into Muhlenburg county, Kentucky, arriving in 1821. There he found German people, who gave him employment by which he was soon able to clothe himself decently, and began to save money. He worked both in wood and stone as the opportunity for either presented itself. Oct. 24, 1824, he was married to Pauline Poley, sister to Joseph Poley. *See his name.* Soon after his marriage he built a sawmill on a small stream, and occasionally worked at his trades, doing a good business. As Mr. Rauch learned more of the influence of slavery, he resolved to seek a free country in which to bring up his family. He accordingly removed with his wife and two children, to Illinois, arriving Oct., 1829, in Sangamon county. In December he bought three-fourths of section thirty-three, which is the southern tier of sections in this county. It is in Auburn township, between the towns of Auburn and Virden. The stream called Sugar creek ran through his land, and among the first things he did was to build a saw and grist mill, and for many years Rauch's mill was known far and near, and hundreds of weary emigrants found rest under his roof, his house being on the road from Springfield to St. Louis. After arriving in Illinois, seven children were added to the family. Of their nine children—

ANDREW, born Aug. 11, 1825, in Kentucky, was married June 13, 1854, in Sangamon county, to Margaret E. Cassity, a native of Kentucky. They have five living children, FRANK, CLARA, EMMA, ELMER and A. LEE. Andrew Rauch and family reside in the vicinity of the old homestead, in Sangamon county, near Virden, Macoupin county, Illinois.

CHARLES, born Dec. 28, 1827, in Kentucky, was married Dec. 18, 1859, in Sangamon county, to Mary Brooks, a native of Delaware. They have four children, LOUISA, JENNIE, JAMES and JOHN, and reside at the homestead, in Sangamon county, near Virden, Macoupin county, Illinois.

ELIZABETH, born April 25, 1830, in Illinois, died in childhood.

SAVILLA, born Feb. 3, 1832, in Sangamon county, married Hiram Orr, and died five weeks later, at her mother's house.

JAMES, born Oct. 5, 1833, in Sangamon county, was married, April 3, 1863, to Jennie B. Goss, who was born August 25, 1837, at Littleton, Grafton county, New Hampshire. They moved to California, and James Rauch died there, Nov. 12, 1864, leaving a widow, who returned to Illinois, Oct. 26, 1865, and is now —August, 1876—residing in Virden, Illinois.

JACOB, born Aug. 16, 1835, in Sangamon county, was married, Oct. 27, 1859, to Emma C. Cassity. They have three living children, ADA, EFFIE and BYRON, and reside in Virden, Illinois.

FRANKLIN, born Oct. 11, 1847, died Dec. 17, 1848.

REBECCA, born Nov. 6, 1839, in Sangamon county, was married, Oct. 26, 1869, to John McGlothlin. They have three children, LOUELLA, HORACE and CHARLIE A., and reside five miles southwest of Auburn, Sangamon county, Illinois.

BARBARA A., born June 2, 1842, in Sangamon county, married Matthew Patton, Jun. *See his name*. They do not live in Chicago, as stated in connection with his name, but now—Sept., 1876—reside three miles southeast of Auburn, Sangamon county, Illinois.

John Jacob Rauch died Nov. 23, 1843, where he settled in 1829. His widow, Mrs. Pauline Rauch, resides there with her son Charles. It is in Sangamon county, near Virden, Macoupin county, Illinois.

Mr. Rauch left his family with the title to a sufficient quantity of land to make a good farm for each one; with a large amount of personal property, and his children are among the most respected citizens of the county. When we consider that he was twenty-two years of age at the time he came to America, without a knowledge of our language, compelled to lose so much of the best time of his life to pay for the privilege of coming, and that he died before he was fifty years of age, his success was wonderful, and it is highly probable that his early death was caused by over exertion. Although he had been so treacherously dealt with on coming to the country, and for the first three years after his arrival; yet his abhorrence of anything like repudiating a contract was such, that he charged his sons if the duplicate to the contract by which he was robbed of his three years time, should ever be presented, they should pay the whole seventy dollars, for the reason that he had not rendered the last six months service, and *that* because it was physically impossible for him to endure it. In the later years of his life, when pondering on the hardships and indignities he had endured, he wrote in German on the margin of the contract quoted, "Jacob Rauch says this indenture was not good." He doubtless alluded to the fact that it was not binding because it was never signed by himself. The back of the indenture bears an inscription, also in German, in his own handwriting. It appears to have been more intended as an expression of a sentiment than an address to any particular one of his children. It is in these words:

"DEAR CHILD, you had better remain in a low station of life; the higher you stand the more you may be humbled; and the Lord will love you better, for He is the Most High, and does great things by means of the lowly.

"JACOB RAUCH."

RAY, THOMAS, was born Jan. 28, 1794, in Gallatin county, Ky. He was married, Feb. 22, 1816, to Polly Furnish, a native of the same county. Mrs. Ray died, Sept. 21, 1820, leaving one child. He then married Susan Ray, who was born April 20, 1798. They had one child in Kentucky, and the family moved to Sangamon county, Ill., arriving October, 1824, in Island Grove, south of Spring creek, and the next spring moved north of Spring creek, in what is now Gardner township, where they had three living children. Of their five children—

SAMUEL E., born Dec. 25, 1817, in Gallatin county, Ky., married in Sangamon county, Sept. 20, 1838, to Elcy Jane Robison. They had four children—SUSAN J., born July 21, 1839, in Washington county, Iowa, where her parents lived one and one-half years. She was married, march 12, 1856, to Isaac Gregory. *See his name*. She died, Nov. 19, 1864, leaving twins. POLLY A., born May 6, 1842, in Sangamon county, married, Jan. 17, 1861, to John Swarens. They have five children, ELLA, FRANK, CLARENCE, LORA and HATTIE, and live one and one-half miles north of Bradfordton. ELCY C. died in her third year. EMMA M., born March 23, 1852, lives with her parents, half a mile east of Bradfordton, Sangamon county, Illinois—1874.

JOHN G., born Aug. 20, 1824, in Kentucky, married in Sangamon county, Feb. 1, 1855, to Abigail Van Gilder, and he died March 25, 1855.

MARGARET A., born Nov. 16, 1832, in Kentucky, married in Sangamon county, June 24, 1852, to Seth W. Wickham. He was one of three children born of the same mother, Oct. 30, 1824, in Muskingham county, Ohio. Of the other two: Elmus died in his tenth year, and Louisa married S. P. Weaver, and died in Ohio, in her twenty-first year, two weeks after she was married. Seth W. Wickham and wife had one child, THOMAS W., and she died April 7, 1867. He was married, Dec. 31, 1868, to Mrs. Cornelia A. Large, whose maiden name was Frazee. *See Frazee*. They have one child, MINNIE L., and reside one mile southeast of Farmingdale, Sangamon county, Illinois—1874.

SUSAN P., born March 26, 1836, married Thomas Johnson, had one child, and she died in 1856. Her son, Charles Johnson, lives with his uncle, Thomas B. Ray.

THOMAS B., born March 10, 1841, married, Feb. 23, 1865, to Charlotte Brown. They had one child, CHARLOTTE, who lives with her grandfather, Rezin D. Brown. Mrs. Ray died Jan. 5, 1866, and T. B. Ray lives at the homestead settled by his father in 1825, in Gardner township, Sangamon county, Illinois.

Mrs. Susan Ray died Dec. 15, 1859, and Thomas Ray died Aug. 24, 1871, both in Gardner township.

William Ray, the father of Thomas, came to Sangamon county, and after a few years sojourn, returned to Kentucky, and died there.

RAY, REASON or REZIN, was born in Maryland, went to Kentucky, where he married Sarah Walters. They had four children, and came to Sangamon county in 1823, settling in Gardner township. His daughter—

LAVINA, born in Kentucky, in 1822, married in Sangamon county, to Ezekiel Drennan. *See his name*.

Mrs. Drennan remembers the "deep snow." She was eight years old, and was helping her father gather corn, and slipped into a whirlpool that formed around a hill of corn. She went under the snow, and her father happening to see her go down, drew her out in time to save her from suffocating.

RAY, SAMUEL. His daughter—

ELIZABETH, born Aug. 5, 1833, married, Dec. 2, 1852, to Robert Haggard, in Sangamon county, and died July 22, 1867, in Labette county, Kansas, leaving six children.

REDMAN, JAMES B., was born in St. Louis county, Mo., and commenced learning the trade of a blacksmith in St. Louis with Rames & Owens, moved with them to Springfield, Illinois, in April, 1830, and later was four years engaged in the same business with Nathaniel Rames, as Rames & Redman. He then returned to St. Louis county, and was there married, in 1834, to Martha A. Graham, and had two children—

MARY E., born near St. Louis, married John O. Rames. *See his name*.

MARGARET married William T. Henly, and resides near St. Louis.

Mrs. Redman died, and James B. Redman is living with his third wife, at Baden, St. Louis county, Mo.

REDMAN, WILLIAM E., was born May 15, 1815, in Maryland, eight miles north of Washington City. He was married, Jan. 6, 1840, in Hagerstown, to Catharine Wolgamot, and moved with her father to Sangamon county, Ill., arriving May 31, 1840, in what is now Woodside township. They had eight children in Sangamon county, five of whom died under seven years. Of the other three—

ISABEL O., born July 16, 1843, married Dec. 19, 1865, to Daniel Keller. She had one child, MARY, and died in Chatham, Illinois.

CATHARINE F., born March 18, 1842, married Nov. 11, 1872, to Daniel Keller, also. They have three children, HETTIE, HARRY and CHARLEY, and live in Chatham, Illinois.

CHLOE ANN E., born March 20, 1847, married Oct. 15, 1867, to D. F. Brewer. They have four children, KATIE E., ADAM POE, JOHN M. and CHLOE B., and reside in Springfield, Illinois. Daniel F. Brewer was born April 26, 1842, in West Chester, Butler county, Ohio, enlisted Sept. 4, 1861, at Cincinnati, Ohio, in the 11th Independent Battery, served until Nov. 5, 1864, when he was honorably discharged, and came to Chatham in 1865.

William E. Redman enlisted June 28, 1861, in Co. F, 21st Ill. Inf., for three years, at Springfield. Although he was past the age to be subject to military laws, he went to the field under Col. Ulysses S. Grant, served until April 28, 1864, when he was honorably discharged on account of physical disability. He was employed for a few months after that in the quartermaster's department. Mrs. Catharine Redman died Dec. 31, 1874, and Wm. E. Redman resides in Chatham, Sangamon county, Illinois.

REED, JAMES E., was born July 14, 1810, in Wayne county, Ky. His father died when he was four, and his mother when he was seven years old. He came to Springfield, Ill., in the fall of 1828, was in the Black Hawk war from Sangamon county in 1831, and again in 1832. He was married July 6, 1837, to Eliza A. Kendall. They had two children—

MARY A., born Feb. 27, 1838, married March 4, 1858, to Josiah B. Morgan. They have four children, and live near Neode-ha, Wilson county, Kansas.

SUSAN F., born March 12, 1839, married Feb., 1858, to Edward S. McMurry. They have three children, and live at Leghorn, Pottawatomie county, Kansas. He is Postmaster there.—1874.

Mrs. Eliza A. Reed died Sept. 22, 1847, and James E. Reed was married Nov. 6, 1847, to Mrs. Susan Ralston, who had previously been Mrs. Earnest, and whose maiden name was Kendall. They had two children—

SARAH E., born Dec. 21, 1848, lives with her parents.

BURZILLA K., born Nov. 20, 1850, married Oct. 16, 1873, to William T. Simpson. *See his name.*

J. E. Reed and wife reside five miles west of Springfield, Sangamon county, Illinois.

REID, SAMUEL H., was born in 1781, near Richmond, Virginia. His parents moved, when he was a young man, to Davidson county, Tenn., near President Jackson's country seat, the Hermitage; and from there to Warren county, Ky. While visiting his brother, Judge Alexander Reid, at Shelbyville, Samuel H. became acquainted with Elizabeth Roberts. They were there married, and lived near Bowling Green, Warren county, until six children were born. Mrs. Reid and three of the children died there. Mr. Reid was married in Warren county to Jane Gott, and moved at once to Sangamon county, Ill., arriving in Sept., 1827, and settled on a farm he had previously purchased, three miles west of Springfield, where they had four children. Of his seven children—

SAMUEL H. and *SARAH J.*, twins, born May 20, 1818, in Warren county, Kentucky.

SAMUEL H. married Oct. 20, 1840, in Sangamon county, to Elizabeth Davis. They had three children—SARAH J., born Oct. 27, 1841, married, April 19, 1858, to Thomas L. Conner, who was born Sept. 1, 1832, in Allegheny county, Penn. They had four children, SAMUEL R. died young. WILLIAM L., MARGARET E. and SARAH J. live with their parents in Springfield, Illinois. DAVID A. died in infancy. ROBERT S., born Oct. 12, 1848, married, Oct. 20, 1869, to Olive M. Cross, who was born Nov. 22, 1850, in Christian county, Illinois. They have one child, SARAH E., and live one and one-half mile west of Springfield. Samuel H. Reid, Jun., and wife now—1876—reside three miles west of Springfield, Illinois, on the farm settled by his father in 1827.

SARAH J. married David A. Reid, a distant relative, had one child, and mother and child died, in Lincoln county, Missouri.

DAVID A., born April, 1822, in Kentucky, raised in Sangamon county, and died March, 1840, in Lincoln county, Missouri.

By the second marriage—

ADALINE, born in Sangamon county, married Thomas Reid, had two children, and she died Jan., 1855, in Lincoln county, Missouri.

WILLIAM M., born in Sangamon county, died, aged eighteen years, in Lincoln county, Missouri.

LUCINDA died, aged fourteen years, in Lincoln county, Missouri.

JAMES, born and died in Sangamon county, aged four years.

Samuel H. Reid, Sen., was a ruling Elder in the church organized by Rev. John G. Bergen, the first ever organized in Springfield, now the First Presbyterian church. He afterwards became a ruling Elder in the Second Presbyterian church, and continued to the end of his life. He died Sept., 1836, and his widow died sixteen days later, both in Sangamon county.

REED, JAMES FRAZIER, was born Nov. 14, 1800, in county Armagh, Ireland. His ancestors were of noble Polish birth, who chose exile rather than submission to the Russian power, and settled in the north of Ireland. The family name was originally Reednoski, but in process of time the Polish termination of the name was dropped, and the family was called Reed. James F. Reed's mother's name was Frazier, whose ancestors belonged to Clan Frazier, of Scottish history. Mrs. Reed, and her son, James F., came to America when he was a youth, and settled in Virginia. He remained there until he was twenty, when he left for the lead mines of Illinois, and was engaged in mining until 1831, when he came to Springfield, Sangamon county, Ill. He served in the Black Hawk war, and at its termination returned to Springfield, where he engaged in mercantile pursuits, made money, and bought a farm near the latter city. Mr. Reed was for several years engaged in manufacturing cabinet furniture at a point on the Sangamon river, seven miles east of Springfield. He employed a large number of men, and a village grew up there, which, in honor of his first name, was called Jamestown. It has since been twice changed, first to Howlett and then to Riverton, the present name. He was married, in 1834, to Mrs Margaret W. Backenstoe, whose maiden name was Keyes, a daughter of Humphrey Keyes. *See his name.* Mrs. Reed had one child by her first marriage. In Apr., 1846, Mr. and Mrs. Reed, with many others, started overland for California. *See Reed and Donner party.* Mr. Reed settled at San Jose Mission, California, and invested in land from time to time. He was among the first who tried their fortunes at gold hunting, in which he was very successful. Of Mrs. Reed's child by a former marriage—

VIRGINIA E. Backenstoe, born in Sangamon county, Ill., was married in San Jose, California, in 1850, to John M. Murphy, who was born Jan. 8, 1824, in Canada, and went to California in 1844. They had nine children, three died young. Of the other six: MARY M., born Oct. 1850, in San Jose, was married there, in June, 1869, to P. McAram. They have two children, THOMAS P. and MARY V. Mr. McAram is a Banker in San Francisco, California, and resides there. JOHN M. was born March, 1858; VIRGINIA, born April, 1860; JULIA A., born Feb., 1866; DANIEL J., born Dec., 1867, and THADEUS S., born July, 1874; they are natives of San Jose, California, and the five latter live there with their parents. Mrs. Virginia E. Murphy writes me, in Dec., 1875, that she never was taught or made to feel, during Mr. Reed's lifetime, that she was a step-child or half-sister, and that he was the most loving and indulgent step-father that ever lived. So thoughtful was he of her feelings that he took occasion, after the death of her mother, to assure her of his continued affection, and that he knew no difference between herself and his own children, as she came to him with her mother, a little babe. He made no distinction between Mrs. Murphy and his own children in his will.

Mr. and Mrs. James F. Reed had six children; one died in infancy. Of the other five—

MARTHA J., born Feb. 26, 1838, in Springfield, Illinois, accompanied her parents to California, and was married there, at Santa Cruz, Dec. 25, 1856, to Frank Lewis, who was born in Lancaster, Worcester county, Mass., Sept. 15, 1828. They had eight children; one died in infancy. KATE, born Oct. 6, 1857. MARGARET B., born June 6, 1860. FRANK, Jun., born March 22, 1862. MARTHA J., born April 6, 1864. JAMES F., born August 25, 1866. CARRIE E., born September 15, 1870. and SUSAN A., born Dec. 31, 1873, live with their mother, in San Jose, California. Mr. Lewis enlisted, in 1846, in the 1st Massachusetts Vol. Inf., for the Mexican war, and served to its close. He spent the next two years in New Orleans, and three years in Central and South America, went to San Jose, California, in June, 1852, and was for many years a member of the city council of that place. He was a wholesale and retail grocer, and died June 18, 1876, mourned by a large circle of acquaintences. The Mayor and city council acted as pall bearers at his funeral.

JAMES F., Jun., born March 26, 1841, at Springfield, Ill., accompanied his parents to California, and has been engaged in mining in Idaho, Nevada and California, until the last two years. He lives now—1876—in San Jose, California.

THOMAS K., born April 2, 1843, in Springfield, Illinois, accompanied his parents to California, has been engaged in mining, is unmarried, and lives in San Jose, California.

CHARLES C., born Feb. 6, 1848, under the Mexican flag, in San Jose, California, was married there, Aug. 12, 1872, to Imogene Bergler. They have two children, CHARLES C., Jun., and WILLIE F. Charles C. Reid is a farmer and stock raiser, and resides in San Jose, California.

WILLIANOSKI YOUNT, born Dec. 12, 1850, in San Jose, Cal., died June 12, 1860.

Mrs. Margaret W. Reed died Nov. 25, 1861, and James F. Reed died July 24, 1874, both in San Jose, Cal. He was a man of great energy, warm and genial in his friendships, social and entertaining in his family. He made money fast, and used it liberally. He was one of the most active men in trying to make San Jose the capital of the State, circulating documents and trying to impress the members elect to the State Convention, of the importance and value of that place as a seat of government, and spent not less than twenty thousand dollars in behalf of that place. Mr. Reed left his family in good circumstances, with a possibility of immense wealth for them in the future, as he owned mines in Idaho, on Reese river, and at White Pine. For a more full account of his sufferings and almost superhuman efforts to relieve others, see the following sketch of the *Reed and Donner emigrant party.*

REED AND DONNER. A party was organized in the vicinity of Springfield, Sangamon county, Ill., and started from that city, April 14, 1846, for California and the Pacific coast. It has always been spoken of by the people of Sangamon county as the "Reed and Donner emigrant party." They were not lured there on account of gold, for it had not then been discovered. When they left Springfield the company numbered thirty-four persons. Of the two newspapers published in Springfield at the time—the *Journal* and *Register*—each have the identical number missing that should have contained information about them. The following are the names as near as I have been able to determine, of the persons composing the company:—

James F. Reed and Mrs. Margaret W. Reed, his wife, with their four children, Virginia E. B., Martha J., James F., Jun., and Thomas K.; also Mrs. Sarah Keyes, the mother of Mrs. Reed.

George Donner and Mrs. Tamsen Donner, his wife, with their five children, Elitha C., Leanna C., Francis E., Georgiana and Eliza P.

Jacob Donner and Mrs. Elizabeth Donner, his wife, with their five children, Isaac, Lewis, Samuel, George and Mary; also William and Solomon Hook, children of Mrs. Donner by a former marriage.

There were also Milford Elliott—often mentioned as Milton Elliott—James Smith, John Denton, Eliza and Bayless Williams, Walter Herron and Hiram O. Miller. There were some others, but I have been unable to learn their names.

Leaving Springfield, their first point of destination was Independence, Missouri, where they were to make the final preparation for crossing the Plains. They were joined at various points by parties from other places, as follows:—

From Lacon, Illinois: Jay Fausdick and Mrs. Sarah Fausdick, his wife. Mr. and Mrs. Graves, with their eight children, Frank, Mary, William, Ellen, Lavina, Nancy, Jonathan and Elizabeth. Mrs. Fausdick was a daughter of Mr. and Mrs. Graves.

From Iowa: Patrick Brien—spelled, in some places, Brein and Breen—Margaret Brien, Margaret J., John, Edward, Patrick, Jun., Simon, James and Peter Brien, and Patrick Dolen.

From Belleville, Illinois: J. P. Eddy, Mrs. Eddy and W. H. Eddy.

From St. Louis, Missouri: William Foster, Mrs. Foster and George Foster; and from Ray county, Missouri: William McCutchen, Mrs. McCutchen and Harriet McCutchen.

From Tennessee: Lemuel Murphy, Mrs. Murphy, Lander, Mary, William

—76

and Samuel Murphy; William Pike, Cynthia Pike and N. Pike.

From Germany: Mr. and Mrs. Kiesberger, or Keysburg, B. and L. S. Keysburg, Mrs. Wolfinger, Mr. Rinehart, Mr. Spitzger and Carl Berger.

From Springfield, Ohio: Samuel Shoemaker, and—

From Chicago, Illinois: C. T. Stanton.

Others are mentioned on the road, incidentally, but this sketch is only intended for those who left Sangamon county. At Independence, Mr. Reed loaded eight wagons with provisions and supplies of various kinds. The Donners made similar preparations, as also the other members of the party. They, of course, had a sufficient number of oxen to haul all their wagons. It was absolutely necessary that emigrants, at that time, should travel in large bodies as a safeguard against the Indians on the Plains. It was never safe to start until the grass had made sufficient growth to afford sustenance for the cattle. This company of eighty-one persons, thirty-four of whom were from Sangamon county, left Independence early in May, for their long, tedious and perilous journey across the Western Plains. All went well until they approached the Big Blue river, four miles above its mouth, where Manhattan, Kan., now stands. They found the stream quite full, and the whole party camped and commenced building boats and rafts for crossing. Just before reaching there, Mrs. Keyes, the mother of Mrs. Reed, showed signs of failing health under the fatigue and discomfort of travel in unpleasant weather. While in camp she grew worse, and on the morning of May 29, 1846, breathed her last. Work was suspended, and each vied with every other in rendering the last tribute of respect to her remains. A neat coffin was made of timber, split, hewn and planed, from a cottonwood tree near by. The remains were placed in it and buried on a beautiful elevation, near an upland burr oak. Religious services were conducted by a Cumberland Presbyterian minister. The grave was sodded, and the tree made to serve the purposes of a head board. On it was cut the following inscription:

"SARAH KEYES, AGED 70 YEARS. DIED 29th MAY, 1846. FROM SPRINGFIELD, ILLINOIS."

At the foot a coarse white stone, resembling marble, was placed, containing the words:

MRS. S. KEYES, AGED 70 YEARS.

Flowers and young Cedars were planted at the head and foot.

Between Independence and Blue river the Reed and Donner party fell in with Col. W. H. Russell and company, who had left Independence a few days before them. Passing Blue river, they all traveled together until they reached Little Sandy river, where a separation took place, the majority of them going to Oregon, Col. Russell heading the latter. The day after the separation the Reed and Donner party elected George Donner Captain, and from that time it was known as the "Donner Company." They continued their journey up the valley of the Platte river, passing Fort Laramie and crossing the Rocky Mountains to Fort Bridger without any serious mishap. This had occupied the entire summer. They tarried at the Fort four days. Parties who had gone before, learned the dangers, and knowing the Donner party were coming, left letters, directed to Mr. Reed, with Mr. Vasques, the partner of Bridger, for whom the fort was named, advising him by no means to take what was known as the Hastings cut off, but to go by the Fort Hall route. The latter was an established route, and well known, but it required a detour to the northwest, whereas the Hastings cut off, passing through Webber canyon to the south end of the great Salt Lake, about where Salt Lake City now stands, made the route more direct, and doubtless was three hundred miles shorter, which was the inducement to take that route. Vasques being interested in having all travelers go that way, withheld the letters from Mr. Reed, and he never knew, until his arrival in California, that any such letters had been left for him, and they unfortunately took what they supposed would be the more direct road.

Approaching the mouth of the Webber canyon, they found a letter sticking in the top of a sage bush. It was from Hastings, the discoverer of the new route. He was then piloting a company through, and proposed to the Donner Company that, if they would send messengers for him, he would return and pilot them through a better way than the one given them. Messrs. Reed, Stanton and McCutchen, of the Donner Company, went to Mr. Hastings, and, after going back part of the way with Mr. Reed—he having procured a fresh horse—Mr. Hastings gave him directions, and leaving him about where Salt Lake city now stands, returned to the first party he was piloting. Mr. Reed returned east to the Donner Company, all hands went to work, and by digging and cutting timber, made a road passing to the south end of Salt Lake, crossing the outlet to the lake—now called the river Jordan. Passing to the northwest, around the lake, they were detained a few days by the death, from consumption, of one of the company, a Mr. Halloran. A few more days' travel brought them to the Springs where they were to provide water and grass for crossing what was called Hastings' desert, an alkaline region destitute of water or vegetation. They were led to believe that it was less than fifty miles across, but it proved to be nearer eighty. It was understood they must travel day and night, stopping only to feed and water the cattle. When about two-thirds of the way across, the stock manifested signs of being exhausted, and the company requested Mr. Reed to go forward until he found water and report. He did so, reaching it in about twenty miles, and returning, met his teamsters about 11 o'clock at night driving the cattle, having left their wagons. After directing them how to proceed, he went on to meet his family and the remainder of the company. Soon after leaving his teamsters, one of their horses sunk down in the road, and while they were endeavoring to raise it, the cattle scented the water, scattered, and nine yoke were never found, leaving one ox and a cow only; his wagons and family, with all their supplies, out on a desert, hundreds of miles from any human habitation, and winter close upon them. The mistake of his teamsters—and one he would not have permitted had he been present—was in leaving the wagons so soon.

The Donners and other members of the company drove their teams much further before leaving their wagons, and some few succeeded in taking them the entire distance.

We will return to Mr. Reed, who was seeking his family twenty miles in the desert. He reached them about daylight the next morning. Not knowing that his cattle were lost, he waited with his family all day, expecting some of his men to return and haul them to water. Not receiving any information, and their supply of water being nearly gone, he started with his family on foot, carrying the youngest child in his arms, and in the course of the night the children became exhausted. They spread a blanket on the ground; all lay down on it, and covered themselves with shawls; but a cold hurricane commenced blowing soon after, and he could only keep the children warm by having their four dogs lie down against them, outside the shawls. About daylight they moved on, and soon came to a wagon, which belonged to Jacob Donner, and contained his family. Mr. Reed left his family with Mrs. Donner. Mr. Donner returned from the water with his cattle, and took his own and Mr. Reed's families to the water, where they remained in camp about a week, hunting for their cattle. Mr. Reed never found any of his; the Indians had made sure work, and secured all except the two previously mentioned. He then divided his provisions, except what he could haul in one wagon, borrowed another yoke of oxen, and, leaving his seven wagons in the desert, moved on with the company,—all the others having found a sufficient number of their oxen to haul their wagons. After a few days' travel, the party who had loaned him the yoke of oxen needed them, when another neighbor loaned him a yoke.

Some days further on it was found that provisions were running short. An estimate was made of the quantity it would take for each family. Mr. Reed then proposed that if two men would go forward to Captain Sutter's in California, he, Reed, would write him a letter, asking for the whole amount, and would become personally responsible for the pay. Mr. William McCutchen, of Missouri, and Mr. Stanton, of Chicago, volunteered to go. The progress was slow, and weeks passed without any tidings from McCutchen and Stanton.

It was suggested that Mr. Reed go in advance to see what had become of them, and hurry up supplies. In all cases of that kind those remaining were to take care of the families of those detached for the good of all. The two Donner families were in advance of the main body. Walter Herron was with George Donner, and when Mr. Reed overtook them, Herron volunteered to go with him. Having but one horse, they rode by turns. Their provisions gave out, and they traveled for days without food, except wild geese and other game which they occasionally killed on Truckee river. When they reached the Sierra Nevada mountains, Herron wanted to kill the horse, and Mr. Reed persuaded him from it by agreeing to kill him rather than perish with hunger. That afternoon Herron became delirious for want of food. They found *five beans*. Herron ate three of them, and Reed the other two. The next morning they came upon some abandoned wagons, which they ransacked, but failed to find any food. Taking the tar-bucket from one of the wagons, and scraping the tar from the bottom, Mr. Reed discovered a streak of rancid tallow in the bottom, which he made known to Herron, who swallowed a piece about the size of a walnut without giving it a smell. He swallowed a second piece, and wanted more, which Mr. Reed refused to give him, having himself eaten some which made him deathly sick. They soon after descended into Bear river valley, where they found some emigrants in wagons, who gave them food and relieved their sufferings. They there met Mr. Stanton, and two Indians sent by Captain Sutter to aid in carrying provisions. Mr. Reed was so emaciated that Mr. Stanton did not recognize him until they had conversed with each other several minutes. The next morning, Oct. 23, 1846, each party continued their journey. Mr. Reed went on to Captain Sutter's, where he secured thirty horses, one mule and two Indians to aid him in bringing out the sufferers. He was joined by Mr. McCutchen, who had been separated from Mr. Stanton by sickness. With some flour and beef they started to meet the suffering emigrants in the mountains. After weeks spent in unavailing efforts, they had to return, as men and horses sank out of sight in the snow. It was evident that nothing could be done until spring, the mountaineers all being absent fighting Mexicans, the war with Mexico having commenced the year before, and the natives of Spanish and Indian blood having expressed a determination to exterminate the Americans.

Snow commenced falling the latter part of October, and caught the whole party, not in a body, but scattered along some distance, the extremes being probably a day's journey apart. The following journal kept by one of the sufferers, includes the time from Oct. 31, 1846, to Mar. 1, 1847. This is taken from a copy of the *Illinois State Journal* of Sept. 16, 1847, and is dated:

TRUCKEY'S LAKE, *Nov. 20, 1846*.

Came to this place on the 31st of last month; went into the Pass, the snow so deep we were unable to find the road, and when within three miles from the summit, turned back to this shanty, on Truckey's Lake. Stanton came up one day after we arrived here; we again took our teams and wagons and made another unsuccessful attempt to cross the mountains, as it continued to snow all the time. We now have killed most part of our cattle, having to remain here until next spring, and live on lean meat, without bread or salt. It snowed during the space of eight days, with little intermission, after our arrival, though now clear and pleasant, freezing at night; the snow nearly gone from the valleys.

Nov. 21—Fine morning, wind northwest; twenty-two of our company about starting to cross the mountains this day, including Stanton and his Indians.

Nov. 22—Froze hard last night; fine and clear to-day; no account from those on the mountains.

Nov. 23—Same weather, wind west; the expedition across the mountains returned after an unsuccessful attempt.

Nov. 25—Cloudy; looks like the eve of a snow storm; our mountaineers are to make another trial to-morrow, if fair; froze hard last night.

Nov. 26—Began to snow last evening; now rains or sleets; the party do not start to-day.

Nov. 29—Still snowing; now about three feet deep; wind west; killed my last oxen to-day; gave another yoke to Foster; wood hard to be got.

Nov. 30—Snowing fast; looks as likely to continue as when it commenced; no living thing without wings can get about.

Dec. 1—Still snowing; wind west; snow about six or six and one-half feet deep; very difficult to get wood, and we are completely housed up; our cattle all killed but two or three, and these, with the horses and Stanton's mules, all supposed to be lost in the snow; no hopes of finding them alive.

Dec. 3—Ceases snowing; cloudy all day; warm enough to thaw.

Dec. 4—Beautiful sunshine, thawing a little; looks delightful after the long storm; snow seven or eight feet deep.

Dec. 5—The morning fine and clear; Stanton and Graves manufacturing snow shoes for another mountain scrabble; no account of mules.

Dec. 8—Fine weather; froze hard last night; wind southwest; hard work to find wood sufficient to keep us warm, or cook our beef.

Dec. 9—Commenced snowing about eleven o'clock; wind northwest; took in Spitzer yesterday, so weak that he cannot rise without help, caused by starvation. Some have a scant supply of beef; Stanton trying to get some for himself and Indians; not likely to get much.

Dec. 10—Snowed fast all night, with heavy squalls of wind; continues to snow; now about seven feet in depth.

Dec. 14—Snows faster than any previous day; Stanton and Graves, with several others, making preparations to cross the mountains on snow shoes; snow eight feet on a level.

Dec. 16—Fair and pleasant; froze hard last night; the company started on snow shoes to cross the mountains; wind southeast.

Dec. 17—Pleasant: Wm. Murphy returned from the mountain party last evening; Bayless Williams died night before last; Milton and Noah started for Donner's eight days ago, not returned yet; think they are lost in the snow.

Dec. 19—Snowed last night, thawing to-day; wind northwest, a little singular for a thaw.

Dec. 20—Clear and pleasant; Mrs. Reed here; no account from Milton yet; Charles Berger set out for Donner's; turned back unable to proceed; tough times, but not discouraged; our hopes are in God; Amen.

Dec. 21—Milton got back last night from Donner's camp; sad news; Jacob Donner, Samuel Shoemaker, Rhinehart and Smith are dead; the rest of them in a low situation; snowed all night, with a strong southwest wind.

Dec. 23—Clear to-day; Milton took some of his meat away; all well at their camp. Began this day to read the "Thirty days' Prayers;" Almighty God grant the requests of unworthy sinners!

Dec. 24—Rained all night and still continues; poor prospect for any kind of comfort, spiritual or temporal.

Dec. 25—Began to snow yesterday, snowed all night and snows yet, rapidly; extremely difficult to find wood, offered our prayers to God this, Christmas, morning; the prospect is appalling, but we trust in Him.

Dec. 27—Cleared off yesterday; continues clear; snow nine feet deep; wood growing scarcer; a tree, when felled, sinks into the snow, and is hard to be got at.

Dec. 30—Fine, clear morning; froze hard last night; Charles Berger died last evening about ten o'clock.

Dec. 31—Last of the year; may we, with the help of God, spend the coming year better than we have the past, which we propose to do if it be the will of the Almighty to deliver us from our present dreadful situation; Amen. Morning fair, but cloudy; wind east-by-south; looks like another snow storm; snow storms are dreadful to us; the snow at present is very deep.

Jan. 1, 1847—We pray the God of mercy to deliver us from our present calamity, if it be His holy will. Commenced snowing last night, and snows a little yet; provisions getting scant; dug up a hide from under the snow yesterday; have not commenced on it yet.

Jan. 3—Fair during the day; freezing at night; Mrs. Reed talks of crossing the mountains with her children.

Jan. 4—Fine morning, looks like spring; Mrs. Reed and Virginia, Milton Elliot and Eliza Williams started a short time ago, with the hope of crossing the mountain; left the children here; it was difficult for Mrs. Reed to part with them.

Jan. 6.—Eliza came back from the mountains yesterday evening, not able to proceed; the others kept ahead.

Jan. 8.—Very cold this morning; Mrs. Reed and others came back, could not find their way, on the other side of the mountains; they have nothing but hides to live on.

Jan. 10.—Began to snow last night; still continues; wind west-north-west.

Jan. 13.—Snowing fast; snow higher than the shanty; it must be thirteen feet deep; cannot get wood this morning; it is a dreadful sight for us to look upon.

Jan. 14.—Cleared off yesterday; the sun shining brilliantly renovates our spirits; praise be to the God of Heaven.

Jan. 15.—Clear day again; wind northwest; Mrs. Murphy blind; Lanthron not able to get wood; has but one axe between him and Kiesburg; it looks like another storm; expecting some account from Sutter's soon.

Jan. 17.—Lanthron became crazy last night; provisions scarce; hides our main subsistence; may the Almighty send us help.

Jan. 21.—Fine morning; John Battise and Mr. Denton came this morning with Eliza. She will not eat hides; Mrs. ———— sent her back to live or die on them.

Jan. 22.—Began to snow after sunrise; likely to continue; wind north.

Jan. 23.—Blew hard and snowed all night; the most severe storm we have experienced this winter; wind west.

Jan. 26.—Cleared up yesterday; to-day fine and pleasant, wind south; in hopes we are done with snow storms; those who went to Sutter's not yet returned; provisions getting scant; people growing weak; living on small allowance of hides.

Jan. 28.—Commenced snowing yesterday—still continues to-day. Lewis (Sutter's Indian,) died three day's ago; food growing scarcer; don't have fire enough to cook our hides.

Jan. 30.—Fair and pleasant; wind west; thawing in the sun; John and Edward Breen went to Graves' this morning; the ———— seized on Mrs. ———— goods until they would be paid; they also took the hides which herself and family subsisted upon; she regained two pieces only, the balance they have taken. You may judge from this what our fare is in camp; there is nothing to be had by hunting yet, perhaps there soon will be.

Jan. 31.—The sun does not shine out brilliant this morning; froze hard last night; wind northwest. Lanthron Murphy died last night about one o'clock; Mrs. Reed went to Graves' this morning to look after goods.

Feb. 5.—Snowed hard until 12 o'clock last night; many uneasy for fear we shall all perish with hunger; we have but little meat left, and only three hides; Mrs. Reed has nothing but one hide, and that is on Graves' house; Milton lives there, and likely will keep that; Eddy's child died last night.

Feb. 6.—It snowed faster last night and to-day than it has done this winter before; still continues without intermission; wind southwest; Murphy's folks and Kiesburg say they cannot eat hides; I wish we had enough of them; Mrs. Eddy is very weak.

Feb. 7.—Ceased to snow at last; to-day it is quite pleasant; McCutcheon's child died on the second of this month.

Feb. 8.—Fine, clear morning; Spitzer died last night; we will bury him in the snow. Mrs. Eddy died on the night of the seventh.

Feb. 9.—Mr. Pike's child all but dead; Milton is at Murphy's, not able to get out of bed; Kiesburg ———— gets up; he says he is not able; Mrs. Eddy and child were buried to-day; wind southeast.

Feb. 10.—Beautiful morning; thawing in the sun; Milton Elliot died last night at Murphy's shanty; Mrs. Reed went there this morning to see after his effects; J. Denton trying to borrow meat for Graves; had none to give; they had nothing but hides; all are entirely out of meat; but a little we have; our hides are nearly all eat up; with God's help spring will soon smile upon us.

Feb. 12.—Warm, thawy morning.

Feb. 14.—Fine morning, but cold; buried Milton in the snow. John Denton not well.

Feb. 15.—Morning cloudy until nine o'clock, then cleared off warm. Mrs. ———— refused to give Mrs. ———— any hides. Put Sutter's pack hides on her shanty and would not let her have them.

Feb. 16—Commenced to rain last evening, and turned to snow during the night, and continued until morning; weather changeable, sunshine, then light showers of hail, and wind at times. We all feel very unwell; the snow is not getting much less at present.

Feb. 19—Froze hard last night. Seven men arrived from California yesterday evening with provisions, but left the greater part on the way. To-day it is clear and warm for this region; some of the men have gone to Donner's camp; they will start back on Monday.

Feb. 22—The Californians started this morning, twenty-four in number, some in a very weak state; Mrs. Kiesburg started with them, and left Kiesburg here, unable to go; buried Pike's child this morning in the snow; it died two days ago.

Feb. 23—Froze hard last night; to-day pleasant and thawy—has the appearance of spring, all but the deep snow; wind south-south-east; shot a dog to-day, and dressed his flesh.

Feb. 25—To-day Mrs. Murphy says the wolves are about to dig up the dead bodies around her shanty, and the nights are too cold to watch them, but we hear them howl.

Feb. 26—Hungry times in camp; plenty of hides, but the folks wont eat them; we eat them with tolerable good appetite, thanks be to the Almighty God. Mrs. Murphy said here yesterday, that she thought she would commence on Milton and eat him; I do not think she has done so yet; it is distressing. The Donner's told the California folks, four days ago, that they would commence on the dead people, if they did not succeed that day or the next in finding their cattle, then ten or twelve feet under the snow, and did not know the spot or any where near it; they have done it ere this.

Feb. 28—One solitary Indian passed by yesterday; came from the lake; had a heavy pack on his back; gave me five or six roots, resembling onions in shape; tasted some like a sweet potato, full of tough little fibres.

Feb. 29—Ten men arrived this morning from Bear Valley, with provisions. We all leave in two or three days, and cache our goods here. They say the snow will remain until June.

The above mentioned ten men started for the Valley with seventeen of the sufferers; they traveled fifteen miles and a severe snow storm came on; they left fourteen of the emigrants, the writer of the above journal and his family, and succeeded in getting in but three children. Lieut. Woodworth immediately went to their assistance, but before he reached them they had eaten three of their number, who had died from hunger and fatigue; the remainder Lieut. Woodworth's party brought in. April, 1847, the last member of the party was brought to Cap't Sutter's Fort. It is utterly impossible to give any description of the sufferings of the company. Your readers can form some idea of them by perusing the above diary.

Yours, etc.,
GEORGE McKINSTRY, Jr.
FORT SACRAMENTO, *April 27, 1847.*

The emigrants thus caught in the mountains died, one by one, until thirty-six of the eighty-one who left Independence in the spring with such high hopes, literally starved to death. To make it more intelligible than the journal would indicate, I give the names of those from Sangamon county:—

George Donner and his wife, Mrs. Tamsen Donner; Jacob Donner and his wife, Mrs. Elizabeth Donner; her son, William Hook, sometimes called William Donner; the three sons of Jacob Donner and wife, Isaac, Lewis and Samuel; four unmarried men, Bayless Williams, Milford Elliott, James Smith and John Denton, *making a total of twelve from Sangamon county who perished from exposure and want of food.* For Mr. Elliott's family history, *see page 285.* For the Donner family history, *see page 257.*

I do not think it will be agreeable to the surviving members of the bereaved families, neither is it congenial to my feelings, to dwell on the horrors of that dreary winter among the inhospitable mountains. Those who could have given most in detail, were always reticent on that subject. They doubtless would have regarded it as the greatest boon that could have been conferred upon themselves if every recollection of it could have been erased from their memories. With the exception of the glimpse into the abyss of woe given in the preceding journal, I think it best, now, in this centennial year, after the lapse of the lifetime of one generation, to draw a veil over the horrors of the scene, and only extract such lessons from it as will tend to elevate our common humanity.

Jacob Donner died among the first, if not *the* first. He was a tender-hearted, conscientious man, and it is attested that his death was caused more by grief at the present and prospective sufferings of his family, than from disease or want of food. George and Jacob Donner were members of the German Prairie Christian church. *See what Isaac Taylor says about it.* The five surviving children of George Donner, and the three surviving children of Jacob Donner and wife, with their descendents, are among the most respected citizens of California. A few words more with reference to Mrs. George Donner. She was a native of New England—Maine, I believe—and was a lady in the highest sense of the word. Some of the citizens of Sangamon county remember her especially on account of her perfect self-control and power to govern. She taught school in the vicinity of Auburn when it was more unusual for a lady to teach than it is now. Some almost full grown, rough, uncouth young men were in her school, and yet she would govern them as thoroughly as though they were children. This self-control seems never to have left her. According to the testimony of Mr. Reed, who, after his own family had been rescued, visited the two camps of the Donners, to find Mrs. Jacob Donner and and Mr. George Donner helpless, and no means of removing them. They were prepared to leave provisions, and a man at each camp to care for the sick, and used every argument to induce Mrs. George Donner to go with them, but with the full knowledge of the probabilities that she would lose her own life, she utterly refused, preferring to meet death in the discharge of her duty to her husband rather than save her own life by seeming to abandon him in his hour of peril; and so she died, as truly a martyr as though she had been burned at the stake.

Other acts of heroisms are too numerous to mention all, but we will notice some of them. Hiram O. Miller proved to be courageous and efficient through all. Milford Elliott could have saved his own life, and having neither wife, children, or any other blood relative among the sufferers, no blame could have been laid to his charge if he had saved himself by pushing through, but he would not abandon helpless women and children, and his life paid the forfeit. The Eddy family, of Belleville, Illinois, was totally obliterated.

All that is known of C. T. Stanton is that he was from Chicago, Illinois. In my opinion, history does not record the name of a greater hero. It does not appear that he was in any way related, or even acquainted, with one of the sufferers previous to their departure from the States. He aided many of them on their way, and after their calamities came upon them, pushed his way through the mountains and reached Sutter's fort, where he was absolutely safe; but he knew there were men, women and children perishing with cold and hunger, and knowing this, there was no rest for him. He secured supplies of food and mules, enlisted the sympathies of two of the unlettered children of the forest, and all pushed on days and weeks, through storms and snow-drifts, until even the two savages, prompted by *him*, fell a sacrifice in the cause of humanity. Savages, did I say? I reverently withdraw the word. Their conduct would put to shame thousands who have been reared under the best of christian influences. There can be no more exalted evidence of humanity than to give one life with the hope of rescuing others from impending death. Mr. Stanton was one of the party of fifteen who attempted to pass out of the mountains, starting Dec. 16, 1846. He was weak and emaciated, as all were, and on the twenty-first of December became snow blind, and that night failed to reach the camp. The whole party lay in camp the next day waiting for him, but he never came. A party of men who went in the mountains the next summer to bring out the goods belonging to the Donner and Graves children, found his bones at the very tree where they left him on the twenty-first of December. They were chewed and broken in small pieces. The only way they could recognize them to be Stanton's was by a letter from his sister in one of his pockets, with some tobacco, the latter having prevented the wild beasts from destroying every evidence of identity. There was also a pistol that had been loaned to Stanton by Mr. Fallen, the man who found his remains. No one of those who perished was more sincerely mourned by the survivors than Mr. Stanton. Mr. Reed left this testimony to his worth: "Poor Stanton, who had no relative in the caravan to draw him back, but from the noble disposition he had, and the kind feelings he entertained for myself and family, and another person who had befriended him, induced him to return with provisions, and he lost his life as a noble PHILANTHROPIST. * * * His kindness saved my little ones from starvation."

When we last mentioned James F. Reed, he had been baffled in his attempt to reach the camp of the suffering emigrants, and had returned to Captain Sutter's, where he became satisfied that it would be utterly impossible to do anything more for them until spring. He was advised by Captain Sutter to proceed to Yerba Buena—now San Francisco— and make his case known to the naval officer in command. Arriving at San Jose, he found the San Francisco side o' the bay occupied by Mexicans. Here he joined a company of volunteers, and took part in the battle of Santa Clara; that opened the way to San Francisco. There he was enabled to raise, by voluntary contributions, $1,000 in the town and $300 from the sailors in port, with which he purchased supplies, which were placed on board a schooner, in command of midshipman Woodworth, who took all to the mouth of Feather river, where men and horses were procured for carrying relief to the emigrants. On their way to the camp they met a party coming out with women and children, among them Mr. Reed's wife and two children, his other two children, Martha and Thomas K., having been left in camp in charge of a Mr. Glover of the rescuing party, who volunteered to stay with and care for them, assuring Mrs. Reed that he was a Free Mason and knew her husband to be such, and that he would rescue her children or die in the attempt. He was as good as his word, protected and cared for the children until they were rescued by their father, and soon all the members of the family were re-united and rejoicing over their great deliverance. Mr. Reed's was the only entire family who left Sangamon county, all the members of which lived to reach their destination, and they did it without any one of them being driven to the necessity of eating human flesh. It seems the more wonderful that they should all have lived through, when their natural protector was separated from them so much of the time. Having in my possession sufficient material to make a more thrilling narrative of facts, than anything that could be drawn from the imagination, I feel how utterly futile this attempt to convey an idea of the sufferings of that company of emigrants has been, but want of space forbids that I should say more, and I am compelled to close.

The scene of the great suffering just described began west of the Great Salt Lake, in a salt desert, and extended hundreds of miles westward, over a succession of mountain ranges, running principally north and south, known as the Sierra Nevada mountains. Localities could not then be described, except by natural boundaries, such as mountains and valleys. The territory then belonged to Mexico, and the suffering and destitution that met the emigrants seemed only a realization of what might reasonably be expected in leaving the land of the Stars and Stripes to come under the sway of the benighted Mexican flag. But the old adage that "the darkest hour is just before the break of day," has been fully realized in this case to those who survived. The war they found in the Sacramento valley, waged by Mexico for the avowed purpose of exterminating the few scattered Americans on the Pacific coast, terminated in that whole region of country being ceded to our government. Then followed the discovery of gold, the influx of Americans, and the organization of the States of California and Oregon, and, a few years later, Nevada. The locality of the closing scene, the camp where the Donners died, is marked by a small body of water among the mountains, now known as Lake Donner, in the western part of the State of Nevada.

RENSHAW, WILEY P., was born Nov. 7, 1800, near Salisbury,

Ga., and was taken by his parents to Dickson county, Tenn. In 1817, the family moved to Madison county, Ill. Martha Nesbitt was born Nov. 8, 1794, near Lexington, Ky., and was taken by her parents in 1797 to Sumner county, Tenn. In 1817 they moved to Madison county, and in 1818 to Bond county, Ill. W. P. Renshaw and Martha Nesbitt were married Dec. 31, 1818, in Bond county. They lived in Madison county until one child was born, and moved to Sangamon county, Ill., arriving Feb. 26, 1821, on the north side of Richland creek, in what is now Cartwright township, where they had seven children.

JANE, born Oct. 11, 1819, in Madison county, is unmarried, and lives with her mother.

MARY A., born Oct. 20, 1822, in Sangamon county, married May 11, 1845, to Simeon Q. Harrison. See his name.

MARGARET E., born July 12, 1825, in Sangamon county, married Jan. 18, 1848, to Felix Butler, had one child, and Mrs. Butler died at Decatur in June, 1849. The child died in September following.

JAMES N., born July 16, 1827, died Sept. 1, 1852.

BARBARA A. H., born Sept. 18, 1829, in Sangamon county, married April 17, 1856, to Andrew M. Houghton. They had two children. WILEY P. died in his fourth year. ANNIE M. lives with her parents, in Menard county, seven miles north of Pleasant Plains, Sangamon county, Illinois.

JOHN SINCLAIR, born Dec. 28, 1831, in Sangamon county, married Nov. 17, 1858, to Elizabeth Ogden, who was born May 5, 1835, in Menard county. They have three children, MARTHA J., ABIGAIL L. and MARY A., and reside in Cartwright township, three miles west of Salisbury, Illinois.

WILLIAM P., born Dec. 28, 1833, died Oct. 7, 1852.

GEORGE M., born Aug. 7, 1839, in Sangamon county, married Oct. 22, 1866, to Matilda F. Parker, who was born Sept. 25, 1840, in Robertson county, Tenn. They live at the Renshaw family homestead, near Salisbury, Illinois.

Wiley P. Renshaw died Oct. 27, 1852, in Sangamon county, and his widow resides at the homestead where they settled in Feb., 1821. She has now Sept., 1873—lived more than fifty-two years within less than two rods of the same spot. It is in Cartwright township, three miles west of Salisbury, Sangamon county, Illinois.

Mrs. Margaret Renshaw, mother of Wiley P. Renshaw, came to Sangamon county in 1823, bringing seven children. Her daughter, Margaret H., married Michael Davis, has five children, and lives in Menard county. Delilah married Carroll Archer. See his name. Mrs. Margaret Renshaw died in August, 1842.

Mrs. Jane Nesbitt, the mother of Mrs. Wiley P. Renshaw, came to Sangamon county about 1826, bringing five children with her. Two years later she moved to Morgan county. In 1844 she came back to Sangamon, and died Feb. 14, 1846. Her daughter, Jane, and son, William, reside near Nemaha, Nebraska.

REISCH, FRANK, was born Jan. 24, 1809, in Baden, Germany. He came to America, landing at New Orleans in the winter of 1832, and traveled over the country until 1836, when he made his home in Beardstown, Illinois. The next year he returned to Germany, and was married Nov., 1837, to Susan Maurer, who was born Feb. 11, 1817, in Germany. In the spring of 1838 Mr. Reisch brought his wife to Beardstown, and from there to Richland creek, in Sangamon county, the same year. They had five children there, and moved to Springfield in 1850, where they had two children. Mr. Reisch engaged in the business of brewing, which he continued until May, 1875, when he sold his brewery to his sons. Of the seven children—

FRANK, Jun., born Jan. 19, 1842, in Sangamon county, married in Springfield, Oct. 15, 1865, to Anna Hammon, who was born Jan. 1, 1845, in Winchester, Scott county, Ill. They have three children, CHRISTINA, SUSAN and MARY, and reside in Springfield. Mr. Reisch was elected to represent his ward in the Sangamon county Board of Supervisors for 1871 and '72. He was elected alderman in April, 1873, for three years. He is associated in the brewery business with his brothers George and Joseph, under the firm name of F. Reisch & Bros., since May, 1875, at which time they bought out the interest of their father.

JOSEPH, born in Cartwright township, Sangamon county, was married in Springfield, April 25, 1876, to Mary Stehlin. They immediately left on a tour to Europe. Joseph Reisch is a member of the firm of Reisch & Bros., brewers.

MARY, GEORGE and ELIZABETH were all born in Cartwright township, Sangamon county, Illinois.

SUSIE and LEONARD, born in Springfield. The five latter reside with their mother, George being associated with his brothers, Frank and Joseph, in business.

Mr. Frank Reisch, Sen., was instantly killed by a fall from an upper window, August 18, 1875. He was in the act of pitching a piece of scantling from the window, when a spike in the timber, unobserved by him, caught in his clothing and drew him out. His widow and children reside in Springfield, Illinois.

RENN, HENRY, was born April 8, 1805, in Franklin county, Pennsylvania, came to Sangamon county in the spring of 1840, and bought a farm half a mile east of where Woodside Station now stands. A few years later he returned to Pennsylvania, and married Nancy Smith, who was born August 20, 1807. Their son—

JOHN WESLEY, born Oct. 15, 1847, in Sangamon county, married Jan. 20, 1869, to Laura J. Jones, daughter of Joshua W. Jones. See his name. Mr. and Mrs. Renn have three children, JESSIE A., LAURA S. and EDNA, and now—1876—reside on the farm purchased by his father in 1840. It is half a mile east of Woodside, Sangamon county, Illinois.

RHEA, JAMES, was born June 3, 1780, in Greenbrier county, Va., and when a young man, went to Barren county, Ky., where he was married, Nov. 20, 1801, to Rachel Joliff, who was born Oct. 16, 1783. They had ten children in Kentucky, and the family moved to Jefferson county, Ill., where one child was born, and moved to Sangamon county, arriving in 1827, in what is now Island Grove township. Of their eleven children—

ELIZABETH, born Sept. 25, 1802, in Kentucky, married there to George May. They came with her parents to Sangamon county, had several children, and moved to Mason county, where she died. Mr. May married again, and took their living children to Gentry county, Missouri.

JAMES, Jun., born August 27, 1804, in Kentucky, married in Jefferson county, Ill., to Susan Mattix, moved to the vicinity of Little Rock, Ark., and died there in 1840, leaving a widow and three children.

WILLIAM, born March 10, 1807, in Kentucky, married in Sangamon county, Dec. 11, 1828, to Susan Foutch, and had twelve children, three of whom died in infancy. William Rhea died Feb. 8, 1860, and his widow lives three miles southwest of Berlin, Illinois.

RICHARD, born Jan. 14, 1809, in Kentucky, married Eliza Rhea. They had three children, and Mr. Rhea died. His widow married William Ethridge, and moved to Iowa.

NANCY, born Dec. 24, 1811, in Kentucky, married Hugh Foutch. See his name. He died, and she married and moved to Iowa.

JEHOIDA, born Oct. 11, 1813, in Kentucky, was married in Sangamon county to John Foutch. See his name.

RACHEL, born Sept. 8, 1815, died, aged ten years.

JOHN, born July 14, 1817, in Barren county, Ky., married Nov. 14, 1839, in Sangamon county, to Julia A. Stark, who was born June 21, 1823, in Rutland, Vermont. They had seven children in Sangamon county. JAMES R., born Nov. 2, 1841, married America Montague, in Sangamon county, and lives near Hamburg, Fremont county, Iowa. STEPHEN E., born Nov. 4, 1843, married Lucy Wilcox, have one child, and live near Berlin, Ill. MARY A., born Jan. 6, 1846, married John F. Wilcox. See his name. THOMAS T., born June 10, 1848, married Sallie Williams. They have one child, JOHN W., and live near Berlin, Ill. JOHN H. died in infancy. MATHA E., born May 10, 1852, married R. Smith, and resides near Berlin. ABIGAIL R. died in infancy. John Rhea and his wife live two and one half miles northwest of Berlin, Sangamon county, Illinois.—1874.

MAHALA, born April 25, 1820, in

Kentucky, was married in Sangamon county, Ill., to Joseph Pulsifer. They had twins, and Mrs. Pulsifer died. Mr. Pulsifer is believed to have been murdered while on a business trip to St. Louis, as he was never heard of. Their two sons, NEVO and NEVI, are married, and live in Gentry county, Missouri.

MARY A., born Oct. 27, 1822, in Kentucky, was married in Sangamon county, Ill., to E. R. Alsbury, had one child, LUCINDA, who married James Shull. *See his name.* Mrs. Alsbury died April 28, 1851.

THOMAS F., born July 27, 1824, in Jefferson county, Ill., married in Sangamon county, Oct. 3, 1844, to Lucinda Wilcox. They have five children, ELIZA E. and REBECCA, the third and fourth, died young. ANNA L., KATE and LOU live with their parents in New Berlin, Illinois.

James Rhea died Feb. 12, 1843, and his widow died Oct. 28, 1851, both in Sangamon county. He was a soldier in the war of 1812, from Kentucky, under Gen. Harrison; was on Lake Erie, and saw the British vessels brought in after Perry's victory.

RHODES, RANDOLPH, was born about 1791, in North Carolina, and when he was a young man, went to Barren county, Ky. He was married in the adjoining county of Greene, in Oct., 1820, to Elizabeth Short. They had three children in Kentucky, and moved to Sangamon county, Ill., arriving in the fall of 1826 on Sugar creek, east of Springfield, where four children were born. In the spring of 1838 Mr. Rhodes moved to southwest Missouri, where two children were born, and returned to Sangamon county in the spring of 1845. In 1849 or '50, he moved to Macoupin county, and died there, Dec. 25, 1851, leaving a family near Macoupin station. Of their children—

WILLIAM, born about 1821, in Kentucky, married in Sangamon county to Jemima Center, had three children, and all the family died in Sangamon county.

JOHN T., born Nov. 10, 1825, in Kentucky, married in Sangamon county, March 2, 1848, to Telitha M. Vice. They had six living children, MARY E., married Levi King. *See his name.* LAURA A., CHARLES L., JULIUS W., ANNIE B. and LUCINDA A. live with their parents, four miles northwest of Springfield, Illinois.—1874.

MARY A., born Jan., 1831, in Sangamon county, married, in 1851, to Wm. R. Hammonds. They had six children, and Mr. Hammonds died, leaving his family in Crawford county, Kansas. Two of the children were killed, and two others severely wounded by a tornado, May 22, 1873.

JAMES J., born May, 1837, in Sangamon county, married Mary M. Tibbs, have two children, and live near Cremona, Allen county, Kansas.

RICHARDSON, LEWIS B., came to Sangamon county in 1824, has been twice married, raised a large family, and lives in Auburn township.

RIGG, SAMUEL, was born in Rutherford county, North Carolina, married there to Nancy Vawters. They had two children, and moved in 1816 to Greenup county, Ky., where six children were born; and moved to Sangamon county, Ill., arriving in 1827. Of their children, the eldest daughter married in Kentucky to Wm. Robinson, came to Sangamon county with her parents, and raised a family of seven daughters.

EWELL, born in North Carolina, married in Sangamon county to Sarah Kelly. They had nine children, and Mrs. Rigg died. Their daughter, NANCY E., married John G. Park. *See his name.* Ewell Rigg married Mrs. Sarah Darden, whose maiden name was Bradley. They reside at Macomb, Illinois.

JOHN E., born in Kentucky, married Alice Cox, and raised a family in McDonough county, Illinois.

JOSEPH R., born in Kentucky, married Julia A. Park, had fifteen children, four of whom died young. JAMES S. married and lives in Moultrie county. The ten, THOMAS E., JOHN E., WILLIAM Z., ROBERT R., LEONARD M., NANCY M., HENRY S., SARAH E., BENJAMIN B. and HARRIET O., live with their parents, near Macomb, Illinois.

MARY died, aged twenty-three or twenty-four years.

RUSSELL married Jane Venard, and raised a family near Macomb, Illinois.

ALPHA married Theophilus Mitchell, and raised a family near Macomb, Illinois.

PETER married Lucy Heuston, and raised a family in McDonough county, Illinois.

Samuel and Nancy Rigg both died in McDonough county, Illinois.

RIGGINS, WILLIAM, was born July 28, 1812, in Cape May county, New Jersey, was married Jan. 6, 1834, in Cumberland county, to Martha Mosslander, who was born in that county July 28, 1813. They had one child in Cumberland county, and moved to Cape May county; had one child, and moved to Sangamon county, Ill., arriving October, 1838, in what is now Gardner township, where they had one living child. Of their three children—

CALEB, born Sept. 9, 1836, in New Jersey, died in Sangamon county, aged fifteen years.

ELIZABETH, born Jan. 15, 1837, in Cape May county, New Jersey, married in Sangamon county, January, 1859, to James Tripp; have five children, and reside near Greenview, Menard county, Illinois.

MARY, born April 24, 1840, in Sangamon county, married Dec. 31, 1863, to Franklin H. Wood. They have three children, SEYMOUR, CHARLES and HARRY, and live near Maroa, Macon county, Illinois.

Mrs. Martha Riggins died April, 1844, and William Riggins was married March 6, 1867, to Mrs. Mary Rathsack, whose maiden name was Bohme. She was born Jan. 22, 1827, in Altkloster, Germany. They have two children—

ANNA C. and

WILLIAM H., and reside in Cartwright township, two miles south of Richland station, Sangamon county, Illinois—1874.

RICKARD, PETER, born in 1787, in Loudon county, Va., was there married to Elizabeth Everhart, who was born in 1790 in the same county. They had one child, and the family moved to Fauquier county, Va., where ten children were born, thence to Sangamon county, Ill., arriving at Springfield in the fall of 1830. In the spring of 1831 they moved three miles west of Springfield, and settled in what is now the southeast corner of Gardner township. Of their ten children—

LEWIS, born Oct. 13, 1806, in Loudon county, Virginia, went to Clark county, Ohio, and was there married to Catharine Wood, a native of Virginia. They moved to Sangamon county, Ill., in 1836. In the fall of 1838 they moved to Missouri, and in the fall of 1844 returned to Sangamon county, and nine years later, in the fall of '53, went to Christian county, Illinois. They had nine children—JOHN died in Christian county, aged about twenty-one years. ROBERT, born Feb. 12, 1837, in Sangamon county Ill., served in company I, 41st Ill. Inf., through the war to suppress the rebellion, was with Sherman in his march to the sea. He was married in Kansas, has three children, and lives in Texas. Mrs. Catharine Rickard died in Christian county, Feb. 18, 1866, and Lewis Rickard was married, March 12, 1868, to Susan Wood, at Springfield, Ohio, and reside there.

ELIZABETH, born April 1, 1809, in Fauquier county, Virginia, was married in Sangamon county to William Butler. *See his name.*

CATHARINE, born July 24, 1811, in Fauquier county, Va., was married in Sangamon county, Ill., June 4, 1833, to Dr. Jacob M. Earley. *See his name.* They had two children. GEORGE N., born Feb. 4, 1837, entered the army as assistant surgeon, Nov. 1, 1863, and died June 3, 1864, at Vicksburg, just before the surrender of that place. JACOB M., Jun., born Oct. 26, 1838, entered the army April, 1861, as Lieutenant in the first company raised in Petersburg, Illinois. Served three years, and was honorably discharged. He was married, March 27, 1868, to Caroline Lurton, of Delhi, Jersey county, Illinois. He died June 24, 1868, of consumption, in Petersburg, Menard county, Illinois. Dr. J. M. Early was murdered, March 11, 1838. *See his name.* His widow was married Oct. 1, 1851, at her father's house, three miles west of Springfield, to George U. Miles. They have one child, CHARLES, who lost one hand in firing a salute in 1865. He resides with his parents, in Petersburg, Menard county, Illinois.—1876.

SUSAN, born Aug. 26, 1813, in Fauquier county, Va., was married in Sangamon county, Ill., to David Talbott, Jun. See his name.

NOAH M., born March 20, 1817, in Fauquier county, Va., was married in Sangamon county to Harriet Talbott. They had five living children in Sangamon county. HARRIET E., born Feb. 4, 1839, was married, Oct. 4, 1865, to John Johnson, who was born Nov. 14, 1834, in New York city. They have one child, LAURA R., and reside five miles southwest of Springfield, Ill. Mr. Johnson has a certificate of the honorable discharge of his grandfather from the Revolutionary army, signed by George Washington. MARY F., born Aug. 16, 1840, was married, May 5, 1869, to Daniel G. Jones. See his name. NOAH M., Jun., born March 7, 1845, was married, Dec. 18, 1867, to Mary L. Patteso. They have one child, CHARLES M., and reside one mile southwest of Curran, Sangamon county, Illinois. GEORGE W., born June 13, 1847, was married, March 16, 1871, to Mary L. Gray. They have one child, GEORGE T., and reside at Philadelphia, Cass county, Illinois. SARAH L., born Oct. 23, 1848, was married, Oct. 4, 1871, to Aaron C. Reed, and died Sept. 27, 1872. Noah M. Rickard died Jan. 8, 1849, and widow resides with her daughter, Mrs. Johnson.—1876.

JOHN G., born Oct. 16, 1819, in Fauquier county, Va., raised in Sangamon county, and married July 5, 1859, in Allen county, Kansas, to Elizabeth Broderick, who was born May 21, 1831, in Shelby county, Indiana. They had three children in Kansas, CHARLES B., FREDDIE O. and NOAH FRANKLIN. The latter died in infancy. They reside four miles west of Springfield, Illinois.

SIMON P., born Oct. 16, 1821, in Fauquier county, Va., was married in Sangamon county, Ill., Nov. 12, 1846, to Sophia J. Earnest. They had seven children, three of whom died under five years. LAURA E., born Sept. 6, 1847, was married, Oct. 19, 1871, to Edwin Watts. See his name. HELEN M., born Dec. 6, 1848, was married, May 18, 1871, to Sidney French. They have one child, FLORENCE H., and reside near Frankfort, Ky. THOMAS E., born July 2, 1850, and ALLETTA E. reside

with their parents, two miles west of Springfield, Illinois.

SARAH J., born March 2, 1824, in Fauquier county, Va., was married in Sangamon county, Ill., to Richard F. Barrett. See his name. They reside in St. Louis.

MARY M., born March 16, 1827, in Fauquier county, Va., married Luther Talbott. See his name.

HENRY WASHINGTON, born Jan. 1, 1830, in Fauquier county, Va., was married April 4, 1852, in Sangamon county, Ill., to Sarah A. Sims. They had seven children; one died in infancy. ELIZABETH L. was married Sept. 26, 1872, to Isaac French, a native of Franklin county, Ky. MINNIE A., LEWIS F., WASHINGTON M., ROBERT I. and GEORGE E. reside with their father. Mrs. Sarah A. Rickard died Dec. 21, 1864, and H. W. Rickard was married June 7, 1866, to Henrietta M. Earnest. They have two children, CATHARINE J. and THOMAS E. H. W. Rickard resides on the farm settled by his father in 1831. It is three miles west of Springfield, Sangamon county, Illinois.

Mrs. Elizabeth Rickard died Jan., 1858, at the family homestead. Peter Rickard died Sept. 17, 1860, in Springfield, Illinois.

RIDDLE, DAVID, was born April 20, 1780, in Mifflin county, Pa. He went to Champaign county, Ohio, in 1807. Mary Hamilton was born in Mason county, about seven miles from Maysville, Ky., March 9, 1786. Her mother died when she was quite young, and she went to Champaign county, Ohio, with some friends, and was there married, about 1808, to David Riddle. Six children were born in Ohio, and the family moved, in 1819, to Washington county, Ill., where one child was born, and Mrs. Riddle died there, July 11, 1821. David Riddle was married in 1822, to Mrs. Elizabeth Crocker, whose maiden name was Wakefield, and moved to Sangamon county, arriving at Springfield Oct. 14, 1822, and the next day moved to a farm in Williams township. They had two children in Sangamon county. Of his children—

JOHN, born Jan. 8, 1809, in Ohio, married in Sangamon county, Oct. 2, 1834, to Sarah H. Clark. They had five children. ELIZA C. died, aged twenty-four years. MARY E. married John Tomlinson, have four children, FRANK G., HELEN A., ELMER S. and CLARENCE A., and live near Mt. Pulaski. FRANCIS A. enlisted at Springfield, July, 1862, in Co. A, 130th Ill. Inf., for three years, was promoted to 1st Lieut., and acted as Captain, Major and Judge Advocate, and was honorably mustered out of the service in August, 1865. He was married in Jacksonville, Ill., to Sarah Gallaher. He is a lawyer, and resides in Chicago. SARAH W. is unmarried, and lives with her father. Mrs. Sarah H. Riddle died, and John Riddle married Martha Archer, who was born May 24, 1819, in Greenville, Bond county, Ill. They have one child, NANCY E., who lives with her parents, one mile northeast of Barclay, Sangamon county, Ill. John Riddle remembers that when he was a boy the family found that there was a letter in the postoffice, but they had not the money to pay for it. He gathered a load of corn, took it to town, and sold the whole load for ninety-five cents, paid twenty-five cents for the letter, and returned home rejoicing.

JAMES, born April 30, 1811, in Ohio, was married in Sangamon county to Susan A. Sampson. They had two children. JOHN M. married Sarah M. Woltz. They have one child, CHARLES A., and live one and a half miles north of Barclay, Illinois. DAVID A. lives at DesMoines, Iowa. James Riddle was a soldier from Sangamon county in the Black Hawk war. He died March 4, 1849, and his widow lives with her son, John M.—1874.

MARGARET, born Sept. 25, 1812, in Ohio, married in Sangamon county to Joseph Dement. He died, leaving a widow and four children in Logan county, Illinois.

ABNER, born Oct. 6, 1814, in Champaign county, Ohio, married in Sangamon county to Mrs. Mary A. Pickrell, whose maiden name was Elkin. They had one child, HAMILTON R., born Dec. 9, 1841, in Sangamon county, enlisted Aug. 1, 1862, in Co. B, 130th Ill. Inf., for three years. He was captured, with Bank's Red river expedition, April 8, 1864, imprisoned at Camp Tyler, Texas, thirteen months, and released in May, 1865. While in prison his regiment was consolidated with the 77th Ill. Inf., and he was mustered out as a member of Co. A, of that regiment, June 17, 1865, at Springfield. He was married, Sept. 2, 1868, to Cordelia F. Constant. They have three children, EARL A., ELIZA MAY and WILLIAM E. Hamilton R. Riddle graduated Feb., 1873, at Rush Medical College, Chicago, and is a practicing physician at Mechanicsburg, Ill. Mrs. Mary A. Riddle died, and Abner Riddle married Mary J. Clark. They have ten children. RUSSELL O. married Sabra Constant, have two children, MAY O. and LOVELLA, and live half a mile south of Barclay, Sangamon county, Ill. MARY J. married Samuel McCullough, and lives in Kansas. The other eight children reside with their parents, near Ottowa, Kan.

NANCY, born April 10, 1817, in Ohio, married in Sangamon county to Abraham Bird. *See his name.*

MARY, born May 13, 1819, in Ohio, married in Sangamon county to William H. Fowkes. *See his name.*

ELIZABETH, born June 12, 1823, in Sangamon county, married Alexander Mills, and resides at Lincoln, Illinois.

SARAH A., born Sept. 30, 1826, in Sangamon county, married to Rev. Alexander Semple. They have three children, and live at Decatur, Ill. He is Presiding Elder in the M. E. Church.

David Riddle died August 12, 1846, and his widow, Mrs. Elizabeth Riddle, died in 1854, both in Sangamon county.

RIDDLE, WILLIAM, was born Sept. 1, 1805, in Kentucky. He is a nephew of David Riddle. At six months of age, he was taken by his parents to Logan county, Ohio. Maxamillia Bousman was born in 1809 in Champaign county, Ohio, where they were married in 1826. They had four living children in Ohio, and moved to Sangamon county, Ill., arriving May 31, 1836, in what is now Williams township, where they had five children, and in 1851 moved to Douglas county, Oregon. Of their nine children—

JANE, born April 14, 1828, in Logan county, Ohio, married Jan. 15, 1850, in Sangamon county, to Thomas Wilson, who was born Nov. 4, 1817, in Dumfriesshire, Scotland. They have four living children, born in Sangamon county, namely: JANE F., WILLIAM R., JOHN T. and LILLIAS H., and reside two miles southwest of Buffalo Hart station, Sangamon county, Illinois—1874.

ARTAMESIA, born Oct. 11, 1830, in Sangamon county, married in Feb., 1849, to James P. Chapman, who died, and she married William H. Merriman. See his name.

ISABELLA, born Jan. 16, 1835, in Ohio, came to Sangamon county with her parents; thence with them to Oregon, and was there married to Israel R. Nicholls. They have eleven children, and reside near North Canyonville, Douglas county, Oregon—1874.

WILLIAM H., born March, 1836, in Ohio, came to Sangamon county; thence with his parents to Oregon, and died there in July, 1836.

GEORGE W., born Feb. 22, 1840, in Sangamon county, married Anna Rice, has two children, and live near North Canyonville, Douglas county, Oregon.

ABNER, born in 1842, in Sangamon county, married Alice Rice, has two children, and reside near North Canyonville, Oregon.

JOHN E., born in 1845, in Sangamon county, married in Oregon, and his wife and child were drowned while crossing a stream in a wagon. He is living with his second wife in North Canyonville, Oregon.

ANNA M., born April 8, 1847, in Sangamon county, married Vincent Beal, has one child, and lives in Jacksonville, Oregon.

TOBIAS S., born Aug. 30, 1849, in Sangamon county, married Sarah Smith, has two children, and lives at Harney lake, Oregon.

Mrs. Maxamillia Riddle died August, 1868, and William H. Riddle resides at North Canyonville, Oregon—1874.

RICHARDS, ANDREW, was married in Nicholas county, Kentucky, to Mrs. Rosanna Dinsmore, whose maiden name was McCune, a sister to Gavin McCune. She had one child by her first marriage, and they had five children, all in Nicholas county, Ky. The family moved to Sangamon county, Ill., arriving in the fall of 1832, at Rochester, where one child was born. Of all their children—

CELIA DINSMORE, born in Kentucky, married in Sangamon county to Joseph Clawson. Both died, leaving three children near Taylorville, Illinois.

Of the Richards children—

ROBERT E., born Sept. 16, 1822, in Kentucky, married in Sangamon county, April 15, 1845, to Louisa Stokes. They had two children. ANNA died in infancy. AMANDA, born May 3, 1848, died Nov. 6, 1862. Robert E. Richards died Feb. 15, 1848, and his widow lives at the house of her neice, Mrs. Lawson H. Smith. See Bell family.

JOHN A., born August 15, 1824, in Nicholas county, Ky., married in Sangamon county, March 29, 1846, to Sarah E. Dickerson. They had nine children; three died young. JANE married Scott Clawson, has three children, and lives near Taylorville, Illinois. KATIE M., ELECTA, IDA and EMMA, twins, and JOHN P. live with their parents in Rochester, Sangamon county, Illinois.

WILLIAM M., born in Nicholas county, Ky., was married in Sangamon county, Ill., to Mary J. Menara. They had nine children; one died. Wm. M. Richards and family live near Breckenridge, Sangamon county, Illinois.

BENJAMIN A., born March 3, 1829, in Nicholas county, Ky., was married Oct. 10, 1850, in Sangamon county, to Matilda Hutchings, who was born Feb. 23, 1832, in Rochester, New York. They had ten children; five died young. PHILIP A., WILLIAM T., CHARLES E., LEMUEL C. and MABEL live with their parents. Benj. A. Richards is the proprietor of a book and job printing office in Springfield, Ill., where he now resides.

ANDREW M., born in Nicholas county, Ky., raised in Sangamon county, went to Texas about 1859, married there, has a family, and lives at Wheelock, Robertson county, Texas.

NANCY, born in Sangamon county, married Thomas Dye, has four children, and lives near Bradfordton, Sangamon county, Illinois.

Andrew Richards and Mrs. Rosanna Richards both died in Sangamon county, Illinois.

RIDGELY, NICHOLAS H., was born April 27, 1800, on his father's tobacco plantation in Maryland, near Baltimore; was educated in Baltimore, and was engaged in mercantile business there until April, 1828, when he removed to St. Louis, Mo., and became a clerk in the United States branch bank established there shortly after his arrival. He continued in this position until May, 1835, when he was appointed cashier of the State Bank of Illinois, incorporated in that year, which office he held until the termination of the charter of the bank, and was one of the trustees who finally closed the business of the bank. While engaged in this closing process, and afterwards, he carried on a private banking business on his own account, and organized "Clark's Exchange Bank of Springfield," and continued his connection with it until it was discontinued, and all its obligations promptly and fully discharged. In 1866 he, in connection with Charles and William Ridgely—his sons,—J. Taylor Smith, and Lafayette Smith, organized "The Ridgely National Bank of Springfield." He became President, and has continued in this office ever since. He has thus been actively engaged in the banking business constantly for forty-eight years. He has been married twice, and has a family of thirteen adult children living, namely:

SARAH married Rev. Richard V. Dodge, and resides in Chicago.

VINCENT is married, and now resides in Adams county, Illinois.

SOPHIA married J. Taylor Smith, of Springfield, Illinois. See his name.

REDICK M. is married, and now resides in Springfield, Illinois.

HENRY married, and now resides in Springfield, Illinois.

CHARLES married, and now resides in Springfield, Illinois.

JULIA married John H. Rea, now of Chicago.

WILLIAM is unmarried, and resides in Springfield, Illinois.

ANNA married James L. Hudson, of Springfield, Illinois.

MARY married Chas. E. Hay, of Springfield, Illinois.

JANE married James T. Jones, of Springfield, Illinois.

HENDERSON is unmarried, and resides in Springfield, Illinois.

OCTAVIA married Charles D. Roberts, of Springfield, Illinois.

N. H. Ridgely and wife reside in Springfield, Illinois.

RIDGELY, REDICK M., was born March 29, 1830, in St. Louis, Mo., and brought by his father (N. H. Ridgely) to Springfield in 1835. He was married July 1, 1850, to Margaret Aitken, who was born March 6, 1835, in Glasgow, Scotland. They have four living children, JANEY H., ALICE M., REDICK and JOHN A. Redick M. Ridgely was City Treasurer from 1851 to 1853, a member of the Board of Supervisors of Sangamon county for two years, and a member of the City Council four years. He was in the Quartermaster's Department in Springfield from 1861 to 1862, and was in the same department in Memphis, Tenn., from 1862 to 1865. He is now — 1876 — Superintendent of all the street railroads of Springfield.

RIDGELY, CHARLES, the eldest son of N. H. Ridgely by the second wife, is a native of Springfield; married Jane M. Barrett, and has several children. Charles Ridgely is President of the Springfield Iron Company, Vice-President of the Ridgely National Bank, and resides in Springfield, Ill.

RIDGEWAY, AUSBURN, brother to Samuel, was born in Berkley county, Va., and married in North Carolina to Jane Phelps. They moved to Lincoln county, Ky., from there to Washington county, in the same State, thence to Sangamon county, Ill., arriving in the fall of 1828, in Buffalo Hart grove. They raised a large family, and the parents both died in Sangamon county. Of their children we will mention four only—

JOHN, born Feb. 23, 1806, in Lincoln county, Ky., came with his parents to Sangamon county, in 1828, and was married, Feb. 12, 1829, to Sarah Bridges. They had seven children, two of whom died young. MARTHA J., born Jan. 3, 1830, married Charles Eckel, and lives near Ottawa, Kansas. ALFRED A., born March 13, 1834, died in 1857. ADALINE and CAROLINE, twins, born Jan. 17, 1837. ADALINE married Benjamin F. Hill, has six living children, and reside near Decatur, Illinois. CAROLINE married Henry Lee, and died Nov. 2, 1864, near Illiopolis. LEVI S., born Sept. 29, 1839, married Rhoda Fletcher. He died, August 2, 1868, in Sangamon

—77

county, leaving a widow and four children, who live near Decatur, Ill. John Ridgeway died Oct. 28, 1858, and his widow married Jonathan Constant. See his name.

PATTERSON, born Nov. 19, 1813, in Lincoln county, Ky., married in Sangamon county to Nancy Huddleston, who died, leaving two children, and he married Mrs. Rhoda J. Walker, whose maiden name was Withrow. They have one child, and live in Cooper township, Sangamon county.

MELINDA married Alexander Dickerson. See his name.

ALEXANDER served three years in the 73d Ill. Inf., has a large family, and moved west after the close of the rebellion.

RIDGEWAY, SAMUEL, was born May 10, 1777, in Berkley county, Va., and was taken by his parents to the valley of the Yadkin river, North Carolina, when he was quite young. He was there married, about 1799, to Elizabeth Caton, who was born August 25, 1775, in Berkley county, Va., also. Shortly after marriage Samuel Ridgeway and wife packed all their worldly goods on one horse, and each rode another. Thus equipped, they set out for Kentucky, and settled near Stanford, the capital of Lincoln county. They had eight children there, and the family moved to Sangamon county, Ill., arriving in Nov., 1829, in what is now Clear Lake township, west of the Sangamon river, and five miles northeast of Springfield. Of their children—

CHARLES, born May 18, 1801, was married in Kentucky to Sally Wilson. They had two children there, and moved to Sangamon county with his parents; lived near Mechanicsburg two years, and returned to his native State. Charles Ridgeway died in 1875, at Danville, Ky., and his family reside there.

AUSBURN, born June 8, 1803, died in Kentucky, August 12, 1826, within two weeks of the time set for his marriage.

PHILIP, born Jan. 1, 1806, in Kentucky, was married in Sangamon county to Margaret Henderson. He died, Sept. 8, 1838, leaving a widow and four children, who moved to Hancock county, Illinois.

JOHN, born March 30, 1808, in Kentucky, was married in Sangamon county, and his wife died within six months. He was married again, moved to Missouri, and from there to Oregon in 1845, and died there in 1872, leaving ten children.

MARY, born Dec. 14, 1811, in Kentucky, was married in Sangamon county to James Watson. See his name.

SAMUEL L., born April 25, 1813, in Lincoln county, Ky., was married in Sangamon county, Ill., Aug. 10, 1837, to Charlotte A. Stout. See Stout family name. They had seven children, and in July, 1872, moved to Maryville, Mo. Of their children, PHILEMON, born May 11, 1839, in Sangamon county, Ill., resides in California. ELIZABETH A., born Oct. 17, 1841, died in her third year. OLIVER, born March 23, 1844, in Sangamon county, Ill., was married to Emma F. Orr, in Adair county, Mo. They have three children, GEORGE, CHARLOTTE and ARTHUR, and reside in Nodaway county, Mo. SAMUEL L., Jun., born March 7, 1847, in Sangamon county, Ill., was married Dec. 26, 1872, to Laura H. Hamlin. They have one child, SAMUEL L., and reside in Nodaway county, Missouri. See Hamlin name. MARY E., born May 11, 1849, was married Jan. 11, 1870, to George L. Drennan, of Sangamon county, Illinois. See his name. ARMENIA J., born June 25, 1851, married Sept. 4, 1876, to Edward Headley, of Sangamon county, Ill. CHARLOTTE EMMA, born Jan. 9, 1853, and FRANCIS, born March 16, 1855, reside with their parents, in Maryville, Nodaway county, Missouri.

BENJAMIN R., born Feb. 5, 1815, in Lincoln county, Ky., was married in Sangamon county June 13, 1839, to Catharine Rape. They had six children. THOMAS J., born Dec. 10, 1846, married Jane Snodgrass, has two children, and live in Springfield. JOHN B., born April 3, 1846, married Lucy E. Cullom, and live near New City, Sangamon county, Ill. ANNA E. married James L. Plummer. They had two children, and Mr. Plummer died April 30, 1871. SAMUEL N. died, aged ten years. NANCY S. died in her sixteenth year. MARTHA F. lives with her parents, near New City, Sangamon county, Ill.

LINDSAY, born Jan. 20, 1818, in Lincoln county, Ky., was married in Sangamon county Dec. 7, 1841, to Lucy M. Dawson. They had five children in Sangamon county. SAMUEL F., born Dec. 25, 1842, enlisted Aug. 12, 1862, for three years, in Co. A, 73d Ill. Inf.; served until March 26, 1864, when he was discharged on account of physical disability. He was married Jan. 2, 1868, in Springfield, to Nancy M. Logan. They have one child, JENNIE MAY, and reside in Springfield, Ill. NANCY S., born Aug. 23, 1845, died in infancy. JOHN D., born July 17, 1848, was married Dec. 24, 1872, to Mary L. McVay, who was born April 7, 1852, in Sangamon county. They have one child, CHARLES ALBERT, and reside five miles east of Springfield, Ill. BERTRAND D., born Dec. 9, 1849, and CHARLES L., born Dec. 14, 1863, both live with their parents. Lindsay Ridgeway and wife reside five miles east of Springfield, on the farm settled by his father in 1829.

Mrs. Elizabeth Ridgeway died Feb. 28, 1847, and Samuel Ridgeway died June 22, 1847, both in Sangamon county, Illinois.

ROBB, DAVID, was born Jan. 24, 1789, in the town of Acworth, N. H. He was there married to Diana Farr, who was born in the same town, May 15, 1791. They had six children in Acworth, and the family moved to West Virginia, and from there to Sangamon county, Ill., arriving in 1830, and settled about two miles south of the present town of Breckenridge. Of their children—

DANIEL, born July 12, 1815, in New Hampshire, married in Sangamon county to Jennie Rogers. They have a family, and reside near Nebraska City, Neb.

LUCY, born July 19, 1816, in Acworth, N. H., married in Sangamon county to Preston Breckenridge. See his name.

JOHN, born May 30, 1820, in New Hampshire, raised in Sangamon county, married near St. Joseph, Mo., to Mary E. Broiles, Oct. 15, 1843. They had two children, and came to Sangamon county, where four children were born. Of their six children: MARY J., born August 12, 1844, in Missouri, married Marshall Raines, have four children, and reside near Xenia, Ohio. DAVID, born Jan. 28, 1846, near St. Joseph, Mo., married in Sangamon county, Nov. 28, 1867, to Ella Gray, have two children, and reside near Breckenridge, Ill. ELIZA E., born and died in Sangamon county, aged ten years. PHŒBE, born Oct. 2, 1850, in Sangamon county, married Andrew J. Poffenberger. See his name. WILLIAM, born Jan. 3, 1844, and JOSEPH, born April 28, 1857, live with their mother. John Robb died August 6, 1858, in Sangamon county. His widow married, Dec. 4, 1860, to Abraham Martin. He died in 1863, and she resides one mile west of Breckenridge, Sangamon county, Illinois.

ELECTA, born Dec. 9, 1821, in New Hampshire, married in Sangamon county to Joseph Clawson. He died, and she lives near Assumption, Christian county, Illinois.

WILLIAM, born Feb. 10, 1824, in New Hampshire, married in Sangamon county to Helen R. McLean. They have five children, and live near Corydon, Iowa.

MARY J., born May 21, 1827, in New Hampshire, married in Sangamon county to Joseph Clawson, had eight children, and she died. Her children live with her sister, Electa, who is their stepmother.

Mrs. Diana Robb died Nov. 4, 1835, and David Robb married Mrs. Elizabeth Graham, whose maiden name was Day. She died in 1856, and David Robb died Nov. 3, 1859, in Sangamon county.

ROBBINS, HIRAM, was born Dec. 26, 1793, in Buncombe county, N. C. His parents moved to Overton county, Tenn., thence to Washington county, Ky., and from there to Vincennes, Indiana Territory. At that place he entered the army, and served six months in the war of 1812 with England. The family after the war, moved back to Tennessee, and from there to Pope county, Illinois, where the father died, and the family moved to Madison county. Hiram Robbins was there married, Dec. 29, 1816, to Elizabeth Dean. They had two children, and moved to Sangamon county, arriving in the summer of 1821 within one mile of where Barclay now stands, and in 1823 moved to what is now Cooper township, where they had six living children. He was a soldier from this county in the

Black Hawk war. Of their seven children—

JOHN was twice married, served three years in the 73d Ill. Inf., and died April 1, 1868.

WILLIAM H., born March 1, 1821, in Madison county, Ill., raised in Sangamon county, married in Greene county, Aug. 11, 1845, to Ann Dodson. She died Aug. 12, 1846. He was married May 14, 1848, to Sarah A. Miller. They had one child, ALICE A., born July 5, 1850, married Benjamin F. Miller, and resides three and one-half miles west of Mechanicsburg, Ill. Mrs. S. A. Robbins died in 1852, and Wm. H. Robbins married, Sept. 4, 1856, to Elizabeth Laswell. They have four children, JOHN W., THOMAS LYON, NANCY E. and ANDREW H., and live near Mechanicsburg, Illinois.

JEREMIAH, born Nov. 29, 1821, in Sangamon county. He has been twice married; served three years in Co. H, 114th Ill. Inf., and lives in Cooper township, Sangamon county.

WILSON, born Jan. 3, 1824, in Sangamon county, married, Oct. 25, 1850, to Susan A. Cantril. They had six living children. ANNA M., born Jan. 1, 1851, married, Dec. 18, 1871, to George Baker, have two children, and live in Cooper township. MARY E., ALBERT S., MARTHA S., JOSEPH E. and ALLEN L. live with their parents, two and one-half miles west of Mechanicsburg, Illinois. Wilson Robbins served one year, from June, 1846, under Col. E. D. Baker, in the war with Mexico.

MARY A., born April 27, 1825, in Sangamon county, married Thomas Simpkins, who died, and she married William Taff. They had one child, THERESA TAFF, who married John Johnson. *See his name.* Mr. Taff died, and she married Joseph Brown, had one child, and Mr. Brown died, and she married Francis Gough, and she died April, 1862.

ELIZABETH A. married E. Taylor, and died in 1847.

HIRAM, Jun., was twice married, and died in McDonough county.

PRUDENCE married M. D. Gough.

ELIZA A., born June 21, 1842, married J. Wesley Veach. *See his name.*

Mrs. Elizabeth Robbins died Aug. 17, 1866, and Hiram Robbins was married to Mrs. Merada Gordon. For a third wife he married, Oct. 1, 1872, to Mrs. Elizabeth E. White, whose maiden name was Strode. They reside in Cooper township, Sangamon county, Ill.

ROBERTS, EDMUND, was born in 1785, in Farmington, New Hampshire. His ancestors were Welsh, and emigrated to New England before the Revolution. They were members of the society of Friends. Forbidden by their principles to take up arms, they, nevertheless, assisted in that struggle as far as they consistently could, by carrying supplies to the army. The subject of this sketch left New Hampshire when a young man, on horseback, for western Pennsylvania. In 1808 an Indian treaty opened the country between the Mississippi and Arkansas rivers, and as far west as Fort Clark now Peoria, Illinois. Mr. Roberts was one of the first eastern men who settled in that country. Steamboats not being used on the western waters then, he made the voyage down the Ohio river in a flatboat, and in 1810 engaged in merchandizing at St. Genieveve, Missouri, as a member of the firm of Keil, Bisch & Roberts. He afterwards removed to Kaskaskia, Ill., where he associated with himself in business, Thomas Mather and James L. Lamb. Mr. Roberts made his trips east on horseback, crossing the Ohio river at Shawneetown, Ill., often sleeping on the ground, with a saddle for a pillow. He was always liable to attacks from Indians and once lost his horse by them, compeling him to walk and carry his saddle until he could buy another. He was married, in 1819, at Mt. Pleasant, Pennsylvania, to Susan Lamb, a native of Chester county, in the same State. She was a sister to his partner, James L. Lamb. *See his name.* After prosecuting business for many years at Kaskaskia and Chester, he removed to Springfield, in the same State, in 1832. Mr. and Mrs. Roberts had eight children, three only of whom survive—

GEORGE L., born March 16, 1821, in Kaskaskia, Ill., was married in Lebanon, Ill., to Virginia E. Horner, a native of the latter place. They had two children in Lebanon, EDMUND and VIR-

GINIA, and reside in Old Mission, Grand Traverse county, Michigan.

JAMES H., born Dec. 12, 1825, in Kaskaskia, Ill., was married Sept. 16, 1863, to Harriet E. Smith, who was born Dec. 6, 1840. Mrs. Harriet E. Roberts died Feb. 28, 1866, leaving two children, LUCRETIA B., born Sept. 6, 1864, and JAMES H., Jun., who died in infancy. James H. Roberts was married Nov. 9, 1870, to Mrs. Susan M. Slater, whose maiden name was Lamb. They have one child, MARY T. J. H. Roberts and family reside in Chicago, Ill. He is engaged in business at 86 Washington street—Sept., 1876.

MARY K., born July 13, 1829, in Kaskaskia, Ill., was married Nov. 11, 1857, to Benjamin M. Thomas, who was born Aug. 10, 1810, in Philadelphia, Penn. They had three children: SUSAN R., born Oct. 25, 1858, in Springfield, Ill.; MARY P., born April 7, 1860, in Chicago, Ill., died July 26, 1863; MORRIS St. P., born Feb. 27, 1862, in Chicago. Mr. Thomas died Oct. 31, 1864, in Vincennes, Ind. His widow and children reside in Chicago, Illinois.

Mr. Roberts was a citizen of Illinois when it contained less than twelve thousand inhabitants. In 1829 he was appointed one of the commissioners on the part of the State of Illinois to determine the route for a canal to connect the Illinois river with Lake Michigan, and lay out town sites; Chicago and Ottawa were two of these towns. Seven years later—1836—ground was broken, and the work of constructing the canal commenced. Mr. Roberts was a firm friend of education, having himself been a teacher in his younger days. He was, in the early history of McKendree college, at Lebanon, Ill., a member of its board of trustees. His two sons were educated there. In 1846 he visited the Eastern States in the interests of this institution, and was successful in supplying it with funds and teachers. From that to the present time, McKendree college has continued to prosper. In consequence of failing health, he retired from active business about 1836, and passed many of his winters in the south, but continued to make Springfield his home.

Mrs. Susan Roberts died Aug. 4, 1844. She had long been a member of the Methodist Episcopal church, loved and revered by all who knew her. In his funeral address on the occasion of her death, Rev. Dr. Akers, describing her influence, said: "She moved among her sisters like the moon among the stars." Her husband never recovered from the shock occasioned by her death, and he died March 28, 1847, both in Springfield, and the remains of both are buried in Oak Ridge Cemetery.

ROBISON, EDWARD, born Oct. 16, 1781, in Loudon county, Va. In 1787 his parents moved to Nelson county, Ky., and a few years later the family moved to Caldwell county, in the same State, leaving Edward at Bardstown to finish his trade as a hatter. He was married in Caldwell county, March 14, 1809, to Jane Hanley, who was born Feb. 29, 1788, in Pendleton District, South Carolina. They had five children in Kentucky, and moved to Pope county, Ill., in 1819, where one child was born. Thence to Sangamon county, Ill., arriving Nov., 1821, near Springfield. After some changes they settled in what is now Gardner township, north of Spring creek, where they had six children. Of all their children—

GEORGE H., born May 9, 1810, in Kentucky; served his country in the Black Hawk war, Mexican war, and about three years in Co. H, 10th Ill. Cav., in the late rebellion. He died unmarried, Dec., 1873, in Sangamon county.

JOHN H., born Oct. 15, 1811, in Kentucky, was married in Sangamon county to Mary A. Duff. They have three children, GEORGE C., JOHN S.; the latter married Sarah Handley; MARTHA married Major Moore. J. H. Robison and family reside near Carleton, Yamhill county, Oregon.

MELISSA, born Nov. 11, 1813, in Caldwell county, Ky., was married in Sangamon county, Ill., to Logan McMurry. See his name.

DAVID P., born March 6, 1816, in Caldwell county, Ky., was married in Sangamon county, Sept. 3, 1836, to Lucy Simms. They had ten children; two died young. LUCINDA J. and EMILY L. died, aged seven years. MARY E. H., or "TIP," born Sept. 25, 1840, was married Sept. 10, 1857, to Thomas A. Sims, who was born Oct. 3, 1835, in Culpepper county, Virginia, and brought up in Muskingum county, Ohio. They have six children, JAMES P., LUCY A., MARY E., JENNIE A., GEORGE J. and MARTHA E., and reside in Gardner township, west of Springfield. MARTHA A. married Edmund McClure. They have four children, JAMES, MARGARET, LEWIS and CLAUD, and live near Linden, Osage county, Kansas. JULIA, born Oct. 30, 1847, was married to Michael Dolan, who was born Dec. 28, 1845, in Galway, Ireland. They have three children, JOHN J., ELLEN and T. EDWARD, and live near Berlin, Sangamon county, Ill. EDWARD J. married Annie Archer. They have one child, and live in Gardner township. GEORGE J., MARION P., KATIE V., and JAMES T. reside with their parents five miles southwest of Springfield, Illinois.

ELIZABETH, born April 21, 1818, in Kentucky, was married in Sangamon county to Richard Hall. They had three children. Mrs. Hall and the youngest child were killed by lightning, April 27, 1845, in Gardner township. This occurred at the house of Mrs. Hall's mother. Three other members of the family were injured seriously at the same time. Of the other two children: WILLIAM E. married Miss Lowery, in DeWitt county. He was a soldier in an Illinois regiment, and died in the army. MELISSA married James Moore. They have six children, two of whom are married, BENTON and CHARLES. James Moore and family live near White Church, Wyandotte county, Kan. Richard Hall was married, in 1847, to Sarah Sanders, of Springfield. They had three children in Sangamon county, and moved to Clinton, Dewitt county, Illinois. Richard Hall died in 1870, near Clinton, and his widow married a Mr. Cobb. They reside near Clinton, Dewitt county, Illinois.

ELCY J., born Oct. 22, 1820, in Pope county, Illinois, was married in Sangamon county to Samuel Ray. *See his name.*

POLLY A., born March 29, 1823, in Sangamon county, married Benjamin Fobes, and died Feb. 24, 1852, leaving one child, SARAH E., who married Jeremiah Messenger, Nov. 21, 1869, and lives in Waverly, Bremer county, Iowa.

MARGARET E., born July 3, 1825, in Sangamon county, married William H. Morgan. *See his name.*

SARAH A. and BARBARA A., twins, born Feb. 1, 1827, in Sangamon county, Illinois.

SARAH A. married Benjamin Kendall. She died Aug. 28, 1851, from injuries received by a runaway team, on the road to Oregon. She left one child—FANNIE, born Nov. 20, 1850, who married Mr. Henkle, and died, leaving one child, near Corvallis, Oregon.

BARBARA A. married Milo Morris. They had two children—GEORGE H., who lives in Butler county, Missouri. WILLIAM lives near Rushville, Schuyler county, Illinois. Mrs. Morris died Aug. 9, 1851, in Loami township.

BURLINDER, born April 20, 1829, in Sangamon county, married Joshua W. Short. They had four children. Mrs. Short and one child died. The other three children—JOHN R. died February, 1876. CHARLES E. married Lola Scripture, in 1873. ANNIE M. lives near Lamar station, Nodaway county, Missouri.

EDWARD J., born May 17, 1833, in Sangamon county, married Sarah Haggard. They have five children, viz: FANNIE, MAY, JENNIE, UMATILLA and KATE, and live near Labette, Labette county, Kansas.

Edward Robison died May 15, 1836, and Mrs. Jane Robison died March 12, 1853. He in Sangamon county, Illinois, and she in Jasper county, Missouri.

Edward Robison was Colonel of a military company, in Kentucky, and was always called Col. Robison. He represented Pope county in the first Legislature of Illinois that assembled at Vandalia. He was justice of the peace twelve or fifteen years in Sangamon county, and solemnized the marriage of James Parkinson and Mahala Earnest, and many others.

ROBISON, JOHN, was born in Virginia, and married in Maryland to Nancy Robbins. They moved to Delaware, where they had four children, and moved to Nicholas county, Ky., where five children were born, and from there to Sangamon county, Ill., arriving in the fall of 1830, in Buffalo Hart Grove. Of their children—

ELIZABETH R., born Nov. 26, 1797, in Delaware, married in Kentucky to Samuel H. Steele. *See name of Elizabeth R. Steele.*

WILLIAM, born about 1799, in Delaware, married in Nicholas county, Ky., to Mahuldah Tarr, moved to Buffalo Hart Grove, Sangamon county, thence to Madison county, where the parents died, leaving several children.

SALLY and NANCY, twins, born about 1801, in Nicholas county, Ky.

SALLY died in Buffalo Hart Grove, about 1835.

NANCY married Hiram Starr. *See his name.*

JOHN W., born about 1803, in Nicholas county, Ky., married in Sangamon county to Lucinda Burns. They had four children, WILLIAM T., born in Sangamon county Aug. 2, 1833, married Dec. 4, 1856, to Julia A. Lunbeck. They had five children; four died under five years. IDA LOU resides with her parents in Springfield. William T. Robison is a clerk in the freight depot of the C. and A. railroad. ELIZABETH M., born April 4, 1835, in Sangamon county, married Dec. 20, 1866, to John Finfrock, who was born July 8, 1833, near Chambersburg, Penn. They have four children, EDGAR H., FRANK R., GRACIE M. and MARY L. Mr. Finfrock enlisted July, 1862, for three years, in Co. I, 114th Ill. Inf.; served until Aug., 1865, when he was honorably discharged. They live three-quarters of a mile north of Buffalo Hart station. MARY J., born April 20, 1837, in Sangamon county, married Sept. 11, 1861, to Joseph W. Martin, who was born Nov. 16, 1838, in Ohio county, Kentucky. They have four children, JESSE W., WILLIAM H., LENA F. and ROBERT F., and live one-half mile north of Buffalo Hart station. JOHN F., born June 20, 1839, in Sangamon county, enlisted July, 1862, for three years, in Co. I, 114th Ill. Inf.; served until Aug., 1865, when he was honorably discharged. He was married March 20, 1867, to Eliza A. Guthrie. They have two children, IVA E. and a babe, and live in Atlanta, Illinois. John W. Robison was killed by lightning at one o'clock on the morning of August 28, 1840, three and a half miles northeast of Buffalo Hart Grove. He was sitting at the bedside of, and was fanning his sick mother, who died two days later. His widow married Sept. 20, 1848, to David S. Warner. She is now a widow, and resides half a mile north of Buffalo Hart Station, Sangamon county, Illinois.

MARY, born and married in Kentucky, to Alexander James. They came to Illinois with her parents, in 1830, but settled in Shelby county. Mr. James died there in the fall of 1871. His widow resides with her son, WILLIAM JAMES who is married, has seven children, and lives near Shelbyville, Illinois.

MILLICENT, born in Kentucky, married in Sangamon county to Amanias Heaton. He died in Madison county, leaving a widow and children.

GEORGE, born in Nicholas county, Ky., came to Sangamon county with his parents, in 1830, married, in 1841, to Caroline Snyder. She died, in 1860, leaving five children. He married Mrs. Jane B⸺, whose maiden name was James. They have two children, and reside in Mt. Pulaski, Illinois.

ELEANOR J., born in Kentucky, married in Sangamon county to Phineas Jordan, had four children, and he died. She married James Hibbs, had one child, and Mrs. Hibbs died in Logan county, Illinois.

Mrs. Nancy Robison died Aug. 30, 1840, and John Robison died in 1841. She in Logan, and he in Sangamon county, Illinois.

ROBINSON, JAMES T., was born Jan. 21, 1808, at New Malton, Yorkshire, England. Of his ancestors, Thomas Robinson, merchant of Malton, England, died Oct. 13, 1779, aged sixty-eight years. His son, Marmaduke, died April 28, 1797, aged seventy-nine. His son, William Barton Robinson, married Alice Blackburn. They had four children. Their two youngest were James T. and Barton, sketches of whom are herewith given. James T. came to New York in 1829, traveled through the Eastern States and Canada, and came to Sangamon county, Ill., arriving in December, 1830, in Buffalo Hart Grove, just in time to witness the "deep snow." He bought land there, and was married Oct. 10, 1832, to Minerva Starr. They had five children in Sangamon county, Illinois.

EMMA L., born Feb. 1, 1834, died, unmarried, Sept. 13, 1868, in Sangamon county.

EDMUND H., born Dec. 31, 1835, was married Oct., 1871, to Harriet Chapman. They reside near Buffalo Hart, Sangamon county, Ill.

WILLIAM B., born May 29, 1838, enlisted July 25, 1862, for three years, in Co. I, 114th Ill. Inf. He was captured at the battle of Guntown, Miss., June 10, 1864, was taken to Andersonville prison, entering about the 18th of June; remained three months; taken to Savannah, thence to Millen; back to Savannah, and from there to Florence, South Carolina, where he remained three months, and on the approach of Sherman's army was removed to Goldsboro', North Carolina, where he was paroled Feb. 25, 1865; released at Wilmington the next day, and honorably discharged at Springfield May 30, 1865. He was married Feb. 21, 1867, to Arminta Burns. They have two children, JOHN B. and ALICE CAREY, and reside two miles north of Buffalo, Sangamon county, Illinois—1874.

JOHN B., born Nov. 21, 1839, enlisted at Springfield July, 1861, in what became Co. B, 11th Mo. Inf., for three years. He was killed in battle at Iuka, Miss., Sept. 19, 1862, and buried on the field.

CHARLES, born Sept. 25, 1845, raised in Sangamon county, spent three years, 1870, '71 and '72, in Oregon, is unmarried, and lives with his mother.

James T. Robinson died Dec. 8, 1871, and his widow resides two miles south of Buffalo Hart station, Sangamon county, Illinois.

Mr. Robinson had business east, and in the spring of 1831 he embarked on the steamboat Talisman, in the Sangamon river, near Springfield, and went as far as St. Louis on that boat, and from there to Pittsburg on another boat, and over the Alleghany mountains, by stage, to Philadelphia. The Talisman was the only steamboat that ever ascended the Sangamon river.

ROBINSON, BARTON, was born May 19, 1819, at New Malton, Yorkshire, England; studied medicine and graduated with the degree of M. D., in London. He came to America, and joined his brother, James T., at Buffalo Hart Grove, in Dec., 1831. He was married in Sangamon county, May, 1833, to Mahala Barber. They had two living children in Sangamon county, and in the year 1836 Dr. Robinson and Jabez Capps laid out the town of Mt. Pulaski, Ill. He moved there, and continued in the practice of medicine. They had two living children in Mt. Pulaski, and in 1858 moved to Lynn county, Kansas, taking their four sons with them, namely—

HERBERT, born in Sangamon county, married in Kansas to Hester Blackburn. They have five children, and live near Farlinville, Kansas.

JAMES, born in Sangamon county, married in Kansas to Cassander Blackburn, has four children, and lives near Farlinville, Kansas.

LANDER, born in Mt. Pulaski, Ill., married in Kansas to Jennie Blackburn, and lives near Farlinville, Kansas.

FREMONT, born in Mt. Pulaski, Illinois, resides with his parents near Farlinville, Linn county, Kansas.

Dr. Barton Robinson and his wife reside near Farlinville, Kansas.

William Blackburn and Alice Southington were married Nov. 30, 1725. They were both of Sneaton, England. They had five children. Their fourth child, John, born at Sneaton, Dec. 15, 1733, O. S., married Oct. 6, 1763, N. S., at Malton, to Bertha Turner. Their fifth child, Alice Blackburn, married William Barton Robinson, at Malton. The names of two of their sons, James T. and Barton, head the preceding sketches.

ROBINSON, WM., R., was born about 1776, in England. When he was ten or twelve years old, his parents came to America, and settled in Virginia. When he attained to manhood he went to Blount county, Tenn., and was there married, in 1808, to Sarah Witcher. They had five children in Tennessee, and moved to Barren county, Ky., where six children were born, and then moved to Sangamon county, Ill., arriving in what is now Williams township, in 1836. One of their children only resides in Sangamon county—

JANE, the third child, born in Tennessee, married in Sangamon county to Abel Yocum. *See his name.*

The children are scattered all the way to the Pacific coast. The family moved to Logan county, where the parents both died in 1860.

ROBINSON, MRS. ANN, whose maiden name was Norris, was born May 5, 1779, in Harford county, Maryland. She was married there, in 1805, to Richard Robinson, a native of the same county. They had two children, and Mr. Robinson died in Baltimore, Nov. 5, 1811. Mrs. Robinson, with two sisters, Temperance Norris, born May 4, 1775, and Elizabeth, born March 22, 1777, and Mrs. Robinson's two children, moved to Springfield, Ill., arriving in March, 1835. Of her two children—

ARNOLD R., born Dec. 10, 1807, in Baltimore, Md., came to Springfield, Ill., in 1835, was married at Jacksonville, Ill., March 19, 1840, to Eliza Robison, who was born July 4, 1822, in the city of New York. Mr. and Mrs. Robinson reside in Springfield, Ill. A. R. Robinson has been for many years an active Free Mason and Odd Fellow, having taken all the degrees in both orders, and always holding some official position. He is Secretary of St. Paul's Lodge of Masons, No. 500; is Grand Tyler of the Grand Chapter, and Grand Council of the State of Illinois. He has been six years in the employ of the United States Government as Custodian of the U. S. Court House and Postoffice, in Springfield, Illinois.

PRISCILLA, born August 9, 1809, in Baltimore, Md., lives with her brother, Arnold R., in Springfield.

Mrs. Ann Robinson died July 30, 1860, in Springfield, Illinois. Of her two sisters who came with her—Temperance died Feb. 4, 1849, and Elizabeth died Dec 20, 1872, both in Springfield, Illinois.

ROBINSON, MRS. MARY, whose maiden name was Mayhew, was born Sept. 9, 1786, at Martha's Vineyard, Mass. Zenas Robinson was born Aug. 1, 1782, in Falmouth, Mass. They were married Sept. 14, 1814, at Cincinnati, O., and had one child there. Mr. Robinson took his family to Big Bone Lick, Boone county, Ky., where he was fulfilling a building contract, and one child was born there. They returned to Hamilton county, O., and had one child near Carthage. Mr. Robinson moved in 1825 to Grand Gulf, Miss., and died there Nov. 8, 1828 or '9. His widow and children returned to Cincinnati to her parents. She remained there until 1836, when she removed, in company with her daughter and son in-law, to Sangamon county, eight miles west of Springfield. Of the three children—

BENJAMIN S., born July 24, 1815, in Cincinnati, O. He studied medicine and attended lectures at the Medical College of Ohio, session of 1839 and '40, and came to Sangamon county, arriving Nov. 3, 1840, at the house of his mother and sister on Spring creek, having taken his last cigar and last glass of intoxicating drink that day in Springfield. Dr. Robinson was married May 20, 1846, to Sophronia Earnest. They had six living children. HELEN F., born March 23, 1849, married September 26, 1872, to Alexander L. Patteson. They have one child, HELEN A., and live two miles southwest of Curran, Sangamon county, Ill. LOUISA, born Sept. 7, 1852, MARY ALLETTA, born April 17, 1854, A. MAYHEW, born June 28, 1856, LIZZIE E., born May 9, 1858, and FREDERICK A., born Jan. 5, 1867. The five latter reside with their parents, two and a quarter miles northeast of Curran, Sangamon county, Ill.

Dr. B. S. Robinson commenced practice in 1841, within two miles of where he now resides. He is now (Nov. 22, 1873,) the oldest practitioner in Sangamon county.

CHRISTIANA M., born in 1818, in Boone county, Ky., married J. Munson Beach. See his name.

CHARLES W., born in 1821, died, aged eleven years.

Mrs. Mary Robinson was married in 1852 to Joshua Brown. See his name. She died May 29, 1861, in Sangamon county, Ill.

RODGERS, ROBERT B., born Aug. 1, 1793, in Westmoreland county, Pa. Catharine A. Huggins was born Feb. 11, 1800, in Liverpool, Perry county, Pa. They were married and had eight children in Pennsylvania, and moved to Medina county, O., where one child was born, and from there to Sangamon county, Ill., arriving in the spring of 1837 in what is now Clear Lake township, east of the river, where two children were born. Of their twelve children—

LUCETTA, born Jan. 1, 1814, in Dauphin county, Pa., married in Wooster, O., to Charles McClure. She died there in 1844, leaving three children.

—79

THOMAS, born April 5, 1816, in Perry county, Pa., married in Sangamon county, to Catharine Hazlitt. They had seven children; two died young. LUCETTA is married, and lives in Iowa. ALFRED, MARY C., LOUISA and THOMAS, Jun., live with their mother. Thomas Rodgers died in 1852, and his widow and children live one and a half miles north of Riverton, Ill.

JANE, born November, 1819, in Perry county, Pa., married in Wooster, O., to William McClure. They died, leaving two children.

REBECCA, born May 30, 1821, in Dauphin county, Pa., married in Sangamon county to James Morton. They have eight living children. THOMAS married Sarah Smith, and lives near Sadoris, Ill. AMANDA married Avery Constant, and lives near Williamsville, Ill. MARY C. married James W. Wilson. *See his name.* CAROLINE married Jefferson Yocom. *See his name.* JOSEPHINE, LUCY J., ANN R. and JAMES W., live with their parents. James Morton and wife reside near Sadoris, Champaign county, Ill — 1874.

AMANDA, born Aug. 17, 1826, in Dauphin county, Pa., married Dec. 11, 1845, in Sangamon county, to William Steele, who was born April 2, 1821, in Carlisle, Ky. They had six children. ELIZABETH C. married Charles Wilkison, who was born Nov. 6, 1838, in Stark county, O. They have two children, WILLIAM and JOSEPHINE, and live in Riverton, Ill. Mr. Wilkison served three months — from April, 1861 — in the 13th Ohio Inf. He enlisted at Springfield, Feb. 2, 1865, for one year, in Co. I, 7th Ill. Cav., served until Nov. 4, 1865, when he was honorably discharged. JOHN H., born Feb. 19, 1846, enlisted Feb. 2, 1865, for one year, in Co. I, 7th Ill. Cav., served until Nov. 4, 1865, when he was honorably discharged. He was married to Euphemia Wilson. They have two children, and live in Riverton, Ill. ROBERT F. married Emily R. Mann, and live in Riverton. HARRIET married John Wood, and died Nov. 20, 1873, having been married but three weeks. GEORGANA married Benjamin F. Flagg in Sangamon county, and lives in Muskegon, Mich. ALFARETTA lives with her mother. William Steele enlisted for three years in 1863, in Co. A, 116th Ill. Inf., and died in St. Louis, March, 1864. His widow resides at Riverton, Sangamon county, Ill.

MARY, born Nov. 17, 1827, in Dauphin county, Pa., married in Sangamon county to J. C. Harris. She had eight children, and died in Christian county, Ill. Robert B. Harris, the last one of her children, was scalded to death at Riverton, Dec. 22, 1873.

JOHN, born July 9, 1830, in Dauphin county, Pa., raised in Sangamon county, enlisted at Springfield, September, 1861, for three years, in Co. A, 3d Ill. Cav., served full term, and was honorably discharged at Springfield, September, 1864. He was married Oct. 9, 1865, at Riverton, to Mrs. Nancy J. Harsh, whose maiden name was Kinder. She was born Dec. 4, 1844, in Wythe county, Va. They have three children, IDAHO, PARLEY and ASA, and reside two miles southeast of Illiopolis, Ill. — 1874.

CAROLINE, born Nov. 24, 1834, in Dauphin county, Pa., is unmarried, and lives with her brothers in Sangamon county.

RICHARD, born June 5, 1836, near Wooster, Medina county, O., married Dec. 25, 1867, in Sangamon county, to Mary A. Major. They have two living children, LOUIS and BYRON, and live in Riverton, Ill.

SAMUEL D., born Nov. 28, 1838, in Sangamon county, enlisted July 25, 1862, for three years, in Co. I, 114th Ill. Inf., served until May 14, 1863, when he was honorably discharged on account of physical disability. He was married Dec. 7, 1865, to Emma Yocom. They have two living children, LEONA and ELLEN MAUD, and reside in Riverton, Sangamon county, Ill. — 1874.

ROBERT, born Sept. 7, 1842, in Sangamon county, enlisted in 1861 in Co. —, 7th Ill. Inf., for three months, and died at Cairo, July 9, 1861.

Robert R. Rodgers died March 25, 1862, and Mrs. Catharine A. Rodgers died April, 1864, both near Riverton, Sangamon county, Ill.

ROGERS, JOTHAM S., was born June 25, 1816, in Bangor, Maine, came to Springfield, Ill., in 1837, and was married to Mary A. Benham, who died without children in 1843. Mr. Rogers was married May 27, 1848, to Sarah

Elder. *See Elder family.* Mr. and Mrs. Rogers had two children in Springfield—

HANSON G. died at eight years of age.

MARY LOUISA, born July 14, 1850, in Springfield, married, May 2, 1868, to Josiah P. Kent, and had one child. Mrs. Kent married the second time, May 29, 1873, to John Hunter. *See the Elder family.* Mr. and Mrs. Hunter moved, in 1875, from DesMoines, Iowa, to Washington, D. C.

Jonathan S. Rogers died July 3, 1857, in Springfield, and his widow was married, Feb. 7, 1859, to Isaac Lindsay. *See his name.*

ROLL, JACOB C., was born April 4, 1782, at Springfield, Essex county, N. J. Sarah Pierson was born July 23, 1786, in the same town. They were there married, Oct. 9, 1810. One child was born in New Jersey, and the family moved, in 1813 to Cincinnati, Ohio, where they had one living child. In the summer of 1825, Mr. Roll loaded a keel boat at Cincinnati with family stores and merchandise. He went down the Ohio to its mouth, and when he had ascended the Mississippi river about thirty miles, his boat sunk. By that accident he lost the principal part of his goods. Securing what he could from the wreck, he continued to ascend the rivers, and reached Sangamo, in Sangamon county, Oct. 10, 1825. There, in connection with Ebenezer Brigham, he commenced merchandising, and at the same time began to improve some land. One eighty acre lot that he broke and fenced, foiled some other man, who was evil disposed, and his fences were destroyed, hay burned and other depredations committed, but the parties who did it all passed away, and he enjoyed the land peaceably for many years after. Of the two children brought to Sangamon county—

PIERSON, born July 31, 1811, in Springfield, N. J., married in Sangamon county, Oct. 12, 1837, to Rachel Carman, who was born Feb. 19, 1814, in New York or Pennsylvania. They had two living children—AMELIA H., born in Sangamon county, March 29, 1838, married, June 7, 1855, to Henry Shoemaker. They had seven children, CHARLES P., SARAH, CHRISTOPHER, MARY, CATHARINE, JACOB and MARGARET A., and reside in Gardner township, six miles northwest of Springfield, Illinois. MARY M., born Nov. 10, 1839, in Sangamon county, married, March 3, 1859, to James Moyer, who was born Sept. 19, 1838, in Lancaster county, Penn. They have four children, SARAH E., CATHARINE, MARY and DRUZILLA, and reside in Gardner township, north of the river. Mrs. Rachel Roll died Oct. 19, 1841, and Pierson Roll was married, May 8, 1845, to Catharine Spencer. They had thirteen children, four of whom died young. Of the other nine—MARGARET A., born Aug. 17, 1846, married, April 29, 1863, to Joshua Jones, who was born Dec. 20, 1840, in Franklin county, Ohio. They had four children, WILLIAM P., JAMES B., WILLARD M. and PERCY MELVILLE; the latter died, aged two years. Mr. and Mrs. Jones live east of the river, in Salisbury township, Sangamon county, Ill. SARAH P., born Sept. 19, 1848, married, May 24, 1866, to William J. Schroyer, who was born Jan. 7, 1836, in Fayette county, Penn. Mr. and Mrs. Schroyer live with her parents. JACOB C. and JAMES B. live with their parents. PHŒBE D. married, Jan. 18, 1876, to John E. Roll, son of Alpheus Roll. *See his name.* ROMOLD, JUDY, WILLIAM N. and JOHN S.; the four latter live with their parents. Pierson Roll and family reside north of the Sangamon river, six miles northwest of Springfield, Illinois.

CHARLES D., born Aug. 28, 1818, in Cincinnati, died in Sangamon county, June 21, 1839.

Jacob C. Roll died Jan. 25, 1849, and his widow died Jan. 28, 1861, both in Gardner township, Sangamon county, Illinois.

ROLL, WILLIAM, was born near Springfield, Essex county, N. J. He engaged in school teaching at Green Village, Morris county, and was there married, Feb. 9, 1809, to Mary Eddy, who was born Feb. 18, 1793. They had eight children, and moved to Sangamon county, Ill., arriving June 7, 1830, at the house of his great-uncle, Jacob C. Roll, near the town of Sangamo, and a few weeks later moved into the town, where they had one child. Of their nine children—

ANN P., born August 11, 1810, in New Jersey, married in Sangamon county, to Alfred Riley. They had four children; one died, aged fifteen. WILLIAM, born April 11, 1835, is married, and lives in Springfield, Ill. LUTHER, born Oct. 10, 1836, is married, and lives in Springfield, Ill. HARRIET lives with her mother. Alfred Riley was run over by a team in the streets of Springfield, and after two days' suffering, died Nov. 23, 1870. His widow lives in Springfield, Illinois.

PHEBE L., born March 1, 1812, in New Jersey, married Thomas S. Edwards, who died in Bureau county. She lives with her brother, John E. Roll.

JOHN E., born June 9, 1814, at Green Village, N. J. came to Sangamon county June 7, 1830, married Jan. 31, 1839, to Harriet Vandyke, who was born Jan. 29, 1815, in New York City. They had three living children in Springfield. WILLIAM V., born November 6, 1839, FRANK P., born March 7, 1852, and JOHN L., born June 25, 1854, all live with their parents. In coming to Sangamon county J. E. Roll walked from St. Louis, with Clawson Lacy and Alfred Riley. While the family lived in Sangamo, Abraham Lincoln built the boat spoken of in his biography. He began in March, 1831, just as the deep snow went off. Mr. Roll made the pins for putting the boat together. They made a canoe to go with the boat as a yawl. John Seaman and Walters Carman got into it to take the first ride. It upset with them, and floated away while they took refuge in a tree. Lincoln saved them by swimming to the tree with a log, having a long rope attached. After getting all on it, those on shore drew it in. J. E. Roll learned the trade of a plasterer and brick mason, and for thirty years followed the business of building and dealing in real estate, having built about one hundred houses, on his own account, in Springfield. He has been in the boot and shoe trade for the last seventeen years. J. E. Roll and family reside in Springfield, Illinois.

MARY C., born Nov. 29, 1816, in New Jersey, married in Sangamon county, May 2, 1840, to John Bagby. They have four children, and lives near Marion Centre, Kansas.

ELIZABETH W., born April 22, 1819, in New Jersey, married in Sangamon county to Isaac H. Smith, who was born either in North or South Carolina, and died in 1851, in Springfield, leaving a widow and five children. Of their children: WILLIAM married Esther R. Brokaw, have three living children, ADA, LIDA and LILLIE, and live in Mason City, Ill. JOHN was killed by a passing train on a railroad, in childhood. ELIZA P., born July 26, 1848, married George E. Mott. *See his name.* Their son, HARRY W., died Aug. 27, 1876, aged six years and five months. JAMES and EDWARD live in Springfield. Mrs. Elizabeth W. Smith resides in Springfield, Illinois.

SARAH and *WILLIAM*, twins, born August 19, 1822, in New Jersey.

SARAH, married in Sangamon county to William P. Short, had seven children; three died young. WILLIAM died in the Union army. William P. Short and family reside near Teheran, Mason county, Illinois.

WILLIAM died in Springfield, Aug. 24, 1839.

NANCY, born March 13, 1828, in New Jersey, married in Sangamon county to Jeremiah Riggins, have five living children, and reside in Mason City, Illinois.

ALPHEUS P., born Sept. 17, 1830, in Sangamo, Sangamon county, Ill., married in Mason county to Mary Mosslander. They have four children. Their son, JOHN E., was married Jan. 18, 1876, in Sangamon county, to Phœbe D. Roll, daughter of Pierson Roll. *See his name.* John E. Roll and wife live near Teheran, Ill. The other three children live with their parents. Alpheus P. Roll and family reside near Teheran, Mason county, Illinois.

William Roll died August 11, 1844, in Sangamon county, and his widow lives with her daughter, Mrs. Riggins, in Mason City, Illinois.

ROSS, MRS. NANCY, was born in 1777, in Essex county, N. J. Her maiden name was Dunn. Her father, Jeremiah Dunn, was captain of a company of New Jersey rangers in the Revolutionary army, and was killed July 28, 1778, at the head of his company, at the battle of Monmouth, N. J. He left a widow with one son and three daughters. The widow never married, although she survived her husband sixty years. Their daughter Nancy, whose name heads this sketch, was married in 1795 to William Ross, who was born in the same county, Feb. 14, 1769. They were married in Essex county, had six children there, and, in 1813, moved to Cincinnati, O., where seven children were born. William Ross died there of cholera, Nov. 18, 1832. Mrs. Nancy Ross moved with some of her children to Sangamon county, Ill., arriving in the fall of 1839 in Round Prairie, four miles east of Springfield, and the next year moved to what is now Cooper township. Seven of her children died young. Of the other six—

HETTY, born in 1796 in New Jersey, married in Cincinnati, O., to Jonathan L. Cory, who died near Natchez, Miss., while there on business. He left one child, WILLIAM ROSS CORY, born March 18, 1823, in Cincinnati, and came to Sangamon county with one of his uncles previous to 1840, and was married in Springfield to Icy Isabel Deck. They had four children, three of whom died under eight years. WILLIAM R., Jun., born Jan. 16, 1847, in Sangamon county, married Sept. 12, 1875, to Annetta Deyo. William R. Cory, Jun., is a teacher, and resides in Rochester, Ill. Mrs. Icy I. Cory died in 1855, and Mr. Cory was married Sept. 22, 1859, to Christiana Clements, who was born July 22, 1836, in Montgomery county, Md. They have five living children, JOHN A., ANNIE I., ALICE A., ELLA L. and CLARA H. William Ross Cory resides in Springfield, Ill. Mrs. Hetty Cory married in Cincinnati to Martin H. Flagg, and moved to Springfield in 1838. They had five children; twins died young; one lives in Cincinnati and two in Minnesota. Mr. Flagg died in 1843 in Springfield, and his widow went to Cincinnati and died of cholera, July 3, 1849.

NANCY, born about 1800 in New Jersey, married in Cincinnati, in 1817, to Bennajh English, born near Philadelphia, and was a soldier in the war of 1812. He died in Cincinnati in 1837, leaving a widow and two children. They came to Sangamon county in 1840. AFFALINDA married John Tunnicliffe, and lives in St. Louis. BENNAJH married Sarah Firey, and lives in Cooper township. Mrs. Nancy English resides with her son in Cooper township, Sangamon county, Ill.

WILLIAM R., born Oct. 3. 1809, in Rahway, Essex county, N. J., married in Cincinnati, O., May 18, 1834, to Ann Flagg. They had two children born in Cincinnati, and moved to Springfield, Ill., in 1838, and from there to Cooper township, where Mrs. Ross died, Feb. 18, 1844. Mr. Ross was married Dec. 28, 1845, to Mary E. Crowl. They had six children. Of his children — LAURETTA, born April 13, 1835, in Cincinnati, married in Sangamon county, Dec. 15, 1851, to Henry O. Stafford. They had four children; two died young, and Mrs. Stafford died Dec. 7, 1859. Of her two children, ORLANDO C. lives with his father in Decatur; LAURETTA A. resides with her grandfather Ross. ADELIA, born in Cincinnati, died in Sangamon county May 22, 1854, in her seventeenth year. By the second marriage—GEORGE R., MORDECAI V. and JOSEPH H., live with their parents. William R. Ross and family reside three miles east of Rochester. Sangamon county, Ill.

ANDREW J., born March 8, 1815, in Cincinnati, was married in Sangamon county June 11, 1843, to Elizabeth Lord, who died Nov. 26, 1865, leaving five children, WILLIM R. ANDRDW J., Jun., LOUISA J., JESSE E. and HENRY H. A. J. Ross married Oct. 10, 1868, in St. Louis, to Mrs. Elizabeth Viler, whose maiden name was Ford. They have three children, RICHARD M., MILES M. and MILTON R., and reside three miles north of Berry station, or Clarksville, Sangamon county, Ill.

CHARLOTTE D., born in 1816, in Cincinnati, married there to W. H. Morris, raised a family, came to Sangamon county on a visit, and died suddenly at the house of her brother, William R. Ross, Aug. 8, 1871. Her remains were taken back for interment in Spring Grove Cemetery, Cincinnati, O.

LOUISA J., born in Cincinnati, married in Sangamon county, Ill., to Milton Ross. He died Aug. 20, 1845, and his widow resides three and three-quarter miles east of Rochester.

Mrs. Nancy Ross died Feb. 24, 1852, in Cooper township. The remains of her husband (William Ross) were removed from Catharine street Cemetery, Cincinnati, by their son, William R., and deposited by her side in Cooper township, in 1870.

ROSS, WILLIAM, was born Jan. 9, 1801, in North Carolina. His father, John Ross, was born in Scotland, and came to America before the Revolution. He was a soldier from North Carolina in the Revolution, for five years, when he was wounded, and thus disabled for further service. He was married in North Carolina, and moved to Adair county, Ky., when the subject of this sketch was a boy. William Ross and Maria Willis were there married, in 1827, and had four children in Adair county. They moved to Sangamon county, Illinois, arriving in Nov., 1836, in what is now Gardner township, where three children were born. Of their seven children—

MARTHA, born Jan. 10, 1829, in Adair county, Ky., married May 13, 1845, in Sangamon county, to Matthias Miller, who was born April, 1819, in Germany. They had five living children—SARAH E., born April 17, 1846, married, May 17, 1860, to John L. Gard. *See his name.* GEORGE W. enlisted April, 1864, in Co. B, 114th Ill. Inf. From over exertion, lack of food and exposure at the battle of Guntown, June 10, 1864, he was sent home on sick furlough, and died Feb. 6, 1865. ALFRED F. lives with his parents. FLORENCE married, Jan. 3, 1871, to Alexander Campbell, have one child, FRANKLIN M., and reside near Farmingdale, Sangamon county, Illinois. VIRGINIA lives with her parents. Matthias Miller and wife reside one and one-half mile south of Salisbury, Sangamon county, Illinois.—1874.

SARAH J., born Feb. 14, 1831, in Kentucky, married James Short, had two children, and he died, and she married Frank Ernst. They have six children, and live one mile north of Farmingdale, Illinois.

ALFRED, born March 18, 1833, in Adair county, Ky., married in Sangamon county, April 2, 1856, to Rachel E. Gard. They have seven children, JASPER N., ANNIE MAY, CHARLES LINCOLN, JOHN WM., ZULAIDA, MARIA JANE and OLIVER F., and live

two miles northeast of Richland station, Sangamon county, Illinois.

JOHN W., born April 24, 1835, in Kentucky, and raised in Sangamon county. He enlisted in 1862, in Co. D, 33d Ill. Inf., for three years, had one leg shot off, in an assault on the rebel fortifications at Vicksburg, June 22, and died in hospital, July 1, 1863.

MARY E., born Oct., 1838, in Sangamon county, married John P. Goodman, have five children, and reside at Monticello, Piatt county, Illinois.

OLIVER M., born in Sangamon county, married Rachel Laborrence, have two children, and reside near McLean, McLean county, Illinois.

JULIA A., born in Sangamon county, married Charles Stough, have two children, and reside in Monticello, Piatt county, Illinois.

WINFIELD S., born in 1851 in Sangamon county, resides with his mother and brother, Oliver M.

William Ross died Oct. 27, 1862, in Gardner township, and his widow resides with her two youngest sons, near McLean, McLean county, Illinois—1874.

ROYAL, THOMAS, was born about 1758, in Manchester, England. He came to America with a comrade about his own age, near the beginning of the war for Independence. They both volunteered in the army of the colonists, and his comrade at his side had his head blown completely off. About the same time Mr. Royal was severely wounded by a charge of buckshot entering his ankle, some of which he carried to his grave. After the Revolution he married a Miss Cooper, in Virginia, and raised a family. Mrs. Royal died, and he married Rebecca Matthews. They moved to Franklin county, Ohio, where Mrs. Rebecca Royal died, leaving one child. Mr. Royal married Mrs. Ellen Brunk. They had one child in Ohio, and moved to Sangamon county, Ill., in company with her sons, George and David Brunk, the Newcomer family, and others, numbering in all sixty-three persons, arriving in the fall of 1824, in what is now Ball township. Thomas Royal brought two children by his first wife—

WILLIAM, born in 1796, in Virginia, entered the ministry in connection with the M. E. church, in Ohio. He came to

Sangamon county in 1826, and after the first three or four years his itinerant connection took him out of Sangamon county, but he remained in Illinois until 1853, when he went to Oregon. He died in Salem, Sept. 29, 1870, leaving a family there.

MARY, born in Virginia, and married in Ohio to Absolom Meredith. *See his name.*

By the second wife—

REBECCA, born July 30, 1812, in Ohio, married in Sangamon county to Jacob Boyd. *See his name.*

By the third marriage—

JOSEPH B., born Nov. 1, 1816, in Franklin county, near Columbus, Ohio, was married in Sangamon county, Aug. 19, 1841, to Louisa Downing. She died Jan. 8, 1853, in Vermont, Fulton county, Ill., leaving four children; two died young. THOMAS M. was married in Washington county, Ill to Sarah M. Kelso, and lives in Chatsworth, Ill. ELEANOR E. married James M. Little, and lives in McDonough county, near Vermont, Fulton county, Ill. Joseph B. Royal was married Oct. 23, 1853, at Vermont, Ill., to Mrs. Elsey McHendry whose maiden name was Boyle. She had one child, SARAH C. McHENDRY, and Mr. and Mrs. Royal have three children, GEORGE A., MOLLIE M. and EUGENE D. The family live at Vermont, Fulton county, Ill. Joseph B. Royal is pastor of the Christian church there.

Thomas Royal died August, 1834, and his widow died September, 1844, both in Ball township, Sangamon county, Ill.

RUCKER, THOMAS, was born Oct. 29, 1807, in Caldwell county, Ky. The first of the name in America was John Rucker, a native of France. On the voyage to America the vessel in which he sailed was wrecked about twelve miles from shore, and nearly all on board were lost. Before leaving the wreck Mr. Rucker took the precaution to tie a couple of large flasks of rum to his neck, which buoyed him up. By that means, and by taking an occasional drink of it, he was enabled to reach the shore. He settled in Amherst county, Virginia, married and raised a family there, from which has sprung, in a larger sense, one of the most numerous families in the United States.

Some of his descendants moved to Caldwell county, Kentucky. Thomas Rucker, whose name heads this sketch, was married in Woodford county, Kentucky, to Diedamia Rucker, who was born in that county Dec. 12, 1805. She was also a descendant of the same John Rucker. Thomas Rucker and wife had one child in Kentucky, and moved to Sangamon county, arriving in the fall of 1832 in what is now Gardner township, where they had five living children. Of their six children—

JAMES H., born June 16, 1832, in Woodford county, Ky., died in Sangamon county, Jan. 17, 1852.

BISHOP EMERY, born Dec. 12, 1834, in Sangamon county, married Lucinda Shaver. They have two living children, and reside near Taylorville, Illinois.

PERMELIA J., born Dec. 12, 1836, in Sangamon county, married George W. Forden. *See his name.*

MARTHA E., born June 2, 1838, in Sangamon county, married Andrew L. Crowl. They have two children, and reside half a mile west of Sangamon Station, Sangamon county, Illinois.

JOSHUA Y., born Nov. 1, 1841, died Nov. 8, 1861.

LUCY A., born July 3, 1843, in Sangamon county, married Thomas Upton, have four children, and live near Summit, Butler county, Neb.

Mrs. Diedamia Rucker died in the autumn of 1863, and Thomas Rucker was married April 7, 1869, to Mrs. Julia A. Leonard, previously Mrs. Boatwright, whose maiden name was Russell. She was born April 7, 1813, in Murray county, Tenn. Her daughter—

MARY E. Boatwright, married John M. Green. They have two children, CHARLES L. and CALLIE M., and live in Springfield.

Thomas Rucker and wife reside near the west end of Monroe street railroad, Springfield, Ill.

RUCKEL, DANIEL E., was born May 5, 1811, in New York City. Catharine V. G. Forbes was born Feb. 8, 1812, in the same city. They were married, April 22, 1834, and had one child there. Mr. Ruckel came to Springfield in the fall of 1836, and his wife and child came the next spring with his brother

Jacob. Mr. and Mrs. Ruckel had three children in Sangamon county. Of their four children—

CATHARINE F., born Feb. 23, 1835, in New York City, brought up in Springfield, Ill., and married in her native city, Feb. 23, 1859, to Curtis H. Hall. They have two living children, MINNIE and THOMAS, and reside at Senaca Falls, New York.

EDGAR W., born Jan. 22, 1839, in Springfield, Ill. He was in New York City when Fort Sumter was fired upon, and enlisted on the first call for 75,000 men, April 16, 1861, in Co. H, 8th New York Inf., for three months, and served full term. He enlisted August 22, 1861, in Co. A, 6th New York Inf., for two years; served full term, being on duty in New York City at the time of the great riots in July, 1863, and was honorably discharged at the expiration of his term of service soon after. Since that time, Springfield, Ill., has been his home. He is not yet married.—Sept., 1876.

MATILDA B., born Nov. 22, 1841, in Springfield Ill., married March 3, 1863, in her native place, to William D. Ward, who was born Aug. 10, 1826, in Reading, England, and was brought by his parents to America in 1830. They settled at Zanesville, Ohio, and died there. William D. Ward came to Springfield in 1854. They have two living children, GRACE V. and LIDA F., and reside in Springfield, Ill. Mr. Ward is engaged in the business of a watchmaker and jeweler.

ELIZABETH C., born July 29, 1844, in Springfield, Ill., married Richard H. Dawson. *See his name in connection with the Meacham family.*

Daniel E. Ruckel died in Springfield, April 9, 1854, and Mrs. Ruckel was married March 17, 1857, to E. G. Johns. He was accidentally killed by a falling derrick while passing the corner of Fifth and Monroe streets, Springfield, August, 1863. Mrs. Johns resides with her daughter, Mrs. Ward, in Springfield, Illinois.

RUCKEL, JACOB, was born Oct. 27, 1815, in New York city, and came to Springfield, Ill., in the spring of 1837. He was married near Farmington — now Farmingdale—to Laura A. Stone. They have five living children, namely—

SAMUEL, FANNY A., WALTER B., JOHN H. and JOSEPH B., who live with their parents.

When the two brothers came to Springfield they engaged in cabinet-making, and about 1840 went to Sangamo, where they run a saw mill and manufactured cabinet furniture, which they continued about three years, and returned to Springfield. Jacob Ruckel afterwards changed to upholstery, and is now dealing in paper hangings of every variety, and resides in Springfield, Ill.

RUSK, BENJ. D., was born in Virginia. His father was killed in the Revolutionary army. His son—

ARCHIBALD H., born Nov. 20, 1833, in Sangamon county, enlisted on the first call for 75,000 men, April, 1861, in Co. E, 7th Ill. Inf., for three months; served full term, and was honorably discharged. He enlisted in August, 1861, in Co. A, 3d Ill. Cav., for three years; served until May, 1862, when he was discharged on account of physical disability. In June, 1863, he was received into Co. E, 114th Ill. Inf., in place of his brother, David L. Rusk, who was discharged in consideration of that exchange. In 1865 he was transferred to Co. A, 58th Ill. Inf; served until April, 1866, when he was honorably discharged at Springfield, and lives in Cotton Hill township.

DAVID L. was one of the Supervisors of Sangamon county from Cotton Hill township.

RUTH, REUBEN F., was born Aug. 26, 1815, in Wrightsville, York county, Penn. He came to Springfield in April, 1839, and engaged in the business of a saddle and harness maker. He was married Aug. 11, 1840, in Philadelphia, Penn., to Maria W. Diller, who was born July 20, 1817, in Lancaster county, Penn. They had two children—

J. DILLER, born June 14, 1841, in Springfield, was married in Petersburg, Illinois, to Anna Bacon. They have one child, GEORGIANA. Mrs. Anna Ruth and her daughter reside in Springfield, Illinois.

R. FRANCIS, born May 8, 1856, in Springfield, lives with his father.

Mrs. Maria W. D. Ruth died May 28, 1870, in Springfield.

R. F. Ruth was a member of the firm of Ruth & Hurst, dry goods merchants, fifteen years, terminating in 1875. He served one term as alderman, and four years as Water Works Commissioner. In 1868 he became President of the Marine and Fire Insurance Company Bank, and now—1876—occupies the same position, and resides in Springfield, Illinois.

Roland W. Diller, a brother of Mrs. Ruth, was born Oct. 5, 1822, in Chester county, Penn. He came to Springfield in 1844, and worked one year as a printer in the *Register* office. In 1849 he engaged in the drug business as a member of the firm of Corneau & Diller. He is now—1876—in the same business, on the same ground—east side of the court house square—and is the oldest druggist in Springfield. Mr. Diller was married Oct. 30, 1850, in Philadelphia, Penn., to Esther C. Ridgeway, a native of that city. They have three children, all born in Springfield. Emma married David B. Ayers, of Jacksonville, Illinois. They have one child, Marshal Roland, and reside on a farm near Homer, Champaign county, Ill. Isaac R. is in the drug business with his father and lives in Springfield. Essie lives with her parents. R. W. Diller and family reside in Springfield, Illinois.

S

SACKETT, CLAUDIUS C., was born Dec. 16, 1813, in that part of Portage which is now Summitt county, Ohio, with Akron as the county seat. Mr. S. came to Waverly, Ill., in the fall of 1836. During the winter and spring of 1836 and '7 he chopped wood and made rails, and with the money thus earned he walked to Springfield, changed it into silver, entered eighty acres of land in what is now Loami township, and returned to Waverly. Mr. Sackett went back to Ohio in the fall of 1837, and came to Sangamon county again in the fall of 1839. He was married Dec. 2, 1843, at Waverly, to Sarah Heaton, of Pennsylvania. They had two living children—

EMILY and *ANNA*, who live with their father. Mrs. Sarah Sackett died December, 1847, and C. C. Sackett was married Jan. 10, 1849, to Mrs. Juliette Coe, whose maiden name was Shumway. She was born Jan. 25, 1823, in the town of Canisius, Livingston county, N. Y. They have two children—

—80

ROSCOE J. and *CLARA A.* reside with their parents in Loami township, Sangamon county, three miles northeast of Waverly, Morgan county, Ill.—1874.

In 1841 Mr. Sackett raised some wheat of a superior quality, and the following winter he sent a young man to St. Louis with a load of it to sell. He engaged to take a trunk through, for which he was to receive $5.00. The team was gone just one week, and when it returned the young man had exactly the amount received for carrying the trunk, the money obtained for the wheat having been expended in defraying expenses. From this an idea may be formed of the markets for farm products at that time.

SACKETT, THOMAS, was brought up near Hamilton, Butler county, Ohio, and was there married to Peggy Martin. They had six children in Ohio, and moved to Sangamon county, near Sangamo, previous to 1830. Of their children—

DORCAS, born in Ohio, married in Sangamon county to Levi Batterton. *See his name.*

PHEBE married Miles Goodman, and moved first to Iowa, and then to Oregon.

MARY married A. Clay Gaines. *See his name.*

HARRIET married Thompson Crider, and died.

JOHN, married and moved to Missouri.

SAMUEL married Cyrena Goodman, and moved to Missouri.

Mrs. Peggy Sackett died, and Thomas Sackett was twice married. After the death of his third wife he moved to Missouri with his sons and died there.

SAFLEY, ADAM, was born in Loudon county, Virginia, and was married to Melinda Ferrell, a native of Virginia also. They had one child in Ohio, and came to Sangamon county, Ill., arriving in 1820 on Lick creek, where they had ten children. We have sketches of three only of them—

STEPHEN, born in Ohio, married in Sangamon county to Nancy Prunk. They have a family, and live near Chesnut, Logan county, Ill.

LUCINDA M., born in Sangamon county, married William Poffenberger. *See his name.*

MARY R., born July 7, 1832, in Sangamon county, married William P. Matthew. See his name.

Mrs. Melinda Safley died, and Adam Safley married Mrs. Nancy Spicer, whose maiden name was Clifton. Adam Safley died January, 1870. Mrs. Nancy Safley lives with her son, John Spicer. See his name.

SANDERS, ELISHA, was born Jan. 16, 1801, in Green county, Ky. He was married Jan. 17, 1824, in the same county, to Jane Faucett. They had three children there, and moved to Sangamon county, Ill., arriving Dec. 16, 1829, and stopped two miles west of Springfield. In 1832 he bought land on Brush creek, fifteen miles south of Springfield, where Timothy Meader now lives. In 1836 he sold out there, and bought land on Horse creek, four miles east of the latter place. They had ten children in Sangamon county. Of their thirteen children—

ROBERT E., born May 26, 1825, in Green county, Ky., married in Sangamon county, April 1, 1846, to Eliza Funderburk. They had two living children. ELISHA, born April 26, 1848, married Sept. 30, 1869, to Mary E. Fry. They have one living child, JULIUS O., and live five and a half miles southeast of Pawnee, in the corner of Sangamon county. MARY E., born April 8, 1850, married Oct., 1867, to George Payn, have three children, ROBERT L., HARRIET M. and JOHN H., and live in Cotton Hill township, on the Vandever place, east of New City. Mrs. Eliza Sanders died Dec. 27, 1852, and Robert E. Sanders married July 12, 1853, to Isabel Bridges, daughter of James. They had six children. MARGARET A., born May 5, 1854, married William T. Beam. See his name. ELIZA J., born Oct. 8, 1856, married Oct. 28, 1873, to James H. Beam. See his name. SUSAN A., born Oct. 11, 1857, died April 6, 1865. JOHN E., THOMAS E. and JAMES W. live with their father. Mrs. Isabel Sanders died August 1, 1865. R. E. Sanders was married May 31, 1868, to Sophia Porter, who was born Feb. 10, 1842, in Belmont county, Ohio. They have two living children, SARAH R. and ROBERT W. live with their parents. Robert E. Sanders resides three miles northeast of Pawnee, Sangamon county, Illinois.

JOHN H., born June 26, 1827, in Green county, Ky., married in Sangamon county, Feb. 25, 1847, to Martha Funderburk. They had four living children: MARY E., born Jan. 6, 1848, married Nov. 23, 1867, to John L. Ludwick, who was born June 6, 1846, in Rockbridge county, Va. He served from August, 1864, to July, 1865, in Co. A, 147th Ohio Inf. They have two children, MARTHA E. and CHARLES H., and live near Pawnee, Ill. VIENNA M., born April 4, 1851, married Oct. 23, 1866, to Joseph Halloway, who was born Jan. 16, 1837, in Hardin county, Ky. They live two and a half miles northeast of Pawnee. SARAH F., born Sept. 24, 1858, and CHARLES T., born Dec. 14, 1859, live with their mother. John H. Sanders died March 7, 1865, in Pawnee, and his widow resides in Christian county, three miles northeast of Pawnee, Sangamon county, Ill. John H. Sanders was in the store of James Bodge, in Pawnee, on the evening of March 7, 1865, when two men entered it, ostensibly with the view of trading, but really with the view of robbery. Mr. Sanders passed out of the door, and as he did so, was shot by an accomplice of the robbers, stationed on the outside, to prevent his giving the alarm. He died before any of his friends could reach him. Two of the robbers, James P. Lemon and Barney B. Vanarsdale, were arrested, the former in Missouri and the latter in Iowa. They were tried, convicted April 25, and hung at Springfield, July 20, 1866. The other, —— Ballard, was hung in Missouri by a mob, but confessed that he assisted in the murder of Mr. Sanders.

MARY A. F., born Oct. 18, 1828, in Kentucky, married in Sangamon county to Rape Funderburk. See his name. She died June 8, 1848.

ELISHA T., born July 2, 1830, in Sangamon county, married Dec. 15, 1850, to Barbara Proctor. They had eight children: JOHN T., ELIZABETH A. and EMMA died under six years of age. Of the other five: LOUISA, born Oct. 15, 1851, was married Jan. 31, 1869, to Edward Tilley. They have two living children, ANDREW J. and EDWARD, and live in Pawnee, Sangamon county, Ill. HARRIET A., born August 16, 1853, was married July 7, 1872, to William R.

Galyen, who was born March 15, 1844, in DeKalb county, Tenn. They have two children, JESSE M. and GEORGE EDWARD, and live in Cotton Hill township. MARTHA I., LEONARD F. and PHILEMON S. live with their parents, two miles east of Pawnee, Sangamon county, Ill. Elisha T. Sanders was ordained a Predestinarian Baptist minister, June 20, 1874.

WILLIAM M., born Jan. 10, 1832, in Sangamon county, married Ellen Peak. They have four living children, SARAH, SINAI, TYRA and ETTIE. William M. Sanders and family reside in Christian county, nine miles east of Pawnee and eight miles west of Taylorville, Illinois.

GEORGE W., born April 16, 1835, in Sangamon county, married, June 15, 1856, to Lucinda Proctor, had one child, MARY E., and Mrs. Sanders died Sept. 12, 1863. Mr. Sanders married, Feb. 25, 1864, to Mrs. Margaret McLaughlin, whose maiden name was Henwood. They have three children, JOSEPH W., WILLIAM E. and ELI PRESTON, and reside two and one-half miles northeast of Pawnee, Illinois.

HARRIET A., born May 25, 1836, in Sangamon county, married, August 17, 1856, to William J. Wheeler, who was born Feb. 21, 1835, in Gibson county, Indiana. They had nine children, seven of whom died under six years of age. MADELON and WILLIAM A. reside with their parents, half a mile northeast of Pawnee, Sangamon county, Ill. Mr. Wheeler has been acting as justice of the peace since April, 1872, and is elected to serve until April, 1877. He was ordained, June 20, 1874, at the Horse creek Predestinarian Baptist church, as a preacher of the gospel.

ANDREW J., born April 22, 1838, in Sangamon county, married, October 7, 1858, to Sarah Lambert, who was born Jan. 30, 1843, in Greene county, Indiana. They had four children, two of whom died, JAMES R. and EMMA died under four years. MILTON J. and FLORA live with their parents, one and one-half mile northeast of Pawnee, Ill. He was ordained June 20, 1874, at the Horse Creek Predestinarian Baptist church, as a preacher of the gospel.

TIMOTHY E. M., born June 2, 1841, in Sangamon county, married, August 28, 1864, to Elizabeth Tilley, who was born April 10, 1844, in Kentucky. They had four children—WILLIAM died in infancy. ALBERT M., CALVIN and EFFIE E. live with their parents, one and one-half mile northeast of Pawnee, Illinois. Mr. Sanders was ordained, Oct. 18, 1873, as deacon of the Horse creek Predestinarian Baptist church.

ELIZA ANN, born Sept. 17, 1842, in Sangamon county, married, Oct., 1860, to Dr. Charles Kerr. They had two children, EDWARD EVERETT and ELIZA ANN. Mrs. Kerr died, Feb. 3, 1865, and Dr. Kerr was married, Sept. 13, 1866, to Melissa McMurry. *See McMurry family*. Dr. Kerr was assistant surgeon of the 59th Ill. Inf., appointed Feb. 18, 1865, was promoted to Major Surgeon of the 10th Ill. Cav., Oct 23, 1865. That regiment was mustered out in November, when he returned to the 59th, and was mustered out with it, at Springfield, in January, 1866. He is now a practicing physician in Pawnee, Sangamon county, Illinois—1876.

JOSEPH W., born Oct. 16, 1844, in Sangamon county, married, Nov. 2, 1865, to Mollie E. Sanders, who was born October 25, 1845, in Kentucky. They have three children, AMANDA M., WILLIAM T. and CHARLES ARTHUR, and reside two and three-quarter miles east of Pawnee, Sangamon county, Illinois.

NANCY ANN, born Dec. 14, 1845, in Sangamon county, married, Jan. 17, 1865, to John Faucett, who was born Nov. 23, 1840, in that part of Green which is now Taylor county, Ky. They have three children, ELISHA M., FANNY M. and JASPER J., and reside one and one-quarter miles east of Pawnee, Sangamon county, Illinois.

STEPHEN A. D., born December 9, 1852, in Sangamon county, married, Dec. 7, 1871, to Amanda A. Womack, who was born Oct. 12, 1853, in Sangamon county. They have one child, MANFORD W., and reside two miles east of Pawnee, Sangamon county, Illinois.

Mrs. Elizabeth Sanders died, June 30, 1865, and Elisha Sanders was married, February 20, 1866, to Nancy Jane Faucett. They have two living children—

ELIZABETH F., and MARTHA E., who live with their parents.

Elisha Sanders was for many years a licensed preacher, previous to May, 1863, when he was ordained, at Horse creek, regular Predestinarian Baptist church, and is now pastor of that church.

This sketch was completed in June, 1874.

Rev. Elisha Sanders says, that although he came into the county ten years after settlement commenced, yet he found houses very scarce. His brother-in-law, Wm. Crowder, and himself, in December, 1829, cut down oak trees, split them in halves, built a cabin west of Springfield, covered it with clapboards, chinked it with wood, and, instead of lime, made mortar of the rich black soil, and plastered the cracks. The plastering was done in freezing weather, but they kept up a fire on the inside until it was dry. The chimney was made of sticks and plastered in the same way, and when it was dry, the prints of their fingers could be seen all over in the plastering. Mr. Sanders now lives in a house much better than the average farm houses in the county, but he says he never felt so rich as when he moved into that cabin plastered with the mud.

Mr. Sanders remembers that the "deep snow" of 1830-'31 was about three and one-half feet deep on a level. He had to gather his corn twice. The first time he took all the ears on a level with and above the snow, and after it went off he went over again and gathered nearly as much more. He saved a cow and calf from perishing by taking them in with his family and keeping them in one corner of the house.

SANDERS, ROBERT W., was born April 10, 1815, near Harper's Ferry, Virginia. His father died when he was a child, and his widowed mother, with her eight children, moved to Rutherford county, Tenn., in 1827. Robert W. was married there, in 1834, to Keziah Johnson. They had two children in Tennessee, and moved to Sangamon county, Ill., arriving in the fall of 1838 in what is now Cotton Hill township, where two children were born. Mr. Sanders assisted in quarrying the stone for the State House, then in course of construction at Springfield. His family suffered greatly from sickness, and in 1840 he returned to Tennessee, where he died May 31, 1857, leaving a widow, nine sons and one daughter. Robert W. Sanders was a minister in the Baptist church for thirteen years previous to his death. The widow felt that some great calamity was about to befall that part of the country where she lived, and without any definite idea of what it was, she meditated long upon the subject, and when her children were wrapped in slumber she resolved, if possible, to take them again to Illinois as a place of safety. She wrote at once to her eldest son, who had returned to Illinois soon after the death of his father. He was glad to give them such aid and encouragement as he could, and they all arrived in Sangamon county Oct. 10, 1859, just in time to understand the situation of the country and add five soldiers to the Union army. Of Mrs. Sanders ten living children—

STEPHEN N., born March 16, 1835, in Rutherford county, Tenn., studied medicine in Sangamon county, Ill., enlisted there in Co. K, 124th Ill. Inf., was elected Captain of same company and twice wounded—once severely. He was acting assistant aid-de-camp on Gen. J. B. Coats' staff a portion of the time; also assistant government marshal of the provisional encampment at Vicksburg, Miss., during the winter of 1864 and '5; served three years and was honorably discharged Aug. 12, 1865. He was married at Loami, Sangamon county, Ill., to Mary J. Smith. They had two children; one died; the other, NORA, lives with her grandmother Smith in Christian county. Mrs. Mary J. Sanders died May 28, 1868. S. N. Sanders was married Nov. 23, 1871, to Susan Elliott, at Wilmington, Ill. He is a practicing physician at Arcola, Douglas county, Ill.

GEORGE W., born Dec. 8, 1838, in Cotton Hill township, Sangamon county, was married near Auburn, Ill., to Elizabeth Bremer. They have two children, CLARA A. and IDA B., and reside in Auburn, Ill.

THOMAS J., born Aug. 23, 1840, in Cotton Hill township, Sangamon county, brought up in Tennessee, and enlisted in Co. K, 124th Ill. Vol. Inf., in 1862, for three years; was elected sargeant, served full term, and was honorably discharged

Aug. 12, 1865. He was married February, 1875, to Maggie Hackley, and resides in Auburn, Ill.

MARTIN L., born Feb. 8, 1842, in Rutherford county, Tenn., enlisted April, 1864, in Co. K, 124th Ill. Inf., served one year and eleven months. He was honorably discharged at the close of the rebellion, and was married at Mechanicsburg to Mary J. Sparrow. They have two children, VIRGIL H. and JAMES H., and reside at Lincoln, Ill.

JOHN F., born Nov. 4, 1844, in Rutherford county, Tenn., enlisted in Co. K, 124th Ill. Inf., April, 1864; served eleven months, and was honorably discharged November, 1865. He was married in Auburn, Sangamon county, Ill., to Jennie Wallace. They have one living child, CLYDE. J. F. Sanders is a practicing physician at Sullivan, Moultrie county, Ill.

ANDREW D., born Oct. 14, 1846, in Tennessee, enlisted in Co. K, 124th Ill. Vol. Inf., for one year, served eleven months, and was honorably discharged at the close of the rebellion. He was married Sept. 22, 1872, to Susan A. Ballenger. They have one child, WILLIAM A., and live in Auburn, Sangamon county, Ill.

CLEMENT J., born Nov. 27, 1848, in Tennessee, was married Sept. 23, 1871, to Ella Watson. They have two children, GUY and a babe, and reside in Auburn, Sangamon county, Illinois.

CHRISTOPHER H., born Oct. 14, 1850, in Williamson county, Ill., is unmarried, and practicing medicine in Covington, Moultrie county, Ill.

HENRY J., born Jan. 18, 1852, in Williamson county, is unmarried, and resides in Auburn, Sangamon county, Ill.

ELLA, born Nov. 17, 1855, in Davidson county, Tenn., was married in Auburn, Ill., to Charles Tomlinson. They live at Butler, Indiana.

Mrs. Keziah Sanders went to Nashville, Tenn., in March, 1873, to visit her relatives and acquaintances, but returned to Illinois in the fall of the same year, and now resides with her daughter in Butler, Ind. She often says that when she left Tennessee in 1859, it was the best move she ever made.

SAUNDERS, GUNNELL, was born July 27, 1783, in Loudon county, Virginia, of English ancestry. His parents emigrated to the vicinity of Lexington, Ky., and a year or two later moved to Fleming county, in the same State. Mary Mauzy was born April 15, 1784, in Fauquier county, Virginia. Her parents, who were of French descent, moved to Bourbon county, and from there to Fleming county, Ky. Gunnell Saunders and Mary Mauzy were there married about 1801, and had seven children there. He was a soldier from Fleming county in the war of 1812, and afterwards moved his family to Sangamon county, Ill., arriving May 10, 1828, and settled four miles northeast of Springfield. Of their children—

JONATHAN R., born Feb. 17, 1802, in Fleming county, Ky., was married there Dec. 18, 1823, to Sarah McKinnie. They moved to Sangamon county, Ill., arriving Nov. 28, 1824, at Springfield. He entered the land on which the Sangamon county fair is held, two miles north of Springfield, and moved there in 1828. They had six children in Sangamon county. GUNNELL A., born Jan. 13, 1825, died in his second year. LEWIS A., born Dec. 27, 1826, in Springfield, was trained to mercantile pursuits in Col. John Williams' store, in Springfield. When gold was discovered in California, he formed a partnership with Samuel Fisher, who for several years had lived with Mr. Saunders. Lewis A. Saunders and Samuel Fisher left Springfield early in 1849, as part of a company of sufficient magnitude for safety. They reached their destination and engaged in mining and selling provisions to the miners on South Feather river. Mr. Saunders wrote to his parents regularly once a month. In a letter written to them early in April, 1850, he reported himself well and in a prosperous condition. That was the last communication his friends ever received from him. His partner, Mr. Fisher, went to Sacramento on business for the firm, and Mr. Saunders was last seen by a Rev. Mr. Mayfield, and a blacksmith from St. Joseph, Mo., April 8, 1850. Neither of those men could say whether it was before or after his partner left for Sacramento. All that his parents ever received from his effects was about two hundred dollars in gold dust, much less than he took with him. Samuel Fisher returned a few months later, and is now—1874—a wealthy farmer and manufacturer at Brooklyn, Schuyler county, Ill. AS-BERRY H., born Nov. 7, 1828, in Springfield, was married Oct. 20, 1856, at Mt. Pleasant, Iowa, to Marcia E. Underwood, who was born Feb. 7, 1837, at Portage, Ohio. They had four children; three died young. HELEN, born June 2, 1863, lives with her father. Mrs. Marcia E. Saunders died Sept. 30, 1874. Mr. Saunders has farming done in Arkansas, and lives in Springfield, Ill. MARTHA A. and FRANCES died in infancy. MILTON, born Oct. 3, 1836, near Springfield, was married Jan. 3, 1861, to Anna E. Edwards, who was born April 29, 1840, in Salem, N. J. They had three children. CORA died in infancy. Mrs. Anna E. Saunders died June 30, 1863, leaving two children, NELLIE E. and FRANCES S., who live with their father. Milton Saunders was married Aug. 28, 1872, to Martha E. Beeley, who was born of English parentage, Aug. 31, 1842, at Concord, Morgan county, Ill. They have two children, LILLIE and MARCIA. Milton Saunders and family live at his father's house, two miles north of Springfield—1874. Mr. Saunders is a deaf mute, caused by disease, and his present wife was so from her birth. They were both educated at the State Institution at Jacksonville. All his children can hear and converse. Jonathan R. Saunders was a lieutenant in a light-horse company from Sangamon county in the Winnebago war of 1826 and '7, and captain of the same company in the Black Hawk war of 1831. He was one of the board of officers who made the treaty with Black Hawk, which the latter violated and caused the war of 1832. J. R. Saunders and wife reside two miles north of Springfield, Ill., and have lived within two miles of their present residence 52 years.

NANCY, born about 1804, in Fleming county, Ky., was married there to Amos Locke, and moved to Bloomington, Ind., and from there to Sangamon county in 1830. The deep snow of 1830 and '31 discouraged them so much that they returned to Bloomington in 1832, and both died there, leaving six children, all of whom moved to Iowa. Two of the sons were killed in the Union army while assisting to suppress the great rebellion.

PRESLEY, born in Fleming county, Ky., came to Sangamon county, Ill., in 1827, and married Edith Cooper. They had three children in that county, who all died young. They moved in 1834 to Iowa, and Presley Saunders laid out the town of Mt. Pleasant. Of their two children born in Iowa, AMANDA married Dr. J. D. Harper, and died in Mt. Pleasant. [See Dr. Harper's name in connection with the Mitchell family.] MARY married in Mt. Pleasant to John McCoy, and lives in Denver, Col. Mrs. Edith Saunders died in Mt. Pleasant, and Presley Saunders married Huldah Bowen. They had four children, and all are married. Presley Saunders is President of the First National Bank at Mt. Pleasant, Iowa, and resides there—1875.

FRANCES, born in Fleming county, Ky., was married in Sangamon county, Ill., to David K. Mackey. They had one child, and Mr. Mackey and the child died. Mrs. Frances Mackey was married to Rev. Arthur Miller, who died, and she died Sept. 24, 1876, in Mt. Pleasant, Iowa.

GEORGE M., born Oct. 6, 1811, in Fleming county, Ky., was married April 9, 1833, to Maria L. Sampson, who was born April 5, 1811, in Fleming county, Ky. They had four children. EVELINE M., born March 4, 1835, married Dr. William Logan. They have one child, and live in Oconee, Shelby county, Illinois. JAMES W., born March 24, 1837, and served three months in the beginning of the rebellion, in an Illinois regiment. He married Sarah Dorrell, and lives in Mason City, Ill. JOHN S., born May 2, 1840, enlisted for three years, in 1861, in Co. G, 10th Ill. Cav., served three years and four months, and was honorably discharged. He was married August 4, 1866, to Cordelia Montgomery. They have two children, ARAMINDA and LEWIS L., and live two miles north of Springfield. DAVID S., born June 17, 1842, enlisted in 1861, in the 2d Ill. Art., for three years, and died at Fort Donelson, May 3, 1864. Mrs. M. L. Saunders died Nov. 29, 1847, and George M. Saunders was married March 9, 1849, to Nancy A. Offill, who was born May 4, 1826, in Bath county, Ky. They had seven living children. ALVIN L., born Feb. 4, 1850, enlisted in 1862, for three years, in Co. C, 115th Ill. Inf., was transferred to the 121st Ill. Inf., served to the end of the rebellion, and was honorably discharged.

He married Mary J. Shaw. They have one child, and live two miles north of Springfield, Ill. JULIA E., SARAH J., EDWARD L., ETNA A., MARY E. and HARVEY E., live with their parents, four miles north of Springfield, Illinois.—1874.

ALVIN, born July 12, 1817, in Fleming county, Ky., came with his parents to Sangamon county, Ill., in 1828, drove an ox team in breaking prairie and hauling wood to Springfield. He remained with his father until 1836, when he joined his brother Presley at what is now Mt. Pleasant, Henry county, Iowa, then part of the territory of Wisconsin. There were but four families, and not more than a dozen houses in the town. He first hired to a farmer, but soon after found employment as a clerk in a small dry goods store. His education was too limited for the latter position, so he attended night school, and in this way improved himself, and retained his position as clerk. He was the first Postmaster at Mt. Pleasant, and continued in that position seven years, during which time he was in a partnership with his brother Presley, in mercantile business. He was a member of the constitutional convention of Iowa, under which that State was admitted into the Union, and was elected State Senator in 1854. He was a delegate to the first Republican convention of Iowa, which met Feb. 22, 1856. Alvin Saunders was married March 11, 1856, in Washington, D. C., to Marthena Barlow, who was born Oct. 24, 1834, at Greencastle, Ind. She is a niece of Mrs. Senator Harlan. They have two children. CHARLES L., born Dec. 23, 1856, and MARY A., born Nov. 16, 1860, live with their parents. In 1858 Mr. Saunders was elected his own successor to the State Senate. He was a delegate to the National Republican Convention of 1860, which nominated Mr. Lincoln as a candidate for President of the United States. He and Mr. Lincoln became acquainted in Sangamon county, Ill., when both were unknown. During Mr. Saunders' second term as State Senator of Iowa, Mr. Lincoln appointed him, early in 1861, Governor of Nebraska Territory, a position he held for six years, and until Nebraska was admitted to the Union as a State, which he officially announced by proclamation, March 27, 1867. When the Union Pacific Railroad bill passed congress, Gov. Saunders was appointed by that body one of the commissioners to give practical form to the measure, and on Dec. 2, 1863, ground was broken at Omaha by his moving with his own hands the first spadefull of earth for the construction of that great thoroughfare. When he was appointed Governor, Nebraska Territory was in debt equal to two dollars per head for every man, woman and child within its limits, and when she was admitted as a State, and Governor Saunders retired, there was sufficient money in the treasury to pay all indebtedness, including the expense of furnishing Nebraska's quota of troops to suppress the great slaveholders' rebellion. Ex-Gov. Saunders resides in Omaha, Nebraska, and is President of the State National Bank of that place.

WILLIAM A., born in Fleming county, Ky., came with his parents to Sangamon county, in 1828, and afterwards went to Mt. Pleasant, Iowa, where he was married to Louisa Dickey. All their children died young, except one. Mr. Saunders died in 1863, and his only child, WILLIAM, born after his father's death, lives with his mother, in Mt. Pleasant, Iowa.

Gunnell Saunders and his wife moved from Springfield, Ill., to Mt. Pleasant, Iowa, in the summer of 1846. Hon. E. D. Baker, of Ball's Bluff fatal memory, with whom Mr. Saunders was on terms of most intimate friendship, visited Mt. Pleasant, and made a speech in favor of the election of Gen. Taylor. Mr. Saunders took Col. Baker in his carriage to Ottumwa, and on the morning of Oct. 26, 1848, bade him adieu and left for home. He was found about two miles from Ottumwa, in his carriage, dead, with the lines so adjusted as to bring the carriage on a cramp. Gunnell Saunders was about sixty miles from home, but his remains were taken to Mt. Pleasant for interment. His widow continued to live there until Oct. 18, 1851, when she died from the effects of a dose of arsenic carelessly put up by a druggist in place of morphine.

SATTLEY, ROBERT, was born Oct. 27, 1788, in the vicinity of Vergennes, Vermont. He and his brother Archibald went with the family of Mrs. Lovina Hawley, a widow lady with two daughters and three sons, to White county, near Carmi, Ill., in the fall of 1818. He was there married, February, 1819, to Eliza Hawley. She was born March 7, 1801, near Vergennes, Vt. Mr. and Mrs. Sattley moved to what became Sangamon county, Ill., arriving in June, 1819, and settled about half a mile north of where Rochester now stands. They had eight children in Sangamon county—

AARON, born Jan. 25, 1820, in Sangamon county, married March 4, 1858, to Delilah Shaver, who was born Feb. 9, 1835, in Ohio. They have seven children, JOSEPHINE, ROBERT H., RALPH D., LOVINA A., WILLIAM A., MARY E. and HARRIET, and reside one mile west of Sangamo station, Sangamon county, Ill.—1874.

RALPH, born Nov. 1, 1821, in Sangamon county, was drowned June 15, 1844, in South Fork, after having saved the life of another young man who was bathing.

HARRIET, born Nov. 27, 1823, in Sangamon county, married Jan. 3, 1849, to George M. Greene. *See his name.*

JULIA, born Sept. 6, 1825, in Sangamon county, married Horace Collins, a native of Ohio. They have seven living children, and reside near Solon, Johnson county, Iowa.

LOVINA, born Sept. 14, 1827, in Sangamon county, married Charles Fairchild. *See his name.*

EMILY, born Oct. 22, 1829, in Sangamon county, died Dec. 15, 1851.

ALFRED died in infancy.

ELIZA J., born June 15, 1834, married John A. Twist. *See his name.*

ROBERT H., born Sept. 18, 1837, in Sangamon county, married Nov. 7, 1860, to Margaret J. Greene. They had four children. The eldest and youngest died in infancy. MARY E. and EMMA J. live with their parents, three miles south of Rochester, Sangamon county, Ill.

Robert Sattley died March 27, 1842, and Mrs. Eliza Sattley died June 13, 1860, both in Rochester, Sangamon county, Ill.

SATTLEY, ARCHIBALD, born Oct. 8, 1794, near Vergennes, Vermont, was married Feb. 13, 1819, near Carmi, White county, Ill., to Harriet Hawley, who was born March, 7, 1801, in Vermont. She was a twin sister of his brother Robert's wife. They moved to what became Sangamon county, arriving in June, 1819, and settled half a mile north of where Rochester now stands. They had eight children in Sangamon county, two of whom died young. Of the others—

MELVINA, born Sept. 3, 1819, married John C. Miller. *See his name.*

ALBERT, born April 10, 1821, in Sangamon county, was married, Sept. 21, 1853, in Springfield, to Susan C. Torrey. They had six children, three died young. The others live with their parents, in Taylorville, Illinois. Albert Sattley is one of the firm of Sattley Bros., Taylorville, Illinois, and resides there.

MARY, born Dec. 31, 1822, in Sangamon county, was married Jan. 16, 1845, in Rochester, to Thomas Cheney. They had four children, two died young. JENNIE married Dr. Henry Jayne, and lives in Taylorville. *See his name.* CHARLES, born Oct. 9, 1850, in Taylorville, was married there, Jan. 30, 1872, to Jennie Murphy, who was born July 1, 1850, in Christian county, Illinois. They live in Taylorville, Illinois. Thomas Cheney died Sept. 6, 1854, and his widow married Matthew E. Long. *See his name.*

ELIZA, born Nov. 11, 1824, in Sangamon county, married Isaac H. Firey. *See his name.*

MARSHALL, born Oct 24, 1831, in Sangamon county, was married, Nov. 5, 1857, to Ruth A. Prather, who was born July 22, 1838, in Washington county, Maryland. They have one child, MYRTLE, and live in Taylorville, Illinois. He is one of the firm of Sattley Bros.

EDMUND was killed by a loaded wagon running over him, in Rochester, at the age of five years.

Mrs. Harriet Sattley died Oct. 13, 1833, in Sangamon county, and Archibald Sattley was married in March, 1834, to Julia E. Sherman, a native of Vermont. They had three children in Rochester.

HENRY, born Sept. 25, 1835, was married Feb. 29, 1861, in Taylorville, to Mary Thompson, a native of Virginia. They had four children, three died young. ELIZA lives with her parents in Taylorville.

ARCHIBALD, Jun., born Sept. 2, 1837, was married Oct. 25, 1860, to Martha J. Ferguson. They have five children, CLYDE A., JAMES F.,

FREDERICK L., HIRAM L. and LUCY. A. Sattley, Jun., is of the firm of Sattley Bros., Taylorville, Illinois.

CHARLES, born Feb. 12, 1839, was married Feb. 15, 1862, near Taylorville, to Clara A. Ferguson. They have five children, LULIE, EMMA, OSCAR, MAUDE, and a babe, and live near Willey station, Christian county, Ill.

Archibald Sattley, Sen., died March 16, 1842, in Rochester, and his widow, Mrs. Julia E. Sattley, was married there to Lewis Thompson. They had two children—

VICTORIA, married J. E. Davis, and lives at Brookton.

ALICE married Harry Smith, and lives in Chicago, Illinois.

Mrs. Julia E. Thompson died in 1865, in Springfield, Ill., and Lewis Thompson died in 1872, near Taylorville, Illinois.

SAYRE, JOHN, was born Oct. 12, 1762, near Bridgeton, Cumberland county, New Jersey, and was married there, August 20, 1792, to Catharine Teel, who was born May 3, 1774, near Bridgeton, also. They had eleven children in New Jersey, and the family moved to Green county, near Xenia, Ohio, in 1822, and from there to Sangamon county, Ill., arriving in the fall of 1834, in what is now Cartwright township, south of Richland creek. Of their children—

JOHN, Jun., born July 18, 1795, in New Jersey, was married in Ohio to Nancy Maxwell. They had three children. He came on a visit to his relations, and died Dec. 31, 1870, in Springfield. He was buried in Cartwright township, and his two daughters are both married. One lives in Iowa and the other in Missouri.

DAVID, born August 2, 1797, was married in New Jersey, and never moved west.

MARGARET, born Feb. 22, 1800, near Bridgeton, Cumberland county, N. J., was married there to Constantine Foster. See his name.

THOMAS, born Dec. 14, 1802, in Cape May county, N. J., married in Sangamon county, June 23, 1836, to Effie Waggoner. They had eight living children—JOHN, born Jan. 11, 1838, died unmarried, Oct. 7, 1865. MARY ARMINDA, born Nov. 1, 1839, married William T. Pirkins. See his name. JAMES T. born June 6, 1841, and GEORGE W. born Aug. 11, 1843, lives with their mother. ELIZA JANE, born Oct. 4, 1847, married Aug. 10, 1871, to James W. Shoup, who was born July, 1846, in New York city. They live near Richland Station. CHARLES C., ANN E. and MARGARET E. live with their mother. Thomas Sayre died Jan. 23, 1861, and his widow resides now (1876) on the farm where he settled on coming to the county. It is two and a half miles northeast of Richland Station, Sangamon county, Ill.

ELIZA, born August 26, 1806, in New Jersey; was married in Sangamon county to Rolla Morgan. They had eight children, moved to Iowa, and Mrs. Morgan died there. The family started over the plains, and Mr. Morgan and one of the children died on the road. The others continued their journey, and reside in Portland, Oregon.

FOSTER, born July 8, 1809, in New Jersey, died in Ohio, July 22, 1836, from injuries received in a well.

EDMOND, born Dec. 2, 1812, in New Jersey, is unmarried, and lives in Cartwright township, Sangamon county, Ill., now, 1876.

MARY, born June 16, 1814, near Bridgeton, New Jersey, was married Sept. 15, 1842, in Sangamon county, Ill., to John H. Beaumont. They had one living child, FANNIE, who married Dr. Harrison Withrow. See his name. They live in Petersburg, Ill. Mr. Beaumont died May 3, 1870, at Pleasant Plains, Sangamon county, and his widow lives at Petersburg, Menard county, Ill.

CLARISSA, born Oct. 31, 1816, in New Jersey, was married in Sangamon county, Ill., to Jordan Simpson. See his name.

Mrs. Catharine Sayre died Sept. 18, 1835, and John Sayre died Dec. 27, 1835, both near Richland creek, Sangamon county, Ill.

SCOTT, DALLAS, was born April 6, 1791, in Cumberland county, Ky. Sarah Foster was born May 1, 1793, in the same county. They were there married in 1815, and had two children in Kentucky, and the family moved to Sangamon county, Ill., arriving Nov. 1, 1819, on Richland creek, three miles east of the present town of Pleasant Plains, where six children were born. Of their eight children,

ELIZABETH, born Nov. 13, 1816, in Kentucky, married in Sangamon county to Travis Elmore, and live near Ashland, Cass county, Illinois.

GEORGE M., born July 18, 1819, in Kentucky, married in Cass county, Ill., to Margaret Whitmire. They had two living children. He was a physician, and died June 13, 1851, at Lagrange, Missouri. His children live with their mother, who married, and lives near Sidney, Ohio.

CINTHELIA, born Sept. 10, 1821, in Sangamon county, married Feb. 9, 1841, to Valentine C. Cartwright. See his name.

MILTON M., born Feb. 24, 1824, in Sangamon county, Ill., married in Kentucky to Jane Scott. They have one child, and live in Crawford county Mo.

JOHN F., born April 6, 1826, in Sangamon county, married, has five children, and lives near Omaha, Nebraska.

MATTIE J., born April 24, 1829, in Sangamon county, is unmarried, and lives with her sister, Mrs. Cartwright.

HATTIE N., born December 4, 1831, in Sangamon county, married Amos Dick, has one child, EMMA, and lives near Wapella, DeWitt county, Illinois.

FRANCIS M., born April 26, 1835, in Sangamon county, married January 17, 1858, to Mary L. Brockman, who was born Oct. 1, 1836, in Morgan county, Ill. They had seven children. HARRIET E., the third child, died at four years, and AMOS, the seventh child, died Sept. 4, 1873, in his second year. The other five, GEORGE D., CYNTHIA A., JOHN L., JAMES H., and EUGENE, live with their parents. F. M. Scott resides at the homestead where his parents settled in 1819. It is in Cartwright township, three miles northeast of Pleasant Plains, Sangamon county, Ill.

Dallas Scott died June 18, 1841, and his widow died Feb. 4, 1862, both in Cartwright township, Sangamon county, Ill.

SCOTT, JAMES, was born Oct. 22, 1797, in Culpepper county, Va. His father moved to South Carolina, thence to Rutherford county, Tenn., and from there to Caldwell county, Ky., all when James was a boy. Mary Woods was born Feb. 29, 1804, in Georgia, and her parents soon after moved to Caldwell county, Ky. James Scott and Mary Woods were there married May 6, 1819. They had 6 children in Kentucky, and moved to Missouri, crossing the Mississippi on the ice in the winter of 1827 or '28. After four weeks, they went to Morgan county, Ill. In the spring of 1828 they returned to Kentucky, and in the fall of 1829 moved to Morgan county, Ill., where nine children were born, in all fifteen children, namely—

EVELINE, born March 8, 1820, in Caldwell county, Ky., married Henry N. Hamlin. See his name.

ELIZABETH, born April 20, 1821, in Caldwell county, Ky., married in Morgan county, Ill., to John H. Ham. They have a family, and reside near Decatur, Ill.

FRANCIS M., born March 27, 1823, in Caldwell county, Ky., married Mrs. Sarah Burch, and reside near Franklin, Morgan county, Ill. They have five children, viz.: MINERVA E., GEORGE, MARTHA, WILLIAM H., and SARAH F.

LUCY, born March 3, 1825 in Caldwell county, Ky., married in Morgan county Ill., to Samuel O'Neal. See his name.

MARY A., born Dec. 9, 1826, in Kentucky, married George G. Harnsburger, and resides near Decatur, Ill.

SARAH, born Oct. 9, 1828, in Kentucky, married in Sangamon county, Ill., to Joseph Stickel, and reside near Hillsboro, Montgomery county, Ill.

MINERVA J., born April 2, 1830, in Morgan county, Ill., and was married there to William R. Ford. See his name.

MARTHA E., born Feb. 13, 1832, in Morgan county, Ill., was married in Sangamon county to Hiram W. Walker. See his name.

NANCY M., born in Morgan county, died aged 6 years.

THOMAS J., born Dec. 9, 1835, in Morgan county, Ill., married Fannie Bird, and for his second wife, married Mary Ford. They have one child, LUTHER D., and reside at Virden, Macoupin county, Ill.

WILLIAM F., born April 9, 1838, in Morgan county, married April 9, 1862, in Sangamon county, to Matilda Headley, who was born Sept. 27, 1838, in Parke county, Ind. They have four living children, HELEN, THALBERG W., CHANNING H., and LAUREL. Their second child, EDNA, died Sept. 9, 1865. The following lines written by the mother, and published in the Illinois *State Journal* expresses her feelings at the time:

IN MEMORIAM.

Sleep, little baby sleep,
Not in thy mother's arms or cradle bed,
But in the grave forever with the dead
To sleep thy last long sleep.
My precious child! alas, no longer mine.
Earth holds no form so dear to me as thine.

Rest, little darling, rest,
Thy mother's heart is breaking o'er the loss
Of thee, sweet baby! O, the bitter cross
Is hard to bear—what joys what hopes are hid
Forever underneath thy coffin lid!
Yet rest thee, darling, rest.

Could I again behold
Thee, baby, as when living, my delight,
Thy beauteous face so fair, thine eyes so bright,
Thy hair of sunny gold,
How would it ease this aching, longing pain,
Could I but clasp thee to my heart again!
BALL, ILL., March, 1872. M. S.

William P. Scott resides in Ball township, about two hundred yards north of where Robert Pulliam built the first cabin in the county.

HARRIET A., born May 6, 1840, in Morgan county, married in Sangamon county to David Pyle. *See his name.*

JULIA, born in 1842, died in 1857.

NANCY ANTIONETTE, born April 13, 1845, in Morgan county, married in Sangamon county to Fletcher A. Stickel, and resides in Centralia, Kansas.

JAMES R., born Dec. 9, 1847, in Morgan county, married in Sangamon county, in 1872, to Mary R. Patterson. They have one child, CLARA ETTIE, and live in Ball township.

James Scott and wife reside in Ball township, three hundred yards east of where Robert Pulliam built the first cabin in Sangamon county, in the autumn of 1817. Mrs. Scott's youngest child has witnessed more returns of his birthday than she has of her own. *See date of her birth for explanation.*

SCOTT, JOHN, was born about 1734 in Pennsylvania. His father, Andrew Scott, emigrated from Scotland and settled in Pennsylvania about 1725. John Scott was a soldier in the American Revolution, and was married about 1756 to Anna Crayton. They had one child—

ELIZABETH, who married James Maston.

Mrs. Anna Scott died and John Scott married Nancy Keith. They had twelve living children. The family moved to Sangamon county in 1824, and settled at Island Grove. Of his children—

ANDREW, born Nov. 21, 1786, in North Carolina, was married May 28, 1808, in Jackson county, Tenn., to Anna Longest, who was born in 1791 in South Carolina, near the sea coast. They had seven children there, and moved to Sangamon county, Ill., first stopping east of Springfield, thence to Richland creek, and from there to Island Grove, arriving in 1824. Four children were born there. Of their eleven children, GADDIAL, born Aug. 9, 1809, in Jackson county, Tenn., was married July 25, 1833, at Island Grove, Sangamon county, Ill., to Susan Sexton, who was born May 25, 1810, in Knox county, Kentucky. The moved to Knox county, Ill., settling four miles north of Knoxville, Oct. 6, 1834. They had six living children, WILLIAM M., born July 21, 1834, died July 18, 1863. JOHN W., born March 26, 1836, died Oct. 6, 1862. ELIZABETH S., born April 27, 1839, died Feb. 22, 1864. ENOCH S., born July 25, 1841, near Galesburg, was married July 4, 1863, to Mary R. Grant. They had two living children, *John W.* and *Clarence R.*, and live at the homestead near Galesburg, Ill. JAMES M., born May 5, 1843, in Knox county, was married Feb. 23, 1870, to Della Lotts. They had two children, *Forrest L.* and *Olive P.*, and live at the homestead near Galesburg, Ill. JACOB A., born Oct. 14, 1846, died May 3, 1865. Mrs. Susan Scott died Jan. 22, 1875, and Gaddial Scott resides near Galesburg, Ill. NANCY, born Feb. 22, 1811, in Lincoln county, Ky., married in Sangamon county to John Slatten. They moved to DeWitt county, Ill., and from there to Des Moines, Iowa, in 1856, where they now reside. They have seven children. JAMES L., born Jan. 12, 1813, in Giles county, Tenn., came to Sangamon county in 1824, and was married in Iowa to Mary A. Gilmer. They have eight children, and reside near Des Moines, Iowa. ELIZABETH A., born Jan. 20, 1815, in Harrison county, Ind., came to Sangamon county with her father's family and married John Maxwell, of Macon county. They have five living children, and reside near Waynesville, DeWitt county, Ill. ANNA, born Jan. 21, 1817, in Orange county, Ind., married Tilford Gilmer. They have one child, and reside near Glasgow, Jefferson county, Iowa. WILSON A., born Nov. 20, 1818, in Crawford county, Ind.; came to Sangamon county, Ill., in 1824, was married in Iowa to Mrs. Louisa Jayne. Wilson A. Scott went to Fort Des Moines and traded with the Indians there until they were removed west. He accompanied them but returned to Des Moines, laid out the town on the east side of the river, and it was largely through his influence and contributions that the capital was built on that side. He went to California, returned to Des Moines and contributed two or three years to the building up of the city; started to Pike's Peak and died at Fort Laramie in 1859 His remains were buried at Des Moines. CALEB L., born Dec. 22, 1821, in Sangamon county, Ill., spent ten years, from 1850 to 1860, in California, was married Oct. 21, 1860, in Jefferson county, Iowa, to Charlotte K. Templeton, who was born Oct. 9, 1827, in Wayne county, Ohio. They came at once to Island Grove township, Sangamon county, Ill. They had five children, CHARLOTTE J., ANN M., JOHN H. C., HENRY W., and EDNA E., and reside adjoining Berlin on the east. JOHN W., born June 3, 1824, at Island Grove, was married Sept. 7, 1848, to Martha Yates. They had nine children, three died in infancy, MINNIE died in her eighth year. The other five, HENRY A., LOUISA, RICHARD V., JOHN W., Jun., and THOMAS Y., reside with their parents in Berlin, Illinois. DORINDA, born Dec. 12, 1828, in Sangamon county, was married to William T. Hughes, who was born in Adair county, Ky. They have two living children, MARY L. married Samuel Mendenhall, and lives at Elkhart, Ill. ADA M. resides with her parents. William T. Hughes and family live at Elkhart, Logan county, Ill. LUCINDA, born April 17, 1830, in Sangamon county, married Stewart Goodrell. They had three children, MARY, STEWART, Jun., and ANNA. Mr. Goodrell died in 1872; his widow and children reside at Des Moines, Iowa. Stewart Goodrell represented Polk county, Iowa, in the State Legislature several years, and was pension agent at the time of his death. MALINDA, born May 2, 1832, in Sangamon county, married Thomas B. Reed. They had one child, WILSON T., and Mr. Reed died at Island Grove, Ill. His widow and son reside at Des Moines, Iowa. Mrs. Anna Scott died and Andrew Scott married Mrs. Maxwell, whose maiden name was Ellis. He died in 1859 and his widow died in 1861. He was a minister in the Christian church.

ALEXANDER, JOHN, WILSON, WILLIAM, JAMES, MARTIN, SAMUEL, RUTH, ANNA and NANCY, all these brothers and sisters named above, settled in DeWitt county, Illinois; none came to Sangamon county.

SEELEY, BISHOP, born Feb. 10, 1794, at Williston, Chittenden county, Vt. Betsy Brush was born Oct. 18, 1795, at Waltham, Vt. Her father was a Colonel in the Revolution. Bishop Seeley and Betsy Brush were married Aug. 14, 1816, at Madrid, St. Lawrence county, New York, and their six children were born there. The family moved to Sangamon county, Ill., arriving Nov. 13, 1835, in the Farmington settlement, in what is now Cartwright township. Of their children—

SUSAN P., born Aug. 8, 1818, was married in Sangamon county, Illinois, Dec. 25, 1838, to Robert B. Zimmerman. See his name.

LUCIUS A., born Aug. 10, 1820, was married in Sangamon county, Oct. 16, 1844, to Sophia H. Buckman, and moved to Oregon in 1850. They have ten living children, and reside near Portland, Oregon.

JOSEPH S., born Oct. 20, 1824, in St. Lawrence county, N. Y., was brought up in Sangamon county, Ill., went to Oregon in 1848, was married there, had two children, and lives in Wasco county, Oregon.

GEORGE B., born June 8, 1829, in New York, was married April 26, 1850, in Sangamon county, Ill., to Mary L. Child. They are without family, and reside, at Abilene, Kansas.

STEPHEN B., born May 29, 1832, in New York, was married in Tazewell county, Ill., Oct. 1, 1854, to Agnes R. Powers, who was born in Hardy county,

West Va. They have three living children, LUCIUS A., GEORGE B., and FANNIE, and reside adjoining Pawnee, Sangamon county, Ill.

JANE L., born Sept. 20, 1834, in New York, was married March 19, 1856, in Sangamon county, Ill., to James McCoy. *See his name.* They have four living children, HARRIET, ROBERT B., SEELEY and MARTHA, and reside in Topeka, Kansas.

Bishop Seeley moved in 1853 from Farmingdale to Springfield, where he and his wife now reside—1876.

SELLS, DANIEL K., was born Aug. 22, 1800, in Ross county, Ohio, and came with his brother-in-law, Christopher Newcomer, to Sangamon county in 1824, and taught school at Rochester in 1825. He enlisted at Columbus, O., and served through the Mexican war. Has traveled all over the American continent. He lives with his nephew, Dow Newcomer. *See his name.*

SHANE, JOHN, was born in Kentucky, near the mouth of Kanawha river, and was there married and moved to what is now Loami township in 1828; raised a large family and died there in 1847-8. His widow and all except three of his children moved to Harrison county, Missouri.

EDWARD, married Mary A. Withrow, raised a family and died at Mechanicsburg, Ill.

ELIZA, married Emanuel Jones. *See his name.*

EMELINE, married John Jones. *See his name.* After his death she went to Missouri and died there.

SHELLHOUSE, LYDIA, was born in Georgia. Her maiden name was Leadbetter. She married Daniel McDowell, and had three children. Mr. McDowell died, and she married Lewis Shellhouse. Leaving her three children with their relatives in Georgia, she and Mr. Shellhouse moved to Kentucky, where they had four children, and Mr. Shellhouse died there.

The widow and her two youngest children came to Sangamon county, Ill., arriving in what is now Ball township in the fall of 1830, just in time for the "deep snow." Of her four children—

CASWELL, married in Kentucky, to Elizabeth Laughlin, came to Sangamon county several years later than his mother, and died in Ball township.

REBECCA, married in Kentucky to Joseph Laughlin, moved to Christian county, Ill., and both died there.

WILLIS, born in Kentucky, came with his mother to Sangamon county in 1830, married Sarah Easley, had six children, and she died. He married Martha Nuckolls. They had four children, namely: JOHN H., resides with his mother. CHARLES M., married Milly A. Blount, and lives in Christian county, Ill. WILLIAM B., married Amanda M. Lockridge, who died July 28, 1873, and their only child, JENNIE F., died a month later. Mr. Shellhouse lives in Ball township. LYDIA A., married James H. Pulliam. *See his name.* Willis Shellhouse died Oct. 24, 1852, and his widow resides near the centre of Ball township, four and a half miles southeast of Chatham Illinois. The house she lives in was built by Robert Pulliam in 1820. It was built of round logs, and hewn or scutched after it was put up. Being but one story high, no upper floor was required, but three heavy beams, about six by eight inches, serve as joists. On top of these there is a covering of two-inch plank, all hewn from solid logs, because there was not at that time a saw-mill so far north in Illinois. The interior is neatly whitewashed, and with the blazing wood in the wide, open fire-place has every appearance of quiet comfort. It is, beyond a doubt, the oldest dwelling house in Sangamon county.

ORLENA, born in Kentucky, married in Sangamon county to Clark Nuckolls. *See his name.*

Mrs. Lydia Shellhouse died in 1842, in Ball township.

SHELTON, STEPHEN, was born about 1777, in North Carolina, married there to Lydia Heath, and at once moved to Ohio, near the mouth of Sciota river, where two children were born, and the family moved across the Ohio river into Cabell county, West Virginia, where seven children were born. He was a soldier from Virginia in the war of 1812, and from there moved to Sangamon county, Illinois, arriving in May, 1826, in what is now Curran township, where two children were born. Of their eleven children—

WILLIAM, born March 18, 1807, in Ohio, married in Sangamon county, Feb. 11, 1830, to Prudence Neal. They had five living children. JOHN R. enlisted Sept. 1862, in Co. B, 130th Ill. Inf., for three years, served until late in 1863, when he was detailed to the Chicago Mercantile Battery, which was captured and he was returned to his regiment, which was afterwards consolidated with the 77th Ill. Inf. He was honorably discharged in August, 1865. J. R. Shelton married Eliza Kinney. They had five children. WILLIAM A. died Sept. 23, 1876. JAMES R., LUELLA, CHARLES and MARGARET C., the four latter, live with their parents near Atwood, Moultre county, Illinois. AMARINE married Richard C. Smith. *See his name.* DANIEL M. married Nancy A. Dodd. They have three children, and live near Chatham, Illinois. JAMES M. married Louisa McComas. They have three living children, MARY S., IDA E., and SMITH, and live in Chatham. ZARILDA married James Worth. They have six children, and live near Taylorville, Illinois. William Shelton and his wife live in Chatham, Sangamon county, Ill. He was at work in the Galena lead mines when the Winnebago war broke out in 1827, and volunteered in a company raised at the mines. When it was over he remained at Galena until 1830 when he returned to Sangamon county. His recollection of the "deep snow" is that it was four feet on a level in the timber. Corn shocks showed eighteen inches above the snow. He also remembers the sudden change of Dec. 20, 1836, and that geese and chickens froze fast in the slush. Water froze in ripples.

SOPHIA, born in 1809 in Ohio, was married in Sangamon county to Elisha McComas. *See his name.*

NANCY, born in Cabell county, Va., married in Sangamon county to David McComas. *See his name.*

JAMES, born in Cabell county, West Virginia, married in Sangamon county Sally A. Beckelheimer, who died, and he married Letitia Wyckoff, who died, and he married a third time. He had seven children. He had two sons, JASPER and NEWTON. The former was killed at the battle of Chickamauga; the latter was wounded at the same battle, had a leg amputated and died in consequence of it nearly five years later. James Shelton resides in Texas.

MORRIS, born in West Virginia, was a soldier in an Illinois regiment in the Mexican war, and was killed on a scout the day before the battle of Cerro Gordo in 1847.

JOHN, born in West Virginia, was in the same company and regiment from Illinois, in the Mexican war, fought through the battle of Cerro Gordo, came home, married Nancy Bogby, had eight children, and lives in Kansas.

ELEVEN, born in West Virginia, married in Sangamon county to Martha Bogby, have six children, and lives in Kansas.

SALLY, born in West Virginia, married in Sangamon county to Thomas Wyckoff, and both died without children.

LUCINDA, born in West Virginia, married in Sangamon county to Samuel Clarke. They have nine children, and reside at Butler, Bates county, Mo.

ELEANOR, born in West Virginia, married in Sangamon county to Mordecai Howard, had three children, and both died.

ZERILDA, born in Sangamon county, married Jesse Mitts, have six children, and live in Montgomery county.

ELISHA, born in Sangamon county, married Esther Murphy, had four children, and she and two of the children died, and he married Leathy Tongate. They have one child, and reside in Wayne county, Iowa.

Mrs. Lydia Shelton died Nov. 20, 1830, and Stephen Shelton was married in April, 1831, to Judith Neal. They had five children born in Sangamon county.

MARY, married Francis Reed, and died leaving four children in Iowa.

REBECCA, married James Stamper. They have eight children, and reside in Curran township.

AMANDA, married William Jones, have five children, and live in Iowa.

MANVILLA, married Elisha Harbor, had six children, and she died. He married and resides in Montgomery county.

MARTIN, born March 22, 1844, in Sangamon county, enlisted June 6, 1862, in Co. B, 7th Ill. Inf., for three years, was honorably discharged Oct. 3, 1862; enlisted Oct. 5, 1864, in Co.

B, 13th U. S. A., for three years, and was honorably discharged July 27, 1867, in Montana Territory, married in Sangamon county, June 24, 1868, to Sarah J. Dill, have two children, WILLIAM DALLAS and LOUIS W., and reside in Chatham township.

Stephen Shelton died Jan. 22, 1859, in Sangamon county, and his widow resides with his son, William, in Chatham.

SHEPARD, LEWIS M., was born July 31, 1817, near Green village, Morris county, N. J. He came to Sangamon county with his aunt Phœbe Mesler, wife of Cornelius Mesler, in the fall of 1834. He is not yet married and resides with his aunt Mesler, three miles northeast of Berry Station. *See her name.*

SHEPHERD, the origin of this family in America was with Thomas Shepherd, a native of Wales, who came to Virginia long before the thirteen colonies declared themselves independent of the British crown. He settled on the south bank of the Potomac about ten miles west of the Blue Ridge and the mouth of the Shenandoah river. According to the custom then prevailing, he tomahawked, or "blazed" the trees around a tract of land, including several thousands of acres, all lying south of the Potomac. The recording of the description of this land secured to him the title. He laid out and named for himself Shepherdstown. In order to encourage settlement he sold lots—generally half an acre each—at nominal prices, but required an annual quit rent of five shillings to be paid perpetually. That rent is still being paid by owners of the lots, who have not bought off. He acquired other landed property by purchase, and at his death, Thomas Shepherd left a will, a copy of which is in possession of Thomas B. Shepherd, of Sangamon county, the fifth Thomas Shepherd in a direct line from Thomas Shepherd, of Wales. By that will he bequeathed some land, declared to have been deeded to him June 12, 1751, by the Right Hon. Thomas, Lord Fairfax. The will is dated Aug. 20, 1776, and bequeaths to his sons, Thomas, William, John, Abraham and David, lands and a saw-mill in the county of Berkley, Virginia, and lots in the town of Mechlenburg, same county. To his daughters, Susannah, Mary, Martha, Sarah and Elizabeth, he bequeaths money and some personal property. The will covers some eight pages of fools'-cap, and in its metes and bounds is quite a curiosity. Two of the sons of the original Thomas Shepherd were soldiers in the Revolutionary army. One of them, Captain Abraham Shepherd, was captured and held on board a British prison ship until he came near losing his life. The eldest son, or Thomas No. 2, married Susan Hulse, and raised a family of eight children. His eldest child, or Thomas No. 3, was born Nov. 3, 1774, and was married Oct. 15, 1805, to Mary Byers, who was born Dec. 13, 1779, in Shepherdstown, also. They had eight children in Shepherdstown, and Thomas No. 3 died Nov. 9, 1832, in his native town. Eight of his children came to Sangamon county, namely—

SHEPHERD, THOMAS C., or Thomas No. 4, born June 28, 1806, in Shepherdstown, Jefferson county, Va., was married in his native town July 3, 1834, to Ellen Miller, who was born June 24, 1813, in Shepherdstown, also. They made their home at Blackford's Ferry, Washington county, Md., until one child was born, and on the death of his father, Thomas C., took charge of the family, and with his mother, sister and two brothers, moved to Sangamon county, Ill., arriving Nov. 17, 1836, at a farm six miles south of Springfield, that Thomas C. had purchased the spring before. They moved in wagons, and were six weeks on the road. Thomas C. and wife had four children in Sangamon county, namely—

THOMAS B., or Thomas No. 5, born Sept. 28, 1835, in Washington county, Md., was married in Sangamon county, Oct. 26, 1859, to Arminda Pyle. They have three children, THOMAS A., or Thomas No. 6, ANN E. and MARY E., and live three miles northwest of Pawnee, Sangamon county, Ill.

JOHN H., born Feb. 21, 1838, in Sangamon county, was married Oct. 6, 1869, to Ann Pyle. They have one child, ARMINDA M., and live one and a half miles southeast of Pawnee, Sangamon county, Ill.

WILLIAM B., born Jan. 6, 1840, in Sangamon county, married Oct 22, 1867, to Elizabeth K. Brown, who was born Oct. 20, 1848, near Wheeling, West Va. They have one child, ALICE VIR-

GINIA, and live near Woodside, Sangamon county, Ill.

CHARLES M., born Nov. 18, 1841, in Sangamon county, Ill., enlisted at Springfield, July 20, 1861, in what became Co. B, 11th Missouri Inf., served three years and twenty days, and was honorably discharged Aug. 10, 1864. He was married Nov. 11, 1869, to Sarah E. Ford. They have one child, CHARLES RAYMOND, born Sept. 26, 1875, and live six miles south of Springfield, Ill.

MARY E., born Jan. 5, 1849, married Lawson Pyle. See his name. They have one child, MILDRETH.

Thomas C. Shepherd and wife reside where they settled in 1836, six miles south of Springfield, Sangamon county, Ill.

SHEPHERD, HENRY, born Dec. 3, 1807, in Virginia, went in 1830 to Chillicothe, Ohio, and was married there to Margaret Peaff. They came to Sangamon county in 1838. In 1849 he went to California, and died in Sacramento, in the autumn of 1850, leaving a widow and one child—

HARRIET, who married George Metlin. He died in 1872.

The mother and daughter, both widows, live in Petersburg, Menard county, Ill.

SHEPHERD, SUSAN, born in 1809, in Virginia, married George R. Weber. See his name.

SHEPHERD, MARY, born Oct. 31, 1813, in Shepherdstown Virginia, married Nov. 15, 1833, in Sharpsburg, Maryland, to S. B. Smith, who was born June 10, 1810, in Martinsburg, Virginia. They had thirteen children, six of whom died under two years. Of the other seven—

ANDREW, born August 3, 1837, in Pickaway county, Ohio, was in Berkley county, Va., at the beginning of the rebellion, and voted against the ordinance of secession. He was forced into the rebel army by receiving a severe bayonet wound, but refused to take the oath of allegiance or perform military duty. Some whisky was offered him which he could not be induced to drink. It was carelessly left in the way of one of their own men, who drank it, not knowing that it was poisoned, and he died in two hours. Andrew Smith escaped from the rebels, entered the Union army at Washington, D. C., and after a brief term of service was discharged on account of physical disability. He is now—1876—engaged in mercantile business at Boise City, Idaho Territory.

WILLIAM, born Jan. 5, 1839, in Allegheny City, Penn., enlisted in 1862, for three years, in Co. I, 29th Ill. Inf., served six months over time, and was honorably discharged. He was married Sept. 5, 1866, to Lou Ray. They have three children, LILLIAN, GRACE and JESSIE, and live in Champaign City, Illinois.

HENRY H., born Oct. 10, 1840, in Pittsburg, Penn., brought up in Sangamon county, enlisted in April, 1861, on the first call for 75,000 men, but was rejected on account of physical disability, went to the gold regions of the Pacific in 1862, was married Nov. 14, 1864, at Three Mile Creek, Utah, to Mrs. Lovina Wakley, who was born July 25, 1843, in Hancock county, Illinois. They have three children, MARY P., FRANCES A., and GEORE W., and live at Corinne, Box Elder county, Utah Territory.

JOSEPH S., born Jan. 23, 1844, in Allegheny City, Penn., brought up in Sangamon county, was married Feb. 15, 1872, in Springfield, Ill., to Mary J. Craig. They have one child, and live near Morrisonville, Illinois.

THOMAS C., born March 31, 1848, in Sangamon county, and is the seventh son in succession. He was married Jan. 12, 1876, to Annie Craig, and lives three miles south of Rochester, Sangamon county, Illinois.

AMANDA L., died Nov. 19, 1869, in her twenty-first year.

MARY P., died Oct. 4, 1869, in her seventeenth year.

S. B. Smith was four times Sergeant-at-Arms, as assistant and principal, in the Illinois Legislature, from 1850 to 1854. Mr. Smith and his wife now—1876—reside three miles south of Rochester, Sangamon county, Illinois. He was four times Sergeant-at-Arms as assistant and principal in the Illinois General Assembly from 1850 to 1854.

SHEPHERD, JOSEPH, born July 11, 1816, in Shepherdstown, Virginia, came to Sangamon county Nov. 17, 1836, was married March 16, 1848, to Fanny Smith, who was born Oct. 25, 1818, in

Franklin county, Penn. They had six living children in Sangamon county—

J. THOMAS, born Jan. 18, 1849, was married September 4, 1872, to Amanda Whitecraft, and lives in Christian county, six miles east of Pawnee, Sangamon county, Ill.

JAMES H., born Oct. 19, 1850, was married Sept. 10, 1874, to Jessie F. Winchester, who was born Oct. 3, 1856, in New Jersey. They live four miles southeast of Springfield, Ill.

FANNY A., died in her 16th year, Dec. 14, 1869.

SALOME C., JOSEPH J. and AMANDA E., live with their father.

Mrs. Fanny Shepherd died Feb. 19, 1863, and Joseph Shepherd was married to Mrs. Lydia Haggard, whose maiden name was Byers. She has one child, MARGARET C. Haggard, by the first marriage, and Mr. and Mrs. Shepherd have two children, WILLIAM C. and LYDIA.

Joseph Shepherd and family reside four miles southeast of Springfield, Ill.

SHEPHERD, AMANDA, born Nov. 8, 1812, in Virginia, married Philip Weber. *See his name.*

SHEPHERD, JOHN J., born in 1821 in Virginia, was married in Sangamon county to Susan Pettus, sister to Thomas P. Pettus. *See his name.* She died without children, and he married Mrs. Ann Lewis, whose maiden name was Wright. They are without family and live in Lincoln, Ill.

SHEPHERD, SARAH C., born July 5, 1823, in Shepherdstown, was married there in the fall of 1836 to Dr. E. C. Williams. They have several children, and reside in Martinsburg, Va. Their son, LEWIS, was in Sangamon county, when the rebellion commenced, and enlisted on the first call for 75,000 men in the 7th Ill. Inf. for three months. He enlisted for three years in the 29th Ill. Inf., re-enlisted as a veteran in 1864, and was honorably discharged at the close of the war. He is now married, and lives in Texas.

Mrs. Mary Shepherd, whose maiden name was Byers, came to Sangamon county with her son, Thomas C., in 1836, and died in the house of her son-in-law, Philip W. Weber, Nov. 25, 1870, aged ninety-one years. John Miller, of Shep-

—82

herdstown, father of Mrs. Thomas C. Shepherd, visited them, and died at their house Sept. 29, 1860, in his 77th year.

SHEPHERD, JOSEPH H., was born in 1812 in Ohio, and came to Sangamon county about 1833, and was married to Nancy Center, a native of Ohio also. They had six children in Sangamon county, namely—

JAMES M., born Jan. 15, 1834, enlisted April 16, 1861, in Co. G, 7th Ill. Inf. for three months, served full term, enlisted Aug. 9, 1862, in Co. K, 115th Ill. Inf. for three years, served until after the battle of Chickamauga, at which his lungs became diseased from exposure, in consequence of which he was discharged in May, 1865, and died in Williams township Sept. 2, 1869.

WILLIAM R. and HENRY F., twins, born March 11, 1836.

WILLIAM R., married Clarissa Huffman, have two children, and live in Menard county, Illinois.

HENRY F., married Louisa J. Overstreet, and both died, leaving one child.

OSCAR F., born May 15, 1839, in Sangamon county, enlisted April 16, 1861, on the first call for 75,000 men, in Co. G, 7th Ill. Inf., served three months and was honorably discharged. Enlisted Aug. 9, in 1862, in Co. K, 115th Ill. Inf., served until Feb. 13, 1863, when he was discharged at Nashville on account of physical disability. He was married March 1, 1865, to Arminda Thaxton, have two children, EDWIN and PERRY, and live in Sherman, Ill.—1874.

ANNA M., born April 16, 1841, married Harry L. Morris, and died at Davenport, Iowa, in 1870, leaving three children.

SEBASTIAN B., born May 12, 1844, enlisted Aug. 9, 1862, in Co. K, 115th Ill. Inf., for three years, served full term, and was honorably discharged June 23, 1865. He was married Dec. 25, 1866, to Elizabeth Overstreet. They have three children, LOUISA S., EMMA L. and LAVINA G., and live near Cantrall, Ill.

Mrs. Nancy Shepherd died in 1845, and Joseph H. Shepherd died in 1851.

SHIELDS, ALEXANDER, born in 1797 in Franklin county, Pennsylvania. After three years spent in the Western University of Pennsylvania, at Pittsburgh, he graduated there in 1824 or 1825. In 1832 he graduated in the medical department of the University of Pennsylvania, at Philadelphia. He practiced medicine in his native county, and in April, 1835, started west, visiting St. Louis and Palmyra, in Missouri; Alton, Beardstown, Jacksonville, and lastly Springfield in Illinois, arriving May 15, 1835. He intended stopping in Springfield, but he said it rained forty days and nights, and in hopes to escape so much water he went to Tremont to wait until the shower was over. He returned to Springfield in about two weeks and engaged in the practice of his profession. He was married in Springfield in 1837 to Mrs. Ann Salisch, whose maiden name was Capps. *See Capps family.* Dr. Shields moved to what is now Ball township, south of Sugar Creek, near Crow's Mill, in 1845. They had four children.

THOMAS A. died unmarried Sept. 29, 1862, aged twenty-four years.

MANT J., born in Springfield, Ill., was married Nov. 27, 1867, to Henry Sanders. She died March, 1868. Mr. Sanders married Miss Riddle, and lives in Springfield.

SUSAN A., was married Oct. 22, 1873, to Virgil Downing. They have one child, GERALDINE, and live near Cotton Hill P. O.

BENJAMIN F. lives with his parents.

Dr. Shields and family live near Cotton Hill P. O., Sangamon county, Illinois.

SHINKLE, CHRISTIAN, (a brother to Mrs. Mary M. Shinkle) was born in Berks county, Pa., and taken by his parents to Brown county, Ohio. Melinda Judd, sister to Rezin Judd, was born in Maryland, and taken to Brown county, Ohio. Christian Shinkle and Melinda Judd were married and had four children in Ohio, and moved to Sangamon county, Ill., arriving October, 1826, in what is now Mechanicsburg township, where one child was born. Of their five children—

CHRISTIAN, born October, 1813, in Ohio, married in Sangamon county, to Silbeth Carrico, have six children, and live near Fullerton, DeWitt county, Ill.

EZEKIEL, born April 26, 1816, in Ohio, is living with his third wife, and has seven children. They reside near Fullerton, Ill.

MATILDA A., born June 24, 1821, in Brown county, Ohio, married in Sangamon county to David S. McDaniel, who died in less than three months after marriage, and she married Aaron Morgan. *See his name.*

JAMES, born September, 1823, in Brown county, Ohio, raised in Sangamon county, married in DeWitt county, to Martha McCord. They have three children, and reside near Twin Springs, Linn county, Kansas.

JOHN J., born Nov. 11, 1832, in Sangamon county, married in DeWitt county to Sarah A. Barnes. They have four children, and live near Twin Springs, Kansas.

Mrs. Melinda Shinkle died April, 1842, and Christian Shinkle died March 3, 1849, she in Sangamon, and he in DeWitt county, Ill.

SHINKLE, JOHN, was born in February, 1783, in Berks county, Penn., and when he was a boy his parents moved to Brown county, Ohio. Mary M. Shinkle was born Nov. 12, 1784, in Berks county, Penn. In May, 1805, her parents moved to Brown county, Ohio. John Shinkle and Mary M. Shinkle were there married Nov. 7, 1805. They had ten living children in Brown county. The family moved to Sangamon county, Ill., arriving December, 1826, in what is now Clear Lake township, north of Sangamon river, where one child was born. Of their eleven children—

DANIEL, born August 17, 1806, in Ohio, married in Sangamon county to Nancy Owens, moved to the vicinity of Maquoketa, Iowa, had several children, and Mrs. Shinkle died. He was married to Elizabeth Simons and he died in 1872.

SARAH, born Sept. 1, 1807, in Ohio, married in Sangamon county to Clinton Wilson. *See his name.*

JAMES, born May 2, 1810, in Ohio, married in Sangamon county, to Rebecca Williams. They had five children, one died in infancy, and one, JOHN, died in the Union Army. James Shinkle and his wife reside near McConnell's Grove P. O., Stephenson county, Ill.

ELIZABETH, born May 22, 1813, in Ohio, married in Sangamon county to David Worley. They have a family, and reside near Ottawa, Kansas.

THOMAS, born June 12, 1815, is a cripple, and resides in Dawson, Illinois.

CHRISTIANA, born May 20, 1817,

in Ohio, married in Sangamon county to Jeremiah Smith. They had two children. ZACHARY T. lives at Marion, DeWitt county, Ill.; HARRIET A. married A. Herrol, and lives near Twin Springs, Kansas. Jeremiah Smith died in 1849, and his widow lives with their son, Zachary, T., in DeWitt county, Illinois.

JOHN, Jun., born Oct. 21, 1819, in Ohio, married Oct. 4, 1851, in DeWitt county, Illinois, to Martha Miller, who was born there Aug. 28, 1830. They have four children, MARY KATE, CYRUS L., IDA MAY and LINCOLN A. Mr. Shinkle lived on the farm where the family settled in 1826, three miles southwest of Dawson, until 1875, when he moved to Springfield, Ill.

GEORGE, born Nov. 7, 1821, in Ohio. He enlisted at Springfield in 1862 in Co. C, 124th Ill. Inf. for three years, and died of disease at St. Louis, Oct. 8, 1864. His remains were brought home for interment.

BARBARA, born March 12, 1823, in Ohio, married in Sangamon county to Joseph Prokopp. They have one child and live near Riverton, Ill.

REBECCA, born Oct. 21, 1824, died in her fifteenth year.

LEWIS, born March 5, 1827 in Sangamon county, lives at the old homestead, near Dawson.

John Shinkle died August, 1827, in Sangamon county, less than one year after his arrival in the country. His widow raised her family on the farm where they settled, and now resides there. It is three miles southwest of Dawson, Ill. She is 92 years old, and has been a widow nearly half a century.

SHIPLEY, RICHARD A., was born Jan. 15, 1812, in Baltimore county, Md., and was married August 6, 1835, in Washington county, in the same State, to Ellen Albert. They had one child, and moved to Springfield, Illinois, arriving May 20, 1837, where they had six children, three of whom died young. Of their four children—

McKENDREE, born April 7, 1836, in Washington county, Md., raised in Springfield, spent fourteen years in Texas, and died August, 1872, in Springfield.

MARY E., born September, 1838, in Springfield, died in her seventeenth year.

RICHARD A., Jun., born April 8, 1840, in Springfield. He enlisted in 1862, in Co. —, 130th Ill. Inf., served three years and was honorably discharged. He was married in 1862 to Laura Stall. They have one living child, WILLIAM R., and resides in Springfield.

WILLIAM H., born April 8, 1842, in Springfield. He enlisted in 1862 for three years in the Chicago Board of Trade Battery of Artillery, served full term and was honorably discharged in 1865. He was married in 1867 to Ann Johnson. They have one child, ALBERT R., and live in Springfield.

Richard A. Shipley and wife reside at 1108 Monroe street, between Eleventh and Twelfth, Springfield, Ill.

SHORT, JAMES, was born Feb. 5, 1776, in South Carolina, and was one of six sons of Hezekiah Short, who died in South Carolina in 1803. The ancestors of this family came from Scotland. James, the subject of this sketch, was married in South Carolina in 1800, to Lucretia Tennyson, a native of that State. They had two children there, and moved to Greene county, near Greensburg, Ky., in 1804, where five children were born. Mrs. Lucretia Short died Sept. 14, 1817, in Kentcky, and James Short was married there in 1818 to Mrs. Margaret Wright, whose maiden name was Strater. They had two children in Kentucky, and moved in the spring of 1822 to Sangamon county, Ill., settling at the junction of Salt creek and Sangamon river, in what is now Menard county. In the spring of 1827, they moved to Sugar creek, settling three and a half miles southeast of Springfield, where eight children were born. Of the seven children of James Short by his first marriage, two died young. The other five are—

IGNATIUS T., born Nov. 28, 1801, in South Carolina, was married in 1820 at Columbus, then in Pulaski, but now in Hickman county, Ky., to Mary Arnett, who was born in 1802 in South Carolina, also. They moved from Kentucky to Sangamon county, Ill., on horseback, in 1823, settling near Springfield. He was a soldier in the Blackhawk war from Sangamon county. They moved to Macoupin county, Ill., in 1830. Of their six children who lived to maturity, RANSOM A., born Oct. 8, 1824, near Springfield, was married July 20, 1845, at Edwardsville, Madison county, Ill., to Orlean M.

Cread. He enlisted in 1846 in the Mexican war, and died at Monterey, Mexico. LOUISA M., born Nov. 27, 1828, was married in 1844 in Madison county, Ill., to George Woodward, who died in 1846. Mrs. Woodward was married in 1847 to Levi Gimlin. They had one child, ZACHEUS, who was born Jan. 12, 1850, and was married in 1871 to Mary A. Parks. They have two children, *William W.* and *Winnie A.*, and reside near Carlinville, Macoupin county, Illinois. Levi Gimlin died July, 1850, and Mrs.Gimlin was married in 1852 to Charles Emrick. They had five living children. ELNORA, LAURA, THADDEUS D., JERUSHA E. and FANNY live with their mother. Charles Emrick died Jan. 15, 1874, and Mrs. Emrick resides near Carlinville, Ill. MARTHA A., born Jan. 20, 1831, was married in 1849 in Macoupin county, Ill., to Edward Miller. They had one child, MARTHA A., born Jan. 1850, and married Jan. 4, 1867, in Cass county, to George W. Zircles. They have one child, *Ada C.*, and live near Ashland, Ill. Mrs. Martha A. Miller died Jan. 22, 1850, and Edward Miller died in 1851, both in Macoupin county, Ill. WILLIAM HENRY, born March 16, 1840, died unmarried in December, 1856. MARY ELIZABETH, born March 30, 1842, died in November, 1856. HEZEKIAH M., born Feb. 14, 1845, in Macoupin county, enlisted May 12, 1864, for 100 days in Co. G, 133d Ill. Inf., served until Sept. 24, 1864, when he was honorably discharged with the regiment. He entered McKendree College in the fall of 1867, and graduated there in June, 1874. In September, 1875, he united with the Illinois Conference of the Methodist Episcopal Church, and isnow—September, 1876—preaching on the Chatham circuit, and is not yet married.

Ignatius T. Short died in 1853, and Mrs. Mary Short died in 1855, both near Carlinville, Macoupin county, Ill.

ELIZABETH, born May 12, 1804, in South Carolina, was married in Greene county, Ky., to Randolph Rhodes. See *his name*. She lives with her son, John T. Rhodes.

ANNA S., born Jan. 3, 1810, in South Carolina, married Andrew McCormick. *See his name*.

CASSANDRA, born in 1813 in South Carolina, married Harvey E. Armstrong, of Waverly, Morgan county, Ill. She died in 1838, without children.

LUCINDA B., born Oct. 5, 1815, was married to James Q. Wills, of Sangamon county, Ill., June 23, 1836. They had two children, LUCRETIA C., born April 16, 1837, married James Bracken. Mrs. Bracken died Nov 2, 1860, leaving two children. JAMES D., born April 1, 1841, enlisted in Co. A, 10th Ill. Cav., and died in the army, May 21st, 1862. James Q. Wills died July 3, 1845, and his widow was married April 20, 1849, to B. Y. Singleton, of Sangamon county. They have three children. MARGARET L., born April 23, 1850, married at Petersburg, Ill., Nov. 1, 1871, to James A. Robb. They have two children, EVA MABEL and LESLIE ELBERT, and live near Walshville, Montgomery county, Ill. BENJAMIN Y., Jun., and WINFIELD S. Singleton live with their parents. B. Y. Singleton lives near Petersburg, Ill.

Of James Short's children by his second marriage four died young.

JOHN W., born Dec. 21, 1821, in Kentucky, was married Nov 4, 1852, in Sangamon county, Ill., to Nancy E. Billings. *See Billings family*. She died Aug. 20, 1865, leaving one child, MELISSA E., who was born May 7, 1856, and lives with her step-mother. John W. Short was married Aug. 27, 1866, to Mrs. Eliza Dalaney, whose maiden name was Potts. Mr. Short died March 15, 1876, and his widow and daughter reside near Jamestown, Clinton county, Ill.

MARTHA, born in 1822, in Menard county, Ill., married John Potts, of Sangamon county. They had five children, and both died near Jamestown, Clinton county, Illinois.

DORINDA, born in 1824, in Menard county, Ill., married James Tibbs. They had five children, MARGARET, MARY, MARTHA, AMANDA and NETTIE. Mr. Tibbs died in 1856, and his widow lives near Rochester, Ill.

WILLIAM S., born in 1826, in Sangamon county, was married there in 1847, to Harriet Wilson, who was born April 26, 1829. They had three children, OLIVE C., born July 11, 1848, was married November 14, 1868, to Robert Atkinson, and live in Rochester, Illinois. AMANDA M., born Oct. 12, 1850, died young. WILLIAM T., born Nov. 21,

1855, lives with his father. Mrs. Harriet Short died July 6, 1865, in Chatham, Ill., and William S. Short resides near Chanute, Neosho county, Kansas. Mr. Short served in Co. C, 2d Ill. Light Art., from Jan. 4, 1864, to Aug. 3, 1865, when he was honorably discharged.

MARGARET C., born in 1828 in Sangamon county, married Edward Neener. They have three children and live near Chanute, Neosho county, Kansas.

AMANDA M., born Oct. 28, 1830, in Sangamon county, married Jonas L. Fletcher. *See his name.*

James Short died June 7, 1836, and Mrs. Margaret Short died Dec. 25, 1850, both at the homestead where they settled in 1827, three and a half miles southeast of Springfield, in Sangamon county, Ill.

SHORT, JOSHUA, was born as early as 1760 in Virgiana, was a soldier from that State in the Revolution, and after the war for Independence, married there, and moved with his family to Green county, Kentucky, near Muldraugh's Hill, which gave the name to one of the battles fought in suppressing the rebellion. He came with some of his children to Sangamon county, Illinois, arriving October, 1825, on Spring creek, six miles west of Springfield. If there was any relationship between him and James Short, who came from South Carolina, through Green county, Kentucky, their descendants seem not to be informed of it. Joshua Short is remembered as one of the aged men who rode in a canoe, mounted on wheels and rigged as a ship, in the procession at the Whig or Harrison political gathering at Springfield in 1840. He was then more than eighty years of age, and died a few years later in Menard county, Illinois. Some of his children came to Sangamon county, but I have sketches of two only, James and Caleb.

JAMES, born about 1787, either in Virginia or Green county, Kentucky, was the captain of a company and was about marching from that latter county to the scene of conflict when the war of 1812 and '15 closed. He was married, had some children there, and brought his family to Sangamon county, Illinois, in 1825, in company with his father, bringing his family and worldly goods in a cart. James Short died in 1827 at a place called Turkey Point, about five miles west of Chatham, Sangamon county. I have the sketches of two only of his children, Allen and Susan C. ALLEN, born Feb. 6, 1816, in Green county, Kentucky, was brought by his father to Sangamon county in 1825, and left an orphan and a cripple at eleven years of age, with younger brothers and sisters, whom he aided all he could. When he was ten years of age he says he had heard but one sermon, had only seen one pair of boots, and had never seen a newspaper, tract or pamphlet. He was married in Sangamon county to Margaret A. Campbell, daughter of Rev. Thomas Campbell. *See his name.* They had three children in Sangamon county. JAMES L., born Jan. 4, 1839, in Sangamon county, enlisted at the first call for 75,000 men in Co. G, 7th Ill. Inf., for three months in April, 1861, served full time and was honorably discharged. He enlisted again Sept. 20, 1861, in Co. B, 10th Ill. Cav., served until Dec. 20, 1862, when he was discharged on account of physical disability. He was married Feb. 17, 1863, to Mrs. Nancy H. Hudson, whose maiden name was Park. They have one living child, *Hugh Francis*, and live in Lincoln, Illinois. EDWARD J., born Oct. 18, 1840, enlisted Sept. 20, 1861, in Co. B, 10th Ill. Cav., for three years, re-enlisted as a veteran, January, 1864. He was captured July 8, 1864, at Bayou Des Arc, was kept under guard three weeks, paroled and exchanged January, 1865. He was mustered out with the regiment at San Antonio, Texas, in November, 1865, and was married May 6, 1869, to Sarah C. Dial, who was born Sept. 17, 1850, in Morgan county, Illinois. They have two children, *Nellie* and *Minnie*, and live four miles northwest of Chatham, Sangamon county, Illinois. WILLIAM, H. H., born June 29, 1843, enlisted August, 1862, in Co. B, 10th Ill Cav., for three years, served full term, and was honorably discharged June, 1865, at New Orleans, and was married Oct. 26, 1871, to Martha E. Robertson. He died June 2, 1873, at New Berlin, Illinois. Mrs. Margaret A. Short died Sept. 23, 1845, and Allen Short was married to Harriet A. Park, sister of John G. Park. They had nine children, three died young. Of the other six, THOMAS N. lives in Auburn (with Mr. Morse). The other five live with their parents at Columbia, Marion county, Iowa. Allen Short is now a minister in the Cumberland Presbyterian Church. SUSAN C., born in 1819 in Green county, Kentucky, married in Sangamon county to John A. Campbell. See his name. Mrs. Susan C. Campbell died April 3, 1852.

CALEB, born April 19, 1790, in Green county Kentucky, was married there May 26, 1814, to Elizabeth Walters, who was born in that county Feb. 13, 1798. They had three children, and moved to Sangamon county, Illinois, in 1823, and settled in what is now Curran township, south of Spring creek, where they had three children. Of their six children, PAULINE, born March 15, 1815, in Green county, Kentucky, married in Sangamon county to William Henton. See his name. JAMES, born Nov. 23, 1816, in Green county, Kentucky, married in Sangamon county, Illinois, April 4, 1844, to Mary McPherson, niece of Robert Euchus. See his name. Mr. and Mrs. Short had five living children in Sangamon county. SARAH A. married April 10, 1873, to Martin I. Webb, who was born Nov. 12, 1844, near Cazenovia, New York. They live in Loami, Illinois—1874. ROBERT E. married Oct. 7, 1873, to Ollie A. Dawson. See her name with the Meacham family. Mr. and Mrs. Short have one child, Olive I., and live near Loami, Sangamon county, Ill. CAROLINE, ELIZABETH and WILLIAM live with their mother. James Short died, and his widow and children now—1876—reside two miles northeast of Loami, Sangamon county, Ill. JANE, born Sept. 5, 1819, in Kentucky, married in Sangamon county to Thompson Renshaw, and died leaving two children. LUCILLE, born Feb. 9, 1823, in Green county, Kentucky, married in Sangamon county July 2, 1840, to George W. Foster. See his name. He was born May 11, 1817, near Winchester, Kentucky. She died at Kirksville, Mo., leaving four children. Mr. Foster lives at Louisiana, Mo. JOSHUA W., born May 25, 1825, married in Sangamon county, Illinois, to Berlinder Robison. See her name. They had four children. Mrs. Short and one of the children died. JOHN R. died February, 1876, in Missouri. CHARLES E. married in 1873 to Lola Scripture, and live in Missouri. ANNIE M. lives near Lamar's Station, Missouri. Joshua W. Short married ——— Carson, and reside near Maryville, Nodaway county, Mo. ROWAN J., born March 10, 1827, in Sangamon county, was a soldier from that county in the Mexican war, and died in 1847 in the army. Mrs. Elizabeth Short died Nov. 1, 1856, and Caleb Short died Sept. 18, 1863, both in Sangamon county, Illinois.

SHORT, SAMUEL, was born March 10, 1792, in Botetourt county, Va., of German parents. His father died when he was quite young, and at the age of 15, he went to East Tennessee, remained two years, went to Bourbon county, Ky., back to Virginia, and thence to Mechlenberg county, Ky., where he was married Dec. 1, 1814 to Rebecca Strong, who was born Dec. 24, 1787, in Frederick county, Va. They moved to Sangamon county, Ill., arriving in September, 1836, in what is now Auburn township. Mrs Short died in September, 1869. They never had any children, but raised four orphans. Mr. Short married again when he was over 80 years of age, and moved back to Kentucky.

SHOUP, JACOB, born May 9, 1780, in Huntington county, Pa., was married there May 25, 1802, to Sarah Downing, who was born Aug. 13, 1782, in the same county. They moved to Pickaway county, Ohio, where they had sixteen children, each one of whom lived to be twenty-six years of age and over. The family moved to Sangamon county, Ill., arriving in what is now Ball township, in the autumn of 1831. It was then called Cotton Hill Precinct. Of their sixteen children—

JOHN, born May 31, 1803, in Ohio was married there to Hannah Martin. They both died in Logan county, Ill. leaving six children, near Lincoln.

MARY, born Sept. 5, 1804, in Ohio was married in Sangamon county, Ill., to James Fletcher. He died, leaving a widow and two children, near Lincoln, Ill.

JACOB, born Sept. 17, 1805, died unmarried in Pickaway county, Ohio, in the twenty-seventh year of his age.

SARAH, born May 12, 1807, in Ohio died in Sangamon county, Ill., unmarried in the sixty-first year of her age.

THOMAS, born Dec. 19, 1808, in Ohio was married there to Rachel Anderson They had six children, and Thomas

Shoup died in Logan county, Ill. His widow and children live near Lincoln, Illinois.

ELIZA, born Feb. 27, 1810, in Pickaway county, Ohio, was married in Sangamon county, Ill., to William Gulliford. They moved to Oregon in the spring of 1852, and both died there, leaving nine children.

MARIA, born Jan. 30, 1812, in Ohio, was married in Sangamon county, Ill., to David Brunk. See his name.

TIMOTHY, born March 12, 1813, in Ohio, was married in Sangamon county, to Mary Keys. They had five children. JACOB, died in his tenth year. ELIZABETH J., married James Crawley. They have two children, MARY E. and JOHN E., and live in Ball township, near Cotton Hill postoffice, Sangamon county. James Crawley enlisted Oct. 5, 1861, at Springfield, in Co. I, 7th Ill. Inf., for three years, re-enlisted as a veteran Jan. 1864, was captured at Allatoona Mountain, Georgia, Oct. 5, 1864, within one hour of three years from his first enlistment. After spending five months in prison, he joined his regiment, was commissioned First Lieutenant Nov. 1, 1864, served to the close of the rebellion, and was honorably discharged July 12, 1865. ISAAC F., married Maria N. Byers, a native of Madison county, Ohio. They have four children, LILA A., LEWIS, JOHN T. and JESSE E., and live one and a half miles east of Cotton Hill postoffice, Sangamon county, Ill. ALEXANDER F., born March 3, 1844, married Arthalinda Bell. They have three children, MINA, ADALEE and SAMUEL B., and live near Bell's mill, seven miles southeast of Springfield, Ill. JOHN H., born July 11, 1847, was married in October, 1868, to Rachel Bell. They have one child, WILLIAM, and live near Zion's Chapel, and New City, Sangamon county, Ill. Timothy Shoup died Feb. 28, 1850, at Crow's mill, which he then owned. His widow lives with her son-in-law, James Crawley, near Crow's mill, or Cotton Hill, postoffice, Ill.

ELIZABETH, born May 9, 1815, in Ohio, was married in Sangamon county, to Barrett Ramsey. They moved to the Pacific coast in 1852, have five children, and live at Marysville, Baker county, Oregon.

DELILAH, born April 27, 1817, in Ohio, was married in Sangamon county, to Elijah Bradshaw. She died without children. Mr. B. was married again in the winter of 1875, and lives one mile east of Cotton Hill postoffice, Sangamon county.

ALEXANDER, born Feb. 23, 1819, in Ohio, was married in Sangamon county to Mary J. Wilkinson. They had five children, and Mr. Shoup was accidentally killed while pressing cider, in the fall of 1856. His widow married Mr. Brown, and lives in St. Joseph, Missouri.

DORCAS, born Jan. 28, 1821, in Ohio, was married in Sangamon county to Thomas Lovelock. They had six children, JOSEPH, ALEXANDER, THOMAS, SAMUEL, GEORGE and MARY. Mr. Lovelock died, and his widow lives in Ray county, Mo.

HENRY, born May 4, 1822, in Ohio, was married in Sangamon county to Ruth Knotts. They have seven children. ELBERT W., married Martha A. Sanders. They have one child, CHARLES L., and live near Cotton Hill. SARAH E., married James Milliner, and lives near Cotton Hill. JACOB, ELIJAH, LEANDER, SAMUEL and DELILAH live with their parents. Henry Shoup lives on the farm where his father settled in 1831, in Ball township, east of Crow's mill, or Cotton Hill postoffice, Sangamon county, Ill.

NANCY, born May 8, 1824, in Ohio, was married in Sangamon county to Joseph Penn. They have five children, SARAH, JOHN, ROSY, HENRY and GEORGE, and live near Lancaster, Dallas county, Texas.

SAMUEL N., born May 16, 1827, in Pickaway county, Ohio, was married Nov. 18, 1857, in Sangamon county, Ill., to Alice J. Mourer. They had seven children. JOHN CARROLL, the fifth child, died July 24, 1874, from injuries inflicted by being thrown from a buggy attached to a runaway team two days previous. SALLIE IRVING, the sixth child, died August 13, 1874. WILLIE H., ETTIE MAY, HARRY S., LUELLA M. and LUCY live with their parents. Samuel N. Shoup has had an eventful life. He accompanied two of his sisters to Oregon in 1852 and returned in 1855. He went with another sister to Texas in the fall of 1855 and returned in 1856. When the rebellion began he raised a company which became Co. E, 114th Ill. Inf., and was elected and commissioned captain at its organization, was promoted through the different grades to colonel of the regiment, and was in command at the close of the rebellion. He was elected Sheriff of Sangamon county in 1866 for two years. Col. S. N. Shoup and family reside in Ball township, near Cotton Hill Post Office, Sangamon county, Illinois.

MELISSA, born March 15, 1827, in Ohio, was married in Sangamon county to Philemon Stout. See his name.

Jacob Shoup died Dec. 19, 1849, and Mrs. Sarah Shoup died April 20, 1850, both on the farm where they settled in 1831, in Sangamon county, Illinois.

SHRYER, EPHRIAM, was born Nov. 1, 1813, in Christian county, Kentucky. He came to Springfield, Illinois, April 1, 1837, lived there about one year, went to Taylorville, from there to the Galena lead mines, and from there to the mines in Lafayette county, Wisconsin, where he was married March 15, 1843, to Mary A. Tolley. He came back to Sangamon county, where they had eight children, namely—

SARAH, married Robert Campbell, has one child, JAMES E., and lives near New Berlin, Illinois.

JAMES H. unmarried and resides in Dallas county, Texas—1873.

KATE E., married Reuben Skeen, have two children, WILLIE and EPHRIAM, and live in Island Grove township.

JULIA M. died aged twelve years.

JOHN T. lives near New Berlin, Illinois.

HARVEY W., ELLA MAY and *EMMA R.* reside with their parents. Ephriam Shryer and family live near Loami, Sangamon county, Illinois.

SHUFF, MRS. HANNAH H, was born April 18, 1784, in Greenbrier county, Virginia. Her father, Anthony Houston, when she was a child, made up his mind to emigrate west. There were no wagon roads and but few wagons. He provided himself with a large number of pack-saddles, and loaded thirty-two horses with household goods, farming implements, and his family, and moved to what became Scott county, Kentucky. There he settled in a cane brake among the Indians, raised a family of thirteen children, and lived to be nearly one hundred years old. Two of his sons became Methodist preachers and one a lawyer. Ex-Governor Sam. Houston, of Texas, now deceased, was his nephew. His daughter, Hannah H., whose name heads this sketch, was married Nov. 5, 1806, in Scott county, Kentucky, to Jacob Shuff. They had three children in Scott county, and the family moved to Gallatin county in the same State, where Mr. Shuff died August 24, 1824. Mrs. Shuff moved with her family to Sangamon county, Illinois, arriving in the fall of 1833 in Island Grove, three miles west of Berlin. Of her three children—

JOHN W., born August 28, 1807, in Scott country, Kentucky, married in Gallatin county, in the same State, to Angeline Lindsay. He came with his mother to Sangamon county, and in 1835 moved to Morgan county, Illinois, five miles east of Jacksonville. They had nine children. Mr. Shuff died in May, 1872, while sitting at a table with a friend, drawing a map of a road. A few days after his death, his fifth son, JAMES, was drowned while bathing. His widow and children, nearly all of whom are married, reside near Jacksonville, Illinois.

MARY ANN, born August 9, 1809, in Scott county, Kentucky, married in Gallatin county Feb. 1, 1831, to Henry Yates. See his name. She died May 11, 1835.

ANTHONY H., born August 18, 1811, in Scott county, Kentucky, married in Sangamon county, Illinois, Feb. 23, 1837, to Siron Foutch. They had eight living children. MARY A. P. married J. W. Walker. WILLIAM H. H. resides with his father. JOHN W. married Mary Mendenhall and died April 2, 1872. JAMES A. married Lucinda Alsbury and lives one mile west of Berlin, Illinois. NANCY H. and THEOPHILUS A. are unmarried. CAROLINE married A. Shultz, and lives at Carthage, Illinois. MILLARD F. lives with his father. Mrs. Siron Shuff died June 4, 1868. Anthony H. Shuff was married March 17, 1873, to Mrs. Elizabeth A. Phelps, whose maiden name was Townsend, a native of Ithica, New York. She has one child by her first marriage, ANNIE PHELPS. A. H. Shuff and wife reside on the farm where the family settled in 1833. It is three miles west of Berlin, Sangamon county, Illinois. Mr. Shutt has been a cripple for more than forty years, caused by having taken eleven doses of calomel in 1835, and without proper attention afterwards, the greater part of it remained in his system, and it seems wonderful that he could endure what he has, and live.

SHUTT, HENRY, was born July, 1763, in Pennsylvania. His parents dying when he was a child, he went when a young man to North Carolina, and was married there to Elizabeth Groves. They had four children, and moved about 1810, to Muhlenberg county, Ky., where they had three children, and moved to Sangamon county, Ill., arriving October, 1829, in what is now Auburn township. Of their children—

CHRISTIANA, born in North Carolina, married in Sangamon county to Peter Dick, moved to Cass county, Ill., and both died there.

ELIZABETH, born in North Carolina, married in Sangamon county, Ill., to Green Dukes, who died near Auburn, and she went to Kentucky and died there.

JACOB, born in North Carolina, went with his parents in 1810 to Muhlenberg county, Ky., and married there to Elizabeth Wagner, who was born July 31, 1799. They moved, in company with his father, to Sangamon county in 1829. They had thirteen children, including two pairs of twins. Three of their children died, including one pair of twins. Of the other ten, JOHN H., born Jan. 29, 1822, in Muhlenberg county, Ky., married Elizabeth Baldwin, and had seven children. Mr. Shutt died April 3, 1872, leaving his widow and children in Macoupin county, six miles south of Auburn, Sangamon county, Ill. GREEN B., married Elizabeth J. Wimer, who died, and he married Matilda Caroline Stout, and lives in Virden, Ill. MARTHA A., married Elias Owen, and for her second husband married William Luth. They live five miles south of Auburn, Ill. ELIZABETH J., married William Foster. See his name. LOUISA C., married Samuel Hurst, who died, and she married Richard Hughes, has several children, and resides in Virden, Ill. MELINDA E., married James F. Miller. See his

—85

name. JACOB W. and MICAJAH, twins. Jacob W. married Susan C. Gates, a native of Muhlenberg county, Ky. They live five miles south of Auburn, Ill. Micajah lives in Nevada—1874. DAVID M., married Nancy E. Lowdermilk, and live one mile east of Auburn. NANCY C., married John Miller, has two children, and lives near Auburn, Ill. Jacob Shutt died March 17, 1859, and Mrs. Elizabeth Shutt died Oct. 9, 1859, both i Sangamon county.

JONATHAN, married Elizabeth Gates, and remained in Kentucky.

JOSEPH, born in Kentucky, married in Sangamon county to Rachel Long, and lives in Iowa.

HENRY, Jun., was born July 19, 1814, in Muhlenberg county, Ky., and came in 1829, with his father, to Sangamon county. He was married in 1835 to Sarah Long. They had eight children. CHRISTIANA, married Isaac Landers, and lives in Iowa. WILLIAM R., married Miss Lowdermilk, and for his second wife married Miss Edwards, and lives near Auburn, Ill. MATILDA, married John Shutt, and lives in Kentucky. SARAH ANN and MARY ANN, twins. Sarah Ann married Andrew Pickens. She died Feb. 5, 1876, near Auburn, Ill. Mary Ann married Thomas Smith, and lives in Macoupin county. BETSY, married William H. Owen, and died. DAVID H. married Miss Stamper, and lives in Auburn township. RACHEL, married John Orr, and died. Mrs. Sarah Shutt died March 27, 1853, and Henry Shutt was married Sept. 22, 1853, to Charity J. Stamper. They live where he settled in 1829, one and a half miles southeast of Auburn, Ill.

Mrs. Elizabeth Shutt died in 1840, and her husband, Henry Shutt, Sen., died in 1852, both in Auburn township, Sangamon county, Ill. He was in his eighty-ninth year.

SIMPSON, JAMES, was born about 1785 in Maryland, and went to Washington county, Kentucky, when he was a young man, and was there married to Mary A. Boone. They had five children, and she died. He married Monica McAtee, had six children in Kentucky, and the family moved to Sangamon county, Illinois, arriving in the fall of 1828. He located about three hundred yards southeast of where St. Bernard Catholic church now stands, in Ball township, where two children were born. Of their children—

MATILDA married John Burtle. See his name.

James Simpson moved his family to Randolph county, Illinois, in April, 1838. He and his wife both died there. Part of their children live in that county and part in Missouri.

SIMPSON, RICHARD, brother to James, born in 1790 in Maryland, went when he was a boy, with his parents to Washington county, Kentucky. He was there married to Monica Higdon. She had six children, and died, and he married Ann Vinson, had three children in Kentucky, and moved to Sangamon county, Illinois, arriving in 1830, in what is now Ball township. After a stay of but one year in Sangamon county, Richard Simpson moved his family to Christian county, and both died there. Of their children who remained in Sangamon county—

LOUISA married Thomas Burtle. See his name.

MARY married James R. Durbin. See his name.

SIMPSON, JOHN P., was born Oct. 17, 1794, in Somerset county, New Jersey. Mary J. Cross was born Jan. 13, 1793, in New Jersey. They were there married and had fourteen children, some of whom married in New Jersey. The remainder of the family came to Sangamon county, Illinois, arriving Nov. 8, 1839, at Springfield, and the next year settled in what is now Williams township. Of their children—

SAMUEL married in New Jersey to Mary A. Benjamin, and came with his father to Sangamon county. He went to Texas before the rebellion, leaving his family at Canton, Missouri. They have never heard of him since.

CLEMANTINE married James C. Sutton. They have five children, and live in Springfield, Illinois.

BENJAMIN is unmarried and lives in Kansas.

THOMAS L., born in New Jersey, married in Sangamon county to Fanny Halbert. She died in 1853, leaving one child, GEORGE W. He was married in Sangamon county to Alice Booth, have

two children, and live near Lincoln, Benton county, Missouri.

SUSAN A. married James Riddle. See his name.

JOHN died aged two years.

AGNES married Harvey Darnall. See his name.

JAMES is unmarried, and lives in Montana.

MARY E., unmarried, and lives in Springfield, Illinois.

CAROLINE married Dennis Taylor. He died, leaving a widow and four children in Iowa.

HENRY died in Galveston, Texas, aged twenty-seven years.

Mrs. Mary J. Simpson died Feb. 14, 1842, and her husband, John P. Simpson, died Feb. 27, 1842, both in Sangamon county, Illinois.

SIMPSON JOHN, was born Sept. 30, 1801, in Tennessee, and when a young man went to St. Clair county, Illinois. Mary Taylor was born August 25, 1803, in Georgia, and when a child was taken to Lookingglass Prairie, St. Clair county, Illinois. They were married there in 1821, and moved to Shelby county in the same State, where they had one child, and from there to Sangamon county, arriving in 1824 in what is now Williams township, where they had two living children. Of their children—

CHARLES, born Aug. 25, 1823, in Shelby county, Illinois, brought up in Sangamon county, married in White Water, Wisconsin, to Mary Bothrell. Mr. Simpson enlisted in 1862 in the 19th Wis. Inf. for three years, and died August 22, 1864, at Pine Bluff, Arkansas, leaving a widow and six daughters at White Water, Walworth county, Wisconsin.

PERMELIA A., born April 14, 1825, in Sangamon county, married William Correll. See his name.

SILAS B., born Oct. 10, 1831, died June 18, 1851.

John Simpson died Feb. 2, 1835, and Mrs. Mary Simpson died Feb. 25, 1864, both in Sangamon county, Illinois.

SIMPSON, JORDAN, was born July 19, 1808, near Lexington, Ky., came to Sangamon county, 1833, and was married Oct. 27, 1835, to Clarissa Sayre. They had eight children in Sangamon county, namely—

JAMES W., born Sept. 8, 1836, married Nov. 6, 1867, to Julia B. Butler (a daughter of Stephen H. Butler). They have three children, WILLIAM E., SALLIE E., and MARY E., and live in Pleasant Plains, Ill.

ISAAC N., born Nov. 26, 1838, enlisted October, 1861, in Co. G, 10th Ill. Cav., served three years, and was honorably discharged. He was married Dec. 14, 1865, to Lucinda Laswell, had one child, ISAAC N., and Mr. Simpson died Feb. 24, 1866.

WILLIAM J., born April 24, 1841, is a student at Normal University—1874. He is engaged in teaching in the public schools.

CATHARINE B., born Aug. 18, 1843, married Dec. 28, 1864, to Benjamin Watts, a son of Nicholas Watts. They have three children, and live near Warrensburg, Macon county, Ill.

MARY M., born April 6, 1848, married Nov. 20, 1867, to Morris Hillyard, have three children, and reside near Climax, Greenwood county, Kansas.

JEMIMA J., born Oct. 25, 1850, married in 1869 to David Gibson, has two children, and lives near Bolckow, Andrew county, Missouri.

JULIA A., born March 5, 1863, lives with her sister, Mrs. Watts.

LUCY M., born Aug. 20, 1857, lives with her aunt, Mrs. Beaumont, in Petersburg, Ill.

Jordan Simpson, died Dec. 23, 1872, at Pleasant Plains, and Mrs. Clarissa Simpson lives with her son, James W. Simpson, in Pleasant Plains, Ill.

SIMPSON, WILLIAM, was born in 1808, in Simpson county, Ky. He came to Sangamon county, Ill., in 1829, and was married to Elizabeth Willis, who was born May 17, 1806. They had six children in Sangamon county, namely:

MARTHA, born Aug. 6, 1837, married May 8, 1861, to Joel H. Ellis. *See his name.*

MARGARET J., born March 10, 1839, is unmarried, and lives at the southeast corner of Gardner township, at the homestead.

HENRIETTA, born Jan. 10, 1841, is unmarried, and lives near Sidney, Champaign county, Ill.

MARY, born March 24, 1843, married April 24, 1873, to Miller Winston, and lives near Sidney, Champaign county, Illinois.

NANCY, born Aug. 30, 1845, married Sept. 28, 1859, to John Spinning. They have one child, WILLIAM S., and live in Bloomington, Illinois.

WILLIAM T., born April 5, 1852, married Oct. 16, 1873, to Burzilla K. Reed, and lives at the family homestead, three and a half miles southwest of Farmingdale, Sangamon county, Ill.

Mrs. Elizabeth Simpson died Feb. 17, 1860, and William Simpson died March 30, 1872, both in Sangamon county, Ill.

SIMS, JAMES, was born in Virginia, taken by his parents to South Carolina, where he was married to Dolly Spillers. They had four children there, and moved to Logan county, Kentucky, where they had one child, and from there to Caldwell county, where three children were born; thence to St. Clair county, Illinois, and from there to Sugar Creek, Sangamon county, arriving in the spring of 1820 in what became Ball township, Sangamon county. He built a horse mill there to run by bands. He quarried stone of the same kind of which the first State House in Springfield was built, and by the aid of his brother-in-law, William Spillers, made the burrs for his mill. He was the first Representative from Sangamon county in the State Legislature. He moved to Rock Creek in what is now Menard county, and from there to Morgan county. He was a Methodist preacher, and formed the first circuit ever organized in Sangamon county. Of his children—

BETSY married James Black in St. Clair county, raised a large family, and died August, 1872, in Mason county, Illinois.

LUCY married Henry Morgan, raised a large family south of Richland creek in Sangamon county. He died there in 1867, and she died in Kansas two or three years later.

POLLY married in Morgan county to George Wolf. They had seven sons. JOHN is a lawyer in Champaign City, Illinois. THOMAS is a lawyer in Paxton, Ill. JAMES was clerk of Macoupin county one term. Mrs. Polly Wolf died December, 1872, and George Wolf died in 1873, both near Girard, Macoupin county.

MATILDA, married John Kirkpatrick, raised a family, and moved to McDonough county, where he died.

AGNES, born June 7, 1807, in Logan county, Kentucky, married in Sangamon county, April, 1827, to Reuben Bryant. They had six children. One son lives in California. THOMAS married a grand-daughter of Rev. John Berry, and lives in Clinton, Illinois. R. Bryant died and his widow married William McMurry, Sen. *See his name.*

WESLEY married, raised a family and lives near Manchester, Scott county, Illinois.

VIZILLA married Thomas Dunwoody, raised a large family and he died. She lives near Arcadia, Morgan county, Illinois.

CECELIA married James Dougherty, had four children, and died in Morgan county, Illinois.

BLACKMAN, L., married four times, raised a large number of children, and resides in Naples, Illinois.

SIMS, WILLIAM, (uncle to John Sims) was born in Virginia, taken when young to South Carolina, married there to a Miss Welch. He came to Sangamon county among the earliest settlers, and raised a family of nine children, none of whom now live in the county. He was for many years a pioneer local Methodist preacher of limited education, but remarkable for piety and good common sense. He died in Knox or Henry county, Illinois, in 1859.

SIMS, JOHN, was born Sept. 13, 1799, in Spartanberg county, S. C. His father died and his mother married again and moved to North Carolina, thence to Tennessee, and from there he went to live with his uncle, James Sims, in Logan county, Ky. His uncle moved to Caldwell county, and from there to St. Clair county, Ill., in 1815. John Sims and Lucinda Duff were there married Jan. 13, 1819. They moved, with his father-in-law, to what became Sangamon county, arriving in April, 1819, and settled south of Spring creek, in what is now Gardner township, four miles west of Springfield. They had seven children in Sangamon county, namely—

LUCY, born Oct. 8, 1820, married David P. Robison. *See his name.*

EMILY J., born April 27, 1824, married John Skipton. *See his name.*

VERLINDA, died aged seven years.

CAROLINE, born Jan. 21, 1828, in Sangamon county, married James A. Patterson. They have nine children. EMILY A. married William W. Morgan. *See his name.* VIRLEY A., married John R. Henton, and lives near Linden, Kansas. The other seven live with their parents, five miles southwest of Springfield, Ill.

SARAH A., born Nov. 15, 1830, in Sangamon county, married Henry Washington Rickard. *See his name.*

JOHN M., born Aug. 12, 1833, married Mary Kendall, and both died.

GREEN VIRGIL, born Nov. 15, 1835, in Sangamon county, married Mary McClure, has five children, and resides near Linden, Osage county, Kansas.

JAMES B., born April 13, 1838, married December 29, 1864, to Mary F. Massie. They have three children, JACKEY E., CARRIE A., and LILLIAN G. and resides four miles west of Springfield, Illinois.

Mrs. Lucinda Sims died Sept. 26, 1864, and John Sims resides at his old homestead four miles west of Springfield, Ill. *See page 71*, for Mr. Sims statement concerning the honesty of the early settlers.

SKEEN, JAMES, was born March 29, 1811, in Lancaster county, Pennsylvania. Lydia A. Moore was born Feb. 13, 1813, in Lycoming county, Pennsylvania. Her parents moved to Lancaster county, when she was a child. James Skeen and Lydia A. Moore were married November, 1834, and had two children in Lancaster county, and moved to Sangamon county, Illinois, arriving May 15, 1838, at Springfield. A few days later they moved twelve miles west of Springfield and south of Spring creek, where they had seven children, namely—

ELIZA J., born Sept. 21, 1825, in Pennsylvania, married in Sangamon county to William Parsons. They have six children, and reside near Decaturville, Camden county, Missouri.

SAMUEL, born Dec. 7, 1837, in Pensylvania, died 1838 in Sangamon county.

SARAH A., born Feb. 26, 1840, in Sangamon county, married John Allen, had one child, ELIZABETH, and the parents both died.

MARY S., born Dec. 19, 1843, married Moses O. Booker. They had one child, MARY O., and Mr. Booker enlisted August, 1862, for three years, in Co. A, 106th Ill. Inf. He died Sept. 17, 1863, at Paducah, Kentucky. His widow married James Davenport, had one child, ELIZA J., and the mother died April 26, 1870.

NANCY, born June 23, 1845, married Feb. 17, 1869, to Bryant Fay. They have one child, and live in Berlin, Illinois.

REUBEN, born Jan. 4, 1847, married Catharine E. Shryer, April, 1868. They have two children, WILLIE and EPHRAIM, and reside near Bates, Illinois.

LYDIA C., born Nov. 23, 1849, married John Davenport, have one child, and live near Berlin, Illinois.

WILLIAM F. and *ISABELLA*, (twins) born March 29, 1853. She died in infancy, and he lives with his mother.

AGNES J., born March 18, 1858, lives with her mother.

James Skeen died Oct. 12, 1859, in Sangamon county, and his widow resides five miles east of Berlin, Sangamon county, Illinois.

SKIPTON, DANIEL, came from Muskingum county, Ohio, to Sangamon county with his wife, Susan, and one or more children, previous to 1840. He stopped first on Archer's creek, and later settled four miles west of Springfield. Of their children—

JOHN, born in Muskingum county, Ohio, came with his parents to Sanagmon county, and was married about 1838 to Emily J. Sims. They had seven children, namely, JOHN S., born Dec. 28, 1840, Married Feb. 9, 1864, to Susan A. Williams, has one child, FREDDIE R., and live six miles west of Springfield, Illinois. LUCY A. married J. W. Gaines, has three children, and lives near Cayuga, Livingston county, Illinois. MARY J. married Henry Hays, has three children, and live near Cayuga, Illinois. LUCINDA died aged fourteen years. JAMES V., DANIEL and EMILY A., live with their parents near Odell, Livingston county, Illinois—1874.

ANN married Vinson Singleton, has three children, and lives at Mason City, Illinois.

MARY married Samuel Scott. They have five children, and live near Havana, Illinois.

JAMES K. has been married three times, and lives near Mason City, Illinois.

SALLY married Isaac Lane, and lives near Havana, Illinois.

MATILDA married Wilson Logue, and live in Sidney, Iowa.

DANIEL, Jun., married Jane Sims, has eight children, and lives in Kansas.

LUCINDA lives with her sister, Mrs. Sykes.

SUSAN married Edward Sykes, and lives near Mason City, Illinois.

WILLIAM died aged twenty-four years.

Daniel Skipton died in Mason county in 1842, and his widow lives with her daughter, Mrs. Singleton, in Mason City, Illinois, aged seventy-nine years —1874.

SLATER, ELIJAH, was born Dec. 8, 1775, in Wyoming county, Penn. His parents, Samuel and Sibyl Slater, were among the few who escaped the historic massacre of Wyoming in 1778, during the bloody years of the American Revolution. They had barely time to save their lives, each carrying one of their two children on horseback until they reached their friends in Massachusetts. Samuel Slater was killed by a falling tree, and his son and daughter were brought up in Massachusetts. Elijah Slater was married in West Stockbridge, Mass., in 1797, to Olive French. They moved in a few years to Great Barrington, where he engaged in the mercantile business. In 1813 the family moved to Pennsylvania, and occupied the house from which Mr. Slater's parents fled many years before. He left the farm for Kingston, Pa., where he opened a store; from there he moved to Ithica, New York, and continued merchandizing. In 1817 he visited the West, selected Milton, near Alton, Ill., for his residence, and returned to New York for his family. Soon after their arrival at Milton they moved to Sangamon county, settling on Sugar creek, in 1818, where they lived until Springfield was laid out, when he moved there in 1821 or '2, among the first settlers. Elijah Slater and wife had seventeen children—

SAMUEL, born Jan. 27, 1798, in West Stockbridge, Mass., lived with his parents until 1818, when he left Ithica, New York, and came West, landing at Shawneetown, and traveled through Illinois to St. Louis on foot, joining his father at Milton, where he clerked in a store for a short time, and afterwards took charge of a store at Hunterstown (now lower Alton), for Major C. W. Hunter, a merchant of St. Louis. The goods were brought up the Mississippi river on keel boats from the latter city, as there were few steamboats, and they seldom went above St. Louis. Mr. Slater's health failed, and he went north to the "Sangamo" country, where his father had bought some land. His favorable report of the country induced Major Hunter to fit him out with a stock of merchandize for a store on Sugar creek. There was only one other store in the country, and that was kept by John Taylor, farther up on the same stream. Mr. Slater found an empty log house on the farm of Isaac Keys, just below the mouth of Lick creek, which he occupied, and among his stores were medicines and *whisky*, the latter being indispensible. He remained on Sugar creek until 1821, when he went as supercargo to New Orleans for Major Hunter, with some flat boats loaded with oak staves, in 1823. He went again with a lot of bacon, and remained in New Orleans during the winter, at which time he took a lot of hogs to Havana, Cuba, and returned with the proceeds in coffee. Found a clerkship at fifteen dollars per month, with board, for three months. Afterwards, his salary was raised to five hundred dollars per year and board. He visited his friends in Illinois, and was married at Alton, Oct. 27, 1831, to Mary W. Avis. He returned to New Orleans, where they resided until 1839, he moved to Galveston, Texas, and was book-keeper a portion of the time in the United States custom House there. His health failing, he removed in 1848 to his land in the northern part of same State, where he had ten thousand acres. They remained there twelve years. In 1860 he sold the most of his land, determined to move where there was a railroad. He went to Tyler, to settle some business preparatory to leaving, and found the people greatly excited by the news of the general elections and the success of the Republican party. Mr. Slater was told by a friend that the Vigilance Committee was trying to find something out against *him*, that it had been reported he was about leaving the country, and would take a great many negroes with him. Mr. S. intended leaving town that night, but concluded it was safer to remain, as the mob might follow him, so he reported himself to the Vigilance Committee, saying he was willing to appear before them and answer any questions they might ask, thinking that would end the matter; but not so, they cited him to appear at the court house. He did so, and found there about forty men, self elected jurors. There was no charge made against Mr. Slater and of course no witnesses, but a little lawyer said: "*I'll fix him!*" and the trial began. After questioning him some time about where he was born, and the different places he had lived before coming to Texas, they dispatched two men twenty-five miles to search his house for abolition documents, keeping him under guard at Tyler during the time. The two men returned next day with large bundles of the New York *Observer*, which they called those abolition documents. The trial was opened next day, and a Methodist preacher, whom Mr. S. considered his friend, and who secretly was one, was called on to testify. He stated that a third person had told him that Mr. Slater was an abolitionist, and *he* believed it. This settled the question. The trial closed and he was sent to the Vigilance committtee of his own county for punishment, but before arriving at his destination the guard told him of a plan they had formed for his escape. A man who owed Mr. Slater met them at this point and paid him five hundred dollars, besides giving him a good mule to make out his team. He found his wife had made all preparations, and they started Aug. 17, 1860, and traveled ten miles through the woods that night. One of the guard told Mrs. Slater that the committee would have hung her husband the first day had it not been for the Methodist minister, who only testified against Mr. S. to save his own life, and was secretly doing all he could to save Mr. Slater. Some of the guard traveled with them two days and then returned. They made good marches, resting every Sabbath, and arrived at Alton in October of the same year Mr. Slater was in the Quartermaster's department early in the late war to suppress the rebellion, and subsequently mail agent, in place of his son, who enlisted and went as orderly sergeant. Samuel Slater resigned his position as mail agent in 1868, and purchased land in Bates county, Missouri, where he is cultivating a farm, and enjoys better health than when he left New Orleans, in 1839.

Samuel Slater and wife attended a meeting of the early settlers of Sangamon county, held on Sugar creek, in 1874, near where his father settled in 1818, but was unable to find a single person who knew him, and felt as though they thought he was trying to deceive them. He was the Rip Van Winkle of the occasion. Mr. and Mrs. Slater had nine children. THOMAS AVIS, born February 12, 1833, in New Orleans, Louisiana. In 1855 went to Alton, Illinois, to attend Shurtleff College. He studied law, and was admitted to the bar, and soon after received an appointment in the Land Office at Washington, D. C. By too close attention to business lost his health, and died at his father's house in Brighton, Illinois, Sept. 13, 1865. SAMUEL N., born Jan. 15, 1836, in New Orleans, Louisiana, attended school at Alton, enlisted May 15, 1861, in Co. I, 4th Reg. Mo. Vol. Inf., for three months, went out as Orderly Sergeant, served full time and was honorably discharged. He was substitute for his brother in the Land Office at Washington, and afterwards, through the influence of Governor Yates, was sent with appointment in the Custom House to New Orleans, remained there a year or two and returned, was appointed in the Agricultural Department at Washington, D. C., where he remains. He married Ida V. Tramell Nov. 16, 1871. They have one child, OLIVE MAY, and reside in Washington, D. C. MARY O., born Nov. 18, 1839, in Galveston, Texas, attended school in Springfield, Illinois, and Monticello Seminary, and was married August 13, 1873, to William Page, who attended college in Chicago, and graduated in the Law School of Michigan University, at Ann Arbor. He is a practicing attorney, and resides in Butler, Bates county, Missouri. JAMES H., born March 3, 1842, in Galveston, Texas, enlisted in Missouri in the same company with his brother, Samuel N., for three months, served full time, re-enlisted in August, 1862, for three years in Co. D, 122d Ill. Inf. He was honorably discharged July 18, 1865. In 1868 he was appointed Postal Clerk on the Chicago and Alton Railroad, in place of his father, (who had just resigned) which position he still retains. WILLIAM A., born Dec. 29, 1844, in Galveston, attended school in Springfield, and in March, 1865, enlisted in Co. D, 18th Ill. Inf., went out as a drummer boy, was taken sick and died at Pine Bluff, Arkansas, Oct. 20, 1865, and was buried there. MARTHA, born Feb. 21, 1847, at Galveston, attended school in Springfield, Illinois, and Monticello Seminary two sessions. She resides with her parents. CHARLES M., born Sept. 19, 1849, in Henderson county, Texas, was sent in 1861 to Boston, Massachusetts, at his uncle Charles' request, to be educated by him. He is now, and has been for several years, a traveling agent for a business house in New York City. His route is as far west as Omaha and as far south as New Orleans. JOSEPH B., born Nov. 21, 1852, in Henderson county, Texas, resides with his father. PERRY J., born Sept. 21, 1854, in Starrville, Smith county, Texas, is a dentist, and lives in Butler, Missouri. Samuel Slater and family reside near Butler, Bates county, Missouri.

HENRIETTA MARIA was born in 1800 in Berkshire county, Massachusetts. She was married in Madison county, Illinois, to Rev. Thomas Lippincott, and died in 1820. Mr. Lippincott was the father, by a subsequent marriage, of General Charles E. Lippincott, present Auditor of State for Illinois, who resides in Springfield—1876.

OLIVE, born in 1801 in Berkshire county, Massachusetts, was married in Ithica, New York, to Joseph Torrey. See his name. They settled on Sugar creek, Sangamon county, Illinois, where she died in August or September, 1820.

SIBYL, born in 1807 in Berkshire county, Massachusetts, was married Dec. 22, 1842, in Springfield, Illinois, to Dr. Gershom Jayne. See his name.

C. PERRY, born September, 1823, in Springfield, Illinois, studied medicine with Dr. Jayne, spent three years in California, returned and was married in 1854 to Susan Mather Lamb. He was a practicing physician, and died in 1858 in Springfield,

Illinois, leaving a widow and one child, HANNAH M., who was married in Chicago, Sept. 27, 1876, to Walter Trumbull, eldest son of Hon. Lyman Trumbull. They reside in Chicago. C. P. Slater's widow married James H. Roberts, a lawyer, and resides in Chicago, Illinois.

Elijah Slater and wife were two of the original members of the first Presbyterian church of Springfield, Illinois, formed by the Rev. J. G. Bergen. Mr. Slater was distinguished for his energy and upright life, and died July, 1836. His widow died in November, 1844, and both were buried in Springfield, Illinois.

SLATER, JAY, born Feb. 25, 1795, in Massachusetts, was married March 12, 1826, in Sangamon county, Ill., to Lucretia Carman, who was born in 1806, in New York. They had six living children in Sangamon county—

JAMES HARVEY, born Dec. 28, 1826, nine miles south of Springfield, left home March 28, 1849, driving an ox team over the plains, and arrived in California Sept. 11, of that year. In the autumn of 1851 he went to Oregon, and was one of the delegates to the territorial legislature of Oregon, also a member of the constitutional convention. He was married there in 1853 to Elizabeth Gray, a native of Georgia. They had nine children. James Harvey Slater was elected in 1870 to represent Oregon in the United States Congress. He lives at LaGrande, Union county, Oregon.

LYMAN BEECHER, born Aug. 7, 1828, in Sangamon county, was married April 28, 1853, in Mt. Auburn, Christian county, Ill., to Angeline Bodkin. She died July 30, 1854. Lyman B. Slater graduated in the medical department of Missouri State University, in St. Louis, in 1855. Dr. Slater was married Oct. 4, 1855, to Sarah Stockwell, who was born July 15, 1830, in Vermont. They have six children, MARGARET, LYMAN T., EMMA, ALICE L., MARY T., and JAMES H., who live with their parents. Dr. L. B. Slater is a practicing physician, and resides at Taylorville, Ill.

JULIA, born Sept. 26, 1833, in Sangamon county, married William Campbell. They have three children, MARY, OLIVE and CHARES.

JOHN M., born Aug. 26, 1835, in Sangamon county, was married April 30 1856 to Leah Campbell, daughter of Lewis Campbell. They had eight children, LEWIS J. and IDA C., died young, LAURA L., CHARLES GRANT, LYMAN H., JOHN A., NORA E. and ROBERT O., live with their parents, half a mile north of Cross Plains postoffice, Sangamon county, Ill.

OLIVE J., born Nov. 8, 1838, in Sangamon county, was married March 2, 1858, to Samuel P. Stevens. They have four children, ENOS, SAMUEL, MARIETTA and LYMAN, and live near Arvilla, Jasper county, Missouri.

SOPHRONIA P., born Jan. 19, 1845, was married in 1865 to William Neer. They have two children, and live four miles west of Grove City, Christian county, Illinois.

Mrs. Lucretia Slater died July, 1853, and Jay Slater was married March 15, 1854, to Lavina Alkire, who was born Oct. 6, 1823, in Westmoreland county, Pennsylvania, and came to Springfield in 1838. Mr. and Mrs. Slater had two children, one died in infancy.

ALBERT J., born Dec. 19, 1856, in Sangamon county, is a student—1874.

Jay Slater died July 19, 1860, in Sangamon county. Mrs. Lavina Slater was married Oct. 19, 1863, in Sangamon county to Frederick G. Tabler, who was born Sept. 2, 1827, in the Kingdom of Wurtemburg, Germany, and came to America in 1857. Mr. and Mrs. Tabler have two children.

GEOGE F., born Sept. 10, 1864, and MARY E., born Dec. 15, 1866. The two latter reside with their parents, one and a half miles northwest of Bradfordton, Sangamon county, Illinois.

SMITH, JAMES D., born Dec. 5, 1805, in Harrison county, Kentucky, was married at Cynthiana, in that county, in 1829, to Ruth Ann Brown. They had one child in Kentucky, and Mr. Smith visited Missouri and Illinois in 1832. He purchased land in Sangamon county, and moved with his father-in-law, Colonel William Brown, arriving in the fall of 1833 at Island Grove, where nine children were born, three of whom died in infancy. Of their children—

WILLIAM B., born Dec. 6, 1832, in Harrison county, Kentucky, brought up in Sangamon county, was married near Burlington, Vermont, Oct. 13, 1873, to

Julia B. Kinney, who was born near Burlington in 1845. They live two miles southwest of Berlin, Illinois.

JOHN P., born July 25, 1835, in Sangamon county, was married near Lexington, Kentucky, April 28, 1864, to Anna P. O'Bannon. They have six children. HATTIE B., the fifth child, died Oct. 12, 1873. RUTH W., O'BANNON, ELIZA, JAMES D. and ANNIE P. live with their parents four miles west of Berlin, Sangamon county, Illinois, within one mile of where Mr. Smith was born.

JAMES D., Jun., born Dec. 20, 1837, in Sangamon county, was married at Jacksonville, Illinois, Sept. 29, 1864, to Elizabeth B. Brown, who was born April 2, 1842, in Boonville, Missouri. They have four living children, ELISHA B., JAMES D., MARY B., and HALLIE, and live at the homestead, three miles west of Berlin, Illinois.

HATTIE B., born July 27, 1844, in Sangamon county, was married May 27, 1865, to Samuel S. Deweese. They have two children, ELIZA S. and JAMES SMITH, and live one mile north of Alexander, Morgan county, Illinois.

MARTHA D., born March 26, 1847, in Sangamon county, was married Feb. 20, 1872, to George Prewitt, have one child, HALLIE, and live in Georgetown, Kentucky.

RUTH ANN, born Jan. 25, 1850, in Sangamon county, was married Sept. 24, 1874, to James G. Kelly. They have one child, CONWAY, and live in Georgetown, Kentucky.

LLOYD B., born Sept. 24, 1852, in Sangamon county, was married at Alexander, Morgan county, Illinois, to Lulu B. Alexander, daughter of John T. Alexander, Esq.

"On the afternoon of Tuesday, Nov. 7, 1871, James D. Smith, an old and honored resident of Island Grove, Sangamon county, Illinois, was thrown from his buggy and killed whilst returning alone to his home from the town of Berlin. On the afternoon of the Thursday following, the large concourse of people, from town and country for miles around, which gathered at his grave, spoke impressively of the high esteem in which he was held by all who knew him. In 1833, in company with his father-in-law, Col. William Brown, he emigrated to Illinois and made his home on the farm from whence he was borne to the grave. Shunning public life, though often urged to accept positions of trust and honor by his friends, he but once yielded his personal feelings to their solicitations, and was elected and served as a member of the Constitutional Convention of 1862. During the whole of his life in Illinois, he was a member of the Methodist Episcopal Church, and with his brother-in-law, Captain James N. Brown, who, just three years in advance of him, went into the better land, was the founder and most liberal supporter of Island Grove station, *the first* rural station established in Illinois Conference. An active, earnest, humble christian, he was peculiarly free from sectarian prejudice, and although warmly attached to the church of his choice, regarded with fraternal feeling every follower of his Master. Eminently domestic and social in his nature, and urbane in manner, the loved and honored companion of childhood and youth, as well as of those of mature years, his time outside the requirements of large farming and stock operations, was devoted to his family, his kindred and his neighbors, in whose welfare he ever felt the deepest interest. As illustrative of his character, it might here be stated that early in his life at Island Grove he was commissioned Justice of the Peace, and during the whole time he held that office he had but one suit brought in his court to come to trial, having in every other case, by his personal influence with the parties, and efforts in the true interests of peace, affected an amicable settlement of differences. Decided in his convictions, and uncompromising as to the right, yet the intercourse with his fellow men was marked by the exercise of judgment so unwarped by selfishness, and was softened by such abounding charity, that he lived without an enemy. With him benevolence was an ever present sentiment, falling like the gentle dew into the every-day acts of life, manifesting itself alike in the sacred precincts of his family, in his dealings with the many in his employ, and in an open hand to the poor, the needy, the sick, and the stranger. Of *him* it may be truly said, "*He was a good man*," one whom the church, the state and society could illy afford to lose. Living, he was the embodiment of every domestic virtue;

—84

dying, he has left his stricken family a treasure more valuable than his ample fortune—the priceless heritage of a well spent life."

His widow, Mrs. Ruth A. Smith, survived her husband exactly ten months, and died Sept. 7, 1872. The remains of both are interred in Wood Wreath Cemetery, near where they spent so many years of their lives.

SMITH, GEORGE M., was born April 23, 1785, in Virginia. His parents moved when he was a child to Henry county, Ky. Matilda Dowdall was born in Culpepper county, Virginia, Feb. 18, 1793. Her mother died when she was two years old, and her grandfather Holmes soon after moved to Shelby county, Kentucky, taking Matilda and another sister and brother with him. George M. Smith and Matilda Dowdall were married Aug. 14, 1810, in Shelby county, and afterwards lived some time in Henry county, Ky., where they had four children and moved in 1824 to Jennings county, near Vernon, Indiana, where one child was born, and they returned to Henry county, where one child was born. They then moved to Sangamon county, Ill., arriving in March, 1834, in what is now Island Grove. Of their eight children—

JACOB H., born Dec. 23, 1815, in Henry county, Ky., came to Sangamon county, Illinois, with his parents in 1834, and was married in Hennepin, Ill., Dec. 19, 1838, to Joanna Higgins. They moved to Saline county, Missouri, and had five children there. JACOB H. SMITH and his eldest son, GEORGE, were both soldiers in the Union army. They reside at Marshall, Saline county, Missouri.

JOHN W., born July 10, 1818, in Henry county, Ky., was married in Sangamon county June 1, 1845, to Ann E. Fox, who was born June 7, 1827, in Loudon county, Virginia. She was the eldest daughter of Dr. J. B. Fox, lately deceased, in Springfield. Mr. and Mrs. Smith had eight children in Sangamon county, three of whom died young. Of the other five, AMANDA was married Sept. 14, 1871, to George Parish, and lives in Oskosh, Wisconsin. MARY M., JOSEPH B., WILLIE and CARRIE live with their relatives. Joseph B. Smith is a clerk in a mercantile house in Quincy, Illinois. Mrs. Ann E. Smith died May 21, 1871, in Springfield. John W. Smith filled many important positions of honor and trust in Sangamon county. He discharged the duties of census commissioner in 1845, by appointment from the county court. In 1848 he was elected one of the representatives of Sangamon county in the State Legislature, and was again census commissioner in 1855. He was elected sheriff of the county in 1860 for two years, and mayor of the city of Springfield in 1863. He was appointed by the United States government, commissioner on the board of enrollment for military duty for the eighth congressional district in 1864, but soon resigned to accept the position of collector of internal revenue for the same district. He was one of the commissioners named in the law of Feb. 25, 1867, to manage the building of the new state house, and remained on the board until the laws of March 11 and 27, 1869, reduced the number from seven to three. He was elected Mayor of Springfield in 1871, and re-elected in 1872. He was appointed by Gov. Beveridge in 1873 warden of the state penitentiary at Joliet. While discharging the duties of that office he was on his way from Chicago to Joliet on the night of Saturday, Aug. 16, 1873. The train on which he was traveling collided with a freight train near Sag Bridge, a few miles southwest of Chicago. He was in the smoking car at the time and was terribly scalded by the escaping steam from the broken pipes. He, with a number of others, were taken to Chicago, and died there at eight o'clock on the morning of the 18th. His remains were brought to Springfield and buried at Oak Ridge cemetery, Aug. 19th.

ELSIE A., born Dec. 30, 1821, in Henry county, Ky., was married in Sangamon county to Stephen Butler—brother of William Butler, recently deceased—in Springfield. They have ten children, two of whom are married. The family reside at Mondamin, Harrison county, Iowa.

THOMAS D., born Aug. 24, 1823, in Henry county, Ky., was married in Sangamon county Jan. 1, 1851, to Julia A. Maxwell. They had seven children in Sangamon county, and moved from Berlin to Humboldt county, Kansas in 1869. T.

D. Smith died there March 10, 1873, and his family reside there.

MARY J., born April 24, 1825, near Vernon, Indiana, was married in Henry county, Ky., Dec. 21, 1847, to Owen T. McCormick. They lived in Shelby county, Ky., until November, 1849, when they moved to Island Grove, Sangamon county, Ill., and had five children there. SARAH A. was married Oct. 29, 1842, to Benjamin R. B. Weber. See his name. JOSAPHINE A., OWEN T., Jun., MOLLIE E. and GEORGE R. live with their mother. Owen T. McCormick, Sen., died Oct. 27, 1865, and Mrs. McCormick resides at Pawnee, Sangamon county, Ill.

MARTHA M., born Dec. 24, 1827, in Henry county, Ky., was married April 12, 1849 to John Foutch. See his name.

HARRIET O., born Sept. 19, 1830, married Addison Gibson, of Gallatin county, Ky. They left there in July, 1864, on account of the rebellion and came to New Berlin, where Mrs. Harriet O. Gibson died April 24, 1865, leaving six sons, all of whom live with their father in Kentucky.

GEORGE W., born May 10, 1833, in Kentucky, brought up in Sangamon county, went to Weston, Missouri, married Fannie King, and died there.

George M. Smith died Feb. 27, 1842, at Island Grove, and his widow lives with her children.

SMITH, GREENBERRY, was born Feb. 5, 1793, in Washington county, Kentucky, and was married there to Nancy Killen, who was born in 1800 in the same county. They had one child there, and moved to Sangamon county, Illinois, arriving in the fall of 1830, in what is now Springfield township, where they had one child. Of their two children—

ETHELINDA J., born Dec. 21, 1826, in Washington county, Kentucky, married Nov. 21, 1844, in Sangamon county to John Prince. They had six children, WILLIAM P., JAMES L., NANCY J., GREENBERRY, JOSEPH and CHARLES, and live in Springfield, Illinois.

LAFAYETTE, born Nov. 21, 1834, in Sangamon county, married Jan. 1, 1857, in Springfield to Harriet A. Buchanan. They had seven children, two of whom died in infancy, and ALBERT G. died at fourteen years of age. FRANK B., EDWIN F., HARRY L. and FREDERICK WORRALL, reside with their parents in Springfield, Illinois. Lafayette Smith is the senior member of the firm of Smith & Hay, wholesale grocers, in Springfield.

Greenberry Smith died April 23, 1871, and Mrs. Nancy Smith died May 21, 1873, both in Springfield, Illinois.

SMITH, JONAS, was born April 10, 1810, on Long Island, New York. His father moved to Monroe county, Illinois, about 1820. In 1831 Jonas visited his sister Mrs. Ebenezer Colburn at Loami, and in July, 1836, came from Cincinnati to put up and run mill machinery for William and Ebenezer Colburn. He has been engaged in milling from that to the present time as owner and builder of mills on Lick creek and other parts of the country. Jonas Smith was married in 1839, at Loami, to Charlotte Colburn. They had six children, two of whom, Adam L. and Millard F., died young. Of the other four—

MARY J., born Dec. 27, 1842, married Dr. Stephen N. Sanders. See his name. She died in 1867, leaving one child, ANNA.

NOE N., born Nov. 24, 1845, enlisted May 2, 1864, in Co. E, 133d Ill. Inf., for one hundred days, served until Sept. 24, 1864, when he was honorably discharged, and died at Loami, Nov. 3, 1864, of disease contracted in the army.

JULIA A., born March 25, 1848, and ADNA J., born August 6, 1854, live with their parents.

Jonas Smith and wife reside at Loami, Sangamon county, Illinois.

SMITH, JOHN, was born June 23, 1812, in Hartford, Connecticut, and at six years of age he was taken by his parents to Ontario county, New York, and from there to Michigan in 1830. John Smith went to St. Louis, Missouri, in February, 1840, and was there married Jan. 11, 1841, to Charlotte Getchel, who was born Nov. 5, 1812, in Maine. They came to Sprinfield, Ill., in February, 1841, where they had one child, and moved to Chatham, where four children were born. Of their children—

MARY E., born Oct. 5, 1841, in Sprinfield, died Nov. 6, 1853.

BENJAMIN F., born Jan. 12, 1843, in Sangamon county, enlisted Dec. 8, 1863, in Battery A., 3d Ill. Art., served to the end of the rebellion, and was honorably discharged in Springfield. He was married in 1869, in Lynn county, Missouri to Elizabeth Dustin. They have four children, and live near North Salem, Lynn county, Missouri.

GEORGE W., born May 3, 1845, in Sangamon county, enlisted Dec. 8, 1863, in Battery A, 3d Ill. Art., served to the end of the rebellion, and was honorably discharged in Springfield. He was married April 22, 1872, in Missouri to Mrs. Elizabeth Britton. They live near North Salem, Lynn county, Missouri.

EDWARD, born Oct. 19, 1847, in Sangamon county, died Aug. 30, 1870, about seventy miles below St. Louis, on the Mississippi river.

ANNIE L., born April 7, 1851, in Sangamon county, died Oct. 22, 1865.

Mrs. Charlotte Smith died Feb. 2, 1853, in Sangamon county, and John Smith was married Oct. 2, 1860 to Elizabeth Trumbo, They have two children—

ADAM T., born July 14, 1861, and *EMMA L.*, born Feb. 11, 1866, live with their parents, three-fourths of a mile south of Woodside, Sangamon county. Ill.

SMITH, JOHN M., born Aug. 11, 1813, in Sanbornton, New Hampshire, spent six years as clerk in Boston, and married there to Almyra Andrews. They had three children and moved to Sangamon county, Illinois, arriving at Springfield May 4, 1839. Of the three children—

SARAH A., born in Boston, married in Sangamon county to James A. Poor. *See his name.* He died and she married James McCausland, and live near Curran, Illinois.

EMILY married Thomas Springhall, and resides in Springfield—1874.

JOSEPH E., is married and lives in Kansas.

Mrs. Almyra Smith died and he was married in 1844, to Julia A. Duff. She died and J. M. Smith married May 4, 1846, Harriet Baldwin. They have three children—

WILLIAM W., *JOHN E.* and *NANCY E.*, and live half a mile north of Curran, Sangamon county, Illinois.

SMITH, JOSEPH, was born in Loudon county, Virginia. His parents moved to Harrison county, Ky., when he was seven or eight years of age. At the age of fifteen he entered a store in Paris, Ky., as clerk, and afterwards became a merchant in Frankfort. He was married April 9, 1822, in Franklin county, near Frankfort, to Sally Taylor. She was born Nov. 22, 1807, in that part of Gallatin that afterwards became Trimble county, Ky. The family residence at the time was on a very elevated site opposite the city of Madison, Indiana, and was called Mount Bird. It afforded a fine view of the city and of the Ohio river, with its passing steamers. Her father, John Taylor, was a native of Virginia, and entered the Baptist ministry in that State. He became acquainted in Virginia with the father of General who was afterwards President, Zachary Taylor. Both moved to Kentucky, and although they were not related to each other, they married step-sisters and continued their intimacy during their lives. Miss Sally Taylor, now Mrs. Smith, was named for the mother of President Taylor. Joseph Smith and wife had four children in Franklin county, Ky., and moved to Sangamon county, Ill., arriving in October, 1834, and settled on Richland creek, in what is now Cartwright township, where two children were born. Of their six children—

TEMPLE, born Jan. 21, 1823, was drowned in Kentucky at ten years of age, by his horse falling while crossing a stream.

J. TAYLOR was born March 6, 1825, in Frankfort, Ky., came so Sangamon county with his parents in 1834. In 1844 he engaged in the mercantile business in Springfield. J. Taylor Smith was married March 27, 1850, to Sophia N. Ridgely. They had four children in Springfield, one of whom died in infancy. JULIA V. born March 31, 1851, died Aug. 27, 1873. FRED. E. was born July 18, 1853. In June, 1872, he entered the United States Military Academy, at West Point, N. Y., graduated there in June, 1876. He is lieutenant in Co. D, 13th U. S. Inf., and is now—Oct. 1876—at New Orleans, La. JESSIE T., born Oct. 9, 1864, resides with her parents. Mr. Smith was in the mercantile business in Springfield from 1844 to 1874, when he retired. During that time he has dealt in lands and stocks, and is now a director in the Ridgely National Bank, and resides in Springfield, Ill.

JOSEPH S., born July 21, 1827, in Kentucky, is an extensive farmer and stock raiser at Bates, Sangamon county, Illinois.

ELIZA J., born Jan. 21, 1830, in Kentucky, married David A. Brown. See his name.

BRADFORD T., died in infancy.

M. W. DeWITT, born Dec. 12, 1844, in Sangamon county, married Sept. 1, 1864, to M. Adelia McConnell. They have three children, ANDREW SYDNEY, ELIZABETH ADELIA and TEMPLE. M. W. DeWitt Smith is a farmer and stock raiser at Bates, Sangamon county, Ill.

Joseph Smith prosecuted the business of farming, and at the same time was in the mercantile business in Springfield, in connection with James M. Bradford. He also represented Sangamon county in the State Legislature. He died August, 1862, on the farm where he settled in 1834. His widow, Mrs. Sally Smith, resides with her son, Joseph S., at Bates, Sangamon county, Illinois.

SMITH, PHILIP, was born about 1790 in Montgomery county, North Carolina. He was married there to Nancy Cooper. They had seven children, and moved to Sangamon county, Illinois, arriving in 1822 in what is now Cooper township, and the next year moved to Williams township, where five children were born. Of their children—

EPHRAIM, born in North Carolina, has been twice married, and lives in Putnam county.

TILGHMAN, born in North Carolina, married in Sangamon county to Nancy Doughty, have several children, and live near Burlington, Iowa.

ELIZABETH married Andrew Sutton. Both died, leaving one child, WILLIAM I.

PHILIP Jun., born May 13, 1813, in North Carolina, married in Sangamon county July 17, 1834, had ten children. MARY A. married William Dolvau, have two children, and live at Elkhart, Illinois. JOHN enlisted in 1862 in Co. C, 114th Ill. Inf., for three years, served until June, 1864, when he was discharged on account of physical disability, married Martha Williams, have two children, ULYSSES F. and IDA BELL. Mrs. Smith died March 13, 1872, and he resides with his parents—1874. NANCY J. married Sylvanus Tuttle, had one child, RALSTON. Mr. Tuttle enlisted in 1862 for three years in Co. C, 114th Ill. Inf., and was killed at the siege of Vicksburg, May 19, 1863. His widow married William H. Smith. They have two children, PHILIP and IVY MAY, and live in Williamsville, Illinois. WILLIAM O. enlisted August, 1862, in Co. C, 114th Ill. Inf., came home on sick furlough and died Oct. 13, 1862, in his 21st year. HENRY T. married Harriet Kinnaman, have two children, and live in Williams township. REZIN married Izora Fisher, and lives in Williams township. JULIA F. married Edward Clapman, and live in Williams township. LAURA L. and SUSAN C. live with their parents, four and a half miles southeast of Williamsville, Illinois.

LEVI married Eveline Darnall. They have eleven children, and reside in Henry county Iowa.

CELIA married Joseph Hill. Both died of cholera and left four children.

JOHN, married Martha Brown, had two children, JOHN W. and ROMULUS, and Mrs. Martha Smith died. He married Elizabeth Hendrix. They had three children. SUSAN married in 1860 to William H. Smith, had one child, FLORA F., and Mrs. Susan Smith died. ALICE A. married William T. Ham. See his name. JENNIE married George Strawn, and lives in Williamsville, Illinois. John Smith died and his widow married Stephen King. See his name.

EDA married George Sutton, have six children, and reside near Lincoln.

NANCY A. married William McDaniel, had two children, and he died, and she married William Starr, had three children, and he died and she married Mr. West, and lives near Riverton, Illinois.

MARY A. married Charles Kinnaman and had nine children. CELIA J.; ANTHONY W. served three years in Co. C, 114th Ill. Inf. He married Emily Blue, has two children, and lives in Williamsville, Illinois. GEORGE W. lives in Palmer, Christian county, Illinois. All the other members of the family live at Clayton, Adams county, Illinois.

LOUISA married William House, who died, leaving one child, and she married Joseph Young, and lives in California.

IRVIN M. married Jennie Holt, and lives in Louisa county, Iowa.

Mrs. Nancy Smith died in 1854, near Barclay, and Philip Smith died in 1860 in Christian county, Illinois.

SMITH, THOMAS, was born in 1769 in Virginia, and went with his parents when he was a young man to Washington county, Kentucky. He was there married to Elizabeth Peter, who was born in 1772, she was an aunt of Zachariah Peter. They had nine children in that county. In the fall of 1819 they moved to Madison county, Illinois, and from there to Sangamon county, arriving in February, 1822, in what is now Curran township, north of Lick creek. Of their children—

MARGARET married Thomas Cummings. See his name.

RICHARD, born June 6, 1795, married in Kentucky, Dec. 22, 1816, to Elizabeth Hart, who was born near Richmond, Virginia, May 11, 1798. They came to Madison county, Illinois, and from there to Sangamon in 1823. They had seven children. Richard Smith died Feb. 2, 1859, and his widow resides with her son, Thompson, at Clinton, Illinois.

THOMAS, Jun., born in Kentucky, married in Sangamon county to Mary Cooper. They had six children, and Mr. S. died in 1838, two miles east of Springfield, Illinois. Of the children, JORDAN P., died in 1848, aged twenty-one years. LUCY M., born Nov. 30, 1830, married Thomas Smith of Lick creek. See his name. The other four children and mother reside in DeWitt county, Illinois. She is now—1874—the wife of Samuel Smith.

HANNAH, born in Kentucky, married in Sangamon county to Henry Whitlock. They had ten children, and he was murdered in the spring of 1871 in Green county, Illinois, and his widow and children live there.

ELIZABETH, married Augustus Kirkpatrick, had nine children. She and nearly all her children died at Camp Point, Illinois. Mr. Kirkpatrick lives there.

JOHN, born March 18, 1805, in Washington county, near Springfield, Kentucky, came with his parents to Sangamon county, Illinois, in 1822, and was married June 23, 1825, to Jane G. Drennan. They had six children. WILLIAM C., born March 24, 1826, was married June 16, 1844, to Rebecca J. Walker. They had eleven children, the three eldest died under four years. JOHN D. married Martha Alsbury. They had three children, Anna L., Clemantine and Bertie. Mrs. Martha Smith died April 20, 1875, leaving an infant that died in October, 1875. John D. Smith lives near Woodside, Sangamon county, Illinois. WILLIAM J. married Eliza J. Cloyd. They have one child, Jesse N., and live near Chatham, Sangamon county, Illinois. RICHARD P. was married Sept. 16, 1875, to Marion E. Patteson, and live two miles south of Curran, Sangamon county, Ill. The other five, HIRAM N., JOSEPH E., MARTHA L., MARY C. and THOMAS E., live with their parents. William C. Smith and family live one and a half miles south of Curran, Sangamon county, Ill. THOMAS, born April 4, 1827, married Lucy M. Smith. They have seven children. LOUISA married Dallas Davis. See his name. JOHN JORDAN was married Sept. 7, 1876, to Sadie Dennis, and lives near Curran, Sangamon county, Illinois. LAURA B., MARY A., THOMAS and RICHARD live with their parents. Thomas Smith resides three miles east of Curran, Sangamon county, Illinois. In order to distinguish himself from others of the same name, he is accustomed, in business transactions, to sign his name Thomas Smith, Lick Creek. REBECCA A., born Oct. 21, 1828, married William Barbre. See his name. ELIZABETH, C. born March 25, 1830, married William Poor. See his name. LUCY M., born April 17, 1831, married William Barbre. See his name. RICHARD C., born Feb. 12, 1833, married Amarine Shelton. They had eight living children, WILLIAM T., JOHN R., MARIA E., JAMES A., RICHARD E., CHARLES E., FLORA J. and FREDERICK H., live with their parents. Richard C. Smith lived in Chatham township, Sangamon county, until 1874, when he moved to the vicinity of Tolono, Champaign county, Illinois. Mrs. Jane G. Smith died Sept. 16, 1833, and John Smith was married Oct. 6, 1834, to Rebecca Enochs. They have two children, MAHALA J., born Dec. 21, 1841, married David Miller, who was born Jan. 28, 1838, in Coshocton county, Ohio. They have three children, JOHN M., THOMAS E. and LILLIE M., and live near Curran, Sangamon county, Ill. MARTHA H., born Jan. 13, 1847, married Andrew J. Drennan. *See his name.* John Smith and his wife live three miles southeast of Curran, Sangamon county, Illinois.

He says that two thousand Indians, camped on Lick creek, soon after the arrival of his father's family there in 1822, and remained about two weeks. They were very friendly. He also says that the first time he saw Springfield was in February, 1822. Elijah Iles was keeping store in a very small cabin built of round logs and covered with clapboards held on by weight poles. There was not a nail used in the building. Mr. Iles had sold out nearly all his goods and gone to St. Louis for more. The hotel consisted of a double log cabin, and was kept by Dr. Gershom Jayne and his wife. The store, hotel and blacksmith shop constituted the town.

RUTH married Andrew P. Drennan. *See his name.*

MARY Married William Withrow. *See his name.*

SARAH died aged forty years.

SAMUEL, born in Kentucky, was married in Sangamon county to Mrs. Mary Smith, whose maiden name was Cooper. They had two children, JOHN H. and AMANDA C., and live in Clinton, DeWitt county, Illinois.

Thomas Smith, Sen., died Jan. 28, 1841, and his widow died Feb. 1, 1852, both in Curran township, Sangamon county, Ill.

SNODGRASS, JAMES. The place of his birth is not known, but he was married in Cocke county, Tenn., to Elizabeth Snodgrass. They had eleven children in Tennessee, and moved to Sangamon county, Ill., arriving about 1820, in what is now Cotton Hill township. Of their children—

MARGARET, born in Tenn., married in Sangamon county, in 1821, to Thomas Howey.

JAMES, Jun., born in Cocke county, Tennessee, about 1785, married there to Mary Martin. They had two children in Tennessee, and moved to Madison county, Ill., where one child was born and from there to Sangamon county, arriving in 1820 in what is now Cotton Hill township, where three children were born. Of their six children, SAMUEL D., born Sept. 22, 1812, in Tennessee married in Sangamon county, April 12, 1832, to Nancy W. Haines. They had seven living children, MARY J. born Dec. 7, 1834, died March 1, 1852. MYRAH, born Jan. 22, 1837, married Daniel Rape. *See his name.* MELVINA, born Feb. 25, 1842, married Francis M. Rape. *See his name.* GEORGE W., born Sept. 7, 1844, enlisted in August, 1862, for three years in Co. —, 114th Ill. Inf. His father dying a few days later, he was released from military duty, as the only support of his mother. He died at home April 12, 1863. AUSTILLIA J., born Dec. 25, 1846, married Nov. 2, 1865 to William H. Park, who was born Oct. 11, 1839, in Hampshire county, Va. They have two children, *Alice J.* and *Alvin L.*, and reside at Rienzi, near New City, Sangamon county, Illinois. JOHN S., born April 22, 1853, and SAMUEL N., born Dec. 16, 1857, reside with their mother. Samuel D. Snodgrass died Aug. 31, 1862, and his widow, Nancy W., resides one mile east of New City, Sangamon county, Ill. JAMES A., born April 25, 1814, in Tennessee, married in Sangamon county to Telitha Pippin. She died and he was married Aug. 16, 1837, to Mary A. Wise. They had six children. REBECCA J., born April 15, 1839, married Thomas J. Hardin and the second time married Daniel Rape. *See his name.* MELISSA, married Jackson Brent or Bunce, and died in one year after. JOHN W., ANDREW J., and NANCY all died under fourteen years. ZACHARY T., born Aug. 11, 1844, married Sarah E. Rape. They have two living children, *Ada A.* and *Lola B.*, and live four miles southwest of Edinburg, Christian county, Ill. James A. Snodgrass died Feb. 18, 1849, and his widow died March 8, 1872, he in Sangamon and she in Christian county, Ill. ELIZABETH, born Feb. 1, 1819, in Madison county, Ill., married in Sangamon county to John Rape. *See his name.* JOHN, born in Sangamon county in 1821, married Polly Bird, has five children, and lives near Ashley, Washington county, Ill. GEORGE was twice married, and died, leaving a widow and a son, GEORGE, near Stonington, Christian county, Ill. NANCY, married John Morris, has five children, and lives in Missouri. Mrs. Mary Snodgrass died Aug. 31, 1835, in Sangamon county, and James Snodgrass, Jun., married Mrs. Nancy Wilkison, whose maiden name was Moon. They had two children. WILLIAM H. Snodgrass, born Nov. 27, 1842, in Sangamon county, married Jan. 2, 1862, to Sarah S. Hall. They have five living children, IDA J, DORA B., REUBEN E., MARY E. and NANCY B., and live near New City, Sangamon county, Ill. LEVINA J., born Oct. 18, 1838, married Oct. 17, 1856, to James L. McKee, who was born Nov. 13, 1831, in Frederick county, Va. They have six living children, NANNIE A., JAMES WILLIAM, CHARLES L., VIRGINIA A., NOAH MATHENY, and CLARKE M., and live near New City, Sangamon county, Ill. James Snodgrass, Jun., died Jan. 27, 1864, and his widow lives—May, 1874—with her son, William H. James Snodgrass, Jun., was captain of a company from Sangamon county in the Blackhawk war.

FANNY, born in Cocke county, in Tennessee, married in Sangamon county to Henry Crull. They had seven children, four of whom are living. NANCY, born Aug. 17, 1835, in Sangamon county, married Oct. 18, 1858, to Philemon H. Plummer, who was born Aug. 5, 1834, in Richland county, Ohio. They have five children FANNY E., JAMES P., LAURA D., SAMUEL N. and OLIVE W., and reside—1874—at Breckenridge, Sangamon county, Illinois. CATHARINE married Mr. Poor; MARY married Mr. Martin; Mr. and Mrs. Crull are both dead.

ELIZA, born in Tennessee, married Peter Rape. See his name. They died without children.

POLLY, born March 29, 1813, in Tennessee, married Henry Rape. See his name.

JANE born June 13, 1815, in Tennessee, married in Sangamon county to Henry Funderburk. See his name.

ROBERT, born in 1808, in Tennessee, married in Sangamon county to Elza Martin. They had six children, ISAAC, born in Sangamon county, married Sarah C. Ward. They reside in Springfield. JAMES and DALLAS, died in the army. Mrs. Eliza Snodgrass died, and Robert Snodgrass married Sept. 15, 1854, to Mrs. Mary Ward, whose maiden name was Shivers. Robert Snodgrass died February, 1856, and his widow married Lemuel Hall. See Ward.

James Snodgrass, Sen., died Feb. 11, 1836, and his widow died July 7, 1854, both in Cotton Hill township, Sangamon county, Ill.

SNODGRASS, JOSEPH, brother to James, Sen., with whom he came to Sangamon county, in 1820. He was a wheelwright on Horse creek for about fifteen years, and moved to the vicinity of Bloomington.

SOUTHWICK, JESSE, was born about 1762 near Lebanon, Conn. Nancy Moore was born Jan. 17, 1770, in Connecticut, also. They were married and moved to Oneida county, New York, where they had four children, all died of the disease called cold plague. They then moved to Junius, Seneca county, in the same State, where they had seven children. The family embarked at Olean Point, on the Allegheny river, in a family boat, and arrived at Shawneetown, Illinois, in December, 1819. He was in company with James Stewart, and they moved in wagons from Shawneetown to a village called Milton, near Alton, where they halted until March, 1820, and then moved to Sugar creek and settled in what is now Woodside township, six and a half miles southeast of Springfield. Sarah Pierce, a niece of Mr. Southwick, came with them, also Joseph Inslee. The two latter were married in Sangamon county. Of the seven children of Mr. Southwick—

ORPHA, married in New York to Abram Pease. See his name. They came to Sangamon county in 1820 with her father. They both died in Sangamon county, leaving three sons. Brigham is married and lives in Ball township.

ELECTA, born and married in New York to Marquis Martin, and died there, leaving one child.

EUNICE, married in 1819 in New York to Patrick Lynch, and came to Sangamon county with her father. Mrs. Lynch died in Sangamon county October, 1820, leaving one child, JESSE LYNCH, who is a practicing lawyer at Chenoa, Ill. P. Lynch married again, moved to Naples, Ill., and died there.

ADALINE, born July 29, 1803, mar-tied in New York, August 1819, to Fortunatus Bailey, came to Sangamon county with her father, had three children, moved to Wisconsin, where both parents died.

LUCINDA, born 1805 in New York, married in Sangamon county late in 1823, to William Hawes, who was born Sept. 23, 1801. She died without children. Mr. Hawes married again, and lives at Magnolia, Putnam county, Ill.

WILLIAM, born Feb. 9, 1807 at Junius, New York, married September, 1831, in Sangamon county, to Louvicy Proctor, who was born Nov. 23, 1811, at Charleston, Clarke county, Ind. They had seven children in Sangamon county. NANCY E., born may 1, 1833, married Feb. 7, 1851, to Jerome Duncan. They have three children, MARY, WILLIAM D. and CHARLES, and live in Taylorville, Ill. EUNICE, born Aug. 19, 1835, married July 4, 1855, to Craven O. Fox, who was born Aug. 29, 1825, in Loudon county, Va. He died Jan. 20, 1873, leaving a widow and four children, T. C. BOND, MARY O., MATTIE V. and LUETTA, live in Springfield, Ill. DAVID, born July 23, 1839, enlisted in 1861 for three years in Co. A, 3d Ill. Cav., served full term, and was honorably discharged in 1864. In 1866 he went to Montana, and from there in the fall of 1870, to Cerbat, the county seat of Mohave county, Arizona, where he now lives—1874. JAMES W. born April 20, 1842, enlisted for three years, Aug. 1862, in Co. E, 114th Ill. Inf., served full term and was honorably discharged in 1865. In 1867, he became a clerk in the quartermaster's department, was at Fort Harker, while it was being built. He was employed in connection with the building of the Central Pacific Railroad, until it was opened. He is now—Feb. 1874—at Amarilla, New Mexico. JOHN H., born Feb. 14, 1844, left home Dec. 31, 1861, and enlisted at Camp Hall, Ky., in Co. —, 7th Ill. Inf.; was at the siege and capture of Fort Donelson, was in hospital at Pittsburg Landing, during the battle, and was discharged on account of physical disability after four months service. He is now of the law firm of Stevens & Southwick, at Onawa City, Monona county, Iowa. PHILIP S., born Feb. 22, 1847, lives with his father. LAURA A., born July 28, 1851, married March, 1873 to Henry A. Stevens, and

—85

have one child. Mr. Stevens is of the law firm of Stevens & Southwick, Onawa City, Iowa. William Southwick and wife reside on the farm where they settled in 1820. It is six and a half miles southeast of Springfield, Ill.

JAMES L., born Jan. 16, 1814, in New York, married in Sangamon county, July 29, 1832, to Louvicy Trumbo, who was born April, 29, 1815. They had 13 children; four died young. JESSE, born May 12, 1833, married Theodosia Raney, have six children, and live near Oceola, Missouri. WILLIAM H, born Sept. 4, 1834, married Sarah J. Brunk, and live near Cotton Hill, Ill. HARNESS, born Nov. 3, 1837 has been for several years a member of the Sangamon county board of supervisors. He lives in Woodside township, seven miles south of Springfield. CAROLINE S., married H. Payne, have four children, and resides near Connersville, Missouri. ADAM, enlisted in the 1st Ill. Cav., and died at Rolla, Missouri, May 1, 1862. AMANDA, married William Butler, and lives in Macoupin county, Barr's Store postoffice. MARTHA lives with her mother. ANDREW, married Ann M. Brunk. They have one child, JOHN, and live near Cotton Hill postoffice, Illinois. OLIVE M., lives with her mother. James L. Southwick died Jan. 26, 1868, and his widow resides seven miles south of Springfield, Ill.

PAULINA, married Mr. Fields, had two children, and died in Carlinville, Illinois.

Jesse Southwick died Sept. 25, 1826, and his widow died in 1845, he in Sangamon, and she in Putnam county, at the house of her daughter, Mrs. Hawes.

SOWELL, STEPHEN, was born February, 1785, on the river Roanoke, Charlotte county, Virginia. Jane Hannah was born Sept. 12, 1795, in that county. They were there married and had three children, and moved to Rutherford county, Tennessee, about 1817, where three children were born, and moved to Sangamon county, Illinois, arriving April, 1828, in what is now Chatham township, thence to Cooper township, and from there to Loami township in 1830, where three children were born. Of all their children—

MARTHA, born Jan. 22, 1812, in Virginia, married in Sangamon county to

William Eustace, have three children, and live in Jefferson county, Wisconsin.

THOMAS, born July 15, 1814, in Charlotte county, Virginia, married in Sangamon county, Nov. 10, 1836, to Theresa Barger. They had two children, MARTHA A. married William T. Graham, had three children, and Mr. G. died in April, 1871. The widow and children live near Chatham, Illinois. JOHN H. enlisted in Colorado in a cavalry regiment. He was wounded, after two years service, by six shots in his body, from rebel bushwhackers in Missouri, and was honorably discharged on account of physical disability in the spring of 1865. He was married in Sangamon county, August 26, 1866, to Maggie Post. They have one child, and live in Osage county, Kansas. Mrs. Theresa Sowell died Dec. 4, 1846, and Thomas Sowell was married April 20, 1848, to Jane E. Lansden, who was born April 21, 1817, in Wilson county, Tennessee. They have one child, THOMAS A., and reside in Loami, Sangamon county, Illinois.

JANE, born in Virginia, married Hollister Burr, and lives in Cherokee county, Kansas.

MELINDA, born in Tennessee, married in Sangamon county to Schuyler Goodell, have eight children, and live in Miami county, Kansas.

MACCA M., born Sept. 16, 1822, in Tennessee, married July 28, 1844, in Sangamon county to Adna P. Colburn. See his name.

SALLY, born April 18, 1824, in Tennessee, married in Sangamon county to Willis Goodell, had one child, and Mr. Goodell died. The widow married William R. Goodell. They have seven children, and live in Harrison county, Missouri.

NANCY, born in Sangamon county, married James E. McElvain. See his name.

ANGELINE A., born in Sangamon county, married William A. McElvain. See his name.

WILLIAM H., born in Sangamon county, married Maria N. Campbell. They have five children, and live at Macon Station, Macon county, Illinois. W. H. Sowell enlisted in 1861 for three years in Co. B, 30th Ill. Inf., served full term, and was honorably discharged in 1864.

Stephen Sowell died June 11, 1863, and his widow resides with her son, Thomas, in Loami, Illinois—1874.

SPATH, GEORGE, was born April 8, 1816, in Baden, Germany. He came to America and arrived at Alton, Illinois, in April, 1837, and in May, 1838, came to Springfield. He had learned the trade of cabinet maker in his native country and when he came to Springfield soon found employment at his trade. He was married in Springfield Nov. 3, 1843, to Mary Mischler, a native of Germany, also, and sister of Philip Mischler. They had eight children in Springfield.

GEORGE, born July 25, 1844, died March 1, 1873.

MARGARET, born Feb. 14, 1847, married in Springfield, Feb. 10, 1868, to Charles Bouchert. They have one child, GEORGE, and reside in St. Charles, Missouri.

BARBARA, born Feb. 3, 1849, lives with her father.

ELIZABETH, born March 25, 1850, married to Adolph Daiken, and live in Springfield, Illinois.

JOHN, born Feb. 4, 1855; lives with his father.

ANNIE, born May 23, 1857, married Jan. 15, 1875, to John Auger, and live in St. Charles Missouri.

CATHARINE and JULIA live with their father.

Mrs. Mary Spath died Sept. 1, 1872, and George Spath married Mrs. Gertrude Meisenbach, whose maiden name was Wise. She was a native of Baden, Germany, also. They reside in Springfield, Illinois.

SPENCER, JOHN, was born about 1800 in Adair county, Ky. Cynthia Harvey was born in the same county, and they were there married and had three children. The family moved to Sangamon county, Ill., arriving August, 1836, in what is now Salisbury township, where two children were born. Of their five children.

CATHARINE, born Aug. 29, 1830, in Adair county, Ky., married in Sangamon county to Pierson Roll. See his name.

NANCY, born in Adair county, Ky., married in Sangamon county to Isaace Miller. They have six children, and live in Pike county, Missouri.

DIANA, born in Adair county, Ky., married in Sangamon county, to John Shanahan, have three children and live at Point of Rocks, Wyoming Territory.

MARY E., born in Sangamon county, married Eli Drone. They have four children, and live in Pike county, Ill.

JOHN W., born in Sangamon county, married Mary Clements, and live in the southeast corner of Macoupin county, Ill.

John Spencer died September, 1863, and Mrs. Cynthia Spencer died Nov. 26, 1869, both in Sangamon county, north of the river.

SPICER, LEMUEL, was born about 1770 in Kent county, Delaware, and was there married to Sarah Johnson, a native of the same county. They had one child there, and moved to Scott county, Kentucky, thence to Fayette county, in the same State, and from there to Clarke county, Indiana. In the spring of 1833 he moved to Sangamon county, Illinois, and settled in what is now Cotton Hill township. Of their only child—

UPSHEAR D., born Sept. 24, 1795, in Kent county, Delaware, married in Fayette county, Kentucky, April 27, 1816 to Nancy Clifton. They moved to Clarke county, Indiana, where they had seven children, and moved to Sangamon county, Illinois, arriving in the fall of 1833, in Cotton Hill township, where they had five children. Three of their children died young. Of the other nine, ELIAS S., born May 2, 1818, in Clarke county, Indiana, married in Sangamon county to Lucinda Kent. They both died; Mr. Spicer, Dec. 28, 1872, in Sangamon county, leaving three daughters in DeWitt county, and a son in Iowa. MINAS B., born July 12, 1820, in Clarke county, Indiana, married in Sangamon county to Mary Miller. They have four living children, and reside near Clinton, DeWitt county, Illinois. MARY P., born February 20, 1823, in Clarke county, Indiana, married in Sangamon county to Joseph Beam. *See his name.* THOMPSON C., born Dec. 1, 1825, in Clarke county, Indiana, married in Sangamon county Jan. 18, 1848, to Melvina Vigal. They had seven children, two of whom died under four years, of age. MARY J., born Nov. 2, 1850, married Oct. 3, 1869, to Aaron C. Colean, who was born March 4, 1848, in Jersey county, Illinois. They have one living child, *Etta Alice*, and live two miles west of New City, Sangamon county, Illinois. OLIVER A., ALICE H., EMMA L. and CHARLES R., live with their father. Mrs. Melvina Spicer died Dec. 9, 1873, and Thompson C. Spicer resides one and a half miles west of New City, Sangamon county, Ill. GEORGE W., born July 15, 1832, in Indiana, married in Sangamon county March 5, 1854, to Caroline E. Britton. They had four children, WILLIAM B., died aged ten years, BENJAMIN O., CHARLES F., and GEORGE W., Jun., live with their mother. George W. Spicer died Nov. 26, 1862, and his widow married August 8, 1866, to Nathan S. Plummer, who was born March 15, 1836, in Richland county, Ohio. Mr. and Mrs. Plummer have four children, IDA E., CARRIE A., OSCAR V. and MARGARET A., and live near New City, Sangamon county, Illinois. SARAH and SOPHIA, twins, born August 18, 1834, the former died in infancy and the latter in her ninth year. JOHN, born May 21, 1838, in Sangamon county, married Mary E. Porterfield, and for his second wife married, March 4, 1871, Mrs. Mary J. Dee, whose maiden name was Waker. Her first husband, John C. Dee, was a member of the 44th Ohio Inf., and was killed at the battle of Fort Donelson, Feb. 14, 1862. Mr. and Mrs. Spicer live near Cotton Hill P. O., Sangamon county, Illinois. ROSEANN, born Oct. 13, 1840, died June 26, 1856. EMILY, born August 13, 1843, in Sangamon county, married Oct. 27, 1864, to David Marshall, and have one child, MARY FRANCES. They live in Cotton Hill township. Upshear D. Spicer died Feb. 15, 1855, and his widow married Adam Safley. *See his name.*

Mrs. Sarah Spicer died Nov. 6, 1837, and Lemuel Spicer married a second time. He died March 31, 1842, both in Sangamon county, Illinois.

SPRINGER, Rev. FRANCIS, D. D., was born, March 19, 1810, at Roxburry, Franklin county, Pa. When a young man, he learned the business of sign and ornamental painting. He received his literary education in Pennsylvania College, and his theological studies were pursued at the Theological Seminary of the Lutheran church, both located at Gettysburg, Pa. He also studied under two distinguished ministers, one at Otsego, and the other at Schohaire, N. Y. He paid his expenses by occasionally working at his trade, and teaching school. He was licensed to preach by the Evangelical Lutheran Synod of Maryland, Oct. 18, 1836, and was ordained by the same body Oct. 17, 1837. He was married April 11, 1837, to Mary Kriegh, at Clear Springs, Washington county, Md. She was born Feb. 28, 1815, in that county. He taught school and preached in that vicinity from October, 1836, for about two and a half years. They had one child in Maryland, and moved to Springfield, Illinois, arriving May, 1839, where four children were born. In 1847 he moved to Hillsboro, Ill., where they had two children, and in 1855 moved back to Springfield, where they had one child. Of their children—

MARY E., born March 25, 1838, in Maryland, lives with her parents.

PHIL. M., born July 15, 1840, in Springfield, is unmarried, and is of the firm of Springer Bros., stock breeders, in the southeast corner of Clear Lake township, Sangamon county. Their address is Springfield. Phil. M. Springer is Treasurer and Assistant Secretary of the American Berkshire Association. Office in Springfield, Ill.

IDA M., born March 11, 1842, in Springfield, married Henry L. Sanford. They have three children, MARY S., ANNIE E. and FRANCIS S., and live near Elkhart, Logan county, Ill.

JOHN G., was born March 13, 1844, in Springfield. He enlisted Sept. 20, 1861, for three years in Co. B, 10th Ill. Cav., was appointed sergeant major and commissioned second lieutenant of Co. I, March, 13, 1862, and commissioned first lieutenant May 10, 1864, and commissioned quartermaster of the regiment Dec. 31, 1864. At the expiration of his first term, he re-enlisted as a veteran, was with the regiment at San Antonio, Texas, when it was discharged, in November, 1865, and received his final discharge at Springfield in February, 1866. He was in the third district internal revenue department of Arkansas, as clerk and assistant assessor from December, 1866, to June, 1873, and was married at Fort Smith, Arkansas, September 29, 1868, to Frances A. Stratton. They have three children, FRANCIS S., JOHN P. and MIRIAM ESTELLA, and reside at Fayetteville, Arkansas. He is still in the government employ.

CHARLES W., born Oct. 5, 1846, in Springfield, enlisted May 11, 1864, in Co. A, 133d Ill. Inf. for one hundred days. He served until Sept. 24, 1864, and was honorably discharged. Is unmarried and is a practicing lawyer at Hillsborough, Ill.

FRANCIS K., born Dec. 21, 1848, at Hillsboro, Illinois, married in Sangamon county, Feb. 20, 1872, to Eveline II. Nesbitt. They have two children, HENRY and SAMUEL FRANCIS and live in the southeast corner of Clear Lake township, Sangamon county, Ill. Is of the firm of Springer Bros.

LAURA L., born Nov. 20, 1850, in Hillsboro, died Oct. 25, 1860, at Springfield, Illinois.

ANNIE G., born Aug. 1, 1858, in Springfield, lives with her parents.

Rev. Francis Springer commenced teaching soon after his arrival in Springfield, and continued to teach and preach until 1847, when he moved to Hillsboro, Ill., as President of Hillsboro, College. That institution was moved to Springfield in 1852, as Illinois State University. These were both under the direction and patronage of the Lutheran church. He resigned in 1855. He was afterwards school commissioner of Sangamon county, and was superintendent of schools for the city of Springfield, which position he resigned, and became chaplain of the 10th Ill. Cav., soon after the beginning of the rebellion in 1861. A short time after the battle of Prairie Grove, Ark.—Dec. 7, 1862—he united with Dr. James Johnson in raising a loyal regiment in Arkansas, of which he became chaplain. It was the 1st Ark. Inf. He was appointed in 1863 post chaplain at Fort Smith, which he held until 1867, when he resigned, and returned to his family, at Springfield. In 1870 he moved to Irving, Montgomery county, Ill., and continued preaching until the fall of 1873, when he was elected superintendent of schools for Montgomery county, with his office at Hillsboro, Ill. He continues to preach, as opportunity offers, and fully believes that the only reforming influence in the world is Christianity. Rev. Francis Springer is a man of lively sympathy with the rest of mankind, without regard to race, color, nationality or religion. He has large faith in the perfectability of the human race by means of the labors and experiences of the life that now is, and the hereafter. His orthodoxy, as a religious man, does not descend to the minute particulars of a creed, but confides mainly in the cardinal fact of Christianity, that the only true ennobling of the race must be wrought out under the recognized leadership of the word's Redeemer "the Christ of God."

The degree of Doctor of Divinity was conferred on Rev. Francis Springer in 1869 by Wittenburg College, Springfield, Ohio.

ST. CLAIR, LEVI H., was born May 6, 1800, in New York, near Lake Champlain, and there married to Lorinda Spaulding, a native of the same State. They had four children in New York, and moved to the vicinity of Cleveland, Ohio, where one child was born, thence to Sangamon county, Illinois, arriving June, 1833, in what is now Rochester township, where two children were born. Of their seven children—

H. CICERO, born July 18, 1825, in Essex county, New York, was married in Sangamon county, Illinois, Nov. 6, 1851, to Eliza E. Neal. Mrs. St. Clair died near Rochester, Illinois, Sept. 27, 1854, leaving one child, MINNIE, who was born in Mt. Pulaski, Illinois, and resides with her grand-mother, Neal. H. C. St. Clair was married Oct. 7, 1858, to Katie Ring at Lancaster, Ohio. He enlisted at Mt. Pulaski in 1862 in Co. G, 35th Ill. Inf., for three years, was commissioned as second lieutenant, and after serving one year was transferred to the quartermaster's department, in which he served the remainder of the three years. Mr. St. Clair lived in Logan and Macon counties until 1871, when he moved to Belle Plain, Sumner county, Kansas, where he was elected county commissioner in 1873, and state senator in 1874. H. C. St. Clair and family reside at Belle Plain, Kansas.

HELEN, born Sept. 24, 1826, in Essex county, New York, was married in Sangamon county, Illinois, Feb. 21, 1850, to George L. Ormsby. He died in August, 1868, leaving a widow and one child, ALBERT, in Decatur, Illinois.

MARION J., born Sept. 18, 1828, in Essex county, New York, was married in Sangamon county, Illinois, Oct. 19, 1852, to S. D. Fisher, who was born March 7, 1822, in Charlotte, Chittenden county, Vermont, brought up in Essex county, New York, and came to Sangamon county in 1844. Mrs. Marion J. Fisher died Nov. 10 1867, and he married E. M. Benton. They reside at Atlanta, Illinois. S. D. Fisher was elected in 1872 for four years to represent the thirteenth district in the State Board of Equalization. He served four years, from 1870, as a member of the State Board of Agriculture, and was elected January, 1875, for two years as secretary of the same, with his office in Springfield, Illinois.

MARY, born Oct. 11, 1829, in Essex county, New York, was married in Sangamon county, Illinois, to Francis J. Taylor. *See his name.*

OSCAR L., born Jan. 31, 1832, in Cleveland, Ohio, was married in Sangamon county, Feb. 10, 1853, to Nancy E. Neal. O. L. St. Clair died Oct. 15, 1853, in Mt. Pulaski, leaving a widow and one child, OSCAR C., born May 6, 1854. They reside at the Neal family homestead, one mile west of Rochester. O. C. Neal is clerk in the State National Bank, Springfield, Illinois—1875.

MORTIMER, born Oct. 11, 1839, in Sangamon county, married Lizzie Kimball. She died suddenly July, 1869, near Rochester, leaving two children, MAGGIE L. and LEWIS S., who reside with their grand-mother, West, in Springfield, Illinois. Mortimer St. Clair resides at Belle Plain, Sumner county, Kansas.

AMELIA, born April 8, 1843, in Sangamon county, was married there to Calvin C. Johnson. *See his name.* They have two children, EMMA FAY and O——, and reside in Chicago.

Mrs. Lorinda St. Clair died Feb. 21, 1853, near Rochester. Mr. St. Clair was married in Springfield, Illinois, to Mrs. Eliza Rague. He died in April, 1866, near Rochester, Illinois, and his widow resides in Madison, Wisconsin.

STAFFORD. It has long since passed into history that a conspiracy, known as the Gun Powder Plot, was to have culminated in blowing up the English Parliament buildings, on the assembling of that body Nov. 5, 1605. The plot was frustrated by an anonymous letter, advising Lord Monteagle, a Roman Catholic member, to absent himself at that time. That letter led to an investigation on the evening of November 4th, when thirty-six barrels of powder was found in a mine under the Parliament houses. Guy Fawkes was arrested at the entrance, and boldly avowed it as his purpose to have fired the train at the time set. He, with seven of his confederates were tried, convicted and executed.

Another conspiracy, known as the Popish Plot, occurred nearly three quarters of a century later. Titus Oates, who claimed to be a Catholic, pretended to divulge a plot in 1678, on the part of the Jesuits, to murder the King and subvert the Protestant religion. Many prominent Catholics were arrested, tried and convicted of conspiracy, or being concerned in the plot. Titus Oates was afterwards convicted of perjury, and there were many reasons to believe that instead of revealing a plot he and his confederates were conspiring against those they accused. Among their victims was William Howard Stafford, an English statesman, who was born Nov. 30, 1612. As the successor of his uncle on his mother's side he became Baron Stafford, and in 1640 Viscount Stafford. On the oath of Titus Oates he was committed to the Tower of London, October 30, 1678. Witnesses on the trial testified that Lord Stafford had incited them to assassinate the King, and he was condemned and executed Dec. 29, 1680, on Tower Hill, London. The sympathy felt for Lord Stafford turned the tide against Oates, and there were no other executions. His brother, Edward Stafford, being also suspected, fled from England to America and settled in Rhode Island. The only representative of the family left in England was a younger brother, who inherited the property and titles of the family. The Duchess of Sutherland, who died in England but a short time ago was a descendant of that brother.

On his arrival in America. Edward Stafford abjured the Roman Catholic religion and embraced that of the Friends, or Quakers. He was married in Rhode Island to Margaret Green. They had three children. Rebecca and Edward died young. Joseph married Orpha Sweet. They had three sons, John Joseph and Stephen. The eldest and youngest died without children. Joseph married Nancy Green. Their eldest son, Joseph, was born April 25, 1759, in Coventry, Kent county, Rhode Island, and although his parents were Quakers he became a soldier in the American Revolution. He was under his relative, General Greene, from that State, who was also of a Quaker family, and of whom it is said that his mother, when she became satisfied that she could not change his determination to go in the army, said: "If thee must go, I do not want to hear of thee being shot in the back." After the Revolution, Joseph Stafford was married to Orpha Sweet, being the second couple bearing similar names. They had ten children, James, Job, Diadema, Caleb, Oliver, Jewett, Prudence, Christopher B., Moses and Joseph. Four of them came to Sangamon county, namely—

STAFFORD, CALEB, was born June 22, 1789, in Coventry, Kent county, Rhode Island, went with his father, Joseph Stafford, in 1804, to Essex county, New York, where he was married in 1810 to Rebecca Eggleston. He was a soldier in the war of 1812, and was in the battles of Plattsburg, Sept. 17, 1814, Bouquet river, and others in New York. Mr. and Mrs. Stafford had eleven living children in New York, and moved to Sangamon county, Illinois, in 1836, settling near Rochester. Of their children—

DIADEMA, born Dec. 25, 1812, in Essex county, N. Y., married there Dec. 25, 1833, to Gardner T. Bruce, born in 1806, in Keene, N. H., and came to Sangamon county, in 1842. They had three children, namely, GARDNER AUGUSTUS, of Watson, now Buffalo, Sangamon county, Ill., became second lieutenant of Co. L, 10th Ill. Cav., April 8, 1862; was promoted to 1st lieutenant Sept. 29, 1862, promoted to captain July 13, 1864, transferred to captain of Co. A, the same regiment in Jan. 1865, when it was consolidated with the 15th regiment. He was honorably mustered out Nov. 22, 1865, at San Antonia, Texas. G. Augustus Bruce was married to Susan Constant, daughter of Jacob D. Constant. *See his name.* Mr. and Mrs. Bruce have two children, ADELAIDE and WILLIAM, and live at Corinne, Box Elder county, Utah. CHAS. T., has been a soldier in the U. S. army since 1859, and is now—1876—with the army in San Antonio, Texas. HELEN, died at Mechanicsburg, Ill., aged eighteen years. Mrs. Diadema Bruce died at Mechanicsburg, Ill., and Gardner T. Bruce married Mrs. Eliza Lyon, whose maiden name was Correll. See Correll and Lyon families. Gardner T. Bruce and wife reside in Atchison, Kansas.

THOMAS D., born Nov. 14, 1814, in Essex county, New York, and married there to Polly Fisher. They came to Sangamon county in 1836, and had three children. ELIZA married George Flagg, at Rochester, and now lives at Galesburg, Ill. CECELIA married Neely Wood, and lives in Galesburg. NELLIE lives with her father. Mrs. Polly Stafford, died in 1872, and T. D. Stafford married Mrs. Dutcher. They live in Galesburg, Ill. He has been totally blind for several years.

ORSON N., born Sept. 11, 1816, in Willsboro, Essex county, N. Y. In 1829, he went to sea and led the life of a sailor until 1835, when he was disabled by a shipwreck, making him a cripple for life. In 1837 he was attached to a government surveying party, on the northern lakes, charged with the duty of selecting sites for light-houses. At Chicago—in his own words—not finding that terrible monopoly, the railroad, to bring him here in eight hours, for six or seven dollars, he had the privilege of paying twenty-five dollars in gold for a stage ticket, enjoyed the luxury of eight days' jolting, and arrived at Springfield, Nov. 29, 1837. He was married in Rochester, Ill., Aug. 29, 1841, to Eliza A. Sherman, a native of Addison, Vermont. She is a direct descendant of Roger Sherman, one of the signers of the Declaration of Independence. They had one child, EMMA E., born May 23, 1854, and died March 30, 1855. O. N. Stafford has been in different kinds of business. He has sold dry goods, built and remodeled eighteen houses in Springfield, has been connected with the Illinois *State Journal* at various times for several years, was elected a member of the city council of Springfield for 1854 and 1855. He considers Springfield his home, but spends the greater part of his time at St. Augustine, Florida, engaged in the cultivation of oranges, lemons and other tropical fruits.

AMANDA MALVINA, born in 1818, in Essex county, N. Y., married in Rochester, Ill., to Dr. Samuel D. Slater. They have five living children. ALBERT S., married Miss Lee, and is a physician and druggist at Wataga, Knox county, Ill. AMANDA M., married Frank M. VanPelt, and lives in Atlanta, Georgia. ANNA E., married Mr. H. H. Harsh, a banker of Creston, Union county, Iowa, and resides there. FRANK, married Carrie Dutcher, and lives in Galesburg, Ill. MINNIE married Dr. Herbert Judd, and lives in Galesburg. Dr. S. D. Slater resides in Galesburg, Ill.

AMOS, born in 1824, in Essex county, N. Y., came with his parents to Sangamon county, in 1836, and married Sarah Johnson. They had three children. ADA A. married and lives in Galesburg, Ill. EVA J. and Edward live at Maroa, Ill. Mrs. Stafford died Sept. 26, 1867, and Amos Stafford died Nov. 26, 1867, both in Decatur, Ill.

HIRAM P., born in Essex county, New York, married in Sangamon county to Mrs. Eunice Black, whose maiden name was Eggleston. They had five children. FRANCES, the third child, died young; LUCINDA, MOSES, WILLIAM and MINNIE live with their parents. H. P. Stafford lived in Decatur, Illinois, until the fall of 1876, when he moved to Carrollton, Missouri.

HENRY H., born July 16, 1829, in Essex county, New York, brought up in Sangamon county, was married Dec. 7, 1851, to Lauretta Ross. They had two children, and moved to Decatur Sept. 16, 1856, where they had one child. Of their children, ADELAIDE died Dec. 21, 1859, aged seven years and four months. ORLANDO C., born Jan. 11, 1856, in Sangamon county, is a steam engineer in an oil mill at Decatur, Illinois. LAURETTA A., born Nov. 8, 1859, lives with her grand-father, Ross. Mrs. Lauretta Stafford died Dec. 7, 1859, in Decatur and Henry H. Stafford was married Aug. 6, 1863, in Jamestown, now Riverton, Ill., to Lydia A. Wright. They had five children, CELESTIA M. and EFFIE G., the second and fourth, died young. MARY E., GRACIE H. and DAISY L. live with their parents. Henry H. Stafford is an engineer, and has been running stationary engines for twenty years. He resides in Decatur, Illinois.

LUCINDA M., born Sept. 10, 1826, in Essex county, New York, married in Sangamon county to John W. Priest. *See his name.* She died Sept. 10, 1851.

MARY E., born Sept. 11, 1832, in Essex county, New York, married in Sangamon county to James Ransdale, and died in Rochester, Illinois.

LOUISA, born in Essex county, New York, married in Sangamon county to James Matthew McCoy. *See his name.* He died and she married James Huston, and lives near Carrollton, Missouri.

RODNEY NELSON, born Oct. 2, 1834, in Essex county, New York, brought up in Sangamon county, and married in Rochester, Ill., April 2, 1857, to Sarah M. VanOrmann. They moved to Decatur, October, 1858, and had six children. HENRY O., was killed on a railroad Nov. 19, 1873, aged about fifteen years. AMOS A., died young. MARY L., WILLIAM N., REUBEN C. and ARTHUR C., the four latter live with their parents. When R. N. Stafford was about fifteen years of age he was run over by a wagon loaded with railroad ties, by which he came near losing his life. He enlisted Aug. 6, 1862, in Co. A, 116th Ill. Inf. He was wounded three times at the siege of Vicksburg, was with Sherman on his "march to the sea," and served until the close of the rebellion, when he was honorably discharged with the regiment, June 7, 1865, at Washington, D. C. Soon after his discharge he came near losing his life by the explosion of a boiler. He became a Christian in January, 1876. R. N. Stafford and family reside in Decatur, Ill.

Mrs. Rebecca Stafford died June 21, 1843, and Caleb Stafford died May 7, 1855, both at Rochester, Sangamon county, Illinois.

STAFFORD, OLIVER, was born in Coventry, Kent county, Rhode Island. He was married in Addison county, Vermont, to Polly Sattley, and came to Rochester, Sangamon county, in 1825. They had six children, namely—

DANIEL SATTLEY, born in Addison county, Vermont, married in Sangamon county to Mattie Parker. They had one child, CLARA A., born April 2, 1836, in Rochester, Illinois, married Jan. 2, 1856, to John H. Brown. *See his name.* Mr. Brown died April 11, 1866, and Mrs. Brown was married May 5, 1869, to Dr. Justus Townsend. Dr. Townsend and wife reside in Springfield, Illinois, where he is engaged in the practice of his profession. Mrs. Mattie Stafford died in 1838. D. S. Stafford married for his fourth wife Eliza Patterson. They had two living children, EDWARD R. is in the United States Army; MATTIE married a Mr. Black, and lives in Decatur, Illinois. D. S. Stafford died Feb. 4, 1866, in Decatur, and his widow resides there.

PRUDENCE A., born May, 1812, in Addison county, Vermont, married in Sangamon county, Ill., to Jabez Capps. *See his name.*

JANE, born in Vermont, married in Sangamon county to Dr. Franklin Dickinson, and had several children. Their son John married Elizabeth Young, who was born in Anderson county, Ky. They have three children, and live near Rochester, Ill. Dr. Dickenson and his wife both died in Rochester.

WILLIAM P., born near Vincennes, Indiana, brought up in Sangamon county, married in Whiteside county to Susan Coffman, and died there, leaving a widow and children.

OLIVER C., born July 1, 1826, in Rochester, Sangamon county, Ill., married in 1847 to Kitty A. Baker. They have three living children, CHARES, NETTIE and MARY, and live in Mt. Pulaski, Logan county, Ill.

JOSEPH, born in Rochester, Illinois, married Mitylene Ann G. Bowling. They have two children, BURT and FRANK, and live in Galesburg, Illinois.

Oliver Stafford, Sen., died, and Mrs. Polly Stafford died July 4, 1863, both near Rochester, Sangamon county, Illinois.

STAFFORD, JEWETT, was born Jan. 13, 1795, at Coventry, Kent county, R. I., was taken by his parents in 1804, to Essex county, N. Y. In 1812 he went as a soldier from that county in the war with England, was in the battle of Plattsburg, Boquet river, near Willsboro, his home. Jewett Stafford was married in 1818 to Harriet Eggleston, in Essex county, New York. She was born there March 4, 1802. They had two living children in that county, and moved to Sangamon county, Illinois, arriving July, 1825, where Rochester now stands, and had one living child in Sangamon county. Of their three children—

CHARLES, born Oct. 12, 1820, in Essex county, New York, married in Sangamon county, March 21, 1847, to Julia A. Stafford. They had one child, JULIA A., born Dec. 6, 1847. She married Mitchell Lickerson. They have two children, and live near Rochester, Illinois. Mrs. Julia A. Stafford died Dec. 17, 1847, and Charles Stafford was married Sept. 27, 1848, to Mrs. Sarah A. Stafford, widow of John Stafford. Her maiden name was Wallace. She was born Dec. 24, 1822, in Culpepper county, Virginia. They had four children, MARY A., born Feb. 12, 1854, married George W. Boyce, has one child, and lives near Clarksville, Sangamon county, Illinois. ALBERT R., born Sept. 17, 1856, lives with his parents. IDA L., born Jan. 4, 1860, died May 26, 1874. WILLIAM W., born April 6, 1868, lives with his parents at Clarksville, Sangamon county, Illinois.

HORACE, born June 23, 1822, in Essex county, New York, raised in Sangamon county, married in Taylorville, Illinois, Dec. 9, 1850, to Mary A. Gessner, who was born Nov. 1, 1834, in Fredericktown, Maryland. They had three children, CHARLES J., the second one, died in infancy. MARIA L., born Feb. 27, 1852, and EDMUND W., born Oct. 7, 1855, live with their parents. Horace Stafford and family reside at Clarksville, Sangamon county, Illinois. He is postmaster there, of Berry post office.

AMANDA, born May 9, 1826, in Sangamon county, died April 11, 1837.

Mrs. Harriet Stafford died May 3, 1835, in Sangamon county, and Jewett Stafford married Mrs. Elizabeth Steele, whose maiden name was Robison. She had one child.

HARRIET A., born June 28, 1838, and married Nov. 10, 1860, to William E. Hill, who was born Nov. 9, 1839, in Macon county, Illinois. They had four living children, LAURA E., CARRIE F. and HARRY W. Mrs. Hill died in 1876, and William E. Hill and his children live at Clarksville, Sangamon county, Illinois.

Mrs. Elizabeth Stafford died March, 1842, and Jewett Stafford was married November, 1845, to Mrs. Prudence Stafford, whose maiden name was Putnam. Jewett Stafford died August 12, 1862, and his widow lives one mile southeast of Rochester, Sangamon county, Illinois.

STAFFORD, CHRISTOPHER B., was born July 22, 1797, at Coventry, Kent county, Rhode Island. He was married in Essex county, New York, in 1820 to Laura Eggleston, who died in one year, and he married her sister, Sophronia Eggleston, and moved to Sangamon county, Illinois, arriving July 25, 1824, at Rochester, where they had five children, two of whom died young. Of the other three—

MOSES, born in Sangamon county, Illinois, is married, has children, and resides at Decatur, Illinois.

OSCAR C., born near Rochester, Sangamon county, is married has children, and lives in Minneapolis, Minnesota.

PRUDENCE ANN, born near Rochester, Sangamon county, and now lives at 925 east Carpenter street, Springfield, Ill.

Mrs. Sophronia Stafford died and he was twice married after that. His two last wives were sisters, by the name of Shelton. Christopher B. Stafford was an ordained preacher in the Baptist church more than forty years. Thirty years of that time he was a Justice of the Peace, or rather a peace maker, as it is said of him that he used his office to settle difficulties without law, although by that way of doing business he generally deprived himself of fees. He died March 17, 1870, near Rochester, Illinois, and his widow resides in Iowa.

STAFFORD, JOB, brother to Caleb, Oliver, Jewett, Christopher B., etc., never came to Sangamon county; but his son,

HENRY C., born in 1804 in Essex county, New York, came with his uncles to Sangamon county, arriving July, 1825, at Rochester. He was married Dec. 27, 1827, to Clara Ann Gregory. See Gregory family. They had one child, ALFRED, born Jan. 31, 1829, in Sangamon county, and married April 27, 1856, to Lucy A. Foss, who was born Oct. 7, 1839, in Medina county, Ohio. They have one living child, CHARLES W., and reside near Rochester. Henry C. Stafford died Feb. 2, 1834, in Sangamon county, and his widow married David Crouch. See his name.

STAFFORD, WILLIAM, was born 1799 at Coventry, Kent county,

Rhode Island. He was a son of John Stafford, consequently a cousin to Caleb, Oliver, Jewett, and Christopher B. William Stafford was married in Essex county, New York, to Prudence Putnam, who was born March 19 1801, at Lewis, in Essex county. She was a lineal descendant of Israel Putnam. William Stafford and wife had two children in New York, moved to Ohio, and three years later to Sangamon county, Illinois, arriving Jan. 1, 1834, at Rochester. Of their children—

JOHN W., born in Essex county, New York, brought up in Sangamon county, and died March 21, 1870, at Havana, Mason county, Illinois.

JULIA A., born in Essex county, New York, married in Sangamon county to Charles Stafford. *See his name.*

William Stafford died in 1840, and his widow married Jewett Stafford. *See his name.* Mrs. Prudence Stafford now—September, 1876—resides near Rochester, Sangamon county, Illinois.

STALEY, DANIEL, was born Feb. 11, 1799, in Jefferson county, Va. His father moved to Cabell county, West Virginia, when he was a boy. He was married there in February, 1821, to Rebecca Bowen, who was born Jan. 9, 1802, in Guilford county, North Carolina. She was sister to Zaza Bowen. They had two children in Virginia, and the family moved to Sangamon county, arriving in the fall of 1826, in what is now Loami township, where seven children were born. Of their nine children—

SUSANNAH, born Aug. 12, 1822, in Virginia, married in Sangamon county to Levi Campbell. *See his name.* He died and she married William B. McCray, and lives near Loami, Ill.

ELIZABETH, born in Virginia, married in Sangamon county to George Owens, and she died Sept. 29, 1844.

MINERVA J., born in Sangamon county, married George Owens. They have seven living children, and live in Macoupin county, near Scottville, Ill.

BARBARA F., married William Russell, and lives in Newton county, Missouri.

REBECCA, married James F. Ward. They had eight children, and Mrs. Ward died. The family live near Trenton, Grundy county, Missouri.

STEPHEN, born March 2, 1835 in Sangamon county, married March 15, 1855, to Isabel Jacobs. They have six children, MARY E., SARAH A., LIZZIE M., SUSAN, STEPHEN D., and DANIEL, and live two and a half miles west of Loami, Sangamon county, Ill.

MARY C., born Jan. 4, 1838, married Williamson M. Nipper. *See his name.* She had one child, NANCY M. F., and died March 6, 1857.

DANIEL, born Feb. 10, 1841, in Sangamon county, married March 7, 1861, to Elsa J. Hudson. They had five children. ALICE D., the third child, died young. The other four, ADA L., ARNO V., WILLIAM Y. and JOE D., twins, live with their parents on the farm where his father settled in 1826. It is two miles west of Loami, Sangamon county, Ill.

SARAH M., died aged four years.

Mrs. Rebecca Staley died Nov. 24, 1847, and Mr. Staley married Mrs. Hepsey Nipper, whose maiden name was Gibson. She died March 8, 1873. Mrs. S. resides two and a half miles west of Loami, Sangamon county, Ill.

STANLEY, THOMAS, was born March 23, 1790, in Virginia, and was taken by his parents to Ohio. Elizabeth Centre was born June 22, 1790, in New York. She was married there to Andrew Campbell. He was a soldier in the war of 1812, and was killed at the battle of Fort Meigs, leaving a widow and two children. Thomas Stanley was a soldier in the war of 1812 also, and after the war was married to Mrs. Elizabeth Campbell. They had four living children in Ohio and moved to Sangamon county, Ill., arriving in the fall of 1829. Of their children—

ABRAHAM Campbell, born in 1811 in Ohio, came in 1829 to Sangamon county and married Phœbe Shepherd. He is a traveling preacher in the M. E. Church. They have four living children. JOHN W. is a physician. SOPHRONIA, MELISSA and WILLIAM are all four married and live in Illinois. Rev. Abraham Campbell lives now—1876—at St. Elmo, Fayette county, Ill.

SARAH Campbell, born Sept. 14, 1813, near Columbus, Ohio, and came in 1829 to Sangamon county, married John D. Swallow. They had three children. DANIEL E., born Jan. 11, 1844, in

Menard county, married Cornelia Day. They have three children, EFFIE M., MAMIE K. and ELSIE M. D. E. Swallow is a printer and lives in St. Louis, Missouri. SAMUEL M., born Jan. 27, 1846, in Mason county, married Mary K. Allen. They have two children, WILLIAM A., and JULIA K. S. M. Swallow is a printer and lives in Mexico, Missouri. HESTER, born Sept. 17, 1849, is unmarried and lives in Springfield. Mrs. Sarah Swallow lives in the latter city.

Of Thomas Stanley's children—

LEONORA, born in Ohio, was married in Sangamon county, to George Neal. They had four living children, and Mrs. Neal died. George Neal married again and lives west of Springfield, Illinois.

DAVID, died aged fourteen years.

CURRENCY, born in Ohio, was married in Sangamon county to Joseph VanNatten. *See his name.*

AQUILLA H., born in Sangamon county, Ill., enlisted in 1862 for three years in the 100th Ill. Inf., served about six months, and was discharged on account of physical disability. He married Elizabeth Dooley. They have five children, MARGARET, MATILDA, CHARLES, FRANK, and CORNELIA. Aquilla Stanley and wife live northeast of Lincoln, Ill.

Thomas Stanley died in 1837 in Sangamon county, and his widow lives with her daughter, Mrs. Joseph VanNatten, north of Springfield, Ill.

STARR, ADAM, was born about 1777, in Culpepper county, Va., and went with his parents to Bourbon county, Ky., when he was a young man. He was married in Clarke county to Mary Carson, a native of Baltimore, Md. They had eight children in Clarke county, Ky., and moved to Sangamon county, Ill., arriving in the fall of 1828 at Buffalo Hart Grove. Of their children—

HIRAM, born in Kentucky, married in Sangamon county to Nancy Robinson, had seven or eight children, moved to Pike county about 1858, and the parents died. Their children live near Rockport, Pike county, Ill.

DIANA, born in Kentucky, was married in Sangamon county, Ill., to Riley Barber. They had six children, and moved to Kansas in 1856. The parents and three of the children died. One son, HENRY, was killed in Arkansas by guerrillas during the rebellion. DEMETRIUS married Mary Griffith, and lives near Farlinville, Kansas. AMANDA married James Bastion, and lives in Farlinville, Linn county, Kansas.

BARTON, born in Kentucky, was married in Sangamon county in 1835 to Rebecca Patterson. They had four children. Mrs. Starr died near Mt. Pulaski, and he died at Little Rock Arkansas.

SHELBY, born October, 1813, in Kentucky, was married in Sangamon county, Ill., in 1844, to Nancy Groves. They had five children, MARY, ALBERT, JOSIAH, LEANDER and SHELBY, Jun., who live with their mother in Vermillion county, Ill. Shelby Starr died Aug. 8, 1855, in Sangamon county.

MINERVA, born Jan. 9, 1815, in Clarke county, Ky., married in Sangamon county to James T. Robinson. *See his name.*

WILLIAM, born 1817, in Kentucky, married in Sangamon county to Mrs. Nancy McDaniel, whose maiden name was Smith. They had two children, and he was drowned in 1860 in Sangamon river, near the crossing of the G., C. & S. R. R. The family live at Riverton, Ill.

AMANDA, born May 26, 1820, in Kentucky, married Sept. 26, 1840, to Benjamin Bell. *See his name.*

MARY ANN, born Oct. 25, 1822, in Kentucky, married in Sangamon county March, 1842 to William A. Constant. *See his name.* He died, and she married Casper Byerline, and lives near Buffalo Hart, Sangamon county, Ill.

Adam Starr died August 15, 1839, and his widow died in 1852, both at Buffalo Hart grove, Sangamon county, Ill.

STARR, ANDREW, was born Jan. 27, 1795, in Bourbon county, Ky. He was a brother to Adam Starr, and was married in Kentucky, Dec. 27, 1821, to Mary Neal. They had two children in Kentucky, and the family moved to Sangamon county, Illinois, arriving in the fall of 1830, in what is now Chatham township, where three children were born. Of their five children—

WILLIAM M., born Jan. 17, 1823, in Kentucky, married in Sangamon county to Amanda A. Withrow. They have two children. MARY A., married Oct. 9, 1865, to Edward W. Lucas. See *his name, in connection with the Colburn family.* ADDISON B., lives with his parents. William M. Starr and his wife reside at Loami, Sangamon county, Ill.

BARBARA ANN, born May 19, 1825, in Kentucky, married William V. Greenwood. *See his name.*

JOHN ALFRED, born March 22, 1831, in Sangamon county, was married Sept. 20, 1854, to Marion Gould, who was born April 23, 1836, in Jefferson county, New York. They have six children. MARY C., born June 26, 1855, was married March 23, 1871, to Robert T. Hardin. They have three children, JOHN W., IDA MAY., and WILLIAM SHERMAN, and live near Sweetwater, Menard county, Ill. LILLIE L., WILLIAM A., THOMAS S., ANNIE F., and CARRIE A., live with their parents, three and three-fourth miles west of Chatham, Sangamon county, Ill., on the farm settled on by his parents in 1830. John A. Starr is now—1876—plowing his thirty-sixth season in succession on the farm where he was born, and has no recollection of a physician ever having been called to see him.

MARY J., born July 3, 1834, married Sept. 5, 1851, to Dr. A. M. Browning, and died six weeks later. Dr. Browning is a practicing physician in Loami, Sangamon county, Ill.

GEORGE W., born Feb. 3, 1836, married Sarah O. Kelly, and lives in Green county, Missouri.

Andrew Starr died May 5, 1851, and his widow died Aug. 28, 1856, both on the farm where they settled in 1830, near Chatham, Sangamon county, Ill.

STEELE, Mrs. ELIZABETH R., whose maiden name was Robison, was born in Delaware, and taken by her parents to Nicholas county, Ky., where she was married to Samuel H. Steele, who was born in Ohio. They had six children in Kentucky, and Mr. Steele died in Natchez, Miss., of cholera, while on business there in 1832. His widow and children moved to Sangamon county, arriving December, 1833, in Buffalo Hart Grove, where her father, John Robison, had moved three years before. Of her six children—

WILLIAM M., born April 2, 1820, in Nicholas county, Ky., married in Sangamon county, to Amanda Rodgers, and had six children. Mr. Steele enlisted in 1862 for three years in Co. E, 116th Ill. Inf. He died March, 1864, in military hospital at St. Louis, Missouri. *See the Rodgers family name.*

JOHN R., born in Kentucky, came to Sangamon county in 1833 with his mother, went in 1842 to Arkansas, married there to Martha J. Hendris. Being a Union man, he was killed by rebel bushwhackers in the fall of 1863, leaving a widow and three children.

NANCY A., born April 10, 1825, in Bath county, Ky., was brought by her mother to Sangamon county in 1833, married Aug. 4, 1844, to Wesley Lanham. *See his name.* He died Aug. 26, 1861, and she was married Jan. 29, 1868, to William Graham, who was born Jan. 13, 1808, in Lincoln county, N. C.; lived in Todd county, Ky., from 1827 to 1839, when he moved to Morgan county, Ill., thence to Sangamon county in 1858. He has three children by a former marriage. MARY M., born Dec. 30, 1840, in Morgan county, married John Churchill. *See his name.* NANCY J., married B. M. Wood. *See his name with the Burns family.* JOHN F., is unmarried and lives near Illiopolis. William Graham and wife reside near Illiopolis, Sangamon county, Illinois.

ELIZABETH J., born April 4, 1827, in Kentucky, married in Sangamon county in 1845 to John M. Crary. They had two children. ANNIE E., married Isaac Newton Ransom. *See his name.* GEORGE E., lives in Wisconsin.

JULIA A., born October 16, 1829, in Kentucky, died in Sangamon county, aged thirteen years.

GEORGE R., born December, 1831, in Kentucky, raised in Sangamon county, went to California in 1849, and lost his life by the caving in of a mine.

Mrs. Elizabeth R. Steele was married in 1836 to Jewett Stafford. *See his name.* She died March 29, 1842, near Rochester, Illinois.

STEPHENSON, JAMES, was born July 3, 1482, in South Carolina. His parents moved about 1800 to Caldwell county, Ky. Margaret Clinton was born in North Carolina, and when she was about thirteen years old her parents moved to Caldwell county, Ky. James Stephenson and Margaret Clinton were there married, and had six children in that county, and the family moved to Wayne county, Ill., where two children were born, and moved to Sangamon county, arriving in 1825, on Sugar creek, southeast of Springfield, where three children were born. Of their children—

PENINAH, born in Kentucky and died in Illinois in 1845.

WILLIAM C., born in Kentucky, raised in Sangamon county, and was a graduate of the Medical College of Ohio. He married Mrs. Diana Ruble, whose maiden name was Bowen. Dr. William C. Stephenson died at Mt. Pleasant, Iowa, leaving a widow, but no children.

HANNAH A., born in Kentucky, raised in Sangamon county, married Jacob Zwingle. They have two children, MARTIN LUTHER and WILLIAM MELANCTHON, and live near Athens, Menard county, Ill.

JAMES W., born in Kentucky, raised in Sangamon county, married Mary Allen, and have seven children. James W. Stephenson was a soldier in an Illinois regiment, and now lives at Mexico, Andrain county, Missouri.

FINNIS E., born in Kentucky, raised in Sangamon county, and maried Maria Houghton. They had two children. FRANK died in infancy, and CHARLES lives with his father. Mrs. S. died November, 1857. F. E. Stephenson was sergeant of Co. K., 33d Ill. Inf. He lives at Chandlerville, Ill.

ALEXANDER, died at seventeen years of age.

BENJAMIN F., born Oct. 3, 1823, in Wayne county, Ill., and raised in Sangamon county. He graduated Feb. 7, 1850, at Rush Medical College, Chicago, and was married in Sangamon county March 30, 1855, to Barbara Moore. She was born in 1828, in Woodford county, Ky. They had three living children, BENJAMIN M., MARY H. and CARRIE A. Dr. B. F. Stephenson was surgeon of the 14th Ill. Inf. He died August 30, 1871, and his widow and child reside in Menard county, three miles north of Salisbury, Ill.

ELVIRA A., born Dec. 7, 1824, in Wayne county, Ill., raised in Sangamon county, married May 29, 1854, to Aaron R. Houghton, who was born Dec. 9, 1855, in Menard county, Ill., and served one year as a soldier in the Mexican war. They have three children, JAMES F., CHARLES W. and MARY A., and live six miles south of Petersburg, Menard county, Ill.

MARY E., died March 2, 1848, at nineteen years of age.

HARRIET, born Oct. 5, 1830, in Sangamon county, married Nov. 14, 1860, to William N. Spears, who was born Nov. 12, 1826, in Menard county. They had four children. WILLIAM F., died at five years old. EMMA M., RUTH S. and VIRGINIA live with their mother. William N. Spears died in Menard county, Ill., March 28, 1868, and his widow and children reside at Lincoln, Logan county, Illinois.

James Stephenson died Dec. 29, 1867, and his widow died October, 1868, both in Menard county, Ill.

STEVENSON, MILES, was born in Tennessee, and came to Sangamon county about 1822, in what is now Cartwright township. He was married to Deborah Irwin. They had one child in Sangamon county, and moved to Menard county, where six children were born. Of their seven sons—

JAMES M., born Nov. 7, 1829, near what is now Richland Station, Sangamon county, Ill. He was married May 4, 1856, to Martha A. Loving, of Logan county. They have two children, MINERVA J. and SOPHRONIA A., and live near Salisbury, Sangamon county, Ill.

SAMUEL L. and *WILLIAM A.*, died aged about seventeen years each.

DAVID F., is unmarried, and lives with his brother, James M.

JOHN, enlisted in 1862 for three years in Co. F, 114th Ill. Inf. He was captured at the battle of Guntown, Mississippi, June, 1864, was in Andersonville prison pen until the end of the rebellion, and came very near losing his life. He was honorably discharged in 1865, married Mary Loving, has two children, FRANLIN C. and MATILDA, and live near Salisbury, Sangamon county, Illinois.

ALBERT, died young.

WESLEY, married Effie Sharp, has two children, and lives near Cantrall, Illinois.

Mrs. Deborah Stevenson died Decemher, 1852, and Miles Stevenson died May 14, 1868, both in Menard county, Ill.

STEWART, JAMES, was born Sept. 28, 1777, at Fort Ann, Washington county, New York. That was in the very height of the conflict for American Independence, and at times all the families in the neighborhood were compelled to take refuge in the fort. On one occasion, when the men had gone for provisions, Indians entered the fort and found the subject of this sketch at his mother's breast, as she lay sick in bed. One of them took him by the heels and was about to dash his brains out, when she made the savages believe that she was in the act of summoning the white men. He dropped the infant and fled. James Stewart grew to manhood in that region, and followed the business of a lumberman on the Hudson river. He was married in 1803 in Bloomfield, Ontario county, to Roxana Stillman, and in 1806 moved to Buffalo, in the same State. In 1810 Mr. Stewart moved his family back to Bloomfield, thence to Junius, Seneca county. They had six living children in New York. In the fall of 1819 they embarked at Olean Point, on the Allegheny river, in a boat prepared for the purpose. Two other families, those of Joseph Inslee and Jesse Southwick, each occupied a boat. The three united in the purchase of a boat for the conveyance of their horses, wagons, and household goods. The whole party landed at Shawneetown on the last day of 1819. They made their way through the mud and water of the sloughs and running streams, all unbridged, until they reached Sugar creek, about eight miles south of the present city of Springfield, Ill. Each of the families commenced improvements by building cabins. A few weeks later, the mother-in-law of Mr. Stewart—Mrs. Stillman—arrived with her family. Mr. and Mrs. Stewart started to accompany them to the north side of the Sangamon river. After seeing that part of the country they determined to settle there also. Mr. Stewart returned to Sugar creek, and moved his family and property, arriving in the spring of 1820, in what is now Williams township, where three children were born. On coming to the country, there were so small a number before them, that it was almost impossible to obtain food. Mr. Stewart rode two days in search of provisions, and all he could obtain was a bushel or two of frost-bitten corn—for which he paid two dollars per bushel—and a few pounds of rusty bacon, at twenty-five cents per pound. The nearest postoffice was at Edwardsville, seventy-five miles south, and they had to pay twenty-five cents for a letter from their friends. Of their nine children—

JANE C., born Oct. 2, 1804, in New York, married in Sangamon county to Oramel Clark. *See his name.*

BENJAMIN H., born March 22, 1806, at Bloomfield, Ontario county, New York, married Margery Morgan, and had four children. Mrs. Margery Stewart died, and he married Nancy Hall. They had three children. Benj. H. Stewart died in 1871 in Missouri. His son, WILLIAM A., born Aug. 16, 1836 in Sangamon county, married Sept. 27, 1858, to Sarah L. Schick, a native of Danville, Pa. He enlisted Aug. 14, 1861, in Co. A, 3d Ill. Cav. was discharged on account of physical disability, Dec. 30, 1861. He enlisted Jan. 20, 1864, in Co. A, 34th Ill. Inf., served until April, 1865, when he was discharged on account of physical disability. He was appointed postmaster at Williamsville, April 8, 1869, and died April 18, 1870. His widow, Mrs. Sarah L. Stewart was appointed as his successor April 20, 1870.

WILLIAM A., born May 24, 1809, in Buffalo, N. Y. He was brought by his parents to Sangamon county in the spring of 1820. He was captain of a Sangamon county company in the Blackhawk war of 1832, and was in command of a supply train under his uncle, Isaiah Stillman at the time of his defeat on Rock river. Mr. Stewart taught school on Fancy creek for a time after the Indian war, and still later became a steamboat clerk on the Illinois river, and rose to the positions of pilot and captain. He was engaged in navigating the Illinois, Mississippi, Ohio and other western rivers, with his home at Cincinnati, until the breaking out of the great rebellion. William A. Stewart was married at Cincinnati October 14, 1841, to Elizabeth Haman. They had one child, JAMES E., born May 10, 1843, in Cincinnati. He had just completed his literary studies and graduated at Delaware, Ohio, when the rebellion broke out. His home was in Cincinnati, but he went over the river and enlisted on the eighteenth anniversary of his birth, May 10, 1861, in Co. D, 2d Ky. Inf., for three months, and re-enlisted for three years in the same company and regiment. He carried his musket for nineteen months, passing through Pittsburg Landing and many other battles. He was promoted August, 1862, to second lieutenant. In May, 1864, he was commissioned captain of Co. A, 167th Ohio Inf., and March 13, 1865, promoted to Colonel of United States Volunteers. In October, 1865, he engaged in the practice of law at Cincinnati. In October, 1869, moved to Springfield, Ohio, where he succeeded to his father's interests, and was elected Vice President of the Republic Printing Company, publishers of the *Daily Republic;* is also a member of the City Council of Springfield. Colonel James E. Stewart was married April 3, 1874, at Mount Vernon, Ohio, to Mary E. Durbin, and resides at Springfield, O., 1874. Mrs. Elizabeth Stewart died at Cincinnati August 26, 1860, and W. A. Stewart was married in the same city Sept. 14, 1864, to Mrs. E. W. Hall, whose maiden name was Norton. They moved to Springfield, Ohio, in July, 1866. He died there July 21, 1869, and his widow resides there.

Of the public services of W. A. Stewart I can only make a very brief statement. When the rebellion burst upon the country he was engaged as an expert as one of a committee appointed by the United States Government to ascertain the channels and bearings of the Mississippi river. Whilst he was at Washington making his report in July, 1861, he witnessed the battle and defeat at Bull Run. He superintended, under direction of Commodore Foote, the fitting out of the gunboats Carondelet and Mound City, and was on the latter in its engagement with the rebel ram Van Dorn; also in the battles of Fort Henry and Island No. 10. He was pilot of the United States Monitor Osage at the battle of Fort Durussy, in April, which was his last service in the war. He was appointed in April, 1864, United States Inspector of Steamboats at Cincinnati, which he resigned in 1867. While in the naval service he and Commodore Foote co-operated with each other in holding religious services on the gunboats, on all suitable occasions. He was a member of Park Street M. E. Church and Sunday School, at Cincinnati, and of the High Street M. E. Church, Springfield, Ohio; also of the Masonic Fraternity.

ABIGAIL C., born May 16, 1811, in New York, married to Ossian Stone. *See his name.*

MARY M., born April 6, 1813, at Inions, New York, married in Sangamon county to Nathan E. Constant. *See his name.* Mr. Constant died August 25, 1843, and his widow married Miletus W. Ellis. *See his name.*

ROXANA, born Sept. 8, 1818, in Bloomfield, Ontario county, New York, married in Sangamon county, Jan. 30, 1873, to Ira Knights, a native of St. Lawrence county, New York. They reside at the family homestead, where her father settled in 1820, two and a half miles west of Williamsville, Sangamon county, Ill.

MARTHA B., born March 10, 1821, in Sangamon county, married George W. Constant. *See his name.*

JAMES O., born Oct. 20, 1822, in Sangamon county, died June 6, 1849, at Paducah, Kentucky, of cholera, and was brought home for interment.

JOSEPH B., born July 4, 1825, died in the 22d year of his age.

Mrs. Roxana Stewart died Nov. 11, 1833. James Stewart married Mrs. Phœbe Twist. She died Jan. 11, 1836, in Sangamon county. *See the Twist family name.*

The last years of his life James Stewart required a great deal of care, which was freely bestowed by his faithful daughter, Roxana, who declined very advantageous offers of marriage, expressing her determination to remain unmarried as long as he required her attention, and most faithfully and lovingly did she discharge the self-imposed duties. Mr. Stewart died April 16, 1872, in the 95th year of his age, and on the farm where he had spent more than half a century of his life.

STILLMAN, Mrs. ABIGAIL, widow of Benjamin Stillman, came to Sangamon county, Ill., arriving in the spring of 1820, in what is now Williams township, accompanied by three sons and three daughters, all unmarried. She had a son and daughter married, the daughter came with the family, being the wife of James Stewart. The son came two years later. The descendants of Benjamin and Abigail Stillman do not know where they were born or married, but they lived in Massachusetts until four children were born. They moved in 1793 to Bloomfield, Ontario county, N. Y., where four children were born, and Mr. Stillman died there. The family moved to Morganfield, Union county, Ky., where Philo Beers became acquainted with the family. They moved from there to Sangamon county, Ill. Of their eight children—

STEPHEN, born in Massachusetts, came with the family to Sangamon county, selected the land where they settled in what is now Williams township, one and a half miles west of Williamsville. There was a beautiful natural grove on the land, which he called Fancy Grove. A postoffice was established there and called Fancy Grove postoffice, Mr. Stillman being postmaster. It was the first postoffice north of the river. The name has since been applied to a stream of water, and to a township. Stephen Stillman died in Peoria, between 1835 and '40.

JOSEPH B., born in Massachusetts, came with his mother to Sangamon county, and soon after went to the West India islands, and died there in 1825. He was a physician.

RONALVA, born March 22, 1786, in Massachusetts, married James Stewart. See his name.

ISAIAH, born in Massachusetts, married in New York State to Hannah Sherwood, came to Sangamon county, about 1822, and settled on the farm now owned by B. F. Fletcher, one and a half miles southwest of Williamsville. They had three children, two daughters and a son, HENRY, who is a lawyer, and resides at Canton, Fulton county, Ill. Isaiah Stillman was in command of a body of soldiers, as General Stillman, and was defeated at Rock river in 1832, in the war against the Indians, under their chief, Blackhawk. After the war, General Stillman moved to Canton, Ill., and died there in 1865 or '6. His widow still resides there.

MARY, born in New York, died unmarried at Tremont, Ill., in 1862 or '3.

MARTHA, born in Bloomfield, New York, and came with her mother to Sangamon county. She was married Nov. 2, 1820, to Philo Beers. See his name.

HENRY, born in New York, married in St. Louis, and died at Peoria, between 1860 and '65.

CAROLINE, born in New York, married in Peoria to Peter Menard. Both died at Tremont, Ill., leaving four children.

Mrs. Abigail Stillman moved with three of her children to Peoria in 1828, and died there in 1830.

STITT, WILLIAM, was born August 12, 1820, near Lebanon, Warren county, Ohio. He left home quite young, and traveled by water down the Ohio and up the Mississippi and Illinois rivers to Beardstown, Illinois, in company with William W. Wykoff. They started from Beardstown with one horse to ride and tie. When within about fifteen miles of their destination, Mr. Wycoff mounted the horse, gave Mr. Stitt particular directions about the road, and forgot to tie any more, for which he was excused by Mr. Stitt, because he was so near his family, from whom he had been absent several months. This caused Mr. Stitt to arrive on foot, alone, tired and hungry, at the south side of Richland creek, in what is now Cartwright township, in 1838. William Stitt was married Sept. 5, 1847, in Sangamon county, Illinois, to Elizabeth Hardin. They had five children in Sangamon county. The fourth child died young.

WILLIAM WALLACE was married March 9, 1875, to Julia F. Hurt. They live in Cartwright township, Sangamon county, Illinois.

HELEN A., *LAURA L.*, and *EDITH BELLE* live with their parents, three and one-fourth miles southwest of Richland Station, Sangamon county, Illinois.

Isaac Stitt, the father of William, was born in 1779, in Pennsylvania, and married there to Elizabeth Phillips, who was born July 9, 1780, in New Jersey. They had nine children, and Mr. Stitt died in October, 1825, in Ohio. In 1845 Mrs. Stitt, her son, David and family, and her daughter, Elizabeth, came to Island Grove, Sangamon county. David moved the next year to Peoria county, and died there June, 1865, leaving a widow and two children. Elizabeth married Joshua Butler. See his name. Mrs. Elizabeth Stitt died March 10, 1871, at the residence of her son, William.

STONE, ASAHEL, was born Sept. 25, 1780, in Chesterfield, New Hampshire. His father, Colonel William Stone, was born in Groton, Mass., and was second in command at the taking of Crown Point, by Ethan Allen. He was a prisoner at Ticonderoga at the time of its evacuation by the British, immediately after Burgoyne's surrender. Col. Stone's wife was Submit Ward. At the time of his imprisonment, they had two children, aged respectively two and four years. The day before Col. Stone was to leave for Great Britain to be tried for high treason, Mrs. Stone left these two children at home alone and went to the fort, twelve miles distant, in a canoe, accompanied by her brother, David Ward, aged ten years—who was afterwards a Baptist minister and grandfather of Captain E. B. Ward, the late detroit millionaire. They reached the fort late in the afternoon, but the officer in command refused to admit her, notwithstanding all her pleading, and compelled her to wait all night in the boat. On returning home she found her children safe. The next day her husband was liberated. The rapid advance of our troops up the country having compelled the British to leave without being able to provide transportation for their prisoners.

Asahel Stone, whose name heads this sketch was a graduate of Dartmouth College, in the same class with Daniel Webster. He was married February, 1805, in Bridport, Addison county, Vt., to Laura Culver They came to Sangamon county, Ill., Nov. 1831, and entered the land now owned by Hiram E. Gardner six miles west of Springfield. They had six children, viz:—

WHELOCK, S., born Nov. 28, 1805, in Madrid, St. Lawrence county, N. Y. He was a classmate of Dr. Hatfield, of New York city; Dr. J. J. Owens. Prof. Cozzens and D. B. Tower, at Middlebury College, and graduated there in 1828 with the second honors of his class. He afterwards became a minister of the gospel. He was married September, 1832, to Martha Storrs and died at Mobile, Alabama, in 1837, of yellow fever.

OSSIAN L., born May 24, 1807, in Madrid, N. Y., was brought up in Vermont. He came to Sangamon county with his father in 1831 and was married October 29, 1835 in Sangamon county, to Abigail C. Stewart, who was born in Junius Seneca county, N. Y., May 16, 1811. *See James Stewart.* They had four living children, namely: LAURA L., born June 7, 1840, in Sangamon county, was married March 30, 1858, to Jacob Gregory. *See his name.* They have two children, MARY and GEORGE, and reside in Decatur Illinois. JAMES A., born May 6, 1842, in Sangamon county, married September 26, 1866, in Morgan county, to Eliza Allyn. They have three children, JESSIE, PERCY A., and JAMES R. J. A. Stone owns and resides with his family on the farm entered by his father in September, 1834, the patent for which was signed by Andrew Jackson. The farm joins that entered by his grand-father, Asahel Stone. HENRY A., born April 3, 1844, in Sangamon county, died April 21, 1861. CHARLES O., born May 4, 1847, in Sangamon county, is unmarried and resides in Springfield, Illinois. Ossian L. Stone died in 1850 and Mrs. Abigail Stone was married March, 1862, to Aaron Thompson and died in Springfield, Ill., Feb. 15, 1875. Mr. Thompson is one of the firm of Thompson & Newman, planing mill.

THEDA S., born Dec. 14, 1808, in Madrid, N. Y., died at Bridport, Vt., March 31, 1820.

FRANCES S., born Dec. 17, 1813, in Bridport, Vt. Came with her father's family to Sangamon county, and was married at their farm residence Feb. 13, 1840, to Jonathan C. Bancroft. *See his name.* Rev. Dr. A. P. Happer, of the Chinese Mission, was groomsman at their wedding.

PHILIP Z., born Dec. 16, 1816, in Bridport, Vt., was married Feb. 1843, to Julia McCarty in Sangamon county. She died in 1852, while on their way to Oregon. P. Z. Stone resides in St. Louis, Missouri.

LAURA A., born April 10, 1821, in Bridport, Vt., was married at her father's farm residence in Sangamon county, Ill., April 21, 1842, to Jacob Ruckel. *See his name.*

Mrs. Laura Stone died June 21, 1845, and Asahel Stone was married September, 1846, in Springfield, Ill., to Lucretia Dresser. He died there Oct. 2, 1871. His widow resides in Springfield. Asahel Stone was the last survivor of the class in which he graduated in Dartmouth college, of which it has already been stated that Daniel Webster was a member.

STONE, DAN, was born March 13, 1800, in Monkton, Addison county, Vermont, and graduated at Middlebury College, in his native State, in 1818. He went to Cincinnati and studied law with his uncle, Ethan Stone, and was married in that city in 1824 to Augusta M. Farnsworth, who was born March 8, 1808, in Vermont, also. Mr. Stone practiced law in Cincinnati a few years, and during that time was a member of the State Legislature of Ohio, and four years a member of the City Council. He moved to Springfield, Illinois, in 1834, and in 1836 was elected one of the Representatives of Sangamon county to the Legislature of Illinois. He was, consequently, one of the "Long Nine." *See sketch under that heading.* While a member of the Legislature he received the appointment of Judge of the Circuit Court, and was assigned to the district in the extreme northwestern part of the State, and moved to Galena. In 1838 he rendered a decision, with reference to the vote of an alien, that was distasteful to the Democratic party—he being a Whig. That decision led to a reorganization of the judiciary system of the State. The Supreme Court then consisted of four Judges. In February, 1841, the Legislature added five to the Court, all Democrats, and made it the duty of the nine judges composing the Supreme Court to act as Circuit Judges, also. Judge Stone, finding himself thus legislated out of office, soon left the State, and a few years later died in Essex county, New Jersey.

His son, Henry S., is unmarried and lives in San Francisco. His daughter, Jennie A., now the wife of Josiah Paul, lives in Cincinnati. His widow resides in Cincinnati, Ohio, also—1876.

STOKES, JOHN, was born April 14, 1796, in Nicholas county, Kentucky. He was married in that county April 15, 1819, to Deborah Dickerson, who was born Feb. 4, 1798, near Hagerstown, Maryland. They had four children in Kentucky, and moved to Sangamon county, Illinois, arriving in the fall of 1830, in what is now Rochester township, where four children were born. Of their eight children—

SUSAN, born Sept. 13, 1822, in Nicholas county, Kentucky married Isaac B. Bell. *See his name.*

LOUISA, born June 22, 1825, in Kentucky, married Robert E. Richards. *See his name.*

BENJAMIN F., born Nov. 27, 1827, in Nicholas county, Kentucky, married in Sangamon county to Malvina C. Cooper. She died and he married Elzirah C. Cooper. They had four living children, JOHN W., JACOB F., MINNIE M. and GABRIEL, live with their parents in Christian county, near Edinburg, Illinois.

WILLIAM, born Jan. 30, 1830, in Kentucky, raised in Sangamon county, went to California in 1852, and died there December, 1862.

ELIZABETH A., born August 6, 1832, in Sangamon county, married Robert E. Berry. *See his name.*

JOHN, born April 19, 1835, in Sangamon county, married April 18, 1858, to Drada Lovelace, who was born August 7, 1840, in Shelby county, Illinois. They have three living children, CHARLES H., IDA A., and HARRIET A., reside with their parents near Edinburg, Christian county, Illinois.

THOMAS, born Nov. 4, 1837, in Sangamon county, married Priscilla Jones. They had three children, two of whom died young. Thomas Stokes enlisted August, 1862, in Co. E, 114th Ill. Inf., was taken sick at Camp Butler, conveyed home, and died Oct. 28, 1862. His son, HERSCHEL V., resides with his mother, who is now the wife of James Layard. They reside near Sunny Side, Montgomery county, Kansas.

EMILY, born April 14, 1840, in Sangamon county, married Samuel Hedrick, and died August 25, 1867, leaving two children, who live with their father near Morrisonville, Christian county, Illinois.

John Stokes died March 15, 1853, and Mrs. Deborah Stokes died Feb. 12, 1870, both in Sangamon county, Illinois.

STOUT, the origin of this family in America is quite romantic. The principal points in their history may be found in Benedict's History of the Baptists. Some of his statements are based on the writings of an earlier historian. The following embraces all that is known on the subject:

Some time during the seventeenth century, probably about 1680 or '90, a young couple just married in Holland, embarked on a vessel bound for America. The voyage was prosperous until they were nearing the port of New Amsterdam, now the city of New York. The vessel was wrecked off what is now the coast of New Jersey, and nearly all on board drowned. The young couple of Hollanders, escaped drowning and with a small number of the passengers and crew succeeded in reaching the shore. Upon landing they were attacked by Indians, who lay in ambush awaiting their arrival. The whole party were tomahawked, scalped and otherwise mutilated, and left for dead. All were dead except the wife, from Holland. She alone survived, and although her scalp was removed and she was otherwise horribly mangled, she had sufficient remaining strength to crawl away from the scene of the slaughter, and secreted herself in a hollow log which was concealed by underbrush. She lay there a day or two, during which time her mental and bodily suffering may be imagined but cannot be described. She finally made up her mind that there was no possibility of her escaping with life; that if she remained quiet she would certainly die of hunger and thirst, and if she attempted to seek sustenance, that would expose her to the Indians, who would be sure to kill her. At this juncture, a deer, with an arrow sticking in its body, ran past where she was. This led her to believe that Indians were near, and she reasoned that it would be a much easier death to let them kill her, than to endure the pangs of starvation by remaining where she was. She then summoned all her remaining strength and dragged her body out to an open space that the Indians might see her should they pursue the deer. In a short time three of the savages appeared on its trail. Two of them rushed upon her with uplifted tomahawks, but the third one, a chief, restrained them and saved her life. It was not humanity, but gain that prompted him to this act of mercy. He took his prisoner to New Amsterdam and there received a ransom for her. That placed her in the hands of friends who gave her the proper surgical treatment and nursing as she recovered. The name of her husband is not known, neither is her own family name, nothing but her first or given name, Penelope; a name that has stood for more than twenty-five centuries, in tradition and literature, as the highest ideal of a true and loyal wife. It will readily be understood that I allude to one of the creations of Homer, the father of Greek poetry. A brief statement of the case, gleaned from his works will not be out of place here.

When the Greeks declared war against Troy, in consequence of the abduction of Helen, the wife of Menelaus, a Greek chieftain, it was found that one of their number, Ulysses, although a soldier by profession, and a farmer in time of peace, manifested great reluctance to leaving his young and beautiful wife, Penelope, and their infant son, Telemachus, for the purpose of engaging in the war. He feigned insanity, by sowing salt instead of wheat. As a test of his sanity, Nestor, whom all respected for his wisdom and probity, proposed that the infant son of Ulysses should be laid in the furrow in front of the oxen with which he was plowing. The device was successful, and caused him to throw off the disguise by saving his child. It was expected that the war would be brief, but it was extended to a long series of years, and of those who finally returned, Ulysses was the last, after twenty years's absence. Meanwhile, he was supposed to be dead, and many suitors for the hand of Penelope, pressed their claims, and a simple "No" from her was not taken for an answer. The very thought of marrying again, especially while the fate of her husband was in doubt, was peculiarly revolting to her and she announced her intention of choosing a husband among the suitors, when she had completed the weaving of a shroud for her father-in-law. Her ardent suitors waited with all the patience they could command until it was discovered that she undid at night what she had woven through the day. She was then obliged to proceed with her work when the long absent Ulysses returned just in time to save her from what seemed a horrible fate.

This modern Penelope had no such doubts to contend with. The death of her first husband was only too sure, having been witnessed by her own eyes.

After her recovery, she became acquainted with and married an Englishman by the name of Richard Stout. They then went over into New Jersey, made themselves a home and raised a family of twelve sons. One of them, Jonathan Stout, and his family, were the founders of the Hopewell settlement, in Hunterdon county, New Jersey, where Hopewell Baptist Church was afterwards constituted. Of the first fifteen members, nine were Stouts. The church was organized at the house of a Stout, and for forty years their meetings were held chiefly at the houses of the Stouts; after which they erected their first house of worship. In 1790, two of the deacons and four of the elders were Stouts. Jonathan Stout lived until his descendants were multiplied to one hundred and seventeen. Another one of their sons, David, had a son Benjamin, born in 1706. He had a son, Jediah, born April 10, 1757. His son—

STOUT, PHILEMON, was born May 15, 1785, in New Jersey, and in 1789 was taken by his parents to Fayette county, Kentucky. He was married Feb. 8, 1810, in Woodford county to Penelope Anderson, settled in Scott county in the same State, and in 1820 moved back to Fayette county. They had seven children who lived to maturity. The family moved to Sangamon county, Illinois, arriving Oct. 5, 1836, in what is now Ball township. Of their children—

JACKSON, born August 6, 1814, in Kentucky, married Jan. 8, 1838, in Sangamon county, to Matilda Willian. He died Feb. 24, 1839. His widow married Samuel Haines. See his name.

ELIHU, born Jan. 30, 1816, in Scott county, Kentucky, was married in Sangamon county, Illinois, August 30, 1839, to Rebecca A. Patton. They had three children, JAMES M., born June 15, 1840, married Mollie A. Mason. They have two children, JAMES WILLIAM and JOHN PHILEMON, and live two miles south of Chatham, Sangamon county, Illinois. PHILEMON, born Feb. 22, 1842, married Mary Abernathy. They have two children, WILLIAM ADOLPHUS and MARTHA ANN, and live in Auburn, Illinois. Mrs. Rebecca A. Stout died Sept. 21, 1852, and Elihu Stout married Mrs. Sarah J. Moore, whose maiden name was Williams. They had two living children, THOMAS ELIHU and CHARLES H., who live with their father. Mrs. Sarah J. Stout died Sept. 17, 1866, and Elihu Stout was married June 18, 1867, to Mrs. Margaret E. Davis, whose maiden name was Williams. They reside three miles southeast of Auburn, Sangamon county, Illinois.

CHARLOTTE A., born Oct. 13, 1817, in Kentucky, was married in Sangamon county, Illinois, August 10, 1837, to Samuel L. Ridgeway. See his name.

PHILEMON, Jun., born April 19, 1822, in Fayette county, Kentucky, was married in Sangamon county, Illinois, Sept. 7, 1848, to Melissa Shoup. They had four children, three of whom are dead. Her only living child, SAMUEL J., born August 22, 1849, was married July 30, 1871, to Emma L. Brasfield. They had one child, EDNA MAY, who died in infancy. Mrs. Emma L. Stout died Dec. 20, 1875. S. J. Stout lives in Ball township, two miles south of Cotton Hill P. O., Sangamon county, Illinois. Mrs. Melissa Stout died February 26, 1855, and Philemon Stout, Jun., was married Oct. 26, 1856, to Louisa P. Brasfield. They have three living children, JAMES B., JOAB PHILEMON and MELISSA J., live with their parents. Philemon Stout, Jun., lives one mile southwest of Cotton Hill P. O., Sangamon county, Illinois, where his father settled in 1836. He has represented Ball township, in the County Board of Supervisors for many years, and is one of the most extensive farmers in Sangamon county.

MARY, born Feb. 22, 1825, in Fayette county, Kentucky, was married in Sangamon county, Illinois, March 25, 1841, to Dickson Hall, who was born June 15, 1813, in Ohio county, West Virginia. They had six children, one of whom, CHARLOTTE, died in August, 1849. They moved to Christian county, Illinois, in 1849. Of their five children, ELIZABETH E., born March 1, 1842, in Sangamon county, was married Sept. 6, 1870, to Abner Bond, who was born August 11, 1832, in Belmont county, Ohio. In 1838 he was taken to Indiana, and in 1855 came to Christian county. Mr. and Mrs. Bond have three children, ELBRIDGE, MAY and NELLIE STOUT, and live near Taylorville, Illinois. FANNIE H., born August 6, 1843, in Sangamon county, was married in Christian county, March 1, 1870, to George A. Kautz, who was born Jan. 23, 1833, in Brown county, Ohio. They have one child, DICKSON, and live in Moweaqua, Shelby county, Illinois. WILLIAM W., born Nov. 30, 1847, in Sangamon county, brought up in Christian county, was married May 28, 1874, in Waukegan, Illinois, to Sarah L. Stewart, who was born there. They live in Taylorville, Illinois. MARY N., born Dec. 31, 1849, in Christian county, Illinois, was married Sept. 15, 1875, to William M. Dalbey, who was born Feb. 28, 1838, in Pickaway county, Ohio. He came to Sangamon county, Illinois, in 1862, and is a stock raiser in Christian county, five miles west of Edinburg, Ill. EMMA S., born in Christian county, lives with her mother. Dickson Hall died June 23, 1854, and his widow lives near Taylorville, Christian county, Illinois.

ELIZA P., born Sept. 25, 1827, in Kentucky, was married Sept. 21, 1848, in Sangamon county to William Forbes, who was born in Hardeman county, east Bolivar, Tennessee, where they had four children. Mr. Forbes was murdered there in time of the rebellion, but not connected with it. The widow and four children came to Sangamon county. Her son, John P., lives near Oswego, Labette county, Kansas. ROBERT lives with his mother, MATTIE married Joseph Drennan. *See his name.* MOLLIE lives with her mother. Mrs. Forbes lives eight miles south of Springfield, in Woodside township, near the line of Ball. Her postoffice is Woodside, Sangamon county, Illinois.

MARTHA A., born May 1, 1830, in Kentucky, was married Dec. 3, 1847, in Sangamon county to Robert G. Simpson, who was born May 6, 1826, in Fayette county, Kentucky. They have three living children. ELLEN R., was married Oct. 24, 1872, to William S. Richardson. They have one child, CHARLES M., and live in Taylorville, Illinois. RANDOLPH J. is one of the firm of Barnes & Simpson, druggists, Taylorville, Illinois. Mr. Barnes, his partner, is a son of Ezra Barnes. *See his name.* WILLIAM R. lives with his parents in Ball township.

Philemon Stout, Sen., died Jan. 31, 1846, and his widow died Nov. 23, 1860, both in Ball township, where they settled in 1836.

The Stouts very justly take pride in their family history, and being mostly Baptists, they take pride in their Baptist history also. When they meet a stranger by the name of Stout, who manifests a disposition to claim relationship, they apply one test only in their family history. They do not ask him to pronounce the word Shibboleth, but ascertain if he has any knowledge of PENELOPE, and if he knows nothing of her, they know nothing of him. In other words, they do not cultivate his acquaintance, in the direction of relationship, any further.

STOVER, SAMUEL, was born Nov. 10, 1810, in Franklin county, Pa. He was married Oct. 26, 1837, in Washington county, Md., to Elizabeth Wolgamot. In the following spring they went to Pittsburg, and from there by water, down the Ohio, and up the Mississippi and Illinois rivers to Peoria, thence to Springfield in a wagon, arriving in June, 1838. He settled six miles south of Springfield, and had two children there, namely—

SUSANNAH, born Jan. 17, 1841, married May 31, 1864, to John Brotherton, a native of Franklin county, Pa. They had two children, SAMUEL S. and MAUD, and Mr. Brotherton died Dec. 3, 1867, in Springfield. He was a druggist. His widow and children reside with her parents in Springfield.

JOHN, born March 28, 1844, married Sept. 15, 1871, to Emma Wagner, of Ogle county. They had two children. He died July 15, 1875, in Springfield.

Samuel Stover and wife lived on the farm where they settled in 1838, until January, 1875, when they moved to Springfield, Illinois, where they now reside—November, 1876.

STRAWBRIDGE, THOS., was born March 13, 1755, in county Donegal, Ireland. Jane Mitchell, was born in the town of Ballykelly, county Derry. Her mother's maiden name was Strawbridge, a second cousin to her father. The Strawbridge family was of English origin. Thomas Strawbridge and wife had seven children in county Donegal, and Mrs. Jane Strawbridge died in 1809. The family came to America, landing at Baltimore in May, 1810, and went to Northumberland county, Pa. In the fall of

1811, they moved to that part of Champaign, which is now Clark county, O. From there they moved to Sangamon county, Ill., arriving October, 1823, in what is now Fancy Creek township, near Cantrall. Of the seven children—

MARGERY, married in Baltimore to Hugh Jack, a sea captain. He abandoned the sea, and was about taking his wife back to Ireland, when she died in Baltimore.

JOHN, was drowned in the Muskingum river, Ohio. He was about twenty-seven years old, and unmarried.

JAMES, born Aug. 29, 1792, married October, 1839, in Springfield, to Mrs. Elizabeth McDonnald, whose maiden name was Iles. They had two children. MARY E., married John W. Melton, have one daughter, and live in Jacksonville, Ill. ELIZA J., lives with her sister, Mrs. Melton. Mrs. Strawbridge died, and James Strawbridge died October, 1868, both in Jacksonville, and both were buried at Oak Ridge Cemetery, Springfield, Ill.

WILLIAM, born June, 1794, came to Sangamon county in 1823, married in 1831, in Jo Daviess county, Ill., to Mrs. Mary Ames, whose maiden name was Mitchell. They lived in Sangamon county until 1838, and moved to Jo Daviess county, where he prosecuted the lead smelting business until 1849. He then went to California, was returning to his family, and died December, 1851, in New York city, leaving a widow and four children at Elizabeth, Jo Daviess county, Illinois. Of the children, MARY J., married John W. Shaffer. He was appointed Governor of Utah territory. Mrs. Shaffer died June, 1869. Gov. Shaffer died in office at Salt Lake city, Oct. 31, 1870, and was buried at Freeport, Ill. They left three children, who live in New York city with their uncle, William F. Shaffer. MARGARET S., married Col. William F. Shaffer, a banker of New York city, and reside there. WILLIAM, Jun., married Miss Coulter, and lives in Ottawa, Kansas. THOMAS, lives in Burlington, Kansas. Mrs. Mary Strawbridge, widow of William Strawbridge, resides with her daughter, Mrs. Shaffer, in New York city—1874.

JANE, born Dec. 25, 1796, married in Ohio to John McCain. They had one child, and Mr. McCain went to New Orleans on business, and is supposed to have lost his life there, as he was never heard of. His widow came to Sangamon county in 1823. Her daughter, MARGERY married in Sangamon county to Cyrus G. Saunders. Mrs. McCain died Aug. 2, 1848, near Woodside, Sangamon county, Illinois.

THOMAS, Jun., born Feb. 8, 1798 in county Donegal, Ireland, came with the family to America and to Sangamon county in 1823. He learned saddle and harness making at Lebanon, Ohio, and engaged in that business in the fall of 1823, in Springfield, the first in that line in the place. He consequently made the first saddle in Sangamon county and central Illinois. He has for many years been engaged in farming, is unmarried, and reside five miles southeast of Springfield, Illinois.

MARY, born Nov. 30, 1800, in Ireland, married in Sangamon county, April, 1824, to David Anderson, a native of York county, Pa. He died July 16, 1825, in Morgan county. His widow married October, 1839, to Samuel Lyons, who was born near Belfast, Ireland. He died Oct. 12, 1842, in Sangamon county. Mrs. Lyons had no children by either marriage. She lives with her brother, Thos. Strawbridge, Jun., five miles southeast of Springfield, Ill.

Thomas Strawbridge, Sen., died Sept. 24, 1834, in what is now Fancy Creek township, Sangamon county, Ill., in his 80th year.

STRICKLAND, GEORGE, was born March 29, 1812, in Amherst, Massachusetts. He was married May 30, 1836, in Northampton, Massachusetts, to Sarah Little—sister to Thomas S. Little and Mrs. Sophia Phelps. Mrs. Strickland was born Nov. 21, 1814, in Northampton. They had one child, and moved to Springfield, Illinois, arriving in August, 1837. They had five children in Springfield, two of whom died young. Of their four children—

EDWARD P., born May 14, 1837, in Northampton, Massachusetts, and raised in Springfield. He enlisted in the first call for 75,000 men in April, 1861, for three months, in Co. I, 7th Ill. Inf., served full term and was honorably discharged. He again enlisted for three years in 1862, in Co. B, 114th Ill. Inf., and commissioned as first lieutenant at the organization of the company. After the capture of Vicksburg he was promoted to captain. The regiment was put on provost duty at Memphis, Tennessee. He was sent on an expedition and was taken prisoner in June, 1864. He was part of the time at Macon, Georgia, and part of the time at Charleston, South Carolina, where he was with other Union prisoners, placed by the rebel authorities under the guns of the Union army, in order to protect the city. He was moved from Charleston to Columbia, South Carolina, from where he escaped, and, with his first lieutenant, traveled thirty-five days, making a distance of between four and five hundred miles, on foot, to Knoxville, Tennessee, without seeing a white man, neither did they wish to. They traveled at night and subsisted on what they could obtain from the negroes, arriving Dec. 31, 1864. They were sent from Knoxville to Louisville, Kentucky, furloughed home, returned to the regiment, and was with it at the capture of Mobile, after which he was breveted major. He served until the fall of 1865, when he was honorably discharged. He now resides in Springfield, Illinois.

SARAH S., born Sept. 12, 1842, in Springfield, married Oct. 4, 1859, to Jesse D. Lloyd, a native of Springfield, also. He enlisted in 1861 in the 11th Mo. Inf., was commissioned as first lieutenant at the organization of the company, and promoted to captain. He served to the end of the rebellion and died April 10, 1865, leaving his widow and two children, WINFIELD S. and FRANK M., residing in Springfield, Illinois.

HELEN C., born July 16, 1847, in Springfield, and married in her native city May, 1874, to Newell Sturtevant, a native of Maine. They reside in New York City.

THOMAS S., born Oct. 14, 1853, in Springfield, is a printer, and resides with his parents in Springfield, Illinois.

Mr. George Strickland and wife are both living and reside in Springfield, Illinois.

STRINGFIELD, JAMES, was born about 1765 in Buncombe county, North Carolina. His parents moved to Warren county, Kentucky, when he was a young man. He was there married to Nancy Simmons who was born in Roanoke county, Virginia. They had ten children in Kentucky, and moved to Sangamon county in the fall of 1820 in company with their son-in-law, John Strode. Of their children—

MARY, born August 12, 1796, in Warren county, Kentucky, married John Strode. *See his name.*

ROLAND resides near Williamsville. Their other children are scattered and many of them dead.

James Stringfield died in 1835, and his widow died a year or two later, both in Sangamon county, Illinois.

STRODE, JOHN, was born March 13, 1790, in Greenbrier county, Virgiana. His parents moved in 1804 to Warren county, Kentucky. He volunteered in a Kentucky regiment in the war of 1812 and served three months on Lake Erie. After Perry's victory he was honorably discharged, again enlisted, and was in the battle of New Orleans, Jan. 8, 1815. He received a land warrant for his services but never drew a pension. The papers were all burned at Bowling Green, Ky., in 1863. John Strode and Mary Stringfield were married August 14, 1815, in Warren county, Kentucky. They had three children there, and moved to Sangamon county, Illinois, arriving in October, 1820, in what is now Fancy creek township, where eight children were born. When they came, there had been such an extensive and long continued drouth that they could walk across Sangamon river on the stones. They lived four weeks in a tent, while their house was building. Of their children—

NANCY, born June 28, 1816, married William Hargis. *See his name.*

JAMES E., born March 28, 1818, in Kentucky, was married August, 1845, to Susan Hargis. They had eight children. WILLIAM R. enlisted in February, 1864, in Co. G, 10th Ill. Cav., for three years, served until the close of the rebellion, and was honorably discharged November, 1865, at San Antonio, Texas. He married Lucetta Plunkett, and lives in Springfield township. JOHN T. enlisted in Springfield May 14, 1864, in Co. I, 133d Ill. Inf., for one hundred days, served full term and was honorably discharged Sept. 14, 1864. He lives with his mother

—1874. AMANDA married John Miller. They have one child, and live in Fancy Creek township. MARY married Clarence Mallory. *See his name.* BARBARA and ELIZA live with their mother. James B. Strode enlisted in 1862, for three years, in Co. K, 115th Ill. Inf., and was orderly sergeant. He was killed at the battle of Chickamauga, Tennessee, Sept. 20, 1863. His widow lives near Cantrall, Sangamon county, Illinois.

SARAH S., born Feb. 3, 1820, in Kentucky, married in Sangamon county to Ira Judd. She died March 28, 1865, leaving one child, MARY.

ELI, born March 29, 1823, in Sangamon county, married Diantha Strode—a distant relative—and lives near Nickerson, Reno county, Kansas.

BARBARA, born April 13, 1825, in Sangamon county, married Jan. 25, 1864, to John H. Cannon, who was born June 20, 1837, in Jefferson county, Tennessee. They had two children, WILLIAM H. and LEONARD B., both died in infancy. Mr. and Mrs. Cannon live near Cantrall, Illinois.

ELIZABETH, born June 30, 1829, resides with her mother.

ROLAND B., born March 24, 1831, married Lutitia Weese. They have five children, MARY E., CHARLES A., JAMES R., EMMA J. and MINNIE E., and live at the family homestead, near Cantrall, Ill.

JOHN A., born Jan. 4, 1824, married Letitia Gilmore. They have four children, ALICE, MINNIE E., VICTORIA, and EVA M. John A. Strode enlisted at Springfield in 1862 for three years in Co. K, 115th Ill. Inf. He was at the siege and capture of Fort Donelson, was soon after sent to hospital and discharged on account of physical disability. He lived at Brookfield, Mo., a few years, but now lives near Cantrall, Illinois.

WILLIAM H., born July 19, 1836, in Sangamon county, married June 4, 1863, to Henrietta F. Strode, a distant relative. They had six children, NIREM P. and CORA BELL died under four years, LUZETTA A., THOMAS J., ELIZABETH and J. MAUD live with their parents near Cantrall, Sangamon county, Illinois.

JOEL B., born March 7, 1839, married Mary E. King. They have three children, JACOB E., MAGGIE M. and JOHN E., and live at the old homestead, seven miles north of Springfield, near Cantrall, Ill.

MARY C., born in 1841, died in her seventh year.

John Strode died Nov. 27, 1866, and his widow resides on the farm settled by them in 1821. It is in Fancy Creek township, eight miles northwest of Springfield, Illinois.

STUART, JOHN T., was born Nov. 10, 1807, in Fayette county, Ky., seven miles east of Lexington. His father, Robert Stuart, was born of Scotch-Irish parents, in Rockbridge county, Virginia. He was a Presbyterian minister, but went to Lexington, first as professor of languages in Transylvania University. He was there married to Hannah Todd, daughter of General Levi Todd. *See sketch of the Todd family.* Rev. Robert Stuart, while connected with the University, became pastor of the Presbyterian church, at Walnut Hills, seven miles east of Lexington, where the subject of this sketch was born. John T. Stuart graduated at Centre College, Danville, Ky., in the fall of 1826, studied law with Judge Breck in Richmond, Ky., and came to Springfield, Illinois, arriving Oct. 25, 1828. He traveled on horseback and was ten days on the road. He at once engaged in the practice of his profession, and when the Indian troubles came on, that culminated in the Blackhawk war, Mr. Stuart became the major of the battalion in which Abraham Lincoln commanded a company. In 1832 Mr. Stuart was elected one of the Representatives of Sangamon county in the State Legislature. In 1834 he was re-elected. Abraham Lincoln was elected that year, also, and they roomed together at Vandalia. While they were taking a morning walk during that session, Mr. Lincoln asked Mr. Stuart his opinion in regard to his studying law. Mr. Stuart advised him to begin at once, proposed to loan him the necessary books and act as his preceptor, all of which was gratefully accepted by Mr. Lincoln, and when he was qualified for practice he gladly accepted the offer of his preceptor to become his partner. In 1836 Mr. Stuart was a candidate for Congress, but was defeated, as he expected to be, his object being to keep the Whig party—which was largely in the minority in his district—in order for future campaigns.

John T. Stuart was married Oct. 25, 1837, at Jacksonville, Ill., to Mary V. Nash, a daughter of General Frank Nash, of St. Louis county, Missouri, and a niece of the late Judge Lockwood, of Illinois. They had six living children—

BETTIE, born July, 1838, in Springfield, married Christopher C. Brown. *See his name.* She died, and the Bettie Stuart Institute was named in honor of her memory.

JOHN T., Jun., born Dec. 16, 1842, in Springfield, was married there Sept. 6, 1866, to Emily W. Huntington. They have four children, GEORGE H., MARY V., ELIZABETH H. and EDWARD S. BROWN. John T. Stuart, Jun., is a merchant in Chicago, and, with his family, resides there.

FRANK N., born in Springfield, Ill., is running a ranch in Plum Valley, near Sedalia, Colorado.

VIRGINIA L., HANNAH and *ROBERT*, all born in Springfield, live with their parents.

John T. Stuart was elected to Congress in 1838, defeating Stephen A. Douglas, when the partnership between him and Mr. Lincoln ceased. He was again elected in 1840, served that term, and in 1843 formed a partnership with Benjamin S. Edwards, under the firm name of Stuart & Edwards. It is the oldest law firm in the State, and with one exception, Mr. Stuart is the oldest practicing attorney in the State. He was elected in 1848 State Senator for four years for the district composed of Sangamon, Menard and Mason counties. He was out of politics after that until 1862, when he was elected to Congress, serving one term. In 1866 he was elected President of the Springfield City Railway Company, President of the Springfield Watch Company, President of the Bettie Stuart Board of Trustees, and is one of the three commissioners for building the new State House. As Chairman of the Executive Committee of the National Lincoln Monument Association, it devolved upon him to do more than any other one man, in superintending the erection of that monument to the memory

of his legislative colleague, law student and partner, and life-long friend—Abraham Lincoln. The law firm of Stuart & Edwards was changed in 1858, by admitting C. C. Brown, to that of Stuart, Edwards & Brown.

STUBBS, ROBERT L., was born Dec. 24, 1813, in Virginia, taken by his parents to Greene county, Kentucky, and came to Island Grove, Sangamon county, Ill., in the fall of 1832. Martha Ann Smith was born Dec. 5, 1818, in Greene county, Kentucky. Her parents were from the vicinity of Nashville, Tenn., and both died in Kentucky; the father in 1823, and the mother in 1826. She came to Sangamon county in 1834, with the family of Dr. Richard Barrett. R. L. Stubbs and M. A. Smith were married August 4, 1836, and had fourteen children in Sangamon county.

MARY E., born June 11, 1837, married Sept. 11, 1856, to Samuel Clawson, have two children, WILLIAM H. and MARTHA M., and live near New Home, Bates county, Mo.

JAMES T., born March 5, 1839, married Oct. 29, 1867, to Hannah F. Robeson, who was born Dec. 12, 1840, in Morgan county. They have three children, ALBERT L., ELIZABETH A. and JAMES T., and live three and one-half miles east of Berlin, Sangamon county, Ill.

SARAH E., born Dec. 3, 1840, married March 18, 1858, to A. Jackson Rude, have one child, EDWARD E., and live five miles west of Chatham, Ill.

NANCY H., born Sept. 30, 1842, married Sept. 10, 1862, to James Campbell. *See his name.*

ELIZABETH A., born March 13, 1844, married Jan. 29, 1870, to Edmund T. Miller. *See his name.*

GEORGE W., born August 23, 1846, married Sept. 15, 1870, to Eliza Miller. They have one child, GEORGE R., and reside four miles west of Chatham, Ill.

WILLIAM S., born Jan. 7, 1851, married Nov. 6, 1872, to Annie A. Johnson, have one child, JAMES G., and live two miles west of Berlin, Sangamon county, Ill.

MARGARET J., born June 6, 1853, married Dec. 29, 1870, to Dayton LaDue, have two children, and reside near Arthur, Moultrie county, Ill.

ROBERT L., Jun., MARIA M.

PETER G., DOLLIE T. and *CHARLES E.* reside with their mother.

Robert L. Stubbs died Sept. 7, 1871, and his widow resides four miles east of Berlin, Sangamon county, Ill.

SWEET, JOSEPH, was born March 15, 1789, in Otsego county, New York. He was there married to Abigail Neal, who was born Oct. 30, 1793, in Hartford Connecticut. They had eight children in Otsego county, and moved to Sangamon county, Illinois, arriving in the fall of 1830 at Lebanon, now Loami, where two children were born. Of their children—

ASENATH, born Nov. 11, 1813, married in Sangamon county to John Kinney, had three living children, and reside at Linden, Osage county, Kansas.

MANASSEH, born August 10, 1815, married three times, had one child by the first, and three by the second wife. He died in 1872, in Canton, Missouri.

EUNICE, born Sept. 9, 1817, married Jacob Markle, has several children, and lives in Omaha, Nebraska.

FRANCIS, born March 13, 1819, married Phebe Morton, who died, leaving one child, and he married again, and lives in Lewis county, Missouri.

CORDELIA, born June 14, 1822, married Jacob Weidner, has ten children, and lives in Lewis county, Missouri.

JOSEPH, born March 25, 1824, in Otsego county, New York, married in Sangamon county to Lola Hinman. They live in Chatham, Illinois.

IRA, born May 2, 1826.

VERMELIA A., born Feb. 5, 1828, the last birth of the family in New York, married in Sangamon county to Washington Clawson, had two children, and Mr. C. died and the widow married Theodore Watson, had one child, and lives in Waverly, Illinois.

ARABELLA I., born March 18, 1831, the first birth of the family in Sangamon county, married August 22, 1848, in Springfield to Ebenezer B. Watson, who was born Nov. 21, 1819, at East Windsor, Connecticut. They had ten children, six of whom are dead, namely, ALICE died March 10, 1864, in her fifteenth year, PHILIP, GRACE A., HENRY, ARABELLA and MARY R. died under three years. The other four, ANNA, SERENA, EBINEZER B., Jun., and ARABELLA L. live with their parents in Talkington township, three miles east of Waverly, Illinois.

SARAH T., born Sept. 25, 1833, in Sangamon county, married Samuel Brown and moved to Texas.

Joseph Sweet moved to Scyene, Dallas county, Texas, in 1852, and soon after became postmaster, and died in office in 1864. His wife died the same year.

SWEET, ROBERT, was born in 1791, in Otsego county, N. Y. He was married to Sarah Parker, and they had five children in that county. They embarked at Olean Point, in a family boat, and floated down to Shawneetown in May, 1820, and engaged in farming until the spring of 1824, when he moved to Diamond Grove, near Jacksonville, and from there to what is called Sweet's Prairie, in consequence of their being the first settlers there. It is about five miles west of Manchester, Scott county, Ill. In 1830, he moved back to Diamond Grove, and in 1837 moved to Loami, Sangamon county. They had four children in Illinois. Of their nine children—

DANIEL, born June 19, 1809, in New York, married Elecy Sweet. They had four children, and Mrs. Sweet died in 1849. He resides at Chenoa, Ill.

ALVTA, born July 1, 1811, in New York, married, had fourteen children, and resides at Cedar Rapids, Iowa.

MORRIS, born April 8, 1813, in Otsego county, New York, married in Sangamon county May 2, 1839, to Olivia Barger. They had nine children, SOPHRONIA I., married William McKee. *See his name.* SYLVESTER H., born August 12, 1841, enlisted August 12, 1861, in Co. C, 11th Missouri Inf. for three years, re-enlisted as a veteran January, 1864, and died of disease April 17, 1865, at Memphis, Tenn. MONTGOMERY Z., enlisted August, 1862, in the same company and regiment, was wounded at the battle of Iuka, Mississippi, Sept. 17, 1862, and discharged on account of physical disability. Resides at Loami. LETHE M. married Haskell Jones, had two children and mother and children died. MARCELLA and LORENTINE C. reside with their parents. LUCINDA married John Brash and reside in Loami. MARGARET J. and LUELLA reside with their parents in Loami, Sangamon county, Ill.

JONATHAN, born March 1, 1815, in New York, married Phebe Weaver. She had one child, and mother and child died. He resides at Chenoa, Ill.

LOUISA M., born April 5, 1817, married in Sangamon county to Adna P. Colburne. *See his name.*

LORENTINE, born Jan. 21, 1821, near Shawneetown, married Sarah A. Sweet. He died in 1851, leaving a widow and one child. They have since died at Waverly, Ill.

MARY J., born Dec. 2, 1824, married Benjamin Fry, has three children, and lives at Hinsdale, Dupage county, Ill.

HIRAM K., born Feb. 25, 1828, married Julia A. Ayers, has four children and lives at Forest, Livingston county, Ill.

CAROLINE A., born August 5, 1831, married Joseph S. Snell, have five children, and live in Winchester, Illinois.

Mrs. Sarah Sweet died Nov. 22, 1846, and Robert Sweet died July, 1861, both in Sangamon county, Illinois.

SWEET, THEOPILUS, a cousin to Joseph and Robert, was born and married in Otsego county, New York. Had children born there, and moved to Morgan county, Illinois, and from there to the vicinity of Loami, Sangamon county, in 1826. They brought six children and three were born in Sangamon county. I have not a full history of his children. His eldest son—

LEVI, born in New York, married in Sangamon county in 1832 to Lucy Colburn, a daughter of Isaac Colburn, who died at Louisville, Kentucky, in 1820. They had five children, moved in 1853 to Sevene, Texas, and Mr. S. died there in 1863, leaving his family there. Levi Sweet was a preacher in the Christian Church before he went to Texas, and continued to preach as long as he lived.

ADONIRAM married Abigail Greening. He died and she married again and lives in Waverly, Illinois.

ANSEL married Elizabeth Anderson in Morgan county, Illinois.

The wife of Theopilus Sweet died at Loami and he married Lucinda B. Harrison. He moved with part of his children to Scott county, and died about 1860 at Winchester, Illinois. His widow died August 20, 1873, on Richland creek, at the residence of her nephew, John H. Harrison. Theopilus Sweet was a preacher of the Old School Baptist Church when he came to Sangamon county, and soon after changed to the Christian, or what is called Campbellite. He preached in Sangamon about eighteen years, and was then the principal mover in organizing a phalanx of Fourierites at Loami in 1844. That was disbanded in two or three years. Mr. Sweet joined the Missionary Baptists two or three years before his death.

EXPLANATION.

For the convenience of those consulting this volume, the explanation is again inserted, by which it may be known what generation of a family any person belongs to, by the kind of type used in printing his or her name. Original early settlers or heads of families are in LARGE LETTERS; second generation, *ITALIC CAPITALS*; third, in CAPITALS; fourth, in SMALL CAPITALS; fifth, in *Italics*.

T

TAFT, MRS. PHŒBE, whose maiden name was Davis, was born June 5, 1780, in Vermont. She was married there to Josiah Taft. They had eleven children, and Mr. Taft died Sept. 17, 1838, in Vermont. Mrs. Taft and some of her children came to Sangamon county, Illinois, part before and part after her arrival. She and two of her daughters arrived at Rochester in the fall of 1839. Of the five who came to Sagamon county—

WILLIAM W., born Sept. 7, 1803, at Vergennes, Vermont, came to Rochester, Sangamon county, in 1833 or '34, and was married Feb. 1, 1838, to Eliza Delay. They had seven children, near Rochester, namely, JOSIAH, born Nov. 12, 1838, died Oct. 21, 1866. JOHN, born March 14, 1840, died June 10, 1860. CAROLINE born Nov. 9, 1841, and HATTIE, born August 25, 1843, live with their mother. WILLIAM and ELIZA, twins, born Nov. 23, 1846. William lives with his mother. ELIZA married Dec. 18, 1873, to Dr. R. J. McNeill. *See his name.* HENRY, born July 20, 1850, lives with his mother.

William W. Taft died Feb. 16, 1855, and his widow resides on the farm where they settled in 1838. It is one mile west of Rochester, Sangamon county, Ill.

SARAH, born August 13, 1805, in Vermont, married in Sangamon county to Caleb Sherman, and both died; she in Sangamon county and he in Iowa.

ANN, born April 10, 1812, in Vermont, married Mr. Tracy. He died and she married Munson Carter, and resides in Rochester, Ill.

NANCY, born Sept. 5, 1819, in Vermont, married in Sangamon county to Henry Pier. They reside at Belvidere, Ill.

HARRIET, born April 18, 1822, in Vermont, married Josiah Adams. They reside near Harrel, Christian county, Ill.

Mrs. Phœbe Taft died April 2, 1861, in Rochester, Sangamon county, Ill.

TALBOTT, DAVID, was born Jan. 6, 1786, in Baltimore county, Maryland. "There is a tradition that has been handed down to the Talbotts in this country, that prior to, or about the year 1700, three brothers came over from England, two of whom settled in Virginia and one in Maryland. They seem to have visited and continued their acquaintance, and in the course of time united in looking up up their old-fashioned silver plate, of which they appear to have had a considerable quantity. After a general consultation, they decided to return this silver plate to England for remodeling. It was consequently shipped for that purpose, but the vessel in which it was sent was never heard from." The above was taken from a letter written by Thomas E. Talbott, of Dalhoff, St. Charles county, Mo., to his cousin, Thomas Talbott, of Sangamon county. He facetiously adds: "Perhaps some of the Spirit Rappers might call up the spirit of the captain of that old ship and ask him the name of the shippers of this precious plate." He thus disposes of the effort to trace the geneology of the three brothers, but at the same time makes it quite plain that the one who settled in Maryland was named John. He had a son Edward who married an English lady by the name of Margaret Slade. Edward Talbott died soon after marriage. A son, Edward, was born April 6, 1764, after the death of his father, on what was called "My Lady's Manor," in Baltimore county, Maryland. This Edward Talbott was married in 1783, in Harford county, Maryland, to Elizabeth Standiford. They had twelve sons and one daughter. It was their second son, David, whose name heads this sketch. When David Talbott was about ten years old his father moved to Shelby county, Kentucky. He was there married Dec. 4, 1806, to Harriet Harding who was born Dec. 25, 1787, in Berkley county, Virginia. Her father, Nathan Harding, moved to Shelby county about 1802. David Talbott and wife had twelve living children in Shelby county, Kentucky. The whole family, with the exception of the eldest son, moved to Sangamon county, Illinois, arriving April 16, 1835, in what is now Curran township, south of Spring creek. In the fall of that year they moved north of Spring creek, in what is now Garden township. Of their children—

LUCINDA, born Dec. 14, 1808, in Kentucky, is unmarried, and resides with her brother Thomas, at the family homestead.

FLETCHER, born March 24, 1810, in Shelby county, Kentucky, commenced the study of medicine in 1832, with Dr. Hanson Harding, in Shelbyville, Kentucky, attended lectures at Transylvania University, Lexington, Kentucky, in the winters of 1834 and '5, and in the spring of the latter year commenced practice in Spencer county, Kentucky. He came to Springfield, Illinois, in the autumn of 1836, where he practiced medicine one year and returned to Lexington, Kentucky, attended a second course of lectures and graduated in March, 1838. He returned to Springfield in May and continued there until September, when he moved to the country a few miles west of Springfield, where he has continued practicing his profession until the present time. Dr. Fletcher Talbott was married in Morgan county, Illinois, June 18, 1839, to Ruth R. Gatton. They had seven children. WILLIAM T., born July 6, 1841, in that part of Morgan which is now Cass county, Illinois, was married November 2, 1864, in St. Louis county, Missouri, to Sarah F. Gardner, a daughter of Thomas Gardner. She was born April 6, 1842. They have five children, THOMAS G., JOHN F., NETTIE E., MABEL and CHARLES D., the latter born May 13, 1876, is the "centennial" of the family. William T. Talbott is one of the neatest farmers I have found in Sangamon county, or any other place. That he is thoroughly posted on all the latest improvements in agriculture, a visit to his farm, "Elder Grove," will convince the most casual observer. He has an extensive library, a large collection of minerals, fossils, copper coins, etc., etc. Mr. Talbott and family reside at "Elder Grove," two miles northwest of Farmingdale, Sangamon county, Ill. David C., born August 1, 1843, in Sangamon county, was married Oct. 28, 1868, to Elizabeth A. Pirkins. They have three children, namely, WALTER, CARLTON and HENRY FLETCHER, and reside in Curran, Sangamon county, Illinois. JAMES L., born April 25, 1846, in Sangamon county, was married June 19, 1873, to Jennie Gill. They have two children, ROSE and JOHN GILL, and live two miles west of Springfield. FLETCHER H., born October 28, 1848. MARY R., EDWARD R. and CHARLES R. live with their parents. Dr. Fletcher Talbott and wife reside six miles west of Springfield, Illinois.

ELIZABETH, born Oct. 14, 1811, in Kentucky, was married in Sangamon county, to Noah Mason. See his name.

DAVID, Jun., born July 22, 1813, in Shelby county, Kentucky, was married in Sangamon county, Oct. 3, 1850, to Susan Rickard. They had one child, ELLA BELLE, who was born July 5, 1855, and died August 20, 1875. David Talbott and wife reside six and one-half miles west of Springfield, Illinois.

ARSENETH, born Nov. 12, 1814, in Kentucky, was married in Sangamon county to James M. Bradford. See his name.

THOMAS, born Feb. 21, 1816, in Kentucky, is unmarried and lives at the homestead, where his parents settled in 1835, six and a half miles west of Springfield, Illinois.

HARRIET, born Jan. 31, 1818, in Kentucky, was married in Sangamon county March, 1838, to Noah M. Rickard. See his name.

LUTHER, born Feb. 11, 1820, in Shelby county, Kentucky, was married in Sangamon county, Illinois, June, 1851, to Mary M. Rickard. They have eight children, namely, CHARLES W., CATHARINE L., ELIZA F., THOMAS F., ARSENETH H., CAROLINE L., DAVID K. and EMILY BELLE. Luther Talbott and family reside near Harristown, Macon county, Illinois.

MARY R., born Jan. 2, 1822, in Kentucky, was married Dec. 9, 1858, in Sangamon county, Illinois, to Rev. Moses Summers, of the M. E. Church. They have two children, EMILY F. and MOSES W., and live two miles north of Curran, Sangamon county, Illinois. Rev. Moses Summers was born Sept. 11, 1818, in Onondaga county, New York. He came to that part of Morgan county which has since been added to Cass county, Illinois, arriving Nov. 3, 1838. He was there married to Eleanor Yaples. They had three daughters. AZUBA R. lives with her father, MARY E. married Preston H. Gibson, and lives at Brownsville, Nebraska. SARAH C. married Irwin B. Towl, and lives in Lincoln, Illinois. Mrs. Eleanor Summers died Oct. 5, 1857.

EMILY, born Oct. 21, 1823, in Kentucky, was married in Sangamon county to George Brunk. See his name. He died and she married Lindsey H. English, and resides two miles southeast of Springfield, Illinois.

CAROLINE, born August 24, 1825, in Kentucky, died April 22, 1875, at the family homestead, unmarried. Her death was the first of the twelve children David Talbott brought to Sangamon county, forty years before.

SARAH, born May 1, 1827, in Kentucky, was married in Sangamon county, Oct. 12, 1847, to H. K. Cooper, who was born Jan. 5, 1820, in Mercer county, Pennsylvania. They had two children, ROSE H. married William E. Pirkins. See his name. WILLIAM K. married Kate S. Van Patten. They live one and a half miles northwest of Bradfordton, Sangamon county, Ill. Hugh K. Cooper died Sept. 7, 1850. Mrs. Cooper was married Sept. 5, 1858, to William J. Shaver, who was born May 10, 1834, in Rensselaer county, New York. They had three children, JAMES A., and THOMAS T., the eldest and youngest died under four years. GEORGE D. lives with his mother. Wm. J. Shaver died Jan. 25, 1864, and Mrs. Sarah Shaver lives in Gardner township, one and a half miles northwest of Bradfordton, Sangamon county, Ill.

David Talbott died Oct. 31, 1867, and

Mrs. Harriet Talbott died Dec. 22, 1867, both in Gardner township, Sangamon county, Ill.

TALBOTT, BENJAMIN, was born June 19, 1798, in Fairfax county, Virginia. He went to Kentucky, where he was married Jan. 21, 1808, to Mrs. Frances Lumsford, whose maiden name was Johnson. Her former husband, Mr. Lumsford, was an overseer and was poisoned by negroes in Kentucky. They had three children in Kentucky, and Mrs. Frances Talbott died Nov. 17, 1817. Benjamin Talbott was married April 8, 1818, to Elizabeth Johnson, sister of his first wife, and a native of North Carolina. They had two children. Benjamin Talbott moved to Springfield, Illinois, in 1826. Of their children—

HANNAH, born Dec. 14, 1808, in Kentucky, was married there to Alexander Harrower. She died April 28, 1859. Mr. H. resides in Athens, Illinois.

HARVEY, born March 14, 1810, in Kentucky, died in Springfield Oct. 8, 1832.

WILLIAM H., born August 10, 1817, in Kentucky, was married Dec. 3, 1838, in Sangamon county to Matilda Enyart. They had six children, four died young. Of the two living children, CHARLES H., born May 13, 1845, in Springfield, is a merchant in Burton View, Logan county, Illinois. BENJAMIN F., born Feb. 10, 1848, in Springfield, is a printer and stockholder in the Springfield Printing Company. He is also Superintendent in the job department, and resides in Springfield. Mrs. Matilda Talbott died March 16, 1855, and William H. Talbott was married Oct. 2, 1856, to Mary Winters, who was born August 2, 1824, in Franklin county, Penn. They had two children, MARY E. and WILLIAM H., Jun. The latter died March 14, 1871, aged 11 years. William H. Talbott, Sen., died Jan. 21, 1874, and his widow resides in Springfield, Illinois. He was at the time of his death engaged in the business of carriage and wagon making, and had been for many years.

MARTHA, born March 8, 1824, in Kentucky, was married in Springfield Oct. 27, 1842, to Daniel W. Witmer. They have one child, MARY E., born July 21, 1843, was married May 11, 1863, to Reuben M. Huckey. They have two children, MATTIE R. and DANIEL W., and reside in Springfield. Mr. and Mrs. Witmer reside in Springfield, Illinois.

ROBERT A., born Nov. 5, 1826, in Springfield. He was married December, 1851, in Menard county, to Eveline Robinson. They had five living children, J. HARVEY, BENJAMIN S., CLARA W., BETTIE N. and ROBERT W., reside with their parents in Logan county, six miles west of Lincoln, Illinois. In the fall of 1874 R. A. Talbott was elected to represent Logan county for two years in the Legislature of Illinois.

Benjamin Talbott died April 29, 1858, and Mrs. Elizabeth Talbott died March 29, 1870, both in Springfield, Illinois.

Soon after Benjamin Talbott came to Springfield, in 1826, he acted as deputy sheriff and assessor, and filled other minor offices until 1836, when he was elected county recorder, which office he held until 1848, when, under the constitution adopted that year, the office of recorder was merged into that of circuit clerk. He was elected to the latter office four years, and after that had charge of the recorder's branch until his death.

TAYLOR, FRANCIS, was born August 23, 1797, in Shelby county, Kentucky. Nancy Jackson was born March 18, 1795, in the vicinity of Richmond, Virginia, and was taken by her parents to Shelby county, Kentucky, when she was a child. They were married October, 1821, in Spencer county, where they had two children, moved to Oldham county, where three children were born, and then returned to Spencer county, where they had twins, one of whom died in infancy. The family moved to Sangamon county, Illinois, arriving Oct. 13, 1834, at what is now Sangamon Station. Of their six children—

JULIA F., born and died in Kentucky at ten years of age.

PERMELIA A., born May 16, 1824, in Spencer county, Kentucky, married in Sangamon county April 16, 1840, to Benjamin West. See his name. He died and she married Erastus Woodruff, of Orange county, New York. (His son, Augustus Woodruff, by a former wife resides near Sangamon Station.) Mr. and Mrs. Woodruff had one child, MARY E., born August 1, 1853, married Oct. 22, 1873, to Frederick D. Wilson, a native of St. Lawrence county, New York. They reside four miles northwest of Illiopolis. Erastus Woodruff died of cholera Oct. 30, 1854, on Round Prairie, five miles east of Springfield. Mrs. Permelia A. Woodruff married John North. See his name.

PHILIP W., born March 16, 1826, in Oldham county, Kentucky, married Ann M. Connelly. They had eight children, and live at Clinton, DeWitt county, Ill.

FRANCIS J., born March 14, 1828, in Oldham county, Kentucky, married in Rochester, Illinois, to Mary T. St. Clair. They have five children, and reside at Decatur, Illinois.

FANNY, born August 7, 1830, in Oldham county, Kentucky, married in Sangamon county June 22, 1848, to Rev. Robert F. Shinn, of the Protestant Methodist Church, and resides in Quincy, Illinois.

JOHN S., born Jan. 13, 1834, in Spencer county, Kentucky, married Julia Mills. They had two children, and Mr. Taylor was drowned near Henry, Illinois, Feb. 22, 1860.

Francis Taylor died March 21, 1841, and his widow died Nov. 21, 1852, both in Sangamon county, Illinois.

TAYLOR, EDMOND, was born Oct. 22, 1785, in Christian county, Kentucky, married there to Mary Pugh, had five children, and she died. He married Constant Blakey, who was born June 22, 1791, in Georgia. They moved to what became Sangamon county, arriving in the fall of 1819, on Sugar creek, and in 1822 or '23 moved to the south side of Spring creek, four and a half miles west of Springfield. They had eight children in Sangamon county, three died young. Of his ten children—

JOHN, born in Kentucky, raised in Sangamon county, married in 1829, in Pike county, to Eveline McIntire. They have seven children, and live in Seneca, Nemaha county, Kansas.

EDWARD, died in Sangamon county, aged thirteen years.

ELIZABETH, born in Kentucky, raised in Sangamon county, married Samuel McClure, have nine children, and resides near Macomb, Illinois.

ELLEN, born in Kentucky, married in Sangamon county to Martin L. C. Kendall.

JAMES, born in Kentucky in 1818, raised in Sangamon county, became sheriff of Menard county, and died in office, unmarried, about 1848.

By the second wife—

WILLIAM, born in Sangamon county, died in Iowa, aged twenty-one years.

NANCY, born in Sangamon county, married Benjamin R. Kendall, have seven children, and live in Jefferson county, Kansas.

SUSAN, born in Sangamon county, married John Archer. See his name. They reside near Macomb, Illinois.

DANIEL, born Nov. 28, 1829, in Sangamon county, married Oct. 12, 1858, to Nancy A. Ralston. They have six children, WILLIAM E., JAMES H., FANNIE E., LAURA A., JOHN G. and JANE K., and reside on the farm where his parents settled in 1822 or '23. It is four and a half miles west of Springfield, Illinois.

AMERICA A., born Nov. 18, 1831, in Sangamon county, and married John Vulgamott. They have nine children, and reside near Oakley, Macon county, Illinois.

Edmond Taylor died August 20, 1866, and Mrs. Constant Taylor died Sept. 17, 1872, both in Sangamon county, Illinois.

TAYLOR, JOHN, was born May 1, 1772, in Maryland. Three brothers, Isaac, James and William Taylor, came from England to America long before our Revolution. Where James and William settled is unknown to the decendants of Isaac, who settled in Maryland, and who was the father of John, whose name heads this sketch. The parents of John Taylor emigrated when he was quite young to Chester district, South Carolina, where John was married to Susan Mobley. They had seven children there, and moved in 1805 to that part of Barren which afterwards became Hart county, Kentucky, where one child was born, and Mrs. Susan Taylor died there in 1808 or '9. John Taylor was married in that county in 1816, to Susan Trotter. They had one living child there, and the family moved in 1818 to White county, Illinois. In the spring of 1819 they moved to Wayne county, where five children were born, and from there to Sangamon county, arriving in May, 1829, on Wolf creek, in Williams township, where three children were born, making a total of seventeen children. John Taylor spent six years in Sangamon counly, and then moved to Moultrie county Illinois. In 1849 he settled in Davis county, Iowa. He left home in Davis county to tend a religious meeting in the adjoining county of Appanoose, and died there Nov. 7, 1856. His widow now resides with some of her children near Drakesville, Davis county, Iowa. Of all the children of John Taylor, three only settled permanently in Sangamon county. Simeon, the eldest, James, the fifth, and Isaac, the eighth, all by the first marriage. Of the other fourteen I shall speak first.

ELIZABETH, born Sept. 27, 1796, was married in Kentucky to David Garrison. They moved to White, and from there to Wayne county, Illinois, brought up a family, and both died there.

MARY, born March 5, 1798, in South Carolina, was married in Hart county, Kentucky, to George Coats, and still lives there, near Mumfordville.

NINIAN, born Dec. 19, 1799, in South Carolina, was married in Kentucky, brought up a large family, and died there in 1862.

NANCY, born Oct. 4, 1803, in South Carolina, was married in Wayne county, Illinois, to James Bowling, moved to Moultrie county, brought up a large family, and lives near Sullivan, Illinois.

JOHN M., born April 24, 1805, in South Carolina, was married in Kentucky to Nancy Wilson, moved in 1849 to Appanoose county, Iowa, brought up a large family, and died there.

HARRISON, born about 1817 in Hart county, Kentucky, came to Sangamon county with his parents, and was married in Moultrie county, Illinois, to Eliza Killian. They moved to Appanoose county, Iowa, and he enlisted in the 37th Iowa (Graybeard) Regiment. Harrison Taylor died in Iowa, a member of that regiment, leaving a large family near Drakesville, Davis county, Iowa.

ANN, born in Wayne county, Illinois, was married in Moultrie county to Albert Killian, and died in Appanoose county, near Drakesville, Iowa.

MELINDA, born in Wayne county, Illinois, was married in Moultrie county to John Fleming, and both died in Davis county, Iowa.

CHESTER, born in Wayne county, Illinois, was married in Davis county, Iowa, and still lives near Drakesville.

DENNIS, born in Wayne county, Illinois, was married in Sangamon county to Caroline Simpson, and died in Davis county, Iowa, leaving a widow and four children, one of whom died young. Of the other three, PASCO, in stepping from one railroad car to another, fell through and was killed instantly, in June 1875. ADDIE and LULA live with their mother near Drakesville, Iowa.

HENRY, born in Wayne county, Illinois, was married in Davis county, Iowa.

LUCINDA, born in Sangamon county, Illinois, was married in Davis county, Iowa, and died there.

ALVIN S., born June 19, 1834, in Sangamon county, was married there August 7, 1856, to Louisa J. Wilson. They had two children in Sangamon county, and moved in 1860 to Drakesville, Davis county, Iowa, where two children were born, one died in infancy. Mr. Taylor enlisted August 9, 1862, in Co. B, 30th Iowa Inf., for three years, was appointed first sergeant at the organization of the company, promoted to first lieutenant, but before receiving his commission, was promoted to captain and commissioned by Governor Kirkwood, to take rank from May 30, 1863. He entered upon its duties in Mississippi, Sept. 2, 1863, and was mortally wounded May 13, 1864, at Resacca, Georgia. He died there in military hospital, June 7th. Of his three children, CHARLES W. died Jan. 22, 1876. The other two, S. LESLIE and NELLIE A., live with their mother, half a mile south of Barclay, Sangamon county, Illinois.

FOSTER, born in Sangamon county, was married in Davis county, Iowa, and moved farther west in the same State.

Of the three sons of John Taylor who settled permanently in Sangamon county:

TAYLOR SIMEON, born May 10, 1795, near Chester Court House, Chester district, South Carolina, was married March 5, 1817, in Hart county, Kentucky, to Sarah Sturgeon. They had one child there, and, in company with his father's family, moved, in 1820, to Wayne county, Illinois, where two children were born. Mr. and Mrs. Taylor, with their children, returned to Kentucky on a visit, and Mrs. Taylor died there August 19, 1824. In September, Mr. Taylor returned with his three children to Wayne county, where he resided until the spring of 1829, when, in company with his brother James and family, he moved to Sangamon county, and settled in what is now Williams township. Of his three children—

JAMES S., born May 29, 1818, in Hart county, Kentucky, was married Feb. 25, 1841, in Sangamon county, to Sarah Halbert. They had five living children. SIDNEY E., born Feb. 26, 1842, married James W. Jones. See his name. MARGARET J., born Dec. 9, 1843, was married March 1, 1866, to John L. Wright. They have one living child, SARAH H., and reside five and one-half miles southeast of Williamsville, Sangamon county, Ill. SUSAN C., born Nov. 22, 1848, was married March 29, 1869, to Benjamin F. Cleverly. They have one child, LENA, and live at Illiopolis, Sangamon county, Ill. DRUSILLA, born Oct. 28, 1851, married Mr. Hunter, and lives at Riverton, Sangamon county, Ill. ANNIE, born Feb. 6, 1854, lives with her parents, three-fourths of a mile south of Barclay, Sangamon county Illinois—1874.

ELIZABETH, born March 31, 1821, in Wayne county, Illinois, married Hugh L. Cooper. See his name.

SUSANNAH, born Jan. 27, 1823, in Wayne county, Illinois, was married in Sangamon county to John Webb. See his name. They have six children, and live in Ioka, Keokuk county, Iowa.

Simeon Taylor was married the second time August 9, 1832, in Sangamon county, to Jane Blue. They had seven children, namely:

JOHN B., born Nov. 2, 1833, married Anna Thompson, who had one child, JANE M., and Mrs. Anna Taylor died. John B. Taylor married Jane Dickerson. They have one child, JOHN W., and live five miles southeast of Williamsville, in Logan county, Illinois.

NANCY, born Nov. 23, 1834, was married August 17, 1854, to Adam Braughton, who was born June 1, 1829, in Franklin county, Ohio. They had nine children, three of whom died under nine years of age. JAMES A. died August 19, 1872, in his tenth year, caused by the kick of a horse. WILLIAM M., GEORGE W., ADELBERT C., EMELINE and ETHEL live with their parents, two miles west of Barclay, Sangamon county, Illinois.

NINIAN, M., born Dec. 26, 1835, was married Jan. 15, 1857, to Elizabeth P. Constant. She died Feb. 2, 1858, and N. M. Taylor was married Jan. 11, 1859, to Mahala E. Lard. They have four children, SIMEON W., CHARLES A., NINIAN L. and LORIN O., and live four miles southeast of Springfield, Illinois.

MARY, born April 16, 1837, in Sangamon county, and

EMILY, born August 16, 1838, are unmarried, and live with their father.

CAROLINE, born Jan. 20, 1839, was married August 28, 1857, to John Hendrix. See his name. They live near Dawson, Sangamon county, Ill.

WILLIAM L., born Nov. 13, 1842, is unmarried and lives with his father.

Mrs. Jane Taylor died Feb. 23, 1843, and Simeon Taylor was married April 15, 1850, to Susan Hendrix. They had one child, SIMEON, which died in infancy, and Mrs. Susan Taylor died July 11, 1852. Simeon Taylor resides on the farm where he settled in 1829, three-fourths of a mile north of Barclay, Sangamon county, Ill.

TAYLOR, JAMES, born Nov. 2, 1801, in Chester district, South Carolina, moved with his parents to Hart county, Kentucky, and thence to Wayne county, Ill., where he was married to Mary Kelly, who was born in Hart county, also, and taken by her parents when young to Wayne county. They had five children, and moved to Sangamon county in the spring of 1829, settling in what is now Williams township, near Barclay, where seven children were born. Of their nine children who lived to any considerable age:

ZERELDA, born in Wayne county, Illinois, married James W. Cooper. See his name.

NINIAN R., born Feb. 13, 1825, in Wayne county, Illinois, was married April 1, 1847, in Sangamon county, to Catharine (Kittie) Halbert. They have five living children. JOHN B., born May 22, 1851, was married Dec. 2, 1873, to Miranda Turley, and lives in Williamsville. LEWIS C., born April 9, 1854, graduated at Bellevue Medical College, New York, March 1, 1875, and is practicing medicine at Auburn, Ill. ELLEN, EMMA and FRANK H., live with their parents. Ninian R. Taylor was elected in 1870 to represent Sangamon county, in the twenty-seventh General Assembly of Illinois, for two years. He and his family reside at Williamsville, Sangamon county, Ill. He is a merchant there.

JOHN was drowned, aged ten years. He and Eli Wilson were skating and both were drowned.

RHODA, born in Wayne county, Illinois, was married in 1848 in Sangamon county, Ill., to Wm H. White. She died of cholera in 1851, leaving one child, BERTRAND D. WHITE, who lives near Gibson, Ford county, Ill.

ISAAC J., born Oct. 12, 1830, in Sangamon county, married Margaret Halbert. They had two children, ALEXANDER D., born May 9, 1854, graduated at Rush Medical College, Chicago, in 1875, and is practicing medicine at Cotton Hill, Sangamon county, Ill. MARY ETHEL, lives with her father. Mrs. Margaret Taylor died May 16, 1863, and I. J. Taylor was married May 27, 1864, to Mary A. McGinnis. They have two children, JOHN E. and LEONARD R., and reside two and a half miles southeast of Williamsville, Sangamon county, Ill.

JAMES H., born Dec. 25, 1832, in Sangamon county, was married Jan. 5, 1855, to Rachel C. Groves. They had six children. JAMES A. died in his fourth year, BARBARA A., MARY E., DORA B., GERTRUDE C. and WILLIAM H. live with their parents. James H. Taylor moved his family to Danville, Illinois, Nov. 28, 1868, and now—1876—reside there.

SIMEON M., born Feb. 2, 1835, in Sangamon county, married Louisa Buchanan. They have one child, MARY K., and reside on West Monroe street, Springfield, Illinois.

FRANCIS K., born June 14, 1840, in Sangamon county, was married Oct. 24, 1861, to Elizabeth Kalb. They had three children, FLORA L., died Nov. 18, 1875, in her thirteenth year; NELLIE F. died Nov. 25, 1875, in her tenth year, and JAMES C. died Nov. 14, 1875, in his sixth year, all of malignant diptheria. F. L. Taylor and wife reside at the homestead where his father settled in 1829, three-fourths of a mile north of Barclay, Sangamon county, Illinois.

MARTIN V., born March 22, 1842, in Sangamon county, married Mary Buchanan, a native of Brown county, Illinois.

They have three children, JESSE O., WILLIAM A. and JENNIE L., and live near Barclay, Illinois.

Mrs. Mary Taylor died July 27, 1852, and James Taylor died July 27, 1857, both where they settled in 1829, near Barclay, Sangamon county, Illinois.

TAYLOR, ISAAC, born Feb. 9, 1807, in Hart county, Kentucky, came with his father to White county, and from there to Wayne county, Illinois. He came alone in 1828 to Sangamon county, being the first of the family to arrive. In February, 1829, he went to the Wisconsin lead mines, and returned in September of that year, entered land and made some improvements near where German Prairie Station now stands. He enlisted in 1831 under Captain, now General, Moses K. Anderson, in the Blackhawk war, but their services were not needed. In the spring of 1832 he passed through Blackhawk's army at Dixon, on his way to to the lead mines, and was in great danger, as hostilities commenced soon after. He volunteered at the mines and served until the close of the war, returning home in December, 1832. He was married Feb. 13, 1834, to Sarah M. Elliott, at Springfield, Illinois. They had thirteen children. Of their eleven living children—

MARY J., born Dec. 11, 1835, in Sangamon county, was married Feb. 9, 1854, to William H. White. They have seven living children, CHARLES, FLORENCE, MARTHA, GEORGIA, MARY A., EMMA and NELLIE, who live with their parents near Gibson City, Ford county, Illinois.

ZILPHA A., born May 27, 1838, in Sangamon county, was married there in July, 1856, to James S. Halbert. They had two living children, M. ESTELLA and ROSELLA. Mrs. Halbert then married James H. Cartwell. *See his name.* They have one child, LESLIE G.

SARAH E., born July 19, 1840, married Isaac Wilson. *See his name.* They have five living children, KATE, ALBERT, ELMER, ELIZA and NORA.

DAVID A., born July 16, 1842, in Sangamon county, was married January, 1866, to Mary C. Constant. She died August 21, 1874, leaving three children,

OTTO, EMMA H. and JIMMIE H., who live at present—1876—with their grand-papa Taylor. David A. Taylor lives near Gibson City, Ford county, Ill.

NANNIE E., born March 13, 1864, and

AMANDA M., born June 4, 1846, reside with their parents.

JOHN W., born March 1, 1848, in Sangamon county, was married Jan. 17, 1872, in Springfield, Illinois, to Lydia A. Claspill, who was born Nov. 5, 1849, at Moore's Hill, Dearborn county, Indiana. They have two children, CLARA MAUD and NELLIE M., and reside on the farm where his father settled in 1830. It is near German Prairie Station, Sangamon county, Illinois.

ISAAC H., born March 16, 1850, in Sangamon county, graduated at Rush Medical College, Chicago, Illinois, February, 1871, and was married Jan. 16, 1872, to Irena Constant. They have one child, PERCY L. Dr. I. H. Taylor is a practicing physician, and resides at Barclay, Sangamon county, Illinois.

JAMES L., born Feb. 7, 1853, in Sangamon county, and attend lectures at Rush Medical College, Chicago, Illinois, during the winter of 1875 and '76.

C. L. ROSCOE, born April 8, 1855, in Sangamon county, and

WALTER C., born Dec. 28, 1856, live with their parents.

Isaac Taylor and family reside one and three-quarter miles west of Dawson, Sangamon county, Illinois. Mr. Taylor says that Jacob Donner and wife were members of the Christian Church, that then worshipped near German Prairie Station. Mr. Taylor being clerk, gave them letters, by order of the church, when they left for the Pacific coast, and to the horrible doom that awaited them. His recollection of Jacob Donner is that he was a model Christian gentleman.

TAYLOR, JOHN, was born in Danville, Ky. He came when a young man to Madison county, Illinois, and was there married to Elizabeth Burkhead, who was born near Charleston, South Carolina. They returned to Kentucky, and had three children there, and moved to Edwardsville, Illinois, where they had one child, and from there to what became Sangamon county, arriving in 1819 on Sugar creek, in what is now Ball township, where they had two children, and in 1822 moved to Springfield, where they had two children. When Sangamon county was organized, in 1821, John Taylor was elected sheriff, and by re-elections held the office about six years. He was afterwards appointed receiver of the United States Land Office at Springfield, was one of the original proprietors of the town, and did much in the way of improvements to advance its interests. Of his children—

HANNAH, born Jan. 27, 1811, in Kentucky, was married in Springfield April, 1832, to S. M. Tinsley, a native of Virginia. They had eleven children in Springfield. Mr. Tinsley was for many years one of the leading merchants of the city, and died in 1867. Mrs. Hannah Tinsley died in July, 1869.

MARGARET, born Dec. 28, 1813, in Kentucky, was married Sept. 28, 1829, in Springfield, Illinois, to Edmond Dick Taylor, who was born October 18, 1804, at Lunenburg Court House, Virginia. His father's name was Giles Taylor, and his mother's maiden name was Sina Stokes. They moved to Lexington, Kentucky, in 1806, and two years later to Hopkinsville, in the same State. In 1814 they moved to Gallatin county, Illinois, where Mr. Taylor was for several years engaged in the manufacture of salt. Edmond D. Taylor came to Springfield in the fall of 1823, and went into general merchandising, with Colonel John Taylor, who afterwards became his father-in-law. In 1832 he was elected to represent Sangamon county in the Illinois Legislature, his opponent being no less a personage than Abraham Lincoln. He can justly boast of being the only man that ever defeated Mr. Lincoln in an election. In 1834 he was elected to the State Senate. In 1835 he resigned his seat in the Senate to accept the appointment from President Jackson as receiver of public moneys in the United States land office in Chicago, and opened the first land sale ever held there, in June, 1835. In forty days he found himself in possession of $493,000. When he reported it to the Secretary of the Treasury, that officer responded with the exclamation, "Is this not fiction?" Colonel Taylor's bond was only $30,000. He was for many years actively engaged in politics as a leader in the Democratic party. He has been engaged in banking and land speculations all his life. He lost several thousand dollars in the Chicago fire, but is still very wealthy and full of business. Colonel E. D. Taylor and wife had thirteen children, six only of whom are living. One daughter married S. Snowden Hayes, and lives in Chicago. Colonel Taylor's business is largely in Chicago, but he resides at Mendota, Illinois.

JAMES, born Jan 27, 1814, in Christian county, Kentucky, was brought up in Springfield, Illinois. He was a soldier from Sangamon county in the Blackhawk war. His sister, Mrs. Hurst, remembers that herself and some other school girls went into a bakery and assisted in preparing crackers for the soldiers, at the time her brother went. James Taylor was married in Springfield July 25, 1837, to Eliza C. Bryan, daughter of Nicholas Bryan. *See his name*. They had six living children, MARY E., born June 14, 1839, in Petersburg, Illinois, married in Springfield June, 25, 1874, to James M. Barclay, a native of Kentucky. They have one child, LOUAN E., and live in Cairo, Illinois, ELIZA B., born Dec. 9, 1841, in Petersburg, Illinois, was married March 19, 1863, in Beardstown, Illinois, to Robert W. Miller, of Sangamon county. They have four children, WINLOCK W., JEANNETTE, ROBERT TAYLOR and MARY B., and live at Cairo, Illinois. HANNAH T., born Oct. 15, 1843, was married in Springfield April 17, 1867, to James M. Epler. They have three children, ANNIE LOU, HANNAH T. and JAMES T., and live in Jacksonville, Illinois. ANN M., born Oct. 1, 1845, in Springfield, lives with her mother. JOHN C., born Nov. 10, 1847, in Bath, Mason county, Illinois, was married in Clinton, Illinois, Sept. 24, 1873, to Mary Jane Bryan, a native of Pennsylvania. They have one child, JOHN CLAY, and live in Springfield. JAMES S., born August 16, 1855, at Beardstown, Illinois, lives with his mother. James Taylor went to Petersburg soon after marriage, and sold goods there five years. He afterwards moved to Springfield and remained five years, thence to Beardstown, where he was sheriff of Cass county from 1850 to 1859, and four years circuit clerk. He returned to Springfield in 1863 and acted as deputy sheriff one year. He died July 26, 1873, and his widow resides in Springfield, Illinois.

EDWARD J., born in Edwardsville, Illinois, brought up in Springfield, is unmarried, and lives now—1876—in Maryville, Missouri.

JANE E., born June 27, 1820, in Sangamon county, was married in Springfield to David Kriegh, a native of Hagerstown, Maryland. They live in Chicago, Illinois.

ANN, born April 3, 1822, in Sangamon county, was married in Springfield to Charles R. Hurst. *See his name*.

WILLIAM W., born October, 1820, in Springfield, Illinois, died in 1853.

ANDREW J.

John Taylor died at Beardstown May 12, 1849, on his way to New Orleans. Mrs. Elizabeth Taylor died July, 1855, in Springfield, Illinois.

TAYLOR, JOHN, was born Sept. 1, 1804, in Tennessee, and when quite young was taken by his parents to Cape Girardeau county, Missouri. Mary Thomas was born Nov. 14, 1799, in Bracken county, Ky. Her parents moved to Lebanon, Ohio, and from there to St. Genevieve county, Mo., and then to Cape Girardeau county. She was there married to Samuel Cupples, had three children, and Mr. Cupples died in 1828. Mrs. Cupples was married March 22, 1834, to John Taylor. They had two children in Cape Girardeau county, and moved to Sangamon county, Illinois, arriving in the spring of 1837, west of Springfield, and early in 1838 moved to a farm he purchased, in what is now Gardner township, north of Spring creek, where three children were born. Of all her children—

MARY Cupples, born Dec. 8, 1821, in Missouri, is unmarried, and lives with her mother.

FRANCES T. Cupples, born March 9, 1823, in Missouri, married Sept. 28, 1847, to Lysander Root, and she died Feb. 16, 1850.

ROSETTA C. Cupples was born Nov. 11, 1826, in Missouri, married April 9, 1844, in Sangamon county, to Jesse M. Shepherd. They have three living children, and reside at Baker City, Oregon. He is a practicing attorney, and editor of the Bed Rock *Democrat*—1874.

Of the Taylor children—

ANN E., born Nov. 25, 1834, in Missouri, died in Sangamon county, Feb. 6, 1850.

ADALINE C., born August 8, 1836, in Missouri, married in Sangamon county, March, 1854, to John P. Attix. They have three children, and live near Keosauqua, Iowa.

RICHARD S., born May 25, 1838, in Sangamon county, married in Iowa, Dec. 25, 1867, has two children, and lives at Oswego, Kansas.

MARGARET A., born June 18, 1840, in Sangamon county, lives with her mother.

JOHN W., born August 10, 1842, in Sangamon county, was married Feb. 25, 1864, to Margaret L. Stevenson. They had three children, LOTTIE B., JESSE B. and CLARA L. Mrs. Margaret L. Taylor died July 6, 1872, and John W. Taylor married in 1874 Nancy E. McKinnie. They have one child, WILLIAM, and live near Bradfordton, Sangamon county, Ill.

John Taylor died April 22, 1853, in Sangamon county, and his widow resides where they settled in 1838. It is one and three-fourth miles southwest of Bradfordton, Sangamon county, Ill.

TAYLOR, JOHN WICKLIFFE, was born April 21, 1798, in Boone county, Kentucky, nearly opposite Lawrenceburg, Indiana. In 1802 his parents moved to that part of Gallatin which is now Trimble county in the same State, opposite the city of Madison, Indiana. *See sketch of his two sisters*, Mrs. Jane E. Elliott, widow of James Elliott, and Mrs. Sally Smith, widow of Joseph Smith. J. Wickliffe Taylor was married June 1, 1820, in Tremble county, Kentucky, to Jemima Gray, who was born there Feb. 8, 1804. They had one child there, and moved to Springfield, Illinois, early in 1833. In April, 1834, they moved to what is now Cartwright township, ten miles west of Springfield, where they had three children. Of their four children—

JOHN P., born April 10, 1821, in Kentucky, died there July 19, 1832.

BENJAMIN P., born and died in Sangamon county, aged three years.

WILLIAM H., born August 2, 1838, in Sangamon county. He has spent the last two years in Colorado, and has just returned to Sangamon county, and lives near Wheatfield.

SALLIE JANE, born August 12, 1843, and died April 18, 1858.

Mrs. Jemima Taylor died in 1874, near Wheatfield. Since her death Mr. Taylor has lived with his sister, Mrs. Smith, at Bates.

J. W. Taylor was elected in 1852 Judge of the Sangamon county court, and served four years.

TAYLOR, WILLIAM, was born in Bath county, Kentucky, married there to Mrs. Patrick, and brought his family to Sangamon county, Illinois, arriving in 1835 in what is now Cotton Hill township. His son—

EDWARD, born in Bath county, Kentucky, married in Sangamon county to a daughter of Isaac Martin, who was a brother to Abraham Martin. His daughter, MELISSA, born in Sangamon county, Jan. 8, 1845, married Sept. 27, 1866, to John W. Wigginton, who was born Jan. 12, 1835, in Trimble county, Kentucky, and came to Sangamon county in 1866. They reside at Breckenridge Sangamon county, Illinois.

TAYLOR, WILLIAM B., was born Dec. 25, 1800, near Salem, New Jersey. Beulah Smith was born Dec. 19, 1810, in Cape May county, New Jersey. They were married Jan. 4, 1830, in Cape May county, and had three living children in New Jersey. They moved to Sangamon county, Illinois, arriving May 16, 1838, in what is now Gardner township, one and a half miles north of Farmingdale, where they had five children. Of their eight children—

JOHN L., born Oct. 13, 1830, in New Jersey, raised in Sangamon county, and started April 4, 1851, to California. He has not been definitely heard from by his friends since 1857.

BEULAH ANN., born August 10, 1835, in New Jersey, married in Sangamon county, in 1857, to Isom Bolin. They have six children and live in Sangamon county, Illinois.

ROXANA S., born Oct. 22, 1837, in New Jersey, is unmarried, and resides with her brother, William B., Jun.

VICTORIA M., born Dec. 28, 1839, in Sangamon county, lives with her brother, William B., Jun.

JOSEPHINE M., born March 3, 1840, in Sangamon county, married Nov. 11, 1858, to Sidney Robins, had one child,

CHARLES, and for a second husband married, August, 1867, to Geo J. Fiddler. They have one child, JACOB BEN., and live in Mason City, Illinois.

WILLIAM BIDDLE, Jun., born June 1, 1842, in Sangamon county, and resides four miles north of Farmingdale, Sangamon county, Illinois—1874.

ABIGAIL B., born March 20, 1845, in Sangamon county, married April 6, 1865, to Thomas Maylor, and lives near Coyville, Wilson county, Kansas.

ZACHARY, born Oct. 23, 1846, in Sangamon county, and died Oct. 15, 1864.

William B. Taylor, Sen., died May 26, 1852, and his widow died August 22, 1860, both in Sangamon county. He was related to Nicholas Biddle, who was associated with the first United States bank.

THAYER, JOSEPH, was born June 30, 1786, at Amherst, Massachusetts. He moved to Springfield, Illinois, in 1834. He is the father of Rev. Erastus W. Thayer, of Chatham, Illinois, and of Edward R. Thayer, one of the oldest merchants of Springfield. Joseph Thayer is in his ninety-first year, and resides in Springfield, Illinois. His brother, Asahel, resides in Waverly, Illinois. His brother, Martin, was the father of William P. Thayer. *See his name.* Joseph Thayer's brother, Stephen, was the father of Henry Thayer, of Chatham, Illinois. *See Huston.*

THAYER, ASAHEL, born Feb. 10, 1790, in Amherst, Massachusetts, was married May, 1813, to Mary Cannon, of Greenwich, Massachusetts. They had eleven children, five of whom died young. They moved to Chatham, Sangamon county, Illinois, May 14, 1839, thence to Morgan county, Illinois, in 1846. Of their children—

LOIS K., born in 1814 in Amherst, Massachusetts, was married in February, 1839, to George W. Crooker. *See his name.* Mrs. Lois Crooker died suddenly at Taylorville, Illinos, July 5, 1876, after the Crooker family sketch was printed. *See sketch of G. W. Crooker.*

ASAHEL E., born in 1821 in Amherst, was a member of the junior class in Amherst College, when he came to Illinois with his father, began the study of medicine with Dr. J. B. Lewis, of Chatham, and died in his twenty-first year.

GUSTAVUS H., born in 1825, in Amherst, is a graduate of Illinois College, and at one time a minister in the M. E. Church. He is unmarried, and resides with his father.

HELEN, born in 1827, in Amherst, died in her twenty-eighth year.

EMMA, born in 1832, in Amherst, was married January, 1850, to T. Milton Metcalf. He is now county clerk of Macoupin county. They have an adopted daughter, and reside in Carlinville, Illinois.

FRANCES A., born in 1834 in Amherst, resides with her father.

Mrs. Mary Thayer died May, 1866, in Waverly, where Asahel Thayer now resides—1876.

THAYER, WILLIAM P., was born March 15, 1815, in Petersburg, Virginia. His father, Martin Thayer, was a native of Amherst, Massachusetts, and when a young man went to Petersburg, Virginia, where he engaged in business, and was there married to Mrs. Mary C. Mason, whose maiden name was Russell. When the subject of this sketch was about seven years old, his mother died, and his father closed his business and returned to Amherst, Massachusetts, where William P. remained until he was fifteen years old, when he went to New York city as clerk in a dry goods house. About a year later his father engaged in the dry goods business in Philadelphia, and William P. joined him there as clerk. In 1835 the latter went to Newville, Cumberland county, Pennsylvania, and began merchandizing on his own account. He was there married, Jan. 4, 1837, to Mary Huston, who was born in Newville, Jan. 21, 1817. Mr. Thayer closed his business there, and started Jan. 31, 1838, for the west; accompanied by his wife, babe and servant girl. They traveled in a two-horse wagon, fitted up with a stove, and windows on the sides, so that the family might be comfortable, and also see the country as they passed along. After six months travel and many hair-breadth escapes from icy roads and high water, they arrived in Springfield, Illinois, March 13, 1838, and came very near stalling, with his wagon to the axles in the mud, near the southeast corner of the State House Square. They had seven children in Sangamon county. Of all their children—

JAMES H., born Sept. 19, 1837, in

Pennsylvania, died July 25, 1861, in Sangamon county, Illinois.

SARAH J., born Sept. 2, 1839, in Sangamon county, was married Oct. 14, 1857, to Thomas P. Boone, who was born June 27, 1833, in Elton, Todd county, Ky. He is a distant relative of Daniel Boone, the famous hunter and Indian fighter. Mr. and Mrs. Boone had seven children. WILLIE I. died in his seventh year, MARY E. died in infancy, MARTIN R., CHARLES H., FRANKIE F., and HARRY F., live with their parents. The youngest died in infancy. Mr. and Mrs. Boone reside in Springfield, Illinois.

MARTIN R., born Feb. 27, 1842, was married Sept. 19, 1867, to Harriet Melvin, a native of Beaver county, Pennsylvania. They have three children, MAUD, LILLIAN and RUSSELL, and live in Chatham, Sangamon county, Illinois.

WILLIAM P., Jun., born Jan. 10, 1846, was married at Paris, Ill., June 26, 1873, to Mollie E. Patton, who was born August 21, 1854. They reside in Springfield, Ill.

ARCHIE F., EDWARD R., and BERTIE reside with their father.

DOLLIE, next to the youngest child, was married in Chatham in September, 1873, to Joseph Hudson, an agent of the Chicago and Alton Railroad, and resides at Chenoa, Illinois.

Mrs. Mary H. Thayer died June 10, 1872, in Chatham, Ill., and William P. Thayer, Sen., was married Dec. 31, 1873, in Springfield, to Elizabeth Dresser. See sketch of Rev. Chas. Dresser and family. Wm. P. Thayer, Sen., is, in connection with his son, Martin R., proprietor of the Chatham flouring mill, and resides in Springfield, Ill.

THAXTON, JAMES H., was born Oct. 28, 1823, in Allen county, Kentucky. He came to Sangamon county, arriving in the fall of 1839, in what is now Fancy Creek township. He was married in 1845 to Margaret Huffman. They had six living children in Sangamon county, namely—

ARMINDA, born in Sangamon county, married Oscar F. Shepherd. See his name.

MARY A. married James B. Van Meter. See his name.

CLARINDA, LEWIS, CAROLINE and RHODA live with their parents near Sherman, Sangamon county, Illinois—1874.

James H. Thaxton had a sister who married Thomas Brown. See his name.

THOMPSON, JOHN, born March 28, 1783, in Dauphin county, Pennsylvania, left Harrisburg in 1802 for Grant county, Kentucky, and was married there January 9, 1810, to Sarah Points, who was born Feb. 12, 1791. They had two children, and Mrs. Sarah Thompson died Feb. 21, 1815. John Thompson was married Nov. 13, 1817, in Montgomery county to Elizabeth Ferguson, who was born June 18, 1791, in that county. They settled in Bourbon county, Kentucky, and had five children there. They returned to Montgomery county, where four children were born, and moved from there to Sangamon county, Illinois, arriving Oct. 8, 1836, near Springfield, and a few weeks later moved to a farm adjoining Mechanicsburg on the west. Of their eleven children—

JAMES, born Nov. 7, 1810, in Kentucky, married a Miss Black and moved to the vicinity of Greencastle, Indiana, in 1835, and died there soon after.

JOHN, born August 1, 1813, in Kentucky, died in Sangamon county, Nov. 16, 1837. The children by the second marriage are—

MARY G., born Oct. 1, 1818, in Bourbon county, Kentucky, was married in Sangamon county May 30, 1837, to Benjamin B. Branson. See his name.

HARVEY, born Feb. 2, 1820, in Bourbon county, Kentucky, was married March 4, 1844, in Sangamon county to Mary B. Hughes, a native of Bourbon county, Kentucky, also. She died in November, 1864. He was married May 6, 1851, to Mary A. Patton, who was born April 9, 1832, in Pike county, Missouri. They had one child, EDWARD P., born Feb. 24, 1852, and Mrs. Mary A. Thompson died. Harvey Thompson was married Sept. 9, 1869, at Pittsfield, Pike county, Illinois, to Mrs. Ruth A. Hubbard, whose maiden name was Davis, a native of Scott county, Illinois. She had two children by a former marriage, MARY L. and THOMAS J. HUBBARD, who live with their mother. Mr. and Mrs. Harvey Thompson reside in Mechanicsburg, Sangamon county, Ill.

WILLIAM F., born April 21, 1821,

in Bourbon county, Kentucky, was married in Sangamon county, Illinois, to Margaret Vanderen. They had two children, one of whom died young. ELIZA F. lives with her mother. W. F. Thompson died Sept. 23, 1851, and his widow married Louis Johnson. *See his name.*

JOSIAH M., born Oct. 11, 1822, in Bourbon county, Kentucky, was married in Sangamon county, April 13, 1860, to Maggie Munce, who was born Jan. 17, 1837, at Rising Sun, Indiana. They have three children, ELIZA, JOHN A. and THOMAS M., who live with their parents in Mechanicsburg, Illinois.

PRISCILLA M., born April 22, 1824, in Bourbon county, Kentucky, was married in Sangamon county to John R. Grove. *See his name.* John R. Grove died Sept. 20, 1849, and his widow married Rev. Joseph M. Grout, who was born near Boston, Massachusetts. Mr. Grout was pastor of the Presbyterian Church at Shelbyville, Illinois, and died of cholera, August 7, 1855, giving his life as a sacrifice in his efforts to relieve the sick. His widow died at Mechanicsburg, Dec. 2, 1855. They left two sons, WILLIAM T., born March 12, 1853, in Mechanicsburg, Illinois, was married Oct. 20, 1875, in his native place, to Georgie E. Hall, daughter of David S. Hall. *See his name.* William T. Grout is cashier in Thompson & Bro's bank, and resides in Mechanicsburg, Illinois. JOSEPH M. Grout, born Sept. 21, 1855, in Mechanicsburg, Illinois, was brought up by his aunt, Mrs. Branson, graduated at Illinois College, in Jacksonville, June, 1876, and is now—November, 1876—a law student in Springfield, Illinois.

ANDREW TODD, born Jan. 30, 1827, in Bourbon county, Kentucky, was married Dec. 19, 1850, to Elizabeth C. Grove. They have three living children, WILLIAM W., LAURA B. and MAGGIE E., who live with their parents in Mechanicsburg, Illinois.

SALLY A., born July 10, 1828, died in Kentucky.

ELIZABETH A., born April 11, 1830, in Montgomery county, Kentucky, was married in Sangamon county to Peter L. Earnest. *See his name.*

HENRY CLAY, born August 10, 1833, in Montgomery county, Kentucky, was married at Brighton, Illinois, to Maggie E. Johnson. They have three children, ADDIE L., HENRY R. and ZOIE, and reside at Boulder City, Colorado.

John Thompson died Oct. 14, 1855, and his widow died Nov. 22, 1868, both at Mechanicsburg, Sangamon county, Ill.

THOMPSON, ROBERT B., born March 17, 1795, at Saratoga, N. Y., came to Springfield in the autumn of 1824. He was a carpenter by trade, and found work immediately. It is believed that he nailed on the first shingles, and hung the first panel door in Springfield. He was married Jan. 13, 1825, to Mary Matheny, sister of Noah, Charles, James and Cook. They had ten children, namely:

LUCY M., born August 26, 1826, in Springfield, was married Nov. 12, 1850, to George Shake. They have four children. GEORGE A. is a dry goods clerk in Palmer, Ill. CHARLES L., LUCY M. and ANNA M., the three latter reside with their parents, near Palmer, Christian county, Ill.

MELVINA A., born August 24, 1828, in Springfield, was married there Feb. 14, 1856, to Colby Smith. They have three children, NOAH M., CLARA C. and ALMA L., and reside at Fort Scott, Kansas.

JOSEPH R., born August 9, 1830, died in his twentieth year.

MARTHA C. J., born Aug. 20, 1833, in Springfield, married Sept. 12, 1852, to William F. Hill. They have one child, WILLIAM A., who resides with his parents, near Joplin, Jasper county, Mo.

GEORGE R. S., born Dec. 2, 1835, in Springfield, married Martha T. Miller, and died in January, 1853, leaving one child, GEORGETTA. Mrs. Martha T. Thompson married J. S. Robinette, and resides in Springfield, Ill.

MARY E., born Feb. 8, 1838, in Knox county, Ill., died Jan. 7, 1845.

CHARLES R., born March 29, 1840, in Knox county, Illinois, married Elizabeth A. Sears, of Humboldt, Kansas. They have seven children, MARY W., HARRISON S., MATILDA, ANNA, MARTHA, CHARLES S., and ALMA, who reside with their parents, near Golden Gate, Chautauqua county, Kansas.

JAMES M., born Nov. 27, 1841, in Warren county, Illinois, died in April, 1860.

ISABELLA F., born March 29, 1844, in Sangamon county, married B. F. Watts, Nov. 8, 1867. They have three children, ROBERT T., MARY M. and VIOLA I., who reside with their parents, near Palmer, Christian county, Ill.

NOAH A., born August 5, 1847, in Sangamon county, died in his eighth year.

Robert B. Thompson died March 9, 1853, two and a half miles northeast of Chatham, and Mrs. Mary Thompson, died July 30, 1872, in Christian county. Both were buried in Sangamon county, Illinois.

THOMPSON, SAMUEL M., was born Feb. 12, 1801, in Davidson county, eighteen miles west of Nashville, Tenn. He educated himself, and, in connection with General Moses K. Anderson, taught a military school, having branches in Davidson and Dickson counties. Mr. Thompson came to Sangamon county, Illinois, arriving in the fall of 1828 in what is now Cartwright township. He returned to Davidson county, Tennessee, and was married in February, 1831, to Cynthia McCrary. He returned to Sangamon county in the spring of that year. Mr. Thompson volunteered in 1832 for the campaign against the Indians under their chief, Black Hawk. He was in the company of which Abraham Lincoln was Captain, and was elected First Lieutenant at the time the company was organized, on Richland creek. Lincoln was elected Captain at the same time and place. That company united at Beardstown with another from Sangamon county, under Captain Gooding. They were ordered from Beardstown to Rushville, and were consolidated with two other companies to form the 4th Reg. Ill. Vols. Lieutenant Thompson was elected Colonel of the Regiment. He was thus promoted over Captain Lincoln. The latter, however, it should be said, was not a candidate for the office of Colonel. The call was for thirty days, expecting the Indians would retreat across the Mississippi river as they had done the year before. The savages did not retreat, and the regiment was out about sixty days without an engagement. It was disbanded and mustered out of service at Ottowa, June, 1832, by Colonel Zachary Taylor, afterwards President of the United States. Colonel S. M. Thompson and wife had one child born in Sangamon county, and moved to Beardstown in the fall of 1832,

—90

where one child was born. In 1836 Colonel T. moved to Burlington, Iowa, where three children were born, all of whom died in infancy. Of the two eldest—

ALETHIA A., born Feb. 13, 1832, in Sangamon county, Illinois, was married July 31, 1848, in Monroe county, Iowa, to Isaac Hittle, Dec. 7, 1849, in Rush county, Indiana. They had eleven children. One died in infancy. CYNTHIA E., born Feb. 5, 1851, was married Feb. 15, 1865, to John Blakeley. They reside near Williamsburg, Franklin county, Kansas. CLARISSA A., born May 15, 1853, was married August 12, 1875, to David Horbison, and reside in Howard county, Kansas. WILLIAM H., SAMUEL A., LIDA M., SABINA, MARY A., ISAAC O., JAMES A. and ROSA A., reside with their parents near Hillsdale, Miami county, Kansas.

ZANE E., born May 18, 1834, at Beardstown, Illinois, was married May 4, 1851, at Eddyville, Iowa, to William Briggs, of Ohio. They had seven children, MAHLON S., OLIVE, JULIA, ANNIE, CHARLIE, GEORGE and GRANT. Mr. Briggs lost his life in attempting to rescue his son from a coal bank infected with fire damp. He failed in his efforts, and a third man, who came to their assistance, lost his life. This accident occurred in 1870 or '71. Mrs. Briggs by that calamity was incapacited from taking care of herself and the children reside near Eddyville, Iowa.

Mrs. Cynthia Thompson died in October, 1843, near Burlington, Iowa. Colonel Thompson was married in 1855 in Mahaska county, Iowa, to Mrs. Nancy Waldon, whose maiden name was Sullivan. She was a native of Davidson county, Tennsee, also. They reside in Osage county, near Williamsburg, Franklin county, Kansas.

Colonel Thompson has always heard that railroad trains were swift, but he was able to keep ahead of them until November 26, 1874, when he entered a car for the first time at Garnet, Kansas, to visit his old friends in Illinois.

THOMAS, Mrs. FRANCES, was born in Culpepper county, Virginia, moved to Kentucky, thence to Missouri, and to Sangamon county in 1837, with her daughter—

MARY, who married William B. Taylor. See his name. Her son *JESSE B.* Thomas, was one of the two first United States Senators from Illinois.

Mrs. Frances Thomas died in Sangamon county in 1855.

THORNTON, WILLIAM, was born Jan. 17, 1789, in Caroline county, Virginia. He was married Sept. 6, 1808, to Judith P. Thornton, who was born in the same county, June 28, 1788. Soon after they were married they moved, in company with her father, to Bourbon county, Kentucky, where they had seven children and moved to Harrison county, where two children were born. They moved to Montgomery county in the same State, and from there to Sangamon county, Illinois, arriving in the fall of 1834, stopping one year in what is now Woodside township, and in 1835 moved on land Mr. Thornton had previously entered, in what is now the town of Chatham. Of their children—

MILDRED R., married in Kentucky to Rev. Dewey Whitney. They came to Sangamon county with her parents, and had two children. Mr. Whitney was pastor of the Second Presbyterian Church in Springfield a few years, when he abandoned the ministry in consequence of failing health, studied medicine, and after practicing at different places in New York, moved to Yazoo county, Mississippi, where he was killed by a fall from a horse in 1856. Their daughter, JULIA O., married George O. Allen and lives in St. Louis, Missouri. WILLIAM D., married in Brandon, Mississippi, to Mrs. Rebecca Carroll, whose maiden name was Calhoun. They both died leaving one child. Mrs. Mildred R. Whitney died June 17, 1871, at the house of her daughter, Mrs. Allen, in St. Louis, Missouri.

MARY E., married Samuel N. Fullinwider. See his name.

EMMA D., married John R. Duryee, and had two children. JOHN W., married Lucy M. Whitney and lives at Marshalltown, Iowa. MARY L., lives with her mother. Mr. Duryee died Jan. 31, 1860, and his widow and daughter reside in Chatham, Sangamon county, Illinois—1874.

MARTHA W., married Rev. Josiah Porter. See his name.

WILLIAM N., married Jan. 1, 1838, to Roxana Lyman, and he died June 11, 1838, less than six months after he was married. His widow married Aaron Palmer, moved to Chicago, and died there in 1871.

ELIZABETH W., is unmarried, and lives at Chatham, on the homestead settled by her parents in 1835.

LUCY D., married Francis Conway Thornton, had two children. He died June 26, 1844, and his widow married William K. Hardin. They have three children and live in Virden, Illinois.

JUDITH P. is unmarried, and lives at the homestead in Chatham, Illinois.

LYMAN T. died in Kentucky at three years of age.

Mrs. Judith P. Thornton died Dec. 29, 1851, and Colonel William Thornton died May 7, 1871, both at Chatham, Sangamon county, Illinois. Mr. Thornton was a Lieutenant in the war of 1812 from Kentucky.

The Misses Thornton remember that on the day of the "sudden change," Dec. 20, 1836, a man by the name of Lucas, who lived about a mile and a half northeast of Chatham, rode to their house. It was raining when he started, and when he had got half the distance the cold wave struck him. His overcoat was frozen to his saddle, his feet frozen in the stirrups, and he so chilled as to be helpless. Their father (Mr. Thornton) had to knock the ice from the stirrups before he could be taken from the horse.

TIPTON, DAVID B., born May 4, 1799, in Blount county, Tennessee, was married there to Rebecca Jones, who was born in 1802 in Carter county, in the same State. They had three children in Tennessee, and the family moved in 1837 to Clarke county, Illinois, and a year later moved to Sangamon county, arriving October, 1838, in what is now Chatham township, where they had five children. Of their children—

WILLIAM J., born Oct. 1, 1830, in Blount county, Tennessee, married in Sangamon county, Feb. 26, 1852, to Martha Fordner, who was born March 15, 1833, in Green county, Tennessee. They have seven children, JAMES, TEMPERANCE, LEWIS H., MARGARET J., DAVID B., MARY A.

and MATTIE, and live near Curran, Sangamon county, Illinois.

PHEBE A. married Charles Ferguson, have three children, and their residence is not known.

LAVINA married John H. Large, who enlisted in Co. B, 30th Ill. Inf., and died in 1863 in Mississippi. She married Philip Fordner, had three children by each marriage, and lives near Curran, Illinois.

TENNESSEE, born 1840 in Sangamon county, married Peter Large, and live in Morgan county, Illinois.

ELIZA, born 1842, married Theodore Leggett. He died, leaving a widow and one child in Curran township.

MARY A. married Joseph Large, has two children, and lives in Fort Scott, Kansas.

DAVID E., born Feb. 12, 1847, married Ellen Large, Feb. 20, 1867, and had one child. He served four years and eight months in Co. B, 11th Ill. Cav. He is in Santa Fe, New Mexico—1873.

Mrs. Rebecca Tipton died in March, 1849, and David B. Tipton died January, 1863, both in Curran township, Sangamon county, Illinois.

TODD. The first of this family in America came from the north of Ireland, and it is known that they were originally from Scotland. A man by the name of Todd—it is thought that his first name was David—was married in Ireland to Hannah Owen, and came to America, with other members of the family, previous to the American Revolution. They settled at Pequea, Lancaster county, Pennsylvania, and had three sons, John, Robert and Levi. They were educated by their uncle, parson John Todd, who conducted a literary institution in Virginia. These three brothers emigrated about 1778 or '79 to what became Fayette county, Kentucky. They were all influential men in the Indian wars, and in forming the institutions of that State. The eldest:

John Todd, under commission from Patrick Henry, Governor of Virginia, dated Dec. 12, 1778, at Williamsburg, then the capital of the State, was authorized to establish the county of Illinois. He was styled in his commission the County Lieutenant Commandant. As such he organized the county and thus became in fact, though not in name, the first Governor of Illinois. *See page 28.* His first act was to issue a proclamation with reference to land titles, June 15, 1779. Nearly three years later he had been to Virginia, and on his way back made it convenient to visit his family in Kentucky. While at Lexington, news came that the Indians west of the Ohio river were crossing over into Kentucky. Colonel Todd, as one of the commanders, was slain at the battle of Blue Licks, August 18, 1782.

Robert Todd, the second brother, acquired the title of General in connection with the Indian wars, and later military operations in Kentucky. None of his descendants ever came to Illinois. One daughter became the wife of General William O. Butler, of Carrollton, Kentucky.

Levi Todd, the youngest of the three, was engaged in the early Indian wars in Kentucky, and was a lieutenant under Colonel Clark in the expedition that left Corn Island, opposite Louisville, and captured Fort Gates and the village of Kaskaskia, July 4, 1778. M. Rocheblave, the commander of the fort, was so mortified at his having been surprised and captured without firing a gun, that he would not accept any courtesies from his captors, and was sent under a military guard to Virginia. Lieutenant Levi Todd commanded the squad of soldiers who took the prisoner back. He afterwards acquired the title of General, was clerk of the circuit court of Fayette county, Kentucky, the greater part of his life, and lived and died in Lexington. General Levi Todd's daughter, Hannah, was the mother of Hon. John T. Stuart. *See his name.* His son, Robert Todd, was the father of Mrs. Ninian W. Edwards, Mrs. Dr. William S. Wallace, Mrs. C. M. Smith and Mrs. Abraham Lincoln, all of Springfield, Illinois. One only of his children became an early settler of Sangamon county, of whom the following is a sketch:

TODD, JOHN, was born April 27, 1787, near Lexington, Fayette county, Kentucky. He was among the earliest graduates of Transylvania University at Lexington. He next entered the Medical University of Philadelphia, Pennsylvania, and graduated there. Dr. Todd was married July 1, 1813, in Lexington, Kentucky, to Elizabeth Smith, daughter of Rev.

John Blair Smith, D. D. She was born April 18, 1793, in Philadelphia. Her mother was a daughter of General Nash, a leader in the American Revolution from Virginia. Dr. Todd was appointed Surgeon General of the Kentucky troops in the war of 1812, and was at the battle and massacre of the River Raisin in Canada, where he was captured. After the war he returned to Lexington and practiced there. He was for a short time at Bardstown, Kentucky, and from there, in 1817, moved to Edwardsville, Illinois. In 1827 he was appointed by President John Quincy Adams, Register of the United States Land Office, at Springfield, and at once moved there. He remained in office until he was removed solely for political reasons, by President Jackson in 1829. Dr. John Todd and wife had six living children. Of their children—

JOHN B. S., born April 4, 1814, in Lexington, Kentucky, came with his parents to Springfield in 1827, and July 1, 1833, entered the United States Military Academy at West Point, New York, and graduated there July 1, 1837. He was assigned to duty as second lieutenant in the 6th U. S. Inf., promoted to first lieutenant, Dec. 25, 1837, and promoted to captain in 1843. After more than eighteen years active service, during which time he was in almost every frontier fort, and served through the Mexican war, Captain Todd resigned his commission Sept. 16, 1856, and entered into mercantile business. In the summer of 1861 he was elected the first Delegate of Dakota in the United States Congress. He was commissioned September 19, 1861, by President Lincoln, Brigadier General of Volunteers, and in 1862 commanded the 6th Division of the Army of the Tennessee. He was re-elected Delegate to Congress and served until March 4, 1865. He was elected in 1867 to the Territorial Legislature of Dakota, and was Speaker of the House at the session of 1867 and '8. General J. B. S. Todd, then a Captain in the United States army, was married March 25, 1845, at Fort Smith, Arkansas, to Catharine S. Hoffman, a daughter of Colonel William Hoffman, of the United States army. They had nine children. The second and third both died in infancy. Of the other seven, KATE H., born in 1845, at Fort Gibson, Arkansas, married March, 1869, at Yankton, Dakota to Edward F. Higbee. They have one child, JOHN TODD, and live in Yankton. FANNIE A., born in 1852, at Fort Ripley, Minnesota, was married June, 1873, to J. B. Van Velsor, at Yankton, Dakota, where they now reside. JOHN, born in 1854, at Fort Ripley, Minnesota, married August, 1875, to Mary F. Hughes, at Yankton, Dakota, where they now reside. DANA, born in 1857, at Springfield, Illinois. MARY H., born in 1859, MATILDA C., born in 1861, SOPHIA J., born in 1864, the three latter at Fort Randall, Dakota. General J. B. S. Todd died Jan. 5, 1872, at Yankton, Dakota, and his widow and four minor children reside there.

FRANCIS WALTON, born April 17, 1816, at Bardstown, Nelson county, Kentucky, and brought by his parents to Springfield, Illinois, in 1827. He was educated at Jacksonville, and graduated in medicine at Cincinnati Medical College in 1838. He was appointed surgeon in the United States army while in the City of Mexico, in 1846. In 1849 he went to California, and was married there in March, 1851, to Mrs. L. M. Jackson, nee Bullitt, of Nachitoches, Louisiana. They have no children. Dr. Todd is a member of the California State Board of Health, President of the Stockton Board of Health, and Secretary of San Joaquin County Medical Society. He resides at Stockton, California.

WILLIAM L., born April 14, 1818, at Edwardsville, Illinois, and brought up in Springfield, where he learned the business of a druggist. He went to California in 1845, before the Mexican war or the discovery of gold and was there when the survivors of the Reed and Donner party arrived; so many of whom starved to death as they were snow-bound in the mountains. William L. Todd was married April 14, 1868, in California, to Mrs. Clarissa J. Pike, whose maiden name was Chase. She was born in 1823 in Duchess county, New York. Mrs. Todd died childless in March, 1874, in Sacramento. Mr. Todd resides at Los Angelos, California.

ELIZABETH J. was born January, 1825, at Edwardsville, Illinois, married in Springfield July 21, 1846, to Harrison J. Grimsley. They had two children. JOHN T., born Feb. 3, 1848, in Springfield, married Dec. 12, 1871, in Summerfield, New

Jersey, to Cornelia Meesler, daughter of Rev. A. Meesler, D.D., pastor of the Dutch Reformed Church of that place. They have one child, MARY SWIFT. John T. Grimsley is a partner in the mercantile firm of Herndon & Co., and resides in Springfield, Illinois. WILLIAM L., born March 17, 1852, is a clerk with Herndon & Co., and resides in Springfield, Illinois. H. J. Grimsley died in 1865, and his widow married in January, 1867, to Rev. John H. Brown, D.D., pastor of the First Presbyterian Church in Springfield, and later of the Thirty-first Street Presbyterian Church of Chicago. Dr. Brown died Feb. 23, 1872, in Chicago, and was buried in Oak Ridge Cemetery, Springfield. His widow resides in Springfield, Illinois.

LOCKWOOD M., born June 17, 1826, in Edwardsville, raised in Springfield, studied medicine and graduated in St. Louis in 1851. He was with Sherman as commissary in his march to the sea. He married Emily Husband, and lives in Virginia City, Montana Territory.

FRANCES S., born Dec. 19, 1832, in Springfield, Illinois, married there Dec. 18, 1849, to Thomas H. Shelby, of Lexington, Kentucky. Mrs. Shelby died in Springfield Feb. 1, 1851, leaving one child, JOHN TODD Shelby, born Jan. 25, 1851, in Springfield, Illinois. He was brought up near Lexington, Kentucky, graduated at Princeton College, New Jersey, in the class of 1870. married November 7, 1872, in St. Louis, Missouri, to Lizzie M. Craig. They have one child, THOMAS HART. John T. Shelby is a practicing lawyer in Lexington, Kentucky. Soon after the death of his wife, Thomas H. Shelby, with his infant son returned to Kentucky, and is now an extensive farmer near Lexington. He is a grandson of Isaac Shelby, the first Governor of Kentucky, and on his mother's side, a grandson of Edmond Bullock, Speaker of the first Kentucky House of Representatives.

Dr. John Todd and wife celebrated their golden wedding July 1, 1863. He died Jan. 9, 1865, and she died March 11, 1865, both in Springfield, Illinois. Dr. Todd was a Ruling Elder in the First Presbyterian Church in the city at the time of his death.

TOLLEY, ISOM, was born about 1754 in Virginia, went to Bourbon county, Kentucky, when he was a young man, and was there married to Isabel Whitesides, had six children in Kentucky, moved to St. Clair county, Illinois, thence to Morgan county, and from there to Sangamon county, in what is now Loami township in October, 1823. Of their children—

DANIEL, married Jane Bailey and left Sangamon county soon after.

ELIZABETH married John Weir, and moved to Iowa in 1843 or '4.

JAMES born in Bourbon county, Kentucky, and married Elizabeth Mace. They had eight children. SAMUEL was killed by lighting on Spring creek in 1840, aged twenty years. LUCINDA married Arthur Davenport. They have seven children, and reside near Berlin, Sangamon county, Ill. MARY A. married Ephraim Shryer. *See his name.* MARTHA J. married Aaron Van Patton. *See his name.* KATE or (CATHARINE E.), born August 27, 1828, was married Jan. 8, 1845, in Sangamon county, to William W. Beerup. *See his name.* They had three living children. SOPHIA, born Feb. 25, 1849, married John K. Shumate, and lives in Springfield, Illinois. ROSETTA, born Sept. 8, 1855, died March 19, 1861. ADALINE, born Dec. 18, 1858, resides with her parents one and one-half miles south of Farmingdale, Sangamon county, Illinois. ELIZABETH married Charles Myers. He died leaving a widow and six children at Middletown, Logan county, Illinois. MATILDA married Harris Elliott, has two children, and lives at Middletown. SUSAN married William Douglas. *See his name.* Mrs. Elizabeth Tolley died in 1838, and James Tolley married America Kelly. They moved to Kansas, and he died there.

NANCY married John Porter. She died leaving one daughter in Clear Lake township, Sangamon county, Ill.

JOHN married Susan Washburne, who died. He married again and lives near Salisbury, Illinois.

UNITY died unmarried, aged about twenty-five years.

Mrs. Isabel Tolley died aged about ninety-six, and John Tolely died, aged about one hundred and six years, both in Sangamon county, Illinois.

TOMLIN, ALMARIN, was born July 28, 1800, in Cape May county, New Jersey. Rhoda Smith was born

June 15, 1802, in the same county. They were there married January 11, 1821, and had seven children in New Jersey. The family moved to Sangamon county, Illinois, arriving October, 1837, in what is now Cartwright township, where five children were born. Of their children—

EMELINE, born in 1822 in New Jersey, married Samuel Sutton, a native of New Jersey, also. They have three children, HENRIETTA, JOSEPH and CHARLES N., and reside three miles north of Salisbury, Menard county, Ill.

LOUISA, born April 4, 1824, in New Jersey, married William B. Quinn. They have one child, ALMARIN, and live near St. Paul, Minnesota.

EDWIN, born July 29, 1826, in New Jersey, was married April 5, 1854, in Sangamon county, to M. Margaret Correll. They had nine children. FANNIE, the second, died in infancy. EVA H. was married March 16, 1876, near Pleasant Plains, Illinois, to William Sinclair, of Cass county, Illinois. THOMAS A., CHARLES S., LEE C., SALLIE, JACOB, ANNIE and ISAAC F. The seven latter live with their parents on the farm settled by Mr. Tomlin's father in 1837, and is one and one-fourth miles northwest of Pleasant Plains, Sangamon county, Illinois.

JEREMIAH T., born Oct. 5, 1828, in New Jersey, married Jennie Richmond of the same State. They had four children, and Mrs. Jennie Tomlin died in 1869. J. T. Tomlin was married to Mrs. Belle Newman, whose maiden name was Hall, and moved to Quincy, Illinois.

HARRIET, born August 27, 1832, married Josiah Reed. They have eleven children, and live near Circleville, Ohio.

JAMES S., born Oct. 19, 1834, in New Jersey, married in Sangamon county to Anna Townsend, of New Jersey. They have ten children, and reside near Wichita, Kansas—1873.

LYDIA H., born Sept. 11, 1836, married Josiah Alkire. They have three children, and reside in St. Louis, Missouri.

MARY and *MARTHA*, twins, born Sept. 11, 1839, in Sangamon county.

MARY, died in her thirteenth year.

MARTHA is unmarried and lives with her mother at Jacksonville, Illinois.

RACHEL and *RHODA*, twins, born January, 1842, in Sangamon county.

RACHEL married Monroe Rankin. They have two children, and live in McLean county, Illinois.

RHODA married Stephen Capps. They have four children, and live at Jacksonville, Illinois.

Almarin Tomlin died April, 1859, and his widow resides at Jacksonville, Illinois.

TOMLINSON, ELIZABETH, whose maiden name was McKinnie, was born in Orange county, on the Shenandoah river, Virginia. She was taken by her parents to Fayette county, Kentucky, and was there married to Elijah Tomlinson, a native of Virginia, also. They had ten children in Fayette county, and Mr. Tomlinson died about 1812. Mrs. Tomlinson with her children came to Sangamon county, arriving in the fall of 1829, three miles northwest of Springfield. Of their children—

WILLIAM raised a family and died in Kentucky.

CATHARINE died in Kentucky, aged twenty years.

MARTHA married Andrew McKinnie. *See his name.*

CHARLES F. went to the Galena lead mines when a young man, and died of cholera in 1833, at Mineral Point, Wisconsin.

LOUISA, born April 16, 1801, in Kentucky, married there to Nathaniel Hurst, and came to Sangamon county in 1829, and died in Springfield many years later.

NICHOLAS, born in Kentucky, married in St. Louis county, Missouri, to Nancy Davis, and came to Sangamon county in 1845. Mrs. T. died leaving seven children, and he married Mrs. Sarah Brady, and both died in Springfield, leaving four children. Their son, Charles Tomlinson, lives in Springfield.

REBECCA married C. Hendricks and remained in Kentucky.

LEWIS.

ANDREW, born in Kentucky, went to the Galena lead mines in 1827, and died there in 1828 or '9.

JAMES M., born May 20, 1809, in Fayette county, Kentucky, came to Sangamon county with his mother in 1829. He spent five years in the lead mines, went to Kentucky, and was married April 30, 1837, in Fayette county, to Louisa Hurst, who was born Jan. 1, 1809, in Ohio. They had one child in Kentucky, and came to Sangamon county in 1838, where they had four children. Of their five children, MARTHA E., born Jan. 31, 1838, in Kentucky, married March 6, 1866, to John W. Hurst, has three children, and lives in Galena. ELIJAH and ELISHA T., twins, the former died in infancy. Elisha T. enlisted in November, 1861, in Co. G, 10th Ill. Cav. for three years, re-enlisted January, 1864, served to the end of the rebellion, was honorably discharged in January, 1866, and lives with his parents. JOHN B. and THOMAS H. B., twins, born July 5, 1841. The former died in infancy. T. H. B. served from August 7, 1862, to the end of the rebellion in Co. I, 7th Ill. Inf. He married Mrs. Sarah Shufelt, whose maiden name was Meadow, and lives near Lafayette, Indiana. ANDREW J., born April 16, 1843, enlisted September, 1861, in Co. I, 39th Ill. Inf. for three years, re-enlisted as a veteran, was wounded August 16, 1864, at Deep Bottom, Virginia, and died Sept. 14, following, from the amputation of a leg. NICHOLAS B., born June 24, 1845, married Sarah Gilbick, have one child, and live in Springfield. James M. Tomlinson and wife reside three miles northwest of Springfield.

Mrs. Elizabeth Tomlinson died at the house of her son, James M., Dec. 31, 1850, near Springfield, Illinois.

TORRENCE, WILLIAM, was born in Hampshire county, Virginia, and married there to Margaret Chambaugh. They had seven children, and Mrs. T. died in that county. Mr. Torrence was married to Celia Sheriff and had two children in Virginia, and the family moved to Sangamon county, Illinois, arriving in the fall of 1834, in what is now Rochester township, and two years later moved into Cotton Hill township. Two children were born in Sangamon county. Of all his children—

JOHN, born in Hampshire county, Virginia, married in Sangamon county to Sarah Donner, (a sister to George and Jacob Donner.) They had five children. GEORGE is married and lives in Taylorville; SUSAN married Henry Baker and lives near Medoc, Missouri; MARGARET married Edward Todd, and lives in Springfield; WILLIAM, married, and lives near Atlanta, Illinois. John Torrence and wife died in Atlanta.

ABSALOM, born in Virginia, died in Sangamon county, August, 1835.

ROBERT, born in Hampshire county, Virginia, came to Sangamon county with his parents, married in Iowa, and lives near Medoc, Missouri.

NANCY, born in Virginia, was married in Sangamon county to John Adams. They had three children.

SAMUEL, born May 7, 1819, in Hampshire county, Virginia, was married January 7, 1841, in Sangamon county, to Polly Delay. They had eight children in Sangamon county. GREENBERRY, born Dec. 8, 1842, is proprietor of Cotton Hill mills, formerly the old Breckenridge mill, and lives in Cotton Hill township, Breckenridge postoffice. ELIZA, born May 8, 1844, married H. Peddicord, and died August 15, 1873, leaving three children in Champaign City. CHARLES, born August 22, 1846, married Josephine Peddicord. They have one child and live near Taylorville, Illinois. ELIZABETH, born Sept. 13, 1848, married Edgar Eggleston, and lives near Taylorville, Illinois. JENNIE, born March 22, 1850, married James Shaw. They have one child, and live near Taylorville. JOHN, EMMA and ANNA live with their mother. Samuel Torrence was killed by being thrown from a wagon attached to a runaway team, Sept. 21, 1875. His widow and children live two miles south of Rochester, Sangamon county, Illinois.

WILLIAM, born in Hampshire county, Virginia, came to Sangamon county with his parents and is living with his third wife near Taylorville, Illinois. He has one child by his second marriage.

SILAS, born in Virginia, raised in Sangamon county, married in Iowa, and lives near Winona, Minnesota.

JANE, born in Virginia, married in Sangamon county to Harvey Fasset, and lives near Winona, Minnesota.

By the second wife:

EMANUEL, born in Virginia and died in Sangamon county at about twenty-one years of age.

JOSEPH, born in Virginia, raised in Sangamon county, and is living with his second wife in Taylorville, Illinois.

ISAAC, born in Sangamon county, is unmarried, and lives near Decatur, Illinois.

MARGARET, born in Sangamon county and died at fifteen years of age.

William Torrence died in 1841 in Cotton Hill township, Sangamon county, and his widow married John Davis. He died, and she lives in Taylorville, Illinois.

TORREY, JOSEPH, was born March 25, 1788, in Connecticut, came to Madison county, Illinois, and was there married to Olive Slater. They moved to Sangamon county, and settled on Sugar creek, where she died in 1820. Joseph Torrey returned east and was married Jan. 17, 1828, at Millbury, Mass., to Abigail Sibley, who was born Nov. 29, 1804, in Massachusetts. They had four children there, and moved to Springfield, Illinois, arriving in 1836, where three children were born. Of their seven children two died young.

ELIZA A., born March 2, 1829, in Massachusetts, was married July 3, 1851, in Springfield, Illinois, to John C. Moses. They had two children. ABBIE, born August, 1832, was married in Taylorville, Illinois, to David Hay. They reside at Wichita, Kansas. JOHN C., lives in Taylorville. Mr. Moses died May 16, 1860, and Mrs. Moses resides with her sisters, Mrs. Sattley and Mrs. Rockwell.

SUSAN, born March 18, 1831, in Massachusetts, married, Sept. 21, 1853, to Albert Sattley. *See his name.*

ABIGAIL E., born Sept. 10, 1833, in Massachusetts, was married in Springfield, Illinois, Oct. 7, 1856, to Sylvester Paden. He died August 15, 1860. She was married July 7, 1869, to Humphrey H. Hood. They have one child, HARROLD, and reside in Litchfield, Illinois.

ELLEN, born April 4, 1841, in Springfield, was married Dec. 29, 1858, in Taylorville, to Charles V. Rockwell, who was born in Richland county, Ohio. He came to Chicago in 1848, and from there to Decatur, Illinois, in 1850, studied medicine, and attended one course of lectures at St. Louis Medical College. In 1854 he located and practiced medicine at Taylorville. He graduated at St. Louis Medical College in 1858. They have five children, LULU, SUSAN E., GERTRUDE, ESTELLA and GRACIE A., who reside with their parents at Taylorville, Illinois.

JOSEPH S., born Feb. 8, 1844, in Springfield, was married Oct. 27, 1868, in Centralia, to Elizabeth H. Sloan, who was born Nov. 27, 1844, in Rockwood, Randolph county, Illinois. They have three living children, JULIA E., LEWIS E. and MABEL. J. S. Torrey resides in Taylorville, Illinois.

Joseph Torrey was in the boot and shoe business for a short time, afterwards engaged in hotel keeping, and subsequently in pork packing with James L. Lamb. He died on a farm near Illiopolis, Illinois, Sept. 2, 1845. Mrs. Torrey died in Taylorville, Sept. 10, 1857.

TRAYLER. Three brothers, William, Henry and Archibald Trayler, were born of respectable parents, in Green county, near the line of Adair county, Kentucky. They came to Illinois about 1829. William settled near Greenbush, Warren county, more than one hundred miles northwest of Springfield. Henry married a sister of Eli C. Blankenship, a merchant of Springfield, and settled at Clary's Grove, about twenty miles northwest of Springfield. It was then in Sangamon, but now in Menard county. Archibald was unmarried, and engaged in business in Springfield, as a carpenter and builder, in partnership with Reuben Radford, the latter of whom went out of the business, when Mr. Trayler associated himself with a Mr. Myers, under the firm name of Trayler & Myers. Mr. Trayler owned the lot on which the Episcopal Church now stands, at the corner of Adams and Third streets. He had a dwelling house there, and Mr. Myers, having a family, kept the house. Mr. Trayler boarded in his own house, with his partner. William Trayler was somewhat given to telling marvelous stories, and a little inclined to boasting. With that exception, the three brothers were sober, industrious and retiring men. For ten or twelve years after coming to the State, nothing occurred in their lives unusual to the settlers in a new country.

It has become a proverb that "truth is stranger than fiction." This was never more completely verified than in the events I am about to relate, concerning these three brothers, who became victims to the most remarkable case of circumstantial evidence on record, one that would, if given in proper terms, be of absorbing interest to the legal profession. I must, from necessity, make my statements as concise as possible. Hon. William Butler, deceased, is my authority for what I have said of the birth and parentage of the brothers. I have gathered all the other information from the older citizens of Springfield, files of the *Journal* and *Register* newspapers, and from an elaborate article that first appeared in the Quincy *Whig*, and copied into the Springfield *Journal* of April 23, 1846. The latter is principally true, but contains some glaring errors, which, by the aid of men who took part in the proceedings, I have been able to avoid.

A man about fifty years of age, by the name of Archibald Fisher taught school in Monmouth, Warren county, Illinois, and in that vicinity. He also worked at odd jobs when he was not regularly employed. He was unmarried, economical in his habits, and lived in the families of the people wherever his business called him. In that way he had saved a few hundred dollars, and at the beginning of the events I am about to relate was making his home with William Trayler, who was then a widower, with several children.

Mr. Fisher, wishing to enter some land, he and Mr. Trayler started for Springfield together. They set out in a buggy without springs—called a Dearborn wagon—drawn by one horse. On Sunday evening they reached the house of Henry Traylor, and the next day all three came to Springfield, Henry riding on horseback. They arrived about noon, Monday, June 1, 1841, and stopped at the house where Archibald Trayler boarded. After dinner the three Traylers and Fisher left the boarding house in company, for the purpose of looking about the town. At supper time the three brothers returned, but Fisher, having stepped aside, as they were passing along a foot path among the trees in the northwestern part of the city, did not appear. After supper all the others went in search of him. One by one they returned, as night approached, but without any tidings of Fisher. The next morning the search was continued, and up to noon was still unsuccessful. William and Henry, having expected to leave early that morning, expressed their intention to abandon the search and start for home. This was objected to on the part of the boarders, because it would leave Fisher without any means of conveyance. They continued to search the remainder of that day, but at night William, who evidently felt greatly disappointed at being detained so long, hitched up his buggy and started without the knowledge of his brother, Archie, who, missing him, followed on foot, and overtook him just as he was entering the water at Hickox mill, on Spring creek, near where the O. & M. railroad now crosses. Archie called to William, and remonstrated against his going until the mystery was cleared up. William turned around in the water, and they both returned to Springfield. Notwithstanding all this, William and Henry started for home the next day. The mysterious disappearance had to that time attracted but little attention. Three or four days later, Henry returned to Springfield for the purpose of making a more diligent search, and with his brother, Archie, and some of the boarders, another day was spent, and he returned home. On Friday, June 12, James W. Keyes, the postmaster in Springfield, received a letter from Mr. Tice, the postmaster of Greenbush, Warren county, saying that William Trayler had returned home, and was circulating the report that Fisher, the man who had left there with him for Springfield, was dead, and with something of a boastful manner, stated that Fisher had willed his money to him, and that he had gained about fifteen hundred dollars by it—a much larger sum than Fisher was supposed to possess. Postmaster Tice requested the Springfield postmaster to give him all the information on the subject that he could. The contents of that letter were made public, and the excitement became widespread and intense. Springfield had, only the year before, adopted a city organization, with about two thousand inhabitants. The mayor, William L. May, and Josiah Lamborn, the attorney general of the State, headed the movement to ferret out the mystery. Men were formed into squads, and marched about in all directions, so as to leave no spot unsearched. Examinations were made of wells, and every conceivable place where a body might be concealed.

A club was found with some hair attached to it. It was confidently believed that the murder had been committed with that weapon, but it was afterwards demonstrated that the hair was from a cow.

This search was continued until Saturday afternoon, when it was determined to arrest William and Henry Trayler, and officers started for them on Sunday morning. Henry, being nearest, was brought to Springfield on Monday. The mayor and attorney general took him in hand and used every device to elicit information of the supposed murder, but he protested his innocence of any knowledge on the subject. He was reminded that the circumstantial evidence was so strong that he, with his two brothers, would certainly all be hung, and that the only chance to save his own life was for him to become a witness on the part of the State. He withstood all the pressure until Wednesday, the seventeenth of the month, when, protesting his own innocence, he stated that his brothers, William and Archibald, had murdered Fisher, by hanging him to a tree, without his knowledge at the time, that they had temporarily concealed the body, that immediately preceding the departure of himself and William from Springfield, on the second or third of June, William and Archie communicated the fact to him, and engaged his assistance in making a permanent concealment of the body; that at the time he and William left, ostensibly for home, they did not take the direct road, but, wending their way through the streets, entered the woods at the northwest of the city, and that on approaching, where the body was concealed, he was placed as a sentinel. He then entered into a minute description of the murder, going into the smallest details. He said that his brothers entered a thicket of underbrush, where the body was concealed, placed it in the buggy, moved off with it in the direction of Hickox mill pond on Spring creek, and soon after returned, saying they had put it in a safe place; that Archibald went back to town, and that William and himself found their way to the road, and proceeded to their homes.

Until that disclosure was made, the character of Archibald was such as to repel all suspicion of his complicity in the matter, but he was at once arrested and hurried to jail, which was probably the best thing that could have been done for him, for he was in great personal danger from the infuriated populace. Search then commenced anew for the body. The thicket was found, and indications of a struggle under a small tree, bent over as though the hanging might have been done there. A trail was also visible, as though a body had been dragged to where the tracks of a buggy were to be seen, tending in the direction of the mill pond, previously spoken of, but could not be traced all the way. At the pond, however, it was found that a buggy had been down into the water and came out again. Hundreds of men were engaged in dragging and fishing for the body. Becoming impatient, the dam was cut down on Thursday morning, the eighteenth of June, and the water drawn off, but no body found.

About noon that day the officers, who had gone to arrest William Trayler, returned with him in custody, accompanied by a gentleman who called himself Dr. Gilmore. Then it was ascertained that William Trayler had been arrested at his own house, on Thursday, the sixteenth of the month, and started for Springfield, stopping at Lewiston, Fulton county, for the night. Late in the night Dr. Gilmore arrived there and told the officers that Fisher was alive and at his house; that he had followed them to give the information so that the prisoner might be released without further trouble. The deputy sheriff—James Maxey—very properly refused to release him on the word of an entire stranger, and they continued their journey to Springfield.

Dr. Gilmore told the officers that when he heard of the arrest of William Trayler for the murder of Fisher, he was a few miles from home; that when he returned to his own house he found Fisher there; that he would have taken Fisher with him in pursuit of the officers with the prisoner, but that the state of Fisher's health would not admit of it. The doctor further said that he had known Fisher for several years, and that he was subject to fits of temporary derangement of mind in consequence of an injury to his head, received in early life. The doctor still further stated that Fisher told him that the first he knew after visiting Springfield, he found himself in the vicinity of Peoria. Being nearer to his home than to Springfield, he proceeded at once to Warren county, without the slightest thought of his acts leading to the injury of any other person. On their arrival at Springfield,

Dr. Gilmore's statement was made public, and at first the people seemed to be struck dumb with astonishment. When the news was communicated to Henry Trayler, in the jail, he, without faltering, re-affirmed his own story about the murder of Fisher. The idea was at once taken up by the crowd that Dr. Gilmore was in collusion with the murderers, and that he had invented that story as a ruse to secure their release and escape. The Doctor was permitted to remain at liberty, but was regarded with strong suspicion. About three o'clock that afternoon Mr. Myers, the partner of Archibald Trayler, started with a two-horse carriage, accompanied by Egbert M. Mallory, to ascertain whether Fisher was alive or not, and if so to bring him back to Springfield.

Without waiting for the return of Myers and Mallory, the Traylers were brought before proper officers for preliminary examination, on the charge of the murder of Archibald Fisher. Henry Trayler was introduced on the part of the State, and on oath testified that his brothers, William and Archibald, had murdered Archibald Fisher, re-affirming all the minutia of his former statements, and at the close bore a rigid cross examination without faltering or exposure. It was also proven by a respectable lady, who was well acquainted with Archie, that on the Monday afternoon of Fisher's disappearance, she saw Archibald Trayler and another man, who she identified as William Trayler,—then present—and still another, answering the description of Fisher, all enter the timber at the northwest of town, and an hour or two later, saw the two former return alone. Many other witnesses were examined, giving a combination of testimony that seemed to weave a net-work of circumstances about the prisoners, from which it would appear to any other than a legal mind, to be utterly impossible to extricate them. It was also proven that Archibald Trayler had passed an unusual number of pieces of gold coin. The buggy tracks in the mill pond were unexplained, as the prisoners were the only persons who could give any light upon that subject. The evidence of a struggle in the thicket, under the bending tree, where the hanging was supposed to have taken place, was unexplained, although it was afterwards proven that school children had been using the tree as a support to a swing. These and many other points of evidence, the intricacies of which space forbids that I should follow out, were before the court.

When the prosecution had introduced all their evidence and rested the case, one of the attorneys for the defense, Hon. Stephen T. Logan, arose, and with every eye turned towards him, said that on the part of the defendants, he would introduce a single witness only.

Archibald Fisher, in full life and proper person, was then conducted slowly into the presence of the court. Messrs. Myers and Mallory had returned late in the evening before—June 21st—with Fisher, and the friends of the prisoners kept him secreted until the proper time. The effect may be imagined, but can not be described. A gentleman who was cognizant of the proceedings from beginning to end, and who is now a judge of one of the courts of Illinois, describing the appearance of one of the prisoners in the court room, says: "Archibald Trayler was as fine looking a man as I ever saw. When his own full brother was testifying that he was a murderer, he stared at him with a look of astonishment, settling into an appearance of stoical indifference, that seemed to say, 'there is no hope of relief, therefore I must calmly endure the worst;' but when the man he was accused of having murdered was led into his presence, he broke down and gave vent to his feelings in a flood of tears, followed by uncontrollable fits of sobbing and moaning."

By this time it began to dawn on the minds of the people that the threats of death to all three of the brothers had so wrought on the mind of Henry Trayler as to destroy his competency as a witness. A feeling of indignation immediately sprung up against May and Lamborn, who had led in the prosecution, and it only lacked a bold leader to mob and hang them. The feeling was so intense that Judge Logan, who had defended the prisoners, felt it his duty to come to the rescue of their prosecutors. He made a pacific speech, in which he exhorted all to abide by the laws. It had the desired effect, and all dispersed without violence.

A public meeting of the citizens of Springfield was held on the evening of

June 22, 1841, to express sympathy with the brothers, who had passed through that worse than firey ordeal, and particularly with their fellow citizen, Archibald Trayler, whose character had never been tarnished with the slightest shadow of reproach. That sympathy was of little avail. His fine, manly countenance was never again lighted up with a smile. He made some feeble attempts at business, but wandered about, avoiding all society, pined away, and died in less than two years. One who knew him well, says: "If ever a man died of a broken heart it was Archibald Trayler."

William Trayler died in less than a year after the trial.

Henry Trayler lived several years after the death of his brothers, but was never known to speak of the mournful event after his departure from Springfield at the close of the trial. He died in Menard county, and one of his sons, if not more, are among the most respected citizens of the county. It is said that the three brothers never met after they passed out of the court room.

If the unhappy and afflicted being who was the innocent cause of all the trouble, had wandered away and died on the open prairie, much of which had not then been trod by the foot of man, William and Archibald Trayler would, beyond a reasonable doubt, have been executed as his murderers, and that upon the force of surrounding circumstances and the testimony of their own brother, who would doubtless have become hopelessly insane, caused by threats to make him confess a crime never committed, and afterwards by the appaling effects of his own testimony. The world would probably have looked on and called it retributive justice. Such may and doubtless has been the effect of circumstantial evidence, in cases where the truth was never known.

Thus ended one of the most remarkable affairs of its kind on record. Many points and circumstances connected with the case are yet enshrouded in mystery, and will ever remain so.

TRIMBLE, GEORGE, was born April 22, 1814, in Montgomery county, Kentucky. He was married August 23, 1836, to Lydia Shumate, who was born in that county August 15, 1815. They started the next morning after marriage for Sangamon county, Illinois, and arrived in September, 1836, in what is now Curran township. They had six children in Sangamon county, namely:

HUGHEY F., born June 2, 1837, died in his seventh year.

WILLIAM H., born Dec. 31, 1839, married October, 1864, to Nancy A. Gibson. They had two children, John died in infancy, and ANNA E. resides with her father. Mrs. Trimble died Feb. 9, 1869, and Mr. T. was married Oct. 14, 1869, to Helen J. McGraw. They have one child, DORA BELL, and live two miles south of Curran, Sangamon county, Illinois.

ELIZA J., born March 28, 1840, married F. M. Miller. *See his name.*

ELIZABETH, born April 27, 1842, married Edmund T. Miller. *See his name.*

JAMES A., born July 27, 1846, married Mary A. Barbre, and reside in Curran township.

GEORGE C., born Sept. 28, 1849, died Nov. 21, 1870.

Mrs. Lydia Trimble died Dec. 3, 1866, and George Trimble was married Dec. 5, 1867, to Rebecca Drennan. They reside two miles southeast of Curran, Sangamon county, Illinois.

TROTTER, GEORGE, was born about 1782, in Dunbarton, Scotland. He went to the West Indies about 1801, and came to the United States at thirty years of age. About 1813 he was married in Hartford, Connecticut, to Catharine Imlay, who was born in that city Oct. 29, 1786. Soon after marriage Mr. Trotter went to New York city and engaged in the mercantile business. They had one child, and Mrs Catharine Trotter died there, April 1, 1832. Mr. Trotter was married in New York July, 1835, to Mary Ward, a native of Longford, Ireland. They moved to Springfield, Ill., arriving in the fall of 1835, where they had three children. Of his four children.

AGNES D., born Feb. 15, 1825, in New York city, married in Springfield to Zimri A. Enos. *See his name.*

JOHN E., born August 10, 1838, in Springfield, was married Sept. 14, 1865, to Martha L. Slates, who was born July 19, 1844, in Zanesville, Ohio. They had six children, five of whom died young. CLARA A. resides with her parents in Springfield.

GEORGE H., born Nov. 17, 1840, in Springfield, was married in his native place to Ellen Tague, who was born August 5, 1841, in Peterborough, Canada. They have seven children, GEORGE T., MARY E., JOHN E., LOUISA S., WILLIAM A., FRANCIS J., and BERTHA C., and live in Springfield. G. W. Trotter has been three years on the police force.

MARY D., born April, 1842, in Springfield, resides with her mother.

George Trotter was engaged in land speculating from the time he came to Springfield until his death, which took place in May, 1842. His widow resides with her son, John, in Springfield, Illinois.

TROTTER, JAMES, born about 1770, in Culpepper county, Virginia. He was taken by his parents, about 1792, to Bourbon county, Kentucky, and was there married to Elizabeth Kenny, who was also a native of Virginia. They had eight children born in Bourbon county, and moved to Sangamon county, Illinois, arriving in the fall of 1826, and settled on Round Prairie, four miles east of Springfield. Of their children:

JOSEPH died aged 19 years.

JAMES A., born Feb. 19, 1799, in Bourbon county, Kentucky, married there March 22, 1823, to Mary A. Daubinspeck, who was born Feb. 24, 1800, in the same county. They had two children, and moved to Rush county, Indiana, where one child was born, thence to Sangamon county, Illinois, in 1827, one year later than his father. Six children were born in Sangamon county. Of their nine children, ELIZABETH, born Jan. 2, 1824, in Kentucky, married in Sangamon county, June 21, 1849, to Stephen Lawyer, a native of Guernsey county, Ohio. They had seven children, four of whom died young. Mr. Lawyer enlisted August 10, 1861, at Anamosa, in what became Co. L, 1st Iowa Cav., and died Nov. 14, 1863, at Little Rock, Arkansas. The three children, ROBERT, ELIZABETH A. and STEPHEN reside with their mother in Clear Lake township. WILLIAM, born March 15, 1825, in Kentucky, enlisted September, 1862, in Co. I, 114th Ill. Inf. for three years, and died of disease March 17, 1863, at Memphis, Tennessee. JANE, born Feb. 2, 1827, in Rush county, Indiana, married Henry R. Clark, had two children, and her second husband is William A. Butler. See his name. NANCY, born Dec. 8, 1829, in Sangamon county, married Feb. 24, 1848, to Hiram Lawyer, who was born Dec. 11, 1823, in Guernsey county, Ohio. They had nine children, three of whom died young. AMANDA married Mahlon Geathard, has four children, and lives near Rochester. GEORGE W. resides with his parents. ELIZA J., married James Burch. WILLIAM T., ADA A. and EVELINE reside with their parents two miles northeast of Sangamon station, on the farm where her parents settled in 1827. JAMES born Jan. 2, 1831, in Sangamon county, married Dec. 24, 1857, to Elizabeth Burch. They had five children. WILLIAM A. died aged two years. PHILEMON, LUETTA, GEORGE and MARY E. reside with their parents two miles northeast of Sangamon station. JULIA A., born April 20, 1833, in Sangamon county, married James Lawyer, and died January, 1864, leaving three children, two of whom reside with their father, near Salisbury, and Charles lives on Round Prairie. MARY, born August 6, 1835, in Sangamon county, married Thomas W. Long. She died leaving one child, EDWARD, who lives with his father in Taylorville. GEORGE, born Dec. 14, 1839, in Sangamon county, married Eliza Brown, who died, and he enlisted August, 1862, in Co. I, 114th Ill. Inf. for three years, served full time and was honorably discharged. He was married Nov. 23, 1864, to Mary E. Griffiths, who was born Oct. 29, 1846, in Madison county, Indiana. They had one child, JANE, born Nov. 3, 1866. George Trotter died Jan. 21, 1867, of disease contracted in the army. His widow married March 6, 1873, to Burgess Taintor, a native of New York. He has one child by a former marriage, ELLA MAY. Mr. and Mrs. Taintor have one son, and reside two miles north of Springfield, Illinois. CATHARINE, born Jan. 8, 1840, in Sangamon county, married Willis Wilson, has three children, and resides in Tazewell county, Illinois. James K. Trotter died Dec. 27, 1839. His widow resides with her son James, on the farm where she and her husband settled in 1827, two miles northeast of Sangamon station, and five miles east of Springfield, Illinois. When James K. Trotter was moving to the country, in 1827, he had to cross the Sangamon river three miles from his father's house. He left his team and family in safe hands and was about to enter a canoe to cross the river when he saw the two dogs his father brought with him the year before, at the time they all moved from Kentucky. These dogs were sitting on the opposite bank apparently waiting for him. He called and they plunged in and swam to meet him with every appearance of pleasure. He took them across in the canoe and then halloed, supposing that his brothers were hunting near by. The dogs paid no attention to his call, but ran back and forth along the road, and in that way conducted him to the house, when he learned that none of the family had been near the river for several days. Three questions naturally suggest themselves: Why were the dogs there? Did they know he was coming? If so, how? Perhaps they could be answered by some writer on the higher life of animals.

JOHN, born about 1800, in Bourbon county, Kentucky, married Isabel Brazzle, and moved to Wisconsin, where the parents died leaving four children, all married.

MARY, born Nov. 19, 1802, in Bourbon county, Kentucky, married Thomas J. Turley. *See his name.*

NANCY, born Feb. 14, 1805, in Bourbon county, Kentucky, married in Sangamon county, to Edward Clark. *See his name.*

JANE, born April 18, 1807, in Kentucky, married in Sangamon county, to Samuel Williams. *See his name.*

GEORGE, born June 13, 1809, in Bourbon county, Kentucky. In 1826 he accompanied his parents from Bourbon county to Sangamon county, Illinois. They settled on Round Prairie. He remained at home ten years. In 1831 he left for the Wisconsin lead mines, worked in them that summer, returning home in the fall. He served in the Black Hawk war, and was married March 24, 1833, in Sangamon county, to Sarah Chilton, who was born Dec. 19, 1816, in Madison county, Illinois. They had two children in Sangamon county, and in 1836 moved to Stephenson county, locating near what is now Orangeville. Twelve children were born in Stephenson county, three of whom died in infancy. Of their eleven children, THOMAS, born July 1, 1834, in Sangamon county, married, and in 1857 emigrated to Missouri, in 1858, was married there to Mrs. Martha Clemens, formerly Miss Myers, who was born in Missouri. They had three children, namely, NANCY, JOHN and GEORGE. Mrs. Martha Trotter died in 1865, and Thomas T. returned to Illinois. He was married in September, 1867, to Mrs. Sarah Seidel, formerly Miss Woodring, of Pennsylvania. In the spring of 1868 he returned to near Barnard, Nodaway county, Missouri, where they still reside. Of his children by the third marriage, namely: ELIZABETH, born Nov. 7, 1835, in Sangamon county, married July 4, 1858, to Joseph Vanmeter, of Ohio. They had two living children, GEORGE and HENRY, and reside near Onero, Stephenson county, Illinois. JAMES, born March 27, 1837, in Stephenson county, was married in 1860 to Sarah Riem, a native of Pennsylvania. They had five children, ESTHER, ELMER, CHARLES, FRANK, and ARCHIE. He enlisted in the 16th Ill. Vet. Vol. Inf. in January, 1864, and served until the close of the war when he was honorably discharged. In 1869 he moved with his family to Nodaway county, Missouri, where they still reside. WILLIAM, born September 19, 1839, in Stephenson county, Illinois, married in December, 1864, to Emily J. Lorch, who was born in 1840 in Springfield, Illinois. In 1865 they moved to Orangeville, where they had three children, WILLIAM, ANNA MAY and MELVIN. In 1875 the family moved to Polo, Ogle county, Illinois, where they now reside. GEORGE, born July 1, 1841, in Stephenson county, enlisted August 28, 1861, left home Sept. 10, 1861, served two and a half years, was promoted from the ranks to life major of the regiment. Re-enlisted Dec. 6, 1863, at Camp Cowan, Miss., came home on a furlough, returned, was struck by lightning March 16, 1865, while at Dauphin Island. He reluctantly returned home May 21, 1865, where he died March 25, 1866. URANIA, born February 24, 1843, in Stephenson county, married there Oct. 1, 1863, to David W. Scott, a native of Ohio, and a graduate of Cincinnati Eclectic Medical College. Is at present practicing medicine in Buena Vista, Stephenson county, Illinois, where they reside. They have two children, MINNIE and MYRON. MARY A., born Dec. 27, 1844, in Stephenson county, died April 11, 1868. MILLARD F., born May 25, 1850, in Stephenson county, resides with his parents. SARAH J., born May 24, 1852, in Stephenson county, died December 8, 1870. LUCY C., born July 30, 1854, in Stephenson county, married there December 21, 1873, to Woodbury Robey, who was born in the same county. They have one child, LEROY, and reside in Stephenson county. JOHN C., born Sept. 4, 1857, lives with his parents at Orangeville, Stephenson county, Illinois.

ELIZABETH, born in Kentucky, married William Graham. *See his name.*

Mrs. Elizabeth Trotter died March 4, 1825, before the family left Kentucky, and James Trotter died Sept. 26, 1839, in Sangamon county, Illinois.

TROXELL, Mrs. SARAH, whose maiden name was Rouk, was born in Washington county, Maryland, and was there married to Abraham Troxell, a native of the same county. They had ten children in Maryland, and Mr. Troxell died there, March 4, 1824. His widow and some of her children came to Sangamon county in 1836, and the others came later. Of her children—

ELIZABETH, born Jan. 19, 1815, in Washington county, Maryland, was married there to Perry Prather. They had twelve children, and the family moved to Sangamon county, Illinois, in 1850. Of their children, ABRAHAM went to California in March, 1859, and after a few years absence was not heard of until 1875. He now lives in Prescott, Arizona. SARAH E., married Harvey N. North. *See his name.* RUTH A., married Marshal Sattley. *See his name.* WASHINGTON B. was a soldier in an Illinois regiment, and aided in suppressing the rebellion. He lives with his mother. WILLIAM D. is in Prescott, Arizona. MARY C. married Jacob C. Miller. *See his name.* KITTURAH, SAMUEL J., ISAAC R., RACHEL F., JEMIMA J. and JOHN L., the six latter, live with their mother, except Isaac R., who is a telegraph operator. Perry Prather died, and his widow lives four miles east of Rochester, Sangamon county, Illinois.

DAVID, born Jan. 15, 1815, in Washington county, Maryland, came to Sangamon county, Illinois, in the autumn of 1835, settling in what is now Cooper township. He was married in Macon county to Lucinda Dickey. They had two living children, JAMES B., married Harriet Jones, and lives near Argenta, Macon county, Illinois. JOHN was stabbed in the heart, when about fifteen years of age, by a southern refugee, during the time of the rebellion. They were at work together in a field, and although others were near them, the murderer escaped and has never been heard of. The stabbing was done without provocation or warning. Mrs. Lucinda Troxell died Jan. 8, 1875. David Troxell left Argenta March 10, 1874, intending to visit his brother, Peter. Having to pass through Decatur, Illinois, he was seen there the day he left home, and that is the last that is certainly known of him by his relatives. He was a sober, honest and substantial farmer, and his fate is enshrouded in the most profound mystery.

PETER, born May 2, 1816, in Washington county, Maryland, and came to Sangamon county, arriving October, 1836, in what is now Cooper township, south of Sangamon river. He was married in Sangamon county, Feb. 18, 1841, to Susan Firey. They had twelve children. Abraham died in his eighth year. GRANT E., next to the youngest, died in infancy. MARY E., born Jan. 14, 1844, was married Feb. 23, 1865, to John W. North. *See his name.* SARAH E., born Feb. 1, 1847, was married Sept. 1, 1870, to Henry C. Neer, who was born Jan. 6, 1842, in Loudon county, Virginia, and brought by his parents to Sangamon county in the fall of that year. He enlisted in August, 1862, for three years, in Co. I, 114th Ill. Inf., and was taken prisoner at the battle of Guntown, Miss., June 10, 1864. He was imprisoned, at Andersonville, Georgia, and other places, until April 4, 1865, when he was released, and was honorably discharged May 8, 1865. H. C. Neer and wife live three miles north of Breckenridge, Sangamon county, Illinois. ANNIE was married Feb. 22, 1876, to J. Henry Ross, and live near Breckenridge, Sangamon county, Illinois. RUTH E., ISAAC H., WILLIAM P., JOHN J., GRACE E., PHOEBE J. and MARTHA A; the seven latter live with their parents at Edgewood farm, five miles east of Rochester, Sangamon county, Illinois.

WILLIAM, born Nov. 12, 1817, in Washington county, Maryland, came to

Sangamon county in 1836, is unmarried, and lives at the house of his niece, Mrs. North.

JOHN, born July 8, 1819, in Washington county, Maryland, came to Sangamon county in the fall of 1836, and was married Nov. 18, 1857, to Mary S. Firey. They had one child, MARY, who was married August 9, 1876, to Alexander Anderson, and lives in Pana, Illinois. Mrs. Mary S. Troxell died Nov. 16, 1859, and John Troxell was married Nov. 19, 1862, to Cynthia Willy. They have six living children, EVA R., ABRAHAM P., LUCINDA A., ELIZA J., JOHN W. and LUTHER, and reside near Grove City, Christian county, Illinois.

MARY, born Feb. 2, 1821, in Maryland, died in Sangamon county, aged eighteen years.

ABRAHAM and ISAAC, twins, born Nov. 2, 1824, in Washington county, Maryland. The former died in infancy. ISAAC came to Sangamon county in 1836, and married Eliza J. Hazlett. They had two children in Sangamon county. WILLIAM was married Nov. 19, 1874, to Jemima Prather. They have one child, DELBERT, and live near Edinburg, Christian county, Illinois. GEORGE was married Nov. 26, 1874, to Annie Foster, and live in Missouri. Mrs. Eliza J. Troxell died in Christian county, Illinois, and Isaac Troxell lives in California.

SARAH, born Jan. 1, 1823, in Washington county, Maryland, came to Sangamon county in 1836, and was married in DeWitt county to Ralph Rosencrans. She died November, 1867, leaving one child, SARAH, who married James Powell. They live near DeWitt, DeWitt county, Illinois.

JAMES, born Sept. 16, 1827, in Maryland, came to Sangamon county in 1836, enlisted in 1846 in the 4th Ill. Inf., served one year in the Mexican war, under Colonel E. D. Baker, and died in 1847, in Sangamon county, of disease contracted in the army.

Mrs. Sarah Troxell died March 27, 1844, and was buried in Cooper township, Sangamon county, Illinois.

TRUE, Mrs. SUSANNAH, whose maiden name was Williams, was born about 1782 near Richmond, Virginia. Her parents moved to Woodford county, Kentucky, and she was there married to Ezekiel True. They had eleven children in Kentucky, and moved to Morgan county, Illinois, in 1825, and in 1827 moved to Randolph county, Missouri, where Mr. True died, and Mrs. True, with four of her children, moved to Springfield, Illinois, in 1832. Of their children—

WILKINS raised a family in Kentucky and resides near Oconee, Illinois.

PATTY, born in Kentucky, married in Morgan county, Illinois, to Moses Pilcher, and died in 1840 at Springfield. Her son, JEPTHA, resides in Springfield, Illinois.

GREEN B., died in California.

WILLIAM married in Kentucky. Residence not known.

LEWIS lives near Moberly, Missouri.

MATILDA married in Springfield to Mossman Ballard, and died in California.

JAMES married in Chicago, and lives at Durant, Illinois.

LUCINDA was born August 19, 1823, in Woodford county, Kentucky, came to Sangamon county in 1832, married in Springfield Nov. 12, 1843, to Willis H. Johnson. He was born Sept. 18, 1818, in Wilson county, Tennessee, and brought up in Davidson county in the same State. He came to Springfield, Illinois, in the spring of 1843. They had nine children. Three died young. WILLIAM T., born Aug. 25, 1844, enlisted February, 1862, in Co. G 5th Ill. Cav. for three years, re-enlisted as a veteran in January, 1864, served until November, 1865, and was at the capture of Helena, Arkansas, siege of Vicksburg, and capture of Jackson, Mississippi. He was honorably discharged, and was married May 8, 1867, to Margaret A. Hillman. They have two children, KATIE and ALBERT PALMER. William T. Johnson live in Springfield, Illinois. MARY F., born Feb. 10, 1847, was married Feb. 19, 1868, to L. Herbert Spaulding, who was born near Hudson. New York, Aug. 14, 1849, came to Springfield with his father in 1858. They have three children, CLARA L., WILLIE J. and L. DANA, and live in Springfield, Ill. GEORGE W., born June 15, 1848, was married Nov. 28, 1872, to Helen Maxon, in Bloomington, Illinois, and lives there. JOHN M., DRUSILLA J. and CHARLES H., live with their parents in Springfield, Illinois. Willis H. Johnson was the pioneer machinist in Springfield, so far as doing all kinds of work to supply the country. He also established the ten hour system, by making a pattern with his own hands, casting a bell, and having it rung at regular hours. That was in 1845 or '46.

JANE, born Feb. 10, 1826, in Kentucky, married in Springfield to George Anderson, who died May 15, 1856, in Springfield, leaving a widow and four children, who now live in Omaha, Nebraska.

Mrs. Susannah True died August, 1834, in Springfield, Illinois.

TRUMBO, ADAM, was born May 6, 1790, in Bourbon county, Kentucky. Mildreth Foster was born February, 1790, in the same county. They were there married, had ten children, and moved to Sangamon county, Illinois, arriving in November, 1828, about six miles south of Springfield, in what is now Woodside township, where two children were born. Of their children—

JOHN married Ellen Haley and died in 1848 or '49, and his widow married Milton Bridges. See his name.

MELINDA married Jeremiah Adams. She died, leaving four children near Galena, Illinois.

JACOB died at seventeen years of age.

LAVICA married James L. Southwick. See his name.

HARNESS, born Oct. 9, 1816, in Bourbon county, Kentucky, married in Sangamon county, July 15, 1838, to Elizabeth Hall. They had eight children. WILLIAM, born April 10, 1840, died Sept. 14, 1862. SARAH C., born Jan. 26, 1843, lives with her parents. JAMES P., born Jan. 27, 1845, married Dec. 25, 1870, to Anna Staley. They have one child, WILLIAM, and live one and one-half miles west of Chatham, Illinois. JACOB, born July 2, 1848, lives with his parents. MARIA L. died at five years of age. HARNESS, Jun., born Nov. 15, 1854, and OSCAR, born Feb. 7, 1856, live with their parents. ANDREW J., born August 25, 1861, died Sept. 23, 1875. Harness Trumbo lives six miles south of Springfield, near where his father, Adam Trumbo, settled in 1828.

LOUISA J. married Thomas Chord, had ten children, and Mr. Chord died Jan. 20, 1874, leaving his family near Petersburg, Illinois.

NANCY married Joseph Scales. They have ten children, and live in Wisconsin, near Galena, Illinois.

ELIZABETH, born March 10, 1823, in Kentucky, married in Sangamon county to John Smith. See his name.

ANDREW F., born in Kentucky, raised in Sangamon county, and married in Missouri to Mary Flernoy, has three children, and lives near Barr's Ridge P. O., California.

REBECCA married Mitchell Graham. See his name. She had one child, REBECCA, who married Mitchell Lawson, and lives near Johnstown, Bates county, Missouri.

ISAAC H., born March 13, 1830, in Sangamon county, married Emma Bridges. They had three children. The second one, AMANDA J., died, aged seven years. ALMA and ARABELL live with their parents, one mile north of Chatham, Sangamon county, Illinois.

GEORGE W., born Nov. 28, 1832, in Sangamon county, married March 29, 1865, to Mary F. Malone, who was born Feb. 24, 1844, in St. Louis county, Missouri. They had four children, twins, died in infancy. EUGENE L. and ARTHUR A. live with their parents. G. W. Trumbo resides where his parents settled in 1828, and where he was born. It is six miles south of Springfield, Illinois.

Mrs. Mildreth Trumbo died April 20, 1835, and Adam Trumbo married Mrs. Hannah Hall, whose maiden name was Cunningham. He died Oct. 6, 1856, and she died January, 1872, both in Sangamon county, Illinois.

TURNER, ARCHIBALD, was born June 11, 1750, in Ireland. He was the youngest of twelve children, all the others having died in infancy. He came to America when he was more than thirty years of age, and was married about 1790, on James River, Virginia to Rachel ———. They had five children in Virginia, and Mrs. Rachel Turner died July 29, 1818. He moved with his children to the Wabash valley, Indiana, where he was married to Catherine White, also a native of Ireland. They had two children in Indiana, and the family moved to Sangamon county, Illinois, arriving in 1820 or '21. Of his children—

MARY, born Nov. 8, 1797, in Virginia, married in Indiana to William Harvey, moved to Christian county, Illinois, raised a family, and she died about 1869.

JOHN, born Oct. 7, 1799, in Virginia, married in Sangamon county to Esther McMurry. They had seven children, and he died. Their son, Archibald Turner, lives in Springfield, Illinois.

ESTHER, born August 21, 1801, in Virginia, married in Indiana to Daniel McCaskill, moved to Brown county, Illinois, where the parents died, leaving a large family. Their son, JOHN, is a physician in Colorado, and their son, ARCHER, is a Methodist preacher.

MARK, born Oct. 3, 1803, in Virginia, married in Sangamon county to Elvira Bell. They had three children, moved to Decatur, where he died about 1855, and his widow died the next year.

ARCHIBALD, Jun., born July 1, 1808, in Virginia, married in Sangamon county to Elizabeth Lemons, moved to Washington county, Illinois, and died there in 1871. He was a local preacher in the M. E. church.

By the second wife:

HUGH, born February, 1816, in Indiana, married in Christian county, Illinois, to Elizabeth Stokes, and had eight children in Sangamon county. DAVID A., born Sept. 28, 1839, married Elizabeth Littrell, had one child, EDWARD, who died, aged seven years. They live near Pawnee, Illinois. JAMES W., born Dec. 20, 1841, married Lutheria Huston, and live six miles west of Springfield, Illinois. SARAH C., born April 14, 1844, married William M. Young, have five children, and live near Elkhart, Logan county, Illinois. GEORGE W., born March 21, 1847, lives near Edinburg, Illinois. ELIZA J., born Feb. 9, 1849, married Nov. 25, 1868, to Charles W. Ewell. See his name. JOHN H., born Jan. 21, 1851. ROBERT, born July, 17, 1853. ELIZABETH, born April 7, 1857, and MARY A., born April 30, 1859, reside at the family homestead, four miles west of Springfield, Illinois. Mrs. Elizabeth Turner died April 7, 1870, and Hugh Turner died Dec. 14, 1872.

JAMES, born Jan. 26, 1818, in Indiana, married Oct. 25, 1848, in Sangamon county, to Elizabeth A. Earnest. They had two children, SALOME O., born Nov. 10, 1849, married Jacob E. Ingalls. See his name. NOAH H., born Nov. 7, 1851, lives with his mother. James Turner died Oct. 22, 1853, and his widow married Henry B. Chambers. See his name.

Archibald Turner died June 29, 1855, aged one hundred and five years and eighteen days. His widow, Mrs Catherine Turner, died May 10, 1870, both near where they settled in 1820 or '21, four miles west of Springfield, Illinois.

Archibald Turner was raised by Presbyterian parents, and was thoroughly trained in the Westminster Confession of Faith and larger Catechism. He became dissipated in early life, but while living in Indiana he was converted at a camp-meeting, and for the last fifty years of his life was a devoted Christian. Near the close of his pilgrimage of more than a century his memory failed on all current events, but he could repeat correctly passages of the catechism, and the prayers that his mother had taught him in childhood.

TURPIN, Mrs. ELIZABETH, whose maiden name was Isom, was born about 1775, in Kentucky, and married there to Philip Turpin. They had twelve children, and Mr. Turpin died in Kentucky. Mrs. Elizabeth Turpin, with six of her children, came to Sangamon county in 1831 or '32, and settled two miles southeast of Loami. Of her children—

WOODFORD married in Kentucky, moved to Missouri, and afterwards to Sangamon county. His son, JAMES M., born May 10, 1848, in Howard county, Missouri, married Charlotte Webb. See Webb family. Mr. Turpin is a merchant in Loami, Sangamon county, Illinois.

SARAH married in Kentucky to John Clements, and she died there.

Of the six children who came to Sangamon county—

ELIZABETH, after the death of her sister, Sarah, married John Clements and came to Sangamon county. See his name.

WILLIAM, born in Kentucky about 1797, died unmarried in Sangamon county, Oct. 2, 1865.

CELIA married William Withrow. See his name.

URIAH, born in Kentucky, died in Sangamon county, aged twenty-two years.

MARTHA, born in Kentucky, married in Sangamon county to Absalom Stine, had eight children, and he died. The widow and some of her children live in Missouri.

NANCY, born in Kentucky, married Jefferson Back. They had nine children. The parents are dead. Their daughters, ELIZABETH married George J. Walker. *See his name.* They live in Loami, Illinois. CAROLINE married D. Rose, and live in Loami, Illinois. MIRANDA married David D. Martin, and resides in Auburn, Illinois. He is a carpenter and builder there.

CHARLES I., born Nov. 28, 1818, in Kentucky, came with his mother to Sangamon county in 1831 or '32, married August 11, 1836, to Sarah Jarrett. They had eight children. They moved to Missouri and returned. Some of their children were born in each State. REBECCA A., born August 9, 1837, in Sangamon county, married Aaron Hall, Jun. *See his name.* WILLIAM A., born August 29, 1839, in Lewis county, Missouri, enlisted August, 1862, for three years, in Co. I, 73d Ill. Inf. He died Dec. 26, 1862, at Nashville, Tennessee. His remains were brought home and buried in Sulphur Springs Cemetery, near Loami, Illinois. ELIZABETH, born Feb. 8, 1841, in Missouri, married Hugh A. Park. *See his name.* JONATHAN J., born July 7, 1842, in Missouri, married in Sangamon county to Sarah E. Cloninger, who was born August 12, 1841, in Cabell county, West Virginia. They have three children, WILLIAM A., CHARLES L, and SARAH M., and reside one and one-half miles southeast of Loami, Sangamon county, Illinois. CHARLES I., Jun., born Feb. 24, 1849, enlisted in Co. E, 133d Ill. Inf., for one hundred days, and was honorably discharged, with thanks of President Lincoln, Dec. 15, 1864. He was married June 27, 1867, to Eliza Jane Hays, who was born March 24, 1849, in Macoupin county. They reside two and a half miles south of Loami, Illinois. DENNIS, born Sept. 19, 1851, married Dec. 21, 1870, to Caroline F. Hays, who was born May 21, 1853, in Macoupin county, Illinois. They live two miles south of Loami, Illinois. JAMES F., born Sept. 11, 1853, lives with his mother—1874. Charles I. Turpin, Sen., died April 1, 1869, in Sangamon county, and Mrs. Sarah Turpin resides one and one-half miles southwest of Loami, Sangamon county, Illinois.

LUCINDA, born in Kentucky, married in Sangamon county to George Taylor, has five children, and resides in Christian county, Illinois.

Mrs. Elizabeth Turpin died in 1860 in Sangamon county, Illinois, aged eighty-five years.

TURLEY, THOMAS J., was born May 7, 1802, in Montgomery county, Kentucky. His parents had fourteen children, seven of each sex, all born in the same county. The parents, with part of their children, came to Logan county, Illinois, about 1823, and there are many of the name in that county, as the whole fourteen children raised families. The eleventh child, being the youngest son, is the one whose name heads this sketch. He came from Logan to Sangamon county, and was married Sept. 27, 1827, to Mary Trotter. They had ten children, all born in Sangamon county. Two died young. Of the other eight children—

ELIZABETH, born June 8, 1828, in Sangamon county, married Nov. 7, 1850, to William Kenney, who was born in 1827, in Harrison county, Kentucky, was a soldier from DeWitt county, Illinois, for one year, from June, 1846, in Co. E, 4th Ill. Inf., in the war with Mexico, and came to Sangamon county in 1849. Mr. and Mrs. Kenney had five children, MARY A. died in her second year. JOHN B., VICTOR, SARAH F. and WILLIAM live with their parents, two miles west of Mechanicsburg, Illinois.

AGNES J., born Nov. 18, 1829, married Nicholas B. Whitesides. *See his name.*

BOLIVAR, born August 12, 1831, in Sangamon county, married in the same county, Jan. 22, 1857, to Maria Wilson, who was born Nov. 15, 1831, in New Hampshire. They had five children, one died in infancy, and ALBERT J. died in his third year. GEORGE LINCOLN, NICHOLAS IRVING, and HENRY ELMER live with their parents on the farm where his parents settled in 1828.

It is two miles north of Sangamon Station, and four miles east of Springfield, Illinois.

JAMES, born May 4, 1833, married Oct. 20, 1853, to Mary B. Kenney. They had six children, JAMES T., AMBROSE, ADA BELLE, LAURA C., CHARLES H. and ELIZA A. Mr. Turley died August 26, 1862, and his widow and children reside five miles east of Springfield, Illinois.

HENRY D., born Feb. 3, 1836, in Sangamon county, married Sept. 10, 1856, in Logan county to Eliza J. Scoggin, who was born in that county Dec. 12, 1840. They had nine children, four died under two years. FANNIE A., MARY A., CHARLES L., MAGGIE MAY and CHLOE E. reside with their parents, five miles east of Springfield, Illinois.

THOMAS J., Jun., born Jan. 20, 1838, married May 20, 1858, to Rebecca Barr. She died Feb. 14, 1874, leaving five children, ALVAN, ELIZABETH, FLORA A., JAMES and ELIZA A. Mr. Turley was married a second time, and resides three miles east of Springfield, Illinois.

WILLIAM, born Oct. 16, 1840, in Sangamon county, enlisted July 25, 1862, in Co. I, 114th Ill. Inf., for three years, served until the end of the rebellion and was honorably discharged July 4, 1865. He was married August 10, 1865, in St. Louis, to Ellen Curran, who was born April 7, 1842, in Glasgow, Scotland. They had two children, JOSEPH W. and MARY E., and Mrs. Ellen Turley died August 8, 1872. Mr. T. and his children live with his mother, five miles east of Springfield, Illinois—1874.

MARY, born Dec. 11, 1842, in Sangamon county, married Dec. 28, 1864, to Quintus Embree. They had one child, FANNIE A., born Nov. 4, 1865. Mrs. Embree was married Feb. 20, 1875, to William D. Henry. They have one son, WILLIAM D., Jun., and reside five miles east of Springfield, Illinois.

Thomas J. Turley died Sept. 7, 1852, and his widow resides with her children, near where she and her husband settled in 1828, five miles east of Springfield, Illinois.

TWIST, JOHN, was born in Cambridge, Massachusetts, went to Seneca Falls, when a young man, and was there married to Phœbe Russell, who was born in Newark, New Jersey. They had two children at Seneca Falls, and moved to Sangamon county, Illinois, arriving in 1821, in what is now Woodside township, six miles southeast of Springfield, where they had two children. Mrs. Twist made cheese and her husband hauled it to St. Louis on an ox wagon, where he found a market for it. In that way they raised the money to buy their first eighty acres of land. Early in 1826 they moved to a place on the Sangamon river, two miles northeast of Rochester, and about eight miles east of Springfield. Mr. Twist, in connection with Dr. Darling, of Springfield, built a saw and grist mill further up the river, four miles northeast of Rochester. It required all the men within a radius of ten or twelve miles to raise the mill. Mr. and Mrs. Twist had two children near the Sangamon river. Of their six children—

THADDEUS, born in New York, died in Sangamon county, aged fifteen years.

CICERO, born in 1820 in Seneca Falls, New York, married in Sangamon county, Illinois, May 21, 1845, to Sarah A. Barieman, and moved in August, 1848, to DeWitt county, Illinois. They had ten children, CICERO S., the sixth, and SARAH P., the eighth, died young. Of the other eight, NORVILLA A. was married Sept. 20, 1866, to John W. Dunn, has one child, JAMES E., and lives in Macon county, Illinois. LOUISA was married June, 1872, to James Long, has one child, CHARLES, and lives in McLean county, Illinois. MYLO lives with his father. EVAN A. was married Feb. 19, 1874, to Jane Bennett. MARY E., WESLEY W., ADELIA E., and JOANNA live with their father. Mrs. Sarah A. Twist died Jan. 10, 1867, and Cicero Twist was married Nov. 3, 1867, to Sarah Enos, and resides near Weldon, DeWitt county, Illinois.

JOANNA, born Feb. 26, 1822, in Sangamon county, married Henry Johnson, See his name.

MYLO, born in 1824 and died, aged seven years.

JOHN A., born Nov. 12, 1826, near Rochester, Sangamon county, Illinois, was married Nov. 26, 1856, in Rochester, to Eliza J. Sattley. They have six children, IRA F., RALPH S., MARY A.,

ELLA R., ELIZA J. and JOHN A., Jun., and reside in Rochester, Illinois.

John Twist died July 13, 1831, at his mill, on the Sangamon river, north of Rochester. His widow married James Stewart. They had one child.

EMELINE Stewart, born in Sangamon county, and married Addison Foley. They have two children, and live at Hay Market, Prince William county, Virginia.

Mrs. Phoebe Stewart died Jan. 11, 1836, in Sangamon county, Illinois. *See name of James Stewart.*

U

UNDERWOOD, REUBEN, was born March 17, 1798, in Nicholas county, Kentucky. He was married in Bracken county, Kentucky, December 5, 1822, to Margaret Dawson, a sister of John Dawson. *See his name.* She was born August 31, 1796, in Fairfax county, Virginia. Mr. and Mrs. Underwood lived for some time in Harrison county, Kentucky. Then moved with four children to Sangamon county, Illinois, arriving in the fall of 1833 in what is now Mechanicsburg township. Of their five children—

ELIZA, born Sept. 7, 1823, in Kentucky, died Sept. 28, 1825.

JOHN H., born July 31, 1825, in Harrison county, Kentucky, was brought up in Sangamon county, and married in 1859, at Rushville, Illinois, to Jane E. E. Smith. They had six children, CHARLES E., JOHN R., SARAH M., ADELIA E., ARTHUR A. and ALBERT E., the latter twins. J. H. Underwood and family reside at Carrollton, Green county, Illinois.

WILLIAM D., born Jan. 14, 1828, in Kentucky, died in Sangamon county, August 4, 1835.

THOMAS J., born Oct. 30, 1829, in Harrison county, Kentucky, was married at Mechanicsburg, Sangamon county, Illinois, Oct. 28, 1858, to Margaret D. Bondurant. They reside at the homestead, where his parents settled in 1833. It is three miles southeast of Dawson, Sangamon county, Illinois. Thomas J. Underwood enlisted August 6, 1862, for three years, in Co. I, 73d Ill. Inf. He was elected second lieutenant, on the organization of the company. After the battle of Perryville he resigned in consequence of failing health.

ADELIA, born Feb. 29, 1832, resides at the family homestead.

Reuben Underwood died Feb. 10, 1844, and his widow died Jan. 9, 1875, both at the homestead where they settled in 1833. Reuben Underwood's widowed mother came with him to Sangamon county, he being the only child. Her maiden name was Sarah Conway. Her parents were among the earliest settlers in Kentucky. They had taken refuge from the Indians either in Randall's or Martin's station, and when those fortifications were captured and destroyed, June 22, 1780, by the combined forces of the British and Indians, she was separated from her parents and adopted by an Indian and his squaw. She was then about seven years old. They took her to Detroit, Michigan, and after a search of three years, her father, learning where she was, secured an order from the British officers for the Indians to restore her to her father. They also advised Mr. Conway to make the Indian a present to prevent his injuring her. Acting on their advice, he paid them forty dollars. She died at her son's residence, Sept. 19, 1845, aged about seventy-three years.

UNDERWOOD, JOHN, was born about 1785, in North Carolina. Went to Sumner county, Tennessee, when a young man, was there married to Clarissa Cook, and had eleven children in Tennessee. The family moved to Sangamon county, Illinois, arriving November, 1829, in what is now Island Grove township, where one child was born. Of their children—

GEORGE, born Jan. 27, 1811, married in Sangamon county to Elizabeth Sweet, had six children, and she died, and he married Ann Campbell, had four children, and the parents died, leaving their children near St. Joseph, Missouri.

LAWRENCE, born August 5, 1812, in Davidson county, Tennessee, married in Sangamon county, April 9, 1835, to Abigail Colburn. They had fourteen children, four of whom died under nine years. Of the ten, ACHSA, born May 6, 1836, married Nov. 24, 1854, to William Huffmaster. *See his name.* They have ten children, and live at Owaneco, Christian county, Illinois. NATHAN T.

born October 1, 1837, married Mary L. Dorrance, have six children, and live near Loami, Illinois. AZUBA, born April 18, 1839, married August 13, 1862, to Benjamin F. Weeks, who was born July 6, 1841, in Belmont county, Ohio. They have two children, AMY A. and LAURA A., and reside in Loami, Illinois. Mr. Weeks enlisted August 2, 1862, in Co. F, 51st Ill. Inf., for three years, served until June 29, 1865, when he was honorably discharged. He was in the dispensing druggists' department the last year. CLARISSA, born Jan. 4, 1841, married April 14, 1859, to Samuel M. Neal, have three children, and live near Springfield, Missouri. BARTON W., born Sept. 26, 1842, lives near Springfield, Missouri. JESSE T., born Sept. 4, 1847, married June 25, 1868, to Abigail M. Kinney, and live at Linden, Osage county, Kansas. LAWRENCE T., born July 31, 1849, married July 8, 1869, to Martha J. Weir, have two children, and reside two miles west of Loami, Illinois. LUCY, born August 9, 1853, married June 16, 1870, to Scott Carter, who died, and she lives with her parents. DAVID O. and FANNY live with their parents, near Bois D'Arc, Greene county, Missouri.

MARTHA A., born April 10, 1814, married Abel Jones, had several children, and both died in Lewis county, Missouri.

EMELINE, born July 20, 1816, married March 6, 1842, to William Hammond. See his name.

MATILDA, born March 29, 1818, married December, 1842, to Thomas Deaton, have nine children, and reside near Jacksonville, Illinois.

PRESLEY, born Sept. 11, 1819, died unmarried at thirty years of age.

TURNER, born Jan. 14, 1822, married Mary Harbour, had four children, and he died, leaving his widow and children at Hamburg, Iowa.

WILEY, born May 16, 1823, died 1858.

TABITHA, born Oct. 23, 1824, married John Morgan. They live in Atchison county, Missouri.

LOUISA, born May 29, 1826, in Tennessee, married in Sangamon county to Milton Douglas. See his name. Her name is erroneously printed Eliza.

JAMES T., born Oct. 9, 1830, in Sangamon county, was married Jan. 29, 1866, near Chambersburg, Pennsylvania, to Elizabeth Coble, a native of that place. James T. Underwood was for several years assessor of Island Grove township. He was elected in 1861 to represent that township in the board of supervisors of Sangamon county. He is now—November, 1876—a Justice of the Peace, and resides in Springfield, Illinois.

John Underwood built a horse mill in Island Grove, soon after his arrival. It was the first in that part of the county. The settlers came from twenty to thirty miles to do grinding with their own teams. He died Oct. 27, 1866, in Island Grove, where he settled in 1829. His widow died Jan. 18, 1866, at Loami, Sangamon county, Illinois.

UNDERWOOD, WILLIAM, was born and married in Kentucky, and brought his family to Sangamon county, arriving about 1834 at Berlin. They had three children, one of whom died, aged ten years, and Mrs. Underwood died. Their two sons, CHARLES and LYCURGUS, went to their friends, in Kentucky, and went from there, as soldiers, in the Mexican war. William Underwood married for his second wife, Eliza Lemon, and he died in 1840. His widow married John Churchill. See his name.

UTTERBACK, ELIJAH, was born in Culpepper county, Virgiana, Sept. 25, 1776. When he was a young man he went to Henry county, Kentucky, and was there married to Susan Bice—a sister to John Bice. They had three children born in Kentucky, and moved to Sangamon county, Illinois, arriving in October, 1835, in what is now Williams township, where one child was born. Of their four children—

MARY D., born April 12, 1824, in Henry county, Kentucky, married in Sangamon county to Peter Braughton. See his name.

ELIZABETH C., born in Kentucky, married in Sangamon county to James Dode. They have six children, and live in Lafayette county, Missouri.

NANCY A., born in Kentucky, married in Sangamon county to Jacob Lucas. They have six children, and live in Fremont county, Iowa.

ADALINE S., born in Sangamon county, married James Henry. They have two children, and live in Bourbon county, Kentucky.

Mrs. Susan Utterback died August 19, 1841, and her husband died March 3, 1862, both in Sangamon county, Illinois.

V

VANCIL. This name—Vanzael, anglicised—is quite common in Germany, especially among the soldiers of the fatherland. The circumstances which led to its being transferred from Prussia to America were somewhat peculiar. A young man bearing the name, put to death a valuable dog belonging to an old German husbandman. This was deemed a grave offense, and he was called up by his father for trial. The boy plead guilty, but justified his actions. The venerable parent decreed that he should be severely chastised or leave the country. The proud spirited stripling chose the latter, immediately embarked for America, and settled in Virginia. Nothing is known of his marriage, but his son, John Vancil married Mary Penrod. They had a large family, consisting in part of six sons, five of whom were over six feet high, and weighed upwards of two hundred pounds each. While these were yet children, John Vancil joined a company of rangers —the first military organizations at the beginning of our troubles with the mother country—and sent his family into Maryland. One of his sons—

VANCIL, SAMUEL, born about 1768, was but six years of age at the beginning of the American Revolution, when his father separated his family upon going into the army. Samuel was placed in a family of Germans, who, from their religious convictions were opposed to war. At the close of the war John Vancil collected his family in Patrick county, Virginia, where Samuel was married about 1795 to Mary Peckelheimer, and moved to Montgomery county, in the same State, where they had two children, and then moved to Logan county, Ky., where they had one child, and moved back to Virginia, where two children were born, and then moved to Lincoln county, Ky., and from there, in 1811, to Warren county, Ohio, where one child was born; from there to Franklin county, Indiana, and after a stay of five years, moved to Union county, Illinois, where he left his family, and with several others rode up to Sugar creek, and selected a tract of land about one mile southeast of where Auburn, Sangamon county now stands, where he arrived with his family late in November, 1818. They lived in their wagons until cabins could be built. Their only neighbors were the Drennan and Dodds families. *See their sketches.* Game being abundant, they lived largely on wild meat and honey. The Kickapoo Indians were quite numerous, though friendly. Of the six children of Samuel Vancil—

BETSY, was born in 1796, in Montgomery county, Va., married in Warren county, Ohio, to John Walker, and came with her parents to Sangamon county, where she died in 1830, leaving five children, three of whom, when last heard from, were living in Texas.

PENROD, born in 1797, in Montgomery county, Va., married in 1819, in Preble county, Ohio, to Elizabeth Houston. They had eight children, five of whom lived to maturity, namely: JAMES, married Martha A. Gatton. They had eight children, and she died. He married Sarah E. Greenawalt. He died February, 1872, in Virden, Ill., leaving his widow and children there. NANCY, married Jacob B. Vancil *See his name.* ELIZABETH, married Abner Hayden. They had six children. WILLIAM D., married Mrs. Melvina Vancil, and live in Montgomery county, Ill. SARAH E., married Noah Greenawalt, and lives near Cerro Gordo, Piatt county, Ill. NANCY J., married James Cruise who died, and she lives in Piatt county. MARY J., married Francis M. Rape. *See his name.* EMILY E., married Francis M. Cross. *See his name.* EMILY E., lives with her sisters. Abner Hayden died, and his widow has since been married, but is now a widow living with her children, near Cerro Gordo, Ill. MARY married A. Henderson. He died and she married William Forsythe. *See his name.* She lives at German Prairie Station, near Springfield, Ill. GEORGE W., married Melvina Gatton, and died in May, 1872, leaving several children. Penrod Vancil died in 1865, and his widow died in 1868, both near Auburn, Sangamon county, Ill. SARAH, born about 1800, in Logan county, Kentucky, married in Franklin county, Indiana, to John Houston. She died in Preble county, Ohio, leaving four children, one of whom lives in Iowa. GIDEON, born Feb. 1, 1802, in Montgomery county, Virginia, married in Sangamon county, Illinois, March, 1820, to Feraba Wilson, believed to have been the first marriage ever solemnized in the what is now Sangamon county. They had eleven children, all born in Sangamon county. CLARINDA, born in 1821, married in 1835, to Henry Duke. They had several children, all of whom died except one, who is married and lives in Dallas county, Texas. Mr. Duke died in 1864, and his widow lives in Dallas county, Texas. MARY J. is unmarried, and lives in Lawrence county, Missouri. ADAM, born August 16, 1826, died in Logan county, Illinois, Jan. 18, 1849. AARON BRYANT, born July 9, 1828, married in 1852 to Elizabeth Scott, have one child, and reside six miles southwest of Waverly, Illinois. JAMES M., born June 13, 1830, married in 1865 to Isabel Morland, have two children, and live in Camanche county, Texas. ELIZABETH, born May 26, 1832, married in 1850 to George W. Foster. He died in Texas, leaving a widow and two children, who live in Lawrence county, Missouri. GIDEON H., born May 23, 1835, married in 1862 to Martha A. Severe. They have four children, and live in Lawrence county, Missouri. SARAH A., born Nov. 13, 1837, married Dec. 4, 1851, to Robert Scott, have one child, and live in Carroll county, Missouri. THOMAS J., born Nov. 17, 1841, and died June 26, 1866. BENJAMIN F., born Nov. 7, 1843, is unmarried, and lives in Lawrence county, Missouri. MINERVA C., born Feb. 4, 1846, married J. C. Jenkins, and died in Texas, May 21, 1873. Gideon Vancil lived four miles southwest of Auburn, Sangamon county, Illinois, until 1847, when he moved to Hopkins county, Texas, where he lived until the close of the rebellion, when he moved to Missouri. Mrs. Feraba Vincil died in 1866, and Gideon Vancil resides with his children, near Mount Vernon, Lawrence county, Missouri.

SIMEON, born Jan. 1, 1805, in Montgomery county, Virginia, came to Sangamon county, Illinois, in 1818, with his father, was married March 16, 1826, to Mary Black. They had two children, WILLIAM, died in infancy; JACOB B., born August 11, 1828, married Nancy Vancil. They had three children, all died young. J. B. Vancil died in 1873. His widow is married and lives near Auburn, Illinois. Mrs. Mary Vancil died in 1830, and Simeon Vancil was married Jan. 19, 1832, to Mary A. Gates. They had eight children, three of whom died young. Of the other five, CORNELIUS P. married Emily J. Pritchard. They have three children, and live four miles south of Auburn. Illinois. PAULINE C. married Robert Hudgen. They have one child, OWEN, and reside near Cerro Gordo, Piatt county, Illinois. FRANCIS M., born Jan. 29, 1840, in Sangamon county, Illinois, took a select course at Shurtleff College, and studied law. In 1869 he moved to Brownsville, Nebraska, and engaged in a newspaper enterprise there for two years. He was married October, 1870, to Emma Argo, of Vermont, Illinois, who was born September, 1851, in Jersey county, Illinois. They have two children EARLE FRANCIS and EMMA LEOLA. In 1872 Mr. Vancil initiated the movement and assisted in laying out the town of Bloomington, Franklin county, Neb. He resides there; is engaged in the practice of law and stock raising. MARGARET J., born Jan. 15, 1842, married George W. Cray. They have four children, and reside two miles northwest of Virden, Illinois. MARY A. married Andrew Eagen. They have two children, and live three miles north of Virden, Illinois. Mrs. Mary A. Vancil died Feb. 3, 1873, and Simeon Vancil died April, 1875, both at the homestead where they had lived more than half a century. It was three and a half miles southwest of Auburn, Sangamon county, Illinois.

Mr. Simeon Vancil was very fond of conversing on subjects connected with the early history of the country. Speaking of the "deep snow" of 1830 and '31, he said that it was about three and a half feet deep on a level, but that it drifted to a depth of eight or ten feet. After it became sufficiently hard by thawing and freezing on the surface to bear his weight, he remembered attempting to walk across a ravine where the snow brought all on a level. The crust was weakened by hazel brush that came up through it, and at the deepest place he went down, quick as thought. When he brushed the snow from his eyes and looked up, he found the crust at least three feet above his head. It required a long time for him to work his way out, but he finally succeeded by using his gun to break the crust over his head. He said that after the snow disappeared the stumps from which they had cut the trees for fuel were from six to ten feet high. He said that from the Indians who were here at the time, he learned that a deep snow had fallen about thirty years before, and that the buffalo, unable to find food, would collect on the highest points, where the snow was thinnest, and remain huddled together until they died of hunger and cold. He said their account of it was corroborated by large quantities of buffalo bones being found on nearly all those high places. Simeon Vancil was a man of strong mental capacities, hospitable and kind. With one exception, he was for many years the oldest settler of Sangamon county. That exception was William Drennan. They have both passed away.

REBECCA, born in Warren county, Ohio, was married in Sangamon county to Henry Landis, of Logan county, Illinois, and died there a few years later without children.

Mrs. Mary Vancil died in 1822, and Samuel Vancil married a Mrs. Wakefield. He died in 1828, both near where they settled on coming to the country. They were buried in the Wimer grave yard, southeast of Auburn, Sangamon county, Illinois.

VAN DEREN, BARNARD, born May 22, 1789, in Harrison county, Ky., was married there May 27, 1813, to Eliza McKee, who was born May 16, 1795, in the same county. They had nine children in Kentucky, two of whom died here. The family moved to Sangamon county, Ill., arriving June 12, 1835, in what is now Curran township. When they came to the county the greater part of it was flooded with water. Barnard VanDeren was never a strong man physically, and the over-exertion and anxiety connected with bringing his family to so new a country brought on disease. There was not sufficient vitality left to counteract it, and he died July 6, 1835, less than a month after their arrival. Of their seven children—

CYRUS W., born May 6, 1815, in Kentucky, was married there April 2, 1835, to Margaret Patton, and came to Sangamon county, Ill., in 1838, three years later than the other members of the family. They had three living children. ELIZA J., born March 7, 1836, in Kentucky, was married Nov. 21, 1855, in Sangamon county, to Jesse F. Taylor, who was born Jan. 2, 1828, in Clarke county, Ky. They have three children, CYRUS W., LITTLEFIELD and JESSE F., the first born in Jackson county, Missouri, and the last two in Helena, Montana Territory, where Mr. Taylor and his family reside. MARTHA S., born in Woodside township, Sangamon county, married John M. Taylor. They have three children, GEORGE WILLIAM, FREDERICK and LUELLA, and live in Chatham, Illinois. MARY L., lives with her parents in Chatham, Sangamon county, Ill. Cyrus W. VanDeren was for a number of years a justice of the peace, and before the township organization, he was one of the Sangamon county judges, and was elected state senator in 1856, serving one term.

BARNARD A., born May 11, 1819, in Kentucky, was married in Sangamon county, Ill., Nov. 7, 1839, to Mary J. McGinnis. They had two living children. MARY J., died aged 12 years. JOHN D., married Lydia A. Smith, and lives in Oswego, Kansas. Mrs. Mary J. VanDeren died in July, 1852, and Barnard A. VanDeren was married Nov. 8, 1853, to Mary A. Baker. They had two children, THOMAS N. and MAGGIE L. B. A. Van Deran died Feb. 25, 1866 and his widow married John Lowry. They had two children. BARNARD A. died in infancy. MARY LOUISA lives with her parents. John Lowrey and family live near Loami, Sangamon county, Illinois.

MARTHA J., born Oct. 24, 1821, in Kentucky, was married in Sangamon county, Illinois, Nov. 3, 1842, to Lewis Johnson. See his name.

DAVID M., born Feb. 12, 1824, in Kentucky, was married June 17, 1851, to Margaret Evans. Mrs. Margaret Van Deren died in December, 1853, and D. M.

VanDeren was married Dec. 8, 1859, to Rebecca M. Kinney. They had one child, MAGGIE E., and D. M. VanDeren died Feb. 15, 1874, in Springfield, where his widow and daughter still reside.

MARGARET W., born June 9, 1828, in Kentucky, was married in Sangamon county, March 13, 1849, to William F. Thompson. See his name. They had one living child, ELIZA F., who lives with her mother. William F. Thompson died, and his widow was married July 18, 1854, to Lewis Johnson. See his name.

ARCHIBALD J., born Jan. 15, 1831, in Kentucky, brought up in Sangamon county, was married there May 22, 1866, to Mary W. Lloyd. They have four children, LLOYD, JOHN JAY, MARY and ARCHIE ALEXANDER. A. J. VanDeren and family live in Central City, Colorado. He was Grand Master of the Grand Lodge of Free Masons of Colorado in its early history, and was a member of the territorial legislature of Colorado for 1863.

JOHN M., born May 26, 1833, in Kentucky, brought up in Sangamon county, was married there Sept. 8, 1864, to Louisa M. Coe, who was born April 18, 1838, in Waterbury, Connecticut, and raised in Morgan county, Illinois. They have five children, ARCHIE C., FRANK W., HELEN, CHARLES W., and JOHN E.; the latter died in infancy. John M. VanDeren and family now—September, 1876—live in Chatham, Ill., but expect soon to move to Boulder City, Colorado.

As an illustration of the slovenly manner farming has been done in Sangamon county, J. M. VanDeren says he has seen the corn on land that produced from fifty to sixty bushels to the acre stand in the field until time for planting again. Then they would knock down the stalks of corn and burn all together to clear the ground for planting a new crop. As already stated, Barnard VanDeren died within one month after bringing his family to the county in 1835. His widow, Mrs. Eliza VanDeren, thus left alone in the prime of life, has remained a widow now more than forty years, and still lives with her children in Chatham.

On the 6th of June, 1874, just as she entered her eightieth year, a family reunion was held at the house of her son where she lives. There were present seven of the ten children of David and Jane Wallace—McKee, of Harrison county, Ky. The parents and three children are dead. The seven present were Mrs. Eliza Van Deren, of Chatham, Ill., aged seventy-nine, Mrs. Nancy McClintock, of Huntington city, West Virginia, seventy-two, Miss Margaret McKee, of Catlettsburg, Ky., aged seventy-one, Rev. D. D. McKee, of Hanover, Indiana, aged sixty-nine, Mrs. E. G. Hamilton, of Vinton, Iowa, aged sixty-seven, Mrs. Cynthia A. Reynolds, of Murrayville, Ill., aged sixty-six, Elder W. McKee, of Mexico, Missouri, aged sixty-four.

VANDEVER, AARON, born Feb. 7, 1785, in Virginia, was married in Henry county, Kentucky, in June, 1805, to Nancy French, who was born Nov. 19, 1789, in North Carolina. They had six children in Kentucky, and moved in 1814 to Washington county, Indiana, where four children were born, thence to Sangamon county, Illinois, arriving in October, 1829, where they had one child. Of their children—

SARAH, born June 1, 1806, in Kentucky, married and died in Indiana.

CAROLINE and *ELIZABETH*, twins, born March 2, 1808, in Kentucky, both married, and died in Indiana.

SOPHRONIA, born Feb. 14, 1811, in Kentucky, was married in Washington county, Indiana, to Barnett Davis. They have a large family, and live near Taylorville, Christian county, Illinois.

THOMAS L., born July 25, 1813, in Kentucky, died there.

HORATIO N., born March 1, 1816, in Washington county, Indiana, came with his parents to Sangamon county, October, 1829. He was married in June, 1840, in Christian county, Illinois, to Mary J. Rucker, who was born in Kentucky. They have three children, WILLIAM T., born August 22, 1842, and EUGENE A., born August 27, 1853, are bankers in Taylorville, Christian county, Illinois. ELIZABETH, born Feb. 6, 1859, lives with her parents.

H. N. Vandever resided in Sangamon county until the organization of Christian county, in March, 1839, when, without moving, he was placed in Christian county, the dividing line being near his farm. At the first election which occurred, in March,

1839, he was elected recorder for Christian county, and appointed clerk of the circuit court, also, holding the office until 1847. He was elected representative to the state legislature in 1842, raised a company for the Mexican war, but the quota was full. He was appointed by President Polk quartermaster, with the rank of captain, served two years, and during that time was at the battle of Buena Vista. In 1849 he was elected judge of the Christian county court, and filled the office by re-election two terms of four years each. He represented Christian and Montgomery counties in the state legislature for 1861-2. He was a member of the constitutional convention, and in 1862 was elected state senator. In 1870 he was elected judge of the circuit court to fill a vacancy, re-elected in June, 1873, and is now—1876—in office. H. N. Vandever and family live in Taylorville, Illinois.

WILLIAM B., born in February, 1818, in Indiana, died in Illinois.

HARRIET, born Feb. 22, 1822, in Indiana, died in Illinois.

AARON S., born Nov. 10, 1824, in Indiana, died in Illinois.

ZIPPORAH, born in May, 1827, was married March 25, 1847, to William T. Duncan. Mrs. Zipporah Duncan died Dec. 31, 1849, leaving one child, AMANDA, who lives in Montgomery county, Illinois.

LAVINA, born May 21, 1834, in Sangamon county, married Ransom Hargis. She died Sept. 20, 1858, leaving two children, WILLIAM R. and MARY J., living near Taylorville, Illinois.

Aaron Vandever died April, 1857, and Mrs. Nancy Vandever died Aug. 7, 1871, at Taylorville, Christian county, Illinois. Rev. Mr. Vandever was a distinguished minister of the Old School Baptist Church, known as the Regular Baptists.

VAN DOREN, JOSEPH, was born February, 1790, in Somerset county, New Jersey. Maria Conover was born March, 1792, in the same county, and they were married there about 1809. They had three children in that county, and moved, in 1824, to Warren county, Ohio, and from there to Sangamon county, Illinois, arriving May 22, 1839, in what is now Curran township. Of their three children—

WILLIAM L., born February, 1810, in New Jersey, married in 1832 in Warren county, Ohio, to Sarah Hagaman, had one child, and moved to Sangamon county, Illinois, arriving in the fall of 1834, in what is now Curran township, being the first of the family to settle in the county. They had six children born in Sangamon county, and in 1845 moved to St. Louis, Missouri, where Mrs. Van Doren died, in October, 1848. In the spring of 1850 he went to California, and there married, in 1853, to Cornelia Fulkerson. He came to Springfield and kept the Chenery House from 1866 to 1868, and in August of the latter year returned to California, and resides in Petaluma. His son, JOHN S., lives in Petaluma, and his daughter, ANNA married John Rogers, and resides near Petaluma Sonoma, county, California.

ABRAHAM, born March, 1814, in New Jersey, married in 1837, in Warren county, Ohio, to Delilah Jack. They had one child in Ohio, and moved to Sangamon county, Illinois, arriving July, 1838, in Curran township, where five children were born. The family moved to DeWitt county in 1855, and he died there in the fall of 1858, leaving a widow and two children, who reside near Clinton, Illinois.

PETER C., born April 11, 1818, in Somerset county, New Jersey, married Oct. 11, 1837, in Warren county, Ohio, to Margaret Hathaway, who was born in that county, April 13, 1820. Her great-grand-parents, on the mother's side, bore the name of Rogers. They emigrated from Ireland, and soon after the vessel sailed Mr. Rogers died at sea. A violent storm caused the destruction of the ship's stores, and in order to sustain life, three of the passengers were in turn killed and eaten. Mrs. Rogers had been selected by lot, as the next one to be slain. She asked for one hour to pray, which was granted, and all the preparations made for taking her life, the ship, meanwhile, carrying signals of distress. When but a few minutes of the time remained, the sound of a cannon came booming over the waters, conveying the glad tidings that they were discovered, and her life was spared. On arriving in America she settled in Warren county, Ohio, with her only daughter, Elizabeth, who married Patrick Meloy. Their daughter, Amy Meloy, married Ebenezer Hathaway, and *their* daughter, Margaret Hathaway, married Peter C. Van Doren. Mr. and Mrs. Van Doren had one child in Ohio, and moved to Sangamon county, Illinois, arriving May 22, 1839, in what is now Curran township, where eight children were born. Of their nine children, SARAH A., born Dec. 4, 1838, in Ohio, married in Sangamon county, Feb. 20, 1861, to Samuel Gibson, have three children, EMMA M., PETER V. and WILLIAM L., and reside at Monticello, Piatt county, Illinois. JOHN M., born Jan. 15, 1841, in Sangamon county, married Jan. 1, 1865, to Mary E. Sappington, have one child, CHARLES L., and reside at Waynesville, Illinois. EBENEZER H., born Sept. 5, 1843, in Sangamon county, enlisted Aug. 20, 1862, for three years, in Co. B, 130th Ill. Inf., served until August 15, 1865, when he was honorably discharged at New Orleans. He was married Nov. 13, 1867, to Frances I. McComas, and resides two and a half miles south of Curran, Sangamon county, Illinois. CORNELIUS P., born May 22, 1846, married Sept. 30, 1868, to Eliza Stubbs, who was born April 11, 1845, in Warren county, Ohio. They have one child, NETTIE, (WILLIE died in infancy) and resides three miles northwest of Curran, Illinois. HANNAH M., born Nov. 20, 1848, in Sangamon county, married Sept. 28, 1868, to William C. Nixon, have two children, FRANK V. and JOHN, and live on the farm adjoining that on which her father was raised, in Warren county, Ohio. MARGARET H., born March 27, 1851, lives with her parents. WILLIAM L., born Feb. 20, 1853, married Dec. 16, 1873, to Emma S. Darneille. MARY E., born Dec. 3, 1856, married March 9, 1873, to Hiram Alexander. *See his name.* AMY J., born March 10, 1860, lives with her parents. Peter C. Van Doren and wife reside on the farm where his father settled in 1839. It is three miles northwest of Curran, Sangamon county, Illinois.

Joseph Van Doren died August 30, 1845, and Mrs. Maria Van Doren died May 1, 1864, both on the farm where they settled in 1839. He was a soldier in a Light Horse company from New Jersey, in the war of 1812, and although he was about fifty-five years of age, he went as a teamster in the Mormon war of 1844 and '45, in Illinois, was present and saw the Mormon Prophet, Jo. Smith, and his brother, Hyrum, shot dead.

VANHOFF, HENRY, was born in 1804, in the city of Philadelphia, and came to Springfield, Illinois, in the spring of 1838. He was for many years engaged in the wagon and carriage making business, with Obed Lewis. It was one of the first establishments of the kind in Springfield. Henry Van Hoff was married in Springfield, March 4, 1840, to Susan A. Lewis. They had six children in Springfield.

MARY A., born March 10, 1842, and died Nov. 3, 1859.

HENRY L., born August 10, 1843, enlisted April, 1861, on the first call for seventy-five thousand men, for three months, in Co. —, 7th Ill. Inf., served full time, re-enlisted August, 1862, in Co. G, 114th Ill. Inf., for three years, was commissioned first lieutenant and promoted to adjutant of the regiment in 1864, served until August, 1865, when he was honorably discharged. He was married Oct. 26, 1871, in Laporte, Indiana, to Anna M. Fraser, who was born March 6, 1847, in Washington, D. C. They reside in Springfield, Illinois.

ANNA, born July 9, 1845, resides with her sister, Mrs. Hayden.

ADDIE, born July 20, 1847, was married June 7, 1871, to Mifflin Bell, who was born Oct. 20, 1847, in Birmingham, Chester county, Pennsylvania. They have two children, SUSAN A. and MARY E. Mr. Bell is an architect, and is now—1876—assistant superintendent at the new state house. He resides in Springfield, Illinois.

JULIA A., born August 26, 1849, was married Sept. 15, 1870, to Albert C. Hayden, who was born April 23, 1850, in St. Louis, Missouri. They have two children, WILLIAM H. and LEWIS VAN H. Mr. Hayden is a member of the firm of Lord & Hayden, china and glassware merchants, Springfield, Illinois.

LIDE J., born Feb. 9, 1851, and died Oct. 8, 1875, in Springfield, Illinois.

Henry Van Hoff died Dec. 20, 1854, in Springfield, and his widow was married Nov. 19, 1857, to Rev. John G. Bergen, D. D. *See his name.* He died, and she resides in Springfield, Illinois.

VANMETER, ABRAHAM D., was born Nov. 9, 1801, in Hardy

county, Virginia. When he was a boy his parents moved to Champaign county, Ohio. He came to Sangamon county in the spring of 1829, on business, expecting to make but a temporary stay, but he was married in 1830 to Nancy A. Hussey, and settled in what is now Fancy Creek township. They had seven children, namely

HENRY, born July 8, 1831, in Sangamon county, married March 16, 1854, to Mary G. Council. They had two living children, CHARLES F. and THOMAS D., and Mrs. Mary G. Van Meter died April 5, 1862. Henry Van Meter studied medicine and graduated at Rush Medical College, Chicago, at the session of 1854 and '55. He commenced practice at Williamsville, in the spring of 1855, and continued until after the death of his wife. September 1, 1862, he was commissioned assistant surgeon to the 114th Ill. Inf. December 8, 1863, he was promoted to surgeon of the regiment. He commenced his duties before the regiment was organized, and was never on detached duty, but remained with it until August 3, 1865, when he was mustered out at Vicksburg. Dr. Van Meter resumed practice at Williamsville, and was married Feb. 13, 1867, to Mary F. Zane. They had three children, JOHN R., ARTHUR L. and HENRY Z. Dr. Henry Van Meter died after a very brief illness, May, 1873. His family resides in Williamsville, Sangamon county, Illinois.

MARY H., born in Sangamon county, married Dr. Hiram J. Van Winkle, of Morgan county. In the spring of 1864 he became assistant surgeon to the 10th Minn. Vol. Inf. He was with the regiment in the field, taken sick, ordered home, arrived at Williamsville, Feb. 27, and died March 1, 1865. His widow, having no children, resides in Williamsville, Sangamon county, Illinois.

MARGARET A. married Thomas W. Dean, and died Sept. 14, 1858.

HARRIET E. married June 13, 1866, to Oren S. Webster, who was born Jan. 9, 1831, in Tompkins county, New York, came to Sangamon county in 1861, and in 1862 enlisted in Co. B, 130th Ill. Inf., for three years. He was detailed as chief clerk in the military postoffice, at Memphis, Tennessee, and remained there until he was mustered out in February, 1865. He was elected in November, 1865, for four years,, as superintendent of schools for Sangamon county. They reside in Williamsville, Sangamon county, Illinois.

CAROLINE died April 8, 1848, in her sixth year.

JANE E. died July 29, 1853, in her ninth year.

JAMES B. married Mary A. Thaxton. They have one child, JAMES E., and reside in the southeast corner of Menard county, Illinois.

WILLIAM E. married Martha E. Lester, and reside three and a half miles northwest of Williamsville.

CHARLES C. resides with his parents—1874.

Abraham Van Meter and his wife are both living and reside in Fancy Creek township, on the farm settled by her father, Nathan Hussey, March 10, 1819. It is five miles west of Williamsville, Sangamon county, Illinois.

VAN METER, SEYMOUR, was born Feb. 14, 1807, in Champaign county, Ohio, came to Sangamon county in the fall of 1830, and lived in the family of his brother, Abraham. He was a soldier from Sangamon county in the Blackhawk war of 1831 and '32, and afterwards returned to Ohio, where he was married August 5, 1834, to Catherine Bishop, who was born April 8, 1810, in Clarke county, Ohio. He came to Sangamon county with his bride, in the fall, and settled in Fancy Creek township, where they had four children, namely,

JAMES H. died in his second year.

JOHN R., born Dec. 15, 1837, married Jan. 22, 1872, to Elizabeth J. Cresse, of Menard county. They have one child, SEYMOUR, and reside on the farm settled by his father in 1834, five miles west of Williamsville, Sangamon county, Illinois—1874.

WILLIAM H., born Oct. 28, 1839, enlisted in 1862, in Co. F, 73d Ill. Inf., for three years. In consequence of impaired health he was transferred in 1863 to the Veteran Reserve Corps, in which he served to the end of the rebellion and was honorably discharged. He married Kate Clarey. They have one child, ABRAHAM, and live three miles northwest of Elkhart, Logan county, Illinois.

CHLOE, born Jan. 6, 1843, married George Prescott. They have one child,

MARY E., and live four miles northwest of Elkhart, Logan county, Illinois.

Mrs. Catharine Van Meter died April 2, 1858, and Mr. Van Meter was married April 3, 1860, to Mrs. Mary A. E. Whitmore, whose maiden name was Kaizer. Seymour Van Meter died in Fancy Creek township, Sept. 4, 1866, and his widow resides in Logan county, Ohio.

VAN NATTEN, DANIEL, was born March 3, 1800, in Fleming county, Kentucky. He was married Dec. 25, 1818, in Bath county, to Deborah Ferguson. They had one child in Fleming county, and the family moved to Sangamon county, Illinois, arriving in the fall of 1825, in what is now Fancy Creek township, where five children were born. Of their six children—

JOSEPH, born March 10, 1821, in Fleming county, Kentucky, married in Sangamon county, April 7, 1842, to Currency Stanley. They had nine children all born in Sangamon county. NORMAN A. enlisted in 1862 in Co. G, 73d Ill. Inf., for three years, served full term and was honorably discharged. He was married after the war to Clarissa Tufts, and lives in Fancy Creek township. THOMAS M. enlisted for one hundred days in Co. I, 133d Ill. Inf., served five months and was honorably discharged. He married Annie Renney, and died May 4, 1872, leaving a widow and two children near Springfield, Illinois. EMILY J. married James Renney and resides in Sangamon county. WARREN O. married Christiana Bowen, and lives in Fancy Creek township. MARTHA A., DANIEL W., JOHN N., JOSEPH J. and CLARISSA O. live with their parents, seven miles northwest of Springfield, Sangamon county, Ill. JOSEPH Van Natten enlisted in 1862, for three years, in Co. G, 73d Ill. Inf., served full term, and was honorably discharged at the close of the rebellion.

ELIZABETH, born in Sangamon county, married Joseph Van Natten—a relative of the family—have one child, and live near Edina, Knox county, Missouri.

NELSON, born in Sangamon county, married Elizabeth Patterson. He served three years in a Missouri Union regiment, was honorably discharged, and lives in Knox county, Missouri.

DEBORAH, born in Sangamon county, married Benjamin Ferguson, and died in Fancy Creek township.

EDNA, born in Sangamon county, and died in Texas at nineteen years of age.

DANIEL, Jun., is married and lives in Knox county, Missouri. He served three years in a Missouri Union regiment to aid in suppressing the rebellion.

All the Van Natten family moved to Texas in 1858, and all the living returned to Knox county, Missouri, in 1859, except Joseph, who returned to Sangamon county in 1860.

Daniel Van Natten died Oct. 16, 1869, and his widow died March 4, 1871, both in Knox county, Missouri.

VAN PATTEN, MINDERT, was born Jan. 20, 1793, in Scoharrie county, New York. Hannah Cooper was born March 13, 1796, in Pennsylvania. They were married Jan. 7, 1815, in Somerset county, New Jersey, and had ten children there. The family moved to Sangamon county, arriving at Springfield August 9, 1838, and soon after moved to what is now Curran township. Of their ten children—

MARY A., born Oct. 3, 1815, in New Jersey, married there to Joseph Rockafellow, came to Sangamon county with her parents, and went to Fairview, Fulton county. They have seven children.

SARAH, born Jan. 26, 1818, in New Jersey, married there to Henry S. Frazee. See his name.

CAROLINE, born Oct. 14, 1820, married in Sangamon county to Ezra C. Lyman. See his name.

AARON, born Nov. 17, 1822, in Somerset county, New Jersey, married in Sangamon county Nov. 28, 1844, to Martha J. Tolley, who was born Jan. 11, 1826. They had seven children. JAMES M., born Sept. 2, 1845. CARRIE M., born Nov. 1, 1848, married Feb. 17, 1870, to Edward T. Bradford. See his name. KATIE S., born March 7, 1851, married Sept. 9, 1870, to Knox L. Cooper. See his name, in the Talbott family sketch. CHARLES M., WILLIAM H., MARY E., and LEIGH R. resides with their mother. Aaron Van Patten died Sept. 12, 1870, in Sangamon county, Illinois, and his widow resides in Lincoln, Illinois.

ELIZABETH, born March 26, 1825,

in New Jersey, married in Sangamon county to William Pursell. *See his name.*

JOHN, born and died in New Jersey, aged four years.

NICHOLAS, born June 28, 1829, in New Jersey, died in Sangamon county, Sept. 24, 1844.

JOHN C., born Jan. 21, 1832, in Somerset county, New Jersey, married in Sangamon county Dec. 28, 1853, to Rachel McCoy. They had six children, two died under four years. EDWIN, FRANK, EZRA and WILLIE live with their parents. Rev. J. C. Van Patten is connected with the Cumberland Presbyterian Church. He resides one and a half miles south of Farmingdale, Sangamon county, Illinois.

JAMES L., born Sept. 15, 1834, in New Jersey, died in Sangamon county, March 26, 1857.

HANNAH H., born July 15, 1837, in New Jersey, died in Springfield, Illinois.

Mrs. Hannah Van Patten died Jan. 9, 1861, and Mindert Van Patten died Aug. 17, 1861, both in Sangamon county. His death was caused by being thrown from a horse.

VAN NORSTRAND, WILLIAM, born about 1774, in Somerset county, New Jersey, was married there to Adaline Van Liew, who was born Dec. 24, 1777, in the same county. They had five children, and Mrs. Adaline Van Norstrand died in 1824 in Somerset county. William Van Norstrand came to Sangamon county on a visit to his son, Cornelius, and daughter, Margaret A., and died in Springfield, Dec. 22, 1839. Cornelius Van Norstrand returned to New Jersey and brought his sister, Maria, and his brother, Frederick. Of the five children of William and Adaline Van Norstrand—

MARIA, born Sept. 12, 1803, in Middlesex county, New Jersey, is unmarried, and resides with her brother, Cornelius.

CORNELIUS, born Dec. 3, 1807, in Somerset county, New Jersey, came to Sangamon county, Illinois, arriving in July, 1837, and settled on Round Prairie, four miles east of Springfield, Illinois. He is unmarried and lives on the farm where he settled in 1837.

MARGARET A., born Oct. 4, 1810, in Somerset county, New Jersey, was married in New Brunswick, New Jersey, to Thomas Lewis. *See his name.* They came to Sangamon county with her brother, Cornelius, in 1837.

ISAAC, born May 29, 1813, in Middlesex county, New Jersey, went to Louisiana in 1832 or '33, and was last heard from in April, 1842, at New Orleans, *en route* for Cuba. He was unmarried, and is supposed to be dead.

FREDERICK, born August 9, 1817, in Middlesex county, New Jersey, came to Sangamon county with his brother, Cornelius, in 1841, and was married May 22, 1850, in same county, to Margaret J. Blandon, who was born Sept. 6, 1827, in Warren county, Pennsylvania. They have four children, WILLIAM, MARIA, MAGGIE and ADDIE, and reside four miles east of Springfield, Sangamon county, Illinois.

VEATCH, WILLIAM, born about 1810, in Harrison county, Kentucky, and was married there to Ursula Foster. They came to Sangamon county in company with her brother, Evan Foster, in 1830, and lived on Lick creek until 1847, when they moved to Mechanicsburg. They had eight children, all born in Sangamon county, Illinois.

MARY, died at 19 years of age.

MARTHA, was burned to death by her clothes taking fire, when she was a child.

J. WESLEY, born Nov. 7, 1836, in Sangamon county, married April 11, 1860, to Eliza Robbins. They have five children, JOHN H., URSULA E., ANN M., GEORGE T. and SARAH F., and reside three miles southwest of Mechanicsburg, Illinois.

WILLIAM, born in 1839, married Sarah Anderson, have four children, and live near Sweet Home, Nodaway county, Missouri.

SAMUEL, born in Sangamon county, enlisted in the fall of 1861, in Co. B, 30th Ill. Inf. for three years, re-enlisted as a veteran, served to the end of the rebellion, was honorably discharged, and died January, 1867, in Sangamon county, Illinois.

JAMES F., born in Sangamon county, enlisted in 1861, in Co. B, 30th Ill. Inf. and died of disease at Vicksburg, in July, 1863.

SARAH A., born Feb. 4, 1845, in Sangamon county, married Thomas Alsbury, has six children, and lives near Sweet Home, Missouri.

JOEL M., born in 1847, in Sangamon county, enlisted in 1864, in Co. B, 10th Ill. Cav., and was killed in the battle at Little Rock, Arkansas, in the same year.

William Veath died March, 1852, and Mrs. Ursula Veatch died in 1868, both in Sangamon county, Illinois.

VIGAL, MATHIAS, was born August 28, 1779, in Westmoreland county, Pennsylvania. His father died, and his mother married Adam Mung. They moved to Jefferson county, Kentucky. Mary Roney was born March 13, 1777, on the eastern shore of Chesapeake Bay, Maryland, and was taken by her parents to Jefferson county, near Louisville, Kentucky. Mathias Vigal and Mary Roney were married and had four children in that county. They moved in 1820 to Clark county, Indiana, and from there to Sangamon county, Illinois, arriving in the fall of 1830 in what is now Cotton Hill township. Of their four children—

ELIZABETH, born July 9, 1801, in Kentucky, was married in Indiana to Samuel Slake. They had three children and moved to Springfield, Illinois, in the fall of 1828. In the spring of 1829 they moved to what is now Cotton Hill township, where four children were born, and Mrs. Slake died there July 25, 1855. Of their children, three only are living. WILLIAM is married, and lives in Taylorville, Illinois. JOHN and GEORGE are both married and live near Palmer, Christian county, Illinois. Samuel Slake is blind, and lives with his son, William, in Taylorville, Illinois.

RACHEL, born in 1803 in Kentucky, died in Indiana, aged sixteen years.

WILLIAM W., born May 14, 1805, in Jefferson county, Kentucky, came to Sangamon county first in 1828. Since that time he has lived in Springfield, and Cotton Hill township, in the latter of which he now lives, and is yet unmarried.

JOHN T., born April 8, 1808, near Louisville, Kentucky, was married March 10, 1830, in Clarke county, Indiana, to Hannah Coble, who was born in that county May 20, 1811. They moved, in company with his father, arriving in the autumn of 1830, in what is now Cotton Hill township, between Brush and Horse creeks. They had nine children in Sangamon county. MELVINA, born May 22, 1831, married Thompson C. Spicer. *See his name.* Mrs. Melvina Spicer died Dec. 9, 1873. WILLIAM H., born Jan. 22, 1833, was married Oct. 31, 1855, to Sarah A. Willian. They have six children, MARCIA A., EVERETT A., METTA E., WILLIAM M., FREDERICK H. and ERMIN CARROLL, and live in Cotton Hill township, one and a half miles south of New City, Sangamon county, Illinois. W. H. Vigal was a member of Sangamon County Board of Supervisors in 1862, and is at present a member. He has been township treasurer since 1858. ALFRED, born April 28, 1835, was married Dec. 17, 1857, to Diana Carpenter, who was born Feb. 6, 1831, in Delaware county, Ohio. They had six children, CLARA E., JOHN E., ADALINE, the latter died Jan. 19, 1875, aged twelve years, ANTONIO, EDWIN ULYSSES GRANT, and MARY L., and live near New City, Sangamon county, Illinois. MARY A., born April 30, 1837, married William H. Boyd. *See his name.* JOHN F., born July 11, 1839, in Sangamon county, enlisted August, 1862, for three years, in Co. E, 114th Ill. Inf., and was killed in battle at Tupelo, Mississippi, July 15, 1864. SARAH J., born August 25, 1841, died June 22, 1864. NANCY C., born Oct. 20, 1843, died aged ten years. DAVID M., born Nov. 2, 1846, is a teacher, and lives near New City, Illinois. CHARLES E., born March 10, 1852, was married Jan. 7, 1875, to Mary A. Miller. They have one child, LUTHER L. Mrs. Hannah Vigal died May 12, 1853, and John T. Vigal, lives where he settled in 1831, in in Cotton Hill township, near New City, Sangamon county, Illinois.

Mrs. Mary Vigal died March 13, 1837, and Matthias Vigal died Dec. 25, 1862, both in Cotton Hill township, Sangamon county, Illinois.

VINEY ABRAHAM, born in 1781, in Greenbrier county, Virginia, was married, either in that state or Kentucky, to Rebecca Skiles, who was born Nov. 11, 1781, in Pennsylvania. They had one child in Virginia, and moved to Warren county, Kentucky, where seven children were born, thence to Sangamon county, Illinois, arriving in the autumn of 1819, on the south fork of Sangamon river, fifteen miles south of where Springfield now stands. Of their children—

SARAH, born July 2, 1803, in Greenbrier county, Virginia, was taken by her parents to Warren county, Kentucky, at two years of age, and brought by them to Sangamon county in 1819, where she was married to Edward Clarke. See his name.

WILLIAM S., born in Kentucky, married Margaret Laughlin, and lives in Iowa.

MARY, born in Kentucky, was married in Sangamon county to Ezekiel Drennan. See his name. They moved to Missouri and both died there.

AMANDA A., born March 2, 1810, in Warren county, Kentucky, was married in Sangamon county to Mathew P. Kenney. See his name. She died July 9, 1876, in Sangamon county, Illinois. Her son, Ninian C. Kenney, was married Nov. 15, 1876, to a daughter of F. Ewing Dodds. See Dodds in Omissions.

CYNTHIA A., born in Kentucky, died in Sangamon county, Illinois, aged twenty-three years.

JOHN N., born July 13, 1813, in Kentucky, was married in Sangamon county to Nancy Black, and both died. His death occurred Jan. 5, 1871. He was a preacher in connection with the Cumberland Presbyterian church.

REBECCA, born in Kentucky, married in Sangamon county to Amos Richardson, and both died.

HENRY, born in Kentucky, married in Sangamon county to Catharine Kessler and lives in Macoupin county, Illinois.

Abraham Viney died August 24, 1820, and his widow married in 1823 or '24 to Thomas Black, Sen. See his name.

VREDENBURGH, JOHN S., was born March 11, 1809, in Somerset county, New Jersey. The family moved in 1821 to New York city, where he was married, Sept. 22, 1832, to Ann E. Doremus. She was born there Oct. 12, 1810. They had two children in New York, and moved to Sangamon county, Illinois, arriving July 20, 1835, in what is now Curran township, where they had two children. In 1837 they moved to Springfield, where they had four children. Of their children:

MARIA V. D., born June 28, 1833, in New York city, was married March 22, 1853, in Springfield, to Edward R. Ulrich, who was born Oct. 10, 1829, in Duchess county, New York. They had eight children, LOUIS, ANNA V., EDWARD R., Jun., CATHARINE, CHARLES, HENRIETTA, PAUL and MARIA. Anna V. died March, 1876, in her nineteenth year. All the living children reside with their parents in Springfield. Edward R. Ulrich came to Springfield in 1841, and was for many years a lumber merchant there. He has since been engaged in stock and grain dealing.

FRANCES D., born April, 1835, in New York city, lives with her parents in Springfield, Illinois.

PETER, born Feb. 7, 1837, in Sangamon county, was married Dec. 27, 1866, to Mary A. Canfield, daughter of Rev. Josiah Canfield. She was born in New Jersey. They live one and one-half miles northwest of Curran, Sangamon county, Illinois.

THOMAS D., born March 15, 1841, in Sangamon county, was married in Warsaw, Illinois, May 22, 1866, to Maria Reynolds. They have one child, WILLIAM R. T. D. Vredenburgh is with his father, in the lumber business, and resides in Springfield, Illinois.

JOHN S., Jun., born Sept. 1, 1844, in Springfield, Illinois, was married Oct. 15, 1868, to Elizabeth H. Kilman, who was born August 2, 1845, in Godfrey, Madison county, Illinois. They have two adopted children, and reside in Chicago, Illinois.

ANN E., born April 19, 1850, in Springfield, was married May 6, 1874, to James Partridge. They live in Springfield, Illinois.

MARGARET lives with her parents.

LA RUE, born in Springfield, Illinois, is attending college in New Brunswick, New Jersey—1876.

John S. Vredenburgh was formerly a farmer, but has been engaged in mercantile pursuits in Springfield nearly forty years, and is now in the lumber trade. He served two terms as alderman, and one term, from April, 1864, to April, 1865, as mayor of the city. He now—November, 1876—resides in Springfield, Sangamon county, Illinois.

W

WADSWORTH, DANIEL, was born May 15, 1799, in Winthrop, Maine. He was married Dec. 3, 1823, to Margaret F. Goodwin, who was born Oct. 3, 1801, at Freeport, Maine. They

—94

had two living children in Maine, and moved to Sangamon county, Illinois, arriving in Auburn Nov. 17, 1840, where they had two living children. Of their four children—

EMILY N., born Oct. 3, 1824, in Maine, married in Sangamon county, Oct. 12, 1843, to Jehu Harlan, who was born June 11, 1818, near Hopkinsville, Kentucky. They had four children, two of whom died under ten years. EDWARD T. died in 1873, aged twenty-four years. MARGARET H., born August 31, 1851, in Sangamon county, married August 16, 1870, to John H. C. Irwin, who was born in Ballinasloe, Connaught, Ireland, July 1, 1845, and is third son of the late Rev. Canon John Irwin, D. D., who after a long service as clergyman in the Anglican church, and the Protestant Episcopal church in America, died in Canada, Feb. 12, 1874. Mr. and Mrs. Irwin have two living children, GERTRUDE H. and GRACE MAYNARD, and reside in Springfield, Illinois. Mr. Irwin is city editor of the *Illinois State Journal*. Jehu Harlan died Nov. 23, 1851, and Mrs. Emily N. Harlan was married Nov. 13, 1853, to William M. Corzine, who was born March 14, 1834, in Marion county, North Carolina. They have one child, FRANKLIN W., and reside in Auburn, Sangamon county, Illinois.

MOSES G., born Feb. 3, 1826, in Hallowel, Maine, married in Sangamon county, Sept. 23, 1847, to Elizabeth F. Wheeler. They had five children. EUGENE W., born July 11, 1848. MARGARET C., born Sept. 1, 1850, married D. H. Tomlinson, and died March 15, 1875, at Butler, DeKalb county, Indiana. FLORA E., born Dec. 5, 1852, married Jerry Ballenger, and resides in Auburn, Illinois. SUSAN E. M., born Jan. 14, 1855, married W. W. Lowry, of Carlinville, Illinois. They have one child, MINNIE, and reside in Auburn, Illinois. JAMES F. D., born April 6, 1857. Mrs. Wadsworth died May 4, 1857. Moses G. Wadsworth was married Nov. 16, 1862, to Mary E. Day. They had six children, two of whom died young. HARRIE E., CHARLES L., MARY F. and ADA C. reside with their parents in Auburn, Sangamon county, Illinois. M. G. Wadsworth was elected clerk of Auburn township at its organization, and served four years, was township collector four years, has been secretary of Ark and Anchor Masonic Lodge, 354, five years, and is editor and proprietor of the *Auburn Citizen*, one of the best weekly newspapers in the State.

SARAH A., born Sept. 19, 1841, at Auburn, married March 26, 1861, to John N. Williams, who was born March 1, 1839, in Indiana. They have four children, REMIE A., SARAH A., MAUD B. and CHARLES N., and reside in Auburn, Illinois. Mr. Williams is a merchant in that place.

ABBIE J., resides with her parents in Auburn.

Daniel Wadsworth has been a member of the Masonic fraternity since 1821. He assisted in organizing the first Masonic Royal Arch Chapter in the State of Illinois, that of Springfield No. 1. He has been a member of the M. E. church since 1822, and was postmaster many years in Auburn. He is now—1876—in his seventy-eighth year.

WADDELL, JOSIAH, was born Sept. 26, 1804, in Ohio county, West Virginia. He was there married, Jan. 11, 1831, to Elizabeth Hall, of West Alexander, Washington county, Penn. She was a native of Virginia also. They moved to Sangamon county, Illinois, arriving March 1, 1835, in what is now Cotton Hill township. He spent twenty years in farming there. They have no children. They have since 1855, and now live in Springfield, Sangamon county, Illinois.

WAGGONER, GEORGE, was born in Pennsylvania, and when a young man went to Licking county, Ohio. He was married at Newark to Judea Wertzbaugh, who was born in Canada. They had eight children in Ohio, and moved to Sangamon county, Illinois, arriving in October, 1822, in what is now Gardner township, south of Prairie creek, where three children were born.

JOHN born in Ohio, married in Sangamon county to Julia A. Clark, had eight children, and both died in Mason county, Illinois.

ELIZA, born in Ohio, married in Sangamon county to James Darrell, had eight children, and he died and she married Halsey Smith, who died and she married Freeman Marshall, and lives in Havanna, Illinois.

ALFRED, born in Ohio, married Jane Hinsley, have five children, and live at Petersburg, Illinois.

OZIAS, born in Ohio, married Rebecca J. Shepherd, had five children, and she died, and he married Hannah Leonard, had four children, two of whom died young. Ozias Waggoner lives in the southwest part of Springfield, Illinois.

JULIA A., born in Ohio, married in Sangamon county to John Carman, had nine children, and Mr. Carman died in March, 1866, in Christian county. His family live near Nokomis, Montgomery county, Illinois.

EFFIE, born Jan. 28, 1818, in Ohio, married in Sangamon county, to Thomas Sayre. *See his name.*

ELIZABETH, born in Ohio, married in Sangamon county to Martin S. Morris, have ten children, and live in Savannah, Missouri.

HARRIET married Zachariah Clarey, have eleven children, and live in Kansas.

SARAH married Stephen Ewbank, had eight children, and he died leaving his family near Girard, Illinois.

GEORGE C. married Louisa Fuller, and live near Cerro Gordo, Piatt county, Illinois.

Mrs. Judea Waggoner died Jan. 3, 186- or '4, and George Waggoner died. Both buried at Petersburg, Illinois.

WALLACE, JAMES was born in 1776, in Pendleton district, South Carolina, of Scotch Presbyterian parents. They being Whigs were driven from their home by the British and Tories previous to his advent in the world, and he was born in a camp. On arriving at the age of manhood he went to Nova Scotia, and was there married to Ann Doole. About 1816 he moved back to South Carolina. Having lived where all men were free, on his return to his native State, it appeared to him as though slavery was indeed "the sum of all villanies," and he determined to seek a land of freedom in which to bring up his family. He accordingly moved to Sangamon county, Illinois, arriving November 3, 1822, in what is now Auburn township, one mile south of the present town of Auburn. Of his five sons and six daughters, three only remained in Sangamon county, namely:

JOHN and *WILLIAM*, twins, were born June 17, 1808, in Nova Scotia, and came, in 1822, with their father, to Sangamon county.

JOHN, was married August 5, 1830, in Sangamon county, to Eveline Rieger. They had ten children in Sangamon county. GEORGE W. married Charlotte Dilner, who died, and he married Sarah Arnet, and lives in Missouri. ELIZABETH A. married Jonathan S. Frazier, who died leaving a son, CHARLES E. Mrs. Frazier married Joseph H. Lockridge. *See his name.* MARY J. married Thomas Black. *See his name.* ELIZA married William Crane, and lives in Elco, Nevada. AMANDA married John N. Kenney. *See his name.* WILLIAM and JAMES, twins. The former married Minerva Cox, and lives in Chatham, Illinois. The latter married Jennie Chapman, and lives near Auburn, Illinois—1874. MARGARET C. and DAVID F., twins. The former married C. Columbus Cannon, and lives in Auburn, Illinois. The latter married Mary Kessler, and lives near Auburn, Illinois. JOHN B. lives at Placerville, California—1874. John Wallace died Nov. 20, 1854, and Mrs. Eveline Wallace died Aug st 20, 1876, both near Auburn, Illinois.

WILLIAM, was married in 1832 in Sangamon county to Amanda Rusk. They had four children in Springfield, namely: BENJAMIN F., married Mary Gregory. They have two children, GRACIE and STELLA, and live in Keokuk, Iowa. JOHN L., JANE E., and ADA ANN live with their father. Mrs. Amanda Wallace died in 1848, and William Wallace was married in 1849 to Mrs. Allender, who died in 1864. Mr. Wallace was married in 1865 to Mrs. Eliza J. Gard, a native of Clark county, Ohio. They reside in Springfield, Illinois.

MARY ANN married Benjamen Kessler. They brought up a family of several children, and reside in Auburn, Sangamon county, Illinois.

James Wallace moved in 1835 from Sangamon to Macon county, Illinois, taking three sons and five daughters with him. He died there about 1845.

WALLACE, JAMES, was born between 1780 and '85 in South Carolina. He was no relation to the other James Wallace from the same state. He was married there to Francis A. Benison. They moved to North Carolina, thence to northern Indiana, and from there to Henry county, Kentucky. In 1818 they moved to Shawneetown, Illinois, and in the spring of 1819 he moved to what became Sangamon county, settling on Lick creek. They brought nine children, namely,

JOHN, married Minerva Myers, and died in 1843 or '44, leaving a widow and four children near Decatur, Illinois.

WILLIAM married Elizabeth Miller. He died in Arkansas, leaving a widow and three children.

ROSE ANN married Randall Davis, who died in 1867 or '68, leaving his family in Macon county, Illinois.

ELIZABETH, born in South Carolina, came with her father to Sangamon county, was married in Macon county to Edward Turpin. They have four children, and live near Hopewell, Macon county, Illinois.

SARAH died unmarried in Sangamon county in 1831.

ISAAC and *MELINDA*, twins, born August 22, 1815, in Indiana.

ISAAC was married April 13, 1837, in Springfield, to Mrs. Eliza Hawker, whose maiden name was Lindsay. They had four living children, namely, SAMUEL, married Frances Grissom, and lives in Springfield, Illinois. HELEN married F. M. Scott has four children and lives in Mechanicsburg, Illinois. FRANCES married Emery Mayfield, has one child, and lives near Auburn, Illinois. ALICE married Benjamin Kessler, Jun., and live in Auburn, Illinois. Isaac Wallace and wife reside in Springfield, Illinois.

MELINDA married in Macon county to William Hanks, and both died there.

SAMUEL, born in Kentucky, is married, and lives near Tower Hill, Shelby county, Illinois.

James Wallace died in Sangamon county in 1822, and in 1832 his widow, with some of her children, moved to Macon county, where she died.

WALLACE, WILLIAM S., was born August 10, 1802, in Lancaster county, Pennsylvania, and graduated April 8, 1824, at Jefferson Medical College at Philadelphia. Dr. Wallace came to Springfield, Illinois, in 1836, and at once engaged in the practice of his profession. He was married May 21, 1839, in Springfield, to Frances J. Todd, who was born in 1817 in Lexington, Kentucky. *See sketch of the Todd family.* Dr. Wallace and wife had six children in Springfield, namely—

ELIZABETH, died in infancy.

MARY J. was married Nov. 15, 1865, in her native city, to Colonel John P. Baker, who was born July 24, 1838, at Kaskaskia, Illinois. Colonel and Mrs. Baker have five children, MARY, WALLACE F., FRANCIS J., MABEL and FLORENCE, and reside in Springfield, Illinois. John P. Baker graduated in 1856, at Shurtleff College, at Upper Alton, Illinois. He read law three years with his father, Hon. David J. Baker, and was admitted to the bar. In March, 1861, he was appointed by President Lincoln, second lieutenant, in the 1st United States dragoons, placed on duty in Washington City, and was at the battle of Bull's Run, July 21, 1861. He served on staff duty at the headquarters of the 6th Army Corps in the Army of the Potomac, also on staff duty as Inspector General of Savannah, Georgia, in the early part of 1865. Lieutenant Baker was promoted July 17, 1862, to captain in the 1st United States Cavalry, brevetted April 9, 1864, major in the regular army for gallantry and meritorious service at Pleasant Hill, Louisiana; also, brevetted lieutenant colonel for gallant and meritoritous services during the war. After the suppression of the rebellion he served with his regiment at the headquarters of General Sheridan in Louisiana, and in 1865 was ordered from there to the Pacific coast, spending three years in Nevada and Oregon, campaigning against the Indians. Colonel Baker returned to Springfield and resigned his commission in July, 1868. He then became one of the proprietors and associate editor with his brother, E. L. Baker, of the *Illinois State Journal*. He withdrew from the *Journal* in 1872, and has since held the office of United States assistant assessor and United States gauger for the Eighth district of Illinois.

WILLIAM F., *FRANCES* and *EDWARD D.* live with their mother.

CHARLES E. died young.

Dr. William S. Wallace continued in the practice of medicine a full quarter of a century in Springfield, never making any distinction between the rich and the poor in his attentions. In 1861 he received from the hands of his brother-in-law, President Lincoln, the appointment of

Paymaster in the United States Army. He was on duty part of the time in Springfield, Illinois, then in the department of Missouri, and the remainder of the time at the front on the lower Mississippi river. By exposure and exhaustive service in the south he became debilitated and never regained his former vigor. After the suppression of the rebellion he was placed on the retired list and died May 23, 1867, in Springfield, Illinois. His widow, Mrs. Frances J. Wallace, resides in Springfield.

WALL, ISAAC, was born about 1790, near the line between Virginia and North Carolina. He was married in North Carolina to Nancy Duncan, and moved to Rockingham county, Tennessee, and from there to Sangamon county, Illinois, in what is now Auburn township, in 1830. They had four children—

ELIJAH married Margaret Jones, and died.

WILLIAM, born in Tennessee, married Nancy Haines, in Sangamon county, joined the Mormons, moved to Salt Lake, became one of the twelve apostles, took more wives, and raised a large family.

JOHNSON C. married four times, and each wife died without children. He enlisted in the 1st Ill. Cav. in 1861, was captured at Lexington, Missouri, was released, and in 1863 he enlisted at Springfield, in Vaughn's Battery, and died at Little Rock, Arkansas, April 5, 1864.

RICHARD C., born March 15, 1829, in Rockingham county, Tennessee, married Oct. 16, 1845, in Sangamon county, to Mary Jones. They have six children. SARAH married Green Dallas, has three children, and lives in Cotton Hill township. NANCY D., MELINDA A., EVELINE E., MARTHA A. and ANDREW C. live with their parents three and a half miles north of Pawnee, in Cotton Hill township, Sangamon county, Illinois.

Mrs. Nancy Wall died in 1833 or '34. Isaac Wall is married again, and lives in Missouri.

WALKER, DANIEL, was born about 1781, in Fauquer county, Virginia, and was married about 1809, in Loudon county, in the same state, to Sarah Bail, a native of Chester county, Pennsylvania, and of a Quaker family. They had four children in Virginia, and moved to Ohio, where four children were born, and moved to Sangamon county, Illinois, arriving in the spring of 1835, and settled on Horse creek, in what is now Pawnee township. Daniel Walker returned to Ohio on business and died there in the fall of 1835. Of their children, the eldest son—

HAMPTON married in Ohio and moved to Kentucky.

HIRAM, born April 10, 1811, in Loudon county, Virginia, came with the family to Sangamon county in 1835, and on the death of his father he assumed the care of the family and prosecuted the business of farming, part of the time in Christian county. He continued in that business until December, 1845, when he moved to Springfield, Illinois. He has for several years been engaged in the business of dealing in real estate.

HARRIET married James Elder. See his name.

LYDIA A. married Je H. Kent. See his name.

WALKER, SAMUEL, was born Dec. 8, 1777, in Campbell county, Virginia. He was there married to Martha Hannah, who was born March, 1790, in the same county. They had three children in Virginia, and the family moved to Rutherford county, Tennessee, in October, 1816, where four children were born, and moved to Sangamon county, Illinois, arriving October, 1828, in what is now Loami township, where they had two children. Of the nine children—

WILLIAM S., born Nov. 2, 1811, in Virginia, married in Loami, Dec. 4, 1831, to Clarissa Colburn. They had thirteen children, four died under three years. ACUSA J., born April 28, 1834, married April 1855, to N. G. Estes, have six children, and live in Loami, Ill. SAMUEL S., born April 22, 1836, enlisted August 6, 1862, in Co. F, 51st Ill. Inf. for three years, was wounded at the battle of Chickamauga, Sept. 19, 1863, recovered, served full term and was honorably discharged June 16, 1865. He was married May 1, 1870, to Catharine Conrad, and lives in Loami, Ill. WILLIAM H. H., born August 3, 1840, enlisted May 1, 1864, in Co. E, 133d Ill. Inf. for one hundred days, served full term and was honorably discharged. He was married Jan. 10, 1867, to Elizabeth Swink, have one child, SAMUEL S., and live one and a half miles northwest of Loami, Illinois. ELI J., born Oct. 1, 1842, married Sarah Swink, have one child, and live one and a half miles northwest of Loami, Illinois. EUNICE M., born Jan. 22, 1845, married John G. Kelly, have three children, and live in Loami, Illinois. ELMINA F. and LUCY A. live with their parents. REBECCA A., born March 29, 1854, married Alfred Davis February 19, 1871, have one child, and live in Loami, Illinois. LEVI F. lives with his parents at Loami, Sangamon county, Illinois.

JAMES R., born August 13, 1813, died at eleven years.

THOMAS J., born in Virginia June 2, 1816, married Elizabeth Denton, have six children, and live in Cedar county, Missouri.

GEORGE J., born July 29, 1819, in Tennessee, married in Sangamon county, Oct. 22, 1843, to Elizabeth Back, who was born Dec. 25, 1827, in Garrard county, Kentucky. They had eight children, four of whom died in infancy. AMARINE, born Jan. 7, 1854, married Robert J. Collins, have one child, ALONZO D., and live at Loami, Illinois. GEORGE W., LUELLA and JOHN B. live with their parents in Loami, Sangamon county, Illinois.

SAMUEL C. died at twenty-one years of age.

BEVERLY W., born Feb. 8, 1825, in Tennessee, married in Sangamon county to Elizabeth Cooley, have five children, and live in Douglas county, Kansas.

THEOPHILUS, born in Tennessee, married in Sangamon county to Rhoda J. Withrow, and died.

REBECCA, born August 12, 1829, in Sangamon county, married William C. Smith. *See his name.*

HIRAM W., born April 3, 1832, in Sangamon county, married Martha E. Scott, have three children, MARY, LUCY A. and CHARLES F., and reside near McMurray Chapel, in Ball township, four miles southeast of Chatham, Sangamon county, Illinois.

Samuel Walker died August 31, 1834, and his widow died April, 1852, both in Sangamon county, Illinois.

WALTERS, LYDIA, (widow of James Walters), was born in December, 1783, near Salem, Rowan county, North Carolina. Her maiden name was Donner. She was sister to George and Jacob Donner. Her parents moved to Jessamine county, Kentucky, about 1811. She was there married to James Walters. They had nine children in Kentucky, and in 1829 the family moved to Decatur county, Indiana. James Walters died there in June, 1830. In 1839 Mrs. Walters moved her family to Sangamon county and settled in Auburn township. Of her children—

NOBLE married in Kentucky to Elizabeth Davis, moved to Sangamon county, and died in 1859.

GEORGE went to Texas and died there.

MATILDA is a cripple and blind, and lives at the family homestead, in care of her brother, Pollard K.—1873.

POLLARD K. is unmarried, and lives at the family homestead in Auburn township, near the line of Macoupin county—1876. He lost a leg by a reaping machine many years ago.

JOHN went to California and died there.

JAMES married Nancy Baldwin, and lives in Virden, Illinois.

WILLIAM T., born April 21, 1822, in Kentucky, was married Jan. 17, 1858, to Sarah Green. They have four living children, WILLIAM A., CHARLES H., LYDIA MAY and JOHN CARROLL, and live two and one-half miles southwest of Lowder, Sangamon county, Illinois—1874.

MARY ANN married James Clack, and lives in Virden, Illinois.

Mrs. Lydia Walters died July 1, 1871, in Auburn township, in the eighty-eighth year of her age.

WALTERS, GREEN B., was born Oct. 28, 1808, in Jefferson county, Kentucky, and was taken by his parents to Decatur county, Indiana, when he was about thirteen years of age. He came to Sangamon county, Illinois, on a visit, arriving Sept. 15, 1829, at the house of his uncle, George Donner, and remained fourteen months, shaking with the ague. He returned to Indiana and was married Dec. 25, 1833, to Elizabeth Griffiths. He came to Illinois, first stopping in Logan county, and then came to Sangamon county, in 1840, and had nine living children—

MARTHA was drowned, aged twelve years.

MARIA J. married George Walters, and died, leaving one child, RHODA A.

RACHEL C. married John Penick, and lives in Missouri.

JAMES W. is married and lives in Indianapolis.

EMILY A. was married Oct. 22, 1861, to Leonard Ledbrook, who was born at Tipton, Staffordshire, England, and came to Sangamon county in 1859. They have one living child, MINNIE. Mr. Ledbrook is a druggist in Chatham, Illinois, and, with his family, resides there.

MARY N., GEORGE W., JOHN F. and EDWARD BAKER live with their mother.

Green B. Walters died April 12, 1875, and his family lives two miles east of Chatham, Sangamon county, Illinois.

WARD, JOHN, was born July 19, 1810, near Romney, Virginia. Mary Shivers was born Feb. 8, 1814, near Fredricktown, Maryland, and taken by her parents, in 1830, to Virginia. John Ward and Mary Shivers were married near Romney, August 15, 1833. They had two children in Virginia, and moved to Sangamon county, Illinois, arriving Oct. 2, 1838, in what is now Cotton Hill township, where five children were born, the four youngest died under seven years. Of the other four—

SARAH C., born June 22, 1835, in Virginia, married in Sangamon county to Isaac Snodgrass. See his name.

HARVEY, born Jan. 22, 1838, in Virginia, died in Sangamon county in his fifteenth year.

EMILY J., born June 28, 1842, in Sangamon county, married Alfred N. Funderburk. See his name.

John Ward died Nov. 8, 1852, and his widow married Robert Snodgrass. See his name. He died and she was married Sept. 15, 1859, to Lemuel Hall, as his second wife. Lemuel Hall was from Ohio. His daughter, Sarah S., born Feb. 19, 1844, is the wife of William H. Snodgrass. See his name.

Lemuel Hall and wife reside in Cotton Hill township, near New City, Sangamon county, Illinois.

WASH, MILTON H., born March 16, 1819, in Todd county, Kentucky, and came to Springfield, Illinois, in 1839, where he was married July 23, 1840, to Mary J. Bryan. See Bryan sketch. They had two children in Springfield, and moved to St. Joseph, Missouri, arriving Oct. 1, 1844, where they resided until 1859, when they moved to Memphis, Tennessee, and from there to St. Louis, Missouri, arriving August 9, 1862. Milton H. Wash and wife had seven living children. Of their children—

JOHN M., born May 11, 1841, in Springfield, Illinois, was married Dec. 23, 1860, in Missouri, to Belle Townsend. They had one daughter, R. E. LEE. J. M. Wash was again married, Nov. 20, 1874, to Mrs. Matilda Webb, of Baltimore, Maryland. They reside at No. 731 South Seventh street, St. Louis, Missouri.

GEORGE B., born August 17, 1843, at Springfield, Illinois, died in his fourth year.

KATE A., born Dec. 23, 1845, at St. Joseph, Missouri, died there in her fifth year.

BENJAMIN S., born July 26, 1851, at St. Joseph, Missouri, was married Feb. 22, 1875, to Sallie E. Kempland, of St. Louis. They have one child, MARY AMELIA, and reside at 1205 Wright street, St. Louis, Missouri.

FRANK H., born August 8, 1853, in St. Joseph, Missouri, was married Oct. 1, 1874, in St. Louis, to Fannie L. Thornburgh. They reside at 1925 Carr street, St. Louis, Missouri.

AMELIA A., born June 15, 1855, at St. Joseph, died at St. Louis, Missouri, July 13, 1867.

MARY W. died in her third year.

Milton H. Wash and wife reside at 1205 Wright street, St. Louis, Missouri.

WASHBURN, WILLIAM, was born Jan. 24, 1813, at Westminster, Windham county, Vermont, and was raised in Orange county, in the same state. In 1832 he went to Seville, Medina county, Ohio, and taught school there one year, and in 1833 went to Shelby county, Kentucky, where he taught nearly seven years. He was married there August 20, 1839, to Elizabeth R. Harding, who was born in that county August 27, 1820. She is a niece of Mrs. Harriet Harding Talbott. See Talbott. Mr. and Mrs. Washburn had one child in Kentucky, and moved to Sangamon county, Illinois, arriving Nov. 1, 1840, in what is now Gardner township, where five children were born. Of their children—

OLIVIA R., born August 20, 1840, in Kentucky, died in Sangamon county, aged two years.

WILLIAM H., born July 9, 1842, in Sangamon county, was married there Dec. 21, 1875, to Alice Jane Hurt, and lives in Philadelphia, Cass county, Illinois.

LUCIUS H. lives with his parents.

JAMES OTIS died Feb. 9, 1861, in his fourteenth year.

MARY L. and *HARRIET E.* reside with their parents, two and one-half miles southwest of Farmingdale, Sangamon county, Illinois.

The Washburn family in the United States all come from John Washburn, who emigrated from Eversham, Worcester county, England. He was in Duxbury, Massachusetts, as early as 1632, and returning, sailed from England with his family April 12, 1635, O. S. He brought two sons, John, Jun., and Philip. John, Jun., married in 1645 to Elizabeth Mitchell. They had seven sons and four daughters. It is from these that the whole Washburn family in the United States sprang. William Washburn has the genealogy of his own branch of the family in a continuous line from John Washburn, of Eversham, England, to his son, John, Jun., and his son, Joseph, first, and his son, Joseph, second, and his son, Seth, first, and his son Asa and his son, Seth Washburn, second, who was twice married, and had eight sons by the first, and seven by the second marriage. William Washburn, whose name heads this sketch, is his second son by the first wife. William's brother, Asa R., married in Morgan county, Illinois, to Barbara Craig, moved to Sangamon county in 1852, and died at Putney, Vermont, Sept. 12, 1867, while there on a visit for his health. He left a widow and three children in Curran township, Sangamon county, Illinois.

WATSON, ARTHUR, was born in 1770, in Berkley county, Virginia, and when a young man went to Mason county, Kentucky. Temperance Robinson was born August, 1774, in Baltimore county, about twenty miles from the city of Baltimore, Maryland, and in 1794 her parents moved to Mason county, Kentucky. Arthur Watson and Temperance Robinson were married about 1796 in Mason county, and had ten children there, the eldest and youngest of whom died in Kentucky. In 1812 Mr. Watson went from Mason county as a soldier in the war with England. The family moved to Sangamon county, Illinois, arriving April 10, 1825, at Springfield. Mr. Watson soon after entered the land now occupied by the water works, watch factory, rolling mill, north coal shaft, and Oak Ridge cemetery. Of their children—

HIRAM A., born May 14, 1799, in Mason county, Kentucky, died there in 1823.

SANFORD, born Jan. 28, 1801, in Mason county, Kentucky, married in Sangamon county, June 3, 1833, to Betsy Ann Stevenson. They had one child, and the mother and child died September, 1835. He was married in 1842 in Morgan county to Maria Elder, and in 1849 moved to Oregon. Mr. Watson died July 6, 1870, leaving a widow and four children, near Bethel, Polk county, Oregon.

MEDALINE, born May 18, 1803, in Mason county, Kentucky, married in Sangamon county October, 1825, to William Alvey. *See his name.*

ANN R., born August 19, 1805, in Mason county, Kentucky, married in Sangamon county October, 1825, to James C. McNabb. *See his name.*

JAMES, born Feb. 29, 1808, in Kentucky, married in Sangamon county, February, 1833, to Mary Ridgeway. They had five children, and the family moved in 1847 overland to Oregon. Mr. Watson died in 1861, and his widow died in 1873. Four of their children reside near Kings Valley postoffice, Benton county, Oregon.

LUCRETIA, died July 13, 1810, in Mason county, Kentucky, married in Sangamon county, Jan. 20, 1846, to James W. Simpson. They had two children. LAFAYETTE married Jennie Combs, and resides at Tallula, Illinois. CLIFTON L. resides with his mother. James W. Simpson died in August, 1862, and his widow resides near Tallula, Menard county, Illinois.

WILLIAM H., born Dec. 15, 1812, in Kentucky, married in Sangamon county, in 1838, to Agnes Lloyd. He died Sept. 26, 1842, near Middletown, Logan county, Illinois.

AMANDA P., born April 10, 1816, in Mason county, Kentucky, married Wm. S. Pickrell. *See his name.*

JOHN N., born Oct. 22, 1818, in Kentucky, died in Sangamon county June 16, 1835.

Arthur Watson died Sept. 29, 1827, and Mrs. Temperance Watson died Sept. 11, 1837, both near Springfield, Sangamon county, Illinois.

WATSON, JOHN B., born Feb. 10, 1800, in York District, South Carolina, and came to Illinois with his father, settling somewhere in Randolph county. He was married in Kaskaskia, April 9, 1829, to Mary Gillis, who was born in Wilmington, Delaware, Jan. 31, 1814. They moved to Springfield, soon after they were married, Mr. Watson having been to Sangamon county, in 1827, to look at the country. Of their seven children, all born in Springfield, the eldest died in infancy.

MARGARET, born May 28, 1833, died in Springfield August 11, 1852.

MARY L., born June 30, 1836, has been a school and music teacher for twenty years. She is teaching at present—1875—near Petersburg, Menard county, Illinois.

JANE E. died in her sixth year.

ANNA L., born Sept. 11, 1842, is a music teacher in Springfield, Illinois.

ELLEN C., born April 25, 1845, died August 11, 1852.

JAMES G., born April 24, 1848, was married Sept. 2, 1875, to Lucy A. Montgomery, who was born Feb. 1, 1856, on Fancy creek, Sangamon county, Illinois. J. G. Watson, formerly a farmer, is now residing in Springfield, Illinois.

J. B. Watson taught school the first year he resided in Springfield. He was afterwards county surveyor and engineer of the Great Western railroad. He went to California in 1849 and returned in 1852. Mr. Watson and his two daughters died of Asiatic cholera, August 11, 1852. Ellen C. died at half-past one o'clock A. M.; Margaret at half-past seven o'clock A. M., and their father died at half-past nine o'clock P. M. Mrs. Mary Watson's mother, Elizabeth Gillis, belonged to the Society of Friends, and she resided with her daughter in Springfield from about 1830 until her death, which occurred in August, 1852. She was buried at Oak Ridge Cemetery. John B. Watson's mother resided with her daughter-in-law in Springfield from 1854 until her death, which occurred in August, 1860. She was also buried at Oak Ridge Cemetery.

—95

Mrs. Mary Watson was married Dec. 16, 1863, in Springfield, Illinois, to Hon. S. W. Robbins, a prominent lawyer and temperance advocate. They had two children, who died in infancy. About 1860 Hon. S. W. Robbins and wife moved to their farm, seven miles northwest of Springfield, where he died, June 19, 1871, and she died Jan. 29, 1874.

WATSON, WILLIAM M., was born Oct. 16, 1807, near Vincennes, Indiana. He was married June 14, 1831, in Jefferson county, Indiana, to Sarah Talbott, who was born August 5, 1814, in Millersburg, Kentucky. They moved to Shelbyville, Illinois, where they had one child, and moved to Springfield, arriving Sept. 24, 1834, where they had eight children. Of all their children—

JAMES W., born Dec. 8, 1833, in Shelbyville, Illinois, married in Springfield, Jan. 16, 1856, to Angeline Cook, who was born Sept. 3, 1833, in Butler county, Ohio. They have one child, OSCAR A., born in Springfield, Nov. 5, 1856. He is an accountant. James W. Watson is a boot and shoe maker, and since 1871 has been Tyler for the Masonic bodies in Springfield, Illinois.

JULIETT died in 1843, aged ten years.

MARY A., born and married in Springfield to Edward Miles. He was killed by an accident on the Toledo, Wabash and Western Railroad in 1865. She resides with her parents in Springfield.

CHARLES H., born Dec. 11, 1839, in Springfield, married Sept. 14, 1874, in Gibson, Illinois, to Mrs. Mary Waddell, whose maiden name was Whitely, a native of Little Rock, Arkansas. Mr. Watson is an artist and lives in Springfield, Illinois.

SARAH lives with her parents.

DAVID died, aged thirteen years.

HESTER died, aged six years.

THEODORE resides with his parents.

EMILY J., born May 20, 1852, in Springfield, married Dec. 22, 1870, to Mervin B. Converse, and resides in Springfield.

William M. Watson and wife reside in Springfield, Illinois.

WATSON, WILLIAM W., born April 1, 1794, in Sussex county, New Jersey, went in 1817 to Lexington, Kentucky, and was there married, March 15, 1818, to Mrs. Maria Humerickhouse, whose maiden name was Cape. She was a native of Lexington. In the autumn of 1818 they moved to Nashville, Tennessee, where they had five children, and Mrs. Maria Watson died there July 17, 1834. The family soon after moved to St. Louis, Missouri, where Mr. Watson was in business about two years, and in the autumn of 1836 moved to Springfield, Illinois. Of his five children—

BENJAMIN A., born Dec. 9, 1818, in Nashville, Tennessee, was married in Springfield, Illinois, Feb. 11, 1845, to Emily R. Planck. They had seven living children, all except the youngest, born in Springfield. WILLIAM W., born May 13, 1847, was married Oct. 25, 1871, in St. Charles, Illinois, to Augusta C. Tolman. They have two children, WILLIAM W., jun., and a boy babe. W. W. Watson transacts business in Chicago, and with his family resides at Washington Heights, Illinois. EMILY, born Oct. 12, 1849, was married Nov. 24, 1870, at Perry Springs, to Dr. A. B. Carey. They have one child, ALBERT WATSON, and reside at Pittsfield, Pike county, Illinois. JULIA, HATTIE CAPE, MOLLIE L., FANNIE and HARRY live with their father. Mrs. Emily R. Watson died July 30, 1871, at Perry Springs, Pike county, Illinois. Mr. Watson, with his unmarried children, resides there. Benjamin A. Watson was one of the ten young men who in 1840 traveled from Springfield, Illinois, to Nashville, Tennessee, to hear Henry Clay make a speech. See page 480.

ABIGAIL, born Nov. 5, 1822, in Nashville, Tennessee, was married in Springfield June 27, 1843, to John G. Ives, and resides in Springfield, Illinois.

ANN MARIA, born Dec. 5, 1824, in Nashville, Tennessee, was married in Springfield, Illinois, to Thomas S. Little. See his name.

HESTER, born July 21, 1826, in Nashville, was married in Springfield, Illinois, to Thomas Billson. They had three children in Springfield. CORDELIA married George Wass, and lives in Painesville, Ohio. WILLIAM W., was married in Portland, Maine, to Alice Harford, and lives in St. Paul, Minnesota. BELLE F. lives with her brother William W. Thomas Billson went from Springfield to California in 1849, and died there in 1850. Mrs. Hester Billson was married in Springfield, Illinois, about 1856, to Chas. Reeves, of Cleveland, Ohio, and went there to reside. They had two children, GEORGE, now living with his father in Cleveland, and EDWIN C., who lives with his aunt, Mrs. Thomas S. Little, in Springfield. Mrs. Hester Reeves died March 26, 1862, in Cleveland, Ohio.

CORDELIA, born March 16, 1828, in Nashville, Tennessee, was married in Springfield, Ill., to Noah Divelbiss. See his name.

William W. Watson was married May 19, 1842, in Springfield, Illinois, to Mrs. Sarah Mottashed, whose maiden name was Wiley. He died Nov. 2, 1874, in Springfield, and his widow lives in Decatur, Illinois.

WATTS, BENJAMIN, born Nov. 22, 1769, at Warwick, Franklin county, Massachusetts, was the eldest child of Nicholas Watts and Eunice Newton, his wife. Mary Barbour was born Jan. 4, 1771, in Warwick, Massachusetts. Benjamin Watts and Mary Barbour were there married and moved to Shoreham, thence to Windham, Vermont, and from there to Lyman, Grafton county, New Hampshire. They moved to Sangamon county, Illinois, in the fall of 1837. Of their sixteen children six died young. Of the other ten who came to Sangamon county—

JOSEPH, born Sept. 1, 1793, in Vermont, was married in Lyman, New Hampshire, to Mahala Smith, came to Sangamon county in 1838, and moved to Menard county, Illinois, where they both died, leaving five children. ALONZO is married and lives in Iowa. GEORGE, BENJAMIN, NEWELL and AUSTIN.

LYDIA, born July 9, 1798, in New Hampshire, married Gideon Tripp. She is a widow and lives near Farmingdale, Illinois.

SALLY, born Jan. 26, 1800, in Lyman, New Hampshire, married Joel Buckman. See his name. Their only child, BENJAMIN, is married, and lives near Farmingdale, Illinois.

NICHOLAS, born Dec. 31, 1801, in New Hampshire, married Elizabeth Pallady. They have one child, BENJAMIN, who is married, and lives in Macon county, Illinois. Nicholas Watts and family came to Sangamon county in 1842, where he died May 9, 1843. His widow married again.

CHARLES, born Jan. 11, 1804, in Lyman, Grafton county, New Hampshire, was taken by his parents to St. Lawrence county, New York, in 1821. He was married at Brasher, in that county, Nov. 22, 1823, to Elizabeth Innes. They came with one child, in a colony of fifty-two persons, arriving in the fall of 1833, at Old Sangamo. July 4, 1834, they moved to a place one-fourth of a mile south of the present Farmingdale station. Of their ten children, ALEXANDER J., born Oct. 29, 1831, in St. Lawrence county, New York, brought up in Sangamon county, Illinois, left for Oregon in 1851, returned to Sangamon county in 1866, and was married April 4, 1867, in Jacksonville, Illinois, to Alexina J. Lander. They left the same month for Oregon. Mrs. Alexina J. Watts died May 15, 1868, near Applegate, Jackson county, Oregon. Alexander G. Watts resides there, and is county surveyor—1874. ANN JANE, born Dec. 31, 1833, in Sangamon county, was married there Nov. 10, 1853, to Thomas P. Stacy, who was born May 2, 1827, in Hopkinsville, Kentucky. They have seven children, ELIZABETH A., MATHEW K., ALEXINA J., WILLIAM H., SALLIE M., THOMAS E. and GATES, and reside in Jacksonville, Ill. CHARLES H., born Dec. 2, 1836, in Sangamon county, lives near Farmingdale. EDWIN, born June 14, 1839, in Sangamon county, was married Oct. 19, 1871, to Laura E. Rickard. They have one child, and live five miles southwest of Farmingdale, Sangamon county, Illinois. ALBERT B., born Oct. 23, 1841, in Sangamon county, was married Nov. 19, 1867, to Amelia L. Dustin, who was born June 20, 1847, in Jacksonville, Illinois. They have four children, ANNA J., LUCRETIA, CHARLES and JAMES, and live three-fourths of a mile northwest of Farmingdale, Illinois. SAMUEL W., born Aug. 14, 1844, in Sangamon county, lives with his parents. RICHARD N., born Jan. 13, 1848, in Sangamon county, was married Jan. 19, 1871, to Ellen F. McDermott. They have two children, and live in Shelby county, near Assumption, Christian county, Illinois. THOMAS B., WILLIAM and MARY E. live with their parents adjoining Farmingdale, Sangamon county, Illinois, on the south. Mr. and Mrs. Watts counted twenty-nine of the fifty-two persons forming the colony in which they came to Sangamon county. About half of this colony of fifty-two are now living—1876.

ISAAC and BENJAMIN, twins, born Nov. 26, 1808, at Lyman, New Hampshire.

ISAAC was married in St. Lawrence county, New York, Nov. 28, 1833, to Jemima Nevin, who was born June 5, 1815, in county Down, Ireland. They had two children in New York, and moved to Sangamon county, Illinois, arriving Oct. 7, 1838, in what is now Cartwright township, where two children were born, one of whom died in his fifth year. Of the other three, GEORGIE K., born Nov. 10, 1834, in New York, was married in Sangamon county, August 10, 1864, to Andrew Wilson. See his name. RUSSELL, born August 24, 1836, in New York, was married August, 1871, in Iowa, to Mary E. Hardin. They have one child, ISAAC, and live at North Platte, Nebraska, on the Union Pacific railroad. JOHN N. Isaac Watts resides two miles southwest of Farmingdale, Sangamon county, Illinois.

BENJAMIN, Jun., was married in St. Lawrence county, New York, to Calista Jacobs, came to Sangamon county in the fall of 1838. Their only child died young, and Mrs. Watts died in 1840 or '41. Benjamin Watts was married in 1842 to Orpha Bates. They had four children, one of whom died young. CALISTA P. and JAMES A. live with their mother. BENJAMIN O. married Sept. 26, 1876, to Miss Brown at Pleasant Plains. Benjamin Watts, Jun., died February, 1862, and his widow lives three miles west of Pleasant Plains, Illinois.

IRENA and RUSSELL, twins, born June 15, 1813, in New Hampshire.

IRENA married Isaac Holmes and he died, leaving two children. His widow married James Bates. See his name.

RUSSELL came to Sangamon county in 1835, and was married March, 1839, to Diantha Holmes. They had three children, and moved in 1847 to Calapooga, Lynn county, Oregon, where Mr. Watts died Dec. 11, 1854, leaving five children. His widow has since married.

Benjamin Watts, Sen., died Sept. 11, 1838, and Mrs. Mary Watts died two days later, Sept. 13, 1838, both in Sangamon county, Illinois.

WAY, JOHN, was born Sept. 11, 1793, in Lancaster, Pennsylvania. His half sister, Rebecca Way, six years younger than himself, married Joseph Taylor, and they are the parents of Bayard Taylor, the world-renowned author, historian, poet and traveler. The mother of John Way died when he was a child, and his grandfather Ash brought him up in Chester county, Pennsylvania. Ann St. Clair was born in Chester county, August 16, 1803. John Way and Ann St. Clair were there married in the spring of 1823. They had two children in that county, and moved to Philadelphia, where two children were born, two of the four children died in infancy. In the spring of 1838 Mr. Way took his family to Chester county, and left them there while he visited the western country. He decided to make Springfield his home, and wrote to his wife to come on with the family. She fortunately learned of a gentleman by the name of Clendening who was coming west to visit a married daughter. He drove a light wagon, and Mrs. Way made arrangements to come and bring her two children. Mr Way rode on horseback to Paris, Edgar county, Illinois, and met them there. The whole party arrived at Springfield in November, 1838. Mr. Way was a plasterer, and the public buildings and other improvements here called for his services. Some of his work in the Marine Insurance Company's bank building, Springfield, is likely to stand for many years to come. They had six children in Springfield. Of their eight children—

REBECCA, born May 11, 1828, in Chester county, Pennsylvania, died Feb. 9, 1846, at St. Louis, Missouri, while visiting a relative of the family.

RACHEL E., born June 19, 1824, in Philadelphia, Pennsylvania, married Dec. 31, 1851, in Springfield, Illinois, to Christian Schwarberg. They have four children. EDWARD J. married Emma Kidd, and lives near Springfield. ANNIE, GUSSIE and FRANK V., live with their parents four and a half miles northwest of Springfield, Illinois.

HARRIET S., born Oct. 7, 1839, in Springfield, Illinois, was married there Sept. 27, 1855, to John C. Stansbury, who was born April 12, 1834, at Basking Ridge, Somerset county, New Jersey, and came to Springfield, June 27, 1854. They have four children, ANNA M., was married Sept. 24, 1873, to Arthur C. Hammond. They have one child, WILLIE T., and live in Loami, Illinois. CHARLOTTE E., ADA B. and FRANK H., live with their parents. Mr. Stansbury is engaged in the business of carriage and wagon manufacturing in Loami, Sangamon county, Illinois, and resides there.

CHARLOTTE E., born Dec. 20, 1841, in Springfield, married January, 1863, to George Riley Stevens. They have three children, ANNA, HARRIET and FRANK, and live in Montgomery county, Illinois.

JOHN C., born Feb. 25, 1844, in Springfield, enlisted August, 1861, at St. Louis, in what became Co. B, 11th Mo. Inf. for three years, was discharged on account of physical disability March, 1862. He re-enlisted June, 1864, for 100 days in an Illinois regiment, went to Rock Island to guard prisoners, acted as commissary clerk, served full time and was honorably discharged, and lives in Montgomery county, Illinois.

MARY T., born Feb. 19, 1846, in Springfield, married July, 1865, to Preston H. Souther. They have three children, viz: MAUD, MABEL and HOWARD, and reside at Topeka, Kansas.

EMMA T., born March 20, 1848, is unmarried and resides at Glasgow, Missouri.

JULIA A., born June 20, 1850, married November, 1865, to August Schwarberg, who died March, 1866. His widow married November 10, 1869, to Benjamin Vanderver. They have one child, GRACIE, and reside at Coatsville, Pennsylvania.

Mrs. Ann Way died May 12, 1864, in Springfield. John Way was married in 1869, to Mrs. Coverdill. She died August, 1871, and he died suddenly Jan. 18, 1875, at Gerard, Illinois.

WEAVER, LEWIS, was born August 8, 1798, near the river Rhine, in Germany. He came to America when a young man, and was married in Franklin county, Pennsylvania, to Savilla Earhart, a native of Maryland. They had four children in Pennsylvania. He started to move to Jefferson City, Missouri, but changed his mind and came to Sangamon county, Illinois, arriving in 1838 or '39, near Springfield, where four children were born. Of their children—

FREDERICK, born Sept. 23, 1829, in Pennsylvania, died in Sangamon county, Sept. 23, 1842.

LEWIS, Jun., born July 17, 1832, in Pennsylvania, died in Sangamon county, July 3, 1842.

SAMUEL, born Oct. 16, 1834, in Franklin county, Pennsylvania, married Feb. 14, 1860, in Sangamon county, to Maria Jane Lake, who was born March 13, 1843, in Knox county, Ohio. They have six children, RACHEL L., JACOB F., MARY C., PHILIP L. and JESSIE E., and live in Cooper township, four miles southwest of Mechanicsburg, Sangamon county, Illinois.

JOHN H., born June 13, 1837, in Pennsylvania, married and lives near Illiopolis, Illinois.

ELI, born Jan. 15, 1840, in Sangamon county, married near Chatham to Anna Haddon. They have one child, MARY A., and live near Blue Mound, Macon county, Illinois.

LOUISA, born Jan. 19, 1843, in Sangamon county, married William R. Parker, have two children, and live near Eugene City, Oregon.

ELIZABETH, born Nov. 9, 1845, in Sangamon county, married Henry M. Johnson, and lives near Blue Mound, Macon county, Illinois.

DANIEL, born Sept. 22, 1849, in Sangamon county, lives with his brother, Samuel.

Lewis Weaver died April 22, 1853, and Mrs. Savilla Weaver died Oct. 14, 1864, both in Sangamon county, Illinois.

WEBB, HIRAM LUTHER, was born Nov. 12, 1799, in Rockingham, Vermont. The Webb family was a very old one in London and Weymouth, England, at the time the Plymouth colony was settled in Massachusetts. Two of them, Francis and Thomas Webb, were active members of the colony before it left England, but it is not certain that they came to America. Christopher Webb, of Weymouth, came to America previous to 1645, and settled in Braintree, Massachusetts. The name of his wife is not known, but they had six children. His eldest son, Christopher, born probably in England, about 1630, married Jan. 18, 1654 or '55, to Hannah Scott, lived in Braintree, Massachusetts, and had nine children. Their third child, Samuel, born August 16, 1660, married December, 1686, to Mary Adams, had four children, and moved to Windham, Connecticut, in 1707, where they had one child. Their second child, Samuel, born May 14, 1690, married Oct. 8, 1711, to Hannah Ripley, grand-daughter of Governor William Bradford. They had four children. Their fourth child, Joshua, born Feb. 9, 1721, married May 28, 1744, to Hannah Abbey. They had four children in Windham, Connecticut, and moved to Bellows Falls, Vermont, about 1751, where they had seven children. The father, mother and eleven children lived until the youngest was forty-four years old. Joshua Webb, being one of the first settlers in Vermont, took an active part in the movement for erecting it into a separate state, and was a member of the state legislature for the first twelve years of its existence. His tenth child, Luther, born Oct. 24, 1763, following the example of several of his elder brothers, eagerly enlisted as soon as he was old enough to be received in the army of the Revolution, and served until Independence was achieved. One of his brothers was a colonel and another a captain, but Luther, being the youngest, served as a private. They all lived to be very old, and were entitled each to a pension, but declined to apply for it, saying they had fought for freedom and not for money. Luther was married Feb. 9, 1792, to Dorothy Wheelock, and had seven children. The fourth child, Hiram Luther, whose name heads this sketch, was married Dec. 15, 1823, in the town of Walpole, New Hampshire, to Martha B. Bates. She was born Sept. 30, 1799, in the town of Jeffrey, Cheshire county, New Hampshire. They made their home in Rockingham, Vermont, until five children were born, and started west, moving in wagons, and at the end of six weeks, which was the shortest trip made by any one from that region of country, they arrived in Sangamon county Nov. 13, 1834, and settled one mile west of the present Farmingdale Station, where two children were born. Of their children—

MARTHA B., born Dec. 6, 1824, in

Rockingham, Vermont, resides with her mother.

HARRIET J., born Feb. 26, 1827, in Rockingham, Vermont, married in Sangamon county, August 9, 1848, to Joseph E. Cobbey, who was born November, 1824, in Ohio. They have three children, JOSEPH E., Jun., THOMAS D. and JAMES W., and live at Vinton, Iowa.

JANE G., born Feb. 18, 1829, in Vermont, married in Sangamon county, Jan. 1, 1857, to Edgar A. Kincaid, who was born in 1825, in Kentucky. They have four children, FRED L., MATTIE A., ALBERT E. and DICK BATES, and reside near Athens, Menard county, Illinois.

JOHN W., born Nov. 24, 1830, in Vermont, died in Sangamon county, Oct. 22, 1847.

JAMES, born Jan. 12, 1833, in Rockingham, Vermont, is unmarried, and resides on the farm settled by his parents in 1834. It is one mile west of Farmingdale, Sangamon county, Illinois.

JOSEPH L., born August 1, 1837, in Sangamon county, graduated at the Eclectic Medical College, of Cincinnati, Ohio, married Oct. 30, 1873, in Beatrice, Nebraska, to Louisa Kate Shepherd, and is a practicing physician there.

HIRAM P., born March 14, 1842, in Sangamon county, graduated at the State University of Indiana, at Bloomington, in the class of 1865, graduated in law in 1867, and was admitted to practice in Springfield, Illinois, went to Nebraska and was elected treasurer of Gage county in 1869, '71 and '73 for two years each term. He is also engaged in the practice of law and in banking in Beatrice. He was married Oct. 20, 1873, to Jenett Maxfield, in Beatrice, Nebraska, and resides there.

Hiram L. Webb died Oct. 21, 1847, and his widow resides one mile west of Farmingdale, Illinois, where the family settled in 1834. Mr. Webb sold the first corn he raised in the county at eight cents per bushel in trade. He made several trips to Chicago, one hundred and eighty-five miles, with a wagon load of butter and bacon, exchanged them for stores and hardware, which he sold on his return home, after supplying his own needs. James says that *his* first business transaction, for himself and one of his brothers, was to sell eggs at three cents per dozen, and buy each of them a jack knife.

WEBB, JAMES G., was born Feb. 3, 1792, near Winchester, Clarke county, Kentucky. Elizabeth Petty was born May 3, 1795, in the same county. They were there married, and had two children, and the family moved to Sangamon county, Illinois, arriving in the fall of 1826 in what is now Loami township, south of Lick creek. In 1829 he sold his farm and moved to Buffalo Hart Grove, and in 1831 bought the same farm and moved back to Loami township. Five children were born in Sangamon county. Of the seven children—

WILLIS R., born Sept. 18, 1830, in Kentucky, married in Sangamon county, to Emily Darneille. They had three children, and the whole family died in Loami township.

JOHN H., born Feb. 10, 1834, in Kentucky, raised in Sangamon county, married Mary Ream, a native of Maine. He went to Iowa and enlisted in 1861 in a cavalry regiment for three years. He was wounded in Arkansas in 1862 or '63, and was honorably discharged on account of physical disability occasioned by his wounds. They live at Abington, Jefferson county, Iowa.

ELIZABETH, born August 9, 1827, in Sangamon county, died unmarried, Sept. 14, 1854, in Christian county, Illinois.

CHARLOTTE, born Jan. 14, 1830, in Loami township, Sangamon county, Illinois, married Oct. 3, 1848, to James M. Turpin, who was born May 10, 1828, in Howard county, Missouri, and came with his parents to Sangamon county in 1845. He was a soldier in the Mexican war. He enlisted in August, 1862, in Co. I, 73d Ill. Inf. for three years, was elected second lieutenant at the organization of the company, promoted to first lieutenant Dec. 6, 1862, served until after participating in the battle of Chickamauga, when he resigned on account of business engagements at home. Mr. Turpin is now a merchant in Loami, Illinois. He has represented his township in the Sangamon County Board of Supervisors.

ADIN, born July 12, 1833, in Sangamon county, is unmarried, and resides near Winchester, Kentucky.

CAROLINE, born Oct. 11, 1834, died Sept. 30, 1853.
JAMES G., Jun., born August 9, 1840, in Sangamon county, died January, 1859, at Decatur, Illinois.

Mrs. Elizabeth Webb died Sept. 10, 1843, and James G. Webb died March 12, 1844, both in Loami township. He was a soldier from Kentucky in 1812, and taken prisoner at the battle of River Raisin.

WEBB, WILLIAM, was born about 1773 in Virginia, went to Tennessee, and was married to Jane Hillis, in Warren county. They had ten children. The family moved to Petersburg, Illinois, in the fall of 1830, and in 1835 moved to Spring creek, eight miles west of Springfield. Of their children—

ROBERT, born in Tennessee, married there to Elizabeth Lofton, came to Sangamon county with his father, has seven children, and lives near Oskaloosa, Iowa.

SALLY, deaf and dumb, lives with her brother Robert.

ELIZABETH, married in Tennessee to Samuel Neal, and both died, leaving three children.

WILLIAM, married in Sangamon county to Innocent Brown, had five children, and all moved west.

ISABEL married Samuel Blue. See his name.

JANE, died in Petersburg, aged sixteen years.

JOHN married Susannah Taylor in Sangamon county, have six children, and live near Ioka, Keokuk county, Iowa.

ANN, went to Iowa, married Calvin Tandy, has six children, and live in Oskaloosa, Iowa.

FANNIE, born July 26, 1826, married David H. Blue. See his name.

ISAAC, married Ellen Osborn, have ten children, and live in Jefferson county, Iowa.

Mrs. Jane Webb died in Petersburg, Illinois, and William Webb went to Keokuk county, Iowa, and died there in 1848.

WEBER, GEORGE R., born May 29, 1808, in Baltimore, Maryland. His parents moved while he was an infant to Shepherdstown, Jefferson county, Virginia, their former home, and where they were married. George R., whose name heads this sketch, was married in Shepherdstown, May 1, 1832, to Susan Shepherd. They soon after moved to New York city, where Mrs. Susan Weber died. G. R. Weber returned to Shepherdstown, Virginia, and from there came to Springfield, Illinois, arriving April 15, 1835. He was married in Springfield, Illinois, September, 1836, to Catharine Welch. They had eight children in Springfield.

MARY E., was married in Springfield, to Jacob English. They have six children, and live in Howard county, Kansas.

EMMA, was married in Springfield to Frank Child.

CATHARINE C., born Oct. 4, 1844, was married in Springfield, April 11, 1874, to Isaac Short, who was born Sept. 5, 1839, in South Bloomfield, Ohio. They reside in Springfield, Illinois.

ANNA M. lives with her parents.

GEORGE W., born Nov. 27, 1850, in Springfield, Illinois, was married April 27, 1876, in Taylorville, to Nemmie Shumway, daughter of the late Judge Shumway. George W. Weber is the editor and publisher of the Taylorville *Democrat*, and resides in Taylorville, Illinois.

JOHN R. and *NORVAL W.* reside in Springfield, and are conducting a job printing office.

George R. Weber formed a partnership with John S. Roberts in April, 1835, for the publication of the *Illinois Republican*. When the state capital was removed from Vandalia to Springfield, the *State Register* office came with it, and that paper and the *Illinois Republican*, being both democratic, were consolidated in 1839, the proprietors becoming partners under the name of Walters & Weber. This partnership continued until 1846, when Mr. Weber sold out to Mr. Walters, and enlisted in Co. A, 4th Ill. Inf., under Colonel E. D. Baker. While encamped on the Rio Grande, in Mexico, news of Mr. Walters' death reached there, and Mr. Weber being interested in the state printing, it was necessary for him to return. He accordingly was detailed to return home with those soldiers who were unfit for duty, and was never recalled. After the time expired for which he was elected public printer, he severed his connection with the office, and moved to his farm. He, however, contributed articles which appeared both as editorial and communicated to the columns of the *Republican*. Mr. Weber was also elected major in the Mormon war. He served six months as state commissary in our late civil war, and was appointed by President Lincoln as commissary at Camp Butler, which position he retained until the close of the rebellion. George R. Weber has now retired from business, and resides in Springfield, Illinois.

WEBER, JOHN B., born April 7, 1810, in Shepherdstown, Virginia, was there married Sept. 23, 1832, to Sarah A. Woltz, sister of John Woltz. *See his name.* She was born in Shepherdstown, March 20, 1812. They had two children in Virginia, and moved to Springfield, Illinois, arriving April 16, 1836, and had eight children in Sangamon county. The eldest died, aged two years.

ANDREW J., born Sept. 9, 1840, in Springfield. At the first call for seventy-five thousand men, by President Lincoln, in April, 1861, he, with other young men of Sangamon county, organized a company, but the quota of Illinois was already full. Andrew J. Weber was elected captain, and the company was sworn into the United States service as the 1st Reg. U. S. Rifles. After a number of changes it became Co. B, 11th Mo. Inf. More than nine-tenths of that regiment were Illinois men. Company B united with the regiment at St. Louis, July 20. 1861. It was fully organized on the sixteenth of August, and was in the battle of Fredericktown, Missouri, Oct. 21, 1861. Captain Weber was promoted April 21, 1862, to major of the regiment. In the absence of higher officers he was in command of the regiment at the battle of Iuka, Sept. 17, and the battle of Corinth, Oct. 3 and 4, 1862, in which General, since Governor, and now United States Senator Oglesby, was shot and thought to be mortally wounded. General Rosecrans, in his report, says that the 11th Missouri, under Major Weber, led the skirmish which opened the battle, October 3, and also led the charge that drove the last rebel from the field on the fourth. Major Weber was promoted and commissioned lieutenant colonel, March 20, 1863, and commissioned colonel May 15, 1863. All his commissions were signed by Governor Gamble, of Missouri. Colonel Weber was wounded in the head by a cannon ball, while on duty, on the Peninsula, in front of Vicksburg, June 29, 1863. The wound at first was not thought to be mortal, but he died the next day, June 30. According to military usage a single regiment only would have acted as an escort, but after the capture of Vicksburg, July 4, the whole brigade turned out and escorted his remains to the steamer, by which they were brought up the river, conveyed to Springfield, and deposited in Oak Ridge Cemetery, July 9, 1863. His native city may well cherish, with pride, the memory of this young hero, who rose by talent, energy and industry to a position far above his years, and yielded his young and gifted life, a willing sacrifice on the alter of his country. He was but twenty-two years, eight months and seven days old when he was commissioned colonel of his regiment in the face of the enemy; an incident unparalleled in the history of our country.

GEORGE P., born Dec. 2, 1842, in Springfield, Ill., enlisted at the same time and in the same company with his brother, Andrew J. He was elected and appointed orderly sergeant. When his brother was promoted to the office of major, he was promoted to second lieutenant of Co. B, and after that promoted to first lieutenant and adjutant of the regiment, the latter of which he did not accept, being physically unable to discharge its duties, which prevented his re-enlisting as a veteran with the regiment. He was honorably discharged at St. Louis, May 1, 1864. George P. Weber was furloughed home with the remains of his brother, Colonel Weber, and was married July 28, 1863, to Vienna Meader. They have four children, MIRIAM M., SARAH A., TIMOTHY and ELI, and resides four miles west of Pawnee, Sangamon county, Illinois.

It is worthy of remark that when the 11th Missouri Infantry, composed as it was of Illinois men, went through St. Louis in 1861, stones and other missiles were thrown at the soldiers from the windows. When they returned on furlough, after re-enlistment, they were greeted with bouquets of flowers, a grand banquet, and were presented by the citizens of St. Louis with a magnificent stand of colors.

JAMES W. was born November 10, 1844, in Springfield, Illinois, enlisted Nov. 12, 1864, for one year, in his native city, in the 10th Ill. Cav., served full term and was honorably discharged Nov. 12, 1865, at

San Antonio, Texas. Three days after his discharge he started to come home on horseback, in company with two other members of the same regiment, William M. Brown, of Sangamon county, and John Ingalls, of Madison county, Illinois. They were followed from San Antonio, and on the 24th of November stopped at the house of a man named Deason and obtained their dinners. That was in Rusk county, a few miles from a very small village bearing the local name of Rakepocket, but the post-office is Pine Hill. After taking their dinners they continued their journey, and having passed through the village were followed by four men, also on horseback, who, after keeping near them about one mile, to the vicinity of Sharon, in Panola county, pretending to be in a hurry, the four men rode rapidly, overtook and passed the three travelers, when the four suddenly wheeled their horses, and each presenting a revolver, called on the travelers to surrender, which they did. Just at this moment a lad on horseback, who had been to mill, came near the parties, and seeing the men arrayed facing each other, and all on one side with deadly weapons drawn, paused to see if he could ascertain the cause of the strange spectacle. The boy was then ordered by the desperadoes not to remain any longer at the peril of his life, and he moved on quickly. Passing a turn in the road he halted and saw the four drive the three off the road into the woods. In a few moments more he heard the report of fire arms, followed by piercing screams, and then all was still. The boy reported that night to his parents, and the next morning upon search being made the three bodies were found, and decently buried. The assassins obtained three horses and equipments, and from a memorandum found it was thought they also got $2,100 in money. The four inhuman wretches were a one-armed desperado named A. J. Smith, a man by the name of Blackstock, and John and Jerry Deason, the two latter sons of the man at whose house the murdered men had taken their last dinner.

A few months after this occurrence John Deason came home sick and was secreted in his father's house. He was discovered and intelligence given to the soldiers at Shreveport, when a small band of them came upon and killed him on the spot.

—96

Jerry was afterwards killed in Leon county, Texas. Blackstock was killed in Robertson county, Texas. Smith fled to Mississippi, and his fate is unknown. These facts were obtained from a former citizen of Sangamon county, who was at the time living in the vicinity where the tragedy was enacted, and into whose hands one of the early sample sheets of this work had fallen, and in which he saw the name of James W. Weber.

BENJAMIN R. B., born in Sangamon county, married Oct. 29, 1872, to Sarah McCormick. They had one child, LALLAH ANN, who died in 1875. They reside near Pawnee, Illinois.

CHARLES E., born in Sangamon county, lives with his father.

Mrs. Sarah A. Weber died August 5, 1866. John B. Weber was married Nov. 28, 1867, to Mrs. Nancy J. Drennan, whose maiden name was Dodds. They reside adjoining Pawnee, Sangamon county, Illinois.

John B. Weber was engaged in the manufacture of cabinet furniture in Springfield and at Howlett, now Riverton, from 1836 to 1841, when he lost his left hand by a buzz saw. He was appointed by the legislature of 1842 and '43 to copy the land records of the state in numerical order, which kept him employed until 1849. He then went to California, and returned in 1851. He was quartermaster in the last expedition of the Mormon war of 1846. He was clerk in the commissary department in raising the first six Illinois regiments for the suppression of the rebellion. He was elected sheriff and collector of Sangamon county, and served from 1854 to 1856.

WEBER, PHILIP W., was born near Shepherdstown, Virginia, Jan. 28, 1812. He went south in 1835, built a mill in connection with others at Raymond, Mississippi, sold out there and came to Springfield in the Spring of 1837. He was married in Springfield June 18, 1839, to Amanda M. Shepherd. She was born Nov. 8, 1811. They have six children, all born in Sangamon county, namely—

JOHN P., born March 19, 1840, unmarried, and resides with his parents, near Pawnee, Illinois.

MARY E. lives with her parents.

WILLIAM S., born March 11, 1844, enlisted August, 1862, at Springfield, in one of two companies which were consolidated to form Co. K, 124th Ill. Inf., but was left out on account of his being young and small of his age. He went to St. Louis in 1863, and made another unsuccessful attempt. He was married Jan. 1, 1867, to Henrietta Lough. They have two children, FRANK and ANDREW J., and reside in the extreme southeast corner of Pawnee township, Sangamon county, Illinois.

AMANDA, born March 3, 1846, married May 9, 1867, to John W. Blakey. They have one living child, EDGAR L., and live in Pawnee, Illinois. Mr. Blakey is a merchant there,

SARAH C. married Dec. 12, 1867, to Badam N. Brown. They have two children, IDA BELL and FANNY MAY, and live near Pawnee, Illinois.

EMMA S. lives with her parents.

Mr. Philip W. Weber went to California in 1849 and returned in 1859, and soon after, in connection with his brother, John B., bought land and engaged in farming. He now—November, 1876—resides on his farm, adjoining Pawnee, Sangamon county, Illinois.

WEBER, JACOB J., was born February, 1815, in Frederick City, Maryland. He came to Springfield in the fall of 1837. He afterwards went to Fulton county, where he engaged in business and married Miss LaMasters. He came back to Sangamon county in 1855 and engaged in farming in Ball township. They had six children—

JOHN H. died Sept. 11, 1874, at Beatrice, Nebraska, in the twenty-seventh year of his age.

MARY married Dec. 5, 1867, to James T. Lamb. *See his name.*

VIRGINIA married Charles L. Megredy. *See his name.*

CARRIE lives with her uncle, John B. Weber.

JOSEPH lives with his uncle, Philip W. Weber.

Mrs. Weber died, and Jacob J. Weber died suddenly, both on the farm in Sangamon county, Illinois.

WEBER, PETER S., was born in 1817, in Frederick City, Maryland. He came to Springfield in 1837, being the fifth brother, no two of whom came together. He was married in Springfield to Miss Adams. They removed to LaSalle, and his wife died soon after while on a visit to Springfield. He was married in LaSalle twice, and moved to St. Louis about 1850, and from there to New Orleans. He died in that city of yellow fever, August 25, 1853, leaving a widow and one son, GEORGE W. They soon after returned to her former home at LaSalle, Illinois.

WEBER, Mrs. ELIZABETH, whose maiden name was Shutt, came from Virginia to Springfield in 1844. She was the mother of George R., John B., Philip W., Jacob J. and Peter S. Weber. She died Jan. 27, 1868, at the house of her son, Philip W., which had been her home for twenty years previous.

WEST, BENJAMIN, born May 15, 1812, in Boston, Massachusetts. He was educated at Harvard College, and came to Sangamon county, Illinois, about 1835, and settled at Rochester. He was married April 16, 1840, to Permelia A. Taylor. They had three children in Sangamon county, namely—

LOUISA, born Jan. 30, 1841, married Benjamin T. Rice, a native of Cambridge, Massachusetts. They have two children, HELEN W. and NATHAN, and reside at Millbury, Massachusetts—1874.

FANNY, born May 2, 1843, died Dec. 11, 1861, caused by swallowing her false teeth, while asleep, on the night of the 9th of the same month. She died at the house of her mother, Mrs. John North, near Mechanicsburg, Illinois.

BENJAMIN, Jnr., born Jan. 30, 1845, in Sangamon county, and was educated in the Lutheran College at Springfield. He went to New Hampshire to visit his father's relatives, and from there embarked on board the ship Syren, Nov. 16, 1861, at Boston, for San Francisco. The voyage was made around Cape Horn, arriving at the latter city in March, 1862. Captain Green, of the Syren, determined to sail for the Phillippine Islands. On arriving at the port of Manilla, the captain interested himself in the welfare of young Mr. West, and secured for him a situation in the shipping house of Russell & Sturgis, of Boston. That was in July, 1862. After spending a year in their house at Manilla he was placed in charge of a branch house 150 miles distant on the island of Yoilo. Soon after his arrival at the latter place, he went in a pleasure boat with a small party of friends to a neighboring island, and on their return the wind capsized the boat some distance from the shore. His comrades expected him to cling to the wreck until they, who were more experienced, could go to shore and bring assistance. He attempted to swim to shore also, and when they returned no vestige of him could be found. He had gone down alone and unseen. That was on December 25, 1863.

Benjamin West was a lawyer, and was one of the representatives of Sangamon county in the state legislature at the session of 1846 and '47. He died at Rochester June 23, 1847, and his widow married Erastus Woodruff, who died and she married John North. *See his name.*

WEST, SAMUEL, was born Nov. 8, 1813, in Boston, Massachusetts. He came to Sangamon county, Illinois, arriving in 1834 or '35 at Rochester. He returned to Boston on a visit, accompanied by Mrs. Lucetta Stevens, whose maiden name was Putnam. Her husband, Samuel Stevens, having died in Rochester, she was returning to her friends in New Hampshire. Samuel West and Mrs. Stevens were married July 7, 1840, at Unity, New Hampshire. They returned to Rochester soon after. She had one child by her first marriage, namely,

SAMUEL P. STEVENS, born Oct. 27, 1838, in Sangamon county, married at Rochester March 2, 1858, to Olive J. Slater. They live at Avilla, Jasper county, Missouri.

Mr. and Mrs. West had six children in Rochester, namely—

BENJAMIN P., born June 15, 1841, died, aged eight years.

SAMUEL F., born May 28, 1843, married Nov. 6, 1867, in Rochester, to Margaret E. Barr. They have two children, NELLIE E. and CHARLES F., and reside near Pawnee, Sangamon county, Illinois.

MARTHA S., born Feb. 22, 1846, married Dec. 7, 1865, to William Jamieson Cooper. *See his name.* She had four children, and died April 26, 1873.

CHARLES, born August 16, 1848, in Rochester, Illinois, married in 1872 to Gertrude D., and lives near Avilla, Jasper county, Missouri.

LUCY, born Oct. 4, 1850, married June 8, 1870, in Rochester to William Everhart, who was born May 1, 1843, in Loudon county, Virginia. They have two children, FRED B. and NORA, and reside in Rochester, Sangamon county, Illinois.

LOUISA, born April 30, 1854, married Charles Barr. They live in Rochester, Sangamon county, Illinois.

Mrs. Lucetta West died Oct. 14, 1859, in Rochester, Illinois. Samuel West was married July 29, 1860, to Mrs. Zilpha Kimball, whose maiden name was Putnam. He died Sept. 2, 1868, and his widow resides in Springfield, Illinois.

WEST, ELIJAH, was born July 30, 1786, near Carlisle, Nicholas county, Kentucky. He married Elizabeth Henderson, had nine children in Kentucky, and moved to Macoupin county, Illinois, and from there to Sangamon county, arriving in 1835, in Auburn township. Of their children—

JESSE B. married Eliza J. Peebler, in Iowa, and lives there.

MAHALA married Davidson Smith, and lives in Wisconsin.

ELIJAH A. was married in Sangamon county to Atha Organ. They had four children. ATHA A. married Scott Bumgarner, and lives in Auburn township. WILLIAM T., ELIJAH A., Jun., and MARGARET A. live with their mother. Elijah A. West died Nov. 20, 1855, and his widow lives in Auburn township, Sangamon county, Illinois.

JOHN H. died unmarried.

NATHAN A. went to Iowa, and married Mary Peebler. They live in Oregon.

SARAH A. married John Allsbury, and died in Piatt county, Illinois.

WILLIAM M. married Hannah J. Landers, and lives in Auburn township, Sangamon county, Illinois.

MILTON M. died unmarried.

ELIZABETH lives in Piatt county, Illinois.

Elijah West died Jan. 8, 1840, and his widow died also, both in Sangamon county, Illinois.

WHITED, JAMES, was born Sept. 8, 1804, in Virginia. His parents moved when he was an infant to Fentress county, Tennessee. Lucy Thurman was born in that county, August 23, 1811. They were there married March 5, 1828, had three children in Tennessee, and came to Sangamon county, Illinois, arriving March

28, 1838, in what is now Woodside township, where nine children were born, two of whom died under thirteen years of age.

RICHRD E., born in 1830, married Mary Grissom, had three children, and he was stabbed to death at a convivial party in Sangamon county, Jan. 17, 1860. His widow and children live at Albia, Monroe county, Iowa.

MARY H. married Thomas W. Newlun, have three children, and live in Ball township.

SUSANNAH died in 1850, aged 18 years.

JEANETTE, married Joseph Newlun, have six children, and live near Woodside, Illinois.

JAMES V. married Miriam A. Tucker and lives at the homestead near Chatham, Illinois—1874.

LUCY A. married William Knotts, have five children, and lives in Chatham, Illinois.

RUHAMA M. married William Carter, and died Oct. 10, 1872, leaving two children near Woodside, Illinois.

ROBERT H., born Dec. 9, 1851, married, August 25, 1869, Agnes J. Showers, have one child, CHARLES E., and live near Woodside, Sangamon county, Illinois.

THOMAS A. and JANE R. B., live near Woodside, Illinois.

James Whited died April 19, 1870, and his widow died January, 1873, both in Ball township, half a mile south of where they settled in 1838.

WHITESIDES, CHARLES, born 1785 in Virginia, and taken by his parents to Fayette county, Kentucky. They traveled in boats from Pittsburg down the Ohio river to Limestone—now Maysville—Kentucky. Charles Whitesides was married in 1810 in Fayette county, Kentucky to Elizabeth Graves, who was born in 1788 in that county. They had five children in Fayette county, and in 1819 moved to Cumberland county, same state, where five children were born, and the family moved to Sangamon county, Illinois, arriving June 30, 1831, in Springfield. In 1833 they moved to the vicinity of Williamsville, and in 1835 moved to German Prairie, northeast of Springfield. Of their children—

JOHN M., born April 11, 1811, in Fayette county, Kentucky, was married in Cumberland county, same state, to Elizabeth Dawson. They had five children, and Mrs. Whitesides died in Kentucky. He and his children came to Sangamon county in 1844, and now reside in Linn county, Kansas.

EMILY, born in 1813 in Kentucky, died in Sangamon county in 1833.

WILLIAM A., born Nov. 5, 1815, in Fayette county, Kentucky, was married in Sangamon county, Illinois, Feb. 19, 1846, to Honor A. Branch. They had two children, ALBERT, born Dec. 27, 1846, died Dec. 7, 1860; LOUISIANA, born Sept. 11, 1849, was married Oct. 13, 1870, to Edmond Miller. See his name. She died Nov. 23, 1871. Mrs. Rebecca Branch, the mother of Mrs. Whitesides, died at their house July 25, 1876. She spent the last sixteen years of her life in their family. William A. Whitesides and family reside two miles northeast of Rochester, Sangamon county, Illinois.

THOMAS H. born May 12, 1817, in Kentucky, was married to Mary Randolph. They went to Pike's Peak, where Mrs. Whitesides died, leaving four children, two of whom have since died. T. H. Whitesides resides near Mt. Pulaski, Logan county, Illinois.

CHARLES H. born March, 1819, in Fayette county, Kentucky, was married in Springfield to Emeline Sargent. They had five children, and moved to California in 1850. The last heard from them, in 1872, they were in the Sandwich Islands.

NICHOLAS B., born April 18, 1821, in Cumberland county, Kentucky, was married in Sangamon county, April 8, 1847, to Agnes J. Turley. They had five children, two of whom died young. EMILY C., born March 4, 1850, resides with her father. MARY E., born March 11, 1854, was married Jan. 19, 1873, to Wilson W. Yates, and resides near Plato, Iroquois county, Illinois. IDA A., born April 19, 1862, resides with her father. Mrs. Agnes J. Whitesides died May 19, 1863, and N. B. Whitesides resides four miles east of Springfield, Illinois.

GEORGE G., born Feb. 23, 1824, in Cumberland county, Kentucky, brought up in Sangamon county, Illinois, and married Elizabeth A. Berks. They had four children, SARAH E., ROBERT F., JOHN M. and WILLIAM A. Mrs. W. died, and G. G. Whitesides married Mrs. A. Benton, whose maiden name was

Copeland. They had one child, MAGGIE R. Mrs. G. G. Whitesides had two children by her first marriage, LYDIA A. and EUNICE E. Benton. G. G. Whitesides and family reside in Logan county, north of Illiopolis, Illinois.

MARGARET C., born March 15, 1826, in Kentucky, died in Sangamon county, in 1845.

MARY E., born May 15, 1828, in Cumberland county, Kentucky, raised in Sangamon county, was married March 1, 1855, to Andrew Buckles. They had seven children, two died young. MARY T., FLORA A., EMMA L., HENRY S. and ROBERT E., and reside near Mt. Pulaski, Illinois.

MARION F., born August 28, 1830, in Cumberland county, Kentucky, was married in Sangamon county, Jan. 1, 1852, to Anna E. Black. They had four children, three died in infancy. MARY, the eldest, resides with her parents. M. F. Whitesides and wife reside in Springfield, Illinois.

Charles Whitesides died March 31, 1836, four miles northeast of Springfield, and his widow died June 25, 1855, in Logan county, Illinois.

WIKOFF, WILLIAM W., born March 23, 1808, in Monmouth county, New Jersey. His parents moved to Warren county, Ohio, in 1810. He was there married Dec. 24, 1829, to Sarah C. Sinnard, who was born in the same county Oct. 5, 1810. They moved to Sangamon county, Ill., arriving June 19, 1837, on Richland creek, and in 1838 to Island Grove township, and in 1864 into what is now New Berlin township. They brought three children from Ohio, and had six in Sangamon county. Of their nine children—

ALBERT G., born Dec. 6, 1830, in Warren county, Ohio, married in Sangamon county, Dec. 14, 1854, to Ann E. Allen, who was born Dec. 14, 1837, in Morgan county, Illinois. They had five children. THOMAS J. died aged three years. CORDELIA K., DORA BELL, EDWIN A. and ALONZO H. live with their parents one and three-quarter miles southeast of Berlin, Sangamon county, Illinois—1874.

WILLIAM S., born Feb. 18, 1832, in Ohio, married in Sangamon county, Sept. 18, 1853, to Mary E. Allen. They have eight children, and live near Hamburg, Fremont county, Iowa.

ALONZO H., born Oct. 16, 1835, in Ohio, married Dec. 24, 1857, to Ella McDonnell, have four children, and live in Hamburg, Iowa.

CATHARINE F., born July 24, 1839, in Sangamon county, married Dec. 24, 1861, to Thomas W. Taylor, and resides in Berlin, Illinois.

PETER P., born Oct. 10, 1841, in Sangamon county, married May 20, 1872, to Mary A. Cox, and live in Hamburg, Iowa.

THOMAS J., born July 4, 1844, died May 10, 1864.

JOHN M., MARY M., and *MARTHA C.*, reside with their parents near New Berlin, Sangamon county, Illinois.

W. W. Wikoff was keeping tavern at Palmyra, now called Mason, Warren county, Ohio, at the time of the sudden change, Dec. 20, 1836. He remembers that the cold wave arrived there about nine o'clock P. M. When he came to Illinois and conversed with the people, he found that the change took place here about one o'clock P. M. It had taken about eight hours to travel 350 miles. *See sudden change, page 65.*

WYCKOFF, SAMUEL, born in 1781, in Loudon county, Virginia. He moved in company with his parents to Bourbon county, Kentucky, in 1808. He was there married in 1812 to Rebecca Darneille, who was born at Bryan Station, Kentucky, in 1787. They had seven children in Kentucky, and moved to Sangamon county, arriving Oct. 12, 1822, in what is now Chatham township, where two children were born. Of all their children:

JULIA A., born in 1813, married Stephen B. Neal. *See his name.*

JOHN THOMAS, born 1814, married 1837 to Sarah Shelton, who died, and he married Amanda Jacobs, and she died and he married Jane Foster. She died and he died in 1856, leaving one child.

SUSANNAH H., born July 7, 1815, married Washington Hall. *See his name.*

MAHALA J., born 1817, died aged twenty-seven years.

LORENA, born 1818 in Kentucky, married in Sangamon county to Allen Snyder. They have nine children, and live at Mowequa, Shelby county, Illinois.

BENJAMIN F., born July 19, 1819, married Delilah Harbour, had one child, and Mr. Wyckoff died August, 1843.

ASHER P., born Nov. 28, 1821, in Kentucky, married in Sangamon county, Oct. 15, 1840, to Sarah M. Gibson, who was born April 24, 1817, in Todd county, Kentucky, and came to Sangamon county with her mother in 1828. The mother died March 12, 1859, at Wyandotte, Kansas. Mr. and Mrs. W. had ten children, among them three pair of twins. Six of their children died under seven years of age. Of the other four, JOHN W. lives in Kansas. HENRY C. lives near Chatham, Illinois. They were both soldiers in an Illinois regiment. MARY A. married James Eaman, and lives in Ottawa, Kansas. WINFIELD S. was a soldier in an Iowa regiment. Asher P. Wyckoff and wife live in Kansas.

EMELINE, born in Sangamon county in 1824, married Henry Hall in 1843, and both died leaving five children, near Loami, Sangamon county, Illinois.

CHARLES H., born 1826, married Emeline Rude, and live in Cedar county, Missouri.

Samuel Wyckoff died March 18, 1850, and his widow in March, 1853, both near Chatham, Sangamon county, Illinois.

WILCOX, JOHN, was born in Maryland on the eastern shore of the Chesapeake Bay. His parents died when he was quite young, and to keep from being bound out, he ran away, embarked on a sailing vessel and went to the West India islands, returning to Maryland, and when he was sixteen or seventeen years old went with a family to Virginia, and from there to the vicinity of Danville, Kentucky. He was married in Oldham county, Kentucky, to Lucinda Oglesby. She was born in Loudon county, Virginia, and her parents moved to that part of Shelby which afterwards became Oldham county, Kentucky. Her father, William Oglesby, was a soldier in the Revolution. John Wilcox and his wife had two children in Oldham county, and moved to Davidson county, Tennessee, where one child was born, and then moved to Logan county, Kentucky, where eight children were born. In 1818, the family moved to St. Clair county, Illinois, and from there to what became Sangamon county, arriving in the fall of 1819, about six miles east of where Springfield now stands, and settled between the mouths of Sugar creek and the south fork of Sangamon river. Of their eleven children—

MAHALA, born in Kentucky and married Thomas Moore. They had three children, and she died August 18, 1855, and Thomas Moore died April 28, 1866, both near Berlin, Illinois.

STEPHEN, born in Kentucky, married in 1824 to Harriet Newell. They had eight children. He died March 22, 1858, and his widow lives with her youngest son, STEPHEN, near Blue Mound, Macon county, Illinois.

ELLIS, born in Davidson county, Tennessee, about 1790, married Feb. 24, 1824, in Simpson county, Kentucky, to Ann Lewis, who was born Dec. 21, 1800, in Pendleton district, South Carolina. They had two children in Kentucky, and moved to Sangamon county, Illinois, arriving in 1828, in Island Grove, where they had five living children, namely, LUCINDA, born February 15, 1825, in Simpson county, Kentucky, married in Sangamon county to Thomas Rhea. *See his name.* NERIAH L., born in Kentucky, died in Sangamon county, aged ten years. THOMAS, born June 28, 1831, in Sangamon county, married Catharine Ruble. They have eight children, CHARLES L., ALBERT N., BENJAMIN F., MARY A., WALLACE B., FRANCIS, CLARENCE and RUTH S., and live in Morgan county, six miles west of Berlin, Sangamon county, Illinois. JOHN F., born Feb. 12, 1836, in Sangamon county, married July 24, 1863, to Mary A. Rhea, had one child which died in infancy, and Mrs. Wilcox died May 16, 1865. He was married August 7, 1866, to Fanny Scott. They have three children, IVY GALE, N. ELLIS and NELLIE, and live three-quarters of a mile northwest of Loami, Illinois. CHARLES H., born May 19, 1838, married Sept. 11, 1864, to Caroline Caruthers, have two children, and lives with his father. SAMUEL M. died Jan. 29, 1863, in the twenty-third year of his age. JOSIAH L., born Nov. 26, 1844, in Sangamon county, married May, 1861, to Alice V. Parker. They had one child, JOE A., and Mrs. Wilcox died Jan. 29, 1862. Dr. Joe L. Wilcox was appointed, May 19, 1862, second assistant surgeon of the 11th Ill. Cav., was promoted May 19, 1863, to first assistant surgeon, served to the end of the rebellion, when he was mustered out with his regiment, October, 1865. He was married Nov. 9, 1865, to Jean F. Patteson. They have three children, DWIGHT, AUGUSTUS P. and ANNIE. Dr. Wilcox was elected, November, 1874, as one of the representatives of Sangamon county in the twenty-ninth general assembly of Illinois, and is a practicing physician at Loami, Sangamon county, Illinois. Ellis Wilcox and wife now—1876—reside where they settled in 1829. It is five miles west of Berlin, Sangamon county, Illinois.

MARTHA died in her fourteenth year.

EDITH, born in Kentucky, married in Sangamon county to Duke Chilton, and died, leaving her husband and two children at Oneco, Stephenson county, Illinois.

ELIZABETH died, aged twenty-two years.

NANCY married Andrew Stice, and died August, 1871, leaving her husband and four children at Jacksonville, Illinois.

ELIZA married William Oglesby and died in 1843, leaving two sons, JOSEPH and STEPHEN, near Belleville, Illinois.

WILLIAM, born August 9, 1813, in Logan county, Kentucky, raised in Sangamon county, was a soldier in the Blackhawk war, married Nov. 8, 1835, in Oldham county, Kentucky, to Nancy Ellis, had five children, and Mrs. Wilcox died Oct. 2, 1852, leaving two children, ELLIS O. and GEORGE W. He was married Nov. 9, 1856, to Mary Wilbourne. They have two children, CHARLOTTE and WILLIAM BEN. E., and reside three miles west of Berlin, Sangamon county, Illinois.

JOSHUA, born in Kentucky, raised in Sangamon county, married twice, and lives west of Berlin, Illinois.

FRANCES is unmarried and lives with her brother-in-law, Stice, at Jacksonville, Illinois.

John Wilcox died about 1823, and his widow died in 1842, both in Sangamon county, Illinois.

WILCOCKSON, WILLIAM, born August 8, 1789, in Rowan county, North Carolina. Mary England, sister to Rev. Stephen England, was born March 14, 1786, in Virginia. Her parents moved to Bath county, Kentucky, when she was quite young. William Wilcockson and Mary England were there married, had seven children, and moved to Sangamon county, Illinois, in the fall of 1821, in company with their son-in-law, George Power. They settled in what is now Fancy creek township, where two children were born. Of their children—

DAVID died in Kentucky, aged seven years.

NANCY, born June 13, 1804, in Bath county, Kentucky, married there to Geo. Power. *See his name.*

MELINDA, born in Kentucky, was twice married, is now a widow, Gibson, and resides in Woodford county, Illinois.

JOHN married Caroline Spears. He died leaving a widow and nine children in Christian county, Illinois.

STEPHEN E., born in Bath county, Kentucky, married in Sangamon county to Mary J. Lake. They have eight children, BAYLESS L., LUCY J., ELIZA A., EMELINE F., CHARLES H., JAMES E., ELIZABETH C. and JOHN S. The second and third are married, and reside in Henry county, Missouri. All the others reside with their parents near Elkhart, Illinois.

LUCY married Hiram Powell, and both died without children.

ELLEN married John Morgan, had twelve children, and lives in Iowa.

WILLIAM B., born Oct. 15, 1822, in Sangamon county, married September, 1848, to Clarinda Claypool, who was born Nov. 17, 1823, in Champaign county, Ohio. They had four children, and Mr. Wilcockson died very suddenly, April 26, 1856, near Athens, Illinois. Of their children, LEVI C. lives with his mother and manages the farm. THOMAS R., is a student at Ann Arbor, Michigan—1874—with the intention of making the law his profession. JOHN W. and MARY E. reside with their mother, two miles north of Cantrall, Sangamon county, Illinois.

GEORGE H., born in Sangamon county, married Susan Brown. They had seven children, and live in Lawrence county, Missouri.

Mrs. Mary Wilcockson died August 10, 1860, and William Wilcockson died July 24, 1864, both in Fancy creek township, Sangamon county, Illinois.

WILEY. The origin of the family in America was through a man of that name who lived and died in the county of Armagh, Ireland. His first name is not preserved. It is not certainly known, but believed by his descendants, that he was a native of Scotland. He possessed considerable property, and died early in life, leaving as the executor of his will a brother, who defrauded the children of their property. Five of the children—probably all there were—emigrated to New York city in 1734 or '35. One of his sons, who, it is thought, bore the name of Alexander, was born in 1711 in county Armagh, Ireland, married in New York city to Jane Bell. They had ten children, five of whom, two sons and three daughters, grew to be men and women. Their eldest son, Alexander, born Feb. 6, 1745, in New York, was eleven years old when his father died, about 1756, one year after Braddock's defeat. He was apprenticed by his sister Elizabeth—older than himself—to a tailor, and continued in that business thirty years. He married Elizabeth Carr, who was born May 19, 1752. They had ten children. He died Feb. 29, 1824, and she died Dec. 23, 1834. The eldest child, Alexander C., born June 22, 1770, in New York city, married August 27, 1795, to Sarah Coe, who was born Dec. 9, 1774. They had ten children, six sons and four daughters. Their daughter Sarah, born Nov. 24, 1802, married July 4, 1824, to Jonathan Mottashed, in New York city. He died there April 1, 1832, and she married William W. Watson. *See his name.* They had a son, Alexander Wiley, also, but he never came west. Their son—

WILEY, EDMUND. R., born Feb. 18, 1808, in New York city, was married there August 3, 1830, to Catharine Beach. They had three children in New York, and came to Springfield, Illinois, in 1835, where six children were born. Of all their living children—

FRANCES, born July 29, 1831, in New York, resides with her mother.

EDMUND R., *Jun.*, born June 20, 1833, in New York, read law in Springfield, Illinois, and was admitted to the bar. He practiced his profession in Decatur for a short time and returned to Springfield. In 1861 he was appointed adjutant of the 62d Ill. Inf, and served one year. He was major of 61st (colored) Inf. for sixteen months, lieutenant colonel of 3d Colored Heavy Art. about six months, and colonel of the 88th (colored) Inf. one year. Colonel Wiley was clerk of Arkansas county from Nov. 5, 1867, to Oct. 7, 1871, represented said county in the state legislature of 1871 and '72, was elected sheriff in the autumn of 1872, and served until October, 1874. Colonel E. R. Wiley was married in Dewitt, Arkansas, Sept. 29, 1868, to Ladora E. Rice, who was born Oct. 3, 1852, at Springfield, Conway county, Arkansas. They have four children, ALFRED R., ANDREW E., CATHARINE and DORA E., who reside with their parents. E. R. Wiley is a farmer, and lived in Dewitt, Arkansas, until 1876, when he moved to Danville, Illinois.

MARY A. resides with her mother.

AMELIA, born Jan. 17, 1837, in Springfield, Illinois, was married there May 3, 1866, to George White, who was born July 2, 1840, in Pottsdam, New York, and came to Springfield, Illinois, in 1865. They have three children, EDMUND R., GEORGE F. and HOWARD W., and reside in Springfield, Illinois.

ALEXANDER C. born Nov. 9, 1838, in Springfield, enlisted in Co. G, 114th Ill. Inf., was in the siege of Vicksburg, served seventeen months and was appointed lieutenant of Co. E, 61st United States Colored Infantry. He was in the battle of Tupello, Mississippi, served nine months and was honorably discharged Oct. 5, 1864, at Washington, D. C. Lieutenant Wiley was deputy circuit clerk of Arkansas county for six years. He was married April 17, 1871, in DeWitt, Arkansas, to Jennie Quertermous, who was born in Hardin county, Kentucky. They have two children, ROBERT E. and FREDERICK H., who reside with their parents in DeWitt, Arkansas county, Arkansas.

RICHARD B., born Jan. 15, 1841, in Springfield, Illinois, enlisted in an Illinois regiment during the rebellion; is distinguished for his musical talent, and is organist in the Chestnut street Presbyterian church, Louisville, Kentucky.

NETTIE, born in 1844, in Springfield, Illinois, is unmarried, and resides with her mother.

ALFRED, born Sept. 7, 1848, in Springfield, Illinois, was married near Williamette, Arkansas, Sept. 7, 1876, to Pattie M. Hubbard, daughter of Dr. B.

C. Hubbard. Alfred Wiley was a farmer and lived near DeWitt, Arkansas until 1876, when he moved to Starr City, Lincoln county, Arkansas, and engaged in the practice of law.

Edmund R. Wiley, Sen., was in the clothing business in Springfield, until his death, which occurred July 19, 1864. His widow and daughters live in Springfield, Illinois.

WILLARD, ALEXANDER P., born April 8, 1815, in Vernon, Oneida county, New York. He was married June 3, 1837, in Chemung county, in the same state to Louisa L. Higgie. They came the same year to Springfield, Illinois, where they had two children, one of whom died young.

LUCY E., was born March, 1839, in Springfield, married in her native city to William D. Richardson. They have two children and reside in Springfield, Illinois. Mr. Richardson at the time of his marriage was engaged in railroading. After that he became a contractor and builder. Among his largest contracts was the brickwork on the Macoupin county court house, the entire work of building the national Lincoln monument, and the greater part of the brick and stone work on the new state house of Illinois, on which he has been engaged from 1871 to the present time—November, 1876.

Alexander P. Willard was in partnership for a short time after coming to Springfield with E. G. Johns. In 1841 he formed a partnership with Robert B. Zimmerman. *See his name.* They continued in the business of painters and glaziers, and dealers in materials connected with their business until the death of Mr. Willard, which occurred very suddenly, May 5, 1865, in Springfield. Mrs. Willard resides with her daughter, Mrs. Richardson, in Springfield, Illinois.

WILLIAMS, EDWARD, was born June 3, 1789, in Hardin county, Kentucky. Margaret Neal was born April, 1788, in Nelson county, Kentucky. The places of their birth were only about six miles apart, and the parents of both moved when they were children to Ohio county, where they were married about 1806. They had five children in Kentucky, and moved to Sangamon county, Illinois, arriving December, 1826, in what is now Gardner township, where two children were born, one died young. Of their six children—

NANCY C., born April 4, 1808, in Kentucky, married Dec. 19, 1872, in Sangamon county to Christopher Atterberry, and lives in Menard county, Illinois.

SAMUEL N., born in 1810 in Kentucky, married Margaret Martin, and she died. He married Mrs. Margaret D. Ralston, whose maiden name was Peak. They had four living children. Mr. W. died Jan. 9, 1866, and his family lives in Edinburg, Illinois.

CHARLES M., born April 8, 1815, was helpless from youth, and died at fifty-two years of age.

JOHN F., born in 1818, married Elizabeth J. Pierce. They have six children, and reside near Taylorville, Illinois.

EDWARD L., born in 1824, in Kentucky, married Susan H. Pearce in Sangamon county, and had four children. The parents and three of the children died. Their only living child, REBECCA A., married Samuel Cully, has one son, and lives near Taylorville, Illinois.

STEPHEN W., born Feb. 9, 1827, in Sangamon county, married July 25, 1850, to Abigail J. Fry, who was born July 22, 1827, in Smith county, Tennessee. They had two children, EDWARD H. and NANCY J., and Mrs. W. died Nov. 8, 1857. He was married June 30, 1859, to Elcy Davidson. They have five living children, JOHN D., MARY M., MICAJAH, FRANCES M. and MARTHA A., and reside in Christian county, near Pawnee, Sangamon county, Illinois.

Mrs. Margaret Williams died April 2, 1859, and Edward Williams died June 29, 1871, both in Gardner township, Sangamon county, Illinois.

WILLIAMS, ELIAS, born Feb. 27, 1770, near Clarendon, Vermont, was married in that state to Mary Boynton, who was born July 19, 1773, at Plymouth, Windsor county, Vermont. They had four children there, and the family moved to Essex county, New York, about 1804, where two children were born, thence to Hamilton county, Ohio, where one child was born, and from there to Butler county, in the same state, where three children were born. In 1819 the family moved to Wayne or Henry county, Indiana, and from there to Sangamon county, Illinois, arriving in February, 1822, in what is now Cotton Hill township, and the next spring into what is now Rochester township. Of their children—

POLLY and LYDIA died under four years.

SAMUEL, born April 24, 1800, in Windsor county, Vermont, came to Sangamon county, Illinois, before the family arrived in the autumn of 1821, and was married April 5, 1832, to Jane L. Trotter. They had five children in Sangamon county, NANCY T., born Feb. 26, 1833, married Henry P. Clark. *See his name.* JANE L., born June 1, 1835, married Charles F. Humphreys. *See his name.* ELIZA, born Feb. 12, 1837, and HENRY H., born July 30, 1840. The two latter live with their father. WILLIAM T. died in his second year. Mrs. Jane L. Williams died Oct. 11, 1865, and Samuel Williams lives one and a half miles southeast of Rochester, Sangamon county, Illinois. Mr. Williams became a member of the Christian church, June 29, 1817, in Ohio, and when he came to Sangamon county, there being no church of his own denomination, he united with the Methodists, with the understanding that he should sever the connection when a suitable time came for organizing one of his own. He united with others in 1832 in consituting the South Fork Christian church. About that time he commenced preaching, and has continued to do so to the present time. He has received between one and two hundred persons into the church, and has baptized about five hundred, including his assisting other ministers. He has probably married one hundred couple, and taught school in Rochester, Illinois, between the years 1831 and 1837.

ELIAS, Jun., born Feb. 15, 1802, in Vermont, was married in Sangamon county, in 1831, to Polly Baker, daughter of Isaac. They had eleven or twelve children, and moved to Kansas, thence to the vicinity of Nashville, Barton county, Missouri, where they now live.

JOSEPH, born Oct. 2, 1804, in Essex county, New York, was married in Sangamon county, Illinois, to Judith Delay. They had two children, who both died young. Joseph Williams died Oct. 14, 1850. His widow lives in Cotton Hill township.

MARY, born Dec. 18, 1806, in Essex county, New York, was married in Sangamon county in 1824 to Richard E. Barker. They had one child, ELIAS, who married Dorothy Bound. He died in March, 1873. His widow and children live near Clarksville, Illinois. R. E. Barker died and his widow married Andrew Johnson. *See his name.* He died and she married Greenberry Baker. *See his name.*

ISIAH BOYNTON, born June 20, 1810, in Hamilton county, Ohio, was married in Sangamon county April 1, 1833, to Phebe Baker. They had eleven children, two died under five years. SUSAN, born Jan. 19, 1834, in Sangamon county, was married Nov. 10, 1853, to George W. Whitecraft, who was born Sept. 26, 1830, in Bath county, Kentucky, and brought by his parents, in 1835, to what is now Christian county, Illinois. In 1873 he moved to Springfield, where he now resides. MARY married James Martin. *See his name.* JAMES H. married Caroline Hedrick. They have three children, and live near Taylorville, Ill. HARRIET married George Boyd. They had two children, and live near Taylorville, Illinois. MARTHA married A. M. Council, has two children, and lives near Edinburg, Illinois. AMOS S. married Jane Hatler. They have one child, and live in Cotton Hill township. SANFORD, EDWARD and ABRAHAM L. live with their parents in Cotton Hill township, east of New City, Sangamon county, Illinois.

SUSANNAH, born March 2, 1815, in Hamilton county, Ohio, died in Sangamon county, April 12, 1834.

AMOS, born May 10, 1818, in Butler county, Ohio, was married in Sangamon county to Caroline Dearborn. They had two children. ELIAS enlisted in the 16th Ill. Cav., in 1862, for three years, and was captured at Cumberland Gap. He was several months in Andersonville prison, was exchanged, and died a few days later. ISAIAH B. married and lives in Cincinnati, Appanoose county, Iowa. Amos Williams went to California and died there in March, 1850. His widow lives with her son, Isaiah B., in Iowa.

Mrs. Mary Williams died May 15, 1850, and Elias Williams died August 25, 1853, both in Sangamon county, Illinois.

WILLIAMS, JAMES M., was born April 30, 1810, in Rutherford

county, North Carolina. He is a nephew of Andrew Elliott. He came to Sangamon county in company with Terry Bradley, arriving at Springfield, Oct. 13, 1834. He was married October, 1851, to Mary Reford. They had six children in Sangamon county.

MARY E. married Luther Jones, has two children, CHARLES and MINNIE F., and live near Salisbury, Sangamon county, Illinois.

ELLEN J., married May 23, 1872, to William F. Irwin. *See his name.*

CHARLES HENRY, lives with his father.

JAMES A., died aged fourteen years.
MARY A. died aged eight years.
MARTHA died aged two years.

Mrs. Mary Williams died Nov. 28, 1866, and J. M. Williams lives northeast of the Sangamon river, in Salisbury township.

Mr. W. went hunting soon after coming to the county, lost his way, and was escorted to camp about nine o'clock P. M. by a pack of howling wolves.

WILLIAMS, JOHN, was born Sept. 11, 1808, in Bath county, Kentucky. His ancestors came from Wales and settled in Greenbrier county, Virginia. James Williams was born in that county and married Hannah Moppin, who was born in 1776, near Pittsburgh, Pennsylvania, of Scotch-Irish parents, who were Presbyterians. James Williams moved to Bath county, Kentucky, and after partly raising his family, moved to that part of Sangamon which is now Menard county, Illinois, arriving in 1823. James Williams and wife lived and died in Menard county. Their son, John, whose name heads this sketch, attended school in a log school house during the winter, and in the summer labored on his father's farm until 1822, when he obtained a situation in a store in Owensville, Kentucky. At the end of two years he came with some of his father's former neighbors to Illinois, and after spending two weeks with his parents he came to Springfield, Oct. 11, 1824, and entered into an agreement to clerk for one year in the store of Major Elijah Iles for ten dollars per month. At the end of the year Mr. Iles gave him $150, being thirty more than the contract called for. His salary was raised to $200 and board, which was continued without change for five years. At the end of that time his savings amounted to three hundred dollars. Mr. Iles, wishing to retire from business, offered to sell his stock to Mr. Williams, and give him one year's time without interest. Mr. Williams preferred dividing it into four equal payments. Having previously visited St. Louis, on business for Mr. Iles, he became acquainted with the wholesale merchants there, which he afterwards found to be quite advantageous. That, with his three hundred dollars, enabled him to keep up his stock. By honorable dealing he retained all the former patrons of Mr. Iles, and met every payment promptly.

John Williams was married March 31, 1840, in Springfield, to Lydia Porter, who was born August 28, 1821, in Lima, Livingston county, New York. The wife of Major Iles was her half sister. Mr. and Mrs. Williams had six children in Springfield, all now living, namely—

LOUISA ILES, ALBERT PORTER, JOHN EDWARD, JULIA JAYNE, GEORGE and *HENRY CARTER.*

LOUISA I., born Dec. 22, 1840, was married in her native city, in 1859, to George N. Black, who was born March 15, 1833, in Lee, Berkshire county, Mass. Mr. and Mrs. Black have three children, and reside in Springfield, Illinois.

George N. Black came to Springfield in October, 1850, and engaged to clerk for Colonel John Williams at fifteen dollars per month, and board himself. In 1856 he was admitted as a partner in the firm of John Williams & Co., dry goods merchants, and has continued to the present time. In addition to his mercantile business, Mr. Black has been one of the most persistent and efficient workers in originating and prosecuting enterprises calculated to advance the interests of Springfield. Among the enterprises in which he has taken an active part, was the organization of the Leland hotel company; the Pana, Springfield and Northwestern railroad company, of which he became a director and secretary. That became part of the S. & I. S. E., and is now part of the O. & M. railroad. He was one of the projectors of the G., C. & S. railroad, and was one-tenth owner of the same. He was one of the principal movers in the Springfield and Northwestern railroad, and in 1875 was appointed receiver of the same. He is now—November, 1876—in charge of the road. He is one of the principal stockholders of the First National Bank, and was cashier during the first year of its existence. He was one of the stockholders who organized the Springfield City railway company, March 3, 1866; was elected treasurer, and continues to hold that office to the present time. He was one of the original movers in the Springfield Watch company, organized Jan. 26, 1870, and was elected treasurer of the same, etc., etc.

JULIA JAYNE was married in her native city to Alfred Orendorff. *See his name, in the Omissions.*

Colonel John Williams was nominated as a candidate for congress in 1856, and supported by the combined influence of the remnant of the old Whig party, under Fillmore, and of the newly organized Republican party, under Fremont; but was defeated, as he expected to be, his object being to strengthen the state ticket, with Governor Bissell at its head. He was for six years treasurer of the Illinois State Agricultural Society. In 1857 he became treasurer of the Illinois Stock Importing company, for the introduction of blooded stock. At the outbreak of the rebellion, Colonel Williams was appointed, by Governor Yates, commissary general of Illinois, and discharged the duties of that trust for years. He was appointed, by President Lincoln, disbursing agent of the United States government during the building of the United States court house and postoffice at Springfield. About three hundred and twenty thousand dollars passed through his hands in connection with that trust. After the death of President Lincoln, Mr. Williams was appointed one of the escort. He at once proceeded to Washington and accompanied the remains to Springfield. He was one of the original members of the National Lincoln Monument Association, and is now a member of its executive committee. He has been identified with the building of all the railroads to Springfield, but more particularly with the Gilman, Clinton and Springfield, and the Springfield and Northwestern railroads, the latter of which was built mainly through his exertions. He is now president of the Barclay coal mining company, and also owns and operates a farm of over one thousand acres, near Indian Point, Menard county, Illinois.

He commenced private banking in connection with his store, by his customers depositing with him. The business grew gradually for several years. When the national banking law was enacted he united with others in organizing the First National Bank of Springfield, Dec. 12, 1863, and opened its doors for business May 1, 1864. He became president of the bank at its organization and continued in that office ten years. For more than fifty-two years he has been in the mercantile business in Springfield, and is now in his sixty-ninth year, still at the head of the mercantile firm of John Williams & Co. He has for many years been a member of the First Presbyterian church of Springfield, Illinois.

WILLIAMS, JOSEPH, a younger brother to Colonel John Williams, was born in Bath county, Kentucky, and with his parents came to Sangamon county, Illinois, in 1823. After his brother John went into business on his own account, he entered his store as a clerk, and a few years later went into the mercantile business for himself at Decatur, Illinois. He was married Nov. 10, 1836, in Springfield to Huldah Francis. *See Francis family sketch.* They had six sons, and Mrs. Williams died Dec. 10, 1848, in Menard county. Mr. Williams, with his sons, started April 3, 1851, overland for Oregon, and arrived there late in the fall. While exploring the country in May, 1853, he was killed by the Rogue river Indians in Oregon. His children were all brought back to Springfield by their uncle, Colonel John Williams. Of the six—

JAMES E., born July 8, 1838, in Springfield, Illinois, was married August 8, 1865, to Roscia King. They have three children, JOSEPH, FRANCIS and MATILDA. They lived at Irish Grove, Menard county, Illinois, until 1876, when they moved to Maryville, Nodaway county, Missouri.

JEREMIAH H., born Nov. 14, 1839, in Decatur, Illinois, was married Sept. 6, 1866, to Cynthia Scott. They have two children, SAMUEL and JOHN. Mr. Williams is a stock raiser, and resides near Sweet Water postoffice, Menard county, Illinois.

SIMEON F., born July 12, 1841, in Menard county, Illinois, and after the death of both his parents he went to live with his uncle, Charles Francis, at Laporte, Indiana. He enlisted in 1861 in the 20th Ind. Inf., and died April 17, 1863, at Laporte, of disease contracted in the army.

WILLIAM BUCK, born May 29, 1843, in Menard county, Illinois, was married Nov. 1, 1870, to Ann M. Whitney. They have two children, ANNIE I. and WILLIAM H. W. B. Williams was engaged in farming and stock raising near Middletown, Logan county, Illinois, until March, 1876, when he moved to Maryville, Nodaway county, Missouri.

NEWTON A., born Oct. 17, 1845, in Menard county, Illinois. He was married Oct. 17, 1871, to Mary C. Cox. They have two children, CHARLES and LYDIA, and reside near Maryville, Missouri.

JOHN C., born Dec. 28, 1846, in Menard county, Illinois. He is a shipper and resides at Indian Point, Sweet Water post office, Menard county, Illinois.

WILLIAN, THOMAS, was born Feb. 21, 1797, in Kent county, Delaware. When he was two years old his parents moved to Green county, Kentucky. He was there married March 18, 1819, to Mary Crowder. They had two children in Kentucky, and moved to Sangamon county, Illinois, arriving late in 1829, first stopping where the family of Hon. Jesse K. Dubois now resides, west of Springfield. He entered land on Horse creek, in what is now Cotton Hill township, and moved on it in 1831. They had three children in Sangamon county. Of their five children—

MATILDA J., born Dec. 21, 1819, in Green county, Kentucky, was married in Sangamon county to Jackson Stout. See his name. He died, and she was married May 10, 1842, to Samuel Haines. See his name.

WILLIAM C., born Jan. 4, 1822, in Green county, Kentucky, was married Oct. 27, 1858, in Sangamon county, Illinois, to Samantha C. Chapman, who was born July 5, 1828, at Elsworth, Trumbull county, Ohio. William C. Willian died Feb. 19, 1875, and Mrs. Samantha C. Willian died April 1, 1875, both in Cotton Hill township, Sangamon county, Illinois. They left an adopted son, EDWARD L. WILLIAN, who lives in Cotton Hill township.

SARAH A., born August 29, 1833, in Sangamon county, married William H. Vigal. See his name.

NANCY J., born March 4, 1837, in Sangamon county, was married Sept. 12, 1861, to Walter J. Barnes. They have five children, namely, LOUIS M., CAREY E., THOMAS W., WILLIAM J. and MARY O. W. J. Barnes and family reside near Edinburg, Christian county, Illinois.

THOMAS J., born June 25, 1840, in Sangamon county, Illinois, enlisted April, 1861, in Co. G, 7th Ill. Inf., for three months, on the first call for 75,000 men, and served full time. He re-enlisted August, 1862, for three years in Co. K, 124th Ill. Inf., and was commissioned first lieutenant at the organization of the company. He was taken sick at Camp Butler, and died in Cotton Hill township, Nov. 5, 1862.

Mrs. Mary Willian died July 29, 1856, and Thomas J. Willian married Sarah Lambert. They have one child.

CHARLES ALBERT was born Oct. 7, 1861, in Sangamon county, resides with his sister, Mrs. Barnes, near Edinburg, Christian county, Illinois.

Mrs. Sarah Willian died Oct. 30, 1868, in Christian county, Illinois, and Thomas Willian lives with his daughter, Mrs. Barnes, near Edinburg, Christian county, Illinois.

Day Willian, the father of Thomas Willian, and Day Willian's brother, John, came to Sangamon county with their families about 1829, remained a year or two, became dissatisfied and returned to Kentucky.

WILLIS, Mrs. HENRIETTA, whose maiden name was Earnest, a sister to Jacob and Thomas Earnest. She was born Sept. 15, 1783, in South Carolina, and married in Simpson county, Kentucky, to William Willis. They had seven children, and Mr. Willis died in Kentucky. Mrs. Willis, with her children, came to Sangamon county about 1825. Of her children—

RICHARD, spent ten or twelve years in Sangamon county, and went to Iowa. He left there in 1849 or '50, and was last heard from in California.

ELIZABETH, born in Simpson

county, Kentucky, married William Simpson. *See his name.*

STARLING, born in Kentucky, married in Sangamon county to Sarah Halliday, had children, moved to Knox county, Illinois, and from there to Oregon.

WILLIAM went from Sangamon county to Wisconsin, married there, and died from injuries by a threshing machine.

MARTHA married in Sangamon county to Samuel Jones, moved to Knox county, had three children and he died. She married Benjamin Sims, and she died.

THOMAS went from Sangamon county to Iowa on business, and died there.

DRUCILLA, born in Kentucky, married in Sangamon county to Asher Simpson. They have eight children, and reside near Clinton, Dewitt county, Illinois.

Mrs. Henrietta Willis died August 10, 1846, in Sangamon county, Illinois.

WILLIS WILLIAM, was born Sept. 23, 1775, in North Carolina. His father, Jacob Willis, was born in Wales, but whether he was married before or after coming to America is not known to his descendants. He enlisted in the Revolutionary army and was killed in battle about 1780, leaving a widow and the son, whose name heads this sketch. His widow married James Phillips, and about the year 1783 moved to the vicinity of Crab Orchard, Kentucky, taking William with them. He grew to manhood there, and then went to Adair county, Kentucky, where he was married to Elizabeth Steel. They had eight children, and Mrs. Willis died October, 1822. Mr. Willis was married to Martha Morrison. They had three children, and moved to Sangamon county, Illinois, arriving in the fall of 1830 in what is now Gardner township. He brought all his children except the three eldest sons. Of all his children—

HENRY, born April 20, 1803, in Kentucky, married June 7, 1825, to Rhoda Cooley, had six children, and came to Sangamon county in the fall of 1836. He moved back to Kentucky one year later, had three children there, and all returned to Sangamon county in 1848, except their only daughter, who died young. Of their eight sons, JACOB married, and he and his wife died, leaving a son, now in Texas. JOHN married, has five children, and lives in DeWitt county, Ill. GEORGE W. went to California in 1852, and has not been heard of in eight years. WILLIAM T., born Feb. 6, 1834, enlisted August, 1862, in Co. B, 114th Ill. Inf., for three years, was wounded at the battle of Guntown, Mississippi, June 10, 1864, and died ten days later. EDMOND, born Nov. 18, 1835 married June 7, 1869, to Ellen M. Pitcher, have two children, ADAM F. and CARLOS E., and live near Salisbury, Illinois. JAMES D., born June 10, 1838, enlisted in Co. D, 33d Ill. Inf., August, 1861, for three years, served full term, re-enlisted as a veteran in 1864, married Elizabeth Hall, and died on shipboard May 15, 1865, between Mobile and New Orleans. ADAM C., born Jan. 10, 1840, enlisted August, 1861, in Co. D, 33d Ill. Inf., for three years, served full term, re-enlisted as a veteran January, 1864. He was wounded by a railroad accident near New Orleans, March 1, 1865, and died March 5, 1865. About three hundred Union soldiers were killed and wounded at the same time. PARKER H., born Nov. 19, 1842, married Mary A. R. Ward, have three children, and live in Salisbury township. Henry Willis and wife reside near Salisbury, Sangamon county, Illinois.

LAVINA, born March 31, 1805, married in Kentucky to John Cooley. They came to Sangamon county with her father and had eight children. Two of their sons, WILLIS and JOSEPH Cooley, were soldiers in the 114th Ill. Inf., and both died of disease in the army at Memphis, Tennessee. Three sons and three daughters, all married, live in Kansas. John Cooley died in Sangamon county, and his widow lives with her children in Kansas.

JACOB, born Jan. 24, 1807, in Adair county, Kentucky, married there Jan. 29, 1828, to Lucinda T. Barger, a sister to Rev. John S. Barger, of Bloomington, Illinois. She was born May 20, 1814, in West Virginia. They had two children in Kentucky, and they moved to Sangamon county, Illinois, arriving Oct. 8, 1833, in what is now Gardner township, between Richland and Prairie creeks, where they had seven children. Of their children, ANN E., born Nov. 4, 1829, married James R. Stone, have four children, and reside at Wichita, Kansas. JAMES S. B., born July 9, 1833, in Kentucky, married in Sangamon county to Mary A. Campbell. They have four children, and live near Clinton, Illinois. SARAH E., born May 30, 1835, married Jason Miller. *See his name.* FRANCIS M., born Oct. 30, 1837, married Milicent Ann Turner, have two children, and live at Wapella, DeWitt county, Illinois. JOHN W., born July 10, 1842, married Danelia W. Sayre, have two children, and live near Wapella, Illinois. LAURA B., born Feb. 9, 1844, married William B. Capron, have three children, and live near Wapella, Illinois. MARY A., born Oct. 9, 1846, married Henry C. Porter, have three children, and live near Clinton, Illinois. VINCENT H., born Oct. 9, 1846, married Helen M. Wadleigh. He is a traveling preacher in the M. E. church, and was on Twin Grove circuit, near Bloomington, in 1873. ELBERT F., born Jan. 15, 1851, married Oct. 8, 1872, to Laura A. Jameson, have one child, and live in Gardner township. Mrs. Lucinda T. Willis died Oct. 20, 1866, and Jacob Willis was married June 29, 1869, to Mrs. Charlotte R. Laborence, who was previously Mrs. Capron, and whose maiden name was Dodge. She was born April 7, 1814, at Albany, New York, and came to Sangamon county in 1854. She had three children by her first marriage, and five by her second. Of her children, CATHARINE D. Capron married Jacob Perlier, have six children, and lives near Wapella, Illinois. WILLIAM D. Capron married Laura B. Willis, and resides near Wapella. CHARLES S. Capron married Mary Batterton, and lives near Palmer, Illinois. RACHEL Laborence married Oliver Ross. *See his name.* CHARLOTTE D. married Edward East. They had one child, and Mrs. Charlotte D. East died Jan. 2, 1874, in Bates county, Missouri, and her remains were brought to Salisbury, Illinois, and buried there. John A. Laborance lives at Colorado Springs, California. Laura W. married David East, and lives in Missouri, near Metz, Kansas. Annie E. Laborance was married Feb. 17, 1875, to Charles V. Durgy, and lives ten miles south of Bloomington, Illinois.

Jacob Willis died March 31, 1876, and his widow lives at the homestead near where Mr. Willis' father settled in 1833, in Gardner township, near Cross Plains post office, Sangamon county, Illinois.

WILLIAM, Jun., born May 22, 1809, married Melinda Thurman. They had seven children, and she died March 24, 1852, and he married Tasty Daniels. They had ten children, and he died. The family reside in Logan county. William Willis, Jun., has but one child living in Sangamon county, namely, NANCY J., by the first wife, married Asa W. Plunkett. *See his name.* His son, JOHN M. Willis was a soldier in Co. F, 114th Ill. Inf., and died at Memphis, Tennessee.

ELIZABETH, born Oct. 27, 1812, married James M. Brown. *See his name.*

CLARISSA, born Dec. 28, 1814, married Lewis Campbell. They have eight children. Their daughter LEAH married John Slater. *See his name.* Lewis Campbell and family live near Athens, Menard county, Illinois.

JOHN, born Jan. 5, 1818, married Caroline Pierce, had eight children, and lives near Kirksville, Wapello county, Iowa.

NANCY, born Nov. 20, 1820, married C. R. Pierce, have ten children, and lives at Greenview, Menard county, Illinois.

MARY, born May 3, 1824, married Joseph Staklin, and she died at Beardstown, Illinois, in 1846.

JANE, born July 19, 1825, married Archie Town, have five children, and live near Lincoln, Logan county, Illinois.

PARTHENIA, born April 15, 1827, married John Moore, have three living children, and live at Wichita, Kansas.

MARIA MORRISON, step daughter to William Willis, Sen., married in Kentucky to William Ross. *See his name.*

Mrs. Martha Willis died in 1842, and William Willis, Sen., died July 9, 1866, both in Garden township, Sangamon county. He was ninety years, nine months and sixteen days old.

WILLS, JOHN Q. Benoni Bell married his daughter, and she died. Dr. Jones married another, and she died. Another daughter, Mrs. Inslee lives in Sangamon county.

WILSON, ROBERT L., was born Sept. 11, 1805, in Washington county, Pennsylvania. His parents were Scotch-Irish, their ancestors having emigrated from Scotland and settled near the city of Belfast, soon after the conquest of Ireland by Oliver Cromwell in the sixteenth century. In 1778 they sailed for America, settling in York county, Pennsylvania,

In 1782 they moved to Washington county, Pennsylvania, on pack horses, as there had not then been any roads made across the Allegheny mountains. From Washington county, where the subject of our sketch was born, the family moved in 1810 to the vicinity of Zanesville, Ohio, where his father died in 1821, and Robert L., then sixteen years of age, determined to educate himself. He first qualified himself for teaching a country school, and taught until he laid up some money with which he entered Franklin College, Ohio. He sustained himself during his college course in the same way, and graduated in four years. In the fall of 1831 he went to Kentucky, where he taught an academy and studied law. He was married March 28, 1833, in Sharpsburg, Bath county, Kentucky, to Eliza J. Kincaid, and admitted to the bar as an attorney at law. They soon after moved to Sangamon county, Illinois, arriving in the fall of 1833 at Athens. That not now being a part of Sangamon county, he would not properly be included as an early settler of this county, but his having been one of the "Long Nine" is a sufficient reason for including his sketch here. Mr. Wilson was elected in August, 1836, as one of the seven representatives of Sangamon county, who, with the two Senators, made up what was known as the "Long Nine" who served in the legislature of 1836 '37, and secured the removal of the capital of Illinois from Vandalia to Springfield. *See sketch "Long Nine."* He moved with his family from Sangamon county in 1840, to Sterling, Whiteside county, where they now reside. Mr. and Mrs. Wilson had six children.

MARY JANE died, aged seven years.
SILAS R. died, aged thirty-four years.
LEE died, aged seventeen years.
ANN ELIZA, born Dec. 20, 1841.
EMMA E., born Nov. 10, 1843.
ROBERT H. born Nov. 27, 1847.
The three latter in Sterling, Illinois, where they now reside.

Soon after Mr. Wilson moved to Sterling he was appointed clerk of the circuit court, to which office he was elected five times, serving continuously until Dec. 1, 1860. Eight years of that time he served as probate judge. He was in Washington, D. C., when Fort Sumter fell, and enlisted as a private in a battalion commanded by Cassius M. Clay, and called the Clay Guard. It numbered four hundred, mostly non-residents, and acted as night police, guarding the city at the most critical time in its history. As soon as the New York 7th regiment reached Washington, the Clay Guard was relieved and mustered out. Mr. Wilson returned to Sterling, Illinois, and assisted in raising Co. A, 34th Ill. Inf., and was elected captain, but declined in favor of the first lieutenant. He started for Washington on the 4th of July, and called on President Lincoln on the 7th to tender his services in any capacity where he could be useful. Mr. Lincoln said he had made out a list of his old friends before leaving Springfield, that he might appoint them to office, and said, "I have appointed all down to your name. Now, what do you wish?" Mr. Wilson said he thought he could discharge the duties of quartermaster. Mr. Lincoln said, "I can do better than that for you," and made him paymaster. His appointment was made out on the 6th, and he was confirmed by the senate August 7, 1861. He was placed on duty at Washington City, and was soon after ordered to St. Louis. In the two succeeding years he paid out nearly four million dollars, principally in the west and south. After the fall of Vicksburg he was ordered to Springfield, Illinois, and promoted to the rank of colonel for meritorious services. He was mustered out Nov. 15, 1865. During his four years and four months service he received and disbursed about seven million dollars, to near one hundred thousand soldiers, without a shadow of suspicion against his character.

On the 10th of May, 1875, he started alone on a trip of observation and sight-seeing in Europe. He left New York on the steamer Rhein, one of the Bremen line. He arrived at Southampton May 20th, and in London the same day, where he spent one week visiting objects of interest. From London to Dover, crossing the Straits to Calais, France, thence by way of Bologne and Amiens to Paris, with its three millions of inhabitants. He spent three weeks in Paris, sight-seeing and gleaning knowledge from every source. From Paris he went by way of Fontainbleu up the river Seine, through Mount Cenis tunnel to Turin, Italy, and through Genoa, Pisa, Leghorn and other Italian cities to Rome, where he spent two weeks visiting objects of historic interest. From

Rome he went south to Naples, passed Appi Forum and the three taverns. He visited Mount Vesuvius, and looked into its crater of boiling lava. Spent one day each at Pompeii and Herculaneum, and returning to Rome, went to Florence, where he spent a few days. Crossed the Appenines to Venice, the city built two miles from the shore, in the Adriatic sea. Ascended the river Po, through Lombardy, and the city of Verona, to Milan. Crossed the Alps by way of the Simplon Pass, reaching an altitude of twelve thousand feet above the sea. Descended the river Rhone, and Lake Geneva to the city of Geneva and Berne, the capital of Switzerland. From there he returned to Paris, thence to London, where he spent two weeks more. Visited other parts of England, thence to Edinburg, Stirling and many points of interest in Scotland. Went through Ireland and Wales, thence to Liverpool. Sailed on the steamer Baltic to New York and home. He was four months out, at a total cost of seven hundred and fifty dollars.

Hon. Robert L. Wilson is now—1876—engaged in a work similar to this—that of writing a history of Whiteside county, Illinois.

WILSON, JOHN L., was born March 6, 1816, in Bedford county, Tenn. In the fall of that year his parents moved to White county, Illinois, and after that to Bond and Montgomery counties. John L. came to Mechanicsburg in 1839, and was married in Sangamon county, June 18, 1843, to Margaret Gragg. They had four children in Sangamon county.

JAMES N., born March 25, 1844, died in his sixth year.

JOHN W., born April 30, 1847, lives with his parents.

MARTHA, born Jan. 17, 1850, married Clifton H. King. *See his name.*

JASON, born Oct. 7, 1853, lives with his parents.

Elder John L. Wilson was ordained as a minister of the gospel by the Mechanicsburg congregation of the Christian Church in 1852. He served the church at Mechanicsburg half his time for the first two years, and the other half labored as an evangelist. For several years he has been wholly engaged as an evangelist, at the present time (1874) in Macon county. His family resides four and a half miles east of Mechanicsburg, Sangamon county, Illinois.

WILSON, SAMUEL M., was born Sept. 30, 1806, in Harford county, Maryland. He received his literary education at Jefferson College, Cannonsburgh, Pennsylvania, graduating there in 1831. He pursued his theological studies at Princeton College, New Jersey, and in April, 1836, was licensed to preach by the Presbytery of New Castle, Pennsylvania. In June, 1836, he took charge of the Presbyterian Church at Lithopolis, Fairfield county, Ohio, and was ordained by the Presbytery of Columbus, Ohio, in September, 1837. Jane Elder was born March 1, 1814, in Centre county, Pennsylvania. Rev. Samuel M. Wilson and Jane Elder were married Dec. 27, 1836, in Franklin county Ohio. They had seven children at Lithopolis, Ohio, and after a pastorate of twenty-two years over that church, moved to Clinton, Dewitt county, Illinois, in response to a call from the Presbyterian Church at that place. In August, 1858, Rev. Mr. Wilson received a unanimous call to the Centre Church in Sangamon county, Illinois. He accepted the call, removed thither and entered upon its duties. Of their children—

MARGARET E., born March 8, 1838, in Ohio, married in Sangamon county, September, 1859, to Rev. C. W. Finley, of New London, Ohio. She died March 15, 1861, while on a visit to her parents in Sangamon county.

ANDREW, born Oct. 1, 1839, in Ohio, married in Sangamon county, August 10, 1864, to Georgie K. Watts. They have four children, WILLIAM E., M. ANNIE, JENNIE and ANDREW, Jun., and reside at Kingsville, Shawnee county, Kansas—1874.

WILLIAM E., born May 28, 1841, in Ohio, died Feb. 17, 1866, from injuries received by an accident on the Toledo, Wabash and Western Railroad, at Meredosia, Illinois.

THOMAS and *MARTHA* reside with their father.

MARY J., died Dec. 6, 1848, in her fourth year.

JANE died Feb. 3, 1861, in her eleventh year.

Mrs. Jane E. Wilson died July 29, 1868, in Sangamon county, and Rev. Samuel M. Wilson resides three and a half miles south of Pleasant Plains, Sangamon county, Illinois.

The Society of Old Settlers of Sangamon County elected Rev. S. M. Wilson as president of the society at their annual meeting at Pleasant Plains August 29, 1873. He served one year and until his successor was chosen at Crow's Mill, in September, 1874. He thus became an old settler by brevet.

WILSON, SAMUEL, was born May 22, 1778, in Virginia. His parents moved to Kentucky, and he was married in Clarke county to Catharine McFaran. They had two children in Kentucky, and moved to Clarke county, Ohio, where five children were born. They moved to Sangamon county, Illinois, arriving in the fall of 1828. Of their seven children—

CLINTON, born Nov. 30, 1806, in Clarke county, Kentucky, was married in Sangamon county, December, 1831, to Sally Shinkle. They had four children in Sangamon county. LOUISA J., born Sept. 13, 1832, married Alvin S. Taylor. See his name. JAMES W., born Dec. 28, 1835, enlisted July 20, 1861, at Springfield, in what became Co. B, 11th Mo. Inf., for three years. Mr. Wilson in company with Andrew J. Weber and Jesse D. Lloyd, raised the company, and when it was mustered in, August 3, 1861, at St. Louis, Weber was elected captain, Lloyd first, and Wilson second lieutenant. Mr. Wilson was promoted April 21, 1862, to first lieutenant. In November, 1862, Lieutenant Wilson was detailed as signal officer. He was on duty at Vicksburg, Mississippi, at the time the rebels surrendered, July 4, 1863, and sent the following dispatch, the original copy of which he has in his possession. It is written in pencil, on a piece of printing paper, in General Grant's own hand:

"GRANT'S HEADQUARTERS, July 3.

"Admiral Porter:

"The enemy have asked armistice to arrange terms of capitulation. Will you please cease firing until notified, or hear our batteries open. I shall fire a national salute into the city at daylight if they do not surrender.   U. S. GRANT,
"Major General."

The result of that dispatch has gone into history. Lieutenant Wilson served in the Signal Corps until the expiration of his term of service, and was honorably discharged, August 15, 1864. He was married September 29, 1864, in Sangamon county, to Mary M. Morton, and resides one and one-quarter miles southeast of Barclay, Sangamon county, Illinois. MARY E., born March 6, 1838, married Alfred S. Constant. See his name. CLINTON, Jun., born Nov. 29, 1841—after the death of his father—enlisted August 12, 1862, in Co. C, 114th Ill. Inf. He was severely wounded May 20, 1863, at Vicksburg, recovered, served to the end of the rebellion, and was honorably discharged with the regiment. He was married Oct. 18, 1866, in Sangamon county to Rebecca J. Bales, a native of Madison county, Ohio. They have three children, DORA M., JAMES A. and WILLIAM O., and reside in Murry county, Minnesota, near Worthington, Noble county, in the same state. Clinton Wilson was killed May 21, 1841, by lightning, in Sangamon county, while on an errand to the house of a neighbor. His widow resides with her son, James W., near Barclay, Sangamon county, Illinois—1874.

ELIZA, born March 11, 1809, in Kentucky, married in Sangamon county, to Ambrose Cooper. See his name.

ROBERT, born Feb. 17, 1811, in Ohio, died in Sangamon county, Nov. 27, 1829.

SABRIANA, born Oct. 16, 1815, in Ohio, came to Sangamon county, with her parents, went to Kentucky on a visit, was there married to John McFaren, and died leaving two children.

ISAAC C., born April 11, 1817, in Clarke county, Ohio, married in Sangamon county March 6, 1857, to Sarah E. Taylor. They have six living children, CATHARINE, ALBERT, ELMER E. ELIZA E., NORA M., and ISAAC T. and reside one and a quarter miles southeast of Barclay, Sangamon county, Illinois.

MELISSA, born Dec. 7, 1820, in Ohio, raised in Sangamon county, went to Missouri on a visit, was there married to Reuben L. Davis, and died there Sept. 30 1848, leaving one child, JAMES H., born Sept. 21, 1848, near Rolla, Missouri. He resides with his relatives near Barclay, Illinois.

ELI, born March 25, 1827, in Ohio,

was drowned in Sangamon county, Dec. 16, 1834.

Mrs. Catharine Wilson died March 20, 1834, and Samuel Wilson died Oct. 21, 1858, both in Sangamon county, Illinois.

WILSON, THOMAS, was born in 1785 in Buncombe county, North Carolina. Elizabeth Gardner was born in 1786 in Patrick county, Virginia. Her parents moved to Buncombe county, North Carolina, when she was a child. Thomas Wilson and Elizabeth Gardner were there married about 1804 and had two children in that county. They then moved to Warren county, Tennessee. The earthquake of December, 1811, on the Mississippi river so alarmed them that early in 1812 they returned to North Carolina. The government having purchased the lands of the Cherokee Indians in East Tennessee, they removed to Monroe county, near Philadelphia, Loudon county, in 1818, and soon after moved a short distance into Roane county. They moved from there to Sangamon county, Illinois, in the spring of 1830. Five children were born in Tennessee. Of the seven children—

GEORGE, born in Buncombe county, North Carolina, Nov. 27, 1806, married in Tennessee to Elizabeth McCoy, came to Sangamon county, went to Missouri, and from there to Texas.

RACHEL, born in 1809, in North Carolina, married in Sangamon county to Martin McCoy. They had three children, JOSEPH, THOMAS and MARY. Mrs. McCoy died in Springfield, and he near Auburn, Illinois.

MARY, born Jan. 3, 1812, in Buncombe county, North Carolina, married in Sangamon county to Dr. Charles D. Nuckolls. *See his name*.

JACKSON, born in North Carolina, married Susan Martin. They had one child, WILLIAM, who married Adaline Martin in Christian county, and now lives in Missouri. Mrs. Susan Wilson died in Christian county, and Jackson Wilson lives in Texas.

NANCY, born in Tennessee, married in Sangamon county to David Drennan. *See his name*.

WILLIAM, born Jan. 18, 1819, in Tennessee, raised in Illinois, married in Missouri to Mary Murray, and lives in Texas.

JAMES, born April 22, 1822, in Monroe or Roane county, Tennessee, came to Sangamon county in 1834, married Margaret Nuckolls, who died, and he married Elizabeth Courtney, who was born in Jacksonville, Illinois, Feb. 25, 1838, and they reside in Ball township, Sangamon county, Illinois.

Thomas Wilson died in the fall of 1830, and his widow died September, 1845, both in Sangamon county, Illinois.

WIMER, GEORGE, was born near Philadelphia, Pennsylvania, and came to what is now Auburn township, Sangamon county, in 1818, brought up a family, and lives now—1873—in Auburn, Sangamon county, Illinois.

WINCHELL, IRA, was born March 22, 1818, in Franklin county, New York. His parents died about 1825, and he went to St. Lawrence county, and lived a few years with a family near Potsdam, and then spent a few months in Potsdam, all without any guardianship, after the death of his parents. He then engaged to come west with a Mr. Ira Brown, who had a large family of twelve persons. They moved in two road wagons and a one-horse wagon. Mr. Brown stopped to visit a friend at Kirtland, Ohio. It was just at the time of the Mormon hegira from Kirtland to Nauvoo, Illinois. There was great prejudice against the Mormons, and Mr. Brown's large family and general outfit looked so much like that of a Mormon, as to cause him great inconvenience in obtaining supplies. Mr. Winchell's recollection of events connected with the journey are quite interesting and amusing, although the trip was very laborious. They were nine weeks on the road, arriving in Springfield in December, 1831. Mr. Winchell traveled in different parts of the country for ten or twelve years, but always regarded Springfield as his home. Ira Winchell and Alice Huddlestone were married Feb. 18, 1842, in Macoupin county. She was born May 29, 1823, near Columbus, Ohio. Her parents moved from Greenbrier county, Virginia, to Columbus, Ohio, thence to Newport, Indiana, and from there to Macoupin county, Illinois, before the "deep snow." Mr. and Mrs. Winchell have one son—

DELMER, born August 22, 1856, in Gardner township, Sangamon county, and resides with his parents.

Mr. Winchell moved from Springfield, March, 1845, to a place one and a quarter miles north of Farmingdale, Sangamon county, Illinois, where he resides now—1876. He has been engaged in farming and blacksmithing to the present time.

WINEMAN, PHILIP, born Sept. 9, 1801, in Botetourt county, Virginia, came to Sangamon county, Illinois, in the fall of 1823, settling in what is now Auburn township. He was married to Jane Crow, August 11, 1825. She was born in Kentucky. Of their children—

AMERICA, born August 16, 1826, in Sangamon county, married John R. C. Jones. They both died leaving one son, PHILIP Jones, who married Mollie Johnson, and lives one mile southeast of Auburn, Illinois.

SYLVANUS J., born March 23, 1828, in Sangamon county, married Mrs. Margaret E. Kessler June 11, 1862. They have one daughter, MARY A. DILLER, and Mr. W. died in 1875. His widow lives one and a half miles west of Auburn, Illinois.

JAMES P., born Jan. 2, 1830.

WILLIAM H., born Nov. 3, 1832, married Nancy Johnson, and lives one-half mile east of Auburn, Illinois.

HAYDEN S. B., born Nov. 15, 1834, married Rhoda Evans, and lives one mile east of Auburn, Illinois.

VIRGINIA E., born Oct. 19, 1836, married George Bigler, and lives two miles east of Auburn, Sangamon county, Illinois.

MARGARET C., born Feb. 4, 1840, married Jordan B. Organ. *See his name.*

Mrs. Jane Wineman died May 19, 1849, and Philip Wineman married Sarah A. Morrell March 23, 1853. She was born July 4, 1822, in Maine. Of their children—

GEORGE F., born March 6, 1854.

CHARLES H., born Sept. 1, 1855, live with his parents.

VIOLA M., born May 27, 1857, died May 10, 1864.

MILLARD F., born Dec. 27, 1858, died Sept. 13, 1868.

Philip Wineman and family reside near Auburn, Sangamon county, Illinois.

WISE, FREDERICK, born Oct. 15, 1797, in Nelson county, Kentucky. In 1814 he went to the Southern part of Illinois, and in the spring of 1820 came to Sangamon county in company with Mason Fowler and his two sons, and all worked to prepare a home. Mr. Fowler returned for his family, and brought them to Horse-creek, Sangamon county, in the fall of that year. In October, 1820, F. Wise was married to Rebecca Fowler. The day had been fixed for the marriage, and a messenger went to Vandalia for the license. By some unavoidable delay he did not return in time. A justice of the peace by the name of Clawson was ready to solemnize the marriage. Wishing to accommodate the young couple and the invited guests, Mr. Clawson took the resssponsibility to marry them, and when the license came it was properly endorsed and returned to the office where it was issued, and all was right. They had six children, and all except one born in Sangamon county. Of their children—

REBECCA A., born August 31, 1821, in Sangamon county, married August 10, 1837, to James Snodgrass. *See his name.*

JACOB M., born Feb. 7, 1827, in Sangamon county. He enlisted in Springfield in June, 1846, in Co. A, 4th Ill. Inf., served until October, 1846, when he was discharged on account of physical disability at Matamoras, Mexico; married Dec. 13, 1846, in Springfield, to Nancy J. Millstead. They had three children. AMANDA A., married Dec. 7, 1873, to T. H. Gray. She lives in Illiopolis. ALVIN A., married Sept. 25, 1872, to Mary Mitchell, and lives in Illiopolis. GEORGE lives in Illiopolis. Mrs. Nancy J. Wise died June 28, 1858. J. M. Wise was married to Nancy E. Grider, and for his third wife married May 2, 1866, to Mrs. Lydia Griffith, whose maiden name was Bechtel. She died July 18, 1868. J. M. Wise was married Dec. 8, 1868, to Martha F. Griffith. They have three children, MAY, MASON and EDDIE, and reside in Illiopolis, Sangamon county, Illinois. J. M. Wise enlisted February, 1865, in Co. K, 152d Ill. Inf. for one year, served until the end of the rebellion, and was honorably discharged with his regiment.

SARAH E., born August 23, 1831, in Madison county, Illinois—the family having moved there and returned before the birth of the next child. She married in Sangamon county, October, 1848, to Chas. A. Sponsler, and has three living children. ALICE A. married George Washburn, and lives in Mount Pulaski. ARTILLA J. and GEORGE live with their parents in Mount Pulaski, Illinois.

FRANCIS M., born Feb. 8, 1834, in Sangamon county, died in Macon county, in May, 1859.

JOHN T., born July 16, 1840, in Sangamon county, enlisted July, 1861, in Co. A, 21st Ill. Inf., and was killed Dec. 31, 1862, at the battle of Stone river, Tennessee.

LOUISA J., born Feb. 6, 1843, in Sangamon county, married May 13, 1863, in Springfield, to William Boring, who was born Dec. 20, 1837, in Triadelphia, West Virginia, and came to Sangamon county in 1860. He enlisted April 23, 1861, in Co. I, 7th Ill. Inf., under the first call for seventy-five thousand men for three months. He served his full term, and re-enlisted in the same company and regiment for three years. He was wounded Feb. 15, 1862, at the battle of Fort Donaldson, which terminated in the amputation of his right leg above the knee. Mr. and Mrs. Boring have three children, SARAH J., ELLA and NELLIE, the two latter twins, and reside in Hoopolis, Illinois.

Mrs. Rebecca Wise died Feb. 27, 1849, and her husband, Frederick Wise, died August 16, 1850, both in Springfield, Illinois.

WITHROW, JOSEPH, was born about 1772 in Pennsylvania. His parents moved when he was a young man to Botetourt county, Virginia. He was there married to Elizabeth McMullin. They had eight children in Virginia, and in 1811 moved to Washington county, Kentucky, near Muldraughs Hill, where two children were born. Mrs. Elizabeth Withrow died there, and Joseph Withrow married Susannah Landis. They had one child in Kentucky, and moved to Sangamon county, Illinois, arriving in 1825, in what is now Woodside township, where they had one child. Of all their children—

MARGARET, born in Virginia, was married in Kentucky to Timothy Hays. They moved in 1824 to Vandalia, Illinois, and the next year to Sangamon county, where they both died, leaving several children.

WILLIAM, born Oct. 14, 1793, in Botetourt county, Virginia, was married in 1818, in Washington county, Kentucky, to Rhoda B. Prather. They had twelve children, and moved with Thomas Cloyd, in 1824, to Fayette county, Illinois, thence to Sangamon county, in 1825, and settled in Curran township, where two children were born. Their only living child, R. HARVEY, born June 18, 1825, in Vandalia, Illinois, was married June 18, 1849, in Sangamon county, to Sarah E. Barbre. They have nine children, JAMES W., SARAH C., ANN M., LUELLA, LYDIA E., EMMA E., MARTHA C., GEORGE H. and FANNY MAY, and live in Cooper township, two and one-half miles southwest of Mechanicsburg. Mrs. Rhoda Withrow died in 1827, and William Withrow married Polly Smith. They had two children. RHODA J. married Theopholus Walker, who died, and she married Patterson Ridgeway. *See his name*. Mrs. Polly Withrow died and William Withrow married Celia Turpin. They had eight children, and Mrs. Celia Withrow died, and William Withrow married Mrs. Ann Barbre. They had two children, and Mrs. Ann Withrow died. His two sons, ISAAC T. and NOAH W., are married and reside near Mechanicsburg. William Withrow resides two and a half miles southwest of Mechanicsburg, Sangamon county, Illinois.

ANNA, born Dec. 29, 1795, in Virginia, married Thomas Cloyd. *See his name*.

JOHN died, aged twenty-three years.

ROBERT, born Jan. 27, 1800, in Botetourt county, Virginia, was married in Sangamon county, Illinois, Sept. 10, 1826, to Mary T. Peter. They had five living children, AMANDA A., born Sept. 1, 1829, was married Nov. 11, 1847, to William M. Starr. *See his name*. COLUMBIA, born Nov. 11, 1831, was married Feb. 6, 1851, to Francis M. Johnson. *See his name*. They moved from Onarga to Streator, Illinois, where they now reside—1876. GEORGE, born August 29, 1836, married Mary Bridges. They have six children, and live near Clinton, Henry county, Missouri. SANFORD, born April 20, 1839, married Melissa E. Davis. They have four children, NINA, CHARLES, GEORGE, and GUY, and live in Springfield, Illinois. HARRISON, born Nov. 2, 1841, in Sangamon county, Illinois, enlisted July 20, 1861, at Springfield, Illinois, in what became Co. C, 11th Mo. Inf., for three years, was promoted to second lieutenant in 1863, served full term, and was honorably discharged in 1864. He studied dentistry, and was married Dec. 23, 1875, to Fannie Beaumont, in Springfield. Dr. Withrow is practicing his profession in Petersburg, Illinois, and resides there. Robert Withrow died Oct. 3, 1842, and Mrs. Mary T. Withrow was married August, 1844, to Samuel Graham, who was born in 1811, in Pennsylvania. They had three children, LEE R., born July 19, 1845, in Sangamon county, enlisted at Chicago, August 15, 1862, in Co. F, 51st Ill. Inf., for three years, served until the close of the rebellion, and was honorably discharged June 16, 1865. He was married August 7, 1867, in Sangamon county, to Martha J. Darneille. They have one living child, MAUDIE, and live at Loami, Sangamon county, Illinois. MARY F. was married August, 1874, to William N. Richardson, and lives at Streator, LaSalle county, Illinois. ZACHARIAH S. was married November, 1875, in Springfield, to Susan Babcock, and live in Decatur, Illinois. Samuel Graham died Oct. 1, 1850, and Mrs. Mary T. Graham was married August 23, 1854, to Joseph McKinley. She resides in Loami, Sangamon county, Illinois.

POLLY died in Kentucky, aged about twenty years.

MATHEW, born in Kentucky, married Amelia Knotts. They have one child, ELIZABETH, married William Cox, and lives in Virden, Illinois. Mathew Withrow lives eight miles west of Virden, Macoupin county, Illinois.

SARAH married Dr. John Sudduth. They have one child, and live at St. Charles, Minnesota.

JAMES H., born in Botetourt county, Virginia, Jan. 15, 1811, was married in Sangamon county, Illinois, to Maria R. Beauchamp. They had eight living children. HARRIET J. married Charles Yeamans, and died, leaving one child, ANNIE M, who lives with her grandparents. MARTHA S. married L. Dow Cantrill. They have three children, and live at 112 West Allen street, Springfield, Illinois. JULIETTE married David D. Cooper. *See his name.* WILLIAM C., born Feb. 15, 1842, was married Oct. 5, 1865, to Arvilla Bissell, who was born in Lewiston, Fulton county, Illinois, June 29, 1844. They live two miles east of Sherman, Sangamon county, Illinois. ISAAC N. married Eliza Laswell, who died, leaving two children, and I. N. Withrow married Mary Crow. They have two children, and reside at 509 South Ninth street, Springfield, Illinois. NANCY A. married Richard Laswell, who died, and she married Thomas Keagle. They have three children, and live in Williams township. MATHEW lives with his parents. James H. Withrow lives between Sherman and Barclay in Sangamon county, Illinois—1874.

TABITHA was married in Sangamon county, Illinois, to Alvah Graves. They both died, leaving several children in Macoupin county, Illinois.

CAROLINE married Edward Shane. They both died, leaving three children.

ELIZABETH, the eldest by the second marriage, was born in Kentucky, and married Joseph Drennan. *See his name.*

ALMIRA, born in Sangamon county, Illinois, married Israel Coverdell, and lives in Gerard, Macoupin county, Illinois.

Mrs. Susannah Withrow died in 1844, and Joseph Withrow, Sen., died in 1850, both in Sangamon county, Illinois.

WOLGAMOT, JOHN, born in Pennsylvania, and was married there Oct. 28, 1819, to Susannah Martin, a native of Maryland. They had three children, and Mrs. Wolgamot died. John Wolgamot was married August 2, 1827, to Mary A. Firey, a native of Maryland, also. They had three children in Maryland, and moved to Springfield, Illinois, arriving in 1837, where they had three children. Of his nine children—

NICHOLAS M., born August 12, 1820, in Hagerstown, Maryland, was married there to Sarah Angle. They reside in Fairview, Fulton county, Illinois.

ELLENORA, born Nov. 14, 1822, in Maryland, was married in Springfield, Illinois, to William Kreigh. She died, and Mr. Kreigh resides at Farmington, Illinois.

SUSANNAH, born Dec. 12, 1823, in Maryland, came to Springfield with her father, and was married Nov. 27, 1845, at Fairview, Fulton county, Illinois, to William Davis, who was born Nov. 10, 1823, in Huntingdon county, Pennsylvania, and moved to Fulton county, Illinois, with his father in 1837. They had seven children. SARAH R., born Oct. 29, 1847, near Fairview, Illinois, was married in Prairie City, Sept. 20, 1867, to Samuel Barber. They have four children, MINNIE B., LETITIA E., ANNIE and MARY E., and live in Peoria, Illinois. JOHN E., born March, 8, 1851; SIMON G., born August 1, 1853, WILLIAM H., born Sept. 10, 1855, died June 23, 1857; GEORGE H., born Dec. 14, 1857; EDWARD, born Dec. 28, 1859, and MATTIE, born June 26, 1862. All the living reside with their parents. Mr. and Mrs. Davis reside near Ludlow, Champaign county, Illinois.

MARY ELIZABETH, born Jan. 28, 1829, in Hagerstown, Maryland, came to Springfield with her parents in 1837, and was married there August, 1849, to Dr. Henry Wohlgemuth. They had six children, two of whom died young. MARY ELLEN died in her twenty-second year. HENRY, WILLIAM and MINNIE reside with their parents in Springfield, Illinois. Dr. Wohlgemuth was born May 22, 1822, in Hanover, Germany. He commenced the study of medicine there, and after coming to America, and his arrival in Springfield, in November, 1845, continued his studies and commenced practice in Springfield in 1846. He graduated in 1854 at the Eclectic Medical Institute at Cincinnati, Ohio. At the organization of the State Eclectic Medical Association of Illinois, he was elected president of the same, and is also a member of the National Eclectic Medical Association. He was elected city physician of Springfield in 1856, and in 1861 and '62 county physician. In 1863, '64 and ,65 he was a member of the city council, and was a member of the board of education for 1866. In 1865 and '66 Dr. Wohlgemuth, Colonel John Williams and Charles W. Matheny composed the board of commissioners who constructed the Springfield water works. Dr. Wohlgemuth was a member, and most of the time president, of the board of managers of Oak Ridge cemetery for twelve years, and it is but simple justice to say that it is largely owing to his persevering and intelligent labors that this piece of land has been changed from a rough and forbidding harbor for wild animals to one of the most beautiful cities of the dead in all our country.

JACOB H., born Jan. 21, 1831, in Maryland, died March 2, 1862, in Springfield, Illinois.

WILLIAM JOSHUA, born Nov. 5, 1835, died Feb. 15, 1837.

MARGARET A., born April 18, 1838, in Hagerstown, Maryland, was married in Springfield to Judge John Race. They reside in Decatur, Illinois.

JOHN F., born August 5, 1842, in Springfield, was married Dec. 1, 1864, to Virginia A. Sperry, who was born Sept. 15, 1847, in Rushville, Illinois. They have one child, MARY A., and live in Springfield, Illinois.

CHARLES W., born Feb. 22, 1851, in Springfield, died there Nov. 16, 1861.

EMERY, born April 28, 1853, in Springfield, was married Feb. 23, 1876, to Anna M. Fosselman, daughter of J. B. Fosselman—druggist—of Springfield. Mr. and Mrs. Wolgamot live in Springfield, Illinois.

John Wolgamot and Mrs. Susannah Wolgamot both died in Springfield, Ill.

WALGAMOT, SAMUEL, born in 1776, in Washington county, Maryland, was married there to Mary Beard, who was born Jan. 12, 1791, in the same county. They had four children in Maryland, and moved across the state line into Franklin county, Pennsylvania, where three children were born. They returned to Maryland, and from there came to Sangamon county, Illinois. They were seven weeks on the way, arriving May 30, 1840, in what is now Woodside township. Of their children—

ELIZABETH, born Jan. 5, 1812, in Maryland, was married November, 1837, to Samuel Stover. See his name.

MARY, born March 3, 1813, in Maryland, was married April, 1840, to George Baugh, and died Oct. 24, 1840, in Sangamon county, Illinois.

CATHARINE, born Dec. 1, 1815, in Pennsylvania, was married in Maryland, January, 1840, to William E. Redman. See his name.

JOHN R., born April 5, 1819, in Franklin county, Pennsylvania, was married in Sangamon county, Illinois, Jan. 19, 1843, to Anna M. Todd. They had one living child, MARY J., born Jan. 5, 1844, in Sangamon county, was married Oct. 26, 1869, to John M. Baugh, who was born Jan. 14, 1847. They had two children, MILTON A. and BRYAN G. Mr. Baugh was killed by lightning, May 28, 1874, while working in his cornfield, near Woodside, Sangamon county, Illinois. His widow and children reside there. Mrs. Anna M. Wolgamot died July 28, 1846, and John B. Wolgamot was married Oct. 24, 1854, to Emily E. Wood. They had seven children, three of whom died under seven years of age. ANNIE M., ELIZABETH E., JOHN R. and BARBARA reside with their father. Mrs. Emily E. Walgamot died Feb. 21, 1869, and John B. Walgamot was married Aug. 18, 1874, to Mrs. R. J. Widup, and resides at Woodside, Sangamon county, Illinois.

BARBARA, born March 25, 1820, in Pennsylvania, was married in Sangamon county, Illinois, to Adam Johnson. See his name in Omissions.

SAMUEL, Jun., born Feb. 12, 1823, in Pennsylvania, married Lydia Cressy, who died, and he married Eliza Mahar. They have one child, KATE, and reside near Ottawa, Kansas.

ISABEL, born May 1, 1825, in Pennsylvania, married Seldon C. Whitney. They have five children, BARBARA A., DAVID S., BETTIE, KATIE and MAY, and reside near Ottawa, Kansas.

Samuel Walgamot died Sept. 3, 1868, and his widow died Jan. 21, 1873, both in Woodside township, Sangamon county, Illinois.

WOMACK, GEORGE B., was born December, 1817, in Butler county, Kentucky, and brought by his parents to Wayne county, Illinois, in 1829. He came to Sangamon county in 1839, and married Jane Inslee. They had two children in Sangamon county—

NANCY C. resides with her sister, Mrs. Bell.

LOUISA L. married Stephen Bell. See his name.

Mrs. Jane Womack died in Sangamon county, and John B. Womack returned to Wayne county, married Susan Brown and had four children. He died in Wayne county about 1859.

WOLTZ, JOHN C., was born June 5, 1818, in Shepherdstown, Virginia. He started west partly to visit his sister, Mrs. John B. Weber. He traveled by stage to Pittsburg, thence by water the whole length of the Ohio river, up the Mississippi river to St. Louis, thence to and up the Illinois river to Naples, where he ate his first meal in Illinois of corn bread and venison, which he thought was the best food he ever tasted. He traveled on the first railroad built in Illinois to New Berlin, and walked from there on the timbers, four inches wide, laid ready to receive the flat rails, to Springfield, arriving Nov. 7, 1840. Before he obtained employment his finances were reduced to three ten cent pieces. He worked nearly two years at carpenter and cabinet work, mostly at Riverton, without receiving a cent of money, all the time vowing that when he did obtain enough he would leave the country, but an arrow from cupid's bow wounded him before he obtained the requisite amount, and he is now one of the successful farmers of Sangamon county. John C. Woltz was married Dec. 7, 1843, to Sidney R. Halbert. They had seven living children, namely—

VIRGINIA C., born Nov. 26, 1844, in Sangamon county, married March 2, 1865, to William T. Summers, who was born May 15, 1845, in Bracken county, Kentucky. They have one child, WALTER, and reside two miles northwest of Dawson, Illinois.

SARAH M., born Oct. 19, 1846, married Dec. 24, 1869, to John M. Riddle. See his name.

JULIA E. resides with her parents.

JAMES P. died April 17, 1869, in his sixteenth year.

J. CHARLES, MAGGIE H. and *ALICE IDA*, reside with their parents nearly equi-distant from Barclay, Dawson and Riverton, Sangamon county, Illinois—1874.

WOOD, SENECA, was born Oct. 1, 1806, in Springfield, Massachusetts, and came to Island Grove, Sangamon county, Illinois, in the fall of 1831. He was married there in January, 1834, to Sarah M. Todd, who was born in 1817, in Bourbon county, Kentucky. They had eight children, four of whom died young. Of the other four—

CLARA L., born in 1837, married William Wardell. He died, leaving one child. Mrs. Wardell and her daughter, ALICE, reside in Buffalo, Sangamon county, Illinois.

SENECA W., born March 7, 1840, in Sangamon county. He was married December, 1868, to Molly J. Allgate.

She died Nov. 17, 1872, and he was married Dec. 14, 1873, to Mary J. Allgate. They live in Springfield, Illinois. Mr. Wood is conductor on the Capital street railroad.

LEWIS ARTHUR, born in 1846, in Sangamon county, married Elizabeth Hillman. They have two children, FRANK and LEWIS, and live in Springfield, Illinois.

KATIE resides with her parents.

Seneca Wood spent a few years in farming, then kept a hotel and stage stand in Berlin, was postmaster there five years, and justice of peace four years. In 1848 he moved to Springfield, where he now resides—1876.

WOOD, WILLIAM, was born October, 1794, in Knox county, Tennessee. He went to Madison county, Illinois, when he was a young man, and was there married, in 1814, to Polly Cox. They moved to what became Sangamon county, arriving in the fall of 1818, in what is now Auburn township. They had ten children—

LUCINDA married Andrew Gates. See his name.

JOHN married Rebecca Bowen, moved to Texas, and died there.

JAMES went to Texas, married Electa Jenkins, and lives there.

EDWARD married Amanda Pitzer, and died in Illinois.

SALLY married Peter Gates. See his name.

GILBERT, married, and lives in Missouri.

MARGARET married Joseph Campbell, and lives in Virden, Illinois.

WILLIAM married Jane Bristow, and lives in Iowa.

GEORGE married Isabella Easom, and lives in Virden, Illinois.

EVA died in Virden, unmarried.

William Wood and his wife both died in Sangamon county, Illinois.

WORKMAN, JOHN, was born about 1787 or '88, in Allegany county, Maryland, married in Tennessee to Lydia Bilyeu. They had twenty-two children, two of whom died in infancy. They were nearly all sons. Some of the children married in Tennessee. The family became Mormons and all moved in a body, the parents, their twenty children, and nearly as many grandchildren, through Sangamon county to Nauvoo, Illinois, about 1842. Some of the children left the Mormons at Nauvoo, but the principal part of the family went to Salt Lake city. Five of the sons became Mormon preachers, have been missionaries to England, and are yet with the Mormons.

WORKMAN, STEPHEN born in 1797, in Allegany county, Maryland. He went with his parents to Bourbon county, Kentucky, and there married Effie Maddox, moved to Overton county, Tennessee, with three children, about 1827. In 1829 he moved with his brother William to Sangamon county. In 1831 he moved to Kentucky, and in 1834 returned to Sangamon county, and settled one and a half miles south of Loami, and a few years later to Christian county, Illinois.

WORKMAN, WILLIAM, brother to John, Stephen, David and James. He was born April 8, 1799, in Allegany county, Maryland, and was taken by his parents about 1809, to Bourbon county, Ky. He was married March 23, 1819, in Overton county, Tennessee, to Sarah Bilyeu. She was born Nov. 26, 1801, in Green county, Kentucky. They had four children in Tennessee, and moved to Sangamon county, Illinois, arriving Oct. 1, 1829, in what is now Loami township, south of Lick creek, where seven children were born, two of whom died young. Of the other nine—

PETER, born May 24, 1820, in Tennessee, married in Sangamon county, Jan. 28, 1841, to Sally Jane Taylor. They had thirteen children, five died young. NANCY married Samuel Workman. He enlisted August, 1861, in Co. B, 30th Ill. Inf., and died at Cairo, Feb. 13, 1862, leaving one child, SAMUEL M. His widow married Jasper Bilyeu, and lives in Christian county, Illinois. LOUISA J. married David Hays, has three children, and lives in Christian county. SIMON P. married Fanny J. Short. He is in Co. H, 16th U. S. Inf. His wife and two children live with their grandmother, Huggins—1874. MARY E. married Samuel Harbour. See his name. They live near Loami, Illinois. JACOB W., ALMYRA, STEPHEN and CAROLINE live with their parents, two miles south of Loami, Sangamon county, Illinois.

JACOB, born Dec. 8, 1822, in Tennessee, married in Sangamon county, March 19, 1846, to Nancy Taylor. They have eight children. WILLIAM S. married Elizabeth Williams, has two children, and lives in Shelby county, Illinois. JACOB H. married Nancy Harbour, have one child, DENNIS, and live near Loami, Illinois. STEPHEN, GEORGE P., PETER D., JOHN H., NANCY J., and CHARLEY, reside with their parents, two and three-quarter miles south of Loami, Illinois.

JOHN, born July 6, 1824, in Overton county, Tennessee, married in Sangamon county, Sept. 23, 1850, to Caroline Campbell. They had nine children, two died young. SARAH E. and JOHN W. reside with their parents. KATIE A. married Simon P. Campbell. *See his name.* JOSIAH W., LUCINA, LILLIE C. and MARY live with their parents, five miles west of Chatham, Illinois.

STEPHEN, born Jan. 20, 1827, in Tennessee, married in Sangamon county, Feb. 22, 1847, to Mary S. Hays. He enlisted August, 1861, for three years, in Co. B, 30th Ill. Inf., was discharged on account of physical disability, December, 1862. He moved to Harrison county, Missouri, in September, 1865. He was preparing to return to Illinois, and was murdered April 2, 1869. The object of the murderer was robbery, but he failed in that. Mr. W. left a widow and seven children. SALLY married George Ray, and died in Missouri. ELIZABETH married George C. Dean, a native of Saratoga county, New York. They have one child, CHLOE M., and live in Loami township. Mr. Dean served eighteen months in Co. F. 1st Reg. Mich. Sharpshooters, and was honorably discharged July 28, 1865. ADDISON B., PETER, SOPHRONIA, EMILY and STEPHEN D. live with their mother, near Loami, Sangamon county, Illinois.

DAVID, born March 22, 1829, in Sangamon county, married Feb. 6, 1849, to Julia Bilyeu, and died March 16, 1849. His widow married Richard Workman.

ELIZABETH, born May 23, 1831, in Sangamon county, married Josiah W. Campbell. *See his name.*

ISAAC, born August 7, 1834, in Sangamon county, married Feb. 14, 1856, to Elizabeth Workman. They had three children. SALLY married Peter Harbour. *See his name.* JOHN and MARTHA reside with their father. Mrs. W. died Sept. 25, 1860, and he was married June 29, 1862, to Martha A. Wedding, and have six children—WILLIAM H., ISAAC, MAYHEW, JOSEPH, MARY A. and ELIZABETH and reside two miles south of Loami, Sangamon county, Illinois.

WILLIAM B., born August 14, 1837, in Sangamon county, married May 22, 1857, to Lydia Bilyeu, who was born May 5, 1845, in Overton county, Tennessee. They had seven children. The first, third and fifth died, SUSAN, in infancy, ALICE, at five, and POLLY, at two years of age. SARAH A., WILLIAM F., CAROLINE and FRANCES reside with their parents, one mile south of Loami, Illinois. By comparing dates it will be seen that Mrs. Workman was only twelve years and seventeen days old when she was married. Their first child was born Sept. 22, 1858, when she was thirteen years and four months old. Miss Sarah A., their eldest daughter, has quite a talent for music and plays well on the piano—1874.

SAMUEL, born Oct. 17, 1845, married Oct. 16, 1863, to Emily Hays. They had two children. She and the children died, and he married March 4, 1867, to Anna Harbour. They have two living children, JENNIE MAY and KATIE, and reside one mile south of Loami, Illinois.

William Workman and wife live on the farm where they settled in 1829. It is one mile south of Loami, Sangamon county, Illinois.

WORKMAN, DAVID, born Sept. 10, 1804, in Alleganey county, Maryland, raised in Bourbon county, Kentucky, and married in Overton county, Tennessee, to Lydia Bilyeu. They had two children in Tennessee, moved to Sangamon county, in 1829, and settled near his brother William in what is now Loami township. They had twelve children in Sangamon county. Of their fourteen children—

DIANA, born in Tennessee, married in Sangamon county to Benjaman Workman (no relative), have five children, and reside near Fort Scott, Kansas.

JACOB, born in Tennessee, married in Sangamon county to Anna Harbour, have ten children, and live near Fort Scott, Kansas.

NANCY, born about 1830, in Sangamon county, married John Bilyeu. They have several children, and live near Scio, Linn county, Oregon.

MICHAEL, born 1831 or '32, in Sangamon county, married Mrs. Julia A. Workman, whose maiden name was Bilyeu. She had four children, and died Jan. 12, 1859. He married Hannah Workman, a distant relative. They have five children, and live in Christian county, near Mowequa, Shelby county, Illinois.

MINERVA, born Oct. 23, 1833, in Sangamon county, married William P. Carson. See his name.

SARAH married Sampson Bilyeu, and died, leaving one child.

ELIZABETH married John Carson. See his name. They have several children, and live near Fort Scott, Kansas.

PETER, born in Sangamon county, married Martha Workman. He enlisted in 1861 for three years in the 11th Mo. Inf., was accidentally shot through the body in camp, and died at home in Sangamon county, Nov. 18, 1865, leaving a widow and three children, who reside in Christian county, Illinois.

DAVID, born in Sangamon county, married February, 1861, to Amelia Bilyeu, in Sangamon county, moved at once to Overton county, Tennessee, was there pressed into the rebel army, and was placed in command of a wagon train. Watching his opportunity, he cut four mules from a wagon, swam three of them across Green river, and succeeded in reaching the Union lines. He visited his old home in Sangamon county, enlisted in Co. B, 30th Ill. Inf. for three years, in August, 1862, and died at Jackson, Tennessee, Oct. 22, 1862.

LYDIA married in Sangamon county to Thomas Large, have several children, and live near Fort Scott, Kansas.

MARY died, aged nine years.

WILLIAM R., born Sept. 10, 1849, in Sangamon county, married Sept. 16, 1869, to Elizabeth J. Shubert. She was born Feb 11, 1855, in Ripley county, Indiana. They have two children, DAVID E. and JAMES M., and live near Loami, Illinois.

HANNAH, born in Sangamon county, married Robert Wilson, have two children, and reside near Fort Scott, Kansas.

ISAAC, born in Sangamon county, lives with his brother, Michael.

David Workman died Feb. 20, 1865, and Mrs. Lydia Workman died Nov. 26, 1866, both in Sangamon county, Illinois.

WORKMAN, JAMES, born Dec. 17, 1806, in Alleganey county, Maryland, was taken about 1810 to Bourbon county, Kentucky, by his father, Abraham Workman, who was an elder brother to John, Stephen, William and David. When James was a young man he went from Bourbon county to Overton county, Tennessee, and was there married to Elizabeth Bilyeu, had one child, and moved to Sangamon county, Illinois, arriving in the fall of 1830, in what is now Loami township, where one child was born. In 1831 he returned to Tennessee, where one child was born and Mrs. Workman died. Mr. W. married there to Lydia Bilyeu. He moved in 1841 to southwest Missouri, and in 1843 returned to Tennessee, where his wife died without children. Mr. Workman married there to Eliza Rayburn, returned to Sangamon county, and settled where he did in 1830. At the close of the rebellion he returned to Tennessee. Three years later he came back to Sangamon county. He had seven children by his third wife. Three died young. Of his children by the first marriage—

JAMES ABRAHAM, born Dec. 16, 1827, in Overton county, Tennessee, raised partly in Sangamon county, married in Tennessee, May 29, 1847, to Jemima Kitchen, and had four children, JAMES M., SARAH E., THOMAS C. and JEMIMA E. Mrs. Jemima Workman died Nov. 10, 1858, and Mr. W. was married May 20, 1860, to Adaline Buck. They have five living children, WILLIAM D., NANCY A., REBECCA A., EMMA E. and GEORGE H. Mr. Workman was a justice of the peace and tax collector in Overton county. Many of his loyal friends had been killed, and his own life threatened by the Ku-Klux, so he left there and returned in 1866 to the vicinity of Loami, Sangamon county, and now—1871—lives in Christian county, near Mowequa, Shelby county, Illinois.

REBECCA, born August 16, 1830, in Sangamon county, married Sept. 13, 1849, to Solomon Shetter, had eight living children. WILLIAM was killed, aged 15 years, by a fall from a horse. ARISSA married James Stanton, and resides near Loami, Illinois. NANCY E., MINIZA I., ANNA I., ELIZA A., ALBERT A., and EPSEY C. reside near Loami, Illinois.

SAMUEL E., born Feb. 9, 1833, in Tennessee, married Nov. 13, 1851, to Isabel Kitchen, and have seven children, SARAH E., LYDIA J., JAMES D., NANCY A., ISABEL and MARY L., and reside one mile south of Loami, Illinois. The living children of the third wife, GEORGE W., WILLIAM B., BARNEY and DELIA A. M. reside with their parents.

In 1872 James Workman and wife, with their four children, moved to Christian county, near Mowequa, Shelby county, Illinois.

WRIGHT, CHARLES, was born July 21, 1799, at Bernardstown, Massachusetts, brought up in Vermont, and came with his brother, Erastus, to Springfield, arriving Nov. 21, 1821. He taught school a few years in Sangamon county, at one time in the neighborhood of the Drennans, on Sugar creek.

He obtained a contract for surveying government lands on the Wachita river, went south, and worked at it two years. He had his contract almost completed, when he died of malignant billious fever, at Monroe, Louisiana, Sept. 14, 1828.

WRIGHT, ERASTUS, was born Jan. 21, 1779, at Bernardstown, Massachusetts. The family is a very ancient one for New England. Erastus left a history of the family, which he always kept written up, giving the genealogy of the family for nearly two and a half centuries, beginning with Deacon Samuel Wright, who came from England and settled at Springfield, Massachusetts, in 1641.

The parents of Erastus Wright left Bernardstown, Massachusetts, and went to Derby, Vermont, in 1802, that being at the time pioneer ground. Erastus remained with his father on the farm, with no other advantages for education than the country schools afforded, until the spring of 1821, when he started west, in company with his brother, Charles. They traveled by such means as the country afforded before the days of canals and railroads, until they reached Buffalo, New York. There they embarked on a schooner for Fort Dearborn, now Chicago, Illinois. From Fort Dearborn they started on foot, making a preliminary survey of the route now occupied by the Illinois and Michigan canal, touching the Illinois river near where LaSalle now stands. They then descended the Illinois river to Fort Clark, now Peoria, and from there to Elkhart Grove, where Judge Latham resided. On their way south they stopped on Fancy creek, in what is now Sangamon county, at the house of John Dixon, who was one of the earliest settlers in this county, but who afterwards went north and laid out the town, now city, of Dixon, on Rock river. From there they came to Springfield, arriving Nov. 21, 1821. It had been selected as the county seat on the 10th of April before, but there had not then been any town laid out. A log court house had just been completed. Mr. Wright describes the town, as it first appeared to him, in these words:

"Elijah Iles had about five hundred dollars' worth of goods in a log cabin, ten by fourteen; Charles R. Matheney and Jonathan Kelly lived in log cabins not a quarter of a mile distant. The Indians—Kickapoos and Potawatamies—often came along in squads, and when others had built cabins near, called the pl ce 'log town.'"

Mr. Wright went with Judge Latham from Springfield to Elkhart Grove and taught school there during the winter of 1821-2. He bought a claim of Levi Ellis and entered it as soon as it came into the market in 1823. From notes on the flyleaf of a New Testament, in the handwriting of Mr. Wright, he says: "I built the first frame house in what is now the city of Springfield."

In 1824 he built a park, and traded eighty acres of land in Schuyler county for an elk. Old citizens remember that Mr. Wright rode that elk, and drove it in harness, the same as a horse, although he says in a note that he was rough to ride, and not very kind in the harness. Mr. Wright spent three or four years in the lead mining region of Illinois and Wisconsin, and while there laid out the town of Mineral Point, Wisconsin, using a bed cord for his chain. He was married June 15, 1831, in Fulton county, to Jane Gardner, whose parents were from Saratoga, New York. Mr. and Mrs. Wright had three children.

ELIZA ANN, born July 2, 1833, in Springfield, was married Oct. 20, 1858, to Rev. John A. Hamilton, of the Congregational Church, and a native of Chester, Massachusetts. They have one child, JENNIE LOUISE, born August 26, 1859, at Keene, New Hampshire, at which place Mr. Hamilton spent the early part of his ministry, and was afterwards in charge of the Congregational church at Davenport, Iowa, which he resigned to make the tour of Europe and the Holy Land, in 1873. He is now—1875—settled as pastor of the Congregational Church at Norwalk, Connecticut.

JAMES G., born March 20, 1835, in Springfield, married Sarah A. Wilbourn, of Mason county. He died Nov. 16, 1858, at Lincoln, Ill., leaving a widow and one child, the latter has since died.

MARIA JANE, born Nov. 14, 1837, in Springfield, was married Dec. 23, 1856, to Robert P. Johnston, who was born April 30, 1828, at Halifax, Nova Scotia, and came to Springfield in 1851. Mr. and Mrs. Johnston had two children, LLOYD ERASTUS and JAMES WRIGHT. Mrs. Maria J. Johnston died very suddenly August 16, 1862, in Springfield. The sons reside with their father, who was married Feb. 22, 1865, to Isabella Muirhead, of Greenock, Scotland. They have four children, MARGARET A., ISABELLA, SUSIE and ROBERT P., Jun. R. P. Johnston was for many years a partner of P. C. Canedy, in the drug business, and is now Assistant Secretary of State of Illinois. He and his family reside in Springfield, Illinois.

Mrs. Jane G. Wright died Jan. 24, 1841, and Erastus Wright married Lucy Barrows, who died without children, April 22, 1867. Erastus Wright was married March 23, 1868, to Mrs. Lucy F. Carpenter, whose maiden name was Johnson. She was born and educated in Vermont, and married Mr. Thomas Carpenter at Lancaster, Erie county, Pennsylvania, where she buried her husband and only child, ARTHUR. She was married to Mr. Wright at Lincoln, Illinois. He died in Springfield, Illinois, Nov. 21, 1870, on the forty-ninth anniversary of his residence in that city. His widow visited Europe in 1873, and now—1874—resides in Springfield, Illinois.

Erastus Wright was one of the earliest teachers in Sangamon county, and taught for many years. For ten years he filled office of school commissioner of Sangamon county. During that time a large amount of money, derived from the sale of government land for school purposes, passed through his hands. He was one of the earliest Abolitionists, and was always fearless in advocating its doctrines. He acquired considerable wealth, and was liberal towards all benevolent objects, and every public enterprise was sure to elicit his co-operation.

WRIGHT, DOCTOR N., is a son of Samuel Wright, an elder brother to Charles and Erastus. The Doctor is not an early settler, as he came to Springfield August 12, 1842. He has a family, and is a practicing physician in Chatham, Sangamon county, Illinois.

Y

YATES, HENRY, was born October 29, 1786, in Caroline county, Virginia. Dr. Michael Yates, a native of England, emigrated to America before the Revolution and settled in Caroline county, Virginia. He there married Martha Marshall, a sister of John Marshall, afterwards Chief Justice of the United States. Their son, Abner, born in Caroline county, married Mollie Hawes, daughter of Thomas Hawes and Elizabeth Fisher, his wife. They had two children, Henry, whose name heads this sketch, and Martha, who married Henry Ellis. *See his name.* Henry Yates was taken by his parents, in 1788, from Caroline county, Virginia, to Fayette county, Kentucky, where his father died. The family moved to Woodford, thence to Scott, and from there to Gallatin county, in the same State, in 1804. Henry Yates, Henry Ellis, and Colonel Robert Johnson laid out a town on the Ohio river, and Colonel Johnson named it Fredericksburg, in honor of his native city of that name in Virginia. It was at a later period changed to Warsaw, and is the county seat of Gallatin county. Henry Yates returned to Caroline county, Virginia, and was there married, July 11, 1809, to his cousin, Millicent Yates, who was born May 15, 1791. They went to Gallatin county, Kentucky, where they had eleven children, five of whom died young, and Mrs. Millicent Yates died April 19, 1830. Henry Yates married Mary A. Shuff, and moved to Sangamon county, Illinois, arriving in May, 1831, at Springfield. In November, 1832, they moved to Island Grove, where Berlin now stands. They had one child there, and Mrs. Mary A. Yates died May 11, 1835. Henry Yates was married Sept. 28, 1835, to Elizabeth McMillan. They had six children, one of whom died in childhood. Of his twelve children, including the six brought from Kentucky—

THOMAS, born March 14, 1811, in Gallatin county, Kentucky, was married March 29, 1837, at Berlin, Sangamon county, Illinois, to Nancy Higgins, who was born May 23, 1816, in Cumberland county, Kentucky, and came with her parents to Sangamon county in 1836. Thomas and Nancy Yates had ten living children. MARY F. married Anthony A. Rhodes, and lives in Berlin, Illinois. JAMES, born April 19, 1841, married Barbara Dibert, and lives near New Berlin, Illinois. ANN married Davis Henderson, and lives near Berlin. MARTHA M. married Nathan Elliott, and lives near Berlin. GEORGE H. died in his fifteenth year. SARAH lives with her father. CATHARINE married Hugh McLaughlin, and lives near Berlin. JANE, JOANNA and EMMA live with their father. Mrs. Nancy Yates died Dec. 15, 1860, and Thomas Yates resides one mile northwest of Berlin, Sangamon county, Illinois.

RICHARD, born Jan. 18, 1815, in Warsaw, Gallatin county, Kentucky, was educated at Miami University, Oxford, Ohio, Georgetown College, Kentucky, and graduated at Illinois College, Jacksonville, Illinois, being the first graduate of that institution. He studied law at Jacksonville, and attended lectures at Transylvania University, Lexington, Kentucky. Richard Yates and Catharine Geers were married at Jacksonville, Illinois. They had five children. WILLIAM was killed by lightning at twelve or fourteen years of age. MARY died young. HENRY, CATHARINE and RICHARD, Jun., live with their mother. Richard Yates was elected Governor of Illinois in 1856. At the end of his term he was elected United States Senator, serving six years. He died suddenly, Nov. 27, 1873, at Barnum's Hotel, St. Louis, Missouri, and was buried Nov. 30, at Jacksonville, Illinois. His widow and children reside there.

ABNER, born August 4, 1819, in Warsaw, Kentucky, brought up in Sangamon county, was married in 1851, in Jacksonville, Illinois, to Mary Geers. They have two children, MARY and WILLIAM, and reside in Jacksonville, Illinois.

MARTHA, born July 9, 1823, in Warsaw, Kentucky, was married in Sangamon county, Illinois, to John W. Scott. See his name.

JANE, born Oct. 23, 1825, at Warsaw, Kentucky, was married Dec. 10, 1846, in Sangamon county, to John F. Elliott, who was born April 14, 1823, at Upper Sandusky, Ohio. They had five children. MILLICENT, the fourth child, died in infancy. PHOEBE L., HENRY Y., CHARLES Y. and JOHN Y. reside with their parents in New Berlin, Sangamon county, Illinois. Mr. Elliott has for the last few years represented Berlin township in the Sangamon County Board of Supervisors. He is one of the most substantial farmers in the county.

MILLICENT, born Sept. 25, 1827, in Warsaw, Kentucky, brought up in Sangamon county, and married Wesley Matthews. They have one child, MARY E., and reside in Jacksonville, Illinois.

The children of the second wife were—

HENRY, Jun., born March 7, 1835, at Berlin, Sangamon county, Illinois, married June 17, 1856, at Arenzville, Cass county, Illinois, to Louisa Arenz, daughter of Hon. Francis Arenz. She was born June 14, 1836, at Beardstown, Illinois. Henry Yates, Jun., and wife had five children. NELLIE died in her ninth year. GRACE A. died in her fifth year. HENRIETTA, MARY L. and LAURA live with their mother. Henry Yates, Jun., was a merchant in Berlin, sold out in order to enter the army, and raised a company in 1862, which became Co. A, 106th Ill. Inf. He was commissioned captain Sept. 17, 1862, promoted to lieutenant colonel, April 10, 1863, to colonel, April 8, 1864, and brevet brigadier general, August 26, 1866. He was accidentally shot in 1863, sun-struck at Little Rock, and never regained his health. General Henry Yates died Aug. 3, 1871, at Berlin. His widow and children reside in Berlin, Sangamon county, Illinois.

Children by the third marriage—

WILL, born June 11, 1837, at Berlin. He enlisted in 1862 in the 11th Mo. Inf., and was transferred to a cavalry regiment, became lieutenant, and was in Grierson's raid. Mr. Yates came home sick and died Oct. 14, 1864.

JOHN, born Feb. 1, 1839, in Sangamon county, was married Oct. 8, 1864, to Olivia Williams, who was born August 6, 1845, in Warsaw, Kentucky. They had five children. OLIVIA, the fourth child, died Nov. 10, 1872, in her third year. MARY E., WILLIAM H., THOMAS W. and JOHN reside with their parents, one mile north of New Berlin, Illinois.

HAWES, born Oct. 4, 1840, in Sangamon county, was married March 7, 1867, to Mary R. Bevans, and resides in New Berlin, Sangamon county, Illinois.

MARY, born August 1, 1842, in Sangamon county, died unmarried at Jacksonville, Illinois, August 30, 1873.

MARSHALL, born May 23, 1845, in Sangamon county, enlisted in 1862 in Co. A, 106th Ill. Inf., for three years, served his full term and was honorably discharged. He was employed in the custom house, and died of apoplexy April 20, 1867, at New Orleans, Louisiana.

Mrs. Elizabeth Yates died August 12, 1862, and her husband, Henry Yates, Sen., died Sept. 13, 1865, both at New Berlin, Sangamon county, Illinois.

Henry Yates, Sen., having been one of the proprietors of Warsaw, Kentucky. He laid out the town of Berlin in 1833. After the railroad was built, he laid out the town of New Berlin, also.

YOAKUM, WILLIAM, was born in 1791 in Virginia, and when he was an infant his parents moved to Claihorn county, Tennessee, where his father died. His mother moved her family, about 1810, to Madison county, near Edwardsville, Illinois. They moved next to Montgomery county, and then to Sangamon county, arriving June 10, 1819, at the north side of Richland creek, in what is now Salisbury township. William Yoakum was married in 1821 to Sarah Simmons. They had eight children—

JOHN W., born in 1825, started to California in 1849, and died on the way.

MARY A., born in 1827, married William Penny, had six children, and he died in Missouri. She lives near Salisbury, Illinois.

GEORGE H., born in 1830, is unmarried, and lives near Salisbury, Illinois.

MARTHA J., born Dec. 30, 1852, married Francis M. Duncan. See his name.

JAMES C., unmarried, and lives in Menard county, Illinois.

ISAAC R. is unmarried.

JESSE J. married Sarah Miller, and lives at the family homestead, four miles west of Salisbury, Illinois.

Mrs. Sarah Yoakum died in 1863, and William Yoakum was married January, 1868, to Mrs. Letitia Henderson, whose maiden name was Rice, and lives near Salisbury, Illinois. The mother of William, James and Mathias Yoakum died in Salisbury township.

YOAKUM MATTHIAS, brother to William and James Yoakum, was born either in Virginia or Claiborn county, Tennessee, came to Sangamon county, Illinois, in 1819. He married Elizabeth McHenry, and had eight children—

HIRAM married Catharine Elmore, and died in 1856, leaving one child, WILLIAM.

MARY married Eli Yoakum, and lives in Crawford county, Kansas.

JESSE, born Nov. 10, 1831, in Sangamon county, married Jan. 10, 1856, to Margaret Thompson, and has five children, GEORGE C., FRANKLIN T., WILLIAM R., MARY C. and EDMUND, and live east of the Sangamon river, near Salisbury, Illinois.

CATHARINE married Z. S. Cogdal, has four children, and live near Salisbury, Illinois.

ELIHU B. married Mary A. Cogdal, has one child, and lives in Menard county, Illinois.

THOMAS C., born August 14, 1840, married May 17, 1865, to Barilla Hoag. They had one child, MAUD. Mr. Yoakum is postmaster at Salisbury, Sangamon county, Illinois, is also a merchant, and resides there.

ROBERT C. lives with his mother.

Matthias Yoakum died August 27, 1857, and his widow lives in Menard county, Illinois—1874.

YOAKUM, JAMES, brother to William and Matthias, was born in Virginia or Claiborn county, Tennessee, and came with his mother to Sangamon county. He married Julia Owens, and had eleven children in Menard county, Illinois. His sons—

GEORGE and NELSON were soldiers in the Mexican war, and both lost their lives there in 1847.

WILLIAM was married June 16, 1836, to Priscilla Batterton. See Batterton sketch. They have one son, WILLIAM F., who married May Adams, and lives near Salisbury, Illinois.

JOHN lives in Menard county, Illinois.

ISAAC lives in Iowa.

James Yoakum died in Menard county, Illinois.

YOCOM, JACOB, was born Dec. 17, 1787, in a fort or block-house in Bourbon county, near where the city of Lexington, Kentucky, now stands. Mary Booth was born Feb. 11, 1791, in the same county. They were there married Nov. 15, 1810, and went to Montgomery county, in the same State, where eleven of their children were born. They moved in 1827 to Marion county, Illinois, and from there to Sangamon county, in the same State, arriving Nov. 2, 1828, in what is now Williams township, one and a half miles east of Sherman, where three children were born. Of their children—

WILLIAM, born Sept. 18, 1811, in Montgomery county, Kentucky, came to Sangamon county with his parents in 1828, and served three months as a soldier in a Sangamon county company in the Black Hawk war of 1831-32. He was married Dec. 17, 1834, in Sangamon county, Illinois, to Sarah J. Merriman. They had eleven children. GEORGE S. enlisted August, 1862, in Co. B, 130th Ill. Inf. for three years, was taken prisoner April 8, 1864, with General Banks, up Red river, and was thirteen months a prisoner at Camp Ford or Tyler, Texas. He was released at the close of the rebellion, and honorably discharged June 17, 1865. He married Nancy Wimmer. They have two children, MATILDA and MARY ELLEN, and live two miles south of Williamsville, Illinois. MARY A. married Perry Sapp, a native of Knox county, Ohio. They have one child. LYMAN, and live near Williamsville, Illinois. Mr. Sapp enlisted August, 1862, in Co. B, 130th Ill. Inf. He was at home on recruiting service when his regiment was captured, and thus escaped thirteen months of imprisonment. He was honorably discharged at New Orleans, August 22, 1865. JACOB enlisted August, 1862, in Co. B, 130th Ill. Inf., with his brother, George S., and experienced all that his brother did by imprisonment. See his name. Jacob Yocom married Susan Lanterman, and has three children, LULA, MARY A. and SUSAN G., and live two miles south of Williamsville, Illinois. SARAH married Jacob Y. Hussey. See his name. LYMAN M. died Jan. 19, 1863, in his nineteenth year. ELVIRA J. died March 9, 1863, in her fifteenth year. MADISON M., CORDELIA E., REBECCA C., WILLIAM F., and CHARLES E. reside with their parents. William Yocom resides two miles east of Sherman, Sangamon county, Illinois.

SAMUEL, born Dec. 28, 1812, in Kentucky, was married in Sangamon county, Illinois, Feb. 15, 1838, to Ann Cooper, who was born July 18, 1818. They moved overland to Oregon in 1851, and returned by water in 1853. Of their seven children three died in childhood. ALIDA, born Sept. 6, 1840, married Clifton H. King. See his name. She died March 27, 1866. WILLIAM, born Nov. 13, 1843, enlisted August, 1862, in Co. C, 114th Ill. Inf., for three years, served full term and was honorably discharged August 15, 1865, at Camp Butler. He was married Sept. 22, 1869, to Mary Oliver, who was born April 10, 1850, in Ross county, Ohio. They have one child, JOHN W., and reside one and a half miles northwest of Dawson, Sangamon county, Illinois. REBECCA, born Feb. 6, 1846, married John Horn. See his name. THOMAS lives near Barclay, Illinois. Mrs. Ann Yocom died Nov. 21, 1858. Samuel Yocom was married October, 1861, to Mrs. Nancy Shepherd, whose maiden name was Langston. She died November, 1867. Samuel Yocom was married March 18, 1869, to Mrs. Jane Hillman, widow of Richard S. Hillman. Her maiden name was Williamson. They reside at Barclay, Sangamon county, Illinois.

GEORGE W., born Feb. 18, 1814, in Kentucky, was married Jan. 22, 1835, to Margaret J. Cooper. They had fourteen children, one died in infancy. Of their thirteen children, JAMES E. died aged seventeen years. MARY A. married Henry F. Brown, a native of Putnam county, Indiana. They had four children. WILLIAM S. died in his fourth year. ALBERT W., JOHN H. and FRANKLIN CARROLL live with their parents, near Williamsville, Illinois. Mr. H. F. Brown enlisted on the first call for seventy-five thousand men, in 1861, in Co. H, 10th Ind. Inf., served three months, enlisted August 8, 1862, in Co. C, 114th Ill. Inf., for three years, served full time, and was honorably discharged August 15, 1865. AMANDA J. married William Brown. They had one child, ALICE. Mr. Brown enlisted August, 1862, in Co. C, 114th Ill. Inf., and died without leaving Camp Butler. His widow was married Oct. 8, 1874, to John Smith. EMELINE was married November, 1865, to Samuel D. Rodgers. *See his name.* JEFFERSON enlisted August 12, 1862, in Co. C, 114th Ill. Inf., for three years. He was detached and placed in Co. E, 1st Ill. Light Artillery, served fifteen months, returned to the 114th, served until August, 1865, when he was honorably discharged. He married Caroline Morton. They have one child, and live near Williamsville, Ill. ROBERT F. enlisted in the 2d Ill. Light Artillery, served one and a half years, and was honorably discharged. He married Nancy J. Smith. She died Sept. 15, 1875, leaving two children. He lives near Mt. Pleasant, Henry county, Iowa. JESSE V. married Marion Huston, a native of Scotland. They have two children, and live near Williamsville, Illinois. JOHN W. and POLLY L. live with their mother. NETTIE V. died Nov. 4, 1875. CLARA E. died Oct. 28, 1875, and MINNIE M. died Nov. 14, 1875. ELIZA R. died, aged eleven years. George W. Yocom died March 3, 1875, and his widow resides three miles south of Williamsville, Sangamon county, Illinois.

JESSE, born June 19, 1815, in Kentucky, was married in Sangamon county, Illinois, to Minerva Cooper. He moved in 1847 to the Pacific coast. They have ten living children. JAMES A. married Elizabeth Murray, and has seven living children. ZACHARIAH married Ellen Benyfield, and has five children. CAROLINE married George Y. Davis, and has eight children. OLIVER married Ann Robison. MARY married Levi Zumwalt, and had four children. She and the youngest child died. NANCY married Lyman M. Noble. TOMPKINS is unmarried. MARTHA married Campbell Hendrix. KITTIE married John Dempsey. NETTIE V. lives with her parents. Jesse Yocom and wife reside near Lafayette, Yamhill county, Oregon.

SARAH, born Oct. 17, 1816, in Montgomery county, Kentucky, married William S. Hussey. *See his name.*

STEPHEN, born Nov. 16, 1817, in Kentucky, was married Dec. 28, 1843, in Sangamon county, to Martha A. Council. They have four living children. STEPHEN H., Jun., died, aged fourteen years. MARY S. is unmarried, and lives in Williamsville, Illinois. WILLIAM J. enlisted April 30, 1864, in Co. I, 133d Ill. Inf., for one hundred days, served more than one hundred and forty days, and was honorably discharged Sept. 24, 1864. He resides with his parents—1874. GEORGE W. C., was married July, 1873, to Laura Young, and lives near Chesnut, Logan county, Illinois. JESSE F., resides with his parents. Stephen Yocom and family reside four miles south of Williamsville, Sangamon county, Illinois.

ABEL, born Jan. 2, 1819, in Kentucky, was married in Sangamon county to Jane Robinson. They had three children. JAMES W. enlisted Aug. 5, 1862, in Co. B, 130th Ill. Inf., for three years, served full time, and was honorably discharged August, 1865. He married Mary F. Madden. They have three children, EDGAR E., ERNEST L. and MINNIE E., and reside near Illiopolis, Illinois. SARAH A. married George A. Leigh. They have three children, HATTIE L., NETTIE L. and HARRY, and reside corner Twelfth and Carpenter streets, Springfield, Illinois. JOHN H. married Lottie Richmond, has two children, LILLIE and GILBERT E., and lives near Illiopolis, Illinois. Abel Yocom died March, 1874, and his widow resides near where Mr. Yocom's father settled in 1828, near Williamsville, Illinois.

FRANKLIN, born July 30, 1820, in Montgomery county, Kentucky, was married in Sangamon county, Illinois, to

—100

Nancy J. Darnall. They had nine children. ALLYN, born Nov. 12, 1843, in Sangamon county, was married Nov. 29, 1865, to Evaline Lady. They have three children, and live near Sheridan, in Polk county, Oregon. EVALINE, born Jan. 24, 1845, in Sangamon county, was married Nov. 30, 1864, to James Brown. They have four children, and reside in Sheridan, Yamhill county, Oregon. MARILLA J., born April 2, 1846, in Sangamon county, was married May 7, 1868, to David A. Carter. They have four children, and live in Brownsville, Lane county, Oregon. ELIZA L., born Nov. 25, 1848, in Sangamon county, and lives near Salem, Oregon. REBECCA H., born March 2, 1851, was married Dec. 20, 1871, in Oregon, to John W. Minto. They have two children, and live in Salem, Oregon. MATILDA, born April 20, 1855. JONAH, born Nov. 8, 1856, in Oregon, was drowned in the Williamette river, March 19, 1873. RETTA L. and HARVEY. The last four were born in Polk county, Oregon, and the unmarried children reside with their parents in Salem, Marion county, Oregon.

ELIJAH, born Oct. 26, 1821, in Montgomery county, Kentucky, was married Jan. 7, 1852, in Petersburg, Menard county, Illinois, to Caroline A. Higgins. They moved to McLean county, and from there to DeWitt county, near Waynesville, Illinois. They have three living children, ALBERT L., ANNIE R. and ELIJAH LINCOLN. Elijah Yocom died Feb. 2, 1873, of spotted fever, and his widow and children resides on their farm near Waynesville, DeWitt county, Illinois.

REBECCA, born March 11, 1826, in Kentucky, was married June 1, 1848, in Sangamon county, Illinois, to Clement Passwaters. They removed to McLean county, April, 1849, where seven children were born. Of their six living children, EMILY J., born May 2, 1849, was married March 11, 1871, to Samuel Miller, has two children, and lives near Heyworth, Illinois. STEPHEN H., born Dec. 1, 1850, was married Feb. 8, 1873, to Sarah Lee, has two children, and live near Heyworth, Illinois. WILLIAM F., ENOCH D., JAMES C. and JOHN L. reside with their parents, near Heyworth, McLean county, Illinois.

THOMAS J., born Nov. 2, 1828, in Sangamon county, emigrated to California in the spring of 1847, spent eleven months in the gold mines. He was married in Polk county, Oregon, in the spring of 1851, to Elizabeth Tharp. They had ten living children. MARGARET died aged about thirteen years. SARAH married John Thornton, and has two living children. MARY married Robert Griffith, and has one child. The other seven living children of T. J. Yocom reside with their parents near Bellevue, Yamhill county, Oregon.

JAMES P., born April 11, 1830, in Sangamon county, Illinois. He left for Oregon overland in the spring of 1851, accompanied by his mother, two brothers and his brother-in-law, William S. Hussey, and arrived at their journey's end Oct. 4th, of the same year, and was within three days of being six months on the road. He settled on a donation land claim Oct. 8, 1851, in Yamhill county, Oregon. J. P. Yocom was married in the latter county June 18, 1857, to Emeline Hussey, who was born in Sangamon county, Illinois, Jan. 1, 1841. They had three children. HENRIETTA, born Dec. 2, 1858, died Dec. 4, 1874. MIRANDA died in her seventh year. STEPHEN H., born Oct. 14, 1862, resides with his father. Mrs. Emeline Yocom died April 23, 1863, and James P. Yocom was married May 3, 1865, to Mrs. Martha E. Potts, whose maiden name was Beaman. She was born Sept. 11, 1836, in Pettis county, Missouri. They have six children, all born in Yamhill county, Oregon, ANNIE M., FRANKLIN B., VIRGINIA B., MARY, GRANT and MINNIE, who reside with their parents. J. P. Yocom left Oregon Oct. 29, 1875, with his family, going by the steamship Ajax to San Francisco, thence by railroad to Bloomington, Illinois, arriving Nov. 13, 1875, and now reside four miles northeast of Heyworth, McLean county, Illinois.

HATHAWAY, born Oct. 31, 1831, in Sangamon county, Illinois, emigrated over to Oregon in the spring of 1850, was married there March 7, 1852, to Mary Tharp. They have six children. ELIZABETH P. married Linsday Delashmint, and has three children. CEMMONT, CAROLETTA, JOSEPH M., WILLIE and EDDY, and live with their parents in Bellevue, Yamhill county, Oregon.

Jacob Yocom died March 8, 1848, in

Sangamon county, Illinois, and Mrs. Mary Yocom died Dec. 23, 1864, in Lafayette, Yamhill county, Oregon. She was buried at Pleasant Hill Church, Polk county, Oregon.

YOUNG, EZEKIEL, was born about 1795, in Trigg county, Kentucky. He was married in North Carolina to Sarah Coleman. They had five children in Kentucky, and moved to Sangamon county, Illinois, arriving in 1827 on Richland creek, where one child was born. Two of their children only are in Sangamon county.

LUCINDA married Samuel Beardon. See his name.

ARCHIBALD, born April 21, 1828, in Sangamon county, married Nov. 18, 1850, to Elizabeth Wood, born in Sangamon county, (sister to Mrs. Wolgamott.) They had four children. EMMA died January, 1868, in her fourteenth year. LAURA died July, 1869, in her fourteenth year. MARY E. and IDA BELLE reside with their parents, near Woodside, Sangamon county, Illinois.

Ezekiel Young died May, 1853, and his widow died in 1864, both in Cass county, Illinois.

YOUNG, CASPER, was born June 8, 1798, at Hazelloch, on the river Mayn, Hesse Darmstadt, Germany. Susan Boll was born in 1802, in the town of Florsheim, in Nassau, on the opposite side of the Mayn from Hazelloch. Casper Young and Susan Boll were married in Florsheim in 1821. They had four children in Germany and emigrated to America in 1835. They were seven weeks on the passage from Amsterdam to New York. Their first stoppage was at Coshocton, Ohio. From there they went to St. Louis, Missouri, by the Ohio and Mississippi rivers, and tarried one year in St. Clair county, Illinois. In the fall of 1837 they arrived in Sangamon county, in the southeast corner of Woodside township, where three children were born. Of their seven children—

MARGARET, born in Germany, married in Sangamon county to Frank Schick. They had two children. G. Schick was a professor in a college in St. Louis. He is a lawyer. Mrs Schick died in Mt. Pulaski, Illinois.

GARRED—called Charley—was born Dec. 17, 1825, at Florsheim, Nassau, Germany. He was married in Sangamon county April 18, 1852, to Mrs. Sally White, whose maiden name was Gatton, a daughter of Charles Gatton. She had one child by her first marriage, MARY ANN, who is now the wife of Mr. Lyman, of Pana. Mr. and Mrs. Young had three children, REBECCA, WILLIAM R. and CATHARINE, and Mrs. Sally Young died Feb. 2, 1863. Mr. Young was married February, 1864, to Ellen Abell. She died without children, Nov. 4, 1866. Mr. Young was married Oct. 1, 1867, at Lebanon, Kentucky, to Maggie E. Buckman. They reside one and a half miles north of Pawnee, Sangamon county, Illinois. Mr. Young has represented Pawnee township several terms in Sangamon county Board of Supervisors, and is one of the many successful farmers of Sangamon county.

MARY, born in Germany, married Henry Harschlier, has seven children, and lives in Mt. Pulaski, Illinois.

CATHARINE, born in Germany, married Frank Schick. They have six children, and live in Mt. Pulaski, Illinois.

MARY EVE, born in Sangamon county, married Philip Schwigead. They had two children, and Mr. S. Died. The widow married Jacob Hundt, and lives in Mt. Pulaski, Illinois.

Casper Young moved to Mt. Pulaski in 1855. Mrs. Susan Young died June, 1867. Casper Young died Sept. 27, 1875, both in Mt. Pulaski, Logan county, Ill.

YOUNG, JAMES, was born Dec. 19, 1788, in Wilkes county, North Carolina. His parents moved to Montgomery county, Kentucky, when he was a young man. He was there married Feb. 10, 1822, to Lucinda R. Cuming, who was born August 12, 1804, in the same county. They had seven children in Kentucky, and moved to Sangamon county, Illinois, arriving in the fall of 1838 in what is now Curran township, where three children were born. Of their children three died under five years. Of the other seven—

VIRGINIA, born Jan. 15, 1823, married John P. Lindsay, had six children, and died May 2, 1850, near Springfield. See his name in Omissions.

WILBOURN, born Oct. 23, 1824, is unmarried, and resides at the family homestead near Curran, Illinois.

ELIZABETH, born Oct. 21, 1826, married Wade Burch. See his name.

JAMES, born August 20, 1831, married Catharine Foster, have eight children, SILAS A., MARGARET, JAMES M., EUGENE, FRANCIS, ALBERTUS, NANCY and EMMA, and live near Chatham, Illinois.

SILAS J., born March 1, 1834, is unmarried, and lives in Fayette county, Illinois.

ANN E., born Oct. 15, 1837, married William B. Greenwood. See his name. He died and she married Benjamin Easley. See his name.

MARTHA C., born June 6, 1841, married Feb. 22, 1865, and has three children, FATIMA, ARTHUR and LEONA MAY, and live with their mother.

James Young died March 11, 1870, aged eighty-two years, and his widow resides on the farm where they settled in 1838, near Curran, Illinois—1874.

Z

ZANE. Three brothers of that name emigrated from England and settled in Gloucester county, New Jersey. It is not known whether or not they were related to Jonathan and Ebenezer Zane, who explored the country about Wheeling, West Virginia, in 1769, and founded Zanesville, Ohio. Of the three brothers who settled in New Jersey, the first names are not preserved, but one of them had a son, Simeon. His son, Andrew, married Mary Franklin, a distant relative of Benjamin Franklin. They brought up a large family in New Jersey. Their eldest and youngest sons came to Sangamon county, namely—

ZANE, JOHN, born Nov. 8, 1806, in Gloucester county, New Jersey, but was brought up in Cumberland county, in the same State. He was married Feb. 3, 1833, in Cape May county, to Elizabeth Smith, who was born in that county April 13, 1812. They moved to Philadelphia, where they had one living child, returned to New Jersey, where they had one child, and moved from there to Sangamon county, Illinois, arriving Oct. 15, 1839, in what is now Cartwright township, where they had nine children. Of their eleven children—

JAMES S., born July 10, 1836, in Philadelphia, Pennsylvania, married in Sangamon county June 14, 1860, to Maria Rachel Purviance. See Purviance or Purvines family. They have four children, SAMUEL S., JOHN N., FRANKLIN H. and MARY E. James S. Zane was elected in the fall of 1872 sheriff of Jasper county, Missouri, and resides at Carthage, the county seat.

RHODA S., born Sept. 13, 1838, in Cape May county, New Jersey, married in Sangamon county, April 21, 1859, to John T. Epler. She died March 21, 1871, leaving four children, CHARLES L., GEORGE A., MARY J. and RHODA E., who live with their father. John T. Epler is married again and resides two and a half miles south of Pleasant Plains, Sangamon county, Illinois.

MARY E., born March 25, 1841, in Sangamon county, married Feb. 13, 1867, to Dr. Henry VanMeter. See his name.

ELLEN S., born Dec. 20, 1842, in Sangamon county, married July 31, 1861, to Benjamin F. Jones. She died May 25, and he died August 27, 1867. They had two children. MARY J. died, aged three years. JOHN W., born Dec. 12, 1864, lives with his grandfather Zane.

ELIZABETH S., born May 7, 1844, married Dec. 28, 1871, to William S. Bullard. See his name.

ANDREW, born August 20, 1846, in Sangamon county, married Feb. 27, 1873, to Mary J. Hamilton, near Pleasant Plains, Illinois. They reside in Carthage, Jasper county, Missouri.

JOHN W., born Oct. 31, 1848.

JEREMIAH F., born Nov. 26, 1850.

HANNAH M., born Dec. 25, 1852.

ROBERT H., born March 3, 1855;

ALICE B., born April 25, 1859, the five latter live with their parents.

John Zane and wife reside four miles east of Mechanicsburg, Sangamon county, Illinois—1874.

ZANE CHARLES S., brother to John Zane, was born March 2, 1831, in Cumberland county, New Jersey. In the spring of 1850 he came to the vicinity of Pleasant Plains, Sangamon county, Illinois, where he worked at farm labor by the month. He afterwards attended McKendree college, at Lebanon, Illinois, teaching school in different parts of the State at intervals until July 15, 1856, when he came to Springfield. Having previously commenced the study of law, he continued and was admitted to practice in the spring of 1857. He was three times elected city attorney, in 1858, 1860 and in 1865. In June, 1873, he was elected Judge of the judicial circuit, of which Sangamon county is a part, and is now—December, 1876—in office. He was married in 1859 to Margaret D. Maxey. They have six children, *FERNETTA M., CHARLES W., JOHN M., OLIVER W., MARGARET, FRANKLIN A.* and *HERBERT S.*

Judge Charles S. Zane was elected in November, 1876, a member of the National Lincoln Monument Association. He, with his family, resides in Springfield, Sangamon county, Illinois.

ZIMMERMAN, ROBERT B., was born Oct. 5, 1811, in Centre county, Pennsylvania, and went from there to Elmira, New York, where he learned the business of a painter and chair maker. In the summer of 1835 he started west, traveling by stage, he missed his connections at Terre Haute, Indiana, and there being but one stage a week, rather than remain idle he and one or two others started on foot. Arriving at the Okaw river in Illinois they found a company of emigrants from Tennessee, numbering one hundred and twenty wagons, with a corresponding number of men, women and children, all waiting until the men could construct a bridge for the teams to cross. They remained with the emigrants, riding and walking alternately, and reached Springfield Nov. 18, 1835. R. B. Zimmerman was married Dec. 25, 1838, at Farmington, now Farmindale, Sangamon county, to Susan P. Seeley. Mrs. Zimmerman died Oct. 30, 1840, leaving one child—

SUSAN L., born April 17, 1840, in Springfield, Illinois. She was married April 17, 1860, to Eugene L. Gross, who was born Dec. 25, 1836, in Starkville, Herkimer county, New York. Rev. Alba Gross, the father of Eugene L., is a preacher in connection with the Baptist Church, and came to Fulton county, Illinois, in 1841, but now resides in Chatham, Illinois. E. L. Gross studied law at Knoxville, was admitted to the bar, and practiced a short time at Mount Sterling, and came to Springfield, in 1858. He revised and published the ordinances of the city of Springfield in 1865. In January, 1868, he compiled and published a digest of the criminal laws of Illinois. In February, 1868, he, in connection with his brother, Colonel William L. Gross, began their compilation of the Statutes of Illinois, which were published in the fall of the same year. Their last volume was published in 1869. The same year they published an index to all the laws of the State. In 1872 they compiled and published the second volume of Gross' Statutes. E. L. Gross, finding his health impaired, closed up his business, and in the spring of 1873 started on horseback and traveled through the Indian nation, thence to the Pacific coast, and returned by railroad, but that relentless destroyer, consumption, could not be induced to release its grasp. After returning home he lingered until June 4, 1874, when he breathed his last, leaving a widow and four children, LEIGHLA, FRED, SUSIE and BESSIE, all residing in Springfield, Illinois.

Robert B. Zimmerman was married Oct. 2, 1845, in Springfield, to Mary C. Townsend, who was born Nov. 7, 1821, in Caledonia county, Vermont. They had two children, both died young. In November, 1849, Mr. and Mrs. Zimmerman adopted a daughter, LIZZIE, when she was but three months old. She was married Feb. 26, 1875, in Springfield, to Martin V. Smith. They reside in East St. Louis, Illinois.

Robert B. Zimmerman and Alexander P. Willard were in partnership as painters and dealers in painters' stock twenty-four years, and until the death of Mr. Willard. *See his name.* Mr. Zimmerman is yet in business in which he has been more than forty-one years actively engaged in Springfield. He has seen it grow, and had much to do with its growth, from a very small village to a city of twenty-five thousand inhabitants, and from a county seat to be the capital of the fourth State in the American Union. He has been an active and efficient officer of the Second Presbyterian church for many years; and in proportion to his ability he has probably been the most liberal contributor to its funds. R. B. Zimmerman and wife reside in Springfield, Illinois.

THE END

www.ingramcontent.com/pod-product-compliance
Lightning Source LLC
Chambersburg PA
CBHW052106010526
44111CB00036B/1488